BYZANTINE
ART AND ARCHAEOLOGY

BY

O. M. DALTON

WITH 457 ILLUSTRATIONS

DOVER PUBLICATIONS, INC.
NEW YORK

Published in the United Kingdom by Con-
stable and Company Limited, 10 Orange Street,
London, W. C. 2.

This new Dover edition, first published in
1961, is an unabridged and unaltered republica-
tion of the first edition published by the Oxford
University Press in 1911.

Manufactured in the United States of America

Dover Publications, Inc.
180 Varick Street
New York 14, N. Y.

PREFACE

THE purpose of this book is to provide something in the nature of a general introduction to the art and antiquities of the Christian East, which, until the publication of Prof. Diehl's admirable *Manuel d'art byzantin*, had not been treated in a single volume incorporating the results of recent investigation.[1] The work was almost finished when the *Manuel* appeared, and had it not been that the arrangement which I had adopted was different from that of Prof. Diehl, I might have hesitated to proceed further. But, upon consideration, it seemed that there was still room for a volume like the present, in which the attempt has been made, by means of copious references, to indicate exact sources and acquaint English readers with the latest Continental research. At one time I had contemplated including Architecture, the exclusion of which is assuredly a matter for regret. But, on the one hand, the material most nearly connected with my own studies alone bade fair to exceed the limits of a single volume; on the other, it seemed clear that the Mistress Art could only be treated in an adequate manner by one brought up in her tradition or admitted to it in virtue of a wide practical experience. I can lay claim to neither advantage, and therefore abstain from a task beyond my powers, hoping that the issue of this book may suggest to some qualified scholar a volume restating those architectural problems of which the importance is paramount to the study of Byzantine art.

The bulk of the book consists of plain descriptions based upon the work of the chief authorities and intended for reference rather than for continuous reading. Two introductory chapters have however been placed at the beginning, and two chapters on special subjects at the end, while each main division has a short introduction of its own. It is hoped that these additions may make the contents of the several sections more intelligible, and perhaps mitigate in some degree the austerity of a method which follows the unbending lines of a directory.

The period covered is that between the fourth century and the close of the fifteenth; it is, roughly, the duration of the Byzantine Empire. But the limits have not been very strictly drawn; many things have been considered which are not 'Byzantine', some which are not even East-

---

[1] M. Ch. Bayet's *Art byzantin* is favourably known to all students of Byzantine art, but it is restricted in size and in the number of its illustrations. M. Gabriel Millet's chapters on Byzantine Art in A. Michel's *Histoire de l'Art* have not been separately printed.

Christian in their origin. Of the term Byzantine, I have said something at the beginning of the first chapter; the word is adopted on the title-page, and retained in other places, rather by sufferance than by predilection. For the present it seems almost indispensable, as the one adjective which is individual and suggestive of an atmosphere; if it suggests either too little or too much, it is possible for each to protect his orthodoxy by his own reservations, and there is so much essential work waiting to be done, that it seems idle to waste time over a point of terminology. In the discussion of works of art created during more than a thousand years, questions arise which are necessarily controversial or unripe for final settlement. In some cases I have been content merely to state opposing theories; where I have taken a side, I have endeavoured to do justice to the views not adopted. The opinions given on many problems are admittedly tentative, and liable to revision in the light of new research. Such are those regarding the mutual influence of Byzantine industrial art and that of Central or Further Asia, which may prove to require modification when we have before us the full material gathered by the British, German, and French expeditions to Turkestan. Other questions of pre-eminent interest to Byzantine studies, though not directly within our scope, have only received incidental mention; among these are the genesis and affinities of the earlier Mohammedan or Saracenic art, a subject fortunately now in the forefront of inquiry.

Of the numerous defects which mar the scheme of the book as originally conceived, I am but too well aware. There are shortcomings in interpretation; faults of proportion; sins of omission and commission, including, I doubt not, inaccuracies meriting hard censure. Complete success in such an undertaking as the present is for those who are masters of their time; who are able to pursue and classify new developments without delay, and at leisure co-ordinate old and new into an organic whole. For myself, I soon realized that the ideal of including everything was beyond possibility of attainment: the multitude of facts was too great, their mass too ponderous. And yet, compared with others which could be mentioned, this is a restricted field. The lot of one who in our time would keep abreast of any progressive subject grows more arduous year by year; to-day we at least skim a profuse literature; our successors to-morrow will employ professional digesters and trained artists in abridgement — content themselves with the prefaces and titles of the unnumbered books which shall be written. The tide of printed matter flows so strongly that only the determined student can make head against it, happy if no τρικυμία from the unknown deep break at the last moment, and confound the nice order of his argument. For even while a work is in the press, the processes of supersession go on,[1] and many a book at the moment of its birth is already in some measure out of date. I cannot pretend to have always stemmed the flood which pours out of the European press, but if I must admit a partial failure, I have not succumbed without a struggle : the references with which the following pages are loaded bear witness at least to a pertinacity of resistance. I have availed myself of sources published in all the countries active in Byzantine studies, not forgetting those Russian books which are often of the first importance, but, through expression in a difficult tongue, too frequently inaccessible to English students. I cannot pretend to have seen with my own eyes all the monuments described, but I have made acquaintance with considerable numbers as my opportunities have allowed. I have visited the great museums, including those at Constantinople and Cairo, and many libraries and churches ; by travel in Italy, Sicily, and Cyprus, I have endeavoured to learn something at first hand of the mosaic art.

The numerous blocks in the text are intended to show the character of the monuments and objects discussed in the several chapters. It was impossible that they should be exhaustive, or that they should provide the minute detail which may be expected in a monograph, but they should enable readers without access to large libraries to form some notion of the art which they represent.

My general obligation to contemporary writers must find acknowledgement in the Index of Authorities. The debt to the earlier writers is taken for granted ; their names occur in references in the text, but have not swelled the proportions of the index. With the exception of Mr. Warwick Wroth, who has treated the coinage of the Byzantine Empire, British writers on East-Christian archaeology have chiefly been concerned with architecture.[2] Of scholars in other countries to whom I have owed most, I may mention : in France, Bayet, Diehl, Millet, and Schlumberger ; in Germany, Haseloff, Krumbacher, and Wulff ; in Austria, Wickhoff, Riegl, and Strzygowski the most indefatigable of pioneers ; in Italy, Muñoz and Venturi ; in Greece, Lambros, Antoniades, and Papadopoulos Kerameus ; in Russia, Ainaloff, Riedin, Schmidt, Smirnoff, and, above all, Kondakoff, who in a long career has touched all branches of a complex subject, and none without distinction. The *Byzantinische Zeitschrift* and the *Vizantieski Vremennik* have throughout been unfailing sources of instruction.

---

[1] To quote a simple instance : M. V. de Grüneisen's important book on Sta Maria Antiqua has appeared while the present work was in the press.

[2] Especially Prof. W. R. Lethaby, Mr. R. W. Schultz, Miss G. L. Bell, and Dr. E. Freshfield.

More particular acknowledgements are due to the Trustees of the British Museum for the use of numerous blocks employed in the *Catalogue of Early Christian and Byzantine Antiquities*, and the *Guide* to the same subject; to the Society of Antiquaries of London for permission to make electrotypes from blocks in their *Archaeologia* and *Proceedings*; to Sir Gaston Maspero, Chief of the Service des Antiquités in Egypt, for the loan of blocks from Prof. Strzygowski's Catalogue *Koptische Kunst*, written for the Cairo Museum; to M. Gustave Schlumberger and his publishers MM. Hachette, for permission to borrow illustrations from *L'Épopée byzantine au Xme Siècle*; to the Imperial Academy of Sciences at Vienna for leave to reproduce two illustrations, after Herr Mielich's drawings, in the publication *Kusejr 'Amra,* by Dr. A. Musil, Prof. Karabaček, and others; to Mr. N. H. J. Westlake for numerous blocks from his *History of Design in Mural Painting*; to Mr. Quibell for the kind gift of photos from Saqqara; to Mr. Henry Wallis for photographs made for him in Rome by permission of the Librarian of the Vatican, of textiles from the Sancta Sanctorum; to Dr. J. Hampel for photos of enamels in the Museum at Budapest; to Prof. Marc Rosenberg for photos of objects in the Treasury of S. Marco at Venice; and to Messrs. Methuen for the use of several photographs prepared for the illustrated edition of Gibbon's *Decline and Fall*. Lastly, my especial thanks are due to the Delegates of the Clarendon Press, by whom publication has been made possible; to M. Gabriel Millet for most kind assistance in procuring photographs from the negatives in the Collection des Hautes Études, generously placed at the disposal of students from all countries; and to my colleagues Mr. J. A. Herbert and Mr. G. F. Hill, the former for reading the proofs of the chapter on MSS., the latter for going through almost the whole book, and aiding me at all times by encouragement and advice.

O. M. D.

BRITISH MUSEUM,
   October, 1911.

CONTENTS

CHAPTER X

CHAPTER XI

CHAPTER XII

CHAPTER XIII

INDEXES

LIST OF ILLUSTRATIONS

THE locality of the object represented follows the description. The source of the photograph or drawing is given in brackets.

The abbreviation H. E. signifies the collection of photographs at the École Pratique des Hautes Études, Sorbonne, Paris. Most of them are from photos contributed to that collection by M. Gabriel Millet, Maître de Conférences at the School, and wherever the letters H. E. occur alone the photo is understood to be his. Where a photograph borrowed from the same collection has been given by another donor, his name follows the letters H. E.: thus 'H. E.: N. Kondakoff' means that the photo reproduced is from the collection of the Hautes Études, to which it was presented by Prof. Kondakoff.

B. M. signifies the British Museum.

B. M. Catalogue = British Museum, *Catalogue of Early Christian and Byzantine Antiquities*, 1901.

B. M. Guide = British Museum, *Guide to the Early Christian and Byzantine Antiquities*, 1903.

V. and A. M. = the Victoria and Albert Museum.

K. F. M., Berlin = the Kaiser Friedrich Museum, Berlin.

The illustrations from objects in the Cairo Museum attributed to the Service des Antiquités are borrowed, as stated in the Preface, from the Cairo catalogue entitled *Koptische Kunst*.

LIST OF THE PRINCIPAL ABBREVIATIONS

Austrian *Jahrbuch* = *Jahrbuch der kunsthistorischen Sammlungen des allerhöchsten Kaiserhauses*, Vienna.

Ath. Mitth. = *Mittheilungen des kaiserlich deutschen archäologischen Instituts, Athenische Abteilung*, Athens, 1876, &c.

Bayet, *Recherches* = C. Bayet, *Recherches pour servir à l'histoire de la peinture et de la sculpture en Orient avant la querelle des Iconoclastes*, Athens, Bibliothèque de l'École française, Fasc. 10.

B. C. H. = *Bulletin de Correspondance hellénique*.

B. D. = *Byzantinische Denkmäler*, a series of volumes published in connexion with the *Byzantinische Zeitschrift*.

B. Z. = *Byzantinische Zeitschrift*, Leipsic, 1892, &c.

Diehl, *Manuel* = Ch. Diehl, *Manuel d'art byzantin*, Paris, 1910.

Garrucci, *Storia* = R. Garrucci, *Storia dell' arte cristiana*, Prato, 1872–80.

H. E. = *Collection chrétienne et byzantine des Hautes Études*, École pratique des Hautes Études, Sorbonne, Paris.

Jahrbuch K. D. A. I. = *Jahrbuch des kaiserlich deutschen archäologischen Instituts*, Berlin, 1886, &c.

Kraus, *Geschichte* = F. X. Kraus, *Geschichte der christlichen Kunst*, Freiburg, 1896.

Mon. Piot = *Monuments et mémoires publiés par l'Académie des Inscriptions et Belles-Lettres*, Paris, 1894, &c.

O. C. = *Oriens Christianus*, Rome, Priestercollegium des deutschen Campo Santo, 1901, &c.

Prussian *Jahrbuch* = *Jahrbuch der königlich preussischen Kunstsammlungen*, Berlin, 1880, &c.

R. Q. = *Römische Quartalschrift für christliche Altertumskunde und für Kirchengeschichte*, Rome, 1887, &c.

Repertorium = *Repertorium für Kunstwissenschaft*, Stuttgart-Berlin, 1876, &c.

Rev. arch. = *Revue archéologique*, Paris, 1844, &c.

Röm. Mitth. = *Mittheilungen des kaiserlich deutschen archäologischen Instituts, Römische Abteilung*, Rome, 1886, &c.

Strzygowski, *Koptische Kunst* = J. Strzygowski, *Koptische Kunst, Catalogue général des Antiquités Égyptiennes du Musée du Caire*, Nos. 7001 ff., Vienna, 1904 (Service des Antiquités de l'Égypte).

Venturi, *Storia* = A. Venturi, *Storia dell' arte italiana*, Milan, 1901, &c.

V. V. = *Vizantieski Vremennik*, St. Petersburg, 1893, &c. (Published by the Imperial Academy of Sciences.)

Vöge, *Berlin Catalogue.* = W. Vöge, *Beschreibung der Bildwerke der christlichen Epochen*, zweite Auflage. *Die Elfenbeinbildwerke*, Berlin (Königliche Museen), 1902.

Wulff, *Berlin Catalogue* I, II = O. Wulff, *Beschreibung der Bildwerke*, &c., &c., Band III, *Altchristliche und mittelalterliche byzantinische und italienische Bildwerke*. Teil I, *Altchristliche Bildwerke*; Teil II, *Mittelalterliche Bildwerke*. Berlin (Königliche Museen), 1909 and 1911.

Fig. 1. Head-piece from a manuscript of the Homilies of St. Gregory in the Vatican Library. (*Hautes Études* : G. Millet.)

CHAPTER I

INTRODUCTORY : GENERAL CONSIDERATIONS

It must be a subject of consideration to any writer on the archaeology of the East-Roman Empire whether to retain or discard the long-familiar epithet 'Byzantine'. In recent years the term has been employed more cautiously than heretofore, for reasons which may not be lightly disregarded. It seems to infringe the rights of Syria, Anatolia, and Egypt ; it concedes to the city of Constantinople an artistic hegemony which she did not at first possess; it gives no hint of the debt which Byzantium owed to the non-Christian East beyond her frontiers. On the other hand, it has the merits of terseness, and of consecration by long usage, while the difficulty of finding a satisfactory substitute has necessarily favoured its survival. East Roman, Later Roman, Romaic, may be preferable in political history, but in the history of art they are misleading. They lend the city of Rome a predominance even less easily justified than that which 'Byzantine' lends to Constantinople ; they too are question-begging epithets. The most practical course is perhaps to retain the familiar word with reservations, for the earlier period restricting it as far as possible to that which is directly associated with Byzantium, for the later allowing it a wider connotation. Where the term is ambiguous or obviously mis-

Fig. 2.   Interior of Sta Sophia, Constantinople.   (Sébah and Joaillier.)

leading it is often possible to substitute the paraphrase East-Christian, which, colourless though it is, may negatively serve a useful purpose.

The antiquities of the Christian East have achieved recognition very late in the history of art, though they were already in some degree familiar to scholars and travellers four hundred years ago. But the Renaissance rejected them; from the first they were displaced in the favour of an awakening Europe by the monuments of pagan civilization.[1] There seems indeed something of ingratitude in the exclusive zeal of the Renaissance for Roman remains and the literature of pagan Greece, when the Christian East had done so much for mediaeval Italy, and the work of Byzantine painters had proved so useful to the reviving art of Tuscany. But in that hour of revival all that bore the style and fashion of mediaevalism was flung aside as an outworn garment; men were aggrieved at the mere thought of old routine, very impatient of austerity, and of what they deemed unnatural restraints. What were the pomps of the Byzantine princes to the victories of Julius, or the homilies of Gregory of Nazianzus to the new-found dialogues of Plato? Old Rome regained from the East the empire which she had lost more than a thousand years before; first Italy and then Europe called with an insistent voice for the literature and the art of paganism. Against that demand the mediaeval spirit of the Eastern Empire availed nothing; its artists lost their influence; its men of letters kept in favour by teaching the classics of antiquity. Even if the Italians of the fifteenth century had known that art of the Christian East with which travel and exploration have made us now acquainted, the revulsion of feeling had risen too high to permit a just appreciation. If Mantegna had seen the frescoes of Mistra, would he have painted one Roman triumph the less? If Alberti or Michelozzo had studied the churches of the East, would they have found in them an inspiration more powerful than that which came to them from more ancient buildings upon Italian soil? The Turkish conquests concealed much of the greater work from the view of Europe, and the Empire which had produced it was half forgotten. In the seventeenth century a Ducange might devote a life of learning to Byzantine studies, but the French scholar moved in a backwater where few cared to follow; the stream flowed past and left his work unnoticed. Succeeding epochs of war and revolution, of expanding commerce, had no sympathy with such learning; the age of Pompeian discovery, of Winckelmann and Lessing, had even less. If a writer required an epithet for all that was obsolete or unenlightened, he found it in the word Byzantine; if such an author had the ear of Europe, he could pervert history with a phrase. A single barbed epigram of Voltaire discredited all the vast erudition of Ducange.[2]

---

[1] For a comparison of antique and Byzantine elements affecting the Renaissance see Krumbacher, *B. Z.* xiii, 1904, pp. 275–6.

[2] On this subject see Ch. Diehl, *Études byzantines*, and *Introduction à l'histoire de Byzance*. The judgements of recent centuries upon Eastern mediaeval art are of the same character as those formerly passed upon that of our own Middle Ages. The strictures of Voltaire have been too often quoted to bear repetition; they are conceived in the same spirit as that which led him to remark of mediaeval building: 'what unhappily remains of the architecture of those times' (*Œuvres*, xiii. 474). Many will recall the petulant outburst of Rousseau, condemning Gothic cathedrals as 'a disgrace to those who had the patience to build them' (Letter on French Music). Even the weighty President de Brosses was not more sympathetic (*Lettres familières*, i. 174). The mind of Shelley, so open to impressions of natural beauty, per-

Hardly less mischievous than these committed injuries was the sin of omission of which our great English historian cannot be wholly acquitted.[1] Three-quarters of Gibbon's memorable work are occupied with the period between the Antonines and Heraclius; for all the remaining centuries one-quarter must suffice.   The iconoclasts, the regenerator Basil, the great fighting emperors Nicephorus Phocas and John Zimisces, receive almost the same short measure as Michael the Drunkard and Constantine Rhino-tmetus.   It must be remembered in palliation that before the days of dispassionate historical analysis, each age read the past in the light of its especial interests, too prone to dwell upon all that accorded with its own opinions, unduly blind to the importance of that which contradicted them. Voltaire and Gibbon led an assault upon beliefs and institutions which they regarded as obstacles to progress; in their eyes Byzantium stood for all that was effete in politics and noxious in religion.   They could not maintain a judicial attitude of mind ; they did not subordinate themselves to facts, but used facts upon principles essentially forensic ; the govern-ment and society of the East-Roman Empire served them as a foil to the institutions of a practical and enlightened age.   The influence of this scornful attitude on the part of the old historians was not easily destroyed; it outlasted the general introduction of scientific historical methods ; and it was not until the second half of the nineteenth century that a more impartial judgement became possible.   It was perhaps not altogether an evil that an enthusiasm for Greek and Roman antiquities should have come first, and an interest in the art of our Western Middle Ages second, leaving the third place for the archaeology of the Christian East.   For Byzantine studies attained recognition only when a developed critical sense had established a scale of relative values; they could thus from the first be pursued in the light of experience gained in related fields of knowledge.

The periods into which the history of Byzantine art may be divided will vary according to the importance assigned to different lines of cleavage.   For general purposes the simplest system is the best ; much subdividing may here and there increase precision, but there is often a corresponding loss in comprehensiveness and breadth of outlook.   If we omit the years of the Latin occupation in the thirteenth century, the following division may be found convenient :—

I. From the foundation of Constantinople to the outbreak of iconoclasm.

II. The iconoclastic period.

---

ceived no charm in the mosaics in the mausoleum of Galla Placidia at Ravenna.   In all this we are reminded of eighteenth-century judgements on earlier literature ; of Goethe finding the *Inferno* abominable, the *Purgatorio* dubious, the *Paradiso* tiresome ; of Goldsmith's belief that Dante owed his reputation to his obscurity and to the barbarism of the times in which he lived ; of Horace Walpole's foolish dictum upon the same poet ; of Voltaire's remark that the reputation of the great Florentine will continue to increase because he is never read.   It was Voltaire who described Shakespeare as ' un sauvage ivre, sans la moindre étincelle de bon goût'

[1] See Prof. Bury's Introduction to vol. i of his edition of the *Decline and Fall*.

III. From the accession of Basil I (A. D. 867) to the sack of Constantinople in A. D. 1204.

IV. From the Restoration to the Turkish Conquest.

The principal characteristics of these periods may be very briefly stated.

The first period was a time of growth and development during which the various elements which contributed to the formation of a new art were blended into an organic whole. The foundation of the Eastern metropolis is more or less arbitrarily chosen as a starting-point; in a sense it is too early for the actual beginning of a new artistic era. But the mediaeval

Fɪɢ. 3. Part of the Gallery, Sta Sophia, Constantinople, showing marble revetment and false doors. (Sébah and Joaillier.)

spirit undoubtedly appears in literature in the fourth century;[1] and no other event makes so conspicuous a landmark in the debatable ground between the Middle Ages and Antiquity. Decentralization is the keynote of this period, which culminates during Justinian's reign in what has been described as the 'First Golden Age of Byzantine Art'. The Empire, politically one, was artistically a group of almost independent units: Syria, Egypt, and Anatolia were first the teachers and then the rivals of Constantinople. In the second part of this introduction something will be said of the causes which rendered the position of the Eastern provinces so

[1] Krumbacher, *Geschichte der byzantinischen Litteratur*, 2nd ed., pp. 2, 14.

influential (pp. 46–76). Here it need only be noted that even in the time of Justinian the primacy of the capital was but recently established and perhaps not universally acknowledged. The Persian and Arab wars of the sixth and seventh centuries put an end to this rivalry on the part of Syria and Egypt, but the spirit of the conquered territories had left so strong an impress upon Christian art that their power continued to be felt centuries after they themselves had been absorbed in the Mohammedan dominions (cf. p. 55). Later chapters will show how in this early period the activity of the Eastern provinces stimulated the growth of all the arts and enlarged the domain of iconography: in sculpture, in painting, in ornament, in the introduction of new types, their influence was universal and decisive. There are, however, certain general consequences of their predominance during these centuries which may more fitly be treated in the present place. As the seed-time of a later harvest both within and without the frontiers of the Byzantine Empire, the first period is more significant than any other in the artistic history of the mediaeval world.

The position of Rome with regard to the evolution of Christian art is the first point to be considered, and immediately the Byzantine question rises before us, *pugnax et spinosa*, the most inevitable and persistent of archaeological problems. Italy or the Christian East, the Orient or Rome,[1] which had the pre-eminence in the first critical centuries of our era? which controlled the destinies of Christian art? The nature of the controversy is now familiar; we have watched the brilliant assaults upon the Roman citadel and the stubborn resistance of its defenders. To which party has victory inclined? which of the two shall ascend the Capitol in triumph? It would now appear to be established that the claim set up on behalf of Rome that the art of Christianity was chiefly formed in Italy can hardly be maintained; and that from the second half of the third century to the sack by Alaric she was but one among several centres of an essentially Hellenistic art. Few who have endeavoured to enter into the spirit of pagan Rome will deny to her art at its best a power and individuality which may not always charm, but is irresistibly impressive. We may not accept in its entirety Wickhoff's theory of a Roman ascendency, reaching its zenith in the third century,[2] yet while the fortunes of the Empire were at their highest there did exist an imperial Roman style, distinct from the Hellenistic art which had called it into being. This Roman art has the august qualities of Roman law; it may be cold, and in detail uninspiring; it may be a *Soldatenkunst*, too military to be often free or graceful; but the co-ordination of the whole is itself akin to a work of creative genius. The constituents and motives are unoriginal; but a fabric has been erected distinct from any other structure; the spirit of a logical and masterful race has passed into it and given it individual life. In a sense, even the

---

[1] The phrase is, of course, suggested by Strzygowski's now well-known book *Orient oder Rom*, in which the claims of the East were brilliantly upheld.

[2] Franz Wickhoff, *Die Wiener Genesis*, 1895; E. Strong, *Roman Art*.

finest Roman art owed everything to the aid of other peoples; but no other people could have produced it.   Almost all the elements are foreign; they can be detached and analysed, but the result is Roman and nothing else.   We think of Virgil borrowing here from Homer, there from the Alexandrine authors, from Greek fable and from Latin legend, and from these most diverse sources constructing his national and Roman epic. While Rome was still the world's head, expressing her will to a score of obedient provinces, she imposed her art with her law; it was the outward symbol by which her dominion was asserted.   But the very close-ness of its connexion with imperial administrative power lent it an official

Fig. 4. Capitals and architrave in the Church of SS. Sergius and Bacchus at Constantinople
(now the mosque Kutchuk Ayia Sophia). (Sébah and Joaillier.)

taint which prevented it from winning the hearts of strangers ; it belonged too closely to the mechanism of government to stand alone when the machinery ceased to move.   It was too political to be popular with other peoples, and it had an effective life of less than three centuries.   An art of this kind, so sumptuous, so short-lived, so intimately dependent upon a system of government, could no longer lead when Rome herself was once dethroned : as soon as decadence set in, the underlying Hellenistic elements came to the surface, and with them in all the provinces those indigenous features by which the latest phases of Hellenic art had been corrupted. Such an art bore no longer the authentic signature of Rome.   The political decline of the city began before the third century closed ; even in the life-time of Diocletian she was no longer the sole seat of empire.   When

Christianity became a recognized and official religion, the speed of the decline was inevitably hastened. The public life of Rome was so bound up with pagan tradition that it was almost impossible to control a Christianized empire from such a centre. Constantine cut the Gordian knot, broke with tradition, and founded a new city where religious conservatism should place no further impediments in his way. He took with him many of the wealthiest families; he carried off great numbers of skilled craftsmen. The corporations of artisans remaining in Rome were weakened:[1] they declined with the waning patronage upon which they were dependent, though the city remained wealthy even after the exodus to Constantinople.[2] Rome, uneasy and discontented, would not renounce her pagan sympathies; but throughout the higher orders of society there was a sense that the glory was departing. Other cities, Milan and Ravenna, became the capitals of the West: Rome, superseded and disillusioned, was little minded to express her mood by artistic creation. Beautiful things were still made within her walls down to the close of the fourth century, but imitative things instinct with a Greek and not a Roman spirit. With the disasters of the fifth century, the workshops were closed and the artists fled; there was a sequence of catastrophes for which intervening periods of revival could never wholly compensate. In A. D. 410 Alaric took Rome; nearly fifty years later she was sacked by Gaiseric. New buildings were still erected in this century, and old monuments restored, but the work was now done from without rather than from within. Rome accepted alms, and lived on the patronage of absentee emperors or their families. Much was done for her by Galla-Placidia, and the eastern sentiment which dominated the art of Ravenna made itself felt in the work for which Ravenna paid. Thus the mother of many provinces became provincial. She bowed before barbarian rulers; and Theodoric, the noblest among them, imposed upon her the half-Syrian art of his capital upon the Adriatic. There followed the ruin of the Gothic wars, plague, famine, flood, disaster upon disaster, destroying the old opulent life, scattering the last wealthy families, and leaving the city of Romulus to begin a new existence in poverty and destitution. The men who helped her most in the task were the orientals who, in the preceding century, had firmly established themselves within her walls. All the culture and art of the fallen city was now Eastern, and remained so for two hundred years (see p. 78).

If the question 'Orient or Rome' only implies that the elements of Roman Christian art were not indigenous to Italian soil, if it only assumes that for their due development a continued foreign influence was necessary, the answer must be given in favour of the East with its army of Greeks, Syrians, and other peoples acting as interpreters of oriental ideas (pp. 77, 87). Where the Early Christian art of Rome is picturesque it is Alexandrian;

---

[1] For the influence of these corporations see Dr. A. L. Frothingham's *Monuments of Christian Rome*, 1908.

[2] A great proportion of the Roman sarcophagi are of the fourth century; the fact is in itself a proof of wealth, as these sculptured marbles must always have been costly.

where it is monumental, it is so not in the Augustan or the Flavian spirit, but rather in that of Hither Asia or of Egypt. In literature and art the Romans had always been a receptive people; it is inherently improbable that in the hour of their decline they should have reversed those habits of assimilation which had made them what they were. The researches of recent years in Anatolia, in Syria, and Egypt have enabled us to adjust

Fig. 5.   Portrait of Justinian I, in S. Apollinare Nuovo, Ravenna.   (Ricci.)

more nicely the balance between the East and Rome. The Eastern scale sinks lower with the growth of knowledge; when Mesopotamia has been explored it must sink lower yet.

A second question concerns New Rome, which also had to reckon with the Eastern provinces. We do not know what lies beneath the soil of Constantinople; as at Antioch and Alexandria, many disasters have conspired to conceal the evidence which we seek. But it seems improbable that the decline of Old Rome as a centre of the arts should

have entailed the immediate succession of Constantinople. If there was
a transference from one city to the other, it was a transference of artistic
patronage, the new capital enlisting in its service craftsmen from all
accessible centres of culture. It may fairly be urged that the credit of
the work created by such men must be ascribed in the first instance to
the regions in which they were trained. Only an eclectic art could have
arisen in the Constantinople of the fourth century, and eclectic arts
seldom lead to great developments. For a long time the disadvantages
of Byzantium were hardly less than those of the Italian city. She too
was an emporium and clearing-house for the world's ideas; for many
years she could not acquire the character and individuality which belong
to a capital of ancient standing. Deprived by circumstance of the slow
and ordered growth upon which a national sentiment depends, she had
to form her character out of the various elements composing her motley
population. Greeks of Asia Minor and Alexandria, Syrians, Jews, Armenians, Persians, immigrant artists from the Roman guilds, all entered
her service and persuaded her to different ends; in the distraction of their
counsels she lacked what each group among them severally possessed,
a clear consciousness of purpose and direction. The art of the Asiatic
Greek and Syrian was established upon old foundations; it had behind
it for base-lands Mesopotamia and Iran, rich with the inherited traditions
of many ages. The Eastern provinces knew themselves, and expressed
their ideals in their own style and language. But Constantinople had
no established pre-existing culture to resist or to control the influx of
exotic forces: she had first to balance and assimilate new influences,
a task which required at least a hundred years. It was thus a natural
consequence that long after the new foundation neither of the two world-
capitals enjoyed an undisputed hegemony in the arts. There was an
interregnum of indeterminate length during which the leadership was
held by the great provincial cities alone qualified to exercise it. Suppose
a Venice, suddenly enriched and without individual tradition, opening her
gates not to one or two foreign artists, but to a host, a *colluvies pictorum*,
from any quarter where a vigorous art flourished, and you have some
parallel to the position of Constantinople in the fourth century. As the
art of her early years would be essentially a foreign art, in like manner
the earliest art of Christian Byzantium was foreign. It remains to determine
at what period the state of pupilage was ended. Though the most
complete and characteristic expression of Byzantine art is hardly found
before the Macedonian revival, yet by Justinian's reign the capital had
attained a full self-consciousness; it had assumed to itself a directive
power; and this epoch has been justly described as the First Golden Age
of Byzantine Art. It has been remarked that in literature the fourth
century witnessed the first signs of a spirit distinct from that of antiquity
(p. 5); probably the change from classic to Christian forms was later
in development, but the brilliant reign of Theodosius may well have been

distinguished by an art of no less enterprise. The ravages of time have left a material too small to form the basis of a final judgement; but the fifth century is represented by a building (the Church of St. John of the Studium), in which new elements are boldly treated, and it seems reasonable to assume in other branches the simultaneous growth of a truly metropolitan art. It must however be remembered that until the Arab conquests had robbed the Empire of its Eastern provinces this art did not stand alone; it was not the unchallenged representative of East-Christian art as a whole. While Syria and Egypt and Northern Mesopotamia were still Christian countries they did not intermit their active rivalry.[1]

It would thus appear that in the earlier centuries of our era the Eastern provinces occupied a privileged position due to geographical and other advantages briefly discussed below (p. 46). A few of these advantages which are of a more general character may be indicated in the present place. Before the rise of Rome they had gained much by the ethnical and political conditions resulting from the reforms of Alexander the Great and his successors. The happy effects of a conciliatory policy continued when the Hellenistic states became the inheritance of the Roman Empire; the year of division in A.D. 476 found them more homogeneous and more contented than the Western provinces. Taxation was less harshly imposed and aroused less fierce resentment. In parts of Gaul the population welcomed the barbarian invader, preferring to stake all upon the possibility of better usage than longer to endure the fiscal tyranny of the past; but at the conclusion of one of the Persian wars, certain cities on the frontier which had been ceded to the Persian made passionate appeal against the treaty, imploring the Emperor not to abandon them to a foreign allegiance. The two episodes are instructive by their contrast: the stability, the contentment which favour artistic growth are wholly upon the side of the East.

The Eastern provinces contained the cradle of the Christian religion. From the time of the Invention of the Cross and the dedication of the seven sites in the Holy Land the influence of Syria-Palestine upon Christian art and iconography became signally important. The memorial churches erected by Constantine at the Holy Places were the lodestars of Christian pilgrimage; all that wealth and power could bestow was lavished upon their decoration. The best architects, sculptors, and workers in mosaic were summoned to Jerusalem and Bethlehem; their highest efforts were exerted to make the least among the cities of Judah more venerable than

---

[1] Opinions as to the rôle of Constantinople before the sixth century have considerably varied. Strzygowski, who formerly (*Byz. Denkmäler*, ii, p. 207) ascribed to her a creative influence in the Theodosian age, has more recently deposed her to the position of a secondary centre hardly more influential than Rome (*Denkschriften der k. Akad. der Wissenschaften*, iii, pp. 88-9. Vienna, 1906). Most scholars would probably concede a primacy to Constantinople in the reign of Justinian; some would make the metropolis the centre of a new imperial art analogous to that which Wickhoff ascribed to Rome three centuries earlier. (See especially A. Heisenberg, *Grabeskirche und Apostelkirche*, vol. ii, concluding chapter. Leipsic, 1908.)

the capitals of the world. The greater work of these years has mostly perished. But almost contemporary products of minor arts still exist to furnish a clue to its character and to prove that its inspiration was derived less from Rome and Constantinople than from Egypt, Syria, or from Mesopotamian Persia : such objects as the metal ampullae at Monza, the enamelled cross from the treasure of the Sancta Sanctorum in the Vatican, and certain ivory carvings, survive to prove the quarters from which inspiration flowed. The rich ornament of animals and foliage

in which the Syrian took delight, the oriental treatment of reliefs in which gradation of planes is abandoned in favour of contrasting light and shadow, all these things came out of Asia, and were eagerly adopted in the West. The bearded oriental type of Christ is but the most conspicuous of the iconographic forms which the world inherited from the Christian East during these centuries ; the solemn monumental attitudes, the formal groupings of the figures in larger compositions, were borrowed from the same source : the Persian costumes rich with pearls and stiff embroideries came into the Byzantine world through her provinces of the East.

Fig. 6.   Bronze steelyard-weight in the British Museum, perhaps representing the Emperor Phocas.

Yet another cause increased the influence of these favoured provinces. When the power of Rome declined, in all the distant regions subjected to her rule there was a revival of native sentiment in revolt against an imposed and alien art. Everywhere the signs of this recrudescence are apparent; from Gaul to Egypt there is a reassertion of indigenous taste. We need not underrate the significance of this movement within the actual limits of the Christian East, but we must not fail to notice its influence in Western Europe. The decorative art of the barbaric tribes who had overrun the Roman Empire was based upon the same principles as that of Syria and Egypt : they were oriental principles. As will be seen below, this community of feeling was of much service to the spread of Christian art among these peoples; but the most active disseminators of that art were orientalizing Greeks and Syrians (see pp. 23-7).

All these points speak strongly in favour of the paramount place of the Eastern provinces in the first period of Byzantine art. It seems probable that as evidence accumulates and excavations are extended, the tentative decisions in their favour will only be confirmed. For the moment we must remember that, owing to the comparatively small number of monuments yet investigated, much is still a matter of anticipation. Anticipations, in the Baconian sense, are not without their dangers: 'for the winning of assent they are more powerful than interpretations, ... they straightway touch the understanding and fill the imagination.' In the present case they have been valuable aids to discovery. But while Alexandria, Antioch, Seleucia, Nisibis, and many other important sites remain unexplored, a certain moderation is imposed even upon the most enthusiastic of pioneers.

II. *The Iconoclastic Period*, A. D. 726-842.

Brief as its duration was, this epoch is of great importance to Byzantine art.[1] It is commonly included with the preceding period; but as in many ways it marked a new departure, it is desirable to give it prominence by assigning to it a more independent position.

The immediate cause of the iconoclastic movement was a general revulsion of feeling against the superstitious reverence for pictures, precipitated by the success of the Arab arms. The Mohammedan, who abjured ikons, had been triumphantly victorious; the men who had been driven back before him now anxiously inquired whether the nature of the victor's faith had contributed to his triumph, and whether the abuses of their own had contributed to their humiliating defeat. The question was the more easily answered since in many parts of the East the ancient hostility to the representation of sacred persons had continued down to the sixth century, more especially in Syria, and the influence of the austere Paulicians had further strengthened the forces now aroused against the 'slaves of images'. The Syrian adversaries of ikons doubtless proclaimed the loss of their country to Christianity a judgement against an impious practice; and as iconoclast emperors were themselves connected with Syria, the opposition to images could hardly fail to issue in energetic action.

Political causes reinforced those of an ethical and religious character. The growth of monastic influence and the increase of ecclesiastical wealth had begun to constitute a positive danger to the State. At a time when the Empire needed all its manhood, thousands of men in the prime of life were attracted within the charmed circle of the monastery walls. The

---

[1] The present view of the artistic significance attaching to this period is that recently expressed by Diehl (*Manuel*, ch. X, pp. 334 ff.). For the general effects of the period upon the Empire the reader may consult the papers by M. Louis Bréhier in the *Revue des cours et conférences*, &c., noticed in *B. Z.* x. 696 ; xiii. 533 ; xiv. 353.

waste of power from this single cause might of itself have determined rulers concerned for the political future to encourage a movement which bade fair to strike a blow at monasticism. The imperial connexion with iconoclasm began with the edict of Leo III in A. D. 726. Constantine V proceeded to extremes, and it was in this reign that the greatest destruction of 'images' took place; mosaics were torn down, frescoes defaced, pictures and manuscripts burned. This violence was followed by a short reaction: for a while the Empress Irene restored the cult of images. But under later emperors, especially Leo the Armenian and Theophilus, the campaign of destruction was renewed. On the death of the last emperor his widow Theodora once more restored the cult, which from this time forward remained the usage of the Eastern Church.[1]

Fig. 7.   The Emperor enthroned, with guards : part of the Consular diptych of the 5th–6th century in the Cathedral of Halberstadt.   (From *Archaeologia*.)   P. 197.

It may at first sight appear strange that a movement to outward seeming so largely negative should have exerted a lasting influence on the course of Byzantine art. But iconoclasm had its positive side; there is a sense in which it may be called constructive. It must not be confounded with a puritanical hatred of all forms of art: its fury was directed against religious art of a specific kind, and of all that lay beyond this it was widely tolerant. It was far from causing a general artistic stagnation. Damming a single stream, but opening a wider channel for many others, it maintained a wholesome movement of the waters. Its violence is to be deplored; its vandalism impoverished not only the centuries in which it was exercised but those in which we ourselves are living. But it had its stimulating and creative side upon which it is necessary to insist.

This positive influence of iconoclasm upon art was of a twofold nature : it caused a return to Hellenistic models, especially those of Alexandria ; it aroused a frank enthusiasm for the purely oriental decoration which the

[1] Diehl, *Manuel*, pp. 339 ff.

victorious Arabs were now adopting from Persia. The Hellenistic revival was principally concerned with the human figure and with the genre subject; the oriental importation consisted of conventional designs; in each case the models attained a wide popularity and testify to the abounding activity of the age. The new constructions of Theophilus at the sacred palace were enriched with mosaics in which trees, animals, and other motives were displayed upon a gold ground; there were frescoes similar in composition; there were revetments of coloured marbles. It has been well remarked that all this found its parallel in the palaces of Bagdad, where Harun al Rashid amazed all Western envoys by the splendour of his habitations. For a while in the Byzantine Empire religious subjects were relegated to the background; the first place was occupied by a purely secular and official art.

The greater work of this period is almost all lost: the portrait-medallions in St. Demetrius at Salonica, the apse-mosaic of Sta Sophia in the same place, and that of St. Irene in Constantinople may fall within its limits, but they tell us less of the spirit of those times than the productions of the minor arts. The group of ivory caskets with motives from the chase, from war, but above all from classical mythology, probably had its origin in an epoch when scenes of this kind were purposely substituted for sacred subjects; in them the Hellenistic style of Alexandria, never quite forgotten, returned once more to popular favour. The older examples, such as the Veroli casket in South Kensington (p. 215), may well be of the ninth century. Two diptych-leaves now in the Bargello at Florence and the Museum at Vienna appear to represent an empress of this time. They are in the style neither of the sixth or any earlier century, nor of the third period which began with Basil the Macedonian; they seem therefore of necessity to fall within the intervening years of iconoclasm. In manuscripts the influence of the new movement is very marked. Books of science with illustrations drawn from Hellenistic models are conspicuous. Volumes of the Fathers are illustrated from their secular or classical allusions rather than from their theological content. It has been conjectured with much probability by Kondakoff that the zoomorphic initials and rich foliate ornament which flourished in the succeeding period were introduced at this time from oriental sources. Among the illuminators, monks in the monasteries, especially the great monastery of Studium, the resistance to iconoclasm breathed a new spirit into religious art. Psalters with marginal illustrations, intended to appeal to the people, and rich both in symbolical and topical motives, became the vehicles of the monastic thought and policy. Hatred of iconoclastic principle, a fierce determination to secure the triumph of ancient custom, inspired in the monkish artists a creative energy which astonishes by its vigour and the scope of its invention. In this varied illustration there is little of classical serenity, but much life and character. Like the official art of the palace, the art of the monasteries was the better for the hard forces which drove it into new paths of development. Diehl has well summarized the effects of this short but stormy period:—

It was to the time of the iconoclasts that the Second Gold Age owed its essential characters. . . . From the iconoclastic epoch proceed the two opposed tendencies which mark the Macedonian era. If at that time there flourished an imperial art inspired by classical tradition with a developed interest in portraiture and real life, imposing upon religious art the influence of its dominated ideas; if in opposition to this official and secular art there existed a monastic art more severe, more theological, more wedded to tradition; if from the interaction of the two there issued a long series of masterpieces, it is in the period of iconoclasm that the seeds of this splendid harvest were sown. Not merely for its actual achievement but for its influence upon the future, this period deserves particular attention among those which compose the history of Byzantine art.

Of the indirect influence exerted by iconoclasm on the art of Europe by driving Byzantine craftsmen into exile something is said in the section devoted to Italy.

III. *The Macedonian and Comnenian Periods.*

The three centuries from the accession of the Macedonian dynasty to the sack of Constantinople in A.D. 1204 were as brilliant and prolific as any period in the history of Byzantine art. Under the Macedonian and Comnenian rulers the Empire was powerful and prosperous; commerce flourished; industries developed; wealth was widely distributed. As the epoch of Justinian has been described as the First Golden Age of Byzantine Art, so the name of the Second Golden Age has been suggested for this period, especially for the earlier half of it, when the spirit of revival and a renewed consciousness of strength encouraged activity in all departments of life. It will be seen from the examples considered in the later part of this book that every branch of art was now illustrated by important works, and that the repute of Byzantium was raised to a height never previously excelled. In mosaics, in architecture, in painting, in almost all the minor arts, the period was one of prolonged and distinguished achievement.

The tendencies which had arisen under iconoclasm were now developed to their logical conclusion. The secular 'imperial' art patronized by the court received unprecedented opportunities of expansion. The buildings of Basil I and of the Comnenian princes were sumptuously adorned with mosaics and frescoes, in which the historical element was conspicuous (p. 261); both in these and in the miniatures of the manuscripts painted for the several emperors imperial portraits are frequent. The representation of exploits in the history of various princes, with their necessary introduction of contemporary persons and costumes, involved a further advance upon the path of realism. New varieties of feature diverging from the conventional classical types appear with increasing frequency. At the same time the study of

Hellenistic art of which iconoclasm had been a determinant cause was steadily maintained; Greek models were never more prized or more sedulously copied. In the mosaic picture or the miniature, in the ivory

Fig. 8.   Diptych of the Consul Boethius (A.D. 487): Museum of Brescia.   (Alinari.)   P. 197.

carving and the fine enamel, the gestures and attitudes are constantly reminiscent of the fourth century: the folds of the drapery have the dignity and grace of Hellenic inspiration. In the same way the decorative style of the non-Christian East retained the place which it had won; in illuminated ornament, in the figured textiles, it established for itself a definitive and permanent position.

What is true of the secular field is equally true of religious art, which was subjected to similar influences. The same tendency to realism, to the representation of observed facts and features, is reflected in the work of ecclesiastical artists. Secular motives derived from the antique, allegorical figures, personifications and the like, are seen on every hand ; antique gestures, antique draperies, were continually reproduced. The religious art of this time shared both the imitative and the original tendencies of the secular ; for a time it indulged an almost equal freedom, and the tenth century is marked by the growth of a new iconography, in which, side by side with inherited subjects, fresh compositions are not infrequent. Such was the striking motive of the *Anastasis* ; such the solemn Last Judgement ; such the Death of the Virgin, with its dignified and impressive harmony of line. But as the period advances the monastic

FIG. 9.   Side of the ivory casket from the Cathedral of Veroli (ninth-tenth century) in the Victoria and Albert Museum.   P. 215.

influence which had been the principal factor in the defeat of iconoclasm asserted its superior strength. In the eleventh century we already mark a decline in the feeling for the antique ; natural freedom gives place to formalism ; the theological intention becomes more obviously the end for which the work is undertaken. The expression of dogma, not the realization of beauty, is made the first preoccupation of the artist. The elaborate iconographical system according to which the later Byzantine churches were decorated belongs to this period, and each subject within the great symbolic whole contributed to a general scheme of edification.

The Second Golden Age was without doubt an age of copyists and imitators ; in this, representative art followed in the steps of literature. The writers of this age sought inspiration in every branch of ancient literature, not excepting satire upon the model of Lucian. The names of Bryennios, Cinnamos, Nicetas Akominatos, Anna Comnena, lend lustre to a period of praiseworthy activity. But it is as it were a lunar lustre, borrowed from without and not resulting from an inward fire. A similar weakness often impresses us as we study much of the art produced in this period ; it is finished and careful ; it may be of supreme technical perfection; yet it is without the fire of creative genius. But the East was a more valuable ally to art than to letters; it communicated its sense for colour by means of which much that would else be cold and academic is clothed with a splendour of life, compelling admiration even when the forms are poor and the compositions ineffectual. There are no passages in the poetry or the history of the Byzantine Empire which seize and hold the imagination like parts of the mosaics of Daphni or of Cefalù.

The tendency towards routine was partly checked by the absolute necessity for invention. New subjects for which ancient models did not exist now demanded illustration. Menologia, homilies, hymns in honour of the Virgin, required fresh compositions; there was continual scope for original design. The many-sided life of the capital, the eventful fortunes of a wide empire, could not but awaken the interest of the draughtsman and the painter, before whose eyes there passed a procession of the most varied types of humanity. The encouragement to observation thus afforded tended at least in part to counteract the indolent acquiescence which followed the habit of slavish copying. Men strove to rejuvenate as they reproduced; to impart into the scenes which they depicted something of actuality from the stirring world around them.

IV. *Period of the Palaeologi.*

No period of Byzantine art has been more generally misunderstood than that which lies between the restoration at the close of the thirteenth century and the fall of the Empire in A.D. 1453. Until recent years, it was customary to regard the whole epoch as one of almost continuous decadence, in which all the art which survived was lifeless, gloomy, and hieratic, all figures emaciated, all colours sombre and depressed. If at any time during these two hundred years a work was produced which, like the mosaics of Kahrié Djami at Constantinople, plainly contradicted the prevailing theory, its redeeming qualities were ascribed to some hypothetical influence from Italy; they could not by any possibility be indigenous; they could only have been created under the influence of the Italian followers of Giotto. In a word, nothing good could come out of Byzantium; if good there was, it must have been introduced from without.

Recent research has fundamentally modified these views.[1] It has been discovered that the examples of a really admirable art are not isolated exceptions to be easily explained away, but members of a sequence, appearing in more than one region, and everywhere betraying the same qualities. What Constantinople began with the mosaics of Kahrié Djami

---

[1] M. Gabriel Millet, to whom we owe the publication of the churches at Mistra, has described the characteristics of this period with sympathy and penetration, in the chapters on Byzantine art contributed by him to André Michel's *Histoire de l'Art depuis les premiers temps chrétiens*, vol. iii, pp. 941 ff.

was continued in the Morea with the frescoes of Mistra (p. 293), and in Macedonia and Servia by those of Nerez and other places (p. 296); the series closes upon Mount Athos, where the name of Manuel Panselinos is associated with the last phase of a memorable revival. For memorable it may fairly be called when we contrast the resources and opportunities of this period with those of the preceding epoch. Then all the commerce of the East flowed into the Byzantine state; the treasures of the emperors were richer than those of Solomon. The splendid objects of which we read in the pages of Constantine Porphyrogenitus might seem the creations of a fairy story had we not the confirmatory evidence of the crusaders, who piled precious reliquaries and vessels of gold and silver into heaps and divided a booty unparalleled in the history of spoliation. Then the churches and the palaces were adorned with the costliest inlaid marbles and mosaics; carved ivories and sumptuous enamels abounded; whether for the honour

Fɪɢ. 10.   Panel from the ivory casket from the Cathedral of Veroli in the Victoria and Albert Museum.   Ninth century.   P. 215.

of the church or for the luxury of their own homes, men shrank from no expense of gold or labour; they were the citizens of the richest city of the world. It might fairly seem to one who compares the spacious Macedonian and Comnenian times with the straitened epoch of the Palaeologi, that there could be no effective rivalry between the art of the two periods; that the impoverished and despoiled empire, its commerce gone and its prestige diminished, could achieve nothing more than delay the victorious advance of the Turkish armies. Yet strange as it seems a rivalry in fact exists; and if the creations of this latest Byzantine phase do not displace the great work of the earlier epoch, they are not unworthy to stand very near them. If the later artists had worked in the same costly materials, it might be hard indeed to award the palm of merit. They had to adopt the economical medium of fresco and, except at Kahrié Djami, did not know the glow and mystery of mosaic. They seem to have made few ivories and enamels, substances of intrinsic value were less frequently at their disposal. But they worked in a great style, new and distinctive of their time.

If the question is considered more closely, the rise of a brilliant art in these lean and unfavoured years is less anomalous than might at first sight appear. Constantinople was still a great centre of religious and intellectual activity; down to the fifteenth century she was still the greatest centre in the world. In teaching and research she still excelled all other cities. The way for humanism was prepared by her scholars, who before carrying their knowledge into the West must surely have derived full advantage from it themselves. The intellectual and artistic activity of Byzantium in the thirteenth century was remarkable for a city which had known the experience of an alien domination. Is it conceivable that the Eastern artists who had long been teaching the painters and mosaic workers of Italy (see pp. 81, 263) should in the very next century be stricken with such a paralysis that they were unable to execute any considerable work without Italian aid? Did the great city which yet fermented with ideas so absolutely need the foreign leaven? At the first glance a vague similarity between the late Byzantine work and that of the Tuscan schools might tempt us seriously to consider the theory of an Italian influence. But matured reflection will probably correct this premature conclusion. Similarity there may be; but the cause lies less in the dependence of one art upon the other than in the development of both along parallel lines. The whole of Europe, both East and West, was stirred at this time by the breath of new ideas: the resulting movements were not confined to either region alone. There is no need for us to deny the original merit of the first Tuscan schools; they early broke free from pupilage and rapidly produced a native Italian art. But at present there is more evidence of influence exerted from Constantinople westward than of influence exerted in the contrary direction. And Constantinople began to move first. If, moreover, we examine compositions in detail, we find in subjects common to East and West features of striking originality which the Italians neither devised nor followed. Such, to take a single example, is the treatment of the Virgin in the Annunciation at Kahrié Djami. This agitated form, expressive of a nervous and emotional personality, is no less different from the placid Virgins of an Angelico or a Filippo Lippi than from those of the earlier Byzantine art. It is a new and independent creation.

There is a second hypothesis with regard to the sources from which the art of this period was influenced; that, namely, which insists upon its frequent relation to ancient Syrian models. There can be no doubt that Syrian influence persisted late in Byzantine art, and that in the case of Kahrié Djami the cycle of the Virgin is based upon early writings of Syrian origin. Strzygowski and others have rightly pointed to this relation, establishing the probability that the Syrian models continued to be copied as late as the fifteenth century. But convincing as it may be in regard to individual monuments, the criticism hardly affects the independence of late Byzantine art as a whole. As Diehl has urged, such a theory does not explain the real brilliance of execution, the remarkable skill and feeling, which are manifest in so many compositions of the time. It does not explain such original features as the Annunciation to which we have already referred—a scene alien in sentiment to earlier Syrian or monastic art. Upon the whole it is preferable to adopt the theory of Millet that in many cases where Syrian influence survives so late the motives have been modified in their passage through Constantinople.

Side by side with this living art expressing all that was best in this latest period, there naturally existed an art of ikon-makers to which the old criticisms may fairly be applied. In this there is indeed much of the hieratic spirit; there are present many of the unlovely features which our predecessors described by the term Byzantine, the elongated forms, the grim faces, the stern ascetic character. But we do not look to

Fig. 11. Side of the ivory casket of the eleventh century in the Cathedral of Troyes. (From an electrotype.) P. 231.

this art to represent Byzantine achievement in the fourteenth century. For a fair embodiment of contemporary ideals at their highest, we turn rather to the living pictorial art of which we have made mention—the art of Constantinople, of Servia, of the Morea. It is by the creations of this art that the epoch must be judged, by this that it is saved from the unmerited reproach of earlier criticism. It was not the classic Byzantine age ; that name belongs rather to the tenth and eleventh centuries, when a fine austerity of sentiment was embodied in forms of almost Hellenic dignity. It was more quickly responsive to changed conditions, more emotional, less reticent in feeling. While it was more devoted to ritual, it was also more sensitive to the fascination of ordinary life, adding to the older iconography those little touches of reality which lend to the sacred scene the interest of human things. For these reasons its study is no less essential to the comprehension of Byzantine art as a whole than that of any earlier period.

It has become a truism to say that Byzantine art sprang from the union of the oriental with the Hellenistic spirit.   Like Poros and Penia in Plato's myth of the youth of Love, the two parents exercised an opposing influence, each attracting the child in turn, the one by the grace of measure and restraint, the other by the brilliance of an exuberant nature.   Such conditions of life were little favourable to a homogeneous development.   Yet they brought about a compromise most profitable to the world at large, enabling an art still rich in Greek tradition to expand with the growth of the Christian religion, and so fulfil a wider destiny than might otherwise have fallen to its lot.   It was the remarkable fortune of Hellenism in its decadence to be associated with two great proselytizing creeds, Christianity and Buddhism, neither of which possessed, though both equally required, an art capable of rendering the human figure.   The latest phase of Hellenistic art was still sufficiently Greek to perform the service thus demanded, already sufficiently orientalized to have lost the old exclusiveness.   Hellenism in its decay expanded its sphere of action both in Asia and in Europe, whereas in the years of its prime it had made little headway either north of the Alps or east of the Taurus.   Under the Achaemenian dynasty of Persia, Hellenic art had indeed penetrated to Susa and Persepolis. But it had remained a superficial fashion; it did not change the spirit by which Persian art was informed.   The unshaken philosophy and religion of Iran had always imposed their ancient types and forms upon the foreign artist, who was powerless to divert the deep and steady stream of old tradition.   The circumstances were changed after Alexander's expedition had opened a wider road into the heart of Asia.   About the beginning of our era, Buddhism, rapidly spreading through the continent, felt the need of an art which could lend attractive expression to its legend.   It found what it sought in Syria and Anatolia, and thus Hellenistic art came to exert an influence far into Central Asia, while that of Scopas and Praxiteles had no such distant range.   Had it not been for the existence in China of a greater figure-art, Hellenistic influence might have achieved even more than this: it might have trained the representative art of China and Japan.   But in Turkestan it met and was defeated by an art of ancient lineage and greater vitality, truly Asian, and already in the full strength of its maturity.   Even the advantage of its alliance with the Buddhist faith could not bring it victory against so powerful an adversary.

Just as Hellenistic art penetrated inmost Asia as the ally of Buddhism, so it made its way into the Europe of the barbarian conquerors in the train of Christian missionaries.   It obtained unchallenged entry into Italy, Gaul, and Spain because it served the religion which the Goth, the Lombard, and the Frank had adopted as their own.   Had there been no barbarian conversions, had the gods of Valhalla prevailed against the Gospel, the growth of a worthy representative art in Europe might have been long delayed.   For here all effective figure-art was in the hands of Christians, as in the East it was controlled by Buddhists; it was the orientalizing Greek art of the Gentiles to whom St. Paul delivered his message; and it finally succeeded, where Greece and Rome had failed, because it served a successful missionary Church, while classical art had no such fortune. At the time of the barbarian invasions, this association of late Hellenistic

FIG. 12.   Carved ivory panel of the twelfth century in the Museum of Ravenna.   (Ricci.)

art with a living spiritual force was a momentous fact for the future civilization of the European continent.   For here were being established the peoples of the future, the barbarians whose fathers had never under-stood Hellas, the men who were to lay the foundations of our mediaeval communities.   They had the youthful vigour; they had the political instinct which was one day to consolidate great states; they had national sagas and poetic traditions; but in art they had not advanced beyond a decorative and conventional use of animal forms.   The Celts whom they had driven before them were equally devoid of the power to represent the human figure and thus appeal to the deeper emotions.   If these peoples were to rise to greater expression, it could only be by the help of a teacher possessed of the Greek tradition in however decadent a form; but to the Greek tradition these lovers of conventional design were all instinctively opposed.   There was but one way in which it could be made acceptable in their sight, and that was by its partnership with a spiritual force compelling their moral assent; without this union of ethical and aesthetic influences they would never have accepted it at all.   And though in course of time they might have evolved a figure-art of their own, unaided by suggestion from without, the process would have been infinitely slow, the failures more numerous and more disheartening.   The great needs of the Western world were now an art of Greek derivation, but less inimitable than that of Hellas, and a more austere morality than that of fallen Rome.   Eastern Christianity supplied this twofold need, and hastened by several centuries the artistic enlightenment of the West.   Without this timely aid in the early mediaeval centuries, the West of Europe might have developed on more purely oriental lines.   For the aesthetic ideas of the barbaric West were at this time so essentially akin to those of the Nearer East, that but for some such intervention European art might have remained enslaved to animal ornament and conventional design.   They were so fundamentally Eastern that the teacher from the East was less purely oriental in spirit than those whom he came to instruct in so far as the culture which he represented was in part Hellenic.   Through their maintenance of Greek tradition, in however debased a form, East-Christian artists could appeal to the religious emotions by representation of the human face and form; they could depict the Gospel scenes and represent the action and features of sacred persons. But the peoples of Western Europe were still in a stage of artistic development in which human suffering or joy found no adequate representation in art.   Even the gifted Celtic tribes, with their imaginative symbolism and their fine decorative sense, were helpless in the delineation of the human figure.   They could satisfy the eye with intricate combinations of line, but they had no equal message for the soul of man; they could not stir the deeps of universal human feeling.   Though long ago their fathers had borrowed and transformed ornamental motives from Greece, the higher achievements of the Hellenes were beyond their powers of imitation.   If this is true of the Celts, it is more obviously true of the rougher Teutons, with their Asiatic jewellery, their designs of dismembered monsters and interlacing animals.   This relationship of barbaric Europe with Asia was a natural result of circumstances.   At the beginning of the Dark Ages, Europe had an ornamental art, one in principle with that of the Nearer East. For Northern Europe was in direct contact with the art of Persia at the time when the Goths were settled on the Black Sea; and long before the coming of the Goths, the steppes had formed a channel of communication between the two continents by which ideas and artistic motives flowed from one into the other. Through this great northern zone a long line of tribes maintained an unbroken contact; in aesthetic feeling Europe and Asia were one. Decorative pattern was the ideal of both, and neither could assimilate from the storehouse of ancient art anything beyond its fantastic monsters or here and there some feature of its floral ornament.

Fig. 13.   The Entry into Jerusalem : ivory panel of the eleventh century in the British Museum.

It was only when the barbarians had adopted a religion to which the presentation of the human figure was essential, that such an art had any chance of prospering among them. In the fourth and fifth centuries no other force than Christianity could have exerted this influence, and the most active pioneers of the new faith were then Christians of the Eastern provinces. The Christian East, half Hellenic half oriental, laid the foundations of the structure which in a later century Charlemagne was destined to erect.

To recapitulate the foregoing paragraphs. Before the fall of the Roman Empire in the West, Europe was overrun by barbarians whose artistic ideas were akin to those prevailing in the Nearer East. They loved pattern and contrasted colour; they could not represent the human figure. Neither in West nor the Nearer East was there any seed or principle out of which a great figure-art could arise. The only hope lay in the Byzantine Empire, which through the Hellenized cities of the Eastern provinces and the half-Syrian city of Ravenna transmitted to the barbaric world motives and methods of composition, debased, indeed, and without originality, yet still in the true line of descent from Greek antiquity. In after years the Byzantine Empire continued its educative work. It consistently taught a respect for fine craftsmanship and the virtues of discipline and restraint. At the close of the tenth century its models were imitated by the handicraftsmen of the Rhine; its ivories and miniatures inspired the sculptors of the Romanesque period (pp. 119, 236); under the Comnenian dynasty it assisted the growth of Italian painting. After the sack of A.D. 1204 the spoils of Constantinople provided many a model for the French or German craftsman and stimulated the development of the minor arts. But as impressions of early youth are the most indelible, so the lessons which Europe learned from the Empire of Justinian had perhaps a deeper influence than any others. Europe was not alone in the advantage of this intercourse. The art of Islam from the beginning derived from the Christian provinces of the East much that was essential to its growth.

It is necessary to insist upon the indestructible influence of Hellenism, because the activity of recent research in the rich treasure-chambers of the East has somewhat tended to obscure it.[1] We sometimes forget that there was no gap or breach between pagan and Christian art; we speak as if the new faith had made immediate revolution among old forms. This was not the case; iconography was changed, but the Christian figure received the pose and gesture of the pagan god, philosopher, or muse. It is perfectly true that almost from the first the East exerted an irresistible charm, inspiring the Greek with its luxuriant taste in ornament, love of colour, its feeling for the solemn and the supernatural in monumental or commemorative art. The spirit of Byzantium is often more oriental than Greek. But the Hellenic element was never overwhelmed, its power was constantly reasserted. As the metaphysics of Christian theology remained Greek, for all the embroideries of Eastern fancy, in like manner no opulence of oriental ornament or colour can conceal the Hellenism at the core and centre of Christian art. That art was inevitably and by the conditions of its birth of a dual nature; to forget this is a heresy no less vain than those of monophysite or monothelite in the history of Christian dogma. Whatever we may therefore think as to their relative importance in different regions and at different periods, we must mete equal measure to both strains alike; the very obscurity of our imperfect

---

[1] It is the merit of Ainaloff to have insisted upon the Greek element at the foundations of Byzantine art in his valuable and suggestive work *The Hellenistic Origins of Byzantine Art*, St. Petersburg, 1900 (Russian).

knowledge should prevent prejudice against either. There was an old story that the Court of the Areopagus decided its cases in darkness, in order that no distracting influences might pervert the course of justice. The imperfection of our knowledge, perforce condemning us to a like obscurity, should encourage us to maintain the same dispassionate mood.

If such were the conditions under which East-Christian art developed, what was the distinctive character of its maturity? What are its defects and what its merits? What is its position among the other great arts of the world?

If we begin with its defects, we may say that it often became un-

emulous and self-centred; it lacked the fire and fury of creative ideas; it was so conservative that sometimes its revivals seem little more than retrospects. It was too subservient to prescription, and too constantly preoccupied by the didactic purpose. It was limited in its scope by the early abandonment of greater sculpture. It was apt to be unobservant, copying and recopying old designs with too little thought of nature. It depends too much upon an atmosphere and an environment. Its virtues are in part the qualities of these defects. It is admirable in technique, jealous for the repute of a fine tradition in craftsmanship. It preserves seemliness; it does not tolerate the harsh, the vulgar, or the eccentric. In the earlier centuries it gave evidence of a genius for assimilating and developing foreign ideas almost equal to a power of original creation; adapting after wise experiment the ancient inventions of the East, it perfected the architecture upon which its claim to absolute greatness is so largely based. In later centuries it applied

Fig. 14. Leaf of an ivory triptych of the twelfth century: St. John the Baptist and an episcopal saint. (British Museum.)

the same genius to the renovation and development of its own more ancient work. Reserved and circumscribed in other ways, it was grand and opulent in colour: even in its severest hours it contrived so to blend austerity with splendour that as a decorative system it holds a unique place in history.

Gibbon, in a well-known passage, exposes one of the causes which weakened the fibre of the East-Roman Empire. 'Alone in the universe,' he says, 'the self-satisfied pride of the Greeks was not disturbed by foreign merit; and it is no wonder that they fainted in the race, since they had neither competitors to urge their speed, nor judges to crown their victory.' If this criticism is to be applied not to political but to artistic life, it must be considerably modified; but it will be found to contain indisputable

elements of truth. In the Middle Ages, Western Europe held Constantinople a place possessed, as it were by divine right, of acknowledged
pre-eminence in the arts. The city suffered from this subtle flattery;
the consciousness of old prerogative blinded her to the need for enterprise. She condescended to the West; and all the while the West
was rising to higher fortunes than her own. The result of this attitude
is a certain high tranquillity of mood; until the latest period there
is little that surprises or disconcerts; if there is movement, we know
in advance the lines which it will follow. The revolutions which have
affected the history of the arts in the West were impossible for Byzantium.
She witnessed no such change as that from the grim and monster-loving
art of Italy in the eleventh century to the human art which succeeded

FIG. 15.　Ruins and capitals of the sixth century at El Khargeh, Egypt.

the teaching of St. Francis. She knew no such revulsion as that which
changed the character of English literature when the exuberance of the
seventeenth century passed into the restraint of the 'Augustan' age.
The feuds of classic and romantic never reached her ears; no disputes
of realist and impressionist disturbed the still atmosphere which she
breathed in her seclusion. Only in the last centuries of her existence
did she fully awaken to the possibilities of naturalism in art. But it
was then too late for her to gather in the harvest. The kingdom was
departing: the Turk was already at the gates.

　　The most striking exceptions to these conservative tendencies are to be
sought in the enfranchised art of iconoclasm, in the 'imperial' art of the
Macedonian revival, and in those episodes and phases of common life
which, especially in MSS., enrich the scheme of illustration. In these
expressions of the secular spirit the Hellenistic model is often paraphrased
in accordance with a new conception; aspects of common life, seized by

a genuine power of observation, enliven the dullness of old tradition. In our day the secular side is regarded as the least part of Byzantine art—perhaps it was always so—and though it has suffered a disproportionate loss compared

FIG. 16.   Sculpture on a sixth-century ambo in the Cathedral of Ravenna.   (Ricci.)

with the side which was dedicated to religion, it may well be that at no time was it represented by such numerous examples. As with the mediaeval art of the West down to the fourteenth century, as with Buddhist art at all periods, it was an art made tongue-tied by authority. The third period was still young when the chilling influence of prescription began to spread in the work alike of the greater and the minor artist; before that period

closed, it had become a power to which resistance was but rarely offered.
The Gospels and other books which had in earlier times been illustrated
with a certain richness of invention were gradually restricted to a stereo-
typed scheme of miniatures from which the life and vigour of the past have
all departed. It could not be otherwise when the subjects and the manner
of treating them were indicated in advance; the artist was never wholly
free to recompose or introduce a fundamental change. Under the conditions prevailing in the Eastern Church the genius of a Giotto or a
Masaccio would hardly have reached maturity. The Byzantine Greeks
regarded painting as a sacred art (p. 248), and it sometimes impresses us as

if it were indeed a ritual
exercise. It is true that
the Italians of the thir-
teenth and fourteenth
centuries adhered to
types of composition
which were hardly less
monotonous. But they
grew discontented with
the limits of their science
and technique ; they ex-
perimented with per-
spective, with effects of
light and shade, and
with spatial relations;
until at the close of the
fifteenth century they
were able entirely to re-
construct the traditional
religious subjects. Per-
haps if the Turk had
stayed his hand the By-
zantine painters might
have moved in a similar

Fig. 17. Part of an ambo of the fifth century from
Salonika, now at Constantinople. Cf. Fig. 84. (*Hautes Études* :
G. Millet.) P. 145.

direction ; the mosaics and frescoes to which we have already alluded seem to
indicate no less. But without the stimulus of close contact with the West
the movement might have slackened and lost significance for Europe as
a whole.   The retarding influence of orthodox prescription would perhaps
have hindered progress until the West had long ago discovered all there
was to know. How strong that influence was becomes clear to us
when we study the religious art of Eastern Christianity as it became
after the fall of Constantinople, spiritless, submissive to encroachment,
unquickened by the personal hope, lost to the saving graces of imagination.
Despite its frequent inclination towards realism, Byzantine art as
a whole lived too much indoors for rapid improvement in theory or

practice; it was too incurious, too indifferent to the study of nature and the human model: it grew short-sighted by poring over copies and cartoons instead of seeking familiarity with life and growth. While the contemporary art of China and Japan was searching for the harmony between nature and the soul of man, and developing a landscape of supreme quality, the Byzantine schools were handing down their copies of old Hellenistic conventions, trees of strangest vegetation, plants of no species, and dark prism-shaped mountains unrecognized in nature (p. 244). It is remarkable that while both in the Far East and in the Byzantine Empire monastic artists formed a high proportion of the whole, the oriental monk divined the central secrets of the natural world in its relation to mankind, while the Christians are almost children in comparison. The love of animals, trees, and flowers was perhaps more vital to Buddhism than to Christianity, and this may partially explain the difference. Yet, even if we make this concession, there remains a superiority on the oriental side almost humiliating to the European for the first time confronted with the great landscape art of the Sung dynasty in China.

Like other eclectic systems, Byzantine art had few enthusiasms; were it not for the glow of its colour it would often fail in its appeal. It was not quickened and inflamed by a national ideal of beauty; its force was dissipated in the expression of serious generalities. It never passed through an archaic stage, or ripened to excellence through suffering and disillusion. At the beginning it was too richly endowed to strive; like the Church which it served, it lost no less than it gained by the gifts of Constantine. It is a commonplace that a comfortable inheritance will often stifle genius, and the art of Eastern Christianity had never to work for the means of existence. Its constituents were brought to it as it were already fashioned; the forms which we see were not moulded in the fury of the creative hour; they are without the signature of the individual character.

Like much Western mediaeval art, the art of the Christian East depends constantly upon the support of its original surroundings. The Olympian gods were dethroned before the dawn of our era, but even under a grey northern sky a fine Greek statue or vase will compel to instant admiration: such things have an absolute inevitable beauty independent of creed or fashion. It is not quite the same with Byzantine movable works of art. They may be admired for their colour, for their sumptuous effect, for particular technical qualities, but not for the supreme harmony, the rhythm, the perfection of form which alone command a universal homage. Even the greater work, which cannot be transported, may owe more than we think to instinctive religious sympathy and historical interest; it gains by the dim light of the sanctuary; it does not always bear the searching light of day. It may seem superfluous to judge Byzantine art by the Hellenic standard; but this must be done if its place among the great arts of the world is to be fairly estimated; to aim lower would be to pay an equivocal compliment, and to assume it an art unworthy to be measured by the highest canons we possess.

The position of Byzantium in the general history of the arts in some ways resembles that of scholasticism among the philosophies. We find the same peculiar strength, the same undeniable weakness. There is the same dependence upon Greek forms at second hand, in both there is the austere reserve which does not court approval. But there are also the noble qualities which earned for Aquinas his title of angelic doctor. By virtue of the Hellenic and oriental elements of which it is composed, the art of

FIG. 18.   Limestone capital of the fifth century in the Cairo Museum.
(*Catalogue général : Koptische Kunst*, No. 7345.)

the Christian East is a great religious and a great decorative art. As decoration it is often of an unrivalled majesty ; as interpretation of human and inanimate nature it was too imitative to attain supreme success. Its forms do indeed evoke and quicken the sense of life, but it is a life elect and spiritual, and not the tumultuous flow of human existence. They are without the solidity of organisms which rejoice or suffer; they seem to need no sun and cast no shadow, emerging mysteriously from some radiance of their own. Byzantine art is unsurpassed as the interpreter of a common faith; but by its very elevation it evades the warmth of human passion. For when it would depict the life of real, breathing, sinful beings, its academic proficiencies often play it false ; its traditional shapes will not live and move as sincerity would have them. The artists of the Christian East regarded their art as a means rather than as an end in itself, sharing in this the feeling of their contemporaries of the Western Middle Ages; but since theirs was a Church more exacting in its control than that of Rome, a Church altogether hostile to monumental sculpture, they lacked the opportunities afforded by the development of the plastic sense. The free play of the intellect was too constantly excluded from their life; how superfluous to think out problems, when all was happily defined by narrow, if not immutable, precepts! In this fidelity to sacro-

Fig. 19.   Capital of the fifth century, Mosque of Eski-Djouma, Salonika.
(*Hautes Études*: G. Millet.)

sanct tradition Byzantine art is not without analogy to that of ancient Egypt. It had infinite decorative charm, but it grew languid for want of living ideas; it too readily abandoned initiative, to live content in 'the narrow proficiency of perpetual iteration'.[1]

We have dwelled upon the deficiencies of Byzantine art because the reaction against the old injustice has provoked a counter-reaction, and there are many who neutralize the good results attained by using a language of unqualified eulogy. By this insistence upon its weaknesses, are we insensibly reverting to the injustice of Voltaire? Are we taking our stand on the side of those who see in Byzantine art nothing more than a grandiose hieroglyphic system, differing in degree, but not in kind, from

[1] The phrase is that of a writer in the *Edinburgh Review* who criticizes Egyptian civilization upon the lines indicated above (No. 430, October, 1909, pp. 400 ff.).

that of ancient Mexico? To do so would be to ignore qualities which might redeem more serious defects. If the art of the Christian East is lacking in freshness and enthusiasm, it is spared solecisms and 'uncertainties of inspiration'. The restraint of an ever-present law may impoverish imagination, but it forbids rhetoric, and lends to the artistic language the stately grandeur of a liturgy. The mean and trivial accidents of life do not intrude into the sphere of these high abstractions; the vulgar and the foolish thing does not come nigh them; there is immunity from the dangers which beset unbalanced and impetuous natures. This art avoids false pathos, false unction, feeble sentiment. It is neither over-violent nor over-sweet; it has no place either for a Caravaggio or a Guido Reni. Perhaps it was after all a happy destiny which held the East-Christian art of the Middle Ages in a servitude so august and transcendental. Freed from the exalting attraction of the ideal type, it might never have risen above mediocrity. It is greatest, it is most itself, when it frankly renounces nature; its highest level is perhaps attained where, as in the best mosaic, a grave schematic treatment is imposed, where no illusion of receding distance, no preoccupation with anatomy, is suffered to distract the eye from the central mystery of the symbol. The figures that ennoble these walls often seem independent of earth; they owe much of their grandeur to their detachment. They exert a compelling and almost a magical power just because they stand upon the very line between that which lives and that which is abstracted. The constant repetition of designs and methods which have acquired a kind of sanctity or prescriptive right has another compensating advantage. It is in the art of the most conservative civilizations that the most refined and conscientious craftmanship is often found; what is true of dynastic Egypt is also true of the Macedonian and Comnenian dynasties of Byzantium. What does not Europe owe to the finished carvings in ivory, the delicate enamels, the admirable textiles, which travelled westward in the Middle Ages? Under what a debt do her illuminators and painters lie to the miniatures and panel paintings which held before their eyes the classical virtues of reticence and sobriety? The artistic influence of the Byzantine Empire is due in no small degree to those minor arts of which the very name has a certain depreciatory sense. Few peoples have done more than those composing that empire to correct the error thus implied. The effect of these lesser arts on the development of culture is often of a high significance; and as there is truth in the saying that the ballads of a nation may contain the key to its history, in like manner it might be maintained that from what remains of its minor arts it is possible to divine its achievement in the most diverse fields of action.

In two directions Byzantine art achieved no relative or qualified success, but the triumph of positive and acknowledged mastery: in the skilled use of colour, and in architectural construction; in both cases it owed much to the Eastern strain in its composition. There is little need to dilate upon the skill, the fine responsive feeling, with which these artists conceived and executed their schemes of colour; both in the major and the minor arts there survive documents sufficient to prove their perfect competence. In the flowing tones of a rich mosaic which seem to well up from infinite deeps the eye finds the same solace, the heart the same satisfaction, as in the canvases of Titian and Giorgione, those citizens of a half-Byzantine city.

But it is in architecture, the art with which this volume is not directly concerned, that Eastern Christianity finds its grandest expression; in

FIG. 20.   Capital of the sixth century : Cathedral of Parenzo.   (Alinari.)

architecture it attains to absolute greatness. The Byzantine architect perceived the majesty of great curves; he freed construction from the visible tyranny of mass. His domes were symbols of the overarching heaven in which Christ Pantokrator might fitly establish his throne. The eye follows the aerial lines with consummate satisfaction; they entrance by suggestions of infinity; they go forth and return upon their appointed course, until in the contemplation of their infallible perfection all sense of superincumbent mass is overcome. There is no dome which floats like that of Sta Sophia; it is poised rather than supported; the last thing of which the spectator thinks is the enormous thrust and pressure which for fifteen hundred years has urged upon the masonry below. The audacity of the conception is forgotten in the apparent ease of the achievement. The ideal of Byzantine construction was the close-knit organism sufficient to itself, bearing its own burden by the nice balance of counteracting forces. The churches stand lightly, rising in a natural grace ; they do not lean upon buttresses or painfully display the struggle and stress in which all buildings live. After the time of Anthemius and Isidore, there was no further attempt to construct upon so grand a scale as that of Justinian's great cathedral. Byzantine churches are usually of moderate proportions ; some, and those not the least beautiful, are very small indeed. But all have their majesty of curved line which seems to bear the soul away, and is congruous with the mood of still devotion.

The absolute greatness of Byzantine art will be affirmed or denied in proportion as the relationship of art to ethics is regarded as near or remote. The Emperor Marcus Aurelius expressed one truth when he said that everything which is beautiful is beautiful in itself and terminates in itself. But to the artists of the Middle Ages, whether in East or West, this was false doctrine. To them the individual was nothing, the immanent idea or *eidos* was both a type and an ensample. The form, the image, were but means and semblances created to exalt the soul to the contemplation of immortal things.[1] If the function of great art is to enhance the sense of life, the theory which sets ennoblement before all things will never lack defenders, because, after all, it is founded upon another truth no less essential than the first. In its theory Byzantine art is at one with our great mediaeval art ; in its practice, though upon different paths, it attains an equal level of achievement.

[1]   'Αλλὰ καὶ εἰκὼν
            ἐς νοερὴν ἀνάγει μνῆστιν ἐπουρανίων.
                    Nilus, *Anthology*, vol. i, p. 10, Leipzig, 1819.

CHAPTER II

In the foregoing chapter the attempt has been made to indicate in outline some of the more general characteristics of Byzantine art and to estimate the influence which it has exerted in the world. The purpose of the present chapter is to supply something in the nature of a geographical basis, and to illustrate the importance of the several areas; it may thus be regarded as complementary to the first. Since it must necessarily be restricted to the limits of a summary, only salient facts and features have been included; but the references to early or recent works of a more special application will enable all desirous of entering into further detail to obtain information from ampler and more authentic sources.

The imperial provinces and those regions of Asia with which they were most intimately connected have been placed first upon the list, those parts of Europe which lay beyond the Byzantine frontiers last; but the space allotted to the latter is equally extensive. Two reasons may be given for this apparently paradoxical treatment: the position of the Eastern provinces has been exhaustively discussed in comparatively recent works by Strzygowski and other writers; the influence of East-Christian art in Western Europe in the early centuries of the Middle Ages is an essential part of its greatness and cannot be too strongly emphasized.

The Balkan Peninsula ; Greece ; The Islands ; Russia.

In a sense, the Balkan peninsula was the hinterland of Constantinople, and as such was open to the influence of Byzantine art. The permanent occupation of great territories by half-civilized peoples might check this influence, but did not destroy it, because the conversion of the Bulgarians and the Servians to Christianity favoured the introduction of Byzantine culture.

Thrace, with its chief city, remained Byzantine almost from first to last. Salonica was always predominantly Greek. Though it suffered much in early centuries from the neighbourhood of barbaric tribes, its early churches, especially those dedicated to St. George and St. Demetrius, show that by the time of Justinian it must have been very rich in important monuments. Between the seventh and ninth centuries it was troubled by incursions of Slavs and Bulgars, only preserving itself by gifts which almost amounted to a tribute. During the iconoclastic dispute its clergy declared against the innovators, and as a principal centre of resistance it grew in ecclesiastical importance. In A.D. 886, 904, and 912 it was attacked by the Mohammedans, and in 1185 was sacked by the Normans of Sicily. In A.D. 1204 it passed under the authority of a Frankish ruler, but became once more Byzantine in A.D. 1328, falling at last to the Turks in the fifteenth century.

The significance of Mount Athos [1] for Christian art begins in the tenth century, when the earliest of the great monasteries were founded; from that time to the present day the cloister-covered headland has been the

FIG. 21.   Limestone niche of the sixth–seventh century in the Cairo Museum.
(*Catalogue général : Koptische Kunst*, No. 7300.)

Holy Mountain of the Christian East. The monks who sought its shelter and seclusion were natives of the most varied regions, coming from Servia, Georgia, and Russia, no less than from Greece and the Levant. Preserving traditions handed down from a very early period, they have often succeeded in lending to their frescoes and works of art a greater appearance of antiquity than they in fact possess. The artists were naturally in sympathy with the monastic art of Syria, Mesopotamia, and Egypt; and in MSS. of quite a late date the influence of Syrian prototypes is manifest. Little is now preserved of a date earlier than the fifteenth century, and most of the frescoes are later (p. 302). The art

---

[1] Brockhaus, *Die Kunst auf den Athos-Klöstern*; N. Kondakoff, *Monuments of Art on Mount Athos* (Russian), 1902.

of the Athonite monks is imitative and eclectic. No new school was founded in their midst; the promontory has always been a place of memories rather than the home of quickening ideas. One great name, that of the painter Manuel Panselinos, is associated with the Holy Mountain (p. 263).

BULGARIA AND SERVIA.

The Bulgarians, a people of Turco-Finnish stock, became Christian in the ninth century. From the close of that century down to about A.D. 930 they enjoyed a brief period of national glory, and their manners were refined by relations, peaceful and hostile, with the rulers of Constantinople. Their nobles were educated in the Greek capital; their famous Tsar Simeon, who exchanged the monk's for the soldier's habit, is said to have studied the works of Demosthenes and Aristotle. He defeated the Byzantine armies and besieged the Emperor Romanus in his capital, exacting from him terms of friendship and alliance.[1] But after his death Bulgaria declined, until the Emperor Basil II, surnamed the Slayer of the Bulgarians, broke its power and removed it from the number of independent states.[2]

The importance of Servia[3] to East-Christian art begins in the thirteenth and culminates in the following century. The Servians were a Slav people, allies of the Avars, who occupied Balkan territory in the seventh century, the Emperor Heraclius ceding them lands on condition that they acknowledged the suzerainty of Byzantium. In the time of the great Simeon (see above) Servia was dominated by the Bulgarians; it was not until the rise of the Nemanja dynasty at the close of the twelfth century that the country assumed an international position, and began to assimilate the culture of her eastern neighbours.

The third son of the first Nemanja prince, born in A.D. 1169, travelled in the Holy Land, and studied on Mount Athos as a monk under the name of Sava; there the Servian monastery of Chilandari was founded, becoming a channel through which the influence of East-Christian art penetrated into the Slavonic kingdom.[4] The first period of Servian art ended with Stephen Urosh II, Milutin (A.D. 1282–1321). During this period certain influences from the West (Dalmatia) are apparent.[5] The fourteenth century was the great Byzantine period. Milutin, the famed soldier and church builder, married a daughter of the Emperor Andronicus II; his son Stephen (A.D. 1321–31) followed in his steps and built the famous

---

[1] Gibbon, *Decline and Fall*, ch. lv. The chief Byzantine historians are Cedrenus and Zonaras.

[2] Vol. x of *Izviestiya* of Russ. Arch. Inst. of Cple., Sofia, 1905.

[3] Kondakoff, *Macedonia*; Miklosich Stojanović; Strzygowski, *Denkschriften* of the Vienna Academy, vol. lii (Phil.-hist. Classe), 1906, pp. 89 ff.

[4] G. Millet, *Recueil des inscriptions chrét. du Mont Athos*, i, has published inscriptions illustrating the relations between the Holy Mountain and Servia.

[5] Architectural ornament akin to Romanesque initials in the Miroslav Gospel (Facsimiles by L. Stojanović, 1907) influenced by Romanesque style.

monastery of Dečani. Under Stephen's son Dushan (A.D. 1331–55) Servia attained the summit of her power. This king took Macedonia in 1345, and conquered Thessaly, Epirus, Aetolia, and Acarnania, leaving to Byzantium only Thrace and Salonica. Decadence began on the death of this founder of Great Servia. His son Urosh (A.D. 1356–72) was unequal to the task imposed upon him. Under Lazarus (1372–89) and his son Stephen Lazarevič (1389–1427) the political centre was removed from Uskub and Macedonia to the region about the confluence of the two Moravas. The connexion with Constantinople was maintained by both rulers even though the second was actually a vassal of the Sultan. The close of the fifteenth century saw the final establishment of Turkish rule.

Fig. 22. Sandstone niche of the seventh century in the Cairo Museum.
(*Catalogue général*: *Koptische Kunst*, No. 7297.)

The Nemanja period is rich in monuments of Servo-Byzantine art. The church of Studenitsa shows Romanesque as well as Byzantine features. Gradats dates from A.D. 1314, in the reign of Milutin: another foundation of this king is Gratchanitsa, and in both Byzantine influence predominates. Ravanitsa dates from A.D. 1380; Kalenitsa and Manasseya from the late times of Stephen Lazarevič.

The most important artistic remains, apart from the buildings, are the frescoes and the MSS. The former follow Byzantine traditions and share the late Renaissance of the fourteenth century, to which the mosaics of Kahrié Djami and the wall paintings of Mistra in the Morea bear such conspicuous evidence (see p. 293).

In the MSS. similar tendencies are found; but here the influence of the monastic art of Mount Athos is also apparent (see above).

Strzygowski has argued that Servian art was affected by old Syro-

Mesopotamian traditions which never passed through Constantinople, but had been transmitted directly from the East to the Holy Mount.

GREECE AND THE ISLANDS.

Greece does not loom large in the history of the arts during the early Byzantine period. The country had always been discontented under Roman sway; in the days of Pericles it had been spoiled once and for ever for a subordinate destiny; the epigoni could not forget, and were embittered under the discipline of Rome. It was not with them as with the inhabitants of the Greek cities of Asia Minor and the East. These already learned under the Diadochi what it meant to have a master; when Rome came with a measure of communal liberty as an immediate gift and the enduring *pax Romana* in prospect, they accepted the new yoke without reluctance, and despite the exactions of provincial governors achieved a rapid prosperity. But the same yoke galled the necks of the Greeks in Hellas and filled them with a sullen despair. Independence was gone, economical prosperity was upon the wane. The Roman Empire controlled the most productive countries of the Western world; a land like Spain, rich in minerals, cattle, wool, and fish, could supply all needs at lower rates, and undersell the Greeks in their own markets. The world was no longer Hellenocentric; the people of Hellas, resentful and impoverished, kept aloof, and guarded the illusion of national importance. Athens was full of philosophers walking in the porch or the garden and attracting to their lectures students of many nations; she remained the inner citadel of intellectual paganism, tenaciously holding the last strongholds against Christianity. Here in the fifth century Artemis, Athene, and Asklepios still had their worshippers; yet to all but Athenian eyes the metropolis of a lost cause was growing obviously provincial; she depressed the stranger with a sense of vanity and desolation. Synesius of Cyrene, who visited the city in A. D. 416, found dilapidation everywhere, and perhaps recalled the remark of Apollonius of Tyana: 'I became provincial (ἐβαρβαρώθην) not by absence from Athens, but rather through making a sojourn within her walls.' But Athens was not suffered to defy the spirit of the age with impunity; the foundation of the university of Constantinople under Christian auspices dealt her a sensible blow and diverted the stream of students to the East. Her philosophers still professed, but they felt that the future was not with them; their cause was lost long before Justinian closed the schools of Athens. One of them, Leontius, gave an empress to Constantinople in the person of his daughter Athenais, who, under the new name of Eudocia, became the wife of Theodosius II.'

In a word, Greece was fatally loyal to her old traditions. Christianity made way slowly, and was at first almost confined to the walls of Corinth. The country was singularly free from wars and bloodshed, for though in A.D. 395 Alaric the Goth penetrated as far south as the Morea, his was but a temporary raid which brought no permanent exhaustion. Greece was ruined by poverty and old memories, not by armed oppression: the land of Pericles and Thucydides now neither made history nor wrote it. Progress was to come not from rhetoric or poetry but from the prose of a reviving commerce. After Justinian had introduced the culture of the silkworm into the empire (see Ch. X) Greece became a great centre of weaving, and her textiles were famous in Europe. The solid compensations of prosperity led men to forget that the city of Corinth, once famed in all the arts, now gave its name to currants. The silk industry flourished

Fig. 23.   Carved limestone frieze of the fourth–fifth century in the Cairo Museum.
(*Catalogue général : Koptische Kunst*, No. 7308.)

not only in Euboea but in Thebes and in the Morea; and when the Norman princes wished to establish silk manufacture in Sicily, it was to Greece that they sent for workmen. In the tenth and eleventh centuries numerous churches and monasteries were erected, many of graceful construction, and adorned with mosaics and frescoes of remarkable beauty: the monastery of Daphni in Attica and the great Church of St. Luke of Stiris in Phocis retain to this day much of their original splendour. Oriental features in architectural construction, and ornamental motives, both zoomorphic and alphabetic, show that at this period a strong Mohammedan (Perso-Mesopotamian) influence affected the art of Greece,[1] possibly initiated by migrant artists from Hither Asia who followed the Bulgarian armies. The Frankish occupation of the thirteenth century only partially

---

[1] A fragment of an Arabic inscription found on the Acropolis at Athens in 1888 suggests the actual presence of Mohammedans in the eleventh or twelfth century (Van Berchem and Strzygowski, *Amida, Beiträge zur Kunstgeschichte . . . von Nordmesopotamien*, p. 372).

interrupted the peaceful progress of art and industry.[1] Thebes continued to manufacture silk; Halmyros and Chalcis were busy emporia; the plains of Thessaly exported corn to Constantinople, the vineyards of Pteleon sent their wine. Monemvasia in the south furnished our own ancestors with the Malmsey to which mediaeval records refer so often. The close of the thirteenth century, which witnessed the fall of the Frankish principality of Achaia, saw the Byzantine Empire re-established in the Morea. Mistra, close to the site of the ancient Sparta, became the seat of a new and flourishing province, which waxed as Constantinople waned, and, but for the Turks, might have continued to prosper for centuries. Here lived Gemistios Plethon the Platonist, here members of the imperial family made their residence; and the churches, with their beautiful frescoes, all the work of the fourteenth and fifteenth centuries (see p. 293), are the most conspicuous examples of the last revival of Byzantine art (see above, p. 19). The fatal year A.D. 1460 put an end to Greek sovereignty in the Morea; and from that time till our own day the art which had done so much to redeem the failure of mediaeval Greece lay once more under eclipse. To the formation of East-Christian art Greece had contributed little or nothing: its last great phase might have been peculiarly her own had destiny spared her the miseries of Turkish misrule.

The Islands prospered during the imperial expansion of the middle period, and retained much of their importance after the Latin occupation. The Cyclades (Dodekanesos) by the thirteenth century had grown somewhat insecure through the prevalence of piracy, but they were still populous and important, lying as they did on the route from Constantinople to Italy.[2] Naxos, the Queen of the Cyclades, had a fortified castle at Apaliri; Chios had Nea Moni with its fine mosaics; on Andros was the Panachrantou monastery attributed to Nicephorus Phocas, and the small church of St. Michael at Messaria, dating from the time of Manuel I; Paros has its churches, of which detailed accounts have yet to be published. Cyprus was the seat of wealthy Greek communities in the sixth century: the discoveries of jewellery and silver plate in the island attest its prosperity at that time. Crete is very rich in Byzantine churches, mostly of the later centuries,[3] though one at least described by Mr. Fyffe, St. Titus at Gortyna,[4] dates from the first millennium. In the last centuries of the Byzantine Empire Greek painters of reputation were born in Crete (see p. 264).

RUSSIA AND THE CRIMEA.

The Greek cities of the Crimea had preserved late Hellenic civilization through Roman times, but had suffered the barbarian yoke under the Huns.

---

[1] See W. Miller, *The Latins in the Levant*, 1908, and *Journ. Hellenic St.* xxvii, p. 229; Sir Rennell Rodd, *The Princes of Achaia.*

[2] W. Miller, as above, p. 25. For the history of the Islands under the Franks, see ibid. ch. xvii and xviii.

[3] G. Gerola, *Monumenti Veneti nell' isola di Creta*, vol. ii, 1908. The churches are of the ordinary *Kreuzkuppel* type. [4] Theodore Fyffe, *Architectural Review*, Aug. 1907, pp. 60 ff.

They were brought within the influence of Byzantium by Justinian, who made the city of Bosphorus an imperial dependency.[1]   In the seventh century Cherson still preserved its old Greek traditions and municipal organization, a privilege granted by Diocletian and Constantine in return for aid against the peoples of the interior; it emerges from obscurity in the eighth century as the place which received and ejected Justinian II,[2] most intractable of imperial exiles.   The region is interesting as the home of the Tetraxite Goths, a remnant which remained behind when their countrymen moved westward, preserving their name and speech till after the fall of Constantinople.[3]   They had been converted to the Christian faith, presumably in the fourth century, and two centuries later petitioned Justinian for a bishop. Russian archaeologists have discovered remains of early Byzantine

Fig. 24.   Limestone frieze of the fourth–fifth century in the Museum at Cairo.
(*Catalogue général : Koptische Kunst*, No. 7302.)

churches,[4] and the Crimea possessed a mint at which copper coins were struck.

The real significance of Russia for Christian art does not begin until the conversion of the Russian princes to Christianity in the tenth century. When Kieff became a Christian city, artists from Constantinople were invited to decorate the walls of its churches with frescoes and mosaics; in the eleventh and twelfth centuries, the period between the introduction of the new faith and the Mongol invasions, the South of Russia was the home of many arts; and Russians had not only become skilled in mural decoration, but also in goldsmith's work and in enamelling. The Mongolians checked this peaceful development; the seat of government was transferred to northern centres more remote from the Black Sea and more

[1] Bury, *Hist.*, i. 470.   [2] Ibid. ii. 263.   [3] Bradley, *Goths*, p. 363.
[4] D. Ainaloff, *Monuments of the Christian Chersonese*, i ; Tolstoy and Kondakoff, *Russian Antiquities*, iv, St. Petersburg, 1891 ; A. L. Berthier de La Garde, in *Materials for Russian Archaeology*, xii, St. P., 1893 ; *Izviestiya* of the Imperial Arch. Commission, 1900, &c. ; *Compte rendu* of the same, 1888-1904 ; V. Latysheff, *Greek Inscriptions of the Christian Era*, St. P., 1896. (All Russian except the *Compte rendu*.)

amenable to European influence. The time when Kieff was the first city of Russia is the most interesting of all for the student of Byzantine culture; it is fortunate that enough remains of the period survive to permit some estimate of its achievement. It is an interesting fact that the influence of Armenia (p. 56) can be traced in Russian architecture; and it is probable that Armenians were active in introducing Christian art into the valley of the Dnieper. Since the sixteenth century Russian art has incorporated much that is Western and has attained a new individuality of its own. Yet amid all changes it bears upon it the unmistakable marks of its origin, and has preserved, with a certain barbaric grandeur, much of the Byzantine spirit. Like the mother art, it rejected the plastic

Fig. 25.   Limestone frieze with animals, sixth–seventh century, in the Cairo Museum.
(*Catalogue général: Koptische Kunst*, No. 7320.)

representation of the human figure upon a large scale, and its sculpture is chiefly confined to the ornamental carving of the non-Byzantine area. It owed much to Mount Athos, with which its relations have been long and continuous, one of the monasteries bearing the Russian name. The most remarkable monument of Byzantine art in Russia is the Cathedral of Kieff, which is adorned with mosaics and frescoes of the eleventh century.

THE EAST-CHRISTIAN WORLD

Anatolia.

Asia Minor has always been a country of ethnical and geographical contrasts. Her coasts and the valleys of her greater rivers have been accessible to maritime influences; on the other hand, her plateau has preserved primitive and indigenous traditions. Along the littoral and the chief water-ways Hellenistic culture was more strongly represented than in any other province; here were to be found in their purest form the latest manifestations of the Greek spirit. It was no small thing that in the region nearest to Constantinople, in the home-province of Byzantine civilization, the principles of Hellenism should have survived with less modification than elsewhere; it is a fact which helps us to understand the stubborn resistance of the Greek element in Byzantine art to the influence of the East. Great cities like Ephesus, Smyrna, and Miletus,. lesser cities like Sardis, Tralles, or Magnesia, were strongholds of Hellenism whose wealth and commercial importance enabled them to maintain a high position among the towns of the East-Roman Empire. The character of their population, their wide resources, the communications which they maintained with Asia and with other provinces, combined to maintain the prestige of Asia Minor as the first representative of late Greek civilization.[1] The cities upon the Euxine shore of Anatolia were in the earlier centuries under the influence of a Hellenic, in the later of a Byzantine Greek culture. There were Christian monuments in Trebizond before the sixth century; Sinope was a considerable port connecting the interior with Constantinople. Though Trebizond had already profited by the revival under the Macedonian dynasty, and some of her principal churches were built between this time and the occupation of Constantinople by the Latins, yet it was this latter event to which she owed her period of greatness. In A. D. 1204 Alexius Comnenus founded in this part of Asia Minor the Empire of which she was the capital; the abandonment in the same century of the route to the East by the Red Sea and Syria diverted the oriental trade to the Euxine and rapidly turned to her advantage. The Genoese and Venetians settled here; the revenues derived by the Comnenian emperors from this source enabled them to become the generous patrons of architects and painters until their prosperity waned and their dominion was overthrown in the second half of the fifteenth century.[2]

In the interior, upon the plateau, away from the moving currents of new ideas, the conditions of life were different. Here old customs and modes of thought, established before the coming of the Greeks, continued to pursue their ancient way indifferent to the various dominations which had in turn held rule over the peninsula. When in A. D. 133 Rome had become an Asiatic power, she did indeed extend her sway over that Anatolian plateau which neither Persian nor Macedonian had ever fully

---

[1] It should be unnecessary to refer the reader to Sir William Ramsay's various works on Asia Minor, the last, *The Thousand and One Churches*, written in collaboration with Miss Gertrude Bell. Among books and treatises in other languages, Strzygowski's *Kleinasien ein Neuland der Kunstgeschichte* has aroused widespread interest by its attractive statement of original views. In Diehl's review of the book in the *Journal des Savants*, 1904, pp. 239 ff., mention is made of the German, Austrian, and Russian work in Anatolia. Miss Bell's earlier work among the ruined churches is published in the *Revue archéologique*, where there is also an article by M. Millet (1905, Pt. I). The work of Dr. Hans Rott and others is mentioned in the chapter on Painting.

[2] Finlay, *History of Greece from its conquest by the Crusaders to its conquest by the Turks*, &c., and *Mediaeval Greece and Trebizond*; Fallmerayer, *Geschichte des Kaiserthums von Trapezunt*; G. Millet in *Bull. de Corr. hell.*, xix, 1895, pp. 419 ff. For the coins see references on p. 626.

controlled. But what anthropologists describe as 'regional temperament' was not to be suppressed even by the Roman legions : the deities to which the common people prayed were Asian gods, and the state religion was powerless to evict them. As in Syria and Egypt, the social and religious feeling of the indigenous population reacted powerfully upon art. The idealism of the Greek was less sympathetic to the Anatolian than the realistic manner which had marked the art of the ancient monarchies. The tendency to realism and to a severe monumental style characteristically Asian was here no less marked than in Syria, where the same Mesopotamian influences had penetrated. All the features which mark the monastic art of the Empire, the austerity, the theological preoccupation, the devotion to prescribed form, found here a congenial soil. Cappadocia

Fig. 26. Limestone frieze with mounted saint in the Cairo Museum, sixth–seventh century.
(*Catalogue général : Koptische Kunst*, No. 7284.)   P. 153.

is nearer in spirit to Mesopotamia and Syria than to the Hellenistic cities of the Mediterranean littoral.

The interaction of the oriental and Hellenic elements had nowhere more important results than in Asia Minor. For it was here that forms and methods of oriental architecture were modified with the most fruitful results to meet the needs of the Christian Church. In the art of skilful adaptation the Asiatic Greek was supreme; none so quick as he to accommodate existing features of a foreign art to new uses, combining and transforming by bold and practical experiment. He early perceived the advantages of the vaulted and domical system of construction, appreciating the superiority of buildings so erected over the old basilicas with their monotonous wooden roofs. It is probable that the invention of the pendentive, by means of which a dome may be placed above a rectangular ground-plan, was a Greek solution of an ancient difficulty.[1] The cruciform

---

[1] G. Millet, *Rev. arch.*, Jan. 1905, p. 102 ; G. L. Bell in *The Thousand and One Churches*, pp. 441 and 446.

plan, the two-towered façade, the vaulted basilica, all seem to have dominated in Anatolia.[1] The very use of burned, as opposed to sun-dried, brick may be due to the invention of the Greek builders.[2]

The Greeks of the Hellenistic cities of Asia Minor probably did more to preserve the decaying art of sculpture than any other people in the Byzantine Empire. The traditions of the period when Scopas and Praxiteles had worked on Anatolian soil, the later traditions of Pergamon and Rhodes, were not easily forgotten in the west of the country where the Greeks were in strength and oriental influences remote. The 'Sidamara group' of sarcophagi, visibly inspired by Greek art of the fourth century B.C. yet attracting by a striking originality, may have been produced in Asia Minor, though whether in north or south it is still

Fig. 27.   Limestone reliefs, fifth–sixth century, in the Cairo Museum.
(*Catalogue général : Koptische Kunst*, No. 7638.)

impossible to say (p. 130). The marble quarries of Proconnesos, which supplied the whole Mediterranean area with capitals of columns and closure slabs in the fifth and sixth centuries, may almost be regarded as belonging to the Anatolian province, though here there were numbers of workmen from Syria, Egypt, and other regions.[3] Various reliefs with figure subjects found in Asia Minor would seem to show that the art was widely distributed in this region (p. 153), though after the seventh century it sank into insignificance. From Anatolia the Buddhist sculptors of Gandhâra may have derived their models (p. 130).

The relationships of different schools of painting in the Eastern provinces during the earlier centuries of our era cannot yet be defined with certainty; the surviving material is too scanty; the extent to which the

---

[1] Strzygowski, *Kleinasien*; and article in O. Scheel's *Religion*, pp. 385, 393.

[2] Strzygowski, *Kleinasien*, p. 34. Burned brick, unknown to Vitruvius, was introduced into Rome before the time of Augustus.

[3] O. Wulff considers that the Sidamara sarcophagi may have been produced on Proconnesos (*Berlin Catalogue*, i, p. 15). The possible connexion of Anatolian sculptors with the Christian sarcophagi of Gaul and even of Rome raises interesting questions (p. 133).

different regions borrowed from each other is still too imperfectly known. But there seems reason to suppose that Asia Minor, which from the days of Asterius (see p. 260) had been reputed for her painters, possessed excellent illuminators in the sixth century; the Gospels of Rossano and Sinope are plausibly attributed to her workshops and themselves illustrate the intermingling of Asiatic and Hellenistic sentiment (Ch. VIII). Her advantage in enjoying four centuries of development after the conquest of Syria by the Arabs allowed her to develop the art of mural painting down to the beginning of the second millennium.[1]

Syria and Palestine.

This province was one of the most important regions which contributed to the development of East-Christian art; it connected the culture of Hither Asia and that of declining Hellenism by nearer and more numerous ties than any other part of the Byzantine Empire; it transplanted the mixed art resulting from the connexion to the most distant countries of the West. Syria may be said to lie between two continents; on the west, the Mediterranean keeps it in contact with Europe, while to the east it merges in the continent of Asia, to which it geographically belongs. From this situation the province derived the utmost advantage in the centuries preceding the Arab conquest of A. D. 634. Her people were then the most active traders of the time; they received by land the riches of Inner Asia by the great trade route debouching at Antioch, and from this port they distributed them through the Mediterranean with the products of their own art and industry; the effects of the relations thus established are discussed in the sections dealing with the countries of Western Europe (pp. 78, 87). With Alexandria, and through that city with Egypt, Antioch held uninterrupted communication, and so closely were mutual interests allied that in certain branches of art it is often impossible with certainty to distinguish the work of the one country from that of the other. Ivory carvings and other objects of the fifth and sixth centuries are still variously assigned by different scholars, and attributions remain to a large extent subjective. In both alike we find Hellenistic and Asiatic elements in process of amalgamation, we see the blending of the Greek and oriental spirit.

The chief centre of Hellenic influence in Syria was the great city upon the Orontes. Antioch, which in earlier times had enjoyed a dubious fame as a city of luxury and dissipation, retained to the last many of the characteristics which had rendered her name notorious. The pages of Livy, of Plutarch, of Polybius, of Posidonius of Apamea, reveal to us these Greeks and Hellenized Syrians as a people no less devoted to festivity and social pleasures than to the active business of life. In the time of Justinian, Antioch is described by Procopius as the first of the Roman cities in the

---

[1] The most extensive remains are in the rock-hewn churches of Cappadocia (see p. 267). But the constructed churches, now ruined and decayed, must once have been equally rich.

East.[1] Its situation on the northern slopes of Mount Silpius, its abundant supply of water, its genial climate, all contributed to make it a favourite place of residence. Its streets were broad and lined with splendid buildings ;

FIG. 28.   Limestone relief of the seventh–eighth century in the Cairo Museum.
(*Catalogue général : Koptische Kunst*, No. 8761.)

its theatre on the hill and its amphitheatre in the plain, its baths, and its forum were celebrated in the contemporary world. The suburb of Daphne, with its groves of laurel and cypress, its flowing waters, and its ancient

[1] For Antioch see Ottfried Müller, *Antiquitates Antiochenae* ; R. Förster, *Antiochia am Orontes*, in *Jahrbuch des k. deutsch. arch. Inst.*, xii, 1897, pp. 103 ff. ; Ch. Diehl, *Justinien*.

shrine of Apollo, was as famous as once the vale of Tempe in Greece. The intellectual and religious reputation of Antioch differed alike from that of Alexandria and that of Athens. While the former city early developed a fanatical and violent zeal, while the latter persevered in the paganism of a greater past, the Syrian city pursued a middle path, tolerating heathen ceremony, yet not forgetting that the disciples were first called Christians in Antioch. Temples were converted into churches, magnificent new structures were erected by successive emperors, the seat of a patriarch was established, but in the groves of Daphne there were still priests of the ancient faith and sacrifices were still offered to the pagan gods. The austere Julian might despise the home of dancers and musicians, St. John Chrysostom denounce her Babylonian follies; but Antioch, like the capitals

Fig. 29.   Limestone gable of the fourth–fifth century in the Cairo Museum.
(*Catalogue général: Koptische Kunst*, No. 7285.)   Pp. 152–3.

of modern Europe, had a serious side, and beneath a somewhat frivolous exterior she concealed an energy prolific in many fields of enterprise. Down to the invasion of Chosroes in A.D. 540 only the occasional misfortunes of earthquake or civic disturbance interrupted the course of her prosperity. Even after the first shock of war she enjoyed a respite of nearly a century, and during the whole early period she continued to exert an influence upon the peoples with which she was connected by her maritime trade. The ports of Egypt, Italy, and Gaul received her fleets. Her merchants and her monks were found on the banks of the Tiber, the Rhone, and the Rhine (p. 78). The Hellenism of Antioch was reinforced by intercourse with the Greek cities of Asia Minor. By maritime intercourse Ephesus and Miletus were kept in contact with the Syrian capital; the Cilician Gates secured free access to the province which originated the Stoic philosophy. In the interior, towards the East, were the hundred cities of Northern Syria and the Hauran, since the Arab conquest lying abandoned in their solitude, but before the rise of Islam enjoying a civilization in great part Greek.[1] Though the buildings of these regions were perhaps less important to the development of Byzantine architecture than those of Anatolia, they illustrate in the same way the effect of Hellenistic invention working upon material imported from the East. The problem as to their connexion with Romanesque architecture in Europe, raised by de Vogüé many years ago and again brought into prominence by Strzygowski, can here only receive a passing mention.[2]

Through relations of this kind and the character of her own population the Hellenic element in the art of Syria was necessarily powerful.[3] Antioch, with all its buildings and its greater works of art, has disappeared from the face of the earth, and we can only imagine the nature of its architecture, painting, and greater sculpture. But of the minor arts our knowledge is somewhat more extensive. Ivory carvings and the silver plate which with much probability may be attributed to Syrian workshops remain to show how strong the Greek tradition was between the fourth and seventh centuries (Ch. IV, IX). The influence of Syrian art which we find in the mosaics and sarcophagi of Ravenna and Naples permits us in some measure to surmise the nature of the lost originals. In surviving work from Syria, as from other provinces, we observe a swift degeneration of the Hellenistic types; in the treatment of the human figure, but above all in the changed conception of decorative design, we mark the encroachment of oriental ideas.

For Syria had the Orient at her gates, and that very part of it which from ancient times had been most active in the cultivation of the arts. We know something of Mesopotamia in Babylonian and Assyrian times; our knowledge of the district in the earlier Christian centuries is only now beginning, nor will it be adequate to our needs until excavations have been undertaken upon the sites of many cities which flourished at that time.

---

[1] The importance of these wonderful ruined cities was first realized after the publication of M. de Vogüé's book *La Syrie Centrale* in 1860–61. Since then they have been studied by Mr. H. C. Butler, a member of two American expeditions, in *American Archaeological Expedition to Syria*, Pt. II, *Architecture and other Arts*, New York, 1903, and *Princeton University Archaeological Expedition to Syria*, Pt. II, *Ancient Architecture in Syria*, Leiden, 1908. See also Choisy, *L'Art de bâtir chez les Byzantins*, p. 22, discussed by Diehl in *Journal des Savants*, 1904, p. 243, &c., and *En Méditerranée*, pp. 25 ff. Cf. also Uspensky's account in the *Izviestiya* of the Russian Archaeological Institute of Constantinople, vol. vii, 1902, and N. Kondakoff's *Archaeological Voyage to Syria and Palestine*, St. Petersburg, 1904—these two works in Russian.

[2] De Vogüé, *Syrie Centrale*, p. 18; Strzygowski, *Kleinasien*, B. Z., xiii, 1904, p. 293, and *Neues Jahrbuch für das klassische Altertum*, &c., xv, 1904, pp. 19–33. The theories of these writers are controverted by Rivoira, who, in his suggestive work *Lombardic Architecture : its origin and development* (English translation by G. McN. Rushforth, 1910), derives European mediaeval architecture from Italy, denying the priority of the East in almost all the inventions upon which Strzygowski bases his arguments. Rivoira appears to claim far too much for Italy; at the same time there is much in his main thesis which cannot be lightly set aside. Prof. Lethaby has made some valuable remarks on this subject, from which I transcribe the following : 'A distinction will, I am confident, have to be made between the spirit and the body, between the structural and ornamental elements of the newer style. Much that has been argued as to the non-Roman origin of Byzantine *building forms* will have to be given up, and a part of Rivoira's claims for Rome and Italy will have to be conceded, although he seems to exaggerate in making too much of the metropolis and the home country to the neglect of the Hellenistic cities of the East. There are two great difficulties in the way of any clear statement of Byzantine origins—the tendency to identify Rome the Empire with Rome the City, and the difficulty of separating the expressional content of the newer art from its structural means' (*The Church of the Nativity at Bethlehem*, p. 38, Byz. Research Fund, 1910).

[3] See further A. Baumstark, *Ostsyrisches Christentum und ostsyrischer Hellenismus* in *R. Q.*, 1908, pp. 16 ff.

Through Mesopotamia the art of Persia travelled into Syria, and by its contact profoundly modified Greek ornament, which it found in occupation (Ch. XIII). The Persians were the middlemen who traded with the Farther East; they introduced figured silk textiles into the Byzantine Empire (Ch. X); the neighbourhood of their western province, where in Ctesiphon and Seleucia Greeks and Persians had long lived side by side, was in every way significant for the growth of Christian art. In the substitution of an ornament based upon conceptions alien to those of Greece or Rome and clearly inspired from oriental sources, Syria took an active and important part.[1] The carved lintels and doorways of her ruined cities afford sufficient evidence of her work in this direction; the façade of the palace of Mshatta beyond her eastern frontiers (Ch. XIII) proves the transmission of Perso-Mesopotamian motives far to the south before the seventh century; many sarcophagi at Ravenna attest a Syrian influence in which Hellenism did not participate. The modification of classical ornament was among the

FIG. 30.   Part of a limestone frieze, sixth–seventh century, in the Cairo Museum.
(*Catalogue général: Koptische Kunst*, No. 7340.)

most important effects of Syrian artistic activity, for the models which left her shores found their way to the Adriatic and even further to the west, while the style which she was most instrumental in disseminating was copied in the barbaric kingdoms in the earlier centuries of the Middle Ages. Not only in her carved reliefs, but in the ornament of her early illuminated books, her influence on decorative design was constant and far-reaching (Ch. VIII).

Her influence was no less important in the more general sphere of religious sentiment; an atmosphere of Semitic gravity enveloped the monastic life, subduing the freedom of Greek fancy. The Orient imposed its notion of commemorative art; the love of ceremony, the conscious awe of the superhuman, impart to the figures representing sacred scenes and persons a new aspect of remoteness, half fascinating, half forbidding. With these tendencies was joined an inclination towards a simple realism in detail indispensable to an art which found its chief audience among the people. The illuminated MSS. handed down many compositions for sacred

---

[1] See the works by De Vogüé and H. Crosby Butler already cited, and Diehl, *Manuel*, pp. 24, 37.

scenes which remained almost unaltered as late as the fifteenth century;
the popular illustration of the Psalter has been ascribed to the monastic
illuminators of Syria. The manuscripts of the sixth century were copied in
distant countries and down to latest periods; the type of the Etchmiadzin
Gospel, providing models to Frankish illuminators (Ch. VIII), and the Servian
Psalter at Munich, preserving early Syrian features in the fifteenth century,
attest the zeal with which such books were studied. Even the monumental
art of the last Byzantine period is similarly dependent; the Syrian
inspiration is seen in the narrative mosaics of Kahrié Djami at Constantinople. In this way this provincial art remained a power long after the
country where it flourished had been absorbed into the territory of
Islam. In the sixth century,
not long before its loss to
the empire, it stood at the
height of its vigour and
fertility.

In Palestine [1] the conditions affecting Christian art
differed in many respects
from those which obtained
in Syria. Commerce was less
active, the settled Hellenic
element less powerful. But
the Invention of the Cross
in the fourth century and
the erection of the memorial
churches by Constantine and
Helen transformed the Holy
Land into a great artistic

FIG. 31.   Carved limestone, sixth–seventh century,
in the Cairo Museum.   (*Catalogue général: Koptische Kunst*,
No. 7369.)

centre. Churches were enriched with mosaics and paintings of the highest
order; the most familiar motives were reproduced by the minor arts for the
benefit of returning pilgrims. The demand for mementoes, to which the
steady flow of pilgrims soon gave rise, led to the establishment of workshops where such objects as the metal ampullae now at Monza were
manufactured. It is to be supposed that more costly souvenirs, such as
the enamelled cross of the Sancta Sanctorum (Ch. VIII), produced for the
wealthier visitor, were also made upon the spot; and from the fourth to
the seventh century Jerusalem was probably a considerable centre for
many of the minor arts. In all likelihood the workmen were for the most
part foreigners, attracted to the Holy City by the favourable prospects
which she offered. The artists and artificers who worked for Constantine
were of various races; perhaps a majority were Asiatic Greeks and
Syrians, others came from Constantinople. In process of time craftsmen

---

[1] Kondakoff, *Archaeological Journey to Syria and Palestine*, 1904, and *Journal of the Imp. Russ.
Palestine Soc.*, 1892, pp. 144 ff.

from Armenia and Persia were added to the colony of strangers ; the city of David became a cosmopolitan emporium where people of all races and languages were gathered together.

Under Mohammedan rule the same state of things must have continued. When the conquerors required mosaics for their buildings, they turned to 'Greeks', who by this time had in great measure assimilated the decorative teaching of Persia and Mesopotamia. The ornament of the Dome of the Rock and of the Mosque of El Aksa at Jerusalem betrays these oriental affinities (Ch. VII). It is related that the Caliph Walid, desiring to transform into a mosque the Church of St. John at Damascus and to adorn it with mosaics, applied to the Byzantine emperor, who furnished him with workmen. Beyond the borders of the Holy Land, in the desert palace of an Ommiad prince, we find, as late as the ninth century, frescoes in which the spirit of Hellenistic art survives (p. 278). Under the Latin dynasty of Jerusalem immigrant artists were again employed, as in the case of the Church of the Nativity at Bethlehem.

If we seek the real influence of Judaea upon Christian art, we shall find it more manifest in iconography than in any other direction. The spirit of Judaism was a religious rather than an artistic spirit ; such designs as can be called indigenous—for example, those on the limestone ossuaries of the early centuries of our era—appear to be allied to the family of motives described by M. Courajod as the *grammaire orientale* (cf. Ch. XIII), and are consequently common to Hither Asia rather than peculiar to a single region. A bearded type of Christ is thought to have been disseminated from Palestine, though it may have originated in Persia. But to this and to the grave style demanded by the Semitic temperament the strictly Jewish influence on early Christian art appears to be confined. The Hebrews imposed a mood on art ; they did not enrich it with new forms. The types and subjects which spread far and wide from Palestine through the agency of pilgrims were probably the work of resident aliens and not of the Jewish people.

ARMENIA.[1]

The history of Armenia and Georgia is of great importance to the study of East-Christian art, for this mountainous territory was permeated by Mesopotamian, Syrian, and Iranian influences, assimilating the culture of the regions on its southern and eastern borders, and ultimately returning or transmitting artistic forms enriched by indigenous features. In Achaemenian times Armenia had shared the old Persian religion, and at a later date her history was bound up with that of Parthia and Rome. Christianity, introduced at an earlier period, became the official religion under Tiridates in the fourth century ; but for the next two hundred years

---

[1] Strzygowski has collected the facts bearing upon the artistic history of Armenia in *Byz. Denkm.* v. 81 ff. See also Diehl, *Manuel*, pp. 315 ff. and 441 ff. For Armenian architecture the reader may consult Lynch, *Armenia*, London, 1901 ; Grimm, *Monuments of Byzantine Architecture in Georgia and Armenia*, St. Petersburg, 1901 ; N. Kondakoff and A. Tolstoy, *Russian Antiquities*, vol. iv, St. Petersburg, 1891, from which Diehl gives illustrations.

Christian influence preponderated only in the west; towards the eastern border Persian influence prevailed. The advantage of the Sassanians in this quarter was inherited by the rulers of Mohammedan Iran; for even during the period of Armenian independence (A. D. 859–1045) Persian motives, especially ornamental designs, continued to be absorbed into Armenian art. The early religious influence of Syria had been firmly establishing Syrian iconographic types; down to the end of the sixth

FIG. 32.   Carved wooden chest, about A. D. 600, in the Cairo Museum.
(*Catalogue général: Koptische Kunst*, No. 7211.)

century the Armenian Church had recognized the patriarch of Antioch and her bishops were of Syrian origin. Early Syrian miniatures still preserved in the country show us the nature of the models which the Armenians had to copy (see Ch. VIII), and in all that concerned the representation of the human form they were the pupils of Syro-Hellenic masters. It is worthy of mention that Daniel, the *marmorarius* of Theodoric, is thought to have been an Armenian (p. 141).

The relationship between Armenian and Byzantine art of the Macedonian period presents problems of considerable interest. The study of Armenian architecture shows that as early as the seventh century the Armenians had begun to modify the modes of construction adopted in the Christian East, adding new features of their own. In the third Byzantine period we find them still retaining features proper to the first, and developing a remarkable originality in the conception and execution of their designs. The existence of certain common points in Byzantine and Armenian architecture under the Macedonian dynasty may be explained on the theory of a Byzantine influence on Armenia or an Armenian influence on Constantinople; nor is it easy on present evidence to arrive at a definite conclusion as to which view best suits the facts. It is well known that under this dynasty relations between the empire and Armenia were very close; emperors of Armenian descent sat upon the throne; Armenians settled in numbers in Constantinople. In view of the enterprising character of this people, their readiness to travel, and the admitted capacity of their artists, it is certainly tempting to invert the usual theory, and to suppose that Byzantine art did not always dominate that of Armenia, but was often indebted to it for new ideas. Strzygowski[1] has put forward the hypothesis that the *Nea*, the great church erected by Basil I in the metropolis, was erected according to Armenian plans, and he would assign an Armenian origin to various features in other contemporary churches. Knowing what we do of the initiative displayed by Armenians in many fields of activity, we cannot dismiss the theory as either extravagant or inherently improbable. They certainly played a leading part in the development of Russian art during these centuries, and we hear of their architects and painters in Constantinople and in Egypt (p. 287). But, as Diehl has remarked in this connexion, where two civilizations come in contact, the stronger is apt to teach the weaker; and from the ninth to the twelfth centuries the Byzantine Empire enjoyed a period of unequalled power and magnificence. Unless, therefore, it is demonstrated beyond possibility of contradiction that the features in question could not have reached the metropolis independently of Armenian influence, it is prudent to retain the more conservative view, or at least to suspend the judgement.

It is, however, certain that in less conspicuous provinces than that of architecture the Armenians served as active intermediaries between Persia and Byzantium, enriching Christian art by new importations from the East. The fine arabesques of foliage which form so attractive a feature in the illuminated MSS. or in the metal-work of the period were in all probability transmitted by the agency of Armenians. The distinctive oriental ornament which appears in the mosques and churches of the Holy Land may be due to the same perennial source. It may well be that a more extensive acquaintance with the mediaeval art and industry of Armenia will reveal other instances of the skill and capacity which her people

---

[1] In *Kleinasien*, p. 193, &c.; see also *Der Dom zu Aachen und seine Entstellung.* In these works Strzygowski modifies the views as to Armenia published in his earlier book above cited.

possessed. Enamelling may provide a case in point, for important enamelled ikons still preserved in Georgia seem to be of native workmanship (pp. 528–30), and we have yet to learn when and from what quarter the art was introduced into the country.[1] In the section on glass it is noticed that some of the few Christian glass vessels of the third period may be connected with Georgian industry (Ch. XI). Here again information as to origins is meagre in the extreme. Was there an ancient vitreous art of the Caucasus, as the existence of the Koban enamels might lead us to conjecture (p. 495), or were the methods introduced from the south through Syria or Mesopotamia? Whatever the future may have in store, it is certain that in the ninth century Armenia had a national art both of architecture and painting, an art in which Greek and Persian influences were so skilfully balanced that creative powers of a high order were demanded by the process of assimilation.

THE EAST

The misleading suggestions which have prejudiced the use of the term Byzantine are even more prominent in the case of the word Oriental. We speak of the East after too large and indiscriminate a fashion, as if all were homogeneous in thought and sentiment; we are apt to assume that the whole of Asia, in its action upon the art of Europe, has moved like a glacier in a single mass and in the same direction. In truth the divisions of that vast continent have influenced the West at various times, and the effect of their action has not been uniform. A second fallacy, due perhaps to the habit of regarding the Orient through a certain atmosphere of romance, ascribes to the East all the knowledge and all the mystery, while from the West is deducted such small credit as it was ever allowed to possess. We will not believe that the continent of ancient wisdom can ever have learned from Europe or from its own Mediterranean borders; we live under the obsession of the 'oriental mirage'. Here again there is surely exaggeration. If the East has taught, it has also acquired knowledge. But before we can estimate the mutual influence of East and West, it is essential to define what, for our present purpose, we mean by the East. The best way of doing this is to begin by eliminating those regions which have not yet been shown to have exerted a durable or effective influence.

It has been said that all the great representative art of the world has flowed from two sources, one in Greece, the other in China.[2] In interpreting

---

[1] Strzygowski long ago suggested that Armenia may have been a primary centre of enamelling.

[2] It is not necessary to consider the figure-art of ancient Egypt, Assyria, or Achaemenian Persia. The art of Egypt did not really inspire the Christian art of that country (p. 70). Assyria transmitted certain ornamental motives. Achaemenian Iran learned how to render the human figure from the immigrant Greek artists in her great cities, while Parthia and Sassanian Persia in this respect were even more dependent upon the late Hellenic painters and sculptors living in Seleucia and Ctesiphon, or temporarily visiting the country.

the human figure, in evoking the subtle harmony between man and nature, the Hellenes and the Chinese were supreme; each nation has handed down a tradition which has remained a continuous and inspiring force through all the revolutions of history. To the artists of Japan, and in a less degree of Persia, China is a classic land; it stands to their country in the same relation as that in which Hellas stands to Europe. We have seen how deeply Christian art was indebted to Greece; we have now to ask whether it owed a debt to China, the country of the great T'ang and Sung painters who during many centuries of the Middle Ages stood so far above contemporary artists in other lands. To answer this question it is necessary to survey the state of affairs in Inner Asia, where the outposts of Hellenism and of Chinese culture came into immediate contact.

After the conquests of Alexander and the foundation of the Seleucid dominion, the figure-art of Greece had extended its influence across the Indus. But it did not gain a permanent victory; both in India and

FIG. 33.　Carved wooden lintel of the sixth–seventh century, in the Cairo Museum.
(*Catalogue général: Koptische Kunst*, No. 8781.)

Bactria there was a revival of indigenous feeling which continued down to the beginning of the Christian era. The early Buddhist art of Asoka's time did not favour the representation of the human figure; and when the engravers of the Graeco-Bactrian and Graeco-Scythian coins had lost the first Hellenic inspiration, there remained no representative of Hellenism beyond the Parthian court. But the missionary activity of Buddhism about the beginning of our era brought the culture of India and of Greek Asia once more into close relations; and from a study of the sculptures upon the stûpas and vihâras of Gandhâra it seems probable that at this time the Greek had resumed the part of tutor to the Indian (see p. 115). The sculpture of Gandhâra [1] is the offshoot of the late Hellenistic sculpture of Asia Minor or Syria (see p. 130). Between the third and eighth centuries of our era this art advanced with Buddhist culture across Turkestan to the confines of the Middle Kingdom. But during the same period nothing in the figure-art of the region between the Pamir and the Mediterranean appears to show Chinese influence; that only begins upon a perceptible scale with the westward expansion of the Mongol Empire.

[1] See A. Foucher, *L'Art Gréco-Bouddhique du Gandhâra*, Paris, 1905, and *Mon. Piot*, 1910, p. 275; W. Burgess, *The Gandhâra Sculptures*, London, 1899. For contact between Buddhism and Christianity, see also Kennedy in *Journ. R. Asiatic Soc.*, 1902, pp. 377–415; S. Lévi, *Le Bouddhisme et les Grecs* in *Rev. de l'hist. des religions*, vol. xxiii, 1891.

The idea that China was instrumental in the formation of Christian art in any of its essential features must be dismissed as an emanation from the oriental mirage.[1] For the foundations of Byzantine art were all laid by the time of Basil the Macedonian, and no westerly movement of Chinese models after the twelfth century can have decisively affected its destiny. During the earlier part of the first millennium two great artistic influences met in conflict in Turkestan, and the Chinese, fighting nearer to their base, carried off the victory over an enemy wearied by a long advance. We now

Fig. 34. The Ascension of Alexander: relief of the twelfth–thirteenth century on the exterior of S. Marco, Venice. (Alinari.) P. 159.

know that as early as the fourth century China possessed an art superior to that of contemporary Europe, so superior that it had nothing to learn from the degenerate Greeks of 'Ta Chin' (Syria). Such a genius as Ku K'ai-chih[2] was indeed assured of triumph over any Greek of less merit than a Polygnotus; but the Buddhist missionary art issuing from Gandhâra, with which alone he and his fellows had to reckon, was but a pale reflection devoid of inward strength and fire. As a result, China absorbed such Greek or Graeco-oriental motives as attracted her attention, and though she might have taught the Christian world lessons almost above its comprehension, gave little or nothing in return. Then, as often since,

[1] For the relations of China and the Byzantine Empire, see Bury's edition of Gibbon's *Decline and Fall*, Appendix to vol. iv. See also F. Hirth's *China and the Roman Orient*; O. Münsterberg, *Japanische Kunstgeschichte*, i. 33 ff., 104 ff.; ii. 138 ff.; iii. 256 ff.; J. Dahlmann, *Stimmen aus Maria-Laach*, 1902, pp. 1–36; A. von Le Coq, *Zeitschrift für Ethnologie*, 1907, p. 509.

[2] See L. Binyon, *Painting in the Far East*, ch. iii.

she lived a life self-centred and withdrawn; she did not therefore press her advantage beyond the sphere of her material power, and probably accepted the inferiority of Western art as a fact requiring no demonstration.[1] It was not until many centuries had elapsed, when the Mongols began to invade the regions west of their original seats, that Chinese influence flowed strongly into Persia and beyond. To Gengiz and Kublai Khan in the first place, to Timur in the second, not to the Chinese themselves, was due this extension of their art towards the West. The Mongol schools at Herat and Samarkand taught the miniaturists of Persia how to

FIG. 35.   Carved closure-slabs of the tenth century : Metropolitan Church, Mistra.
(*Hautes Études* : G. Millet.)

draw and paint the human figure; they did not teach the illuminators of Constantinople.

Even in decorative design the influence of China during the first millennium is almost imperceptible. It might have been expected that the land which exported silk to the West for so long a period should have transmitted the favourite patterns with which her own silk fabrics were inwoven.[2] But if Chinese influence can be traced at all in this connexion (see Ch. X) the designs in which it is supposed to appear are of a simple geometrical nature: the peculiar character of Chinese fancy is not impressed upon them; their relationship with the Middle Kingdom hardly

[1] Northern Mesopotamia and East Turkestan may have been connected both by ethnical and religious ties ; the monastic spirit of Buddhism may have influenced the monasticism of early Christianity, while the Manichaeans, who, as the German expedition has proved, were early established in Turfan, may have served as intermediaries between Hither and Central Asia. (See *Amida*, as above, pp. 381 ff., where Prof. von Schröder has collected the principal arguments.) The evidence as at present known seems to prove little with regard to *artistic* influence in pre-Mohammedan times, though the results of the recent expeditions are not yet fully published.

[2] Strzygowski, Prussian *Jahrbuch.*, xxiv, 1903, p. 173. The Chinese silk textile in the Victoria and Albert Museum, found in Egypt, has only an inscription, and was obtained from the late cemetery at El Azam.

appears established. There are none of the monsters and dragons of the archaic Chinese bronzes; there is none of that curliness of line which already marked Chinese decorative designs in the seventh century. The evidence seems rather to favour the theory that during the whole of this period China continued rather to receive than to give. While Byzantium was still a city of small account, she had already begun to borrow ; the use of the vine-scroll in the Chinese art of the Han dynasty followed the intro- duction of the vine itself from Ferghana in the first century before Christ. Not only are typical Chinese motives absent from the early silk textiles of the West, while those of Persia abound, but unmistakable Sassanian types are imitated upon Chinese silks contemporary with the last Sassanian kings (see Ch. X). Instead of flowing westward the current seems to have moved in an easterly direction.

What has been said of China may be repeated of Hindostan. There is little proof that India made any great contribution to East-Christian art.[1] Her own early artistic development shows the clearest traces of a persistent influence from Achaemenian Persia ; Greek influences followed in Bactria ; then came the Graeco-Roman art of Gandhâra, and further influences from Sassanian Persia, with perhaps some reflex action from Turkestan. India was great in philosophy, and her peoples possessed a highly developed religious imagination. But the forms which they conceived were at first expressed by other peoples. The Buddhist iconography of the East was indebted for many types to Hindostan, but the art which best embodied them was first Greek and afterwards Chinese. Indian artists were slow in achieving their independence : when they did achieve it, they produced work of a mysterious charm and power, but apparently without influence upon the contemporary art of the West.[2] We conclude therefore that Central and Further Asia owed as little to the Byzantine Empire as that empire owed to them.

'The East,' then, for us must mean those parts of Asia which lie west of the Pamir. The region which really influenced Byzantine art is neither India nor the Further Orient : it can only be sought in Hither Asia. If this volume were concerned with architecture, the essential truth of this proposition would be apparent, for here the evidence is continually reinforced by the progress of modern research. The great constructive art which achieved its triumphs by the elaboration of the vault was native to Mesopotamia, whence it spread into Syria, Anatolia, and Armenia upon its way to wider conquests beyond the Mediterranean. Many fundamental qualities which distinguish Byzantine architecture were derived from this source ; and though the ingenious and adaptive Greek spirit may have been essential to its ultimate development, yet in its fundamental features the art remains oriental. It belongs to Persia and to those more ancient

---

[1] Such points as Prof. Petrie's discovery in Egypt of a Ptolemaic tombstone with a wheel and *trisula* (*Journ. R. Asiatic Soc.*, 1898, p. 875), are of very great interest from the historic point of view, but prove little with regard to artistic influence.

[2] E. B. Havell, *Indian Sculpture and Painting*, London, 1908.

empires of the Euphrates valley from which the culture of Iran was principally derived. To Hither Asia East-Christian art owes its achievement in the field where it was most creative, and can most clearly establish its claim to a great place among the arts of the world.

Strzygowski has insisted for many years upon the overwhelming significance for East-Christian art of the North Mesopotamian region about the Persian and Byzantine frontiers, where the three towns of Edessa, Nisibis, and Amida (Diarbekr) form a triangle, with the last-named city at the apex. The excavation of the more important sites in this

Fig. 36.   The Adoration of the Magi : Sarcophagus in S. Vitale, Ravenna.   (Ricci.)   P. 138.

region is perhaps the most urgent task of Christian archaeology; but even from the photographs obtained by scientific travellers [1] it becomes more and more clear that Osrhoene was indeed a focus which from the fourth century radiated influence in all directions. Amida became a great centre of Christianity in the time of the Emperor Constantius.[2] The façade of the Great Mosque still incorporates sculptured columns and stones of which the affinities are with the art of that period; and the decorative designs confirm Strzygowski's old hypothesis that the ornament of Egypt and other parts of the Byzantine Empire owes far more to this part of Hither Asia than has hitherto been conceded.[3]

---

[1] Especially General de Beylié and Miss Gertrude Bell.

[2] Van Berchem and Strzygowski, *Amida, Beiträge zur Kunstgeschichte des Mittelalters von Nord-mesopotamien, Hellas, und dem Abendlande,* Heidelberg, 1910, pp. 163 ff. Here the early authorities for the history of the city are all cited.

[3] Miss Bell found that in the Tur Abdin the tradition of a remote connexion between the monasticism of this region and that of Egypt is still general. The tradition may well be founded on fact.

Even more familiar than Amida are the names of Nisibis and Edessa, famous for theological schools of the Nestorians, who in course of time became the predominant Christian sect in Persia.[1] The Persian Church had been founded by Syrian missionaries;[2] its Catholic members acknowledged the patriarch of Antioch, and the Nestorians were bound to Syria by the ties of language and tradition. The reputation of the Mesopotamian schools rose so high that the influence of the monks and scholars of Edessa and Nisibis extended far within the boundaries of the Byzantine Empire. In the sixth century we find more than one trace of the respect in which Mesopotamian learning was held in other countries. It is probable that Cassiodorus maintained relations with this region, and that among the manuscripts copied in his new foundation were books obtained from Persian monasteries. The importance of Mesopotamia as a link between oriental culture and that of the Greeks is well illustrated by the career of Mar Aba, a Persian Magus converted to Christianity. This remarkable man learned Syriac at Nisibis, and studied at Edessa under the celebrated Thomas: in later years he himself established a theological school at Nisibis and became patriarch of Persia (A.D. 536–52).[3] He edited the works of Theodore of Mopsuestia, the true founder of Nestorianism, was a considerable traveller, and during a sojourn at Alexandria became acquainted with Cosmas Indicopleustes, whose *Christian Topography* is described below (Ch. VIII). Cosmas, who styles the Persian Patricius, expresses deep obligation to his learning, and it is clear that both in the theological and the cosmographical part of his work he was under a great debt to this wise man from the East. This is especially true of the theories respecting the formation of the world, which Cosmas himself recognizes as of Chaldean origin.[4] This is a single instance of the manner in which the ideas of East and West were brought into contact through the agency of the Mesopotamian schools; it happens to be recorded in the pages of a famous manuscript and thus arrests the attention of the student. How many similar instances of the interfusion between different religions, philosophies, and arts have lain unnoticed in the pages of less popular writers or are lost through the destruction which has befallen the libraries of those times!

It was in ornament that the influence of the Nearer East upon Byzantine art was most enduring and extensive. Several motives which became popular under Christianity were inherited from ancient Asian art, though sometimes

---

[1] For the school of Edessa, see Assemani, *Bibliotheca orientalis*, ii. 402; iii. 376, 378; iv. 70, 924; and Gibbon's short account in *Decline and Fall*, ch. xlvii. For the relations of Edessa to Constantinople, Baumstark, *R. Q.*, 1908, p. 17. For the school of Nisibis, J. B. Chabot, *Journal Asiatique*, 9e serie, viii, 1896, pp. 48 ff. For the Nestorians, besides Assemani and Gibbon, the reader may consult the useful Introduction of H. Yule's *Cathay and the Way thither* (Hakluyt Soc., 1866), and his Introduction to Wood's *Journey to the Sources of the Oxus*.

[2] But there was probably a monastic influence from Egypt as well. It is observed on a subsequent page that monastic institutions may possibly have been affected by influences from Turkestan.

[3] See Assemani, *Bibl. Orient.*, and Chabot, as above; Wright, *A Short History of Syriac Literature*, London, 1894, pp. 19, 116 ff.

[4] Jensen, *Die Cosmologie der Babylonier*, 1880.

indirectly, through the intermediation of the Greeks.   Among these are the
guilloche, so popular in Assyria, and the elements of the *grammaire orientale*
noticed in another place (Ch. XIII). Almost without exception these motives
appear to belong to the Nearer and not to the Farther East. It was here that
the art of Asia came into most direct conflict with that of Hellas; and since
the love of all-invading pattern entered into the lives of all classes in the
Nearer East, the resistance to the Greek style was universal and invincible.
The greater Greek art had insisted upon a salient central motive, standing
as it were in the open, unconfused by the encroachment of subsidiary
design. It knew the contrasting value of void space, and relegated its
geometrical and floral ornament to borders and places of secondary

Fig. 37.   Christ with St. Peter and St. Paul : Sarcophagus of St. Rinaldo,
Ravenna.   (Alinari.)   P. 138.

importance. But the desire of the West Asiatic, and more especially, it
would seem, of the Mesopotamian, was to escape the void by covering
it with a continuous repeating pattern, a desire the more easily gratified
inasmuch as he took comparatively little interest in the human figure,
preferring among living things the reproduction of animal forms. No
sooner did Hellenic influence wane, about the time of the Christian era,
than the oriental love of diapers covering the whole surface, and tolerating
no central or salient feature, began to win the upper hand. The Greeks
of Asia, now half oriental in their views of life, gave way to it on every
side.[1] Both in the minor arts and in decorative sculpture we see the
rapid triumph of this principle: by Justinian's reign it was definitely
established, and the sculptured foliage in the spandrels of the arcades
in Sta Sophia (Fig. 2) has become the classical example of its adoption.[2]

[1] The spread of Christianity in Persia must have further contributed to the interchange
of artistic motives (J. Labourt, *Le Christianisme dans l'Empire Perse sous la dynastie Sassanide*,
Paris, 1904 ; Max Freiherr von Oppenheim, *Vom Mittelmeer zum Persischen Golf*, i, p. 106, Berlin,
1899).   [2] Riegl, *Stilfragen*, p. 281.

The modification of the late Hellenic floral ornament under the hands, first of the Sassanians, and afterwards of Persians living under the Mohammedan rule, is a study of great interest. We see the beginning of that conventionalized treatment of vine and acanthus which reached its culmination in Saracenic art, and influenced the later ornament of Byzantium.[1] Sassanian Persia evolved a fantastic system of floral decoration in which vases, amphorae, and eagles' wings were introduced amidst a luxuriant foliage. This strange style, which appears on the sculpture of Mshatta in the First Period, was continued in later centuries, and is found in the mural mosaics executed in the Holy Land described below, dating from the eleventh and twelfth centuries. In the earlier centuries the Syrians had been the most active intermediaries between East and West; from about the year A.D. 1000 the Armenians seem to have taken the most prominent place. Under Mohammedan rule Persian Mesopotamia maintained its ancient reputation. It was here, at Mosul, that the art of encrusting bronze with silver reached its great development in the twelfth and thirteenth centuries: the fashion must have been of much earlier date, and

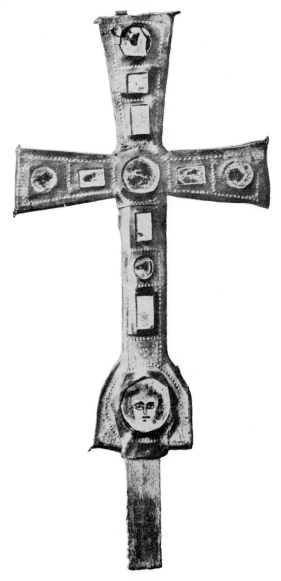

FIG. 38. Wooden cross set with glass pastes, fifth century, in the Cairo Museum. (*Catalogue général: Koptische Kunst*, No. 8804.)

from this part of the world it was probably derived by the Byzantine makers of the encrusted bronze doors of churches and cathedrals. When the Baghdad Railway has traversed this area excavation will probably reveal

[1] Riegl, *Stilfragen*, pp. 297 ff.

its full importance for the history of Christian art. Meanwhile, though the spade has not yet been employed, we are beginning to learn something of the conditions which prevailed under the Seljuk dynasty, and to trace the remote origins of the art of Islam in Asia.[1]

Even more important than foliate or geometrical ornament was the use of conventionalized animals in decoration, a fashion derived by the Achaemenian Persians from Assyrian art, and transmitted westwards by their Sassanian successors through the influence of sculpture and of figured textiles (p. 168). Beasts and monsters attacking each other, or 'heraldically' confronted on either side of a sacred tree, were very popular in these textiles, to which their symmetrical arrangement especially adapted them. Though they were also employed in stone sculpture, ivory carvings, enamels, and other metal-work, it was through their connexion with the silk fabrics of Persia that they gained so sure a foothold in the Byzantine provinces and in the Europe of the Romanesque period.[2] Here again Northern Mesopotamia exerted a preponderating influence lasting into Mohammedan times; the decorative use of Arabic script appears also to have spread from this region.

In figure-art there was no such assertion of oriental supremacy as that which is to be observed in architecture and decorative design. We have seen that in the early centuries of the Christian era China possessed an art of supreme quality, an art of which the influence was felt far to the west of the Middle Kingdom in Turkestan. But we have also seen that many centuries elapsed before the representative art of China was studied by painters beyond Turkestan and the Pamirs: her style of rendering the human figure was as little known as was her profound mastery of landscape. In this branch of representation Hither Asia had been the pupil of Greece long before the birth of Christ, and her ancient dependence remained unbroken until the close of the first millennium of our era. In Achaemenian Persia, the power of rendering the human form without hieratic convention had first been taught by immigrant Greeks from Ionia in Susa and Persepolis; the Parthians boasted themselves philhellenes; and under the later Sassanian dynasty the impress of late Hellenic art upon Persian figure sculpture is very manifest. The Persians did not disdain to learn from the Greeks settled in Seleucia and other cities.[3] When Western Asia became Mohammedan, the old influence long remained in the ascendant. The earlier Moslem princes had recourse

---

[1] Strzygowski and Van Berchem, *Amida*, as above.

[2] For monsters and animals in 'Romanesque' Europe, see below in the section France, and the paragraphs relating to Macedonia in the chapter on sculpture. For metal-work and enamels, see the remarks on the Ewer of St. Maurice d'Agaune and the Pala d'oro at Venice (pp. 496, 512). The Sassanian ewer and textiles in the treasury of Horiuji at Nara in Japan show that this Persian style penetrated to China and Japan in the early Middle Ages. For the textiles, see below, p. 591; for the ewer, L. Gonse, *L'Art japonais*, ii. 36; A. Odobesco, *Le trésor de Pétrossa*, ii, p. 19; Longpérier, *Œuvres*, i. 301, 305; S. Reinach in *Rev. arch.*, 1901, p. 242.

[3] e.g. the figure sculpture of Takh-i-Bostan shows the late Hellenic influence of the Syrian area (Strzygowski, *Hellenistische und koptische Kunst*, p. 25).

to Asiatic Greeks and Syrians in the decoration of those palaces where
the rules of orthodoxy were disregarded; Byzantine forms appear on
their coins; and the frescoes of Kuṣeir ʻAmra, of the later ninth century,
are almost as purely Greek in style as if they had been produced in
Antioch or Alexandria in the time of Theodosius. The dissemination of
oriental costume and Eastern modes of life gradually effaced the old
Hellenic influence as the artists of Damascus, Cairo, and Baghdad worked
their way to independence; but the rise of figure-art in Western Asia
came when Mongol conquerors introduced the Chinese style first into

Fig. 39.   Lead ampullae of the sixth century from the Holy Land, in the Cathedral of Monza :
Scenes from the Gospel, with the Crucifixion.   (*Hautes Études*: G. Millet.)   P. 623.

Samarkand and afterwards into Persia. It has already been urged that
this was at too late a date to affect the destinies of Byzantine representative art.

When we say, then, that Byzantine art is half oriental, we mean that it
is oriental of the Nearer not of the Farther East. Its love of sumptuous
colour and omnipresent pattern, its preference for vaulted buildings, it
derived from Persia and Mesopotamia, not from India or the Middle
Kingdom. So far as Byzantine art was concerned, the supreme qualities
of old Chinese art, the control of sensitive and nervous line and the
emotional rendering of landscape, might never have existed. Ku Kʻai chih
lived about the time of Theodosius. The great landscape painters of the
Tʻang dynasty were contemporary with iconoclasm; the artists of the Sung
dynasty, which closed about the same time as the Latin interregnum of the
thirteenth century, achieved supreme results in floral painting, in the

interpretation of nature, and in the rendering of gods and men, but contemporary Byzantine art reveals no more traces of their influence than if they had lived and worked in another planet.

EGYPT, ABYSSINIA, AND NORTH AFRICA

The influence of Hellenistic Alexandria upon Rome is a cardinal feature in the history of art. Even before the beginning of our era Italy may almost be said to have stood in a state of pupilage to the Egyptian city (p. 76). In sculpture the picturesque relief, in painting the picturesque fresco, were alike of Alexandrian origin; in the earliest illumination of the manuscript (Ch. VIII) as in some of its later developments, in the application of mosaic to new uses (p. 326), in the manufacture of glass and the methods of ceramics (Ch. XI), the debt to the capital of Egypt is obvious and confessed. In literature the place of Alexandria is equally commanding: the Romans adopted her authors as their models; in the fourth and fifth centuries all Greek poets of reputation wrote at Alexandria, and most were born in Egypt; it was here that the Graeco-oriental romance began its wonderful career.[1] The city looms so large in the history of early Christian times that to some[2] it appears the primary source of fertilizing influence, more important than any other to the formation of the new art. In early Christian times the prestige of the Alexandrian artist was such that to the foreigner Alexandria and Egypt must have seemed almost synonymous terms. Yet the art of the city was not in a true sense African: it was but a single phase of a Hellenism common to many regions, and cannot always be readily distinguished from that of Antioch and other Asiatic Greek cities.[3] When, towards the eleventh century, Byzantine and Armenian masters working in the country once more raised figure composition to a higher level, a similar statement may be made of the new time. We find paintings and sculptures which are not distinctively Egyptian, but owe their character to extraneous influence;[4] while architecture preserves Byzantine forms.[5]

[1] For Alexandria in Roman times, see J. P. Mahaffy, *The Greek World under Roman Sway*, pp. 16, 164, and *Greek Life and Thought*, p. 506. The literary debt of Christianity to Alexandria is explained in the pages of Harnack, Usener, and Bigg (*The Christian Platonists of Alexandria*). For the relations of Egypt and Italy, see also p. 76 below.

[2] F. X. Kraus, *Geschichte der christlichen Kunst*, vol. i. Ainaloff, *The Hellenistic Origins*, has insisted upon the importance of Alexandria, tracing her influence in the different branches of art; frequent references to his work will be found in other parts of the present volume. Strzygowski, in his *Hellenistische und koptische Kunst*, distinguishes the influence of the Greek and indigenous elements in Egyptian Christian art, allowing due weight to the former. Diehl, *Manuel*, pp. 54-6, in like manner recognizes the paramount position of Alexandria.

[3] It will be noticed below (p. 183, &c.) how extremely difficult it is to assign ivory carvings, MSS., and other objects in which the Hellenistic element predominates to any of the great Hellenistic centres. Even in the case of the episcopal chair at Ravenna, there is no unanimity of opinion (p. 203).

[4] Cf. the carved wooden doors of Al Mu'allaka (p. 149) and the probable influence of Armenians in later frescoes.

[5] The churches built in Nubia during this period, as revealed to us by the American expedition of Dr. MacIver. retain Byzantine forms. See *Churches in Lower Nubia*, by G. S. Mileham and D. Randall MacIver (Eckley B. Coxe Junior Expedition), Philadelphia, 1910.

But there was another Egypt of which the same cannot be said. From the establishment of a Greek kingdom in the Delta of the Nile, the land of Egypt had begun a silent revolt against the invading culture. The reaction was already powerful under the later Ptolemies; after the seventh ruler of that name, Hellenism declined even in its stronghold of Alexandria, though destined here to flourish, contaminated by oriental influences, almost to the

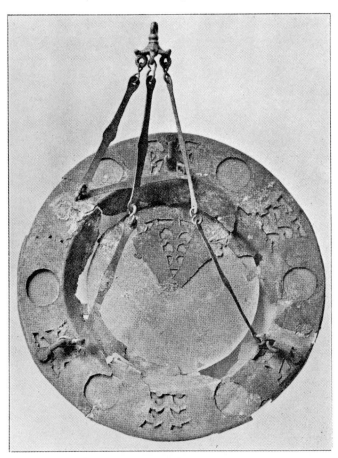

Fig. 40. Silver lamp-disk (*polycandelon*) of the sixth century from Lampsacus. (British Museum.) Cf. Fig. 41. P. 567.

time of the Arab invasion. It was otherwise with the inland country. After the revolt of Thebes in 85 B.C. and the ensuing troubles, Upper Egypt became more and more an agricultural region with no great intellectual or artistic centre. With the growth of monasticism, and the tendency to an austerer view of life, an art more realistic and didactic, more congenial to the Egyptian temperament than that of the Greek decadence, began to replace the art of Alexandria. That reversion of taste to indigenous forms of expression which followed the decay of Roman power in the provinces of East and West was especially strong upon the

Nile,[1] where an ancient civilization and a national art had existed for
several thousand years. It was impossible for Egyptian Christians to
banish the Hellenistic types with which Christian art had from the first
been associated. These types persisted in the frescoes of the sixth and
seventh centuries no less than in the catacombs of Alexandria, though here
native sentiment and old tradition imposed their own peculiar qualities,
the two streams of influence sometimes meeting, as at El-Bagawat, in
a single building. Thus was formed the art which we know as Coptic, an
art which without a Hellenistic base would never have assumed its actual
form, but became so overgrown with local or oriental features that in its
later phases it appears almost independent of Greek tradition. Where
popular fancy wins the upper
hand we find a lapse into the
crudest realism;[2] where the aim
is primarily religious, the conventional forms of a hieratic
symbolism. As the Hellenistic
foundation is forgotten, there is
a progressive loss of life and
natural power, a return, if upon
a lower plane, to the formalism
of the ancient monarchy. In
ornament the losses are less
serious, for here the Copt displays a natural talent; in his
treatment of the acanthus, and in
other ways, he develops styles at
once pleasing and original; in his
textiles he shows a fine sense of

Fig. 41. Restoration of open-work design in
centre of a silver lamp-disk of the sixth century
from Lampsacus. (British Museum.) Cf. Fig. 40.

decoration. But in this field Egypt seems to have early fallen under the
influence of Syria and Persia (Mesopotamia). Glazed pottery of the first
century is ornamented with definitely Persian motives, while in the sixth
century textiles with Persian design must have entered the country in considerable numbers (Ch. X). Syrian motives, among which the vine-scroll
with animals in the convolutions is conspicuous, occur upon Egyptian limestone carvings (Figs. 25, 27, &c.) and ivory carvings; the analogies with the
early ornament of Mesopotamia are noticed elsewhere (Ch. XIII). All this
art is non-Hellenic: the share of Hellenism in the ornament produced in
Egypt in the Christian centuries is comparatively small. The Eastern principle of contrasting light and shadow soon dominated in carved designs and
approximated them to work in colour without relief. Nor was it only in
decorative design that what may be called the oriental spirit is mani-

---

[1] The classical instance of the victory of ancient Egypt over Hellas is afforded by the
frescoes of Kom el-Shugafa, where Egyptian motives are painted *over* others in a 'Pompeian'
style (Strzygowski, *Hellenistische und koptische Kunst*, p. 76).
[2] As in the Leda reliefs in the Cairo Museum.

fested : the subject, as intellectual content, is affected by indigenous modes of thought and religious sentiment. The influence of Egypt upon Christian iconography is very evident. The descent of the typical group of the ' Virgin and Child' from the figure of Isis carrying Horus may be disputed; but the 'equestrian saint', of which the most familiar example is St. George, is certainly of Nilotic origin;[1] the *Anastasis*, one of the most striking subjects in Byzantine art, seems to have been composed from Egyptian elements (Ch. XII) ; it is hardly necessary to add the *ankh*, or sign of life, which, as the *crux ansata*, entered upon a new existence under Christianity.[2]

It is observed elsewhere (p. 98) that the spread of Egyptian influence on iconography must have been favoured by the rapid growth of monasticism, the emigration of Egyptian monks, and the temporary visits of foreign monks to the banks of the Nile. At Lérins (p. 88) and in Ireland the Coptic monk made his presence felt : the Pachomian rule became familiar to men of many nations; as upon monastic use, so upon liturgy, Egyptian influence was striking and persistent.

In architecture there is evidence for the influence of Egypt, though it probably did not equal that of Syria and Asia Minor. Characteristic

Fig. 42. Pound weight of the sixth century, inlaid in silver with figures of military saints. (British Museum.) P. 621.

features such as the trefoil apse are not certainly Egyptian, but appear to have been introduced, like the squinch, from Asia.[3] The subterranean type of cistern supported by a forest of columns was probably imported into Constantinople from Alexandria.[4]

It is probable that upon the higher planes of artistic achievement Anatolia and Syria equalled, if they did not excel, the Nilotic province. But the artists of Christian Egypt had one advantage. They had inherited

[1] Strzygowski, *Hellenistische und koptische Kunst*, p. 24.

[2] P. D. Scott Moncrieff, *Gnosticism and Early Christianity in Egypt*, *Church Quarterly Review,* October, 1909. It is of interest to note that the ankh had been adopted upon Cilician and Cypriote coins before the Christian era. A form like an inverted ankh commonly serves as an initial O in Frankish MSS.

[3] For a *résumé* of the position with regard to Egyptian Christian architecture, see Diehl, *Manuel*, pp. 57–8. To the references there given, viz. C. M. Kaufmann's reports on the excavations at Abu Mina (Cairo, 1906–8), J. E. Quibell, *Explorations at Saqqara*, Cairo, 1908, 1910, and A. J. Butler, *The Ancient Coptic Churches of Egypt*, Oxford, 1884, may be added the paper by C. R. Peers, *On the White Monastery at Sohag*, *Archaeological Journal*, 1904, pp. 131, 198.

[4] Strzygowski, *B. D.*, iii. p. xvi, 1893.

from earlier centuries perfected technical methods which they patiently maintained in a high state of excellence; ancient traditions of craftsmanship made it easy for them to compete with the representatives of other peoples in the domain of the industrial arts. We may take as instances painting by the encaustic method (p. 256), the weaving of tapestry, and perhaps the glazing of pottery in colours (Ch. XI). In such fields the Copts started in the race with advantages which did not belong to others: they never lost a reputation for technical skill and ingenuity. They failed rather in the higher representative art, where mere tradition was of less avail. Though their influence was widely felt in many ways through Western Europe, they remained a race apart, and the true Coptic art was always contentedly provincial.[1] It was through Alexandria that the voice of Egypt reached the outer world, and Alexandria was never all Egyptian.

ABYSSINIA.

This country, which had received its Christianity from Egypt in the fourth century, was in direct commercial relation with the Eastern Empire in the reign of Justinian, who sent a bishop and clergy to Axum.[2]

FIG. 43.   Bronze weight, inlaid with silver, bearing the name of Theodoric.
(British Museum.)   P. 621.

Christian remains of about this time have lately been discovered at Adulis in the Italian colony of Eritrea, and the coinage shows that Greek was known until about the seventh century. But more interesting than these evidences of contact with a higher civilization is the connexion between the iconography of Abyssinian religious art and that of the Christian communities to the north. Types of composition in different sacred subjects still betray this ancient descent, though the influence of the Portuguese missionaries of the sixteenth century introduced new and confusing elements from the West. For us the art of Abyssinia is of small

---

[1] For examples of Coptic art, see Strzygowski's *Koptische Kunst*, 1904, a volume of the *Catalogue général des antiquités égyptiennes du Musée du Caire*, and *Hellenistische und koptische Kunst*; W. E. Crum, *Coptic Monuments*, 1902 (a volume in the Cairo *Catalogue général*, containing the stelae); O. Wulff, *Altchristliche und mittelalterliche byzantinische und italienische Bildwerke*, Teil I, Berlin, 1909 (a catalogue of the Kaiser Friedrich Museum); A. Gayet, *L'Art copte*. Also various articles in the Paris *Annales du Musée Guimet*.

[2] Bury, *History of the later Roman Empire*, i. 469. For early Abyssinian history, see Dillmann, *Abh. der Berliner Akad.*, 1878, pp. 177–238, and 1880, pp. 1–51.

importance; it is too crude and barbaric to need more than a passing notice, though the illuminated manuscripts of the country repay a careful study from other standpoints than that of art.[1]

NORTH-WEST AFRICA.

'Africa,' comprising the old Roman provinces of the North-west, is of less importance in the history of Byzantine art than those eastern regions which have already been passed in review.[2] Beyond it was no continent of Asia rich in ancient civilizations, traversed by trade routes which brought to the Syrian coast the various products of the East, but the Pillars of Hercules, the unnavigated ocean, and the barbarous tribes

FIG. 44.   Bronze weights for one ounce and half-ounce, sixth century.
(British Museum.)   P. 621.

of an unknown interior.   Down to the fall of the Roman Empire in the West the fortune of Africa had been upon the whole prosperous.   The ruins of Roman settlements, explored by the enterprise of French archaeologists, of Timgad, Tebessa, and other towns, reveal an essentially Roman civilization; the city with its forum, its basilica, its temples and paved streets differs in few respects from its Italian prototype: it is an Italian culture transplanted to the land of the Moors.   The pagan and early Christian art of Africa is allied to that of Italy, a natural result of the close and continual relations between the mother country and the colony which served as the granary of Rome, though there are features in the ruins of African churches which suggest an Eastern influence probably transmitted by way of Egypt.   In the main, down to the Vandal invasion of A. D. 435, the culture of Africa was Latin.   After that time the hard Teutonic rule pressed heavily upon the arts, and there remains but little to illustrate their fortunes during the period of Gaiseric's 'Corsair state'. The Byzantine conquest under Belisarius, in A. D. 533, brought the country under the bureaucratic imperial régime; the administration was centralized, great fortresses were erected, and the country assumed the character of a Byzantine province.   To this period perhaps belong some of the interesting mosaics which continued in Christian times the old reputation

---

[1] The reader may form an excellent notion of these from the reproductions published by Dr. E. A. Wallis Budge.   See especially the *Life of Takla Hâymânôt*, 1906.
[2] See Ch. Diehl, *L'Afrique byzantine*, a valuable general account, with references.

of the provincials in this particular branch of art. But tranquillity was soon broken by mutinies of troops, by Moorish raids, and by the exactions of unscrupulous governors. The population decreased, discontent spread, until the invading Arab found a country prepared for almost any change and quite ready to exchange a Byzantine for a Saracenic rule. Neither in the major nor the minor arts was Africa a source of fruitful influence.

THE WESTERN WORLD

ITALY, SICILY, AND DALMATIA.

Any survey of the principal European countries from the point of view of their relation to Byzantium must naturally begin with Italy, which was of all the most directly connected with the East-Roman Empire.

Italy was more fully prepared to receive Byzantine influence than the rest of Europe, because her civilization was more advanced and her art had been more continuously nourished from Hellenistic sources. If we go back beyond Roman imperial times, we recall the ancient ties connecting the peninsula with the Hellenes, from whose activity in colonization the name of Magna Graecia was given to the southern territory. But the period of Greek influence most important for our subject began when the Romans had added to their dominions the kingdom of the Ptolemies and a great part of Hither Asia. From that time onward the Greeks and the partly Hellenized Asiatics of the Eastern Mediterranean became very numerous in Rome and in Campania, and the Hellenistic cities, more especially Alexandria, played a most prominent part in the development of Italian art. In Strabo's time Naples was almost a Greek city, with gymnasia, phratries, and other institutions after the Greek model; Puteoli was an open port for Alexandria; the Alexandrian influence in the art of Herculaneum and Pompeii is universally admitted.[1]

Rome could not have defended herself if she would against the Greek invader: her cultured nobles read the idylls of Theocritus; her colonial governors collected statues; there grew up an irresistible demand for the reproduction of Greek sculpture and Greek painting. In the reliefs of the Column of Trajan the influence of the realistic Alexandrian school is apparent. It was impossible that the continuity of Greek influence should be broken by the triumph of Christianity.

If, in the shortest possible compass, we review the story of Italy from the period of imperial decay, we cannot but perceive how inevitable was her ultimate dependence upon the Christian East. Nothing less than a strong national art, deeply rooted in the affections of the people, could have survived the successive waves of disaster which broke over the country during the fifth and sixth centuries; but Roman art was not national in this sense;

[1] This is now a matter of common knowledge. The reader who wishes a readable and brief statement of the case may consult Mahaffy, *The Greek World under Roman Sway*, pp. 208 ff., 1890; and Boissier, *Promenades archéologiques*, p. 318.

it was perhaps more Italian than the art of Alexandria was Egyptian, but in essential features it also was of foreign introduction; it could not outlive the misfortunes of the Roman Empire. Even in the third century many of the most successful artists (it is significant that they were Greeks) had left Rome in the train of Diocletian. The foundation of Constantinople led to a great emigration of these craftsmen's guilds, upon which the prosperity of metropolitan art so largely depended; the removal of wealthy senatorial families from the Tiber to the Bosphorus reduced the golden stream of patronage.[1] Changes like this had already endangered the position of Rome as the capital of the world; but from the close of the fourth century she ceased to be even the metropolis of Italy. Down to this period she may still have exerted an influence upon provincial art. But from the time of Theodosius the peninsula had no longer a permanent centre of administration; the arts were forced to share the vicissitudes of a migratory court. The emperors retreated first to Milan, next to Ravenna, by the last step placing themselves under the direct influence of a Graeco-oriental culture. It would be an exaggeration to say that Rome was destroyed as an artistic centre by these events; the Campagna was still covered with villas and gardens, there were still great palaces upon the Roman hills. The city of Romulus was of a marvellous vitality; her wealth had been too vast to be so swiftly drained away. She recovered even from the sack of Alaric in A. D. 410; and though the incursion of Gaiseric fifty years later brought ruin to many families, so that not a few palaces now stood deserted, yet it could still be treated as a passing tribulation. Down to the Gothic war Rome remained a majestic and a wealthy city. But she now possessed the shadow only; the substance had passed else-where. The emperors who flitted over her stage were themselves shadows, an Avitus, a Majorian, an Anthemius, figures appearing only to be pro-claimed, chastened by adversity, and forgotten. But in the place of shadows art will not long flourish; she needs a safe tranquillity for her expansion. From the beginning of the fifth century Ravenna became the artistic capital of Italy, Ravenna the port for Eastern ships, the see of oriental bishops, the dwelling-place of Greeks and Syrians.[2] Here the Roman court resided; here social and political influences were centred; here alone was there wealth to be expended in the service of art. In the first half of this century Rome received the largess of Galla Placidia; in the second, she saw her buildings restored by the munificence of Theodoric, an enlightened but yet a barbarian king: in both cases the money and the workmen came from the half-Syrian city on the Adriatic. To this wave of Graeco-oriental influence from the north we may perhaps ascribe

[1] English readers will find the most convenient summary of Roman history during the earlier Christian centuries from the artistic point of view in Dr. A. L. Frothingham's *Monuments of Christian Rome*, 1908, a volume in Macmillans' series of Handbooks of Archaeology and Antiquities.

[2] The influence of the Syrians is early apparent in other parts of Northern Italy. The dedication of a church to Sta Reparata, a Syrian saint, indicates this for the Florence of the fifth century (Davidsohn, *Geschichte von Florenz*, vol. i).

the slight renaissance manifested in mosaics like those in the church of SS. Cosmas and Damian. But the succeeding wars, in which the armies of Justinian and the Goths ravaged the peninsula, were fatal to the conditions of artistic fertility. Belisarius and Narses, Totila and Teia, carried ruin far and wide; after the sack of A. D. 546 Rome stood empty forty days. By all these disasters the continuity of Roman life was at last broken; the old society dispersed, the foundations of a cultured and leisured life were destroyed. Rome was driven to begin life again in squalor and humiliation; the palaces upon her seven hills were abandoned; a new and lowlier city rose along the banks of the Tiber. This was no longer a city of patricians, not even an Italian Rome. Monks and traders from Syria and Egypt occupied whole quarters; the civilization which they represented was that of the Eastern Mediterranean. Sta Maria in Schola Graeca (afterwards Sta Maria in Cosmedin) was built in the sixth century; St. Saba may have been founded about the same time by monks from Jerusalem. From St. Cesareo in Palatio, St. Anastasia, St. Giorgio in Velabro, Sta Lucia de Renatis, the process of orientalization was continued during the century following. Pope Adeodatus (A. D. 672–6) now placed a congregation of Greek monks in St. Erasmo, there to remain until in the tenth century Leo VII replaced them by Benedictines. A succession of oriental popes sat in the chair of St. Peter.[1] The Syrian, Gregory III, was a considerable builder; Paul II (A. D. 757–68) erected SS. Stephen and Sylvester, and introduced more Greek monks. Other monasteries of the eighth century were St. Gregorio, St. Prisca, St. Balbina, and the convent of Sta Maria in the Campus Martius. Pascal I (A. D. 817–24) founded the monastery of St. Praxed.

The position of the Basilian monks was thus already strong when the outbreak of iconoclasm at Constantinople rendered it even more predominant. The fugitives from the Eastern Empire came among their own people; the artists among them found no competitors other than predecessors of the same oriental origin. It was the Rome of this 'Byzantine' period between the sixth and ninth centuries to which the English bishops came for works of art to enrich their churches (p. 102). Between Narses and Charlemagne the art of Rome was no less oriental than that of Ravenna.

From this condition of servitude Italy gradually emerged; the popes, trained in the school of adversity, oppressed on the one side by the rapacious exarchs of Ravenna to whom Rome owed allegiance,[2] on the other by the encroachments of the Lombards, became the leaders in a regenerative movement. They held their own not only against the barbarian princes, but upon occasion against the Byzantine emperors. Though the heretical Constans II had banished one pope to the Chersonese, another had defied

---

[1] Theodore (A. D. 642–9) was a Greek. Of the ten popes between A.D. 685 and A.D. 741, five were Syrians (John V, Sergius, Sisinnius, Constantine, and Gregory III), and four Greeks (Conon, John VI, John VII. and Zacharias). Only one, Gregory II, was a Roman.

[2] Ch. Diehl, *Études sur l'administration byz. dans l'exarchat de Ravenne*, 1888.

the second Justinian, a third received rich gifts from Constantinople. In the eighth century the hold of the East-Roman Empire rapidly weakened, and before that century closed the Byzantine suzerainty was finally brought to a close. Pope Stephen, dreading the Lombard conquest of Rome, appealed to the Emperor Constantine V and appealed in vain. The failure was momen-

Fig. 45. Embroidered dalmatic of the fifteenth century in the Sacristy of St. Peter's, Rome : the Transfiguration. (Moscioni.) P. 600.

tous for Italian history : it thrust the pope into the arms of the Franks, and prepared the way for the triumph of the papacy under Hildebrand. It also prepared the way for new artistic influences. With the growth of Frankish power the influx of orientals into Rome came to an end. But Byzantine influence did not disappear from the art of Rome and the surrounding country : we find it in the mosaics of SS. Nereus and Achilleus and the frescoes of Sta Maria in Cosmedin of the ninth century ; we find it, faint or distinct, obvious or remote, in many a mural decoration of the next four hundred years ; at Sta Maria in Pallara on the Palatine, in the latest of the frescoes of Sta Maria Antiqua (p. 304), at St. Elia near Nepi, at St. Abbondio near Rignano, at St. Urbano alla Caffarella (p. 304), and St. Clemente; at Sta Maria in Trastevere and St. Pietro in Toscanella, in the subterranean church of the Sacro Speco at Subiaco, and the apse of Sta Maria in Toscanella. Sometimes the survival of oriental features may be due to imitation of earlier Roman-Byzantine frescoes—this may be the case at St. Urbano and St. Clemente; at other times the influence of wandering monastic artists from the south of the peninsula may have made itself felt; at other times again a Greek ikon or an illuminated MS. may have proved a source of inspiration. Although the rich decoration of mosaic inlaid in marble, which we know as Cosmatesque, was almost certainly of oriental introduction, Italian art was now moving to a new birth; the eleventh century was a time of revival and reconstruction; with the thirteenth came new suggestions from beyond the Alps; at the end of that century the frescoes of Cosmatus in the chapel of the Sancta Sanctorum prepare the way for the great art of Cavallini, whose style was formed independently of Byzantine influence.

We have now to consider the position of other parts of Italy with regard to the Christian East. Of Ravenna enough has already been said to indicate the oriental character of her art, which will also receive separate notice in the chapters on sculpture and mosaics (pp. 135, 342). Before we pass to Venice and Southern Italy it will be convenient to cast a glance at that trans-Adriatic coast region which in the Middle Ages stood so close to Ravenna, and derived its culture from that city. Istria and Dalmatia, which in earlier times had been prosperous centres of Roman civilization, fell in the fifth century first to Odovakar and then to subsequent rulers of Ravenna: after the Byzantine conquest they were dependent on the exarchs of that city. Their new relations, political and ecclesiastical, with the city of Honorius explain the affinities to Ravennate art which we mark in the architecture and mosaics of their churches. Their connexion with the Roman Empire of the East survived for a short time the extinction of Byzantine power on the Italian shore; but after her conquest by Charlemagne in A. D. 789, Istria became a duchy under the new Western Empire and was gradually withdrawn from Byzantine influences.[1] From the beginning of the second millennium Western culture became supreme; the Church admitted the sovereignty of the pope; monks of the Western orders were established in the monasteries. The monuments of East-Christian art upon the Eastern Adriatic belong therefore, like those of Ravenna, to the early periods; the country was not affected, as was Venice, by the Byzantine renaissance which began with the Basilian dynasty. The mosaics of Parenzo exhibit the closest relationship to the sixth-century work of the Italian city.[2]

---

[1] F. Hamilton Jackson, *The Shores of the Adriatic* : ii. *The Austrian Side*, pp. 188 ff., 397 ff.
[2] The same Eastern influences which affect the art of Ravenna are visible here. Bishop Maximianus of Ravenna was born at Porto Vestre, near Pola.

After the capture of Ravenna by the Lombards in A. D. 753, Venice and its territory, which had elected a duke since about A. D. 700, became the representative of Eastern culture on North-Italian soil, and was destined to hold that position for nearly seven hundred years.[1] Politically dependent upon Constantinople down to the ninth century, she remained faithful in freedom to the old allegiance ; and though, as in the twelfth century, relations were sometimes strained, her traders were too prudent to offend an empire upon whose friendship their prosperity so largely depended. Venice was filled with buildings in the Byzantine style, of which many remain to this day, from the famous Cathedral of St. Mark

Fig. 46.   Silk tapestry of the sixth century from Egypt.
(Victoria and Albert Museum.)

down to the private houses still visible along her canals. Through all these centuries Eastern artists in mosaics and Eastern painters found a home in the city of the lagoons. Venetian sculptors reproduced in stone the motives of Byzantine ivories and textile fabrics. Venice, with the neighbouring Murano and Torcello, stood aloof from the Italian world, and while other towns were striving after a new national life, remained in many ways almost a foreign city. Yet immigrant artists from other parts of Italy were active there in the twelfth and thirteenth centuries, while Venetians sought their fortune on the mainland. The workers in mosaic who decorated the apses of St. Peter and St. Paul at Rome in the times of Innocent III and Honorius III came from Venice. When, in the Comnenian period, Byzantine painting exercised so strong an influence upon

---

[1] Armingaud in *Archives des missions scientifiques et littéraires*, 2ᵉ sér., iv, pp. 299 ff.; E. Lentz, *Verhältniss Venedigs zu Byzanz*, Berlin, 1891. See *Byz. Zeitschr.*, 1893, pp. 6 ff.

Italian art, the Tuscan cities did but follow the Venetian example when they extended hospitality to the artists of the East (see p. 266). The Venetians may have learned from Byzantium the art of damascening in silver on bronze (Ch. XI), though the *azzimini* chiefly belong to the sixteenth century, when models of Saracenic origin had long been plentiful.

After the rupture of political relations between Constantinople and Rome, the great centre of Eastern influence in Italy lay in the south,[1] always the stronghold of Greek culture in the peninsula. We have seen that Southern Italy had maintained close relations with the countries of the Eastern Mediterranean long before the decline of Imperial Rome. M. Bertaux has shown how the geographical position of Calabria, Apulia, Campania, and the Abruzzi separated them by physical barriers from the rest of Italy, and made them, like Sicily, the natural appanage of the power which held command of the sea. With the establishment of Christianity, and after the fall of the Roman Empire in the West, there was probably no break in this old association; it is credibly reported that the bishop of Siponto (A. D. 474–491), a relative of the Emperor Zeno, sent to Constantinople when he needed artists for his church.[2] The Gothic dominion brought scarcely more change to Southern Italy than to the great island across the Strait of Messina: it was in the sixth century that Cassiodorus established his monastery of Vivarium above Squillace. After the wars of Justinian's reign the encroaching Lombard dukes of Benevento were often troublesome neighbours, but Greek influence suffered no serious loss. Otranto remained a Byzantine base, and the fifty thousand fugitives from iconoclasm found a refuge in the southern provinces. Even before the establishment of the Macedonian dynasty in the ninth century, a new Byzantine expansion began when Constantine Copronymus added Calabria to the theme of Sicily. But with the succession of a series of strong Eastern rulers—Nicephorus Phocas, John Zimisces, Basil II—the Byzantine Empire took complete and effective possession of Southern Italy as represented by the 'heel' and 'toe'. From the ninth to the eleventh century Calabria and Apulia were regularly colonized by Greeks from the Peloponnese; cities were founded, monasteries built; the eremites spread through the land, leaving on the walls of their cells abundant traces of contemporary art (p. 308). So complete was the occupation that when, after the eleventh century, all her Italian possessions were lost to the Byzantine Empire, Greek culture was too firmly rooted to be easily displaced. The Basilian monks long held their own successfully against the Western orders, acknowledging the patriarch of Constantinople; Rome was reluctantly obliged to tolerate Eastern ritual. These monks enjoyed the favour of the

---

[1] The principal authorities on Byzantine relations to S. Italy are given by Ch. Diehl in his *L'Art byzantin dans l'Italie méridionale*, ch. i. See also Palmieri in *Viz. Vrem.*, x. 281-303 (1903). J. Gay, *L'Italie méridionale et l'empire byzantin depuis l'avènement de Basil Ier jusqu'à la prise de Bari par les Normands*, Paris, 1904, covers the earlier period.

[2] E. Müntz, *Études sur l'histoire de la peinture et de l'iconographie chrétiennes*, p. 41 (Paris, 1882).

Norman princes, who even built new abbeys for their occupation. Although the Latin orders had triumphed by the close of the fourteenth century, the monastery of St. Nicholas near Otranto maintained its position until the Turkish invasion of A. D. 1480. The Greek tongue was spoken under both Norman and Angevin dynasties, and has lasted in the degraded dialects of Calabria to our own day, though the survival is partly due to a new wave of immigration caused by the Turkish conquest of Greece.

The effect of this abiding Greek connexion upon the arts was naturally very considerable, but from the first it was modified by counteracting forces. In architecture the Byzantine style very early admitted Saracenic elements: the cathedrals of Tarento, Siponto, and Canosa show how far the process of assimilation had progressed in the eleventh century ;[1] La Roccelletta and Sta Maria del Patiro near Rossano reveal the same union of diverse influences. But in course of time the Saracenic style in its turn lost effective support, leaving Byzantine and Western art face to face. Gradually the native Italian element gained the advantage; the power which in the twelfth century was content to exist side by side with that of Byzantium asserted its strength a century later, and soon after that time was assured of a final triumph.[2] The Italian tongue, the Latin monk, the Western ideal in art, henceforward encountered but a feeble resistance in

Fig. 47. Silk textile, with elephants and winged monsters, in the Kunstgewerbe-Museum, Berlin. (From a water-colour in the Victoria and Albert Museum.) P. 595.

the old region of Magna Graecia. But so powerful had been the influence of the Eastern Church and the Eastern monastic tradition that in the early eleventh century St. Nilus, a Basilian monk from Calabria, migrated northward to the neighbourhood of Rome and there founded the monastery of Grottaferrata. The buildings, with their fine mosaics, are still standing to-day as a lasting memorial of Byzantine monastic life and art in Italy.

As an intermediary between Byzantine and Western art in South-central Italy the Benedictine abbey of Monte Cassino in Campania occupies

---

[1] Lenormant, *Gaz. arch.*, 1883, pp. 54–5, 233 ff. For Saracenic influence on the illuminator's art at Monte Cassino, see E. Bertaux, *L'Art dans l'Italie méridionale*, p. 434.
[2] *Gaz. arch.* 1881–2, p. 124.

a position of peculiar interest.[1]   According to a statement by Leo of Ostia,[2] the Abbot Desiderius (afterwards Pope Victor III) introduced Byzantine craftsmen to embellish the monastery with mosaics, because the art of

mosaic had been forgotten. He also caused gold-smith's work, enamels, and ivory carvings for the use of the church to be made by Greek workmen, and imported from Constantinople the great bronze doors in the style of those at Amalfi and Salerno (Ch. XI). The influence of these strangers was no doubt considerable ; they laid down mosaic pave-ments in the later Byzantine style (Ch. VII), and their methods were soon adopted by the monks among whom they had come to live. The illu-minated manuscripts of Monte Cassino show many traces of such imitation (Ch. VIII). But enough has been already said of the condition of the arts in Italy to show that there was no complete stagna-tion at this period, and that in Rome the traditions of Greek religious art still survived, while in Calabria and Apulia there was a vigorous school of fresco-painters among the Basilian monks. The Benedictines of Monte Cassino certainly received instruction from the Greeks, but they were no slavish imitators, and they soon eman-cipated themselves from foreign control. Their art, to which M. Bertaux has devoted especial attention, assumes an individual character and is rich in elements derived from Northern Europe.[3]

The names of numerous artists of Greek ex-traction known to have worked in Italy from the ninth to the sixteenth century have been revealed to us through the researches of Müntz and Froth-ingham. The more prominent are mentioned in

FIG. 48.   Tapestry strip (clavus) from a tunic : Coptic, about sixth century. (Vic-toria and Albert Museum.)

the introductory remarks to the section on painting (p. 263).

The island of Sicily was held by the East-Roman Empire from the sixth century ; a Byzan-tine emperor passed the last three years of his life in Syracuse.[4] But

---

[1] Monte Cassino, founded by St. Benedict, was sacked by the Lombards in A.D. 589, and remained unoccupied for a hundred and thirty years. It was rebuilt in A.D. 720, but its great artistic period did not begin for three centuries.

[2] Schulz, *Denkmäler der Kunst des Mittelalters in Unteritalien*, ii. 117. The original account is in the *Chronicon Casinense* of Leo of Ostia, for which see *Monumenta Germ. Script.*, vii. 718. The French version by the monk Amatus, a contemporary of Desiderius, will be found in Cham-pollion-Figeac, *Ystoire de li Normant*, p. 105, Paris, 1835. In this only mosaic *pavements* are mentioned. The poem of Archbishop Alfanus of Salerno, a friend of Desiderius, speaks of the mosaicists as Thracians.

[3] *L'Art dans l'Italie méridionale*, vol. i.   [4] Constans II, A.D. 665-8.

the Saracens, whose inroads had begun in the seventh century, obtained a firm foothold in the eighth, and by the year A. D. 965 the whole island was in their hands. Mohammedan influence was thus more permanent and widely diffused in Sicily than upon the neighbouring mainland, where the power of Islam was never established upon such wide and lasting foundations. A number of churches remain to attest the Byzantine occupation,[1] and minor works of art discovered in the island are to be seen in the important museums of Syracuse and Palermo. But Byzantine art produced its finest flower under the dominion of the Norman

Fig. 49.   Alabaster chalice ; about the eleventh century : Treasury of S. Marco, Venice.
(Schlumberger-Hachette.)   P. 552.

princes, whose tolerant and eclectic principles permitted Greek, Saracenic, and French civilizations to flourish side by side. The great mosaics of the cathedrals and churches of Northern Sicily are due to their continual munificence, and where not purely Greek are executed in the spirit of the Byzantine tradition. The enterprise of the Normans introduced colonies of silk-weavers from Greece, and the celebrated textile industry of the island was established by their assistance (Ch. X).

France and Spain.

In the early centuries of the Christian era the condition of the Western provinces was less fortunate than that of those in the eastern half of the empire. The emperors, like thriftless landlords, had ruined their own

[1] Orsi in *B. Z.*, vii. 1–28 ; viii. 642 ff.

estate. The oppressive curial system weakened the middle class; the increase of *latifundia* cultivated by slaves drove the peasant from the land. Near the frontiers, the northern barbarians were suffered to occupy whole districts, and the way was thus prepared for the gathering armies of their kinsmen beyond the border. The Roman provinces of Gaul were among the first to feel the effect of these evils, though even in the fifth century the southern half of the country still enjoyed some measure of the cultured rural life so dear to Cicero and Horace. Sidonius Apollinaris, himself a Gallo-Roman, has left many pleasing descriptions of the social intercourse between the wealthy families of Gaul; his older contemporary Ausonius had extolled Arles as a western Rome, and paid his lavish tribute of praise to Trèves, Bordeaux, and Narbonne. But this society rested on no sure foundations: the very generation of Sidonius saw the Vandal, the Visigoth, and the Burgundian herald the coming of the yet more redoubtable Frank. With the entry of the Merovingians into Arles and Narbonne the power of Italy in Gaul became extinct and was never again revived. It was fortunate for the Roman provincial of the South that the Visigoths at least had in their more eastern seats received a tincture of East-Christian civilization, and that when established in Aquitaine they maintained communication with their kinsmen on the southern side of the Alps. Sharing in some degree the ideals of the great Theodoric, they did not desire the complete destruction of Roman culture; and by the distribution throughout the conquered territory of a new peasant class, they diminished the evils which the system of *latifundia* had encouraged. The art of the latest sarcophagi of Gaul, more or less contemporary with the appearance of the Goths, reveals a style allied to the purely ornamental style at Ravenna[1] (p. 135); it has been suggested that the *manus Gothica*, trained in principles originating in the East, was instrumental in keeping architecture alive in France through a critical and unsettled period.[2]

[1] The earlier Christian sarcophagi, chiefly represented by the examples at Arles, are probably related to the late Hellenistic art of Asia Minor (p. 132). The dissemination of oriental motives at this period formed the subject of some of M. Louis Courajod's suggestive lectures (A. Marignan, *Un historien de l'art français : Louis Courajod*).

[2] This position, attacked by Rivoira, is maintained by Strzygowski in *Kleinasien ein Neuland*. See also *B.Z.*, xiii. 293 and xvii. 288. The contention is that the Goths learned the half-oriental architecture of the late-Hellenic world and transplanted it to Gaul independently of Rome. The Church of St. Peter at Rouen is described as constructed *quadris lapidibus a manu Gothica* : so also St. Martin at Tours and St. Saturninus at Toulouse. Many years ago de Vogüé (*La Syrie Centrale*, i, pp. 18-23) had observed the analogies between French Romanesque churches and those of early Christian Syria, suggesting that European schools under East-Christian influence, such as that which erected the tomb of Theodoric at Ravenna, may have acted as intermediaries, while fugitives from iconoclasm may have continued their work. This book is not directly concerned with architectural problems, which will not, therefore, be discussed in the text; but the important connexion between Byzantine and French churches of the eleventh and twelfth centuries must receive some mention here. Opinion as to Byzantine influence on the domed churches of Southern France is divided. It is maintained by de Verneilh (*Architecture byzantine en France* in Didron's *Annales archéologiques*, vol. xi) and also by Choisy, who traces two currents, one more purely Byzantine, passing via Venice to Périgord (resemblance of St. Front at Périgueux to St. Mark's at Venice), the other from Mesopotamia, travelling with the commerce of Baghdad (*Histoire de l'architecture*, ii, p. 253). Dehio would allow only a general acquaintance with Byzantine art on the part of the French architects (*Die kirchliche Baukunst des Abendlandes*, p. 341), and Phené Spiers has argued in favour of relative independence, noting various constructional differences (*Bulletin monumental,*

On the arrival of the Franks in the South the situation changed for the worse. The new-comers, unused to the government of cities, revived many of the worst features of Roman social economy. Education decayed; the succession of cultivated provincials which had included men like Fortunatus and Gregory of Tours now came to an end; in the seventh

FIG. 50. Chalice with enamelled mounts; about the eleventh century : Treasury of S. Marco, Venice. (Schlumberger-Hachette.) P. 552.

century there was little or nothing to choose between the culture of the Frank and that of the Gallo-Roman. Such works of art as now entered the country were introduced by traders from the East,[1] who maintained through the southern ports the old intercourse with the Eastern Mediterranean. The Syrian, the Jewish, and the Egyptian merchant brought in the

1898, and *Architecture East and West*, 1905). Analogies between the French churches and those in Cyprus, especially St. Barnabas, near Famagusta, have also been pointed out (*Repertorium*, xxii, p. 481). Strzygowski (*Der Dom zu Aachen und seine Entstellung*), emphasizing the resemblance between the cathedral at Aix-la-Chapelle and the Church of St. Gregory at Etchmiadzin in Armenia, notes a similarity between the plan of St. Germigny-les-prés and the patriarchal church on the same Eastern site. The above references will suffice to illustrate the difficulty of this question, which can only be solved by architects. On the subject in general, see W. R. Lethaby, *Mediaeval Art*, ch. iii ; Diehl, *Manuel*, p. 674.
[1] For the influx of traders from the East into Western Europe, see L. Bréhier, *B. Z.*, xii. 1 ff.

fine products of artistic industry which were beyond the powers of the Frankish craftsman, for local skill was chiefly confined to the manufacture of weapons, jewellery,[1] and textiles of inferior quality. Under these conditions the Church became the most important patron of this commerce with the East, which provided it with textiles from Tyre and Berytus, manuscripts and ivory carvings from Alexandria and Antioch, carved capitals from Proconnesus; it is probable that down to the time of the Arab conquests these importations were continuous. For the political and social changes in Gaul must have destroyed, or reduced to insignificance, the old provincial workshops. With the exception of the Goths, who could at least appreciate sculpture of the decorative order, the barbaric invaders cared for little beyond the sumptuous and the brilliant; their enthusiasm was for silver plate, bright hangings, and jewels rich with coloured stones. Within the limits which such tastes imposed, they were able to a great extent to satisfy their desires from national sources. They kept goldsmiths in their households whose work was probably in the barbaric style familiar to us through the *orfèvrerie cloisonnée* of our museums. A similar barbaric character probably marked the woven fabrics produced in the gynaecea of the Frankish palaces and villas, though here the influence of imported models may have been more pronounced. Down to the time of Charlemagne such art as retained the traditions of the classical past was preserved by the Church, or produced at her command. The Christian Church was not confined within the frontiers of any single kingdom; it was a great cosmopolitan organization with a wide experience and artistic sympathies beyond the attainment of the isolated barbarian prince. The Church still needed ornaments and sacred utensils of traditional character, and above all she required a figure-art for the representation of sacred subjects. For the satisfaction of these needs she relied in great measure upon the monasteries which were now established in Gaul, and kept the country in continual relation to the Christian East.[2]

The first monasteries known to us are those at Ligugé near Poitiers (about A.D. 360), and at Tours, both founded by St. Martin, the latter when he became bishop of the chief city of Touraine.[3] The most famous and influential community was, however, that of the *Insulani* founded in A.D. 410 by Honoratus on the isle of Lérins.[4] This monastery became the great asylum for literature and science after the irruption of the Goths into Italy. The monks were renowned for their learning, and Arles,

---

[1] The jewellery was of a type introduced from the East by the Goths (Dalton, *Archaeologia*), viii, 1902, p. 267.

[2] See L. Bréhier, as above; R. Rocholl, *Zeitschrift für Kirchengeschichte*, xxv, 1904, pp. 481 ff. The Merovingian MSS., which are chiefly illuminated with decorative ornament and capital letters, exhibit many oriental affinities, amongst which the most notable are the capitals composed of fish and animals, to which there are curious parallels in Armenia. For these MSS. see the Comte de Bastard's Album of reproductions, of which there is a copy in the British Museum.

[3] Dom Cuthbert Butler, *The Lausiac History of Palladius* (vol. vi of *Texts and Studies*, contributions to biblical and patristic literature, ed. by Dr. J. Armitage Robinson), p. 245 (1898).

[4] Comte de Montalembert, *The Monks of the West, from St. Benedict to St. Bernard*, i, p. 346.

Avignon, Lyon, Vienne, Troyes, and Metz took bishops from among their number. The rival of Lérins was the monastery of St. Victor at Marseilles, founded by Cassian, the greatest organizer of monastic life in Gaul.[1] His rules for the government of his community were embodied in his *Institutions* and *Conferences*; the second part of the latter work is dedicated to Honoratus, and to Eucherius, a prominent monk of Lérins.

The significant point with regard to all these early communities in Gaul lies in their direct connexion with Egypt, and their adoption in many cases of the Egyptian eremitic rule. Cassian himself had lived for seven years as a monk in the Thebaid; it was his policy to adhere to Egyptian

Fig. 51. Two-handled chalice : Treasury of S. Marco, Venice. (Schlumberger-Hachette.) P. 552.

precedent; his dedication of the *Conferences* to Honoratus probably implies that his great rival held views analogous to his own. Literary evidence proves that some of the earliest monks established on Gaulish soil were, like the first monks of Italy, immigrants from the East. Sidonius Apollinaris relates the death near Clermont of a Syrian hermit from the Thebaid.[2] Gregory of Tours speaks of the austere eremitic life led by the monks of Auvergne.[3] In the fifth and sixth centuries Gallic monasticism was clearly Egyptian both in theory and practice. The influence of similar Eastern connexions upon the Church in England and Ireland is noticed below (p. 97).

With the Carolingian period the influence of East-Christian art in the West was undiminished, though it entered upon a new phase. Education was now a chief concern of government; the monastic artists were taught to seek good models wherever they could be found; and many of those

[1] Montalembert, i, p. 355.　　　　　　　[2] *Epistolae*, vii. 17.
[3] In his *Liber vit. patrum.* See Butler, as above, p. 247.

which were most readily available were among the works of art previously imported from Syria and Egypt. Studied by trained and intelligent men filled with a new spirit of emulation, these models now for the first time began to exercise their proper influence, the effects of which are very conspicuous in Carolingian manuscript illumination (Ch. VIII). After the ninth century there was a time of comparative slackness in the North of France. But with the dawn of the Romanesque period the southern French provinces began to teach the rest of Europe how to revive the lost art of monumental sculpture. This they did partly through the imitation of models upon the monumental scale, but more extensively through

FIG. 52. Bowl of a chalice with gemmed mounts in the treasury of S. Marco; about the eleventh century. (Schlumberger-Hachette.) P. 552.

copying illuminated manuscripts and ivory carvings of the Macedonian Renaissance, which now entered Western Europe in great numbers. Vöge has observed that the well-known tympanum at Vézelay may be an attempt to render a Pentecost such as that in the first cupola of the Cathedral of St. Mark at Venice,[1] and Viollet-le-Duc had remarked at an earlier date that this work and the almost equally remarkable tympanum at Moissac were really paintings translated into stone. The clearest proof of the influence exerted upon major sculpture by Byzantine ivory carvings is to be found in Germany (p. 238); but France, to which the German sculpture of the period was deeply indebted, undoubtedly copied similar models. Such are the figures of Our Lord on the tympanum of Saint-Étienne at Cahors;[2] such a Christ and Cherubs in Saint-Sernin at Toulouse. In the sphere of mere ornament instances of imitation are very frequent, especially in Languedoc and Provence, where foliate and animal designs allied to those seen on Eastern textiles are of comparative frequency.[3]

[1] *Repertorium* xxii 1899 p. 99.   [2] A. Michel, *Histoire de l'art*, i, Pt. II, p. 628.
[3] Cf. Diehl, *Manuel*, p. 677.

With the thirteenth century France developed a great national art which owed little or nothing to foreign influence.

In Spain, from the fourth to the eighth century, the influence of the East was less important than in the country conquered by the Franks. Gaul was on the direct route from the Eastern Mediterranean to the North-west; Spain lay apart from the great artery of commerce which followed the valley of the Rhone. When the Suevi and Vandals, and after them the Visigoths, made themselves masters of the Iberian peninsula[1] the Roman provincial culture was gradually transformed, though, as in France, the Gothic princes maintained a barbaric civilization of their own, not without dignity and splendour. The official and ecclesiastical language was Latin, and the numerous inscriptions preserved in the country contain little which points to any considerable intercourse with the East. After the conquest of Italy by the generals of Justinian, the Byzantine Empire obtained a temporary hold upon the Mediterranean coast, including Malaga and Cartagena; but the population were not eager to pass under the exacting imperial rule, and in A. D. 584 Leovigild the Visigoth recovered all that had been lost. Byzantine art in Spain is directly represented by a few capitals of the sixth century, of the types made in Proconnesus and exported to all the coasts of the Mediterranean. After the Arab conquest the art of the country was more deeply imbued with the oriental spirit than that of any other part of Europe; but both motives and technical methods had been modified by transmission through Saracenic hands.

GERMANY.

Although 'Germany' and France were under a single government in the time of Charlemagne, it has been convenient to treat the eastern part of the Frankish dominions in a separate section, anticipating the division which took place after the great emperor's death. Only a small part of Germany, that lying to the west about the valleys of the Rhine and the Moselle, had been influenced by Christian art in the first centuries of our era. Several examples of Roman provincial art in this area, such as the sepulchral monuments at Neumagen, appear to be affected by late Hellenistic types like those which found their way into Central Syria.[2] The ubiquitous Syrians had reached Trèves in Roman times: the position of the city in the fourth century as an imperial residence ensured their continued presence; the first bishop of Trèves was Agritius of Antioch (A. D. 328). There still exist several gravestones of immigrants from the East in these early times. One is to the daughter of a Syrian; another to Azizos, son of Agrippa, a Syrian from the region of Apamea; a third to Ursikonos, an

---

[1] The Vandals first occupied Spain in A.D. 409.

[2] Sir Charles Newton has observed this in his discussion of the Mausoleum of Halicarnassus. See also Strzygowski, *Der Dom zu Aachen und seine Entstellung*, 1904, pp. 44-5. For Syrians in Mainz, see *B. Z.*, xv, 1906, p. 415, and for other Graeco-Syrian influences, J. Poppelreuter, *Bonner Jahrbücher*, Hefte 114-15, pp. 344 ff., and *B. Z.*, xv, 1906, p. 703.

Anatolian; two more to natives of Adana in Cilicia. Works of art confirm the statements as to early relations with the Christian East. The ivory panel in the cathedral treasury, with a scene depicting a transportation of relics (p. 211, and Fig. 127), may have entered Germany by the Rhone Valley or through Italy. The Barberini diptych, now in the Louvre (p. 199), must have been preserved in Germany at a very early period, for

Fig. 53.　Paten of about the eleventh century : Treasury of S. Marco, Venice.　P. 552.

among the names written in ink on the back are those of four archbishops of Trèves living between the fourth and sixth centuries,[1] with those of two bishops of Metz. It may have been carved in Alexandria, to which city an early ivory pyxis with Nilotic scenes now at Wiesbaden, but formerly at Trèves, may also be ascribed.

Other Christian works of art of an oriental origin are at Aix-la-Chapelle, perhaps imported in the time of Charlemagne, perhaps already

[1] Agritius, Anastasius, Rusticus, Sabaudus.

in the country at an earlier date. The ivory panels now inlaid in the pulpit of the cathedral are mentioned in another place (p. 212), where it is pointed out that several subjects appear to indicate an Alexandrian influence; the form of the cathedral itself is that of an oriental *Martyrion*.[1] The ancient silk textiles in which were wrapped the remains in the reliquaries at Aix and at Cologne (Ch. X) are in an early Persian or Byzantine style. These examples tend to show that the influences from the Christian East continued from Roman times to those of the Carolingian Empire.

Germany east of the Rhine had no Christian art until the latter part of the tenth century. In the earlier Carolingian period the population of this region was still pagan: Charlemagne spent years of his life in combating the heathen Saxons of Hanover and Oldenburg; Boniface and his missionaries laboured among the Frisians and other tribes; Emmeram, Rupert, and Corbinian devoted themselves to the conversion of Bavaria. But the rise of the Saxon dynasty of the Ottos in the tenth century was accompanied by a rapid growth of Byzantine influence in Northern Germany. The three emperors of this name all entertained friendly relations with Constantinople; they even adopted the costume of the Byzantine court, with the long tunic reaching to the feet. Presents were sent from Constantinople to Otto the Great on more than one occasion;[2] and Widukind says of this prince that he received from 'Romans, Greeks, and Saracens' vessels of gold and silver, glass, bronze, ivory, and other materials, ornamented with animals hitherto unseen.[3] The Saxon emperors maintained a regular intercourse with Venice; treaties of commerce were signed, and gifts exchanged with the rulers of the Adriatic city. Such being the relations of the Germans to the Byzantine Empire and the North-Italian representative of its culture, it was natural that the marriage of the young Otto II to the Byzantine princess Theophano should have produced a considerable effect upon German industrial art. The ground was already prepared; there was not so much a sudden importation of work absolutely new and strange as a reinforcement of models already known and appreciated. The princess brought with her *innumerae thesaurorum divitiae*, which must certainly have included jewels and figured silk textiles; nor is it improbable that her suite included persons themselves skilled in diverse arts of luxury.[4] The growth of a Rhenish school of cloisonné enamellers in the time of Archbishop Egbert of Trèves at the close of the tenth century (A. D. 975–93) was certainly the result of Byzantine influence (see Ch. VIII); at the same time Byzantine floral

---

[1] Strzygowski, *Dom zu Aachen*, has summarized the evidence proving the existence of an East-Christian influence in the art of Gaul and Germany in the first seven centuries.

[2] G. Humann, *Repertorium für Kunstwissenschaft*, xxv, 1902, 17. In the reign of Otto took place the embassy of Luitprand to Nicephorus Phocas, from which we learn interesting details with regard to the manufacture of silk textiles (p. 587).

[3] *Res gestae Sax.*, iii, c. 56.

[4] On the question of Byzantine artists working in Germany in the second half of the tenth century and later, see E. Müntz, *Rev. de l'art chrétien*, 1893, pp. 181 ff.

ornament makes its appearance in German works of art [1] and Byzantine influence may be observed in the illumination of manuscripts.

The intimate relations between Germany and the East did not cease in the eleventh century. Conrad II sent an embassy, with gifts, to Constantinople; Henry III did the same, and received a mission from the Eastern court in return. Henry IV received many Byzantine gifts, a golden altarpiece, a pectoral cross of gold and pearls, a cup of sardonyx, and costly textiles. Irene, consort of John Comnenus, sent to her niece Uhhilde, Duchess of Bavaria, a gold cross enriched with gems.[2] Wibald of Stablo visited Constantinople in A. D. 1155 and A. D. 1157, when he probably brought back examples of enamel work and other precious objects.[3]

FIG. 54.   Crystal paten with gemmed mounts: Treasury of S. Marco, Venice.
(Schlumberger-Hachette.)   P. 552.

It is not to be supposed that the influx of these splendid objects provided no stimulus to the industrial art of the West. In addition to these imperial gifts, the wealthy and powerful pilgrims who visited the Holy Land before the crusades brought back many Byzantine works of art; after the crusades there was importation *en masse* into the important cities of Germany and France. The scanty remains of the pillage of

[1] Humann, *Beiträge zur Geschichte von Stadt und Stift Essen*, 1898, pp. 100–1 ; Vöge, *Ergänzungsheft* vii of the *Westdeutsche Zeitschrift*, p. 357.   Some works of art may have been imported into Germany by maritime commerce.   The monk of St. Gall says that there were Greeks on the Oder in the tenth century (*De Carolo magno*, lib. ii, c. 16, in *Mon. Germ. hist.*, ii, p. 737).
[2] For the above gifts, see Humann, p. 114.
[3] J. Janssen, *Wibald von Stablo und Corvey*, 1854, pp. 199 and 208 ; *Archaeologia*, lxii, p. 26.

Constantinople now at Limburg, Aix, Hildesheim, Halberstadt, Augsburg, Munich, and other towns show how very great the riches of the Eastern capital must have been.[1]   And when we think of the constant movement of treasured objects through the custom of making gifts, through bequests, through loans for purposes of copying, and through exchange, it is easy to imagine how strong an influence the fine Byzantine craftsmanship

Fig. 55. Silver dish of the sixth century in the museum at Nicosia, Cyprus. P. 574.

may have exerted upon the industrious artists of the German monasteries.[2] The embossed metal-work on the shrine of St. Felix at Aix-la-Chapelle, with foliate ornament of evident Byzantine parentage, is but one among many objects which furnish the proof of this supposition.[3]   Illuminated MSS. written at Regensburg in the early eleventh century show in many ways a Byzantine influence. This was only to be expected, since Re-

---

[1] Riant, *Exuviae Sacrae Constantinopolitanae.*
[2] Humann, *Repertorium,* xxv, 1902, pp. 19–20.
[3] S. Beissel, *Kunstschätze des Aachener Kaiserdomes,* Pl. X.

gensburg was at this time a principal centre of German art, while it lay upon the trade route connecting the South of Germany with Italy and Constantinople.[1]

German art of the Romanesque period is so permeated by Byzantine influences that by the thirteenth century we find a general absorption of oriental iconographical types rather than the patient imitation of particular features. German individuality asserts itself in the treatment of details, and there is a difference in feeling which is usually quite distinctive: this is evident in manuscript illuminations, where the material for comparative study is considerable (Ch. VIII). In ivory carvings the imitation is sometimes very close, as in the case of a panel with the Crucifixion in the British Museum.[2] Byzantine miniatures and ivory carvings continued of great importance to the development of Northern art; sometimes they reached Germany indirectly, through the influence of the Southern French

FIG. 56. Monogram and inscription in niello on a silver spoon of the sixth century from Lampsacus. (British Museum.) P. 567.

sculpture which they had originally inspired, sometimes directly by the copying of manuscripts and minor sculptures imported from the East-Roman Empire. The choir-sculptures in Bamberg Cathedral present affinities to the reliefs of Moissac, Vézelay, Toulouse, St. Julien de Joncy, and Ste Croix at Bordeaux.[3] German ivory carvings now at Berlin and Munich, probably in like manner produced at Bamberg,[4] bear a similar relationship to French sculpture, suggesting that French influence on German plastic art may first have been exerted through the medium of ivories. The current which flowed thus early into France probably pursued its course almost immediately into Germany, and the reliefs at Bamberg afford early evidence of its passage. Its effects continued for many years, for the later Bamberg sculptures, and even those of Strasburg Cathedral, show traces of the original Byzantine inspiration.[5] A more northern school of German sculpture reveals a similar influence of the ivory carving. The figure of Our Lord on the tympanum of the Church of St. Godehard at Hildesheim is so close to the style of tenth-century Byzantine ivory reliefs as represented by an example in the Victoria and Albert Museum, that a direct imitation of the type is almost certain.[6] For in the sculpture at Hildesheim there is a marked and very sudden

[1] G. Swarzenski, *Die Regensburger Buchmalerei des 10. und 11. Jahrhunderts*, Leipsic, 1901.

[2] *Catalogue of the Ivory Carvings of the Christian Era*, 1909, No. 58.

[3] A. Weese, *Die Bamberger Domskulpturen*, 1897, and *Der Dom zu Bamberg*, 1898; Dehio, *Repertorium*, xxii, 1899, p. 133; W. Vöge, *Repertorium*, xxii. 94 ff., and xxiv. 195 ff.

[4] Vöge, *Repertorium*, xxii. 96.

[5] Vöge, *Repertorium*, xxiv. 200. Cf. the 'Death of the Virgin' at Strasburg with that of a Byzantine ivory at Munich (Library, Cim. 58).

[6] A. Goldschmidt, Prussian *Jahrbuch*, xxi, 1900, p. 233. For the ivory see W. Maskell, *Description of the Ivories, &c.*, p. 110; H. Graeven, *Elfenbeinwerke in photographischer Nachbildung*, Ser. 1, No. 61.

advance in plastic skill within the short space of twenty years (A. D. 1190–1210), a period too brief for any gradual evolution of indigenous art. It is safe to conclude that the improvement is due to extraneous influence, and that this influence was probably exerted through the agency of the minor arts: as suggested elsewhere, the case is perhaps a parallel to that of the Northumbrian sculpture of an earlier date (p. 238). The head of Bishop Adelog in the cathedral crypt at Hildesheim also recalls the modelling of a head of St. Stephen upon another Byzantine ivory at South Kensington. At Halberstadt the drapery of the figures of apostles in the choir suggests a Byzantine model.

It will be gathered from the above instances that, though they began later, the effects of Eastern influence on German mediaeval art were hardly less profound than in the case of France.

The British Isles.

The affinities between insular and continental types of weapons dating from the remote Bronze Age indicate a connexion between Ireland and Spain even at that period.[1] In Roman times geographers regarded Ireland as midway between Spain and Britain, a fact which proves continued intercourse between Irish and Spanish ports. Although the island was never conquered by Rome, the existence of Ogam stones, apparently earlier in date than the fifth century, tends to prove that Latin must have been known at that early time: the discovery of coins of the Republic and early Empire may point to some intercourse with the Roman provinces.[2] Tacitus also notices the trade between the Empire and the island. The story of St. Patrick shows that in the first part of the fifth century commercial relations were still maintained: the saint escaped from his first captivity in Ireland in a ship carrying the highly valued Celtic hounds to some port north of the Loire or Garonne, possibly Bordeaux.[3] Christianity had reached Ireland before Patrick. The election of Palladius as bishop points to the early existence of Christian communities. The Paschal system which prevailed in Britain down to the seventh century was probably introduced before Patrick's mission. The saint had sojourned at the half-oriental monastery of Lérins (see above, p. 88), and had been trained at Auxerre;[4] he used the Gallican liturgy, which differed from that of Rome and was connected with liturgies of the East. The story of St. Patrick shows us how intimate must have been the relation between the earliest culture of Christian Ireland and the East. The fact explains the learning

---

[1] Especially obvious in the bronze halberd-blades.
[2] For these facts see Prof. Bury's *Life of St. Patrick* (1905), pp. 12, 185, 288, 312.
[3] Bury, p. 340.
[4] Ibid., pp. 49, 152, 296. Patrick's visit to Rome dates from A. D. 441–3. He brought back relics of St. Peter and St. Paul. The cult of relics steadily increased in importance between the fourth and seventh centuries; see H. Zimmer, *Celtic Church*, pp. 119 ff. ; and Victricius, Bishop of Rouen, in Migne, *Patr. Lat.*, t. xx (Bury, p. 152).

of the later Irish monks, which gives them such an honourable place in the history of civilization in the dark ages.

No artistic remains of the first Christian centuries in Ireland have survived: it is only from the seventh century at earliest that material exists for the study of Celtic Christian art. This material confirms the historical statements as to the connexion of the Irish Church with the orientalized Gallican Church. The Irish illuminated MSS. contain seated figures of Evangelists writing which can only have been derived from East-Christian illuminated gospels of the sixth century, for such types were unknown elsewhere, and no other Western region can well have

Fig. 57.   David killing the bear : silver dish found near Kyrenia and now at Nicosia.

supplied the models. The earliest example of such a seated Evangelist known to us is the St. Mark of the Codex Rossanensis (see Ch. VIII), and the type is derived from pagan forms based in the first instance on Hellenistic bas-reliefs. The figures of angels have probably the same origin ; in fact all the scenes including human figures, however fantastic they may sometimes appear, are probably distorted versions of compositions first popularized in the Christian East.[1] Some of the subjects which occur upon the high crosses and other monuments of the period from the tenth to the twelfth centuries are probably late versions of such early introductions. Diminished skill in figure-sculpture and successive copying have rendered the course of their development obscure : sometimes we seem to trace motives definitely suggested by Egyptian models.[2] But in all this later work a Scandinavian influence is apparent, and this intrusive force has modified

[1] The Durham Book (Lindisfarne Gospels) in the British Museum affords a proof of the oriental origin of the Evangelist types, for the figures are accompanied by their names in Greek, written in Latin character, O Agios Markos, &c. The book, though written at Lindisfarne, is still strongly under the influence of the Irish school.

[2] e.g. the representation of Christ with two wands, one over each shoulder, like Osiris with his sceptres, a motive which reappears in the Alfred Jewel (Proc. Soc. Ant., xx. 71).

or replaced many elements of Southern or Eastern origin. As it was with the figures so it was with the ornament. Although certain of the pagan Celtic motives survived to a late date, the introduction of Christianity brought an influx of designs previously unknown in the West of Europe; a number of these can be traced in the first instance to Syria and Egypt, though they may often have been mediately derived from Rome and Ravenna, themselves at this period outposts of oriental art (see pp. 77, 78). The interlaced and plaited designs are more probably reintroduc-

Fig. 58. David and the lion : silver dish of the sixth century from Cyprus.
(Collection of J. Pierpont Morgan, Esq.)

tions from these sources than deliberate imitations of the borders on local Roman mosaic pavements. In Ireland they were certainly imported after the Roman occupation of England had come to an end, and were ultimately developed into intricate forms of knot-work.[1] The fret-patterns, though set out diagonally in a manner as yet without precedent in the East, came in at the same time, and are foreign to the old Celtic art:[2] the step-patterns may possibly prove of like descent. Whether their origin is to be

[1] The late J. Romilly Allen traced the evolution of these designs in his *Celtic Art in Britain.* Interlacings appear at an early date upon mosaic pavements, which perhaps were the first works of industrial art to adopt them from textiles or basket-work. They appear in the Hellenistic area, from which they were imported into Italy and thence into the Roman provinces of the north and west. See also G. Coffey, *Guide to the Celtic Antiquities of the Christian Period, Royal Irish Academy Collection,* Dublin, 1909, pp. 10 ff.

[2] The fret, a very old design (see Ch. XIII), was popular in the first centuries of our era in Palmyra and other Eastern sites. We find tendencies to incline the angles and to form a continuous pattern of several connected rows in the period from the fourth to the sixth century. The Irish diagonal or 'skew' fret may possibly have been anticipated in the East (*Proc. Soc. Ant.,* xxii. 215).

sought in the angular motives of basket-work, or weaving, or cloisonné work in gold, or whether it is connected with the mural crenellations of Hither Asia, which undoubtedly suggested the borders of mosaic pavements at Pergamon and bands of crenellated ornament in other branches of art, they also came into Ireland after the century of St. Patrick.[1] The early Irish metal-work employs the same designs as the MSS., and in some cases the illuminators appear to have borrowed motives which originated in metal.[2] With the sixth century the Irish monks had begun to carry their art into the north of Britain. From their settlements in Iona their influence spread into Northumbria in the early seventh century, when Lindisfarne was founded. In Northumbria, Celtic art met and fused with another art probably originating in centres allied to those which had already modified the designs of pagan Ireland.

The reputation of the Irish monasteries for scholarship stood exceedingly high. Columba, born in West Leinster in A. D. 543, was educated in the great monastery of Bangor in County Down, where we know that Latin was studied and music assiduously practised. The story of his missionary career, first in Britain, then in Gaul, finally in Italy, is the story of other Irish missionaries who in the eighth and ninth centuries introduced the elements of Irish art into the Teutonic kingdoms of Europe. The position of Ireland as a seat of culture in the early Middle Ages is attested by the career of Dagobert, son of Sigibert of Austrasia. In the middle of the seventh century this prince of Austrasia was sent by Grimwald to an Irish monastery, where he remained for seventeen years, returning at the end of that time and enjoying a reign of five years' duration.[3]

Christianity had entered England and Scotland during the Roman occupation, either by a gradual infiltration from Gaul and the lower Rhine, or by direct missionary effort from the (Greek) churches at Lyon and Vienne[4] Monuments of the occupation at this early time are not very numerous. The small church discovered at Silchester[5] is remarkable as being of a type which is not Italian, but oriental. The sacred monogram, in forms used in the fourth and fifth centuries, occurs upon sepulchral stones,[6] and it is to be noted that the form within a circle and having the loop of the *Rho* turned outwards like an R, as seen in Scotland, is common in Ravenna, and has been found on slabs excavated by the French expedition at Delphi.[7] Christian symbols occur upon a few objects of the minor arts of this early period found in Britain. But the

---

[1] Note the bands of inclined crenellation on the Pilastri Acritani at Venice. Also border of mosaic in the house of the Consul Attalus at Pergamon (*Mitth. k. deutsch. arch. Inst.*, Athens, 1907, xxxii, Pl. 17).

[2] J. M. Doran, *Burlington Magazine*, June 1908, p. 138.

[3] Hodgkin, *Italy and her Invaders*, vii. 39.

[4] Warren, *The Liturgy and Ritual of the Celtic Church*, holds the latter view. The former is maintained by H. Zimmer, *The Celtic Church in Britain and Ireland*, p. 2 (1902).

[5] *Proc. Soc. Ant.* xvii. 206.

[6] J. Romilly Allen, *Early Christian Symbolism* and *Early Christian Monuments of Scotland*.

[7] Anderson, *Scotland in Early Christian Times*, 2nd Ser., 1881, p. 274.

traditions of provincial Roman art seem to have died out after the evacuation of the country in the fifth century. It was not pagan Rome which inspired the figure-art of the Anglian or the Saxon.

When we reach Anglo-Saxon times the intercourse between England, France, and Italy was once more continuous, and the indications furnished by the monuments are more precise. The royal houses of our island were now allied by marriage to those of the Franks and Lombards. In the latter part of the seventh century a Kentish princess was the queen of the

Fig. 59. Silver dish of the sixth century from Cyprus, with a scene from the Life of David.
(Collection of J. Pierpont Morgan, Esq.)

Lombard Cunincpert; [1] during the same period Balthildis, an Anglo-Saxon princess, acted as regent for her son in Neustria.[2] English pilgrims were frequently in Rome, and among their number were Coinred, King of Mercia, Offa, Prince of the East Saxons, and Ine, King of Wessex.[3] In the year A. D. 680, at a conference convened by Pope Agatho, Anglo-Saxon delegates had joined in condemning Monothelitism.[4] From this time, and through the eighth century, the English Church was influential throughout Europe. It was the Church of Bede : it sent out the great missionaries Willibrord, Winnifrith, and Boniface to evangelize the pagan Teutons of Europe. The introduction of works of art from the South and East began at an early date. The Gospels of Corpus Christi College, Cambridge, evidently a primitive copy of an East-Christian model perhaps made in

[1] Hodgkin, as above, vi, p. 305.　　　[2] Ibid., vii, p. 42.
[3] Ibid., vi, p. 322.　　　[4] Ibid., vi, p. 344.

the South of Italy (Ch. VIII), may have been included among the numerous
books mentioned by Bede as sent from Rome to Augustine by Gregory
the Great : its antiquity is evident, and it was in the monastery of
St. Augustine at Canterbury between the years A. D. 844 and A. D. 949.   But
in the earliest history of English Christian art under kings of Teutonic
blood Northumbria occupies the most important position.   The conversion
of the country had been effected from two sources.   On the one side was
the early Scoto-Irish Church and the British Church in Wales; on the
other the Roman Church first represented by Augustine.   In the latter
part of the seventh century the agreement was reached between the native

FIG. 60.   The Anointing of David : silver dish of the sixth century from Cyprus.
(Collection of J. Pierpont Morgan, Esq.)

and the Roman Churches, and it is about this time that a great artistic
activity, especially marked by the erection of churches in stone, began in
the North of England.[1]   The famous names connected with this artistic
revival are those of Wilfrid of Hexham and Benedict Biscop of Jarrow,
both frequent visitors to Gaul and Italy, and importers of foreign workmen and foreign works of art.   Eddius relates that Wilfrid introduced
masons (*caementarios*) into Northumberland; Bede, writing in the eighth
century, states that Benedict brought masons from Gaul to build him
a stone church 'in the Roman style'.[2]   With the introduction of an

[1] For what follows the reader should consult the article on this early English sculpture
by Messrs. Prior and Gardner in the *Architectural Review*, xii, 1902 ; also the same authors'
work on English sculpture, now in the press.
[2] Bede's Life of Benedict Biscop, in his *Historia Abbatum Wiremuthensium*, will be found in
Migne, xciv. 713 ; the section about Benedict's artistic activity may be consulted in J. von
Schlosser, *Quellenbuch zur Kunstgeschichte des abendländischen Mittelalters*, where references to
writers on early history of art are given.

ecclesiastical architecture in stone there suddenly appears a stone sculpture of a quality never before equalled in England, and destined to remain unsurpassed for several centuries. The Bewcastle Cross, set up as its runic inscription seems to show 'in the first year of Ecgfrith', and thus dated to A. D. 670, has a figure of Our Lord standing upon the lion and dragon, of peculiar dignity and modelled with a skill which astonishes when it is remembered that at the close of the seventh century monumental sculpture of any merit at all had almost entirely disappeared throughout the whole of Europe and the Byzantine Empire (see p. 110). The Ruthwell Cross,[1] dating from much the same time, has another fine figure of Our Lord standing with a book in his left hand and raising the right in the gesture of benediction, together with other subjects all plastically conceived and far above the standard of a barbaric art. Fragments found near the site of Wilfrid's and Benedict's churches at Hexham and at Jarrow exhibit the same advanced style. Of these the Cross of Acca, Bishop of Hexham (d. A. D. 740), the greater part of which is now in the Cathedral Library at Durham, is remarkable, though without figure subjects;[2] another example is a curious carved stone now in the Abbey Church at Hexham, with the lower part of a nude human figure among vine foliage, the treatment of the limbs showing a considerable knowledge of modelling. Reasons are advanced elsewhere (p. 236) for the belief that this really remarkable sculpture, which decayed almost as suddenly as it arose, must have been inspired from foreign (East-Christian) sources. Its appearance is probably to be explained in a similar way to that of the later sculpture at Hildesheim (p. 96), though the links in the chain of evidence are here by no means so complete.

The minor arts of Northumbria furnish interesting confirmation of this view. It is probable that the 'Franks casket' derives some of its subjects either from illustrations in a manuscript 'Chronicle of the world', of a type first circulated from Alexandria at the beginning of the fifth century (Ch. VIII), or from reproductions of these subjects in wood or ivory.[3] These chronicles contained just such secular subjects as the suckling of Romulus and Remus and the capture of Jerusalem, which we find upon the casket intermingled with episodes from northern legendary cycles. English travellers and pilgrims, often ecclesiastics of wealth and standing like Benedict Biscop himself, may well have brought back ivories or even wooden coffers in addition to MSS., and to the figured silk textiles of which we have record.

---

[1] J. Romilly Allen, *The Early Christian Monuments of Scotland*, pp. 442 ff., and J. Anderson's Introduction, p. xxx. The fragments from Hoddam in the Edinburgh Museum exhibit the same qualities as the figures upon the two great crosses, and must be the work of the same school (ibid., p. 440).

[2] Haverfield and Greenwell, *Catalogue of the Sculptured and Inscribed Stones in the Cathedral Library at Durham*, 1899, pp. 53 ff. The cross at Hilton of Cadboll has foliage containing birds.

[3] British Museum, *Catalogue of Ivory Carvings*, No. 30; J. Strzygowski, *Das orientalische Italien*, p. 18. The flat technique and poor modelling of the casket suggests that the carvers may have worked either direct from a MS. or from a wooden coffer, like that in the Cathedral of Terracina, but with historical subjects instead of merely animals.

The Greek workmen whom these great ecclesiastics employed may have either had ivories in their own possession or have been supplied with them by their patrons. If so, the ivories must have been of fine quality, worthy to rank with the panels of the Ravenna chair.

Between the first half of the eighth century and the second half of the tenth, that is to say for a period of more than two hundred years, the power of rendering the human figure with truth and dignity was almost entirely lost. The Scandinavian raids unsettled the country; elements of Norse ornamental art found their way into North Britain and Ireland, fusing with pre-existing motives, until by the beginning of the eleventh

FIG. 61.   David before Saul : silver dish of the sixth century from Cyprus.
(Collection of J. Pierpont Morgan, Esq.)

century the highly decorative art of the later high crosses had been evolved. With that art we are not here concerned, for the Christian East exerted no further influence upon its development. But the Anglo-Saxon Renaissance in the South of England, which placed the art of Wessex on a level with that of any country in contemporary Europe, claims our most careful attention, though it must at once be said that a direct Byzantine influence is not easy to trace either in the numerous illuminated MSS. of the Winchester school, or in the rarer examples of Saxon sculpture still preserved. In these we once more discover work of a quality unsurpassed for about two hundred years. The sculptors exhibit a capacity for modelling which is in advance of that shown by their successors in the Norman period; they can execute figures in three-quarter profile, and can lend lively expression to the faces. Their monumental work is represented by the large stone roods at Romsey, Hedbourne Worthy, and Little Langford, with the

two angels now set over the chancel arch at Bradford-on-Avon.[1]   If the
two large reliefs now in Chichester Cathedral are of this period, we must
add to the talents of these Saxon sculptors real power in the expression of
emotion and a dramatic conception of traditional subjects.[2]   The rood at
Romsey is not unlike a Byzantine Christ of the tenth or eleventh century,
as represented upon ivory carvings of that period; but the Chichester
work is animated by another spirit, it has almost the realism of South-
German art in the fifteenth century.   Sculpture upon a small scale is well
represented by a few ivory carvings of great interest, chiefly in the British
and the Victoria and Albert Museums.   The figures upon the handle of the
seal of Ælfric are finely modelled;[3] so are those upon the beautiful tau-

Fig. 62.   David receiving Samuel's message : silver dishes of the sixth century found in
Cyprus, now at Nicosia.

cross from Alcester:[4] the carvers who produced this work were sculptors
with a true conception of form and movement.   The large panel at South
Kensington with the Adoration of the Magi is in a more ornate and conventional style; the proportions are unduly elongated and the expressions
monotonous, the whole having in it something which suggests the art of
the early tympana at Moissac and Vézelay.

The fine quality of this Wessex sculpture and its apparently sudden
rise are probably due to the same causes which encouraged the rapid
growth of the art in Northumbria and Northern Germany (pp. 93, 102).   In
the present case, however, much of the inspiration may have been derived

[1] All reproduced by Messrs. Prior and Gardner, *Architectural Review*, as above, pp. 14–15.
[2] Mr. Prior accepts these reliefs as Saxon, and thinks that they may have been brought
not from the Cathedral of Selsey but from the Saxon Church of St. Peter at Chichester.
Others are disposed to place them later, perhaps even as late as the twelfth century.   As
Mr. Prior points out, however, the architecture is exactly that of early eleventh-century
miniatures, while the figures have more movement and the faces more liveliness of expression
than any of those which can be ascribed to the twelfth century.
[3] British Museum, *Catalogue of Ivory Carvings*, No. 31.
[4] Ibid., No. 32.

in the first instance from France, Germany, and Italy, and the Eastern influence may thus have been indirectly exerted. It was not so much contemporary Byzantine work which furnished our artists with models, though in the eleventh century a few ivory carvings may well have been imported into England; the reflection of the East-Christian art of the sixth century reached them especially through Carolingian illuminated books. It has been remarked that it is difficult to trace direct Byzantine influence upon the Anglo-Saxon schools: the most remarkable of these, that of Winchester, exhibits much originality.

In the goldsmith's work of the time the threads which may connect Saxon art with the East are equally difficult to detect. English craftsmen retained under Christianity the skill in which their pagan ancestors had excelled. The gold rings of kings and princesses, the enamelled Alfred Jewel, survive to prove their capacity: the work is in one sense wholly English, but in the models and perhaps in some of the processes we may suspect the influence of a foreign art.[1] The reputation of Saxon workmen was appreciated abroad no less than at home, and several references to metal-work made by our countrymen occur in the pages of the *Liber Pontificalis.*

FIG. 63. Carolingian silver bowl, reproducing early East-Christian motives. (British Museum.)

The popes frequently ordered objects in metal from our shores, especially lamps in silver and bronze.[2] Some are stated to have been ornamented with lions, gryphons, and 'serpents',[3] which suggests that

---

[1] The formal foliage and conventional tree-forms upon some of this goldsmith's work suggest the conventional 'sacred trees' of Persia as seen upon the early textiles. They occur on a background of niello upon a sword of the early tenth century found at Wallingford (*Victoria County History, Berkshire*, vol. i, p. 243 ; *Archaeologia*, l, Pl. XXVIII), and upon the gold ring of Ethelwulf in the British Museum. Cf. also a piece of silver in the Cuerdale hoard (*Arch. Journal*, iv. 190, Fig. 90). The design on the back of the Alfred Jewel in the Ashmolean Museum is also of oriental derivation (*Proc. Soc. Ant. London*, xx. 71).

[2] The extracts from the *Liber Pontificalis* are given by S. Beissel in *Zeitschrift für christliche Kunst*, ix, 1896, p. 364. *Gabatae Saxiscae* are mentioned several times (*Liber Pont.*, Duchesne's edition, ii. 36, n. 27 ; i. 417 (Gregory III, n. 7) ; ii. 79, n. 26 (Gregory IV); ii. 120 (Leo IV); ii. 145, n. 24 (Benedict III) ; ii. 153 ; ii. 74).

[3] 'Storiam leonis, diversas istorias serpentorum,' &c.

oriental textiles had found their way to England, and furnished our crafts-men with new designs. It might be argued that these 'Saxon' objects acquired by the popes were really of German rather than English origin were it not distinctly recorded that Egbert, on his visit to Rome in the middle of the ninth century, brought with him costly gifts for the Church of St. Peter, among which four gilded silver lamps of 'Saxon work' are especially mentioned. In connexion with surviving examples of Anglo-Saxon niello it should be noted that several of these Anglo-Saxon works of art are described as inlaid with that substance.[1] For enamels and niello see below, Ch. VIII.

[1] The silver nielloed bowl in the British Museum (Fig. 63) may conceivably be an example of this English work, though the style of its ornament connects it rather with the Frankish Empire (*Archaeologia*, lxi. 357). Strzygowski (*B. Z.*, xix. 665) suggests a Persian origin for this, arguing from the analogies which the ornament presents to that of Sassanian silver. (Cf. J. Smirnoff, *Oriental Silver*, Pl. LXI, LXIX.) Though actual examples of Caro-lingian silver are far to seek, the resemblances to Frankish ornament are very striking, and the form of the bowl is one known in England and Scandinavia in Viking times. Oriental motives are common in Frankish decorative art, so that a general similarity to Sassanian work is easily explained.

FIG. 64.   Illuminated head-piece from a Gospel of the eleventh century in the British Museum, showing conventionalized vine-ornament.

CHAPTER III

SCULPTURE

1. INTRODUCTORY REMARKS.

THE glyptic art had begun to degenerate throughout the Roman Empire long before the foundation of Constantinople, and the establishment of the imperial city did little to arrest its decay.   The new metropolis enjoyed exceptional opportunities which might almost have led to a revival.   The talent of the Eastern provinces was attracted within her walls; she possessed among her treasures famous works of the Hellenic masters.   But neither the Greek nor the Syrian artist of the fourth century could draw from the statues of Pheidias or Lysippus the inspiration which the Italian of the earliest Renaissance derived from mediocre works of the Graeco-Roman period.   The causes of this disparity in achievement are not very far to seek.   To an instinctive appreciation of beauty in form the Italians added a new joy in life and a new intellectual freedom.   The impulse to create was in them; their imagination was breaking free from ancient fetters. They lived in independent states, each with a character and environment of its own, where personality had scope for development, and prescription was no longer accepted without criticism ; they were thus so well prepared for a new illumination that even the inferior models yielded by the soil of their country sufficed to kindle the creative fire. It would be hard to say what might have happened if, instead of their actual models, they had

FIG. 65. Kairos : limestone relief of the fourth century in the Cairo Museum.
(*Catalogue général : Koptische Kunst*, No. 8757.) P. 158.

disinterred such works as the Athena Parthenos of Pheidias or the Hermes of Praxiteles; if, in place of Roman reliefs, they could have studied the firstfruits of the archaic Greek period or the masculine art of Polyclitus. But the sculptor of the Christian East was without the peculiar advantages of the Hellene and the Italian. He was not a member of a small state governed by men enthusiastic for the arts; his country was incorporated in a uniform political system less favourable to the rise of original genius. The genius of the Empire was bureaucratic; in proportion as the frontiers receded the tendency to centralization increased. The conditions which gave individuality to the Italian commune, to the ancient Greek city, or even to the German *Kleinstadt* of the type of Weimar, were here conspicuously wanting. And throughout the whole dominion the imagination of the artist was seldom suffered to range at will, but often held under the control of a Church which prescribed what subjects might be represented and what treatment each must receive.

These psychological and political causes would in themselves have sufficed to make a Renaissance difficult ; but there was another in reserve which seemed to render it impossible. From the very reign of Constantine the Non-Christian East bore hard upon all the Eastern provinces ; not the East which our times have known, dispirited and misruled; but an Orient at all times formidable, and represented by powerful and militant states. The whole feeling of this East [1] was against the sculpture which renders the human form with delicate gradations of relief; it preferred an art confined to ornament and working by strong contrast of light and shade. It thus compelled the sculptor to produce silhouettes and to elaborate pattern ; it had scant appreciation of skilful modelling. Even before the rise of Islam these ideas had encroached upon the Hellenistic world, driving back the Greek influence which in old days had spread inland from the Ionic colonies, and at a later period followed Alexander to the banks of the Indus. In the course of the third century they reached Rome and affected the later reliefs on the Arch of Constantine. By the sixth century of our era the art of Scopas and Praxiteles, so long traditionally honoured in Asia Minor, had ceased to be the equal companion of architecture ; it sank into a dependent place as the craft of decorators and monumental masons.

The aversion of the oriental from the plastic representation of the human form was a fatal hindrance to the sculptor's art in an empire so largely orientalized as that of Byzantium. It was no longer possible to study the nude as the Greeks had studied it. Almost the only figures which were permitted or profitable in representation were clad persons from sacred story, members of the imperial family, or high officials, some of whom wore forgotten costumes only known from copies, others garments without the Hellenic charm, voluminous, half-Eastern robes, often stiff with embroidery and pearls. Under such conditions as these the greater sculpture which depends upon the living model could not but decay. It was indeed time for it to abdicate, and abandon a position which could no longer be honourably maintained; it was better that in the Christian East the glory of the representative arts should be upheld by the worker in

---

[1] For the sense in which the phrase The East is used in this book see Introduction, pp. 59 ff.

mosaic, of whose craft an advanced convention was a natural and proper attribute. It was more fitting that monumental figure-sculpture should disappear than that it should protract a miserable existence under conditions inimical to a healthy growth.

The sculpture of the Christian East was the direct descendant of the latest Hellenistic sculpture as practised both in and beyond Italy during the first two centuries of our era under the aegis of imperial Rome.[1] There is no breach of continuity between the pagan and the Christian art; the principles remained unaltered, the subjects were gradually modified: it was at first an iconographical rather than an artistic change. Many pagan motives were tolerated by Christians, who interpreted them in a new symbolic sense: the examples of Cupid and Psyche and of Orpheus will naturally recur to the memory. By degrees, designs of a definitely Christian character were substituted for these 'neutral' subjects, until in the advanced fourth century they everywhere became predominant. Under such circumstances it was inevitable that the theory and practice of the pagan workshop should have been inherited without essential alteration. We therefore find Christian sculpture accepting the Graeco-Roman idea of background as penetrable space, instead of conceiving it as an impenetrable plane of vision in the manner of earlier Greek art; we find it even attempting to renew the perspectival effects which had distinguished the reliefs of the Trajanic period. We see this in the ivory diptych of Rufius Probianus (p. 191) and on the embossed silver box from S. Nazaro at Milan. The most important and most durable influence which was to affect the evolution of sculpture for many centuries was one which had begun to make itself felt in Roman art from the time of Septimius Severus. It was an influence which originated in the East.

Eastern taste was indifferent to the delicate effects produced by almost imperceptible transition between plane and plane. The oriental preferred a single plane in a single light upon a single ground of darkness. The procedure which found favour in his sight was to cut the background deeply away, so that the design stood out light upon dark space, the result in either case being really a pattern of rhythmic alternation. The delicate play of light and shade at which fine modelling aims was sacrificed to mere contrast of colour: the effect was no longer sculptural but coloristic; the method was optical and independent of inference from touch. The contrast of black and white is so decided that the eye sees nothing beyond the contour of light masses on dark ground; though the position of the colours is reversed, it is the principle of the maker of silhouettes, of the damascener, and the worker in intarsia. This oriental method had indeed been essayed in a purely experimental manner and for a particular purpose by Greek sculptors before the rise of Rome. In the pediment of the treasury of the Cnidians at Delphi the background behind the upper part

---

[1] See also the remarks below, p. 133, in the section on the Christian sarcophagi at Rome and Arles.

of the figures is deeply cut away, so that they emerge against a depth of blackness: moreover, a point to be particularly noticed, the front surface of the figures is nearly flat. Perhaps the logical Greek mind was quick to perceive the consequences of such a device, and for this reason did not

Fig. 66. The Annunciation: end of the Pignatta Sarcophagus at Ravenna. (Ricci.) P. 137.

repeat the experiment. For in the perfect coloristic design, the pattern must be brought forward to a single plane as near as possible to the eye of the spectator, so that every part of its surface may be equally illuminated; only by this means can the utmost contrast be maintained throughout the whole composition. This plan is effective enough in the case of conventional ornament; it succeeds to perfection in such sculptures as the façade of Mshatta, now at Berlin; but it has a very different effect upon human

forms, especially when grouped together. It compels the perfect alignment of all the figures in the foreground, as if on a sunny day they were
drawn up across the mouth of a cavern. In other words, it means the
reinstatement of 'frontality' and the abandonment of foreshortening.
There is no subtlety of gradation: the transition from one plane to another
is rapid and abrupt. A sculpture conforming to these coloristic requirements is compelled to retrace the path towards a primitive art. The
insistence on a single plane has the same result as the desire of the
primitive mind for the most extended and conspicuous surfaces of the things
to be depicted, those surfaces which crowd all others out of the memory-
picture upon which it depends.[1]

The coloristic method has another inevitable consequence. In Greek
reliefs the plane of the background connects each figure with that nearest
to it, joining the two in the unity of a single organic whole. But when
the background is cut out of sight, or treated as if it did not exist, the
bond of union is broken; the figures stand in what Riegl has called cubic
isolation: the sense of solidity and cohesion is lost. This would be of less
moment if the sculptor confined himself to single figures emerging as it
were from a matrix of darkness. But when a group is represented the
psychological connexion between its members is sacrificed, and the composition is resolved into detached units. When a subject is to be conceived
as a whole, the emotional and psychic unity must be visibly and materially
suggested; but by the coloristic method it is visibly denied. The figures
aligned at the cave's mouth are there by compulsion, not because each
is playing a voluntary part in a common action. They are mere numbers,
any one of which may be withdrawn without essential loss. But when
groups are habitually rendered by this frontal method of isolation even
the artist himself is apt to forget the dramatic significance of his subject.
It is without emotional suggestion; it ceases to be interesting, sinking
to the level of a decorative design. In ceremonial and religious subjects,
where there is no lively action, where the detachment of figure from figure
has a certain propriety, where a symmetrical treatment is often congruous
with the scene depicted, the new style has its own effectiveness. In scenes
involving violent movement and concerted action, on the other hand, it is
necessarily unsuccessful: it destroys the common emotional motive which
gives such compositions their life and interest. This point is well illustrated by the friezes upon the Arch of Constantine (p. 142). Those which
represent the battles of the Milvian bridge and of Verona fail in their
appeal: compared with the spirited combats of earlier Roman reliefs, they
are engagements of disconnected units; there is no interlocking of strained

---

[1] It is unnecessary to enter into any long explanation of the psychological basis of primitive and archaic art now that Prof. Loewy's essay on *The Rendering of Nature in Early Greek Art*
is available in Mr. J. Fothergill's excellent translation (Duckworth, 1907). A definition of
'frontality', a conspicuous feature in primitive art, will be found on p. 45: 'An imaginary
plane taken through the top of the head, nose, backbone, breastbone, navel, and crotch, so as
to divide the body into two symmetrical halves, remains always unchanged, without bending
or turning in any direction.'

limbs, no fury and wrath of battle. With the other two reliefs, which represent the emperor speaking on the rostra and presiding at the *Congiarium*, the effect produced is far more satisfactory. The isolation of the figures befits the leisured ceremonial action; the detachment of the central figure enhances the might and majesty of the imperial office. The transition from such scenes to those of Christian import is a natural

Fig. 67. Impost capital of the sixth century : S. Vitale, Ravenna. (Ricci.) P. 176.

one; had the sculpture of the fourth century been endowed with vitality and endurance it might have travelled far upon the lines thus indicated; it might have achieved those purposed triumphs at which Riegl believed it to have aimed.[1] But the tendencies which the new method represented were decorative tendencies; and in a world in which a Semitic aversion from figure-art grew more and more powerful the glyptic art was condemned to become an art of ornament.

---

[1] Mrs. Strong's discussion of the Constantinian period (*Roman Sculpture*, ch. xiv) is an admirable account of the aesthetic and psychological effects of the coloristic method on figure sculpture, an account doubly valuable inasmuch as it gives in a lucid form the substance so hard to extract from the intricate style of Riegl.

A short digression may perhaps be here permitted in order to recall the affinities which exist between the figure sculpture of the fourth century and that Indian sculpture which relied in great measure upon similar principles. In the reliefs from Gandhâra and Amarâvati (second–fourth centuries A.D.), which are well represented in the British Museum, the influence of the coloristic principle is apparent. Here too there is an evident effort to bring all the figures into one plane, whatever may be their spatial relation to each other or their psychological relation to the action represented, though the reduction to a single plane is not absolute. The artists, intent upon the contrast of light and dark, ignore the method

FIG. 68.   Marble capital of the sixth century in the Cairo Museum.
(*Catalogue général : Koptische Kunst*, No. 7352.)

of creating spatial illusion through perspective and a gradually diminishing relief. Instead of perspective they employ the primitive device of super-position; and though they somewhat reduce the proportions of the upper figures, the diminution is insufficient, and is carried out without system. Yet they give these superposed subsidiary figures an intimate share in the action by making them crane forward out of the background like mediaeval angels issuing from the clouds. The bodies are set at an angle; it is as if they were intended to be regarded from below, like reliefs designed for a higher position, in a temple or in the pendentive of a dome. This device, logical or not, certainly adds to the liveliness of the composi-tion, and its unnatural character is half concealed by the general crowding of the figures. The excessive consideration for the optical principle was not adopted in the early work executed in India under Perso-Hellenic

influence before the Christian era: it seems to come in with the art
of Gandhâra, which sought its models at an already contaminated source,
perhaps in Syria or Anatolia.   This suggests the conclusion that coloristic
treatment, in its uncompromising form, originated not in the Further but
in the Nearer East, perhaps in Mesopotamia, where, as we learn from the
decoration of the Mshatta façade, the system must have been early developed.
The oldest stone sculpture of China, that of the tombs in Shantung (third

Fig. 69.   Marble capital of the fourth-fifth century in the Cairo Museum.
(*Catalogue général : Koptische Kunst*, No. 7350.)   P. 172.

century B.C.), is in very low relief without violent contrasting shadow,
and is based upon a different principle.

There are certain stages which an art must pass alike on its upward
and its downward path: in a decadent age we meet with work of a
technical imperfection, recalling the effort of a young age rich in promise.
In certain Byzantine reliefs, for example, we find methods employed which
remind us of expedients adopted by archaic Greek art or that of the early
Romanesque period.   The men who made them had reached on the
downward path a point level with that long ago attained by others upon
their ascent.   Thus in some of the late sarcophagi at Ravenna the folds
of drapery are no longer modelled, but rendered by a series of incised

lines cut upon a flat surface; the drapery itself envelops or disguises the figure beneath it instead of harmonizing with its structure. Similar methods had been practised centuries earlier by the sculptors who made the seated figures at Branchidae, the early statues found at Delos, and other archaic figures. The folds of the garments are indicated by mere furrows instead of being modelled in relief, and there is a want of harmonious adaptation to the underlying figure. There is no skilful transition from one plane to another; the eyes stare; the faces are broad and heavy. The hair, too, is rendered in a conventional fashion by parallel grooves, through the incapacity of the artist to represent it in a natural manner. All these features find parallels in reliefs from Ravenna and other places which we shall have occasion to mention below. But in spite of the similar technical incapacity the total effect produced is different. The archaic art, whether Greek or Hindu or early mediaeval, is informed with a sincere and eager spirit; it is always groping after an ideal of which it is half conscious; it is for ever learning, selecting, and rejecting, struggling by original effort towards some final canon of excellence. The degenerate art, on the contrary, is for ever forgetting and unlearning; it abides by traditional types and arrangements the spirit of which it does not comprehend; it degrades them by successive copying into lifeless caricatures of the forgotten model. Instead of confidence, eagerness, and sincerity, we find diffidence, apathy, and the scamping hand. We stand below the level even of the negligent production which in a fairly good period supplies a popular demand. Some of the more careless reliefs upon the Attic stelae of the fourth century B.C. are hardly superior in execution to those of Christian sarcophagi dating from about nine hundred years later. They, too, resort to the time-saving of the harassed craftsman working to supply an impatient market; yet even in the worst of them there is a suggestion of latent power, capable under more favourable conditions of producing fine results. In some of the free sculpture at Rome, dating from about the time of Constantine, the abandonment of gradations in relief and the adoption of a stiff frontal pose are not inconsistent with a monumental simplicity, one in kind with that of the impressive Romanesque statues of the Middle Ages. But these are works without immediate successors; in the period of decadence which followed, their greater qualities were lost, their defects were alone retained.

For the above reasons, figure sculpture upon a large scale, which had begun to decline in the fourth century, was moving to its extinction in the fifth: the age of Justinian produced it by exception; in the time of Heraclius it may be said to have existed no longer. After the seventh century and iconoclasm it survived only in miniature, restricted to the compass of the ivory carving or other small relief. In this form it continued to be influenced by antique glyptic art, for when a model for the human figure was required it was sought among works of Hellenistic origin. The diptych of the Symmachi and Nicomachi perhaps occupies an exceptional place

(p. 190); but the figures on the front of Maximianus' chair are still eloquent of a good tradition: in both cases the original was a plastic work of a period already remote. After the iconoclastic disturbance, sculpture in the round was practically extinct and the sources of imitation were largely changed. With the Macedonian Renaissance, carving in ivory received a new impetus and attained qualities of a very high order; but they are no longer the qualities of earlier times. The reflection of a monumental style, as we still see it on the archangel of the British Museum (Fig. 200) or the diptych of Probus at Aosta, has vanished never to return. The plastic sense had grown weak; the dignity of the statue was no longer fully understood. The artist still sought his inspiration among works of antiquity, but the models were more frequently derived from painting than from statues or reliefs. The most conspicuous examples of this diminutive sculpture in ivory are mentioned below (Ch. IV): here it must suffice to indicate the sources from which the more skilful carvers derived their delicate and charming forms. Only in one instance is an antique statue the indirect source of inspiration; in other cases Roman silver plate may have been imitated; but as a rule it was from painting that this minor sculpture chiefly derived the half-classical character which preserves it upon so respectable a level. Like the work of the illuminator which provided it with so many subjects, it is an art of illustration, not passing beyond expressiveness; it achieves grace often and dignity not seldom; it fails in the suggestion of life and vigour. Yet the ivory carvers, thrown back upon classical or sub-classical models, retained in a creditable degree the love of modelling and the feeling for the finer play of light and shade: their subservient but always pleasing art renewed the Greek plastic tradition which the irruption of the coloristic principle had threatened to destroy. When it is considered under what a disadvantage they laboured, compared with their rivals of thirteenth-century France, their achievement is in every sense remarkable. There were no *imagiers* to make every great church a school for sculptors; the influence of a creative spirit was not abroad in their land. They were hardly to blame if the divorce from nature and the too intimate dependence upon pictorial art affected their most finished types with a certain taint of mannerism. The great fault of Byzantine painting is its failure to render life; for lack of observation of the living model the drawing is sometimes incorrect; an expressive face is thrown away upon a body which is not animated by an individual spirit. The same weakness is found in glyptic art. In almost any period of Hellenic sculpture the body alone suffices to convey the artist's meaning: the head may be mutilated or lost, but the intention cannot be misconstrued. But here it is not possible to be sure of the artist's intention without knowing the iconographical type in advance: it is not the limbs that speak, but the iconographic rule. Too often the art betrays itself as a pensioner of antiquity, living upon traditional types, but types originally so good that even in their latest expression they retain

something of their primitive charm.   The same defects which detract from
the merit of the Byzantine miniature are necessarily apparent in the reliefs
which the miniature helped to inspire.

Some errors these ivory carvers avoided, in spite of the temptations to
which pictorial models exposed them.   They usually preserved a simple
background, escaping the fate of their fellow craftsmen in Europe during
the seventeenth century, when the ambition to rival the painter in perspectival effects produced reliefs which lack the simple and essential qualities
of sculpture.   To the last the Byzantine artist gives his figures their due
salience and does not confuse their contours among the intricate lines of

Fig. 70.   Our Lord and Apostles : Sarcophagus in S. Francesco, Ravenna.   (Ricci.)   P. 137.

a pictorial setting.   The persistence of this quality down to the thirteenth
century results from the conservative tendencies in Byzantine painting.
The illuminators of MSS. in the middle period were themselves continually
copying Hellenistic models or early imitations of them, so that a Psalter
belonging to the tenth century may bear the most obvious traces of descent
from a work executed in the fourth.   The ivory carvers, who depended so
much upon the illuminators, were naturally affected by the same preserva-
tive and salutary relation.   The influence of these minute reliefs in ivory
upon the nascent sculpture of France, Germany, and England is noticed in
other sections (pp. 90, 96, 103, 236).   A minor art has rarely won for itself
so honourable a place in the general history of artistic development as the
ivory carving of the Byzantine Empire ; it is the irony of fate that this
refined art contributed to the rise of a greater sculpture in almost every
country but its own.   Down to the thirteenth century, when the example of
Western countries led to the reintroduction of figure reliefs, as at Kahrié
Djami and in the Balkan peninsula (pp. 162-3), the great style lived only in
architecture, in mosaic and in fresco.   Sculpture was reduced to the position

which it held in Western Europe during the Carolingian period, in the representation of the human figure a minor art, in decoration the hand-maid of architecture.

These introductory remarks may be concluded by a short reference to two points as yet unmentioned—the distribution of figure sculpture in the Christian East, and the use of colour to enhance its effect. It seems probable that the greater centres of the sculptor's activity were in Asia Minor, where Hellenistic tradition was strongest, where the neighbourhood of the capital and of the marble quarries of Proconnesus encouraged the practice of a monumental art (p. 49). It will be seen that several of the

Fig. 71. Our Lord and Apostles : Sarcophagus of Liberius in S. Francesco, Ravenna. (Ricci.)   P. 137.

more interesting remains have actually been discovered on Anatolian soil ; [1] it may well be that extended discoveries will provide further evidence in favour of a conclusion already plausible on general grounds of inference. Apart from Antioch, which in great measure shared the Hellenism of the Anatolian Greek cities, Syria for the most part contented herself with decorative designs. The greater sculpture of Antioch is lost; that of inner Syria may have suffered from Arab iconoclasm in the seventh century, but what remains is not of a quality to encourage high expectations with regard to Syrian plastic art as a whole. [2] That art is best represented by the mouldings and carved ornament enriching the ruins of churches and private dwellings in the ruined cities of the interior. In the fourth century Egypt, under the influence of Hellenistic Alexandria, produced remarkable work,

---

[1] To the examples discussed below we may add the St. Michael from the church of Aladja in Lycia (Texier and Pullan, *Byz. Arch.*, p. 184 ; Bayet, *Recherches*, pp. 110–11), and fragments reported from Corycus and Anazarbus in Cilicia (*Rev. arch.*, 1855, p. 129; 1856, p. 365 ; De Laborde, *Voyage d'Asie Mineure*, i, Pl. 63).

[2] Cf. the rudely carved lintels at Khanàsir and Zebed, in which the Virgin and Child in medallions are flanked by hovering angels (H. Crosby Butler, *Architecture and other Arts* (*American Archaeological Expedition to Syria*, 1899–1900), p. 308, New York, 1904) ; sepulchral relief with an eagle at Dana (Christian ?), V. Chapot, *B. C. H.*, 1902, p. 175.

much of it in porphyry (p. 125), but the decay of Greek influence in the country was followed by a rapid deterioration in sculpture. A definitive attribution of the Sidamara group of sarcophagi (p. 128) to Anatolia would further strengthen the claims of that province and provide a direct link between Hellenistic and Christian sculpture on Anatolian soil. The extent to which colour may have been employed in late Hellenic and East-Christian sculpture is still somewhat uncertain.[1] The museum at Broussa possesses a polychrome marble bust of a man in high relief, from Cyzicus, ascribed to the third century.[2] The colours, now faded, must at one time have been brilliant. The background is black, the face and neck are now of a yellowish tint relieved with touches of pink, the lips are red, the eyes picked out with brown and black, the hair brown, the mantle reddish brown. The whole is a work of almost startling realism. One thinks of the polychrome portrait busts of the fifteenth century, of which Donatello's Niccolò da Uzzano is the supreme example.

The stucco reliefs in the Orthodox Baptistery at Ravenna were coloured (p. 151); wooden statues appear to have been gilded (p. 125), and it may further be noted that gilding was applied to the reliefs at Gandhâra[3] probably executed, as stated, under late Hellenistic influence from Syria or Asia Minor. Byzantine ivory carvings, like those of Western Europe, were painted and gilt (p. 189). In purely ornamental sculpture we find a frank concession to the coloristic point of view when the whole ground is filled with a black composition[4] in order to throw the design into more distinct relief.

2. Sculpture now destroyed.

Before attention is directed to the principal examples of East-Christian sculpture it may be of interest to record the fact that numbers of antique statues were imported into Constantinople, especially in the reign of Constantine. The great cities of the western world were laid under contribution,[5] and Athens, Rome, Smyrna, Sardis, Antioch, and Seleucia all paid their tribute in this kind to the new metropolis. It is impossible to say how far the mythological statues mentioned by the Byzantine historians were works of a good period of Greek art, how far they were Hellenistic, or how far Graeco-Roman copies. Perhaps a majority belonged to the second and third categories; but there can be little doubt that the number of really fine statues was not inconsiderable, and in one or two cases we have evidence which seems to justify attribution to particular sculptors. Thus there is good reason to believe that the colossal bronze Athena which was placed on a column in the Forum of Constantine was the very work of Pheidias, and once stood upon the Acropolis

---

[1] It is thought that Christian sarcophagi were partly coloured (Swoboda in *R. Q.*, 1887, p. 100 ; 1889, p. 134 ; J. Ficker, *Altchristliche Bildwerke*, p. 91).

[2] G. Mendel, *Catalogue des monuments, etc., du Musée impérial Ottoman de Brousse* in *B. C. H.*, 1909, pp. 315–17.

[3] Reliefs at Shar i Bahlol, observed by Dr. Brainerd Spooner. The halo of one figure on this site had been first covered with stucco and then gilded (*Pioneer Mail*, August 7, 1907).

[4] This method was employed at Daphni, at St. Luke of Stiris in Phocis, and at S. Marco.

[5] See the list in Codinus, quoted by Unger, *Quellen der byzantinischen Kunstgeschichte*, p. 32.

at Athens.[1] There is literary mention of other work by Pheidias, such as the
statement by Cedrenus[2] that his seated figure of Zeus was placed in the square
known as Amastrianos, but this, like other statements of the same nature, has
no evidential value.   A bronze Hercules in the Hippodrome, destroyed in the
thirteenth century, is, however, considered to have been the Herakles of
Lysippus ;[3] we shall see below that its type was reproduced by the carver of
an ivory casket of the ninth or tenth century (see p. 216).   We read of statues
in marble or bronze of Helios and Selene, of Nike, of Artemis, as to which
nothing definite can be said.[4]   But Cedrenus and Zonaras declare that copies
of the Aphrodite of Cnidus, the Hera of Samos, and the Athena of Lindus
were destroyed by a fire in the library in the year A. D. 476.[5]   The better reliefs
upon the Golden Gate, which Sir Thomas Roe wished to acquire in the seventeenth century, were very likely Hellenistic work.[6]   Roman portrait statues
were certainly numerous : thus Augustus stood in the Hippodrome, Trajan in the
Milion, Diocletian on the Cathisma ; and it can hardly be doubted that members
of senatorial families migrating to Constantinople took the busts or statues of
their ancestors with them.   A curious importation of another kind was a bronze
group representing an ass and its driver, originally set up by Augustus at
Actium, because his meeting with them before the momentous battle at that
place was considered a happy omen.[7]

Turning now to sculpture produced in or after the time of Constantine, we
find frequent mention of portrait statues made in the East-Roman Empire during
the first five centuries after the foundation of Constantinople.   Reserving the
column of Theodosius for description with that of Arcadius, we may cite figures
in marble, bronze, wood, and silver of Constantine (several), Helen, Constans,
Constantius, Constantia, Licinius, Gratian, Valentinian, Julian and Anastasia,
Marcian, Theodosius II, Arcadius and his queen Eudoxia, Justinian and Theodora,
Justin II and Sophia, Justin II, Narses, Jacob the physician of Leo I.   Descending
to an even later date we hear of portrait statues of Phocas, his daughter Domentia
and her husband Priscus, of Philippicus Bardanes, and of Constantine, son of
Irene.   Sometimes in association with imperial statues, sometimes alone, we read
of the Tyche or Fortune of Constantinople.[8]   Some of the types of emperors and
empresses upon the coinage may be inspired by statues.[9]   Among effigies of
fabulous beings were those of sphinxes and syrens.[10]   Of animal figures, chiefly in

[1] H. Stuart Jones, *Select Passages*, &c., No. 101 ; S. Reinach, *Rev. des études grecques*, xx, 1907,
pp. 399 ff.   The evidence is derived from Nicetas Choniata Acominatus.   See also Unger, as
above, p. 147.   The statue was destroyed by the mob in A. D. 1203.   See also *B. Z.*, xviii.
276-7.

[2] Cedrenus, i. 566, translated by Unger, as above, p. 166.   The Pheidian statue of Zeus is
said to have been removed to Constantinople at the end of the fourth century and to have
been burned in the palace of Lausus.   See Bury's edition of Gibbon, vol. iii, p. 498.

[3] A. Furtwängler, *Sitzungsberichte der phil.-hist. Klasse der k. bayrischen Akad. der Wissenschaften*, 1902, pp. 435 ff.   See below, p. 216, where the probable imitation of this statue upon
ivory caskets is mentioned.   Unger, *Quellen*, pp. 317-18, on authority of Nicetas Chon., 859, says
the statue was originally brought from Tarentum by Fabius Maximus, and from Rome to
Constantinople by Julian (see J. Overbeck, *Plastik*, ii. 92).   But Graeven, *B. J.*, Heft 108,
pp. 252 ff., says it remained in Constantinople until 1709.   Nicetas describes it as being
melted down by the Latins.

[4] For these and the following names see Unger, as above, Index, *s.vv.*; A. Van
Millingen, *Byzantine Constantinople*, p. 66.

[5] Cedren., i. 616 ; Zon., xiv. 2.

[6] *Jahrb. des k. deutschen arch. Inst.*, viii, 1893, p. 38.   The subjects were derived from
classical mythology—Prometheus, Endymion, Phaethon, &c.

[7] Nicetas, p. 859, see Unger, p. 318.

[8] References in Unger, *s.v. Tyche.*   On the Tyche of Constantinople see Strzygowski,
Analecta Graeciensia; Graz, 1893, pp. 143-53 ; P. Gardner, *Journal of Hellenic Studies*, ix (1888),
pp. 77-8.   The silver statuette in the British Museum, which forms part of the treasure found
upon the Esquiline Hill at Rome, is reproduced by Gardner, as above, Pl. V, and in the British
Museum *Catalogue of Early Christian and Byzantine Antiquities*, Pl. XX.

[9] W. Wroth, British Museum *Catalogue of Byzantine Coins*, e. g. Justin II and his wife
Sophia, Tiberius II and Anastasia, Phocas and Leontia.

[10] Unger, *s.vv.*

bronze, there is very frequent mention. We read of representations of the following animals, mostly set up in the Hippodrome : boar, elephant, hippopotamus, hyena, ox, wolf, serpent. The Anonymus Banduri says that the elephants erected by Theodosius, with his own statue and a Victory, at the Golden Gate were brought from Athens.[1] As late as the time of Basil I we learn from Constantine Porphyrogenitus and Photius that in the atrium of the new church of that emperor there were marble dragons and bronze rams, goats, and cocks upon the two splendid fountains there erected. A bronze pine-cone from a column in the Hippodrome was broken in an earthquake in A. D. 865 : it is of interest in connexion with the example, still in existence, at the entrance to the cathedral at Aix-la-Chapelle.[2] Such pine-cones were commonly used upon fountains.

Statues of sacred persons or personages from sacred history were made during the same period. Constantine is said to have erected a large statue of Christ in the Chalcé :[3] he also caused figures of Daniel and the Good Shepherd to be placed over the fountains in public squares.[4] There was a bronze statue of the archangel Michael in the Church of All Saints damaged in the earthquake of 1296.[5] There appears to have been no free sculpture in Santa Sophia at Constantinople, but Paul the Silentiary speaks of columns on the capitals of which were reliefs with Our Lord, the Virgin, angels, apostles, and prophets.[6] The marble statue of Christ mentioned by an anonymous Russian of the fifteenth century may have been of very late date.[7] The emblems of the cross or sacred monogram are said to have been associated with several figures of Constantine and Helen.[8] Figures indirectly connected with religion were those of the heretics Arius Sabellius and Eunomius, placed by Theodosius near the ground in the Forum of Constantine in order that they might be insulted by the people.[9]

A number of the statues already mentioned were set upon columns of various height, and we may note that figures in this position are frequently represented in Byzantine illuminated miniatures of the tenth to the thirteenth centuries, both in backgrounds in which cities appear, and in scenes where the gods of the Gentiles play a prominent part. But we have now to speak of a few columns of exceptional size on which imperial statues were placed.[10]

The earliest erected in Constantinople was perhaps that set up by Constantine to receive his own effigy: of this the shaft, much damaged by fire and therefore known to the Turks as the 'burned stone', is still in existence. But the most famous examples were those of Theodosius I and Arcadius, which were decorated, after the manner of the columns of Trajan and Marcus Aurelius at Rome, with a continuous spiral band of sculpture running from the bottom to the top. A silver statue was placed on the Column of Theodosius in A. D. 394 ; that on the Column of Arcadius was set in position by Theodosius II, but fell down in the earthquake of A. D. 740. No trace of either remains ; and the very Column of Theodosius was destroyed in order that the Sultan Bajazet II (A. D. 1481–1512) might build himself magnificent baths.[11] The inscribed base

---

[1] *Anon. Band.*, p. 21 ; Unger, p. 227.
[2] See J. Strzygowski, *Der Dom zu Aachen und seine Entstellung.*
[3] Banduri, *Imperium orientale, sive Antiq. Constant.*, i, p. 21.
[4] Eusebius, *De vita Const.*, iii, ch. 49 ; *R. Q.*, iv, p. 102 ; Bayet, *Recherches pour servir*, p. 31.
[5] Pachymeres, *Andronicus Palaeologus*, iii. 15.
[6] Paulus Silentiarius, *Descriptio*, &c. (Bonn edition), vv. 691–712.
[7] Lethaby and Swainson, *The Church of Sancta Sophia*, p. 109.
[8] Banduri, i, p. 33.   [9] Codin. (Bonn edition), pp. 40, 169.
[10] The columns known as the pillar of the Goths in the Serai, and the Kyz Tash or Column of Marcian near the Mosque of Muhammad the Conqueror, were erected to support statues. The so-called Column of Pompey at Alexandria was also of this class, though it probably dates from the time of the Theodosian family (*B. Z.*, vi, 1897, p. 639). The marble eagles found near the base suggest those of the Column of Marcian.
[11] The literary references for these statues are given by Unger, *Quellen, s.v.* Theodosius, Arcadius. For the Column of Theodosius, see Müntz, *Rev. des études grecques*, 1888, p. 318 ; *La colonne de Th. à Cple.*

of a porphyry column outside the Church of St. Irene refers to a silver statue of Eudoxia, wife of Theodosius II, erected by Simplicius, prefect of the city.[1]

The equestrian statue of Justinian [2] holding the orb of empire, described by Procopius and later historians, survived till comparatively modern times. The fragments were seen in the sixteenth century by Gyllius, who said that the nose was nine inches long, and the leg taller than a man. It originally stood upon a bronze column in the Augusteum, raised upon a base with seven marble steps. We are enabled to form some idea of its character from a drawing of the fifteenth century preserved in the library of the Seraglio at Constantinople and several times reproduced.[3] Perhaps the bronze equestrian statue of Theodoric,[4] formerly

FIG. 72.   Daniel and the lions : end of a sarcophagus in the Museum at Ravenna.
(Ricci.)   P. 139.

in front of the palace at Ravenna, and now also destroyed, was comparable to this monument of Justinian, but it may have been partly inspired by the type of the equestrian saint, or hero of the faith, so popular in the Christian art of Egypt from at least as early as the fourth century.[5]

[1] C. I. G., 8614 ; Unger, p. 136 ; Kaibel, *Epigr. Gr. ex lapidibus collecta*, No. 921 ; *V. V.*, i, p. 778. In the same place there is another base for a statue erected to Porphyrius, a driver, in the Hippodrome (*V. V.*, i. 774 ; *Ath. Mitth.* 1880, pp. 295 ff.).

[2] Procopius, *De Aed.* (Bonn ed.), pp. 181–2 ; Malalas, p. 482 ; Unger, *Quellen*, pp. 145 ff. ; Labarte, *Le palais impérial*, &c., pp. 13, 35–6 ; Paspati, Τὰ Βυζαντινὰ ἀνάκτορα, p. 111 ; Mordtmann, *Esquisse topographique*, pp. 64, 66 ; Unger, *Quellen*, pp. 137 ff.

[3] Mordtmann, as above, p. 65 ; Ch. Diehl, *Justinien*, p. 27 ; Pokrovsky, in *Materials for Russian Archaeology*, vol. viii, 1892, p. 35 (publication of the Imperial Archaeological Commission, St. Petersburg).

[4] J. von Schlosser, *Sitzungsberichte der Wiener Akademie*, Hist.-phil. Klasse, vol. cxxiii, Pt. II, pp. 164 ff., and *Schriftquellen zur Geschichte der karolingischen Kunst*, Vienna, 1892, p. 431 ; F. Bock, *Bonner Jahrbücher*, Heft 50, 1871, pp. 1–53.

[5] Strzygowski, *Hellenistische und koptische Kunst in Alexandrien*, p. 28, Vienna, 1902. For a list of early equestrian statues see J. J. Smirnoff, *Transactions of the Moscow Archaeological Society*,

It is only natural that the wooden statues, often richly gilded, of which we read in historical works should have disappeared in every country except Egypt, where the dryness of the soil and climate have preserved wooden sculpture infinitely older than any with which we are concerned.[1] The fate of the ξόανα of ancient Greece has been shared by the portrait statues of the later time, from that of Constantine downwards. That emperor is said to have erected a statue of himself of gilt wood, holding a Tyche (Fortune) of Constantinople in his hand,[2] and doubtless his example was followed by others.

Wooden sculpture on a small scale was probably continued down to a late date. The rhetor Johannes Eugenicus (fifteenth century) describes in an ἔκφρασις a small carving representing animals round a plane-tree.[3]

In the various sections which follow (Free sculpture, Figure Reliefs other than Sarcophagi, Sarcophagi, Ornamental Reliefs and Capitals), a certain number of conspicuous examples have been chosen : a complete inventory is beyond the compass of the present volume.

3. FREE SCULPTURE.

The bronze horses over the principal door of S. Marco at Venice may receive a passing mention here, though they are of Hellenistic workmanship, and date from before the Christian era.[4]

The attribution of the colossal bronze statue of an emperor now placed near S. Sepolcro at Barletta[5] is uncertain. The name of Heraclius was already associated with it when the Venetians brought it from Constantinople in A. D. 1204, but it appears to date from the fourth century, and to be the work of a Greek sculptor. The vessel conveying it to Italy was lost near Barletta, and the statue, when recovered, lay for a long time neglected on the quay, but has been in its present position since A. D. 1481. In A. D. 1491 the hands and legs were restored by Fabio Alfano.[6] The emperor wears a narrow diadem and the costume of a Roman general, but bears a cross in his raised right hand and an orb in his left.

A small bronze statuette of a warrior in the Berlin Museum[7] is claimed as a representation of a Byzantine bodyguard of the sixth century ; a somewhat similar figure is in the British Museum.[8]

The Cairo Museum contains a colossal statue (Fig. 73) of polished porphyry, representing a seated male figure,[9] unfortunately without the head, arms, and feet, which may either have been intended for a Roman emperor, or for a Christ Pantokrator (Fig. 73). It is still 3,080 metres high, and was found in 1870 at Alexandria[10] on a site where three porphyry columns were to be seen at the time

---

1905 (Russian). M. A. Kirpičnikoff has traced the superstitions popularly attaching to various statues in Constantinople, *Annual of Hist. Philological Soc. of Odessa*, vol. iv, 1894.

[1] The sands of Chinese Turkestan have preserved wooden sculpture for us in much the same way as those of Egypt.

[2] *Chronicon Paschale* (reign of Heraclius), Ol. 277. 3, quoted by Unger, *Quellen*, p. 67.

[3] A. Muñoz, *Nuovo Bullettino di arch. cristiana*, 1904, pp. 225 ff.

[4] They are probably the horses mentioned by Codinus and other writers (see Unger, pp. 299, 300, 322) as having been brought by Theodosius II from Chios to Constantinople, where they stood in the Hippodrome. Cf. also Giusti in Ongania's *Basilica di San Marco*, iii. 423 ff. ; F. Lenormant, *Gazette des Beaux-Arts*, 1883, pp. 387, 388 (Fig.) ; H. W. Schultz, *Denkmäler der Kunst des Mittelalters in Unteritalien*, 1860, Atlas, Pl. 27.

[5] Venturi, *Storia*, vol. i, 414, Fig. 154, p. 164.

[6] F. Hamilton Jackson, *The Shores of the Adriatic*, vol. i, p. 123.

[7] W. Bode, Prussian *Jahrbuch*, 1900, p. xxiii.

[8] H. Walters, British Museum, *Catalogue of Bronzes in the Department of Greek and Roman Antiquities*, No. 1601, p. 261.

[9] J. Strzygowski, *R. Q.*, xii (1898), pp. 4 ff. ; *Beiträge zur alten Geschichte*, ii, 1902, pp. 120 ff. ; and *Koptische Kunst*, No. 7256, p. 3, and Pl. I. The use of porphyry in sculpture is an indication of Egyptian origin. The imperial torso in the Turin Museum, of too early a date to concern us here, is attributed to Egypt (Seymour de Ricci, *Rev. arch.*, Sér. IV, vol. viii, 1906, Pt. II, p. 381).

[10] Neroutsos Bey, *L'Ancienne Alexandrie*, p. 66.

of the French Expedition. The date appears to be the first half of the fourth century, and there seems nothing in the style of the figure to contradict the Christian attribution. The Christ in the interior of the Constantine bowl (Ch. XI) shows that the type was already known at this early period. The treatment of the drapery is not classical; the folds are shallow without effective contrast of light and shadow, and the regular parallel ridges are unpleasing to the eye. In the costume itself we mark the intrusion of new and confusing elements which mar the logical simplicity of the traditional Greek dress. There appear to be three garments, a tunic, a mantle, and a kind of scarf with tasselled ends passing across the breast, the whole producing a strange and somewhat puzzling effect. We seem to be in the presence of innovations in costume, traces of which are visible in other monuments of the same century.[1]

FIG. 73. Porphyry statue of Our Lord (?) of the fourth century: Cairo Museum. (*Catalogue général: Koptische Kunst*, from Fig. 1.)

The porphyry bust of a man in the same museum,[2] found at Athribis, is a work of the same century, probably of the period of Constantine. It represents a man in the prime of life wearing a chlamys fastened on the shoulder by a (broken) fibula of the cross-bow type. The hair and beard are treated in the most mechanical and conventional manner by parallel lines of short vertical strokes; the forehead is deeply furrowed, the eyebrows raised, the eyes dilated in a fixed stare. The whole expression, evidently intended to denote a virile personality, is at once strained and vacuous: the task which the sculptor set himself to perform was clearly above his powers. Those who see in the bust an imperial portrait have identified it with Maximian.

This bust has an especial interest on account of its identity in style with the two porphyry groups, each representing a pair of men embracing each other, at the south-east angle of St. Mark's at Venice,[3] towards the Piazzetta (Fig. 74), and the similar figures in the Vatican.[4] Here we have the same furrowed brows and staring, almost pained expression, the same arrangement of the hair. It has been suggested that these figures may be the so-called *Philadelphis*, or group representing the two sons of Constantine embracing each other, to which Codinus alludes.[5] Although the types of the costume and swords had previously been regarded as indicating that these groups

---

[1] Strzygowski, *Die Calenderbilder des Chronographen vom Jahre 354*, pp. 92 ff. For an ivory relief in the Maspéro Collection with a standing figure of Our Lord in a very similar costume, see *R. Q.*, xii, 1898, p. 22; and Strzygowski, *Orient oder Rom*, p. 63, Fig. 25.

[2] *Koptische Kunst*, as above, No. 2, Pl. II; *Beiträge zur alten Geschichte*, ii, 1902, p. 113; Mariette Bey, *Album du Musée de Boulaq*, Pl. XXXIX.

[3] *Beiträge zur alten Geschichte*, ii, 1902, p. 113; *Koptische Kunst*, as above, p. 7, Fig. 2; L. von Sybel, *Christliche Antike*, ii. 228; Venturi, *Storia*, i, Fig. 166, p. 178; Molmenti, *Storia di Venezia nella vita privata*, p. 51.

[4] H. Semper, *Zeitschrift für christliche Kunst*, 1901, p. 80 (Fig.); A. Venturi, *Storia*, i. 436.

[5] Codin. (Bonn edition), p. 188; Unger, *Quellen*, p. 176.

are copies of earlier work, and executed in the tenth century,[1] there is no certainty that these details are inconsistent with fourth-century fashions, and it seems more reasonable to assign them to the same date as the Cairo bust. The

FIG. 74. Porphyry group, exterior of S. Marco, Venice. (Alinari.)

flat caps, which also occur on ivories and sarcophagi of the fourth century, are probably military. All these examples of the sculptor's art in porphyry were probably produced in Egypt, the country where the stone is obtained. And apart from the material, they all manifest tendencies alien to Hellenistic tradition: the ancient formalism of Egypt seems in them to find a tentative

---

[1] Semper, as above, suggests that the Vatican figures are of the sixth century, and those of Venice a tenth-century copy, perhaps made at Acre.

expression. These 'African' tendencies are accentuated in the rare portrait heads and statuettes in limestone, dating from the fourth to the sixth centuries, of which the Kaiser Friedrich Museum possesses examples.[1]

A bronze statuette in the Bargello at Florence, representing the Good Shepherd, has been claimed as a work of the fourth century.[2]

Two small statues of the same subject,[3] not earlier than the fourth century, are in the Ottoman Museum at Constantinople. One has been known from a considerable time,[4] the other was discovered at a more recent period in the neighbourhood of Broussa.[5] Similar figures of the Good Shepherd are at Athens[6] and Sparta.[7] The example at the Lateran, holding a staff in the left hand, is well known, though it is considered that the left arm is a restoration.[8] Another figure was found near S. Paolo, Rome.[9]

The most perfect of these figures is that from Broussa, which has only lost the left forearm. The others are more seriously damaged, the lower part of the body being incomplete and the left arm broken. The example at Athens has the face mutilated. The execution is in all cases indifferent, but the work appears to be of the fourth century.

4. SARCOPHAGI.

(a) From Anatolia.

An end of a sarcophagus, from Sulu Monastir in the Psamatia quarter of Constantinople (Frontispiece), has a figure of Our Lord, in the attitude of the Lateran Sophocles, beneath a niche on either side of which is an apostle with a scroll.[10] The head of the central figure is surrounded by a cruciferous nimbus, and, though like the others it is somewhat damaged, is clearly of an ideal and un-differentiated character. It is hard to believe that figures of this description, retaining so much Greek feeling, can be later than the fourth century of our era.

The Sulu Monastir sculpture is the only Christian relief among a considerable class of sarcophagi and fragments, known, from the place where one of the most remarkable examples was discovered, Ambar Arassy or Sidamara, as the Sidamara group.[11] The great majority belong to the second and third centuries, and are of a definitely pagan character. To some of these the figures on the Berlin fragment

---

[1] Wulff, *Berlin Catalogue*, Nos. 42 ff.

[2] *R. Q.*, xxii, 1909, 246.

[3] For the Good Shepherd in Christian art, see L. Clausmitzer, *Die Hirtenbilder in der alt-christlichen Kunst*, 1904.

[4] De Rossi, *Bull.*, 1869, p. 47, and Pl. IV, No. 2 ; Garrucci, *Storia*, vol. iv, Pl. 425, No. 6, and p. 35 ; N. Kondakoff, *Monuments of Constantinople*, &c., in Sixth Archaeological Congress at Odessa, 1887, p. 229 (Russian) ; Laurent, in *B. C. H.*, xxiii. 585. The height of the statuette is about fifty-five centimetres.

[5] Laurent, as above, pp. 583-5 and Fig. ; S. Reinach, *Répertoire de la statuaire*, ii. 551, No. 7.

[6] Th. Homolle, *Rev. arch.*, 1876 2, p. 297 ; Garrucci, *Storia*, vi, Pl. 428, No. 7, and p. 35 ; Strzygowski, *R. Q.*, iv, p. 97, and Pl. IV, No. 1.

[7] Milchhoefer in *Ath. Mitth.*, ii, 1877, p. 358 ; Strzygowski, *R. Q.*, iv, p. 98, and Pl. IV, No. 2

[8] Perret, *Les Catacombes de Rome*, iv, Pl. IV ; Roller, *Catacombes*, i, Pl. XL, No. 1 ; Strzygowski, *R. Q.*, iv, p. 99, Pl. V ; Wiegand in *R. Q.*, iv, p. 100.

[9] De Rossi, *Bull.*, 1887, Pl. XI–XII, and *Bull. Comunale*, 1889, p. 131, and Pl. 5–6. The last reference and Strzygowski's article in *R. Q.*, iv, quoted above, will be found useful for the subject of the Good Shepherd in general.

[10] The fragment belongs to the Kaiser Friedrich Museum in Berlin (O. Wulff, *Berlin Catalogue*, No. 26 ; Strzygowski, *Orient oder Rom*, ii. 40–61, and *Byz. Denkm.*, III. xiii ; A. Muñoz, *Nuovo Bullettino di archeologia cristiana*, v. 79 ; D. Ainaloff, *Hellenistic Origins of Byz. Art*, pp. 160-4, and Pl. IV ; *Journ. Hellenic St.*, xxvii, p. 109, Fig. 7).

[11] The best examples of the Sidamara group are of a very remarkable character, Greek motives of the fourth century B.C. being treated with an originality and force recalling the work of the Italian Renaissance. (See Strzygowski's description of the fragments in the Cook Collection at Richmond, mentioned below.)

exhibit close analogies, especially to those on the sarcophagus in the Villa Colonna at Rome, and on that from Selefkieh in the Ottoman Museum at Constantinople, on both of which recurs a youthful long-haired figure closely resembling that of Christ.

The characteristics of these sarcophagi[1] are : the arrangement of the statuesque figures alternately in arched niches and in the narrower unarched interspaces; the employment of peculiar architecture, and the use in the decoration of this architecture of a system in which the chisel is replaced by the drill, and modelling abandoned in favour of contrasting light and shade. The first feature is peculiar to this group, for in the familiar Roman sarcophagi there is a succession of niches, and the interspaces are not employed for figures. The second feature is marked by the interposition between the capitals and the pediments of an impost (probably a survival of an ancient architrave) divided horizontally into two compartments, and decorated with motives which recur with great persistency; by the use of scallop shells in the niches behind the shoulders of the figures; by the regular employment of spirally fluted columns on bases of Hellenistic type; and by the duplication of the volutes at the top of the Corinthian capitals. The neglect of the chisel for the drill in ornament, while it continued to be used with such admirable effect in the accompanying figures, marks the invasion of the field of Hellenistic art by that system of colour contrasts which oriental taste preferred to the finest plastic art (p. 111). Here it is even more pronounced than in rather later Byzantine decorative sculpture in which the chisel was allowed to complete the work done by the borer. On these sarcophagi the drill reigns supreme. The capitals are ornamented with acanthus leaves of various design, but all drilled with a view to coloristic effect. Of the two divisions of the impost, the lower is conventionally treated, giving a central trident-shaped design, really a derivation from the old Lesbian cymation, the upper having in the middle an ove of exaggerated size emerging from a depth of shadow. Between these imposts comes the scallop, and above, the pediment with a moulding of dentils, a broad band of conventional scrolls upon the gable, and scrolled acroteria above all. Such are the features of the most characteristic members of the group, but they are not all present in each example. In some the impost above the capital is not found; in others the scallop is absent, or the niches succeed each other continuously without intermediate spaces, or the character of the acanthus filling the spandrels is of a different character. But in every case the characteristic treatment of the drapery and the spirally fluted columns are constant. The general effect is unmistakable and the group is sharply distinguished from all others. Work of so individual a character suggests the influence of a single centre. Was this centre in Italy or in the East?

Of the total number of sarcophagi and fragments at present known, about half have been found in Asia Minor;[2] a nearly equal number are in Italy[3] (Rome and Florence); a few are at Constantinople, Athens, and in the Cook Collection at Richmond in Surrey. The argument from provenance is rather in favour of an Anatolian origin; for it seems less unlikely that in the period

---

[1] For these sarcophagi the student may consult Strzygowski, *Orient oder Rom*, and *Journal of Hellenic Studies*, vol. xxvii (a paper, translated by Mrs. Strong, describing the examples in the Cook Collection); A. Muñoz, *Nuovo Bullettino di arch. cristiana*, xi, 1905, and *L'Arte*, 1906, 130; G. Mendel, *B. C. H.*, xxvi, 1902, 241 ff. The following are references for the other important examples : Selefkieh, *Orient oder Rom*, Figs. 14–16; Sidamara, Th. Reinach in *Mon. Piot*, 1902, 189; *Byz. Denkm.*, iii. xii; *Journ. Hellen. St.*, xxvii. 100; Ramsay in *Revue des études anciennes*, 1901, 278 and 358; Palazzo Riccardi, Florence, *Orient oder Rom*, 52, Fig. 20; *Nuovo Bullettino*, as above, xi, 1905, Fig. 1, p. 82; Alinari, Photo 3009, Villa Colonna. *Nuovo Bullettino*, as above, 86-7, Figs. 3 and 4; Villa Ludovisi, Garrucci, *Storia*, v, Pl. 362, Fig. 2; *Orient oder Rom*, 50, Fig. 18; Villa Mattei, A. Riegl, *Spätrömische Kunstindustrie*, 78, Fig. 16; Rivoira, *Origini dell' architettura lombarda*, Fig. 297.

[2] In addition to Sidamara and Selefkieh, the chief sites are Isnik, Eski-Bedestan, Uskeles, Ismidt.

[3] The fragment in the British Museum (*Orient oder Rom*, 51, Fig. 19) was obtained in the Roman Ghetto.

from the second to the fourth century sarcophagi should have been exported from Asia Minor to Rome, than that they should have been sent from Rome to comparatively obscure places in Anatolia. The conclusion is supported by the analysis of the marble of which the Selefkieh sarcophagus is composed. Dr. Lepsius pronounces this to be an Asiatic species,[1] and it is improbable that Italian artists should have imported marble of this origin to work up and re-export, when they had an abundant supply in their own country.[2] A minor point in favour of Asiatic origin is the frequent use of the scallop niche, which perhaps originated in Mesopotamia ;[3] while the definitely coloristic method adopted in the treatment of ornamental detail is an oriental feature. It is perhaps a further argument that this school of sculpture appears to have influenced the art of Gandhâra, the district including Peshawar and the valleys to the north of it, formerly a part of the Graeco-Bactrian and Graeco-Scythian dominions. Graeven[4] has pointed out the affinity between the Christ of the Berlin sarcophagus and certain Buddha types from the region in question,

FIG. 75. Sarcophagus of the fourth century, Mas-d'Aire, Landes, France. (After Le Blant).

in which the attitude and treatment of the drapery are repeated. It was perhaps, therefore, through the late Hellenistic sculptors of Asia Minor or Northern Syria that the Apollo type adopted for Buddha was first introduced, a type destined to travel to the furthest limits of Asia, and survive to our own day in Chinese and Japanese art.[5]

Various regions have been suggested as the most probable locality for the production of this distinctive sculpture. Strzygowski inclines to the culture area of Antioch ; Wulff to Cyzicus or Proconnesus. The case for Rome has been stated by Mendel.[6] There is a certain resemblance between the style of examples in the Sidamara group and sarcophagi at Ravenna.[7]

Christian sepulchral reliefs, some of the third century, in Isauria and Phrygia have early symbolic designs in an architectural setting.[8]

---

[1] *Orient oder Rom*, 55.

[2] Anatolian artists are stated to have worked in Italy (*Nuovo Bull.*, as above, 301 ff.), so that even if some of these sarcophagi proved to be of Italian marble they might still be the work of Anatolian sculptors.

[3] *Journ. Hellen. St.*, as above, p. 114. Coins of Byblus of the third century A. D. appear to show a shell niche.

[4] *O. C.*, i, pp. 159 ff. Dr. Graeven shows the similarity between the Christ of the Berlin sarcophagus and a statue of Buddha from Gandhâra also in the German capital.

[5] On the question of an influence from Asia Minor in Graeco-Roman times, especially in sculpture, see Vincent Smith, *Journal of the Asiatic Society of Bengal*, Calcutta, 1900, p. 131.

[6] *B. C. H.*, xxvi, as above.   [7] Cf. Wulff, as above, 15.

[8] A. Margaret Ramsay, *Studies in the History and Art of the Eastern Provinces of the Roman Empire*,. Aberdeen, 1906.

(b) From Egypt.

The great porphyry sarcophagus in the Vatican Museum at Rome,[1] known as the sarcophagus of St. Helena (Fig. 76) and obtained from her mausoleum in the Via Labicana, is probably, like other sculpture in the same stone (p. 125),

Fig. 76.   Porphyry sarcophagus of St. Helena, fourth century : Vatican.   (Alinari.)

of Egyptian origin.   The reliefs upon its sides represent mounted warriors with their captives, a circumstance which has led more than one archaeologist to doubt whether a tomb with such inappropriate subjects can have been really

---

[1]. Helbig, *Führer*, i, p. 241 ; Venturi, *Storia*, i, p. 435, Figs. 172–5 ; Strzygowski, *Orient oder Rom*, pp. 76-7, Figs. 33–4, and *Hellenistische und koptische Kunst*, p. 24 ; A. Riegl, *Spätrömische Kunstindustrie*, p. 96.   The sarcophagus has been considerably restored.

made for an empress.[1] The similarity of the figures to those upon a wood carving found in Egypt and now at Berlin (see p. 149) has led to the conjecture that in both cases the subject may be symbolical, representing the triumph of the warriors of the true faith over unbelievers,[2] in which case its destination would be less unsuitable. Although the comparisons made by Riegl between the warriors and those upon sculpture of the Antonine period are obvious, it must not be forgotten that the similarity to the reliefs on the Constantinople columns of the Theodosian period is equally clear, and that in both cases the same Hellenistic art provided the types.

The porphyry sarcophagus from Sta Costanza, also in the Vatican galleries,[3] having on the sides a decoration of *amorini* gathering and pressing grapes, peacocks, lambs, &c., with ornament of vine-scrolls in bold relief, and on the lid laurel wreaths and masks, may also be assigned to the late Hellenistic art of Alexandria. For although there is nothing in the designs which might not have been produced in Rome, when we find in Alexandria an identical porphyry lid,[4] and in Constantinople a fragment from the side of a porphyry sarcophagus with identical putti and vine-scrolls of the same style,[5] probability seems in favour of an origin in the country where the stone was quarried. And it seems to be increased when we observe a resemblance between the type of a limestone head with curly hair in the Cairo Museum[6] and that of the putti of the sarcophagus. The case is parallel to that of the capitals of Proconnesian marble which were sculptured on Proconnesus and shipped in a finished state to all parts of the Mediterranean, and to that of the marble sarcophagi of the Sidamara type, which, as we have seen, were probably produced in Asia Minor and exported in the same manner.

(c) Rome, Gaul, and Spain.[7]

The sarcophagi in Italy outside Ravenna are chiefly concentrated at Rome, and, with the allied groups in France and in Spain, have a direct relation to our subject in so far as an East-Christian inspiration has been claimed for them. The Christian sepulchral relief was certainly developed by a gradual process out of the earlier pagan relief devoted to the same purpose, such changes as occurred

---

[1] A. Riegl, *Bulletin* of the Second Congress of Christian Archaeology at Rome, p. 165, suggests that the sarcophagus dates from the second century, and that it was made for a general. The mounted figures, he says, resemble those on the base of the column of Antoninus Pius in the Vatican and on the two spiral columns still standing. A. Monachi in *Archivio della R. Soc. Rom. di Storia Patria*, xxii, pp. 570–3, also finds the subjects unsuitable for an empress's tomb, and suggests that Constantius Chlorus may have been buried with Helena.
[2] Strzygowski, *Orient oder Rom*, pp. 65 ff., 81 ff.
[3] Helbig, *Führer*, i, p. 238 ; Garrucci, *Storia*, v, Pl. 305 ; E. Q. Visconti, *Museo Pio-Clementino*, vii. 12 ; A. Riegl, *Spätrömische Kunstindustrie*, p. 86 ; Strzygowski, *Orient oder Rom*, p. 78, Fig. 35 ; Venturi, *Storia*, vol. i, Fig. 171 ; L. von Sybel, *Christliche Antike*, ii. 226–7.
[4] *Orient oder Rom*, Fig. 37, p. 79. The lid is in the museum at Alexandria.
[5] Ibid., Fig. 36, p. 79. The fragment is in the Imperial Ottoman Museum, and was found at Constantinople.
[6] *Koptische Kunst*, No. 7277.
[7] J. Ficker, *Catalogue*, 1887 (with bibliography) ; O. Marucchi, *Guida del Museo Crist. Lateran.*, 1898 ; Garrucci, *Storia*, vol. v ; L. von Sybel, *Christliche Antike*, ii, pp. 42 ff. ; Venturi, *Storia dell' arte italiana*, vol. i. Single sarcophagi and smaller groups are to be found in other cities in the Italian area, as Syracuse (F. Lantieri, *Descrizione di un . . . sarcofago scoperto nelle Catacombe di S. Giovanni*, Syracuse, 1872). Pagan sarcophagi may be studied in Robert's *Antike Sarkophagreliefs*. De Rossi believed that Christian sarcophagi existed from the end of the first century. Figure subjects, other than those of 'neutral' types (e. g. Cupid and Psyche), really begin in the third century, while the mass of specifically Christian examples may be assigned to the century following. Ficker was inclined to date the latter class after the year 359, the year of the inscription upon the sarcophagus of Junius Bassus. But most other critics, including Riegl and Strzygowski, believe that this particular sarcophagus is far earlier, and that, as in so many cases at Ravenna, we have here nothing more than the evidence of a re-interment. Weis-Liebersdorf, *Christus- und Apostelbilder*, 1902, 8–13, 16, 89, assigns it to the Antonine period. See also Wittig, Catalogue of the Sarcophagi in the German Campo Santo at Rome, Supplement to *R. Q.*, 1906, and A. de Waal, *R. Q.*, xxi. 117 ff.

being rather iconographical than artistic, and this, like the other early monumental sculpture in Rome, was at first the work of Greek artists executing
the orders of Roman patrons. The great homes of sculpture in the Hellenistic
period were in Asia Minor and Egypt; in the former country Pergamon and
Rhodes produced the most famous artists; in the latter, Alexandria possessed
a school of which the influence was felt in various directions, reacting even
upon the Anatolian cities.[1] From the school of Pergamon Rome learned the
art of representing scenes of battle; to Alexandria she owed the treatment
of more peaceful subjects, personifications, mythical or legendary figures,
above all, the adoption of a picturesque realism in reliefs depicting features
of landscape and architecture. From the same source she borrowed the graceful
amorini associated with animals and flowers which lend Roman decorative
sculpture under the early empire so much of its delicate charm. The pagan
sarcophagi of Rome are less indebted to the Pergamene than to the Alexandrian school, or perhaps to the art of those Anatolian cities where the
Alexandrian manner became predominant. It was in workshops already influenced by the art of these regions that the first Christian sarcophagi were
produced; and whether the sculptors were actually Greeks, or Romans trained
by Greek masters, the inspiration of the work is Hellenistic.[2]

   As far as this point all are probably agreed. But whereas some consider
that the pagan Roman schools, established under Greek inspiration, produced
the Christian reliefs without breach of continuity, and that it is unnecessary
to postulate any great influx of sculptors from the Christian East in the third
and fourth centuries, others are of opinion that there may have been such
an immigration, and, further, that many sarcophagi were actually imported
in a completed state from the Greek centres of the Eastern Mediterranean,
or perhaps from those quarries of Proconnesus where sculptors from the most
various regions were gathered together.

   It is perhaps impossible to decide a problem of such difficulty upon present
evidence. An exact study of all the sarcophagi of the Roman and Gaulish
groups should first be completed by scholars thoroughly familiar with earlier
pagan sculpture; marble should be subjected to analysis in order to decide
whether it is of Italian or Proconnesian origin; the probabilities for and
against the two theories should be considered in the light of a more extensive
knowledge than we now possess. In the meantime it would appear that, as
in the case of so many controversies, the truth may lie between the two
extremes of opinion. The art is of Greek origin, and the group of foreign
sculptors who commenced the series may well have been reinforced at intervals
by later immigrants. As, however, the art of the sarcophagi as a class is but
mediocre, and required no exceptional talent, local sculptors were probably employed
in considerable numbers; and if a majority of existing examples are their work.
the group as a whole may be claimed for the Italian branch of late Hellenic
art. If iconographical tests are applied, some points at least result in favour
of Western manufacture. For instance, in the Entry into Jerusalem Our Lord
rides astride instead of sideways. It is rash to draw general conclusions
from any iconographical feature; yet the sideways position in this scene is
practically universal all over the Christian East; and if the cross-legged
attitude was represented by a Greek or Syrian, it must have been to the

---

[1] Alexandrian influence has been traced in the work of Archelaos of Priene; and in the
second century of our era Aristeas and Papias of Aphrodisias in Caria were equally affected
by the Hellenistic school of Egypt (M. Collignon, *Hist. de la sculpt. grecque*, ii, pp. 674–6).

[2] For the development of the bas-relief at Rome the reader may consult E. Courbaud, *Le
bas-relief romain*, &c., 1899, and Mrs. Strong's *Roman Sculpture*. M. Courbaud adopts a compromise between the theory of an independent Latin art upon an Etruscan foundation,
adopted by Wickhoff in the introduction to his *Wiener Genesis*, and that of Th. Schreiber,
who derives the very essence of Roman art from Alexandria (*Die Brunnen-reliefs aus Palazzo
Grimani*, 1888).

order of an Italian or a Gaul.　In either case a sarcophagus treated in this
way is more likely to have been produced in the West than elsewhere.　On
the other hand, such resemblances in type as that between the Jonah group
from Tarsus (p. 143) and the similar subject upon a Roman sarcophagus must

Fig. 77.　Porphyry sarcophagus of Constantia, fourth century : Vatican.　(Alinari.)　P. 132.

not be forgotten.　However this may be, these sarcophagi owe their style and
character to late Hellenistic influences, not modified, as were the earlier
historical reliefs, by distinctive Roman qualities, but essentially Greek of the
decadence.　There being no appreciable infusion of the Roman spirit, they
represent a Hellenistic art, not the less Hellenistic for being produced upon
Italian soil.

　　The Gaulish group,[1] as represented by its earlier examples, has evident
affinities to the Roman ; it shows us Christian subjects treated in the old

---

[1] E. Le Blant, *Les sarcophages chrétiens de la Gaule*, and *Gazette archéologique*, 1885, p. 357 ;
L. von Sybel, *Christliche Antike*, ii, pp. 207 ff.

pagan tradition. We find sarcophagi with strigils, with figures in inter-columniations, and with undivided groups of figures like the Roman examples, most of them dating from the period between the third and fifth centuries. After this time the manufacture moved from the lower Rhône (especially Arles) westwards to Toulouse, Narbonne, and Bordeaux ; and a symbolic orna-mental style tends to replace that in which figures predominate.[1] For their general character these later examples suggest analogies with Ravenna, and consequently with Syria, by which the Ravennate ornament was inspired (pp. 53, 77).

The resemblance of the earlier Gaulish sarcophagi to those of Rome has been used in support of the view that both derive from the late Hellenistic East.[2] It is urged that in the third and fourth centuries direct relations between Rome and the South of France were difficult,[3] whereas both the Italian capital and the French ports were in direct maritime communication with Alexandria, Antioch, and Western Anatolia. It has been replied that ships trading from the East hugged the Italian coast, and that they must therefore have touched at Ostia, thereby maintaining a connexion with Rome no less direct than that with East-Mediterranean ports. On present evidence the question is one which can only be decided by a nice adjustment of probabilities. Spanish sarcophagi, as yet imperfectly studied, have a general analogy with the Gaulish group.[4]

(d) Ravenna.

The large and important series of Christian sarcophagi at Ravenna[5] differs in many respects from the Roman and Southern Gallic groups. Their structure, like that of earlier Greek sarcophagi, is more architectural, and more directly suggests a house or dwelling of the dead ;[6] the number of figures is usually less considerable, and a single scene, treated with a rigid symmetry, suffices even for the longer sides. The type in which figures are isolated between the columns of an arcade is common to all areas in which sarcophagi are found ; that in which closely grouped figures occupy the whole surface is hardly represented at Ravenna. The existence of early sarcophagi with subjects not definitely Christian shows that at Ravenna, as elsewhere, the old pagan art was taken under the patronage of the new religion, and that there was no

---

[1] The style is allied to that of the *grammaire orientale*, so brilliantly treated by Courajod. See A. Marignan, *Un historien de l'art français, Louis Courajod.*

[2] Strzygowski, *Kleinasien*, p. 195, and Schiele's *Religion in Geschichte*, i. 383 ; Ainaloff, *Hellenistic Origin of Early Christian Art*, p. 87 ; the latter writer detects Alexandrian rather than Anatolian influences.

[3] Mommsen, *Römische Geschichte*, v, pp. 71 ff., 100 ff.. 104 ff. It has been pointed out by Strzygowski that subjects occur on Gaulish sarcophagi (e. g. scenes from life of Joseph at Le Puy) which do not occur on sarcophagi at Rome.

[4] See the references given by von Sybel, *Christliche Antike*, ii. 219.

[5] Photographs by L. Ricci, Ravenna, and by Alinari. The series is catalogued and dis-cussed by K. Goldmann, *Die ravennatischen Sarkophage*, Strasburg, 1906, and H. Dütschke, *Ravennatische Studien*, Leipzig, 1909. Of these two works, both of which are illustrated from photographs, the latter appears to the writer to be the most valuable, the dating following in the main the lines suggested by A. Riegl, *Spätrömische Kunstindustrie*, pp. 99 ff., though some of the figured sarcophagi are placed earlier than the period usually accepted. The interpreta-tions of Dr. Goldmann appear over-subtle, and he brings down many sarcophagi to too late a date. See O. Wulff, *Repertorium*, xxxv, pp. 281 ff. Shorter notices and illustrations will be found in A. Venturi, *Storia dell' arte italiana*, vol. i ; L. Sybel, *Christliche Antike*, ii. 196–206 ; G. T. Rivoira, *Origini della architettura lombarda*, i, Figs. 164 ff. ; Strzygowski, *Byz. Denkm.*, iii, p. xix ; V. Schultze, *Christliches Kunstblatt*, 1889, pp. 102 ff. ; J. Ficker, *Darstellung der Apostel in der altchristlichen Kunst* ; N. Pokrovsky, *Monuments of Orthodox Iconography and Art*, ch. viii (Russian) ; Ch. Bayet, *Recherches pour servir . . .*, pp. 113 ; Garrucci, *Storia*, vol. iv. Of older books, Ciampini, *Vetera Monimenta* ; Fantuzzi, *Monumenti Ravennati de' secoli di mezzo*, Venice, 1802 ; G. Fabri, *Ravenna ricercata* ; A. Tarlazzi, *Memorie sacre*, 1852, may be mentioned.

[6] This idea is developed by Dütschke, as above, pp. 122 ff.

breach in the continuity of artistic tradition. The relief tends to grow lower than in the Roman group, and in the treatment of more than one example we are reminded of the 'Peter Relief' from Asia Minor at Berlin (Fig. 88), and the fine ivory pyxis from the Christian East at the same place (Fig. 115). The resemblance to the Sidamara group (p. 128) is more remote, but is yet sufficient to suggest that the Ravenna figured sarcophagi may represent a later provincial development of the art which produced the example with the Christ at Berlin and its earlier pagan predecessors. Both in the Sidamara group and at Ravenna we find attitudes recalling Greek sculpture of the fourth century B.C.

The claims of Anatolia are perhaps stronger than those of Syria ; but since in both provinces Hellenistic influences controlled figure-art in the fourth century, while sculptors from both regions were working together in the marble quarries of Proconnesus,[1] it is impossible to discriminate with certainty between their several productions. Whatever doubt may exist with regard to figure subjects, the ornamental motives are certainly derived from Syria and the regions to the north and east of that country. This is what we should expect from the close relations of the Adriatic city with the East and from the number of Syrian bishops who sat upon her episcopal throne. Especially characteristic are the motives in which birds and animals are seen in the convolutions of vine-scrolls, as on the sarcophagus of Theodore and other tombs ;[2] whorl-like designs, as seen on the end of a sarcophagus in S. Apollinare in Classe, remind us of the *grammaire orientale* ; the frequent guilloche is an old favourite from Hither Asia ; the confronted lions on either side of a conventional tree on a child's sarcophagus in the Museo Nazionale[3] recall those Persian motives which the Christian East more especially transmitted to the West by the figures inwoven in silk fabrics. It has been noticed elsewhere that the scallop niche, very frequent in these sarcophagi, may have an oriental origin (p. 130) ; the barrel form of so many lids is associated with Syria.

The earliest of these sarcophagi are evidently those with the finer figure subjects. The latest appear to be those with nothing but decorative and symbolic designs. But the figure subjects, if we may judge from their degeneration, continued down to the sixth century, perhaps in some cases even later ; while ornament, the same in character as that of the later group, appears upon examples which should be of the fourth century. There can be little doubt that in the fifth century the two styles are contemporaneous, and it becomes a question whether they did not overlap at an earlier period. If they did, there must have been a remarkable persistence in the manner of rendering peacocks, vine-scrolls, and other ornaments ; for the peacocks and foliage upon the back of the sarcophagus of St. Rinaldus in the cathedral (p. 138) are of precisely the same character as those upon the late sarcophagus of Archbishop Theodore. A similar difficulty confronts us with regard to the various forms of the sacred monogram and the cross, which would seem to be used indifferently. If we reject the earlier dating of the ornamental work, the only alternative is to suppose that the older sarcophagi were often left undecorated on the ends and backs, and that the ornament of later style appearing on these parts was added later, perhaps when a reinterment was made. This seems a reasonable hypothesis and has been adopted by many. The majority of the figure subjects belong to two classes : isolated figures within intercolumniations or niches, and groups representing Our Lord seated or standing between Apostles. Some versions of the latter resemble the *Traditio Legis* (see Ch. XII) ; others are apparently of a more general type, and form varieties of the *Maiestas Domini*, in which Christ is enthroned in Paradise. Each class is represented by examples of good and indifferent quality.

[1] O. Wulff in *Repertorium*, xxxi. 281 ff.
[2] Dütschke, p. 78, No. 76, Fig. 32. Photos : Alinari, 18015 ; Ricci, 257–8.
[3] Dütschke, No. 38, pp. 35–6, Fig. 15.

Of the sarcophagi with figure subjects, the oldest would appear to be that in S. Francesco, once containing the remains of Liberius (Fig. 71) : this may date, if not from the close of the third, at any rate to the first quarter of the fourth century.[1] A second in the same church,[2] with isolated figures in the same style (Fig. 70), may either be a copy or a second version of a lost original model. The remaining figured sarcophagi, with the possible exception of the most debased, which may be later, should probably be placed in the last three quarters of the century. Prominent among them are the Pignatta Sarcophagus and those of Rinaldus and the exarch Isaac. The first,[3] in S. Francesco, has on the front

FIG. 78. The Pignatta Sarcophagus, Ravenna. (Ricci.)

Christ enthroned, holding a book in his left hand and raising his right to the level of his head (Fig. 78), a vigorously treated figure recalling, like that of the sarcophagus in Sta Maria in Porto (see below), the Christ of the ivory pyxis at Berlin which was probably made in the Christian East (p. 183). His feet rest upon a lion and dragon, while to right and left stand St. Peter and St. Paul, beyond whom are two palm-trees. On the right end, between fluted pilasters, is the Annunciation (Fig. 66), the angel on the right, the Virgin seated and holding the spindle with the wool above the basket ; on the left end is the Salutation, between two cypresses (Fig. 79). On the back, two deer drink from a large amphora filled with water.

[1] Garrucci, *Storia*, 348, 2-5 ; Riegl, *Spätrömische Kunstindustrie*, Fig. 27, p. 102 ; Goldmann, Pl. I; Dütschke, pp. 48 ff. ; Venturi, *Storia*, p. 212, Fig. 198 ; *Gazette archéologique*, 1882, Pl. XV. Photos : Alinari, 18075 ; Ricci, 320-2.
[2] Garrucci, *Storia*, 347, 2-4 ; Riegl, Fig. 28, p. 103 ; Goldmann, Pl. II ; Dütschke, pp. 52 ff.; Venturi, *Storia*, p. 210, Fig. 197. Photos : Alinari, 18077 ; Ricci, 323-4.
[3] Garrucci, *Storia*, 344 ; Venturi, *Storia*, i, Figs. 193 and 214 ; Kraus, *Geschichte*, Figs. 151 and 153 ; Goldmann, Pl. IV ; Dütschke, No. 68, pp. 59-62. Some are inclined to regard this sarcophagus as of the fifth century. The sarcophagus received its name from the Pignatta family, by which it was used ; the word PIGNATORVM is engraved in large letters on the barrel-shaped lid, which bears a cross in relief.

The sarcophagus of St. Rinaldus (Fig. 37) in the cathedral [1] has on the front
Our Lord, beardless and with long hair, seated on a throne with high back, upon
a mount from which issue the four streams.   In his left hand he holds an open
book ; his right arm is extended.   From right and left approach St. Peter and
St. Paul bearing wreaths : beyond are two palms.   Above the head of Our Lord
are conventional clouds, showing that the background is regarded as indicating
depth.   On the back, in lower relief, is a jewelled sacred monogram upon a
medallion, flanked by two peacocks, behind which are conventional plants with
rose-like flowers.   The two ends likewise bear decorative designs with doves
and vase and vine foliage ; the corners have fluted columns, and along the top of
each face runs a Lesbian cymation.   The barrel-lid has a wreath, and a cross
flanked by lambs.   The figure of Christ on this sarcophagus is not without
dignity, but the proportions are inaccurate and the figures of the Apostles are
inferior to those on the tomb of Liberius.   In many respects they recall types
of Carolingian art, and this is not surprising, seeing that both at Ravenna and
in the Frankish Empire the reproduction of the antique was carried on under
similar conditions.

A sarcophagus in Sta Maria in Porto [2] should be compared with that of
St. Rinaldus.   It also has Christ enthroned between Paul, who receives a
book, and a beardless Apostle standing somewhat apart : the places of the palm-
trees are occupied by two other beardless Apostles.   On the back is a cross upon
a medallion flanked by two birds and two palm-trees.   On each end are two
Apostles bearing wreaths.   Spiral columns stand at the corners, and a cymation
runs round the top.   The barrel-lid has at one end a lamb, at the other a vase
flanked by two doves.   The figure of Christ, which has no nimbus, approaches
very nearly that of the Berlin ivory pyxis (p. 183).   A variant of inferior style,
in which Peter and Paul are clearly differentiated and two wreath-bearing
Apostles are added on the front, is in S. Apollinare in Classe. [3]   The figure of
Christ has here long wavy hair and lacks the virile character of the last
example.   At each end are three standing Apostles ; at the back a cross-bearing
medallion, flanked by peacocks and foliage in the same style as the designs on
the backs of the sarcophagi of Rinaldus and Archbishop Theodore.   A cymation
runs round the top and fluted pilasters ornament the angles.   The barrel-top
has a form of the sacred monogram repeated six times in very bold relief : on
each of its ends is a cross flanked by birds which stand on foliage.

The sarcophagus of the exarch Isaac in San Vitale [4] is so called because it
was re-used for the sepulture of a Byzantine governor.   On the front is the
Adoration of the Magi, the Virgin sitting on the extreme left and holding out the
Child to the Magi, who follow each other at intervals (Fig. 36).   On the left side
is the Raising of Lazarus ; on the right, Daniel between two lions.   The back
shows a medallion with the sacred monogram flanked by two peacocks ; behind
each is a date-palm.   The sarcophagus has fluted columns at the corners, and
a Lesbian cymation along the top of all fields except the back.   In this, as in its
larger decorative designs, it resembles the sarcophagus of Rinaldus ; and in both
cases the question arises whether the ornamental part may not be a later addition.

[1] Garrucci, *Storia*. Pl. 345, 1–3 ; Goldmann, Pl. V, 5 ; Dütschke, pp. 13 ff. ; Kraus,
Geschichte, 239, Fig. 194 ; Venturi, *Storia*, i, Fig. 200 ; Riegl, *Kunstindustrie*, Fig. 26 ; Weis-
Liebersdorf, *Christus- und Apostelbilder*, p. 71.   Photos : Alinari, 18089 ; Ricci, 195–6.
[2] Garrucci, *Storia*, 349, 1–3 ; Dütschke, pp. 68 ff. and Figs. ; Goldmann, iii. 3 ; Venturi,
Storia, i, Fig. 196 ; *Bollettino d'arte*, ii, 1908, No. 9, p. 3, Fig. 1.   Photos : Alinari, 18084 ; Ricci,
434–5.
[3] Garrucci, *Storia*, 346, 2 ; Dütschke, pp. 85 ff., No. 80 ; Goldmann, Pl. IV, 4, and V, 4 a.
Photos : Alinari, 18016 ; Ricci, 250, 251, 644.
[4] Ciampini, *Vetera Monimenta*, 1699, Pl. III ; Garrucci, *Storia*, 311, 2 ; Cattaneo, *L'architettura in Italia*. p. 23 ; A. Venturi, *La Madonna*, p. 263 ; Goldmann, Pl. VII ; Dütschke, pp. 9 ff.
The barrel-lid bears a Greek inscription in iambics relating to the exarch, and a Latin prose
translation.   It is worthy of note that Isaac is described as an Armenian.   For a fragment
from another sarcophagus with the Adoration (in S. Giovanni Battista), see Dütschke, p. 63,
Fig. 26.   Photo : Ricci, 459.

The sides with the Raising of Lazarus and Daniel should be compared with those of a sarcophagus in the Museo Nazionale[1] (Figs. 72, 80), which has on the front a version of the *Traditio Legis* or *Maiestas* already noted upon the Pignatta

FIG. 79. The Salutation : end of the Pignatta Sarcophagus, Ravenna. (Ricci.)

Sarcophagus. On the back are two fragments of another sarcophagus,[2] in which the figures were crowded more or less after the Roman fashion : one represents the Sacrifice of Isaac ; the other, five mutilated standing figures. All the sculpture of this sarcophagus should be of the fourth century.

---

[1] Garrucci, *Storia*, 332, 2–4 : Goldmann, p. 10, Figs. 74 and 21 a, b ; Dütschke, pp. 41–3 ; Venturi, *Storia*, i, Figs. 194, 195, 199. Photos : Alinari, 18117, 18118, 18119 ; Ricci, 53–4.
[2] Dütschke, pp. 44–5. To compare are a sarcophagus from Rome in the Louvre, Garrucci, *Storia*, 324, 1–3 ; another in the Vatican, Garrucci, ibid., 327, 2–4 ; and a third from Marseilles, Le Blant, *Les sarcophages*, &c., Pl. XVI, 1.

It would be of little profit to give minute descriptions of all the more debased figured sarcophagi. Mention may, however, be made of those in the cathedral associated with the names of SS. Barbatianus[1] and Exuperantius,[2] but not demonstrably made to contain their remains. The first (Fig. 81) has on the front, under scalloped canopies between columns, three standing figures—the youthful Christ flanked by St. Peter and St. Paul: beyond the figures are two amphorae, each containing a flower; on the back is a disk with the sacred monogram flanked by two lambs; on the ends, candelabra and crosses with monograms. The barrel-lid has jewelled crosses and a monogram within a wreath on one side, plainer crosses and monogram on the other. The sarcophagus of Exuper-

Fɪɢ. 80. The Raising of Lazarus : end of a sarcophagus in the Museum at Ravenna.
(Ricci.) P. 139.

antius also has Our Lord standing between Peter and Paul; but the figures form a group, and there are no columns except at the corners : two palm-trees stand beyond the Apostles. One end has a cross with divergent foliage; the other a sacred monogram within a wreath: the back is not visible. The gestures of the figures recall those of Apostles in the mosaics of the mausoleum of Placidia, while the lambs represent the same symbolism as that of the sarcophagus of Honorius: we may perhaps date the work towards the middle of the fifth century. A sarcophagus in the archiepiscopal palace has on the front a large *tabula ansata* with the name of Seda, a cubicularius of Theodoric.[3] To right and left, beneath two arches, were formerly two figures now broken away, perhaps by orthodox enemies of Arianism. It is a misfortune that the figures are lost, for there is plausibility in Dütschke's suggestion that this tomb

[1] Garrucci, *Storia*, 336, 4 ; 337, 1–3 ; Dütschke, pp. 16 ff. ; Goldmann, Pl. VII ; Venturi, *Storia*, i. 202 ; Baumstark in *O. C.*, iii, 1903, 180, &c. Photos : Alinari, 18088 ; Ricci, 53–4.
[2] Garrucci, 336, 1–3 ; Dütschke, pp. 20–2 ; Goldmann, Pl. II. Photo : Ricci, 198.
[3] Found in the cathedral ; now in the archiepiscopal palace. Dütschke, p. 25 **and** pp. 275 ff. Photo : Ricci, 229.

may represent the style of the *marmorarius* Daniel, to whom Theodoric gave a monopoly for the execution of sarcophagi.[1] Names of artists are so rare in the history of Early Christian art that the loss is doubly to be regretted.

Of the sarcophagi ornamented with nothing but symbolical subjects, the first to be noticed are those in the mausoleum of Galla Placidia. One, traditionally known as the tomb of Honorius, has on the front the Lamb standing under a gabled arch before the Cross, on the arms of which are two doves, while to right and left are crosses between round arches with shell niches.[2] On the other, called the tomb of Constantius, the nimbed Lamb stands on the mount from which issue the four streams: to right and left stand two other lambs, and beyond these two palm-trees. On the corners of the lid of this example

Fig. 81. Sarcophagus of S. Barbatianus in the Cathedral at Ravenna. (Ricci.) P. 140.

appears the sacred monogram in the Constantinian form, though, as in other cases at Ravenna, the loop of the *rho* is continued in a downward direction, giving it somewhat the appearance of a Latin R.[3] There does not seem any valid reason for denying to these two monuments a date as early as the fifth century: Goldmann's attribution to the seventh century will hardly win wide acceptance. A sarcophagus in the museum (No. 495) has two confronted lambs; between is the sacred monogram in a wreath with *lemnisci* converted into tendrils, and beyond, two palm-trees.[4]

[1] Cassiodorus, *Variae Epistolae*, iii. 19 (in *Monumenta Germaniae hist.*, p. 89). Daniel is conjectured to have been an Armenian. Le Blant, in his *Inscriptions chrétiennes de la Gaule*, preface to vol. ii, remarks upon the frequency of Hebrew names in the Christian East, and their comparative rarity in the West. Bayet (*Recherches*, &c., p. 117), in giving this reference, notes that his own experience is confirmatory.

[2] Goldmann, Pl. VIII, No. 11, and p. 56; Garrucci, Pl. 356; Venturi, Figs. 203–4 on pp. 216–17; Dütschke, pp. 4–7. Photos: Alinari, 10313; Ricci, 6213.

[3] Garrucci, Pl. 355; Venturi, *Storia*, i, Fig. 204; Dütschke, pp. 1–3; Goldmann, Pl. VIII, 11. Photo: Ricci, 64–5.

[4] For this conversion of *lemnisci* into tendrils terminating in leaves, see p. 167. Another sarcophagus in the museum (No. 504), which has on one end crosses and on the other the sacred monogram with α and ω suspended from it, has on the lid the sacred monogram in a wreath with tendril-*lemnisci* upon which doves are perched. Yet another sarcophagus in the same place shows this wreathed monogram flanked by two sheep with rosettes above their

The remaining sarcophagi with symbolic ornament are for the most part in S. Apollinare in Classe and in the museum.[1] They bear various subjects, in which confronted peacocks or lambs are associated with crosses, sacred monograms in wreaths, vases, vine-scrolls, and other designs. The execution is always symmetrical, sometimes stiff and heavy, but seldom ineffective, and degeneration is less marked than in the case of the reliefs with human figures. We may especially notice the sarcophagus of the Archbishop Theodore in S. Apollinare in Classe; here we see the monogram flanked by two peacocks, behind each of which is a conventional vine-scroll.[2] Birds peck the grapes in each corner, and before the peacocks' breasts are two rosettes.[3] The ends have vases or crosses with foliage and birds; the back, birds and hares in the convolutions of vine-scrolls. The lid has on each side a row of three sacred monograms in laurel wreaths, that in the centre being of the Constantinian form, the others of the type with straight vertical shaft. Another example in the same church shows two confronted peacocks, and a vase in the centre of an arcade of six arches, each with a scallop niche, the four external arches having beneath them crosses and palm-trees.[4] A similar arrangement is seen on another sarcophagus in the same building, where, however, the central motive consists of a palm-tree between two lambs.[5] The crosses and palms beneath scallop niches occur on a second tomb in this church,[6] which has another late example known as the sarcophagus of the Archbishop Felix. It shows a central niche with gable top, beneath which is the sacred monogram with α and ω suspended from it: this is flanked by two lambs with crosses above their backs; beyond them are two round arches from which *coronae* are suspended; while beyond are candelabra with burning tapers, and fluted pilasters.[7]

5. Figure Reliefs other than those of Sarcophagi.

First and Second Periods.

The later reliefs on the Arch of Constantine at Rome hardly fall within our period, more especially if, as Mr. Wace has suggested, two at least of the larger subjects were executed for Diocletian and only adapted for use upon the monument of his successor by the alteration of the imperial head.[8] But as they illustrate the advance of that coloristic treatment which became characteristic of East-Christian sculpture, and are especially important as transitional monuments between this sculpture and that of imperial Rome, it is necessary to make passing mention of them in the present place.[9] It is of course well known that not all the sculptures on the arch are of the time of Constantine, many being of earlier date. The Constantinian reliefs are the flying Victories of the spandrels

---

hind quarters (Dütschke, pp. 39–40; Goldmann, p. 11, Fig. 19). This wreath is repeated at one end, while the other has an amphora containing a large trefoil. Sheep flank a wreathed cross with tendril-*lemnisci* terminating in vine-leaves on a sarcophagus in S. Apollinare in Classe (Venturi, Fig. 207).

[1] See Dütschke, pp. 72 ff., where all are discussed and many figured.
[2] Goldmann, p. 55 and Pl. VI; Garrucci, Pl. 391, 3; Venturi, Figs. 209 and 213; Dütschke, pp. 82 ff. Archbishop Theodore died in A.D. 688.
[3] Another sarcophagus in S. Apollinare has almost the same design (Venturi, Fig. 211). Peacocks standing upon vine branches, which issue from a vase surmounted by the sacred monogram, appear on a closure-slab in the same church (Venturi, Fig. 210).
[4] Venturi, Fig. 212; Dütschke, p. 81.
[5] Dütschke, p. 82; Venturi, Fig. 205. A similar design ornaments the front slab of a balcony monument in S. Antonio at Padua, only here the central design is the nimbed Lamb in a fluted disk (Venturi, Fig. 208).
[6] Venturi, Fig. 215.   [7] Venturi, Fig. 206; Dütschke, p. 77.
[8] *Classical Review*, xx, 1906, 235; *Papers of the British School at Rome*, iv. 270. Mr. Wace observes that the heads have been chiselled away. As Constantine celebrated no triumph in Rome, the reliefs of the north and west sides may have been executed for Diocletian's triumph of A.D. 302.
[9] The Arch of Constantine was erected in A.D. 315. A detailed description with the necessary references will be found in Mrs. Strong's *Roman Sculpture*, ch. xiv.

of the main arch, with the genii of the Seasons below them; the two medallions with Sol and Luna on the sides; and the long, narrow friezes forming a zone below the medallions on the front and back. The work of the groups, which is all undercut, exhibits that 'cubic isolation' of the several figures which, as already observed, follows from the attempt to reduce all to a single plane upon a background of uniform dark shadow (p. 113).

Fig. 82.   Marble reliefs of the fourth century from the Hippodrome, Constantinople :
Kaiser Friedrich Museum, Berlin.   (Berlin : Königliche Museen.)

A large marble relief with Jonah in the monster's jaws, now at New York, was found at Tarsus in 1876. It is assigned to the third or fourth century.[2]

A white marble relief in the Musée Lavigerie at Carthage (much damaged) represents the Virgin seated with the Child, with an angel near her; and the angel appearing to the shepherds. The relief, which is in a foliate border, and cannot have formed part of a sarcophagus, is in a good style, and the draperies are well rendered. It may perhaps be of the fourth century.[1] Other reliefs and fragments representing the Virgin may also approximate to this date.[3]

---

[1] De Rossi, *Bullettino*, 1884–5, 146 ; J. Delattre, *Culte de la Sainte Vierge en Afrique*, pp. 10 ff. M. Bayet, who saw the relief in 1905, expressed himself in favour of the close of the fourth century (Delattre, p. 13).

[2] W. Lowry, *American Journal of Archaeology*, v, p. 51, 1901.

[3] Delattre, as above, p. 18 ; Rohault de Fleury, *La Sainte Vierge*, ii. 602–6.

The four reliefs on the base of the Theodosian obelisk in the Hippodrome at Constantinople [1] represent an emperor, perhaps Constantine, watching a performance of dancers and musicians and receiving gifts and petitions. The symmetrical treatment of these reliefs is adapted to the ceremonial nature of the subjects, and the general effect is not displeasing (Fig. 83).

The reliefs decorating the sides of a marble block, perhaps used in a ball game, found in the Hippodrome in 1834 and now in the Kaiser Friedrich Museum at Berlin, are probably of the late fourth century.[2] It has on it chariot races in the Hippodrome and a very interesting representation of the lot-casting urn used for deciding the positions of the drivers. It is an interesting fact, first pointed out by the late Dr. Hans Graeven, that this urn, which was fixed to a framework and turned mechanically, was copied by Carolingian artists, probably from a miniature in some very early illuminated MS. It is introduced into the scene of the parting of the garments in the Crucifixion in the Utrecht Psalter and on at least two ivory carvings, one in the cathedral church at Narbonne, the other in the Victoria and Albert Museum.[3] The sculptures, which are of indifferent quality, recall those of the obelisk base and must be of similar date. We may compare those on the marble plinth of the lost bronze statue of Porphyrius, which has circus scenes, a portrait figure, &c., on its sides (see p. 124, n. 1). (Fig. 82.)

The column of Arcadius,[4] like the vanished column of Theodosius,[5] was on the triumphal way between the Golden Gate and the imperial palace, its actual site being the forum known as Xerolophos. It stood until the year 1719, when it was so damaged by an earthquake that the Government ordered its removal. What remains is called the Avret Tash, or Woman's Stone, because there was formerly a woman's market in the neighbourhood. It is in a side street ; and though only the base and lowest part of the shaft still stand, it rises above the one-storied houses which surround it. The square base contains two chambers, on the roof of one of which is a design in relief with the sacred monogram between α and ω, in a lozenge inscribed in a rectangle: the spandrels at the corners of the latter figure contain palmettes and scrolls. Of the exterior only the east side is visible, the other sides being concealed by the structures which crowd round it. The remaining reliefs have suffered severely from the effects of fire and neglect. Hardly a complete figure has survived,[6] and it is impossible to use these damaged remains as the basis for a study of contemporary sculpture.

The column of Marcian was until recently inaccessible, standing as it did within a private courtyard: only the capital at the top could be studied from

[1] Wace and Traquair, *Journ. Hellen. St.*, 1909, 60 ff. ; Hertzberg, *Geschichte der Byzantiner*, &c., pp. 4–5 (Fig.) ; d'Agincourt, *Sculpture*, Pl. X, Figs. 4–7 ; G. Rivoira, *Origini della architettura lombarda*, i, Fig. 18 ; Harbeck, *Jahrb. k. d. A. I.*, xxv. 28.

[2] O. Wulff, *Berlin Catalogue*, i, p. 16, No. 27 ; *Revue archéologique*, ii, Pt. I, Pl. XXVIII (1845). The lot-casting machine also occurs upon a contorniate medal (C. Robert, *Étude sur les médaillons contorniates*, Pl. III, Brussels, 1882).

[3] Dalton, in *Proc. Soc. Ant.*, xxi, 1906, pp. 188 ff.

[4] See J. Strzygowski, *Jahrb. k. d. A. I.*, viii, 1893, pp. 230 ff. The sculpture at the upper end of the spiral was drawn by Melchior Lorch, who was in Constantinople in 1557–9 (A. Michaelis, *Mittheilungen*, as above, 1892 ; Strzygowski, p. 241, Fig. 7): it shows a procession of warriors with their prisoners approaching Arcadius and Honorius. The column, as it was in the early seventeenth century, was published by Sandys in 1610 (reproduced by Strzygowski, as above, Fig. 1 on p. 232). Its appearance at the end of the same century is shown by other drawings (A. Geffroy, *La colonne d'Arcadius à Constantinople d'après un dessin inédit*, in *Mon. Piot*, 1899, pp. 99–130, and Pl. X–XIII. See also E. Müntz, *Revue des études grecques*, 1888, p. 318). A detail by the French artist Cassas (d. 1827) is reproduced by d'Agincourt, *Sculpture*, Pl. XI, Fig. 3 (Strzygowski, p. 235).

[5] Ducange, *Constantinopolis christiana*, i, p. 79 (Fig.), after an early drawing ; also reproduced by d'Agincourt (*Sculpture*, Pl. XI), by Banduri (ii. 509), and by Strzygowski, as above, p. 243. On the shaft were the triumphs of Theodosius: on the base, the emperor receiving homage. See also Unger in *Repertorium*, ii, 1879, pp. 118 ff. ; de Beylié, *L'habitation byzantine*, p. 28.

[6] Strzygowski's Fig. 6 on p. 237 shows some ornamental detail, one complete figure of a man, and fragments of other figures.

the neighbouring streets:[1] earthquakes had shifted the capital from its true position, and large fragments had fallen to the ground. A recent fire has permitted two French scholars to examine the base,[2] only known from the seventeenth-century drawing by Spon.[3] Three faces are carved with large wreaths containing crosses with six limbs: on the fourth, or principal face, were two winged Victories holding between them a wreath with a cross within

Fig. 83.   Reliefs on the base of the obelisk of Theodosius, Constantinople.
(Sébah and Joaillier.)

it. This relief has suffered severe damage, only one Victory now remaining, and that headless. But the general sense of movement, and the skill with which the drapery is executed, show that the sculptors of the period still possessed a good tradition.

Of the sculptured ambos of Salonica only two fragments remain, both now in the Ottoman Museum at Constantinople.[4] Single figures under an arcade

[1] Salzenberg, *Altchristliche Baudenkmale von Constantinopel*, Berlin, 1854, 34–6 ; *Album*, Pl. I, Fig. 5 ; N. Kondakoff, *Byzantine Churches and Monuments of Cple.* (*Proceedings of the Sixth Archaeological Congress at Odessa*, 1887), 214, Pl. XLVII.

[2] MM. J. Ebersolt and A. Thiers. See J. Ebersolt in *Rev. arch.*, July–August, 1909, 1 ff., Figs. 1 and 2.

[3] J. Spon and G. Wheler, *Voyage d'Italie, de Dalmatie, de Grèce et du Levant*, &c., i, p. 134 : the drawing is reproduced in Banduri, *Imperium orientale*, ii, p. 498.

[4] Formerly in the courts of the churches of St. George and S. Panteleemon respectively. *H. É.*, photos C. 671, 674 ; Ch. Bayet, *L'Ambon de Salonique*, in *Bibl. des écoles françaises de Rome*

with scalloped niches make up the subject of the Magi seeking and adoring the
infant Christ.   The Child is on the lap of the Virgin, who is seated full face,
while an angel introduces the worshippers.   Another imperfect figure standing
with crossed legs evidently represents a shepherd.   The spandrels are filled
with eagles displayed, and above is a panel containing vines, vases, &c., within
an acanthus border of a style suggesting the fifth century.   The work betrays
the hand of a meritorious sculptor ; in the figure of the Virgin there is a certain
majesty, and the drapery is carefully treated.   But more than one detail removes
the composition from the earliest period of Christian art.   An angel intervenes
between the Magi and the Child ; the fact that the scene passes indoors is indicated by curtains upon a rod beneath the arches.   M. Bayet remarks that the
appearance of the Virgin, so aloof and detached, recalls the Adoration in
S. Apollinare Nuovo at Ravenna ;[1] while the separation of the actors in a
single scene by the columns of arcade under which they stand is a characteristic
of sarcophagi in the same Adriatic city, perhaps suggested by sculptures of Syrian
origin (p. 135).

The famous carved wooden doors of the Church of Sta Sabina at Rome[2] have
naturally formed a subject of contention between the opposing parties among
students of Early Christian art ; for if it can be shown that they were made in
the Christian East, their resemblances, iconographical and other, to certain
sarcophagi and ivory carvings raise the question whether these objects also
should not be transferred to the oriental side of the account.   The doors in
their present form are a reconstruction, and the carved foliated borders are of
more modern date, though they perhaps reproduce more or less faithfully the
original designs.   But the disposition upon the two valves of eighteen out of an
original twenty panels with carved reliefs, in alternating pairs of larger and
smaller size, is in accord with what we know to have been the ancient arrangement upon folding doors ; and it may be assumed that when they were put in
position this arrangement was followed.

The subjects are such as are commonly found upon Early Christian sarcophagi and frescoes, with the exception of some of the Passion scenes, the
representation of which is a rarity at this time.   The principal subjects are :
the Adoration of the Magi, the Miracle of Cana and Healing of the Blind, the
Transfiguration, the Agony in the Garden, Christ before Caiaphas, the Denial of
Peter, Christ before Pilate, the Crucifixion, the Maries at the Tomb, Christ
appearing to Three Disciples, Christ appearing to the Holy Women, Christ in
Glory ; the Calling of Moses, the Crossing of the Red Sea, the Miracles in the
Desert, the Ascent of Elijah to Heaven, the Calling of Habakkuk.   In the New
Testament series the Annunciation was probably once included : what the other
lost panel contained it is difficult to say.   Several details seem to support the
oriental origin.   The figure of Moses with a scroll resembles the Moses of the

---

et d'Athènes, vol. i, 1876, pp. 249 ff. ; Bayet and Duchesne, Mission au Mont Athos, pp. 249 ff.
and Pl. I–IV, and Recherches pour servir, &c., pp. 105–6 ; Garrucci, Storia, Pl. 426, Fig. 1 ; Rohault
de Fleury, La Messe, iii, Pl. 170, 171 ; G. Rivoira, Origini della architettura lombarda, Fig. 71 ;
Kraus, Geschichte der christlichen Kunst, i, Fig. 189, p. 234.

[1] Cf. also the ivory carving in the British Museum (Fig. 126).

[2] The following are the principal publications of the doors, those of Kondakoff, Wiegand,
and Berthier being the most detailed: Mamachi, Annales ordinis Praedicatorum, i. 569 ff.,
Rome, 1756 ; d'Agincourt, Sculpture, Pl. XXII ; Garrucci, Storia, cdxcix ; N..P. Kondakoff, in
Rev. arch., N.S., vol. xxxiii, 361 ff., Paris, 1877 ; J. B. de Rossi, Musaici, Fasc. iii, No. 5 ; J. J.
Berthier, La porte de Sainte-Sabine à Rome, Freiburg, 1892 ; E. Dobbert, Über den Stil Niccolò
Pisano's und dessen Ursprung, 1873, pp. 87–8, and in Prussian Jahrbuch, i, 1880, p. 43 f. ;
F. Wiegand, Das altchristliche Hauptportal an der Kirche der heiligen Sabina, Trèves, 1900 ; A. Ainaloff,
Hellenistic Origins, ch. ii, and B. Z., xi, 1902, p. 280 ; J. Strzygowski, Prussian Jahrbuch, xiv,
p. 75, Berlin, 1893 ; B. Z., xii, 1903, p. 698 ; G. Millet, in A. Michel, Histoire de l'art, i. 258 ;
A. Venturi, Storia, i. 476, Figs. 308–25 ; G. Stuhlfauth, Elfenbeinplastik, 26, 203 ; H. Grisar,
R. Q., 1894, pp. 1–48 (maintains the Western origin) ; Holzinger, Altchristliche Baudenkmäler,
1899, 45, Fig. 39 ; Journ. Brit. Arch. Assoc., N.S., i, 1895, p. 251 f. ; L. von Sybel, Christliche Antike,
ii. 257–8.

stone relief at Berlin (Fig. 90); the façade of the church with its two lateral towers is of a Syrian or Anatolian and not of an Italian type.[1] The picturesque character of many scenes, recalling Hellenistic genre reliefs of Alexandria, is also an indication of an Eastern origin.[2] Roman sculptors generally renounced picturesque backgrounds after the time of Trajan; but in Syria and Asia Minor there seems to have been a continual tendency to revert to early models, and the appearance of such treatment in the fourth century is perhaps more likely

FIG. 84. Fragment of an ambo of the fifth century, Salonika. (*Hautes Études* : G. Millet.) P. 145.

east of the Mediterranean than in Italy. It may be noted that the picturesque treatment with landscape backgrounds and genre accessories is characteristic of the early Indian reliefs of Bharhût (Barahat) and Sanchi, which are of the first half and middle of the first century B.C., and show signs of Greek as well as Persian influence. A further argument in favour of the oriental origin of the doors is to be found in the existence in Constantinople of doors in marble (Fig. 3) similar in arrangement of the panels to those of Sta Sabina, and in all probability ornamental survivals of earlier doors carved in wood. They are of the first period previous to the outbreak of iconoclasm, and therefore the originals must have dated from an even earlier time. One pair is in the Gynaeconitis in Sta Sophia, where they serve to separate the western and southern portions of the gallery:[3] each valve has five panels with alternately plain and foliated borders, but the carved subjects which remain are ornamental, consisting of

[1] Venturi, *Storia*, i, p. 343.
[2] Ainaloff, see *B.Z.*, xi, 1902, p. 280.
[3] Prussian *Jahrbuch*, xiv, 1893, 75-6, Fig. 4 ; Rivoira, *Orig. d. architettura lombarda*, i, Fig. 72.

foliate designs with a vase and pine-cone. Another pair is in the Kalender Jami, a Byzantine church transformed into a mosque.[1] Here they are merely ornamental reliefs in the form of doors built into the wall of the naos to right and left above the main entrance, and are surmounted by a pediment with acroteria of acanthus leaves: the panels here are alternately small and large as at Sta Sabina, but without figure subjects. A third pair is in the Church of Chora, now the Mosque of Kahrié Djami (p. 416), built into the wall to right and left of the northern lateral entrance leading from the narthex to the

Fig. 85. Wooden sculpture of the fifth century, with saints, in the Cairo Museum.
(After *Koptische Kunst*, Pl. VII.)

wooden gallery. Here again each valve has five panels, alternately low and high, with ornamental borders and filled by figure subjects. These are now much mutilated, but it is possible to identify four: Nativity, Adoration, Baptism, and Ascension, some of which occupy more than one panel. The parallelism with Sta Sabina is here very close.

The date of these Byzantine doors is attested by the similarity of the foliated borders of those in Sta Sophia with those on the consular diptych of Philoxenus (A.D. 525) in the Trivulzi Collection at Milan,[2] by the style of the pediment at Kahrié Djami, which recalls that of the Moses relief at Berlin but is probably considerably older, and by the capitals on the supporting columns, which resemble

---

[1] Prussian *Jahrbuch*, xiv, 1893, p. 77, Fig. 5 ; E. Freshfield, in *Archaeologia*, lv, Pl. XXXVI-XXXVII.
[2] W. Meyer, *Zwei antike Elfenbein diptychen*, &c., No. 27 ; E. Molinier, *Ivoires*, p. 30, No. 80.

those of the propylaeum of the Golden Gate ; further evidence is afforded by iconographical details of the reliefs on the Kahrié Djami doors, for instance the frontal position of the Virgin in the Adoration, which corresponds to that seen on the Monza ampullae (Ch. XI) and the mosaics of S. Apollinare Nuovo (p. 354), and points to the sixth century as the probable date ; lastly, the arrangement of the bronze Byzantine doors of later periods is usually different (Ch. XI).

The other early carved wooden doors in Italy, those of the Church of S. Ambrogio at Milan,[1] which are probably even earlier than those of Sta Sabina, may also be importations of oriental origin : it is singular that all the heads should have been struck off the figures, a fact which may point to Mohammedan fanaticism.[2] The carved scenes are taken from the story of David, a favourite subject in Byzantine art, and there is a rather close analogy between the scene in which the messenger of Samuel comes to the young David among his flocks and the same scene upon a silver dish[3] in the remarkable series found in Cyprus (Fig. 62).

The carved wooden doors of the church of the monastery on Mount Sinai,[4] probably dating from the tenth or eleventh century (Kondakoff), have panels similarly disposed, but the ornament contains no human figures, being entirely floral and animal, and incised, not carved in relief ; they include goats, hares, peacocks, dogs, partridges, vases with vine-scrolls, and birds. In Coptic churches in Egypt there are still wooden reliefs and panels with figure subjects.[5] A frieze in the Church of Al Mu'allaka at Cairo has the Ascension and the Entry into Jerusalem, another the Annunciation and Our Lord ; the door of the Church of St. George has gospel scenes and two angels. The five panels in the British Museum, which also came from Al Mu'allaka, are shown by their ornament to be as late as the thirteenth century.[6]

In the Kaiser Friedrich Museum at Berlin there is a wood-carving of considerable size, probably once surmounting a pilaster, from Eshmuneïn (near Hermopolis Magna) in Egypt, representing warriors mounted and on foot before the fortified walls of a city.[7] One party, consisting of a group of foot-soldiers with tunics of mail and crested helmets, carrying shields, and swords or spears (the latter broken off), is led by two warriors of larger stature in an attack upon mounted enemies in scale armour, one of whom is falling from his horse. At the back, on the left, a standard-bearer raises aloft a *labarum* on which is carved a cross. In the open gate of the city stand other soldiers of the first party, while on the walls to the right three prisoners are hanging with their heads fixed in fork-shaped gallows (*furcae*). On the ramparts above appears a row of soldiers of smaller size ; from the middle rises as it were a precipitous rocky eminence crowned with buildings, while in a central arch stand two figures, one a male in a long mantle, the other apparently a female (the head broken). On the left three large male forms in tunic and pallium emerge like terminal figures from the rock.

The architecture of the buildings resembles that upon the ivory carving in the Louvre representing St. Mark preaching before Alexandria (p. 212), while the warriors in the foreground have more than one point of analogy with the

---

[1] A. Goldschmidt, *Die Kirchenthür des heiligen Ambrosius in Mailand*, Strasburg, 1902. Prof. Goldschmidt believes the doors to have been made in Italy. The monograph is reviewed by Strzygowski (*B. Z.* xi, 1902, p. 666), who insists upon an oriental origin, laying especial stress upon the hint as to provenance given by the mutilated heads. J. Sauer, *R. Q.*, 1902, p. 72, is disposed to question the early date.

[2] The existing heads on various panels are restorations. Against the theory that the removal of the original heads points to an oriental origin it has been argued that it would not have been worth any one's while to bring doors so mutilated into Italy. But the intention of those who brought them may have been to have the heads replaced, an intention which was not fulfilled. [3] *Archaeologia*, lx, pp. 8–10.

[4] N. Kondakoff, *Journey to Sinai*, &c., p. 72 (Russian) ; G. Ebers, *Durch Gosen zum Sinai*, p. 279 ; A. Lenoir, *Architecture monastique*, p. 308.

[5] Strzygowski, *R. Q.*, 1897, *Die christlichen Denkmäler Ägyptens* ; *Orient oder Rom*, p. 73.

[6] British Museum *Catalogue*, No. 986.

[7] O. Wulff, *Berlin Catalogue*, i, No. 243 and Pl. VII ; *Orient oder Rom*, Pl. III, pp. 65 ff. The carving is forty-five centimetres high. It is flat at the back, the section being a half-oval.

figures upon the porphyry sarcophagus of St. Helena (p. 131). Even if the wood-carving had not been found in Egypt, these similarities would 'have suggested such a provenance.[1]

FIG. 86.   Coptic tombstone of the seventh or eighth century.
(British Museum.)

The date of the work is evidently early, perhaps of the fifth century, the warriors in the foreground being well conceived and vigorously rendered. The

[1] The helmets are the same as those on the St. Helena sarcophagus, and one or two of the faces are very similar in type. The treatment of the mounted warriors is also similar.

arms and accoutrements recall those in the Old Testament scenes from the story of Joshua in the mosaics of Sta Maria Maggiore at Rome, and are also similar to those of the Joshua Rotulus (p. 447), though the helmets here have no plumes. These affinities naturally suggest that the subject of the wood-carving may also be derived from the story of Joshua ; but it is impossible to see here the conquest of Jericho or Ai, since the victorious party is issuing from the city and not entering it. Strzygowski's conjecture that the whole symbolically represents the victory of the forces of faith against the infidel is perhaps the most plausible. According to this view the three figures in the forks would be captured infidel captains ;[1] the two figures in the upper archway, the emperor and empress standing as spectators of the triumph in the door of the church ; while the three terminal figures would represent the Trinity,[2] on behalf of which the battle is joined.

The human figures among the stucco reliefs of the fifth century which ornament a broad zone of the orthodox baptistery at Ravenna[3] are coarsely modelled, and appear to have undergone restorations. But the reliefs with ornamental motives have a great charm ; they consist of such designs as confronted animals, peacocks, hares, stags, &c., on each side of vases and baskets of fruit. The figure subjects, which alternate with the others, represent Daniel between the lions, Jonah and the monster, and Christ between the Apostles, all of types familiar on sarcophagi and on the frescoes of the Catacombs. The stucco reliefs in the arches of the nave of the cathedral at Parenzo[4] have similar ornamental motives, though the variety is less abundant (birds, filled baskets, cornuacopiae, floral motives, &c.).

The Ravenna reliefs were coloured. The stucco figures at the west end of S. Maria della Valle at Cividale are either Byzantine or copies of Byzantine models, perhaps, as Bertaux has suggested, in the precious metals. They are assigned to various dates, from the eighth century to the twelfth ; they may possibly be even earlier than the first of the suggested periods.[5] Moulded ornament in stucco, as distinguished from representations of the human figure, remained popular for centuries both with Mohammedans and Christians. The stucco decoration of the Mosque of Tulun at Cairo (ninth century), and that of the Church of El-Hadra in the Syrian Monastery of the Scete Desert,[6] are well known ; but moulded stucco is used in later Byzantine churches, e. g. in the string courses and slabs of the Church of St. Luke of Stiris in Phocis.[7] The decorative use of stucco may be of Mesopotamian origin, as Makrizi (ii. 265) says that Tulun ordered the plan of his mosque from a *Nazrani*.

It is impossible to do more than cast a general glance at the Christian sculpture of Egypt between the fourth and eighth centuries. The plastic art which is described as Coptic[8] began when sculptors who preserved traditions and the hereditary skill of the older Egypt began to treat after their own

[1] The five kings of the Amorites are shown similarly executed in the Joshua Rotulus. Similar forked branches were used in Egypt for executions down to the first half of the nineteenth century (Lepsius, *Briefe*, pp. 209 ff.)

[2] The persons of the Trinity are represented by three bearded figures on the sarcophagus from S. Paolo fuori le Mura now in the Lateran (Garrucci, *Storia*, Pl. 215, Fig. 1).

[3] Ch. Diehl, *Ravenne*, 33, Paris, 1903, and Rivoira, *Origini della architettura lombarda*, i, Fig. 55. These stucco sculptures appear in the photos of the interior reproduced by most writers on Ravenna. Cf. Fig. 208.

[4] C. Errard and A. Gayet, *L'Art byzantin*, Pt. III, *Parenzo*, Pl. VII and VIII.

[5] Venturi, *Storia*, ii. 127, Fig. 102 ; F. Hamilton Jackson, *The Shores of the Adriatic*, Pl. opp. p. 332 ; J. Strzygowski, *Das orientalische Italien* (in *Monatshefte für Kunstwissenschaft*, vol. i), xx ; Diehl, *Manuel*, 362.

[6] J. Strzygowski, *Oriens Cristianus*, i. 356 ff. The ornament which is on the walls of the Haikal is conventional, with architectural and floral motives, but no human figures.

[7] Schultz and Barnsley, *Church of St. Luke*, p. 26 f.

[8] Cairo Museum Catalogues, *Koptische Kunst*, by J. Strzygowski (refs. to his earlier publications), and *Coptic Monuments* by W. E. Crum ; O. Wulff, *Berlin Catalogue*, vol. i, pp. 24 ff. ; see also Kraus, *Geschichte*, i. 254 ; Gayet, *L'Art copte* ; V. Schultze, *Archäologie*, 262, &c.

manner the types introduced for the most part through Hellenistic channels. Where in stone, its material is almost always the soft limestone so easily procured in the neighbourhood of the Nile. It is almost entirely devoted to the decoration of buildings, and like the sculpture of the other Eastern provinces of the empire, it became ancillary to architecture almost from the first.[1] It found a place chiefly in friezes over niches and doorways, especially within the gable-like pediments many of which are preserved in a more or less fragmentary condition. Free sculpture is very rare (see above, p. 128). In the figures and groups of the fourth and following centuries we observe a rapid degeneration in the sense of proportion and the growth of a stiff conventional style, varied by

.Fig. 87.   Orpheus : limestone gable of the fourth century in the Cairo Museum.
(*Catalogue général : Koptische Kunst*, No. 7287.)

occasional extravagances of gesture and attitude which almost recall the fantastic creations of the Hindu sculptor. There is also a coarse delight in representation of undraped figure, far removed from the Hellenic pleasure in the ideal nude ; in certain sculptures, such as the Leda reliefs in the Cairo Museum, at Alexandria, and at Berlin,[2] a naïve realism is pushed to its extreme. In all these works, chiefly produced in Upper Egypt, we may note the reaction of a frankly sensuous oriental taste against the finer sentiment of the Greek.

Coptic art from the fourth century onward produced no figure sculpture even of the second rank. A sufficient idea of its quality may be gathered from the large published collections in the Cairo Museum and the Kaiser Friedrich Museum in Berlin. To the fourth and fifth centuries belong the figures in the

---

[1] The only sculpture which has remained in its place is the relief representing the Coptic type of equestrian saint in the lunette over the courtyard door of the Mosque of Ali at Dashlug (Strzygowski, *Hellenistische und koptische Kunst*, p. 22, Fig. 15 ; *Koptische Kunst*, Fig. 160). All the other examples are detached from their architectural framework.

[2] *Koptische Kunst*, as above, No. 7279 ; *Hellenistische und kopt. Kunst*, p. 45, Figs. 28-31 ; Wulff, *Berlin Catalogue*, i, No. 64, p. 30.

gable-like pediments[1] over doorways to which allusion has been made, in which we see curly-headed *amorini* supporting medallions with the cross, Pan, Orpheus charming the beasts, all framed within borders of interlaced acanthus typical of this period of Egyptian art. With the sixth and seventh centuries the nudities become rarer, the reliefs flatter and more feeble. With friezes with hunting scenes and mounted saints,[2] tympana and niches with figures on a background of vine-scrolls,[3] conventional birds, &c., we are already in the sphere of the familiar Coptic tombstones produced in such numbers between the sixth and eighth centuries,[4] and possessing only an archaeological interest. Sculptures with specifically Christian subjects are rare and usually late. Among the most interesting are the reliefs with a mounted saint (Fig. 26), and the Virgin seated with the Child between two angels, found at Thebes and now at Cairo.[5] The Coptic sculptures at or from Bawît include representations of mounted saints, a mutilated standing figure not without dignity, and a curious bas-relief, apparently representing the monster which swallowed Jonah.[6] (For examples of Coptic sculpture, see Figs. 21–33, 86, 87.)

The Berlin Museum possesses a broken relief of Proconnesian marble (Fig. 88) with two figures, perhaps from the scene of the death of Ananias.[7] It was found at Ajatzam (Alatchan), between Sinope and Amaseia, the ancient seat of a bishopric, a city which from the accounts of Gregory of Nyssa and Bishop Asterius (d. 410) was inhabited in the fourth and fifth centuries by a wealthy and luxurious community. On the right stands an Apostle with a long cross, on the left is a stooping figure in a short tunic, on this theory representing one of the servants who carried Ananias out of the Apostle's presence. The same scene is completely represented upon the ivory reliquary of the fourth century at Brescia (p. 192).[8] This marble relief may have been made in the region of Amaseia; but it is perhaps more probable that it was imported from Constantinople or from Proconnesus. The style of the figures recalls that of sarcophagi of Ravenna, and the modelling of the features and hands that of the busts of evangelists in the Ottoman Museum next to be considered. Probably the date is still within the limits of the fifth century.

The Ottoman Museum contains a large marble medallion, and fragments of three others, with busts in very high relief.[9] In the best example the figure is perfect, and represents a bearded evangelist holding a book with a cross on the cover. From the fact that the relief is highest at the top, it may be assumed that the sculpture was intended to be seen from below, and it is probable that the set of four evangelists once ornamented the pendentives of a church dome, a position where in later times they are found executed in mosaic.

The complete evangelist—perhaps intended for St. Mark—wears a tunic and chlamys, the folds of which are well rendered. His heavy face, with the large eyes, broad nose, and full cheeks, diverges from the typical representations of earlier times and seems to be a portrait. Although the sculptor is familiar with the methods of rendering the eye introduced in Graeco-Roman times, the treatment of the face is distinct from that of the Roman portrait-busts with their finer and more penetrating realism. The likeness is half-way between a type and an individual, as, upon an infinitely higher plane of art, is the bust of Pericles by Cresilas. The work has character, and is executed with sufficient

[1] Examples in *Koptische Kunst*, as above, Nos. 7285 ff., 7292[b].
[2] Ibid., Nos. 7283–4.   [3] Ibid., 7292[a].
[4] Cairo Museum, *Catalogue général, Coptic Monuments*, by W. E. Crum, 1902; Wulff, *Berlin Catalogue*, i, Nos. 73 ff.
[5] Ibid., No. 8704; also figured and mentioned in the later volume of the Catalogue (*Koptische Kunst*, as quoted above), p. 105.
[6] J. Clédat in Cabrol's *Dict. d'arch. chrétienne*, s. v. *Baouït*, Figs. 1266 ff.
[7] J. Strzygowski, Prussian *Jahrbuch*, xxii, 1901, 29 ff. (Fig.); O. Wulff, *Berlin Catalogue*, i, No. 29. Dr. Wulff thinks the subject is part of a scene representing one of Christ's miracles.
[8] Strzygowski, as above, p. 31 (Fig.).
[9] *B. Z.*, i. 355, and Pl. III.

skill to justify its attribution to the fifth century. The treatment of the garments somewhat recalls that of the Archangel Michael on the ivory panel in the British Museum (Fig. 121), and a thick neck is common to both figures. But the bust of St. Mark lacks the ideal feeling of the smaller work.

Fɪɢ. 88.   Marble relief of the fifth–sixth century, with St. Peter : from the neighbourhood of Sinope.   (Kaiser Friedrich Museum, Berlin.)

A fragment with Lazarus [1] in the Ottoman Museum may be compared with the Moses relief at Berlin (p. 160).   Two reliefs representing the Three Children of Babylon are also at Constantinople.[2]   But two marble drums of columns in the same collection [3] are more important as illustrating the condition of Byzantine

[1] A. Muñoz, *Nuovo Bull. di arch. crist.*, xii, 1906, pp. 107 ff.   [2] Ibid. Both from Psamatia.
[3] J. Strzygowski, *B. Z.*, i, 1892, 576 ff. and Pl. I and II ; V. Schultze, *Archäologie*, p. 331, Fig. 102.   The sculpture has been considerably damaged, and many of the heads of the figures are missing.,   The use of the vine-motive for covering the surfaces of columns was of earlier introduction, Constantine the Great having presented *columnas vitineas* from Greece to St. Peter's at Rome (*Lib. Pont. : Vita Silvestri*, § 16).   It also persisted later, for Basil (867–86) set up in the palace known as Kainourgion sixteen columns carved with animals in the convolutions of encircling vines (Theophanes, Bonn ed., p. 332).   The plain 'ivy' scroll encircling the drum (*B. Z.*, i, Pl. I) is of an early type, analogous to bands of ornament found upon nielloed silver of the sixth century (Fig. 360).   It is not characteristic of middle or late Byzantine art.

sculpture about the year A. D. 500, when the power of modelling the human figure was already on the decline, while the execution of floral ornament was

vigorous and masterly. The surface of each is covered by a vine-branch growing spirally upwards : between the leaves are single figures of men and animals, with two groups, one representing the Baptism, the other an altercation between two women, one of whom carries a cock, the other a dog. There is thus a curious mixture of the genre scene with the religious subject ; some of the animals, notably a charging bull, are admirably conceived. The human figures are of different merit : all have certain defects, such as arms disproportionately short where the body is draped, excessively long where it is nude. But in the subjects where pagan or religious models were presumably available, the work has still a certain classical feeling ; the drapery is still skilfully treated, especially in the case of the St. John in the Baptism. In those cases, however, in which the sculptor had to rely upon his own powers, as with the two women, the inferiority is marked. The forms are clumsier, the draperies less natural. The column may be assigned with confidence to the period between the reign of Theodosius and that of Justinian. In the latter period the human figure was already losing its old pre-eminence, and the floral ornament had not yet been excessively conventionalized. The bold natural treatment of these columns could hardly have been possible later than the sixth century.

The two front columns of the ciborium in S. Marco at Venice,[1] brought from the Church of Sta Maria del Canneto at Pola in the thirteenth century, belong to the early sixth century ; the remaining two appear to be later complementary work perhaps of the eleventh or twelfth century. Each has nine zones divided by plain bands bearing Latin inscriptions ; and each zone has a series of figures beneath arcadings of round arches in which are to be seen scalloped niches.

FIG. 89.   Sculpture on column of the ciborium, S. Marco, Venice.   (Alinari.)

[1] Rohault de Fleury, *La Messe*, ii, Pl. CIII ; Garrucci, *Storia*, Pl. 486 ff. ; E. Dobbert, *Über den Stil Niccolò Pisano's und dessen Ursprung*, 1873, p. 88 ; A. P. Zorzi, in Ongania, *La Basilica*

The figures, though for the most part occupying separate niches, form part of groups or subjects illustrating the stories of Joachim and Anna, the Virgin and Our Lord, some of the episodes being derived from the Apocryphal gospels; this treatment recalls that of the ambo of Salonica (p. 145). The relief is high, and Venturi, comparing it with that of the ambo, disputes the oriental origin of the work, believing that in the sixth century, to which he assigns it, sculptured reliefs in the East had already become flatter and more carelessly modelled. He sees in the survival of early types and subjects upon these columns characteristics pointing to a local art which preserved beyond their time iconographic features already abandoned in great centres: such, for example, is the prevalence of the youthful and beardless type of Christ. He thinks that Pola itself may have produced this remarkable sculpture. Strzygowski, on the other hand, considers the columns oriental, and suggests Syria-Palestine as a probable locality.[1] This seems more probable, but whatever the place, the influences which presided over the work must have been oriental. There are distinct analogies between its style and that of the figured sarcophagi of Ravenna; iconographical and ornamental details also point to the East, some subjects, e. g. the death of Judas and the two scenes with Pilate, suggesting comparison with the miniatures of the Codex Rossanensis (p. 452). We may note the sideways position of Our Lord when riding into Jerusalem; the Ascension resembling that of the carved wooden panel in the Church of Al Mu'allaka at Cairo; and the persistent use of the scalloped niche throughout (p. 130). The columns may have been Venetian booty obtained in the East. The best work shows great fertility of invention, and a considerable dramatic sense: gestures are well rendered and the draperies are skilfully disposed.

A marble relief in the Berlin Museum (Fig. 90) formerly built into the inner face of the wall of Constantinople on the landward side, representing the calling of Moses by the Lord,[2] probably dates from the seventh century. It is in flat relief with but the feeblest attempt at modelling, and the folds of the draperies are not modelled, but marked by parallel lines. The work is that of a monumental mason rather than a sculptor, and in fact the relief appears to have been intended to place over a tomb.

In an intercolumniation surmounted by a gable, Moses, turned to the right, extends both hands covered with his mantle to receive a scroll held by the hand of the Almighty; behind him an attendant figure raises his right hand in wonder; before him are flames. In the gable is a cross flanked by peacocks; above it are conventional floral scrolls, and on the architrave is a mutilated inscription.[3]

The motive of the hands covered with the mantle as a sign of reverence is of Eastern origin and appears in Christian art in the fifth century, while the bowed knee of Moses indicates an approach to the Byzantine proskynesis. As

---

di San Marco, vol. iii, No. xiii, pp. 281 ff. ; H. von der Gabelentz, *Die mittelalterliche Plastik Venedigs*, pp. 1 ff. ; Venturi, *Storia dell' arte italiana*, i, pp. 454 ff. and Figs. 219–72. Prof. Venturi thinks they may have been brought from Pola in A. D. 1243. In the dialogues of the Anonymus of Pola, published by Kandler, there is mention of columns taken from the basilica at Pola founded by Bishop Maximianus of Ravenna in the sixth century. The human figures are rougher in the two posterior columns, and the treatment of columns, niches, and ornament is inferior.

[1] *Byz. Zeitschr.*, xii, 1903, p. 433 ; *Die christlichen Denkmäler Ägyptens, R. Q.*, 1897. Cf. also A. Haseloff, *Codex purpureus Rossanensis*, 127, who develops the suggestion of Graeven that the Codex and the columns are inspired by models from the same region (Graeven, *Göttingische gelehrte Anzeigen*, 1897, p. 66).

[2] Wulff, *Berlin Catalogue*, i, No. 32 ; J. Strzygowski, Prussian *Jahrbuch*, xiv, 1893, pp. 65 ff. The parallel scene on the doors of Sta Sabina at Rome, where it is accompanied by Moses among Jethro's flocks and before the burning bush, makes it probable that the episode is not the receiving of the Law, but an event which took place on Horeb. In Byzantine representations of the receiving of the Tables on Sinai Moses always averts his head, whereas here he looks directly at the scroll.

[3] Containing the name John, and apparently part of the word ἰατρός.

this, however, was already represented in its extreme form in the seventh century, we may perhaps place the relief not far from the year A.D. 600.   With this date the style of the ornamental foliage agrees, for it is not that of the period after iconoclasm.   Moreover, we should not expect a gravestone of this kind to have been produced while the religious dispute was actually in progress.

Another marble relief[1] in the Imperial Ottoman Museum at Constantinople. now in a fragmentary condition, and representing two male figures in tunic and pallium separated by a tree, the whole surrounded on two sides by a broad acanthus border, exhibits the same defects and is probably a work of the same period.

Fig. 90.   Marble relief of about A.D. 600 from Constantinople.
(Kaiser Friedrich Museum, Berlin.)

It is interesting to note that the treatment of the acanthus leaf on both these marble reliefs recalls that on the capital with inscription relating to Heraclius, also in the Ottoman Museum (p. 172).

A ciborium with saints and angels in the spandrels, preserved in the same museum, is attributed to the sixth or seventh century.[2]

A relief walled into the north side of S. Marco at Venice[3] represents a throne and nimbed lamb flanked on each side by six other lambs, with the inscriptions: +O ΑΜΝΟC +ΟΙ ΑΓΙΟΙ ΑΠΟCΤΟΛΟΙ.   On the throne are the cloth,[4] cross, diadem, and book of the Gospels.   The relief should not be later

---

[1] Prussian *Jahrbuch*, as above, p. 71, Fig. 2.

[2] Rivoira, *Origini della architettura lombarda*, i, Figs. 274–5.

[3] Ongania, *La Basilica di San Marco*, Pt. III, p. 257, and Pl. XLIV; O. Wulff, *Die Koimesiskirche von Nicäa*, p. 243 (Strasburg, 1903).   It may be noted that Christ and the Apostles under the figure of lambs are to be seen at the Cathedral of Saint Front at Périgueux, a church supposed to be modelled upon San Marco (F. de Verneilh, *Annales arch.*, xiv, pp. 234–6).

[4] As in the mosaic on the triumphal arch in Sta Maria Maggiore at Rome.

than the seventh century, because the Sixth Council of Constantinople forbade the representation of Christ as the lamb. The symbolism is allied to that which found expression in the mosaics of the triumphal arch in Sta Maria Maggiore at Rome, and in several of the sarcophagi at Ravenna.

A bas-relief in the Ottoman Museum, found at Thasos,[1] and probably earlier than the iconoclastic period, represents the youthful winged figure of *Kairos* holding a balance, and with the wheel beneath his feet: to the right are two

FIG. 91.   Marble relief with *Kairos* in the Cathedral of Torcello.   Cf. Fig. 65.   (Alinari.)

draped female figures, *Pronoia* and *Metanoia*. *Kairos* ('Opportunity') was regarded as the type of human life,[2] and continued popular in later periods of Byzantine art; an early example of this figure is found on a limestone relief from Thebes in the Cairo Museum (Fig. 65), dated by Strzygowski as early as the third or fourth century,[3] a later in the relief at Torcello (Fig. 91),[4] formerly

---

[1] A. Muñoz, *L'Arte*, ix, pp. 212 ff., Rome, 1906.
[2] Ibid., *L'Arte*, 1904, p. 135.   [3] Strzygowski, *Koptische Kunst*, No. 8757, p. 103.
[4] R. von Schneider, *Das Kairosrelief in Torcello*, in *Serta Harteliana*, Vienna, 1896, pp. 279 ff.; Cattaneo, *L'architettura in Italia*, Fig. 166; Venturi, *Storia*, i, p. 522–3; *B. Z.*, vi, 1897, p. 211. Representations of Καιρός, Opportunity, with a long forelock and bald behind, began to be popular in the Hellenistic age, when allegory found developed expression in art. The type is said to have been introduced by Lysippus, but the figure became more richly endowed with attributes as time went on. The balance was suspended from a razor's edge (ἐπὶ ξυροῦ

part of the ambo in the cathedral, and probably, like a similar relief with Ixion in the same place, made in the Lagoon region under Byzantine influence at the beginning of the eleventh century or earlier.   On the Torcello *Kairos*-relief, which perhaps dates from about A. D. 1008, the year of the restoration of the church, Opportunity is seen with knife and scales running to left upon two winged wheels, and evading a bearded man who endeavours to seize him.   A youth grasps him by the forelock, and Victory, by his side, hands him a wreath, while a woman at the opposite end of the composition turns away in disappointment; the slab has an interlaced border.   With the slabs with *Kairos* and Ixion may be compared the two slabs let into the façade of S. Marco at Venice, and representing four of the labours of Hercules.[1]   The whole group, like the little panels of the secular ivory caskets (p. 214), suggests the direct imitation of antique models, and such may have been accessible to the sculptors.

Third Period.

Figure sculpture in this period is of little merit and examples are not numerous.   They consist of low reliefs, the best of which, e. g. one or two in S. Marco at Venice, look as if they may have been inspired by carvings in ivory.   It is not easy to be certain in every case whether the work is purely Byzantine, or to what extent foreign influences may have contributed to it.

The stone medallion representing a Byzantine emperor on the wall of a house in the Campo Angaran at Venice, and probably brought from Constantinople in A. D. 1204, is assigned to the tenth or eleventh century.[2]   The relief, which is of no great merit, shows the emperor in his embroidered mantle.

The relief on the north side of S. Marco at Venice (Fig. 34), representing the familiar subject of Alexander's ascension,[3] may be as early, though it should perhaps be rather referred to the Fourth Period.   The king is seen in his gryphon-car wearing a royal mantle of Byzantine character, but a conical cap.

The same church has inset in its walls two reliefs of St. Demetrius and St. George seated and drawing their swords, which, though the accompanying inscriptions are in Latin, are Byzantine at least in inspiration.[4]   In the Church of Agia Paraskevi in Chalcis (Euboea) Strzygowski discovered a relief representing the Virgin as Orans[5] in a style suggesting the Third Period.   The feeble relief without modelling, the schematic composition, and the presence of the monogrammatic letters on either side of the head support the attribution.   Work of this kind differs materially from that of the higher reliefs of the time before iconoclasm.   One example in S. Marco at Venice[6] is probably of Venetian origin as the nimbus is fluted.   The finest relief of this subject is that in Sta Maria in Porto at Ravenna.[7]   A Virgin at Trani is of the eleventh century.[8]

ἵσταται ἀκμῆς), and wings were added to the ankles.   See Baumeister, p. 771 and Figs. 823–4 ; also E. Gardner, *Handbook of Greek Sculpture*, p. 412.   Such a representation of *Kairos* is given in a poem of Theodore Podromos (twelfth century), Krumbacher, p. 753.

[1] The panel nearest the piazzetta is considered to be certainly a late work, the other is held by Saccardo (in Ongania, *Basilica di San Marco*, iii, pp. 260 and 269) to be Roman.   The slabs are reproduced in Ongania, Plate LIII.

[2] Schlumberger, in *B. Z.*, ii, 1903, 192 f., and Pl. II ; P. Molmenti, *Storia di Venezia nella vita privata*, 53.

[3] Ongania, *La Basilica di San Marco*, Pl. LXIV, and text, iii. 254 ; Didron, *Annales archéologiques*, xxv, 1865, 141 ; Venturi, *Storia*, ii. 527.

[4] Venturi, *Storia*, ii, Figs. 370, 371.   For various reliefs in S. Marco see H. von der Gabelentz, *Mittelalterliche Plastik in Venedig*, 1903.

[5] *R. Q.*, 1893, p. 8 ; De Rossi, *Festschrift*, pp. 401 ff. ; Δελτίον τῆς ἱστορικῆς καὶ ἐθνολογικῆς ἑταιρίας, 1889, 717 ff.

[6] Ongania, *La Basilica di San Marco*, ii. 339, Fig. *h*.   A Byzantine origin is claimed for other reliefs in the church representing the Virgin and Child, Our Lord with the Virgin, St. John Baptist, saints, and angels, all approximately of the eleventh century.   Ibid., iii, p. 270.

[7] Diehl, *Manuel*, Fig. on p. 610.   [8] Schlumberger, *Épopée*, iii, p. 253.

A fragment of a relief at Naxos has the Nativity and Flight of the Holy Family.[1]

The Berlin Museum possesses another curious stone relief (Fig. 92) of late date, found in 1895 in the village of Tusla, which is on the line between Gebse and Pendik on the Gulf of Ismid in Asia Minor, and is close to Haidar Pasha on the Anatolian railway.[2] The object, which is imperfect, is a sunk panel on which are two figures with tall conventional plants between them. That on the left is a man with a wolf's or dog's head, that on the right a personage

FIG. 92.   Stone relief from Tusla, Asia Minor, twelfth century (?).
(Kaiser Friedrich Museum, Berlin.)

in a conical helmet with side pieces, the details of his costume being very indistinct.

The Byzantine origin of this relief is confirmed by the discovery in the same year of another somewhat similar but even rougher relief at Hamidieh, about eight kilometres south-west of Eskishehir (Dorylaion). It has upon both sides a nude figure of a man with wolf's or hound's head ; in one case carrying an oval shield, in the other wearing a bridle upon the head. An important point is that the first-mentioned figure has on the border above it an incomplete

---

[1] Ἐφημερὶς ἀρχαιολογική, 1890, 20, and Pl. III.   M. Damirales would ascribe the relief to Early Christian times, but the peculiar convention of the trees suggests a period subsequent to the tenth century. The convention recalls that of Carolingian art and that of the centuries immediately succeeding, and it is possible that the relief may be the work of a Western sculptor.

[2] Prussian *Jahrbuch*, xix, 1898, 57 ff.

Greek inscription terminating in ΚΕΦΑΛΟϹ, probably the second part of such a word as κυνοκέφαλος or λυκοκέφαλος.

The occurrence in Byzantine art of such Cynocephali, recalling the forms of ancient Egypt, is not unprecedented. In the Calendar of A. D. 354 (p. 484), the bust of Anubis is seen near the priest of Isis on the page for the month of November. In the frescoes of Mount Athos St. Christopher is represented with a wolf's or dog's head,[1] though the Painter's Guide describes him as young and beardless, and in paintings he is usually seen in ordinary human form. But in the frescoes of the Monastery of Karakallou dating from A. D. 1717 he is seen in warrior's costume and with an animal head among SS. Theodore, Nestor, Aretas, and Menas. It may be noted that on one of the reliefs the Cynocephalus holds a shield (the lost right hand probably holding a sword or spear), while in the other he appears in association with a warrior.

The Hamidieh relief was found on the site of an ancient Christian cemetery, a fact which suggests the possibility of some funeral cult.[2] But for the inscription upon this relief, it might have been supposed that the figure represented a mime,[3] as performances were given at the Byzantine court in which the actors wore animal masks. Possibly the fresco (p. 301) in the Cathedral of Sta Sophia at Kieff[4] and the early Italian mosaic at Cremona[5] may be brought into connexion with this custom.

Other reliefs with representations of monsters and animals with foliage resembling ivy rather than palm in the background are to be seen in the outside wall of the chief apse of the Church of Skripu (Orchomenus), of the year A. D. 873-4.[6]

Two reliefs in the Central Museum at Athens belong to the same group, and seem to show that in the years following the iconoclastic dispute, when religious sculpture was almost at a standstill, there was a fashion for carving fabulous creatures of this kind, which do not appear to be always connected with the Physiologus. The first shows a combat between a kind of siren and a man armed with sword and shield, a tree with a serpent climbing up it separating the two adversaries. In the second, a beardless centaur plays a guitar, while a small figure in long garments (a dancer?) is seen in the background.[7]

There is a resemblance between the nature of all these subjects and some of those found upon the secular group of ivory caskets (see pp. 214-22), the oldest of which were probably produced in the ninth century. On these caskets centaurs, sirens, and pairs of combatants are all found, and the conclusion is that the rudely carved reliefs and the finer caskets of bone and ivory alike manifest the survival of mythical subjects in Byzantine art.

Bronze figure sculpture of some little merit is not unrepresented in this period, the principal examples taking the form of small cast panels with effigies of saints upon them. The British Museum has such a relief with a standing

---

[1] Prussian *Jahrbuch*, xix, 1898, p. 59; Didron, *Handbuch der Malerei*, &c., ed. Schäfer, p. 316, note 2. See also K. Richter, *Der deutsche St. Christoph.*

[2] Sometimes dog-headed figures are introduced in Byzantine art with the intention of conveying an insult to the persons represented. So in Psalter illustrations the Jews who take Christ prisoner appear in this guise. See J. J. Tikkanen, *Die Psalterillustration im Mittelalter*, 56, and N. Kondakoff, *Miniaturen des Chludov-Psalters*, Pl. XIV.

[3] For the *Ludus Gothicus*, in which these masks and skins were worn at the reception of the emperor, see Constantine Porphyrogenitus, *De caerimoniis aulae byzantinae*, i. 83 (Bonn ed., i. 381, with Reiske's commentary on the passage, vol. ii, pp. 355). The animals mentioned include wolves, bears, boars, and stags.

[4] *The Cathedral of Sta Sophia at Kieff*, Pl. LV, Fig. 2 (publication of the Imperial Russian Archaeological Society); Tolstoy and Kondakoff, *Russian Antiquities*, vol. iv, p. 153 : both works in Russian. The scene represents a man with a beast's head in combat with another.

[5] Demmin, *Die Kriegswaffen in ihren geschichtlichen Entwicklungen*, p. 354, 1893 ; E. Aus'm Weerth, *Der Mosaikboden in St. Gereon zu Cöln*, &c., Pl. VI, Bonn, 1873. Here again two combatants are represented, one labelled CENTAVRVS having what looks like an ass's head.

[6] *B. Z.*, iii, p. 6.

[7] Prussian *Jahrbuch*, as above, pp. 61-2, Fig. on p. 62.

figure of St. Theodore, apparently of the eleventh century [1] (Fig. 93); another, with St. George, at whose feet a donor kneels, is in M. Schlumberger's collection; a third, wi+h three military saints, is at Berlin. [2]

A bronze steelyard-weight with bust of the Emperor Phocas(?) in the British Museum, [3] though of rude workmanship, has some character and individuality.

Repoussé figures in bronze on medallions or other small objects are too numerous to mention : all are on a small scale. For embossed silver, see pp. 563 ff.

Of purely ornamental sculpture in bronze the borders of the panels on the great ninth-century doors at Sta Sophia at Constantinople must be specially mentioned on account of their admirable workmanship (p. 618 and Fig. 391).

FIG. 93.   Gilt bronze plaque of the eleventh century : St. Theodore.   (British Museum.)

Fourth Period.

With the thirteenth century, perhaps as a result of intercourse with the West, there is an increase of sculpture in high relief very different from the shallow reliefs with which the Christian East had contented itself since the seventh century.   Among the more remarkable examples are the tympana with half-figures of Our Lord and angels at Kahrié Djami at Constantinople (Fig. 94).   They were made to ornament the monument of Michael Tornikes, friend of Theodore Metochites (d. A. D. 1328). [4]   Another relief has a half-figure of the Virgin within a rich and finely carved border of acanthus. [5]   The capitals with busts of angels in this church are also of late date. [6]   The style of the mutilated subjects amid the foliage in the Mosque of the Calenders (*Deesis, Etimasia*) has been compared with that of the figures in Kahrié Djami. [7]

A frieze under the arcade of the south door at Sta Sophia, Trebizond, has a relief showing the Temptation and Expulsion from Eden, with angels, symbols of the Evangelists, &c. [8]   It is accompanied by a Greek inscription; the work is very crude.

At Mistra an enthroned Christ in the Museum is in very shallow relief; [9]

[1] *Catalogue of Early Christian and Byzantine Antiquities*, No. 544.

[2] G. Schlumberger, in *Florilegium Melchior de Vogüé*, 560, and *Épopée*, ii, p. 493.

[3] *Catalogue*, No. 485.

[4] Th. Schmit, *Izviestiya* of the Russian Arch. Inst. at Constantinople, xi, 1906, Pl. 83 and 84 ; Diehl, *Études byzantines*, pp. 416–17, 1905 ; D. Pulgher, *Anciennes églises byz. de Constantinople*, p. 31 f. and Pl. XXIII, XXVI, XXVII (Vienna, 1878) ; Freshfield, in *Archaeologia*, lv, Pl. XXXV.   There is a similarity between the angels and others at Bari in the South of Italy, where there are other parallels to these late Byzantine sculptures (see *Byz. Zeitschr.*, xiv, p. 625).   [5] Schmit, Pl. 88.   [6] Ibid., Pl. 85 and 86.

[7] J. Ebersolt, *Rev. arch.*, July–Aug., 1909, p. 22.

[8] Texier and Pullan, *Byz. Architecture*, Pl. LXIV.   According to Millet, *B. C. H.*, xix, 1895, p. 457, Texier s plate is inaccurate.

[9] Millet, *Monuments byz. de Mistra*, Pl. 49, 2.   For parallels between Byzantine and Italian

the style is linear, and the folds of the drapery are represented by mere grooves. An Ascent of Alexander in the Church of Peribleptos is without merit.

Two slabs now in the iconostasis of the church at Chepin in Bulgaria, representing St. Peter and St. Paul, each under an arch with his name by his head, have been assigned to the thirteenth century.[1]

A slab on an ambo at Kalabach in Thessaly is stated to have the Ascension.[2] A St. Michael and a Virgin are at Episkope, and there is a curious relief with many figures at Orminion.[3]

Fɪɢ. 94.   Sculpture in Kahrié Djami, Constantinople ; early fourteenth century.
(Sébah and Joaillier.)

Some of the carved wooden doors from Coptic churches in Egypt fall within this period. The panels from Sitt Miriam (Al Muʻallaka) at Cairo, in the British Museum (Fig. 95),[4] have figure subjects from the New Testament, agreeing in the main with the usual Byzantine types, while ornamental details are borrowed from Saracenic art: they appear to be of the thirteenth century.

Other wooden doors bear figures of men, animals, and monsters, recalling those on contemporary ambos and stone slabs. A notable example is that in

sculpture during this period, see E. Bertaux, *L'Art dans l'Italie méridionale*, p. 446, and Millet, *B. Z.*, xiv, p. 625.

[1] *V. V.*, v, 1898, 612-13, and Pl. III.   St. Paul holds a book, St. Peter the keys.

[2] Kondakoff, *Macedonia*, p. 231 (reference to photos by Smirnoff).

[3] A. J. Wace, *Journ. Hellen. St.*, 1906, pp. 154-9.

[4] British Museum *Catalogue*, No. 987.

the Church of St. Nicholas at Ochrida, apparently dating from the thirteenth or fourteenth century.[1] The door is divided into panels. The two vertical rows in the middle contain equestrian figures of SS. George, Demetrius, and the two Theodores, with a centaur: on the other panels are fish, birds, lions,

FIG. 95. Cedar panels of the thirteenth century, with the Annunciation, Baptism, and Ascension, from the Church of Sitt Miriam, Cairo. (British Museum.)

a gryphon with a serpent, &c. The style recalls that of Russian work at Suzdal, reliefs in the Church of St. Menas at Salonika, and painted designs in Sta Sophia, Kieff. It further has analogies with the well-known cypress coffer in the cathedral at Terracina, exhibited in the Exhibition of Grottaferrata;[2] and there

---

[1] N. Kondakoff, *Macedonia*, pp. 236–7 and Pl. III (Russian).
[2] A. Muñoz, *L'Art byzantin à l'Exposition de Grottaferrata*; Strzygowski, *Das orientalische Italien (Monatshefte für Kunstwissenschaft*, i).

seems reason to believe that this coffer may have been ascribed to too early a date.   Another door in this style is at Vatopedi on Mount Athos.[1]

The iconostasis is often elaborately and finely carved in Greek churches, though the work is usually of a later date than the fifteenth century.   Fine examples are in churches of the Holy Land, and that in the Church of the Nativity at Bethlehem is especially remarkable.[2]

For figures dating from the various periods embossed in silver, see Ch. IX.

6. Ornamental Sculpture.

Carving in stone of a purely decorative character is so abundant in East-Christian and Byzantine art that it will only be possible to indicate its characteristics in a general fashion.   It is for the most part subordinated to architecture, and is employed to enrich the interior or exterior of churches and other buildings : cornices, architraves, and lintels of all periods are embellished in this way.

The designs carved on lintels and friezes, especially in the ruins of churches and other buildings in Syria and Egypt between the fourth and eighth centuries, are of considerable interest chiefly for the variations of scrolled vine and acanthus in which they so abound.   In Egypt there are characteristic methods of treating the acanthus, examples of which are now accessible in considerable numbers.[2]   All this work is more important for its ornament than as sculpture, the relief being flat and the effect coloristic ; something will be said on these designs in the chapter on ornament.   *Mouldings* tended to become less rich with the lapse of time ; in churches depending on mosaics for their interior decoration deep and elaborate mouldings were undesirable.   Classical features such as oves and astragali continue to a late period (Ch. XIII), though such sumptuous effects as those of the mouldings of Mshatta are no longer attempted. Cornices, architraves, iconostases continued to be carved with floral, geometrical, and animal designs in flat relief down to the last centuries of the empire, examples of the latest work being found at Mistra.[3]   But, apart from capitals, the principal field for decorative work was afforded by flat slabs or panels used for various purposes in decoration from the fourth century ; these panels yield the most characteristic examples of sculpture during all periods of the East-Roman Empire.   They are found over a very wide area which extends from Hither Asia across the Balkan peninsula and Italy into Spain.[4]   They range in date from the fifth century to the twelfth or thirteenth, and their ornamentation, which is either symbolic or purely decorative, includes representations of lambs, doves, peacocks, &c., but never admits the human figure.   Many of the motives, as we shall see, are purely oriental, having their origin in Mesopotamia, Syria, and Persia ; and it is from the Orient, with its dislike for high relief, that the whole style is derived (p. 110).   It is probable that the sculptors frequently imitated textile fabrics, the effect of which they desired as far as possible to reproduce.   It is evident from the general uniformity of these slabs, wherever found, that the art here exemplified was dominant from one end of the Mediterranean to the other for several centuries, and that, whether the centres of distribution were few or many, the inspiration was one and indivisible.   New motives were introduced in the Byzantine Empire from the ninth to the eleventh centuries, but the purely ornamental and Eastern character was throughout maintained.

In Italy they first appear at Ravenna ; but by the end of the eighth century they were in general use, and are to be found in numbers in Roman churches.

[1] Kondakoff, *Monuments of Christian Art on Mount Athos*, Pl. XXXVIII (Russian).
[2] Baumstark, *R. Q.*, 1906, 186.
[3] J. Strzygowski, *Koptische Kunst* (Cairo Catalogue) ; J. Clédat in Cabrol's *Dict. d'arch. chrétienne*, s. v. *Baouït*, Figs. 1273–4 ; Wulff, *Berlin Catalogue*.   Syrian friezes and lintels are reproduced by De Vogüé, *La Syrie Centrale* ; H. C. Butler, *Architecture and other Arts* (American Archaeological Expedition).   [3] G. Millet, *Monuments byzantins de Mistra*, Pl. 45 ff.
[4] *B. Z.*, ix, 1900, 718.   The tombstones of Armenia present interesting affinities with the later slabs.

Probably their sudden increase about that time was due to the influx of Greek monks into Rome, in which city and territory sculpture of this kind continued to be produced until the eleventh century.[1] But the carving on the ciborium and choir closures of S. Clemente, executed between A. D. 514 and 535, is a proof of the popularity of the style at an even earlier date.[2] A number of carved slabs, both purely Byzantine and Italo-Byzantine, enclose the galleries in S. Marco at Venice (cf. Fig. 96), which is a veritable storehouse for reliefs of this kind.[3] It is thought that some of them may have originally served as the fronts of sarcophagi.[4]

It has been observed that these slabs were used for various purposes. Most frequently they formed the transennae of choir closures or parapets of galleries ;[5] less frequently they filled the lower part of windows, served as tombstones, were

FIG. 96.   Closure-slabs in the gallery, S. Marco, Venice, eleventh century.
(*Hautes Études* : G. Millet.)

fitted together as sides of sarcophagi, placed upon walls as a revetment or round fountains (*phialae*) ; again, they served to decorate the surfaces of ambos or pulpits. In the latter case they were often smaller, and the panels placed at the sides of the steps sometimes diverged from the rectangular form.

It would be a difficult task to enumerate all the slabs of which records exist ; even the list of sites upon which examples are found would be of considerable

[1] A. L. Frothingham, *Journ. American Arch.*, x, 1895, 183.

[2] Ibid., 173.

[3] Ongania, *La Basilica di San Marco*, text, vol. iii. 262–3, with references to numerous plates in folio v ; Von der Gabelentz, *Mittelalterliche Plastik in Venedig* ; Cattaneo, *L'Architettura in Italia*, &c., reproduces several slabs of Byzantine and Italo-Byzantine origin, cf. Fig. 28, p. 77, &c.

[4] Cf. D. Ainaloff and E. Riedin, *Cathedral of Sta Sophia at Kieff*, p. 52 (Russian).

[5] Examples in the galleries of Sta Sophia, Constantinople (Salzenberg, Pl. X) ; St. Demetrius, Salonika (Texier and Pullan, *Byz. Architecture*, Pl. XVIII, XIX, XXI) ; St. Mark's, Venice, see note above.   *In windows*, St. Luke in Phocis (Schultz and Barnsley, p. 24, Pl. XIII–XV) ; Sta Sophia, Constantinople (Salzenberg, Pl. XVII).   As *transennae of choirs*, S. Clemente, Rome. Round *fountains*, Monasteries of Vatopedi and Lavra, Mount Athos (G. Schlumberger, *Épopée*, i, p. 129 ; ii, p. 521.   Perhaps the slabs now in the floor and on the walls of the metropolitan church at Serres in Macedonia once served this purpose (L. Chesnay, *Mon. Piot*, 1902, Figs. 8–16, p. 134).

length. Some of the more important may, however, be given in a footnote,[1] while in the text the principal styles of design may be briefly discussed.

The excavations of the French on the site of the temple of Delphi have furnished definite information as to the date of slabs with a typical ornamentation found in numerous other places, notably at Ravenna. At Delphi occurs the type illustrated in Fig. 81. Here the original elements were a sacred monogram in a wreath, with two diverging *lemnisci*, with heart-shaped leaves at the ends,[2] and supporting two crosses. In course of time the spaces between the limbs of the monogram become more important than the monogram itself, and there finally resulted a rosette formed of six heart-shaped cavities surrounded by a ring, which gives the whole somewhat the appearance of a wheel; the *lemnisci* become long tendrils issuing as continuations from the ring encircling the rosette. Now a similar 'wheel' to those on the slabs at Delphi occurs on a lintel at Kokonaya in Syria[3] with a sacred monogram in a wreath. The lintel is dated A.D. 431, and it is evident that even at that early period the original design and its degenerate form were in use side by side. A similar design is on a lintel at Assos in a ruined church in which an inscription of the fourth century has been discovered,[4] on a sarcophagus at Panion, where the sacred monogram accompanies an inscription containing the names of Arcadius and Honorius,[5] and on the imperial sarcophagi at Constantinople, some of which at least must be of the fifth century. A cross inscribed in a circle, a design found on the backs of the slabs at Delphi, also occurs on these sarcophagi, as well as on a font at Aladja-Kislé, the acanthus on which is of fifth-century type.[6] We may conclude that the slabs ornamented in this manner, as well as the sarcophagi with the same decoration, belong as a class to the fifth century; and though the motive was imitated as late as the tenth century the slabs of this period are distinguishable from the older examples either by the alteration of the form, by omissions, or by the addition of new elements to the design such as palm-leaves beneath the crosses, rosettes, or candelabra flanking the arms, or a floral border round the whole, instead of the plain margin of the originals. Examples showing these changes are to be seen at Ravenna, in St. Mark's at Venice, at Monza, Constantinople, and the Church of St. Luke in Phocis: in the last-mentioned church the leaves at the end of the *lemnisci* have become serpents' heads. The tomb of Yaroslaff at Kieff is a curious example of various early symbolic motives.[7]

---

[1] In Greece and the Balkan peninsula examples occur at Constantinople (Church of the Theotokos, &c.), at Salonika (St. Demetrius, Texier and Pullan, p. 123), at Athens (*Ath. Mitth.*, 1889, 271 ff.), Káisariani on Hymettus (Strzygowski and Lambros, Ἐφημερὶς Ἀρχαιολογική, 1902, 90), Delphi (*B. C. H.*, xxiii, p. 206 f.), Daphni (G. Millet, *Le Monastère de Daphni*, ch. i), and several sites in the Morea, including Mistra (Millet, *Monuments byz. de M.*), in Servia and Macedonia (Miliukoff, *Izviestiya* of the Russian Arch. Inst. at Cple., iv, 1899, 146; N. Kondakoff, *Macedonia*, 231); at Broussa in Anatolia is a slab with peacocks (Mendel, *B. C. H.*, 1909, 350). On the Adriatic, at Parenzo, Grado, Pola, and Zara (Museum). In Italy, at Rome (S. Clemente, Sta Maria in Cosmedin, S. Saba, Sta Maria in Trastevere, S. Lorenzo, Sta Agnese, S. Sabina, S. Prassede, and other churches) (A. L. Frothingham, *Journ. Amer. Arch.*, x, 1895, 183 ff.), Venice (Ongania, *Basilica di San Marco*, as above), Ravenna (especially in the Museo Civico), Bologna, Ancona, Rimini, Otranto (E. Bertaux, *L'Art dans l'Italie méridionale*, 76, Fig. 15), and Naples. The best discussion of the earlier slabs will be found in J. Laurent's article *Delphes chrétien* in *B. C. H.*, xxiii, 1899, 238 ff. Slabs of the tenth century and later are discussed by O. Wulff (*Die Koimesiskirche in Nicäa*, 164 ff.); examples are well illustrated by Schultz and Barnsley (*The Church of St. Luke of Stiris*, Pl. XIII-XV), and in Ongania, as above. Further illustration will be found in collective works (Garrucci, *Storia*; Venturi, *Storia*, &c.), while the photographs of Alinari and Ricci supply much material for study (the former in V. and A. Museum).

[2] For *lemnisci* with heart-shaped leaves on ivory carvings, &c., see note 3, p. 202.

[3] De Vogüé, *Syrie Centrale*, Pl. XCIX and p. 88. A similar 'wheel' between two crosses occurs on a lintel at Deir Sambil of the date A.D. 421 (ibid., Pl. CLI). The monogram in a wreath flanked by two monogrammatic crosses is found on the part of the Golden Gate at Constantinople which dates from the closing years of the fourth century (Prussian *Jahrbuch*, viii, 1893, p. 234). [4] *C. I. G.*, 8838; W. Ramsay, *The Cities and Bishoprics of Phrygia*, p. 521.

[5] Laurent, as above, p. 245. [6] Petersen and von Luschan, *Lykien*, p. 39.

[7] Ainaloff and Riedin, *Cathedral of Sta Sophia at Kieff*, pp. 52-3. On this monument,

Delphi has also furnished examples of slabs ornamented with a series of interconnected circles containing quatrefoils or whorls of acanthus, and having in the interspaces leaves or fragments of leaves of the same plant, and even animals and birds: in one example two birds are confronted on either side of a central cross.

Motives of this kind are partly of textile origin, and were copied by sculptors and workers in mosaic.[1] They are frequently found carved in stone on lintels and

Fig. 97.   Closure-slab, tenth–eleventh century, in S. Marco, Venice. (Alinari.) P. 166.

cornices in the ruined cities of Syria ;[2] they occur on the capitals of St. Demetrius, Salonika, S. Vitale at Ravenna, and Sta Sophia at Constantinople.[3] A fine panel in openwork at Ravenna (Ch. XIII), from the classical character of its border, is not likely to be later than the sixth century.   Very early examples of such interconnected circles occur in mosaics: òne from Aegina is assigned to the second century ;[4] another, a mosaic from Tyre in the Louvre, is ascribed to the fourth.

But the style is fully developed in sculpture in the fifth and sixth centuries, and to the earlier part of the sixth century most slabs of this type probably belong.[5] To a similar but even earlier date and the same oriental origin must be assigned slabs covered with a diaper of circles in contact, each having four

crosses are flanked by fish, and palm-leaves as well as crosses stand on *lemnisci* which end in leaves.   The authors suggest the seventh century as a probable date.   For the examples in St. Luke's, see Schultz and Barnsley, Pl. XIV. D.

[1] Such motives appear on the robes of consuls upon their diptychs (Molinier, *Ivoires*, Pl. I and Figs. on pp. 18, 19, 21, &c.).

[2] At Béhioh, Moujeleia, Serjilla, &c. (De Vogüé, *Syrie Centrale*, Pl. 137 ; 46, Figs. 2, 4 ; 24, Figs. 1 and 3).   The acanthus rosette is frequent in Syria, and is also found on the Cup of Chosroes in the Cabinet des Médailles, Paris.

[3] Laurent, as above, p. 263.   [4] Le Bas and Reinach, *Les Îles*, Pl. I, p. 140.

[5] An example at Kieff has an eagle, rosette, &c., in the circles (Ainaloff and Riedin, as above, Fig. 53).

almond- or leaf-shaped segments in the interior and in the centre a rosette. This is a rarer style of decoration than the preceding, though represented by a number of examples.[1]

With the full sixth century these sculptured slabs assume another character. Designs are enclosed in geometrical figures, especially lozenges and circles, formed of bold mouldings in high relief, very different from the plain borders of the earlier period.[2] The lozenges and circles are sometimes connected with each other in one design. From the seventh century the field is often continuously

Fig. 98. Closure-slabs of the fountain, Monastery of Lavra, Mount Athos.
(*Hautes Études* : G. Millet.) P. 170.

covered with circles and interlaced designs between which animals, plants, and crosses are distributed. The development was complete in the ninth century, the period when the architectural activity under the Macedonian emperors began. The Church of St. Luke of Stiris in Phocis is rich in examples of the eleventh century, in which interlaced ornament, animals (lions, &c.), floriated crosses, &c., are found.[3] The Church of the Assumption at Nicaea is also rich,[4] and the

[1] Serjilla, fifth or sixth century (De Vogüé, Pl. 49) ; Moujeleia (ibid., Pl. 50, Figs. 1, 4, 5) ; bronze door of the Church of the Nativity, Bethlehem (Owen Jones, *Grammar of Ornament*, Pl. 28) ; marble at Brescia (Cattaneo, *Archit.*, Pl. 137) ; S. Vitale, Ravenna (Ricci, Photo 36) ; Church of St. Ginès at Toledo (De Rios, *Arte latino-bizant. en España*, Pl. III, Fig. 12). The circles enclosing four segments were adopted in barbaric art, and lasted through the early Middle Ages. They are found, for example, in the border of the Book Cover of Theodelinda at Monza.

[2] The ambo of S. Apollinare in Classe has a central panel in this style flanked by two narrow panels, each with a cross standing upon a disk or circle (Laurent, as above, p. 267, Fig. 25) ; a similar combination is seen on closures between the pillars along the front of the gynaeceum or gallery in Sta Sophia at Constantinople (Lethaby and Swainson, *Sancta Sophia*, Fig. 61, p. 261).

[3] For examples of slabs of the later period see Schultz and Barnsley, 26 and Pl. XIII-XV. Some of the slabs in St. Luke's are not carved stone but plaster cast in a mould (Schultz, pp. 26-7) like the string-courses in the same church. Further examples are at Kieff (Ainaloff and Riedin, *Monuments of Kieff: The Cathedral of Sta Sophia*, p. 53). See also Millet, *Le Monastère de Daphni*, p. 14, n. 4 ; Diehl, *Manuel*, 428 ; R. Phené Spiers, *Architecture East and West*, p. 124 ; Salzenberg, *Altchristliche Denkmäler*, Pl. XXXV, 14 ; *Ath. Mitth.*, xxxi, pp. 279 ff. ; 'Εφημερὶς Ἀρχαιολογική, 1902, 92 ; *B.C.H*, Mars–Juillet, 1909, 352.

[4] Wulff, *Koimesiskirche*, 164 ff.

fountain (*phiale*) of the Monastery of Lavra on Mount Athos has good examples.[1] Others are inserted in the façade of Kilissé-Djami at Constantinople.[2]

The survival in new combinations of motives dating from a quite early period is probably due to the fact that these were admirably adapted for the purposes for which they were needed.[3]

In the Fourth Period animal ornament continued popular, but conventional floral designs and interlacings furnish the main motives. The work usually lacks the salience and character of that produced in the earlier centuries.[4]

Fig. 99. Closure-slab of the ninth or tenth century. Metropolitan Church, Mistra. (*Hautes Études*: G. Millet.)

The two pilasters known as the *Pilastri Acritani* in the piazzetta near the south-west corner of S. Marco at Venice may be noticed here.[5] Their ornament of vine-scrolls is characteristically Syrian, and they were probably carved in Syria in the sixth century. They formerly stood near the door of the Genoese citadel at Acre, and were brought to Venice after the Venetian victory over the Genoese in A.D. 1258. The disposition of the ornament is analogous to that seen in contemporary silk textiles from the same region.[6]

We should also notice the elaborate sculpture from the façade of Mshatta (Ch. XIII) with its similar suggestion of textile methods. In this work, the date of which lies somewhere between the fourth and the seventh centuries,[7] classical mouldings are found, but the bulk of the ornament is Persian, a fact which is readily explained if, as Strzygowski holds, the sculptors came from the Persian province of Mesopotamia. Mshatta is not a Byzantine work, but the principle of decoration which it embodies is precisely that which triumphed at

---

[1] Kondakoff, *Monuments of Christian Art on Mount Athos*, p. 42. Some of the slabs on this fountain, with peacocks, beasts, &c., in interlaced borders, are probably later than A.D. 1200, and belong to the Fourth Period.

[2] *Rev. arch.*, July–August, 1909, 33.

[3] In the walls of the Church of the Virgin *Gorgopico* at Athens are slabs with confronted gryphons and vases, confronted birds with snakes, sphinxes, lions, &c. The style is debased, and the work is probably not earlier than the date of the church (Rivoira, *Origini della architettura lombarda*, i, Figs. 278–81).

[4] Slab with gryphons and birds from a fountain near Eski Djuma, Salonika; peacocks, &c., on the old ambo on Sta Sophia, Ochrida, thirteenth-fourteenth century (Miliukoff, *Izviestiya* of the Russian Arch. Inst. of Cple., iv, Pt. I, 1899, 29 and 89; Kondakoff, *Macedonia*, 232), and on remains of a ciborium in the Church of Nerez, near Uskub (Kondakoff, as above, 176). Fountain slabs of Lavra on Mount Athos (Kondakoff, *Monuments, &c., of Athos*, p. 43); and of Kyrk-tchechmé, Constantinople, with peacocks (*Röm. Mitth.*, xviii, 195, Fig. 10; Mordtmann, *Esquisses topographiques de Cple.*, 71); slabs with animals, St. George, Salonika (Kondakoff, *Macedonia*, 82); numerous carvings at Mistra (G. Millet, *Monuments byz. de Mistra*, 1910); others at Trebizond (Millet, *B. C. H.*, xix, 1895, 457).

[5] Strzygowski, *O. C.*, ii. 423, photo.

[6] Prussian *Jahrbuch*, xxiv, 1903, 159.

[7] Strzygowski (*Jahrbuch*, as above, 1904) argues for a considerably earlier date. Diehl (*Manuel*, 48, &c.) is in favour of the fifth or sixth century.

Constantinople in the time of Justinian.[1] Many of the motives which it displays are common to Byzantine and Persian art, and some of them were in later centuries reproduced in the mosaics of the Basilica at Bethlehem (p. 414). Something further is said on this subject in the chapter on ornament.

7. CAPITALS.

(Cf. Figs. 2-4, 15, 18–20, 67–9, 100–5).

The Corinthian capital was the ground-form from which those used in Christian times were developed, and in examples of the fourth and fifth

FIG. 100.   Capitals of the transept, St. Demetrius, Salonika.
(Hautes Études : G. Millet.)

centuries the descent is obvious, despite the varied treatment of the acanthus foliage.[2] There were two principal causes which led to the modification of the earlier Greek type, one based upon structural necessity, the other upon changes in taste and technical methods. To the first is due the substitution of a straight-sided abacus for the old type with incurved sides (e. g. Fig. 69), a change

[1] Diehl compares the general effect of the sculptured ornament in the spandrels of the lower order in Sta. Sophia with that of Mshatta.

[2] A good idea of the various types of capitals in use from the fourth to the seventh century may be gathered from the series in the Kaiser Friedrich Museum in Berlin, illustrated in O. Wulff's catalogue *Die altchristlichen Bildwerke*, &c., i, 1909, pp. 53 ff. and 65 ff. See also G. Millet in A. Michel, *Histoire de l'art*, i. 154 ff. ; Lethaby and Swainson, *Church of Sancta Sophia*, 247 ff. ; O. Wulff, *Die Koimesiskirche in Nicäa*, 47 ff. and 122, and *B. Z.*, 1904, 564 ff. ; Strzygowski, *Kleinasien*, 117 ff. ; *B. D.*, iii. xx. Like the carved slabs, capitals of Proconnesian marble were very widely distributed, being found from Jerusalem (Mosque of Omar) to Kertch, from Alexandria and the Fayûm to Carthage and Kairuan (cf. Diehl, *Manuel*, 169, and, for Kairuan, Saladin, *La mosquée de Sidi Okba à Kairouan*, Paris, 1903). Egypt is very rich in capitals, many evidently imported from Proconnesus, and having parallels in other places, either themselves seaports or accessible from such. Imported forms were copied and modified by Coptic workmen. Fine examples have been found at Ahnas, Bawit, Saqqara, and other sites. For Egyptian capitals see Strzygowski, *Koptische Kunst*, 69 ff., and Wulff, *Berlin Catalogue*, as above, 65 ff. For later development see also M. Meurer, *Vergleichende Formenlehre des Ornaments*, pp. 541 ff., 1909.

which gave a capital better capable of supporting an impost-block (see below);
to the second must be ascribed the disappearance of the plastic treatment of
the leaves in favour of a flat relief in which contrast of light and shade is
obtained by a free use of the drill, or else so far neglected as almost to deprive
the work of plastic value.   At these stages other ornamental motives often
replaced the acanthus, which, however, was never abandoned as long as capitals
of Greek descent were made in the East.   We thus find interlaced 'basket
designs', lozenge diapers, parallel bands of zigzag, or vine foliage, all resulting
from the tendency to reduce the relief to a single plane (cf. Figs. 15, 18, 68).
Doubtless application of new motives to the capital was due in large measure
to the influence of Syria, where they had been adopted upon carved panels in
stone and wood.[1]

An interesting capital in the Imperial Ottoman Museum shows that old
tradition died slowly.   It has an inscription which assigns it to the seventh
century[2] and the reign of Heraclius (A. D. 610–41): it is said to have been
found in Constantinople.   It is so far Greek that the abacus forms a re-entrant
angle on each face instead of a straight line; round the top runs a band of
olive-leaves, while the sides bear in high relief pairs of crossed cornuacopiae
enclosing wreaths, a motive familiar in the mosaics, inlaid marble, and ivory
carvings of the sixth century;[3] above these are pairs of leaves enclosing fruits,
while between the pairs of cornuacopiae, just above the band of oves finishing
off the capital at the bottom, are leaves of acanthus type in low relief.[4]
The survival of a form with such strong reminiscences of the antique is
remarkable when the impost-capital with square top had already long been
popular.   Not less remarkable is the conjunction of very high and bold relief
with relief of a flat and feeble character, and with the most inartistic label
on which the inscription is very ill cut.   The high reliefs are well executed
and show that, at any rate in merely decorative work, the Byzantine sculptor
of the seventh century was by no means contemptible.

The period between the fourth and seventh centuries is the most
important in the development of the Byzantine capital, and in what follows
attention is chiefly directed to this time of growth and adaptation.   The
Macedonian period, a rival of the First Period in so many branches of art,
fell behind it in the decoration of capitals.[5]   After the close of that dynasty
degeneration was rapid.   In the Comnenian period old motives were reproduced; under the Palaeologi, capitals were often taken from earlier buildings
and re-employed, or where new work was done, it lacked character and style.
Nevertheless, many of the capitals at Mistra[6] are not ineffective, the combination of a zone of tall acanthus with a superposed zone of tall leaves (*feuilles
d'eau*) having a certain originality and charm.   But a detailed examination
shows how inferior the work is to that of the fifth or sixth century.

We may now consider some of the principal changes of the First Period
in rather greater detail, noting in the first place the capitals in the Church
of the Nativity at Bethlehem (Fig. 169), which are probably of Constantine's
time, and are still very close to the original Corinthian type (cf. Fig. 69).   Of
the more decidedly modified forms that described by Strzygowski as a Theodosian capital is the most important.   It was produced through a period rather
longer than that covered by the second emperor of that name (A. D. 408–50), and

---

[1] Wulff, *Berlin Catalogue*, as above.

[2] J. Strzygowski in Prussian *Jahrbuch*, xiv, 1893, Fig. 3 on p. 73.   The inscription, which
is on a square label in the middle of one side at the top, runs : ὁ θ(εὸ)s τῶν ἀγίων βοήθι Ἡρακλίῳ
τῷ δεσπότι.   See Curtis and Aristarchis in Ἑλλ. φιλ. Σύλλογος, Παράρτημα, 16, p. 24.

[3] For instance at S. Vitale, Ravenna; Parenzo Cathedral, diptych of Areobindus, A. D. 506.

[4] The treatment of these leaves recalls that of the foliate ornament on the marble relief
with Moses in the Berlin Museum (Fig. 90).

[5] Capitals of the eleventh century in S. Marco, Venice, are reproduced in Ongania, *Basilica
di S. M.* ; and by C. Errard, *L'Art byzantin*, vol. i, *Venise*, Pl. VI.

[6] G. Millet, *Monuments byz. de Mistra*, Pl. 46.

is composite, having two large bands of thorny acanthus (*acanthus spinosa*) and four volutes at the corners. Between the volutes runs a band of single acanthus leaves of five lobes, the whole rising from a torus of acanthus leaves laid obliquely.[1] Examples of this type are in the Piazza Vittorio Emmanuele

FIG. 101. Capital of the fifth century, S. Apollinare in Classe, Ravenna. (Alinari.)

at Ravenna,[2] in S. Apollinare in Classe (Fig. 101), and in St. John of Studium at Constantinople[3] dating from A.D. 463. The capital is thus the prevalent fifth-century type, for the thorny acanthus makes its first appearance on the Golden Gate at Constantinople, which dates from about A.D. 390,[4] while it went out

[1] *B. Z.*, i, 1892, 68 ; *B. D.*, ii, 1893, 241. For examples in the Broussa Museum, see G. Mendel in *B. C. H.*, Mars–Juillet, 1909, 360.

[2] Ricci, photo No. 362 ; J. Laurent, *B. C. H.*, 1899, Fig. 2, p. 209.

[3] Pulgher, *Anciennes églises*, &c., Pl. I, No. 2 ; Salzenberg, *Altchristliche Baudenkmäler*, Pl. III, No. 1.

[4] Strzygowski in Prussian *Jahrbuch*, viii, 1893, 27. For the development of different types of acanthus see the same writer, *Ath. Mitth.*, xiv, 1889, 281–2 ; *R. Q.*, ix, 1891, pp. 1–11, 97–109 ; *B. Z.*, i, 1892, p. 68. Examples of the capital are found at Venice, Rome, Milan, Salonika, Broussa (vestibule of the Green Mosque), Sofia (museum), Mesembria, and Deir Seta in Syria.

of common use towards the end of the fifth century. The period of its chief extension may be placed between A. D. 425 and 475, to which the fragments of ten capitals found at Delphi [1] belong.

The old columns were too small to receive the arch which had to spring

Fig. 102.   Capital of the sixth century ; Ravenna, Museo Nazionale.   (Alinari.)

from them, for they were still of the size and form originally designed to support a plain architrave. An intermediate member had therefore to be devised with a considerably greater area than that of the column: this was the *impost*, a block approximately in the form of a shallow truncated pyramid placed with its base uppermost. Although the impost appeared in the fourth century, when the archivolt succeeded the architrave, comparatively few examples have

[1] Laurent, *B. C. H.*, 1899, 207 ff. For examples of the deeply undercut acanthus at Mir-Achor-Djami (St. John of Studium), Constantinople, see J. Ebersolt, *Rev. arch.*, July-August, 1909, Pl. VI, and Wulff, *Berlin Catalogue*, i, No. 162 ; for those at Kutchuk Aya Sophia (St. Sergius), Ebersolt, as above, Fig. 7, p. 11. Fine undercut acanthus in the Mosque of the Calenders at Constantinople is shown in Dr. Freshfield's plates in *Archaeologia*, lv, Pl. XXXII, &c.

survived of that early date.[1] In the fifth century it was general, and must usually have accompanied the capitals of the Theodosian type.[2] But separate blocks disappear with the beginning of the sixth century, when impost and capital were combined. Fragments found at Delphi have the sacred monogram with an open loop to the *rho*, a feature which is characteristic of the period between about A.D. 375 to about A.D. 450, and is distributed over the whole

FIG. 103. Capital of the sixth century, Monastery of Lavra, Mount Athos.
(*Hautes Études* : G. Millet.)

empire from Syria and Egypt to Gaul and Africa, being found alike in Italy and Constantinople.[3] The examples from Delphi are also ornamented with the *acanthus mollis*, which shows that not only were the two kinds of acanthus used together, but that theories which would confine the *spinosa* to the East and the *mollis* to Italy cannot be accepted without reserve.[4]

For the next stage of evolution in the capital the name of impost-capital is generally accepted, implying the union of the two previously separated parts in one block.[5]

---

[1] The impost was probably invented in Syria (examples in the pretorium at Musmieh. De Vogüé, *Syrie Centrale*, Pl. VII). Examples exist at Rome ascribed to the middle of the fourth century (de Rossi, *Bullettino*, 1880, p. 153). The column of Theodosius at Constantinople had this feature (d'Agincourt, *Sculpture*, Pl. XI, No. 4).

[2] Laurent, *B.C.H.*, 1899, 214, mentions fifth-century imposts as found in the following churches at Rome : S. Stefano Rotondo, S. Lorenzo fuori, Sta Agnese, Sta Maria in Cosmedin (Bunsen, *Basiliques chrétiennes de Rome*, Pl. XIII, XVII, XXI, XIII) ; at Ravenna : S. Apollinare Nuovo, S. Giovanni Evangelista, SS. Nazaro e Celso, S. Apollinare in Classe, S. Vitale, S. Francesco, Sta Agata ; at Naples : S. Giorgio Maggiore (de Rossi, *Bullettino*, 1880, Pl. X and p. 154) ; at Salonika : S. Demetrius, Eski Djuma, Sta Sophia.

[3] Laurent, as above, 217.

[4] Strzygowski, *Ath. Mitth.*, 1889, 280 ; Prussian *Jahrbuch*, 1893, p. 10. Cattaneo (*Architettura*, 37) had hinted at this classification, and Heldreich had suggested it.

[5] Laurent, as above, p. 223. There is an interesting description of the capitals in Sta Sophia in Lethaby and Swainson, 247 ff. ; the capitals in the cathedral are there grouped in seven classes.

This combination was accomplished in the case of all the three varieties of capitals: the composite, the Ionic, and the Doric; in the first case the result was more in the nature of a fusion; in the other two the component parts remained distinguishable. The *composite* impost-capital, extensively used in the time of Justinian, had two principal varieties, the first, of cubic form, partaking more of the character of the old impost, that is to say, forming a reversed truncated pyramid rounded only towards its point of junction with the shaft; the second, conical, and descending more directly from the original capital. It was rounded on all sides, and includes the type commonly described as the 'basket capital'. It was often finished at the corners by eagles, as at St. Demetrius, Salonika, by rams, or by large volutes [1] (Figs. 18, 20, 103).

The relation of these developments to the parent composite capital is less obvious than it would be had not the ornament changed with the form. In early examples, such as one from Delphi probably dating from about A.D. 450, the two superposed rows of acanthus of the classical composite capital are still employed, but later we have a single row, still acanthus but no longer in such high relief, and often divided into half or quarter leaves arranged in series: on the faces are medallions containing crosses or other objects, round which the elements of the foliated design are grouped.

The process of debasement appears to have been somewhat as follows: The leaf becomes shallower, and looks as if it were glued to the block, no longer producing the old contrast of light and shade; this is the *acanthus mollis*, and is found as already noted on the pilasters of the Golden Gate at Constantinople, which dates from A.D. 388–91.[2] Next the interior details of the leaf were accentuated, its edges becoming hard and sharp; thus originated the *acanthus spinosa* or thorny acanthus so popular in the first half of the fifth century. A variety of this is the 'wind-blown acanthus' as seen in S. Apollinare in Classe and elsewhere (Fig. 101). Then the individual leaves tend to merge in the festoons or interlacings which we find on capitals of Justinian's time. The number of varieties of the composite impost-capital dating from the sixth century is considerable. The 'basket' capital, with eagles or rams at the corners, the 'melon', and the various forms of 'Byzantine Corinthian', all belong to this type.[3]

In certain cases the impost-capital did not suffice, the upper surface even now providing an insufficient area for the arch. At S. Vitale in Ravenna there are familiar examples of this (Fig. 67), a second impost being added, of a form very similar to the capital below, and not shallower like the earliest imposts. This continuation of the impost after the middle of the fifth century is characteristic of the Adriatic cities, Ravenna and Parenzo.[4]

---

[1] Basket capitals occur on the columns of the old ciborium of S. Clemente at Rome (Cattaneo, *L'Architettura*, &c., Fig. 7, p. 29), and at Bawit (Clédat in Cabrol, *Dict. d'arch. chrétienne*, s.v. *Baouît*, Fig. 1269), surmounted by eagles (?) and couchant rams. Very plain and rudimentary capitals, such as those in the cistern of Philoxenus (Salzenberg, p. 28), have to be classed with the cubical variety. Both Salzenberg and Laurent (as above, 225) have remarked their close resemblance to the Romanesque cushion-capital. As Laurent points out, numerous intermediaries between these early Byzantine forms and those of Romanesque times can be found in Italy (Cattaneo, *Architettura*, &c., pp. 88, 107, 113).

[2] Strzygowski, *Jahrbuch k. d. A. I.*, viii, 1893, p. 10.

[3] For the sixth-century capitals at S. Marco, Venice, some of which have monograms, see R. Cattaneo in Ongania, *La Basilica di San Marco*, vol. ii, 217 ff. An interesting early capital with rams' heads at the corners and eagles on the four sides is in the Metropolitan Church at Voden (Miliukoff, *Izviestiya* of the Russ. Arch. Inst. Cple., iv, p. 35). It recalls other capitals in St. Demetrius, Salonika, and at Bawit (cf. Figs. 18, 103). For a capital with birds at Mir-Achor-Djami at Constantinople, see *Rev. arch.*, July–August, 1909, p. 6; for one at Broussa, *B. C. H.*, Mars–Juillet, 1909, 361; for an example at Trebizond, *B. C. H.*, xix, 1895, 518; it is almost identical with those in St. Mark's.

[4] Strzygowski, *B. D.*, ii, 212; C. Errard, *L'Art byzantin*, iii (*Parenzo*), Pl. VI. A number of fifth and sixth-century capitals are also reproduced by Rivoira, *Origini della architettura lombarda*, Figs. 26, 29, 32, 35, 64, 89–92, 94–6, 99, 100, 102, 135–8, 140, &c.

The small size of the *Ionic* capital facilitated its combination with the impost. The two could be directly carved from a single block without any extensive modification of form. The two original elements were from first to last readily distinguished.

This convenient quality of the Ionic impost-capital led to its popularity and its long persistence. It began in the fifth century, continuing during the Second Golden Age, from the ninth to the eleventh centuries, and the area of its distribution was exceedingly wide.[1] With the lapse of time it naturally underwent considerable variations. In the fifth century the Ionic portion preserved

Fig. 104. Capital of the sixth century from Salona : Spalato.
(*Hautes Études* : G. Millet.)

the large classical volutes separated by an echinus decorated with oves, while the upper part received a plain decoration of a monogrammatic or other cross, with or without acanthus leaves. With the sixth century the volutes diminished in size, and were so carelessly carved as almost to resemble snail-shells ; the upper part, though occasionally preserving an antique appearance, is generally covered with the scrolls and conventional festoons first common in the period of Justinian. The degradation is complete in the capitals of the cistern at Constantinople known as the Bible House, on which the crosses, birds, and scroll-work are characteristic of the Macedonian period.[2]

The Doric impost-capital is a rarer variety than others and is practically confined to Greece.[3]

[1] Strzygowski, *B. D.*, i, p. 97 ; ii, p. 230, &c. ; *B. Z.*, iii, 1894, 14 ; *O. C.*, 1901, 152. M. Laurent has collected the following examples of the Ionic impost-capital : Fifth century—Etchmiadzin (*B. D.*, i, p. 7), Ravenna (S. Giovanni in Fonte, SS. Nazaro e Celso, Ricci's photo No. 152), Rome (S. Stefano Rotondo, d'Agincourt, *Arch.*, Pl. XXII, and Bunen, Pl. XXI); Chalcis (*Ath. Mitth.*, xiv, 1889, 289, Fig. 6), Venice (S. Marco), Pomposa (Ricci, photo No. 518), Delphi (Laurent, as above, p. 236). Sixth century—Sta Sophia, Cple. (Salzenberg, Pl. XVII, No. 12), and SS. Sergius and Bacchus (Salzenberg, Pl. V, Nos. 3 and 4) ; Delphi (Laurent, as above, p. 235). Seventh and eighth centuries—Cistern at Cple. (*B. Z.*, iv, 1895, 598), Salonika, Sta Sophia (Texier and Pullan, Pl. 39) and St. Demetrius (ibid., Pl. 24), Sheikh-Musa, Syria (*Quarterly Statement*, Palestine Exploration Fund, April, 1899, p. 125). Ninth and tenth centuries—Cisterns at Cple. (*B. D.*, ii, pp. 100, No. 4, and 228; windows of St. Luke in Phocis).
[2] *B. D.*, ii, p. 100, No. 4.
[3] Laurent, as above, 237-8 (Delphi, Aegina, &c.).

Capitals of the first Byzantine period are so widely distributed and so uniform in type that they were probably made in a single centre, almost certainly to be sought in the marble quarries of Proconnesus. From the busy workshops by the quarries they were exported to all the ports of the Mediterranean; they are **found** in Syria in the East, in Cordova in the West. Like the carved slabs and the sarcophagi of similar date, they were a staple export from the Sea of Marmora; the close affinities of specimens now separated by great distances are explained by their common origin.

FIG. 105. Capital of the sixth century from Salona: Spalato.
(*Hautes Études*: G. Millet.)

8. INFLUENCE IN THE WEST.

The probable influence of East-Christian sculpture upon the sarcophagi of Italy, France, and Spain has already been discussed above (pp. 132–5). The short life of monumental figure sculpture in the East put a premature end to its function as an educative power; after the first Byzantine period it ceased to affect the art of Europe. But its place was almost immediately taken by minor sculpture, chiefly in ivory, which early became a most important instrument in the development of European plastic art (p. 236), aided by the illuminations in manuscripts which, with an equal mobility, travelled as far and were no less useful to the artist in search of designs. In France, Germany, and England the influence of the ivory carver's art was a cardinal factor in evolution. In Italy it was chiefly operative in the north-east, in the region of Venice, though the gates of Bonannus at Pisa and other bronze gates further south owe much to this source of inspiration. A kind of hereditary instinct seems to have kept the Italians true to classical models; the sculptors working for Frederick II in Apulia obeyed such an instinct; so did Niccolò Pisano, who borrowed from the pagan art of Rome rather than from that of the Christian era. But even he adopted Eastern iconographical types: in content, if not in style, his subjects betray a dependence upon Byzantine compositions.[1]

[1] E. Dobbert, *Der Stil Niccolò Pisano's und dessen Ursprung.*

Fig. 106. Illuminated head-piece from a Gospel of the eleventh century in the British Museum.

CHAPTER IV

SCULPTURE: CARVINGS IN IVORY AND STEATITE

It has been already stated that the ivory carvings of the Christian East possess a higher relative importance to Byzantine art as a whole than do those produced in the West to occidental art. For while in the West monumental figure sculpture, reappearing in the eleventh century, regained in the twelfth the position which was its due, the Eastern Empire was almost without figure sculptors in stone from the sixth to the thirteenth centuries, while workers in bronze or other metals confined their efforts to a diminutive scale. The Byzantine Empire through the greater part of its history, from the time of Justinian to the period in the thirteenth century when it began to be effectively influenced by Western glyptic art, was in very much the same position as the shorter-lived empire founded by Charles the Great. In the Carolingian period monumental sculpture was also dead; and the ivory carvings which were then produced in considerable numbers acquire in consequence an historical value which under normal circumstances they could not have attained. Some of the causes conducing to this result were similar both in the East and in the West, and are noticed in other places, where stress is laid upon the capital importance of Byzantine ivory carving to the development of monumental sculpture in Europe (pp. 96, 103, 236).

But this position, so exceptional for a minor plastic art, was not immediately attained. So long as monumental sculpture lived, it retained its ancient influence over the destiny of the small relief. The style of the earliest Christian ivories is evidently affected by that of the sarcophagi ; the figures have the same massive character, the same squat proportions ; their relief is often higher than that which obtained in later times. Nor did the ivory carvers confine themselves to the imitation of Early Christian sculpture ; they naturally went back to works of pagan art by which that sculpture was itself inspired. Their debt is especially clear in the case of single figures, such as those of consular diptychs (see below, p. 196), where the derivation from portrait sculpture of the early empire is evident : thus we recognize an imperial statue of a familiar type in the Emperor Honorius in the diptych of the Consul Probus in the Cathedral of Aosta (A. D. 406).[1] Other figures upon these diptychs recall Roman sepulchral monuments ; while the seated consuls, who are represented either as receiving congratulations on their appointment or as giving the signal for commencing the games

FIG. 107. Bone relief of about the third century in the Cairo Museum. (*Catalogue général : Koptische Kunst*, No. 7090.) P. 195.

from their place in the circus, are in like manner derived from the large sculptured portraits of the early empire. From such representations of the Roman magistrate in his official seat descends the type of Our Lord enthroned, or seated in majesty upon the globe or the rainbow. With the book of the Gospels in one hand, and with the other raised in benediction, he resembles the type of which the diptych of Rufius Probianus, vice-prefect of Rome, is so admirable and so early an example.[2] The reversion to pagan models extends even further than to Roman imperial times. We shall see below, in relation to the archangel of the British Museum and the ivory

---

[1] Best reproduction, Molinier, *Ivoires*, Pl. II : references to earlier publications on p. 17.
[2] Molinier as above, Pl. IV ; W. Meyer, *Zwei antike Elfenbeintafeln*, Pl. II ; Labarte, *Histoire des arts industriels*, 2nd ed., vol. i, p. 13. Cf. p. 191 below.

chair at Ravenna, that from the fourth to the sixth century the traditions of the Hellenic age were still respected. Like the sculptors of the sarcophagi of the Sidamara group, the ivory carvers had still a sense for plastic form, they were still above a merely servile imitation. Ivory carving had profited by the general demand for subjects in the Greek manner ; the diptych of the Symmachi and Nicomachi reproduced not without success the motive of an Attic sepulchral relief (p. 190). With the decay and disappearance of monumental sculpture the influence of the greater glyptic art naturally ceased; and though, as on one of the caskets with mythological subjects, we find about the tenth century a representative of the Heracles of Lysippus (p. 216), the work is a curiosity of survival without essential value.

The relations between ivory carving and minor plastic art in other

Fig. 108. Side of a wooden casket with engraved bone panels, about the fifth century, in the Cairo Museum. (*Catalogue général : Koptische Kunst*, No. 7065.) P. 195.

materials may be briefly noted, though here, too, the results were not of primary importance. The ivory carver and the silversmith seem to have reproduced the same subjects in a very similar style: the upper zones of the early consular diptych at Halberstadt (Fig. 7), representing an emperor seated with his guards, recall the group upon the votive shield of Theodosius at Madrid (Fig. 356); the silver disk of Aspar at Florence reminds us of the diptych of Asterius, in which the consul is seated in like manner and holds a scroll ; the embossed silver plaques of the casket at Anagni (p. 557) reproduce the designs of contemporary caskets in ivory. With painting relations were continually close. From the time when illuminated MSS. began to grow common, they provided models for the carver, as was constantly the case in France in the Middle Ages, where the ivories of the fourteenth century are so nearly allied to contemporary miniatures. But more important paintings of purely secular origin were on rare occasions a source of inspiration: thus the figure of Calchas in a picture of Timanthes is held to have been the original of the Abraham on the fine *pyxis* at Berlin (p. 195). Nor should we overlook the effect which the great mosaic compositions of the First Period produced upon the imagination of artists in ivory. It is quite probable that some of the types seen upon Syro-Egyptian *pyxides* and diptychs of the fifth and sixth centuries may copy mosaic originals: it has been conjectured that this was the case with the seated Virgin and Child of certain composite diptychs (p. 210), for which the mosaics on the Church of the Nativity at Bethlehem may have provided the models: the monumental character of these figures is certainly in favour of such a supposition. Several of the angels upon panels of this early period recall types of which examples still survive in mosaic, for instance at Kiti in Cyprus. We must finally notice the influence of textiles, though this influence was probably not exerted much before the iconoclastic period. When the zoomorphic motives of early Persian silk fabrics became popular in the Byzantine Empire, we find them suggesting subjects to the Byzantine ivory carver, as they also did to the Western sculptors in Romanesque times. The designs of certain oliphants are reminiscent of textile patterns; and certain caskets with animals of purely oriental style may be placed in the same category. Possibly the subject on the lid of the casket at Troyes may be derived from a textile design (Fig. 144).

Fig. 109. Figure engraved on bone, about the fifth century, in the Cairo Museum. (*Catalogue général: Koptische Kunst*, No. 7069.)

Ivory carvings naturally reflect the style of models which were popular or accessible at different epochs. In the First Period there is a greater tendency to a broad monumental treatment than in later centuries. The figures are generally larger and the relief more salient. After the iconoclastic dispute and the Basilian revival we notice a change of method. Ivory carving is now consciously a minor art: the monumental gives place to the minute and the highly finished. The ivories of the Third Period charm by an admirable delicacy only equalled by that of the best Gothic ivories of France, but like these they often sink into a mannerism which seems to express some faint reflection of feeling rather than feeling itself. The development was doubtless due to similar causes in East and West, for though the French carvers had abundant models in monumental sculpture, it would appear that with the fourteenth century they resorted more and more to the convenient models presented by drawings or illuminations. Like their Byzantine rivals they travelled away from nature; but being less rigidly restricted in the range of their subjects, they more easily preserved their contact with the world.

The difficulty in deciding the provenance of ivories from the Christian East is especially great in the First Period. At that time the artistic centres were more numerous, and for a while Italy was still a competitor, though on a rapidly decreasing scale. While Syria and Egypt were still within the empire, that is to say down to the first Mohammedan conquests of the seventh century, it was but natural that Alexandria and Antioch, the great artistic and industrial centres where the Hellenistic spirit still survived, should take a leading part in this as in all other branches of art. We shall see below, in treating certain groups of ivories, that this general probability is confirmed by facts, and that the majority of the ivories

Fig. 110.   Side of an ivory *pyxis* of the fourth century in the Kaiser Friedrich Museum at Berlin.   (From a cast.)   P. 195.

dating from the period between Constantine and iconoclasm must be ascribed to the Syro-Egyptian artistic province; but since Egypt and Syria stood in close relation to each other, giving, receiving, and transmitting influence, the task of assigning particular works to one or other of the two countries is almost an affair of divination. The Arab conquest changed the centre of gravity, removing as it did from Byzantine control the very regions which had hitherto been most productive. The empire being now for a while driven back upon an inner line of defence, the capital itself was probably the chief centre of production; and in all likelihood this continued to be the case even after the conquests of Basil, Nicephorus Phocas, and John Zimisces had once more expanded the imperial frontiers. Constantinople then seems to have occupied a position with regard to the ivory carver's art comparable to that of Paris in Western Europe during the thirteenth and fourteenth centuries, and perhaps

encouraged by this concentration, there began in both places the same
process towards a delicate and mannered style. Between the tenth and
thirteenth centuries ivories may have been executed in a few other parts

Fig. 111.   The Baptism : ivory panel of the sixth century.   (British Museum.)   P. 208.

of the empire; but if so they probably copied metropolitan models no less
closely than European mediaeval ivories copied those of Paris.

   The earliest Christian ivories naturally inherited the forms and types
of pagan times : the old shapes were adapted to new uses and ornamented
with subjects from a new iconography. In the first place we may notice
the ivory box or casket. Such receptacles had been used for trinkets by

the. Romans, who did but follow the Greeks and the peoples of earlier civilizations : the fine casket from Enkomi in Cyprus in the British Museum is an ancient example, going back to Mycenaean times. The Romans had especially affected the circular box or *pyxis*,[1] cut from a transverse section of a tusk, using it chiefly for jewels and other valuables of small size. Boxes of this kind had lids and locks ; but an open cylindrical form, the *acerra*,[1] was used for the grains of incense thrown upon the altar in sacrifice. The Christians adopted both the rectangular and the circular type, employing them chiefly as reliquaries, and as *pxyides* in the more restricted sense which the word has now come to bear. In many cases they continued to employ boxes of pagan origin, regardless of the secular scenes upon their sides. But examples of this are comparatively rare ; for as early as the fourth century ivory carvers were already producing both forms with Christian designs. The rectangular caskets had generally a wooden core or *âme*, to which panels were applied.

In the decoration of furniture with plaques of carved ivory, a usage common to the great ancient civilizations, Christian art again followed early precedents. The panels of doors in Santa Sophia, Constantinople, were so enriched,[2] and the adornment of thrones or magisterial chairs in this manner was imitated in the decoration of episcopal chairs, of which a familiar surviving example is that preserved at Ravenna and associated with the name of Archbishop Maximianus (p. 203).

More important than either caskets or plaques for furniture were the diptychs which descended from the ancient writing-tablets, but were more immediately derived from the tablets with ornament carved in relief presented to important personages and friends by the higher Roman officials on their accession to office (p. 196). Although in these the interior was still prepared with wax for writing, the exterior with its representation of the donor gradually became the significant part ; by this change the first step was taken in the transformation of the writing-tablet into the devotional diptychs of later times. Of all the early diptychs those sent by the consuls were the most important, though the rarer commemorative diptychs made for private persons to record events in family history are of even greater interest. To this class belongs the diptych already mentioned as made to commemorate a matrimonial alliance between the families of the Symmachi and Nicomachi, of which one leaf (the finest) is in the Victoria and Albert Museum, the other in the Musée de Cluny at Paris.

---

[1] A number of *pyxides* will be individually mentioned below. But on this form of box in general, the reader may consult E. von Sacken in *Mittheilungen der k. k. Central-Commission*, vol. ii, N. F., Vienna, 1876, 43 ff. ; E. Molinier, *Ivoires*, 55 ff. ; H. Graeven, *Mon. Piot*, vi, pp. 160 ff. ; and *Antike Schnitzereien*, Nos. 1, 17–19. The *pyxides* reproduced in fictile ivory by the Arundel Society are enumerated by Westwood, *Fictile Ivories*, pp. 270 ff. ; while references to others in various collections will be found in his index. Several are reproduced by Garrucci, *Storia*, vi, and by Rohault de Fleury, *La Messe*. See also H. Graeven's *Photographische Nachbildung* (both series), the catalogues of the British, Berlin, and Vatican Museums, of the Louvre, and that of the Basilewsky Collection (now at St. Petersburg) by A. Darcel.

[2] Lethaby and Swainson, *Church of Sancta Sophia*, 160 ; J. P. Richter, *Quellen der byz. Kunstgeschichte*, 14, 64 ; D. Ainaloff in *V. V.*, v. 159.

Diptychs were very early used in those parts of the church ritual in which the names of saints, bishops, and benefactors were publicly recited.[1]

FIG. 112. Ivory reliefs on the episcopal chair at Ravenna ; sixth century. (L. Ricci.)
P. 205.

Consular diptychs were sometimes adapted to this use ; but new panels with religious subjects seem to have been made at least as early as the sixth

[1] As early as the Council of Mopsuestia (A. D. 550) there was a custodian of the diptychs, and reference is made to *diptycha in quibus memoriae sacerdotum istius optimae civitatis scripta continentur vocabula* (Gori, *Thesaurus vet. dipt.*, i. 45).

century. There are no diptychs for private devotional use dating from the First Period, and probably their manufacture does not go back much

Fig. 113. Ivory *pyxides* of the sixth century : Daniel between the lions ; the martyrdom of St. Menas. (British Museum.) Pp. 209, 210.

further than the ninth century: almost all existing examples date from the tenth century and later. The triptych was a natural development from the diptych, and numerous examples are preserved ; but we do not find polyptychs with many leaves, such as those which were produced in the West during the later Middle Ages. The use of carved ivory panels for book-covers was a result of the general introduction in the fourth century of the book or *codex*, succeeding the *rotulus* or roll. The codex required a cover; and this, especially the cover of the liturgical book, offered a large surface for decoration. A carved ivory panel was well adapted to this purpose: hence we find the two leaves of old diptychs early used to decorate the covers of books, or, where only one leaf or panel could be procured, to embellish the upper side only. The large composite diptychs (see p. 197) were better adapted to this purpose than narrow single leaves, because their square form corresponded more nearly to that which had been generally adopted for the codex. After the abolition of the consulship in A. D. 541 this type continued to be made, but directly as book-covers, and no longer as diptychs. The examples mentioned below, the subjects of which are entirely Christian, are sufficient proof of the adaptation (p. 202).

Ivory statuettes were hardly, if at all, made in the Eastern Empire, because sculpture in the round was not favoured by the Church. But they may have been made in isolated cases; for instance, a rhetor named Cyprius is said to have presented to a church an ivory statue of St. Helena.[1] Their absence robs the group of Byzantine ivories of the variety and charm which the Madonnas, saints, and other groups in the round lend to almost contemporary Western work. Byzantine ivory carving further suffers by the absence of objects intended for secular use, such as the mirror-cases and jewel-caskets made in such numbers in mediaeval France. Throughout the whole duration of the empire, the Church possessed the same control which in the West she had exercised down to the end of the twelfth century. The West, under the influence of a literary and scholastic revival, achieved its artistic independence in the thirteenth century, enriching its iconography by an immense variety of subjects derived from the literature of romance. The difference between East and West in this matter is strikingly marked by the fact that though romances were plentiful in the Eastern Empire, and many of the most popular mediaeval stories were of oriental origin, so far as we know they were never suffered to obtain a footing in the decoration of toilet objects or utensils made for domestic use. The exploits of Digenis Akritas are not perpetuated in the same way as those of Parcival or Gawain or Lancelot of the Lake.

Bishops' staves, though in use in the Greek Church under a form approximating to that of the tau-cross, have not come down to us in ivory from early times; the same applies to the handles of the flabella used to drive the flies away from the altar. Here again we find the Byzantine ivory carver indifferent to opportunities of which his Italian and French

---

[1] J. P. Richter, *Quellen der byz. Kunstgeschichte*, Vienna, 1897, pp. 14 and 64. This may, however, have been something in the nature of a chryselephantine statue, and not a statuette.

contemporaries availed themselves to the full, though the flabellum has
continued in the East until the present day, while in Western Europe it
became obsolete at the close of the Middle Ages.

As in mediaeval Western Europe, ivory carvings were generally coloured
and gilded, though few surviving examples have preserved this decoration
in any but the most imperfect
condition. An early example
is the large book-cover from
Murano, of which one half is
in the museum at Ravenna
(see p. 209). In a later period
we have the curious casket,
perhaps of the ninth century
(see p. 221), in the Kircherian
Museum at Rome, where
traces of red and green can
be seen on the garments of
several figures. The Harbaville triptych in the Louvre
(see p. 227) was once partially
gilded, and the letters of its
inscriptions were coloured
red ; the lost panel with the
Deesis, formerly in the Episcopal Library at Vich in
Catalonia, Spain, was treated
in a similar manner. Ivories
were also sometimes stained
purple, the royal colour so
often used to dye the vellum
of MSS. The remarkable
casket at Troyes (p. 231)
affords an example of this
mode of decoration.

A few points of difference
distinguishing Eastern from
Western ivory carvings may

Fig. 114. Central panel from one leaf of a composite diptych of the sixth century. (John Rylands
Library, Manchester.) P. 209.

be noticed. Unlike Western mediaeval ivories, which are hardly ever
decorated behind, Byzantine panels and devotional tablets are frequently
carved on the back, most commonly with a decorative cross. The
architectural canopy which is such a constant feature in the West
during the thirteenth and fourteenth centuries is less conspicuous in the
East. A figure will often be placed under an arch resting on two columns ;
but this is generally of simple construction ; even where, as in numerous
examples of the Third Period, the canopy is pierced, the effect is less

elaborate than that of a fourteenth-century French panel with its intricate crocketed gables and ornamented spandrels. The leaves of the Byzantine triptych are not attached by means of hinges, but turn upon vertical pins in the upper and lower inside corners fitting into holes in projecting bands across the top and bottom of the middle panel.

First Period.[1]

It has been observed that the attribution of ivories belonging to the First Period is a matter of great difficulty ; in the first place the conflicting claims of East and West are by no means easy to decide, especially during the earlier years ; in the second, the close relations maintained between the provinces of the Eastern Empire render the establishment of artistic frontiers a very hazardous proceeding. All that we know of the migratory habits of artists in antiquity further complicates the subject, for there is no reason why carvers in ivory, born and trained in one province, should not have tried their fortune in others, and imported into them the peculiar characteristics of their style. Again, drawings, paintings, and carvings which served as models must have circulated as freely at this period as in later times, introducing persistent foreign influences to disturb the development of local schools. Even when it is granted that an ivory is of East-Christian inspiration there will often remain a doubt whether it is to be ascribed to an Eastern artist working in the East, to an Eastern artist settled in the West, or to a Western artist who had assimilated Eastern methods. There can indeed be little doubt that the majority of ivories dating from the period under discussion are of East-Christian origin, and that for the most part they were made in the Syro-Egyptian artistic province. A general difference of style, a tendency to realism in the human types, and the minute treatment of details marks them off from the Italian work of the late classical period ; while details of iconography in the sacred subjects represented show an increased resort to the Apocryphal writings in which the East delighted. More precise indications are provided by analogies with objects like the ampullae at Monza (see p. 623), known to have come from the Holy Land, and by such examples of conventional ornament as those upon the chair of Maximianus at Ravenna, which are clearly of Syrian descent. But there is a minority which cannot so easily be divorced from the Western soil on which they have been discovered ; and in view of what has been said above, even the presence of details emanating from oriental sources does not prove them to be the work of oriental hands. We may first notice a few of the more important ivories of which the East-Christian origin, even where probable, is not proven ; we may then pass to those which seem undoubtedly to belong to the East.

There seems no valid reason to doubt the Roman origin of the diptych of the Symmachi and Nicomachi, already mentioned as divided between the Victoria and Albert Museum and the Cluny Museum at Paris.[2] The two families are Roman, and the *onus probandi* lies on those who suggest that Rome at the end of the fourth century was incapable of producing such work. That the model

---

[1] In this section the ivory carvings are considered as far as possible according to their artistic affinities ; except in the case of consular diptychs they are not grouped according to their forms (diptychs, *pyxides*, &c.) or to the purposes for which they were used. The latter method of classification has been adopted by Von Sybel (*Christliche Antike*, ii. 228-57), whose list the student will find extremely useful.

[2] South Kensington leaf : W. Maskell, *Fictile Ivories*, 44 ; Gori, *Thesaurus diptychorum*, i, Pl. VI ; A. Venturi, *Storia*, i, Fig. 355. Leaf in Cluny Museum : Molinier, *Ivoires*, p. 43 ; Venturi, Fig. 354 ; L. von Sybel, *Christliche Antike*, ii. 237 ; A. Haseloff, Prussian *Jahrbuch*, 1903, p. 55. The panel of the Lampadii at Brescia is of the same group (W Meyer, *Zwei antike Elfenbeintafeln*, &c., p. 35 ; H. Graeven, *Röm. Mitth.*, vii, 1892, 21 ; Westwood, *Fictile Ivories*, 12).

was Greek has often been remarked, but it was of the fourth century B.C., and not any late Hellenistic work: the types seem to have been suggested by the reliefs upon a sepulchral *stele* such as the artist might easily have studied in the capital of the Western world. The diptych of Rufius Probianus,[1] *Vicarius* of Rome, preserved at Berlin, is still less likely to have been made in any other city. But if these two examples are Roman, then the ivory in the collection of Prince Trivulzio at Milan, representing the Women at the Tomb,[2] should be Roman too, for the palmette border surrounding the door of the sepulchre is identical with that framing the two other diptychs, and not found upon any

Fig. 115. The Sacrifice of Isaac : side of an ivory *pyxis* of the fourth century in the Kaiser Friedrich Museum, Berlin. P. 195.

ivory for which an Eastern origin can be asserted. The Trivulzio ivory should carry with it the fine panel in the Munich Museum[3] on which the scene at the tomb is combined with the Ascension; for here the general treatment is analogous. It also carries with it the set of four panels from a casket in the British Museum, carved about A.D. 400, with scenes from the Passion and after ;[4]

---

[1] W. Meyer, as above, Pl. II; E. Molinier, *Ivoires*, p. 40, Pl. IV; Venturi, *Storia*, &c., i, p. 356 ; Westwood, p. 13.

[2] Molinier, as above, Pl. VI; Garrucci, *Storia*, Pl. 449, Fig. 2 ; Graeven, *Gött. gelehrte Anzeigen*, 1897, 69–72; L. von Sybel, *Christliche Antike*, Fig. 65. Westwood, p. 366, No. 6, describes this panel as Carolingian. M. Diehl gives it to Alexandria (*Manuel*, 73).

[3] H. Graf, *Katalog des bayerischen Nationalmuseums*, vol. v, Pl. VI, No. 157 ; Garrucci, *Storia*, Pl. 459, Fig. 4 ; J. Stuhlfauth, *Altchristliche Elfenbeinplastik*, p. 58 (references to all the literature). Westwood, p. 337, ascribes the panel to the ninth or tenth century.

[4] British Museum, *Catalogue of Early Christian and Byzantine Antiquities*, No. 291, and *Cata-*

here the tomb of Our Lord is similar in construction, differing from the type of the Monza ampullae, while the head and shoulders of one of the women are almost the same. The costume of the soldiers, with their flat caps, tells us little, for it seems to occur in works both of Italian and East-Christian origin (see p. 127). The set of three smaller panels in the British Museum[1] must belong to the same group: some of the costumes are identical, and the figures have the same rather squat proportions.

The chain of affinities thus established is one of the most perplexing with which the student of Early Christian antiquities is concerned; it has been drawn out to some length to illustrate the extreme difficulty of research with regard to Christian antiquities of this period. For if at the beginning the connexion with Rome appears to be obvious, at the end the relationship to the Eastern provinces is almost as prominent, yet there has been no obvious break in the continuity of development. There are good reasons for suspecting that the doors of the Church of Sta Sabina, with their panels carved with Testament subjects, were imported into Rome (see p. 146), and the Crucifixion upon those doors, a subject very exceptional at the beginning of the fifth century, has analogies with the Crucifixion on the British Museum panels. The giving of the Law to Moses on the same doors is moreover iconographically related to a similar subject upon a marble relief of Eastern origin at Berlin (see p. 156). The architecture seen in the Thekla scene on the set of three panels in the British Museum, with its façade flanked by a tower, seems to point to Asia Minor;[2] architecture of similar origin appears upon the Brescia casket, with which these panels are stylistically related—an object also claimed for Asia Minor. This casket[3] presents the same contradictions in an even more perplexing form, for the resemblance to the style of the Roman sarcophagi is conspicuous.

With the ivories just mentioned we enter the fifth century, to which a few diptychs of Roman consuls belong. These differ in style from those of the following century made for consuls of the East; and there seems no particular reason why they should have been made in any other country than that of the magistrates who ordered them. The earliest, that of Probus, consul in A. D. 406, reproduces, as we have already seen (p. 180), an imperial statue and preserves the old classical tradition.[4]

Another ivory carving, perhaps of the fifth century, and showing the same general relationship to Early Christian sculpture in stone and wood, with the same puzzling suggestion of oriental influences, is the diptych with scenes from the Gospels in the treasury of Milan Cathedral.[5] The diptych, also with Gospel scenes, in the Cathedral of Palermo[6] is assigned by Venturi to this early period; and Molinier ascribes a similar date to the panels in the Bibliothèque Nationale at Paris.[7]

The mention in preceding paragraphs of the diptych of the Symmachi and Nicomachi and of that of Rufius Probianus has already brought us into

---

logue of Ivory Carvings, No. 7; H. Graeven, Göttingische gelehrte Anzeigen, 1897, 75; Venturi, Storia, i, Figs. 397-400.

[1] Catalogue of Early Christian Antiquities, No. 292.

[2] Strzygowski, Kleinasien ein Neuland der Kunstgeschichte, pp. 215 ff. This architecture is again found on the Werden Casket in the Victoria and Albert Museum. Arguments derived from such architectural resemblances are not in themselves conclusive; we may compare the occurrence of Italianizing architecture upon the thirteenth-century embroidery known as Opus Anglicanum and certainly made in England.

[3] Garrucci, Storia, vi. 441-5; Graeven, Photos, ii. 11-15; Westwood, Fictile Ivories, 33-8; Venturi, Storia, i, Figs. 273-7; G. Stuhlfauth, Elfenbeinplastik, 41, &c.

[4] Molinier, Ivoires, 17, and Pl. II; Westwood, No. 42.

[5] Garrucci, Storia, vi, Pl. 450; Labarte, Histoire des arts industriels, 2nd ed., i. 32 and Pl. V; Venturi, Storia, i. 508 and Fig. 390; Graeven, Göttingische gelehrte Anzeigen, 1897, 75-7. Some are inclined to place these panels at any rate after the sixth century, as Dr. A. Heisenberg (Grabeskirche und Apostelkirche). Labarte considered it of the ninth century.

[6] Venturi, vol. i, p. 505, and Fig. 382.

[7] Labarte, Histoire, 2nd ed , vol. i, Pl. IV; Molinier, Ivoires, p. 60.

contact with a group of ivory diptychs made to celebrate events in individual life. These commemorated acces-sion to public offices, or domestic occurrences, such as marriage or recovery from dangerous illness. The two diptychs already men-tioned represent the two classes ; but as the domestic class is the smaller, and few of the ivories composing it can be proved Byzantine, we may dismiss it in a very few words. The chief family diptychs appear to belong to the fourth and fifth centuries, espe-cially to the latter. Well-known examples are the diptych from the Mayer Collection in the Free Public Museums at Liverpool, with Aesculapius and Telesphorus, Hygieia and Eros,[1] perhaps as early as the fourth century ; the diptych with the muse and poet at Monza ;[2] that at Brescia,[3] with a male and female figure variously identified ; that at Trieste, with the Dioscuri, Europa and Zeus;[4] that in the Louvre, with poets and muses ;[5] and that formerly in the treasury of the cathedral, now in the museum of Sens,[6] with the Rising of the Sun and Moon under the attri-butes of Bacchus and Diana.[7]

The majority of these works evidently imitate the classical art of an earlier date, and this circum-stance gives them an appearance of superiority over contemporary ivories with Christian subjects, the artists of which had no such models to copy. It also renders even more hopeless the task of discriminating between work produced in Italy and in the Christian East, where the same kind of imitation was in progress. Ornamental and architectural

Fig. 116. Adam in Eden : leaf of a diptych of the fifth–sixth century in the Museo Nazionale (Bargello), Florence. (Alinari.) P. 195.

[1] Pulszky, Gatty, Westwood, *Fictile Ivories*, Nos. 15 and 16 ; W. Maskell, *Description*, &c., p. 166 ; Molinier, *Ivoires*, No. 61, p. 45 ; H. Graeven, *Gött. gel. Anz.*, 1897, 351 ; Venturi, *Storia*, i, Fig. 357 ; W. Meyer, *Zwei antike Elfenbeintafeln*, &c, No. 55.

[2] Molinier, No. 62, p. 45 ; W. Meyer, No. 51 ; Didron, *Annales archéologiques*, xxi. 289, 294 ; Westwood, 21 ; Venturi, *Storia*, i, Fig. 358.

[3] Molinier, No. 59 ; Meyer, No. 57 ; Westwood, Nos. 18, 19 ; Wieseler, *Das Diptychon Qui-rinianum*, Pl. I ; Venturi, *Storia*, i, Fig. 356. The usual interpretations are Hippolytus and Phaedra, and Virbius and Diana.

[4] Molinier, No. 60 ; *Archäologische Zeitung*, N. S. viii, 1876, Pl. XII.

[5] Molinier, No. 63 ; Westwood, No. 25.

[6] Molinier, No. 64 ; Meyer, No. 56 ; Labarte, *Hist. des arts industriels*, 1st ed., Album, vol. i, Pl. I ; Westwood, Nos. 23–4, &c.

[7] A few other ivory carvings of the same date are mentioned by Molinier, *Ivoires*, p. 48.

details often seem to suggest an oriental origin ; one is reminded of the ornamental details upon many sarcophagi to the oriental character of which

Molinier and others have rightly drawn attention. But we cannot say with certainty that the importation of an ornament implies the importation of the object on which it occurs or of the whole art on which it depends. The same remarks apply to the rare diptychs which represent family portraits. Of these the best known is that in the treasury of Monza Cathedral, on one leaf of which is a soldier of rank wearing an embroidered tunic and chlamys and armed with spear and shield, on the other his wife and child.[1] There are various opinions as to the identity of the persons represented, Molinier and Jullian believing them to be Stilicho, Serena, and Eucherius ; whoever they may actually be, the costumes and the quality of the work prove the diptych to be not later than the beginning of the fifth century.

The diptych in the Cathedral of Rouen[2] with SS. Peter and Paul on the two leaves may be as early as the fifth century, for the types resemble those of the sarcophagi. These leaves were employed about the twelfth century to adorn the binding of a manuscript relating to the archbishops of the diocese, and it is probable, as de Linas and Molinier argue, that this was only done when the surfaces of the leaves themselves were overcrowded with names. If this is so, the diptych is one of the few known to us originally made to contain the lists read in church, the diptych in the Cathedral of Tongres being probably another (see p. 208). The figure of St. Peter recalls good Greek models allied to the Lateran Sophocles, which inspired many works of art in the Christian period (p. 128) ; that of St. Paul finds analogies on sarcophagi from Southern France.[3] Molinier, partly in conse-

[1] Gori, *Thesaurus*, i, Pl. VII ; Labarte, *Histoire des arts industriels*, 1st ed., Album, vol. i, Pl. II ; Molinier, *Ivoires*, Pl. II ; Westwood, *Fictile Ivories*, No. 42, p. 14 ; Graeven, *Gött. gel. Anz.*, 1897, p. 354 ; C. Jullian, *Mélanges d'arch. : École française de Rome*, i. 5. The usual alternatives to Stilicho, Serena, and Eucherius are Aetius, Galla Placidia, and the young Valentinian III.

[2] C. de Linas, *Gaz. arch.*, 1886, 25–37, Pl. IV ; Molinier, *Ivoires*, 53 ; Westwood, p. 46 ; Graeven, *Gött. gel. Anz.*, 1897, 71.

[3] E. Le Blant, *Sarcophages chrét. de la Gaule*, Pl. XI, No. 1.

quence of this, believes the diptych to be of Western origin. A diptych in the Louvre,[1] of about the same date, with Apostles and saints, is also assigned by Molinier to Latin art. The famous diptych in the Bargello at Florence,[2] which Graeven would place as early as the fourth century, others as late as the fifth, is in the same uncertain position. It has on one side Adam with the various beasts in the terrestrial paradise, on the other scenes from the life of St. Paul (Figs. 116, 117). In the paradise scene the nude figure of Adam is not without grace, nor is the modelling contemptible, while the animals testify to observation of nature on the part of the artist. The treatment of the figures on the second leaf has a certain sober gravity and restraint; it recalls the work upon a small panel, formerly in the Mallet Collection at Amiens, now in the Kaiser Friedrich Museum at Berlin,[3] which Haseloff, not without reason, ascribes to the Italian art of the fifth century. The representation of the terrestrial paradise upon the back of the consular diptych of Areobindus in the Louvre,[4] with its centaurs, sirens, and gryphons, and its gesticulating Eve, seems to embody the spirit of an altogether later age, and it may be doubted whether it was added at an earlier period than the fifteenth century.

We may now consider the more important ivories of the First Period, the origin of which is almost certainly East-Christian.

The large *pyxis* in the museum at Berlin[5] is distinguished by an almost classical excellence of style and can hardly be later than the first half of the fourth century (Figs. 110, 115). It has upon one side Our Lord seated among the Apostles, on the other the Sacrifice of Isaac. The figure of Abraham in the latter subject may be derived from that of Calchas in a picture of the Sacrifice of Iphigeneia by Timanthes, and the manner of representing the sacrifice appears in monuments associated both with Syria and Egypt, a *pyxis* at Bologna, and a bone carving from Alexandria in the Kaiser Friedrich Museum at Berlin, where the attitude of Abraham is almost identical.[6] Stuhl-fauth's attribution of the *pyxis* to Rome and his date about 400 A.D. are both inacceptable; the work points to an earlier date and to the Syro-Egyptian province, though to which part of it must remain uncertain. The bone carving to which allusion has just been made belongs to a group, once in all probability decorating articles of furniture, found in considerable numbers at Alexandria.[7] These carvings are of interest in relation to the Christian ivory carvings, as the figures upon them, though for the most part purely pagan, have many affinities with those adopted by Christians. In some cases, as on the Berlin *pyxis*, motives are incorporated in Christian ivories which go back to classical originals; another subject of a bone relief, representing Niké holding above her head a medallion containing a bust,[8] is reproduced upon an ivory diptych in the library at Munich (p. 198), though here the ideal classical types have disappeared and a bearded head of oriental type has replaced the youthful head within the medallion.

A large group of the pagan carvings is ornamented with nude figures of classical type, sometimes with a background of water-plants and birds suggesting

[1] Molinier, *Catalogue des ivoires*, No. 2 (figured).
[2] Garrucci, *Storia*, Pl. 451, Fig. 3; Denon and Carrand Collections; Grivaud de la Vincelle, *Monuments antiques inédits*, ii, Pl. XXVIII, p. 232; Molinier, *Ivoires*, 57 ff. and Pl. V, 2; Westwood, *Fictile Ivories*, p. 48; Graeven, *Gött. gel. Anz.*, 1897, 67; Venturi, *Storia*, i, Fig. 385.
[3] A. Haseloff in Prussian *Jahrbuch*, xxiv, 1903.
[4] Molinier, *Ivoires*, Pl. III.
[5] W. Vöge, *Elfenbeinbildwerke* (Catalogue, Kaiser Friedrich Museum), 1902, No. 1; Stuhl-fauth, *Elfenbeinplastik*, p. 18.
[6] Wulff, *Berlin Catalogue*, No. 428; Strzygowski, *Hellenistische und koptische Kunst*, 10; Ainaloff, *Hellenistic Origins*, 45, 59.
[7] J. Strzygowski, *Hellenistische und koptische Kunst in Alexandrien*, Vienna, 1902, and *Koptische Kunst*, 171 ff.; Wulff, *Berlin Catalogue*, i, Nos. 341 ff.; H. Graeven, *Antike Schnitzereien aus Elfenbein und Knochen in photographischer Nachbildung* (Hannover, 1903), Nos. 64–6.
[8] *Hell. und kopt. Kunst*, 6 ff.

oriental inspiration.[1]   The principal example of this work is a bridal casket at
Cairo of similar form to the silver casket of Projecta in the British Museum.[2]

CONSULAR DIPTYCHS.[3]

A definite predominance of an oriental or Byzantine style is shown by the
consular diptychs which were made to the order of consuls on their accession to

Fig. 118.   Part of the consular diptych of the fifth–sixth century in the Cathedral
of Halberstadt : from a cast.   (*Archaeologia*, lvii, p. 164.)   P. 197.

office and were sent by them as complimentary gifts to important personages ;
in the same way in England, if small things may be compared with great, gold

---

[1] *Hell. und kopt. Kunst*, 13–14.   [2] Strzygowski, *Koptische Kunst*, No. 7060.
[3] The best accounts of consular diptychs are given by E. Molinier, *Ivoires*, ch. i;
W. Meyer, *Zwei antike Elfenbeintafeln der k. Staatsbibliothek in München*, pp. 3 ff., Munich, 1879.
Westwood enumerates those reproduced for the Arundel Society in his *Fictile Ivories*, first
section, 'Classical Ivories.'   L. von Sybel, *Christliche Antike*, ii, pp. 232–5, gives a very
convenient list of the precisely dated examples.   The Theodosian code of A.D. 384 prohibited
the presentation of diptychs by any officers other than consuls ; but the prohibition was
ineffective, as ten years later Symmachus in a letter to his brother announces the dispatch
of a diptych on the elevation to the quaestorship of his son (Marquardt, *Römisches Privatleben*,
ii[2], pp. 562, 803; Pauly-Wissowa, *Realencyklopädie*, iv, 1135, and v, article *Diptychon*; Daremberg
and Saglio, art. *Diptychon*, i. 27).

rings were distributed by newly made serjeants-at-law. A considerable number were required by every consul, and the quality of the work varied according to the rank of the recipient. Proof of this is supplied firstly by the manufacture of the great composite diptychs (see below), which appear to have been reserved for imperial persons ; secondly, by the existence of examples in different styles made for the same magistrate. Thus there exist eight diptychs of Areobindus (A. D. 506), four of a more elaborate type, showing the consul seated at the games (see below), the other four with medallions, monograms, and geometrical or floral ornament, which must have been more rapidly executed and cost considerably less. The series of consular diptychs begins about the commencement of the fifth century and ends with the year of office of Basilius in 541, when the consulate was abolished by Justinian. Thirty-seven are identified by inscriptions giving names, or by monograms ; twelve are anonymous. Of these forty-nine examples only six belong to the fifth century, and all these are of Roman consuls. Of the remaining thirty-one only that of Orestes (A. D. 530) belongs to Rome. This diptych (Fig. 120), now in the Victoria and Albert Museum,[1] is so entirely in the style of the contemporary Byzantine examples as to suggest that oriental influence was already paramount in this branch of art.

The usual scheme of decoration shows the consul in the toga picta arranged in the 'contabulated' style, that is to say folded into a comparatively narrow band before it was put on.[2] Sometimes the chlamys with the *tablion* is worn, an imperial and court costume from the fourth century (Fig. 118). In the earliest examples the consul stands (Felix, A. D. 428) or is seated (Asterius, A. D. 449, Boethius, A. D. 487), holding a sceptre in his left hand and either nothing or a scroll in his right. In most of these examples he must be considered as receiving the congratulations of his friends. But as early as Boethius (A. D. 487) there appears in the raised right hand the *mappa circensis*, the napkin thrown down as the signal for the commencement of the games (Fig. 8).[3] That there may be no doubt in the spectator's mind as to the scene depicted, the lower part of the diptych is filled either with charioteers, horses, acrobats, mimes, or with figures of men pouring money out of sacks to signify the largesse of the new-made consul. To right and left of the consul there sometimes appear accompanying figures, either persons of rank, as on the fifth-century diptych in Halberstadt Cathedral,[4] or personifications of Rome and Constantinople, as on the diptychs of Magnus (A. D. 518) and Orestes (A. D. 530), as well as on contemporary coins. With a few exceptions the diptychs had the same design on both leaves.

It has already been remarked that the quality of consular diptychs varied according to the importance of the recipients. As the chief recipient was the emperor, it was necessary to devise for his acceptance a more elaborate type than that presented to less-exalted personages. To meet this need there came into existence very large diptychs ('composite diptychs'), each leaf of which was composed of five parts (cf. Fig. 124). The principal panel was in the centre, flanked by two narrower panels of the same height, while at top and bottom were narrow horizontal panels equal in length to the breadth of the three others combined.[5]

[1] W. Maskell, *Description*, &c., p. 55. This diptych was acquired in 1866.

[2] Wilpert in *L'Arte*, Rome, 1898, and *Die Gewandung der Christen in den ersten Jahrhunderten*, Bonn, 1898 ; O. Wulff, *Die Koimesiskirche von Nicäa*, 204 ff., Strasburg, 1903. The latter adopts a theory based upon that of Bielyayeff, and differing from that of Meyer, who discusses the question of costume on pp. 22 ff.

[3] The action of holding up the *mappa* is found upon coins, from those of Valentinian III to Phocas (Meyer, as above, p. 15).

[4] Graeven (*Gött. gel. Anz.*, as above) ascribes this diptych to the first quarter of the century. It is reproduced among the fictile ivories of the Arundel Society.

[5] On the type, see Graeven, *Gött. gel. Anz.*, as above, 352 ; V. Schultze, *Archäologie*, &c., 273 ; O. Wulff in *Deutsche Literatur-Zeitung*, 1906, 1468.

Two fragments of an example in the Trivulzio Collection at Milan [1] show the nature of the upper and lower plaques. That from the top has two winged figures of Victories holding a wreath containing a female bust (the Tyche of Constantinople), that from the bottom barbarian tributaries. The inscriptions on these two plaques: AC TRIVM-PHATORI + PERPETVO SEMPER AVG; and: VIR ILLVSTR : COM : PROTIC (?) ET CONSVL ORDINAR, leave no doubt that the whole of which they formed parts was intended as a gift to an emperor from a consul. Another upper plaque from a composite diptych is at Basle; [2] with its flying Victories and medallion with female bust it is almost identical with the Milan plaque, and bears the inscription PERPETVAE SEMPER + AVGVSTAE. The royal library at Munich contains two side plaques from such a diptych [3] which Meyer supposes to represent the consul bringing his congratulations for the new year in the presence of imperial guards and an officer of the court; a standing figure of Victory holds up a medallion containing a bearded imperial bust, which is conjectured by Meyer, upon inadequate evidence, to be Julian. [4] If the scene really represents a gift to an emperor, we must suppose that the top and bottom panels were not dissimilar from the examples at Milan and Basle, and that the centre panel represented the emperor himself. This is suggested by the presence of the bodyguard and by the fact that the consul is humbly standing offering a scroll, instead of proudly seated as always in the absence of his sovereign. Whatever the true interpretation, the style of the work suggests the sixth century rather than the fourth.

Fig. 119. Diptych of the Consul Anastasius (A. D. 517). (Victoria and Albert Museum.)

The only comparatively perfect example of a composite diptych possibly made for presentation to the emperor is that now in the Louvre, formerly in

---

[1] Westwood, *Fictile Ivories*, 365, No. 5 ; W. Meyer, as above, p. 50, and Pl. I and II. The winged Victories recall the scheme of two winged genii holding portrait medallions which frequently occur on pagan sarcophagi. See also Strzygowski, *B. D.*, vol. i, *Das Etschmiadzin-Evangeliar*, 31. [2] W. Meyer, 50-1; de Rossi, *Bullettino*, 1878, Pl. I.

[3] Meyer, pp. 51-5 and Pl. III ; Molinier, *Ivoires*, No. 49, p. 39.

[4] Riedin (*Proc. of the Imperial Russian Archaeological Soc.*, N. S., vol. ix, 1897, 201) declares that the scene represented is not a gift made by a consul to an emperor, but the *apokombia*, a gift made to the Church by a high official, perhaps a patrician, when entering upon his (new) rank. He says that the offering is not a scroll, but a bag of money. (See D. Bielyayeff, *Byzantina*, i. 48, 254, ii. 47 and 240; Migne, *Patr. Gr.*, vol. 112, p. 516.) Riedin, like Molinier, declines to accept the fourth century as the date, preferring the sixth, which is certainly more probable. The bust in the medallion, in his view, represents Our Lord.

the Barberini Collection at Rome, and thence known as the Barberini diptych.[1]
Here the emperor, variously supposed to be Constantine or Justinian,[2] is seen
on the central panel, mounted and carrying a lance.   The upper plaque has

Fig. 120.   Diptych of the Consul Orestes (A. D. 530).   (Victoria and Albert Museum.)   P. 197.

Victories holding a medallion containing a beardless bust of Our Lord ; the
lower, barbarians bringing tribute, among them being apparently natives of
India.   Of the two lateral plaques, only that on the left side remains : it bears

---

[1] Gori, *Thesaurus*, ii, Pl. I, 168; W. Meyer, No. 58; Molinier, No. 10; G. Schlumberger,
Monuments Piot, vii. 1 ff.; Westwood, p. 353; A. Venturi, *Storia*, i. 394 (Fig.); Strzygowski,
Hellenistische und koptische Kunst, p. 29, Fig. 17, and *Kleinasien*, 137, 183; E. Strong, *Roman
Sculpture*, Pl. 105; L. von Sybel, *Christliche Antike*, ii. 242, and Fig. 75; Ch. Diehl, *Justinien*
(frontispiece).   M. Molinier, *Ivoires*, p. 10, declines to accept the Barberini ivory as a diptych
because it is devoid of any dedicatory inscription, and it may be, as he suggests, that it
was originally made as a book-cover.   Names written in ink on the back of the Barberini
diptych prove that it was already in Germany in the seventh century.
[2] H. Graeven (*Ath. Mitth.*, xv, 1900, p. 212) and J. Strzygowski (as above, p. 28)
express the opinion that the period of Justinian is too late.   The French archaeologists,
MM. Schlumberger and Diehl, believe that the emperor is Justinian.   So apparently does
Von Sybel, and upon the whole this view appears the most probable.

a warrior offering a figure of Victory. It will be shown below that after the peace of the Church this composite type of consular diptych served as a model for book-covers, the figure of Christ being substituted for that of the emperor, the Virgin and Child for that of the empress, who was probably sometimes represented upon the second leaf (p. 198) (cf. the Basle fragment, with *perpetuae semper Augustae*). As a general rule, the emperor was probably seated after the fashion of the higher magistrates (cf. the diptych of Rufius Probianus, p. 191), and this is the scheme represented on the sarcophagus of Junius Bassus (p. 132, n. 7), on the ivory *pyxis* at Berlin (p. 195), and on various diptychs.[1] Emperors are seen enthroned in the Calendar of A.D. 354 (p. 484), on the votive shield of Theodosius at Madrid (p. 569), and also upon coins.

It has been already observed that the diptychs of consuls and officials passed in considerable numbers into the possession of the Church, where they were used for purposes of commemoration. To this circumstance a number owe their preservation ; and it would appear that in a few cases the carved figures of the consuls were modified in order that the ornamentation might better conform to Christian sentiment. In a diptych at Prague the consul has been transformed into St. Peter ;[2] the *mappa* has become a scroll, the sceptre a key, while a nimbus has been traced round the head. An ivory at Milan shows a consular figure similarly changed into St. Paul.[3] But though modification in these cases cannot be doubted, it is not so easy to explain in the same way the curious diptych in the treasury of Monza Cathedral with figures of David and St. Gregory.[4] It is quite true that the deliberate representation of a pope holding up the *mappa* is peculiar ; but if the very extensive alterations required on the other theory were really made, it is strange that the carver entrusted with the work did not change the *mappa* into a scroll, as was actually done in the Prague panel. This was a far easier transformation than that of the eagle on the sceptre into a cross, and the unnecessary introduction in many places of foliate designs. The differences in the general arrangement, and the position of the space left for the inscription, make this pair of panels very anomalous if they are to be regarded as a sixth-century diptych altered some time after the death of Gregory in A.D. 604. The opinion of Bloch,[5] Westwood,[6] Venturi, and others, that the diptych was made *ad hoc*, and that the preservation of the general consular scheme was partly suggested by the exalted worldly position of the *gens Anicia* to which Gregory belonged, appears to present the fewest difficulties. Both theories presumably attribute the actual work to a Teutonic carver trained in Italy.

The leaf of a diptych in the British Museum (Fig 121), with the standing figure of an archangel,[7] in some respects the noblest ivory in existence, is perhaps allied to the previous group by the circumstance of its dedication. From its exceptional size and beauty as well as from the attitude of the angel, who seems to offer the orb of imperial power, it is supposed to have been made as a present for an emperor, who was represented upon the lost second leaf.[8] The diptych

---

[1] J. Strzygowski, *B. D.*, i, 31.

[2] H. Graeven, *Röm. Mitth.* (Rome), 1892, p. 213 ; Molinier, *Ivoires*, p. 52, and No. 45, p. 38.

[3] Graeven, as above, 213 ; Molinier, 25 ; Venturi, i, Fig. 343. The type resembles that of the diptych of Magnus, A.D. 518.

[4] Graeven, as above, 218, and *Gött. gel. Anz.*, 1897, 77 ; Molinier, No. 84 ; Venturi, i, Fig. 390.

[5] In Daremberg and Saglio, *Dictionnaire des antiquités grecques et romaines*, s. v. *Diptyque*. M. Bloch, however, perhaps inadvertently, assigns the diptych to the fifth century.

[6] *Fictile Ivories*, p. 30 ; Molinier, *Ivoires*, No. 44, p. 37, where other references are given.

[7] British Museum, *Cat. of Early Christian and Byzantine Antiquities*, No. 295, and *Catalogue of Ivory Carvings of the Christian Era*, No. 11, where the principal references to earlier reproductions are given. Cf. also Diehl, *Manuel*, 277.

[8] Stuhlfauth (*Elfenbeinplastik*, 174, and *Die Engel*, 180) argues that the Virgin rather than an emperor was carved upon the second leaf. Venturi (*Storia*, 506) thinks rather a crowd of worshippers. Kondakoff (*Byzantine Churches of Constantinople*, 6th *Archaeological Congress*, Moscow, 116) regards the angelic figure as a personification of Hagia Sophia, or the Divine Wisdom.

is of exceptional importance for the study of early ivories; unfortunately its history and date are not easy to determine with precision.

Strzygowski, in a suggestive paper communicated to the Hellenic Society,[1] notices the analogy between the angel and the inferior but still fine figures on the chair of Maximianus. He shows that the arrangement of the five figures on the front of the chair corresponds to that on the sides of the sarcophagi of the Sidamara type, which he would assign to the art of Antioch. He then brings the angel, the figures of the sarcophagi, and those of the chair into connexion with the decoration of the proscenium wall of the ancient theatre. Here, as we know from a fresco at Pompeii in the Fourth Style,[2] the doors through which the actors entered and the spaces between them are flanked by pairs of columns connected above by rounded arches or by pediments, all united by a continuous entablature as on the sarcophagi. Now the doors are approached by short flights of steps; and it is remarkable that the archangel is made to stand in a very awkward position at the top of a similar flight of steps flanked by projecting columns. If he is represented coming forward from the proscenium wall, as an actor about to descend upon the stage, we

[1] *Journal of Hellenic Studies*, xxvii, 1907, 99 ff. See also the article by Mrs. Strong in the *Burlington Magazine*, May, 1907, p. 110.

[2] Strzygowski, *Göttingische Gelehrte Anzeigen*, 1906, 910 ff. See also Von Cube, *Die römische 'Scenae frons' in den Pompeianischen Wandbildern*, Berlin, 1906. The figure

FIG. 121. Leaf of an ivory diptych, fourth–sixth century, with the Archangel Michael. (British Museum.) P. 200.

standing at the top of the short flight of steps is seen in the stucco decoration of a wall in the Stabian Thermae, and in some paintings in relief now in the Bronze Rooms of the museum at Naples. The doors in the stage wall with their flights of steps may be clearly seen in Von Cube's reconstruction of a Pompeian stage façade, reproduced in *Journ. Hell. St.*, as above, 120.

should have to infer a powerful influence exerted by stage architecture upon the arts of painting and sculpture, and it seems at first sight unlikely that motives with such an origin should have been adopted into Christian art. But the researches of Holl suggest that the *iconostasis* of the Greek Church, with its three doors for ceremonial entries or εἴσοδοι, may have had a similar theatrical descent.[1] When it is remembered that such theatrical influences can only have been exerted in some great centre of population ; that the fourth Pompeian style came from Antioch ; and that the chair of Maximianus, the standing figures on the front of which have analogies to the archangel, has oriental foliated designs and is most probably a work of Antiochene art, it is certainly a defensible hypothesis that the British Museum diptych was also produced at Antioch, possibly at a period not far removed in date from that of the sarcophagus at Berlin, that is to say within the limits of the fourth century. The figure is the work of some school living upon older Greek traditions, and especially distinguished for its masterly treatment of drapery. The belief that this school may have flourished in or near Antioch is supported by the style of the rosettes and leaves in the spandrels above the columns, a style which was much favoured in early illuminated manuscripts painted in Syria, and by the identity of the mouldings of the arch with those ornamenting the large zigzag band, and certain of the rosettes on the façade of the palace of Mshatta.[2] The wreath before the scallop, with its *lemnisci*[3] terminating in leaves, recalls certain slabs and sarcophagi at Ravenna, Delphi, and elsewhere, perhaps imported from the Syrian area.

The Museum panel may therefore represent the art of the Hellenistic ivory carver of Antioch at an earlier and higher stage than the chair and the group of ivories connected with it. Its admirable quality proves the vitality of the Hellenic spirit, which even at this late hour, amid so many influences making for decay, could still give plastic form to a majestic idea ; and it is interesting to remember that at about the same period the best school of ivory carvers at Rome showed a similar appreciation of early Greek sculpture (p. 190). It seems quite possible that this fine work may belong, as Graeven held, to about the time of Theodosius, though others assign it to the fifth, or even the sixth, century.[4]

OTHER IVORIES OF THE FIRST PERIOD.

Book-covers after the model of consular diptychs made for presentation to emperors (p. 197) are among the most important documents for the provenance of the ivory carvings of the sixth century, and most of them were beyond a doubt produced in the Christian East. The only example as to which there is uncertainty is that in the treasury of Milan Cathedral,[5] which is exceptional in many ways. Instead of the flying angels supporting a wreath, which in other book-covers of the class decorate the panel at the top, it has Gospel scenes similar in character to those at the bottom ; while at the extremities of both these panels are figures of the Evangelists within wreaths. The central panels, instead of Our Lord and the Virgin, contain the Holy Lamb in *orfèvrerie cloisonnée* set with coloured stones or glass pastes, and a cross similarly ornamented, each within a wreath : the lateral panels have each three Gospel scenes instead of the usual two.

The following additional ivory carvings are in the same style as the Milan book-cover : three panels from a casket, formerly in the Abbey of Werden in

---

[1] *Archiv. für Religionswissenschaft*, ix, 365 ff. ; *J. H. S.*, p. 119.

[2] Prussian *Jahrbuch*, 1904, 276.

[3] See p. 167. The *lemnisci* are already converted into stems or tendrils by the fifth century, though the ribbons with hearts at the ends persist to the sixth (Wickhoff, Austrian *Jahrbuch*, xiv, p. 196, miniatures in a sixth-century MS.).

[4] Diehl, p. 278, assigns it to the latter period.

[5] Garrucci, *Storia*, vi, Pl. 454–5 ; J. Strzygowski, *Kleinasien*, p. 198, Fig. 144 ; Venturi, *Storia*, i, 424–5, Figs. 388–9. The references to other publications are fully given by Stuhlfauth, *Elfenbeinplastik*, 69, who discusses and gives the references for the other objects belonging to the group.

Westphalia, and now in the Victoria and Albert Museum ;[1] the right-hand lateral leaf of a (lost) composite book-cover, formerly in the collection of M. Mallet of Amiens, but now in the Berlin Museum ;[2] panels in the museums at Toulouse and Nevers ;[3] three *pyxides*, one still at Werden, one in the museum at Rouen, the third in Florence,[4] and perhaps the panel in the British Museum representing Our Lord disputing with the Doctors.[5] Of this group, the panels at Berlin and Toulouse are the oldest, and the *pyxides* the latest examples, the book-covers and other panels occupying an intermediate position.

Although the whole series is less obviously oriental than the groups which we have next to discuss, it may be observed that the following points suggest a doubt as to its origin in the West. The book-cover is very original in its ornamentation, diverging considerably from the usual schemes of Roman-Christian art. The decoration with the jewelled lamb is an orientalizing feature. The figure of St. John the Baptist upon the panel at Berlin is like that of one of the men who carried out Ananias on the marble relief from Asia Minor now in Berlin [6] (Fig. 88). On the Werden casket there is a church the façade of which is flanked by two towers in a style of architecture associated with the Christian East.[7]

On the other side it may be pointed out that in the Nativity the manger is under a shed-like roof. This is a Western feature, for in the East the scene is almost invariably at the mouth of a cave.

With the large number of ivories forming two distinct groups, of which the nuclei are the chair of Archbishop Maximianus and the large composite diptych formerly at Murano and now at Ravenna, we are in the presence of works incontrovertibly of oriental origin. They represent what has survived from the production of at least two schools working in the great cities of the oriental provinces. It has already been said that the artistic and icono-graphical influences in these provinces between the fourth century and the Arab conquests are so confused that the more precise localization of these ivories can only be conjectural.

The famous sixth-century chair known as the chair of Archbishop Maximianus, in the chapel of the archbishop's palace at Ravenna, is of wood covered with carved ivory panels.[8] These are rectangular, and ornamented with figure subjects: between them are narrower plaques forming frames or borders, ornamented with birds and animals in scrolls of foliage. Over the central figure on the front of the chair is a monogram which can be read ' Maximianus ', and

[1] Garrucci, Pl. 447 ; Strzygowski, *Ikonographie der Taufe Christi*, Pl. II, Fig. 3 ; Westwood, *Fictile Ivories*, pp. 41–3 ; Stuhlfauth, *Elfenbeinplastik*, pp. 71 ff. ; Sybel, *Christliche Antike*, ii. 247. The casket is erroneously ascribed by W. Maskell to the eleventh century (p. 67).

[2] A. Haseloff, Prussian *Jahrbuch*, xxiv, 1903, 47 ff., and Plate ; Strzygowski, *Kleinasien*, 198.

[3] A. Darcel, *Trésors des églises et objets d'art français appartenant aux musées exposés en 1889 au palais du Trocadéro*, vol. i, No. 14.

[4] Garrucci, *Storia*, Pl. 438, Figs. 1 and 2, and 437, Fig. 5. Cf. Stuhlfauth, *Elfenbein-plastik*, 79.

[5] British Museum, *Catalogue of Early Christian and Byzantine Antiquities*, No. 293 ; *Catalogue of Ivory Carvings*, No. 9.

[6] The two are figured side by side by Strzygowski, *Kleinasien*, 197.

[7] Ibid., 214. Architecture of a similar origin appears on the Brescia reliquary (p. 192) and one of the early set of casket-panels in the British Museum (*Catalogue of Early Christian and Byzantine Antiquities*, No. 292).

[8] The literature of this chair is too extensive to be given at length. It is illustrated in detail by Garrucci, *Storia*, vi. 414–19, from drawings ; and from photographs, by H. Graeven, Series ii, 41, 62–3 ; Venturi, *Storia*, i, pp. 468 ff., Figs. 278–307 ; C. Ricci in *Arte italiana decorativa e industriale*, vii, 1898, and Molinier, *Ivoires*, p. 67, Pl. VII ; G. Stuhlfauth, *Elfenbein-plastik*, 86 ff. : a full bibliography of the earlier works in which it is described is given by Stuhlfauth ; a less complete bibliography by Venturi, as above, 466. See also Graeven, *Bonner Jahrbücher*, 1900, 159, 162 ; Rohault de Fleury, *La Messe*, ii, 154–5 ; C. M. Kauffmann, *Handbuch*, p. 523 ; Leclercq, *Manuel*, ii, p. 352 ; Strzygowski, *Journ. Hellen. Studies*, 1907, 115 ; H. Dütschke, *Ravennatische Studien*, 1909, 279 ff. ; E. Strong, *Burlington Magazine*, May, 1907, p. 111.

naturally suggests the long-prevalent attribution to the Maximianus (A. D. 545–556) in whose episcopate the Church of San Vitale was dedicated. But recent investigation seems to show that in all probability the chair was never in

Fɪɢ. 122.   Front of the ivory-covered episcopal chair at Ravenna : sixth century.   (Ricci.)

Ravenna at all before A. D. 1001, when it arrived there as a gift of the Doge Pietro Orseolo to the Emperor Otto III, then residing in the city.[1] The gift is recorded by John the Deacon, who says that the doge gave, in return for certain imperial presents, *cathedram elephantinis artificiose sculptam tabulis . . . quam avide suspiciens in eadem conservandam urbe reliquit.* This passage at least

---

[1] C. Ricci, *Arte italiana decorativa e industriale*, vii, 1898, 42 ff. ; for the passage in Johannes Diaconus see Pertz, *Monumenta Germaniae historica*, vii, 104.   See also Venturi, as above, 466.

accounts for the presence of a throne covered with ivory panels at Ravenna, and cannot be explained away as referring to the second ivory-covered chair which was still at Grado in the eleventh century, because the latter is definitely stated to have come from Alexandria, the city of St. Mark, whose life was recorded on the panels.[1]

Fig. 123.   Our Lord and the Woman of Samaria, panel of the episcopal chair at Ravenna.   (Ricci.)

It is usually considered that the panels upon the chair are the work of more than one hand.   The five large panels on the front, with figures of John the Baptist and four Apostles, and the smaller panels on both sides with New Testament scenes, and those fitted into the framework of the back, are all of finer quality than the larger panels decorating the sides, which have scenes from

[1] De Rossi, *Bullettino*, iii, 1865, 29; H. Graeven, *Bonner Jahrbücher*, Heft 105, *R. Q.*, 1899, Pl. 8 and 9, and photos, series ii, 42-8; Strzygowski, *Orient oder Rom*. 34, 74, with Fig. 32; Venturi, *Storia*, Figs. 415-7; Leclercq in Cabrol's *Dictionnaire*, i. 1124, Figs. 274-5.

the history of Joseph.[1] The latter vary in quality, and may themselves be the work of more than one artist. It must not be forgotten, however, that a single artist may have lavished more care on the work placed on the more conspicuous parts of the chair.

Before proceeding to enumerate a number of allied ivories, we must in a few words discuss the probable origin of the chair. The place of residence of the bishop for whom it was made does not necessarily affect the question, for, as in modern times, objects for presentation must have been frequently ordered from without; and as the connexion with Maximianus of Ravenna has been discredited there is no necessity to attribute the work to that city. On the other hand there are definite reasons, already touched upon in connexion with the panel in the British Museum, which point to the eastern shores of the Mediterranean. The choice seems to lie between Alexandria and Antioch. Ainaloff decides in favour of the former city, and Dütschke believes that one of the animals in the scroll-work is a jerboa,[2] but the arguments for a Syrian origin appear to have at least an equal weight. Although Ainaloff finds analogies in the treatment of the figures with the miniatures of the Vatican Cosmas (p. 462) and notes points of resemblance with a painted triptych from Egypt in the Golenisheff Collection,[3] he admits the essentially Asiatic character of the ornamental work, which recalls that of the Mshatta façade at Berlin (p. 170). The opinion of Strzygowski that the chair was produced at Antioch or within its culture area has been confirmed by his investigations on Mshatta[4] and the sculpture on the sarcophagi of the Sidamara group. The statuesque character of the figures on the front of the chair is very marked; they are evidently the work of men still influenced, like the sculptors of the sarcophagi and of the British Museum archangel, by the old Hellenic spirit; and as we have seen reason to believe that these monuments were produced on the eastern littoral of the Mediterranean, there is a presumption in favour of an Asiatic origin. Strzygowski shows that the disposition of the figures on the front of the chair in separate niches of unequal breadth surmounted by scallop canopies corresponds so exactly to the disposition of the pagan figures on the sides of the sarcophagi that the carver of the chair must have had the typical decoration of such a sarcophagus in his mind. Had it not been so he would hardly have crowded five figures into the space at his disposal: three would have served equally well. But as an imitator, and not an original designer, he had to include the two extra figures corresponding to those which in the sarcophagi stand in the narrower inter-spaces. Stryzgowski gives plausible reasons for supposing that the scallop niche is of oriental origin,[5] while there can be little doubt that the fine scroll-work containing birds and animals, deeply cut with dark interstices between every part, is Syro-Mesopotamian and not European in its origin. The interesting theory which accounts for the disposition of figures under unequal niches along the sides of the sarcophagi has been already mentioned in connexion with the British Museum archangel (p. 201). With regard to the treatment of the statuesque figures themselves, Strzygowski urges that they are clearly the work of an artist trained, not in the 'illusionist' school which flourished about

---

[1] Several panels have been removed from the chair, but only two are lost. Those which have been traced are in the Museo Olivieri at Pesaro, in the museum at Ravenna, in the Stroganoff Collection at Rome, in the Museo archeologico at Milan, and the Museo Farnese at Naples. For the Stroganoff panels see F. Hermanin, *L'Arte*, i, Rome, 1898; and E. K. Riedin, *Panel from the Chair of Archbishop Maximianus*, &c., Charkoff, 1893 (Russian).

[2] P. Dütschke, *Ravennatische Studien*, 1909, 279 ff., and Figs. 83 and 84. Diehl, *Manuel*, 281, also decides in favour of Egypt.

[3] *V. M.*, v, Pl. II, and p. 184.

[4] For Mshatta see Prussian *Jahrbuch*, 1904, 299; for the sarcophagi, p. 128 above. It may be noticed that some of the scenes on the chair (e. g. the Baptism) apparently resemble the descriptions left by Constantine the Rhodian and Mesarites of the lost mosaics of the Church of the Apostles at Constantinople (A. Heisenberg, *Grabeskirche und Apostelkirche*, ii. 236 ff.); while the miniatures of the Gospel of Rabula differ in their types.

[5] *Journ. Hellen. St.*, as above, 114-15, and see p. 130.

the beginning of our era, but rather in the principles which dominated Greek sculpture in the fourth century B.C., before the time of Alexander. The fine treatment of the drapery is evidently inspired by such models, and the types of the sarcophagi are purely Greek in origin. As Strzygowski puts it, the sculptors of the sarcophagi, who worked from the first to the fourth century A.D.,

FIG. 124. Ivory book-cover of the sixth century in the Bibliothèque Nationale, Paris. (From a cast.)

were living on the heritage of the period before Alexander and copying ancient types ; it would be natural for ivory carvers to follow their example. It is a further point that the ivory covers of the Etchmiadzin Gospels (p. 208) are stylistically and iconographically related to other panels on the chair.

The best-known members of the group connected with the chair are the two large composite book-covers, each with both leaves intact, at Paris and at Etchmiadzin in Armenia. That preserved in the Bibliothèque Nationale [1] has

---

[1] *Bibl. Nat.*, No. 9384 ; Garrucci, *Storia*, Pl 458, Figs. 1 and 2 ; Lenormant, *Trésor de glyptique*, vol. ii, Pl. 9–12 ; Westwood, *Fictile Ivories*, 45–6 (Nos. 108, 109). For other references see Stuhlfauth, *Elfenbeinplastik*, 97 ff., and H. von Sybel, *Christliche Antike*, ii, Fig. 76.

in the centre of one side Christ, bearded and without nimbus, seated between St. Peter and St. Paul. In the upper plaque two angels, substituted for the Victories of pagan times, hold a wreath containing a cross. The bottom panel shows Christ with the Woman of Samaria and the Raising of Lazarus; on the left lateral plaque are the Healing of the Blind, and of the Paralytic; on the right lateral plaque, Christ with the Woman with an Issue of Blood, and the Healing of the Demoniac.

In the centre of the other leaf is the Virgin seated with the Child between two angels.[1] The top plaque is almost identical with that on the first leaf; that at the bottom has the Entry into Jerusalem. On the left are the Annunciation and Visitation; on the right, the Meeting of Joseph and Mary, and the Journey to Jerusalem. In all the Gospel scenes Christ is represented as young and beardless. The execution is poor throughout.

The book-cover in the Monastery of Etchmiadzin in Armenia[2] also has as central plaques on the two sides, Our Lord seated, and the Virgin seated with the Child. The top plaques are similarly ornamented with flying angels supporting wreaths containing crosses, with the sun and moon in the corners, those at the bottom the Entry into Jerusalem and the Adoration of the Magi respectively. The lateral plaques on the upper leaf, each divided into two compartments, have four miracles of Our Lord, while those on the other leaf have scenes from the life of the Virgin, partly drawn from the Apocryphal Gospels. The iconography of these scenes diverges from that of the Early Christian art of the West; for example in the Entry into Jerusalem the *Tyche* of Jerusalem is introduced, a feature characteristic of East-Christian art. Strzygowski, who assigns the book-cover to the first half of the sixth century, was at first inclined to seek its origin at Ravenna, but has later abandoned this view and believes that all three monuments are more likely to have been produced in the culture area of Antioch.

The following are the principal other ivory carvings belonging to this group: the well-known diptych in the Berlin Museum with figures of Our Lord and the Virgin,[3] the relationship of which to the figures on the front of the chair is unmistakable; a panel in the Stroganoff Collection at Rome, representing St. Peter;[4] a panel in the Provincial Museum at Trèves with Abraham and Melchizedek;[5] the two large panels in the M[c]Clean Collection in the Fitz-william Museum at Cambridge[6] with Apostles and Gospel scenes, and the related diptychs in the Brussels Museum[7] and the Cathedral of Tongres;[8] the Baptism in the British Museum (Fig. 111);[9] a panel with St. Paul in the Musée de Cluny,

---

[1] For the derivation of this type from imperial figures upon Roman medallions showing the empress (e. g. Fausta) enthroned full face, holding her child, see Strzygowski, *B. D.*, i. 39 ff. The figure of Juliana in the MS. of Dioscorides (p. 460) probably shows the style of lost diptychs with figures of empresses. The type of the Virgin and Child flanked by angels was adopted in mosaic art, and was the subject chosen to decorate apses from the sixth century onwards.

[2] J. Strzygowski, *B. D.*, i, *Das Etschmiadzin-Evangeliar.*

[3] W. Vöge, *Beschreibung der Bildwerke*, &c. (Catalogue of Ivories in the Kaiser Friedrich Museum), 1902, No. 2; Graeven, Prussian *Jahrbuch*, 1898, 83; Venturi, *Storia*, Figs. 383–4. These are the panels the authenticity of which was doubted by Didron and Molinier. But on the lower edge of the Virgin leaf are to be seen traces of a monogram similar to that upon the chair, almost destroyed when a piece was sawn off the bottom to shorten it.

[4] Ainaloff in *Archaeological Notes*, St. Petersburg, 1897, 305-9 (Russian); *B. Z.*, vii, 1898, 648.

[5] H. Graeven, in *Bonner Jahrbücher*, Heft 105.

[6] Garrucci, 452, Figs. 1 and 2; Molinier, 78; Graeven, *Bonner Jahrbücher*, 1900, 153 ff.; Dalton, *Catalogue of the Objects in the M[c]Clean Bequest*, No. 31.

[7] J. Destrée, *Musées Royaux*, &c., *Catalogue des ivoires*, Brussels, 1902, No. 1.

[8] Graeven, *Bonner Jahrbücher*, 1900, 152; J. Helbig, *La Sculpture au pays de Liège*, 13; Reusens, *Éléments d'archéologie chrétienne*, Aix, 1885, i, 194, Fig. 195; Rohault de Fleury, *La Messe*, vi, Pl. 437; Molinier, *Ivoires*, 55. This diptych may have been originally liturgical. It has on the back names of bishops of Tongres and Liège, the latest dating from A.D. 959.

[9] *Cat. of Early Christian and Byz. Antiquities*, No. 294.

Paris ;[1] and several ivory *pyxides* : that with the Martyrdom of St. Menas in the British Museum ;[2] that formerly at Lavoute-Chilhac, Le Puy, now in the Louvre,[3] with the scene of Our Lord and the Woman of Samaria ; a fragment in the Berlin Museum with Joseph sold to the Ishmaelites ;[4] a *pyxis* in the Basilewsky Collection in the Museum of the Hermitage, St. Petersburg,[5] with Joseph entertaining his brethren and the money being found in Benjamin's sack ; and a part of another *pyxis* in the collection of M. Novikoff at Kertch.[6]

The difference in merit between these various objects is considerable, making it probable that some are later than others. The inferior workmanship on several of the *pyxides* suggests that they date from the latter part of the sixth century or possibly from the beginning of the seventh.

We now come to another group, clearly made in the Christian East, but characterized by a different and inferior style. The Civic Museum at Ravenna contains one leaf of a book-cover, formerly at Murano, of which the companion leaf is only represented by three plaques now in different collections.[7] On the central panel Our Lord is seated between St. Peter and St. Paul and two angels, while beneath, as it were in a kind of predella, are the Three Children of Babylon in the furnace. The lateral panels have each two miracles of Our Lord, and the bottom panel two scenes from the story of Jonah. The upper plaque has the usual angels bearing the wreath containing a cross. The panels are bordered by bands of ornament formed of vine-scrolls and acanthus leaves, while above the 'predella' of the central plaque is a row of 'billets' (Fig. 210).

The remaining leaf is only represented by three plaques. The central panel, with the Virgin and Child and Magi with the Nativity below, formerly in the collection of the Earl of Crawford, is now in the John Rylands Library at Manchester[8] (Fig. 114). The bottom plaque, with the Annunciation, the Administration of the Oath by water to Mary, and the Journey to Bethlehem, is in the Stroganoff Collection at Rome.[9] The left-hand lateral plaque is cut into two halves, which are in the Botkin Collection at St. Petersburg.[10]

The iconography of the figure-groups is Syrian in character ; but the ornamental borders are closely related to those used about the sixth century in Upper Egypt. As the iconographical types of Syria and the Holy Land were carried by pilgrims into many Christian countries and there reproduced, both Strzygowski and Ainaloff[11] think it probable that the work was executed in Egypt, though under artistic influences emanating from the Holy Land. All the plaques of this leaf retain traces of painting and gilding. Details of ornament, such as the rows of disks like the heads of billets, certainly find parallels in Egypt.[12]

[1] E. Molinier, *Gazette archéologique*, xiv, 1889, Pl. 22.

[2] *Catalogue of Early Christian and Byzantine Antiquities*, 1901, No. 297 ; *Catalogue of Ivory Carvings*, &c., 1909, No. 12.

[3] R. de Fleury, *La Messe*, v, Pl. 366, 367 ; *Les Arts*, 1902, pp. 16–17.

[4] Vöge, *Catalogue*, as above, No. 4.

[5] Garrucci, *Storia*, Pl. 439, Fig. 6 ; R. de Fleury, *La Messe*, v, Pl. 370.

[6] Stuhlfauth, *Elfenbeinplastik*, 93.

[7] Gori, *Thesaurus*, iii, Pl. VIII ; Garrucci, *Storia*, vi, Pl. 456 ; Venturi, *Storia*, i, p. 432.

[8] Strzygowski, *Hellenistische und koptische Kunst*, 87, Fig. 63 ; Ch. Diehl, *Justinien*, 649, Fig. 206 ; D. Ainaloff, *V. V.*, v, 1898, 153 ff., and Pl. I. The facing position of the Virgin, as in this panel and one in the British Museum mentioned below, is found in Syrian art, e. g. on the Monza ampullae, and in one of the miniatures at the end of the Etchmiadzin Gospels (Strzygowski, *B. D.* i, *Das Etschmiadzin-Evangeliar*, Pl. VI). The arrangement with a 'predella' occurs in the Syrian Gospel of Rabula (A. D. 586, see p. 448), where the miniature with the Crucifixion has this peculiarity. [9] Ainaloff, *V. V.*, 1897, p. 128 (Figs.).

[10] Strzygowski, *B. Z.*, viii, 1899, 680–1.

[11] The monumental character of the central groups has suggested to Smirnoff and Ainaloff that they may be inspired by the (lost) external mosaics of the Church of the Nativity at Bethlehem (*Proc. Soc. Bibl. Arch.*, 1904, 212).

[12] Strzygowski, *Hellenistische und koptische Kunst*, 86–7 ; Ainaloff, *Hellenistic Origins*, 54 (Russian). Strzygowski, from comparison with sculptures in Egypt, ascribes the work to the monastic art of Inner Egypt rather than to the Hellenistic art of Alexandria.

The principal ivories connected by style and treatment of individual subjects with this Ravenna book-cover have been enumerated by Stuhlfauth,[1] who, however, includes among them the two large panels in the Fitzwilliam Museum at Cambridge here assigned to the group of the ivory chair (p. 208).   Among

Fig. 125.   Ivory book-cover of the sixth century in the Museum at Ravenna.   (Alinari.)
P. 209.

them are : panels at Bologna and in the Uvaroff Collection at Moscow ; two plaques (one in the British Museum (Fig. 126) and one in the Le Roy Collection at Paris) once forming the central panels of a single composite book-cover, of which the remaining parts are lost ;[2] with a large series of ivory *pyxides* in the Basilewsky Collection in the Hermitage at St. Petersburg and in the following museums : British Museum (*Catalogue*, No. 298, Daniel, &c.), Cluny

---

[1] *Elfenbeinplastik*, 112 ff.

[2] *Proc. Soc. Biblical Archaeology*, 1904, 209 ff. ; R. Koechlin, *La Collection Martin Le Roy*, ii. 1, and Pl. I.

Museum (two), Louvre (from Lavoute-Chilhac), Vienna, Berlin, the Vatican, Darmstadt, Bonn, Pesaro, and Livorno. The group as a whole is inferior to that of the chair, and none of the pieces composing it is of high artistic merit.

We may now briefly mention a few well-known ivories of the First Period, which, though clearly produced in the Christian East, cannot so easily be included in definite groups. The so-called Barberini diptych mentioned above (p. 198) has been affiliated by Stuhlfauth to the school of the chair, but it is not clear that the resemblances on which the opinion is based are sufficient to justify its inclusion : the similarity between the barbarians bringing gifts and figures upon the ivory *pyxides* at Florence, Rouen, and Werden, which are affiliated to the group of the Milan book-cover (see p. 202), tends to increase the suspicion that this group may not really belong to Italy.[1] The panel may well be of earlier date than the chair, though the description of the emperor as Constantine rather than Justinian is doubtful, the general appearance of the sculpture suggesting the art of the sixth century. Whoever the emperor, he is perhaps represented as the Hero of the Faith, mounted on horseback and triumphant over evil. The equestrian saint was a favourite motive in Egypt, and may have been derived from a mounted type of Horus.[2]

FIG. 126. The Adoration of the Magi, part of an ivory book-cover of the sixth century in the British Museum.

The remarkable panel at Trèves, representing the transportation of relics in the presence of an emperor,[3] probably Justinian, seems to have been made in Alexandria, and Strzygowski conjectures that the scene represented is the removal of the remains of the forty martyrs to the Church of St. Irene, Sycae (Constantinople), in A. D. 552[4] (Fig. 127).

An Egyptian origin is suggested by the same writer for the set of carved

[1] Haseloff, Prussian *Jahrbuch*, xxiv (1903), p. 53.
[2] Strzygowski, *Der koptische Reiterheilige und der heilige Georg*, in *Zeitschr. für ägyptische Sprache*, 1902; and *Hellenistische und koptische Kunst*, 21 ff. Examples of mounted saints are a sculpture in a lunette of the Mosque of Ali at Dashlug, an ivory comb from Antinoe (*R. Q.*, xii, Pl. I), &c.
[3] Westwood, *Fictile Ivories*, p. 64 ; *Archaeological Journal*, xx. 149 ; Rohault de Fleury, *La Messe*, v, Pl. 415.
[4] *Orient oder Rom*, 85 ; *Der Dom zu Aachen und seine Entstehung* (1904), 49 ; *Hellenistische und koptische Kunst*, 78.

ivory panels now inlaid in the pulpit of the Cathedral of Aix-la-Chapelle.[1] The equestrian figure is to be compared with the emperor of the Barberini diptych and the other mounted figures represented in Egyptian sculptures already mentioned, more especially the relief in stone at Dashlug (note 2, p. 211): the other panels are figures of Isis and Bacchus, Nereids, and an armed warrior. The evidence for the Egyptian origin of these panels is plausible: a panel representing a nude figure standing with crossed legs before a background of vine-scrolls, just in the manner of the Aix Bacchus reliefs, has actually been found in Egypt.[2] But apart from the particular points which connect them with Egypt the panels as a whole exhibit a general affinity to the earlier Alexandrian bone carvings with classical subjects to which allusion has already been made. Several ivories in various collections recall the style of these pulpit carvings, especially the 'Apollo' at Berlin,[3] the panels representing

FIG. 127.   A translation of relics : ivory carving of the sixth century in the Cathedral of Trèves.   (From a cast.)   P. 211.

Rome and Constantinople at Vienna,[4] and a panel in the museum at Ravenna[5] with Apollo and Daphne.

An ivory relief in the Louvre representing St. Mark seated before the city of Alexandria, surrounded by an audience of thirty-five men each wearing an embroidered mantle, while from the walls and windows in the background interested spectators look down, is ascribed to the beginning of the seventh century and is in all probability Alexandrian.[6] It is of exceptional interest because, in the upper part representing the city, an attempt is made to reproduce streets and buildings in a realistic manner, in this resembling the

[1] *Hellenistische und koptische Kunst*, 19-67 ; *Orient oder Rom*, 85 ff. E. Dobbert, in *Repertorium*, viii, 1885, 174 ff., where references to earlier publications are given. Dr. Graeven believed that three of the panels were made in Constantinople during the First Period, while three are later imitations made in Venice. He believed the whole set to have originally formed part of a throne presented by the Venetians to Otto III.

[2] *Hellenistische u. kopt. Kunst*, 65, and *Koptische Kunst*, No. 7115. Examples at Leipzig, Strzygowski, *Hell. u. kopt. Kunst*, Fig. 47, p. 59.

[3] Venturi, *Storia*, i, p. 402 ; Strzygowski, as above, Fig. 43, p. 53.

[4] Strzygowski, Figs. 34-5, p. 49.

[5] Venturi, *Storia*, i. 339 ; Graeven, photo, ii. 43.

[6] G. Schlumberger, *Mon. Piot*, i. 165-70, Pl. XXIII ; E. Molinier, *Catalogue des ivoires*, No. 3 (MM. Molinier and Schlumberger consider the preacher to be St. Paul) ; J. Strzygowski, *Hellenistische und koptische Kunst*, 79, and *Orient oder Rom*, 71 ff. ; *Byz. Zeitschr.*, ix, 1900, p. 606.

panel at Trèves, with the transportation of relics. But the closest parallel is with the wood carving from Egypt in the Kaiser Friedrich Museum at Berlin (p. 149), where the architecture is very similar, while there are also analogies with the background architecture of the group of ivories illustrating the acts of St. Mark in the Pentapolis, of which the greater number are in the Milan Museum,[1] but one is at South Kensington[2] (Fig. 129). If the thirty-five listeners represent the patriarchs of Alexandria, the ivory cannot be earlier than Anastasius, thirty-sixth patriarch (A. D. 607–9).

The panels in the Bargello at Florence and at Vienna, representing a queen or empress standing beneath a canopy, have been variously identified by different critics. Graeven considered the personage to be the Gothic Queen Amalasuntha;[3] Molinier saw in her the Empress Irene, who was regent for her son Constantine VI in 780;[4] while Modigliani[5] decides in favour of Ariadne, wife of the Emperors Zeno and Anastasius, whose bust appears upon the diptych of the Consul Clementinus. If the latter theory is correct, and it seems not improbable, the panels were executed before A.D. 507, in which year the son of Anastasius and Ariadne died. It seems probable that Molinier's date is too late, and that in spite of the extremely florid character of the ornament and the costume, parallels for the principal features are

FIG. 128. An empress : ivory panel in the Museo Nazionale (Bargello), Florence. (Alinari.)

[1] The architecture on these panels again resembles that in the Ashburnham Pentateuch (A. Sprenger, *Die Genesisbilder*, &c., Pl. II ; Strzygowski, *Orient oder Rom*, Fig. 11, p. 33).

[2] *R. Q.*, xiii, Pl. VIII.

[3] Prussian *Jahrbuch*, xix, 1898, 82 ff. Both panels are figured in Gori, *Thesaurus dipt.*, ii, Pl. 11 and 12. The Vienna panel is also in R. von Schneider, *Album auserlesener Gegenstände der Antikensammlung des a. h. Kaiserhauses*, Pl. 50. For the Florentine panel see Graeven, as above, p. 84 ; Molinier, *Ivoires*, v, Fig. 3.

[4] *Gazette des Beaux-Arts*, Third Period, vol. viii, 1892, p. 337, and *Ivoires*, as above.

[5] *L'Arte*, Rome, 1898, 365–7 ; see also *B. Z.*, viii, 1899, 250.

to be found in the art of the First Period. Among other details may be mentioned the curious wimple which was a fashion with ladies in the sixth century, and was transferred from the representations of secular personages to those of the Virgin Mary.[1] Further, the custom of presenting diptychs with large portrait-figures seems to have fallen into desuetude after the abolition of the consulate in A.D. 541, when consular diptychs ceased to be made.

The ivory vase in the British Museum,[2] formerly in the Maskell Collection, presents problems very difficult to solve. From vases carved at two opposite points on the sides rise formal vine-scrolls, the leaves at the top merging into plain trefoils and quatrefoils; in the interspaces are medallions with busts of angels, and birds with opened wings. This ornamentation is enclosed above and below by bands of maeander, also enclosing birds; the base is calix-shaped, and round it near the bottom is a loose ring of ivory turned from the solid when the vase was made. The lid[3] is carved with a scroll of trefoils.

The ornament on this vase is undoubtedly oriental and of a Syro-Mesopotamian style. Analogous work occurs on smaller *pyxides* of less graceful design in the Victoria and Albert Museum and at Berlin.[4] The date of the whole group lies somewhere between the sixth and the eleventh centuries: the conventionalization of the vine leaves perhaps points rather to the later part of this period. Though the British Museum example was made for Christians, the same origin is not certain in the case of all: the smaller examples may be the work of Mohammedan ivory carvers.

Second and Third Periods.

With the Arab conquest of Syria and Egypt, the Persian wars of Heraclius, and the succeeding iconoclastic disturbances of the eighth century, the art of carving in ivory entered a new phase and found new channels of expression. On the one hand the crusade against images introduced a preference for secular subjects; on the other, the increased knowledge of oriental and especially Persian art led to an increase of Persian motives. The secular figure subjects are found upon a large group of caskets presumably made, like those of mediaeval Europe, for jewels and small objects of value; the oriental motives, principally lions, gryphons, and other beasts, often framed in a diaper of interconnected circles, are found on a few of the caskets, but are more frequent upon the ivory horns commonly known as oliphants. As the horns are less numerous and less interesting from an iconographical point of view than the caskets, they may be briefly treated first, though it may be premised that the dating is in both cases only approximate. It may be assumed that few of either class are earlier than the close of the iconoclastic period, and that the majority must probably be placed between the second half of the ninth century and the twelfth. The secular character of both groups, due to the absence or the unpopularity of religious models, outlasted the causes which had brought it into existence; but while at the end of the ninth century religious subjects reappear upon the caskets, the horns for the most part retain

---

[1] On this fashion see E. Molinier in *Études d'histoire du moyen âge dédiées à Gabriel Monod*, Paris, 1896, 61 ff., and Prussian *Jahrbuch*, as above, 83. Prominent examples of the fashion are to be seen in the mosaics in S. Vitale representing Theodora and her suite; in a marble head in the Palace of the Conservatori at Rome (*Bull. della Comm. arch. Comunale di Roma*, xvi, 1888, Pl. VI); and in the diptych leaf at Berlin representing the Virgin (Vöge, *Berlin Catalogue*, No. 3).

[2] British Museum, *Catalogue of Ivory Carvings*, No. 15; W. Maskell, *Description of the Ivories,&c.*, p. xliv; A. Maskell, *Ivories*, Pl. XVI, Fig. 1.

[3] The workmanship is not quite equal to that of the body of the vase, and it may be a later, though not necessarily a modern, addition.

[4] See British Museum, *Catalogue of Ivory Carvings*, 1909, note under No. 15.

the zoomorphic decoration which best suited their form. It is interesting to compare the beasts represented upon them not only with those on Byzantine caskets with zoomorphic ornament, but also with those upon carved ivory caskets made at the close of the tenth and the beginning of the eleventh centuries

FIG. 129. St. Peter and St. Paul : ivory panel of the sixth (?) century in the Victoria and Albert Museum. P. 213.

for Moorish princes in Spain, which drew upon the same oriental sources for their designs.

Some fifty of the caskets are in existence in public and private collections ; [1] the finest example of all, formerly in the Cathedral of Veroli, is in the Victoria and Albert Museum (Figs. 9, 10, 130, 132). They have upon them groups and

---

[1] See the list given by Graeven in Austrian *Jahrbuch*, xx, 1899, 25 ff. See also A. Venturi, *Le Gallerie nazionali italiane*, iii, 1897, 261 ff. ; *L'Arte*, i, Rome, 1898, 212 ; and *Storia*, i, 512 ff. ; R. von Schneider, *Serta Harteliana*, Vienna, 1896 (*Über das Kairosrelief in Torcello und verwandte Bildwerke*) ; W. Maskell, *Description of the Ivories*, &c., 176 ; Molinier, *Ivoires*, &c. Further references are given by Graeven and Venturi. The following caskets are reproduced in whole or part by M. Schlumberger : in his *Nicéphore Phocas*, p. 175 (Xanten), 647 (Sens) ; in his *Épopée*, i, pp. 59, 113, 185 (Darmstadt), 263, 357, 539, 637 (Veroli, S. Kensington), 281 (Lyon), 348 (St. Petersburg), 349 (Brussels, see also J. Destrée, *Catalogue of Ivories*), 385 (S. Kensington) ; in his *Épopée*, ii. 1, 8 (Carrand), Florence, 201, 271 (Xanten).

single figures, of which a large proportion are derived from classical mythology. The panels on which the figures are carved are framed in borders enriched with rows of very characteristic rosettes, between which are in many cases heads in profile resembling coin types (Fig. 132). The last feature makes it almost certain that pieces of silver plate supplied the carvers with many of their models, for a common method of ornamentation in Graeco-Roman plate was to inlay in the borders of dishes or salvers coins bearing the imperial effigy; while an example is known of a plate to which were applied gold disks with incised busts simulating the coins of earlier work. In addition to this, silver vessels

FIG. 130. End of an ivory casket of the ninth–tenth century in the Victoria and Albert Museum. P. 215.

in the Roman treasures of Boscoreale, Bernay, and Pompeii are ornamented with putti and animals so closely allied to those of the caskets that there can be little doubt as to one at least of the sources whence the ivory carvers derived their inspiration.[1] It is not probable that many carvers resorted to antique sculpture for their models, but the casket at Xanten has on it a figure imitating the Herakles of Lysippus,[2] which stood in the hippodrome of Constantinople. But the centaurs, the genii, Bacchic and Maenad-like figures which constantly recur, speak at every turn of the Graeco-Roman art from which they are derived, and it is unnecessary to specify further instances.[3]

Were these the only relationships which a study of the caskets reveals, the opinion of Venturi that they are products of expiring classical art would meet with a more general agreement. But they have affinities to the eleventh-century sculptured slabs at Torcello with *Kairos* (Fig. 91) and Ixion,[4] to other

[1] Graeven, Austrian *Jahrbuch*, as above, p. 20.
[2] A. Furtwängler, *Sitzungsberichte der phil.-hist. Klasse der k. bayrischen Akad. der Wissenschaften*, 1902, 435 ff.; H. Graeven, *Bonner Jahrbücher*, Heft 108, 252 ff. The statue remained in Constantinople until 1704, when it was melted down. This fact has been considered an argument in favour of Constantinople as the place where the caskets were made.
[3] H. Graeven, *Antike Vorlagen byzantinischer Elfenbeinreliefs*, in Prussian *Jahrbuch*, 1897.
[4] R. von Schneider, as above. The slab in the cathedral at Torcello, with two confronted peacocks, has a border of rosettes like those of the caskets.

slabs with the Labours of Hercules at S. Marco, Venice, and to sculptures found in Asia Minor and Greece[1] (one with a dancer and a centaur playing a lyre); moreover, many of the small and animated figures strongly recall those of illuminated psalters of the Monastic group,[2] the earliest known examples of which do not go back beyond the ninth century (p. 465). It might be possible indeed to explain the resemblance to the Torcello sculptures by assuming that these are themselves mere copies of far earlier originals, but it is not so easy to explain the absurd misunderstanding of common mythological scenes

FIG. 131. Ivory casket of the ninth–tenth century in the Victoria and Albert Museum.

which is a frequent feature upon the caskets. Figures are taken out of their context and inserted where they have no meaning; attributes are misinterpreted or misplaced in so naïve a manner that it is impossible to suppose the artists to have lived at a time when classical mythology was still a familiar subject. Thus Venus and water-nymphs are given torches as attributes; the thyrsus of Dionysus is turned into a whip; wings are applied to figures which have no claim to them; head-dresses are assigned to persons who in ancient art are always bare-headed. We do not find mistakes pointing so obviously to pure ignorance of classical mythology upon any of

[1] Strzygowski, Prussian *Jahrbuch*, xix, 1898, 57 ff. Cf. also his *Amida*, p. 345.
[2] Venturi, *Storia*, 514, compares the style of the figures on the caskets with the art of Roman imperial medals of the late fourth and early fifth centuries. But the almost bulging relief ('*fare rotondeggiante*') may be explained as the result of reproducing by another technique the high relief of embossed metal-work.

the ivories dating from the fourth to the sixth century on which classical subjects are represented: whatever errors the carver commits, he is still clearly familiar with the general trend of the story. This unintelligent treatment of familiar subjects appears an almost conclusive argument in favour of the theory that the carvers cannot have lived before the sixth century. An argument of a more specific kind which must carry considerable weight is that on one of the earliest and best of the caskets, that at Cividale (Museo Archeologico), mounted figures are seen riding with stirrups. Stirrups were not used in Europe before about A.D. 600, and even in the East, where they probably originated, not very much earlier. One small fact like this is more cogent than many abstract arguments. The relationship existing between particular details on the caskets and various illuminated manuscripts is if anything in favour of similar conclusions. Graeven[1] showed that groups of figures correspond exactly to certain groups in the Joshua Rotulus in the Vatican (p. 447), and in one case the men who in the manuscript are stoning Achan are introduced into a panel of the Veroli casket illustrating the story of Europa, where they are entirely out of place. Venturi, however, points out with justice that on his theory the identity is easily explicable, supposing the rotulus and the casket to have both copied antique models of the same character. There is a certain similarity between the rosettes and the busts in medallions which appear among them in the borders of the caskets, and those seen upon the remarkable glass cup in the Treasure of S. Marco at Venice.[2] This cup has a Cufic inscription assigned to the early twelfth century; and as the subjects in the larger medallions upon the sides are derived from classical models we perhaps have here an example of the same kind of copying to which the ivory carvers themselves resorted (see p. 614).

Another indication of later date is furnished by the close resemblance of the nude putti with their characteristic curly hair, so constantly found on these caskets, with the figures representing the dead resuscitated from the Valley of Dry Bones on a panel in the British Museum.[3] This panel, with another of the same kind in the same collection, bears every sign of having been copied from a manuscript, the style of which would in no case point to a date earlier than the ninth century. Caskets with classical figures in repoussé work were produced by silversmiths contemporary with the ivory carvers, and are clearly related to them in style (see p. 557); other silver-work seems to belong to the same group.

Caskets of similar form to those with mythological subjects, and with the same borders of rosettes, but ornamented with animals and monsters of oriental style to the exclusion of the human figure, are represented in England by the example in the McClean bequest to the Fitzwilliam Museum[4] at Cambridge, formerly in the Spitzer Collection (Graeven's list, No. 43). This style, like the other, was probably imitated by Italian ivory carvers in the twelfth century, and the casket in the museum at Pisa is considered to be such an imitation.[5] Another small group of four caskets,[6] in which the rosette borders are a

---

[1] Prussian *Jahrbuch*, xviii, 1897, 1 ff.

[2] Pasini, *Tesoro di San Marco*, Pl. XL; Molinier, *Trésor de Saint-Marc*, 58, and *Ivoires*, p. 90.

[3] British Museum, *Catalogue of Early Christian Antiquities*, No. 299; Graeven, Photos, Series i, 1898, No. 45; W. Maskell, *Ivories*, 152, No. 11; E. von Dobschütz, *Repertorium*, xxvi, 282.

[4] Dalton, *Catalogue of the McClean Bequest*, No. 35. Cf. the other Spitzer casket in the Musée du Cinquantenaire, Brussels, for which see J. Destrée's Catalogue, and Schlumberger, *Épopée*, i, p. 349.

[5] A. Venturi, *Le Gallerie nazionali*, iii, 261, and Pl. IV; H. Graeven, *Adamo ed Eva sui cofanetti d' avorio bizantini*, in *L'Arte*, Rome, 1899, Fig. 1.

[6] At Darmstadt (Graeven, in *L'Arte*, as above, Figs. 2–6; Schlumberger, *Épopée*, i, p. 59), Florence (Bargello: Graeven, Figs. 11–14), in the collection of Monsignor Bethune (South Kensington Loan Exhibition, photographs: Graeven, Figs. 7 and 8), and in a private collection at Rheims (Graeven, Fig. 9). The last is possibly an early Western imitation.

Fig. 132. Side of the Veroli casket, ninth–tenth century,
in the Victoria and Albert Museum.

constant feature, has scriptural or religious subjects carved upon panels usually of small size. On all but one of these the story of Adam and Eve is found; the exception being the example in the Bargello at Florence, which is ornamented with figures of Our Lord, the Virgin, and saints. The borders of rosettes are here more elaborate, and they are sometimes combined with bands of vine-scrolls, either alone or enclosing birds and animals. It is probable that these caskets are later than the iconoclastic disturbance, and belong to a time when the pagan mythologic subjects were less popular. There are several isolated panels in existence which once formed part of caskets now lost. One is in the British Museum,[1] and represents the archangel of the Expulsion from Eden (Fig. 134); another is in the Museo Oliveriano at Pesaro, in which the whole scene is carved.[2] The latter is important with regard to the question of date, for either this or a similar panel, as

FIG. 133. Adam and Eve : end of an ivory casket of the twelfth century.

Graeven was the first to show, must have served Bonannus as a model for the rendering of the same episode on the bronze doors of the cathedral at Pisa : the arrangement and the treatment of the figures are identical, and Adam carries over his shoulder the same bifurcated hoe. The Pisa doors are a few years earlier than those made by the same artist for the Cathedral of Monreale, which are dated A.D. 1186; we may therefore assume that these caskets with religious subjects were already in existence about the middle of the century. As they are related to the class with pagan subjects by their similar rosettes, and since the attitude of a frequently recurring figure of Hercules has evidently influenced that of the Adam, as on the Darmstadt example, we may conclude that as a whole the caskets with Christian subjects are the later. Among the finest examples with the story of Adam and Eve

---

[1] *Catalogue of Early Christian and Byz. Antiquities*, No. 302.

[2] Graeven, Photos, Ser. ii, No. 49, and *L'Arte*, 1899, Fig. 16 A; A. Venturi, *Storia*, ii, p. 610.

are the panels in the Bargello and in the Pulszky and Oppenheim (now Morgan) collections respectively.[1] Probably they belong to the twelfth century, and the close resemblance between the saints upon the example at Florence and those upon a pierced Byzantine panel in the Victoria and Albert Museum (Fig. 142) supports this view, for the panel is probably not older than the close of the eleventh century at earliest. The panels (probably from a single casket) in the British and Berlin Museums respectively, with different scenes from the story of Joseph, are of the same class and period, the costumes and attitudes of the figures being similar. Their existence shows that other Old Testament subjects besides the story of Eden were used to adorn caskets, and perhaps an example of a similar kind was imitated by the sculptor of the remarkable casket at Sens. In these cases the miniatures in the Octateuchs (p. 464) were probably an important source of inspiration.

The curious casket in the Museo Kircheriano at Rome,[2] covered with scenes from the story of David, is clearly related to the caskets just described, in so far as the carver probably saw one of the kind and in general tried to imitate its style. A large number of small figures are displayed in dramatic action, but the types of the faces are notably different, the whole being vigorous but somewhat barbaric in its effect. It may be, as many critics have supposed, that this casket goes back to the second half of the ninth century ; but in this case its inferiority to the finer pagan caskets must be ascribed either to production in some provincial centre or to the work of a school very different from that which produced the casket of Veroli. There are details about it, however, which give rise to reflection, and suggest that it may be considerably later than has usually been supposed. For example, the large conventional leaf between the lower pair of figures on the lid is of a type which is commonest in the art of the twelfth century, and is found upon two ivories to which this date is usually assigned, one in the Museo Cristiano at the Vatican,[3] the other in the Museo Oliveriano at Pesaro,[4] the latter probably a Western imitation of a Byzantine original. This large and massive style of leaf frequently appears in Romanesque art, especially in enamels. The top of the lid, which is a truncated pyramid, is divided into two compartments, in the upper of which Our Lord is seen blessing an emperor and empress, while in the lower stand two adoring figures.[5] An iambic inscription in two verses invokes a blessing upon an imperial pair. The inscriptions round the sides are in even more corrupt iambics, and the lettering on two sides differs from that on the others, the form Σ appearing instead of the usual C. These sides are by another hand, and are probably a restoration : the substance of these lines is a eulogy of the bride and bridegroom. The casket must have been made on the occasion of an imperial or royal marriage. The treatment of the David scenes differs considerably from that usually found in

Fig. 134. The Archangel Michael : panel of the twelfth century, from a casket. (British Museum.) P. 220.

---

[1] Molinier, *Ivoires*, Pl. IX *bis*, Figs. 2 and 3.

[2] G. Schlumberger, *Mon. Piot*, vi, 1900, 191 ff. and Pl. XVIII ; A. Venturi, *Storia*, ii. 599 ff. ; H. Graeven, Photos, Ser. ii, Nos. 57–61 ; Westwood, *Fictile Ivories*, 354.

[3] R. Kanzler, *Avori*, Pl. XVI, Fig. 11 ; A. Muñoz, *L'Art byz. à l'exposition de Grottaferrata*, Rome, 1906, 115.

[4] H. Graeven, Photos, Ser. ii, No. 51.

[5] It has been held that the couple are a king and queen, not the emperor and empress ; and that the selection of scenes from David's life may point to a prince of the same name. As a possible personage the Bagratid prince David, who died in A.D. 894, has been suggested (Strzygowski, *B. Z.*, x, 1901, 729).

the Psalters which inspired other versions in minor sculpture, for instance the set of silver dishes found in Cyprus (p. 574).

Related in some respects to the group of caskets with figure subjects are two panels in the British Museum with the Valley of Dry Bones (Fig. 135),[1] and the Nativity: the treatment of the small nude figures of the rising dead in the former carving with their characteristic curly hair is, as stated, reminiscent of that which is often found in the mythological and other secular scenes. The inaccurate inscriptions give the impression of copies from written words not quite clearly understood, and illuminations in manuscripts may have supplied the carver with his models. In the style of the figures there is a great difference from that of the Harbaville triptych and ivories of its period; there is

Fig. 135.   Ezekiel and the dry bones: panel of the tenth century in the British Museum.

less certainty of execution, a less exquisite finish. If the triptych is of the tenth century, then these panels in the British Museum may be as early as the ninth, for their imperfections are those of an inexperienced rather than those of a decadent art. To the ninth century we may also assign the better among the caskets; but as there is a very considerable difference in the merit of various examples, it may be conjectured that this style of work, once having become popular, outlasted the iconoclastic period, and continued perhaps to the twelfth century, while ivories used for devotional purposes had begun to develop upon independent lines. The caskets may have been made in Constantinople; but there is no convincing evidence in favour of any particular locality. They were no doubt exported in considerable numbers, and seem to have been imitated in Italy. The panels with the Labours of Hercules on the chair of St. Peter in the Vatican appear, as Westwood[2] long ago suggested, to be related to those of the

---

[1] *Catalogue of Early Christian and Byzantine Antiquities*, Nos. 299, 300; *Catalogue of Ivory Carvings*, Nos. 18, 19.

[2] *Fictile Ivories*, p. 341. The argument of Garrucci attributing a Carolingian origin to

caskets, and may even have been derived from a casket. In this judgement Molinier concurred.[1]

The subjects upon the oliphants being largely zoomorphic and without inscription, it is very difficult to decide in particular cases whether they are Byzantine reproducing Eastern designs or whether they are original oriental work. As a class they date from the ninth to the twelfth centuries, a period when oriental motives invaded not only Byzantine art but the Romanesque art of Western Europe, and when the same motive may appear with but slight variation in Constantinople or Italy, in Granada or in France. M. Molinier's study of the oliphants led him to the conclusion that they may be divided into three groups: (1) those which are purely oriental; (2) those made in Constantinople after oriental models; (3) those made in the West in imitation either of Byzantine or oriental originals.[2] The conclusion is in the main accepted by Hampel,[3] who has, however, brought forward some interesting evidence in the endeavour to connect certain oliphants with a particular period of Byzantine art. The town of Jász-Berény in Hungary has 'from time immemorial' possessed

FIG. 136.   Panel from a casket of the eleventh–twelfth century.
(Victoria and Albert Museum.)

a horn on which, with bands of ornament consisting of interlacings, and connected circles containing monsters, birds, and animals of oriental style, there occur representations of acrobatic and other performances which are supposed to have as their scene the hippodrome of Constantinople. The small human figures, especially with their curly hair, recall those on the group of caskets already mentioned; while the conspicuous position given to an eagle possibly suggests a connexion with the symbol of Byzantine imperial power. The connexion with the casket group becomes more probable on comparing the oliphant with the two long panels from a casket in the British Museum, where dancers and acrobats of a not dissimilar character are represented. Another oliphant in the Cathedral of St. Veit at Prague[4] is ornamented with bands of animals somewhat similar to those of the Jász-Berény example, while the central part, instead of combats and acrobatic performances, has two broad bands in which chariot races round the 'Spina' are represented, a form of sport which certainly points to the hippodrome. A third example, in the same cathedral, shows in a broad band of ornament running round the mouth a racing

the chair on the ground that a bust amidst the scroll designs represented Charles the Bald, falls to the ground if Venturi is right in assigning this part of the work to the Renaissance. The panels on the chair are certainly of heterogeneous origin. See Garrucci, *Storia*, vi. 12; Venturi, *Storia*, i. 526 ff.

  [1] Molinier, *Ivoires*, pp. 91–2.

  [2] *Ivoires*, 93.

  [3] *Alterthümer des frühen Mittelalters in Ungarn*, ii. 920 ff.; *Archaeologiai Ertesítö*, N. S., xxiii, 1903, 97 ff. (reviewed, *B. Z.*, xii, 1903, p. 705). Supka, following Strzygowski, connects the Jász-Berény horn with N. Mesopotamia (*Lehel Kürtje Tanulmány*, Budapest, 1910, p. 63).

  [4] Hampel, *Alterthümer*, as above, 921–4, and Pl. 536–7; F. Bock, *Mittelalterliche Kunstdenkmale*, &c., 1860, ii. 136. The casket-panel in the British Museum is No. 301 in the *Catalogue of E.-C. and Byz. Antiquities*.

chariot issuing from an arch, and mounted acrobats. A curious cloisonné enamelled dish in the museum at Innsbruck (p. 500), which if not Byzantine must have been directly influenced by Byzantine models and dates from the tenth century, has also a group of acrobats, three of whom are seen upon a T-shaped apparatus balanced upon the head of a fourth. We thus have at least three oliphants which appear to have a connexion with the civil life of Constantinople; a fourth, formerly in the Spitzer Collection, is carved with bands of animals and conventional ornament like that of other examples, but in the central part with figures of Our Lord, the Virgin, angels, and Apostles, showing it to have been made for the use of Christians. Most of the other horns are ornamented with beasts, huntsmen, &c. Dr. Hampel proposes to amplify the classification suggested by Molinier, and divides them into four instead of three groups: (1) Horns like the two first mentioned, with hippodrome scenes; perhaps used to give the signal for actual performances in the circus. (2) Horns with hunting scenes, used in hunting. (3) Horns with animals, monsters, and floral ornament; these may have been used either for secular or for Church purposes. (4) Horns with religious subjects, used in churches and monasteries. We have already discussed the three horns which compose the first group. The second group is also small, consisting of some five examples, one of which is in the Victoria and Albert Museum.[1] The third group is far the largest, comprising about fifteen specimens. The fourth class is represented by a single horn—that above mentioned, with the figures of Our Lord and the Virgin.

A number of the above oliphants were probably made in Western Europe, some of them perhaps as late as the twelfth century; but for the reasons already stated it is exceedingly difficult in many cases to decide which may have been made in Constantinople and which in other places. There is little in the ornamentation of any examples which affords any precise indication of date: we can only say that characteristics of style place all the horns in the period between the ninth and twelfth centuries. The use of the zigzag band as a border or division and certain details of foliate ornament is common to some oliphants and an inscribed ivory panel (Fig. 138), perhaps part of a cross, now in the Kaiser Friedrich Museum,[2] to which the last quarter of the ninth century has been assigned as a date; but no absolute reliance can be placed upon the relationship, this ornament being of so simple a character. This panel, which is carved on all its sides, has on the front and back, which terminate at the top in a large round arch with scalloped niches, two groups of three half-figures, one of Our Lord between SS. Peter and Paul, the other the Virgin attended by the Archangel Gabriel, and crowning a youthful Emperor Leo; the two medical saints, Cosmas and Damian, are represented upon the narrow sides or edges. A long inscription[3] runs round the large arches and along the architraves; and the age of the emperor represented, together with the style, less finished than that of later work, makes it probable that the emperor is Leo VI, who came to the throne in A. D. 886, and that the cross of which the ivory formed part may have commemorated his coronation. Leo V (d. 820) must be excluded, in his quality of confirmed iconoclast.

Such indications by no means amount to proofs; but for the obscure period between the seventh and tenth centuries they are all the evidence available. It is quite certain that the ornament of the majority of the oliphants, whoever may have executed it, is derived from Eastern sources, and that much of it originally came from Sassanian Persia. The character of the animals, real or

---

[1] W. Maskell, *Description of the Ivories*, 37.

[2] Vöge, *Berlin Catalogue*, i, No. 7; G. Schlumberger, *Gazette des Beaux-Arts*, 1892, Pl. I, 118.

[3] The inscription runs: ΚЄ ЄN TH ΔΥΝΑΜЄΙ COY ЄΥΦΡΑΝΘΗCЄΙ ΛЄШN O BAC(ΙΛЄΥC) ΚΑΙ ЄΠΙ TШ CШTHPΙШ COY ΑΓΑΛΛΙΑCЄTAI CΦOΔΡΑ + ЄΝTЄΙΝON ⚹ BACΙΛЄΥЄ ΛЄШN ANAΞ + ΛΙTΑΙC ΦOΙTHTШN XPΙCT(Є) (H)ΓOY CШ ΔOΥΛШ. The first part is taken from Psalm xxi. 1; the latter part consists of two iambic verses.

fabulous, points in this direction, and so does their disposition in a diaper of interconnected circles such as we find on Sassanian textiles (p. 590).

It would be monotonous to consider in detail the Byzantine ivories of the tenth and two following centuries.[1] At their best they attain a technical perfection only equalled by French ivories of the thirteenth and fourteenth centuries ; and in many of the most beautiful examples there is not only dignity and grace, but the evidence of a fine artistic feeling.   Yet, like their Western analogues, they suffer

FIG. 137.   The Death of Jacob: panel from a casket of the twelfth century.
(British Museum.)   P. 230.

from the taint of monotony ; they express the same spirit too nearly in the same way ; the convention is high and delicate, but it allows too little scope for the intervention of creative genius.   Within the three centuries of their production, those ivories of the maturity are most difficult to date.   Subjective methods of

---

[1] Byzantine ivories of the Second and Third Periods may be studied in all the general works on ivory carvings cited above. Reproductions will be found in the large catalogues of the Kaiser Friedrich Museum at Berlin, the Vatican, and the British Museum ; in the Portfolio of Ivories of the Victoria and Albert Museum ; in the catalogues of the Meyer Collection at Liverpool, by F. Pulszky and C. Gatty ; in H. Graeven's two series of photographs ; in M. Schlumberger's historical works (*Nicéphore Phocas*, and *L'Épopée byzantine*, i and ii), where a considerable number are illustrated ; in the older publications : Gori, *Thesaurus diptychorum* ; Garrucci, *Storia*.   It is impossible to enumerate all the examples of so numerous a class ; but it will be found represented in England in the two great London museums, in the Free Public Museums, Liverpool, in the Bodleian Library at Oxford (Christ enthroned), and the Fitzwilliam Museum, Cambridge.   In France fine specimens are to be seen in the Louvre and the Musée de Cluny, which contain between them perhaps the most important examples of all (Giraudon's photos). The treasury of Troyes possesses the important casket mentioned below (p. 231). In Germany the Kaiser Friedrich Museum has important pieces, all catalogued (see above); the museums at Dresden, Hanover, and Darmstadt contain ivories of exceptional merit.   The treasuries of Aachen Cathedral, Halberstadt Cathedral, Trèves, and Quedlinburg have also ivories of the period.   Austria is not rich in work of this time, but the Imperial Museum possesses a beautiful diptych leaf, the companion to another at Venice (p. 228).   Italy has, besides the Cortona reliquary (p. 227), examples in the museums of the Vatican, Venice, and Florence; other pieces are to be seen in the treasury of Monza, and in private collections so well known as to be almost public—the Barberini and Stroganoff at Rome, the Trivulzio at Milan.   Many of the important Italian ivories are reproduced in Graeven's series.   Russia has various examples in the Hermitage and Stieglitz Museums at St. Petersburg.

appreciation assign the finest to the tenth and early eleventh centuries and distribute the rest over the whole later period from A. D. 1050 onwards. Molinier long

Fig. 138. Coronation of the Emperor Leo VI; Our Lord between SS. Peter and Paul. (Kaiser Friedrich Museum, Berlin.) P. 224.

ago insisted that for such a procedure no certitude can be claimed ; we cannot be sure that inferior workmanship proves a debased period ; it may equally result from the inferior talent of an artist living in a good period, or from the incapacity of a local school. It may be safely assumed that the really admirable work is of the time when the other arts conspicuously flourished under the Macedonian and Comnenian lines ; but in the East-Roman Empire we have not the assistance which in the study of Western mediaeval works we derive from contemporary major sculpture or from progressive changes in architecture and costume. Nor can we be quite sure that the last Renaissance of the fourteenth century altogether neglected this minor art ; some pieces even of great excellence may prove later than has hitherto been supposed, though there is little trace of a change in sentiment such as we observe in the painting of that epoch (pp. 19, 254).

Despite all these uncertainties we are not without some aids which enable us to arrive at an approximate date in many cases. The comparative study of miniatures in illuminated manuscripts is of high importance, for it may be assumed that, as in the West, the relation between the art of the ivory carver and that of the illuminator was particularly close, while the manuscript can more often be assigned to a particular year than is the case with other works of art. In one instance we have an ivory in its original position in an object dated within a few years by an inscription. On the front of a reliquary for wood of the true cross in the Franciscan Church at Cortona in Italy, dedicated, as an inscription on the back explains, by Stephen, a priest of Sta Sophia at Constantinople, in the reign of Nicephorus Phocas (A. D. 963–9), is an ivory panel[1] having at top and bottom two broad bands each containing three medallions with busts of Our Lord between Michael and Gabriel, and Constantine with Helen and Longinus, while the central part has standing figures of the Virgin, St. John the Baptist, St. Stephen, and St. John the Evangelist in the angles of a larger cross. The work is of fine quality, the figures are dignified, the draperies free from stiffness : there is an obvious advance upon the Berlin ivory of the time of Leo VI. But the hopes raised by the approximate dating of this panel are dissipated when we come to examine another ivory which must be a hundred years younger. This is the centre of a triptych[2] in the Bibliothèque Nationale at Paris (Fig. 139) representing Our Lord standing between Romanus (A. D. 1068–71) and Eudocia, to whom he gives his blessing : the names are indicated by inscriptions above the heads of the figures. The style is here the same as that of the Cortona panel, so that the triptych helps us but little for the purpose of dating other ivories with precision. We may mention a third panel bearing historical figures in the Musée de Cluny at Paris.[3] This is similar to that just mentioned, and shows Our Lord blessing Otto II of Saxony and Theophano, the Byzantine princess whom he espoused ; a small figure crouches at the emperor's feet—possibly the author or scribe of the manuscript upon the cover of which the ivory was fixed. This panel is of much poorer execution than the two others, so that if the Cortona relief were not in existence we might form erroneous conclusions as to the capacity of the ivory carver towards the last quarter of the tenth century.

Out of the large number of Byzantine ivories of the Third Period existing in various collections we may now mention a few of special merit or importance. The famous triptych in the Louvre known as the Triptyque d'Harbaville,[4]

---

[1] Gori, *Thesaurus diptychorum*, iii, Pl. XVIII ; G. Schlumberger, *Nicéphore Phocas*, 189 ; Venturi, *Storia*, ii. 578 ff., Figs. 411, 412. Even here there is room for doubt whether the Nicephorus in question may not be Nicephorus Botoniates (A.D. 1078–81). See Diehl, *Manuel*, 619.

[2] Molinier, *Ivoires*, 197 ; Venturi, *Storia*, ii. 583. Older references, Gori, *Thesaurus*, iii. 1 ; Lenormant, *Trésor de glyptique*, Pl. II ; Didron, *Ann. arch.*, xviii. 197 ; *Rev. arch.*, i, Pl. IV.

[3] G. Schlumberger, *Nicéphore Phocas*, 651 ; Louandre, *Les Arts somptuaires*, v. 67, and Plate ; Weiss, *Kostümkunde*, i. See also Westwood, *Fictile Ivories*, 397 ; Cahier and Martin, *Mélanges d'archéologie*, i. 186. The inscription begins OTTO P̄MAN and ends : +ΘΕΟΦΑΝѠ IM̄P ĀḠ, and Γѡ ('Ιωάννης ?) perhaps referring to the smaller figure. The genuineness of this plaque has been questioned, but it was apparently seen by the two Benedictines Martène and Durand at the beginning of the eighteenth century (*Voyage littéraire*, ii. 29) : it was then upon the cover of a Book of the Gospels in the Abbey of Echternach near Trèves.

[4] Best reproduced by Molinier, *Ivoires*, Pl. IX. Cf. also Ch. de Linas, in *Revue de l'art*

perhaps the most finished work of the Byzantine school, has all the elegance of a French ivory of the early fourteenth century and may have been produced in the interval between the date of the Cortona reliquary and that of the panel with Romanus. The rich ornamentation of the back, perhaps representing the triumph of the Cross in the Garden of Eden, has features which reveal the influence of oriental decorative art, and the whole work is instinct with a delicate and sumptuous charm. It is true that formal rows of saints are not a subject which gives scope for composition or inventive power, but in the pose, and in the expression of individual faces, the carver has shown himself to be an artist who appreciated both nature and the antique. The large triptych in the Museo Cristiano at the Vatican is evidently a later reproduction of a similar scheme. But it is difficult to follow French archaeologists in assigning it to so late a period as the fifteenth century : the thirteenth century is perhaps late enough to account for the inferiority of workmanship.[1]

Fig. 139. Our Lord crowning Romanus and Eudocia : centre of a triptych of the late eleventh century. (Bibliothèque Nationale, Paris.) P. 227.

A second large triptych in the Biblioteca Casanatense in Rome[2] follows the scheme of the Harbaville triptych more closely than does the Vatican example, but the figures are heavier and coarser, and the work suggests a later period. But even here the arguments in favour of the fifteenth century do not appear convincing. They are partly based upon the occurrence of the name Constantine in one of the iambic verses carved upon the central band dividing the upper and lower groups in the interior. This has been referred to the last emperor of Constantinople, though the absence of the usual title δεσπότης has not failed to excite remark. But it does not seem necessary to associate the triptych with an emperor at all : it may have been made for any personage of wealth or consequence.

Another ivory of importance is a diptych, probably of the eleventh century, the two halves of which are now separated, one being in the Museo Archeologico

chrétien, 1885 ; G. Schlumberger, Mélanges d'arch. byz., 71 ff. ; Gazette des Beaux-Arts, 3ᵉ Période, v, 1891, p. 294 ; Venturi, Storia, ii. 584 ff. ; R. Kanzler, Gli avori dei musei sacro e profano, &c., Pl. VII and VIII.

[1] Ch. de Linas, in Revue de l'art chrétien, 1886 ; Molinier, as above, p. 104 ; Venturi, Storia, 588 ; A. Muñoz, L'Art byzantin à l'exposition de Grottaferrata, 1906, 103 ff.

[2] Muñoz, Grottaferrata ; De Linas, as above.

at Venice,[1] the other in the Imperial Museum at Vienna.[2] The first has upon it figures of St. Paul and St. John the Evangelist ; the second those of St. Peter and St. Andrew. The Apostles stand with books in their hands, dignified in attitude and expression, their long mantles falling in logical and graceful folds. Their names are carved in intaglio near their heads ; but across the top of each leaf is an inscription in two iambic lines cut in relief. The lines on the Venetian leaf are :

CΚΕΥΟC ΘΕΟΥΡΓΟΝ CΥΛΛΑΛΕΙ ΤΩ ΠΑΡΘΕΝΩ
ΒΛΑΒΗC CΚΕΠΕCΘΑΙ ΔΕCΠΟΤΗΝ ΚΩΝCΤΑΝΤΙΝΟΝ.

Fɪɢ. 140. Triptych of the eleventh century. (Kaiser Friedrich Museum, Berlin.) P. 230.

On the leaf at Vienna is the following couplet :

ΩC ΑΥΤΑΔΕΛΦΟΙ ΜΥCΤΟΛΕΚΤΑΙ ΤΩΝ ΑΝΩ
ΝΕΜΟΙΤΕ ΛΥΤΡΟΝ ΔΕCΠΟΤΗ ΚΩΝCΤΑΝΤΙΝΩ.

The identity of the imperial donor thus twice named cannot be established with certainty on account of the frequent recurrence of the name Constantine in the tenth and eleventh centuries.[3]

---

[1] Gori, *Thesaurus diptychorum*, iii, Pl. XXVIII, XXIX ; G. Schlumberger, *Gaz. des Beaux-Arts*, 3ᵉ Période, xiii, 1895, 379–81 ; Venturi, *Storia*, &c.. ii, Fig. 414, p. 585 ; *C. I. G.* 8784.

[2] In the *Münz- und Antikenkabinett*. Westwood, p. 78.

[3] Gori considered the emperor to be Constantine Porphyrogenitus ; Von Sacken and F. Kenner thought Constantine Ducas (ᴀ. ᴅ. 1059–67) ; M. Schlumberger suggests Constantine, brother of Basil II (1025–28), or Constantine Monomachos, third husband of Zoe (1042–58).

The leaves of another fine diptych, probably also of the eleventh century, are separated in a similar manner. One carved with the *Noli me tangere* and the *Anastasis* is in the museum at Dresden ; the other, with the Crucifixion and Descent from the Cross, is in the Hanover Provincial Museum.[1]

It is impossible to notice individually the numerous ivories of the Third Period, which maintain a high average of excellence : a complete list of such works would be of value, and might bring us nearer to the precision in the dating of Byzantine carvings at present so difficult to achieve. We may specially mention, however, the Virgin and Child in the Stroganoff Collection,[2] the triptychs with the Crucifixion in the Cabinet des Médailles[3] of the Bibliothèque Nationale, Paris, and of the Kaiser Friedrich Museum (Fig. 140) ; the triptych panels with figures of the Virgin at Utrecht[3] and Liége, the seated Christ in the Bodleian Library,[4] and several panels in the Victoria and Albert Museum, one with busts of St. John and four saints upon a pierced ground (Fig. 142). As far as our knowledge goes, those ivories which in correctness of proportion, skilful treatment of drapery, and careful modelling of the extremities approach the excellence of the Harbaville triptych may with probability be assigned to the tenth and first half of the eleventh centuries. Those in which the figures are elongated, the faces monotonous in expression, the draperies poorly rendered, and the extremities out of proportion may be assumed to belong to a later date than the panel of Romanus and Eudocia, and may be conjecturally placed in the twelfth and thirteenth centuries. It has already been stated that careless-ness of finish and inferiority of style need not necessarily imply any great differ-ence in date : these defects may be due to the incapacity of inferior craftsmen turning out to order works of moderate price. We cannot be certain that all the second-rate work is late, though a parallel decadence in illuminated manu-scripts justifies the conclusion in the majority of cases. We seem to trace the existence of different schools even among the ivories of high merit. Those which have hitherto been selected for special mention have been chiefly dis-tinguished by a certain sculptural dignity. But in several panels the aim is picturesque, and the influence of miniatures may be assumed. In the panels with the Ascension in the Kunstkammer at Stuttgart, in the Bargello at Florence,[5] and in the Stroganoff Collection, Rome,[6] and those with the Washing of the Disciples' Feet and the Forty Martyrs in the Kaiser Friedrich Museum,[7] the careful composition of the groups and the tendency to dramatic action suggest the inspiration of pictorial art. Such ivories as the casket panels in the British[8] and Kaiser Friedrich Museums[9] with the Story of Joseph (Fig. 137) were perhaps inspired by illuminated Octateuchs. Of this picturesque group there are also numerous late or inferior examples apparently related to illuminated miniatures : the panel with the Entry into Jerusalem in the British Museum[10] may serve as an illustration of these (Fig. 13).

The great majority of these ivories of the Third Period represent subjects from the New Testament, or figures or busts of sacred persons, saints, and Apostles : in this predilection the Byzantine ivory carver resembled his Western colleague. The destination of diptychs and triptychs as devotional tablets explains the predilec-tion. A certain number of panels are, however, ornamented with subjects from the Old Testament. Of these we may cite the series already mentioned as in the British and Kaiser Friedrich Museums, which once formed part of a single casket, and are carved with the Story of Joseph. Caskets were well adapted for a sequence of historical scenes, and since they were mostly made for secular

---

[1] G. Schlumberger, *Épopée*, ii. 216 and 217 (Figs.).
[2] Graeven, Photos, ii, No. 67. This figure of the Virgin is admirable in its simple dignity.
[3] Diehl, *Manuel*, Fig. 311. The panel is in the Archiepiscopal Museum.
[4] Ibid., p. 624, Fig. 314.   [5] Graeven, *Elfenbeinwerke*, ser. ii, No. 34 (photo).
[6] Graeven, ibid., No. 70.   [7] Vöge, *Berlin Catalogue*, Nos. 8 and 9.
[8] *Catalogue of Early Christian Antiquities*, No. 302ᵃ ; *Catalogue of Ivory Carvings*, Nos. 20 and 21.
[9] Vöge, *Catalogue*, Nos. 13 and 14.
[10] Nos. 302ᵇ and 19 in the two British Museum Catalogues.

purposes they were less rigorously confined to religious subjects.   The well-known casket in the treasury of the Cathedral of Troyes affords an example with secular designs.   It is flat topped, and, originally dyed purple, was probably part of the booty from the sack of Constantinople assigned to Garnier de Traisnel, almoner of the Crusade, who himself died in the East [1] (Figs. 11, 144–5).

On the lid is represented a circular structure surmounted by circular and rectangular buildings with gable and conical roofs, and having in the base a gateway in which an empress (?) stands, holding a diadem (?) in her hands. On each side, facing outwards, is a mounted emperor with a lance, wearing the diadem with pendants and a cuirass of scale armour with a chlamys.   The symmetrical disposition of these figures suggests that they may be imitated from a textile design, and may be intended to represent a single personage. The sides have hunting scenes, full of life and vigour, and the ends birds in foliage.   On the front we see a lion-hunt; on the back, a man on foot attacks with his spear a huge boar assailed from three sides by as many dogs, each of which wears a collar.   The date may be the eleventh century.

The ivory covers of the Psalter written and illuminated for Melisenda, daughter of Baldwin II, King of Jerusalem (A.D. 1118–31), and wife of Fulk, Count of Anjou and King of Jerusalem (A.D. 1131–4), do not represent a pure Byzantine art.[2]   The subjects on the two covers, scenes from the Story of David and the Works of Mercy, are treated in a style which makes it difficult to say whether we are in presence of East-Christian work produced under

Fig. 141.   Our Lord : figure from a panel of the eleventh century. (Victoria and Albert Museum.)

Western inspiration, or Western (French) work strongly affected by an Eastern environment.   Each scene is enclosed in one of a series of interconnected circles, six on each leaf ; the interspaces on the cover with the Story of David are filled with the Combat of the Virtues and Vices, based upon the Psychomachia of Prudentius ; those on the other cover are occupied by spirited representations of struggling beasts and by single birds.   The borders are ornamented with scrolls of vine foliage; enriched upon one side with interlacings, vases, and pecking birds, and (upon the upper band) two fish.   The nature of the figure subjects, and especially their coincidence upon the same work of art,[3] suggest that the scheme is of Western conception : the armour of Goliath appears

---

[1] Le Brun Dalbanne, *Memoires lus à la Sorbonne en 1863*, p. 212, Pl. II ; Molinier, *Ivoires*, pp. 92–3 (Figs.) ; Schlumberger, *Épopée*, i, pp. 673, 714 (Figs.).

[2] The Psalter is in the Department of MSS. in the British Museum, and is exhibited in the Grenville Library.   It is illustrated in the British Museum *Catalogue of Ivory Carvings*, already quoted, Nos. 28–9, Pl. XV and XVI.

[3] The same combination of subjects is found on the Romanesque enamelled crozier in the Bargello at Florence (*Gazette Arch.*, 1887, Pl. XVIII).   Lethaby believes the Melisenda book-covers to have been made in Anjou (*Proc. Soc. Antiq. of London*, 1911.

Fig. 142. Pierced panel of the eleventh-twelfth century: St. John and other Saints. (Victoria and Albert Museum.) P. 230.

to be Western, and all the inscriptions are Latin.   On the other hand, the royal costumes are Byzantine ; the ornament of the borders has far more affinity with Eastern (Armenian) motives than with anything French.   Moreover, the treatment of the beasts recalls that of Mohammedan ivory carvers, especially those who worked for the Moorish princes of Spain, and relationships of the same kind appear in the disposition of the vine border of the lower cover.   We need not suppose that the carver of these panels was influenced from Spain, but

Fig. 143.   The Entry into Jerusalem :   panel of the tenth–eleventh century.
(Kaiser Friedrich Museum, Berlin.)

rather that he drew from the same Asiatic sources from which Spanish-Moorish art derived its peculiar character.   The miniatures within the book are for the most part the work of a Greek painter, Basilius ; and if we recall the mosaics of the Church of the Nativity at Bethlehem (p. 414), executed by Byzantine craftsmen for Latin princes, we may perhaps incline to the opinion that these ivory covers were produced under similar conditions.   But the blending of Eastern and Western elements is so intricate, and the style so exceptional, that it is difficult to pronounce any certain opinion.

Throughout their history, a period of some thousand years, the ivory carvings of the Christian East were imitated by the craftsmen of the West.   The large composite diptychs and the *pyxides* of the fifth and sixth centuries were copied in Carolingian times : well-known examples of copies are the book-covers from the Abbey of Lorsch, now in the Victoria and Albert Museum (Fig. 146),[1] and the

[1] Nos. 138–66, W. Maskell, *Description of the Ivories*, 53 ; and V. and A. Museum, *Portfolio of Ivories.*

Museo Cristiano at the Vatican.[1] The book-cover in the Bodleian with Our Lord trampling on the asp and basilisk,[2] which is of the same period, is an imitation of such a composite work cut from a single piece of ivory, though the model is held by some to have been made in Italy. A single panel of this model has actually been preserved and is now in the Kaiser Friedrich Museum.[3] The British Museum possesses a Carolingian pyxis which must have been inspired from an original of the same kind as those which we have considered above (Fig. 148).[4]

In the South of Italy after the ninth century a school or schools of ivory carvers produced a large number of panels clearly based on Byzantine models. The series on the paliotto at Salerno[5] is the most familiar example ; single panels showing the same peculiarities of style in various stages of decadence are to be found in different collections, e. g. the museums of Berlin and Bologna. One, of a finished but dry style, representing the Raising of Lazarus, is in the

Fig. 144.   Top of the casket of the eleventh century in the Cathedral of Troyes.
(From an electrotype.)   P. 231.

British Museum.[6] It is allied to the group of panels in the Museo Archeologico at Milan,[7] representing scenes from the life of St. Mark and formerly assigned by Dr. Graeven to the sixth century. It seems probable that they are all of later date and of about the eleventh century.

We have seen that the caskets of the ninth and following centuries were imitated in Northern Italy in the twelfth ; other panels were produced there towards the same period. Attention may be drawn to two panels in the Museo Olivieri, Pesaro ;[8] a pair of panels on a MS. in the Barberini Library, Rome, with the Ascension and Pentecost ;[9] a panel in the collection of Count Stroganoff at Rome, with the Nativity.[10] The Byzantine arrangement of busts of saints in interconnected circles or medallions, as seen for instance in a panel in the Museo Civico, Bologna, is imitated on a book-cover in the Cluny Museum at Paris.[11]

Another interesting example of apparent imitation is the casket in the

[1] R. Kanzler, Avori, Pl. IV.   [2] Westwood, Fictile Ivories, Pl. VI, p. 55.
[3] Haseloff, in Prussian Jahrbuch, xxiv, 1903, p. 47.   [4] Catalogue of Ivory Carvings, No. 43.
[5] Arundel Society's casts in Victoria and Albert Museum ; E. Bertaux, L'Art dans l'Italie méridionale, i. 433'; Venturi, Storia, ii, Figs. 458–69 ; Schlumberger, Épopée, ii. 265 ; Westwood, 91.
[6] Catalogue of Early Christian Antiquities, No. 290 ; Catalogue of Ivory Carvings, No. 27.
[7] Graeven, Photo, ii. 42 ff. ; a panel in the V. and A. Museum belongs to this series, No. 270, 1867 ; Portfolio of Ivories, Pt. III.
[8] Graeven, Photo, No. 51 ; E. Modigliani, L'Arte, ii, Rome, 1899, 291 f.
[9] Modigliani, as above, 290 ; Graeven, Nos. 55 and 56.
[10] Hermanin in L'Arte, 1898, 5 ; Graeven, No. 75.   [11] Les Arts, April, 1902, p. 12.

Cathedral of Sens.[1] It is dodecagonal, with a conical lid having the same number of surfaces. The panels covering the body are divided into two horizontal zones, the uppermost surmounted by a tympanum. On the lower zone are scenes from the life of David; on the upper is represented the Story of Joseph. The tympana contain gryphons and beasts of prey, confronted peacocks, &c.; while in the spandrels and along the top of each panel is conventional foliage partly derived from the acanthus. The figure subjects are not unskilfully grouped, and, as Molinier has remarked, some of the details, especially the drawing of the horses, suggest analogies with the casket at Troyes (p. 231). The beasts of prey and monsters are carved in a bold and free style; they may have been derived from textile models, as was probably the case with the oliphants and certain Byzantine caskets already mentioned. But though in the reminiscences of the antique and in details of decoration we trace an influence of Byzantine models, we may agree with Venturi that there is a certain vivacity and absence of convention in the art of this casket which removes it

Fig. 145. Front of the casket in the Cathedral of Troyes. (From an electrotype.) P. 231.

from the company of Byzantine ivories. One scene, a banquet given by Joseph to Jacob, is not to be found in the Bible story; in another, the Anointing of David, Samuel and the young king are alone in the field with the flocks, the scene thus completely diverging from the traditional Byzantine rendering. Again, in the combat of Goliath and David, the giant, contrary to all rule, is mounted on a horse; and throughout the treatment of the costumes is unusual.

Other North-European examples are the three early panels with the Crucifixion at Essen, at Tongres, and in the Musée de Cluny, and another Crucifixion formerly in the Spitzer Collection.[2]

The Bargello at Florence possesses a panel with the Maries at the Tomb[3] which must have been made in Northern Europe, though the Byzantine inspiration is clear; and the group of panels sometimes classified as Rhenish-Byzantine, of which the Victoria and Albert Museum possesses five examples,[4] must be assigned to the artistic centres of the Middle Rhine. Two panels on the covers of a Book of the Gospels at Würzburg closely imitate the Byzantine style of the tenth–eleventh century, and in one the Greek characters of the names are preserved. Both have figures under canopies in open-work.[5] Too much

[1] Millin, *Voyage dans les départements du Midi*, i. 97, Pl. IX and X; G. Schlumberger, *Nicéphore Phocas*, 647; E. Molinier, *Ivoires*, 106; A. Venturi, *Storia*, iii. 367 ff. and Figs. 346–59; Viollet-le-Duc, *Dictionnaire du mobilier français*, i. 80. All sides of the casket were reproduced in fictile ivory by the Arundel Society, and may be seen in the Victoria and Albert Museum.
[2] Molinier, *Ivoires*, 139–40. [3] Graeven, Photos, ii, No. 26; Venturi, *Storia*, ii, p. 625.
[4] Nos. 144-5 (1866), 371 (1871); W. Maskell, *Description*, &c., 63; V. and A. Museum, *Portfolio of Ivories*, Pts. X and XI; Venturi, *Storia*, vol. iii, Figs. 360–2.
[5] J. von Hefner Alteneck, *Trachten, Kunstwerke und Geräthschaften*, &c., i, Pl. 38 and 41.

stress need not be laid upon the importation of Byzantine models by Theophano, the Byzantine princess who married Otto II ; on the other hand. it is an exaggeration to deny all artistic importance to such a marriage. The strong influence of Byzantine art in these regions during the Romanesque period is proved by a study of the illuminated manuscripts (see p. 490). We may suppose it to have been a steady factor in artistic development, not the casual result of any particular historical event. Vöge has shown reason for the belief that even the vigorous but uncouth group of German ivories dating from the tenth century, of which the Crucifixion on the Echternach Gospels at Gotha and other panels at Berlin and Paris are interesting examples, were partly inspired by Byzantine models.[1] It is needless to pursue the subject further : sufficient examples have been adduced to show that, like illuminators of MSS., European ivory carvers between the ninth and thirteenth centuries frequently depended upon models from the Christian East.

It has already been observed that at more than one period the East-Christian carver in ivory exerted an important influence upon the early mediaeval sculpture of Western Europe. It has been suggested (p. 103) that a probable instance of this is found in our own country, where the remarkable stone sculpture of Northern England,[2] dating from the seventh century, can hardly have arisen independently of foreign models, either in the form of illuminations or ivory carvings. This sculpture, best represented by the figures upon the high crosses of Bewcastle and Ruthwell (Fig. 147), appears very suddenly and decays with great rapidity ; its rise and fall are those of an exotic art which flourishes during the persistence of exceptional conditions but is unable to maintain itself when they are withdrawn. The half-figure of Christ at Rothbury, not a hundred years later than the Bewcastle cross, shows all the symptoms of decadence ; the staring eyes, the elongated lips, the drapery channelled rather than modelled, are all evidence of a growing incapacity. Yet even here an ancient type is preserved, one which we also find in Carolingian miniatures of about the same period. But with the crosses of Aycliffe and Ilkley, and the fragment from Gainford, the decay is complete : the human figures have almost sunk to conventional hieroglyphs without pretence to natural truth. It can hardly be doubted, therefore, that this meteoric appearance of a monumental sculpture in Northumbria must be ascribed to external influence.[3] To the question from what quarter this influence proceeded there is only one probable answer: it must in the first instance have come from the East of the Mediterranean. Neither in Ireland, nor in the Frankish dominions, nor in Italy, do we know any sculpture at all comparable with this, or any art in which the human figure is treated with equal ability. But although, by a method of elimination, we are driven to seek the models in the Byzantine Empire, the problem has only lost a part of its difficulty. For in the East at this time monumental sculpture had already ceased to be used upon any extensive scale for sacred subjects ; statues of emperors were still erected (p. 122), but they were probably devoid of merit. It is improbable that either in the East or in Italy there were any contemporary sculptors capable of executing or inspiring work in which the effects of a fine tradition are obvious. The inspiration must have come, as Mr. Prior has already suggested, from the minor arts, and more probably from minor glyptic art than from painting ; in this case the models are more likely to

---

[1] Prussian *Jahrbuch*, xx, 1899, 177.

[2] For a good account of this sculpture see Messrs. Prior and Gardner's articles on English sculpture in the *Architectural Review*, xvi, 281-2, xvii, pp. 87 ff., and their forthcoming book on the same subject.

[3] Rivoira, *Lombardic Architecture*, tr. G. M°N. Rushforth, 1910, concludes that, on account of the beauty of the figures, the Ruthwell cross cannot be earlier than the twelfth century. But the Bewcastle and Ruthwell crosses are of the same age, and the former is dated by the mention of Alchfrith. The Ruthwell runes are accepted by English scholars as late seventh century, or very little afterwards. Runes would have been unintelligible in the twelfth century. Rivoira also doubts the early date of the Acca cross.

have been ivory carvings than metal reliefs. The purely ornamental decoration of the crosses are northern developments of motives, the more conspicuous of

FIG. 146. Book-cover of the ninth–tenth century, carved in the Frankish dominions after an East-Christian model. (Victoria and Albert Museum.) P. 233.

which are probably of Syrian origin, and their tall slender proportions are characteristic of the North.[1]

The probability of inspiration from ivory carvings, even at this early time, is

[1] The custom of setting up over a grave an upright stone carved with a cross was, however, known in Egypt and Armenia.

increased by a parallel case at a later period, where the existence of a model in ivory can hardly be doubted. Vöge[1] had long ago insisted that Byzantine ivories must have helped to inspire the Romanesque sculpture of Southern France. It remained for Prof. Goldschmidt to produce a definite instance in the half-figure of the seated Christ in a tympanum of the Church of St. Godehard at Hildesheim.[2] He showed that in Saxony the sudden change, at the very end of the twelfth century (A. D. 1190–1210), from an 'archaic' to a natural style can only be explained by the sudden intervention of a foreign influence. The comparison which he draws between the Christ of the tympanum and a Byzantine ivory in the Victoria and Albert Museum makes the nature of the model clear. The difference between the Hildesheim sculpture and such an earlier work as the Christ at Gröningen is inexplicable on any other hypothesis. In the same manner, the treatment of the face and hands of Bishop Adelog of Hildesheim (d. A. D. 1190) in his monument in the crypt of the cathedral of that city, shows an enormous advance upon the sculpture of the preceding decades ; it has individuality and a subtle delicacy of expression, the modelling of the features again recalling that of the Byzantine ivory carver. In other figures, as for example the Apostles at Halberstadt, the treatment of the draperies is so close to that which we find upon Byzantine ivories that it is difficult to avoid the theory of a direct influence : the small mannerisms, the arrangement of particular folds in particular positions, are reproduced with great fidelity ; the imitation is especially clear in the case of the folds covering the shoulder.[3] By degrees the Western artist endeavoured to outbid his teachers, exaggerating the number of the folds, suggesting violent movement and unwittingly diminishing the true plastic effect. It is the same phenomenon which made its appearance a little earlier in the case of illuminated manuscripts : modelling is subordinated to the linear and calligraphic style to which artists of inferior training naturally resort. There is an example of a similar proceeding at an earlier period in the case of the group of Carolingian ivories to which the Sneyd *pyxis* in the British Museum belongs (p. 234).

Fig. 147. Sculpture of the seventh century on the Ruthwell cross, influenced by an East-Christian model. P. 236.

[1] *Repertorium*, xxii, 1899, 95 ff., xxiv, 1901, 195 ff.   [2] Prussian *Jahrbuch*, xxi, 1900, 230 ff.
[3] Ibid., pp. 233–5.

It would be possible to draw up a considerable list of Romanesque sculptures in which the influence of Byzantine ivories is highly probable. But the above, which are crucial cases, suffice to prove its existence.[1]

STEATITE CARVINGS.

With Byzantine ivory carvings is closely allied a whole group of minute sculptures in steatite, serpentine, or fine schist.[2] The subjects of these carvings are almost entirely religious, resembling those of the ivories; and though a few are of excellent quality the majority of specimens are of little artistic merit: most are three or four inches in height, but some are as large as ivory plaques of average size. There are traces in some cases of gilding, and it is probable that,

Fig. 148. Ivory *pyxis* of the ninth century, carved in the Frankish dominions after an East-Christian original. (British Museum.) P. 234.

like ivories, they had a polychrome decoration, which has in the great majority of examples entirely worn away. The stone in itself is softer than ivory and suffers more rapidly from attrition. These steatite carvings do not appear to go back beyond the tenth century, most of them dating from the eleventh and twelfth centuries; but many are later still, for this kind of work survived the overthrow of the Byzantine Empire, and examples are found among the products of Russian[3] and modern Greek religious art. A number of spurious examples are said to be in existence.[4]

In the following paragraphs some of the more interesting and accessible carvings in various collections may be noticed.

[1] Cf. also A. Michel, *Histoire de l'art*, &c., i. 597–8.
[2] According to Lapparent, serpentine and steatite are abundant in Greece and Asia Minor. See H. de Villefosse, *Bull. Soc. Ant. de France*, 1900, 317 ff.
[3] Examples assigned to Russian art of the eleventh–thirteenth centuries are in the Khanenko Collection at Kieff. See *La Collection Khanenko*, Kieff, 1902, Livraison V, Pl. XXXVII, Figs. 1303 ff.
[4] J. Strzygowski, *B. Z.*, xv, 1906, 423.

Fig. 149. Panel of the twelfth century, carved in steatite with the 'Twelve Feasts'
of the Church, Toledo. (*Hautes Études*: E. Roulin.) P. 242.

The British Museum[1] has several examples, but none of exceptional merit. Three have half-figures of the Virgin and Child ; three others representations of saints ; two have Gospel subjects, one the Nativity, the second, which is a fragment, the figures of Our Lord and a soldier from the scene of the Passion.

In France the Louvre possesses several steatites with figures of saints (one,

Fig. 150. Panel of the thirteenth–fourteenth century, carved in steatite with the Twelve Feasts: Monastery of Vatopedi, Mount Athos. (*Hautes Études*: G. Millet.) P. 242.

with St. Demetrius, in exceptionally high relief).[2] There is a St. George in the museum at Angers.[3]

The collection of the Comtesse de Béarn[4] contains at least two fine examples, one being especially remarkable. It is a panel with subjects in two zones : at the top the *Etimasia* (Ch. XII) between SS. Michael and Gabriel ; below, four saints (Demetrius, Theodore Stratelates, George, and Procopius) each accompanied by his name, while an inscription in four iambics extols the warrior saints. Other panels have SS. Demetrius,[5] Chrysostom, and George.

M. Schlumberger's own collection contains a panel with Constantine.[6]

Italy is rich in steatite carvings. The Museo Cristiano in the Vatican has several examples. A panel has SS. George and Theodore Tyron on one side and

---

[1] *Catalogue of E. C. and Byz. Ant.*, Nos. 108, 111, 112, 115-19.
[2] G. Schlumberger, *Épopée*, ii. 45, 57 (Figs.), and *Mon. Piot*, ix, 1902, 231, and Pl. XX.
[3] The same, *Épopée*, ii. 132.
[4] The same, *Mon. Piot*, as above, 229 ff., and Pl. XX.
[5] Ibid., 235; *B. Z.*, i, 1892; Diehl, *Manuel*, 627.   [6] G. Schlumberger, *Épopée*, ii. 277.

SS. Michael and Daniel on the other;[1] another S. Theodore Stratelates,[2] probably of the eleventh or twelfth century, and resembling an ikon on Mount Athos; others have a bust of Our Lord, and the Pentecost;[3] a wooden panel[4] is inlaid with a number of steatite carvings, a beardless saint (Panteleemon ?) in the middle, and round the border smaller panels amongst other carvings in ivory.

In the Church of S. Anzano near Florence there is a fine carving of the Archangel Gabriel, partly gilded; at Lentini another, with Constantine and Helena.[5]

In Germany the Kaiser Friedrich Museum possesses several examples. One has St. Therapon, Bishop of Cyprus;[6] another Our Lord between the Virgin and St. John.[7] Spain possesses, in the panel in the cathedral at Toledo, carved with the Twelve Feasts of the Church (Fig. 149), the largest example in existence.[8]

In the Hermitage Museum at St. Petersburg are several plaques.[9] One of about the eleventh century, from Cherson, has SS. Demetrius and George;[10] another from the same site has part of a seated Virgin.[11]

In the Khanenko Collection at Kieff are two plaques with St. George and St. Andrew respectively.[12]

On Mount Athos the Monastery of Vatopedi has a finely carved panel with the Virgin and Child (*Hodegetria*), and another with SS. George, Demetrius, the two Theodores, and other saints, both framed in painted panels: these carvings are probably of the twelfth century, that representing the Virgin going back to a model of about the sixth.[13] There is a larger panel with the Twelve Feasts[14] (Fig. 150); another has a standing figure of St. George.[15]

An example with the 'Twelve Feasts' in the Church of St. Clement, Ochrida, is of rough workmanship and assigned by Kondakoff to about the sixteenth century.[16]

[1] A. Muñoz, *L'Art byz. à l'exposition de Grottaferrata*, 124.
[2] R. Kanzler, *Gli avori*, &c., Pl. XI, Fig. 7.
[3] Muñoz, as above, Fig. 86.   [4] Ibid., p. 120, and Fig. 85.
[5] G. Schlumberger, *Mon. Piot*, iv. 232 ; Salinas, *L'Arte*, vi.
[6] Schlumberger, *Épopée*, ii. 85.   [7] Ibid., 105.
[8] G. Schlumberger, *Épopée*, i. 465 (Fig). A somewhat similar example was in the Carmichael Collection sold at Christie's, May 12 and 13, 1902, *Catalogue*, No. 150.
[9] G. Schlumberger, *Épopée*, i. 539.
[10] Ibid., 13 (Fig.).   [11] Ibid., 152 (Fig.).
[12] *La Collection Khanenko*, Kieff, 1902, Livraison V, Pl. XXXVII, Figs. 1301, 1302.
[13] Kondakoff, *Monuments of Christian Art on Mount Athos*, pp. 147–8 ; Schlumberger, *Épopée*, ii. 273.   [14] Ibid., 524.
[15] *Hautes Études*, photo C. 193 ; *Manuel*, 626.
[16] Kondakoff, *Macedonia*, 1909, 270, Fig. 185.

CHAPTER V

PAINTING: I. MURAL PAINTINGS AND PANELS

It has been stated in an introductory chapter that Byzantine art suffered the disadvantage of never passing through an archaic stage; it inherited too much, and as a result of its rich endowment rendered too unquestioning a homage to tradition. In consequence of this habit of acquiescence it was too ready to accept the copy and cartoon in place of nature; it received too easily that ecclesiastical prescription which gradually assumed over it an excessive control. When, as must have often been the case, the model itself was an academic work of the late Hellenistic period, the Byzantine copyist often stood at a second remove from nature. The Campanian fresco-painters of the earlier empire are found to have taken their figures from one more ancient picture and their background from another,[1] and the practice was not their own invention but widely adopted in the Graeco-Roman world. The model of the Christian artist must often have been itself a cento without organic cohesion; nor is it remarkable to find in Byzantine art, as in literature (p. 18), the effects of this disregard for essential principles of unity. Here and there in the

---

[1] W. Helbig, *Untersuchungen über die Campanische Wandmalerei*, 1873, 348; G. Rodenwaldt, *Die Composition der Pompeianischen Wandmalerei*, 1909, 52, 77, 132.

history of Byzantine painting we find evidence of an interest in nature and a realism apparently based upon intelligent and interested observation. But for the most part, alike in the province of figure painting and that of landscape, the artist sees through other eyes than his own. It must be admitted that the difficulties with which he had to contend were serious. As a rule he was debarred by circumstance from the proper study of the human form, for religious sentiment was averse from the representation of the nude, and religious sentiment was extremely powerful. The conditions of life were altogether different from those which had obtained in ancient Greece. The ascetic or the monk, not the athlete, was held up as the ideal; the nude came to be regarded as something in itself disgraceful; and there is little evidence that even the draped model was generally employed. Figures produced by artists who knew little of anatomy are naturally unconvincing; too often they support their draperies but do not wear them; sometimes the draperies appear to have an almost independent existence. Facilities for study from the life were very restricted, whereas copies were abundant and easily procured. Continued copying checked the growth of a natural or vigorous style, and elementary errors in drawing were often committed whenever a copy was not available. Nevertheless the careful preservation of good tracings and miniatures of a good period, the continuity of tradition, the general obedience to manuals of composition so well studied that they were known by heart, united with the pursuit of sound technical methods and an understanding use of colour to ensure a pleasing effect even in the case of figure subjects.

In the treatment of landscape and architecture there is the same indifference to reality, the same acquiescence in routine, though here the excuse is less obvious.[1] The most characteristic features of Byzantine landscape are hills symmetrically disposed in pairs, with a conventional vegetation of trees or plants, the smaller of which are sometimes dotted over the surface in such a way as to resemble a continuous pattern. The hills are composed of prism-shaped rocks, the tops of which form sloping or horizontal planes, and are strongly lighted, contrasting with the vertical sides remaining in deep shadow.[2] The trees which cling to this barren ground are mere schematic forms of the 'mushroom' and other types, copied and recopied until all connexion with nature is lost: only cypresses, palms, and dead trunks faithfully suggest the vegetation of the actual world. In the foreground a formal band of green is diapered with conventional flowers. The architecture is composed of colonnades, porticoes, and artificial units fantastically but symmetrically arranged, though here there is more observation of reality than in the case of natural objects. Occasionally we recognize a domed church of a familiar type, and habitable houses are depicted.[3] But for the most part the buildings are clearly a congeries of

---

[1] This subject has been excellently treated by Dr. Kallab in the Austrian *Jahrbuch*, xxi, 1900, pp. 1 ff.

[2] Early examples in the Vienna Genesis (p. 444).

[3] The palace of Theodoric in the mosaics of S. Apollinare Nuovo at Ravenna has features

motives handed down from generation to generation, and there can be no
question of an honest attempt to render things actually observed.   If the
scene represents an interior, the fact is merely indicated by accessories
suggesting the inside of a house:[1] thus an arcade with an ambo before it

Fig. 152.   Mural paintings, Sta Maria Antiqua, Rome.   (N. H. J. Westlake,
       History of Design in Mural Painting.)   P. 304.

suffices to indicate the interior of the Temple at Jerusalem.   All the features
of this conventional *mise en scène* point back to Hellenistic art and the
Roman art which its principles helped to form.   The prism-shaped rocks
may be traced through Roman frescoes to Hellenistic bas-reliefs.[2]   The archi-

in common with the ruined houses of Syria, and gives proof of some attempt at realism ; in
MSS. and mosaics of the eleventh and twelfth centuries realistic features such as bulbous domes
are seen (mosaics of Bethlehem).   The Menologium of Basil also appears to represent particular
churches, and M. Millet believes that characteristic local features are thus preserved.   But
here conventional walls and buildings usually close the scenes.

   [1] Examples in the Vienna Genesis (see especially the scene in which Abraham receives
the promise, and that representing the drunkenness of Noah).   The most striking feature in
these indicated interiors is the absence of a roof.   The prison of St. John in the Codex
Rossanensis, and that in which Joseph is incarcerated, in the Vienna Genesis, are like boxes
with the lids off.

   [2] Schreiber, *Die hellenistischen Reliefbilder*, Pl. XC.

tecture descends from that of Pompeian frescoes, through such conventional designs as those in the dome-mosaics of St. George at Salonika, or of the Baptistery at Ravenna.[1] The process of schematization, gradual down to the fifth century, was rapid at a later date. In the earliest monuments there is still an attempt to render a self-contained landscape, as in the mosaics of Sta Maria Maggiore at Rome, the miniatures of the Vienna Genesis, and those of the original of the Joshua Rotulus; whereas in the Ravenna mosaics and the miniatures of the Codex Rossanensis, the Gospel of Rabula, the Vatican Cosmas, freedom and invention already give place to motives of a stereotyped design. The typical Byzantine landscape is fixed by the time of the Menologium of Basil II (tenth century), though a few books of a deliberately archaizing character, such as the Paris and Venice Psalters (see p. 468), reintroduce for a while the features of late Hellenistic art.[2] In the eleventh century the conventional forms win the upper hand, and they are characteristic of the Comnenian period, the art of which directly influenced that of Tuscany. By the thirteenth century they predominated in Italy,[3] and it was only by degrees that the Italian painters of the Trecento emancipated themselves from this Byzantine pupilage. In the work of Duccio and his successors its influence is manifest; it may be seen in the works of other painters, including Lorenzo Monaco; even the fifteenth century shows survivals of the ancient inspiration.[4] Naturally the style penetrated wherever Middle-Byzantine art obtained a firm foothold; it is found in the mosaics of S. Marco at Venice, and in those of Monreale in Sicily, though in the latter case the peculiar motives are treated in a somewhat original manner. Byzantine landscape retained to the last the limitations of the Hellenistic model. The poetical effects produced by the modern power of rendering atmosphere with its varying lights and shadows and vague receding distances were unknown to the antique artist, who depicted everything with a clear contour and ignored the suggestion of things half perceived.[5] The seizure of the evanescent phase, the passing aspect, which depends upon the quick perceptual power of the individual, was not for him; his art is impersonal and unobservant. A gulf separates Byzantine painters from their contemporaries, the great artists of the T'ang and Sung period in China with their penetration of the most intimate secrets of inanimate nature.

[1] For the unreal character of painted architecture, see Rodenwaldt, as above, 124. Festooned drapery on columns and walls connecting one point with another was of Hellenistic origin; it lasted through the Middle Byzantine period, and is nowhere more conspicuous than in the late frescoes of Mistra.

[2] Rodenwaldt argues for the Italian (Roman) origin of developed landscape backgrounds (as above, 27, 77, 132). If Vitruvius is correct, landscape began in the second Pompeian style; at any rate, it was general in the fourth. The famous Odyssey landscapes in the Vatican, which are of a romantic character, are among the oldest in which depth of space is consistently depicted. On these see K. Woermann, *Die antiken Odysseelandschaften*, 1876 ; B. Nogara, *Le Nozze Aldobrandine*, 1907 ; F. Wickhoff, *Wiener Genesis*, 79.

[3] Kallab, as above, 28.

[4] For an example of the Comnenian work which influenced Italian art see the panel in the British Museum mentioned on p. 319 (Fig. 155).

[5] This point is well brought out by Helbig, as above, 353-65.

Wickhoff, in the brilliant introduction to his edition of the Vienna Genesis, has attached much weight to the persistence in the fifth century of an impressionist method of painting which he describes as illusionism. In this style the artist so depicts his subjects that they may appear natural at a certain distance and that distance only. When examined closely, the subject is found to be a crude arrangement of diverse colours placed harshly in juxtaposition; at the calculated distance the colours blend, and the proper effect is produced. That such methods were employed in late Roman or late Hellenistic art is indisputable; they may have developed from scene painting and the scenic Pompeian style; they were always imposed upon the artist in mosaic, where a face or other detail is grotesque at a near view, and natural only when the spectator stands sufficiently far away. But though some early artists practised them, it need not be assumed that they were ever generally representative of East-Christian painting, which both in figure and landscape remained faithful to the contour or the silhouette; there is no merging or 'irradiation', but a clear outline defining each essential form.[1] And the fact that in process of time the artist relied more and more upon pre-existing compositions must have itself proved a sufficient discouragement to illusionism. Didron has described the system of the monk-painter Joasaph in the Monastery of Esphigmenou, as he saw it practised in the year 1839,[2] a system which probably differed little from that of older Greek painters. Elaborate compositions were executed with the utmost rapidity from memory alone, the artist reproducing forms which were not seen but mentally conceived: with the relative and temporary validity of impressions he was not concerned. A consistent illusionism is even less characteristic of Byzantine art as a whole than a consistent realism.

The average painter of the Christian East perhaps knew better how to convey the sense of depth in his composition than the great Apelles, for the power to render receding space came late in Hellenistic times.[3] But, like many artists of the Roman imperial period, he preferred to avoid the greater difficulties, manipulating natural features in order to limit the view by a near or middle distance, which he intended as a scenic background for the figures.[4] In the same way he often draws a screen of walls and buildings across the picture to avoid the necessity of rendering distant objects. Through the prevalence of such methods a conventional and monotonous character is given to the scene in which the figures are

---

[1] For a criticism of Wickhoff's position see J. Poppelreuter, *Kritik der Wiener Genesis*, pp. 26 ff.

[2] *Manuel d'iconographie chrétienne*, 65 (edition of 1845).

[3] Rodenwaldt, as above, 3, 9–10. Wickhoff maintained the limitations of Apelles' art in the representation of depth; his opinion upon this point has, however, been disputed. In any case, distance was well understood at the time when the Odyssey landscapes in the Vatican were painted, though in some examples the view is not carried as far as the horizon. The same applies to the landscapes in the villa of Fannius Sinistor at Boscoreale (F. Barnabei, *La Villa Pompeiana di P. Fannio Sinistore*, &c., Pl. IX, X).

[4] Th. Schmidt, in a paper read before the Russian Arch. Inst. at Constantinople, has attempted to analyse the chief characteristics of Byzantine landscape and trace them to their respective sources. See the notice in *B. Z.*, xix, p. 240.

set, and the tendency to the repetition of stock motives was yet further increased.

It is stated in the Caroline Books that the contemporary Greeks regarded painting as a consecrated art: *dicunt enim artem pictoriam piam esse*, a statement confirmed by much that we know of Byzantine theory and practice. But it must not be inferred from this that there was no important secular art in the Christian East. The wealth and patronage

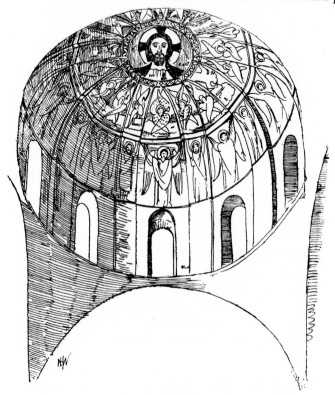

Fig. 153. Painting in the dome of the Church of the Redeemer, Athens.
(N. H. J. Westlake, *History of Design in Mural Painting.*) P. 293.

of the Church, always rivalling those of prince and nobles, in later centuries excelling them, undoubtedly gave to religious art a real and growing preponderance. The vicissitudes of fortune have exaggerated this advantage; for as sacred buildings have survived in far greater numbers than any others, and religious books outnumber the secular in a high proportion, it is easy to overestimate the predominance of the sacred art and the subordination of the profane. In the one case material is fairly abundant; in the other it is even scantier than we might have hoped to find it. The literary references given below (p. 258) would alone suffice to prove that through the mediaeval centuries secular art flourished both in the capital and the provinces, a conclusion which might indeed have been deduced from a general knowledge of social conditions; for down to the later years of decadence, the number of the leisured and wealthy class was always considerable in the East-Roman Empire. We have descriptive notices of the secular style of decorating churches obtaining in early times, and of frescoes and mosaics with historical subjects set up by various emperors and nobles in their palaces, from Theodosius to the Palaeologi, a period covering the whole range of time between the fourth and the fifteenth centuries. The preponderance of sacred over profane subjects was perhaps more pronounced than in the

FIG. 154. The Story of David : illumination from a Psalter of A. D. 1066 in the British Museum. (Add. MS. 19352.)

West, but it was at no time absolute or exclusive.[1] Among the surviving representatives of secular subjects may be specially noted the mosaic pictures representing Justinian and Theodora at Ravenna, that representing Constantine IV in S. Apollinare in Classe, mosaic portrait figures at Salonika and Kahrié Djami at Constantinople (p. 418), frescoes at Kuseir 'Amra (p. 278), Kieff, and Mistra ; illustrations in historical and other MSS. and on coins, ivory carvings, and other minor works of art are numerous. Few though they are compared with subjects of a sacred character, they may at any time be reinforced as a result of new discoveries.

[1] M. Diehl, in his *Manuel d'art byzantin,* has insisted upon the danger of under-estimating the extent and influence of secular art.

With these reservations we may admit that the solemn shadow of the Church lay over Byzantine art, affecting its mood and directing its procedure. In the representation of sacred scenes the Church had the controlling voice. The Council of Nicaea had decreed that the composition of each subject down to the smallest detail was the province of the theologians; the part of the artist was confined to execution. It is difficult in any country to give an individual accent to the works of an idealist art; under the conditions which prevailed in the East-Roman Empire it was perhaps impossible. The conservatism natural to ecclesiastical prescription was not counterbalanced, as in the West, by the growth of independent nationalities with different tastes and sentiments. In the West, during the five centuries between Charlemagne and Charles V of France, there was a succession of artistic styles, each affecting several countries and representing a general change in the feeling for beauty and in the manner of its expression. The sentiment of the Carolingian differed from that of the Anglo-Saxon; that of the Ottonian is even more distinct. Still more striking grow the changes when Romanesque passes into the art of the thirteenth century. Compare a Carolingian with a Gothic version of an identical subject, and the distance between the two is seen to be immense: for good or evil there has been growth and evolution along lines which it would have been hard to prophesy. But compare two Byzantine Crucifixions, one of the ninth, the other of the thirteenth century, and sentiment, conception, and composition will be found essentially the same. Though there may be a difference in quality, the two might almost be the work of a single artist whose life had been miraculously prolonged. For the Eastern Church, beauty of form has always been secondary to the correct and intelligible expression of theological ideas; the painter must be theologian first and artist second. The manuals of the Greeks, from the prototype of the ' Painter's Manual ' discovered by Didron on Mount Athos [1] to the *podlinniks* of the Russians, are concerned with iconography before everything: if the forms employed to express the idea are pleasing, it is well; if not, it matters little, for dogmatic truth must be considered before visible beauty.

With the tyranny of the antique upon one side and the prescription of the Church upon the other, the Byzantine art was often so preoccupied with rules and reasons that it was prevented from following creative lines. The painter was never quite free to choose his own subject and treat it in his own way. Even in the rarer secular motives, such as the hunting scene or the ceremonial group, an antique method, a *mos maiorum*, was always to be considered. In the rendering of animals and sometimes of plants we often seem to mark an independent observation; this is most noticeable in

[1] The age of this book is less considerable than Didron supposed. The monk Dionysius, who wrote it, is now known to have lived late in the fifteenth century. The Russian manuals, of which the earliest go back to the sixteenth century, are partly theoretic, partly pattern-books or collections of drawings. M. Pokrovsky has given an account of both kinds in his *Monuments of Christian Art and Iconography*, but as the book is in Russian the abbreviated version promised by M. Muñoz will be doubly welcome to the English reader. Cf. Didron, *Manuel d'iconographie chrétienne*, 1845 ; Constantinides, Ἑρμηνεία τῶν ζωγράφων, Athens, 1885 ; Diehl, *Manuel*, 774.

Fig. 155. Painting on panel : Annunciation, Nativity, Baptism, Transfiguration :
thirteenth century. (British Museum.) P. 319.

the illuminations of MSS., where the painter was under a less rigid control. But in the more numerous cases where the subject was religious, the consecrated manner of treating it had to be followed. Well was it for Byzantine art that the inventors of the type-compositions representing scriptural and devotional scenes were for the most part the Greek or Hellenizing artists of the Eastern Mediterranean who had still a sense of beauty and were masters of the methods known to Hellenistic times.

From the preceding paragraphs it might perhaps be inferred that Byzantine painting has no proper and intrinsic character, no merits of a quality to justify its high pretence. Such a verdict would be hardly less unjust than that which dismissed all Byzantine history as a tedious and uniform tale of weakness and misery. In spite of its manifest defects, it maintains an honourable place among the arts of the world. To understand its position we must accept it as an art based upon ethical and intellectual foundations; its chief aim is not the expression of personal emotion, but the embodiment of a general human ideal to which it always makes ulterior reference. No individual feeling is ever suffered to interfere with this set purpose of edification; not the feeling of the artist or spectator but the nature of the subject is always the primary aim. But Byzantine art, more especially when it works upon a large scale, is actually exalted by its limitations. Through those very theological restrictions which forbade devotion to created things as objects of beauty only, the artist was held in the path of noble simplicity, and the power of bold and wise renunciation was communicated to his work. He was obliged to paint for the instruction of all whom religion concerned, and therefore for a majority composed of simple people. He was compelled to omit the inessential detail in order not to confuse the story; for the sake of the spectator he must preserve a breadth and simplicity of composition. He dared not confuse his outlined figures by too conspicuous or realistic a background; salience and life must be given not by heavy and graded shadows but by unbroken flat tints in a key which is always clear and brilliant. This method, which is largely oriental, admirably accords with the architecture, itself mainly oriental, to which Byzantine painting in its highest manifestations is so closely allied. As in the case of Western mediaeval art, the very conventions adopted for ulterior aims contribute to a greater majesty of effect. The clearly outlined figures, their contours filled with colour boldly massed, possess a mystical and superhuman quality in presence of which anatomical defects appear of no account. By adopting the natural and inevitable methods of its environment, by fulfilling dominant religious needs, this art, which set out to instruct, achieved an independent value as magnificent and congruous decoration : through renunciation it rose to grandeur.

So far for the redeeming features of theological restriction; those resulting from technical limitation often tend in the same direction. Whether they painted in tempera or in mosaic, the two methods upon which they principally relied, Byzantine artists were impelled to a lofty repose and gravity of style, a convention supremely suited to their purpose, a mannerism at unity with itself. The weakness of tempera painting lies in the difficulty with which deep tones and shadows are produced, those tones and shadows with which lighted and shaded planes are composed into a structure and vitality is most puissantly suggested. They can only be produced by repeated washings and hatchings; the colour dries too fast for blending; touches can only be applied side by side or superposed. It is no process for the inspired fury of creation; but it well accords with the solemnity of a religious art. Its finely luminous tints, contrasted by the skill of the hereditary colourist, will yet evoke the sense of life; above all,

Fig. 156. St. Peter rescued by Our Lord; miniature of a Psalter of A.D. 1066 in the British Museum. (Add. MS. 19352.) P. 470.

of the mystical life essential to the sacred subject, the existence which is simple, renunciant, composed. If this is true of painting, it is yet more true of mosaic, in which a wise convention, a solemn glow of colour, is the one secret of success. Producing results such as those which survive at Ravenna, at Salonika, at Constantinople, and in Attica, the limitations of mosaic may well be described as splendid; the art which brought it to perfection may not be denied the elements of greatness.

Byzantine art may have set small store by personal emotion; it may have cared too little for the immediate aesthetic impression, too much for the ethical content; in the sight of those who dissociate aesthetic from practical feelings it may appear too objective, too didactic, too wedded to the general type. But among systems of artistic expression which achieve greatness by fidelity to a fixed principle of estimation and a theory of values consistent with broad ideals, which reject the precarious impression and hold fast to the enduring symbol, it must stand with the art of the Western Middle Ages in a position which may indeed be assailed but can scarcely be overthrown. It will have the suffrage of all who believe that art for the sake of art is not the final word in criticism; but that some of the power in beauty is drawn from the diffused experience of humanity and rises from the general heart of men.

Byzantine painting was essentially conservative and faithful to the laws of its being. It remains perhaps an open question whether it would have belied its truer nature if it had pursued to the end the innovating path which began in the fourteenth century and was still followed in the Morea when the armies of Mohammed conquered Greece. In this late renaissance it relaxed in some measure its austerity and definitely inclined to the picturesque. The number of the figures in the traditional subjects was increased, accessories became more numerous, the atmosphere was more dramatic; at the same time we miss something of the solemn effect of the earlier figures, the relief and salience, the mystical distinction of their comparative detachment. We seem to discern traces of this changed spirit in the mural paintings of Nerez as early as A. D. 1164 (p. 296): the mosaics of Kahrié Djami (p. 416), but above all the frescoes of Mistra (p. 293), reveal its full development. The new movement must have begun in the capital, whence it spread through the agency of migratory painters carrying the Byzantine manner into the various countries of Eastern Europe. It may fairly be described as Greek; it is unnecessary to suppose a controlling foreign influence from

Fig. 157. The Descent into Hell (*Anastasis*), from a twelfth-century Gospel in the British Museum. (Harley 1810.)

Italy or elsewhere. The literary suggestions in descriptive writers such as Choniates, Manuel Philes, or Eugenikos, who devoted themselves to the principles of Alexandrian aesthetics, would alone almost suffice to explain the new freedom and sentiment which now transformed a traditional art. But the Crusades had brought East and West together, and there resulted a ferment of ideas by which the Byzantine Empire was insensibly affected. The earliest manifestations of the new spirit appeared too soon in the East to owe their existence to a direct influence of Giotto or his followers, nor is it necessary to suppose that in later times particular Greek artists studied Italian work line upon line or precept upon precept. The similarity may perhaps result from a process comparable to that which, in another sphere of knowledge, physiologists describe as germinal interfusion. Under the new tendencies Byzantine art became more emotional; it was more and more devoted to the illustration of hymns and liturgies. Indulgent of episode, prone to luxuriance, it attracts by a pleasing air of opulence and ease; a breath of freedom has passed over it and given it a new but softer life. But for the Turkish conquest the world might have witnessed a development along lines very different from those actually followed in countries obedient to the orthodox Greek Church.

The natural relation between the literature and art of a country is evident in the several Byzantine periods. After the literary revival between the ninth and twelfth centuries, a high level was attained by many authors writing in various fields. But although there is a polished ease of style with a superficial appearance of unity, a closer examination reveals the characteristics of the cento. Poetic flowers of antiquity, Hellenistic innovations, ecclesiastical, official, and technical expressions, all contribute to form a whole which is created by dexterity rather than by genius.[1] But apart from this resemblance, which may be ascribed to the operation of like general causes, we may note a more particular link connecting letters and representative art. As the earlier descriptions or criticisms of works of art by Pliny, Petronius, and Philostratus[2] are of considerable service to the study of Hellenistic and Roman painting, so the later literary descriptions of Christian times are not without their importance. The second book of the Κύκλος of Agathias, an anthology compiled in the time of Justinian, is entirely devoted to epigrams descriptive of works of art. But the writers to whom we are most indebted take as their model the *Imagines* of Philostratus, in which a whole gallery of pictures is described and criticized. The name ἔκφρασις[3] was given to such descriptions whether composed in prose or verse. They continued down to the fifteenth century, and might be of considerable value were it not for our doubts as to the extent to which the author draws on his imagination or parades his accomplishments as a connoisseur. We have an example of late date by Eugenikos in the fifteenth century[4] which might well have been composed for the picture of the burial of St. Ephraim in the Christian Museum of the Vatican.[5] In this case there is a close correspondence between picture and description; and if all other ἐκφράσεις are as conscientious and exact, they throw a certain light upon Byzantine methods of composition. Many

[1] See Krumbacher's remarks, *Geschichte*, p. 30.

[2] W. Helbig, *Untersuchungen über die Campanische Wandmalerei*, 61 ff.

[3] Such works were written by Johannes Mauropus (Euchaites), middle of eleventh century (Krumbacher, p. 740), and Manuel Philes (c. A.D. 1275–1345), who describes works of all kinds, pictures, sculpture, coins, gems, books, &c. (Krumbacher, p. 777). See also A. Muñoz in *Nuovo Bullettino di archeologia cristiana*, 1904, 221; *Repertorium*, 1904, 390; *L'Art byzantin à l'exposition de Grottaferrata*, 35 ff.

[4] C. L. Kayser, *Philostratei libri de gymnastica qui supersunt : Accedunt Marci Eugenici imagines*, &c., Heidelberg, 1840; Muñoz, *Grottaferrata*, 37. For Eugenikos, see Krumbacher, p. 115.

[5] Reproduced by Muñoz, *Grottaferrata*, Fig. 14, p. 33.

modern poets have written verse of a similar tendency. Keats, whose genius was pictorial, has described Titian's 'Bacchus and Ariadne' almost in the manner of an ἔκφρασις, and his ode to a Grecian urn, like several of André Chénier's shorter poems and Rossetti's sonnets, falls within the same descriptive category.

It is clear even from documentary evidence that during the First Period paintings were executed on walls, on canvas, and on panels.[1] In

FIG. 158. Alexander pursuing Darius ; Bellerophon and the Chimaera : miniature from a tenth-century MS. of the Cynegetica of Oppian in the Marciana, Venice (Gr. 479). (*Hautes Études* : G. Millet.)

the last case the encaustic method, of which so many examples have been preserved, was very commonly employed.[2] This is a process which was much practised in Egypt, as the numerous portraits upon late mummy cases now in European collections abundantly prove. The remarkable panels from Sinai described below (p. 316) show that it continued in

---

[1] For the technique of Byzantine painting see E. Berger, *Beiträge zur Entwicklungsgeschichte der Maltechnik*, Munich, 1897.

[2] Διὰ τῆς κηροχύτου γραφῆς, Eusebius, *De vita Const.*, iii, c. 3. Ἐγὼ καὶ τὴν κηρόχυτον γραφὴν ἠγάπησα, Homily of St. John Chrysostom, cited by John of Damascus (Migne, i, p. 1313). Quoted by Bayet, *Recherches*, p. 67. On the encaustic method see Helbig, *Wandgemälde der Städte Campaniens*, pp. x xxx. That the encaustic method was employed upon walls as well as panels appears to be certain ; see Emeric David, *Histoire de la peinture au moyen âge*, pp. 96-7.

favour rather later than was at one time supposed; but it seems to have fallen into disuse by the time of the Macedonian renaissance. For mural decoration both fresco and tempera were used, though the latter was the most in favour.[1] In the former process the colours are applied without a vehicle to plaster still wet, in the latter a medium is used upon a surface which has been allowed to dry; but in both cases the wall is covered with more than one layer, the first being coarse and mixed with straw, &c., the later of finely pulverized lime in which hair or cotton may be added to give cohesion. Vitruvius prescribed the use of no less than six coats of plaster, the first three of sand and lime, the last three of marble pounded with increasing care; the uppermost, upon which the work was done, was polished.[2] The picture was executed in colours mixed with lime, in some cases so thickly applied that the figures seem to stand out in relief. True fresco has the merit of great permanency, due to the formation of carbonates and sometimes silicates of lime after drying.[3] But its scale of colours is more restricted than in the case of tempera, and it requires a rapid and unerring hand, since it cannot be retouched when the plaster is dry. True fresco appears to have been known to Minoan artists, though the Egyptians used tempera.[4] The Greeks and Romans also knew fresco, but frequently painted with a medium, which was commonly made of fig-sap and white of egg.[5]

The majority of East-Christian and Byzantine wall paintings were executed in tempera, the colours being applied to plaster already dry, and mixed with some kind of medium such as glue, size, gum, or white of egg. M. Clédat is of opinion that all the early mural paintings in Egypt are in tempera.[6] In these the vehicle was often weak, with the result that the painting flakes off at a touch, or even under the influence of atmospheric exposure. This is especially the case with greens and blues: reds and ochreous tints are less perishable. As a rule the artist first outlined his subject in yellow or red; the shading was done with a green or blue tone, and the folds of draperies were indicated by red, yellow, or black lines, with high lights in white. The conclusions derived from a study of these ancient Coptic mural paintings prove the great conservatism of East-Christian art; it has been observed that the methods of the monastic painter Joasaph studied by Didron in the Monastery of Esphigmenou on Mount Athos in 1839 very nearly resemble those used by the Copts more than a thousand years earlier. The figures were outlined in red, and green

---

[1] Kuṣeir 'Amra is described as painted in true fresco (p. 280), and some of the work in the Cappadocian rock-cut churches is considered to have been done by this method (p. 267).

[2] See the article by H. Stuart Jones, *Quarterly Review*, No. 419, April, 1909, 436.

[3] For technical information on fresco and tempera see James Ward, *Fresco Painting*, 1909; A. P. Laurie, *Greek and Roman Methods of Painting*, 1910. In ' Fresco secco' the plaster, which has been allowed to dry, is re-wetted with water, and colours without a medium are used; the results are not so permanent as with true fresco. In spirit-fresco the colours are ground in a wax medium and thinned with spirits of turpentine or oil of spike. For historical facts and information of a more general character see also Mrs. Herringham's translation of Cennino Cennini's *Trattato della pittura*. For the artistic qualities of tempera, see R. E. Fry, *Burlington Magazine*, June, 1905, p. 175.

[4] Ward, as above, 11.   [5] H. Stuart Jones, as above, 437.

[6] Article *Baouît* in Cabrol's *Dict. d'arch. chrétienne*, p. 232.

and blue tones were freely used in shading.[1] Joasaph followed the rules given in the Manual, rules which had no doubt come down from ancient times, perhaps from a date as early as that of the paintings at Bawît or Saqqarah. His treatment of flesh is interesting, explaining the sombre and sallow appearance of so many Byzantine faces. A dark colour was first applied by an assistant; the master then added three coats of yellow, allowing each to dry before the next was added; but in the parts to be represented in shadow, the dark was not completely concealed; shading was completed with blue and green pigments, and darkness was counteracted where necessary by the addition of a little more yellow: cheeks and lips were heightened with red. It is interesting to note that the eyes were left to the last. The pupils were added in black upon the original dark ground, the sclerotic in white; a dot of delicate pink as the final touch gave life and brilliance to the expression.

In panel paintings tempera was probably universal, and they must have been executed very much as the Manual directs.[2] The wood was first covered with size, which was allowed to dry. Then three or more coats of fine gesso and size were successively applied. Gilding generally had a ground of ochreous red; upon this gold foil was laid and moistened with alcohol,[3] which caused it to adhere sufficiently to admit of burnishing. If we may judge from the evident traces of red beneath the gilding in MSS., a similar ground was employed in illuminations, though in describing gilding upon paper, Dionysius only mentions gum.[4]

Like the earlier mediaeval painters of Western Europe, Byzantine artists did not paint in oil. It is interesting in this connexion to recall the priority of the Orient in the discovery of oil colours. There is oil painting on the Tamamushi tabernacle in Japan which is dated as early as the sixth century.[5]

Although at Rome, in Egypt, and elsewhere examples of mural paintings of the early period are now becoming known, the literary references to what is lost show how small is the proportion still preserved. The conditions, atmospheric and other, have been adverse to survival, though, as will shortly be shown, the remains which have come down to us are in some cases remarkably extensive and in better condition than might have been expected. M. Bayet and others have published the literary evidence in so accessible a form that it is only necessary to notice some of the more important examples.[6]

The Eparch Olympiodorus, asking the advice of St. Nilus as to the decoration of a church to be erected by him in the fourth century, suggests motives from the chase or country life, such as had been usual up to this time. The saint recommends a series of subjects from the Old and New Testament in chronological order,[7] those of the two Testaments to be kept on opposite sides of the church, as was apparently the case of S. Maria Antiqua at Rome. Paulinus describes paintings of the new Church of

---

[1] Didron, *Manuel*, 65 ff.   [2] Ibid., pp. 26–7.   [3] Ibid., p. 31.
[4] Ibid., p. 46.   [5] Binyon, *Painting in the Far East*, p. 84.
[6] Bayet, *Rècherches pour servir à l'histoire de la peinture*, &c., 60 ff.
[7] *Letters of St. Nilus*, Bk. iv, ch. 61; see Garrucci, *Storia*, i. 593; for the passage in full, and for other references, J. Reil, *Die altchristlichen Bildzyklen des Lebens Jesu*, p. 58.

St. Felix at Nola,[1] and Prudentius, if Prudentius, and not a Carolingian, be the true author, parallel pictures from Old and New Testament for the decoration of church walls.[2]

The triclinium of Bishop Neon, which may have actually adjoined the Basilica of Ursus at Ravenna, was adorned with either frescoes or mosaics

FIG. 159.   St. John the Evangelist dictating to a scribe : miniature from a MS. of Simeon Metaphrastes in the British Museum. (Add. MS. 11870.)   P. 480.

representing the Creation of the World, the Story of Peter, the Psalm *Laudate dominum de coelis,* and the miracle of the Feeding of the Five Thousand.[3]

---

[1] The text and literary references are given by J. von Schlosser, *Quellen zur Kunstgeschichte des abendländischen Mittelalters* (in Eitelberger's *Quellenschriften für Kunstgeschichte*), Vienna, 1896, 13 ; see also J. Reil, *Die altchristlichen Bildzyklen des Lebens Jesu,* 57.

[2] On his *Dittochaeum* see von Schlosser, as above, 3 ff. As to the doubt of authorship see J. Reil, as above, pp. 59–60.

[3] Agnellus, *Liber Pont., Vita S. Neonis* (Migne, *Patr. Lat.,* cvi. 518); F. Wickhoff, *Repertorium für Kunstwissenschaft,* xvii ; E. K. Riedin, *Viz. Vrem.,* ii, 1895, pp. 512 ff.

Asterius, Bishop of Amaseia (d. A.D. 403), gives a lengthy description of mural and other painting in Asia Minor.[1] An epigram in the Anthology describes the Church of St. Polyeuctes, founded in the fifth century, and mentions paintings in the vaults representing episodes in the life of Constantine.[2]

Choricius of Gaza, in the sixth century, describes frescoes in the churches of that city with considerable detail.[3] They were all derived from the New Testament, and included the Passion scenes.

Several epigrams in the Anthology, chiefly by Agathias, who lived in the early part of the sixth century, are descriptive of paintings, though it is not certain that these are all mural.[4]

To commemorate a miracle of the Holy Cross at the time of the capture of Antioch by Chosroes in A.D. 540, the circumstances attending it were painted on the ceiling of the church.[5] Before leaving the subject of the painted decoration of church walls, we may note the existence of similar scenes and cycles in the early mediaeval centuries in the West.[6]

Allusions by St. Basil and St. Gregory of Nyssa to works of art[7] may refer in part at least to panels; the painting representing the martyrdom of St. Euphemia described in one of his sermons by Asterius, Bishop of Amaseia in the fourth century, appears to have been on canvas.

There are other references to what appear to be panel pictures, of which only a few need be transcribed. The death of a blasphemer named Olympius, who lived in the reign of Anastasius, was commemorated by a picture painted by order of the emperor, and suspended in the baths where the sinner was miraculously punished.[8]

Christophoros of Mytilene (d. about A.D. 1050) alludes to a picture of the Forty Martyrs.[9]

It has been already stated that secular subjects, though surviving in comparatively small numbers, were not neglected by the East-Christian artist. The letter of Olympiodorus to St. Nilus (see above) proves that in the first Christian centuries secular designs were used in the decoration even of churches; the mosaics of Sta Costanza in Rome, and the Nilotic scenes in other churches, remain to afford ocular evidence of a widely distributed custom. Some of the frescoes of Kuṣeir 'Amra, probably by a Greek artist (p. 280), perhaps give an idea of this decoration as it

---

[1] Migne, *Patr. Gr.*, xi : Strzygowski, *Kleinasien ein Neuland*, p. 200 ; A. Muñoz in *Nuovo Bullettino di archeologia cristiana*, 1904, p. 222.

[2] Anthology, ed. Jacobs, i. 18.

[3] *Orationes. etc., Choricii Gazaei, fragmenta*, ed. Boissonade, pp. 91 ff. ; Bayet, as above.

[4] See Garrucci, *Storia*, vol. i. In the *Anthologia Palatina*, i. 36, a picture is described in which an angel gives insignia to an official.

[5] Evagrius. *Hist. Eccl.*. iv, c. 26

[6] e. g. Frankish examples by Venantius Fortunatus, Alcuin and Bernowin (Dümmler, *Poetae Lat. medii aeri.* i. 346, 413), Ermoldus Nigellus and Walafried Strabo (Von Schlosser, as above, pp. 37 ff., 126 ff. ; Migne, *Patr. Lat.*, cxiv. 916 ; Garrucci, *Storia,* i, p. 599). On the subject of early Western frescoes see F. X. Kraus, *Die Wandgemälde in der Sankt-Georgskirche zu Oberzell*, p. 13 f.

[7] Both quoted by Bayet, *Recherches pour servir . . .*, 63.

[8] John of Damascus, *Oratio III de imag.*, ed. Migne, i. 1388. See also Garrucci, *Storia,* i. 590.   [9] Krumbacher, *Geschichte*, 2nd ed., 737.

existed in Western Asia in the first millennium of our era. Historical subjects followed. The rhetor Eunapius, in the second half of the fourth century, mentions a representation of victory over barbarians.[1] We read of the mosaics set up by Justinian in the Chalké or vestibule of his palace in Constantinople, representing the triumph of Belisarius over the Goths and Vandals.[2] The warlike exploits of the Emperor Maurice (A.D. 582–602) were painted at Blachernae.[3] Iconoclasm naturally favoured the extension of secular art. In a building used by Theophilus as an armoury were painted all the types of weapons in use; in another building were all manner of animals; fruits and flowers in mosaic, or on a mosaic ground, decorated a third. After the restoration of the cult of images, we read of the remarkable mosaics in the *Kainourgion* of Basil the Macedonian (p. 393), in which battle scenes and the members of the imperial family were represented. In the period of the Comneni, secular art continued to flourish; the exploits of Manuel were depicted in mosaic; probably the pictures with which the same emperor adorned the Palace of Blachernae were also of secular subjects. The pages of John Kinnamos, secretary of Manuel Comnenus, prove that nobles and wealthy citizens in this period followed the example of the imperial house.[4] Nicetas Akominatus (Choniates) (d. about A.D. 1220) describes the works executed for Andronicus Comnenus. At the west end of the Church of the Forty Martyrs this emperor caused to be depicted various episodes of his romantic and eventful life, including the murder of the unfortunate Alexius. In his own residence he had painted series of hunting scenes and further events of his earlier nomadic career; in one place he was seen cutting up and cooking the venison obtained in the chase.[5] The verses of Theodore Prodromos (twelfth century) on the Twelve Months are not without importance in connexion with the pictorial representations of the months and seasons in Byzantine art.[6] Manuel Philes also wrote upon this subject.

Caricature was not unknown in the Byzantine Empire. The representations of iconoclasts in various MSS., including the Chludoff Psalter and the Psalter of Theodore in the British Museum, almost come under this head; and the Emperor Andronicus is said to have ordered the disfigurement of portraits of the Empress Maria in order to diminish public sympathy, which ran strongly in her favour.

[1] Strzygowski, *Orient oder Rom*, 84.

[2] For this and the following references to lost secular works of art, see the article by G. Mavrogiannes in Ἐφ. Ἀρχ., 1893, 23 ff.

[3] Millet notes that the Roman emperors preferred to see their exploits perpetuated in sculpture rather than in painting. Historical painting may have originated under the monarchies of Hither Asia (in A. Michel, *Histoire de l'art*, i, Pt. i, 179–80).

[4] *History of the Times of John and Manuel Comnenus*, Bk. vi. That Kinnamos was interested in art is shown by a surviving essay of his on the following subject : What would a painter say if he had to paint Apollo and Daphne upon a panel of insufficient size ?

[5] This scene may be compared with a similar realistic subject in the frescoes of Kuṣeir 'Amra (p. 282). We may also recall the bone casket of Troyes (p. 231) and other caskets, as well as scenes in various MSS.

[6] Στίχοι εἰς τοὺς δώδεκα μῆνας (Krumbacher, 753).

Portraits of imperial personages were evidently numerous; nor were persons of lesser rank left without memorial. We remember the mosaic representations of Justinian and Theodora, and his large gold medal (p. 629, n. 1); the mosaic with Constantine Pogonatus in S. Apollinare in

FIG. 160.   Martyrdom of Anthimos, Bishop of Nicomedia : illumination of the eleventh-twelfth century in the MS. of Simeon Metaphrastes in the British Museum. ʻ(Add. MS. 11870.)

Classe; the portrait mosaics in St. Demetrius at Salonika (Fig. 198), and in Kahrié Djami at Constantinople; the fresco portraits of the Palaeologi at Mistra and at Trebizond. In illuminated MSS. emperors sometimes appear under conditions which allow us to assume that the features resemble those of the living man. Among such miniatures may be mentioned that of Basil I in the Psalter of the Marcian Library at Venice. Representations of emperors upon ivory carvings (pp. 224, 227) are probably more conventional, as are most of those upon coins (p. 627). In those in enamel the likeness is even more remote.

Names of artists who lived before the thirteenth century have not come down to us in any number. Of those quoted by Unger,[1] one Lazarus, a monk, is simply mentioned as an obstinate opponent of the iconoclastic Emperor Theophilus; another, Andreas, is highly praised by Theophanes and Cedrenus, but has left no works by which his art can be criticized. Ephraim, an historical painter (?) of the twelfth century, is better known as a mosaicist (see p. 415). Manuel Panselinos of Salonika, stated to have also lived in the twelfth century, is one of the first painters to whom existing work is attributed: he is said to be the author of the frescoes in the church at Kares on Mount Athos. His name, 'All Moonlike,' points to the brilliance of his achievement and is familiar to the readers of the 'Painter's Manual', where he is exalted in laudatory terms by the monk Dionysios of Furna.[2]

Müntz[3] and Frothingham[4] have searched for the traces of all the Greek artists whose names are recorded in Italy. Before the ninth century there must have been many, especially among the monks whose communities flourished in Rome under the Greek popes of the seventh and eighth centuries (see p. 78). But it is not until that period that we have references to names—Lazarus, Chrysaphius, Methodius—and these tell us very little. Lazarus was a painter-monk sent to Rome with gifts by the Emperor Michael III.[5] Methodius, perhaps the apostle of the Slavs, executed the wall painting in the narthex of S. Clemente at Rome and painted the famous ikon of SS. Peter and Paul which he gave to the Vatican.[6] Chrysaphius, chamberlain to Leo III, was sent by him to Ravenna to restore the mosaics of S. Apollinare in Classe. Another monkish painter, Theophylactus, has signed his frescoes of the year 959 in a crypt at Carpignano;[7] while the name of Eustathius, with the date A.D. 1020, occurs in the same place. The artists of the twelfth century known to us by name are very few: one is Marcus Indriomeni, who worked on the mosaics of S. Marco at Venice (see p. 399). Of the painters working in Sicily we have no personal record, except of Bion, who cast the great bell for Roger at Palermo in A.D. 1136. But there are known to have been many Greek ateliers in the island, and it is perhaps from them that Theophilus, author of the famous *Schedula diversarum artium*, derived his acquaintance with the methods of Byzantine art. A certain Daniel signed the vault of a crypt of S. Biagio near Brindisi[8] (A.D. 1197). With the thirteenth century we reach the

---

[1] *Quellen der byzantinischen Kunstgeschichte*, pp. 52–4.
[2] Ἑρμηνεία τῶν ζωγράφων (Painter's Manual), 39–41.
[3] *Revue de l'art chrétien*, xxxvi, 1893 ; *Les Artistes byzantins dans l'Europe latine du Vᵉ au XVᵉ siècle.*
[4] *American Journal of Archaeology*, ix, 1894, 32 ff.   [5] *Liber Pontificalis, Life of Benedict.*
[6] Jelic, in De Rossi, *Festschrift*, Rome, 1892, pp. 83 ff.
[7] Ch. Diehl, *B. C. H.*, 1885, 211–13.
[8] Ibid., 1888, 458. A mosaic pavement at Otranto is signed by Pantaleon.

period in which Greek influence began to produce its full effect. Theophanes of Constantinople is believed to have worked in Venice in A.D. 1242, and the mosaicist Apollonius to have taught Andrea Tafi. The painter Melormus, who was working in Tuscany at the very beginning of the century, is regarded as the possible master of Guido da Siena.[1] Another important name is that of Conxolus, who signs his name on the frescoes of the stairs leading from the upper to the lower church of the Monastery of Sacro Speco at Subiaco: the frescoes of the lower church may be in great part due to him. It is clear that this monastery, like Monte Cassino, must have depended very largely upon Greek artists. In this century we have also the first signed panel pictures. Andrea Rico of Candia in Crete signs a Madonna in the Uffizi at Florence[2] as well as panels in the galleries of Naples and Parma. A panel with the Presentation, in the Vatican, bears the name Johannes.[3]

For the fourteenth century we hear of Mark of Constantinople, Demetrius of Pera, and George, working at Genoa; of George Clotzata, who executed a tempera painting of the two Saints Theodore in the Vatican,[4] and of Kyrillos, who signed a triptych with the Trinity and Annunciation,[5] formerly at Palermo. In the Sacro Speco at Subiaco the name of Stamatico occurs in lettering which seems as likely to belong to the fourteenth century as to the sixteenth.[6] A panel picture in the Vatican, representing the Virgin and Child, is signed by Antonios Pampilopos; a cross in the sacristy of the Monastery of Sacro Speco, Subiaco, bears the name of Eutychios.[7] A painter named Eustathios signed a work formerly in the possession of Cardinal Fesch.[8] A panel in the Vatican, with Our Lord and Mary Magdalen in the Garden, is by Donatas Bizamannos of Otranto.

For the beginning of the fifteenth century we hear of George of Constantinople working in Venice and Ferrara: a signed picture of St. Mark by him is in the Brera at Milan; Antonio of Negropont also worked in Venice. The Vatican has a Visitation signed by Angelos Bizamannos[9] of Otranto, and the gallery at Berlin a Crucifixion by the same artist: the painting in the Vatican by Theodoros[10] would appear to be of the sixteenth century.

In the sixteenth century Emmanuel Zanfurnari, a member of the Greek colony in Venice,[11] was active as a painter, and several of his works

[1] H. Thode, *Franz von Assisi*, 84.

[2] Frothingham, as above, Pl. X. Frothingham would identify Rico with the Tafi who executed the mosaics in the baptistery at Florence. A Cretan school of painters is mentioned in the Painter's Manual of Mt. Athos (Didron, Pt. I, Sect. 51). For Cretan painters from the fourteenth to the seventeenth century see also G. Gerola, *Monumenti veneti nell' Isola di Creta*.

[3] D'Agincourt, *Peinture*, Pl. 88.

[4] Frothingham, as above, 48. The picture is signed on the back. See D'Agincourt, Pl. XC.

[5] J. Gambacosta, *Memorie per servire alla storia letteraria di Sicilia*, ii, Pt. iii, 271.

[6] Frothingham, 48.   [7] D'Agincourt, Pl. CXXV.

[8] Emeric David, *Histoire de la peinture au moyen âge*, 129 (1863).

[9] D'Agincourt, Pl. XCIII.   [10] Ibid., Pl. III.

[11] Signor Veludo has given an interesting account of this Greek colony written in modern

are preserved. The researches of Signor Veludo make it almost certain that the well-known picture of the Burial of St. Ephraim the Syrian

FIG. 161. The Death of the Virgin : miniature from a Gospel of the twelfth century in the British Museum. (Harley 1810.)

(in the Christian Museum of the Vatican) is by him, and not by an earlier painter of the name.[1] An Emmanuel Zane was working in Italy in the seventeenth century.[2]

Greek and published in Venice in 1893. For oriental painters in Italy during the Renaissance M. Ch. Diehl's article in *Rev. de l'art ancien et moderne*, xix, p. 143, should be consulted.

[1] A. Muñoz, *L'Art byzantin à l'exposition de Grottaferrata*, p. 34. The picture used to be attributed to much earlier periods, and was traditionally said to have been brought from Greece by Squarcione. The mere fact that it is painted in oil should long ago have disposed of these attributions. [2] *Byz. Zeitschr.*, xii, 1903, p. 702.

It will be seen from the above that information with regard to the First, Second, and Third Periods is singularly scanty, and that names only become frequent when Byzantine art had passed its prime.

The influence of Greek painting in the West was perhaps exerted most effectively through the art of the illuminator. But the monastic artists from the East who decorated the walls of churches and catacombs at Rome between the sixth and tenth centuries (p. 303) often inspired their Italian successors in the metropolis and in Campania; the frescoes with which the Greek monks in the South of Italy decorated their grottoes (p. 308) prepared the way for a native Italian art; and on such work as that of S. Angelo in Formis (p. 316) the Greek foundation is unmistakable. From the time of the Abbot Desiderius in the eleventh century the art of Monte Cassino is largely Byzantine in character, though here, too, the illumination of manuscripts provided the most useful models (p. 486).

From the time of the earlier Comnenian emperors to the close of the thirteenth century Byzantine art was admired and imitated by painters of Northern and Central Italy. The frescoes of the baptistery at Parma have clear Eastern affinities. Byzantine panels came into the country perhaps through Venice; and it is possible to trace their influence in the work of the early Sienese and Florentine painters from the beginning down to an advanced period of the fifteenth century (p. 322). The debt of the painters of the thirteenth and fourteenth centuries is not denied. In the pictures of Duccio di Buoninsegna not only are many of the old Greek compositions repeated, but niceties and mannerisms of treatment are also reproduced. Duccio may himself have visited Constantinople; certainly he had the advantage of more accomplished Eastern masters and more perfect models than contemporary artists in Florence. His work is in close accord with the best Comnenian art; it has the same technical excellence and an equal glow of generous colour. But from the very closeness of the relationship it has many of the same defects, the preoccupation with expressiveness, the defective modelling, the lack of energizing force. Compared with the breathing forms created by Giotto his figures are still hieratic and he himself is still three parts Byzantine. Contemporary Florentines were less docile than their neighbours of Siena, partly perhaps from temperament, partly because their models do not appear to have been of equal value: Cimabue, less accomplished than Duccio, is more forceful and more Italian. In him, as in his pupils, the Byzantine tradition is yet alive, but its still influence is disturbed by the action of an unsubservient and creative nature. Even the original genius of Giotto did not wholly disdain the old allegiance.

I: MURAL PAINTING.

(a) *Asia Minor*.[1]

Mural paintings are still very numerous in the vast and imperfectly explored area of Anatolia, though they have suffered so much from exposure to damp and to other forces of destruction that most of those as to which we possess accurate knowledge are but imperfectly preserved. In most regions heavy storms are frequent, and frescoes have less chance of survival than in the rainless climate of Egypt. In the free-built churches, the roofs of which have almost always fallen in, walls have only retained their decoration in places protected by favourable accident ; and there are few considerable remains belonging to the pre-iconoclastic period. The most numerous frescoes are those in the rock-hewn churches of Cappadocia, which have for the most part remained under cover, and have only suffered from an all-pervading damp. They chiefly date from the tenth and eleventh centuries, some descending as late as the earlier part of the thirteenth. A simple style of mural painting without figure subjects seems to have existed at an earlier date, and traces of it are visible in a number of churches.

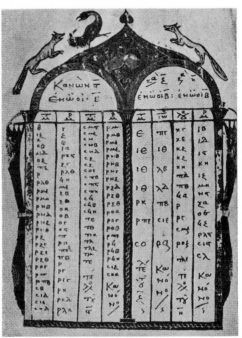

FIG. 162.   Eusebian Canons from a Gospel of the twelfth century in the British Museum. (Add. MS. 35030.)

Few of the Anatolian frescoes rise above mediocrity, though the older work in the Church of St. Stephen on the island of Nis (Pisidia) and the frescoes in several churches at Gereme in Cappadocia are of considerable merit. They have, however, much iconographical importance, as the number of saints represented is large, and the treatment of biblical and symbolical scenes frequently offers points of interest. It would appear that in Cappadocia at least the paintings were executed in true fresco.[2] The plaster was often strengthened by the addition of chopped straw and tow.

In Lycia not very much is as yet recorded. A small church at Kürksass, near Myra, has remains of frescoes including the Nativity, Adoration of the Magi, Last Supper, Crucifixion, and various saints.[3] Traces of painting were also observed in a church at Gagae.[4] At Alaja, in a domed church, the four Evangelists writing, a Virgin enthroned, and several saints are still visible.[5] The frescoes of the Church of St. Nicholas at Myra have greatly suffered, and but little now remains. The Divine Liturgy and figures of saints were distinguished by Rott.[6]

---

[1] H. Rott, *Kleinasiatische Denkmäler*, Leipsic, 1908 ; G. de Jerphanion, *Rev. arch.*, 1908, 1–32, and *Compte rendu de l'Acad. des Inscr.*, 1908, 7–21 ; H. Grégoire, *B. C. H.*, xxxiii, 1909, 1–170 ; Levidis, Αἱ ἐν μονολίθοις μοναὶ τῆς Καππαδοκίας, Constantinople, 1899 ; Diehl, *Manuel*, 533.

[2] H. Rott, *Kleinasiatische Denkmäler*, 126.

[3] Dr. K. Michel, in H. Rott, *Kleinasiatische Denkmäler*, 76.

[4] Ibid., 77.   [5] Ibid., 80.   [6] Ibid., 336 ff.

At Isbarta (Baris) in Pisidia Arundel[1] in the first half of the nineteenth century saw a church 'plentifully ornamented with paintings', but building operations have resulted in their disappearance.[2] The Church of St. Stephen[3] on the island of Nis, in Lake Eyerdirgöll, is covered with frescoes much discoloured by smoke and evidently of two periods. Dr. Rott, by washing the walls with water, was able to identify many of the subjects. Among the earlier series are the Sacrifice of Isaac, the Washing of the Disciples' Feet, the Betrayal, and the Ascension; inscriptions show that these were followed by the Descent from the Cross and two other scenes. In the choir is the Divine Liturgy, a rendering of exceptional merit; on the south wall are a much-damaged Last Judgement and a martyrdom. Among the later work, chiefly on the lower walls, are figures of saints, the Nativity, Presentation, and the Sacrifice of Isaac. This work is perhaps as recent as the thirteenth century, while Rott assigned the earlier frescoes to the ninth at latest.

In Pamphylia, the Church of the Panagia (Djumanin-Djamissi) at Adalia has frescoes of about the thirteenth century, recalling in style those of Suwasa in Cappadocia; but for the most part they have been covered by Turkish whitewash.[4]

With Cappadocia we enter upon a whole series of interesting paintings in rock churches and chapels, which may be compared to the work executed under somewhat similar conditions in the South of Italy (p. 308). The frescoes in the ruined choir of a basilican church between the villages of Göwerdjinlik and Djardaghkoi, near Newshir, are claimed as of pre-iconoclastic date.[5] Three busts of an almost classical style adorn a choir window, while in the apse are thirteen figures of Our Lord and Apostles. All have suffered greatly from exposure, and the principal colours (blue, red, and greenish-yellow) are much faded. At Amos, in a rock-hewn chapel the roof of which has recently fallen in, the decoration may possibly go back to the iconoclastic period, as the palaeography of the inscriptions suggests an early date.[6] In the choir is the Pantokrator between two angels; on the south wall the Annunciation may still be discerned. Elsewhere are the Virgin and Child attended by two angels, and a number of saints, including Michael, Gabriel, Dionysius, Demetrius, Blasius, and Theodore.

In the free-standing stone basilica at Andaval, perhaps erected in the fifth century, are remains of mural paintings of post-iconoclastic date. In the choir are the Pantokrator between angels, and two rows of saints, including Gregory and Epiphanius. In the nave are seen the Adoration of the Magi, and Constantine and Helena.[7]

Rock churches at Semendre, Soandere, and Ulnach, with the addition of a free-standing church at the latter place, have still remains of frescoes.[8] The Münchilkilisse, a two-aisled funerary chapel cut in the tufa,[9] has on one side of the barrel vault of the north aisle the Angel appearing to Zacharias, the Salutation, the scene from the apocryphal *Protevangelium Jacobi* in which Joseph and the Virgin are compelled to drink the water to prove their innocence,[10] and the Journey to Bethlehem; on the other side only the Nativity is visible; the south aisle has no paintings. In the choir is Our Lord in a mandorla surrounded by cherubim, and on the lower wall painted hangings (cf. Kuseir 'Amra, p. 282). In the vestibule are SS. Demetrius and George, and on a tym-

---

[1] J. Arundel, *Discoveries in Asia Minor*, 1834, i. 349.

[2] Rott, as above, 8.   [3] Rott, as above, 86 ff.

[4] Rott, as above, 45.

[5] An accurate plan of the church was made by the Russian archaeologist Smirnoff (Strzygowski, *Kleinasien ein Neuland*, 69 f.). For a brief notice of the frescoes, see Rott, 247-8.

[6] Rott, as above, 108-9.

[7] See Smirnoff's observations incorporated by Strzygowski, *Kleinasien*, 201; and Rott, as above, 108.

[8] Rott, as above, 111-12, 126.

[9] Rott, 128.   [10] Ch. viii. 15, 16.

panum two other saints. In a similar church in the valley of the Balyq,[1] not far away, the mural paintings are numerous and interesting, though not of a high quality. On the vault of one aisle are seen the Annunciation, the Salutation, the 'Water of Oath' as above described, the Journey to Bethlehem, in which the Virgin is seated on the ass in the attitude of an *orans*, and a scene

Fig. 163. The Virgin and Child : fresco in the Crypt of Sta Lucia, Brindisi.
(N. H. J. Westlake, *History of Design in Mural Painting*.) P. 309.

in which a peasant is represented ploughing. On the west wall are the Nativity with the Washing of the Child, and the Sacrifice of Isaac ; in the other aisle are the Last Supper, the Betrayal, the Crucifixion between the two thieves in the presence of the Virgin, St. John, St. Ephraim, Longinus and Stephaton (here described as O ΕϹΟΠΟϹ, or the man who offers hyssop). In the apses are the Virgin between Michael and Gabriel, with seven saints, and Our Lord in glory. A number of other saints are seen in other places, and there is one figure without a nimbus, who may represent a donor : all the scenes are accompanied by inscriptions. A great deal of the work in the chapel is effaced, and the colours are much dimmed, but the effect of the whole in its original state must have been brilliant.

[1] Rott, 129 ff. and Fig. 39 ; Grégoire, *B. C. H.*, 1909, 109–11 (Figs.).

The free-standing Akkilikilisse in the same valley has the figure of the Panto-krator;[1] more important are the frescoes of the Karabashkilisse,[2] a rock-cut monas-tic church in the same region, because the work is accompanied by an inscription stating that it was executed in the reign of Constantine Ducas (A. D. 1059–68) by the monk Nephon and the nun Catherine, with the co-operation (συνδρομή) of Michael the protospatharios, perhaps the divisional commander of the district.[3]

As is usually the case in these Cappadocian churches, the sacred scenes are painted upon the barrel roof, and the lower walls are covered with figures of prophets and saints. In a niche the dedicators of the frescoes, Nephon and Catherine, kneel before a third figure, near which are remains of an inscrip-tion. Catherine is also represented in another niche ; and in another place the monk Basil kneels before a bust of the Virgin. The scriptural subjects are the Nativity with the Washing of the Child and Annunciation to the Shepherds ; the Presentation ; the Crucifixion between the Virgin and St. John ; the Maries at the Tomb ; the *Anastasis*, with Hades in chains ; and (in the choir) the Divine Liturgy. In a chapel, above a large arcosolium grave, is an abbot (Bathistrokos). with other figures in monastic habit. Three rock-cut churches on the other side of the valley, collectively described by Rott as the Belikilisse, are hewn from the heart of the pyramids of tufa.[4] All have frescoes, though many subjects have almost entirely disappeared. Among those still visible may be mentioned the Annuncia-tion, Presentation, Zacchaeus in the Tree, Peter and Paul before Nero, Peter and Paul in Prison, and the same two Apostles with a third figure accompanied by the inscription Κόρη βασιλ(ε)ιος πυρέ(σ)σουσα, John the Baptist in the Wilderness, the Last Supper, Crucifixion (much perished), Flight into Egypt, Adoration of the Magi, Presentation, Water of Oath, and Massacre of the Innocents, with Christ and the Apostles, and a great number of saints. The neighbouring Chanavarkilisse (Wolf's Church)[5] has still the Nativity, Presentation, and a much-damaged Last Judgement, Divine Liturgy, and Christ Pantokrator. The style of these frescoes is rough and conventional.

In a lateral valley leading out of the Soandere valley is the half-ruined Chapel of St. Eustathius[6] with damaged frescoes, beneath one of which, representing a mounted saint, is an inscription not earlier than the eleventh century. At the end of the valley is the Church of St. Barbara,[7] with important frescoes and a painted inscription showing that the decoration was carried out in the reign of Constantine and Basil, therefore between A.D. 976 and 1028. On the roof-vaults are the Annunciation, Salutation (ὁ ἀσπασμός), the Water of Oath. Journey to Bethlehem, Nativity with the Washing of the Child, and *Anastasis*[8] with Hades in chains beneath Christ's feet ; on the lower walls are numerous saints, including Constantine and Helen with the Cross between them. In the choir is Christ enthroned between the symbols of the Evangelists : Adam and Eve approach in adoration, and cherubim veil their faces with their wings. Among them is the tetramorph, a fantastic figure formed of the four beasts of Ezekiel's vision (lion, ox, eagle, and man), and having eyes in its wings. The fiery wheels of the Vision are also indicated.

In the valley of Ortakeui, in the same part of Cappadocia, is the triapsidal Church of St. George with frescoes of two periods, two layers of stucco being in some places visible. The choir has the Virgin and Child ; in addition, the figures of St. Eustathius and another mounted saint, with SS. Gregory and John, may be distinguished. There are tombs with inscriptions of the thirteenth

---

[1] Rott, 132.   [2] Rott, 135 ; Grégoire, B. C. H., 1909, 96.
[3] There are traces of earlier frescoes, so that the present paintings represent a re-decoration.
[4] Rott, 140.   [5] Rott, 144; Grégoire, B. C. H., 1909, 101.
[6] Smirnoff's description incorporated by Strzygowski, *Kleinasien*, 203 ; also separately published in *Journal of the Ministry of Public Instruction*, 1900, 35 (Russian) ; Rott, 144.
[7] Rott, 146 ; Grégoire, B. C. H., 1909, 104 ff. and Figs. For the inscription see Prídik in *Journal of the Ministry of Public Instruction*, as above ; facsimile in Appendix.
[8] Figured by Rott, 148. Christ is in a mandorla, within which rays issue from his body.

century, and the upper frescoes are probably not much older.[1] In the same valley are various rock chapels once richly adorned with frescoes which have suffered from the effects of time and of neglect.

In the region of Susam Bayry near Urgüb, in the rock-hewn Church of St. Theodore, there are again frescoes of two periods, of which the later are inferior to the earlier.[2] Among the numerous scenes represented on the walls

Fig. 164. The Crucifixion : mural painting in S. Urbano alla Caffarella. (Moscioni.) P. 304.

are the Draught of Fishes, Raising of Jairus's Daughter, Crucifixion between the Thieves, a Martyr tortured upon a Wheel, the Flight into Egypt with the Fall of the Idols,[3] the Magi conducted to Christ by an Angel, several of the miracles, Christ and the Samaritan Woman, and the Entry into Jerusalem. On the roof, divided into two longitudinal halves by a row of busts of saints in medallions, are the Annunciation, Salutation, the Water of Oath, John the Baptist in the Desert, the Baptism, the Pursuit of Elizabeth and the infant John by Herod's Soldiers,[4] the Journey to Bethlehem, the Nativity with Washing of the Infant and Annunciation to Shepherds, the Miracle of Cana and the Call of St. Peter.

---

[1] Rott, 149–51.   [2] Rott, 205 ff.
[3] See the apocryphal Gospel *De nativitate Mariae et infantia Salvatoris*, ch. xxiii–iv.
[4] *Protevangelium Jacobi*, xxii–iii.

In the choir is Christ enthroned between the Evangelists' symbols; below him are archangels, cherubim, and seraphim.

The rock-hewn Church of the Ascension at Gereme near Urgüb is among the most important of the painted churches of Cappadocia.[1] The Ascension itself is in a small sepulchral chapel forming a kind of vestibule. Our Lord is enthroned within a mandorla supported by four soaring angels: beneath stand the Virgin between two angels, and the Apostles divided into two groups, the whole recalling the treatment of the same scenes in the dome mosaics of St. Sophia at Salonika (p. 376). The treatment is conventional, but in spite of the damaged surface this fresco is among the best of those in the Cappadocian churches. Other scenes in this antechapel are the Annunciation, and Abraham entertaining the angels. The three-aisled church itself is exceedingly dark, but perhaps for this very reason its frescoes are unusually well preserved. The whole space is decorated, bands of scroll designs and other ornament filling the intervals between the paintings. The subjects comprise: the Baptism, with the personification of Jordan with crab's claws on his head, Transfiguration, Raising of Lazarus, Journey to Bethlehem, Nativity with Washing of the Infant, Adoration of Magi (below which is a large figure of the Archangel Michael), the Betrayal, Crucifixion with the Virgin and John, Longinus and Stephaton (Ο ΕϹΟΠΟϹ), the *Anastasis*, the Three Children of Babylon in the Furnace, the Last Supper, the Four Evangelists at their Desks, Abraham, the Veronica[2] (τὸ ἅγιον μαν(δύ)λι(ο)ν with the head of Our Lord upon it), the *Deesis*, with two adoring figures named by an inscription as Nicephorus and Basil, a number of single figures of saints, the Virgin and Child (in the left apse), the Entry into Jerusalem (vault of nave), the Pantokrator (in the main dome), Christ with a scroll inscribed 'I am the Light of the World' (dome of the presbyterium), a number of prophets of the Old Testament. The sumptuous decoration of this church, executed throughout by careful artists, gives an excellent idea of the monastic style, which even in these remote valleys preserved a character of dignity and distinction. The frescoes, like those of the two churches next to be described, must belong to the tenth or eleventh century.

Fig. 165. An archangel: mural painting in the crypt of St. John, Cafaro. (N. H. J. Westlake, *History of Design in Mural Painting*.)

Gereme possesses several other rock churches and chapels decorated with mural paintings, some of them of a comparatively early date. The small rock-hewn chapel known as the Tcharikilisse[3] has in the apses the Virgin and Child, *Deesis*, and Archangel Michael, below which, in the arches of a painted arcading, are standing figures of saints—Blasius, Gregory, Basil, Chrysostom, Nicholas,

---

[1] Rott, 212 ff., with Figs. 73-5, and Pl. III.
[2] Brockhaus, *Die Kunst in den Athosklöstern*, 76 ff.
[3] Rott, 217 ff.

Hypatius. The principal remaining scenes in the church are Christ adored by three figures named as Theognòstus, Leo, and Michael, the Nativity with Washing of the Infant and Adoration of the Magi, the horses of the three kings visible in the background, the Baptism with Jordan personified, the Raising of Lazarus, the Entry into Jerusalem, Transfiguration, Betrayal, Simon of Cyrene carrying the Cross, Crucifixion without the thieves, *Anastasis*, Resurrection with the angel seated at the tomb, the Ascension, and the Virgin with the Child between Michael and Gabriel. In the principal dome is the Pantokrator, with the four Evangelists in the spandrels ; in a lunette Abraham entertains the angels (ἡ ἁγία τριάς).

The neighbouring Elmalykilisse[1] is again richly covered with paintings of the same school, perhaps by the same hand as those in the two preceding churches. We see here the Nativity with its usual accessory motives; the Flight into Egypt, Baptism, Raising of Lazarus, Transfiguration, Last Supper, Entry into Jerusalem, Betrayal, Christ led Prisoner, Crucifixion, Entombment, Resurrection, and Ascension ; on the lower wall are the Three Children in the Furnace ; in the principal dome is Christ with the Book of the Gospels, the four Evangelists below him in the spandrels ; in the apses are the same subjects as those already described in the Tcharikilisse ; in other parts of the church a great number of saints and prophets.

Not far away is the largest rock-hewn church of Gereme, the Tokaly-kilisse,[2] now very damp and often flooded with water : the rich mural paintings have suffered considerably from this moisture. Near the entrance are John the Baptist, and Our Lord in Glory surrounded by the Apostles seated on thrones. Along the walls are rows of saints. On the two longitudinal halves of the barrel roof are the usual biblical scenes : Annunciation, Salutation, Water of Oath, Journey to Bethlehem, Nativity, Pursuit of the infant John the Baptist by Herod's Soldiers, John called by an Angel to Preach in the Wilderness, John preaching to the Publicans (οἱ τελῶναι) by Jordan, the Baptism, the Marriage at Cana, Entry into Jerusalem, Betrayal, Christ before Pilate, the Adoration of the Magi, Massacre of Innocents, Flight into Egypt (two scenes), Miracle of Loaves and Fishes, Calling of Peter and Andrew, Simon carrying the Cross, Crucifixion without the thieves, Descent from the Cross, Entombment, *Anastasis*, and Ascension. All these frescoes are faded, and appear to be more recent and inferior in style to those of the transept walls and roof, which include a large Ascension, the Annunciation, Adoration, Flight into Egypt, Presentation, Christ in the Temple, the Angel calling John the Baptist, Baptism, Temptation, Matthew at the Receipt of Custom, the Calling of Peter, the Marriage at Cana, Raising of Jairus's Daughter and Healing of the King's Son, Healing of the Paralytic (?), Raising of Lazarus, Entry into Jerusalem, and Last Supper. Elsewhere are the Widow's Mite, the Death of the Virgin, and other subjects, with numerous figures of saints. The choir frescoes are much damaged. In the main apse is the Crucifixion between the thieves, with the Virgin and John, Longinus and Stephaton ; in the north apse is Abraham entertaining the Angels, in the south the Pantokrator between two angels. There are many inscriptions, one naming the painter Constantine. The frescoes of this church, especially those of the transept, the best of which are probably of the eleventh century, are the most remarkable in the Gereme district.

Quite close is the rock-cut Chapel of the Theotokos, also richly decorated.[3] We see here scenes from the life of the Virgin, including the Censing of the Purple Veil of the Temple,[4] the Virgin fed by Angels in the Temple, the Annunciation, the Salutation, the Journey to Bethlehem, Nativity, Crucifixion between the thieves, Entombment, *Anastasis*, St. George being broken on a

---

[1] Rott, 219 ff. In this church there are traces of painting of an earlier date with simply ornamental motives.

[2] Rott, 224 ff. ; H. Grégoire, *B. C. H.*, 1909, 81 ff. and Figs. 13 and 14.

[3] Rott, 229 f.   [4] Cf. Bayet, *L'Art byz.*, Fig. 57, p. 175.

wheel set with knives, the Pantokrator with angels, the Virgin and Child, and busts of saints in medallions, &c. In the neighbourhood are other frescoed chapels.[1] In the first is St. Procopius on horseback, St. Eustathius with the stag, the Pursuit of the infant John the Baptist by the Soldiers of Herod [2] (where we see Zacharias lying slain by arrows before the Temple and Elizabeth with the Child taking refuge among trees against soldiers armed with bows), Joseph's Dream, the Annunciation, Visitation, the Water of Oath, Nativity, Adoration with the old magical inscription **CATOP, APEΠO TENET**,[3] Presentation, Flight into Egypt, Massacre of Innocents, Christ in Majesty with the Evangelists' symbols, personifications of Sol and Luna, and (below) the Twelve Apostles, saints, adoring monks in pointed hoods, &c. Above the figures of saints on the south

FIG. 166.   The Virgin and Child between St. Peter and St. John : S. Urbano alla Caffarella.
(N. H. J. Westlake : *History of Design in Mural Painting*.)

wall is a frieze of animals and birds, hares, cocks, ravens (?) drinking from vases. The frescoes in this chapel are not of artistic merit. Another chapel, noticed by Texier in his *Byzantine Architecture*,[4] has the Nativity. A third, a sepulchral chapel, has large figures of St. Basil and Daniel as *orans* flanked by lions,[5] between them a smaller female figure without nimbus, and at the side, standing figures of Our Lord and the Virgin.

The Hemsbeykilisse in the same district, now inhabited by a colony of doves, has a fuller cycle of frescoes than any church but the Tokaly-kilisse.[6] The dome has the ascended Christ and the Twelve Apostles : in other parts of the church are Joseph's Dream, the Water of Oath, the Salutation, Nativity, Presentation, Flight into Egypt, the Angels giving the Charge to John the Baptist, John adoring Christ, the Baptism, Healing of the Blind Man, Zachariah in the Tree, Raising of Lazarus, Entry into Jerusalem, Last Supper, the Washing of the Disciples' Feet, Christ before Caiaphas, the Betrayal, Denial of Peter, Christ before Pilate, Simon bearing the Cross, two Crucifixions, one with the thieves, the other without, the *Anastasis*, Entombment, Resurrection, Pentecost, Death of the

---

[1] Rott, 230 ff.   [2] Rott, Plate opp. p. 231.
[3] *Sator arepo tenet opera rotas.* An anagrammatic magical formula which occurs frequently in Roman times and was regarded in later centuries as a charm against fever and fire. The words read the same backwards and forwards.
[4] pp. 42, 236, Pl. V. Texier appears to have misinterpreted the scene of the Nativity.
[5] Rott, Fig. 80, p. 232.
[6] Rott, 234 ff. ; Grégoire, *B. C. H.*, 1909, p. 88.

Virgin, and numerous saints. The execution is good throughout, and the frescoes must belong to the tenth or eleventh century. The churches of the Apostles and of the Holy Cross on different sites not far from Sinasos are rich in frescoes ; in the last named figure subjects are, by exception, avoided.[1]

At Aktchik Serai are rock-hewn churches with ruined frescoes, among which are visible the Transfiguration, Ascension, and Constantine and Helena with the Cross between them.[2]

Frescoes in a similar church at Arebsun,[3] on the Halys, are much darkened by smoke, but the Last Judgement with the archangel weighing the souls was visible, and the Baptism, Betrayal, Last Supper, Crucifixion, *Anastasis*, Ascension, and Death of the Virgin are discernible. The style of the frescoes is inferior to that

Fɪɢ. 167.   The Last Supper : mural painting of the fifteenth century in the grotto of the Theoskepastos, Trebizond.   (*Hautes Études* : G. Millet.)   P. 276.

of those at Gereme, and an inscription states that they were executed in the time of Theodore Lascaris in A. D. 1212.

In the free-standing octagonal church at Suwasa,[4] which itself dates from Early Christian times, are remains of other frescoes of the thirteenth century.[4] The Nativity, Raising of Lazarus, Entry into Jerusalem, Last Supper, Betrayal, Crucifixion without the thieves, Entombment, and Ascension can be distinguished. Among single figures are mounted saints (George and Demetrius ?) and the Virgin Hodegetria.

In the free-standing Tchanlikilisse[5] at Tcheltek there are also remains of the Nativity, Baptism, Transfiguration, and Last Supper, with figures of saints.

The larger rock-hewn church at Selme, the Kalekilisse,[6] is much blackened by smoke and otherwise damaged : the decoration of the church was originally extensive. In a church in the side of the dark valley of Peristrema is an animated representation of the Last Judgement by an unpractised hand, with the

¹ Grégoire, as above, 90, 91.   ² Rott, 242.   ³ Rott, 246.
    ⁴ Rott, 251 f.   ⁵ Rott, 260.   ⁶ Rott, 263 f. and Fig. 97.

archangel weighing the souls, and a number of realistic devils tormenting the damned ; the salvation of the blessed is represented by the patriarchs Abraham, Isaac, and Jacob holding the souls in their bosoms. The other subjects are the Flight into Egypt, the Raising of Lazarus, Entry into Jerusalem, Last Supper, Crucifixion with the thieves, the Pantokrator, Virgin and Child, the Apostles and numerous figures of saints, and Daniel in the Den of Lions. The work here is again inferior to that at Gereme. In the Karajedikilisse[1] in the same place the numerous frescoes have greatly suffered. though scenes from the story of John the Baptist and Our Lord, the legend of St. George, and other subjects are visible.

The mural paintings in the churches at Trebizond are of the fourteenth and fifteenth centuries, that is to say of the period of the Comnenian emperors. In the early Church of St. Anne, restored by Basil the Macedonian, are representations of deceased ecclesiastics and others interred within the walls, one kneeling before the Virgin, a St. Michael, a St. John the Baptist, and a Death of Joachim and Anna.[2] The presence, on damaged parts of the wall, of more than one painted stratum all of the same two centuries, indicates that these funerary pictures were frequently renewed.

Low down on the west wall of the Church of St. Eugenius, restored between A. D. 1340 and 1350, are traces of royal personages which were more distinct in Fallmerayer's time than they now are.[3] The same investigator noted frescoes on the outside of the apses at St. Anne and St. Eugenius, of which only traces now remain.[4] In the church of the Panaghia Theoskepastos, on the slopes of Boz-Tépé, the wall dividing the church from the vestibule had on the exterior portraits of Alexius III, his wife Theodora, and his mother Irene ; but these are now covered by modern work.[5] The small rock-cut chapel of the Theoskepastos, probably consecrated to St. Onuphrios, received a rich decoration in fresco in the year A. D. 1411 at the expense of a certain Paraskévas Poutzaris, as is recorded by an inscription[6] (Fig. 167).

(b) Syria—Palestine.

The third-century frescoes at Palmyra discussed by Strzygowski (Orient oder Rom.), though not Christian, may be mentioned here as closely related to Christian art (Fig. 168).

The remains of wall painting in Syria are scanty ; for the most part they represent symbolic or decorative designs, or animal and aquatic motives. On fragments of plaster in tombs in North-Central Syria[7] we see sacred monograms and crosses within circles, the grape-vine, water-birds, and plants.

A rock-hewn tomb at Hammâm id-Djêdj near Shnân has busts from which the faces have been scraped away, and symbols including peacocks and fish.

Other recorded frescoes in this area are of the Third and Fourth Periods. Those in the church of the cloister of the Holy Cross at Jerusalem,[8] though of the seventeenth century, appear to be restorations of models perhaps as early as the eleventh. Their iconography, however, seems to diverge considerably from Byzantine types ; this may be due to the Iberian origin of the artists.

The frescoes in the Church of Abù Rôsh (now restored) are assigned to the period of the Frankish occupation, though they were probably the work of Greek artists. Among the subjects were the Anastasis, the Deesis, a Crucifixion, and a Death of the Virgin.[9]

---

[1] Rott, 275 ff. Other churches in this district are probably decorated with frescoes.
[2] G. Millet in B. C. H., xix, 1895, 435–7.
[3] Orig. Framm., i. 125.   [4] Millet, as above, 458.
[5] Texier, Asie Mineure, 597 and Pl. LXIV, and Byz. Arch., 231 and Pl. LXVI. The fact is also noted by Tournefort and Fallmerayer (Millet, as above, 437).
[6] Millet, 440.   [7] H. C. Butler, Architecture and other Arts, 293–4.
[8] A. Baumstark in Monatshefte für Kunstwissenschaft, i, 1908, 771–84.
[9] A. Baumstark, R. Q., 1906, 157–8.

The faded figures upon the columns of the Church of the Nativity at Bethlehem [1] are of about the same period (Fig. 169). They consist of single saints, including Cnut, with both Greek and Latin inscriptions. The occurrence in association with these figures of kneeling persons and coats of arms suggests that they are votive. The iconography is almost entirely Byzantine, though the donors seem to have belonged to the Frankish nobility. Other frescoes are

FIG. 168.   Paintings of the third century in a sepulchral chamber at Palmyra.
(N. H. J. Westlake: *History of Design in Mural Painting*.)

reported in the monastery church of the Baptist, between Jericho and the Dead Sea, and in the Lavra τοῦ Χοζίβας.[2]

In the Monastery of Màr Sàba some mural paintings may have been originally executed as early as the fourteenth century,[3] though they have been restored in later times. Among the subjects are a Virgin and Child of the *Platytera* type (see Ch. XII), a Virgin holding the Child, recalling the fresco in the Catacomb of Commodilla at Rome in which the lady Turtura is represented (p. 304), a *Deesis*, a bust of Our Lord, angels, and saints. The decoration of the main church, which includes a series of martyrs, has been ascribed to the late fifteenth or to the beginning of the sixteenth century.[4]

[1] Baumstark, 158–9 ; Durand in *Bulletin monumental*, Caen, 1884 ; de Vogüé, *Églises de la Terre sainte*, 70 ; W. R. Lethaby and others, *The Church of the Nativity at Bethlehem* (Byzantine Research and Publication Fund), 1910.
[2] Baumstark, 159.   [3] A. Baumstark, *R. Q.*, xix, 1905, p. 161.   [4] Ibid., p. 162.

The discovery of the mural paintings in the Palace of Kuseir 'Amra, on the edge of the Arabian Desert about the latitude where the Jordan falls into the Dead Sea, was an event of great importance for the study of painting in the second half of the first millennium of our era.[1] The desert east of Moab, in which the earlier Palace of Mshatta (p. 170) is also situated, was a region controlled by various Bedouin tribes which both the Romans and Sassanians found

FIG. 169.   Column of the fourth century in the Church of the Nativity at Bethlehem, with paintings of the twelfth century.   (Byzantine Research and Publication Fund.)   P. 277.

it necessary to conciliate; the most influential were the Lakhm, who received Sassanian support, and the Rassan (Gassan), who were friendly first to the Roman, and afterwards to the Byzantine Empire.   The chiefs of these tribes, who from subsidies and other sources were in possession of considerable wealth, built residences of stone in those desert grazing-grounds where a sojourn of several months in the year is possible; and here they doubtless entertained the envoys both of the Roman and the Persian.   One of the Lakhm entertained a Sassanian prince for a long period in such a palace, which, according to our

[1] *Kaiserliche Akademie der Wissenschaften, Kusejr 'Amra*, Vienna, 1907, by Alois Musil and others.   Professor Musil had visited the site before the final expedition, during which the photographs and water-colour reproductions used in the above volume were taken.

Arab authority, was erected for him by a Greek architect.   Mshatta itself was such a desert residence.

Life in these retreats was luxurious, and diversified with all kinds of amusement: by day there was the chase after the wild ass and the antelope; by night the feast with music and dancing. The Mesopotamian influences revealed in the architecture and ornament of Mshatta show us clearly from what quarter these amenities were introduced into the life of the nomad princes.

When the Arabs advanced into this region, the power of the Rassan was rapidly destroyed. From A.D. 633 the Mohammedans were accepted as the overlords of the Bedouin, who, nominally at least, adopted their belief. The Ommayad khalifs, a tolerant dynasty, disliked at Mecca but popular in Syria, pursued a politic course with the desert tribes; they were in the habit of quitting Damascus in the winter months and transferring their residence to the healthier regions of the desert. Abd el-Malik had numerous Christians in his entourage, while Greeks and Persians were his architects. It was in the reign of Yezid, who acceded in A.D. 720, that the custom of spending the unhealthy summer months in the desert was introduced. But Walid II did more than make the desert his summer quarters: he had resided there for some twenty years before his accession in A.D. 743, leading an existence suggestive of the Arabian Nights. A man of unorthodox habits, he surrounded himself with every luxury which his wide dominions could provide. Wines and silver plate, fine raiment and jewels, were brought to his desert palaces on camels. In his harem were Greek women who bore him sons; about his court were singers and dancers for the entertainment of himself and his guests. A hunter of repute, pursuing the lion and the antelope, he was also a man of taste and education, himself a poet and musician, and familiar with the Greek tongue. These years of splendour were almost all passed before he became khalif in A.D. 743. In the following year he was slain by his rival and cousin Yezid, for his long absence from Damascus had made him unpopular in Syria, the province on which the Ommayad house had hitherto relied as its greatest support.[1] This is the man for whom the Palace of Kuseir 'Amra was probably erected, and the frescoes which adorn it were executed at his command.

Before the various scenes depicted on the walls are shortly described, it will be well to state in what the peculiar importance of these frescoes consists. They show us how absolutely the art of the early Mohammedan period depended upon the Hellenistic art of Syria and Mesopotamia. In the second place they prove how tenacious of life and of its old traditions the Hellenistic art of Hither Asia really was. The survival of a classical spirit in certain MSS. and other works of art in the tenth and eleventh centuries appears much less abnormal now that we have before us these frescoes dated in the middle of the eighth century, works so purely Hellenistic in style that competent observers at first considered them to be some three centuries earlier than they are. Here, as in Constantinople, the old genre scenes retained their popularity, and at once found favour with the luxurious princes of the conquering faith. We now more readily understand how the iconoclastic emperors, when they banished the religious picture, so easily introduced the fishing and the hunting scenes of earlier centuries. The old scenes had survived in Byzantine secular art, and their fresh vogue was encouraged by the knowledge that the triumphant leaders of Islam tolerated the representation of similar subjects. The scenes which St. Nilus had striven to banish (see p. 258) had only been expelled from the Christian churches: in the palaces they had prolonged an uninterrupted existence.[2] There are Persian and Mesopotamian elements in the ornament of Kuseir 'Amra; but the figure

---

[1] The story of the desert palaces and their occupants is excellently told by Dr. Musil, *Kusejr 'Amra*, as above, 123–66.

[2] J. Strzygowski, '*Amra und seine Malereien*, in *Zeitschrift für bildende Kunst*, xviii. 213–18. Hunting scenes illustrating the pursuit of the gazelle, lion, hippopotamus, &c., occur in the funerary chapels at Bawit in Egypt (p. 285).

compositions, which are by far the most important part, are Hellenistic through-out. It is possible that some of the artists who worked here were not of Greek descent ; but the traditions in which they were trained had come down to them almost unimpaired from the early culture of the Hellenistic cities on the Mediter-ranean coast. Elsewhere, as in Egypt, Greek art might be strangled or debased by the recrudescence of local styles, but here it was preserved in a surprising purity.

The buildings at Kuṣeir ʿAmra consist of a great hall covered by three barrel vaults running north and south, with a central niche and two apsed lateral chambers at the south end. Opening out of the east wall is a sequence of small chambers, the first two of which have vaulted roofs, while the third is covered by a dome. It is clear that these chambers were the different apartments of

Fig. 170.   Painting of the eighth century on vault of chamber at Kuseir ʿAmra.
(After *Kusejr ʿAmra*, by A. Musil and others : Vienna, K. Akademie der Wissenschaften.)

baths, and that the first, or cold bath, was beneath the dome and entered through a small court on the east.[1] The great hall may be described as a hall of audience or throne room, the lateral chambers at its south end serving as retiring rooms for the prince.

The walls and vaults of all these rooms are covered with paintings which have unfortunately lost much of their original rich effect. The colours were directly applied to a facing of mortar about three centimetres in thickness, and in the opinion of Austrian chemical experts are to be regarded as fresco rather than tempera, since no traces of size are apparent. The range of colours is limited, those used being bright blue. deep brown, light brown, dull yellow, and a bluish green.[2]   Notwithstanding these limitations, the effect of the whole

[1] Remains of pipes leading from a well north of the building to the domed chamber have been found.   On the Arab baths with their three rooms (*frigidarium, tepidarium*, and *caldarium*) derived from Roman models, see Karabaček (*Kusejr ʿAmra*, p. 227).

[2] The blue is natural ultramarine.   The deep brown is a red produced apparently from oxide of iron, then overlaid with a thin coat of ultramarine.   The lighter brown and the yellow appear to be of ochreous composition containing iron.   The green is produced when the yellow has received a light coating of ultramarine (*Kusejr ʿAmra*, 200-1, results obtained from specimen fragments by Drs. Pollak and Wenzel).

must once have been brilliant ; no such extensive decoration in fresco is known to have survived in any other secular building, or indeed in any building earlier than the Romanesque period.

In the niche at the south end of the great hall is painted a prince enthroned between two attendants. He is bearded and has the nimbus, and may represent either Walid himself, Mohammed, or one of the early khalifs. Round the niche is a row of desert birds ; above the throne is an inscription,[1] and below it a broad zone with a river scene, people fishing in a boat, water-birds, &c. The vault of the niche has semi-nude female figures between spirally fluted columns with curtains, above which are half-figures of larger size. Along the top of the vault is a row of vases, with scrolls. The lateral chambers, which are dark and only entered from the hall, have roofs painted with vine-scrolls.

Fig. 171. Painting of the eighth century in one of the chambers at Kuseir ʿAmra.
(After *Kusejr ʿAmra*, by A. Musil and others : K. Akademie der Wissenschaften, Vienna.)

The most interesting paintings in the hall itself are those covering the west wall. At one end are nude figures exercising after the bath. In the middle is a nude female figure standing on the edge of a bath contained in an octagonal building with round arches and an upper gallery with grilles, from which other women are looking on : the architecture, though without perspective, appears to represent a domed building somewhat in the style of San Vitale at Ravenna. At the opposite end is a group of figures of the highest interest, accompanied in some cases by their names in Greek characters, now partly effaced. They are six in all, and the first four from the left represent princes with whom Islam had come in conflict. On the extreme left is the Byzantine emperor (KAICAP) ; next comes Roderick,[2] king of the Visigoths in Spain ; next to him Yezdegerd, the last Sassanian monarch of Persia ; and in the last place the Negus of Abyssinia, followed by a woman and a boy. The whole of this long fresco is enclosed in a double border of 'rosettes' in circles, reminiscent of those upon the well-known group of carved ivory caskets (see p. 215). On the walls to the

---

[1] Karabaček reads this as an invocation of good fortune in favour of Prince Ahmed (A. D. 862–66), but it is considered earlier by other authorities.
[2] Karabaček (as above, 217) takes Roderick for Theodora, mother of Michael III.

south and north of this west vault are a richly dressed woman under a canopy and a woman standing near sea monsters and a ship. On the east wall is an antelope hunt; on the north wall the capture of antelopes in nets; on the south wall we see the evisceration of the game, above which are allegorical female figures in antique dress, styled ICTOPIA, CKYHC (CKEYIC), and ΠΟΙΗϹΙϹ. The barrel vaults are ornamented with double rows of arcades with gable arches, beneath which are nude figures, men engaged in the operations of the building trade, &c. Above the columns of the arches are birds in pairs. On the spandrels of the great arches of the hall and in other positions are nude female figures under canopies, one richly dressed and reclining on a couch, by which attendants stand, and palm trees. The lower part of the walls is painted to represent hangings, a fashion which appears to have originated in Hither Asia, reappears at Pompeii (House of Pansa), and was continued in Romanesque and Gothic art. The caldarium, or small room opening out of the hall upon the east side, has on its vaulted roof a large lattice, or lozenge-diaper,[1] the contained spaces of which are for the most part occupied by figures of men, wild asses, a bear, a monkey, and cranes; the central row has busts representing the three ages of man (Fig. 170). In the two lunettes are two remarkable pictures, perhaps emblematical of birth and death, the former showing two nude figures, one being a pregnant woman, grouped in a Michelangelesque manner on either side of a window, the latter (Fig. 171) a man looking pensively at a recumbent figure, to which a genius or eros points. The adjoining chamber, or tepidarium, which has a cross-vault apparently with ribs, has three lunettes, with women and children bathing: through the architecture in the background is seen a green meadow and blue water. In the window are vine-scrolls in the convolutions of which men and beasts are symmetrically opposed. The domed third room (the first to be entered by the bather) had its cupola painted with the stars of the northern heavens (the Bears, Erichthonios, Boötes, Ophiuchos, Cassiopeia, &c.), and with the signs of the zodiac.

(c) Egypt.

Work of the First and Second Periods.

The wall paintings in the catacombs of Alexandria[2] discovered in 1864, not far from Pompey's column near the south-western extremity of the old city, are in the vestibule and a square chamber with three adjacent chapels to which the vestibule gives access. They are of importance because they are executed in a similar style to those of the Roman catacombs, and their symbolism is of the same character. There has been considerable restoration at various early periods, but in their original form the symbolic scenes appear to have been painted not later than the first half of the fourth century. They thus illustrate that pictorial art of Alexandria which is known to have exerted so strong an influence in Italy. We may notice in the first place a frieze running round the apse in the vestibule. In the middle sits Christ between standing figures of Peter and Andrew, the latter offering a dish upon which lie two fishes: on the ground are twelve baskets filled with loaves, and doubtless St. Peter was represented as offering loaves, though this part of the subject is damaged. To the right, between trees, recline two persons partly effaced, evidently to be regarded as partaking of the food miraculously provided, the inscription painted

---

[1] Recalling the design of certain early textiles (p. 586).

[2] Nerutsos Bey, L'Ancienne Alexandrie, Paris, 1888, ch. x, xi, xxi ; C. Wescher, Rapport d'une mission accomplie en Égypte in Archives des missions scientifiques et littéraires, 2e Série, i, Paris, 1864, 190 ; Bullettino di archeologia cristiana, iii, 1865, pp. 57–64 and 73–7, and 1872, pp. 21–2 ; Arch. Journal, xxiii, London, 1866, 256–8 ; Garrucci, Storia, ii. 128–31 and Pl. CVb ; C. Bayet, Recherches pour servir, &c., 1879, 18–21, 58 ; V. Schultze, Die Katakomben, 282–4 ; V. Golenisheff, in Proceedings of the Oriental Section of the Imperial Archeological Society, v, St. Petersburg, 1890, 3–4 ; A. Popoff, Jerusalem and Sinai, St. Petersburg, 1878, 8 and 137 (the last two references are in Russian).

above them reading: TAC ЄΥΛΟΓΙΑC ΤΟΥ X̄Ȳ ЄCΘΙΟΝΤЄC. On the left is a group which has suffered even more severely, and of which the details are not easy to distinguish. The head of Our Lord is visible in the middle, with the letters overline IC near it. Close to these is the inscription H AΓΙA MAPIA, and further to the right ΠΑΙΔΙΑ. Below are figures at table, and it seems certain that the subject is the miracle at Cana in Galilee. Thus the frieze presents the two miracles usually symbolical of the Eucharist, which was probably celebrated here.[1]

The figure of Christ between Peter and Andrew, in the middle of the whole composition, bears signs of having been repainted, perhaps in the sixth or seventh century. The figures of saints in the corners and on the walls of the antechamber are probably of similar age. The walls of the principal chamber have also figures of prophets painted over subjects of earlier date, one of which

FIG. 172.   Remains of mural painting, El Khargeh.   P. 286.

may represent St. Peter and the angel at the sepulchre. In a lunette is a figure trampling upon serpents (cf. p. 672). The other lunettes show traces of inscriptions and figures over which have been painted saints of the same type as those covering the walls: among these St. Bacchus is conspicuous, making it certain that St. Sergius was also depicted. Near St. Bacchus is a cross between the letters of the inscription overline IC overline XC NI | KA. On the vault Our Lord is seen adored by angels.

In the churches and cells on the site of the Monastery of St. Jeremias at Saqqara excavated by Mr. J. E. Quibell[2] are many paintings of interest. The monastery is known to have been founded about A.D. 480 and destroyed about A.D. 960, and coins of Heraclius and Phocas have been discovered. Probably the frescoes date from the sixth and seventh centuries (Figs. 173–6). The wall paintings at Bawit,[3] west of Deyrut el-Sherif, are for the most part

---

[1] De Rossi, *Bullettino*, as above, 74.   The Eucharistic subjects may be compared with those in the Catacombs of S. Calixtus at Rome.

[2] J. E. Quibell, *Excavations at Saqqara*, Cairo, 1908 and 1911; *Compte rendu du Congrès international d'archéologie classique*, Cairo, 1909, p. 268.

[3] Jean Clédat, *Le Monastère et le nécropole de Baouit*, in *Mém. de l'Inst. français d'arch. orientale du Caire*, xii, 1904. M. Clédat's excavations were carried out in 1901–2. He has given a further account in Cabrol's *Dict. d'arch. chrétienne*, s.v. *Baouit*. See also Palanque, in *Bull. de l'Inst. français arch. du Caire*, v. There are remains of paintings in the ruined churches at Bawit, the columns having figures of saints; but the church paintings are less important and in worse condition than those of the chapels.

in the series of funeral chapels in the necropolis of the ancient monastery,[1] long
buried under mounds of sand.   Among the most remarkable are the series in
Chapel III representing the story of David, a cycle which was not a favourite
with the earliest Christian artists, but had become popular by the sixth century.[2]
In the seventh chapel is a group of the Virgin and Child surrounded by saints ;
in the fifty-ninth a fine group of the Virgin and Our Lord with a further group
of saints ; in the seventeenth a remarkable Baptism, in which Jordan appears

Fig. 173.   Mural paintings, Monastery of St. Jeremias, Saqqara.
(Photo communicated by J. E. Quibell, Esq.)   P. 283.

to be personified by a female figure, the Temptation of St. Pachomius, mounted
figures of St. Phoebammon and St. Sisinnius, with animals connected with the
myth of Horus ; in the twenty-sixth, Our Lord enthroned between the apocalyptic beasts ; in the twenty-eighth, the Virgin seated holding the Child, who is
surrounded by an oval mandorla.   On either side stand two angels with acerrae
and censers.   In addition to these there are a large number of saints, many of
whom, like St. Apollo, are Egyptian, of single figures, and busts in medallions, &c. ;
we may notice the winged *Pistis*, or Faith, and *Elpis*, Hope, in Chapel XVIII,
where there is also a winged figure personifying dew.   Scenes from the Gospels
are comparatively rare, but in different chapels we see the Annunciation, Nativity,
Visitation, Massacre of the Innocents, Baptism, Miracle at Cana.   Among the

---

[1] For the Monastery of Apa Apollo, see W. E. Crum, *Der heilige Apollo und das Kloster von
Bawit*, in *Zeitschr. für ägypt. Sprache*, xl, 1902.
[2] Cf. remarks on the silver plate from Cyprus (p. 574).

religious subjects occur others of a secular character, for instance the gazelle
hunt of Chapel XXXVII [1] and the hippopotamus hunt of Chapel XXXVI.[2] Like
the similar scenes at Kuṣeir 'Amra (p. 279) they have still much of the life and
grace of late Hellenistic art.   Such figures as that of the child riding the panther
in Chapel XXVIII have all the appearance of fifth- or sixth-century work.   In
Chapel XVIII we see a representation of Orpheus, in another (XLII) of the sibyl.
In some of the faces the artists show real mastery: the demon in Chapel XVII,
with his suggestive and saturnine smile, is worthy of especial mention.[3]   The
walls before the apses have usually a medallion containing a portrait bust,

Fig. 174.   Painting in a niche, Monastery of St. Jeremias, Saqqara.
(Photo communicated by J. E. Quibell, Esq.)   P. 283.

supported by two winged figures ; in the nineteenth chapel two peacocks flank
a central cross.   The paintings in this position have been far more exposed to
destruction than those within the apses, and most of them are in a lamentable
condition.   Some of the early symbolic animals, the hart, peacock, lamb, &c.,
are represented ; while baskets of fruit, birds, and other motives of like character
fill the vacant spaces, and testify to the early date of the paintings as a whole,
which must be for the most part between the fifth and seventh centuries.[4]   The
colour scheme includes green, reds ranging from brown to pink, purple, greyish
blue, yellow, and black.

The method employed by the artists was to sketch the subject in outline,
first in yellow, then in red.   Within the contours, sometimes strengthened with
black, which were left to give precision of line, the body colours were applied.
For hair, beard, &c., and for shading, green was the favourite colour : legs and
hands were left unshaded.[5]

[1] Clédat in Cabrol, s.v. Baouît, coloured plate between pp. 240–1.
[2] Ibid., 238.   [3] Ibid., 239, Fig. 1278.
[4] In some of the larger compositions, however, M. Clédat sees traces of later work of
about the eleventh century, similar to that found in the White Monastery (art. Baouît, in
Cabrol, p. 237).   [5] Clédat, Mémoires, 134.

The funerary chapels in the Christian necropolis on the border of the desert north of El-Khargêh, and known as El-Bagawat,[1] are extensively decorated with mural paintings (Fig. 172). The buildings are of brick, and the walls are covered with a thin coating of stucco upon which the paintings are executed. The style is that of the late Hellenistic art of Alexandria, and the traces of Egyptian influence are insignificant, being confined to details such as the *crux ansata* or ankh, which is freely used with a symbolical meaning. The inscriptions are numerous, and those which are in Greek should be contemporary with the frescoes. These, both from their character and their subjects, would appear to be not later in any case than the seventh century. Among the scenes represented are Adam and Eve, Noah's Ark, episodes from the stories of Jonah, Abraham, Jacob, Susanna, Daniel, the Three Children in the Furnace, and St. Thekla in a Burning Brazier, conversing with St. Paul: most of these belong definitely to the cycles of Early Christian art, though the martyrdom scene points to a date probably not earlier than the fifth century. The personifications of Εὐχή (Prayer) and Righteousness (Δικαιοσύνη) holding scales and cornuacopiae are of especial interest, and recall those of Faith and Hope at Bawît: among other single figures appears the Virgin as *orans*. The ornamental motives, which include vine-scrolls and massive wreaths like those of early mosaics at Ravenna and elsewhere, all point to an early date.

A rock chamber at Athribis, two miles south of the White Monastery near Sohag, has on its whitened walls figures very rudely painted in red.[2] The principal represent figures in the attitude of *orantes* between crosses; one of them, who stands between lions, is probably Daniel. Birds with crosses on their heads, a hunting scene, &c., occupy the less prominent positions, and on one wall is a Coptic inscription. On account of the summary nature of the drawing the date is not easy to determine, but the birds rather resemble those on the Coptic stelae, and the work may be as early as the seventh or eighth century.

The apses and west end of the nave in the older Church of El Hadra at the Syrian monastery by the Natron Lakes[3] are decorated with mural paintings.[4] The subjects are the Annunciation, in which the Virgin stands as in the Etchmiadzin Gospel, the Nativity and the Adoration of the Magi, the Ascension, and the Death of the Virgin. The scheme of the Nativity is simple, neither the ox and ass nor the nurses washing the Child being present: the composition resembles that on the cover of the Etchmiadzin Gospel (see p. 208). In the *Koimesis* the soul of the Virgin held by Our Lord has the form of a diminutive *swathed* figure. These paintings all lie over work of earlier date: the Ascension is superposed on an older representation of the same subject. The upper and more recent work is on a blue ground, and of a formal and conventional character; the lower series is on a white ground, and such parts of it as are visible, especially the faces, indicate a freer and more skilful hand.

The stucco ornamentation in the *haikal* of this church appears to be of the ninth century (see p. 151), and it seems probable that at any rate the early paintings are of this age.

Work of the Third Period.

The White Monastery near Sohag on the border of the Libyan desert, originally dating from the fifth century, contains interesting mural paintings.

[1] Vladimir de Bock, *Matériaux pour servir à l'archéologie de l'Égypte chrétienne*, St. Petersburg, 1901, 7 ff., and Pl. VI–XVI ; A. M. Lythgoe, *Bulletin of the Metropolitan Museum*, New York, 1908, pp. 203 ff. (frescoes with allegorical and biblical persons, and biblical scenes) ; see also Quibell, *Congress of Archaeology at Cairo*, 1909.

[2] V. de Bock, *Matériaux pour servir à l'archéologie de l'Égypte chrétienne*, St. Petersburg, 1901, 68 ff., Figs. 80–5, and Pl. XXIX ; J. Clédat, *Notes d'arch. et de philologie* in *Bull. de l'Inst. français du Caire*, ii, and Cabrol, *Dict. d'arch. chrét.* i, col. 2344 ff.

[3] A plan is given in Butler's *Ancient Churches of Egypt*, i. 321.

[4] J. Strzygowski, *Oriens christianus*, i, 1901, 356 ff. (no illustrations).

In the central apse is a colossal figure of Christ enthroned within a mandorla, holding the book in his left hand and raising his right in benediction.[1] The head is unfortunately destroyed, but to right and left of it are seen the abbreviated forms of Our Lord's name in Coptic and Armenian characters. There is an Armenian inscription below to the left, mentioning a certain

Fig. 175.   Our Lord enthroned : mural painting in the Monastery of St. Jeremias, Saqqara.
(Photo communicated by J. E. Quibell, Esq.)

Gregory as the person who ordered the painting to be executed; he may be a bishop of the eleventh century.[2]   In four medallions to right and left of the lower part of the mandorla are the four Evangelists, each holding a scroll with an Armenian inscription : between them and the mandorla are Coptic and Armenian inscriptions, the former dated A.D. 1124.   In the southern apse a colossal cross with a cloth draped across the arms is supported in a mandorla by two angels : to right and left are the Virgin and St. John the Baptist.[3]   The soffit of the

---

[1] V. de Bock, *Matériaux pour servir*, &c., 58 and Pl. XXI.
[2] One of the Armenian inscriptions shows that Armenian painters were at work in the church at the end of the eleventh century (J. Clédat in Cabrol's *Dict. d'arch. chrétienne*, s.v. *Baouît*, col. 209).   The name of Theodore, painter and copyist, is given, and M. Clédat says that the apses in the White and Red Monasteries have been four times restored.
[3] V. de Bock, *Matériaux pour servir*, &c., Pl. XXII.   De Bock did not photograph the northern apse, nor (apparently) does he describe any paintings in it.

arch before the apse is painted with a series of medallions containing busts of Apostles and rosettes.

The Red Monastery, a few miles to the north-west of the White, contains painted ornament dating from different reconstructions of the building, both on the walls of the church and in the small chambers adjoining the central apse.[1] Some of the work seems to betray the same hands as that in the White Monastery; perhaps the Armenian restorers were at work in both places.

There are mural paintings at the Monastery of the Martyrs near Esneh.[2] In one of the sanctuaries there is upon the wall a group with an archbishop named Gregory, a female *orans*, and another figure, near which the Entombment may have been painted.[3] Above the door is the Virgin enthroned with the Child between two angels, executed in a better style, and probably earlier than the

FIG. 176. Angels: mural painting, Monastery of St. Jeremias, Saqqara.
(Photo communicated by J. E. Quibell, Esq.)

last group: in the dome is an imbricated design. Another sanctuary has in the apse a large figure of Our Lord enthroned, the face unfortunately obliterated.[4] The mandorla is flanked by the four apocalyptic beasts and by two kneeling angels. In the intrados of the arch are St. Peter and St. Stephen on either side of a central cross. In another chamber are the Virgin and two angels, with remains of Coptic inscriptions, the whole rudely executed. Some of the Esneh inscriptions are of the eighth century, though it is doubtful whether any of the wall paintings are so early. There is again an affinity to some of the work in the White Monastery, which, as we have seen, is conjectured to be the work of Armenian restorers at the close of the eleventh century.

The wall paintings in the Monastery of St. Simeon at Assuan are of considerable interest.[5] The east apse of the church shows Our Lord enthroned in a

---

[1] V. de Bock, *Matériaux pour servir,* &c., 66. De Bock does not describe the paintings in detail. What is visible in his plate shows borders of quatrefoils, overlapping circles, &c.

[2] V. de Bock, *Matériaux pour servir,* as above.

[3] Ibid., 76.   [4] Ibid., Pl. XXX.

[5] J. de Morgan, *Catalogue des monuments de l'Égypte antique,* i. 129 ff., Vienna, 1894; A. Gayet, *Le Deir d'Assouan,* 161 ff., 1892; V. de Bock, *Matériaux pour servir,* 81; N. H. J. Westlake, *Mural Painting,* ii. 106–7.

mandorla flanked by two standing angels and other figures.[1] Below, as well as on the walls of a chapel cut in the rock, there are friezes of saints. The ceiling of the chapel is painted with panels and fret-like designs.[2] Relationships with paintings in the White Monastery, and at Esneh, supposed to be of the eleventh century, suggest that the present work is of that date.

Chambers cut in the rock at Deir Abu Hennis, south of the ruins of Antinoe, are ornamented with interesting frescoes representing scenes from the early life of Christ, &c. ; they are in a bad state of preservation.[3] The inscriptions show that they are not in any case earlier than the first half of the seventh century.

Other rock chambers with painted subjects have been noted at Gourneh.[4]

In the second pylon at Philae was a mural painting, and in one of the chambers of the first pylon traces of colour. Frescoes in the apse of the Temple of Luxor are almost effaced. There are also remains at Kalabche, and at El-Azam, near Assiut.[5]

Algeria and Tunis seem to have yielded little or nothing of Christian date. The wall paintings discovered are of the pre-Byzantine period, and do not therefore come within our province. They are few in number, the most remarkable being in a subterranean chapel on the south-east side of the Hill of St. Louis at Carthage.[6]

(d) Constantinople and Salonika, Greece, the Balkan Peninsula, the Islands.

In Constantinople itself the Parekklesion or lateral gallery on the south side of the Mosque of Kahrié Djami (p. 416) contains frescoes of two different periods ; the most interesting and the best appear to date from the early fourteenth century, and are probably contemporary with Theodore Metochites.[7] In the cupola the Virgin is seen accompanied by archangels ; on the side walls are warrior saints, bishops, and ascetics ; above are subjects from the Old Testament. In a niche an indistinct painting seems to represent an emperor with his family, and once had an inscription. The poorer work is chiefly on the east side, and is perhaps of the fifteenth century. An equally late representation of the Virgin and Our Lord side by side is seen in the narthex of the church.[8]

There were late frescoes, perhaps of the time of the Palaeologi, within one of the lateral archways of the Golden Gate.[9]

The Cathedral of Herakleia (the ancient Perinthus), near Constantinople, now half-ruinous, has mural paintings following the later Byzantine tradition.[10]

In Salonika frescoes are visible beneath the Turkish whitewash in the narthex of Sta Sophia ;[11] on a blue ground, Moses receives the tables of the Law, and the Three Children of Babylon are seen in the furnace : there are also figures of saints, and the sacred monogram. On the east wall of the church are busts in medallions, and in the gallery a row of saints, once more on a ground of blue.

In the Mosque of Eski Djuma at Salonika, formerly the Church of Hagia Paraskevi, there are remains of painting, perhaps in true fresco, in the soffits of the window openings.[12] In one is a stiff plant rising from a vase upon a red

---

[1] De Bock, as above, Pl. XXXI.   [2] Ibid., Pl. XXXII ; de Morgan, as above, 135.
[3] Ibid., 84, Pl. XXXIII ; J. Clédat, Bull. de l'Institut français d'arch. orientale du Caire, ii, 1902, 1–30 ; Westlake, as above, 107 ff. Mr. Westlake notes the Egyptian character of the floral ornament.
[4] Ibid., 85 ; Maspero, Revue arch., 1883, Pt. II, 213 ; Sayce, Proc. Soc. Bibl. Arch., viii. 187 ; Bouriant in Mém. de la mission arch. française du Caire, i. 33 ff.   [5] De Bock, 89.
[6] For the literature see Cabrol, Dict. d'arch. chrét., &c., s.v. Afrique, sect. xxvi.
[7] Ch. Diehl, Études byzantines, 416 ff., Paris, 1905 ; Th. Schmit, Izviestiya of the Russian Arch. Inst. at Constantinople, xi, 1906, Atlas, Pl. 81 and 82 ; Pulgher, Anciennes églises byzantines de Constantinople, p. 33 and Pl. XXX.
[8] Pulgher, as above, Pl. XIX, Fig. 1.   [9] Van Millingen, Walls of Constantinople, p. 65.
[10] Jahreshefte des österreichischen arch. Inst. in Wien, i ; Kalinka and Strzygowski, Die Cathedrale von Herakleia.   [11] Smirnoff in V. V., v, p. 369.
[12] The information is derived from Mr. W. George, who has reproduced these designs in colour for the Byzantine Research and Publication Fund.

ground, which appears to belong to an earlier series ; others have thin scroll
designs in dark pigment upon grey or red-brown grounds ; another has a recurrent
design, derived from the palmette, in white upon a parti-coloured ground of
red and green.   These later designs recall the work of the eleventh century.

On the wall of the south gallery next the narthex is a fine sketch of a bird

FIG. 178.   Saints : mural painting in the Parthenon, Athens.
(N. H. J. Westlake : *History of Design in Mural Painting*.)   P. 292.

in brown upon the white mortar jointing of the rubble work.   Other sketches
of birds are also to be seen.

The Byzantine wall paintings in Greece and the Balkan Peninsula are still
numerous, though many have been destroyed or half effaced,[1] while others have
been covered with whitewash or repainted at a more recent date.   The work in
little out-of-the-way churches is often of great interest, and in itself as important
as that in buildings which are better known ; but unless accessible to study by
means of photographs or published reproductions it cannot at present possess

[1] A decree of Otho I, dated May 20, 1836, placed all the ruined churches in Greece at the
disposal of the Ministry of Public Instruction, with unfortunate results from the point of view
of archaeology and art.   Didron, in a passage quoted by Mr. Westlake (*History of Mural Painting*,
ii. 100), described the melancholy state of affairs in 1844.   In numbers of churches frescoes of
considerable age are covered over with one or more coats of whitewash, so that they cannot be
studied : so at Merbaka in Argolis (A. Struck, *Ath. Mitth.*, 1909, 204).

the same value for the general student.[1]   Attention must here be confined to a
limited number of sites which can be made profitable for comparative study.
As a whole the compositions on the walls of these churches are marked by
great uniformity : the artists are obedient to the iconographical canons of their
time, and originality is seldom found either in subject, conception, or in
technique.   Where it does occur, as at Mistra, it is doubly impressive.

At Athens, the Parthenon, which was used as a church from the seventh
century, has important remains of mural painting[2] (Figs. 178, 179).   The oldest
are those on the north wall of the opisthodomos, which in Christian times became

FIG. 179.   Saints: mural painting in the Parthenon, Athens.
(N. H. J. Westlake : *History of Design in Mural Painting.*)

the narthex.   Here there are three tiers of single figures rather above life size,
possessing repose and dignity, and perhaps of the eleventh century : they are in
red outline, directly upon the marble, with slight shading.   In the centre of the
upper zone Our Lord was seen enthroned ; in the middle of the lower the
Virgin with the Child : the other figures are standing saints formerly accompanied by their names.   The painting is now fragmentary, and the work is only
extensive on one side.

The frescoes in the dome of the Church of the *Megalé Panagia*, now destroyed,

[1] Lampakis, Δελτίον τῆς Χριστιανικῆς Ἀρχαιολογικῆς Ἑταιρίας, i, &c. ; Smirnoff, V. V., vi. 323.
Some of the paintings in these churches are dated.   Lampakis (*Mém. sur les antiquités
chrétiennes de la Grèce*, Athens, 1902) mentions several churches with frescoes, some of which,
however, like Kaisariani, are too late for our limit.   Among them are : Asteri, Karea, and
St. John Theologos on Hymettos, the monastic churches of Phaneromeni at Salamis,
Hierothea near Megara, St. George at Phaneas, Corinth, Monemvasia, Calambaca, Zerbitsa,
Golla, &c.
[2] *Scottish Review*, vi, 1885, *Some Christian Monuments of Athens*, by the Marquis of Bute ;
N. H. J. Westlake, *Archaeologia*, li. 173 ff., and *History of Mural Painting*, ii. 90 ff.   Mr. Westlake,
in the latter work, suggests that the frescoes of the north wall may date from before the
time of Basil II, who himself visited the Parthenon.

had in the centre the Pantokrator, and below, in semicircular compartments, the nine orders of the heavenly hierarchy ; below again was a zone representing the firmament, in which were visible the signs of the zodiac. The spandrels probably had the four Evangelists.[1] Between the windows were the terrestrial subjects, the deeps, whirlpools, powers of nature, fruitful hills, &c. The whole composition was intended to illustrate the last three Psalms, which together formed the group known as the *Ainoi*. The Church of St. Andrew has mural paintings conforming to the later Byzantine tradition.[2]

The Church of the Redeemer, now destroyed, had in the dome the Pantokrator, below whom were two zones of seraphs and angels[3] (Fig. 153).

The Church of St. Michael (*Asomatos Taxiarches*), not far from the *Megalé Panagia*, has frescoes which were once of considerable merit.[4] The largest, divided into two vertical halves, represented the Agony in the Garden and the Betrayal, with busts in medallions below. It is rather difficult to judge the date of this work from the reproductions, but it should be later than that in the Parthenon (Fig. 177).

At St. Luke of Stiris in Phocis frescoes have replaced the lost mosaics in the dome of the greater church,[5] while in the crypt of St. Barbara beneath, more modern paintings cover work of an earlier period, probably of the eleventh or twelfth century :[6] in 1839 Didron recorded that the walls of the smaller Church of the Theotokos, now whitewashed, were covered with frescoes.

At Kaisariani in Attica the church is fully decorated with frescoes of the seventeenth century : although late they may be mentioned here, because a scheme of their arrangement has been published,[7] and the arrangement itself is largely traditional.

At Mistra in the Morea[8] (p. 44), the churches of the Peribleptos, Pantanassa, and Panagia of the Brontocheion have still a great part of their original decoration ; traces remain in the church of the two Saints Theodore ; under the whitewash of the Metropolitan Church subsist remains which may represent the earliest art of this region. All the visible work, however, dates from the period of the Palaeologi.

It has been stated that Mistra represents one of the most interesting phases of Byzantine art, a phase which was probably so far original as to have developed without direct influence from the West, whatever indirect benefit Eastern artists may have derived from the contact of East and West during this period (p. 20) (Figs. 180–4).

M. Millet finds at Mistra the work of three schools. Firstly, at the Metropolitan Church there was a school of fine draughtsmen, following older tradition, content with the convention and restraint of the past, but finely expressive in their treatment of the human figure. In the second place stands a school which may be described as impressionist, following the new tendencies towards the picturesque. The artists of this school multiply the personages, enrich the decoration, and create a conventional architecture to enliven their backgrounds. But the figures are powerfully conceived and vigorously modelled ; they are not always vague types, but stamped with the impress of individuality. The work of this school is found in the Brontocheion as well as in the Metropolitan Church. The work of the third school, of which the activity is best seen in the Peribleptos, is elegant and graceful ; its artists love the minute and the finished, as if they were miniaturists at heart and church decorators by accident. They understand the antique ; many of their figures are of a singular if effeminate charm. The

---

[1] *Scottish Review*, as above, 102, 104–5 ; *Archaeologia*, as above, 181 ff. and Pl. VIII ; Westlake, *Hist. of Mural Painting*, 92.　　[2] Millet in *B. Z.*, i, 1892, 646–8.
　　[3] Westlake, *History*, as above, 97. The figure is from a drawing by Mr. T. J. Wilson, done in 1846–7.　　[4] *Archaeologia*, as above, 185 ; Westwood, *History*, as above, 99.
　　[5] Schultz and Barnsley, 65.　　[6] Ibid., 34.
　　[7] Strzygowski and Lambros, 'Εφ. 'Αρχ. 1902, 92 ff.
　　[8] G. Millet, *Monuments byzantins de Mistra*, 1910, and *B. C. H.*, xviii, 1895, 453 ff. ; L. Magne, *Gazette des Beaux-Arts*, Third Period, xvii, 1897, 306 (water-colour drawings by M. Yperman reproduced).

decorators of the Pantanassa (A. D. 1430) are masters of rich colour and precise line ; the picturesque and the pathetic attract them ; they are no longer in accord with the tranquillity and detachment which distinguish the 'old masters' of Byzantine art.

Frescoes of the Comnenian dynasty and later still exist in churches in the islands, though in many cases they have been covered with whitewash. Such covered paintings can be discerned in the exonarthex of Nea Moni on Chios.[1]

Fig. 180.   The Death of the Virgin : mural painting of the fourteenth century in the Church of the Peribleptos, Mistra.   (*Hautes Études* : G. Millet.)   P. 293.

There are no mural paintings of the first two periods in Servia and Mace-donia ;[2] the earliest belong to the period of the Nemanja dynasty (p. 40).   As in Russia, the first masters were Byzantine, but rapidly formed a local school, and in the transitional period it is difficult to say where the work of the masters ceases and that of the pupils begins.   The picturesque style represented in

[1] *Byz. Zeitschr.*, v, 1896.
[2] P. Pokryshkin, *Orthodox Ecclesiastical Architecture of the XII–XVIII Centuries in the Modern Kingdom of Servia*, St. Petersburg, 1906 (in Russian), many plates ; W. Petkovič in *Nowa Iskra*, 1906, *Iconography of the Monastery Churches in Servia* (reviewed, *B. Z.*, xvi. 742) ; Kondakoff (*Macedonia*, St. Petersburg, 1909, p. 65) says that drawings made by Valtrovitch and Miliutinovitch and exhibited at the first Archaeological Congress in Moscow, 1872, remain unpublished.

FIG. 181. Remains of mural paintings of the fourteenth century, Church of the Brontocheion, Mistra. (*Hautes Études* : G. Millet.) P. 293.

mosaic by the cycle in the Mosque of Kahrié Djami at Constantinople (see p. 416), and in fresco by the wall paintings at Mistra (p. 293), occurs early in Servia (see frescoes of Nerez below), and is probably to be ascribed to Byzantine influence: it is also found in the mural paintings at Gradač (middle of the thirteenth century): these analogies lend a peculiar interest to these Servian monuments. In the sixteenth century analogies with the art of Mount Athos are numerous. From this period national Servian features begin.

In the monastery church of Nerez near Uskub (Skopia) are a few frescoes considered contemporary with the building (twelfth century). These are in the *prothesis* and *diakonikon* and the lateral chambers corresponding to them in the north-west and south-west of the church, and in the neighbourhood of the altar, the latter with Greek inscriptions. The subjects are with difficulty distinguished, but the colouring and style are said to differ from those of the remaining frescoes, the earliest of which are assigned to the sixteenth or seventeenth centuries.[1] The style of the earlier work is held to anticipate the manner found in the fourteenth and fifteenth centuries at Mistra.

In the monastery church of Treskaveč, not far from Prilep in Macedonia, two domed lateral chambers have frescoes dating from the end of the twelfth or the beginning of the following century. They represent Our Lord, the Virgin, the Etimasia, and a number of martyrs and saints. These chambers are very dark, and without artificial light the work cannot be properly examined.[2] This church also possesses frescoes of King Stephen Miliutin (A. D. 1281–1322) and a princess, probably Simonida his consort, daughter of Andronicus and Irene.[3] These are of the fourteenth century, and are probably good portraits. Other frescoes in the church are perhaps later reproductions of damaged original designs.

The frescoes of the Kraljeva Crkva at Studenitza of A. D. 1314, with scenes from the life of the Virgin, exhibit a similar treatment to that found in the mosaics of the inner narthex at Kahrié Djami (p. 420) and that in the Monastery of Vatopedi on Mount Athos, all being of about the same period.[4] There is much liveliness and an approach to realism in the work in this church, the Descent into Hell being especially fine. Earlier frescoes at Studenitza, in the church founded about A. D. 1200, include a Crucifixion and Last Judgement.[5]

Ziča, founded A. D. 1222–1228, has frescoes representing the Bearing of the Cross and the Forty Martyrs in an excellent style.[6]

Frescoes in St. John the Evangelist at Ochrida represent Our Lord, prophets, and angels (dome): others, in the body of the church, are overlaid with whitewash.[7]

St. Clement, Ochrida, has Gospel scenes, and an interesting portrait of the dynast Osto Rayakovitch: the inscriptions are Slavonic, and the date the close of the fourteenth century.[8]

The work at Ravanitza, Manassiya, Kalenič, and Liubostynia is ascribed to the fourteenth and fifteenth centuries.[9]

The ruinous Church of Zaum (A. D. 1361), on the south-east shore of Lake Ochrida,[10] has frescoes of the period in very bad condition. Over the principal door is the *Deesis*, on either side of it three figures of saints and royal personages. In the apse is the Virgin with a Greek inscription ((MP) Θ͞V ($\dot{a}\chi\epsilon\iota\rho o)\pi o\iota\eta\tau os$): below her are saints in medallions, and the throne with the lamb and chalice

---

[1] P. N. Miliukoff, *Izviestiya* of the Russian Arch. Institute at Constantinople, iv, Sophia, 1899, 137.

[2] Ibid., 113 ff. For this church see also Antonin, *Travels in Rumelia*.

[3] Miliukoff, Pl. 19 b. This king is represented with Simonida in a fine church at Nagurić, two hours east of Kumanovo (A. J. Evans, *Archaeologia*, xlix, p. 155).

[4] Kondakoff, *Macedonia*, 65–6. See Strzygowski's review of Pokryshkin, *B. Z.*, xvi. 731.

[5] Kondakoff, 65.   [6] Ibid.   [7] Kondakoff, 236.

[8] Kondakoff, 245.   [9] By Petrovič.

[10] Miliukoff, as above, 83–6, and Pl. IX and X.

flanked by four bishops. Other subjects are the Assumption, Our Lord enthroned, the Virgin enthroned, St. Peter of Alexandria before Our Lord, and a series of life-sized saints, including two stylites on columns.

In the fourteenth-century Church of Liubiten, which from its high position looks south towards Uskub, are frescoes[1] representing King Stephen Dušan, his consort Helena, and his son (north wall), while on either side of the chief door

FIG. 182. Part of an Ascension : mural painting of the fourteenth century, Church of the Peribleptos, Mistra. (*Hautes Études* : G. Millet.)

are SS. Michael and Gabriel, and Cosmas and Damian. In the apse Our Lord is seen giving the Communion in both kinds, and there are various saints, with inscriptions in Greek. To right and left of the apse are apostles and saints, also with Greek inscriptions. Other paintings have Slavonic inscriptions. They include a number of Our Lord's miracles, Christ in the Synagogue, Christ and the Samaritan Woman, and various saints. The dome having fallen in, and the roof being now ruined, these paintings are rapidly decaying ; later travellers have noticed deterioration since the visit of Dr. Arthur Evans. Miliukoff is of

---

[1] A. J. Evans, *Antiquarian Researches in Illyricum*, in *Archaeologia*, xlix, p. 93 ; P. N. Miliukoff, *Izviestiya* of the Russian Arch. Inst. at Constantinople, iv. 130–2 (Sophia, 1899) ; N. Kondakoff, *Macedonia*, 177 ff.

opinion that all date from the fourteenth century. Kondakoff notes the
intrusion of naturalistic details into the Byzantine compositions.

The church on the island of Mali Grad in the south-west of Lake Presba is
built within the shadow of an enormous cave.[1] On the exterior, about the
principal entrance, the wall is covered with frescoes : in a tympanum is the Birth
of the Virgin ; about the door, the Last Judgement ; above it the Virgin sits
enthroned between a prince and princess [2] and their children. Of these paint-

FIG. 183. Mural painting of the early fifteenth century, Church of the Pantanassa, Mistra.
(*Hautes Études* : G. Millet.)

ings the upper alone, with the representations of princely personages, are
considered older than the seventeenth century, to which the others are assigned.
The interior is richly decorated. On the triumphal arch is the *Deesis* ; below,
Our Lord in a mandorla supported by angels. In the apse is the Virgin, on
either side angels and saints ; below, a throne flanked by bishops. On the side
walls of the church a lower zone is occupied by life-sized saints ; a higher zone
contains a row of medallions with busts of saints ; above this is a broader zone
embracing on each side half of the barrel-vaulted roof, and covered with Gospel
scenes : Nativity, Salutation, Flight into Egypt, Baptism, Christ before Caiaphas

[1] Miliukoff, as above, 68 ff., and Pl. XX, XXI.
[2] Greek inscriptions give the name of the prince as Novak, who lived towards the middle
of the fourteenth century, a date confirmed by two inscriptions in the church. But an
exterior inscription mentions restoration at the beginning of the seventeenth century ; and it
becomes a question how much of the work was left untouched, and whether even the interior inscriptions have not been repeated.

and Pilate, Christ mocked, the Entry into Jerusalem, the Transfiguration, Betrayal and Crucifixion, the Maries at the Tomb, the *Anastasis*, and Assumption. While the artist adheres in the main to the traditional types, he shows force and originality : the gestures are lively, the grouping in the more complicated scenes is well conceived. In spite of certain features which suggest a later date (seventeenth century), Miliukoff inclines to the belief that the majority of the frescoes are of the fourteenth century.

The Church of St. Spaso, at the village of Boria (*Emporia*), in the valley of Korch, south-west of Lake Ochrida, founded in A. D. 1390 under Amerales, son of Novak, is likewise covered with frescoes.[1] A Greek inscription over the chief door mentions the name of this prince, with those of John V Palaeologus and his son.

On the exterior of the same wall is a Last Judgement ; the interior is covered with frescoes. In the apse is the Virgin as *orans*, with the Child in a medallion on her breast, and the inscription ἡ πάντων χαρά. Below is the Lamb upon a disk placed on a throne with a chalice, flanked by four episcopal saints. On the triumphal arch is the Annunciation ; on its lower parts are St. Cyril and St. Stephen. On the south wall are the Entry into Jerusalem and the Betrayal ; on the north, the Crucifixion and the Maries at the Tomb ; below are full-length figures of saints, including Constantine and Helena. The work in the dome is almost destroyed, but there are traces of the forms of prophets and the Evangelists in the pendentives. These frescoes are inferior to those of Mali Grad (see above).

The wall decoration of the monastery church of Markov to the south of Uskub, though very much has been destroyed, contains some work ascribed to the close of the fourteenth century.[2] This is chiefly the upper part of the walls in the interior. In the bema are the Communion of the Apostles, Last Supper, and Christ appearing after his Resurrection, with Greek inscriptions ; below are subjects with Slavonic inscriptions, two representing adoration of the Virgin. Miliukoff assigns the older work to about the year A. D. 1400.

To about the same period belong the figures of founders on the exterior of the monastery church of the Archangels near Prilep,[3] and in the Church of Matka, where there are a Virgin and Child, an Ascension, saints, and prophets in the bema.[4]

To the fifteenth century belong the mural paintings of St. Peter's, at Presba. Outside, over the door, is the Virgin, with a Greek inscription. The Virgin is repeated within in the apse ; below her is the Lamb upon a throne flanked by two bishops ; near by, on the vault, Our Lord is seen enthroned and in the act of benediction. On the lateral walls are the Baptism, Transfiguration, Presentation of the Virgin, Raising of Lazarus, Maries at the Tomb, Crucifixion, Entombment, and *Anastasis*. In a lower zone are numerous saints. A Greek inscription gives the date of this decoration as A. D. 1410.

A church at Nagorič, apparently dedicated to St. George, has frescoes of later date than the fourteenth century ; but the cathedral of the same place, also dedicated to St. George and founded in A. D. 1330, has mural paintings of exceptional quality.[6] In the five domes are various representations of Christ ; in the apse, the Virgin and Child between angels, and below, the Last Supper. On the walls are Gospel scenes, the Death of the Virgin, the Last Judgement, &c.; in the narthex, in superposed zones, are the lives of SS. George and Demetrius, with numerous saints and prophets. Kondakoff considers the work of the same century as the foundation of the building.

In the church at Mateetz,[7] near Kumanoff, now roofless, are to be seen the

[1] Miliukoff, as above, 75 ff.

[2] Miliukoff, as above, 134 ff. ; A. J. Evans, *Archaeologia*, xlix. 84, 98–9 ; Kondakoff, *Macedonia*, 180 ff. Since the visit of Dr. Evans much vandalism has taken place. The portraits of King Vukasin and his son on the outer wall have disappeared.

[3] Miliukoff, 145. [4] Kondakoff, *Macedonia*, 191.

[5] Miliukoff, 60–62. [6] Kondakoff, 194 ff. [7] Kondakoff, 199 ff.

Communion of the Apostles (in the bema), with large figures of prophets, apostles, and saints. On the west wall is the Death of the Virgin ; on the left side are various members of the Servian royal house, the lower part of the work being damaged. The architecture of the building is of the fourteenth century.

The Church of Grachanitza, founded by Milutin (A. D. 1275–1321), is painted with figures of saints, the lower part being much damaged, the building having been used as a stable by the Turks : on two piers of the central dome are seen Stephan Urosh and his Byzantine consort, Simonida.[1] The work dates from before the close of the fourteenth century, and may be contemporary with the church. In the narthex, which is a later construction, are portraits of St. Simeon

Fig. 184.   The Transfiguration : mural painting of the fourteenth century, Church of the Peribleptos, Mistra.   (*Hautes Études* : G. Millet.)

in monastic dress, and his son, St. Sava, in episcopal vestments.[2] On the west wall is the Death of the Virgin, and above it the Miracle at Cana and the Expulsion of the Merchants from the Temple. In the large dome, Our Lord with the four Evangelists, the type of head recalling that seen at Monreale. Other figures include the Virgin as *orans* between Michael and Gabriel, above her being Christ Emmanuel. Kondakoff finds the work representative of the best late Byzantine manner, ' as if illuminated miniatures had been transferred to the walls.'

Other frescoes of the sixteenth century and later, some in churches already mentioned as containing earlier work, are enumerated by Miliukoff,[3] but cannot be mentioned here.

(e) Mount Athos, Russia, the Caucasus.

The Cathedral of Sta Sophia at Kieff,[4] founded by Yaroslav in the first half of the eleventh century, has in addition to its mosaics (p. 394) an extensive

[1] Kondakoff, *Macedonia*, 205 ff. ; M. E. Durham, *High Albania*, 279 ff., 1909.
[2] Durham, as above, 281.   [3] pp. 145–6.
[4] D. Ainaloff and E. Riedin, *The Cathedral of Sta Sophia of Kieff*, St. Petersburg, 1887, serving as text to the Album issued by the Imperial Russian Archaeological Society, entitled : *Antiquities of the Russian Empire : the Cathedral of Kieff*, St. Petersburg, 1871–87. The most convenient work for a preliminary study is Ainaloff and Riedin's *Ancient Monuments of Art in Kieff* :

series of mural paintings in tempera.[1] These in their origin no doubt go back to the century in which the church was built; but the greater part of them were subjected to drastic restoration between 1843 and 1848, only those in the Chapel of St. Michael remaining untouched, by imperial command. The paintings had suffered very seriously from the various disasters which befell the building during the first five hundred years of its existence. Then in the seventeenth century, during the Uniat occupation of the fabric, they were covered with whitewash, beneath which they were rediscovered in 1843. The restorations followed the ancient work as far as it was possible to trace it, and though they cannot be regarded as absolute reproductions they present the general character of Byzantine religious art at the time of Yaroslav's conversion.

The principal paintings are in the Chapels of SS. Joachim and Anne, St. Peter, St. George, and St. Michael (only those in the latter, as above remarked, remaining in their original condition), in the transept and in the gallery, and on the walls of the stairs leading up to it. The decoration of the stairs is of exceptional interest because it is purely secular in its subjects.

The Chapel of St. Joachim and St. Anne has the various scenes based on the story of the Apocryphal Gospels, including the meeting at the Golden Gate, the Nativity of the Virgin, her life in the Temple, Betrothal to Joseph, Annunciation, and Salutation.

The work in the Chapel of St. Michael is but imperfectly preserved, but there are traces of the Victory over Satan and figures of saints, while the apse contains a fine figure of the archangel with outspread wings. On the roof are remains of scenes in which the angel appears to Joshua, Balaam, and Zachariah. The Chapel of St. Peter contains scenes from the life of the saint, including the Baptism in the House of the Centurion Cornelius and the Delivery from Prison.

In the Chapel of St. George are paintings of a similar biographical nature, the most remarkable being the martyrdom of the saint in boiling pitch.

In the transept the subjects illustrate scenes from the Passion and after: Christ before Caiaphas, the Denial of Peter, the Crucifixion, *Anastasis*, Appearance to the Holy Women, Incredulity of Thomas, the Mission of the Apostles, and the Pentecost. The Crucifixion is of the more elaborate type, with the two thieves, Longinus and Stephaton, the Virgin with three attendant women, St. John, and the centurion and his follower.

In the gallery are scenes from the Old and New Testament: Emmaus and the Miracle at Cana, Betrayal and Last Supper, Sacrifice of Isaac, Abraham entertaining the Angels, the Three Children of Babylon in the furnace. The walls and columns are covered with whole and half figures of saints, almost entirely renovated: among the whole figures may be mentioned Constantine and Helena and Cyril and Methodius; among the latter, the personifications of Faith, Hope, Charity, and Divine Wisdom; names seem to have been somewhat arbitrarily assigned to figures of which little more than the original contour was visible.

The very curious secular paintings on the walls of the staircases [2] represent performances in the hippodrome attended by the emperor and empress, perhaps on the occasion of an important public festival (Christmas?). We see the imperial personages, with their guards and attendants, seated in the *Kathisma*; the charioteers of the four factions behind the barriers ready to start; musicians, dancers, and acrobats,[3] including a man bearing a pole on his shoulder up which a boy is swarming; combats between mounted and unmounted men and beasts;

---

the *Cathedral of Sta Sophia*, Charkoff, 1899, and to this the references in the above brief account are given. See also N. Pokrovsky, *Mural Decoration of Early Greek and Russian Churches*, St. Petersburg, 1890, 45 ff.; Tolstoy and Kondakoff, *Russian Antiquities*, iv. 124. All the works mentioned are in the Russian language.

[1] Ainaloff and Riedin, 27. The colour was applied to the dry stucco by a medium of size or white of egg.

[2] Ainaloff and Riedin, 1899, 45 ff.; N. Kondakoff, *Zapiski of the Imperial Russian Archaeological Society*, iii (3–4 of new series), 287 ff.

[3] These scenes may be compared with those upon ivory carvings (consular diptychs at

single combats between pairs of men, one of the antagonists in one case wearing an animal mask over his head.[1] Some of these hunting scenes have no connexion with the amphitheatre, but are simply illustrations of the chase, as enjoyed by princes of the time.[2] There are trees in the background, and the scene is evidently laid in the open country. As some of the animals, e. g. the panther, are unknown in Russia, and the costumes are oriental, it is probable that the artists were not Russians but Greeks.

An interesting episode represents men carrying a gift of a boar's head and fore-quarter to the imperial palace.[3] An imperial procession is only preserved in a few imperfect figures. There are also the remains of hawks and falcons and of a number of fantastic animals and monsters, including winged lions and gryphons of the usual oriental type.

Russian mural painting in the twelfth century maintained the Byzantine tradition, and it is in some cases a matter of dispute whether a given work was executed by Byzantine or Russian artists. Pokrovsky[4] has traced the history of the art through the period preceding the Mongolian invasion to the Renaissance of the sixteenth century and later times. Some of the older work of the twelfth century may still have been executed by Greek artists, and Pokrovsky holds that this is often the case even where inscriptions are not in Greek, native artists, as in Italy, growing independent of their masters. The style of the work in the Mirojsky Monastir at Pskof (A. D. 1156) is almost purely Byzantine, and that in the Cathedral of St. Demetrius at Vladimir (end of the twelfth century) has been compared to MS. illumination. That at Neredits[5] (A. D. 1199), New Ladoga, in the district of Novgorod, is similar; but in the Cathedral of the Assumption at Vladimir we find a more picturesque and impressionist style analogous to that of the Peribleptos at Mistra.

Down to the sixteenth century old iconographic traditions were followed: there were fewer changes than in Western Europe. This fact, already noticed in connexion with Byzantine art as a whole, is especially conspicuous in the mediaeval art of Russia.[6] In the sixteenth century the Russians again based their art upon the earlier Byzantine models, though introducing changes of detail according with the national idiosyncrasy of taste and belief. In the seventeenth century Western influences made themselves decidedly felt.

With the exception of those in the Chapel of St. George in the Monastery of St. Paul, which date from A. D. 1423 (Fig. 185), the surviving mural paintings on Mount Athos[7] are not earlier than the first half of the sixteenth century. It is true that there is record of work of A. D. 1198 at Chilandari. and in the narthex of Vatopedi in A. D. 1312. But the old Cathedral of the Presentation at Chilandari was destroyed at the close of the thirteenth century; and the other paintings are so drastically restored that the original work is often doubtful. Those of Vatopedi were repainted in the year 1789; assuming the original

Liverpool and elsewhere; panels from a casket in British Museum (p. 223); oliphant of Jász-Berény (p. 223).　　　[1] Ainaloff and Riedin, Fig. 57. p. 48.

[2] The animals pursued are the bear, boar, panther, squirrel (?), &c.

[3] *Mural Decoration of Early Greek and Russian Churches*, ch. iv–viii. These chapters describe the paintings at Novgorod and Vladimir-Suzdal, and the post-Renaissance work at Mount Athos in Greece and Russia down to the eighteenth century.

[4] *Mural Decoration of Early Greek and Russian Churches*, ch. iv–viii.

[5] J. Ebersolt, *Mon. Piot*, xi. 1–23 and Pl.; Pokrovsky, *Mural Paintings*, 172 ff.; Bayet, *L'Art byz.*, 280.

[6] Pokrovsky, *Sketch of the Monuments of Orthodox Iconography and Art*, ch. ix–xi (St. Petersburg. 1891, in Russian). See also *B. Z.*, v, 1896, 599.

[7] N. P. Kondakoff, *Monuments of Christian Art on Athos*, St. Petersburg, 1902, 50 ff.; Pokrovsky, *Mural Decorations of Early Greek and Russian Churches*, as above (both the above in Russian); Bayet and Duchesne, *Mémoire sur une mission au Mont Athos*. Paris, 1876; Didron, *Annales archéologiques*, iv. 133, 223; v. 148; xvii. 72; xviii. 109, 197; xx. 275; xxi. 27, 80, 126; xxiii. 249; xxiv. 177; Didron, *Manuel d'iconographie chrétienne*. Introduction; Diehl, *Manuel*, p. 765. See also Brockhaus, *Die Kunst auf den Athosklostern*. Drawings by the artist Papety are in the Louvre; see also *Revue des Deux Mondes*, 1847; *Archives des missions*, ii, p. 493. For M. Miller's expedition see M. Proust's description, *Le Tour du monde*, 1861, pp. 103 ff.

compositions to have been carefully followed, they are of much interest on account of their similarity to the cycles with the life of the Virgin at Studenitza (see p. 296) and Kahrié Djami (p. 420).

These are the conclusions of the Russian archaeologists who have devoted the most careful study to these frescoes in recent times. Bishop Porphyry, Pokrovsky, and Kondakoff are in general agreement, and the opinions of earlier travellers and archaeologists, ascribing a remote date to many of these mural paintings, can no longer be accepted. The memoir by MM. Bayet and Duchesne, though published many years ago, is a short and scientific account free from

Fig. 185.   Presentation and Death of the Virgin : mural painting of A.D. 1423 in the Chapel of St. George, Monastery of St. Paul, Mount Athos.   (*Hautes Études* : G. Millet.)

the inaccuracies and hasty generalizations contained in the works of many travellers. The existing frescoes of Mount Athos do not therefore come within our limits : it may, however, be stated that the most interesting are those executed by Manuel Panselinos in A. D. 1535–6 in the Church of Protaton. A list of dates of other frescoes from the sixteenth to the eighteenth century is given by Kondakoff.[1] Bayet would assign the frescoes of Lavra to a similar date.[2] Most of the artists whose names are known were not trained on Athos : Panselinos came from Salonika, Theophanes from Crete, Mark from Georgia, and so forth. Panselinos is an interesting figure because he seems to have been acquainted with Italian art of the fifteenth century, and by this knowledge to have given new life to the earlier Byzantine types, to which, however, he remained faithful.

Mural paintings in the later Byzantine style are in the Church of Kékrési in the Caucasus.[3]

(f) Italy.

Artists from the Christian East or their pupils have left their work upon the walls of the Roman Catacombs. In the Basilica of SS. Felix and Adauctus,

[1] *Monuments of Christian Art on Mount Athos*, 53.
[2] Bayet and Duchesne, *Archives des missions*, 1876, 460 ff.
[3] Alluded to by C. de Linas, in *Revue de l'art chrétien*, 1883.

in the catacomb of Commodilla,[1] one painting represents Our Lord seated on the globe between St. Peter and St. Paul (the *Traditio clavium*), another the Virgin enthroned with the Child between SS. Adauctus and Felix, the former saint presenting to her a female figure described as Turtura. These two subjects may go back to the early sixth century. A third fresco with a standing figure of St. Luke is accompanied by an inscription stating it to have been executed in the reign of a Constantine, apparently Pogonatus (A. D. 668–85). The figure of the Virgin has been compared with that in the mosaics of S. Apollinare Nuovo at Ravenna, and the type attributed to Syria;[2] the figure of Christ in the *Traditio clavium* resembles that in the apse of S. Vitale in the same city. Figures of SS. Emerita and Stephen are also in the Ravennate style. In all these frescoes the colour is rich and solid in tone.

The well-known paintings in the catacombs of Ponzianus and Generosa are clearly dependent on Byzantine inspiration.[3] In the cemetery of Generosa are frescoes suggesting an East-Christian influence (Fig. 186).

In the catacombs of Albano, fifteen miles along the Appian Way, there is a bust of Our Lord between busts of the Virgin and S. Smaragdus, similar in style to the work in the catacomb of Ponzianus, but rougher: they may be of the ninth century.[4]

The churches of these early centuries, where they have retained their mural paintings, show an equal dependence upon East-Christian art.[5] Remains of frescoes with Greek inscriptions were found at S. Saba on the Aventine, a monastery founded by Greek monks.[6] Both here, in Sta Maria Antiqua (see below), and in the later work in S. Urbano alla Caffarella, ornamental motives occur which are found in the Codex Rossanensis and in the Gospel of Rabula (see pp. 448, 452); conspicuous among these are the borders formed of overlapping disks tinted in various colours.[7] The frescoes at S. Saba are in the oratory of S. Silvia beneath the larger basilica of the twelfth century. Figures of saints, and a bust of Our Lord, unfortunately damaged, are so finely treated and so nearly allied to East-Christian work that they must be ascribed to Greek artists.[8] A group of monks in a cruder style appears to be later, though also oriental. Scenes from the life of Christ of small size correspond to the work of Pope John VII in Sta Maria Antiqua.

The mural paintings of Sta Maria *in Schola Graeca*, executed during the papacy of Hadrian (A. D. 772–95), are Byzantine in style.[9]

The mural paintings in the Church of Sta Maria Antiqua under the Palatine Hill and adjoining the forum illustrate in the most remarkable manner the art which prevailed at Rome during the Dark Ages.[10] The church, which was

---

[1] J. Wilpert, *Nuovo Bullettino di arch. crist.*, 1904, 161 ff. and Pl. V–VII; A. Muñoz, *Pitture medievali romane*, in *L'Arte*, 1905.

[2] A. Muñoz in *L'Arte*, as above, 55 ff.; *B. Z.*, xiv, 1905, 728.

[3] See J. Wilpert, *Die Malereien der Katakomben*, 255, 257, 258, 262.

[4] *Nuovo Bullettino di arch. crist.*, 1902, 101–2 and Pl. IV. Above the Virgin's head are the words MITER THEV.

[5] Cf. also the *mosaics* of the Triumphal Arch of Sta Maria Maggiore (p. 338).

[6] Grisar, in *Civiltà Cattolica*, ser. 18, ii, p. 589; iii. 719; v. 194. See also *B. Z.*, x, 1901, 714; xi, 1902, 661.　　　　[7] A. Muñoz, *Il Codice purpureo di Rossano*, 22.

[8] Wüscher-Becchi, *R. Q.*, xvi, 1903; *Die griechischen Wandmalereien in S. Saba*. Frothingham, assuming the monastery to have been founded in the sixth century, would ascribe the finest frescoes to about A.D. 600 (*The Monuments of Christian Rome*, 291). Wilpert (*Studi su l'iconografia cristiana*, in *Mélanges d'arch. et d'histoire*, xxvi, 1906) assigns the earliest to the time of John VII, the later perhaps to that of Paschal I (A.D. 817–24).

[9] Frothingham, *Journ. Amer. Arch.*, x, 1895, p. 186.

[10] For the literature down to the year 1905 see C. Hülsen, *Röm. Mitth.*, xx. 84–94. The first comprehensive account in English is that of Mr. G. N. Rushforth in *Papers of the British School at Rome*, vol. i. Wilpert, who criticizes Rushforth on many points, has given excellent reproductions in *L'Arte*, xiii, 1910, 1 ff., and will publish the whole decoration of the church. See also *B. Z.*, x, 1901, 713; xii, 1903, 434; xiv, 1905, 578; xv, 1906, 413; Venturi, *Storia*, ii. 257 ff., 377 ff.; E. Bertaux, *Rome*, ii, 50 ff.; W. von Grüneisen in *Archivio della R. Soc. rom. di storia patria*, xxix, 1906; *Studi iconografici*, &c.; Diehl, *Manuel*, 327 ff.; Photographs by Dr. G. Gargiolli in the *Gabinetto Fotografico* of the Ministry of Public Instruction, Via in Miranda 1.

FIG. 186. Our Lord and Saints: early mural painting in the Cemetery of Generosa, Rome. (N. H. J. Westlake: *History of Design in Mural Painting*.) P. 304.

crushed and buried by the fall of buildings above it in the ninth century, received its decoration at various times between the sixth (possibly even the fifth) and eighth centuries. The oldest work is seen in the lowest layer in the presbytery;

Fig. 187.   Mural paintings in Sta Maria Antiqua, Rome.
(N. H. J. Westlake : *History of Design in Mural Painting.*)

the second layer should not be much later than the middle of the seventh century, as the inscriptions on the scrolls held by the Fathers of the Church are derived from the *Acta* of the Lateran Council of A. D. 649. They may have been executed under Pope Martinus (A. D. 649–53). The third layer in the same place is ascribed to the time of John VII (A. D. 705–7). The work in the Chapel of the Crucifixion is assigned to the time of Zacharias (A. D. 741–52) ; that on the presbytery apse to that of Paul I (A. D. 757–67) ; and that of the right wall of the court to that of Hadrian I (A. D. 772–93). Some of the representations of popes have the square nimbus, an indication that the painting was done in their lifetime.[1] The Chapel of the Forty Martyrs has a figure of St. Leo, medallions with busts of saints, a subject which may have been the *Anastasis*, the Virgin, to whom a saint presents a pope with square nimbus, two large crosses with medallions containing heads of Our Lord and the Virgin, below which are lambs and peacocks, scenes perhaps from the life of St. Anthony, and (in the apse) the Forty Martyrs frozen to death.

The court of Sta Maria Antiqua has on the entrance wall St. Agnes, St. Cecilia, and other male and female saints ; on the right side Pope Hadrian offering a book to the Virgin, St. Silvester, and other saints ; near these figures are a Christ enthroned, St. Anthony the hermit, and a female saint. In the southern corner is a female figure with dedicatory inscription, the name unfortunately destroyed. On the left wall are more recent scenes from the life of St. Anthony ; in the left corner a colossal head of St. Abbakyros, with spatula and medicine boxes. On the wall opposite the entrance hardly anything remains but an inscription giving a year conjectured to be A. D. 792.

In the nave the decoration is largely upon the piers : it comprises a head of the Virgin, Daniel in the Lions' Den, St. Salomone and her Seven Sons (2 Macc. vii), Our Lord enthroned between angels, the Annunciation (two representations, one over the other, of different age), St. Demetrius, Judith with the head of Holofernes, the Virgin with the Child, St. Anne with the infant Virgin and Elizabeth with St. John ; above are scenes from the New Testament, almost totally destroyed, though the Nativity and Adoration of the Magi can be distinguished. The left aisle has Our Lord, with eleven Latin saints on his right and nine Greek saints on his left. Above are scenes from the Old Testament in two rows, the best preserved representing the history of Joseph.

By the entrance into the Chapel of the Crucifixion are two nude figures, perhaps part of the group of the Forty Martyrs ; on piers are Christ between saints, and the Three Children in the Fiery Furnace. In the lunette over the apse is Christ crucified adored by angels, with a long inscription in Greek. Below this are four half-figures of popes each with a rectangular nimbus, one with his name, *S. Martinus p(a)p(a) Romanus*. Below, and immediately to the right of the apse, three layers of stucco are distinguished, and the work may be described as palimpsest. The lowest layer has the Virgin enthroned, adored by angels ; the next, a mutilated Annunciation, in which the heads of the Virgin and the angel remain ; the uppermost, almost life-sized figures of SS. Gregory of Nazianzus and Basil. In the corresponding position to the left of the apse only a nimbus with the name *S. Augus(t)in(u)s* remains. Below the palimpsest only the second layer is preserved, with figures of St. Basil and St. John Chrysostom holding inscribed scrolls ; to these figures correspond those of SS. Leo and Gregory of Nazianzus on the left. The subjects on the upper part of the wall are entirely perished.

In the apse[2] Paul I adores Our Lord, who stands between tetramorphs.

On the upper part of the side walls were continuous series of New Testament scenes in two superposed rows. The story began on the left wall next the entrance, but the only subjects which now remain are the Adoration of the Magi, Christ before Pilate, the Bearing of the Cross, and a figure of the Virgin at the far end ; below is a row of Apostles' heads in medallions. The series is continued on the right wall, but the following alone are distinct : the Incredulity of Thomas, the Appearance of Our Lord on Lake Tiberias, the *Traditio clavium*, and the Appearance of Our Lord in Galilee. Below these are Apostles' heads in medallions corresponding to those on the opposite side. The lower part of the wall is painted to resemble hangings (cf. Kuṣeir ʿAmra, p. 282), but near the door is a figure of a female saint carrying a child.

---

[1] These examples of the square nimbus have given rise to some controversy (see *B. Z.*, xv. 700).   [2] Wüscher-Becchi, *Zeitschr. für christl. Kunst*, 1904, pp. 289 ff.

The left-hand lateral chapel has on the back wall the Crucifixion, below which is a Virgin with SS. Peter, Paul, Quiricus, and Julitta. Other subjects are the founder carrying a model of the church, and three figures of popes. On the side walls are eight scenes from the life of SS. Quiricus and Julitta, and the family of Theodotus (?) adoring (the Virgin ?); on the entrance wall are Theodotus (?) kneeling before SS. Quiricus and Julitta,[1] and other saints.

In the right-hand lateral chapel are figures of various saints.

Fig. 188.   The Crucifixion : mural painting in Sta Maria Antiqua, Rome.
(N. H. J. Westlake : *History of Design in Mural Painting.*)

The frescoes in the lower Church of S. Clemente have affinities with East-Christian art, but can hardly be described as Byzantine.[2]

The earlier wall paintings in the rock-cut oratories and churches of Southern Italy [3] are for the most part the work of Basilian monks who lived as eremites in these regions and gathered at regular intervals to attend services in common.

---

[1] Probable repainting makes the identity of Theodotus uncertain (*B. Z.*, xv. 700).

[2] Wilpert, *Le Pitture di S. Clemente* in *Mélanges de Rome*, 1906. For those in S. Maria in Via Lata, see Cavazzi, *Nuovo Bullettino di Arch. Crist.*, xi, pp. 123 ff. ; of the ninth or tenth century at Vallerano, Calosso, *Gli affreschi della grotta del Salvatore*, &c., 1907. For others in the Cathedral of Anagni, P. Toesca in *Le Gallerie nazionali*, v, pp. 151 ff. Cf. also references in *B. Z.*, xii, 1903, p. 709.

[3] Salazaro, *Studi sui monumenti dell' arte meridionale dal IV° al XIII° secolo* ; Diehl, *L'Art byzantin dans l'Italie méridionale*, 1894, and *Manuel*, p. 542 ; Ch. Bayet, *L'Art byzantin*, pp. 299–301 ; Lenormant, *Notes archéologiques sur la terre d'Otrante* in *Gazette archéologique*, 1881–2.

In many respects these chambers recall those of Cappadocia (see p. 268) decorated approximately at the same time and under similar conditions.

These mural paintings of Calabria and the region of Otranto begin with the tenth century, and the oldest are purely Byzantine, executed in simple tones without bright colours or gilding. In the twelfth century a new art appears, still obeying the old iconographic rules, but marked by a freer style and a richer scheme of colour: in the thirteenth and fourteenth centuries the work of this school was considerable, and is well represented by existing remains.[1] The inscriptions which constantly accompany the paintings are both in Greek and Latin, sometimes in one language alone, sometimes in both; but it hardly appears possible to distinguish between frescoes with Greek and those with Latin inscriptions. At Soleto, SS. Stefani near Vaste, in the crypts of Grottaglie, and of S. Biagio near Brindisi, work which almost seems inspired by the feeling of contemporary Tuscan art is described by Greek legends; conversely, in the crypt of St. John near Brindisi figures conceived in the purely oriental tradition are accompanied by inscriptions in Latin. There was a gradual transition from the Byzantine to the Italian manner; and though Latin tended to predominate from the thirteenth century, the occurrence of Latin inscriptions is not a certain test of indigenous origin.

At Carpignano, north-east of Otranto, in a crypt beneath the Church of Sta Maria delle Grazie, are paintings of various periods. In a niche is a Christ enthroned,[2] with an inscription below it giving the date as the year of the world 6467, corresponding to A.D. 959. This evidence lends this representation of Our Lord an especial value, for as a rule it is only miniatures which can be dated with such absolute precision. The execution is superior and the type is purely Byzantine. In a niche in the right wall Christ is again seen enthroned; here the style is ruder, the elongation accentuated, the hands and draperies ill drawn. An accompanying inscription gives the date as A.D. 1020. In the end wall is an arcosolium with figures of SS. Theodore (?), Nicholas, and the Virgin seated with the Child. The conventionality of the style and the exaggerated length of the faces suggest the twelfth century; in the inscription the date is uncertain, but may possibly be A.D. 1146. On one of the pillars are three saints, perhaps of the thirteenth century. Other figures of SS. Nicholas and Christina are probably not earlier than the fifteenth.[3]

In the crypt of Sta Lucia near Brindisi are niches with a Virgin enthroned with the Child, of the twelfth century,[4] and later figures of SS. Peter, Mary Magdalene, and Nicholas. In the Church of S. Giovanni in Sepolcro, a circular building of the twelfth century, are figures of saints not earlier than the fourteenth century, apparently superposed upon frescoes of earlier date.

In the crypt of St. John, situated in the farm of Cafaro in the same district, a fine figure of an archangel, with orb and staff and wearing richly embroidered robes, is in the style of Byzantine art of the eleventh and twelfth centuries, to which period it appears to belong:[5] the other wall paintings at this place appear to be of the thirteenth or fourteenth century.

The neighbouring crypt of S. Biagio affords excellent examples of the two styles of local art, the Byzantine and the indigenous, painted over frescoes of earlier date. The former are upon the roof, the latter upon the walls of the crypt. The date of the earlier designs (A.D. 1197) is given in an inscription above the entrance doorway. The subjects of the roof, which is divided into five compartments, are the Flight into Egypt (partially over-painted), the

---

[1] Diehl considers this freer style the evidence of reawakening Italian art in the South of Italy; Millet contests this (*B. Z.*, xiv, 1905, 624), pointing out that an equal freedom and vivacity characterize the fine frescoes of Mistra in the Peloponnese (see p. 293).

[2] Diehl, *L'Art byz.*, Fig. on p. 35.   [3] Diehl, as above, 29.

[4] Diehl, p. 47; Salazaro, as above, ii, pp. 30-1.   [5] Diehl, Fig. on p. 49.

Presentation, Annunciation (Fig. 189),[1] and Entry into Jerusalem, the scenes following the usual Byzantine arrangement, and a remarkable figure of Our Lord with the open book containing the text 'I am the Light of the World'. The expression is severe, and on either side of the head are the words 'The Ancient of Days'.[2] The symbols of the Evangelists accompany this figure. The paintings on the walls are for the most part saints, with a fine representation of SS. George and Demetrius on horseback slaying dragons (Fig. 190).[3] The Nativity

FIG. 189.   The Annunciation : mural painting in the crypt of S. Biagio, Brindisi.
(N. H. J. Westlake : *History of Design in Mural Painting*.)

finds a place among the saints. These frescoes appear to be of the fourteenth century.

In the territory of Otranto there are mural paintings of considerable historical importance. In a small basilican church (the grotto dei Santi Stefani), cut in the tufa near the village of Vaste near Otranto, the work of three periods may be seen.[4] The Christ standing upon a footstool between two adoring angels in the right apse,[5] SS. Nicholas, Basil, and Gregory in the corresponding apse on the left, and the neighbouring figure of the Archangel Michael appear to be Byzantine work of the early twelfth century. These paintings are executed upon a coating of stucco applied directly to the wall. Another series of paintings covers a second layer of plaster, laid over the first where the work appeared to need renovation. The most important of this group is a Virgin standing as *orans* in a long red mantle ; a saint (St. John ?) kneels at her right, and draws her attention to four diminutive figures kneeling on the other side, above whose heads is an inscription giving a date—the year of the world 6884 (A.D. 1376). Many other figures of saints upon a similar

---

[1] Busts of David and Isaiah on medallions are introduced into this scene.
[2] 'Ο παλαιὸς τῶν ἡμερῶν.   For the confusion of attributes of the Father and the Son see Ch. XII.   [3] Diehl, 61.   [4] Diehl, 64 ff.   [5] Diehl, Fig. on p. 71.

layer of plaster and of the same style may thus be ascribed to the last quarter of the fourteenth century. Most of these cover the piers and have kneeling worshippers before them, with inscriptions giving their names.[1]

The third series also consists of figures of saints, but these are of more careless execution, and with Latin inscriptions ; they probably date from the end of the fifteenth, or the beginning of the sixteenth century.

The rock chapel of Celimanna, in the south of the Terra d'Otranto, has figures of saints with bilingual inscriptions, apparently of the fifteenth century, while others, with Greek inscriptions only, appear to be earlier.[2] In the crypt of the Church of the Carmine at Ruffano is a St. Peter perhaps as early as the year A.D. 1200.[3] In an early structure known as the Cento Pietre, south of Ruffano, converted into a chapel in the Middle Ages, is a seated female figure with a child on her knees raising his arms in the attitude of an *orans* ; this appears to be a representation of St. Anne rather than of the Virgin, and Diehl considers it as early as the eleventh century.[4] A Virgin and Child, a figure of a saint, and a fragmentary Annunciation appear to be of the same date. Other saints are of the fourteenth century, and most of the paintings are in bad condition.

In the apse of the circular rock crypt dell' Annunziata between Lecce and Tarento[5] is a St. George in a red tunic, carrying his lance. The work, which is much affected by damp, may be as early as the eleventh century. Other figures of saints in a rock chapel near the Lama di Villanova are perhaps a century later. The walls of the Chapel of San Stefano at Soleto in the Terra d'Otranto are covered with paintings, of which only those of the apse are upon the original plaster. The subject in the apse is the Pentecost, represented in a manner which differs in various points from the usual type, and is assigned by Diehl to the twelfth or thirteenth century.[6] At the top of the composition is a bust of the Almighty as the Ancient of Days, with the Son and the dove, representing the Holy Spirit, all within one aureole. The lower lateral walls are covered with figures of saints, above which are on one side scenes from the life of Christ, on the other scenes from the story of St. Stephen. Above the apse is the Annunciation ; on the west wall, in its usual place, is the Last Judgement,[7] the elaborate scheme followed being in the main that adopted at Torcello and at S. Angelo in Formis, though among the damned who are being carried by devils are simple labourers and tradesmen, indicated by the names of their callings. An inscription on the left wall appears to give the date A.D. 1347. Iconographically they are for the most part Byzantine, and the inscriptions are Greek ; but we seem to trace the moving of another spirit.

The oratories and chapels cut in the sides of the *gravine* (valleys with precipitous limestone walls) which cross the plain between the mountains and the sea in the region of Tarento are frequently decorated with mural paintings, though the country is not so rich as that just described. Most of them were the places of worship for communities of eremite monks, whose cells may be seen in the vicinity ; but some were perhaps places of pilgrimage only. In a few cases chapels and cells are cut in the rock which forms the floor of the valleys, and are entered by a stair which descends from amidst the cultivated fields. For the most part they were already abandoned by the sixteenth century : some have altogether disappeared. The more important are situated within a radius of fifteen or twenty miles of Tarento, near the villages of Massafrà, Mottola, Grottaglie, and Palaggianello. In the *gravina di San Marco* near the first-named place, the rock chapel of La Candelora[8] has figures of saints, the Virgin as *orans*, and the scene of the Presentation

---

[1] Many of the names are those of women, showing that this church was used by a mixed congregation.
[2] Diehl, 84. [3] Ibid., 86. [4] Ibid., 87-8. [5] Ibid., 89.
[6] Diehl, 99-101. [7] Ibid., 101 ff. [8] Ibid., 117.

in the Temple, the inscriptions being in Latin, but the style and iconography Byzantine: none of these paintings appear to be earlier than the thirteenth century. In the Chapel of San Leonardo in the same valley, with saints of late date, probably of the sixteenth century, are others, including a St. Stephen, in an earlier style: in the apse is the *Deesis*, but with a Latin inscription: the work may be of the fourteenth century.[1] The Chapel of St. Pantaleon in the same neighbourhood has lost its frescoes.

In the *gravina* of Mottola, the Chapel of the Madonna of the Seven Lamps, which does not appear to have been a monastic church, has figures of saints

Fig. 190. SS. George, Demetrius, and Nicholas: mural painting of the fourteenth century in the grotto of S. Biagio, Otranto. (*Hautes Études*: G. Millet.) P. 310.

and the *Deesis* with Latin inscriptions, probably painted in the fourteenth century.[2] A chapel near the farm of Casalrutta[3] in the same *gravina* has numerous frescoes, apparently of the fourteenth century. The inscriptions are in Latin, but the inspiration and the general scheme are Byzantine. The paintings which are best preserved are in the three apses; one apse has the *Deesis*, another Christ enthroned between St. James(?) and the Virgin, the third Christ standing between Michael and Gabriel. In a crypt below, also at one time entirely covered with paintings, an apse has Our Lord between St. Basil and St. Andrew.

The Chapel of Sta Margherita, in a deserted ravine not far from Casalrutta, has paintings of two periods on different layers of stucco, the later, apparently of the fourteenth century, replacing figures, probably of the same saints, of a century or so earlier.[4] Even the later subjects, though the inscriptions have Latin characters, are inspired by Eastern models, for a St. Demetrius pierces with his lance a small figure in ecclesiastical vestments described as Arius, a subject which is not Western. On the second pillar of the chapel, painted on stucco applied directly to the wall, is a fine St. Michael with spear and orb, and with his name in Greek. In the apse is a *Deesis*; and near it a

[1] Diehl, 123.   [2] Ibid., 124.   [3] Ibid., 124 ff.   [4] Ibid., 137.

Virgin and Child: like the archangel, these two paintings appear to be of the earlier date.

The *gravina* of Grottaglie east of Tarentum has several rock chapels, some of which have been wilfully damaged in the nineteenth century: the principal is known as the Church of Lama di Pensiero.[1] Here the walls have figures of saints, Gospel scenes (Entry into Jerusalem, Last Supper, Christ before Pilate, Crucifixion, Annunciation, Nativity, and Presentation in the Temple (?)). The Virgin is twice represented, once holding the Child, with an archangel in a sumptuous costume holding an orb; a second time, also between angels, with a small figure of a kneeling donor at her feet. The names are in Greek, and a lost inscription is said to have given the date as A. D. 1392.

The *gravina* of Palaggianello[2] has also several chapels, one of which, that of St. Nicholas, is very remarkable. The Chapel of S. Girolamo contains work of two periods, some with Latin inscriptions and apparently of the fifteenth century, others probably older, representing a person in a rich Byzantine costume, and a figure of a prophet. The Chapel of St. Andrea has a mounted St. George, apparently of the fourteenth century, with a Greek inscription: other saints of the same period have in some cases Greek, in others Latin inscriptions, the work being of a uniform character.

The Chapel of St. Nicholas[3] has in the central apse a standing figure of Our Lord between St. Nicholas and the Virgin: on the wall to the right of the entrance Christ is again seen, enthroned in rich apparel; behind him are two angels; at his feet kneels a donor. Other paintings on the walls represent St. Peter and St. Matthew. All have Latin inscriptions and appear to date from the fourteenth century.

The Chapel of St. George,[4] excavated like a crypt in the floor of the valley, has round the walls niches with figures of saints, and Our Lord between St. George and St. Paul, at his feet a kneeling figure of a monk named Paul; the inscriptions are in Latin, but the types, especially that of St. George, are Byzantine. The Chapel of the Holy Eremites,[5] in the flank of the *gravina*, was a monastic church. It contains paintings of purely Byzantine style with Greek inscriptions, perhaps of the twelfth century. On the end wall behind the altar are St. Michael, in jewelled robes, holding a spear and an orb, and St. Eustathius with the stag. near the horns of which are the letters IC. XC, and the inscription ὦ Πλάκιδα τί με διόκις.[6] Between the two is a small niche with a cross between the letters M Γ B X.[7]

The Chapel of St. Nicholas, at the foot of the hill of Mottola, shows work of the same transitional character as that of Sta Margherita near Casalrutta (see above). The plan is Greek, as also are the types of the numerous saints which cover the walls. In some cases Greek names are still visible, though most are Latin; and it is evident that earlier Byzantine figures have been 'Romanized', and the names replaced in Latin; there is only one layer of stucco on the walls. The decoration of the apses remains untouched. In the centre is the bust of the Pantokrator, flanked by St. John the Baptist and the Virgin. On the right is St. Michael, bearing an orb or medallion inscribed XC NIK(ᾶ), and near him the Dream of Zachariah; on the left is Our Lord enthroned with St. Stephen at his feet, and another representation of St. Michael. These earlier paintings are perhaps of the eleventh century, and to this date the original decoration of the whole chapel seems to have belonged. The palaeography of the Latin inscriptions suggests the fourteenth century as the probable period when restoration took place.

[1] Diehl, 127. [2] Ibid., 129 ff. [3] Ibid., 130.
[4] Ibid., 131. [5] Ibid., 132.
[6] St. Eustathius (= St. Eustace and St. Hubert) bore the name of Placidas before his conversion. His story is told in the Golden Legend.
[7] Diehl conjectures as a possible reading: Μήτηρ γεννᾶ βρέφος Χριστόν.

In the district of Matera,[1] which was lost to the empire in A.D. 1041, the influence of Byzantine art had been equally great, though the mural paintings which remain are less considerable. In the *gravina* of Matera, the rock chapels of Sta Barbara and Cappuccino Vecchio have work of the fourteenth century; a Virgin with the Child in that of Santa Sofia may be of the thirteenth. In

Fig. 191.　Mural paintings over the door and over the central arch of the porch. S. Angelo in Formis.　(N. H. J. Westlake : *History of Design in Mural Painting*.)　P. 316.

the Chapel of St. Nicholas, in the southern part of the *gravina*, once the church of a monastic community, little of the once rich decoration remains intact, but an Annunciation can still be distinguished; in the apse a figure of Our Lord is in almost perfect condition, but neither painting is earlier than the fourteenth century. In one of the three oratories known as the Madonna of the Three Doors, there is a majestic Virgin, which in many ways recalls the art of Cimabue and may be of the early part of the thirteenth century. In the Chapel of Cascione, the Greek and Latin rites appear both to have been

[1] Diehl, 151 ff.

used, and the paintings, of which the principal is a Virgin between two saints, have inscriptions in the two languages, which makes it probable that the later part of the fourteenth century is their date. The Chapel of Sta Lucia of Bradano, not explored by Diehl, is said to have a colossal head of Our Lord of the twelfth century.[1]

In Campania the direct influence of Byzantine mosaic compositions introduced by the artists imported by Desiderius is to be inferred in certain cases, as in a church at Foro Claudio, two miles from Carinola on the road to Sessa, where an apse with the Virgin and Child enthroned above the Twelve Apostles

FIG. 192. The Crucifixion : mural painting in S. Angelo in Formis.
(N. H. J. Westlake : *History of Design in Mural Painting.*)   P. 316.

is after a Byzantine model exemplified in the mosaics of Torcello (see p. 402) and Monreale, and in S. Giusto at Trieste :[2] it appears to belong to the latter part of the eleventh century. But as a rule in this region such Byzantine influence as exists appears to have come south from Rome, and to represent the earlier traditions of the eighth and ninth centuries, when the capital was filled with immigrant Greek monks. The colouring of many mural paintings recalls the scheme of the Roman mosaic-workers of that time ; details of dress seem to point in the same direction. The work appears to be earlier than the twelfth century : the Crucifixion, martyrdom, and figures of saints in the Grotta dei Santi[3] (tenth century), the Virgin and saints of the Grotta delle Formelle[4] (tenth–eleventh centuries), the busts of Our Lord, St. Michael, and

[1] Diehl, 159.   [2] E. Bertaux, *L'Art dans l'Italie méridionale,* i. 270.   [3] Ibid., 245.
[4] Salazaro, *Monumenti dell' Italia meridionale,* i. 58.

St. Gabriel, with figures of other saints at S. Biagio near Castellamare,[1] the saints in the chapel on the promontory of Montorso and of the ruined Church of Sta Maria di Trochio near Monte Cassino, all exhibit affinities with the work of the early Roman school. They differ from the frescoes of Apulia and the Basilicata, where Byzantine influence dates from the Basilian revival.

The eleventh-century frescoes of the Church of S. Angelo in Formis have given rise to interminable polemics between those affirming the Byzantine character of the work and those who find in it an almost independent Italian initiative.[2] The principal champions of the latter theory are F. X. Kraus and Caravita; of the former view, Eduard Dobbert and A. Muñoz. There seems to be little doubt that the conception of the subjects is Byzantine ; Byzantine, too, are very many of the facial types and the details of costume. It may be conceded that the greater part of this important mural decoration was executed by Italian artists, but artists trained in Greek methods ; the type of several scenes resembles that of the corresponding subjects in the Codex Rossanensis (p. 452), and the types of the Entry into Jerusalem, Last Supper, Washing of the Disciples' Feet, and Raising of Lazarus are oriental. On the other hand, in many scenes fresh traits are introduced which are certainly of Western origin. We must perhaps imagine a group of painters partly Greek and partly Italian, obeying Byzantine ideals, and working under the direction of Byzantine masters. The state of affairs is in fact analogous to that which obtained about the same time among the mosaicists of Venice (p. 399). The most Byzantine work is in the narthex, where cursive Greek inscriptions are found,[3] and in the apse.

In German countries Byzantine influence is evident in mural paintings as in MSS. It appears, for instance, at Salzburg (Nonnberg), and on Lake Constance.[4]

II. Panel Painting.

Portable pictures, which were introduced in Martyria as early as the fourth century,[5] were usually executed upon wooden panels, and the subjects of those which have been preserved are almost all religious. The study of the earlier periods is rendered difficult by the rarity of surviving works, and by the complete or partial invisibility of many ikons in churches, which are often placed in ill-lighted positions and sometimes partly covered over with silver and gold plates and precious stones.[6]

Out of the darkness enveloping the origins of Byzantine painting a few facts emerge. The earliest surviving work is evidently allied to that of the portraits on the mummies of Graeco-Roman Egypt.[7] The Russian bishop Porphyrius Uspenski brought home from Sinai several panel pictures, now in the Ecclesiastical Academy at Kieff, which make the earliest developments of painting in the East-Roman Empire comparatively clear. They are all on panels, executed like the Egyptian portraits by the encaustic process,[8] and

---

[1] Bertaux, 247 ; Schulz, *Denkmäler der Kunst des Mittelalters in Unteritalien*, ii, 224–6.

[2] Salazaro, *Monumenti dell' Italia meridionale*, fasc. ix and x ; Caravita, I *codici e le Arti a Monte Cassino*, vol. i, p. 259 ; H. W. Schulz, *Denkmäler der Kunst des Mittelalters in Unteritalien*, 1860, Atlas, Pl. LXXI ; F. X. Kraus, Prussian *Jahrbuch*, xiv, 1893, 84 ff., and *Repertorium*, xxiii, 1900, 53 ; E. Dobbert, Prussian *Jahrbuch*, xv, 1894, 221, and *Repertorium*, 1892; see also *Jahrbuch*, xix (1898), remarks in the course of the author's article on the Goslar Gospels ; Ch. Diehl, *L'Art byzantin dans l'Italie méridionale*, 109, and *Manuel*, 681 ff.

[3] Diehl, *Manuel*, 681.

[4] F. X. Kraus, *Wandgemälde der S. Sylvesterkapelle am Bodensee* ; P. Buberl, *Kunstgeschichtliches Jahrb. der K. K. Zentral-Commission*, 1909, pp. 74 ff. (Nonnberg).

[5] Chrysostom, Gregory of Nyssa, and Prudentius. See refs. in Garrucci, *Storia*, i. 467 ff.

[6] This custom, familiar to all who have visited Russian churches, descends from Byzantine times. In the inventories of the eleventh century there is mention of pictures so treated (A. Muñoz, *L'Art byz. à l'exposition de Grottaferrata*, 16).

[7] Examples in the National Gallery and the British Museum, the Musée Guimet, Paris, the Berlin Museums, the Vatican, &c. Two encaustic portraits of rather later date were discovered at Antinoe (*Ann. du Musée Guimet*, 1902, Pl. XI, after p. 140).

[8] Κηρόχυτος γραφή. The description of the process in Pliny is not quite clear. It seems

represent the Virgin and Child in half figure, St. John the Baptist or a prophet, busts of St. Sergius and St. Bacchus side by side, busts of a male and female saint in the same position, and a half figure of St. Panteleemon.[1] The Virgin closely resembles a female sepulchral portrait on linen from Antinoe, painted in the fourth century, and presented by M. Gayet to the Egyptian Museum of the Vatican (p. 318, n. 1). She has the same large black eyes and full lips, and is represented in so naturalistic a manner that without the nimbus she might well represent an Egyptian lady of the Fayûm. This picture of the Virgin is the earliest of the series, though Kondakoff places it as late as the sixth century. The other panels are so conventional in their treatment of faces and drapery that they may be as late as the ninth or tenth ; if these dates are correct, the tradition of encaustic painting must have survived the Arab conquest of Egypt. The other ikons of the group are attributed to the seventh century or even later. Examples of encaustic painting in the Kaiser Friedrich Museum at Berlin establish the Egyptian descent yet more definitely. The principal specimens are a rectangular casket with busts of Our Lord and SS. Luke, Thomas, and Cosmas, and a palette with a bust of the Virgin (?), the one attributed to the fifth or sixth, the other to the sixth or seventh century, and both from Egypt.[2] Another object, a single panel, has busts of a female saint (?) and of St. Theodore.[3]

The process, which long coexisted with tempera, seems to have gradually lost favour with artists, and not to have been common in the Third Period.[4] It was apparently applied upon occasion to canvas or linen. Asterius of Amaseia describes a cycle of four scenes from the story of St. Euphemia in her martyrion at Chalcedon (Kadikeui) which seem to have been painted in this way.[5]

The great majority of East-Christian panel paintings are in tempera. Their number is considerable, and will be increased as well by future discovery as by the scientific examination of ikons now inaccessible in churches. In the present place attention can only be drawn to certain representative examples.

Ainaloff believes that the leaf of a painted wooden triptych in the Golenisheff Collection at St. Petersburg, with two superposed compartments, one with the Nativity, the other with the Baptism, is as early as the sixth century.[6] He compares the type of the Baptism with that of the Etchmiadzin Gospels (p. 450), and notes analogies with the ivory chair of Maximianus (p. 203) and with the central panel of a composite diptych formerly in Lord Crawford's collection (Fig. 114).

The panel painted on linen stretched on wood, with a figure of Our Lord, discovered in the Sancta Sanctorum at the Lateran, was reputed to be of Eastern origin. It is in very bad condition, but Mgr. Wilpert, who subjected it to

---

probable that the painter heated certain spatulate implements (*causeria*) before applying the wax ; a fresco at Kertch (Panticapaeum) shows a painter in the act of heating such an instrument (see H. Stuart Jones, *Quarterly Review*, No. 419, April, 1909, pp. 452-3). According to another theory the wax was liquefied by mixing with oil.

[1] Reproduced by Muñoz, as above, Figs. 3 (two saints), 4 (SS. Sergius and Bacchus), 5 (Virgin and Child). Publications of one or more of these panels by Likhacheff, *Material for the History of Russian Ikon Painting*, i, Pl. I and II ; Strzygowski, *Byzantinische Denkmäler*, i, Pl. VIII, *Orient oder Rom*, 124 ; by Ainaloff, *Encaustic Religious Paintings from Sinai* in *V. V.*, 1902, 343 ff. ; and Kondakoff, *Monuments of Christian Art upon Mount Athos*, Pl. XLIX and L, and Figs. 52 and 53. See also *B. Z.*, xii, 1903, 703.

[2] Wulff, *Berlin Catalogue*, Nos. 1604, 1605 (ref. to earlier publication).

[3] Ibid., No. 1606, ascribed to the sixth–seventh century.

[4] Pictures of saints in the chapels at Sta Sophia, known as the σηκρητά, appear to have been encaustic (J. P. Richter, *Quellen der byz. Kunstgeschichte*, 1897, 59, 92).

[5] Migne, *Patr. gr.*, xl. 333-7. On the text see Strzygowski, *Orient oder Rom*, 118-19, who has drawn attention to the importance of the passage for the history of art. It had been previously cited by Garrucci, *Storia*, i. 471 ; but its significance had not been fully appreciated.

[6] *V. V.*, v. 181 ff. and Pl. II. See also Strzygowski, *Denkschriften der k. Akad. der Wissenschaften*, li, Vienna, 1906, 199. The subjects are painted upon a thin layer of stucco applied to the wood.

a very careful examination, suggests a Roman origin at the end of the fifth or in the earlier part of the sixth century.[1]

Dr. Jelič is of opinion that the panel with SS. Peter and Paul in the Vatican is the work of the missionary St. Methodius, and that it was presented to the Pope during the saint's sojourn in Rome between the years 867 and 869.[2]

The wooden reliquary-box with sliding lid found in the Sancta Sanctorum (Fig. 193) has on the top of the lid a figure of St. John Chrysostom, on the under side of the lid the Crucifixion between the Virgin and St. John, and on the bottom of the interior a cross of double traverse in intaglio, flanked by painted figures of SS. Peter and Paul, busts of Our Lord and the Virgin. and two angels.

FIG. 193. Paintings on a wooden reliquary from the Sancta Sanctorum, Vatican Library. (After Ph. Lauer, *Mon. Piot*, 1907.)

The eleventh century has been suggested as the date of the work, but it may be rather later.[3] A period not much later has been proposed for a small picture of the Crucifixion surrounded by other subjects in the Alexander III Museum at St. Petersburg.[4]

The remarkable series of pictures upon the iconostasis in the Church of St. Clement at Ochrida[5] are evidently early ; most are assigned by Kondakoff to the thirteenth and fourteenth centuries, though two or three are said to be of the twelfth. Among these are a pair of panels, one representing the Archangel Gabriel, the other the seated Virgin, together forming an Annunciation group, perhaps for the two sides of an iconostasis. There are five other pictures of the Virgin, two of the Hodegetria type, one described on the (contemporary) frame

---

[1] *R. Q.*, xxi. 65 ff. and figures. We may note that in Egypt figure subjects of a fine quality were painted upon linen alone. Cf. the already mentioned portrait from Antinoe in the Egyptian collections at the Vatican, of which Diehl gives an illustration (*Manuel*, Fig. 20).

[2] *De Rossi-Festschrift*, Rome, 1892, pp. 83–94. Old tradition ascribed this panel to the age of Constantine. Cyril and Methodius are said to have also painted a fresco in S. Clemente, with representations of themselves as donors.

[3] Ph. Lauer, *Mon. Piot*, 1907, Pl. XIV ; H. Grisar, *Civiltà Cattolica*, year 57, iv. 54.

[4] V. de Grüneisen, in *Rassegna d'arte*, 1904, 138 ff. ; *B. Z.*, xv. 417.

[5] N. P. Kondakoff, *Macedonia*, 248 ff. and Pl. V–XII.

as Peribleptos, and possibly a copy of some famous ikon in the monastery of that name at Constantinople. Another picture, perhaps of later date, represents Our Lord as the Almighty ; the faces are grave and dark, and the Virgin's face is in most cases characterized by a very prominent nose, the cast of features remaining fairly constant in all.

The interesting panel with four subjects in the British Museum (Fig. 155),[1] obtained from the Monastery of the Virgin near the Natron Lakes in Egypt, appears from a comparison with illuminations to date from the thirteenth century. It is rich in colour and rather lighter in tone than most pictures of later date.

It is difficult to be precise as to the date of the well-known ikon of the Virgin in S. Marco at Venice. It is probably less ancient than tradition would have it, but may be at least as old as the British Museum panel.[2]

Another picture of the Panagia τῆς χρυσοπηγῆς at Zacynthus is said to be of a good period.[3]

Other panel paintings do not go back beyond the fourteenth century, and even those of this date are rare. A Transfiguration in the Sterbini Collection at Rome appears to be of this age.[4]

The Virgin and Child enthroned between two standing angels in the Uffizi Gallery at Florence (Fig. 194)[5] has sixteen busts of saints and prophets round the border. It is considered by Muñoz to date from the early fourteenth century, and the dignity of the figures makes this possible. It may, however, be rather later.

Of the fifteenth century, the Sterbini Collection possesses an interesting Nativity,[6] showing in a rocky landscape the Annunciation to the Shepherds and the approach of the Three Kings from the far distance.

The portrait upon the monument (in Santa Maria Novella at Florence) of Joseph, Patriarch of Constantinople, who came to Italy for the Council of A. D. 1438–9 and died there, appears to be a Greek work, perhaps by some artist in the patriarch's suite.[7] The bearded figure in tunic and omophorion stands facing, holding a book ; in the background are two angels and a Greek inscription. It seems unlikely that a work in this formal style should be by an Italian of the Quattrocento.

The Virgin and Child in the Church of the Madonna del Scarpello on an island off Perasto in Dalmatia is said to have been brought from Negropont in A. D. 1452.[8]

A number of Greek panel-ikons in Russia may fall within our Third and Fourth Periods ; they are illustrated in Likhacheff's monumental work.[9] Kondakoff assigns the enthroned Christ of the Uspenski Cathedral at Moscow to the period between the eleventh and fourteenth centuries,[10] as also the Veronica picture in the Monastery of St. Andronicus in the same place. The Virgin Hodegetria at Smolensk was restored in the seventeenth century, but appears to have been originally of the late thirteenth. The bust of Christ in the Alexander III Museum at St. Petersburg is of about A. D. 1360.[11]

A Virgin in the Monastery of Chilandari on Mount Athos is claimed for the fourteenth century, and a Virgin in Lavra is thought by Kondakoff to be

[1] British Museum, *Catalogue*, No. 987 ; *Burlington Magazine*. Jan. 1909.

[2] Ongania, *La Basilica di San Marco*, Pl. XXII and XXIIª. M. Molinier (*Gaz. des Beaux-Arts*, Second Period, xxxviii, 1888, p. 468) is probably right in thinking that it cannot be an original of the fifth century, but is a copy of a later date than the tenth.

[3] G. Mairojani, Βυζαντικὴ τέχνη, 1893, 226–7.

[4] Muñoz, *L'Art byz. à l'exp. de Grottaferrata*, Fig. 16, p. 38.

[5] A. Muñoz in *Rivista d'arte*, 1909, 113–14. Other authorities believe the date to be rather later (cf. *B. Z.*, xix. 243).

[6] Muñoz, *L'Art byz.*, &c., Fig. 18, p. 40.   [7] A. Muñoz in *Rivista d'arte*, 1909, 115.

[8] F. Hamilton Jackson, *The Shores of the Adriatic*, ii, *The Austrian Side*, 374 (no illustration). Another Virgin in the Church of S. Niccolò at Lussin Grande is described as Byzantine; ibid., 182.

[9] N. P. Likhacheff, *Materials for the History of Russian Ikon Painting*, vol. i, Pt. I, 1906.

[10] *Iconography of Our Lord*, Pl. I.

[11] Ibid., Pl. V. A panel in the same museum is described by V. de Grüneisen in *Rassegna d'arte*, 1909.

Fig. 194. Painting on panel: the Virgin and Child, with angels and prophets: Uffizi Gallery, Florence; fourteenth century. (Photo: R. Gabinetto, Florence.) P. 319.

a century older. A few other ikons may be of the fifteenth century, but most are later.[1]

The panel pictures in the churches of Palestine chiefly ornament the iconostasis or are set upon the προσκυνητάριον on the occasion of special feasts. They appear to be almost all later than the sixteenth century.[2]

A very interesting triptych in the possession of the Earl of Crawford, with the Last Judgement and other subjects, may be as early as the sixteenth century.[3]

Fig. 195. Panel from the Maestà of Duccio at Siena : the Flight into Egypt.
(Photo : Alinari.)

The great majority of the panel ikons now in existence are of similar date : most, indeed, are of the seventeenth and eighteenth centuries. The repetition of traditional forms, the adherence to fixed facial types and consecrated attitudes, the predilection for gold backgrounds, combine to lend these pictures, whether Greek or Slavonic, an air of antiquity which they do not really possess. But in many cases the influence of Western art is very obvious, especially when we reach the seventeenth century.

In the eighteenth century we find rococo details introduced ; Theodore Poulaki imitated the designs of Dürer and other artists. The work of these painters falls beyond our limits. The reader will find an interesting account

[1] N. Kondakoff, *Monuments of Christian Art on Mount Athos*, ch. iv.
[2] A. Baumstark, *R. Q.*, xx. 166. The Church of the Nativity at Bethlehem is especially rich.
[3] Described by Lord Balcarres in *Proc. Soc. Ant. London*, xix, pp. 136 ff.

of them in Muñoz' book on the Exhibition of Grottaferrata, to which I am indebted for so many of the facts in the present chapter.

As in the case of illuminations in MSS., so with paintings on panel, the reproduction of East-Christian designs in the West began at an early date.   Interesting examples of the first half of the seventh century are afforded by the Resurrection of Lazarus, and SS. Augustine and Gregory, painted inside the two leaves of the consular diptych of Boethius at Brescia, apparently by a Western hand.[1]   The style of the work closely recalls that of the Codex Rossanensis and the Sinope fragment, which were executed in the Nearer East (p. 452).

It has been stated above that Byzantine panel pictures of the Comnenian period exerted an evident influence upon the early Tuscan schools in Italy. There are in the galleries and churches of Siena,[2] Florence,[3] Assisi,[4] Rome,[5] and elsewhere many Italian pictures of the late thirteenth and fourteenth centuries in which the imitation of Byzantine originals is direct.   But one of the most pleasing examples of such imitation, because the artist at the same time avows his debt and reveals his own power of independent invention, is a small wooden triptych in the collection of the Commendatore Sterbini at Rome, exhibited at Grottaferrata in 1905.[6]   Each panel is divided into two compartments, one above the other.   On the left the Virgin and Child in the pose adopted by the Italian painters of the thirteenth century are seen with St. Joseph, all in half-figure : below them stand St. Laurence, St. Philip, and St. John the Baptist. On the right leaf the Crucifixion with two angels, the Virgin, St. John, and the prostrate Magdalen is at the top ; below are the kneeling St. Francis receiving the stigmata, and St. Louis.   This charming work has been attributed to Duccio, to Cimabue, or to one of Cimabue's pupils.   The painter may have belonged to the Sienese school, but the subject of St. Francis receiving the stigmata is characteristic of Florentine art.   What chiefly interests us here is the close dependence upon the Byzantine manner.   The three saints of the left leaf are oriental in conception ; the wall across the background of the Crucifixion scene is a typical Byzantine feature ; the background behind St. Francis, with its rocks and buildings, might also have come direct from an Eastern miniature.   There could not be a better example of the manner in which Byzantine painting influenced that of Italy in the Trecento, or of the manner in which Italy prepared its swift emancipation.   But the debt of Italy to the art of the Comnenian period is evident and undeniable ; the inheritance of the typical Byzantine landscape (see p. 244) would alone suffice to prove it.[7] In illustration of the latter point a single scene from Duccio's Maestà at Siena is reproduced (Fig. 195).

[1] A. Muñoz, Nuovo Bull. di arch. crist., xiii, 1907, 5 ff., with earlier references.

[2] Gallery, Sala I, Nos. 14, 15, 485, the subjects including scenes from the lives of SS. John the Baptist, Peter, and Francis.

[3] Accademia, Nos. 99 and 100.   The Magdalen with Latin inscription, and St. John the Evangelist with inscription in Greek.

[4] Sacristy of S. Francesco.

[5] Vatican, Museo Cristiano : see Thode, Franz von Assisi, 90 and 110 ff.   The famous Rucellai Madonna in Sta Maria Novella, assigned by Vasari to Cimabue and by later critics to Duccio, is now taken from both and attributed to an anonymous ' Master of the Rucellai Madonna '.   See Suida, in Prussian Jahrbuch, 1905, 28 ff.

[6] A. Muñoz, L'Art byzantin à l'exposition de Grottaferrata, Rome, 1906, 6 (Fig. 1).

[7] For the spread of Byzantine influence in the thirteenth century see Rumohr, Italienische Forschungen, i. 282–355.

Fig. 196. Illuminated head-piece : eleventh century. (British Museum.)

CHAPTER VI

PAINTING: II. MOSAICS

THE general remarks at the beginning of the chapter on painting apply in great measure to mosaics, and to these the reader is referred. But the art of 'painting' in mosaic is by association so peculiarly Byzantine that something further must be said of its nature and development.

The method of decoration by coloured *tesserae*, oriental in its origin, is most impressive when it abides by the decorative traditions of the East. Here, as we have already noticed, the silhouette is all-important; and though the figures may be statuesque in pose, the contour is not plastically conceived. Modelling and structure give place to colour boldly massed, upon the contrasts of which depend the life and significance of the form depicted. There is everywhere a grandeur in simplicity, the charm of a right convention openly avowed. The defects in training and perception observed in other Byzantine methods of painting were here less prejudicial to achievement; the defective sympathy with nature is hardly observed where the atmosphere is almost supernatural; the manipulation of light and shade is of little moment when the wall itself seems to glow and flame with its own light.

The mosaic of Byzantine churches is unsurpassed by any other form of mural decoration practised in the Christian East. Its true rival is not fresco but painted glass. This has been maintained by John Addington Symonds in a picturesque passage which will bear quotation at length:

'The jewelled churches of the South are constructed for the display of coloured surfaces illuminated by sunlight falling on them from narrow

windows, just as those of the North—Rheims, for example, or Le Mans— are built for the transmission of light through a variegated medium of transparent hues. The painted windows of a Northern cathedral find their proper counterpart in the mosaics of the South. The Gothic architect strove to obtain the greatest amount of translucent surface. The Byzantine builder directed his attention to securing just enough light for the illumination of his glistening walls. The radiance of the Northern church was similar to that of flowers or sunset clouds or jewels. The glory of the Southern temple was that of dusky gold and gorgeous needlework. The North needed acute brilliancy as a contrast to external greyness. The South found rest from the glare and glow of noonday in these sombre splendours. Thus Christianity both of the North and South decked her shrines with colour. Not so the paganism of Hellas. With

FIG. 197. Mosaics of the twelfth century in the apse of the cathedral at Cefalù, Sicily. (Westlake : *History of Mural Painting.*)

the Greeks, colour, though used in architecture, was severely subordinated to sculpture ; toned and modified to a calculated harmony with actual nature, it did not, as in a Christian church, create a world beyond the world, a paradise of supersensual ecstasy, but remained within the limits of

the known. Light falling upon.carved forms . . . in simple lustre was enough
for . . . Hellas. . . . Neither the gloomy glory of mosaics nor the gemmed
fretwork of storied windows was needed to attune the souls of Hellenic
worshippers to devotion.'[1] The contrast here put forward between Byzantine and Hellenic art is not without its value. The Greek masters appealed
to the general heart of men; they were classical; their work may be transplanted into almost any environment and everywhere retain its commanding power. The Byzantine mosaicist appealed rather to the individual
emotion aroused by the associations of a particular environment; he had
much in common with the romantic spirit; his work loses more by
transplantation.

Before we consider the principal monuments representative of Byzantine mosaics in the different periods, a brief epitome must be given of the
origin and early history of a style of ornamentation which became so
characteristic of Byzantine art. The principal wall mosaics of the Early,
Middle, and Late Periods may then be mentioned in their turn; pavement
mosaics of the Christian period will follow; and some account will be
given of small portable mosaics executed on wooden panels.

The word mosaic, which is now usually held to have no connexion
either with Moses or with the Hebrew *Maskith*, is probably a derivation
from the root to which $Mo\tilde{v}\sigma\alpha$ belongs, and is thus of the same verbal
descent as music.[2] It signifies a mode of ornamenting a flat surface by
designs formed of small pieces of differently coloured stone or glass,
usually cubical in form, fixed in cement upon a base of brick or stone.
It was employed to ornament both floors and walls, and served both
purposes for a great many centuries; but after the triumph of Christianity attention was chiefly directed to mural decoration, for which cubes
or *tesserae* of glass were almost exclusively employed in place of the stone
and brick cubes used in the manufacture of mosaic pavement. There can
be little doubt that the art originated in the East, and that its earliest
examples must be traced to Mesopotamia, Persia, and Egypt. It was in the
Egypt of Ptolemaic times that it rose to independence, and sent out two
principal branches, one back to the East into Syria, Asia Minor, and
Constantinople, the other to Sicily, North Africa, Magna Graecia, Rome,
and the West. Even before the Peace of the Church different preferences
characterize these regions. The Greek school, reigning in the Hellenistic
East, preferred decorating walls and vaults; the Roman school had
a predilection for tesselated floors. These were not exclusive preferences;
the West decorated wall surfaces in the time of the early empire, while

[1] *Sketches in Italy and Greece*, 1879, pp. 156-7.
[2] See the article, *Musivum Opus*, by P. Gauckler, in Daremberg and Saglio's *Dictionary of Antiquities* (Hachette, 1877, &c.), p. 2088. To this article, which brings our knowledge of Roman mosaics up to date, I am indebted for many of the facts mentioned below. The origin of the art of forming decorative designs with *tesserae* was known in Crete in the second millennium B.C., Dr. Arthur Evans having discovered in a rough stone box in the Lesser Palace at Knossos *tesserae* for mosaic of crystal, amethyst, beryl, lapis lazuli, and solid gold (*The Times*, August 27, 1908). These *tesserae* must have been used for fine work analogous to that of the miniature mosaics described below (p. 430).

the East produced mosaic pavements down to a comparatively late date. In briefly touching upon the different early schools and periods, we may adopt M. Gauckler's triple classification into (1) mosaics of the Alexandrian period; (2) those of the period of the Antonines; and (3) those of the Christian periods inaugurated by the Peace of the Church.

During the first of these periods the influence of Egypt was paramount; and, though most of the earliest surviving examples have been found in

Fig. 198. A portrait head: mosaic of the sixth or seventh century in S. Demetrius, Salonika. (From a drawing by Walter George, Esq.: Byzantine Research and Publication Fund.) P. 381.

Rome and Campania, they bear the visible impress of Egyptian taste. The names of artists, where they occur, are Greek, and are signed in Greek characters; thus two of the finest works at Pompeii are signed by Dioscorides of Samos. Although all the different kinds of mosaic were known in Italy before the time of Augustus, very few existing specimens are earlier than the beginning of the Christian era, a notable exception being the decoration of the House of the Faun and a few other houses at Pompeii, which have by some been placed as early as the second century B.C., by others about a hundred and fifty years earlier.[1] When, from the time of Augustus, the adoption of this mode of decoration became general, the character of the favourite subjects betrayed their Hellenistic and Egyptian descent. The costumes, the landscapes, the flora

[1] Gauckler prefers the later date (p. 2097).

and fauna, the ornamental motives—all are primarily Alexandrian.[1] The
deities, the mythological and historical personages and episodes, are all

Fɪɢ. 199.   The Birth of the Virgin : mosaic of the eleventh century in the Monastery of
Daphni, Attica.   (*Hautes Études* : G. Millet.)   P. 397.

Greek: we see Centaurs, Amazons, Argonauts, the stories of Perseus and
Theseus, the Trojan Cycle, scenes from the Odyssey, the Battle of Issus,

[1] Among examples in Rome are the Isiac mosaic of Prima Porta (*Notizie degli scavi*, 1892,
160 ; *Mélanges de l'École française de Rome*, 1893, 49) ; the mosaic from the Appian Way in the
Museo delle Terme (*Rev. arch.*, 1896, 135).   Outside Rome are the mosaics of Palestrina,
Naples, and Pompeii ; especially noteworthy is the picture representing the Battle of Issus
(*Bullettino arch. napol.*, 1855, Pl. IV ; *Giornale degli scavi*, iii. 9 ; *Gazette arch.*, 1879, p. 80).

and the Academy of Plato.[1] There are genre scenes of all kinds, both sporting and theatrical. Lastly, there are landscapes in the style of the painter commonly called Ludius, Sicilian scenes illustrating the idylls of Theocritus, and the exceedingly popular representations of aquatic life by the Nile.[2] The finer figure or landscape subject—*emblema*—was independently executed and fitted into a prepared cavity in the centre of a composition usually consisting of geometrical and conventional designs. At Pompeii the *emblema* has hardly greater dimensions than a large tile, and was in effect a miniature copying some popular (usually Alexandrian) work of art. Admirable examples are exhibited in the Capitoline Museum at Rome, and these should be recalled in connexion with the diminutive mosaics which we shall have to study later (p. 430).

The material employed for *tesserae* in the first century was principally marble of Greece or Luna, more rarely limestone or schist, hardly ever brick.[3] The scale of colour was thus restricted, and the chief shades, in addition to black and white, were red, yellow, and olive-brown. The ornament, as opposed to the figure subjects, consisted of rosettes, imbrications, interlaced bands, palmettes, ivy leaves, thyrsi, peltae or Amazonian shields, and figures of animals. It has already been stated that these motives were for the most part employed in the decoration of pavements, for which marble *tesserae* were best adapted. But the Augustan age was also familiar with the cubes of glass enamel which were so soon destined to play so prominent a part in Christian mosaic; these were used

---

[1] From Torre Annunziata (*Notizie degli scavi*, 1897, 337).

[2] Nilotic subjects occur in the mosaics of several churches (see below, pp. 332, 338), in the lower part of the Issus mosaic (see note 1 on p. 327), and are also found on products of the minor arts, e.g. a silver dish from Tipasa (H. de Villefosse, *Mélanges d'arch. et d'art*, Paris, 1893, p. 181), and another silver patera (Garrucci, *Storia*, 461–2), on Coptic textiles (Riegl, *Versammlung deutscher Philologen und Schulmänner in Wien*, 1893, pp. 191–7, and *Stilfragen*, p. 38), on the ivory *pyxis* at Wiesbaden, and in the tenth-century Armenian Gospel of Queen Mlke (*B. Z.*, xiv, 1905, 730). Such subjects were evidently popular, and there are references to them in contemporary and later literature. Philostratus (*Imagines*, ed. Boissonade, Paris, 1849, vol. i. 342) describes a picture of this kind called 'The Marsh' in the gallery of a rich man at Naples. Choricius of Gaza, a rhetor of Justinian's time, describes a Nilotic frieze in the Church of St. Stephen at Gaza (*Choricius*, ed. Boissonade, p. 120). Hunting scenes, analogous in character, were a popular decoration in private houses and perhaps also in churches (see the Epistles of St. Nilus, Bk. IV, ch. 61, in Migne, *Patr. Gr.*, vol. lxxix). For further information on this subject see Gauckler, p. 2100; Ainaloff, *Hellenistic Origins*, 138 ff.; Woermann, *Die Landschaft in der Kunst der alten Völker*, Munich, 1876, 303; W. Helbig, *Untersuchungen über die Campanische Malerei*, 101; G. Rodenwaldt, *Die Komposition der Pompeianischen Wandgemälde*, 32.

[3] It may be of interest in a very few words to describe the manner in which cubes of mosaic are made and fixed (see Gerspach, *Gazette des Beaux-Arts*, 1880, 145). In the case of ordinary colours, a mass of glass of the requisite tint is made, and from this rectangular pieces are detached. In the case of gilded cubes, the following procedure is in use at Murano, and is doubtless an ancient method. The workman takes a thin piece of colourless glass shaped like a watch-glass but about ten centimetres in diameter. To the concave side he applies a thin gold foil and subjects the glass to a certain heat. Then he pours into the concave side some fused enamel, generally dark red or bottle-green, flattens the whole, fires again, and allows to cool gradually. When the 'cake' thus formed is cut up, the section shows three layers, transparent glass, gold foil, and enamel body. The transparent covering of the gold foil is apt in process of time to decay and drop off, leaving exposed the dark enamel base, and producing dark patches in the picture. It is a difficult matter to ensure permanency, for in the second firing the workman has to devote his chief attention to ensuring successful results with the gold, which readily blackens if overheated, and fuses at a different temperature from the enamel. The procedure is similar to that employed in the manufacture of the gilded glasses of the Catacombs. The preparation of cements is a matter of prime importance, and experience shows that the most durable mosaics are embedded in the thinnest layer of cement.

to ornament vertical and not horizontal surfaces. Large specimens, if they existed, have been destroyed; but there survive various examples of work upon a small scale from Pompeii, chiefly niches for fountains,[1] *piscinae*, and

Fig. 200. Isaiah and Solomon: mosaics of the eleventh century in the Monastery of Daphni, Attica. (*Hautes Études*: G. Millet.) P. 396.

portions of columns. The tones are few and strongly contrasted, the ground being usually blue; the reds are furnished by pottery cubes, lava, and ferruginous stone: shell was also inserted in these compositions. If gilt cubes were used at all, they were extremely rare.[2]

---

[1] An example from Pompeii in the Victoria and Albert Museum (in the Glass Gallery).
[2] Gauckler, as above, 2107. Müntz (*Bull. de la Soc. des Antiquaires de France*, 1891, p. 266)

In the Antonine period the Romans to a great extent emancipated themselves from Greek tutelage. Roman pupils succeeded their Greek masters, and many subjects were derived from more purely Italian sources. The glass mural mosaic of this period has nearly all perished, but contemporary writers and inscriptions mention chambers so covered.[1] Glass cubes were still rare and costly at Rome and perhaps imported from Egypt. Gold was used, and cubes with traces of gilding have been found

Fig. 201. The Magi before Herod : mosaic of the fourteenth century in Kahrié Djami, Constantinople. (Sébah and Joaillier.) P. 420.

in the Baths of Caracalla. The style of this period naturally influenced that which succeeded it. Among the early mosaics of the age of Constantine, the most conspicuous are those of Sta Costanza (p. 332), and in these mosaics may be traced a clear resemblance to more than one pavement of Antonine times in the Proconsular Province.[2] A similar adherence to earlier tradition seems to be proved in the case of the mosaic pictures on the esplanade of the harbour of Carthage, as described by St. Augustine,[3] which were clearly conceived in the realistic picturesque spirit of the Antonine epoch.

notes that there are no gold cubes at Pompeii, but that these were known in Nero's time, the Golden House being perhaps named from this kind of decoration. See also Artaud, *Hist. abrégée de la peinture en mosaïque*, p. 18.

[1] Gauckler, 2121.
[2] Ibid., p. 2121. The sites are Kurba (Curubio) and Oudna (Uthina).
[3] *De Civitate Dei*.

With the distinctively Christian period which begins with Constantine the simple symbolism of earlier times tends to disappear. The art of mosaic now appeared as the rival of fresco, and assumed something of a monumental style. In North Africa, indeed, the pavements still present the old subjects familiar from the painted decoration of the Catacombs, such as the story of Jonah, the Sacrifice of Isaac, the Good Shepherd;[1] but on the walls of churches these subjects grow rare, so that the Good Shepherd[2] in the (fifth century) Mausoleum of Galla Placidia at Ravenna has almost the air of a survival. Classical personifications of rivers, mountains, and cities lived on to a far later time in manuscripts and in the minor arts; in mosaic there is a personification of the River Jordan in the Orthodox Baptistery.[3] But in a general way the historical treatment supersedes the symbolical, though the two are often combined where historical episodes are intended to convey an allegorical meaning. Cycles from the Bible were produced at great cost, and executed by artists of repute.[4] Of these the Old Testament scenes in the nave of Sta Maria Maggiore at Rome are the best surviving examples (see below, pp. 338–40), while the series in S. Apollinare Nuovo at Ravenna affords a remarkable instance of New Testament illustration (see p. 351). Like the illuminated biblical manuscripts now becoming general, such mosaics were intended to impress the scriptural story upon the mind in a vivid and easily intelligible manner, and it is probable that the arts of the illuminator and the worker in mosaic exerted a reciprocal influence on each other.

Mosaics, like frescoes, are readily damaged, and when once the process of disintegration has begun it advances with deplorable rapidity. The result is bad enough when the natural causes of decay are alone in operation; but it is often hastened by human agency, generally responding to motives of a religious or superstitious character. Thus the Greek peasants in Cyprus desire to possess cubes of ancient mosaic, which they regard as talismans,[5] and a similar desire doubtless explains the disappearance or dilapidation of much mosaic work throughout the Christian East.

FIRST AND SECOND PERIODS

I. Mosaics in Italy and the Adriatic.

(a) Rome.

In the rare mosaics of the Catacombs[6] dating from the fourth and fifth centuries, the transition from the symbolic to the dogmatic treatment of sacred subjects is already marked. The crypt of St. Eusebius had a cantharus flanked

---

[1] Gauckler, as above, 2124.   [2] See Fig. 209.

[3] See p. 345. A personification of Jordan is found on a sixth-century ivory panel in the British Museum representing the Baptism (Fig. 111). The examples in MSS. are comparatively numerous.

[4] The *musivarii* were relieved from public charges by Constantine (*Codex Theod.*, XIII, iv. 2), and occupied a privileged position.

[5] This information I derive from Mr. George Jeffery, Curator of Ancient Monuments in Cyprus.

[6] Less than a dozen mosaics are known to have existed in the Catacombs (E. Müntz, *Bulletin et Mémoires de la Soc. Nat. des Antiquaires de France*, VI° Série, ii, 1891, 294–321). See

by birds; the pavement in SS. Peter and Marcellinus a dove and interlaced designs; a mosaic in S. Calixtus, described by Marangoni in the eighteenth century, represented Christ seated on the globe between SS. Peter and Paul, the Resurrection of Lazarus, and another scene.[1]

Among the more considerable early mosaics in Roman churches those of Sta Costanza take the first place.[2] The present church was built between A.D. 326 and 330 as a mausoleum for Constantia, sister of Constantine the Great, and his daughter Helena, whose sarcophagi (Figs. 76–7), removed from the building, are now in the Vatican Museum. It is a domed circular structure surrounded by a ring-vault, and the interior was once completely decorated with mosaics and marble panelling. At the present time only the mosaics of the ring-vault and those of two of the fifteen niches which surround the interior wall of the rotunda are preserved. These have undergone numerous restorations, which, however, are not considered to have made essential changes in the original designs. The elaborate mosaic decoration of the dome, though much decayed, was still in existence until the first half of the seventeenth century, when all that remained was completely stripped away (A.D. 1620). We can form a general notion of their character from drawings by Francesco d'Ollanda, a Dutch artist resident in Spain in the sixteenth century, from sketches of about the same date in the library of St. Mark, and from descriptions and sketches by Pompeo Ugonio, the friend of Bosio, preserved in the library of Ferrara. The drawing of d'Ollanda, which is in the Escurial, was engraved by Pietro Santi Bartoli, and the lower part was reproduced by Ciampini.[3] The MS. description of Ugonio was first identified by de Rossi; but the discovery that it contained a lengthy description of the mosaics of Sta Costanza is due to Müntz, who patiently deciphered a volume written in a difficult shorthand.[4] From Ugonio's description we know that Bartoli's engraving of those parts of the dome not represented in d'Ollanda's drawing is fantastic.

The decoration of the dome was an important example of the transitional stage of Early Christian art; the conventional motives derived from Alexandrian art were blended with historical scenes from the two Testaments. Round the lower part ran a river scene representing Cupids fishing, similar to those known upon pagan mosaics, in Sta Maria Maggiore, and in the Lateran Basilica.[5] Above

also J. B. de Rossi, *Roma sotterranea*, iii, pp. 582, 592–3 ; F. X. Kraus, *Real-Encyklopädie der altchristlichen Kunst*, ii. 422. Besides the subjects mentioned above, the Roman Catacombs have or had the following mosaics: two portraits (once in S. Cyriaca, now in the Chigi Library) of Flavius Julianius and Maria Simplicia Rustica his wife (see d'Agincourt, *Painting*, Pl. XIII, Figs. 25 and 32 ; de Rossi, *Musaici*; Gerspach, *La Mosaïque*, 43) ; a cock, from the same catacomb, now in the Vatican Library ; Daniel in the Lions' Den (V. and A. Museum, Photo 62,021) and the Resurrection of Lazarus, in the Catacomb of St. Hermes, monograms and inscriptions, &c. The figure mosaics of St. Priscilla are entirely lost (de Rossi, *Bullettino*, ser. IV, vi. 108; d'Agincourt, Pl. XIII, 16).

[1] De Rossi, *Bullettino*, 1866, 86, 95, 99.

[2] Alinari, photos ; de Rossi, *Musaici*; Garrucci, *Storia*, Pl. 204. 4 ; Venturi, *Storia*, i; G. Clausse, *Basiliques et mosaïques chrétiennes*, i. 116 ff., Paris, 1893 ; D. Ainaloff, *Journal of the Ministry of Public Instruction*, St. Petersburg, 1895, 247 (Russian) ; E. Müntz, *Revue archéologique*, 1875, 224, 1878, 351 ; Crowe and Cavalcaselle, *History of Painting in Italy*, new English edition edited by Langton Douglas, i. 9 ; A. Pérâté in A. Michel, *Histoire de l'art depuis les premiers temps chrétiens jusqu'à nos jours*, i. 39 ff., &c.

[3] *Vetera monumenta*, vol. ii. A print from Bartoli's engraving is in the Cabinet des Estampes at Paris; it contains insertions made by Bartoli under the assumption that the church was a temple of Bacchus. It was first published in Pl. II of the Appendix to Bellori's *Picturae antiquae*, Rome, 1819, and has been reproduced by G. Clausse, *Basiliques*, &c., as above, i. 120–1, and Garrucci, *Storia*, Pl. 204. 4.

[4] *Rev. arch.*, xxxv, 1878, 357. In the earlier part of the same article Müntz had described the sketches in the Marcian Library at Venice, which he reproduced on Pl. XI.

[5] These genre scenes of river life, usually associated with the Nile, are found on the mosaic representing the Battle of Issus at Naples, in African pavement mosaics, and in Pompeian frescoes. In the fourth century a frieze of such putti was in the oratory on the Monte della Giustizia, below a scene representing Christ and the Apostles (de Rossi, *Bullettino*, 1876, 50, and Pl. V and VII). The examples in Sta Maria Maggiore and the Lateran Basilica have been considered either thirteenth-century copies of the Sta Costanza work, or careful restorations

this, as it were from the shores of the river, rise a series of caryatid figures each flanked at the base by two tigers or panthers and at the top by dolphins. Above each principal figure was a group of three smaller figures, from which issued foliated scrolls all uniting at the summit of the dome. The interspaces between the large caryatids contained sacred subjects from the Old Testament ; while the cartouches between the small upper groups of three figures were probably ornamented with New Testament scenes, though in Ugonio's time these had already severely suffered, and we have only his rough sketches on which to base a judgement. Of the larger lower scenes mentioned by Ugonio one is conjectured by Ainaloff to represent St. Paul taken to execution,[1] another may have been the Raising of Lazarus. That in the eighth interspace (the first in d'Ollanda's drawing) may be St. Peter with the fish and tribute money, though Ugonio thought of Tobit ; another may have been the Story of Susanna ; in two more, Cain and Abel with their offerings and Moses striking the rock are almost certainly depicted. Of the scenes upon the upper cartouches too little remains to justify much more than conjecture ; in style and conception these lost mosaics must have been closely related to the art of the Catacombs. There is a similar choice of scenes in both cases, a similar concordance of the two Testaments, and a similar use of ornamental designs.

The mosaics of the ring-vault have like affinities (Fig. 202). The birds, flowers, and fruits, the genii, Cupids and Psyches, disposed in compartments divided from each other by garlands or floral bands, suggest the conventions of Pompeian artists. Individual motives coincide with many in the frescoes of the Catacombs ; while the quality of the work and the light backgrounds recall the style of pavement mosaics. The continuous geometrical pattern, formed of hexagons, 'stars,' and crosses, which covers one section finds an early parallel at Amida in Mesopotamia (Ch. XIII) : the design is essentially oriental and the several figures are precisely those used through the mediaeval centuries by the Persian makers of glazed tiles.

The vintage scene, with its genii involved in scroll-work of vine tendrils, suggests an influence from Syria, where motives of this kind seem to have first been popular, passing thence into Egypt and the West. The geometric and diaper designs in other sections suggest a similar influence from oriental textiles. It was the vintage scenes which gave rise to the theory, generally held from the sixteenth century by all except Bosio and Ugonio,[2] that Sta Costanza had been erected as a temple of Bacchus.

The mosaics remaining in two opposite lateral niches in the interior wall of the rotunda, the fourth from each side of the entrance, present figure subjects which have given rise to much dispute. That on the left represents the scene known as the *Traditio legis*, in which Our Lord, standing between SS. Peter and Paul, gives the former the book of the Gospels ;[3] that on the right, which was more seriously damaged and more fatally restored, shows the Almighty or Our Lord seated on the globe,[4] and offering an indeterminate object to a figure who advances with hands veiled beneath the mantle. The subject has been variously interpreted as God giving the tables of the Law to Moses, or Christ giving the keys to Peter or the scroll to John (Rev. i. 19). Ainaloff finds in it a resemblance to the mosaic in S. Vitale, in which Our Lord seated on the sphere

---

of original mosaics of similar style and almost equally early date. Vitet (*Journal des Savants*, 1863, 501, and *Études sur l'histoire de l'art*, i. 298) held the second view, while Venturi (*Storia*, i, p. 237) only accepts S. Giovanni as antique. Ainaloff believes that they are original compositions essentially undisturbed by the artists of the thirteenth century. He notes that such motives were familiar to the Christian East, and quotes the letter of St. Nilus to Olympiodorus (Migne, *Patrology*, Greek series, vol. lxxix—*Nili Epistolae*, Bk. IV, ch. 61), in which similar designs are mentioned. See also Woermann, *Die Landschaft in der Kunst der alten Völker*, Munich, 1876 ; Ainaloff, *Hellenistic Origins*, 138.

[1] He compares the sarcophagus (Garrucci, *Storia*, Pl. 322. 2).
[2] *Rev. arch.*, xxxv. 355.   [3] Photo in Victoria and Albert Museum, 70. 885.
[4] *Rev. arch.*, xxx, 1875, 273 ; photo, V. and A. Museum, 70. 884.

receives the titular saint.[1] In both niches Christ is bearded and is of the 'Nazarene' type, early disseminated through the Christian world as a result of

Fig. 202. Interior of Sta Costanza, Rome, with mosaics of the fourth century.
(Alinari.) P. 332.

pilgrimages to the Holy Land. Opinion seems on the whole in favour of an early date for these two mosaics, either the fourth century or quite early in the fifth. De Rossi, Crowe and Cavalcaselle, Müntz, and Venturi[2] hold this view:

[1] Ainaloff, as above, 267.   [2] *Storia*, &c. as above, i. 241–2.

Ainaloff believes the work to belong to the fifth century.[1] Vitet,[2] Labarte,[3] and Schnaase[4] attributed it to various periods from the sixth to the eighth century.[5] It is true that the figures have a barbaric appearance incongruous with the decorative schemes of the ring-vault. But, as Müntz has pointed out,[6] the designs of the vault are stock patterns, which were copied over and over again until perfection was easy, whereas the figures of the niches represent a new departure in composition. Another point in favour of the early date is the use of a pale background. All the mosaics of Ravenna have backgrounds of blue or gold. Even Sta Pudenziana has the dark ground; and the only other early mosaics which are without it are those in the nave of Sta Maria Maggiore,

FIG. 203.   Our Lord with Apostles and others : mosaic of the fourth century in the apse of Sta Pudenziana, Rome. (Alinari.)   P. 336.

which are considered to be of the fourth century (p. 338). Again, the borders, which consist of garlands, are of the same design as others in the ring-vault. Purple and gold, usually characteristic of mosaics later than the fourth century, do not appear. Finally, the type of the *Traditio legis* is early, and distinct from that adopted from the seventh century onwards.[7]

In the apse at the end of the rotunda, above the principal altar, Ugonio saw a mosaic with Our Lord in the midst of the Apostles, evidently allied to that in Sta Pudenziana, of which it may have been a prototype.[8] In the niches round the gallery was also mosaic decoration representing stars : one of these, which still remains, has in addition the Constantinian form of the sacred monogram.[9]

---

[1] As above, 267.   [2] *Études sur l'histoire*, i. 207.
[3] *Hist. des arts industriels*, iv. 212.   [4] *Geschichte der bildenden Künste*, iii. 567.
[5] H. Parker, *Mosaic Pictures in Rome and Ravenna*, 37 (Oxford, 1866), assigns the work, like Labarte, to the eighth century.
[6] *Rev. arch.*, xxx. 279.
[7] Ibid., 282. Christ stands upon the mount from which issue the rivers, approached from both sides by lambs coming from Jerusalem and Bethlehem. With his right hand he points to a palm-tree in which a phoenix is seated. This type, unknown in the Catacombs, resembles that upon various sarcophagi (Garrucci, *Storia*, Pl. 327. 2, 333, 334. 2, 335. 2), and is distinct from that adopted in the sixth and seventh centuries, when saints and martyrs were introduced. See Ainaloff, as above, 262 ff. De Rossi (*Bullettino*, 1868, 44) has shown that the reading *Dominus pacem dat* is a legitimate variant for the more usual *legem dat*.
[8] *Rev. arch.*, xxxv, 1878, 362; Ainaloff, as above, 260.   [9] Ainaloff, 258.

Sta Costanza had a mosaic pavement with black designs on a white ground, among which were genii making libations, altars, birds, vine scrolls, &c. : it is partly shown in Santi Bartoli's engraving.

The mosaics of the apse of the Church of Sta Pudenziana at Rome [1] (Fig. 203) are hardly less famous than those of Sta Costanza. Onuphrio Panvini, whose manuscript account in the Vatican Library is cited by de Rossi, ascribed a great antiquity to the work ; Bianchini [2] even carried it back to the days of the Antonines. Vitet [3] pronounces in favour of the fourth century, which is also the opinion of de Rossi,[4] of Ainaloff,[5] and of Crowe and Cavalcaselle, F. X. Kraus, and the majority of critics. Schnaase prefers the fifth century,[6] Barbet de Jouy [7] the eighth.

Restorers have been at work on the apse from very early times. Perhaps the first worked for Adrian I, whose monogram was once visible.[8] In 1588 Cardinal Gaetani renewed decayed portions with painted stucco ; between 1829 and 1832 Cardinal Litta caused further renovations to be carried out, this time with *tesserae*. But there is ground for the belief that, except for the loss of two figures of Apostles on the two sides of the picture, the composition has not been modified in any important feature.

The mosaic represents Our Lord seated on a throne amid the Twelve Apostles, St. Peter and St. Paul being on his right and left hand, crowned by two female figures. Behind the group runs a semicircular wall in masonry ; at the back of this a large jewelled cross rises from a small hill. Behind, again. are buildings among which a circular domed structure is conspicuous ; in the sky are the symbols of the four Evangelists. It has been conjectured that a row of lambs, six to right and six to left, flanked a central lamb beneath the feet of Christ.

Bianchini was of opinion that the scene represented the foundation of the building by the Senator Pudens and his daughters Praxed and Pudenziana. The figures represented the family of the founder ; the cross symbolized the Church, and the surrounding architecture the Vicus Patricius. De Rossi, regarding the scene as Our Lord and the Apostles in the celestial paradise, held that the buildings were an adumbration of the heavenly city, *sub specie Vici Patricii* ; the female figures he held, like Bianchini, to represent Praxed and Pudenziana. Ainaloff [9] believes the buildings of the background to represent the surroundings of the Holy Sepulchre at Jerusalem as they grew up after the donations of Constantine and Helen. The circular domed building to the left of the spectator he takes to be the Sepulchre itself (*Anastasis*), which is represented as a circular structure in various Early Christian monuments,[10] and continued in existence down to the time of the pilgrim Arculph in the seventh

---

[1] Photos, Alinari, Victoria and Albert Museum, 70. 697-700. De Rossi, *Musaici*, Fasciculi 13 and 14, and *Bullettino*, v, 1867, 49-60 ; Ciampini, *Vetera Monumenta Romae*, vol. ii ; Garrucci, *Storia*, iv. 208 ; Ainaloff, as above, 272 ; G. Clausse, *Basiliques et mosaïques chrétiennes*, vol. i, p. 144 ; F. X. Kraus, *Geschichte der christlichen Kunst*, vol. i ; Crowe and Cavalcaselle, i. 11 ; Venturi, *Storia*, i. 246, and Fig. 105 ; Pératé in A. Michel, as above, 44 f.

[2] *De vitis Romanorum Pontificum.*   [3] *Journal des Savants*, 1863, 28.

[4] *Musaici*, as above. From Panvini's transcription of a lost inscription de Rossi concludes that the mosaic was dedicated by Leopardus, Ilicius, and Maximus in the time of Bishop Siricius, between A.D. 384 and 398.

[5] As above, 273 ff.

[6] *Gesch. der bild. Künste*, iii. 197.   [7] *Mos. chrét.*, p. 48 (Paris, 1877).

[8] The Liber Pontificalis says that Adrian restored the church. Labarte (*Hist. des arts industriels*, 340-2) thought he could trace these restorations, and argued that the figure of Christ was of the Byzantine Pantokrator type. Restoration has especially affected the right side of the mosaic, though Crostarosa, who examined it closely in 1895, said that the architecture represented was original (*Nuovo Bullettino*, 1895, 67).

[9] As above, 282 ff.

[10] On sarcophagi, Garrucci, *Storia*, v. Pl. 315. 5, 316. 2 ; on the ivory panel from the Trivulzio Collection at Milan, Molinier, *Hist. des arts appliqués à l'industrie*, ii, *Ivoires*, Pl. VI, and Ainaloff, p. 293 ; on a silver medal, Garrucci, vi. Pl. 480. 14. A Russian reviewer of Ainaloff (*V. V.*, iv, 1897, 221) agrees in general with this identification, but holds that much is purely ideal.

century. The cross in the centre of the composition he believes to represent the actual cross erected between the *Martyrion* and the *Anastasis*, and described in the accounts of the early pilgrims.[1] This 'Golgotha Cross' was richly ornamented with precious stones, and the jewelled cross which is so frequent in Byzantine works of art is intended for a representation of it. The presence of the lamb before Christ's throne is an additional proof of the fact that the scene is laid at Golgotha; and in the accounts of the Fathers, which compare the splendours of the earthly with those of the heavenly Jerusalem, he finds additional probability that the Jewish city and not Rome was chosen to symbolize Paradise. The careful perspective and the realism in points of detail make it clear to him that an actual site and not a mere ideal composition is intended.

The two female figures holding crowns are now usually held to be the *Ecclesia ex gentibus* and the *Ecclesia ex circumcisione*;[2] but Mgr. Crostarosa has recently maintained the earlier opinion of Bianchini and de Rossi that they

FIG. 204. Mosaic wreath of the fifth century: dome of St. George, Salonika.
(*Hautes Études* : G. Millet.) P. 374.

represent SS. Praxed and Pudenziana, in whose lifetime and by whose gift the *Domus Pudentiana* became the property of the Church. The architectural background, according to his view, is the Domus itself, which like other large Roman palaces consisted of a large number of buildings of various forms, including a basilica.[3]

Grisar[4] has followed Ainaloff with regard to the principal features, accepting the cross as the Golgotha Cross, and the domed building as the *Anastasis*, but regarding the sigma-shaped arcade as a conventional representation of Jerusalem, since similar arcades are seen in the Madaba mosaic.

Heisenberg[5] has more recently argued that the arcade represents the *atrium* of Constantine's basilica of the Holy Sepulchre. The scene, according to him, is an ideal version of the actual ceremony which took place in this *atrium* on Good Friday, when the bishop's throne was set up before the cross, and he and the presbyters read passages from the Gospels relating to the Passion. He accepts the female figures as Praxed and Pudenziana.

It will be seen that the interpretation of the apse mosaic of Sta Pudenziana remains uncertain; the balance of probability seems to support an East-Christian influence in the work, which was executed in the fourth century.

---

[1] For references with regard to this cross at Golgotha see also O. Wulff, *Die Koimesiskirche in Nicäa*, Strassburg, 1903, p. 223.

[2] Lefort in *Rev. arch.*, 1874 ; *Nuovo Bullettino*, 1896, 174 ff.

[3] *Nuovo Bullettino*, 1895, 58 ff.

[4] *Civiltà Cattolica*, iii, 1895, 722 ff. ; *Analecta romana*, i. 564 ff.

[5] *Grabeskirche und Apostelkirche : zwei Basiliken Konstantins*, i. 141 ff. (Leipsic, 1908).

The surviving ancient mosaics in Sta Maria Maggiore,[1] which have suffered from constant restorations at the most various periods, cover the surface of the triumphal arch and the walls of the nave. The decoration of the apse, with the possible exception of the frieze representing a river scene with genii,[2] is probably of the thirteenth century; while other mosaics, now lost, but alluded to in early manuscripts, represented the Virgin approached by a procession of saints. The position of the lost work is disputed, de Rossi believing that the Virgin was placed in the apse, while the saints were between the upper windows of the nave; Richter argues that the whole subject occupied the west wall above the principal entrance.[3]

The number of the mosaic scenes in Sta Maria Maggiore is so great, and the discussions to which they have given rise are so voluminous, that it is not possible in the present place to do more than indicate their general nature and state the conclusions of the principal investigators who have studied them.

The subjects upon the arch are usually interpreted as the Annunciation, Presentation in the Temple, Flight into Egypt, Adoration of the Magi, Reception of Christ by King Aphrodisius in Egypt (or Christ disputing with the Doctors), Massacre of the Innocents, Magi before Herod, and (in the lower corners) the cities of Jerusalem and Bethlehem. Above the arch is a throne on which are a jewelled cross and crown, having on either side figures of St. Peter and St. Paul and the four apocalyptic beasts, and below, the inscription XYSTUS EPISCOPUS PLEBI DEI.

The subjects of the nave, which are distributed in a long series of panels, represent scenes from the Old Testament derived from the histories of Abraham, Jacob, Moses, and Joshua.[4]

The difficulties which beset the interpretation and proper attribution of the mosaics are, briefly, as follows :—

The work is clearly very old; the grouping, the types of the figures, the iconographical details, the light background, and the absence or great rarity of gold cubes in any original parts[5] all point to an early period, and no critic of authority has attributed any of these mosaics to a later time than the first half of the fifth century. But the general character of the scenes upon the arch is different from those of the nave. The former are obviously of a dogmatic character, and introduce episodes from apocryphal books not known to have

---

[1] Ainaloff, Journal, &c., May, 1895, pp. 94 ff., where the following list of references for these mosaics is given : Paul de Angelis, Basilicae S. Mariae Maioris descriptio, &c., Bk. V, p. 91, Rome, 1621 (illustration of the arch, but inaccurate and worthless); Ciampini, Vetera Monumenta, vol. i, Rome, 1747 (illustration of the arch still of value); Bianchini, Anastasii Bibliothecarii de vitis Romanorum Pontificum, vol. iii, p. 124 f.; Agostino Valentini, La Patriarcale Basilica Liberiana, illustrata per cura Ag. Val., Pl. LXI, Rome, 1839 (many inaccuracies in the rendering of the arch mosaics); Giacomo Fontana, Raccolta delle migliori chiese di Roma e suburbane, vol. iii, Pl. XXVIII, Rome, 1855 (pleasing illustration of arch, but containing inaccuracies afterwards reproduced by R. de Fleury); Garrucci, Storia dell' arte cristiana, Pl. 211-14 (illustrations of the arch are better than any that precede, but introduce new errors); J. B. de Rossi, Musaici cristiani e saggi dei pavimenti delle chiese di Roma anteriori al secolo XV, Fasciculi xxiv, xxv, Rome, 1893. Pending the complete publication by Mgr. Wilpert, the best reproductions are to be found in J. P. Richter and A. Cameron Taylor's The Golden Age of Classic Christian Art, London, Duckworth, 1904. This work deals entirely with these mosaics, and contains the best coloured reproductions of various scenes and groups in nave and on the arch which have yet appeared, together with numerous process and line blocks. Details and isolated scenes are reproduced by d'Agincourt, Histoire de l'art par les monuments, Pt. V, Pl. XVI, Fig. 4, Paris, 1811-23; Rohault de Fleury, La Sainte Vierge, vol. ii, Pl. 85, Paris, 1878; Lehner, Die Marienverehrung in den ersten Jahrhunderten, Pl. III, Stuttgart, 1881; A. de Waal, R. Q., 1887, Pl. VIII-IX; A. Venturi, Storia, i. 252 and Fig. 111.

[2] Ainaloff, in opposition to the general belief, accepts this part of the apse as ancient (see above, p. 332, n. 5).

[3] As above, p. 29.

[4] Richter believes that the pictures of the Joshua series are not in their original places, but were probably moved by Cardinal Pinelli (Second Congress of Christian Archaeology, Rome, 1900). The Joshua pictures have many points of relationship with the same subjects as treated in the Joshua Rotulus in the Vatican Library (see p. 447).

[5] Richter says that none of the gold cubes are original.

been adopted in art before the fifth century.   Moreover, their rendering of familiar scenes, for instance that of the Adoration, where Christ is seated alone upon a very large and massive throne, diverges, apparently of set purpose, from the familiar versions of Early Christian art.[1]   Further, the style and sumptuousness of many costumes is characteristic of the fashions introduced by the Byzantine court from about the time of Theodosius, while the costumes of priests point to a similar oriental origin.[2]   If, then, they are original, and not due to early restorations, it is not easy to place them earlier than the fifth century.   On the other hand, the pictures in the nave are full of movement and more antique in character

Fig. 205.   Interior of S. Apollinare Nuovo, Ravenna : sixth century.   (Alinari.)

than those of the arch, recalling the oldest known illustrated MSS. of the Bible, which, though not earlier than the fifth century, must certainly have had prototypes of an earlier date.

In view of these facts two courses are open to us.   Either we must suppose the mosaics of the nave earlier than those of the arch ; or, considering the work to be all of one period, we must adopt one of two subordinate alternatives.   If we choose the fifth century as the sole date, we must explain the style of the nave pictures by supposing them to be careful copies of older compositions ; if

[1] Smirnoff (*V. V.*, iv, 1897, 14-15) suggests that the infant Christ is placed in solitary grandeur upon the throne because it was inconsistent with his supreme divinity, affirmed at the Council of Ephesus, that any person not divine, even his mother, should be placed on the same level.   It is possible that for a considerable time after the Council the artistic tradition may have been unsettled, and unusual compositions may have been attempted which did not find permanent favour.   Venturi (as above, 255-6) takes a somewhat similar view.   This remarkable feature is discussed by Smith and Marriott, *Dict. of Christian Antiquities*, 84, and V. Schultze, *Archäologie der christlichen Kunst*, 25.

[2] Ainaloff lays particular stress upon these features, and in general regards the mosaics as strongly influenced by the early phase of East-Christian art.   A short but useful abstract of this valuable article upon Sta Maria Maggiore is given by Richter and Taylor, 415-19.

an earlier period, we must find parallels in early work for details which have the air of being late. Ainaloff, Venturi,[1] and Richter concur in the belief that the pictures of the arch and nave are contemporary, rejecting de Rossi's conclusion that the nave was done for Liberius in the second half of the fourth century, while the arch was decorated for Sixtus III, by whom the inscription was composed. But whereas the Russian archaeologist believes that the whole decoration was executed for Sixtus, Richter, basing his arguments on the artistic qualities of the work, on the symbolic tendencies of the whole, and on the theological opinions which in his view they illustrate, declares for the second, or at latest the beginning of the third century. He maintains that work of such quality[2] was beyond the powers of fifth-century decadence, and can only be attributed to the golden age of classic Christian art, that is to say, to a time a hundred years before the conversion of Constantine. For him the scenes upon the arch are not intended, as de Rossi and others supposed, to glorify the Virgin as Theotokos, after the Council of Ephesus, for in individual scenes, as for instance in the Adoration, the Mother is obviously subordinated to the Child ; he rather sees in these compositions the Advent of the Logos, considering them as an antitypical group corresponding to the prototypical scenes of the nave.[3] The latter he consequently regards not as merely historical illustrations in the style of a picture Bible—for they do not observe the strict historical sequence— but as a carefully chosen typological series. The presence of late types of costume upon the arch and of gold cubes throughout he ascribes to restoration. As to the subjects from the apocryphal writings, he argues that though we happen to have no examples in art before the fifth century, this is merely negative evidence. The theological atmosphere of these mosaic scenes is that of Justin Martyr, of the two Clements, of Irenaeus, Hippolytus, and Origen, and not that of Jerome and Augustine or any post-Constantinian writer.

Into the controversy thus raised we cannot here enter ; it can only be decided by the union of both sides in a single view as to what is original work and what is restoration. If, for example, Richter is right in ruling out all the gold cubes and all the 'Byzantine' costumes as later interpolations, then many of Ainaloff's arguments fall to the ground, though serious iconographical difficulties would still remain. For us it is important to notice that Richter admits the probability that the artists may have come from Syria, and suspects in many details of the work the inspiration of the Christian East :[4] this opinion will receive very general support.

In discussing the mosaics of Ravenna we shall have occasion to notice that the subjects of the lost mosaics of Sta Maria Maggiore in that city seem to have coincided with those of the arch in the Roman church, a fact which may perhaps be considered to favour the usually accepted date of the fifth century (see below, p. 365).

Across the wall of the Church of Sta Sabina,[5] founded in the time of Celestine,

---

[1] As above, 266-7.

[2] Richter takes a higher view of the artistic quality of the scenes in the nave than many other critics, some of whom agree with Vitet that though the antique inspiration is undeniable, the execution often leaves much to be desired. They see heads too big for bodies, bodies themselves thick and squat, indecision of line, negligence and clumsiness of detail. Richter, who has been suspended from the roof and carefully examined these high-placed mosaics, has seen them to exceptional advantage, and in his admirable illustrations (by Signor Tabanelli) has enabled others to see them almost as well. But though he has thus increased our admiration for some scenes, notably the parting of Abraham and Lot, he has equally brought into a stronger light some of the elements of weakness mentioned above. He has perhaps too low an opinion of the art of the fifth century and of the last quarter of the fourth, which produced much creditable work.

[3] The close connexion between the subjects of the nave and arch is, however, accepted and explained by those who believe the mosaics to be a pictorial poem in honour of the Virgin and of her son God made man (see Venturi, as above, 271-2).

[4] The Golden Age, &c., 399. Strzygowski (Prussian Jahrbuch, 1903, 151) maintains the existence of oriental influence in these mosaics.

[5] Venturi, as above, p. 275 and Fig. 108 ; G. Clausse, Basiliques, &c., 161.

A. D. 423–32, there is mosaic decoration consisting of a large central inscription between two female figures representing the *Ecclesia ex gentibus* and the *Ecclesia ex circumcisione,* above which in Ciampini's time were still to be seen St. Peter and St. Paul. The costumes, in which purple is conspicuous, the type of the eyes, the border enclosing the work, and the blue background all suggest an artistic affinity with Ravenna,[1] though the figures themselves may descend from those of Roman monumental art. In the chapels of the Lateran Baptistery there are other mosaics illustrating the transitional art of the fifth century. The design of one,[2] with its central medallion containing a nimbed lamb within a wreath, still recalls catacomb art, though the background is here of gold. But the style of certain details (birds and vases, &c.) resembles that of similar accessories in the Mausoleum of Placidia and S. Apollinare Nuovo at Ravenna rather than the work of the first Christian centuries at Rome. The design in the second chapel[3] is divided into two

FIG. 206. Ornament in mosaic, Sta Sophia, Constantinople. (After Salzenberg.)

halves filled by rich acanthus scrolls diverging from a point in the middle of the base. In a border below are a lamb and white doves, representing Christ and the Evangelists; below again is a jewelled cross of the Golgotha form. Though some critics have assigned the mosaics to the twelfth century, Hübsch, de Rossi, Müntz, and Ainaloff all attribute them to the fifth, and probably to the earlier half, for the nearest parallel to such acanthus scrolls is to be found in the Mausoleum of Placidia.[4]

The lost mosaics on the triumphal arch of St. Paul *extra muros,* destroyed in the fire of 1823 and since restored, are said to have still preserved the antique character: they dated from the time of Leo I, and are ascribed to about the year A. D. 450.[5] The scene represented is the apocalyptic vision of the twenty-four elders singing before the throne, or rather before a bust of Christ in a medallion. The mosaics in the apse of SS. Cosmas and Damian[6] were executed under Felix IV about the years A. D. 526–30. They

[1] Ainaloff, *Journal of the Ministry of Public Instruction,* St. Petersburg, July, 1895, 21.
[2] De Rossi, *Musaici,* Fasc. 17 and 18; Garrucci, Pl. 238; Hübsch, *Die altchristlichen Kirchen,* Karlsruhe, 1862, Pl. XXVIII, Fig. 1; Venturi, as above, 244, and Fig. 107; Clausse, as above, 174.
[3] Venturi, 243, and Fig. 106; Pératé in A. Michel's *Histoire de l'art,* 46.
[4] Hübsch, as above, Pl. XXI, Fig. 1; Müntz, in *Rev. arch.,* 1874, 172; Ainaloff, as above, 23.
[5] Vitet, *Journal des Savants,* 1863, p. 346; Venturi, 276, and Fig. 79; Crowe and Cavalcaselle, i. 14, with plate.
[6] De Rossi, *Musaici*; Venturi, as above, 273 ff.; Crowe and Cavalcaselle, i. 15 and 16; Clausse, as above, 184.

represent SS. Peter and Paul presenting the two titular saints to Our Lord: at the sides stand St. Theodore and Pope Felix.   On the external front of the arch is the Lamb between the seven candlesticks, angels, the twenty-four elders, and the symbols of the Evangelists.   Here the influence of the antique tradition is still strong, and the style excellent for work carried out so soon after the sack of Rome.

In the Roman mosaics of the period between the sixth and ninth centuries, with much that is clearly of East-Christian inspiration there is a certain barbaric force which points to the practice of the mosaic art by Western hands.   It is impossible in the present place to do more than notice those churches in which Eastern influence is most evident.   The figures of Apostles and saints in the Chapel of St. Venantius (*temp*. John IV, A. D. 640–2) recall those of S. Apollinare Nuovo, Ravenna.[1]   The cross in the apse of S. Stefano Rotondo (*temp*. Theodore, †649) is of the type seen on the Monza ampullae from the Holy Land. Drawings of the lost mosaics of the Basilica of St. Peter and St. Paul (*temp*. John VII, †707) prove the introduction of oriental iconographic features, such as the Washing of the Child at the Nativity.[2]

The later phase of degradation in Roman mosaic art, as illustrated in St. Praxed and St. Cecilia,[3] finds a parallel in the work of the dome of Sta Sophia at Salonika.   The figures of St. Peter and St. Paul in the Chapel of St. Zeno in St. Praxed, if added to the Apostles of that dome, would hardly excite remark.[4] The Salonika mosaics can hardly be regarded as imitating Roman work, for the types of Christ and of the angels are Eastern, and the treatment of the ground and of the trees is equally Byzantine.   It has therefore been suggested that the mosaics of Sta Sophia are examples of a decadent period in Byzantine art, the earlier illustrations of which have perished ; and that from the close of the seventh century the degradation of the oriental masters was followed step by step by their Western pupils.   The period of decadence would thus coincide with that of the iconoclastic dispute, the results of which may have continued to operate in the provinces even after the establishment of peace in the capital.   It is not necessary to believe that all or even the greater part of the work was executed by immigrant Greeks ; it is natural to suppose that there was on the part of Italians much imitation of Greek models, which the residence in Rome of Greek monks would certainly have encouraged.   The work (St. Cecilia, St. Praxed, St. Maria in Domnica) executed for Pope Paschal, and that in St. Mark for Gregory IV, 830–40, marks the nadir of Italian mosaic art.   The revival began with the importation of Byzantine artists by Desiderius of Monte Cassino (p. 84) in the eleventh century and was continued in Venice (p. 399).   With the thirteenth century Italy produced her own artists, and the names of Jacopo Torriti and Gaddo Gaddi prove her enfranchisement from Greek pupilage.

(*b*) *Ravenna.*[5]

From the time when Galla Placidia returned from Constantinople to Italy and took up her residence on the Adriatic, down to the close of the sixth century, Ravenna was the chief centre of mosaic art in Italy and possibly of the world.   There remain more mosaics of this period in this quiet provincial town than in any other place, for what the East had once to show

[1] S. Beissel, *Zeitschrift für christliche Kunst*, x, 1897, 114 ; O. Wulff, *Die Koimesiskirche in Nicäa*, 281.

[2] Frothingham in *Rev. arch.*, 1883, Pt. I, p. 70 ; Garrucci, *Storia*, Pl. 279 ; *Rev. de l'art chrétien*, xxvi, 1893, 361 ff.

[3] Beissel, as above, 148, 182–4.   For reproductions, de Rossi, *Musaici* ; Venturi, *Storia*, &c.

[4] O. Wulff, *Die Koimesiskirche*, &c., 284.

[5] The mosaics of the churches in Ravenna are reproduced in Alinari's and Ricci's photographs ; Alinari has negatives of all the important subjects.   Most may be seen in the collection of photographs in the Victoria and Albert Museum, series xix a b.

FIG. 207.   Apse of the Cathedral of Parenzo, showing mosaics of the sixth century.
(Alinari.)   P. 373.

of equal age has not been preserved in the same manner. Three great names are indissolubly associated with the art of Ravenna, those of Placidia (†A. D. 450), of Theodoric the Ostrogoth (conquered Odovakar A. D. 493, †526), and Justinian ; and each is commemorated by mosaics which survive to the present day. To the time of Placidia belong the Catholic Baptistery (c. A. D. 430), and the princess's own tomb (now SS. Nazaro e Celso) (c. A. D. 440) ; to that of Theodoric the Arian Baptistery (c. A. D. 500) and most of the work in S. Apollinare Nuovo (A. D. 504) ; to that of Justinian, S. Vitale (A. D. 547) and S. Apollinare in Classe (A. D. 549). To the succeeding period of rapid decadence under the exarchate may be ascribed parts of the decoration of S. Apollinare Nuovo (A. D. 560), S. Apollinare in Classe (A. D. 672), and the archiepiscopal chapel.

We gain but little information as to art from Agnellus' compilation known as the *Liber Pontificalis*,[1] though we learn the names of four mosaic artists : Cuserius, Paulus, Janus, and Stephanus.[2] The question whether the inspiration of the mosaics of Ravenna was or was not continuously oriental has been the subject of much contention in the past. The present writer agrees with those who answer the question in the affirmative. Those who wish to follow the discussion in detail may consult the list of works given in the footnote, which is based upon the bibliography of Riedin.[3] We may now discuss the principal monuments.

The Catholic Baptistery,[4] otherwise known as S. Giovanni in Fonte, and

---

[1] Published in Muratori, *Rerum italicarum scriptores*, vol. ii, p. 1–187 ; Migne, *Patrol. Lat.*

[2] *Liber Pont.*, as above, p. 51 ; S. Beissel, *Stimmen aus Maria-Laach*, xlvii, 1894, 422 ff., 497 ff., and lvi, 1899, 344–9.

[3] (a) Supporting the theory of Eastern Christian influence : Labarte, *Histoire des arts industriels*, &c., Paris, 1873, ii. 349, 358 ; Schnaase, *Geschichte der bildenden Künste im Mittelalter*, Düsseldorf, 1869, i. 211 ; Crowe and Cavalcaselle, *History of Painting in Italy*, i ; Förster, *Geschichte der italienischen Kunst*, Leipzig, 1869, vol. i, p. 106 ; Gregorovius, *Wanderjahre in Italien*, Leipzig, 1871, iv. 11 ; J. P. Richter, *Die Mosaiken von Ravenna*, Vienna, 1878 ; N. P. Kondakoff, *Histoire de l'art byzantin*, i, and *Journey to Sinai in 1881*, Odessa, 1882 (Russian) ; Bayet, *Recherches pour servir à l'histoire de la peinture et de la sculpture chrétienne en Orient*, Paris, 1879, 80, 81, 95, and *L'Art byzantin*, 35 ff. ; E. Müntz, *Études sur l'histoire de la peinture et de l'iconographie chrétiennes*, Paris, 1888, 31 ; E. Dobbert, *Repertorium*, viii, 1885, 163, 173, and xxi, 1898, 1 ff. and 95 ff. ; Ch. Diehl, *Ravenne : Études d'archéologie byzantine*, Paris, 1886, 1, 44, 50, &c. ; J. Strzygowski, *Das Etschmiadzin-Evangeliar*, Vienna, 1891, 50–1 ; V. Schultze, *Archäologie der altchristlichen Kunst*, Munich, 1895, 202, 222, &c. ; D. V. Ainaloff, *Mosaics of the Fourth and Fifth Centuries*, in *Journal of the Ministry of Public Instruction*, St. Petersburg, 1895 (incidental allusions) ; E. K. Riedin, *Journal of the Imperial Russian Archaeological Society*, St. Petersburg, 1897, 41–264 ; N. Pokrovsky, *Mural Decoration of Early Greek and Russian Churches*, 11 ff.

(b) In favour of Western independence, at any rate down to the sixth century : Hübsch, *Die altchristlichen Kirchen nach den Baudenkmalen und älteren Beschreibungen*, Carlsruhe, 1862 ; Kugler, *Handbuch der Geschichte der Malerei*, 1866, 40, 53 ; Didron, *Manuel d'iconographie chrétienne*, Paris, 1845, 46 ; Woltmann, *Geschichte der Malerei*, Leipzig, 1879, i. 167 ; S. Beissel, *Stimmen aus Maria-Laach*, 1894, 344–9 ; F. X. Kraus, *Geschichte der christlichen Kunst*, i. 427–44, Freiburg, 1896.

(c) In favour of a mixed origin, in which Eastern and Western influences almost balance each other, or leaving the question undecided : X. Barbier de Montault, *Revue de l'art chrétien*, vii, 1896, 70 ; F. von Quast, *Die altchristlichen Bauwerke von Ravenna*, Berlin, 1842 ; Garrucci, *Storia dell' arte cristiana*, Prato, 1877, iv.

(d) Early works dealing with these mosaics are : Agnellus, *Liber Pontificalis, sive Vitae Pontificum Ravennatum* (ninth century), printed in Muratori, *Rerum italicarum scriptores*, ii, Milan, 1723 ; Migne, *Patrologiae cursus completus*, Latin series, vol. 106, and *Monumenta Germaniae historica*, *Scriptores rerum longobardicarum et italicarum saec. vi–ix*, Hannover, 1878 (ed. Waitz). From this ancient source all writers have drawn in a greater or less degree ; Tomaso Tomai, *Historia di Ravenna*, Ravenna, 1580 ; Rubens, *Historiarum Ravennatum libri decem*, Venice, 1589 ; F. Fabri, *Le Sagre Memorie di Ravenna*, Venice, 1664 (and his continuator Tarlazzi, *Memorie sacre di Ravenna*, Rav., 1852) ; Ciampini, *Vetera Monumenta*, i and ii, Rome, 1690–9. An account of the recent restorations undertaken by the Commission of Monuments is given by C. Ricci, *Ravenna e i lavori fatti dalla Sovrintendenza dei monumenti nel 1898*, Bergamo, 1899 ; *Ravenna*, Bergamo, 1902, and in *Arte italiana decorativa e industriale*, xiii, 1904, pp. 21–5. Restoration of the apse of S. Apollinare in Classe was in progress in the autumn of 1906.

[4] Richter, as above, 9 ff. ; Riedin, 51 ff. ; Venturi, as above, i. 283–5, and Figs. 114–17 ; G. Rivoira, *Le Origini della architettura lombarda*, i, Fig. 55 ; Crowe and Cavalcaselle, *History of Painting in Italy* (new English edition edited by Langton Douglas, London, 1903), p. 18 and

perhaps built by Ursus (A.D. 400–10), was decorated, according to the *Liber Pontificalis*, by Neon (A.D. 425–30). It is an octagonal building surmounted by a dome, and the interior decoration is divided into four zones, the two uppermost occupying the dome, the two lower ornamenting the two superposed

Fig. 208.   Mosaics of the Catholic Baptistery, Ravenna : sixth century.   (L. Ricci.)

courses of round arches of which the lower part of the structure is composed. In a large medallion at the top of the dome is represented the Baptism.   In addition to the figures of Christ and St. John, who holds a long jewelled cross, there is present a personification of the River Jordan.[1]   The background is gold,

plate opposite ; C. Ricci, *Monumenti Ravennati, Il Battistero di S. Giovanni in Fonte*, and *Ravenna*, Figs. 43–6 ; J. Kurth, *Wandmosaiken von Ravenna*, pp. 65–81 and Pl. XV, &c.

[1] This Baptism scene has been considerably restored. The restorations have affected the heads of Christ and St. John, as well as the garments of the latter. The bowl in the Baptist's hands is not original. See C. Ricci, as above, 38 ; Riedin, 63.

but the nimbus is in each case blue with red borders. The broad zone below has a procession of Apostles bearing crowns to lay at Christ's feet: between each pair rises a tall conventional flower from a green ground signifying that the scene is laid in Paradise. The background is blue, and round the top is a line of looped curtains. The tunics and mantles are alternately white and gold, and the clavi purple. The second narrower zone is decorated with a series of conventional representations of the interiors of churches. These are of two types. In one the centre is occupied by an altar on which lies an open book of the Gospels, while on either side is a jewelled chair; in the other a chair is seen in the centre, while the lateral divisions are closed by *cancelli*. The idea underlying this peculiar decorative scheme is doubtless the glorification of the Church, and the example here seen is the earliest of a series, later instances occurring in the Church of St. George, Salonika,[1] and the basilica at Bethlehem.[2] Riedin thinks that possibly these representations may be intended for parts of the galleries of a church, in which sacred objects were sometimes exposed for veneration.[3]

The uppermost of the two remaining zones contains eight arches, each enclosing three smaller arches, under the midmost being placed the eight windows, while the lateral pairs form niches each occupied by a stucco figure of a prophet holding a book or scroll.[4] Before the restoration of 1889 the background was a dull red, and the reliefs themselves yellow (Ricci, *Il Battistero*, p. 36). Above the figures are pairs of confronted animals and birds (hares, goats, peacocks, vultures, dogs, cocks, pheasants, sheep) divided by baskets of fruit, &c., alternating in four cases with representations of the *Traditio Legis* (see p. 664), Daniel, Jonah, and a youthful figure of Christ without nimbus and carrying a book, walking upon a lion and a serpent. It is held by some that all this stucco decoration is later than the mosaics; but the subjects are characteristic of the earlier date, and stucco had been employed for similar purposes in imperial Roman times. Riedin (pp. 79–80) points out analogies to the subjects in various oriental monuments, among others on certain Ravenna sarcophagi and the Gospel of Rabula, where the decoration of the Eusebian Canons offers points of resemblance. The spandrels between the arches are filled by acanthus designs in mosaic with birds among the leaves.

In the lowest zone, between the arches, are bold scroll designs in green and gold on a blue ground enclosing figures of prophets, Apostles, or saints in white garments heightened with gold lines, after the style seen in the Vatican Virgil and later Byzantine MSS.[5] In four of the arches are exedrae or niches, while the spaces within the remaining four were filled with coloured marbles forming designs, some of which still remain: the lower walls were also covered with marble. Above the arches enclosing the niches were inscriptions in mosaic relating to the use of the building for the ceremony of baptism, and with them the monograms of the bishops Peter, Chrysologus, Neon, and Maximianus.

Oriental elements in the decoration of the baptistery are the presence of the personification of Jordan; the forms of the crowns carried by the Apostles, resembling the diadems of Byzantine emperors; the treatment of the stucco reliefs, recalling that of the reliefs on the base of the obelisk in the Hippodrome

---

[1] Photo, *Hautes Études*, cf. Fig. 221. Texier and Pullan, *Byz. Architecture*, Pl. XXX–XXXIII. The architecture in this case is of a more elaborate character than at Ravenna. For these architectural motives see pp. 374, 414. They perhaps originated in Alexandria, and are found in the wall paintings of the house discovered in 1893 on the Palatine.

[2] De Vogüé, *Églises de la Terre sainte*, 71; Lethaby and others, *The Church of the Nativity at Bethlehem* (Byzantine Research and Exploration Fund), 1910. The Bethlehem mosaics are of the twelfth century, but reproduce more ancient designs.

[3] As above, 54, 74 ff. He quotes Bishop Sophronius of Jerusalem, according to whom the instruments of the Passion were so exposed. Kondakoff has suggested that such an occasion may have suggested the representation of the Throne with the instruments of the Passion (cf. p. 666).

[4] Richter, 17–20; Riedin, 54.   [5] Venturi, i, Figs. 116–17.

at Constantinople.[1] The general type of the Baptism scene is claimed as Byzantine, and compared with the versions on a relief in Constantinople,[2] and of the miniatures in the sixth-century Gospel of Rabula at Florence[3] and the Etchmiadzin Gospel.[4] The solemn ceremonial character of the procession of the Apostles has also been noted as a new element, absent in Early Christian art.[5]

It is the beginning of the formal style, and we already see here the strange fashion of walking, as it were upon the toes, which may be remarked upon later Byzantine monuments, as for instance in the eleventh-century mosaics of Sta Sophia at Kieff.[6] It may be noted in conclusion that the decoration of both the Ravenna baptisteries is less remarkable for the number of subjects represented than other early baptisteries of the fourth to sixth centuries which have either survived or are known to us by description.[7] Such are the lost mosaics of the Vatican and Lateran Baptisteries[8] and the surviving decoration of the Baptistery of Naples (p. 369).

The Mausoleum of Galla Placidia[9] is thought to have been erected by the princess about A.D. 440 in honour of SS. Nazarius and Celsus;[10] she was buried within its walls. Its plan is in the form of a Latin cross such as is seen in almost contemporary crypts in the catacombs of Alexandria;[11] in the centre is a dome on four arches concealed on the exterior by a quadrangular tower with tiled roof. The arms of the cross have barrel vaults, and the whole surface of the interior, except the lower walls, which were formerly faced with marble, is covered with mosaic, the ground throughout being blue. In the vaults covering the eastern and western arms of the cross this blue ground is diapered with gold rosettes, &c.; in the other two are vine scrolls rising from acanthus and enclosing the figures of four Apostles and terminating at the top in the sacred monogram. In the dome a central cross appears in a firmament of stars;[12] in the spandrels between the four supporting arches are the symbols of the Evangelists.

Flanking the four windows under the dome are four pairs of Apostles in bluish tunics and white mantles standing under ornate niches on a green ground; between each pair and below the windows are doves either standing by a fountain or perched upon water vessels (cf. the Capitol mosaic, Woltmann, *Gesch.*, i. 92). The pair above the left transept are St. Peter and St. Paul, St. Peter, almost for the first time in monumental art, carrying a key as a symbol.[13] The heads of these figures, most of which are youthful, are poor and not equal to the drapery, which is executed in a far more skilful manner. The figure to the spectator's left is in each case more successful than that on his right, probably

[1] Richter, 17; Dobbert, *Repertorium*, viii. 164.

[2] Figured, *B. Z.*, i, Pl. II, Fig. 1.

[3] J. Strzygowski, *Ikonographie der Taufe Christi*, Pl. II, Fig. 9.

[4] J. Strzygowski, *Das Etschmiadzin-Evangeliar*, Pl. VI, Fig. 2.

[5] E. Dobbert, in *Repertorium*, viii, 1885, 163.   [7] Riedin, 55–6.

[6] Dobbert, in Prussian *Jahrbuch*, xv. 221.

[8] E. Müntz, *The Lost Mosaics of Rome*, in *American Journal of Archaeology*, ii, 1886, 296.

[9] Alinari and Ricci, photos; Riedin, ch. ii, 89 ff., Pl. I, and Figs. 8–15; G. Rivoira, *Le Origini della architettura lombarda*, i. 45; Kurth, as above, pp. 44–64 and Pl. X–XIV.

[10] *Liber Pontificalis*, p. 28 B. Some have held that the building was dedicated to SS. Gervasius and Protasius (Fabri, *Sagre memorie*, 295; Garrucci, i. 505).

[11] Richter, as above, 24; Riedin, 92.

[12] Riedin, 93. Cf. Baptistery of Naples (p. 369). The cross so placed in the vault or dome was not confined to churches, but also decorated the imperial palaces (Eusebius, *Vita Const.* in Migne, *Patr. Gr.*, xii, c. 49). This motive is mentioned by Paulinus of Nola (Migne. *Patr. Lat.*, lxi. 336, 339; Wickhoff, *R. Q.*, iii. 158 ff.). Sometimes the sacred monogram occupied the place of the cross; so in a fourth-century fresco in Hungary (de Rossi, *Bullettino*, 1874, 169 ff. and Pl. VIII), and in the sculpture in the small chamber in the base of the column of Arcadius at Constantinople (*Ath. Mitth.*, 1893, 230).

[13] St. Peter has keys on the triumphal arch of St. Paul outside the walls at Rome, but these were almost certainly added during one of the numerous restorations which these mosaics have undergone. They are, however, seen upon one of the sarcophagi at Ravenna.

because in attitude it approaches the readily accessible model of the antique orator.

The lunettes of the transepts are ornamented with acanthus scrolls in yellowish green, while in the foreground in each is represented a pair of harts approaching the water (C. Ricci, *Ravenna*, Fig. 39). The most important subjects are those which fill the lunette over the entrance door and that immediately opposite. The first is the famous Good Shepherd,[1] the second possibly the martyrdom of St. Laurence.[2] The Good Shepherd is seated on a boulder in a meadow with a rocky background with bushes, surrounded by his sheep and holding a long gold cross in his hand. He is no longer the herdsman of Early Christian art clothed in short tunic and carrying a simple pedum or crook, but Christ the Lord wearing a gold dalmatic with blue clavi and a mantle of royal purple. Round his head is a golden nimbus, and his oval face is framed in rich brown hair falling in long locks on either side. The type of head has suggested a comparison with Apollo,[3] and finds parallels upon sarcophagi of the fourth century. This picture has been considered the finest example of Early Christian mosaic in existence ; and certainly the ideal treatment, the clever management of lights and shadows, and the opulence of colour combine to place it in the very first rank.

The subject of the Good Shepherd is appropriate to a mausoleum, since the ancient liturgies allude to the departed as sheep taken by the Good Shepherd into the fold (Le Blant, *Étude sur les sarcophages chrétiens*, xxxiii–xxxv ; V. Schultze, *Arch. der christlichen Kunst*, 172). The long golden cross of the Golgotha type (p. 337), which was carried by the emperor in processions at Constantinople (Kondakoff, *Byzantine Enamels*, 291), as well as the purple raiment, are indications of an oriental influence.

The sheep standing in the lower left-hand corner is a restoration later than the time of Ciampini, whose reproduction (*Vet. Mon.*, vol. i, Pl. 66, p. 227) shows the sheep in this place recumbent (see Ricci, *Guida di Ravenna*, 77).

In the opposite lunette a man advances from the right towards a large gridiron, beneath which a fire is burning.[4] He holds over his right shoulder a long golden cross, and in his left hand a red-bound open book, probably the Gospel of St. Mark, for in a cupboard opposite are seen the books of the three other Evangelists, each with its name inscribed. His tunic is blue, his mantle white. The face is fine and aristocratic, the close-cut hair of a chestnut colour, but the type is one which was never adopted in representations of Our Lord : round the head is a golden nimbus.

If the person here represented is really St. Laurence, the occurrence of two such subjects as the Good Shepherd and a Martyrdom in one building of the fifth century is of great interest. In idea at least, the Good Shepherd still belongs to the early symbolic tradition, though the ancient simplicity has already vanished. The other subject would be an early example of realism, though it is still only transitional, the saint enduring no pain. The martyrdom of St. Laurence occurs upon Early Christian minor works of art dating from the fourth to the fifth century.[5] It is well known that representations of martyrdoms

---

[1] Alinari, 11596 (V. and A. Museum, 5223–90) ; Richter, as above, plate opp. p. 28 ; Riedin, Pl. I and Fig. 15 ; C. Ricci, *Ravenna*, Fig. 41 ; Crowe and Cavalcaselle, i, plate opp. p. 20. The picture has been drastically restored (Crowe and Cavalcaselle, i. 21, note).

[2] Kurth, as above, Pl. XIV ; C. Ricci, *Ravenna*, Fig. 40. The figure in this scene was formerly held to represent Christ, but the identification as St. Laurence was suggested by the Abbé Crosnier in 1859 and confirmed by de Rossi in his discussion of the decoration of the Church of S. Lorenzo at Rome. Although this interpretation has found general favour, some are still unable to accept it; for instance, Venturi does not accept this explanation, thinking that the book may be a volume of Manichaean heresy which is about to be cast into the flames (i. 280).

[3] Cf. the Christ on the Lateran sarcophagus (Garrucci, *Storia*, 323. 4), which is also of the type of Apollo.

[4] Alinari, 11595 (V. and A. Mus., 5212–90).

[5] F. X. Kraus, *Realencyklopädie*, s.v. *Laurentius*.

FIG. 209. The Good Shepherd : mosaic of the fifth century in the Mausoleum of Galla Placidia, Ravenna. (Ricci.)

in general did not begin until about this period. A relief of the fourth century has the martyrdom of St. Achilleus,[1] and Roman frescoes of about the same date show that of SS. Crispus Crispinianus and Benedict.[2]

The ornamental motives in SS. Nazaro e Celso are composed of wreaths of fruit and flowers rising from vases, vine scrolls, and bands of maeander.[3] There is a similarity between some of this decorative work and that of the Orthodox Baptistery, which, considered in relation to the more general resemblance in such matters as gradations of colour and the outlining of the figures, has led some critics to attribute the decoration of both buildings to the same hands.[4]

The Arian Baptistery,[5] otherwise known as Sta Maria in Cosmedin, is, like the Orthodox Baptistery, octagonal, and was probably built by Theodoric. The mosaics are confined to the dome, and reproduce the subjects of the Catholic Baptistery. The execution is throughout inferior: the draperies are unskilfully handled and the types of the faces monotonous. In the dome is the Baptism. The figure of Christ is very small and boyish, as is usual before the seventh century, while that of the Baptist is without the nimbus. Above Our Lord's head descends the dove, from the beak of which water issues.[6] To the right is the seated figure of Jordan, represented as an old man with white beard and hair from which issue crabs' claws,[7] nude down to the waist, and below wearing a sea-green cloth with red border. In his right hand he holds a reed, his left is raised in wonder.[8] The lower zone is occupied by the Twelve Apostles divided into two groups, each approaching a throne on which lies a cushion supporting a cross: the throne is not here intended as in the later *Etimasia* as a symbol of the Last Judgement, but simply stands for Our Lord. The Apostles are clothed like the figures in the Mausoleum of Placidia, and each has a pale blue nimbus. Between each pair is a palm-tree to indicate that the scene of the action is Paradise. One group is led by St. Peter, the other by St. Paul, but only the five figures following St. Peter are unrestored. The principal restorations were carried out in 1835 (Ricci, *Guida di Ravenna*, p. 28). The scroll held by St. Paul and the keys in the hands of St. Peter are late additions.[9]

The Church of S. Apollinare Nuovo,[10] built by Theodoric and originally dedicated to St. Martin, only received its present name in the ninth century, when the relics of St. Apollinaris were placed there in safety from the Saracens. The building was probably erected in the first decade of the sixth century: in the time of Agnellus (A. D. 553-66) it was transferred from the Arians to the Catholics.

The mosaics are of two periods corresponding to the two dates already mentioned. To the time of Theodoric belong the series of biblical scenes

---

[1] De Rossi, *Bullettino*, 1875, 8, Pl. IV ; Le Blant, *Les Persécuteurs et les martyrs aux premiers siècles de notre ère*, Paris, 1893, 281–2.

[2] *R. Q.*, ii, 1888, 148, and Pl. VI ; Germano, *La Casa Celimontana dei SS. Martiri Giovanni e Paolo*, Rome, 1894, 325, and Fig. 44.

[3] Von Quast, *Die altchristlichen Bauwerke von Ravenna*, Pl. IV.

[4] Crowe and Cavalcaselle, i. 20, note.

[5] Riedin, as above, ch. i ; Richter, as above, 36 ff. ; Crowe and Cavalcaselle, 22 ; Kurth, 193–200, and Pl. XXVI ; C. Ricci, *Ravenna*, Pl. 52.

[6] This feature, as Riedin notices, probably shows the influence of the so-called Hebrew Gospel (p. 65). See also H. Usener, *Religionsgeschichtliche Untersuchungen*, 60, 34. Cf. the ivory carving in the British Museum (Fig. 111). As a whole, the scene of the Baptism should also be compared with that on an ivory in the Victoria and Albert Museum (Garrucci, *Storia*, 447. 3 ; Strzygowski, *Ikonographie der Taufe Christi*, Pl. II, Fig. 3). Cf. also the versions on a relief on part of a column at Constantinople (*B. Z.*, i.), on the chair of Maximianus (Garrucci, 418. 2), and in the Etchmiadzin Gospel (J. Strzygowski, *Das Etchmiadzin-Evangeliar*, Pl. VI, Fig. 2).

[7] With these crabs' claws should be compared those issuing from the head of the personification of the Sea in the Vienna MS. of Dioscorides (see p. 460). The motive is, however, antique (Riedin, p. 69).

[8] In conformity with the words of the Psalm : ' The waters saw thee and feared.'

[9] Riedin, p. 72.

[10] Richter, 42 ff. ; Riedin, 113 ff. ; C. Ricci, *Ravenna*, Figs. 54–82 ; Crowe and Cavalcaselle, i. 30–5 ; Kurth, 134–92, and Pl. XXV and XXVI ; A. Muñoz, *L'Arte*, 1905, pp. 55 ff. ; &c.

which run along both walls of the nave high up above the windows near the roof, and also the isolated figures between the windows. To the time of Agnellus must be assigned the two long processions of male and female saints

Fig. 210.   The Port of Classe; Apostles : mosaics of the sixth century in the nave of S. Apollinare Nuovo, Ravenna.   (Ricci.)

which occupy the lower part of the walls.[1]   All the mosaics have a gold background.

The twenty-six biblical scenes which represent the Life and Passion of Our

[1] Fabri, Ciampini (ii. 89), Von Quast (p. 19), Crosnier (p. 678), Hübsch (p. 63), and Crowe and Cavalcaselle attributed the whole mosaic decoration to the time of Agnellus.   On the other hand, Riedin (p. 114) thinks that the passage in Agnellus referring to the decoration of S. Apollinare Nuovo (*Monumenta Germaniae historica, Scriptores rerum langobard. et ital.*, &c., p. 334-5) admits of the conclusion that all the mosaics date from Theodoric's time, or at any rate from the beginning of the sixth century.   Kraus (*Geschichte*, i. 434) thinks the two lower zones, i.e. the Apostles between the windows and the processions of martyrs, were both executed after Theodoric's death.   There seems no reason to assume that the Gothic king saw the work completed, and most authorities are unanimous in ascribing the processions to the period of Agnellus.   But the style of the figures of the Apostles is so superior that in the text the view of Rahn (p. 27), Richter (as above, 43), Dobbert (*Repertorium*, xxi, 1898, 100), Diehl (*Ravenne*, p. 54), and others, who consider them of equal age with the scenes from the life of Christ, has been adopted.   The opinion of Richter that the seated figures of Christ and the Virgin, to which the two processions severally move, may be later than Agnellus does not seem to have found acceptance (p. 68).   In addition to carrying out restorations, Agnellus placed on the façade of the church mosaic portraits of Justinian and of himself (*Liber Pont.*, 'Life of S. Agnellus').

Lord are a series of great iconographical importance, and are so arranged that
the subjects from the Life are on the left side from the entrance and those from
the Passion on the right.   Among the principal subjects of the former group
are the Healing of the Paralytic, the Healing of the Possessed, the Division of
the Sheep and the Goats (Matthew xxv. 31–2), the scene used allegorically to
typify the Last Judgement (Fig. 211) and recalling a sarcophagus in the Stroganoff
Collection (Riedin, Fig. 23, p. 141), the Widow's Mite, the Pharisee and the
Publican, the Raising of Lazarus, Christ and the Woman of Samaria, the Woman
with the Issue of Blood (or possibly the Woman taken in Adultery), the Healing
of the Blind, the Calling of Peter and Andrew (or the Miraculous Draught of
Fishes), and the two miracles of the Feeding of the Five Thousand, the Gathering
of the Baskets that remained (or the miracle at Cana : this picture has suffered
restoration).   The thirteen scenes of the Passion are the Last Supper, Christ in
the Garden of Gethsemane, the Kiss of Judas, Christ led Prisoner, Christ before
the Sanhedrin, Christ announcing to Peter that he should betray him, the
Denial of Peter, the Repentance of Judas, Christ before Pilate, the Road to
Golgotha, the Maries at the Tomb, the Way to Emmaus, the Risen Christ among
the Disciples.   These pictures are still under the influence of antique pagan
art, manifest alike in the composition and in the costumes of individual figures.
With the mosaics of Sta Maria Maggiore, the carvings on the doors of Sta Sabina,
the ivory panels of the chair of Maximianus at Ravenna, and the miniatures
of the Codex Rossanensis (p. 452), they are the most important early series of
historical subjects, and are all the more interesting because they are exclusively
derived from the New Testament.   The laws of perspective are imperfectly
understood, but the colour is effective.   The figures in the series upon the left
side of the church recall those of the Early Christian sarcophagi,[1] and the composition of the various scenes is extremely simple, Our Lord being accompanied
by a single Apostle, who serves to convey to the spectator the emotion aroused
by the action, for the Saviour himself looks towards the spectator.   In this
series Christ is beardless, and has the cruciferous nimbus, which here makes an
early appearance in monumental art.   He wears a purple dalmatic, the colour
usual in the art of the Christian East.[2]   An oriental influence may also perhaps
be indicated in the different colouring of the two angels with the two flocks, the
one being depicted as ruddy, the other blue.[3]

In the second series Christ is bearded, the hair and beard being blond.
Although they mark a transition from the old symbolic to the new historical
art they are still far from realism, and both the Flagellation and the Crucifixion
are omitted.   This series seems to show more pronounced affinities to early
illuminated MSS. ; the scene in which Pilate washes his hands, and the Last
Supper, recall the same scenes in the Codex Rossanensis.[4]   The costume of the
high-priest resembles that of the priestly figures in the mosaics of Sta Maria
Maggiore at Rome ; and the sepulchre in the scene of the Maries at the Tomb is
a circular building with cupola, probably reproducing the building over the Holy
Sepulchre at Jerusalem.[5]   Although these two series are the earliest surviving

---

[1] Venturi, *Storia*, i. 288. Richter compares the style of these pictures to that of the
frescoes in the catacombs of Central and Southern Italy (p. 50). For the Gospel pictures see
C. Ricci, *La Vita di Gesù*, in *Emporium, rivista mensile illustrata*, &c., Bergamo, xv. 261–84, and the
same author, *Ravenna*, 21 ff.

[2] e.g. the Gospel of Rabula, the sixth-century Syrian Gospel in Paris (Bibl. Nat., No. 33,
fol. 5 v and 6 v), and the Codex Rossanensis.

[3] Venturi, p. 290.

[4] Ibid., and Riedin, p. 158. Haseloff, however (*Codex purpureus Rossanensis*, 123), shows
that the relations between the mosaics and the miniatures must not be regarded as continuously close. The same may be said with regard to the lost mosaics of the Church of the
Apostles at Constantinople described for us by Mesarites and Constantine the Rhodian
(A. Heisenberg, *Grabeskirche und Apostelkirche*, ii. 249).

[5] See the remarks in connexion with the building represented in the mosaic of
Sta Pudenziana (p. 336).

representations of Gospel narrative in any church, the decoration of walls with such subjects had been usual from the fourth century.[1]

Riedin has noted various points suggesting oriental influence, e. g. the red colouring of the angel who stands by the goats in the scene representing the Last Judgement, which recalls similar treatment in later Byzantine MSS.;[2] the Last Supper is of the familiar type of the later Byzantine period;[3] the bearded type of Christ in the Passion scenes recalls that of the Codex Rossanensis and of the sixth-century Syrian Gospel at Paris (*Bibl. Nat.*, No. 33). Dobbert[4] sees in the general character of all the pictures from the Life of Christ the breaking

Fɪɢ. 211.   The Separation of the Sheep and the Goats : mosaic of the sixth century in the nave of S. Apollinare Nuovo, Ravenna.   (Ricci.)   P. 352.

free of East-Roman art from the traditions of Early Christian times. The stiff treatment of the drapery, the sharp-cut band of ornament below the pictures, and the manner in which hills are represented, recall bas-reliefs, and suggest

[1] We have various literary evidences of this. St. Theodore the Studite says that Sabinus ordered the decoration of his church with Gospel scenes (*Antirrheticus*, Migne, *Patr. Gr.*, vol. 99, p. 388). Scenes from the New Testament adorned the walls of the Church of the Virgin at Blachernae in Constantinople founded by the Empress Pulcheria (Montfaucon, *Anal. gr.*, Paris, 1688, 453–4 ; Garrucci, *Storia*, i. 508–9). St. Nilus, in a letter to Olympiodorus, speaks of nave decorations consisting of scenes from the Old and New Testaments (Migne, vol. 79, p. 578). The decoration of the Church of St. Sergius at Gaza included Gospel scenes, among them being the Crucifixion (Boissonade's ed. of Choricius of Gaza, pp. 91–8). The same was the case with the Church of the Apostles at Constantinople and with Western churches: the Lateran Basilica, the Basilica of St. Ambrose at Milan, St. Felix at Nola, and the Basilica of St. Sylvester built by Pope Celestine. For the above see Riedin, p. 138.

[2] Riedin, pp. 141–2 ; Paris Gospels, *Bibl. Nat.*, No. 74 (eleventh century) ; and Bible in the Laurentian Library, Florence (also eleventh century); in the first of which an angel thrusts an emperor down into hell, while in the second the angel expelling Adam and Eve from Paradise is of a fiery colour. Riedin also compares the mosaics of Sta Maria Maggiore at Rome in the scene where the angels are entertained by Abraham.

[3] This point had previously been brought out by Dobbert (*Repertorium*, xiv. 183, note 23).

[4] *Repertorium*, xxi. 103.

that some work similar to the doors of Sta Sabina, or miniatures influenced by such reliefs, may have inspired the artist.[1] The last pictures of the Passion series, from the Betrayal onward, in which the grouping, the types, and the treatment of drapery differ, suggest that there may also have been other models.

Between the panels with the historical subjects are gold niches with 'scalloped' arches, each surmounted by a cross between two doves, and below these, between the windows, is a middle zone composed of figures of prophets and Apostles, in which Riedin sees a more pronounced Greek influence (p. 137).

Fig. 212.   Christ before Pilate: mosaic of the sixth century in the nave of S. Apollinare Nuovo, Ravenna.   (L. Ricci.)

In the soffits of the windows are diapers of stars, circles, crosses, and other designs.

The long processions of crown-bearing martyrs[2] on the walls of the nave below the windows are represented on green meadows on which grow lilies and palms; the females advance from the town of Classis towards the Virgin throned with the Child in her arms, the males from the city of Ravenna towards an enthroned figure of Our Lord, who is bearded and differs from the symbolic juvenile type of the miracle scenes.[3] Both the Virgin and

---

[1] Riedin, p. 162.

[2] The males are principally saints venerated in the West, and only five are directly connected with Ravenna.   The female martyrs are of Roman or Roman-provincial origin.   The remains of four feet show that two other saints once formed part of the procession.   Several of the same saints in similar costume are represented in the mosaics of the Cathedral of Parenzo (Garrucci, 276. 2).

[3] Crowe and Cavalcaselle, p. 30 (Plate); Riedin, 117–18, Figs. 18, 19.   The representation of the palace, probably the façade, with inscription PALATIVM, is architecturally of interest. The palace was perhaps east of S. Apollinare Nuovo, and the building to the south, now called the Palace of Theodoric, was probably a guard-house.   In the lunette of the gateway in the mosaic representing Ravenna are seen three indistinct male figures in white, one carrying a long cross.   Behind are seen various buildings, among others S. Vitale and S. Apollinare.

Our Lord are attended by angels ; but the Virgin is also approached by the Magi bringing gifts, who thus appear to lead the procession of female martyrs. The figures of the Magi, as at present seen, are all restorations,[1] as also is the left side of Christ's figure and the sceptre or torch which he holds, in place of the original book of the Gospels. The two outer angels attending the Virgin are restored, as also are the angels in the corresponding position attending Our Lord.[2] The figures of the saints have been left untouched. The men, with the exception of St. Laurence and St. Martin, are clothed almost entirely in white, which is thrown into relief against the gold background, producing an inharmonious effect unrelieved by gradations of colour and intensified by the monotonous character of the drawing. Upon their mantles are to be seen in exceptional variety the letters so often found in similar positions in Early Christian art.[3] The procession of women is superior to that of the male saints. These female martyrs are arrayed in gold-embroidered upper garments over white tunics ; they show a greater variety of type than the men and recall the female figures in the ceremonial picture in S. Vitale.[4] They may also be compared with the mosaic picture of St. Agnes at Rome dating from about the year 630. The two throned figures of Christ and the Virgin have given rise to a diversity of opinion ; [5] the Christ recalls the fresco on the roof of the principal chapel in the Catacomb of Peter and Marcellinus at Rome,[6] which is certainly of earlier date. Before leaving the subject of the two processions, we may specially note the introduction of realistic pictures of Ravenna and Classis into a purely ideal subject, the action of which is supposed to take place in heaven.

In the Chapel of Tutti Santi in the left aisle is preserved a fragment of the mosaics formerly ornamenting the entrance wall, consisting of a head (Fig. 5) of the Emperor Justinian,[7] which may be compared with the portrait in S. Vitale. The corresponding figure of Agnellus, who restored the church, has been destroyed.

The Church of S. Vitale[8] was begun under Archbishop Ecclesius (A.D. 524–34) by a certain Julius Argentarius, probably continued under his successors Ursicinus (A.D. 534–9) and Victor (A.D. 539–46), and consecrated under Maximianus in the first year of his office, A.D. 547. It has a dome supported by eight piers, between which, on the ground level, are exedrae, each with two columns, and on a higher level the openings of a gallery fronted with columns in a similar manner. The exterior would be a complete octagon but for the addition, on the side opposite the entrance, of a rectangular

---

[1] Crowe and Cavalcaselle, 49. Agnellus mentions the Magi (*L. P.*, § 38), so that they must have formed part of the original composition.

[2] Richter, 64. There was once a figure of St. Stephen introducing the male saints, but this has entirely disappeared. We learn from a manuscript account by G. F. Malazappi da Carpi that it was still in existence in 1580.

[3] Richter, 66, where there is a reference to the use of letters to symbolize the character of the wearer in Egyptian monasteries.

[4] Crowe and Cavalcaselle, Plate opp. p. 32. Cf. also the figure of the Virgin in the mosaics of Sta Maria Maggiore at Rome (Garrucci, *Storia*, 212. 1 and 2), on the Milan diptych (Garrucci, 447. 1), and the female figures in a seventh-century Coptic MS. in the Library of Naples (No. 1, B 19 ; see Riedin, p. 123).

[5] Richter (p. 68) suggests that they may not have been designed to form part of the composition, and sees in them a certain barbaric influence. Riedin makes a general comparison with the figures in S. John Lateran, S. Cosmas and Damian, Sta Sophia at Constantinople, and the monastery on Sinai, as well as in the miniatures of the MS. of Cosmas Indicopleustes, noting that in all these early representations the aspect is mild, in contrast to the stern expression of the Pantokrator of the tenth and eleventh centuries.

[6] Crowe and Cavalcaselle, i, p. 48 ; Richter, p. 69. The fresco is reproduced by Garrucci, *Storia*, vol. ii.

[7] Kurth, 191 and Pl. XXVI.

[8] Crowe and Cavalcaselle, i. 23–6 ; C. Ricci, *Ravenna*, Figs. 87–101 ; Richter, p. 73 f. ; Riedin, pp. 164 ff. ; Kurth, pp. 88–131 and Pl. XVI–XXIV. For recent restorations see C. Ricci, *Ravenna e i lavori fatti dalla Sovrintendenza dei monumenti nel 1898*, Bergamo, 1899.

room or tribuna, terminating in an apse. The mosaic decoration covers the apse, the tribuna or presbyterium, and the triumphal arch before it.

In the apse a youthful Christ is seen seated on the globe of the world and extending a jewelled diadem to St. Vitalis, who, presented by an angel, holds out his hands covered by his mantle to receive it:[1] on the other side advances Archbishop Ecclesius bearing a model of the church and likewise led by an angel. Beyond are two ceremonial pictures, one representing the Emperor Justinian (clearly a portrait)[2] carrying a gift in the form of a basin probably containing an offering of gold, accompanied by Bishop Maximianus

FIG. 213.   The Empress Theodora and attendants : mosaic of the sixth century in S. Vitale, Ravenna.   (L. Ricci.)

and surrounded by his suite and guards, the other the Empress Theodora bearing a golden bowl or chalice accompanied by her attendants. These two scenes either represent the participation of the imperial pair in the dedication of the church, for which there is, however, no historical evidence, or merely one of the ceremonial entries of the kind described by Constantine Porphyrogenitus.[3] Justinian doubtless contributed to the expense of decoration; he might thus

---

[1] Kurth, Pl. XXI; Riedin, Fig. 38, p. 192, and Pl. II; C. Ricci, *Ravenna*, Fig. 97. For Christ upon the globe, cf. the mosaics of Sta Costanza, Rome (p. 333).

[2] The ceremonial pictures are figured by Du Sommerard, *Les Arts au moyen âge*, Album, 10ᵉ série, Pl. 32, 112; Hefner-Alteneck, *Trachten, Kunstwerke und Geräthschaften*, i, Pl. 3 and 4; *Revue archéologique*, vii, 1850, Pl. 145; Crowe and Cavalcaselle, pp. 24 and 26; J. Kurth, Pl. XXII–IV; C. Ricci, *Ravenna*, Figs. 99–100. Cf. the mosaic portrait in S. Apollinare Nuovo, above, p. 355.

[3] D. Bielyayeff, *Byzantina*, ii, ch. 5. Such ceremonial entries were probably already stereotyped in Justinian's day (*Byzantina*, as above, 46, 153, 160–1).

be regarded as at least intimately concerned with the dedication ceremony, for which he may also have sent a gift of plate. The imperial procession has halted in the narthex, and the emperor has been censed by the Archbishop Maximianus. We know by the fact that the emperor still wears his diadem that he has not actually entered the church, for within the sacred walls the crown was removed.

It is on the walls of the tribuna that what may be called the dogmatic subjects are to be found, the most important scenes occupying a central lunette on either side. On the right hand are Abel and Melchizedek bringing their offerings ; on the left, Abraham entertains the angels and prepares to sacrifice his son. In the spaces between these two pictures and the body of the church are the prophets Isaiah and Jeremiah ; on the spaces towards the apse are : on the right, and next the scene of Abel's offering, Moses represented with lambs like the Good Shepherd of the Mausoleum of Placidia, and Moses and the Burning Bush ; on the left, Moses receiving the tables of the law. Above this series of pictures, on the upper part of the tribuna walls, two on either side, are the four Evangelists accompanied by their symbols, figures which in style recall the mosaics of the Monastery of St. Catherine on Sinai. In the centre of the roof,[1] in a medallion enclosed in a wreath, is the apocalyptic Lamb on a background of blue sprinkled with silver stars. From this radiate four bands of ornament formed of leaves and fruit, &c., and terminating at the lower ends in peacocks and dolphins. These divide the surface into four compartments filled with scroll-work resembling that seen in the Chapel of St. John in the Lateran Basilica, and in the Orthodox Baptistery at Ravenna. Amidst the scrolls in each compartment an angel in white garments stands upon a sphere, with raised arms appearing to support the central medallion, a motive already employed in the decoration of the Orthodox Baptistery and the Mausoleum of Placidia. In the convolutions of the scrolls are various creatures (hare, fish, panther, stork, deer, parrot, peacock, &c.), as seen in the carved scrolls on the ivory chair of Maximianus (Fig. 122) and on numerous other works of art. Above the apse, and above the two lunette pictures, are pairs of flying angels supporting medallions,[2] and in the soffit of the triumphal arch are busts of Christ, the Apostles,[3] and the martyrs Gervasius and Protasius in medallions [3] which again recall the Sinai mosaics.

The principal subjects in this remarkable scheme of decoration must now be described in greater detail. In the right-hand lunette picture [4] Abel and Melchizedek stand on either side of a rectangular table set in a meadow. To the right stands Melchizedek in priestly attire offering bread : a palace is seen behind him. To the left is Abel dressed as a shepherd offering a lamb : the hand of the Almighty appears from clouds above to signify the acceptance of the offering. On the table, which is covered with a white cloth with purple border, is a chalice with handles, and two circular cakes of bread : it is thus evident that it is intended to represent an altar. The offering of Abel is a favourite subject in Byzantine art, but the complementary figure is usually Cain : the two brothers were thus represented in the lost mosaics of Sta Costanza at Rome (p. 333). Melchizedek wears a white tunic confined by a green girdle, and a purple mantle fastened by a gold brooch.[5] On his head is a red cap, on his feet red shoes, and he has a golden nimbus. The figure of the priest-king in Christian art is usually balanced by that of Abraham, as in

[1] C. Ricci, *Ravenna*, Fig. 101 ; Riedin, Fig. 33, p. 166. Compare the decoration of the roofs in the chapels of the Lateran Baptistery (p. 341).

[2] C. Ricci, *Ravenna*, Fig. 98. Cf. the angels on the large five-part diptychs (Fig. 124), and in the mosaics of the Monastery of St. Catherine on Mount Sinai.

[3] The bust of Christ is entirely restored. Such medallion portraits in mosaic are probably descendants of the encaustic portraits of the Fayûm.

[4] C. Ricci, *Ravenna*, Fig. 96 ; Riedin, Fig. 36, p. 171.

[5] This is the traditional priestly costume in Byzantine art ; cf. the costume of the priests in the Passion scenes in the Gospel series of S. Apollinare Nuovo.

the mosaics of Sta Maria Maggiore at Rome and in the miniatures of the Vienna Genesis.

In the opposite lunette we see in the centre a rectangular table beneath a tree, at which three angels are seated,[1] wearing white garments and each having a golden nimbus but no wings. On the table are three circular cakes of bread marked with crosses. Abraham approaches from the left bearing a dish on which lies a calf, while Sarah stands in the door of a hut behind him.[2] Abraham is an old man, wearing a short brown tunic. To the right of the picture Abraham is again represented standing on the grass quite close to the table preparing to strike Isaac, who kneels upon a low altar. Near by is the ram ; above, the hand of the Almighty issues from the clouds. The subject is frequent in the frescoes and on sarcophagi, but is there treated in a more symbolic manner. Above each of the lunette pictures are two soaring angels holding between them a medallion containing a jewelled cross. Of the figures of Isaiah, Jeremiah, and Moses little need be said except to remark their general excellence and to note that the representation of Moses taking off his sandals recalls the same scene in the Roman Catacombs of SS. Nereus and Achilleus and of Calixtus,[3] while in the representation of the Giving of the Law the prophet's attitude and costume suggest those of the crown-bearing Apostles in the Catholic Baptistery. Moses has throughout a golden nimbus, and, as usually in Byzantine art, is without a beard.

In the upper series of pictures the grey-haired Evangelists are seen seated in a green landscape with their Gospels upon their knees : Matthew has a desk and a *scrinium*, or case for manuscripts.

Although the mosaics of S. Vitale are splendid and impressive, they are not equal to the earlier work of Ravenna, such as that of the Mausoleum of Placidia. Many of the figures are feeble and disproportioned ; the passage from light to shade is no longer finely graduated. The important place assigned in these compositions to landscape should be especially noticed ; it is formally treated, without any power of rendering distance. As Richter has remarked, it almost suggests geological sections.[4] The conventional indications in other mosaics such as those of S. Apollinare Nuovo are here replaced by a formal attempt to render scenery. But foregrounds and backgrounds are not distinguished, and black lines are used to emphasize the outlines and features of the figures, defects which are not entirely compensated by the careful drawing or the skill with which the draperies are often arranged. The colour scale is more extensive than in the earlier work, and mother-of-pearl is used to heighten the effect, but brilliance cannot disguise the fact that the principal persons in the ceremonial pictures are arranged in the foreground as if they were hung on wires.[5] The biblical personages wear a solemn and hieratic aspect, different from that of Early Christian art. These changes resulted necessarily less from artistic decadence than from the changed spirit of an age enthusiastic in dogmatic discussions. The mosaics of S. Vitale are indeed a striking example of the dominion which theology now began to exercise over art.

It is generally agreed that the subjects represented in S. Vitale are intended to teach a dogmatic lesson. Some critics have seen in the principal pictures

---

[1] Riedin, Fig. 35, p. 168 ; C. Ricci, *Ravenna*, Fig. 95. The subject of the entertainment of the angels is also found in the mosaics of Sta Maria Maggiore. In later Byzantine art it occurs frequently as an allegorical representation of the Trinity (mosaics of St. Mark, Venice, and of Monreale : miniature of Vatican Octateuch, see J. Tikkanen, *Die Genesis-Mosaiken in Venedig*, &c., p. 61, Helsingfors, 1889).

[2] Crowe and Cavalcaselle notice the antique character of Sarah's figure, which suggests the so-called Pudicitia in the Vatican Sculpture Gallery.

[3] Crowe and Cavalcaselle, 7 ; de Rossi, *Roma sotterranea*, vol. ii, Supplementary Plate B. Cf. also the same scene on the ivory casket at Brescia (Garrucci, *Storia*, Pl. 443).

[4] p. 85.   [5] Venturi, i. 294.

types of the Sacrifice of the Mass, and bring[1] them into connexion with the Roman canon.   This view, stated by Abbot Lambrecht as early as the twelfth century,[2] has most recently been maintained by Kraus[3] and Beissel,[4] who contest the oriental influence in these compositions.   Others, represented by Quitt and Schenkl, argue that the above view does not explain the whole cycle of pictures in the church.[5]   For instance, it gives no special point to the

Fɪɢ. 214.   Portrait of Archbishop Maximianus : mosaic of the sixth century in S. Vitale, Ravenna.   (Ricci.)

Entertainment of the Angels by Abraham, Moses at the Burning Bush, and receiving the Tables of the Law, the prophets Isaiah and Jeremiah, the Evangelists and Apostles, and Christ enthroned.   They hold that the true interpretation must be sought in the Christological disputes of the sixth century, in which the defenders of the Catholic faith crossed swords with the Monophysite followers of Eutyches.   The especial texts illustrated by the

[1] Kugler, *Kunstgeschichte*, i. 269 ; Kondakoff, *L'Art byzantin*, i. 135 ; Richter, *Mosaiken von Ravenna*, 81.

[2] *B. D.*, iii. 75.   [3] *Geschichte der christlichen Kunst*, i. 438.

[4] In *Stimmen aus Maria-Laach*, xlvii, 1894, 503 ; and S. Beissel, *Bilder aus der Kunstgeschichte der altchristlichen Kunst und Liturgie in Italien*, 178.

[5] *B. D.*, iii. 74 ff.

mosaics Quitt finds in the books of Bishop Vigilius of Thapsus against Eutyches, written in the last quarter of the fifth century;[1] and he explains the appearance of such pictorial polemics in the West, where the great controversy entered less into the lives of the people, by the personal intervention of Justinian. The emperor was a theologian and an ardent champion of orthodoxy. He neglected no detail in questions which he regarded as of capital religious importance, and where he contributed funds, was quite likely to dictate the lines which the decoration should follow. Schenkl, agreeing that the inspiration of these pictures did not flow from Rome or the Roman liturgy, thinks it more probable that the text of which they are a commentary should be sought in the works of St. Ambrose, the most prominent defender of the doctrine of the two natures of Christ in the Western Church.[2] The greatest of North Italian bishops was well versed in the writings of the Greek theologians, and was their principal interpreter in his own country. Here, then, was the real source of inspiration, a source which made the pointed defence of dyophysitism on Italian soil perfectly natural, and would be entirely approved by the imperial patron of the church. The influence of Ambrose would further explain the presence of Gervasius and Protasius, two saints held in especial honour at Milan, among the Apostles upon the arch. For why, if Milan had no connexion with the work, should these two saints and these alone be singled out to occupy such a place of honour?

Such arguments carry considerable weight, and the newer theory appears to explain the scheme of decoration more completely than the old. It must also be remembered that the relations of Ravenna and Rome were not always either close or cordial during the Gothic period,[3] nor is it certain that the Roman liturgy had been adopted in Ravenna at the beginning of the sixth century.

The Archiepiscopal Chapel[4] is very richly decorated. A monogram and inscription on a capital in the interior ascribe the completion of the building to a certain Peter, perhaps Peter Chrysologus, bishop in the middle of the fifth century.[5] The busts of Apostles and of Our Lord in medallions on the soffits of the arches nearest the entrance and nearest the altar may be earlier than the other mosaics, though opinion is not unanimous on the point. Here is to be seen the monogram of Bishop Maximianus which occurs in the Catholic Baptistery. The head of Christ is in each case youthful and beardless, the long hair falling on the shoulders; the type is perhaps reproduced from the symbolic pictures in S. Apollinare Nuovo,[6] and also resembles that on the ivory reliquary of Brescia. On the soffits of the two lateral arches are busts of saints in medallions, but the centre at the top is occupied by a sacred monogram between Alpha and Omega: on one arch the names are of male, on the other of female saints.[7] The heads of Apostles are considered by Richter to be earlier and superior in style: the others later and inferior. In the compartments of the vault are the Evangelists' symbols, which have been so extensively restored as to call for little notice; on the ribs are four angels with raised arms, supporting, after the fashion of those in S. Vitale, a medallion with the sacred monogram. These angels have been considerably restored and seem to have impressed observers very differently, for while Richter

---

[1] B. D., iii. 83.

[2] Ibid., 111–18. Cf. B. Z., xiii. 291.   [3] B. D., iii. 113.

[4] Richter, 93 ff.; C. Ricci, Ravenna, Figs. 47–8; Crowe and Cavalcaselle, i, p. 27; Kurth, 225–35 and Pl. XXX.

[5] More than one Bishop Peter occupied the See of Ravenna in the fifth century (Labarte, Hist. des arts ind., ii. 344). Kraus (Real-Encykl., ii. 425) and Gerspach (La Mosaïque, p. 51) are in favour of the fifth century and the period of Chrysologus. Schnaase, Crowe and Cavalcaselle, Rahn (Ravenna, p. 18), Garrucci (Storia, iv. 31), and Riedin (p. 211) prefer the sixth century.   [6] Richter, p. 94.

[7] SS. Sebastian, Fabian, Damian, Cassian, Chrysogonus, Chrysantus; SS. Daria, Perpetua, Felicitas, Euphemia (Eufimia), Eugenia, Cecilia.

thinks them of poor workmanship and not earlier than the seventh century, Riedin finds in them examples of the purest style, comparing them with the caryatid angels of S. Vitale.[1]

In the presbyterium, above the altar, is a standing figure of the Virgin with the hands raised in prayer, originally in the bema of the cathedral; this may be as early as the tenth century.[2] There is also a much damaged and restored figure of Our Lord, of the Emmanuel type, the date of which is difficult to determine; he carries a cross like the Good Shepherd in the lunette of the Mausoleum of Placidia.[3] It remains to mention four single heads in mosaic, also from the cathedral, two being those of SS. Vitalis and Apollinaris, the two others unnamed: they recall the Evangelists on the triumphal arch of S. Apollinare in Classe. Yet a further fragment represents a bearded man in half profile.[4]

FIG. 215.   Mosaic decoration in the bema of Sta Sophia, Salonika.
(*Hautes Études*: G. Millet.)

Architecturally, the chapel resembles the Mausoleum of Placidia. But in the mosaics we notice the method of outlining figures and features in black which is noticeable at S. Vitale as well as in early oriental miniatures, such as the Gospel of Rabula.[5] The medallions with Apostles also have affinities with those in S. Vitale, and those of the martyrs and saints with figures in the processional mosaics of S. Apollinare Nuovo. Such considerations lead to the conclusion that the mosaics of this chapel belong to the same century, if to a rather later period within it.[6]

S. Apollinare in Classe[7] was built at the port of Ravenna in the time of Bishop Ursicinus (A.D. 534–8)[8] and was dedicated under Maximianus (A.D. 549). The mosaics cannot have all been completed in the sixth century, as we learn from the Life of Reparatus (A.D. 672–7) that such work was still being executed in his time.[9]

---

[1] Riedin, 212.
[2] Riedin, 217, who compares the figures of the Virgin as *orans* in Sta Sophia at Kieff, at Nicaea, at Cefalù, at the Gelatsky Monastery, at S. Donato, Murano, and other examples. He rejects Richter's view that this mosaic is Italian work of the twelfth or thirteenth century.
[3] Riedin, 216–17.
[4] Ricci, *Guida di Ravenna*, 200; Richter, 97; Riedin, 219.
[5] Riedin, 213.   [6] Ibid., 214–15.
[7] Riedin, 220 ff. and Figs. 47–54; Kurth, 200-24 and Pl. XXVII and XXVIII; C. Ricci, *Ravenna*, Fig. 109.
[8] *Liber Pontificalis*, p. 101 E.   [9] Ibid., p. 108, note 4.

The mosaics of the triumphal arch are divided into horizontal zones, and in the centre of the uppermost is a medallion with a red ground containing the bust of Our Lord. He is bearded, and recalls to Riedin the types of SS. Cosmas and Damian, the Lateran Basilica, and the MS. of Cosmas Indicopleustes. To right and left, on a blue ground with clouds, are the Evangelists' symbols in the form of winged half-figures holding books, as in the mosaics of SS. Cosmas and Damian at Rome. In the second zone, broken by the arch, on a gold ground also with clouds, are lambs issuing from the two cities of Jerusalem and Bethlehem, the walls of which are golden, with precious stones, and moving upwards towards the portrait of Christ. The third zone consists of two triangular surfaces with blue ground on which are palm-trees, and below on the pilasters are large figures of the Archangels Michael and Gabriel, on a gold ground, wearing white tunics and purple mantles, and holding labara on which are small panels with the word ΑΓΙΟϹ thrice repeated. The nimbus of each is blue.[1] Below again are the busts of St. Matthew and St. Luke on a blue ground, the types recalling those of S. Vitale. The ascetic appearance of the Evangelists, the costume of the angels, and the type of labarum which they carry suggest affinities to later Byzantine art.

The mosaic in the apse is clearly of an earlier date, and represents the Transfiguration treated in a symbolic manner.[2] At the top, on a gold background, appears the hand of the Almighty issuing from clouds; lower down, also emerging from clouds, are the half-figures of Moses and Elias in white garments, both young and beardless as in S. Vitale, and in the finer style of the sixth century.[3] Their eyes are fixed upon the centre of a large jewelled cross in a jewelled medallion strewn with stars on a blue background: in the centre of the cross is a small bust of Our Lord. At the ends of the arms are the letters A and Ω; above the vertical limb is the word ΙΧΘΥϹ and below it the words SALVS MVNDI.

In the lower part of the apse, beneath a horizontal band, is a green landscape, with birds, cypresses, and pines. Here stand three lambs with heads raised, evidently representing the three Apostles present at the Transfiguration on Mount Tabor.[4] The blending of realism and symbolism here observed is more artificial than in the case of the Good Shepherd picture in the Mausoleum of Placidia, where a similar tendency was remarked (p. 349). At the bottom of the picture is a row of twelve more lambs, perhaps Apostles, among them St. Apollinaris standing with arms outstretched in prayer.[5] The saint wears a white dalmatic and a dark paenula and has a golden nimbus. The figure, which has been considerably restored, is not without resemblance to those of the popes in St. Agnes without the walls at Rome, which date from about A.D. 630.[6] Between the choir windows below the apse are the life-sized figures of the four archbishops of Ravenna with their names in Latin

---

[1] Isaiah vi. 3. The lower parts of the angels' figures are restored; Haseloff has expressed the opinion that both the heads are also restorations (O. Wulff, *Die Koimesiskirche von Nicäa*, 278, note 4).

[2] The apse mosaic has recently been restored under the supervision of the *Sovrintendenza*; the left side, which had suffered a great deal, and had been partly replaced by painting in oil, has been re-executed in mosaic to correspond with the right side: all that is new has been enclosed within a dark line. It was found that a part of the clouds above the cross had been already restored in ancient times (see S. Muratori, *L'Arte*, 1910, 60–2).

[3] Riedin, p. 226.

[4] This is a very early representation of the Transfiguration, and is unique in character, though the employment of the cross on a background of stars to represent Christ has already been remarked in the Mausoleum of Placidia and in the Baptistery of Naples. The Transfiguration in the apse of the Sinai Monastery (see p. 383) is of the type adopted by later Byzantine art, Christ himself appearing upon the mountain. [5] p. 228.

[6] Richter, 104. Riedin (p. 228) considers that it is contemporary with the rest of the apse mosaic, and that its commonplace character is due to the employment of inferior artists.

characters,[1] the two earlier alone having the title of saint. Above their heads hang crowns between curtains draped to right and left.

In a line with these portraits are two more elaborate pictures on blue backgrounds, the one ritual, the other ceremonial, both suggested by the earlier work in S. Vitale: in the first we have a combination of the two ritual pictures of that church. A table-like altar is set in the centre, behind which stands Melchizedek, while on his left is Abel. The former wears a purple mantle fastened with a brooch over the breast, and a gemmed fillet in his hair; the

Fig. 216.   Constantine IV, Pogonatus, with Archbishop Reparatus : mosaic of the seventh century in S. Apollinare in Classe, Ravenna.   (Ricci.)   P. 364.

figure of Abel is almost entirely restored.   On the right Abraham leads Isaac to the altar (both figures largely restored), the action taking place before an architectural background, perhaps representing an interior section of a church, as in the ninth-century choir mosaic of S. Ambrogio at Milan.[2]   From curtains in the background appears the hand of the Almighty.   The picture has suffered much from decay, but from what remains of the original work it seems to represent the art of a copyist in a decadent period.   The colours are poor and the drawing is feeble ; critics find it impossible to date such work earlier than the seventh century,[3] and this attribution is borne out by the probable historical explanation of the companion picture, which is in the same style.

[1] Severus (A. D. 346–91), Ursus (400–12), Ecclesius (525–34), and Ursicinus.   The figures, which can at no time have been of great merit, have been restored (Riedin, 234, Fig. 54).   [2] Richter, 105 ; Kurth, Pl. XXVIII.
[3] Richter, 106 ; he thinks that the work is local.

This picture (Fig. 216), representing a ceremonial subject, is on the opposite side.[1] The scene represents a Byzantine emperor and two princes, all with the nimbus, attended by courtiers and a group of clerics. The emperor wears a white tunic and purple chlamys, fastened with a brooch on the right shoulder, but no diadem. The clerics stand on the right, two deacons with censers, two other ecclesiastics, and the Archbishop Reparatus,[2] to whom the emperor presents a scroll labelled (PRIVI)LEGIA. Reparatus (A.D. 672-7) is known to have visited Constantinople and to have received from Constantine IV Pogonatus a grant of privileges opposing the Roman claims to ecclesiastical supremacy.[3] The painted inscription CONSTANTINVS MAIOR IMPERATOR HERACLII ET TIBERII .... IMPERATOR is based upon an original inscription imperfectly recorded by Agnellus,[4] either because in the ninth century it had already been damaged, or because it contained difficult abbreviations. The mosaics of the nave are all lost. The spandrels between the archivolts contain painted emblems which may be copied from earlier work. The style and decorative motives in S. Apollinare in Classe are clearly Eastern; but it seems probable that most of the mosaics were executed by local artists.

The Church of S. Michele in Affricisco, of which now but little remains, was built in A.D. 545 and ornamented with mosaics in the apse and on the triumphal arch.[5] These were sold in 1847 to King William IV of Prussia, and until recent years remained in storage in Berlin. They now form one of the principal features of the Kaiser Friedrich Museum.[6]

In the apse, on a gold ground, Our Lord as Emmanuel[7] stands between Michael and Gabriel: he wears a purple tunic and mantle, and holds in his right hand a long jewelled cross, in his left an open book with the inscription: *qui vidit me vidit et Patrem. Ego et Pater unum sumus* (John xiv. 9, and x. 30). The archangels are in white garments, and hold golden sceptres. Round the upper part of the apse runs a band of floral scrolls, in the volutes of which are doves, while at the top is the Lamb with the nimbus, the whole representing in a symbolic manner Christ and the Apostles. In the spandrels to right and left of the apse stand St. Cosmas and St. Damian. In the centre of a broad zone covering the whole breadth of the triumphal arch above the apse is Our Lord enthroned. He is bearded[8] and wears a golden tunic with purple mantle. In his left hand is an open book of the Gospels, his right hand is raised in the gesture of benediction. To his right and left stand two archangels, one holding a reed with the sponge, the other holding a spear; behind are other angels, four to the spectator's left and three to his right, the last blowing golden horns. About the feet of all are conventional representations of clouds, signifying that the scene is passing in heaven (Rev. viii. 2).

The mosaics above described represent only a part of those which once adorned the churches of Ravenna. To those which have vanished either

---

[1] Garrucci, iv. 91; Riedin, 231 ff.; Kurth, Pl. XXVIII.

[2] This is attested by the fragments of an inscription (Rep)AR(atus) (Epis)COPVS. Some have explained the scene as the dedication of the church in the presence of Justinian.

[3] Agnellus, p. 148 C; Gregorovius, *Geschichte der Stadt Roms im Mittelalter*, vol. ii, p. 163.

[4] The inscription probably ran: *Constantinus maior (natu) imperator, Heraclius et Tiberius fratres imperatoris.*

[5] Riedin, 236 ff.. Fig. 55; O. Wulff, Berlin *Catalogue*, vol. i, Pl. I, and Prussian *Jahrbuch*, xxv, 1904, 374; Crowe and Cavalcaselle, i, p. 26; Kurth, pp. 236-40.

[6] The mosaics were published by Ciampini, *Vet. mon.*, ii, Pl. XVII, and ch. vii. The illustration in Garrucci, *Storia*, Pl. 267. 2, was based upon a cast.

[7] Kondakoff, *Iconography of Our Lord*, Figs. 10 and 10[a]; Kurth, Pl. XXIX. The subject may be compared with that of several sarcophagi (e. g. Garrucci, *Storia*, 325. 1-3), where, however, Christ is flanked not by angels but by Apostles. The archangels in the present case recall those upon the well-known silver dish in the Stroganoff Collection (p. 571), as well as those attending the throned figures of Our Lord and the Virgin in S. Apollinare Nuovo.

[8] Riedin compares the Christ of S. Apollinare Nuovo and of the Vatican MS. of Cosmas Indicopleustes.

through the destruction of the buildings which contained them, or through disasters affecting themselves alone, we have numerous allusions in early writers, especially in Agnellus, but in few cases is the information extensive or precise.[1] The cathedral or Basilica of Ursus was covered with mosaics, and Agnellus has handed down the name of the artists, though he gives no details as to their work.[2] The same authority tells us that in the Basilica of Peter there was over the west door a figure of Christ of extraordinary beauty, and within the building a group of Our Lord, St. Peter, and St. Paul, doubtless the favourite subject of the *Traditio Legis*.[3] In the Basilica of St. Laurence, built in the reign of Honorius, there was rich mosaic decoration of which no details are given,[4] and in the adjoining Oratory of SS. Gervasius and Protasius a group of three youths, either the titular saints with St. Stephen, or else, as Müntz suggests, the Three Children of Babylon in the Furnace.[5] On the triumphal arch of the Church of the Holy Cross, built by Placidia, was a mosaic representing the Baptism, and above the main door Christ upon the Holy Mount whence issued the four rivers.[6] Agnellus relates that in the Church of St. Agatha, by the altar, was a figure of the Archbishop John (A. D. 418–40). In the apse was a figure of Christ the Judge seated on a throne between two angels and holding the scroll with seven seals : it was only destroyed by an earthquake in A.D. 1688 and has been reproduced by Ciampini.[7] The work was evidently fine, and Ciampini considered it to date from the fifth century ; but recent critics think that it cannot have been in any case earlier than the sixth.[8] The Chapel of St. Andrew had over the entrance a mosaic portrait of the founder, Peter Chrysologus.[9] The Church of Sta Maria Maggiore, said to have been erected by Ecclesius in the time of Theodoric, had rich mosaics, destroyed in A. D. 1550.[10] In the apse was the Virgin ;[11] elsewhere, perhaps on the triumphal arch, were scenes from the Life of Christ, the subjects of which recall those on the triumphal arch of Sta Maria Maggiore at Rome.[12] In St. Stephen's, built by Archbishop Maximianus, was an apse mosaic representing the founder,[13] and in SS. John and Paul, also in all probability erected in the sixth century, figures of the titular saints.[14]

Nothing remains of the wall-mosaics placed by Galla Placidia in the Church of St. John the Evangelist in fulfilment of a vow made during a storm which overtook her vessel on the voyage from Constantinople ; they have been described by Rubeus and an anonymous writer in Muratori.[15] On the triumphal arch were Christ in majesty giving a scroll to St. John the Evangelist, a stormy sea with two ships, upon one of which St. John appears to Placidia, the seven candlesticks and other mystic figures from the Apocalypse, portraits of Constantine, Valentinian, Gratian, and other emperors and empresses of the early dynasty. In the apse was a seated figure of Christ on a throne, and, below, the bishop Peter Chrysologus singing the Mass, the Evangelist St. Luke, various imperial personages, and twelve sealed books. Latin inscriptions stated that the church was the

---

[1] On the lost mosaics of Ravenna see E. Müntz in *The American Journal of Archaeology*, i, 1885, 115–30 ; Steinmann, *Die Tituli und die kirchliche Wandmalerei im Abendlande vom V. bis zum XI. Jahrhundert*, vol. i ; Riedin, as above, 243–58 ; Richter, 110–12.

[2] *Lib. Pont., De S. Urso*, xvi, § 23.

[3] Ibid., *De S. Petro*, xvii, § 24 ; *De S. Neone*, xviii, § 28.

[4] Ibid., *De S. Iohanne*, xx, § 36.   [5] As above, p. 118.

[6] Agnellus ; Rubeus, *Hist. Rav.*, 107 ; Fabri, *Sagre Memorie*, 153 ; Garrucci, i. 506 ; Riedin, 250-1.

[7] *Vet. Mon.*, i, Pl. XLVI (reproduced by Kraus, *Real-Encyklopädie*, Fig. 358).

[8] Müntz, as above, 117 ; Riedin, 252.   [9] Agnellus, *L. P., De S. Petro*, xxi, § 50.

[10] Rubeus, as above, Book III, 154 ; Fabri, as above, 214 ; Agnellus, *L. P., De S. Ecclesio*, § 27.

[11] Rubeus says that the Virgin held the Child, and that Bishop Ecclesius approached, offering the model of the church (p. 154).

[12] Riedin, 254.   [13] Agnellus, *L. P., De S. Maximiano*, xxvi, § 72.

[14] Fabri, as above, 216 ; Riedin, 254.

[15] Rubeus, *Historiarum Ravennatum Libri X*, ii. 98 F ; Muratori, *Rerum Italic. Scriptores*, i, Part II, 567-72. Riedin suggests that a miniature in a fourteenth-century MS. in the Ravenna

thank-offering of Placidia and her children Valentinian and Honoria for her escape from shipwreck. The account of Rubeus contains more details than that of the anonymous writer, and Riedin conjectures that these additions, which include the candlesticks and sealed books, may refer to mediaeval restorations or else be due to the writer's imagination. The mosaics now in the church were probably made in the thirteenth century for a pavement.[1] Their subjects are of two kinds: symbolic and physiological, based upon the Physiologus, and historical. Among the creatures represented are the cock, the deer, sphinx, gryphon, siren, unicorn, and panther.[2] The historical part is represented by

Fig. 217. The Incredulity of Thomas: mosaic of the eleventh century in the narthex of St. Luke in Phocis. (*Hautes Études*: G. Millet.) P. 394.

figures of men, ships, and buildings, some of the warriors with the nimbus, some of the buildings described by the word COSTATINOPOLIM: the allusion may be to the capture of Constantinople during the fourth crusade.[3] The workmanship of the mosaics is extremely rude, and if the Eastern Empire furnished the ideas, the West supplied the hands.

Whether the subjects decorating the walls of the triclinium adjoining the Basilica of Ursus, built by Bishop Neon on the model of similar buildings at Constantinople, were mosaics or frescoes is not clear from the description left by Agnellus;[4] they may, however, be conveniently mentioned here. They included

Library, representing Galla Placidia making her vow at sea, may be a copy of one of the mosaic scenes described above (*Journal of Imp. Russ. Arch. Soc.*, 1897, 248, Fig. 57). See also Kurth, as above, Pl. IX.

[1] Richter, 112; Rahn, *Ravenna*, p. 9; Riedin, as above, pp. 246 ff., and *Viz. Vrem.* ii, pp. 327 ff., with Pl. IV-VIII; Garrucci, *Storia*, i, p. 495; Von Quast; Kurth, pp. 41-3; E. Müntz, *Rev. arch.*, 1876; Ricci, *Guida di Ravenna*, 6-7.

[2] Riedin, as above, 329; Kondakoff, *Byz. Churches and Monuments of Constantinople*, 53, 58, 60.

[3] Riedin, 338.

[4] *De S. Neone*, xviii, § 29. The important words *pingere iussit* need not necessarily imply fresco, though it is quite probable that they do. Accounts of the triclinium will be found in *Repertorium*, xvii (F. Wickhoff), *V. V.*, ii, 1895 (E. K. Riedin), and *Journal of Imp. Russian Arch. Soc.*, 1897, 245.

illustrations of the Psalm *Laudate Dominum de Coelis* ; the Flood ; the Creation and the Fall : the Calling of Peter and the sheet let down from heaven (Acts x. 9-16) ; and Christ amid the Apostles, giving the law to Peter.

Having now passed in review the mosaics of Ravenna we may briefly discuss the origin of their art.[1] The arguments in favour of their execution by Byzantine artists are of two kinds, general and particular. In the first place it is argued that probability is in favour of an oriental inspiration. Ravenna was closely connected with Constantinople from the first half of the fifth century down to the fall of the exarchate. Both Galla Placidia and Theodoric had lived in the Eastern capital, and were necessarily affected by its culture. Under the exarchate the two cities were under one emperor ; the fashions and the artistic preferences of Constantinople must inevitably have influenced the life of the Adriatic city. In the second place, the characteristics of the mosaic itself point to the East. Thus the blue and the gold grounds which replace the pale Roman backgrounds are oriental ; the procession of Apostles as seen in the Orthodox Baptistery suggest the ceremonial of Constantinople, the diadems which they carry are of an oriental type. The curious walk of some of these figures, as if their whole weight was supported on their toes, is oriental, occurring for example in the mosaics of Sta Sophia at Kieff. The garments of the prophets in the lower spandrels of the same baptistery, with their close parallel shading of gold lines, recall those of Byzantine enamels and mosaics. The costumes in many of the mosaics are Byzantine, for instance those of the virgins in the processions of S. Apollinare Nuovo and that of the Virgin Mary in the same church. The invariable use of purple in the garments of Christ is also an Eastern characteristic. Other details of the same kind have been noticed in the detailed description of the various churches ; and we may add the identity of the borders surrounding the sacrificial pictures in S. Vitale with a border used in Sta Sophia at Constantinople. Finally, the mosaics of Kanakaria and Kiti in Cyprus (p. 384), which are not at all likely to be in any way connected with Rome, are very like those of Ravenna,[2] the Gabriel of Kiti nearly resembling the St. Laurence of the Mausoleum of Placidia. The mosaics of the Monastery of St. Catherine on Sinai also offer points of analogy.[3] On the other hand, there are undoubtedly points of resemblance between the Ravenna mosaics and those of the Roman churches ; this is especially noticeable, for instance, in the case of the male martyrs in S. Apollinare Nuovo. The occurrence of the Evangelists' symbols also points rather to Western than to Eastern influence (cf. p. 680). The conclusion which upon the whole commends itself is that the mosaics of Ravenna were from the beginning inspired from the Christian East, and that the resemblances which exist between them and those of Rome are largely due to the fact that the Roman mosaics themselves were produced under similar influences. Probably oriental craftsmen were introduced into Ravenna either from Constantinople itself or from the Eastern provinces,[4] and they worked from Eastern designs. Neither Rome nor Ravenna was in a position in the fifth or sixth century to found a vigorous school without external help. But the impulse once given, it is equally probable that Italians were soon trained to the work: men of Ravenna and Rome must have collaborated with their oriental teachers and, as at Venice at a later period, in course

---

[1] The various points here mentioned are brought forward by Dobbert in his review of Riedin, in *Repertorium*, xxi, 1898, 95 ff., in an earlier paper in the same publication, viii, 1885, 166, &c. ; and in the Prussian *Jahrbuch*, xv, in an article on the frescoes in S. Angelo in Formis. See also Riedin, as above, 258 ff. At the beginning of this section, mention was made of the paper by Beissel maintaining the dependence of Ravenna upon Rome, the arguments being in part based upon the recorded movements of workers in mosaic.

[2] Riedin, 262 ; *Repertorium*, 1898, 105.

[3] Ainaloff, *Hellenistic Origins*, 137.

[4] Strzygowski and Ch. Diehl (*Ravenne*, Paris, 1903) hold that the mosaics of the earlier period from Galla Placidia to Theodoric show the influence of an Antiochene school.

of time become masters themselves. In some such way the divergences from
the predominant oriental manner may perhaps be explained.

The difficulty in studying the mosaics of Ravenna is much increased through
the numerous restorations to which the work has been subjected. The more
modern restorations, or those of which there is historical record, may be
detected without difficulty; but those of more ancient date, if carried out with
care, cannot be so easily identified without a minute examination of the walls.
Another difficulty lies in the inability, even of the best photographs, to render
all the details which the iconographer or the critic requires. Until all known

FIG. 218.   Christ Pantokrator : mosaic of the eleventh century in the narthex of the
Church of St. Luke in Phocis.   (*Hautes Études* : G. Millet.)   P. 393.

mosaics have been reproduced upon a large scale the decision of many disputed
questions is impossible.[1]

It may be added in conclusion that the preservation of these ancient mosaics
in the early Middle Ages is at least in part due to the moderation of Charlemagne. The following are the terms of a concession by Hadrian I to the
Frankish king :—

‘ Musiva et marmorea urbis Ravennae tam in templis quam in parietibus et
stratis, tam marmorea quam musivum, caeteraque exempla de eodem palatio
vobis concedimus auferenda.’

Generosity or indifference could go no further; but Charlemagne restricted
himself to the mosaics of the palace, and Aachen was not beautified at the
expense of the Mausoleum of Galla Placidia or of San Vitale.

―――――――

[1] See the remarks in note on vol. i, p. 18 of Crowe and Cavalcaselle.

(c) Other parts of Italy.

Similar affinities with Ravennate art are to be found in the rare Italian mosaics of the fifth century outside Rome. Conspicuous among these is the Baptistery of San Giovanni in Fonte in the cathedral at Naples,[1] a rectangular building with a dome connected with the square plan by an intervening octagon. The baptistery, being entered from the adjoining Church of Santa Restituta, is sometimes called by that name. Here again we meet with the early scheme of a central medallion from which radiate ornamental bands of vases, birds, fruits, and leaves dividing the dome into eight compartments, formerly filled with figure subjects of which only fragments remain. Below, in niches in four sides of the octagon corresponding to the angles of the building, were the symbols of the Evangelists, of which one (the eagle) is entirely destroyed. The medallion contains a monogrammatic cross on a background of stars: round the head of the monogram is a nimbus, and above is the hand of the Almighty. The arrangement recalls the crosses in the Mausoleum of Placidia and the apse of S. Apollinare in Classe : the Church of St. Felix at Nola evidently had a similar subject.[2] It is possible, as Ainaloff suggests, that such crosses as those in the mosaics of the Mausoleum of Placidia have an historical reference to the vision mentioned in a letter to Constantine by St. Cyril of Jerusalem. Cyril declares that a cross appeared in the heavens at the Feast of Pentecost ; and Philostorgius, describing the same vision, adds that it was encircled by a rainbow.[3]

The scenes in the compartments covering the sides of the domed roof are in very bad preservation, and some of them are merely fragmentary. One is the Samaritan Woman at the Well combined with the Miracle at Cana, resembling the same scene on the ivory panel on the chair of Maximianus at Ravenna ;[4] another is the *Traditio Legis*, much as seen in Sta Costanza (see p. 333), only here Christ is not upon the hill but on a globe ; a third is the Miraculous Draught of Fishes, a scene unknown elsewhere except in S. Apollinare Nuovo.[5] Other parts of the mosaic which have fallen down have been replaced by late frescoes.[6]

Above the Evangelists' symbols are graceful pastoral scenes, the Good Shepherd on the hill from which flow the rivers of Paradise between sheep and deer, on a blue ground. Three of the four symbols of the Evangelists survive, the winged man of St. Matthew, the lion of St. Mark, and the bull of St. Luke. These symbols are conventionally executed, and are thought to be perhaps copies from sculptures : the lion resembles types upon sarcophagi.[7]

On the upper part of the walls are four small figures of martyrs bearing wreaths and clothed in white, which suggest the figures in the Mausoleum of

---

[1] A. Sorrentino, *Bullentino d'arte*, iii, pp. 217 ff., 1909 ; Garrucci, *Storia*, Pl. 269 ; Venturi, *Storia*, i. 245 ; E. Bertaux, *L'Art dans l'Italie méridionale*, 43 ff. and Figs. 5–9 ; E. Müntz in *Rev. arch.*, 1883, 16 ff. ; Crowe and Cavalcaselle, i. 10 ; C. Stornaiuolo, *Atti* of the Congress of Christian Archaeology, 1900 (1902), 269 ; G. Galante, *Nuovo Bullettino di arch crist.*, 1900, 99 ff. ; A. Filangieri di Candida, i, 1898 ; G. Clausse, *Basiliques et mosaïques chrétiennes*, i. 355 ; A. Muñoz in *L'Arte*, 1908 ; Diehl, *Manuel*, 117. Müntz notes that in the seventeenth century and even later a few mosaics were still to be seen in the Catacombs of S. Januarius. See also V. Schultze, *Die Katakomben von S. Gennaro in Neapel*, 1877.

[2] *R. Q.*, 1889, iii. 158 ff. A church at Inkermann has in the apse a cross within a circle, but no stars. See A. Strukoff, *Ancient Monuments of the Chersonese*, Moscow. 1876, 26 (Russian). A jewelled cross also ornamented the roof of a hall in Constantine's palace (Eusebius, *Vita Const.*, in Migne, *Patr. Gr.*, xii, ch. 49, p. 1109).

[3] P. Batiffol in *R. Q.*, iii, 1889, 263 f.

[4] Garrucci, *Storia*, Pl. 414. 4.   [5] Ibid , Pl 249. 5.

[6] Müntz held them to be careful copies of the originals, but Ainaloff says that this is not the case.

[7] Garrucci, *Storia*, 295. 2, 334. 3 ; *Mélanges d'arch. et d'histoire*, 1894. Pl. VIII L ke the symbols on the Trivulzio ivory (Molinier, *Ivoires*, Pl. VI) the diptych in M l Cathedral (Venturi, *Storia*, i, Figs. 388–9) and the throne of St. Mark from Grado i t e Tre ury of S. Marco, these symbols have six wings.

Placidia, and in frescoes of the Catacomb of S. Januarius, dating from the fifth century. This baptistery in fact reveals affinities both with the art of the Catacombs and with that of the earliest school at Ravenna:[1] it has been recently restored under the direction of Cavaliere F. Mazzanti.[2] Of the mosaics formerly in the apse of the Basilica of St. Severus at Naples, a building erected in the fourth century, little can be said, as they are only superficially described by Muratori.[3] They represented Our Lord with the Apostles and, below, four prophets.

The Church of St. Priscus at Capua,[4] built between A. D. 491 and 506, has only preserved the mosaics of a lateral chapel; but drawings which have been preserved show that those which have been lost were in the catacomb style, with a central medallion in the domed roof, from which radiated bands dividing the surface into equal compartments. The medallion contained a throne set on a sphere surrounded by stars, and in the compartments were figures of saints carrying wreaths, divided from each other by vases and fruit flanked by birds: round the base was a broad garland of leaves and fruits with small figures of winged genii.

In the apse were processions of saints. The figures in this church were evidently inspired by the same ideas which produced the processions of saints surrounding the domes of the two Ravenna baptisteries, and the massive garland round the dome is of the character of Ravennate work.

Passing now to the chapel, which still retains its decoration, we find a central medallion, now destroyed, to which rise vine-scrolls issuing from vases in the four compartments. One lunette has the throne with cushion and scroll with seals, and a high back, on which a dove is seated; the second is incomplete, but shows the symbol of St. Matthew. It may be noted that it is of the early type seen in Sta Costanza, in which only the upper part of the body is shown: the later type shows the whole body both of the winged human figure and of the three beasts. In the lunette over the west entrance is a bust of Christ between Alpha and Omega[5] which recalls Byzantine figures,[6] and must be later than the mosaics already described: the absence of the cross in the nimbus, the use of A and Ω instead of the later I C. X C, point to the period between the sixth and seventh centuries. The free use of green and gold suggests Eastern influence, and Ainaloff again finds the affinities with the mosaics of Ravenna evident.[7] It has been further pointed out by Bertaux that land communication between Campania and Ravenna was extremely difficult and that the resemblances between their mosaics are best explained by a common Eastern inspiration coming by sea.

In the Chapel of St. Aquilinus in the Church of San Lorenzo at Milan, occupying the upper part of two apses, are mosaics which go back to the close of the fifth century, and may have been executed by command of Theodoric, who in the year A. D. 495 ordered the church to be ornamented with marble and mosaic.[8] The work is in very bad condition and restored by painting. In the apse to the right of the entrance Christ is seated on the hill (or globe ?) between the Twelve Apostles.[9] He is youthful and of antique type, and has the Constantinian

---

[1] Ainaloff, *Journal*, &c., July, p. 36; E. Bertaux, as above, p. 61.

[2] *L'Arte*, 1898, A. Filangieri di Candida : *I Restauri dei musaici del Battistero di S. Giovanni in Fonte.*

[3] *Rerum Italicarum Scriptores*, i, Pt. II, 293-4 ; *Bullettino di arch. crist.*, 1880, 144-6.

[4] Ainaloff, as above, 37. Procopius (*De bello Gothico*, Bk. I, ch. xxiv) mentions a mosaic portrait of Theodoric at Naples, which gradually decayed with the decline of the Gothic fortunes in the peninsula (Muratori, *Rerum Ital. Script.*, i, Pt. I, 269 ; E. Müntz in *Rev. arch.*, 1883, Pt. I, 28).

[5] Garrucci's drawing, *Storia*, 257. 3, is inaccurate and based upon Salazaro, *Studi sui monumenti dell' Italia meridionale*, 48.

[6] e. g. the type in the MS. of Cosmas Indicopleustes (Garrucci, *Storia*, 451. 1), the diptychs in Berlin (ibid., 451. 1) and Paris (ibid., 458. 1), the cross of Justin in Rome (ibid., 265. 1), and the mosaic of S. Apollinare in Classe (ibid., 253).

[7] As above, 44.   [8] Ainaloff, 45 ; Venturi, i. 275 ; G. Clausse, *Basiliques*, i, p. 381.

[9] This subject is very common in the fourth-fifth centuries, being found, for instance, on several sarcophagi, and on the large ivory *pyxis* at Berlin.

monogram between A and Ω inscribed in his nimbus. The group is awkward, and the different Apostles are not characterized. The absence of detail and the general simplicity suggest the practice of earlier art, but the gold background marks a later period than the fourth century.

FIG. 219.   The Annunciation : mosaic of the sixth century in the Cathedral of Parenzo.
(Alinari.)   P. 373.

The second apse has a pastoral scene referred by Garrucci[1] to the story of Jacob, but interpreted by Schnaase as the Annunciation to the Shepherds.[2] In its rather clumsy style, the mosaic is reminiscent of the Vatican Virgil of the sixth century (p. 459).

[1] *Storia*, 224. 2 ; referring to Genesis xxxvii. 3, 23.
[2] *Gesch. der bildenden Künste*, iii. 197.

The Chapel of St. Victor in the Church of St. Ambrose has lost the mosaics of its apse, but retains in part those of its cupola and walls.[1] In the centre of the dome is a half-figure of the saint[2] on a plain gold ground, recalling the medallion portraits in the Ravenna mosaics,[3] but inferior to these in style and execution. The frieze of the cupola is antique in character, and contains cameo-like busts and figures in grey on a red ground, similar in their colouring to the busts of the Evangelists below them. These busts find parallels on sarcophagi, and are among the earliest examples of actual representations in mosaic of the Evangelists, the more ancient custom being to suggest them by means of their symbols.

On the walls are saints specially reverenced in Milan, St. Ambrose between Gervasius and Protasius, and Maternus between Felix and Nabor. These figures, which are on a blue ground, recall the monumental types of Ravenna, but are the work of an inferior artist. They must be ascribed to the fifth century, a period when representations of martyrs began to be common. Mosaics in the Chapel of S. Satiro, now incorporated in the Church of S. Ambrogio, are in the style of the fourth or fifth century.

At Casaranello, in a church resembling in plan the Mausoleum of Placidia at Ravenna, there are some interesting mosaics in the choir and dome. They are remarkable for the absence of human figures and in fact bear a general resemblance to pavement mosaics of Syrian type.[4] In the baptistery at Albenga in Liguria[5] are mosaics with stars, birds, &c., on a blue ground, above which are sheep; they appear to be of the fifth century, and to show traces of the influence which radiated from Ravenna at that period.

(d) Dalmatia.

In the apse of the northernmost of the two churches which form the Cathedral of Trieste[6] are mosaics with Latin inscriptions—the Virgin and Child flanked by St. Michael and St. Gabriel; below these, figures of the Apostles divided by a palm-tree into two groups. The work, which strictly should be mentioned among the later mosaics, is probably an eleventh-century restoration of an older design, again carefully restored in 1863. The types of the Apostles are early, St. Peter and St. Paul having no attributes; the style and colour of their mantles recall the Early Christian manner: between the figures are palm-trees and conventional trees. In the apse of the southern church (S. Giusto), Our Lord treads upon asp and basilisk, while S. Giusto and S. Servolo stand on either side.

The older mosaics of Dalmatia and Istria are contemporary with those of Ravenna and allied to them in style. The Cathedral of Parenzo, a basilica erected on the site of an earlier church by Bishop Euphrasius in the first half of the sixth century, has in the apse mosaics which appear contemporary with the new foundation, and present analogies with those of Ravenna, especially those of the Arian Baptistery.[7] The most recent restorations, undertaken at the beginning of the present century, resulted in the rediscovery, on the wall above the apse, of an upper band of mosaics which had been hidden by a modern ceiling.

---

[1] Garrucci, *Storia*, Pl. 234, 235; Ainaloff, *Journal*, &c., July, p. 48 f.; Venturi, as above, i. 275.

[2] Ainaloff, p. 50, Fig. 27; F. X. Kraus, *Real-Encyklopädie*, ii, Figs. 237–8.

[3] e.g. S. Vitale (Garrucci, Pl. 259. 4, 6, 7); and archiepiscopal chapel (Garrucci, 224. 8). See the essay 'Il più antico ritratto di Sant' Ambrogio' in the volume *Ambrosiana*, published on the fifteenth centenary of the death of St. Ambrose, Milan, 1897.

[4] A. Haseloff, *I Musaici di Casaranello*, in *Bullettino d'arte*, i, 1907, 1–8.

[5] Ainaloff, *V. V.*, viii, 1901 (*The Mosaics of the Ancient Baptistery of Albenga*), Russian.

[6] T. G. Jackson, as above, iii. 362–3; F. Hamilton Jackson, *The Shores of the Adriatic*, ii. 62. Careful copies of the mosaics are in the museum at Trieste.

[7] Photos of Parenzo mosaics by Wlha of Vienna are in the V. and A. Museum, Nos. 1122 et seq., 1903. Others in the collection of the *Hautes Études*. On the cathedral, see T. G. Jackson,

In the apse the Virgin and Child are enthroned upon a gold ground between two angels and various saints, Euphrasius himself standing on one side accompanied by his young son and holding the model of his church.   On the wall spaces beyond the windows are the Annunciation (Fig. 219) and the Visitation,[1] between which, in the spaces between the windows, are an archangel between St. John the Baptist and another saint.   This part of the work has been restored.   Below these mosaics the wall is covered with fine inlaid marbles.   In the upper band of mosaic, much restored, as mentioned on p. 372, note 8, Christ is seen seated on the globe holding the book of the Gospels, while on either hand

Fig. 220.   The Visitation : mosaic of the sixth century in the apse of the Cathedral at Parenzo.   (*Hautes Études* : G. Millet.)

stand six Apostles.   In the soffit of the triumphal arch are busts of female martyrs[2] in medallions, after the style noticed in S. Vitale at Ravenna, St. Catherine's, Sinai, and the Panagia Kanakaria in Cyprus, &c.   Above the triumphal arch a lamb with cruciferous nimbus in a field of stars has replaced the sacred monogram which recently occupied this position, traces of the former design having been discovered during the restoration.   The west front of the

Dalmatia, the Quarnero, and Istria, Oxford, 1887, iii. 316 ff. ; A. Amoroso, *Le Basiliche cristiane di Parenzo*, Parenzo, 1895 ; P. Deperis, *Il Duomo di Parenzo ed i suoi mosaici*, in *Atti e memorie della Società istriana di archeologia e storia patria*, x, 1894, Fasc. 1 and 4 ; C. Errard, *L'Art byzantin*, Part II, Pl. XIV ff. ; G. Boni in *Archivio storico dell' arte*, Rome, 1894, 107 ff. ; O. Marucchi, *Nuovo Bullettino di archeologia cristiana*, 1896, 14 ff. ; Rivoira, *Origini dell' architettura lombarda*, i, Fig. 134 ; F. Hamilton Jackson, *The Shores of the Adriatic*, ii. 113 ff. ; Wlha and Niemann, *Der Dom von Parenzo*.   The restorations, which in the case of the upper band of mosaic formerly hidden by the ceiling were very considerable, led to severe criticism on the part of Signor Boni, and to a polemical reply by Deperis in the second article mentioned above.   Of the groups of Apostles standing on either side of Our Lord only the heads and shoulders remained, and the bodies have been entirely reconstituted.   But a red line has been run across the whole length to mark where the old work ceases and the new begins.   On the restoration, see also *B. Z.*, x, 1901, 719.   Illustrations of the mosaic as restored are given by Boni and Marucchi, as above, and by Diehl, *Justinien*, Fig. 100, p. 273, Fig. 101, p. 278, Fig. 102, p. 279.
   [1] Figured by Diehl, *Justinien*, Figs. 100-2, pp. 273, 278, 279 ; Errard, Pl. XV.
   [2] They are : SS. Agatha, Agnes, Cecilia, Eugenia, Basilissa, Felicitas, Euphemia, Thecla, Valeria, Perpetua, Susanna, and Justina.

cathedral was also covered with mosaics: those on the baldacchino over the altar are of the thirteenth century. The mosaics of the Cathedral of Parenzo should be especially compared with those of S. Vitale at Ravenna, which they resemble both in style and disposition.[1]

II. Mosaics in the Christian East.

The upper part of the dome of St. George at Salonika was partly damaged and covered with whitewash by the Turks. At the top there is a large medallion with a figure of Our Lord surrounded by a wreath of foliage and fruits (Fig. 204). Below the medallion was a zone of figures (Apostles?) now concealed by whitewash.

The lower part of the dome is covered with mosaics on a gold ground divided into eight compartments.[2] The subject in each case presents an elaborate building in two stories in a Pompeian style, with numerous columns between which curtains are suspended: on the top are various birds including peacocks. The buildings are all of similar character, and though 'classical' in style are probably intended as interiors of basilican churches. In the foreground stand saints in the attitude of *orantes*.[3] The vaults of the chapels are ornamented with a diaper of mosaic, the square and octagonal compartments being filled with birds (partridges, herons, ducks, &c.) and fruits (apples, pomegranates, &c.).[4] These motives should be compared with those in Eski Djouma (p. 382) and St. Demetrius.

Although some critics are still doubtful as to the date of the work,[5] others, especially Russian scholars, assign it with confidence to the earliest period (fifth or even fourth century).[6] The architectural ornamentation has already been mentioned in connexion with that seen in the Orthodox Baptistery at Ravenna (above, p. 344), and it may well be that the decoration of the two buildings was not very far removed in time, that of St. George being the earlier. The free use of pearled and jewelled ornament on columns and arches is an oriental feature.

The mosaics of Sta Sophia at Salonika,[7] a church used as a mosque, suffered

---

[1] See p. 355.

[2] Reproduced in colours, but inadequately, by Texier and Pullan, Pl. XXX–XXXIV; a photograph in G. Rivoira, *Le Origini della architettura lombarda*, Fig. 19 (Rome, 1901); N. Kondakoff, *Macedonia*, 1909, 82 ff., Figs. 23–25 and coloured Plate I; J. Kurth, *Mosaiken der christlichen Ära*, i. 16; Ch. Bayet, *Mémoire sur une mission au Mont Athos*, 1876, 319 ff., and *Recherches*, 85. See also N. Pokrovsky, *Mural Decoration of Ancient Greek and Russian Churches*, 24; Woltmann, *Geschichte der Malerei*, i. 176; Ainaloff, *Hellenistic Origins*, 147. The mosaics, which were much damaged (see Kondakoff's Fig. 26), were 'restored' with paint in 1889 by an Italian named Rossi (Kondakoff, 87).

[3] They are SS. Romanus, Eucarpion, Ananias, Basiliscus, Priscus, Philippus (Bishop of Heraclea in the fifth century), Therinus, Leo of Patara, Philemon of Comana, Onesiphorus, Porphyrius, Cosmas, and Damian.

[4] Millet in A. Michel's *Histoire de l'art*, i. 174; Kondakoff, *Macedonia*, 82; Diehl, *Manuel*, 122.

[5] Woltmann, *Geschichte der Malerei*, i. 176, who assigns the work to the time of Justinian. The fantastic character of the architectural motives inclines others to think of an even later date (W. Kallab, Austrian *Jahrbuch*, xxi. 26).

[6] J. J. Smirnoff, *V. V.*, v. 392; Pokrovsky, as above. Kondakoff, *Macedonia*, as above, points to the analogy between the architectural zone in these mosaics, and the architecture of Spalato, or that shown in the Calendar of Filocalus (p. 484). The architectural ornament in the nave mosaics of the Church of the Nativity at Bethlehem is evidently based upon earlier work analogous to that at Ravenna and Salonika (p. 414).

[7] Diehl and Letourneau, *Monuments Piot*, xvi, 1909, 39 ff. and Pl. IV–VI; Ch. Bayet, *Mémoire sur une mission au Mont Athos*, 1876, 325 ff.; *Archives des missions scientifiques*, 1876, 521–8; and *Recherches pour servir*, &c., 1879, 91 ff. (valuable descriptions); N. Kondakoff, *Macedonia*, 89 ff. and Figs. 37 and 38; Texier and Pullan, *Byz. Architecture*, 144–5 and Pl. XXVI, XL, and XLI (the plates not accurate enough to satisfy modern requirements); J. Kurth, *Ath. Mitth.*, xxii. 1897, 463; Labarte, *Histoire des arts industriels*, 2nd ed., 1873, ii, p. 349; Gerspach, *La Mosaïque*, 56; N. Pokrovsky, *Proceedings of the Seventh Archaeological Congress*, Moscow, 1890, i. 158, *Monuments of Orthodox Iconography and Art*, St. Petersburg, 1894, p. 139, and *Mural Decoration of*

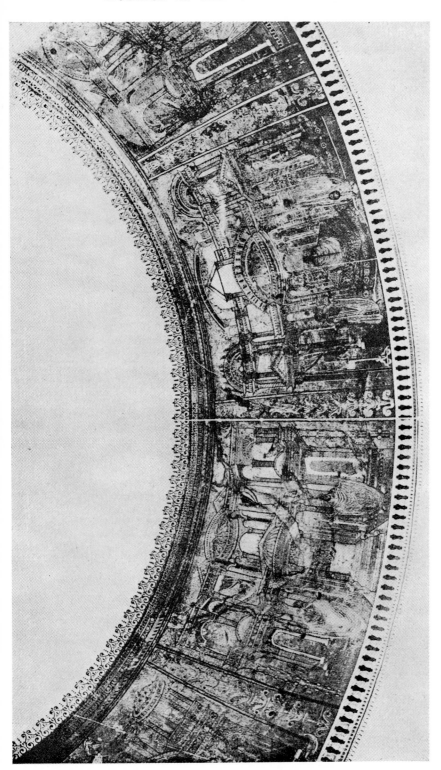

Fig. 221. Mosaics of the dome of St. George, Salonika. (*Hautes Études*: G. Millet.) P. 374.

from the fire which destroyed the quarter of the city in which the building stands in the year 1890. The fire performed, however, one useful service in rendering the church accessible to investigators, and making more visible the interesting mosaic inscriptions, which assist us in determining the date, but the mosaics were not entirely visible until after the work of M. Letourneau in 1907. The mosaics cover the bema and the dome, and in each case there are accompanying inscriptions. Taking those of the bema first, we find a diaper design consisting of gold squares alternately containing silver crosses and vine leaves : in the middle of the vault, on a gold ground, is a circle with a silver ground containing a cross. In the apse is a seated figure of the Virgin with the Child upon her knees : the faces of both, formerly obscured, are now clearly visible. On the gold background can be discerned a cross, now gold on gold and therefore inconspicuous, but perhaps originally outlined with *tesserae* of various colours. It is probable that this cross once formed the sole decoration of the apse, as in St. Irene, Constantinople (p. 387), and that the figure of the Virgin was added at the close of the iconoclastic period.[1]

The inscriptions have been discussed by various scholars, but the most satisfactory readings appear to be those given by Smirnoff.[2] That in the lower part of the conch of the apse reads : ☧ Κ(ύρι)ε ὁ θ(εὸ)s τῶν π(ατέ)ρων ἡμῶν στερέωσον τὸν οἶκον τοῦτον ἕως τῆς συντελε[ίας τοῦ αἰῶνος καὶ σῶσον αὐ]τὸν πρὸς δόξαν σὴν καὶ τοῦ μονογενοῦ(s) σου υ(ἱο)ῦ καὶ τοῦ πάναγίου σου πν(εύματος).[3] An inscription above this contains the fourth and fifth verses of the sixty-fifth Psalm.[4] The inscription on the north and south walls of the bema[5] consists of the words ☧ χὲ βοήθη Θεοφίλου ταπινοῦ ἐπισκόπου, together with six cruciform monograms inscribed in circles, which may be read : Κύριε βοήθει Κωνσταντίνου δεσπότου (for the three monograms on the north wall), and Κύριε βοήθει Εἰρήνης δεσποίνης (for the three on the south wall), the names referring to Constantine VI and his mother Irene.[6] The date would thus be the last quarter of the eighth century, probably not very far from A.D. 785. The figure of the Virgin in the apse would then have been inserted upon the triumph of the image-worshipping party.

The upper part of the dome is filled with a representation of the Ascension on a gold ground[7] (Fig. 222). In a central medallion is Our Lord in a glory supported by angels. In the zone below are the Virgin, as *orans*, between two

Early Greek and Russian Churches, 24 ; O. Wulff, *Repertorium*, xxiii, 1900, 337 ff., and *Die Koimesis-kirche*, 1903 ; E. K. Riedin, *V. V.*, vi, Pl. XII–XVI. The narthex and the body of the church are covered with frescoes, only partially visible beneath the whitewash.

[1] J. Smirnoff, *V. V.*, v. 371–2, and vii. 60. It will be remembered that a similar cross occupied the apse of Sta Sophia, Constantinople. Smirnoff's view is shared by Wulff. Diehl also considers the cross the original decoration, placing it, however, as early as the fifth or sixth century (*Mon. Piot*, as above, 52). The Virgin he assigned to the close of the eighth century. See also his *Manuel*, 345–6, Fig. 170.

[2] Ch. Bayet, *Mission au Mont Athos*, 329 ; P. N. Papageorgiou, Ἑστία, Athens, 1892, 394–5, and 1893, 219 and 317 ; A. Papadopoulos Kerameus, *V. V.*, 1894, 448 ; J. Smirnoff, ibid., v. 365 ff. ; J. Kurth, *Ath. Mitth.*, 1897, 463–72.

[3] Smirnoff, as above, 373 and 392.

[4] Πλησθησόμεθα ἐν τοῖς ἀγαθοῖς τοῦ οἴκου σου, ἅγιος ὁ ναός σου, θαυμαστὸς ἐν δικαιοσύνη. The same inscription, continued at greater length, occupies a similar position in the mosaic decoration of St. Irene at Constantinople (see *V. V.*, i, 1894, p. 781), which Bielyayeff assigns to the iconoclastic period, when a simple cross was preferred to figure subjects (see p. 387).

[5] Smirnoff, 375, 387 ff. (with sketches) ; J. Kurth, as above ; Bayet, as above, 525–6 ; *Repertorium*, 1900, 337 ff.

[6] Bayet read the word ταπινοῦ as Κωνσταντίνου, and took it to refer to a bishop of Salonika living in the sixth century. This early dating he thought confirmed by the use of ☧ instead of a cross at the beginning of the inscription. But it would appear that this monogrammatic cross was not completely displaced by the cross in the sixth century. The reading of Texier is imperfect (*Byz. Arch.*, 145) ; that of Kurth seems less probable than that of Smirnoff given above. Kurth supposes the Constantine to be Copronymus.

[7] Diehl and Letourneau, Pl. IV (the first satisfactory illustration) ; Texier and Pullan, 144–5, and Pl. XI and XII. The mosaics are well described by Bayet, *Archives des missions*, &c., as above, 522 ff., and *Recherches pour servir*, &c., 91 ff. Diehl observes that an interesting comparison may be made between this Ascension and that of one of the cupolas in St. Mark's at Venice (Alinari, photo 13745).

angels, and the Twelve Apostles.　Above the Virgin is the inscription, ' Ye men of Galilee, why stand ye gazing up into heaven,' &c. (Acts i. 11).　The Apostles, who are without the nimbus and separated from each other by trees, carry books or scrolls, and stand in various attitudes on a curious conventional ground of many colours.　The band of fruits and flowers which forms the lower border of the composition is interrupted in two places (beneath the two angels), leaving in each case a rectangular panel with a dark ground on which are inscriptions in white or pale letters.　These have been read as follows : + Μηνὶ Νοεμβρίῳ ἰνδι-κτίονι τετάρτῃ ἔτους ἀπὸ κτίσεως κόσμου ϛ (ἐ)πὶ Παύλου τοῦ ἁγιωτάτο(υ ἡμῶ)ν ἀρχιεπισκόπου ἐγέ(νετο σ)ὺν θ(ε)ῷ τὸ ἔργον τοῦ(το).[1]　Unfortunately the crucial numbers which should have followed the ϛ (6) to compose the date from the creation of the world are invisible.　M. Letourneau, who examined the work from a scaffold, is convinced that the inscription existed before the ornament and was imperfect when it was executed, so that we shall never discover the precise date.　The conclusions of Papageorgiou,[2] who suggested first A. D. 571 and next A. D. 495, were generally adopted until the criticism of Laurent showed them to be un-tenable :[3] it was pointed out that before the seventh century dating from the creation of the world does not occur.　A bishop of Salonika named Paul is mentioned for the year A. D. 649 ; and as the fourth year of an indiction falls in A. D. 645, Laurent conjectured that this is very probably the date of the work.　The church itself may be somewhat earlier, but there is no reason to suppose that it was built in imitation of Sta Sophia at Constantinople.[4]

Riedin, who reproduced the mosaics from a series of photographs,[5] quoted a variety of instances derived from the art of the eleventh and twelfth centuries to which this Ascension scene is allied.[6]　The figure of the Virgin especially is almost the same in all these examples, while in other figures the resemblances are hardly less striking.　If we turn to church decorations of the same period, we find a similar treatment of the subject in S. Marco, Venice,[7] in the Church of St. George at Old Ladoga,[8] in the Church of the Redemption at Nereditsi,[9] and at Monreale.[10]　The figure of the Virgin as *orans* finds near parallels in the mosaics of Sta Sophia at Kieff,[11] and at Ravenna, and not in work of the earlier period.

The appearance of the various figures, their elongated proportions, the close and multiplied folds of the garments certainly seem inconsistent with a seventh-century attribution.　But Smirnoff, in a second article,[12] while admitting that Riedin is right in considering the seventh century too early, argues that the twelfth century is too late.　The work of these mosaics is inferior to that of the fine Byzantine mosaics of the eleventh and twelfth centuries, and details, such as the form of the trees between the Apostles, are incongruous with the style of that period.　Further, the presence of the band of foliage round the base of the

---

[1] Smirnoff, as above, 383 (sketches).　The remains of a *painted* inscription above the wreath are of no archaeological importance.

[2] Ἑστία, 1894, ii. 318.　　　　　　　[3] B. Z., iv, 1895, 431–3.

[4] Smirnoff, as above, 387.　The type of the Pantokrator and of the angels supporting the glory in which he sits is early, and has been rightly compared by Diehl to that of sixth-century MSS. (Rabula, Sinope fragment) and the fresco in the Catacomb of S. Ponzianus at Rome.　The remaining figures, which show a greater freedom of style, resemble the work of the late tenth or of the early eleventh century, at which time they were probably added to replace the damaged figures of an older composition, and M. Letourneau (p. 47) notes that the figures are of a different date from the grounds.

[5] V. V., vi. 370 ff. and Pl. XII–XVI.

[6] The flying angels are compared with those with miniatures in Gospels in the Monastery of Gelat and on Mount Athos (Pokrovsky, *The Gospels in Monuments*, &c., St. Petersburg, 1892, Figs. 200–1), on a relic-case at Shemokmedi (Kondakoff, *Account of the Antiquities in certain Churches and Monasteries of Georgia*, St. Petersburg, 1890, Fig. 63, Russian), and on the bronze doors of St. Paul's, Rome (Rohault de Fleury, *L'Évangile*, vol. ii, Pl. C. 4).

[7] Ongania, *La Basilica di San Marco*, Pl. XII–XIII.

[8] Pokrovsky, *Mural Decorations*, &c., 194 (Russian).　　　　　[9] Ibid., Pl. II.

[10] Gravina, *Il Duomo di Monreale*, Pl. XX.

[11] D. V. Ainaloff and E. K. Riedin, *The Cathedral of Sta Sophia at Kieff*, St. Petersburg, 1889, 44 (Russian).　　　　　[12] V. V., vii, 1900, 60 ff.

dome is reminiscent of earlier times, and does not occur in the renaissance of Byzantine mosaic. Finding that there was an Archbishop Paul of Salonika at the close of the ninth century,[1] he now proposes *c.* A.D. 885 as the probable date.[2]

MM. Diehl and Letourneau agree with Laurent in considering the large zone of figures as of the eleventh century: they assign the figure of Our Lord to an earlier date, perhaps to the seventh century.[3] It appears that a line of division

Fig. 222.   The Ascension : mosaic in the dome of Sta Sophia, Salonika.
(*Hautes Études*: G. Millet.)

between the work of two periods can be distinguished. It seems possible, therefore, that the mosaics of this church represent different centuries.

Recent restorations (1907–8) in the Church of St. Demetrius at Salonika have brought to light a number of most interesting mosaics.[4] They cover the south wall above the arcade dividing the two north aisles, the two piers at the

[1] Le Quien, *O. C.*, ii. 46.
[2] *V. V.*, vii. 67.   [3] *Mon. Piot*, as above, 54 ; Diehl, *Manuel*, 488.
[4] P. N. Papageorgiou, *B. Z.*, xvii. 321–81 ; O. Tafrali, *Rev. arch.*, Jan.–Feb., 1909, 83 ff. ; J. Strzygowski, *Monatshefte für Kunstwissenschaft*, 1908, i, 1019 ff. ; Th. Uspensky, *Izviestiya* of the Russian Arch. Inst. at Constantinople, xiv, Sofia, 1909, 1–61 ; Ch. Diehl, *Manuel*, 190 ff. Uspensky also read an important paper upon them at the Congress of Classical Archaeology at Cairo, 1909, summarized in the *Compte rendu*, 1909, p. 267. The fire referred to in the inscription appears to have taken place about A. D. 634 (see O. Tafrali, as above, p. 95). The date of the church is disputed, but the opinion which ascribes it to the fifth century may be well founded, in which case the Leontius of the inscription might be the prefect of Illyria mentioned in the Theodosian code under the years A. D. 412 and 413 (ibid., p. 101).

entrance to the bema, and an isolated panel above the door leading from the narthex to the inner of the two south aisles. They are clearly of two dates, the later following the fire mentioned in the inscription (see below). The lower part of the long series above the arcade evidently remained undamaged; the newer work comprises all above a line running just above the heads of the figures, with the inscription mentioning the name of Leontius and the mosaics of the two piers.[1] The different sections of the subjects in the long series are indicated by vertical ornamental bands, and the whole is bounded along the top by a broad band of ornament. The upper part, though more recent in date, has suffered more severely from decay than the lower: at the beginning and towards the end great pieces are broken away, while smaller fragments are missing at intervals.

There are several inscriptions along this arcade. Towards the beginning and end an identical dedicatory inscription is repeated.[2] Below the three medallions above the middle arch, representing St. Demetrius and two ecclesiastics, are two iambics referring to Leontius.[3] At the easterly springing of the same arch are the remains of an imperfect inscription,[4] while at the springing of the next arch there is another which is complete.[5] On the south pier of the bema the Virgin holds an inscribed scroll,[6] while beneath the picture is a line of characters almost perfect.[7] Beneath the three figures on the north pier of the bema are four complete iambics.[8]

The first subject along the arcade, beginning from the west, is very badly damaged, but to right and left of the arch two saints, richly clothed in the long chlamys with *tablion*, stand each within a niche with hands uplifted in prayer. The head of the westernmost is lost. Each was approached by a smaller male figure in a deferential attitude veiling his hands beneath his mantle; but of these only the easternmost remains. Above, towards the next arch, is a square frame containing the bust of an aged saint with white beard, wearing a small modius on the head (Zachariah?). The space between the figures is occupied by jewelled columns and foliage. The next subject towards the east is a group of the Virgin seated with the Child upon a high-backed jewelled throne flanked by the Archangels Michael and Gabriel. On the right stands a bearded saint in the attitude of an *orans*, wearing a chlamys; on the left a beardless saint in similar costume ushers a man with hands veiled beneath his mantle. In the upper right-hand corner of the compartment are busts in medallions of a bearded male saint and two female saints— Pelagia and Matrona—below which a diminutive male figure is seen moving to the left towards the throne. In the corre-

---

[1] Mr. Walter George, who was working at the mosaics for a long period in 1909, and has made coloured drawings of them, gives this as his decided opinion. He states the following differences between the old and newer work :—The red of the older work is vitreous and of a carmine tint; that of the newer, bricky and vermilion; the newer black is also more opaque than the older; for the newer white, marble is employed instead of glass, and the same substance replaces silvered cubes for the pear-shaped drops in the darker borders; the gold *tesserae* of haloes, &c., in the lower and older part are set with a forward inclination, while above they are in the plane of the wall. The dividing line between the work of the two periods is conspicuous.

[2] ΥΠΕΡ ΕΥΧΗС ΟΥ ΟΙΔΕΝ Ο Θ̄С̄ ΤΟ ΟΝΟΜΑ+. In the second case only the beginnings of the lines are clear.

[3] +ΕΠΙ ΧΡΟΝΩΝ ΛΕΟΝΤΟС ΗΒΩΝΤΑ ΒΛΕΠΕΙС
  ΚΑΥΘΕΝΤΑ ΤΟ ΠΡΙΝ ΤΟΝ ΝΑΟΝ ΔΗΜΗΤΡΙΟΥ.

[4] ΚΑΙ ΤΗΝ ΔΕСΠΟΙ
  ΝΑΝ ΤΗΝ ΘΕΟΤΟ
  ΚΟΝ ΤΗΝ (?) ΑΓ///.

[5] + ΚΑΙ СΥ ΔΕСΠΟΤΑ ΜΟ(Υ) | ΑΓΙΕ ΔΙΜΗΤ(Ρ)Ι (Β)ΟΗΘΙ ΗΜΙΝ | ΤΟΙС ΔΟΥΛΟΙС СΟΥ ΚΑΙ | ΤΗ ΔΟΥΛΗ СΟΥ ΜΑΡΙ|Α ΗΝ ΕΔΩΚΕС ΗΜΙΝ+.

[6] ΔΕΗСΙС Κ̄Ε̄ Ο Θ̄Ε̄ | ΕΙСΑΚΥ|СΟΝ ΤΗС | ΦΟΝΗС ΤΙС | ΔΑΙΗСΕΩС | ΜΟΥ ΟΤΙ Υ|ΠΕΡ ΤΥ ΚΟ|СΜΥ ΔΕΟ | ΜΕ.

[7] /////// ΙСΙΝ ΑΝΘΡΟΠΟΙС ΑΠΕΛΠΙСΘΕΙС ΠΑΡΑ ΔΕ ΤΗС СΗС ΔΥΝΑΜΕΩС ΖΩΟΠΟΙΗΘΙС ΕΥΧΑΡΙСΤΩΝ ΑΝΕΘΕΜΗΝ.

[8] See below.

sponding position on the left are two busts, one of a male, the other of a female
saint. The next subject occupies the width of four arches. In the middle,
crowning the centre arch, are three busts in medallions; in the centre
St. Demetrius, beardless and wearing a chlamys, on his right and left a bishop
and a lower ecclesiastic holding jewelled books: beneath, on a *tabula ansata*, are
the iambic verses referring to Leontius.[1] The subject proper refers to the story
of a child named Mary. On the left the child and her mother are seen with
St. Demetrius, who is seated before a polygonal building or tent: above, to the
right, are a standing female figure with nimbus, and a damaged bust, apparently
in a medallion: beyond are a rectangular building and a large medallion

FIG. 223.   Part of the Ascension: mosaic in the dome of Sta Sophia, Salonika.
(*Hautes Études* : G. Millet.)

containing the bust of a bearded male saint: next to this is a jewelled ciborium
from which hangs a lamp. Beyond, two angels stand with their hands upon
the shoulders of two figures, one of whom carries a child: in the foreground
stands the Virgin in a purple robe. Next follows the Leontius inscription with
the three medallions, after which we see St. Demetrius standing in the attitude
of an *orans* between two columns and before curtains: to right and left are two
female figures in white, before one of whom stands a child. Beyond again
is a building surmounted by busts of Our Lord and the Virgin in medallions;
then comes the final division of the subject, unfortunately very much damaged.
In a flowery landscape, in which a tomb (?) with columned upper portion stands
apart, three women and a youth conduct a little girl in a long tunic and a dark
mantle semé of red hearts towards a saint (?) in a white chlamys: the girl holds
an offering of two white doves. Below the saint's feet is an inscription ; behind
him are columns with a hanging curtain, below which plants and grass are,
however, visible. Further to the right are the remains of a medallion and of

---

[1] Diehl, *Manuel*, Fig. 169. For the verses see p. 379, n. 3. Cf. *B. Z.*, xvii. 326, and
Pl. III. 6.

a fountain in a garden. The subjects of the arcade are closed on the right by a figure of St. Demetrius in a rich chlamys standing as an *orans* before a scalloped niche from which hangs a curtain semé of hearts. Within the columns a small figure advances from the left with extended hands: beyond them to right and left stand two other male figures, that on the right having near it the second dedicatory inscription, identical with that at the beginning of the series.

The various compartments of the series are enclosed within jewelled borders resembling those of other early mosaics at Ravenna and Parenzo, green, red, and blue stones in rectangular and oval gold settings succeeding each other or alternating with pearls upon grounds of red, purple, &c. The whole group is contained above by a broad band of wavy ribbon in red and green, entirely destroyed in several places. Ornamental details include wreaths of flowers and fruit, and vine-scrolls issuing from vases.

On the two faces of the pier on the north side of the entrance to the bema are two compositions, both presumably belonging to a later period than that of the mosaics just described. In the smaller, St. Demetrius, in his usual rich costume, stands between two small boys[1] whose rank is in each case indicated by the white chlamys with purple *tablion* and the gold fibula upon the shoulder; both veil their hands beneath their mantles: a green wall and canopy form the background. The larger shows the Virgin and a bearded saint standing before a decorated wall, above which is seen the blue sky with a bust of Our Lord in a white segment of radiating light: he extends his hand downwards towards the Virgin, who, wearing a ruddy purple mantle, the upper part of which veils her head, holds in her right hand a scroll with inscription. The saint, in decorated chlamys, stands in the attitude of an *orans*.

The corresponding pictures on the opposite south pier are in the same style. One shows St. Demetrius standing between a bearded ecclesiastic who holds a jewelled gospel before his breast and a bearded official (Fig. 198) in a green *pallium contabulatum* holding a purse in his right hand and a T-shaped staff with a finial and other embellishments in his left. Behind the figures is a wall draped with a green curtain striped with gold, and below is the important inscription of four iambics in two lines stating that the persons represented are the founders of the church.[2]

The second picture shows St. Sergius richly clothed like St. Demetrius, and wearing the gold and jewelled collar marking his rank as captain of the imperial guard.[3] Behind him is a green wall draped with a blue curtain, above which is inscribed the saint's name. The picture above the narthex door shows a beardless saint (again St. Demetrius?) standing as *orans* before a columned niche (Fig. 224). From the right approach two youths of different ages, veiling their hands beneath their mantles. Behind is a landscape with hill and trees, in the foreground of which is a high pedestal or column surmounted by a vase.

The mosaics of St. Demetrius are of exceptional artistic and archaeological importance. The figures are rendered with singular grace; the compositions in the scenes relating to the child Mary possess charm and human interest; the richness of the costumes and the landscape backgrounds are remarkable. By the latter feature we are reminded of such early mosaics as those of the Mausoleum of Placidia or the frescoes of Kuseir 'Amra (see pp. 347, 278), both inspired by the conventional but picturesque landscapes of late Hellenistic art. Some of the heads are clearly portraits: this is evidently the case with the two 'founders' standing to right and left of St. Demetrius. The technical quality of the work is unsurpassed by any other early mosaic.

[1] Diehl, *Manuel*, Fig. 93.
[2]   + ΚΤΙΣΤΑΣ ΘΕΩΡΕΙΣ ΤΟΥ ΠΑΝΕΝΔΟΞΟΥ ΔΟΜΥ
      ΕΚΕΙΘΕΝ ΕΝΘΕΝ ΜΑΡΤΥΡΟΣ ΔΗΜΗΤΡΙΟΥ
      ΤΥ ΒΑΡΒΑΡΟΝ ΚΛΥΔΩΝΑ ΒΑΡΒΑΡΩΝ ΣΤΟΛΩ
      ΜΕΤΑΤΡΕΠΟΝΤΟΣ ΚΣ ΠΟΛΙΝ ΛΥΤΡΟΥΜΕΝΟΥ +.
[3] Cf. the silver dish in the British Museum (p. 575).

Both the general treatment and the details of costume and ornament point to a date not later than the sixth century for the earlier mosaics: the style of the chlamys, the form of the fibula, &c., point in this direction, as do the borders simulating gems and pearls, and the designs of wreaths and vines; these are features which recur in the early mosaics of Ravenna and Parenzo. The presentation of sections by different donors which we find in the mosaics of the nave is, so far as our knowledge goes, confined to this church, among those of the early periods. The custom obtained, however, in the case of mosaic pavements. And in spite of the differences in the colour of the cubes, the restored upper portion of the nave mosaic and the large panels on the piers, presumably contemporary

Fig. 224. St. Demetrius and worshippers: mosaic of the sixth century in St. Demetrius, Salonika. From a water-colour by Mr. Walter George. (Byzantine Research and Publication Fund.) P. 381.

with it, so successfully preserve many features of sixth-century work that they must have been executed before the traditions of that period had been forgotten.

The basilican Church of Hagia Paraskevi, now the Mosque of Eski Djouma, was once richly decorated with mosaics and frescoes. The former are to be found in the soffits of all the arches of the nave, both the lower and upper ranges, the arches between nave and narthex, and those between narthex and exo-narthex. Till recently these mosaics were covered with plaster, the removal of which displayed decorative designs of exceptional charm and remarkable brilliance of colour. They are all of an early style, and cannot be later than the sixth century. Among them we may note vine-scrolls rising from vases, vases filled with lotus and papyrus flowers upon which stand birds (one has in the centre what appear to be ears of corn), interlaced bands formed of flower wreaths rising from fluted bowls, and having in their convolutions white doves on branches and rosette-like ornaments; vases with acanthus leaves and cornuacopiae rising symmetrically from them, and a diaper composed of a silver lattice in the openings of which are blue flowers with long straight stems upon a gold ground; there are also crosses within circles. The borders are of guilloche or of the design representing oval and rectangular jewels in gold settings alternating with pearls upon a red ground such as we have found at St. Demetrius (p. 381). Below some of the designs are votive inscriptions of known types.[1] Nothing in the whole range of Early Christian ornament surpasses these very graceful conceptions, and the richness of the colours is worthy of the designs. Beautiful rich blues, dark and turquoise, fine greens and reds of varying shade, unite with the silver and gold *tesserae* to form a colour scheme of singular charm.

The Monastery of St. Catherine, Mount Sinai, has in the apse of its church a mosaic representation of the Transfiguration which is ascribed to the sixth or seventh century (Fig. 225);[2] above and at the sides of the apse are other mosaics, perhaps of later date.[3] On the two sides are two figures of Moses, one with the Burning Bush, the other receiving the Law. Above are two flying angels, below which are two medallions with silver grounds, one having a male, the other a female bust, and perhaps intended for the Virgin and St. John the Baptist.[4] These medallions are considered by Kondakoff to be in any case later than the twelfth century. In the scene of the Burning Bush, Moses stands undoing his shoe in a rocky landscape; in the corresponding scene the prophet standing between rocks receives the tables from the hand of the Almighty. These scenes have none of the characteristics of early Byzantine art, and must be due to the hand of the restorer: the form of the tables of the Law is that introduced in the sixteenth century.[5]

The Transfiguration is surrounded by a border of medallions with silver backgrounds containing busts of the prophets and Apostles with the addition of David and two personages named John the Deacon and Longinus the Hegoumenos: all have their names beside their heads. Such borders of medallions we already know from the examples in S. Vitale at Ravenna, Kanakaria in Cyprus, &c.

In the Transfiguration,[6] Christ has a pale-hued tunic and mantle with gold clavi, and stands in a blue mandorla of three concentric shades: he holds a scroll in his left hand, and with his right makes the gesture of benediction. His nimbus is silver with an inscribed gold cross, and six rays issue from his body. His hair is a rich brown, and in general type he resembles the Christ of the Rabula Gospel. In the foreground John lies prone, covering his face; James and Peter kneel, the latter upon one knee only.

Below the Transfiguration, and at the right end of the border of medallions, are mosaic inscriptions mentioning the Hegoumenos Longinus and a Presbyter Theodore. In their present form Kondakoff thinks they can give no information of any value as to the date of the mosaics.[7]

In the sixteenth century there still existed other mosaics representing the Virgin and Child between Moses and St. Catherine.[8] Although, as above stated, the principal mosaic is usually considered to be of the sixth century, a later date has been suggested.[9]

[1] e. g. + Ὑπὲρ εὐχῆς Ἀνδρέου (τα)π(ε)ινοῦ +, + Ὑπὲρ εὐχ(ῆς οὗ) οἶδεν + ὁ Θεὸς τὸ ὄνομα, the formulae also occurring at St. Demetrius.

[2] Ainaloff (*Hellenistic Origins of Early Christian Art*, p. 210 (Russian)) claims the apse mosaic for the time of Justinian, though assuming that restorations have taken place.

[3] For illustrations of the Sinai mosaics see De Laborde, *Voyage dans l'Arabie Pétrée*, Pl. XX; Rohault de Fleury, *L'Évangile*, Pl. XLIII. 1, and Garrucci, *Storia*, iv, Pl. 268 (both reproducing De Laborde's drawing). Noroff, *Jerusalem and Sinai*, 1879: a drawing by Polivanoff. Photographic reproductions are given by Ch. Diehl, *Justinien*, 291, Fig. 107, and by Kondakoff. *Iconography of Our Lord and Saviour*. The mosaics are described by Kondakoff, *Journey to Sinai in 1881*, Odessa, 1882, 75 ff. (Russian); G. Ebers, *Durch Gosen zum Sinai*, Leipsic, 1872, 273 ff. ; C. Usoff, *Mosaics of the Church of the Monastery of St. Catherine*, publication of the Moscow Archaeological Society, 1879: illustration based on Polivanoff's drawing; Diehl, *Manuel*, 190. For the date of the building (A. D. 554–62) see H. Grégoire, *B. C. H.*, 1907, 327 ff.

[4] Ebers considered them to be Moses and St. Catherine (as above, 275). Kondakoff (*Journey*, p. 81) considers St. John and the Virgin more probable. Tradition describes the two busts as portraits of Justinian and Theodora. [5] Kondakoff, *Journey*, 78.

[6] This subject is rare in Early Christian art, only occurring in two other mosaics, those of S. Apollinare in Classe at Ravenna and SS. Nereus and Achilleus at Rome.

[7] Kondakoff, 95 ff. [8] Smirnoff in *V. V.*, iv, 1897, 13.

[9] S. Vailhé, *Rev. de l'orient chrétien*, 1907, 96–8. See also *Revue biblique*, 1907, pp. 105 ff.

The most ancient Christian mosaics of the Holy Land have all perished. We know from the words of the pilgrim Abbess Aetheria, who visited the Holy Places at the close of the fourth century, that there were mosaics in the atrium of Constantine's Church of the Holy Sepulchre, and possibly even on the west façade of the basilica.[1] The Church of the Nativity at Bethlehem[2] had rich decoration of early mosaics: on the west façade was an Adoration of the Magi, said to have been spared in the sixth century by the soldiers of Chosroes because the Magi had Persian caps. The dome of the Church of the Holy Sepulchre at

FIG. 225. The Transfiguration: mosaic in the monastery church of Mount Sinai.
(*Hautes Études*: N. Kondakoff.) P. 383.

Jerusalem once possessed a mosaic representing Constantine and Helena holding the Cross between them.[3] We may suppose that almost all the sacred edifices of the Holy Land were adorned with mosaics, and it is superfluous to seek for further instances.

The two examples of early mosaic in the island of Cyprus, published and discussed by Smirnoff,[4] date from the fifth or sixth century. One fills the apse in the church of the Panagia Angeloktistos at Kiti on the southern coast of the island, a few miles west of Larnaca; the other occupies a similar position in the Panagia Kanakaria, the still-used church of an abandoned monastery near the village of Lithrankomé, on the southern slope of the ridge forming the backbone of the Karpass. The existing churches belong to the post-iconoclastic period of Byzantine architecture; but in both cases the venerated mosaics of older buildings seem to have been incorporated in the new structures.

[1] *Ornavit auro musivo et marmore.* Aetheria, in Geyer's *Itinera Hierosol.*, 76. 17.
[2] For the mosaics of this church see below, p. 414.
[3] P. Horn, *Ichnographia Locorum et Monumentorum Veterum Terrae Sanctorum*, 96 (ed. Golubovich). See A. Baumstark, *R. Q.*, xx, 1906, 169.   [4] *V. V.*, iv, 1897, 1–93.

In the Kiti mosaic the Virgin is seen standing on a footstool, with the Child on her left arm, between the two archangels Michael and Gabriel, who hold in their right hands orbs, in their left wands or sceptres.   All the figures have the nimbus, which, however, is not gold but very dark in the central part and in the outer part formed of bands of dark blue and a paler tint:[1] it is doubtful whether there was ever any cross in the nimbus of the infant Saviour.   The exact shade of the garments of Christ and the Virgin is difficult to determine, but those of the Child are of the paler tone.   The Virgin wears a long-sleeved tunic and a mantle, the angels white tunics with gold clavi, white mantles (*pallia*) on

Fig. 226. Cross and ornamentation in mosaic of the eighth century in the apse of St. Irene, Constantinople. (Byzantine Research and Publication Fund.)   P. 387.

which are seen the letters H and Γ.   Their wings are executed in imitation of those of peacocks with 'eyes',[2] and they stand upon a green ground.   On either side of the Virgin's head, on a band of pale cubes set in the gold background, is the inscription +H AΓIA | MAPIA+, while below, between her and the angels, may be read in vertical lines, on the left MIXAHΛ, and on the right ΓABPIHΛ.   Below the composition is an ornamental border of rosettes.

The use of the form 'Saint Mary' instead of the usual 'Mother of God' ($\overline{MP}$ $\overline{ΘY}$, or ΘEOTOKOC) points to an early date,[3] in any case not removed

[1] The colours are obscured by accumulations of dust and smoke, while the faces of the Virgin and Child have in addition traces of dull red paint. Of the figure of Michael, only the head, the right hand, and the lower part of the body remain, and the missing parts are filled in with stucco.

Smirnoff notes that the mosaic at Kiti appears to be mentioned in a synodal letter to the Emperor Theophilus written from Jerusalem in A. D. 836. The letter mentions a number of wonder-working ikons, and this occurs among the number.   It is published by J. Sakellion : Ἐκ τῶν ἀνεκδότων τῆς Πατμικῆς Βιβλιοθήκης: Ἐπιστολὴ συνοδικὴ . . . πρὸς Θεόφιλον αὐτοκράτορα Κωνσταντινουπόλεως.

[2] The only analogy for this kind of wing in the case of angels (not seraphim) appears to occur in the Sinai mosaics. See N. Kondakoff, *Journey to Sinai*, 79 (Russian).

[3] These words occur, but in monogrammatic form, on the Trivulzio ivory with the Annunciation (Garrucci, *Storia*, Pl. 453. 1 ; G. Schlumberger, *L'Épopée byz.*, &c., 1896, 48).

by more than a century from A.D. 436, the year of the Council of Ephesus. That the date is later than this council is certain from the presence of the two archangels as a celestial guard, for before the solemn proclamation of the Virgin as the Mother of God and Queen of Heaven such representations were unknown.[1] The Virgin herself resembles the type known as the *Hodegetria* (Ch. XII), which may well have been introduced into Byzantine art about the middle of the fifth century from one of the oriental centres, perhaps Jerusalem or Antioch.[2]

The execution of the Kiti mosaic is remarkably fine, as fine as anything in Rome or Ravenna. The manner in which the transitions from dark to light shades are managed differs from that employed in those cities, but has an analogy in a Roman pavement found near Constantine in Algeria,[3] a fact which suggests that the school of mosaicists to which Kiti work is due was affiliated to Alexandria. It was evidently not identical with the school which worked at Salonika, and its style is distinct from that of the later schools of the eleventh and twelfth centuries. It is possible that the Sinai mosaics, when properly published, may afford a clue to its origin. We know that there were mosaic workers in Syria and Palestine in the First Period, because the decoration of the Church of the Holy Sepulchre was restored at some time before the year A.D. 862, possibly after the Persian invasion, by a monk Thomas of Damascus.[4] The synodal letter of A.D. 836 already quoted (p. 385, n. 1) mentions the lost mosaic of Justinian's time, representing the Adoration, on the exterior of the basilica at Bethlehem.[5] This mosaic, spared by the Persians under Chosroes because of the Persian costume of the Magi, was possibly the model copied by the makers of the Monza ampullae (see p. 623), some of which have this subject.[6] In these ampullae, as in the Kiti mosaic, the Madonna looks straight forward at the spectator, not at the Child ; there may here be an indication of a dominant Syrian type.

On iconographical and stylistic grounds Smirnoff assigns the Kiti mosaic to the close of the fifth or early part of the sixth century.[7] The absence of the title MP ΘY, or ΘEOTOKOC, has been already noted as evidence of an early origin ; on the other hand, the work can hardly have been done before A.D. 436. The fact that the nimbi are not gold is also in favour of an early date, the nearest parallels being found in the niche mosaics of Sta Costanza (p. 333) and in Sta Maria Maggiore. Further, it is unlikely that such admirable quality should have been done in Cyprus in the period between the middle of the seventh century, when the Arabs took the island, and its reconquest by the Byzantines in A.D. 964. The year A.D. 650 would thus be the latest possible limit.

The mosaic in the Panagia Kanakaria[8] also represents the Virgin as Queen of Heaven between two angel guards. She is seated on a throne surrounded by an oval glory of dark blue between two palm-trees, and wears a purple tunic and blue mantle : the Child wears a blue tunic and white mantle, and has a golden cruciform nimbus. The picture has suffered greatly from time, and the lower part is all lost except the central portion representing the Virgin's knees and feet. One angel has almost entirely disappeared, while of the other

---

[1] Archangels holding orbs are seen on the famous British Museum diptych with St. Michael (p. 200), and on the large diptych at Ravenna (p. 209), though in the last instance the chlamys replaces the pallium. It may be recalled that on consular diptychs personifications of Rome and Constantinople hold orbs. None of these are later than the beginning of the seventh century.　　　　　　　　　　　　[2] Smirnoff, as above, 54.

[3] V. Delamare, *Exploration d'Algérie*, Pl. 141–2. The method consists in the employment of alternating dark and light cubes placed in a single line (Smirnoff, 64).

[4] This fact is derived from a contemporary metrical postscript to a Psalter of the year A.D. 862, ending with the lines :—

Τέτευχε τήνδε λαμπρὰν ὑελουργίαν
Θῶμας μωνάζων, ζωγράφος, Δαμασκόθεν.

See Smirnoff, 90.

[5] The existing mosaics in Palestine are all of the later date (p. 414).

[6] Bayet, *Recherches pour servir*, &c., 72 ; Smirnoff, 91–2.　　　　　　[7] p. 65.

[8] Smirnoff, as above, 65 ff. ; figure on p. 73.

only the upper half of the body remains. It can be seen that this angel holds a sceptre or wand in the left hand, though the hand itself is lost. He wears a blue tunic with yellow clavi and a white mantle: the feathers of his wings are dark blue, light blue, and a lilac shade. His nimbus is of a colour not easy to determine, but certainly not golden.

The whole group is enclosed in a mosaic border composed of a series of medallions representing the Twelve Apostles, six probably being placed on either side of a central medallion of Christ. Only a few of these medallions are now distinguishable, and these only in part. Each Apostle was accompanied by his name, but not many letters are now visible.

Smirnoff remarks that the mandorla surrounding the Virgin is a unique feature in early Byzantine art, and its presence lends these mosaics a peculiar interest. This dark-blue glory recalls early examples of the nimbus in which gold is not employed of which mention has already been made, the blue aureole of Christ in the Sinai mosaics,[1] and that in the manuscript of Cosmas Indicopleustes. The rainbow-tinted or irisated border enclosing the mandorla gives no definite clue to date, for it occurs on monuments of very various age.[2] The series of Apostles in medallions may be compared with the heads of those of the Orthodox Baptistery at Ravenna, those of the lost mosaics of St. Agatha in Suburra (Garrucci, *Storia*, Pl. 240. 2), those of the triumphal arch in S. Vitale and the archiepiscopal chapel at Ravenna, and those of the Sinai mosaics. There is a general resemblance to the work at Parenzo, but it is difficult to find any very close analogy among published mosaics. There is a difference in technique between the Kanakaria work and that at Kiti, which makes it probable that there was more than one school of mosaicists in Cyprus. Kanakaria indeed seems to stand nearer to Ravenna and Rome than to Kiti, though even there too the types of faces are different.

Smirnoff places the mosaics of Kanakaria slightly later than those of Kiti, assigning them to the period between the beginning of the sixth and the middle of the seventh century.[3]

Another mosaic reputed to be of similar early date is reported from the Church of Παναγία τῆς Κύρας, also in the Karpass. It is said to represent the Virgin and to be in a rather dilapidated condition, but up to date I have obtained no full description of it.

The mosaics of St. Irene at Constantinople, the fine church used by the Turks as an armoury, cover the apse and the triumphal arch, but are obscured by whitewash.[4] The subject in the apse is a large cross of dark blue on a gold ground (Fig. 226), while on the arch there appears to be nothing but ornamental designs with two mosaic inscriptions (Fig. 227).[5] Bielyayeff is inclined to ascribe these mosaics to the iconoclastic period when the building was last restored, a conclusion supported by the examination made by Mr. Walter George in the past year (1910) and by epigraphic and literary evidence adduced by M. Millet.[6] Inscriptions associated with simple representations of crosses in

[1] Kondakoff, *Journey to Sinai*, 87 (Russian).

[2] In mosaic, in the dome of St. George, Salonika, on the vault of the presbyterium in Sta Sophia, Salonika, round the bust of the Virgin in Sta Sophia, Constantinople ; in MSS., e.g. in the Vienna Dioscorides and in the Etchmiadzin and Florentine Gospels (J. Strzygowski, *B. D.*, i. 57). [3] As above, 89.

[4] D. Bielyayeff, *V. V.*, i. 780 ff. Photographs of the interior of the church, from both ends, in G. Rivoira, *Le Origini della architettura lombarda*, i, Figs. 289, 290. Mr. Walter George has studied the church on behalf of the Byzantine Research and Publication Fund (1910).

[5] The first inscription is: οἰκοδομῶν εἰς τὸν οἶκόν σου καὶ ἀνάβασιν αὐτοῦ καὶ τὴν ἐπαγγελίαν τοῦ ἁγίου πνεύματος ἐ(ἰς ἡ)μᾶς ἠλπείσαμεν εἰς τὸ ὄνομα αὐτοῦ. The second is Psalm 65. 4 and 5 : Πλησθησόμεθα ἐν τοῖς ἀγαθοῖς τοῦ οἴκου σου· ἅγιος ὁ ναός σου, θαυμαστὸς ἐν δικαιοσύνῃ. Ἐπάκουσον ἡμῶν, ὁ θεὸς ὁ σωτὴρ ἡμῶν, ἡ ἐλπὶς πάντων τῶν περάτων τῆς γῆς καὶ τῶν ἐν θαλάσσῃ μακρά(ν) + . The same inscription is found in Sta Sophia, Salonika (p. 376). Mr. George reads the first word differently.

[6] *B. C. H.*, 1910, 96 ff. M. Millet cites iconoclastic poems quoted by Theodore the Studite relating to the veneration of the Cross.

Cappadocian chapels belong to the ninth century ; and it seems probable that these chapels were decorated in this manner as a result of iconoclastic sentiment. The cross was the symbol of the iconoclasts, who even falsified letters of the Fathers to prove that it should form the sole mural decoration of churches. Traces of mosaic in the narthex, with conventional ornament, have also been observed.

The mosaics of the Church of the Assumption at Nicaea [1] were partly ruined by the collapse of the dome, which probably contained the figure of the Panto-

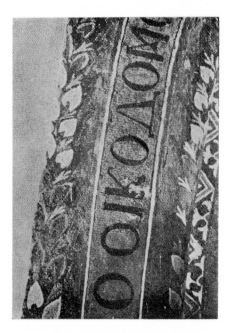

FIG. 227. Mosaic with inscription of the eighth century : arch of the apse of St. Irene, Constantinople. (Byzantine Research and Publication Fund.)

krator. The bema and narthex have mosaics of different dates, but the body of the church was ornamented with frescoes.

The great arch has in the centre a medallion containing the *Etimasia* (p. 666), here a throne with cushion and veil, supporting a book and a cross, and placed in a dominating position, as at Daphni, Monreale, and in the Cappella Palatina at Palermo. On each side is a pair of angels wearing imperial costume and holding disk-like orbs in their hands. Their long purple tunics are adorned with figured gold bands : their wings and the fillets in their hair are white. They are described by inscriptions as representatives of Ἀρχαί, Δυνάμεις, Κυριότητες, and Ἐξουσίαι, and under the two to the right are the words : Καὶ προσκυνησάτωσαν αὐτῷ πάντες ἄγγελοι. The words Εὐφράνθητε οὐρανοὶ ἅμα αὐτῷ must have once occupied the corresponding position under the two left-hand figures. On the gold background between the wings of the two angels on the south side is a mosaic inscription : στηλοῖ Ναυκράτιος [2] τὰς θείας εἰκόνας. The use of the word στηλοῖ suggests a connexion with the festival known as Ἀναστήλωσις τῶν ἁγίων εἰκόνων, which celebrated the triumph of the orthodox party at the close of iconoclasm. This word, with the addition of the adjective θείας, may be taken as indication of a date closely following the iconoclastic persecution.

In the apse is a standing figure of the Virgin on a gold ground.[3] She wears a purple mantle covering her head, and ornamented with a gold border and tassels. In her arms is the Child, who wears a gold garment and raises the

---

[1] O. Wulff, *Die Koimesiskirche in Nicäa und ihre Mosaiken*, Heft XIII of *Zur Geschichte des Auslandes*, Strassburg, 1903, 194 ff. and Pl. I–III ; Ch. Diehl, *Mosaïques byzantines de Nicée*, B. Z., i, 1892, 75 ff., revised and reprinted in *Études byzantines*, Paris, 1905.

[2] Wulff and Diehl believe that Naukratios may be the mosaicist; others think this improbable, and would refer the name to the donor of the mosaics. But the monograms in the church, which do refer to the donor, do not appear to stand for the name Naukratios. The absence of any title and the inconspicuous position of the inscription are also against the attribution to a donor.

[3] The type—a standing figure holding the child in one arm—is not that usually found in Byzantine mosaics, the two nearest examples being in S. Marco, Venice. As a rule the Virgin, when standing, has a medallion containing the Child represented on her breast. The type in the present case may be a variation of the seated Virgin and Child already adopted by the seventh century.

right hand in the act of benediction. Above her head are a semicircle and two concentric bands, representing heavenly zones ; and from the semicircle issue three rays, that in the middle descending to her nimbus. Across them runs an inscription from Psalm 110. (109.) 3 (Septuagint version): ἐκ γαστρὸς πρὸ ἑωσφόρου γεγέννηκά σε, referring to the celestial birth of the Son: the three rays are intended to represent the Trinity. Round the top of the apse runs the inscription : τῷ οἴκῳ σου πρέπει ἁγίασμα Κ(ύρι)ε εἰς μακρότητα ἡμερῶν (Psalm 92 (93). 5), within borders of geometrical and formal ornament of an early character.[1] The type of the *Etimasia* is also early.[2]

The mosaics of the apse and the bema are related to each other as two parts in the expression of one theological design—the declaration of the Trinitarian idea in its relation to the Incarnation and the divine motherhood of the Virgin, as expressed in the first chapter of the Epistle to the Hebrews.[3]

The iconographic and dogmatic character of the mosaics suggests that they date from the same period as the church. They must be connected with the iconoclastic struggle, and may be assigned to the sixty years between the second Nicene Council in A. D. 789 and the middle of the ninth century ; after the definite triumph of the orthodox party in A. D. 842 there would be no need for such solemn emphasis on the sacred character of the figures. The beginning of this period seems to commend itself as the more probable date. The figure of the Virgin, though somewhat elongated and no longer showing the large and simple treatment of the sixth century, is yet of a grave and majestic dignity ; the draperies are well designed and the colours rich. The angels likewise preserve something of the serene beauty of a period in which classical tradition was yet alive.[4] The mosaics of the narthex,[5] which only survive in part, are in a later style. Over the central door is a mosaic inscription : Κ(ύρι)ε βοήθει τῷ σῷ δούλῳ Νικηφόρῳ πατρικίῳ πραιποσίτῳ βέστῃ καὶ μεγάλῳ ἑταιριάρχῃ. The inscription on a later fresco has preserved the information that this Nicephorus lived in the time of an emperor named Constantine. From the fact that Constantine VIII appointed one of this name a Protovestiarius, and that a lead bulla, apparently of the period, gives the same name as that of a Great Hetairiarch, it is conjectured that this may be the Constantine in question. Epigraphy confirms this conclusion : there are accents, which are not found over uncials on monuments before the tenth century, whereas in the mosaic inscriptions of the eleventh they are common.[6]

In the tympanum over the royal door is a half-figure of the Virgin as *orans*, which with its grave expression, natural treatment, and fine colouring is a beautiful example of the mosaic work of the period.[7] The type may be derived from that of the Virgin placed by Basil I in the church of the new palace at Constantinople as described by Phocas.[8] In the roof, which has a gold ground,

---

[1] Wulff, as above, Fig. 41, p. 199.

[2] Ibid., 243–4. A similar inscription occupies the same position in the Church of St. Luke in Phocis.

[3] vv. 3–6. 'Who . . . sat down on the right hand of the Majesty on high ; being made so much better than the angels, as he hath by inheritance obtained a more excellent name than they. For unto which of the angels said he at any time, Thou art my Son, this day have I begotten thee? And again, I will be to him a Father, and he shall be to me a Son. And again, when he bringeth in the First-begotten into the world, he saith, And let all the angels of God worship him' (Wulff, p. 274).

[4] Wulff, 297 ff. Opinions are not unanimous, though most are inclined to place these mosaics within the first millennium. See Diehl, as above, 78, and *Le Monastère de St. Luc en Phocide*, 62 ; Strzygowski, *B. Z.*, i. 340, *Archäologische Ehrengabe zu de Rossi's 70. Geburtstag*, 398 ; J. Smirnoff, *V. V.*, iv. 87, note 1.

[5] Wulff, as above, 301 ff. The only objection to the acceptance of this date is that in the reign of Constantine X (Ducas) a severe earthquake visited Nicaea, as recorded by Michael Attaliotes. Possibly the Nicephorus of the inscription may have lived in the latter part of the eleventh century (Diehl, 3 ff.). [6] Ibid., 305.

[7] G. Schlumberger, *L'Épopée byzantine*, iii, 1905 ; Diehl, *Études*, 265 (after Schlumberger).

[8] *Novae ecclesiae descriptio*, 199. Diehl (*Études*, &c., p. 367) remarks the popularity attained by this type in Byzantine art during the tenth and eleventh centuries (coins of Leo VI,

is a jewelled sacred monogram (of the type formed by two Greek crosses placed one over the other) in a blue medallion of different shades, upon which are gold stars representing the heavenly spheres: this motive occurs in numerous mosaics of the eleventh and twelfth centuries.   The mosaics of the narthex also include figures of Christ, St. John the Baptist, the Evangelists, St. Joachim, and St. Anne.   In technique these mosaics may be compared to those of Daphni

FIG. 228.   Our Lord : the Virgin and Child : mosaics of the eleventh century, Church of St. Luke, Phocis.   (*Hautes Études* : G. Millet.)   P. 393.

(p. 396), and the transitions from one tone to another are gradual and delicate. Black outlines are used to give the figures relief against the gold ground, or, in the case of flesh tones, against hair or garments.   The features and details of hands and feet are rendered by red cubes.   There is a certain fondness for greenish tints.   As a whole, the work is more delicate than that in the bema and commands a greater variety of tones.

John Zimisces, and later emperors).   He further notes its resemblance to the Virgin in the mosaics of the cathedral at Torcello.
    [1] In the vault of the Diakonikon at Nea Mone, Chios, in the narthex at St. Luke in Phocis, at Daphni, and at Kieff.

THIRD AND FOURTH PERIODS

The mosaics of the great Church of the Divine Wisdom at Constantinople are only in part visible, the rest having been covered with whitewash by the Turks. In the year 1847 restorations were carried out in the cathedral, and many mosaics were uncovered by Fossati, the architect employed for the purpose. These restorations afforded an opportunity for reproduction, and to them we owe the illustrations of Fossati himself and of Salzenberg.[1] We do not know either the character of the entire decoration as it at first subsisted, or the certain date of all the work that was uncovered in 1847 ; the reproductions then published were neither complete nor sufficiently accurate for a definite judgement. From the analogy of the Church of the Holy Apostles, described by Constantine the Rhodian and by Mesarites, we may infer that there was once a whole cycle of Gospel scenes, such as is found in later churches like that of the Monastery of Daphni in Attica ;[2] but it is worthy of remark that neither Paul the Silentiary nor Procopius nor the Anonymus Banduri[3] make any mention of mosaic pictures. It has, however, been urged that this negative evidence is not conclusive,[4] and Wulff follows Kondakoff in assigning some of the known mosaics to the age of Justinian, the rest, with the exception of mere ornamental designs, being admitted to be in no case earlier than the ninth century.[5]

Among those by some assigned to Justinian's time are the Cherubim in the pendentives of the great dome, which are of an early type, the angel with orb and sceptre on the south side of the apse, and the remains of the Pentecost ornamenting the western cupola in the central part of the south gallery.[6] The other mosaics known to us, which are but the *disiecta membra* of a cycle still unknown, are as follows : In the dome is the Pantokrator,[7] in the apse the Virgin (Blacherniotissa) enthroned with the Child ; along the north and south walls saints and prophets, among which are identified Anthemius of Nicomedia, Basil, Gregory the Theologian, Dionysius the Areopagite, Nicholas, Gregory of Armenia, Isaiah, Jeremiah, Jonah, and Habbakuk ; on the great eastern arch beneath the dome is the *Etimasia* in a medallion flanked by the Virgin and St. John the Baptist, and, below, the portrait of John Palaeologus.[8] These mosaics are thought to have been originally due to Romanus (eleventh century)

[1] Fossati, *Aya Sofia*, London, 1852 ; W. Salzenberg, *Die altchristlichen Baudenkmäler*, &c., Berlin, 1854 ; E. M. Antoniades, Ἔκφρασις τῆς ἁγίας Σοφίας, Athens, 1907 ff. Other works which should be consulted are Kondakoff, *The Churches of Constantinople*, in the Proceedings of the Sixth Archaeological Congress at Odessa, 1887 (in Russian); Lethaby and Swainson, *The Church of Sancta Sophia* ; N. Pokrovsky, *Mural Decoration in Ancient Greek and Russian Churches*, 25 ff., and *Outlines of the Monuments of Orthodox Iconography*, &c., ch. v (Russian); G. Millet in A. Michel's *Histoire de l'art*, i, Pt. I, 190. For various references to mosaics in Sta Sophia in Byz. literature, see J. P. Richter, *Quellen der byz. Kunstgeschichte*, 1897, index, s.v. *Mosaiken*.

[2] On the walls between the windows there were probably figures of saints. For the lost mosaics of the Church of the Apostles see the description of Constantine the Rhodian edited by E. Legrand, *Revue des études grecques*, ix, 1896, pp. 32 ff. For Mesarites' description (late twelfth century) see A. Heisenberg, *Grabeskirche und Apostelkirche*, ii, pp. 3 ff.

[3] The title of the Anonymus' work is : Διήγησις περὶ τῆς οἰκοδομῆς τοῦ ναοῦ τῆς μεγάλης τοῦ θεοῦ ἐκκλησίας τῆς ἐπονομαζομένης Ἁγίας Σοφίας.

[4] O. Wulff, *B. Z.*, v. 218.

[5] Fossati and Salzenberg were inclined to ascribe all mosaics to the sixth century. Labarte, Bayet, and Woltmann excepted the lunette mosaic in the narthex. The opinion of many writers now is that the archangel is the only figure mosaic earlier than iconoclasm. See Lethaby and Swainson, as above, and Th. Preger in *B. Z.*, x, 1901, 458.

[6] Antoniades, 312 ; Salzenberg, 29. Some would include the Virgin and Child in the apse among the earliest mosaics (*B. Z.*, v. 219). Smirnoff (ibid., iv. 49) doubts the antiquity of the angel.

[7] This subject perhaps dates from the restoration carried out by Basil II after the earthquake of A.D. 975 ; some consider that the great cherubim of the pendentives are not earlier than this period.

[8] Other portrait mosaics reproduced by the brothers Fossati included Constantine, Zoe, Alexius and John Comnenus, and Irene. Fossati saw over the south portal a mosaic of the Virgin receiving the Church of Sta Sophia from Justinian, and the city of Constantinople from Constantine.

and to have been restored in the fourteenth century by John Cantacuzene.   On
the opposite western arch are the Virgin and Child in a medallion between
St. Peter and St. Paul,[1] mosaics perhaps to be ascribed to Basil I, and restored
by Basil II.   The Pentecost, already mentioned, concludes the list of the
identified subjects within the building.   Above the royal doors of the narthex
is the figure of Our Lord enthroned, adored by an emperor, perhaps Leo VI the
Wise (A. D. 886–911), perhaps a later monarch : on either side are busts which
are variously interpreted as the Virgin and an archangel, personifications of
Light and Peace, &c.[2]

Fig. 229.   Christ washing Peter's feet : mosaics of the eleventh century in the narthex
of St. Luke in Phocis.   (*Hautes Études*: G. Millet.)   P. 393.

The roof of the narthex and side aisles is decorated with mosaic ornament
of geometrical and floral design, interconnected medallions, &c., among the
details being heart-shaped figures, lozenges, and swastikas.   The vaults of the
galleries had rich mosaic diapers, now in great part destroyed[3] (Fig. 3).

It may be of interest, in connexion with Sta Sophia, to touch briefly upon
the lost mosaics of the Church of the Apostles at Constantinople, as described
by Mesarites.   These have recently been discussed by Heisenberg, who has

[1] Salzenberg, p. 102 and Pl. XXXII.
[2] Ibid., p. 101 and Pl. XXVII ; Antoniades, Pl. opp. p. 168 ; Labarte, *Hist. des arts indus-
triels*, 2nd ed., ii, Pl. LVIII.   The description as Leo is adopted by Kondakoff, *Byzantine
Churches of Constantinople*, 115.   Labarte thought the emperor Heraclius, Woltmann Basil I ;
Millet considers him a ruler of the Macedonian period.   Bayet (*L'Art byzantin*, 3rd ed., 52)
calls the emperor Andronicus II ; Oman (*Byzantine Empire*, p. 317) follows him, and Wroth
(*Imperial Byzantine Coins*, Introduction, p. lxx) notes the resemblance to coins of that emperor
(Pl. LXXXIV, Figs. 10-12).   Other attributions to Justinian and Constantine Pogonatus are
no longer entertained.   The female bust has by some been regarded as the Divine Wisdom
represented under the form of the Virgin.   In churches dedicated to Ἁγία Σοφία the Virgin is
usually represented in the apse (e. g. here, at Salonika, and in the church dedicated by
Ecclesius at Ravenna in the sixth century, on which see Agnellus, ed. Bacchini, ii. 38).
[3] Salzenberg, 98 ; Antoniades, Figs. on pp. 196-200, 206, 278, 286, 312.

conjecturally assigned each subject its position in the building.[1]   On the walls
were numerous scenes from the Gospel and figures of Apostles ; round the
domes a continuation of the same ; in the centres of the domes the Pantokrator,
Crucifixion, Pentecost, Transfiguration, and Ascension.

There are general resemblances between the compositions as described by
Mesarites and those of the Codex Rossanensis, though the differences of detail
are considerable.   The resemblances with objects probably originating in the
Holy Land, as the ampullae at Monza, are very frequent, while the divergence
from the Syrian types in the Rabula MS. is equally remarkable.   For these
reasons Heisenberg is inclined to assign the mosaics to the sixth century, though
they are commonly attributed to the Macedonian period.

The Church of the Peribleptos on the Propontis was richly decorated with
mosaics of the eleventh century.[2]

The imperial palaces at Constantinople were richly decorated with mosaics.
Especially brilliant was the ornament of the Kainourgion, erected by Basil I.
Here the emperor was several times represented, now among his generals, now
enthroned by the side of the Empress Eudocia surrounded by their children,
now again adoring the cross with his family.[3]   Manuel and Andronicus Comnenus both followed this example, which Basil himself had inherited from
earlier times.[4]

The larger of the two churches of the Monastery of St. Luke at Stiris has
still a complete scheme of mosaic decoration covering the whole interior, and
affording, like Daphni, a fine example of the system followed in Byzantine
churches from the eleventh century :[5]   the pictures are of one period though the
work of more than one artist, and show the influence of the monastic spirit.
They are clearly related to the miniatures of the Menologium of Basil in the
Vatican Library, in which their qualities of rich colour, skilful handling of
drapery, and frequent nobility of expression, as well as their occasional defects
of composition, inaccurate drawing, and ignorance of anatomy are equally conspicuous.[6]   The Menologium was executed in Constantinople for the Emperor
Basil II : the mosaics are of the early eleventh century.   The general effect of
the interior is brilliant, though numerous windows have been filled up in
consequence of the damage done to the fabric by earthquake.   In the dome is
Christ Pantokrator surrounded by the Virgin, St. John the Baptist, the archangels,
and (lower) by the prophets and Evangelists.   In the apse is the Virgin seated
with the Child ; and on the sides of the bema the great doctors of the Church.
The walls, vaults, and pendentives of the church are decorated with the Gospel
scenes corresponding to the great ecclesiastical feasts, and an array of saints in
order of their importance ; near the west end, monks and ascetics, then martyrs ;
near the altar, bishops and deacons ; in the arms of the cross warrior-saints
take their place in attendance upon the majestic Christ of the dome above.

The narthex is also richly decorated with mosaics.   In an apse at its north
end is the scene of the Washing of the Feet ('O Νἱπτηρ) (Fig. 229), and in the

[1] A. Heisenberg, *Grabeskirche und Apostelkirche : Zwei Basiliken Konstantins*, ii, Leipzig, 1908,
ch. v, 140.   Mesarites also mentions mosaics in the Mausoleum of Constantine and in that of
Justinian.

[2] For references see J. P. Richter, *Quellen der byzantinischen Kunstgeschichte*, 1897, 235.
Other references to mosaics in the capital will be found in the same work.   See Index,
s.v. *Mosaiken*.

[3] Constantine Porphyrogenitus, *Life of Basil*, ch. 89; see J. P. Richter, *Quellen der byzantinischen Kunstgeschichte*, 1897, 363 ; Diehl, *Manuel*, 375-6.

[4] The authorities are Nicetas and Kinnamos : Diehl, as above.

[5] Ch. Diehl, *L'Église et les mosaïques de Saint-Luc en Phocide*, *Gazette des Beaux-Arts*, 1897
(reprinted in his *Études byzantines*, Paris, 1905, 382 ff.), *Monuments Piot*, 1897, and *Manuel*, 476 ;
Schultz and Barnsley, *The Monastery of St. Luke of Stiris in Phocis*, 66 ff. and Pl. 36-55 : Plate 34
gives a plan of the mosaics marking the position of each subject ; numerous coloured plates
illustrate the general effect.   M. Diehl's article in the *Monuments Piot* is illustrated by photo-
gravures.   G. Schlumberger, *L'Épopée*, i, Figs. on pp. 120, 161, 341, 729 ; ii. 197, 329, 545.

[6] Diehl, *Études*, 390.

opposite apse the Incredulity of Thomas (τῶν θυρῶν κεκλεισμένων, John xx. 26). In the centre of the east wall is a half-figure of Our Lord with a book, flanked by the Crucifixion and the *Anastasis*: the remaining surfaces are covered by figures of saints.

The monastic influence, with its tendency to produce stiff and severe figures,

FIG. 230. St. Sergius : mosaic of the eleventh century in the Monastery of Daphni, Attica. (*Hautes Études* : G. Millet.) P. 397.

is most marked in the work of the artists who executed the ascetic saints and bishops. The archangels and warrior saints are less remote from the classical tradition, and still have something of the spirit of earlier centuries. On the other hand, the figure of the Virgin, for all its dignity, has not the grace of the older conceptions of the Mother of God ; and the Pantokrator. if august, is hard and stern. In the Gospel scenes and in more than one saintly figure there is evidence of an attempt at individual treatment: the artists are not yet en-slaved by formulae. The whole church, like that of Daphni, is a fine example of the systematic decoration according to an accepted scheme.

The mosaics of Sta Sophia at Kieff,[1] a church founded by Yaroslav in

[1] D. Ainaloff and E. Riedin, *Ancient Monuments of Art in Kieff: The Cathedral of Sta Sophia*, Charkoff, 1899 (illustrated) ; the same authors' earlier work, *The Cathedral of Sta Sophia at*

A. D. 1037, are in great part of that date, but the damage caused at various times by fire and pillage has necessitated considerable restoration. Some of them were for a long time covered over when the building was in the hands of the Uniats. The mosaics in the dome, which were still to be seen in the first half of the seventeenth century, were thus concealed, and part of them were only rediscovered in 1885.[1] In the centre is Christ as Pantokrator,[2] within a medallion, the figure almost perfect ; below this is a figure of an archangel,[3] perfect down to the knees, holding a labarum and an orb. On the east side of the dome is St. Paul, similarly imperfect. High up on the inner surface of the triumphal arch, to the left of the spectator, is Aaron in high-priest's vestments, and carrying a censer. In the seventeenth century the whole series of mosaics about the dome was visible—Christ surrounded by angels and the Twelve Apostles, with the four Evangelists in the pendentives.

On the two piers of the triumphal arch are the angel and the Virgin of the Annunciation,[4] the latter erect and holding the purple thread and the spindle. Within the bema, forming the lower zone of ornament, are standing figures of saints in an admirable style,[5] the faces having the character of portraits : only the upper parts of the figures are original. Above the saints is the Communion of the Apostles :[6] in the centre is an altar standing before a ciborium, and on each side of it an angel serving as subdeacon to Our Lord, who is twice represented. On the right he stands at the end of the altar, offering the cup to a group of six Apostles ; on the left he occupies a similar position, offering the bread. Above, in the upper part of the apse, is a standing figure of the Virgin as *orans*, draped in purple, and wearing the red shoes which mark royal rank. The Virgin in the apse of a church, especially when in the attitude of prayer, was regarded as the personification of the Church on earth, for which she intercedes, as Christ Pantokrator in the dome represents the Church in heaven.

In the four arches beneath the dome were originally medallions containing busts of the Forty Martyrs of Sebaste, but only fifteen of these now remain, coloured with fine rich tones.[7] At the top of the triumphal arch are three medallions containing the three persons of the *Deesis*[8] (p. 664). Above the eastern and western arches of the dome are the remains of figures of Christ as Emmanuel with a scroll and of the Virgin. Of the four Evangelists once in the pendentives only St. Mark remains ; he is seated on a folding chair before a desk, writing his Gospel.

The tones of the mosaics in different positions in this church are of a different character ; those of the dome and the bema, with the exception of the figures of the saints, are lighter than the rest. The drapery is broken into numerous folds and there is apparent an effort after effect which perhaps points to the influence of the metropolis, where changes of style were initiated at this period. On the other hand, the figures of saints and busts of martyrs illustrate a more traditional character. These differences may point to a division of labour in the decoration of the building. It is known that artists from Constantinople were employed at Kieff ; but as there was a great deal of mosaic work being

---

Kieff, St. Petersburg, 1899, itself without illustration, serves as the text to the fine plates by Th. Solntseff, published by the Imperial Russian Archaeological Society of St. Petersburg between the years 1871 and 1887 under the title *Antiquities of the Russian Empire : The Cathedral of Sta Sophia at Kieff* ; Kondakoff and Tolstoy, *Russian Antiquities*, iv. See also N. Pokrovsky, *Mural Decorations of Ancient Greek and Russian Churches*, 41 ff. ; N. Kondakoff, *Macedonia*, 151 ; Bayet, *L'Art byzantin*, 275 ; Schnaase, *Geschichte der bildenden Künste*, iii, 1869, 365 ; G. Schlumberger, *L'Épopée*, i, Figs. on pp. 57, 73, 373, 537 ; ii. 212 ; and *Nic. Phocas*, 353.

[1] Ainaloff and Riedin, *Ancient Monuments*, &c., 10.

[2] Ibid., Fig. 15, p. 23.   [3] Ibid., Fig. 14, p. 22.

[4] Ibid., Figs. 4 and 5, p. 12.

[5] SS. Epiphanius, Clement, Gregory, Theologus, Nicholas, Stephen, Laurence, Basil the Great, John Chrysostom, Gregory of Nyssa, and Gregory the Wonder-worker (Ainaloff and Riedin, Figs. 6 and 7).   [6] Ibid., Figs. 8–11.

[7] Ibid., Fig. 16, p. 24. Bust of St. Severianus.   [8] Ibid., Fig. 17, p. 24.

executed at this time in various parts of the empire it is unlikely that they were sufficiently numerous to undertake the whole of it. In all probability they employed such local talent as was available to carry out the work in the less important positions. The work as a whole stands between that of St. Luke and Daphni: it is more advanced in its treatment than the former, 'plus varié, plus souple, plus pittoresque.'[1] The cubes of mosaic employed at Kieff, as in other places, were composed of glass and of opaque stone. The latter were chiefly used for the uncovered parts of the body—face. hands, &c.—and were of smaller size than the vitreous cubes which formed the background and the garments of the figures.

The mosaics of the Monastery Church of St. Michael at Kieff, among which the Communion of the Apostles is the most important, are more definitely Russian in character, though closely following Byzantine models.[2]

The church of the Monastery of Nea Moni in the island of Chios [3] suffered severely in 1881 from earthquake, when the dome was destroyed with all its mosaics. These represented Christ Pantokrator surrounded by nine angels and (on a lower level) the Twelve Apostles. When its whole decoration was complete, the interior deserved comparison with Daphni and St. Luke in Phocis, so extensive was the cycle which it contained. The date is considered to be a little earlier than those of Daphni,[4] perhaps the period of Constantine Monomachos (A.D. 1042–54). When examined by Dr. O. Wulff in 1897, the surviving mosaics were found to have suffered considerable deterioration.

In the main apse is the standing figure of the Virgin as *orans*; in the lateral apses busts of St. Michael and Gabriel. In the church are seven out of eight scenes from the life of Christ: the Annunciation, Presentation in the Temple, the Baptism, Transfiguration, Crucifixion, Deposition, and *Anastasis*: only the Nativity is lost, the other scenes being under the circumstances fairly well preserved. The inner narthex has mosaics in bad condition. The subjects include scenes from the life of Christ (the Raising of Lazarus, the Washing of Peter's Feet, the Entry into Jerusalem, Pentecost, Ascension, and another scene), the Virgin, military saints, SS. Joachim and Anna, Stephen Martyr and Pante-leemon, two pairs of Stylites, Daniel and Isaiah, and fourteen busts of other saints in medallions. The exonarthex was adorned with frescoes which, however, have been largely covered over with whitewash. The colours in these mosaics are very rich, but subdued in tone; there is an absence of the greens which are characteristic of the later work at Bethlehem and Kahrié Djami. The drapery is disposed in longitudinal unbroken folds. The figures are seen against gold, standing upon a greyish-green ground often diversified with flowers. Accessories are limited in number. We mark a further stage in the advance towards the elegant and the picturesque treatment seen at its best in the work next to be described.

The church of the Monastery of Daphni, not far from Athens, was erected in the second half of the eleventh century, and the mosaics with which the interior was covered are held to be almost contemporary with the building.[5] They are the finest mosaics of their period, characterized by such an elegance of design, richness of colour, and skill of composition that they command universal admiration. They mark the culminating point attained in the Third Period, when the artist had learned to express his idea with an astonishing refinement and grace of style.

[1] Diehl, *Manuel*, 482.   [2] Ainaloff and Riedin, 1899, 55-7.
[3] J. Strzygowski, *B. Z.*, v. 1896, 145 ; *V. V.*, vi, 1899, 300 ff. ; V. G. Barsky, *Trans. Imp. Russian Palestine Society*, 1886, ii. 200 ff. ; O. Wulff, *Izviestiya* of Russ. Arch. Inst. Cple., iii, 1898, 206 ff. (no illustration) ; Diehl, *Manuel*, 485.
[4] *V. V.*, as above, 300.
[5] G. Millet, *Le Monastère de Daphni*, Paris, 1899, 183. M. Millet's photographs form part of the Collection des Hautes Études at the Sorbonne. Figures illustrating the mosaics are also given by M. Schlumberger, *L'Épopée*, i, pp. 265, 569, 680, 741 ; ii. 384, 396, 512, 629. See also Ἐφ. Ἀρχ., 1894, 111 ff. and 149 ff. ; G. Lampakis, Χριστιανικὴ ἀρχαιολογία τῆς Μονῆς Δαφνίου, Athens, 1889, and Ἡ Μονὴ Δαφνίου, &c., Athens, 1899 ; and Diehl, *Manuel*, 491, &c.

The interior of the church, with its great number of isolated figures and biblical scenes arranged according to a regular scheme, is at once splendid and impressive.   In the dome is a colossal bust of the Pantokrator, round whom, at a lower level and occupying the spaces between the windows of the drum, stand sixteen prophets (Fig. 231).   In the vault of the bema is the *Etimasia*, and in the two niches at the sides the Archangels Michael and Gabriel.   In the apse is the Virgin seated.   The prothesis originally had John the Baptist with Aaron and Zachariah ; but the two latter figures have been removed to niches in the body of the church.   The two lateral figures in the diaconicon, St. Gregory Thauma-

Fig. 231.   Christ Pantokrator : mosaic in the dome of the Monastery Church of Daphni in Attica.   (*Hautes Études* : G. Millet.)

turge and St. Gregory of Agrigentum, have in like manner been removed, leaving only St. Nicholas.   Under the arches of these two lateral chapels are figures of saints.   In the transepts to north and south of the central dome are two groups of martyrs commemorated in the Menologia : in the north SS. Probus, Tarachus, and Andronicus (Oct. 12), in the south SS. Samonas, Gourias, and [Abibos] (Nov. 15), the last figure destroyed.   Above the two side doors leading into the narthex are the busts of St. Sergius (Fig. 230) and St. Bacchus ; while the rest of the western portion of the church is decorated with busts and standing figures of other saints.   A number of figures once decorating the roof of the narthex and the great arches beneath the dome have been entirely destroyed.   The Gospel scenes are in the transepts, the pendentives of the dome, and in the narthex.   In the church itself are : Birth of the Virgin (Fig 199), Salutation, Nativity, Adoration of the Magi (Fig. 232), Presentation in the Temple (lost), Baptism, Transfiguration, Raising of Lazarus (fragmentary), Entry into Jerusalem, Crucifixion (Fig. 418), Descent into Hell (*Anastasis*), Incredulity of Thomas, Death of the Virgin ; in the narthex : the Betrayal, Christ Washing the Disciples' Feet, the Last Supper, the Prayer of Joachim and Anna, the Blessing of the Virgin by the Priests, and the Presentation of the Virgin in the Temple (the head of Joachim in this scene restored). These narthex mosaics are in two groups, the first four in the northern, the remainder in the southern half.

The Metropolitan Church of Serres in Macedonia has in the apse a zone of mosaic representing the Communion of the Apostles,[1] as in two cases at

FIG. 232.   The Adoration of the Magi : mosaic of the eleventh century in the Monastery of Daphni, Attica.   (*Hautes Études* : G. Millet.)   P. 397.

Kieff (Fig. 233).[2]   The mosaic suffered greatly as a result of a fire in 1849 and has been badly restored in paint.   Christ, represented twice, stands under a ciborium, and delivers the wine and the bread to two groups of Apostles approaching from right and left.   The work, where it remains intact, is of considerable merit, and may well be, as Diehl supposes, of the end of the eleventh century, though Kondakoff is inclined to ascribe it rather to the

[1] L. Chesnay, *Monuments Piot*, 1902, 126 ff., Figs. 4 and 6, and Pl. XII ; N. Papageorgiou, Αἱ Σέρραι ; N. Kondakoff, *Macedonia*, 151–3, Figs. 91 and 92 ; Diehl, *Manuel*, 490.

[2] Ainaloff and Riedin, 289 ff.   The earliest examples of this subject date from the eleventh and twelfth centuries.   It is common in frescoes of the Greek Church in the fifteenth and sixteenth centuries.   References to frescoes on Mount Athos, at Mistra, &c., are given by Chesnay, as above, 129.

second half of the thirteenth, suggesting that cartoons of the best period may have been used by later artists.

The mosaics of S. Marco at Venice [1] are only in part Byzantine: the famous church is a museum for the mosaic of all periods between the eleventh century and modern times, many of those of the sixteenth century and later reproducing the style of celebrated painters. The result is distracting to the eye, and the original harmonious impression is lost.

It was the Doge Domenico Selvo who commenced the decoration of the interior with mosaics in 1071; the chronicle of Bemba relates that they were

FIG. 233. Part of the Communion of the Apostles: mosaic of the eleventh century, apse of the Metropolitan Church of Serres. (*Hautes Études*: Perdrizet-Chesnay.) P. 398.

completed in 1094; but Saccardo doubts whether the work referred to extended beyond the pavement and the apse. Whenever the general decoration of the roof and walls was commenced, doubtless in the early eleventh century, it is probable that Byzantine artists were employed. For on the one hand the message asking for mosaic artists sent to Constantinople by Desiderius, abbot of Monte Cassino, implies that native workmen could not be obtained, and on the other the close commercial relations of Venice and Constantinople and the presence of Greek painters in the former city in the twelfth century make it more than probable that the republic began the ornamentation of its great church under Greek tuition, if not by the aid of Greek hands. A document of 1153 mentions the name of Marco Greco Indriomeni, artist in mosaic,[2] and the presence of this Greek master at so advanced a period

[1] P. Saccardo, *Les Mosaïques de Saint-Marc à Venise* (Venice, 1897), and in Ongania, *La Basilica di San Marco*, iii, pp. 301 ff; J. J. Tikkanen, *Die Genesismosaiken von San Marco in Venedig*, &c., in *Acta Societatis Scientiarum Fennicae* (Helsingfors), vol. xvii, pp. 207 ff.; C. Neumann, *Die Marcuskirche in Venedig*, Prussian *Jahrbuch*, 1892; A. Venturi, *Storia dell' arte italiana*, ii, 1902, 418 ff.; C. Errard and A. Gayet, *L'Art byzantin*, Part I, *Venise*, Pl. XIV–XXIV; Diehl, *Manuel*, 502 ff.; G. Clausse, *Basiliques et mosaïques chrétiennes*, ii. 164 ff.; N. Pokrovsky, *Mural Decoration of Early Greek and Russian Churches*, 29 ff. (in Russian); S. Beissel, *Zeitschrift für christliche Kunst*, vi, 1893, 231, 267, 363.

[2] Saccardo, p. 23.

in the century seems to show that indigenous workmen were not yet competent to stand alone. It would seem probable that Venice, always more directly subjected to oriental influences, was less swift to develop an indigenous school of mosaicists than other parts of Italy; and this state of tutelage may have prevented the rise of a Jacopo Torriti, an Andrea Tafi, or a Gaddo Gaddi within her territory. The Italian spirit did not completely triumph until the middle of the fifteenth century.[1] There was then a great revival, and from that time until our own day an almost continuous series of masters worked upon the decorations of the church, infusing into their mosaics the spirit and style of the centuries in which they lived. In the sixteenth century the old independence of mosaic came to an end, and with the work of the Zuccati, Rizzio, Bianchini, Marini, Salviati, and others it entered into complete subjection to the art of painting in oil.

M. Diehl, the latest authority to resume what is known of the mosaics in S. Marco,[2] accepts as early the following subjects in the interior: Christ between the Virgin and St. Mark in the tympanum over the entrance door,[3] the Pentecost of the western cupola, the Ascension of the central dome, the Christ Emmanuel with prophets of the eastern cupola, the Feasts of the Church, the Miracles of Our Lord, and the Life of St. Mark in the vaulting of the great berceaux supporting these three cupolas and along the upper part of the walls; all these he assigns to the close of the eleventh century, remarking their affinity in variety of composition and colour to the mosaics of the Monastery of Daphni. In certain features they diverge from contemporary Eastern work: Western saints are introduced, unusual personifications occur; Latin inscriptions explain the subjects; but the general character is the same. The work of Italian pupils of Greek masters begins in the thirteenth century: it is found on the façade, where the Translation of the body of St. Mark over the left door is alone original,[4] and in the narthex (see below). Saccardo assigns the decoration of the Chapel of St. Zeno to this date. To the fourteenth century belong the partly restored mosaics of the baptistery, which are still Byzantine in conception, and those of the Chapel of St. Isidore, which are influenced by the art of the Giottesques. The two angels above the treasury door are early, but not likely to date from before the fire which damaged this part of the building in A.D. 1231.

In some respects the most interesting of all the earlier mosaics are those of the narthex or vestibule. This is due to the fact, first noted by Tikkanen,[5] that their subjects, derived from Genesis and Exodus, were clearly copied from an early illuminated Bible of the same group as the Cotton Bible (p. 446). Tikkanen believed that the series of pictures covering the domes and vaults of the western or entrance section of the vestibule are of the early part of the thirteenth century and perhaps by Byzantine masters, while those of the northern section date from its second half, and are the work of Italian pupils. Decorative as they are, the mosaics as a whole fall far behind the illuminations, in comparison with which they are stiff and formal. As far as may be judged from the miniatures which have survived, the imitation is faithful, the only great difference lying in the free introduction of architectural backgrounds where none originally existed, and the changing of blue grounds into gold.

It seems quite possible that the whole series is the work of Italian pupils

[1] Saccardo, 32.   [2] *Manuel*, 503.
[3] But see Saccardo, 23; and Tikkanen, 297.
[4] The bronze horses (p. 125), which came from Constantinople in A.D. 1204 but were not erected for some time, appear in this subject (Saccardo, 26; Tikkanen, 298–9).
[5] As above, especially 303 ff. It is not asserted that the mosaics need have copied the actual book known as the Cotton Bible, but a Bible of its type, which had probably become the standard for Bible illustration of the period (p. 320). The Genesis mosaics are reproduced in Naya's photographs (Nos. 3552, &c.), which are to be seen in the Victoria and Albert Museum, Nos. 1351–1906 et seq.

of the Byzantine masters in mosaic. But whatever were the hands that produced them, they draw their inspiration immediately from oriental sources, and are the creation of the Byzantine mind.

When compared with other mediaeval Genesis cycles, the series in S. Marco seem to stand somewhat alone.[1] The group of Carolingian miniatures on the one hand, and on the other an early Italian group, including the mosaics at Palermo and Monreale, the carved ivory paliotto of Salerno, the mosaics of the baptistery at Florence, the Cimabuesque frescoes at Assisi, and the embossed reliefs upon a silver cross in the Vatican, all derive from ancient

Fig. 234.   Joseph and his Brethren : mosaic of the thirteenth century in the narthex of S. Marco, Venice.   (Alinari.)

traditional models, but these belong to a different class from that in which the Cotton Bible was included.

The principal subjects of the vestibule mosaics, which fill the cupolas, vaults, and tympana, range from the Creation, through all the principal Genesis stories, Adam and Eve, Cain and Abel, Noah, Abraham, and Joseph, down to Moses and the events in the wilderness, which occupy the northern or later section.

The fine old Basilica of Torcello, on an island reached from Venice in a few hours, is known to many who have never visited it from Ruskin's description in the *Stones of Venice*. The island began to be inhabited in the seventh century, when Paul, Bishop of Altino, transferred his see there and built his cathedral in A.D. 641. The building was altered after the lapse of about fifty years, and again partly reconstructed and restored in A.D. 1008 by Bishop Orso Orseolo, son of the doge of Venice.

The mosaics[2] in the cathedral occupy the apses at the east end, and the

[1] Tikkanen, pp. 346 ff.

[2] Alinari's and Naya's photos: P. Molmenti, *Le Isole della laguna veneta*, Bergamo, 1904 (Series *Italia Artistica*, ed. by Corrado Ricci), 117 ff. ; P. Saccardo, *Les Mosaïques de Saint-Marc de*

interior of the great western wall. The Virgin standing with the Child in her arms above the Twelve Apostles occupies the central apse (Fig. 235) and is the oldest mosaic in the building.[1] The date is probably the earlier part of the eleventh century, and the work is contemporary with that of St. Luke

Fɪɢ. 235.   The Virgin and Child, with the Apostles : mosaic of the eleventh century in the apse of the Cathedral of Torcello.   (Alinari.)

in Phocis (p. 393), with which it shows affinities of style and treatment. The subject in the right lateral apse, that of the Chapel of the Holy Sacrament, is Christ seated on a throne holding a book of the Gospels and flanked by Michael and Gabriel (Fig. 236): below stand SS. Nicholas, Ambrose, Augustine, and Martin.[2] Above, and beyond the apse, four angels support on four sides

---

Venise, Venice, 1897, pp. 19-22 ; A. Renan in *Gazette des Beaux-Arts*, Second Period, xxxviii, 1888, 407 f., Fig. on p. 409 ; G. Clausse, *Basiliques et mosaïques*, &c., ii. 142 ; L. Testi, *Storia della pittura veneziana*, 1909, 75-7.

[1] Saccardo, ·p. 21, compared the work to that of Parenzo, and apparently held it to belong to the First Period.   Bayet (*L'Art byz.*, 304) and Molmenti speak rather of the twelfth century. The opinion expressed above is that of Diehl (*Manuel*).   The small half-figure below the window in the middle of the apse represents Bishop Heliodorus.

[2] Naya's photo, 3752, V. and A. Museum, No. 1419, 1906 ; Molmenti, 127.   Bayet (as above, 304) sees in this apse traces of Italian collaboration.

a central medallion containing the Lamb.[1]   Two of the angels kneel, the others
stand erect upon globes. This work is later than that of the central apse,
and may date from the end of the eleventh century or rather later.

Fig. 236.   Our Lord between archangels, and saints : mosaic of the twelfth century in the
lateral apse of the Cathedral of Torcello. (Alinari.)

To the same period and the same artists may be ascribed the decoration of
the west wall,[2] [though it has sometimes been assigned to the close of the

---

[1] Molmenti, 128 ; Testi, 75.
[2] Naya's photo, 3764, is in the V. and A. Museum (No. 1422, 1906).   Molmenti, *Le Isole*,
&c., 125 (photo) ; N. Pokrovsky, *Proceedings of the Sixth Archaeological Congress at Odessa*, 1884, iii,
published at Odessa, 1887, 285 ff. and Pl. LXXIV ; Testi, 76 (large photo by Naya).

twelfth century.[1] At the top is the Crucifixion between the Virgin and St. John; below are five successive zones diminishing in breadth from top to bottom: the two lowest are broken by the west door, in the round tympanum of which is a half-figure of the Virgin.

The zone below the Crucifixion bears a representation of the *Anastasis*, and is flanked by two large figures (restored) of Michael and Gabriel holding orbs and staves and trampling on serpents. The next zone begins the subject of the Last Judgement. In the centre Christ is seen in a mandorla between the Virgin and St. John the Baptist (the three forming the *Deesis*), behind whom are two angels. On either side are seated Apostles, behind whom are visible a crowd of nimbed heads, many restored. From the mandorla issues a stream of fire descending to the right and traversing the lower zones. Two small wheels appear to support the mandorla; on either side of these are cherubim with eyes in their wings; on the top of each of the four wings appears an Evangelist's symbol.

The following zone contains the throne, on the cushions of which lies a closed book: before it is a carpet, behind it are the instruments of the Passion guarded by two angels. Two kneeling figures, male and female, adore the book, which represents the apocalyptic Book of Life. To right and left angels are blowing curved horns, while beasts vomit out bodies and fragments of bodies: those on the left are land animals—lion, tiger, elephant; those on the right sea monsters. On one of the latter rides a kind of nereid holding a large fish, from the mouth of which a human figure issues. An angel standing near those who blow the horns carries a scroll covered with stars and scatters stars abroad with his right hand.

In the middle of the succeeding zone appears an angel holding a balance, the scales of which flying devils attempt to depress with spears. On the left advance the elect in four groups. On the right two angels with pikes thrust down the damned into the fiery river. In the corner Lucifer, seated on a two-headed dragon, holds the small figure of Antichrist upon his knees.

The next zone, which is interrupted by the door, has on the right side six compartments. In one the luxurious are seen up to the waist in flame; in another the violent walk naked in darkness; then follow the lazy in a bog; those who sinned with their eyes are represented by skulls into the hollow orbits of which serpents enter; those who sinned with their ears have heads with incandescent earrings on a fiery ground; those who sinned by touch are depicted as masses of skulls and bones.

On the left of the door is Eden. A marble gate leads into a garden, and to the right of it are an angel and St. Peter: to the left stands a figure holding a two-armed cross. To the left again is the Virgin with raised hands, and beyond her is St. Nicholas carrying a child in his right arm and surrounded by other children.

This elaborate representation of the Doom merits a detailed description, and should be compared with occidental versions of the same subject (cf. p. 667).

The Virgin in the apse of the Church of S. Donato at Murano is considered to be Byzantine.[2] She stands without the Child, wearing a severe expression; the figure is probably later than that in the apse at Torcello, perhaps by nearly a century. In two chapels in the Church of St. Just at Trieste there are apse mosaics of a similar period, one representing Our Lord with martyrs.[3]

---

[1] Venturi would place it as early as the ninth century (*Storia dell' arte italiana*, ii. 429).

[2] Naya's photo, 3711, in the V. and A. Museum, S. Kensington (No. 1408, 1906); Bayet, *L'Art byzantin*, 304.

[3] G. Clausse, as above, ii. 162-4.

The mosaics of Sicily[1] and Southern Italy belonging to the period of the Norman princes are partly the work of Greek artists, partly of their Western

FIG. 237.   Mosaics of A. D. 1143 in the Martorana, Palermo.
(*Hautes Études*: G. Millet.)   P. 410.

pupils. The conditions affecting the art were similar to those obtaining in Venice and Torcello ; but as restorations and substitutions have here been less

---

[1] Photos, *Hautes Études*, Alinari and G. Brogi ; D. Marzo, *Delle belle arti in Sicilia dai Normanni sino alla fine del secolo XIV* ; A. Springer, *Die mittelalterliche Kunst in Palermo* in *Bilder aus der neueren Kunstgeschichte*, 1886 ; G. Clausse, *Basiliques et mosaïques chrétiennes*, 1893 ; Bayet, *L'Art byzantin*, 298 ; Ch. Diehl, *L'Art dans l'Italie méridionale*, ch. vii, and *Manuel*, 513.

extensive, the effect of the Sicilian churches is more harmonious than that of
S. Marco.   The mosaics in the Chapel of the Royal Palace (Cappella Palatina)
and the Church of Santa Maria dell' Ammiraglio (the Martorana) at Palermo, and
the Cathedral of Cefalù on the coast to the east, date from the second quarter of
the twelfth century; those of Monreale Cathedral, a building begun in A.D. 1174,
were completed in A.D. 1182 and represent a later style.   The mosaics on the
mainland have been less perfectly preserved.

The mosaics of the Cathedral of Messina, consecrated under Roger II
about A.D. 1130, had already suffered from fire and earthquake before the final
disaster of 1908, so that little of the original work remained.[1]   This was to be
found in the three apses, though even here the old design was early modified.
The restorations rendered necessary by the earthquake of A.D. 1232 began at
the end of the thirteenth century, and were carried out by Frederic II of Aragon
and his successors.   In the principal apse Christ was enthroned between
Michael, Raphael, the Virgin, and St. John.   At his feet knelt three small
interpolated figures representing Frederic, Peter, and the Archbishop Guidotto.
In the left apse was the Virgin seated with the Child between two angels, the
dove descending above her head.   Beyond the angels, on the right and left,
were the kneeling figures of Eleonore queen of Frederic and Elizabeth queen of
Peter, represented on the same scale as the angels.   In the right apse the
central figure was St. John (IOANOC), seated with the book of his Gospel between
St. Nicholas and Bishop Mino.   To right and left were intercalated two small
kneeling figures of the young King Louis, successor of Peter II, and his tutor
John of Randazzo, Duke of Athens.   The early restoration of these lateral apses
was more fundamental than that of the central apse, and they were practically
reconstructions.   The church of the former Monastery of San Gregorio at
Messina had in the apse a Norman-Byzantine mosaic[2] representing the Virgin
seated with the Child, with St. Gregory kneeling with a scroll.

At the entrance to the Cathedral of Capua is a mosaic with the Virgin and
Child and St. John the Evangelist with their names in Greek characters.[3]   The
work has, however, been mended at various times and has been allowed to fall
into disrepair.

The Cathedral of Salerno[4] has in the lunette over the entrance door a figure
of St. Matthew holding a book with the first words of his Gospel in Latin.
It is of fine workmanship, and has been assigned to the eleventh century.
One of the apses has the remains of what was probably a Baptism.   In the
corresponding apse is a mosaic originally dedicated by John of Procida, friend
of King Manfred and originator of the Sicilian Vespers.   It still preserves the
original arrangement, but a restoration was carried out in 1867.   At the top
stands an archangel in imperial costume holding orb and labarum ; below him
St. Matthew is seen seated between the standing figures of SS. Fortunatus,
John, James, and Laurence, while the diminutive figure of John of Procida
kneels in the foreground.   The names are given in Latin, and below is a Latin
inscription.   It probably dates from the close of the eleventh century, and is
Byzantine in conception.   The other mosaics in the cathedral have been destroyed, except those of an ornamental character.[5]

The Cappella Palatina, or Chapel of the Royal Palace at Palermo,[6] was built

[1] Clausse, *Basiliques,* &c., ii. 115 ff., Figs. on pp. 121, 123, 125 ; Venturi, *Storia,* ii. 412.
[2] Clausse, ii. 128–9, Fig. on p. 129.
[3] Venturi, *Storia,* ii. 416.
[4] Clausse, *Basiliques,* 16–20 ; Venturi, *Storia,* 414–16.
[5] Venturi, Figs. 295–6, pp. 429 and 431.
[6] Domenico Lo Faso Pietrasanta, duca di Serradifalco, *Il Duomo di Monreale,* &c., 24–8,
Pl. XVI–XVII ; Buscemi, *Notizie della basilica di San Pietro, detta la Cappella Regia,* Palermo,
1840 ; Terzi, *La Cappella di San Pietro nella Reggia di Palermo,* &c., Palermo, 1873–85 ; Venturi,
Storia, ii. 395 ff., Figs. 279–85 ; Clausse, *Basiliques,* &c., ii. 60 ff. ; A. Pavlovsky, *Rev. arch.,*
3ᵉ sér., xxv, 1894 (iconography of the mosaics); *Mosaics of the Capp. Pal.,* St. Petersburg, 1890;
Kondakoff, *Hist. de l'art byzantin,* ii, p. 20; Diehl, *Manuel,* 519.   Restorations at various times
have chiefly affected the western wall and the central and left apses.

by Roger II and consecrated in A. D. 1140, though the decoration of the interior
was not completed until about 1160, in the reign of William I, when the nave
and aisles received their decoration.   The effect produced by this church is one
of extraordinary magnificence, covered as it is in almost every part above the
marble revetment of the lower walls by brilliant mosaics on a gold ground.   The
Saracenic ceiling of the nave, with its painted scenes of festivity, animals, and

FIG. 238.   Mosaics of the twelfth century, Martorana, Palermo.
(*Hautes Études* : G. Millet.)   P. 410.

monsters, and the oriental character of many details hardly detract from the
harmony of a whole, the dominant note of which is splendour.   No less than
a hundred and thirty-four mosaic pictures, a hundred and ten single figures, and
thirty-eight medallions containing busts follow each other in unbroken succession over apses, arches, walls, and embrasures.   The subjects in the choir and
nave are Byzantine, and accompanied by Greek inscriptions.   In the upper part
of the apse is a great half-figure of Christ, holding the book of the Gospel and
raising his right hand in benediction.   Below is the seated figure of the Virgin
between SS. Mary Magdalene, John the Baptist, James, and Peter, but none of
these figures are in their original condition.   At the top of the triumphal arch are
the throne with the instruments of the Passion (*Etimasia*); below are the Archangels Michael and Gabriel, and SS. Gregory and Sylvester, the last two figures
being of post-Norman date.   The two   secondary   apses   contain   busts   of

Christ and the Virgin, representations of the Nativity and Adoration, and busts of St. Peter and St. Paul. In the dome is Christ Pantokrator[1] in a medallion surrounded by a Greek inscription, 'The Almighty said: "The heaven is my throne, the earth is my footstool".' Below him are

FIG. 239. The Admiral George of Antioch at the feet of the Virgin : mosaic of the twelfth century in the Martorana at Palermo. (Brogi.) P. 410.

the four archangels, each holding a labarum, and four angels in imperial garb. In the drum stand David, Solomon, Zachariah, and St. John the Baptist ; in the niches at the corners are the four Evangelists writing at their desks. In the spandrels between the larger figures are eight busts of prophets of the Old Testament. Round the base of the dome runs a dedicatory inscription of

[1] Venturi, Fig. 279, p. 397 ; Kondakoff, p. 19.

the church by Roger to St. Peter, giving the date as the year 6651, which corresponds to A. D. 1143.

The mosaics in the choir and transepts represent the Gospel scenes relating to the twelve Feasts of the Church year, among which the Entry into Jerusalem,[1] above the sacristy door, deserves especial mention. Figures of the minor prophets complete the scheme of decoration. The mosaics of the nave and aisles

Fig. 240.   Christ Pantokrator : mosaic of the twelfth century in the dome of the Martorana, Palermo. (Brogi.)   P. 410.

represent scenes from the Old Testament, those of the aisles scenes from the Acts of the Apostles : in the soffits of the arches are medallions with busts of saints. These mosaics, as already observed, are by later hands than those of the choir, and may be described as Siculo-Byzantine.

The Cathedral of Palermo has lost, through restorations, all its old mosaics but one over one of the doors representing the Virgin enthroned with the Child upon her knees, which appears to belong to the Norman period.[2]

Santa Maria dell' Ammiraglio[3] was erected in A. D. 1143 in honour of the

[1] Venturi, Fig. 283 ; Clausse, Fig. on p. 69.   [2] Clausse, as above, 58.
[3] G. Clausse, vol. ii, pp. 39 ff. ; A. Venturi, *Storia*, vol. ii, pp. 404 ff. ; Tchukareff, in *Proceedings of the Imperial Russian Archaeological Society*, new series, iv, pp. 50-67 (Russian).

Virgin by George of Antioch, admiral of Roger II; its other name of La Martorana is derived from Aloisia Martorana, foundress of the adjoining convent, to which the church was annexed in A. D. 1433. Though the central apse was destroyed in the sixteenth century in the construction of a more commodious choir, there still remains a great part of the mosaic decoration.

In the dome is the Pantokrator[1] surrounded by a Greek inscription (Fig. 240); beneath are angels, and, round the drum, Evangelists and prophets; on panels flanking the steps to the high altar are the Archangels Michael and Gabriel in royal raiment and each holding a labarum. Elsewhere are medallions with busts of saints, while the vaults, in addition to large figures of saints with their names in Greek characters, are enriched with scenes from the life of the Virgin of great merit, especially that representing her death.[2]

Near the west end of the church are now placed two mosaic pictures, which, in spite of repeated restorations, still retain great historic interest. One represents the founder, George of Antioch, prostrate at the feet of the Virgin (Fig. 239) in a similar attitude to that of the emperor in the mosaic over the door of Sta Sophia at Constantinople;[3] in the other, which is of slightly later date, Christ is seen crowning King Roger II.[4] In the former picture the Virgin holds a scroll with a Greek inscription containing a supplication on behalf of the admiral to Christ, whose figure appears in the right-hand upper corner emerging from the heavens.

The mosaics of this church, like those of Cefalù, next described, are purely Byzantine in style and follow the iconographic rules of the Third Period.

At Cefalù, on the north coast between Palermo and the eastern extremity of Sicily, King Roger II in the first half of the twelfth century built a cathedral similar in plan to that at Monreale, with three aisles and a transept, with three apses corresponding to the aisles at the east end. The church was sumptuously adorned within and without with mosaics,[5] of which many are now lost. For example, the façade once bore pictures of Roger II, William I, William II, the Empress Constance, and the Emperor Frederick II, all of which are now destroyed.[6]

In the finely proportioned interior the mosaics are confined to the choir, and the effect is therefore more simple and severe than in the Cappella Palatina or at Monreale. At the top of the apse is a great bust of Christ; in the hemicycle below are the Virgin between four archangels; in the second and third tiers are ten Apostles and the Evangelists Mark and Luke. The decoration of the choir wall is similarly disposed in four zones, filled by standing figures of saints. The group containing the Greek Saints Basil and Chrysostom is of especial excellence both for drawing and colour,[7] and must be ascribed to Byzantine masters. The mosaics of the vaulted roof representing four archangels and four cherubim, though also of admirable workmanship, are by some considered to be of the thirteenth century[8] (Fig. 241). The inscriptions accompanying the mosaics in this church are both Greek and Latin. Six Latin verses in honour of King Roger, running round the apse, give the date 1148.

The Cathedral of Monreale is magnificently decorated with a series of mosaics forming an organic whole and upon a most imposing scale.[9] But as the work must have been done in great haste, the whole building being completed in

[1] Venturi, Fig. 288, p. 415.
[2] Ibid., Fig. 292, p. 423; Diehl, Manuel, 517.
[3] Clausse, Fig. on p. 49.
[4] Venturi, Fig. 291, p. 421; Clausse, Fig. on p. 47; Diehl, Manuel, 519.
[5] G. Clausse, Basiliques, &c., ii. 110 ff.; A. Venturi, Storia, 402 ff.; Diehl, Manuel, 515.
[6] But described in a MS. at Palermo dated 1329 and reproduced by Pirri.
[7] Venturi, Fig. 287, 413.
[8] Ibid., Fig. 286, p. 411.
[9] Domenico Gravina, Il Duomo di Monreale, Palermo, 1859 (folio); Pietrasanta, duca di Serradifalco, Il Duomo di Monreale, &c., Palermo, 1838, 1-22 and Pl. I-XV; G. Clausse, Basiliques et mosaïques, ii. 81 ff.; A. Venturi, Storia, ii. 410 ff.; Diehl, Manuel, 524 ff.

eight years (A.D. 1174-82) by William II, perfection of detail was probably
sacrificed to grandiose effect, and much of the work is conventional and lifeless.
Though the majority of the inscriptions are in Latin, and most of the decoration
must be the work of Sicilians, the iconography is Byzantine, and probably

FIG. 241.   Mosaics of the twelfth century: Cathedral of Cefalù, Sicily.
(*Hautes Études*: G. Millet.)   P. 410.

a part of the mosaics, notably that in the choir, was executed by Greek hands.
The number of subjects is too vast even for enumeration here, and only those
of especial interest can be mentioned.[1]   In the upper part of the main apse
is a colossal bust of Christ holding the book, below him in two zones are the
Virgin enthroned with the Child attended by archangels and saints.   In the
lateral apses are the Apostles Peter and Paul and scenes from their lives;
in the aisles are Gospel scenes, in the nave, scenes from the Old Testament.
In the soffits of the arches are busts of saints in medallions, and in spaces
between the larger subjects, standing figures of saints and Apostles.   In the
choir, on the lower part of the first two piers, are two historical subjects.   On
the right, looking towards the altar, the king, William II, is seen offering
a model of the church to the Virgin, who is seated, while above are two

---

[1] Almost everything is reproduced in the ninety plates of Gravina.   Clausse (p. 90
gives a list of the subjects in the nave, and mentions the principal subjects of the aisles.

angels and the hand of the Almighty: by the king's head is the inscription
REX GVLIELMVS SCŌS. On the left, Christ enthroned full-face lays his
right hand upon the head of the king, who stands, a smaller figure, at his side
with the same inscription about his head. By the head of Christ are the words,
MANVS ENĪ MEA AVXILIABITVR EI. The features of the king in both
these pictures seem to indicate an attempt at portraiture.

In such a blaze of splendour as that of Monreale particular defects pass out
of focus and at first appear of no importance. But upon a closer scrutiny the
inferiority of style to that of Cefalù and the Martorana becomes manifest:
the nearest parallel is to be found in the decoration of the aisles in the Cappella
Palatina.

Of the Palace of the Zisa, built by William I (A. D. 1154–66) at the extremity
of the old royal park, in a quarter beyond the walls, there remains a chamber
adorned with mosaics. Above a mural fountain are three connected medallions
upon a background of floral scrolls, containing trees, in two cases flanked by
peacocks, in the third and central example by men shooting with bows at birds
seated on the branches. Above and below the medallions are ornamental
borders of Byzantine character.[1] The work is in a good style and by artists
equal to those who decorated the royal chapel.

The Basilian Abbey of Grottaferrata near Rome, founded by St. Nilus the
younger at the beginning of the eleventh century, has two mosaic compositions,[2]
generally accepted as of Byzantine workmanship. One is over the triumphal
arch, and represents the Pentecost flanked by the Apostles enthroned in two
equal groups with rays of light descending upon their heads (Fig. 243).[3] The
colours in this composition are brilliant and the drapery well executed. These
qualities also mark, though in a less degree, the second picture over the principal door. Here Christ is seen enthroned between the standing figures of the
Virgin and St. John the Evangelist (the *Deesis*),[4] while to the right of the
throne stands a diminutive figure of a Basilian abbot. This work is generally
attributed to the eleventh century, but Venturi considers it a copy of later date
derived from a Byzantine model. It was restored by the pontifical government
in 1858.

A brief mention may here be made of the mosaics in the dome of the
baptistery at Florence,[5] which have been recently restored. They are for the most
part the work of Andrea Tafi (b. A. D. 1213), who brought the Greek mosaicist
Apollonios from Venice to help him in the work. Greek influence is clear, but
the frequent clumsiness of treatment must be ascribed rather to the inexperience
of Tafi and his Tuscan pupils. The mosaics in the apse are signed by a Franciscan
named James, the date being given as A.D. 1225. The uppermost zone contains
angels, archangels, principalities, and powers, and Our Lord between four
seraphim ; in the lower zones are the Last Judgement, with a colossal figure of
Christ ; scenes from Genesis from the Creation to the Deluge ; scenes from the
life of Our Lord, and of St. John the Baptist.

Various mosaics in the Holy Land, by Byzantine masters, belong to the
Third Period.

The mosaics of the Mosque of Omar (Dome of the Rock, *Kubbet es-Sakrah*) at
Jerusalem [6] are of two periods, but in both cases the mosaicists were Christians.

---

[1] Venturi, 408, Fig. 293 on p. 425 ; Clausse, ii, p. 75.

[2] A. L. Frothingham, *Les Mosaïques de Grottaferrata* in *Gazette archéologique*, 1883, Pl. LVII,
LVIII ; A. Venturi, *Storia dell' arte italiana*, ii. 416–18 ; G. Clausse, *Basiliques et mosaïques*,
i. 423 ff.

[3] Schlumberger, *L'Épopée*, ii, Fig. on p. 289.

[4] Ibid., i, Fig. on p. 581.

[5] A. Pérate in *Les Arts*, February, 1908, 8 ff. (with illustrations) ; G. Clausse, *Basiliques*,
ii. 219 ff.

[6] De Vogüé, *Le Temple de Jérusalem*, pp. 83 ff. and Pl. XIX–XXIII ; Kondakoff. *Archaeological
Journey to Syria and Palestine*, 1904, Pl. XLVI and XLVII (text in Russian) ; A. Baumstark,
R. Q., 1906, 143 ; Clermont-Ganneau, *Archaeological Researches in Palestine*, i. 190.

FIG. 242. Mosaics in the Cathedral of Monreale near Palermo.
(*Hautes Études*: G. Millet.) P. 410.

Those of the body of the building, decorating the wall above the columns, are probably contemporary with the mosque itself, and date from the end of the seventh century. Those in the dome and on the sides of the drum belong to the restoration of A.D. 1027, when the mischief done by the earthquake eleven years earlier was repaired. In both cases the motives consist of conventional floral and geometric designs on a gold ground, no human figures being introduced. In the lower mosaics fantastic formal 'trees' built up of foliations, vase-like figures, pairs of wings, &c., recall the designs of the later work in the Mosque of El-Aksa and at Bethlehem. Some of these figures are enriched with gems and even pieces of jewellery; [1] from their sides diverge vine-scrolls with bunches of grapes. In the drum of the dome between the windows somewhat similar 'trees' rise from vases, while a lower band has vases connected by vine-scrolls of a style recalling that of Early Christian art: the dome itself is covered with

Fig. 243.   The Pentecost: mosaics of the twelfth century at Grottaferrata.
(*Hautes Études*: G. Millet.)   P. 412.

a diaper of foliage. The borders are partly floral, partly geometrical: those round the dome contain Arabic inscriptions giving the date of the work. Whatever may be the precise date of the older mosaics in the Dome of the Rock, their prototypes must belong to the First Period.

The mosaics of the Church of the Nativity at Bethlehem [2] occupy the walls of the nave and transepts: they are but the residue of a complete and splendid decoration still in great part existing at the close of the sixteenth century, when it was described by Quaresmius.

At the west end of the church was the Tree of Jesse, now entirely destroyed. On the walls of the nave were busts in medallions of the ancestors of Our Lord in a long line above the architrave; above these, between foliate designs in which Persian influence is apparent,[3] were conventional churches and architectural tables containing Greek inscriptions relative to the oecumenical and provincial Councils; above, again, between the windows, was a procession of angels advancing towards the east. Of this decoration only four complete and three incomplete Councils, six angels, and seven busts survive. The mosaics

---

[1] De Vogüé, Pl. XXI.

[2] *The Church of the Nativity at Bethlehem* (Byzantine Research and Publication Fund, London, 1910); G. Millet in A. Michel's *Histoire de l'art*, i. 166; Diehl, *Manuel*, 527; Baumstark in *R. Q.*, 1906, 145. The older books are C. J. M. de Vogüé, *Les Églises de la Terre sainte* 1860; Quaresmius, *Terrae Sanctae Elucidatio*, ii; Ciampini, *De sacris aedificiis*, 1793, 150 ff.

[3] The Sassanian eagle's wings occur as part of conventional tree-like forms built up of leaves, vases, &c., as they do at Mshatta and in the Dome of the Rock (p. 412). For Mshatta see Strzygowski, Prussian *Jahrbuch*, 1904; the wings are there discussed on p. 320.

once visible in the grotto beneath the church are all lost except for insignificant fragments, as are those of the exterior.[1]

In the transepts, of many subjects from the life of Our Lord, only the Entry into Jerusalem, Incredulity of Thomas, Ascension, and Transfiguration are represented, the two last by fragments only. In the choir are a fine band of interlaced ornament and an important inscription assigning the mosaics to the time of Manuel Comnenus (A. D. 1169), and to the hand of an artist named Ephraim. The statement of this inscription is probably correct, and the scheme of decoration to which the remaining fragments belonged was no doubt executed at the time when Jerusalem was in the hands of Western princes. But the artists, of whom there must have been several, came from the Christian East, and worked under the supervision of Western ecclesiastics : by one of the angels of the nave we note the name of one *Basilius*. It may well be that in a general way pre-existing designs of an earlier period were reproduced :[2] the architectural ornament of the nave recalls the fashion illustrated in St. George at Salonika and the Orthodox Baptistery at Ravenna, and the ornament in the same place has affinities with earlier art. But in details the work suggests the Third Period : the final Councils are too late in date to have been included in a scheme executed in the First ; the colour-scheme, in which green is very conspicuous, is not that of any early mosaics ; the iconography of the scriptural scenes is that of later Byzantine times. De Vogüé's view that the mosaics as we see them formed part of a decoration carried out in the time of the Crusaders, when for a short time East and West worked in harmony, may therefore be regarded as most probable. The Persian character of the ornament, also conspicuous in El-Aksa and the Dome of the Rock, may possibly be due to Mesopotamian or Armenian influences.

The mosaics of the Mosque of El-Aksa at Jerusalem date from the time of the restoration under Saladin A. D. 1187.[3] The conqueror of Jerusalem resorted to East-Christian artists,[4] who decorated the dome with a diaper of conventional floral scrolls, and the drum with fantastic formal 'trees' composed of foliations, vessels, columns, pairs of wings, &c., in a Perso-Mesopotamian style like that observed at Bethlehem.

In this work both mother-of-pearl and silvered cubes are employed to render high lights, as at Bethlehem.

The monasteries of Mount Athos were all in existence in the tenth century, and during the next few centuries their churches were enriched with numerous mosaics.[5] Most of this work has perished, but a little is still to be seen at Vatopedi and Xenophon.

In the former church there is a representation of the *Deesis*, Christ enthroned between the Virgin and St. John the Baptist in the tympanum of the royal door ;[6] on each side of this door are the Angel Gabriel and the Virgin,[7] representing the Annunciation, while the same subject is repeated upon spandrels in the interior.

In the tympanum of one of the lateral doors leading to the first inner narthex is a damaged figure of St. Nicholas. The monks state that other mosaics formerly covered the other parts of the church, but this is disputed by Kondakoff.

---

[1] J. Wilpert, *Rassegna Gregoriana*, 1909, p. 25.

[2] It is known that in the First Period the church was decorated with mosaics. On the exterior, at the west end, was the Adoration of the Magi, said to have been spared by the soldiers of Chosroes because the Magi wore Persian caps.

[3] De Vogüé, *Le Temple de Jérusalem*, 1864, 101.   [4] Ibid., 101.

[5] Didron, *Annales archéologiques*, v. 152 ; C. Bayet and Duchesne, *Mémoire sur une mission au Mont Athos*, 1876, 310 ff. ; C. Bayet, *L'Art byzantin* ; N. Kondakoff, *Monuments of Christian Art on Mount Athos*, St. Petersburg, 1902 (Russian) ; G. Clausse, *Basiliques*, &c., i. 453 ; Diehl. *Manuel*, 490.

[6] Kondakoff, Fig. 47, 101 ; Schlumberger, *L'Épopée*, ii, Fig. on p. 560 ; Diehl, *Manuel*, Fig. 239

[7] Kondakoff, Figs. 48 and 49, pp. 103 and 105 ; Schlumberger, *L'Épopée*, ii, Fig. on p. 140 ; ii. 345. The lower part of each figure is concealed by a modern picture.

An inscription refers to the restoration of the mosaics in the time of a certain Higoumenos named Joannikios. The *Deesis* and Annunciation are by some considered as early as the close of the eleventh century; the others are perhaps later.

The mosaics in the new catholicon of Xenophon were removed from the old church. They form two panels: on one is St. George, on the other St. Demetrius; the work is of good quality. All these mosaics are on a gold ground, and most are inferior to the finest work of the eleventh century. In the *Deesis* Kondakoff notes deviations from the classical Byzantine type.

The mosaics of Kahrié Djami [1] at Constantinople adorn the inner and outer narthex of the church built for the monastery known as Μονὴ τῆς χώρας near the Adrianople gate. The name, which is equivalent to 'without the walls', implies the great antiquity of the foundation, as the walls within which it now stands were built by Theodosius II in the first half of the fifth century. The church, however, was rebuilt for the second time by Maria Ducas, a princess of the imperial family, at the beginning of the twelfth century, the period when the household moved to the neighbouring palace of Blachernae at the Golden Horn. It suffered during the Latin assault and occupation, and after the return of the Greek princes was restored and decorated by Theodore Metochites, minister of Andronicus Palaeologus (1282–1328), between the years A. D. 1310 and A. D. 1320. The mosaic picture (Fig. 245) over the tympanum leading from the inner narthex into the church (Schmidt, Pl. 57 and 58) represents Theodore in a high turban-like white head-dress striped with red, a gold tunic, and flowered green mantle. kneeling with a model of the church in his hand before Christ enthroned. The inscription records his title of grand logothete, and describes him as 'founder' (κτήτωρ) of the church. The claim of Theodore to have carried out extensive restorations is supported by Nicephorus Gregoras, his pupil and friend,[2] and is asserted by himself in his own poems.[3] From these passages it would certainly be gathered that not only a great part of the structure, but also the entire mosaic decoration is due to the munificence of Theodore. But Kondakoff argues that except in the case of the tympanum with the portrait, the figures of St. Peter and St. Paul, the *Deesis*, and the decoration of the cupolas in the second narthex, the mosaics are works of the Comnenian period which Theodore at best can only have restored. This theory is in harmony with the old traditional belief that Byzantine art produced no work of real merit after the beginning of the thirteenth century. Yet the arguments against a twelfth-century date appear to be very strong. In the mosaics of Daphni and in the miniatures of MSS. we have actual examples of the manner in which many of the same subjects were treated at that period, and notice marked divergences. While the fourteenth century seems most probable for the execution, there seems reason to believe that the compositions go back to early Syrian types.[4]

The mosaics at Kahrié Djami consist of two cycles representing the life of

[1] Sébah and Joailler, photos; Ch. Diehl, *Les Mosaïques de Kahrié-Djami*, *Gazette des Beaux-Arts*, 1904–5, reprinted in *Études byzantines*, Paris, 1905, 392 ff.; N. Kondakoff, *Proceedings of the Sixth Archaeological Congress at Odessa*, 1887, vol. iii, p. 165 ff., and an earlier work, Odessa, 1881; Th. J. Schmidt, *Izviestiya* of the Russian Archaeological Institute at Constantinople, viii, 1902, 119–52—these and *Izviestiya* as above, xi, 1906, text and album of ninety plates; A. Leval, *Les Principales Mosaïques, Peintures et Sculptures existant à Kahrié-Djami à Constantinople*, Cple., 1886; O. Wulff, *Litterarisches Centralblatt*, lviii, 1907, No. 45–6; Pulgher, *Les Anciennes Églises byz. de Constantinople*, with Plates XVIII–XXX, 1877.

[2] Bk. VIII, ch. 5, and IX, ch. 13.

[3] Ed. A. Treu, A. 1004 ff., B. 222 ff.

[4] Schmidt, as above, 116 ff.; possibly the models were the frescoes executed for the (Syrian) Abbot Syncellus at the close of the iconoclastic dispute. Strzygowski (*Die Miniaturen des serbischen Psalters in München* in *Denkschriften der kaiserlichen Akademie der Wissenschaften*, vol. 52, 1906, 87 and 129) points out that both the miniatures of the Vatican copy of Jacobus Monachus and the Kahrié Djami mosaics show clear traces of inspiration from early Syrian art, and that many of the types are Syrian. For Kahrié Djami he cites the Immaculate Conception over the door of the exonarthex, where the Virgin is seen in half-figure as *orans* between two angels with the medallion containing the Child over her breast.

FIG. 244. The high-priest gives the wool to the Virgin : mosaic of the fourteenth century in Kahrié Djami, Constantinople. (Sébah and Joaillier.) P. 416.

Christ and that of the Virgin, and are confined to the inner and outer narthex, as the decoration of the church itself has either been destroyed or hidden beneath thick coats of whitewash.   At Daphni there are three episodes from the life of the Virgin, the Prayer of Joachim and Anna, the Virgin's Nativity, and the Presentation in the Temple, which may be compared with the same subjects at Kahrié Djami ; but though the main outlines are the same, the Constantinople

Fig. 245.   The founder offering the church to Our Lord : mosaic of the fourteenth century at Kahrié Djami, Constantinople.   (Sébah and Joaillier.)   P. 416.

mosaics are more picturesque and fertile in invention.   They also show a more skilful composition, and a broader conception of landscape than the work of the Greek monastery church.[1]   The manuscript appears to afford even clearer evidence to the same effect.

The difficulty of accepting a fourteenth-century date for the whole of the mosaics has lain in the general reluctance to admit that any good thing could come out of Byzantium after the Latin conquest.   M. Diehl has rightly insisted upon the exaggeration which this view implies.   He cites the frescoes in the churches of Mistra and on Mount Athos, also dating from the fourteenth

---

[1] Diehl, *Études*, &c., 421-2.

century, where we find the same powers of composition, the same sense of the picturesque, the same movement and power of expression (cf. p. 19 above). He further cites a MS. in the Bibliothèque Nationale (Gr. 1242), painted by Manuel Tzykandilos for John Cantacuzene, in which the same feeling for colour and for the natural rendering of familiar scenes is no less clearly apparent. There is

FIG. 246. The Annunciation : mosaic of the fourteenth century, Kahrié Djami, Constantinople. (Sébah and Joaillier.) P. 416.

therefore no need to assume Italian intervention, however close may have been the relations of the court of the Palaeologi with the Italian peninsula.[1] The evidence accumulates in favour of a late Byzantine renaissance in the fourteenth century. Contact with the West may have had its indirect effect upon the social and artistic movements of the day, but there seems no proof of the direct intervention of Western artists. There are attitudes and groupings of figures which

---

[1] Strzygowski and Millet (in A. Michel's *Histoire de l'art*) repudiate any Western influence. They also agree in assigning all the mosaics to the fourteenth century.

appear to find no parallel in Italian art, but offer evidence of a real originality ;[1] the architecture and the ornamental borders in which the mosaics are framed are almost entirely Byzantine,[2] and so is the conventional landscape. The excessive and inappropriate use of curtains in unnatural positions on the exterior of buildings is an Eastern and not an Italian feature.

The most important subjects represented by the mosaics are, in the inner narthex, the cycle of the history of the Virgin, inspired by the apocryphal *Protevangelium* of James, which it follows scene for scene ; and in the outer narthex, a series of scenes from the life of Christ. These last do not include the Passion or the events after the Crucifixion, which were probably represented in the interior of the church. In addition to these two cycles there are a bust of Christ over the entrance door, opposite it the Virgin between two archangels, and over the door leading into the nave, Theodore Metochites offering his church to Our Lord, as already described. There are also a number of individual figures of saints and Apostles.

The mosaics of Kahrié Djami suffered less than the structure from the earthquake of June 1884. The damage thus caused was not made good until 1898–9.[3]

The central cupola in the funerary chapel of the Mosque of Fétiye-Djami (Church of the Pammakaristos), which dates from the early fourteenth century, has in the centre a bust of Our Lord holding the Gospel and blessing with his right hand.[4] Below, round the curve of the dome, stand the Twelve Apostles. The expression of the Christ is mild and gentle ; the attitudes of the Apostles are skilfully varied. The quality of the work affords another proof that originality and individual artistic feeling were not destroyed at one blow by the sack of A. D. 1204.

The mosaics in the dome of the Church of the Paregoritissa at Arta, representing Our Lord with prophets below him, are ascribed to the thirteenth century and adhere more closely to tradition.

At Trebizond there is little mosaic, most of the mural decoration being painted. But a fragment *outside* the apse of the Metropolitan Church of Panagia Chrysokephalos in the citadel is still to be seen beneath a covering of whitewash. Fallmerayer claims to have seen an Annunciation here.[5]

MOSAIC PAVEMENTS.

The custom of covering floors with *tesserae* forming patterns and figure subjects was so universal during the First Period that only a few remarkable examples can be noticed.[6] It was practised in all the provinces, and the greater proportion known from certain districts is chiefly due to the greater progress of excavation in these regions. Conspicuous among them is Syria-Palestine.[7]

---

[1] The Distribution of the Wool in the Temple (Fig. 244) and the Healing of the Sick are finely composed. The arrival of the Magi at Herod's Court (Fig. 201), the Massacre of the Innocents (Schmidt, Pl. XXXVII), the Miracle of the Loaves and Fishes (Pl. XLIV), contain figures which are full of life and character. In the Annunciation (Fig. 246) the attitude of the Virgin diverges from known types.

[2] A band of interlocking acanthus leaves, however, round one of the cupolas is of a type very common in Central and Western Europe in the Romanesque period (Schmidt. Pl. XLVI). The ciborium with trefoil arch (in the Temptation, Schmidt, Pl. XLIII) suggests a Western form.   [3] *V. V.*, i, 1894, 792–3, and vi. 322.

[4] J. Ebersolt, *Rev. arch.*, July–August, 1909, 37 ff. and Pl. IX ; Diehl, *Manuel*, 742. The mosaics are also described, though not reproduced, by N. Kondakoff, *Churches of Constantinople* (Sixth Arch. Congress, Odessa), 208 (Russian).

[5] *Orig. Framm.*, i. 120 : see G. Millet in *B. C. H.*, xix, 1895, 458.

[6] The subjects of floor mosaics are geometrical, animal, or symbolic. Where they contain figures, these are mythological or secular : sacred subjects could not be placed where they would be trodden underfoot.

[7] See Jacoby, *Das geographische Mosaik von Madaba*, 1905 (lists) ; Strzygowski, *Zeitschrift des deutschen Palästina-Vereins*, xxiv : Baumstark, *R. Q.*, 1906, 139 ff. The Dominicans of the École Biblique at Jerusalem have the material for a Corpus of these mosaics.

We may notice in the first place the mosaic discovered at Serjilla in Central Syria by the American Expedition,[1] because although its subjects are the common hunting scenes, it has in the centre a long inscription with an

Fig. 247. The Orpheus Mosaic, Jerusalem : sixth century.
(N. H. J. Westlake : *History of Design in Mural Painting.*) P. 422.

indiction-date giving the year A. D. 472–3. We may next notice the examples from the neighbourhood of Tyre and Sidon discovered by Renan during his mission in Phoenicia. At Kabr Hiram, a suburb of Tyre, a ruined church

[1] *Rev. arch.,* 1901, Pt. II, 62 ff. and Pl. XII.

was found to possess an elaborate mosaic floor in good preservation.[1] The nave has a series of medallions enclosed by vine-scrolls issuing from vases in the four corners. They contain animals either alone or pursuing each other, with scenes from pastoral and country life. In the aisles are further series of medallions with personifications of the months, seasons, and winds, subjects already known upon pavements in North Africa.[2] In narrow panels between the piers of the aisles are more animals and scrolls. The date of the whole may be the beginning of the sixth century, though de Rossi was inclined to place the central portion as early as the fourth.[3] Even better preserved was a second pavement discovered by Renan in a church in the neighbourhood of Sidon.[4] It has a number of animals in a series of medallions, as well as vases and flowers. An inscription gives the date as the end of the sixth century. The pavement is now in the Louvre.

Jerusalem and its neighbourhood have furnished many mosaics.[5] One of the most interesting (Fig. 247) is that discovered in 1901 north of the Damascus Gate, and known from its principal subject as the Orpheus Mosaic.[6] The rectangular floor which it decorates is perhaps that of a sepulchral chapel, for Orpheus, like Jonah, is associated in Christian as in pagan art with death and the life to come, a fact which explains his appearance in monuments of Early Christian art.[7] Of some fifty mosaic pavements with this subject in Algeria, Tunis, France, Switzerland, Germany, Austria, and England almost all are of pagan origin; the Jerusalem example is therefore of especial interest. The musician occupies a large panel surrounded by a broad margin in which busts and figures of animals are enclosed in acanthus borders: near him are a centaur, Pan or a satyr, an eagle, a bear, a serpent, and other creatures. Below this large panel are two rows of smaller rectangular compartments, one in the first row partly covered by a pillar. The other two compartments in this row contain two nimbed female figures described by inscriptions as *Theodosia* and *Georgia*; the three compartments of the lowest row are filled by a small figure of a nimbed hunter with a spear, a lion, and a panther. Theodosia and Georgia have been variously regarded as historical persons (foundresses) or as allegorical figures; perhaps the former alternative is the more probable. The date of the mosaic may be the fifth century.[8]

Two mosaics with Armenian inscriptions and symbolic ornament, perhaps of the sixth century, were discovered, one on the Mount of Olives,[9] the other west of the Cave of Jeremiah outside the Damascus Gate.[10]

The town of Madaba has proved exceedingly rich in mosaics, but we need only mention the now famous pavement with a map (Figs. 248 and 249) of part of Egypt, Syria, and the Holy Land.[11] The erection of a new church upon

---

[1] Renan, *Mission de Phénicie*, 607 ff. and Atlas, Pl. XLIX; Didron, *Annales archéologiques*, xxiii. 278–82; Bayet, *L'Art byzantin*, 31; V. Schultze, *Arch. der christlichen Kunst*, 201.

[2] *Gaz. arch.*, 1879, Pl. XXII; *Mon. Piot*, iii, 1896, 202. See also *Archaeologia*, xxxviii, 1860, 202 ff.

[3] *Revue biblique*, vii. 424; *Compte rendu de l'Acad. des Inscr. et Belles-lettres*, 1862, 161 ff.

[4] Renan, *Mission*, 511–13.

[5] Jacoby, as above, 13 ff.; *Palestine Exploration Fund*, 1891, 19–20, 309–10; 1893, 139–40; 1895, 86, &c.; *Revue biblique*, v, p. 122; vii, p. 254.

[6] J. Strzygowski, in *Zeitschrift*, as above, xxiv. 139 ff.; *Revue biblique*, 1901, 436 ff., 1902, 100 ff.; *Palestine Exploration Fund*, 1901, 233 ff.; Marucchi, in *Nuovo Bullettino di archeologia cristiana*, 1901, 217 ff. The mosaic has now been removed to Constantinople.

[7] e.g. sculptures in the Central Museum at Athens and the Ottoman Museum at Constantinople; ivory *pyxides* at Florence and Bobbio, &c. See Heussner, *Die altchristlichen Orpheusdarstellungen* in *R. Q.*, iv. 104.

[8] References to allusions to mosaics in the description of the early pilgrims to Jerusalem are given by Jacoby, *Das geographische Mosaik von Madaba*, p. 17.

[9] *Palestine Expl. Fund*, 1893, 139–40; *Revue biblique*, vi. 241; *Mitth. des deutschen Palästina-Vereins*, 1895, 51.

[10] *Pal. Expl. Fund*, 1895, 257; *Zeitschrift des deutschen Pal.-Vereins*, xviii. 88.

[11] The now considerable literature is quoted by A. Jacoby in his monograph, *Das geographische Mosaik von Madaba*, Leipsic, 1905. See also Diehl, *Manuel*, 211. English accounts

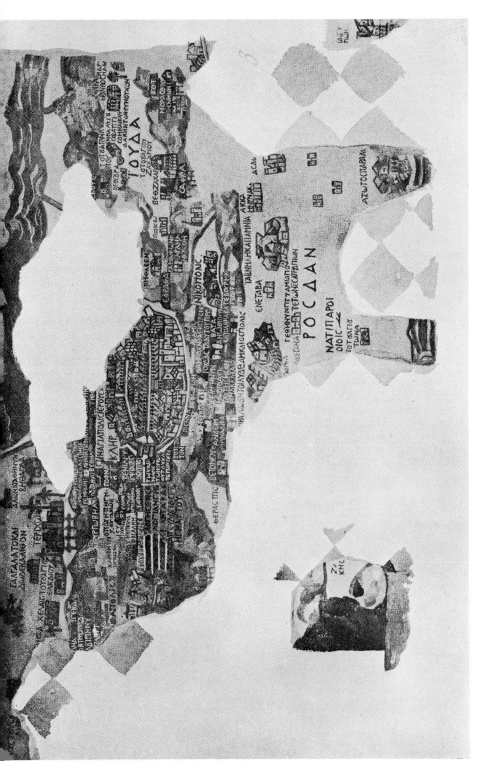

the old site resulted in the mutilation of the map, which is now imperfect on the left side and has lost fragments on the right. It now begins with the lower part of Jordan near its outlet into the Dead Sea, and ends with the mouths of the Nile. Towns are represented as clusters of buildings usually accompanied by their names in Greek ; and it is plain that the principal object is to celebrate those which were visited by pilgrims. Although the work is not of the highest order, it gives evidence of the same lively spirit of observation and feeling for nature which we find in other mosaics of better quality and earlier date.[1] Fish are seen swimming in the rivers ; there are ships on the Dead Sea ; palm-trees occur here and there, and in one place a gazelle is seen flying from a lion. The date appears to be the first half of the sixth century, and the mosaic is the oldest example of a true geographical map. The artist was evidently acquainted with the Ὀνομαστικὸν περὶ τῶν τοπικῶν ὀνομάτων of Eusebius, and with the Διαμερισμὸς τῆς γῆς which has come down to us through several channels, among others through the Chronicon Paschale.[2] He seems, however, to rely in part upon his own local knowledge.

Among the Egyptian towns recorded is Athribis, the seat of a bishopric and of the famous sanctuary of St. Menas ; among those of Philistia, Gaza, where the dome of a great church brings to mind that St. Sergius which Choricius has described. In the Holy Land itself the chief interest centres in the representation of Jerusalem, for it is certain that the artist intended to depict the principal features of the city as it was before its capture by Chosroes. It is elliptic, surrounded by walls with towers and gates at intervals : within these some of the principal buildings and streets are visible. On the north side is the Damascus Gate, from which a broad street, the *Via recta*, flanked by arcades, runs to the opposite end of the city. Another arcaded street runs south-east and south, and from it branches in an easterly direction to the gate of St. Stephen a further street identified as the *Via dolorosa*. To the south of the gate of St. Stephen is another entrance which appears to be the Golden Gate. The most interesting feature of all is the Church of the Holy Sepulchre,[3] visible on the west side between the *Via recta* and the walls. The church is entered by steps leading to the three doors mentioned by Eusebius in his Life of Constantine (iii. 37). To the west of it are the Anastasis, or circular Church of the Resurrection, and the place of Golgotha. The details of the several buildings are not very clear in the map, and the rounded space which some have taken for the dome of the Anastasis may be simply intended for an open space behind the basilica. One of the two large buildings on the opposite side of the *Via recta* may represent the praetorium of Pilate, later the Church of Sta Sophia. Among other sites marked upon the map may be mentioned Rama, Gerizim, Sichem, Jericho (surrounded by palms), and Bethabara, where the Baptism is said to have taken place.

The mosaics discovered in the ruined cities of North Africa are very numerous, but for the most part the subjects are not distinctively Christian. Exceptions are found in the case of a pavement at Hemhir Msâdine in a funerary chapel, where Daniel in the Den of Lions occurs above the tombs of a Bishop Vitalis, a Blossus, and a Victor ; in another pavement in the neighbourhood, Jonah and the Monster are seen among acanthus scrolls with peacocks, ducks, and other birds.[4] Africa, where inscriptions are constantly in Latin, and even after the conquest of Justinian religious interests were attracted to Rome, betrays its relation to the Byzantine Empire less in its pictorial art than in

of the mosaic will be found in the *Palestine Exploration Fund*, Quarterly Statement, 1899, 316, and in the *Proceedings of the Society of Biblical Archaeology*, 1897, 308 ff.
　　[1] Ainaloff, *Hellenistic Origins*, &c., 214.
　　[2] Jacoby, as above, 33–4.
　　[3] See Guthe in Hauck's *Realencyklopädie*, vii. 44 ; A. Heisenberg, *Grabeskirche und Apostelkirche*, Leipsic, 1908 ; A. Jacoby, as above, 75.
　　[4] *Rev. arch.*, 1902, Pt. II, 406 ; R. Cagnat, *Bulletin critique*, 1895, 358, 378. Daniel is also represented at Bordj-el-Youdi, Tunis, *Bull. arch. du Com. des travaux hist.*, 1898, 335.

its architecture. The symbolic motives of Early Christian art were long retained, and new features have a local character little affected by the influence of Syria and Egypt. African mosaic pavements are thus less important for the purposes of the present volume than those of the Eastern provinces, though for their intrinsic merits they deserve the careful study which the excellent French publications of recent years have rendered possible.[1]

The curious tombs covered with mosaic, with figures of the deceased

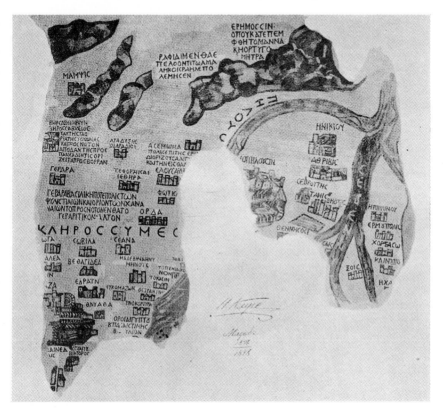

Fig. 249. Part of a map of the Holy Land : mosaic pavement of the sixth century from Madaba, Palestine. Cf. Fig. 248. (*Hautes Études* : Société orthodoxe palestinienne.)

between candelabra, doves and vases, vine-scrolls, &c., discovered in various sites, especially at Tabarka (Thabraca), may be conveniently mentioned here. Their date is thought to lie between the fourth and sixth centuries.[2]

The mosaic pavements of Asia Minor only require excavation to prove as numerous and interesting as those discovered in other parts of the Christian world. A few examples are mentioned in the footnote.[3]

[1] See the papers and monographs by Gauckler, de la Blanchère, Gsell, H. de Villefosse, Cagnat, and others, a large number of which are quoted in P. Gauckler's article *Musivum opus* in Daremberg and Saglio's Dictionary of Antiquities, and in Cabrol's *Dictionnaire d'archéologie chrétienne*, article *Afrique*, section xxv. It may be noted that some of the interesting mosaics from Carthage representing the months and seasons, now on the staircase at the British Museum, were published by Mr. Franks in *Archaeologia*, vol. xxxviii. 222 ff.

[2] For the literature, and for figures of six of these tombs, see Cabrol, as above, 715-20.

[3] Miletus and Didyma (stags drinking, other animals : early type), see Wiegand, Suppl. to *Abh. der k. preuss. Akad. der Wiss.*, 1908, 1-46 ; Ephesus, R. Heberdey, *Jahreshefte des oest. arch. Inst.*, x, 1907, *Beiblatt*, 61-78 (in basilica).

The dating of the earliest of the Christian pavements in *opus vermiculatum*,
which are to be found in Italy and the region of Istria, is a matter of great
difficulty,[1] and in regions where the East-Christian art of Ravenna extended it
is not always easy to say at what point 'Byzantine' influence is lost in the art
of the Western Middle Ages.   In few branches of art was antique tradition so
persistent and so continuous as in that of floor mosaic : features like the disposition of animals in medallions or separate compartments were reproduced down
to the close of the twelfth century.   Müntz inclines to place those of Grado

FIG. 250.   Mosaic pavement, Jerusalem.   (*Hautes Études* : Société orthodoxe palestinienne.)

as early as the sixth century, as well as others at Inzino and Trieste.[2]   Most of
the mosaics with votive inscriptions he attributes to a similar early period,[3] and
some at least of the fine pavements at Parenzo, Ravenna, Pomposa, and Venice
must belong to the time of the Greek domination.[4]   In Central and Southern
Italy we find numerous instances of mosaic floors which must belong to the
period of Byzantine occupation between the tenth and twelfth centuries.   Those
with which Desiderius decorated the floor of his church at Monte Cassino were
chiefly geometrical, the lines filled with cubes of coloured marble.   Before the

---

[1] E. Müntz, *Rev. arch.*, xxxiii, Pt. I, 42 ff.   The fragment from Sta Maria di Capua Vetere,
assigned to the sixth century and representing an eagle seizing a quadruped (E. Bertaux,
L'Art dans l'Italie méridionale, i. 64–5 and Fig. 13), is the same in style and colouring as similar
designs at Pomposa.   This affords a clue to date for the latter.

[2] Ibid., 45.

[3] Ibid., xxxii, Pt. II, pp. 402 ff.   Persons of moderate means were in the habit of giving
quite small sections of pavement to their churches, and recording the fact with their names.

[4] C. Errard and A. Gayet, *L'Art byzantin*, &c., Pt. I (Venice), Pt. XIX ; Pt. II (Parenzo),
Pl. XXVIII-XXXI ; Pt. III (Ravenna, Pomposa), Pl. X–XII.   Some of the pavements at
Parenzo have votive inscriptions in Latin.   For mosaics of the fifth century at Salona see
F. Hamilton Jackson, *The Shores of the Adriatic*, ii. 312.

high altar were slabs of marble with figures of animals, the silhouettes being cut out of the base and filled with a chequer of squares of coloured marble.[1] The rare mosaic pavements of the eleventh and twelfth centuries preserved in the East have only geometrical designs, as at St. Luke in Phocis, Palermo, Iviron on Mount Athos, and Trebizond[2] (Fig. 251).

The remains of a pavement in the Church of the Pantokrator at Constantinople

FIG. 251.   Pavement of the eleventh century in inlaid marble and other stone :   Church of St. Luke, Phocis.   (After Schultz and Barnsley : *The Church of St. Luke of Stiris in Phocis.*)

have in the interspaces between the disks of oriental marble bordered with glass cubes, genii, the Labours of Hercules, and figures of eagles in *opus sectile*,[3] but these recall, as M. Bertaux has remarked, rather the technique of marble encrustations of the walls of Sta Sophia, or the basilica of Parenzo (Fig. 253), than that of the ancient floor mosaics.   Yet figure subjects were certainly used in the Eastern Empire, if we are to believe the accounts of the

[1] E. Bertaux, *L'Art dans l'Italie méridionale*, Fig. 74, p. 176.   Similar animals are to be seen in the pavement of Sant' Adriano, near San Demetrio Corona, Calabria (ibid., Fig. 209, p. 484).

[2] For St. Luke in Phocis, see Schultz and Barnsley, *Church of St. Luke*, Pl. XXX.   For the geometric pavement in the apse of the Chrysokephalos at Trebizond, G. Millet, *B.C.H.*, xix, 1895, 458.   For those of Sta Sophia, Trebizond, Texier, *Arch. byz.*, 229.   For Iviron, Schlumberger, *L'Épopée*, i, p. 453.

[3] Salzenberg, *Altchristliche Baudenkmale von Constantinopel*, Pl. XXXVI.   The pavement of San Miniato, Florence, is in *opus sectile*, as also the decoration on the façades at Pisa and Lucca (Bertaux, 485).

chambers in the palace of Basil I and of his new church (see below). Those parts of the pavement in S. Marco at Venice which go back to the eleventh or twelfth century show both geometrical designs and medallions in pairs, between palmette-like foliage, containing figures or animals in *opus vermiculatum.*[1] Here again we find also animals sunk in champlevé in slabs of marble and filled in with a chequer of coloured cubes, as at Monte Cassino and S. Adriano.[2] In the nave of the Church of Sta Maria del Patir near Rossano is a pavement[3] with medallions containing animals and monsters (lion, gryphon, unicorn, centaur-sagittary), the interspaces being filled with palmette-like foliage ; all the animals have on their fore-quarters and flanks rosettes of oriental character. Decorative work of the same character, though more elaborate, ornaments the pavement of the Abbey Church of Tramiti,[4] where a multiple border of zigzags surrounding the figure of a gryphon recalls a border surrounding a marble disk in the pavement of the Pantokrator (see above). It would seem that these Apulian and Calabrian pavements represent a system of oriental floor decoration of which no complete example survives in the East. In another pavement of this region, in the Cathedral of Otranto,[5] among figures of animals we find groups of human figures, one representing Alexander's ascent in the gryphon-car[6] (cf. Fig. 34). Other pavements, now destroyed or mutilated, show that the South was as rich in work of this kind as the Lombard plain. They once decorated churches at Tarento,[7] Lecce,[8] Trani,[9] and Brindisi.[10]

The Byzantine mosaics with geometrical designs in which interlacing bands or variegated borders enclose disks ($\ddot{o}\mu\phi\dot{a}\lambda\iota\alpha$) of precious marbles were introduced into Italy by the mosaicists summoned to Monte Cassino by the Abbot Desiderius (see p. 84). The interlacing bands were formed as a rule of cubes of variegated marble, not with cubes of coloured glass,[11] and in the earlier Italian imitations, e. g. the closure panels of the choir of Salerno Cathedral, set up by Archbishop William (A.D. 1137–54), the same procedure was adopted, though the plane was now vertical instead of horizontal.[12] Simple geometrical figures in the same style were also adopted by the Cosmati of Rome,[13] who remained faithful to the designs of the pavements without introducing the more intricate motives suggestive of intarsia in wood and ivory. The new style superseded the carved slabs in low relief (p. 165), and sometimes, as in Sta Maria in Cosmedin, the encrusted ornament covers the back of a carved slab which has been reversed in order to receive it.

In the last third of the twelfth century the marble ambos, paschal candelabra, and closure-slabs of the Campanian churches and cathedrals were decorated with mosaic encrustations in which cubes of coloured and gilded glass were profusely used. The designs are purely geometrical and consist of interlacing bands, of which those occupying large panels are usually circular in contour after the Byzantine manner, while those of the borders and friezes form broken and angular lines with sequences of polygons and stars after the Mohammedan fashion.

[1] U. de Gheltof in Ongania's *Basilica di San Marco*, Pt. II, folio, No. 5.

[2] Ibid., Nos. 6 and 9. Somewhat similar treatment of animals in remains of the choir-pavement in the Cathedral of St. Nicholas at Bari (Bertaux, 486).

[3] Ch. Diehl, *L'Art dans l'Italie méridionale*, 195–7 and Fig. ; E. Bertaux, as above, 484 ff.

[4] Bertaux, 487.

[5] Schulz, i. 261–7. The mosaic is signed by a priest Pantaleon, and was executed between A.D. 1163 and 1166.

[6] For these mosaics see E. Müntz. *Rev. arch.*, xxxii–xxxiii, as above.

[7] E. Aar. *Gli studi storici in Terra d'Otranto*, Florence, 1888, 124.

[8] Ibid., 125.   [9] Sarlo, *Il Duomo di Trani*, 10, No. 2.

[10] Schulz, as above, 303–6 ; Bertaux, 492 ff. Drawings taken by Millin in 1812 are in the Cabinet des Estampes, Paris (G. b. 63).

[11] Transennae now in the walls of S. Marco at Venice, and believed to have come from Constantinople, have geometric designs reserved in the marble on a background of cubes of glass as well as of marble (Boito in Ongania's *Basilica di San Marco*, Plates ; and Bertaux, p. 497).   [12] Bertaux, as above, 503.

[13] M. Bertaux believes that the style of encrustation which we know as Cosmati work was

This combination was introduced into Italy from Palermo, where it had resulted from the contact of Moslem and Byzantine art. Fine early examples are at Salerno and Ravello.

Among the most remarkable secular mosaic pavements, now lost, were those on the floor of the sleeping-chamber of Basil I in the part of the imperial palace

FIG. 252. Mosaic and marble covering of the walls in the Church of St. Luke in Phocis : eleventh century. From a drawing by R. W. Schultz, Esq. (N. H. J. Westlake : *History of Design in Mural Painting*.)

known as the Kenourgion, described by Constantine Porphyrogenitus in his life of that emperor. In the centre was a peacock within a circle of Carian marble ; in the spandrels were four eagles, and the ground seemed to 'flow with streams' of the green marble of Thessaly.[1]

The covering of the lower part of church walls with a casing of different coloured marbles was general in the East ;[2] proofs of its extensive use remain at Constantinople and in Greece ;[3] it was adopted in those parts of Italy influenced

introduced into Rome from Campania and not into Campania from Rome. For the Cosmati see also G. Clausse, *Les Marbriers romains*, and A. L. Frothingham in *Journ. American Arch.*, x, pp. 189 ff., 1895.

[1] The passage is quoted by Labarte, *Le Palais impérial de Constantinople*, p. 79. Cf. J. P. Richter, *Quellen der byz. Kunstgeschichte*, 364.

[2] Eusebius mentions it in the case of the Martyrium at Jerusalem (iii. 36).

[3] Sta Sophia (cf. Fig. 3) ; Kahrié Djami, Mosque of the Calenders. The new church of

from the East, especially in Palermo, Ravenna, and Parenzo.[1] In the latter place we have good examples of wall revetment inlaid with designs in stones of various colours (Figs. 207, 253).

Fig. 253.   Ornament in inlaid marbles of the sixth century : S. Vitale, Ravenna.   (Ricci.)

MINIATURE MOSAICS.[2]

It has been already noticed (p. 328) that the *emblemata* of Roman mosaics were separately made, often at a distance from the place where they were finally to be used.   Sometimes, but rarely, they were carried from place to place : Suetonius says that Caesar took pavements with him upon his campaigns.   But about the twelfth century, if we may judge from surviving monuments, it became the fashion in Constantinople to have small pictures in mosaic for devotional use.   M. Kondakoff has explained that they were venerated upon the days of

Basil I was sumptuously decorated in this style.   In Greece the most perfect example is St. Luke in Phocis (Fig. 252).   Daphni was also thus covered with marble, and so was Nea Moni on Chios.

[1] F. Hamilton Jackson, *The Shores of the Adriatic*, ii, p. 114 ; C. Errard and A. Gayet, *L'Art byzantin*, Pt. III, Pl. X ff. ; de Beylié, *L'Habitation byzantine*, Pl. I ; C. Diehl, *Justinien*, p. 576 and Pl. VII.   The materials are green and red porphyry, dull red marble, greenish marble, stones of purple, yellowish green, and blue, and inlays of vitreous paste (Jackson, p. 114). A fragment of later date, with interlacing broken lines, is in the Campo Santo at Pisa (E. Bertaux, *L'Art dans l'Italie méridionale*, i, Fig. 220, p. 498).

[2] E. Müntz, *Les Mosaïques byzantines portatives* in *Bulletin monumental*, Caen, 1886, 223 ff. ; Labarte, *Histoire*, 2nd ed., ii. 352 ; Diehl, *Manuel*, 530.   There were no less than twenty-five of these mosaics in the collection of Paul II (Müntz, *Les Arts à la Cour des Papes*, ii, pp. 143, 203).

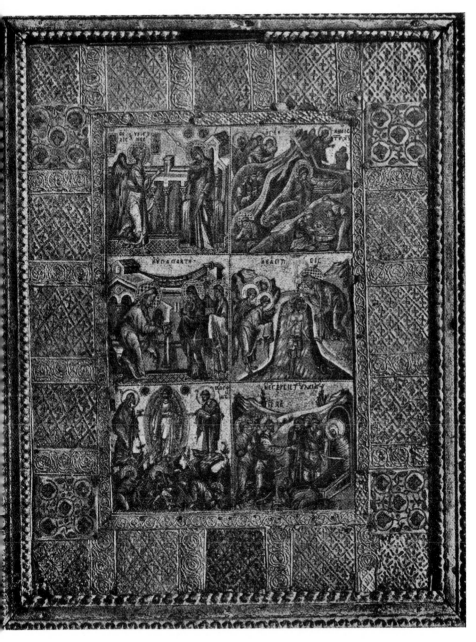

Fig. 254. Portable mosaic of the thirteenth century in the Museum of Sta Maria del Fiore, Florence. (Alinari.) P. 432.

the saints depicted: they are mentioned by Constantine Porphyrogenitus among the most precious objects in the imperial throne room.

The base of these mosaics is of wax, in which very small cubes or cut strips of glass, stone, and metal are fixed. So fine is the work, especially in the faces of human figures, that in some cases it is almost impossible to see the points of contact, while the effect is heightened by the use of gold and silver for high lights, or to accentuate the principal divisions.

The number of portable pictures in mosaic now surviving is small. The following list is based upon that of Müntz, but includes a few additional examples.

ITALY.

Rome. Vatican Library: St. Theodore, thirteenth to fourteenth century.[1]
Borghese Palace: The Virgin and the Apostles, perhaps fourteenth century.[2]
There was a portable mosaic, with a figure of Our Lord, in the Church of St. Praxed as late as the sixteenth century; twenty formerly belonged to Cardinal Pietro Barbo (Paul II); others were bequeathed by Cardinal Bessarion (d. 1472) to the Basilica of St. Peter.[3]

Florence. In the Museo di Santa Maria del Fiore are two mosaic pictures of extraordinarily minute workmanship (Fig. 254). The ground is formed of microscopic golden *tesserae*: the subjects are the Feasts of the Church, and the date is perhaps the thirteenth century.[4] The collections of the Medici family, dispersed at the revolution of 1494, contained several examples, mentioned in the inventory of Lorenzo the Magnificent.[5]

Venice. The treasury of S. Marco contains a picture representing St. John the Baptist.[6] Another mosaic, in the Church of Sta Maria della Salute, represents the Virgin and Child.[7]

At *Sassoferrato* there is a picture of St. Demetrius.[8]

FRANCE.

Paris. The Louvre has a picture with the Transfiguration[9] and a circular medallion with St. George slaying the dragon.[0] St. George is mounted, and rides to right, transfixing the dragon with his lance: the cubes of the mosaic are of marble, glass, and silver. The date is probably the thirteenth century.

ENGLAND. In the Victoria and Albert Museum is a fine mosaic with the Annunciation,[11] with Greek inscriptions. The ground is of gold *tesserae* fixed in wax, and the same metal is used to delineate the architecture and other features. Silver is employed to give richness and variety to the ornament, while lapis, verde antico (?), and rosso antico unite with glass cubes to enhance the effect.

BELGIUM. A small mosaic picture with a bust of Christ is in the Church of SS. Peter and Paul at Chimay.[12]

---

[1] Barbier de Montault, *La Bibliothèque Vaticane*, 122; A. Muñoz, *L'Art byzantin à l'exposition de Grottaferrata*, Rome, 1906, 169–70, and Fig. 136.

[2] Barbier de Montault, in *Revue de l'art chrétien*, xviii, 1874, 152.

[3] Müntz, as above, 229–33.

[4] Alinari, photos; Gori, *Thesaurus diptychorum*, iii. 320 ff. and Pl. I and II; Müntz, 233; F. X. Kraus, *Zeitschrift für christliche Kunst*, iv, 1891, Pl. VIII; Bayet, *L'Art byzantin*, 150; Rumohr, *Italienische Forschungen*, i. 304–6.

[5] Müntz, 234.

[6] Durand in *Annales archéologiques*, xxi. 102–3; E. Molinier, *Gazette des Beaux-Arts*, Second Period, xxxvii, 1888, 391, and *Le Trésor de Saint-Marc*.

[7] Durand, as above.

[8] *Byzantinische Zeitschrift*, ix, 1901, p. 718. Described by Professor Savignoni at the Second Congress of Christian Archaeology, Rome, 1900.

[9] Labarte, *Histoire des arts*, &c., 1st ed., Pl. 120; Schlumberger, *L'Épopée*, iii, p. 449.

[10] Müntz, as above, Plate opposite p. 225; Courajod and Molinier, *Donation du Baron Davillier*, No. 274, Paris, 1885; *Gazette des Beaux-Arts*, 2nd series, vol. xxviii, 1883, 205; G. Schlumberger, *Nicéphore Phocas*, p. 415.

[11] *Gazette des Beaux-Arts*, 1859, i. 157 (A. Darcel). This mosaic was acquired in 1859.

[12] W. H. J. Weale and J. Maes, *Instrumenta ecclesiastica, Choix d'objets d'art etc. exposés à Malines*, 1864, Pl. IV, No. 54, Brussels, 1866.

GERMANY. The Abbey of Burtscheid possesses a mosaic with a figure of St. Nicholas of Myra in episcopal vestments.[1] The picture in the Monastery of the Holy Cross at Donauwörth is considered by Durand to have been enamel.[2]

RUSSIA. In the Basilewsky Collection at the Hermitage Museum, St. Petersburg, is a picture with Samuel, above whom is seen the hand of the Almighty. The same museum has a half-figure of a military Saint (Schlumberger, *L'Épopée*, i, p. 309).

FIG. 255. St. Anne and the Virgin : portable mosaic of the eleventh or twelfth century, Monastery of Vatopedi, Mount Athos. (*Hautes Études* : G. Millet.)

Another example in the same collection represents St. Theodore Stratelates, half-figure, standing armed with shield and lance.[3] In the museum at Kieff is a St. Nicholas.[4]

Mount Athos. In the Monastery of Vatopedi there are a Crucifixion between the Virgin and St. John,[5] a half-figure of St. John Chrysostom,[6] and a standing figure of St. Anne (Fig. 255) with the Virgin.[7] At Esphigmenou there is a full-length figure of Our Lord (Fig. 256),[8] at Chilandari a Virgin and Child.[9]

---

[1] Bock, *Die Reliquienschätze der ehemaligen gefürsteten Reichsabteien Burtscheid*, &c., Cologne, 1867, 16–17 ; Schlumberger, *L'Épopée*, ii, Fig. on p. 121.   [2] *Ann. arch.*, xxi. 103.

[3] A. Darcel, *La Collection Basilewsky*, 25 ; Schlumberger, *L'Épopée*, i, Fig. on p. 309.

[4] Likacheff, *Materials for the History of Russian Painting*, i, Pl. III, 4.

[5] Kondakoff, *Monuments of Christian Art on Mount Athos*, Pl. XIII ; Didron, *Annales archéologiques*, xxvii, 261–3, and xxi. 176.

[6] Kondakoff, as above, Pl. XVI.   [7] Ibid., Pl. XII.

[8] Ibid., Pl. XI.   [9] Ibid., Pl. XV.

An ikon of St. Nicholas, of which only the head is visible, in mosaic, is in the Church of Stavro-Nikita.[1]

The picture representing St. John Chrysostom, formerly in the Monastery of Vatopedi, is now in the collection of M. de Nelidoff.[2] It is of the twelfth century.

SPAIN. In the Episcopal Library at Vich in Catalonia there was formerly a portable mosaic representing St. Nicholas, which has now been stolen.[3] It is attributed to the thirteenth century.

FIG. 256. Our Lord : portable mosaic of the eleventh or twelfth century in the Monastery of Esphigmenou, Mount Athos. (*Hautes Études* : G. Millet.)

The style of these works should be compared with that of contemporary panel ikons and miniatures ; but the medium of mosaic is not adapted to work on this diminutive scale, and the result is seldom quite successful. The finest examples are said to be the St. Nicholas at Stavro-Nikita, the Crucifixion of Vatopedi, and the panels at Florence.

[1] Kondakoff, as above, Pl. XIV.
[2] Ibid., Pl. XVI ; Ainaloff in *V. V.*, vi, 1899, 75 ff. and Pl. XI ; A. Muñoz, *L'Art byzantin à l'exposition de Grottaferrata*, Rome, 1906, p. 170 and Pl. III.
[3] E. Roulin, *Monuments Piot*, 1900, 95 and Pl. XI ; Kondakoff, Fig. 50, p. 108 ; A. Muñoz in *B. Z.*, 1905, 575, and *L'Art byzantin*, &c., Fig. on p. 178.

ΕΙϹΤΗΝΓΕΝΕΘΛΙΟΝΗΜΕΡΑΝΤΚΥΗΜΙΥΧΥ

FIG. 257. The Nativity : head-piece from the twelfth-century Homilies of Gregory of
Nazianzus in the monastery on Mount Sinai. (*Hautes Études* : N. Kondakoff.)

CHAPTER VII

PAINTING : III. ILLUMINATED MANUSCRIPTS[1]

THE great series of illustrated manuscripts ranging over a period of about
a thousand years offers for comparative study a material more accessible than
that at our disposal in the case of any other branch of Byzantine art.

The remarks which were made at the beginning of this section apply
to the miniature no less than to other forms of painting : there is
a certain uniformity of treatment, a permanence of tradition which at
times appears monotonous ; the main causes are the same : fidelity to
early models, obedience to ecclesiastical rule. In mediaeval Europe, from

---

[1] General surveys of Byzantine illuminated MSS. will be found in N. P. Kondakoff's *Histoire
de l'art byzantin*, in G. Millet's chapters in A. Michel's *Histoire de l'art*, and Ch. Diehl's *Manuel*,
Bk. II, ch. iv, III, ch. vii, and IV, ch. iv. Two chapters in J. A. Herbert's forthcoming volume
on Illuminated Manuscripts (in Methuen's Connoisseur's Library) will deal comprehensively
with the subject.

Italy to England, there were at least five well-marked changes within the space of a single millennium. To the art of the Christian Celts and the Merovingian Franks succeeded that of the Carolingian Renaissance. There followed the German style of the Ottonian period, and the Anglo-Saxon art of Southern England. Next came the Romanesque in all its varieties, and finally the fully developed Gothic itself with its various subdivisions. Every one of these changes brought with it some modification in sentiment, in colour, in iconography, in technique. Even if we leave on one side the highly original art of the Celts and the vigorous outline-drawings of the Anglo-Saxons, we still find illustrated MSS. separated by comparatively short periods of time, but infinitely remote in the scheme of their colour and in the style of their ornamentation. An illuminated book of the eleventh century, with its hard greens and reds and its almost total neglect of gilding, creates a very different impression from a book of the thirteenth century, with its rich gilding and its sumptuous blues and crimsons. Nor do the changes affect practice only : they extend to the sphere of sentiment as well. The accepted type of the Virgin with the Child about the year A. D. 1300 is far removed from that which prevailed only two hundred years earlier : a new feeling modified the old austere conception of the divine. The change of manners and social institutions was more rapid among the Western peoples, with their divergent national temperament and their numerous centres of art and industry, than it was in the Eastern Empire, especially after the loss of Syria and Egypt. And the Roman Catholic Church never exerted so rigid a control over the individuality of the artist as the Orthodox Church of the East.

In the Eastern Empire, after the First Period, the divergence between localities or epochs is seldom so pronounced. A Byzantine MS. of the fourteenth century may differ in power and quality from a book dating from the tenth; but the two will be nearer to each other in spirit than Western MSS. of the same two periods. In the latter case each illuminator obeys one law; and though the interpretation may not be the same, the identity of the law is at once discerned. As with feeling and conception, so it is with technique and with schemes of colour. If not invariable, they suffer no violent or radical alterations. There are fewer breaks in continuity, fewer losses of technical knowledge, fewer bold experiments in harmony or composition. In no part of the empire, and in no country within the radius of its artistic influence, could we imagine the rise of so original an art as that of the Anglo-Saxons.

As far as figure-art is concerned, this unity of Byzantine illumination arises from a faithful adherence to Hellenistic tradition. Whenever there was a revival in Byzantine art the antique model emerged into greater prominence; even if a Syrian influence is apparent, it must be remembered that Christian Syria itself drew largely from the Hellenistic source. In the time of Basil I and his immediate successors such a dependence surprises us little : it appears natural that the fine copy of the

Homilies of Gregory of Nazianzus in the Bibliothèque Nationale, with its personifications, its classical architecture, its pastoral landscapes, should reproduce in a later age the picturesque sentiment of ancient Alexandria; it was this very age which preserved for us the greater number of our classical Greek texts. In the general progress of the empire between the ninth and twelfth centuries, the arts were cultivated with renewed vigour; the number of antique models preserved in Constantinople and in the monasteries must still have been very large; the distance in point

Fig. 258. Paul on the road to Damascus: miniature of the seventh century in the Vatican MS. of Cosmas Indicopleustes. (*Hautes Études*: G. Millet.) P. 447.

of time between the fourth and the ninth centuries was still not wide enough to prevent the maintenance in a conservative society of an almost consecrated tradition. But when we find classical features reproduced in books illustrated half a millennium later, we recognize a loyalty which would commend itself to the religious artists of the Buddhist East. An example of this late period may be quoted from a MS. in Paris, which shows us the two poets Dosiades and Theocritus making offerings to Apollo and Pan, both gods being of a purely Hellenistic type.[1] The illuminators

---

[1] H. Omont in *Monuments Piot*, xii, 1905. Another interesting example of such survival is a medical MS. of the ninth or tenth century in the Laurentian Library at Florence. It is a Hippocrates Περὶ ἄρθρων. with commentary by Apollonius of Citium, and contains nude figures recalling those of the Calendar of Filocalus (J. Ebersolt, *Rev. arch.*, 1905, 68). Cf. also the MSS. of the Cynegetica of Oppian (Marciana 479, tenth century, Bibl. Nat., Paris, fifteenth century), and the eleventh-century Paris Nicander.

of Western Europe in the fourteenth century had emancipated themselves from many old traditions and developed a style of their own : they looked forward or around them, not backward ; conventional though it was, their art was a more complete expression of contemporary life. Where the treatment of the human figure is less immediately concerned, the fidelity is the same, but the sources are different. The Early Christian art of Syria and Mesopotamia, which had grafted upon ideal Hellenic types its own more realistic sentiment, found imitators equally obsequious. It had been

FIG. 259.   Solomon and David, the Baptism, Nativity, &c. : page from the Syriac Gospel of Rabula, A.D. 586, in the Laurentian Library, Florence. (*Hautes Études* : A. Venturi.) P. 448.

no less predominant in the monasteries than the Hellenistic style at the court; and since monasticism outlasted the empire, its influence survived the fall of Constantinople. A striking example of this long persistence is a late Servian Psalter at Munich;[1] the earlier Armenian Gospel of A.D. 902 in the Lagoon Monastery at Venice shows it no less clearly.[2]

It need not be supposed that this loyalty to tradition was inconsistent

[1] See p. 473. Both Strzygowski and Millet agree on the antique influence, though they differ as to the channels by which it reached Servia. Millet considers that it may have passed through Constantinople ; Strzygowski, that it issued in the last resort from Mount Athos, a great centre of Syrian tradition.

[2] In the Gospels of Mlke, Queen of Armenia (early tenth century). The canons are in the style of those in the Gospel of Rabula and its congeners. The miniatures with the Ascension and the Evangelists betray similar influences (P. Alishan, *Die Miniaturen des Evangeliars der Königin Mlke*, Venice, S. Lazzaro, 1902).

with a lively appreciation of the realities of life. A feeling for the expressive, for the characteristic, maintained its place by the side of the feeling for inherited types and repeatedly manifested its power in the history of Byzantine art. Realism was always latent, and sometimes hardly less free and animated in expression than that of Carolingian and Anglo-Saxon illumination. Even in mosaics, where the artist conforms more strictly to the

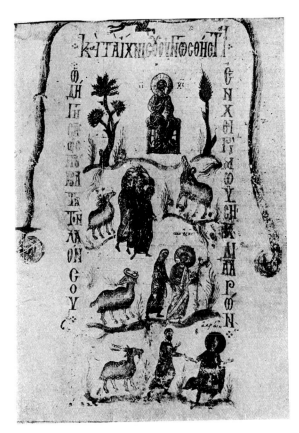

FIG. 260. Illumination from the Psalter of A. D. 1066 in the British Museum.
(Add. MS. 19351.) P. 470.

requirements of an ordered scheme, we see the portrait at times emerge from the impersonal type. The heads of Justinian and Archbishop Maximianus at Ravenna will at once recur to the memory in this connexion (Fig. 5). But the same character is found in the ascetic saints of St. Luke in Phocis, which are of the eleventh century; while two hundred years later, at Kahrié Djami, the scenes pass in an atmosphere of actual life. It is the same with frescoes, where again the real and individual takes its place by the side of the typical and ideal. The paintings on the staircase at Kieff (p. 301) show that the genre scene might be introduced even within the precincts of a cathedral; and if we had preserved to us many frescoes from palaces or private dwellings we should doubtless find a far fuller expression of the realistic spirit. But in MSS. there was a wider scope for such freedom : the illuminator was less constrained, and stood in a more personal and intimate relation to the spectator ; his work was less in the public eye, less bound by the proprieties of iconographical convention. Then, too, the book had margins and head-pieces, and pages for Eusebian Canons, where floral and animal ornament, or little scenes from the chase, agriculture, or war could be introduced without offence. Thus illumination affords a deeper insight into life under the Eastern Empire than any other branch of art. The more rapid technique and the comparative abundance of space in a book of many leaves permitted the illuminator to indulge his fancy, where the worker in ivory or metal remained faithful to a traditional type, or owed his apparent originality to direct imitation of a manuscript. It was the illuminator who multiplied subjects and invented varieties of composition : the other minor arts looked to him for guidance. There were other causes which increased the illuminators' influence. Throughout the whole duration of the empire they enjoyed the patronage of the imperial house, and of the noble and wealthy classes. At quite an early period it was the fashion for ladies to possess finely illuminated volumes; we may compare the Books of Hours of the Western Middle Ages.[1] Juliana Anicia, daughter of Galla Placidia, for whom the Vienna Dioscorides (see below, p. 460) was painted, is represented receiving an illuminated codex of the same work from a personification of *Phronesis*, it being the evident intention of the painter to illustrate her patronage of his branch of art.[2]

The earliest form of illustrated book was a long scroll or roll of papyrus, for the home of the art of illuminating was ancient Egypt. At first such scrolls were of a strictly religious character ; but in Ptolemaic times literary and scientific works were enriched with a pictured commentary. Alexandria, the seat of Hellenistic culture in Egypt, gave the world the earliest illuminated manuscripts; the Alexandrian artists who migrated to the new imperial metropolis in the north must have included illuminators among their company, and at an even earlier date such artists were probably established at Antioch and in the other Hellenistic cities of the Mediterranean. Two streams of influence appear to have converged to produce the illuminated book of the Middle Ages.[3] The first was that of the painter upon papyrus, the material upon which the earliest illuminations of the Christian era are executed. The illustrator confines himself to the elucidation of the text without apparent care for the artistic quality of his work. As in the papyri of pagan Egypt, the figures are set in lines like parts of a diagram ; there is no indication of depth or of light and shade to suggest solidity ; the only ornamental decoration consists of plant forms used as divisions : we have before us merely a primitive kind of coloured drawing. From the Egyptian papyrus scroll developed the scroll illustrated by Hellenistic

---

[1] St. Jerome fulminated against this kind of extravagance (E. Preuschen, *Zeitschrift für Neu-Testamentliche Wissenschaft*, iii, 1902, 253 ff. ; Krauss, *Geschichte*, i. 447).

[2] A. von Premerstein in Austrian *Jahrbuch*, xxiv, 1903, 106 and 123.

[3] See Strzygowski in *Denkschriften der k. Akad. der Wissenschaften*, Vienna, 1905, li. 169 ff.

artists, whose methods are represented by the Joshua Rotulus in the Vatican, perhaps an exact copy of a scroll dating from about A. D. 300 (see p. 447).

Perhaps in the fourth century, perhaps even earlier,[1] the Hellenistic scroll based upon Egyptian prototypes found a rival in the *codex* or paged book of vellum, the home of which may with probability be sought in Mesopotamia.[2] In these books appear formal compositions surrounded by borders and possess

FIG. 261. The Crucifixion : miniature from a twelfth-century Gospel in the British Museum.
(Harley 1810.)

ing as it were an individual existence : the scheme of colour is also more comprehensive, for instead of the prevailing red and yellow of Egypt, we find purples and blues with enrichment of gilding. Illustration is granted the right to a position more independent of the accompanying text; for the first time one might conceive a man buying a book as much for the pictures which it contained as for the written matter. There is now a deliberate effort to beautify the page ; ornament as ornament is recognized as a worthy adjunct to the book. The earliest pictures painted in books were probably portraits of the authors: Martial alludes to one in a MS. of Virgil.[3] The oldest surviving example appears to be that in the Vienna Dioscorides (see p. 460), painted about the year A. D. 512 ;[4] and the fashion was almost

---

[1] St. Jerome alludes to parchment as a substitute when papyrus could not be obtained.
[2] Strzygowski, *Denkschriften*, as above, p. 169.   [3] xiv. 186.
[4] Vienna *Jahrbuch*, xxiv, 1903, 124. The type, which also occurs on a sarcophagus from Konia, may be of Anatolian origin (J. Strzygowski, *B. D.*, 39 ff. ; *Orient oder Rom*, 47).

at once adopted in illustrated Gospels, in which each Evangelist is seen at the beginning of his Gospel, usually writing at a desk.[1]

The Asiatic ornamental system rapidly prevailed, and was adopted by the monkish artists, to whom the earliest art of illumination owed so much. In this style the monk Rabula illuminated the Gospels known by his name at Zagba in Mesopotamia in the year A.D. 586 (see p. 448). Probably he copied an earlier book of the fifth, or even of the fourth century, perhaps nearly contemporary with the Calendar of Filocalus (see p. 484). The combination of Greek and oriental sentiment which marks all East-Christian art is manifested in the illustration of these early parchment books: in Rabula's work oriental affinities are evident. But in the Vienna Dioscorides Hellenistic feeling predominates, and in the fine books of the eleventh century, executed for imperial or noble personages, an influence almost purely Hellenistic is apparent.

The illustrated codex may have first become familiar to Europe through Cassiodorus, in whose Monastery of Vivarium near Squillace the transcription of MSS. was a regular occupation. There is nothing improbable in the supposition that he maintained relations with the scholars of Edessa and Nisibis,[2] who were masters of the art which he desired to introduce into Italy.

The miniatures of Byzantine illuminated books painted on vellum are in colours mixed with gum or size. But the priming is usually inferior to that of contemporary Western manuscripts. While a French, English, or German book of the thirteenth century will often have preserved its miniatures in a comparatively perfect condition, even when the thumbed corners of the pages testify to continuous use, a Byzantine book of the same age will almost certainly be much abraded. The inferiority is even more marked in the case of the gilding. The Western book will frequently present a wealth of gilded surface, highly burnished, and as brilliant now as on the day when it was first applied. The Eastern manuscript seldom approaches this perfection.

It is perhaps unsafe to generalize about the methods employed by illuminators within the wide limits of the Eastern Empire; but in several cases the abrasion of the surface colour has enabled us to follow the procedure of the artist with some certainty, and it is probable that the methods thus observed were of general application.[3] Several pages of a Gospel in the Library at St. Petersburg (No. 21), held by some to be of the ninth century, pages in the Paris Psalter of the tenth century (MS. gr. 201), in the twelfth-century Gospel in the same collection (No. 54), in another Gospel of the same period in the Royal Library at Berlin (No. 66),

---

[1] B. D., iii. 38 ff.   [2] Strzygowski in *Jahrb. für klassisches Alterthum*, xv, 1905, 29.
[3] See Ch. Diehl, *Notice sur deux mss. à miniatures de la Bibliothèque de l'Université de Messine*, *Mélanges d'arch. et d'histoire*, viii, 1888, 321 ff., and *L'Art dans l'Italie méridionale*, ch. viii; J. Tikkanen in *Acta societatis scientiarum Fennicae*, xix, No. 2, Helsingfors, 1890; *Eine illustrierte Klimax-Handschrift*, &c.; N. Pokrovsky, *The Gospel in the Monuments*, &c., 228; E. Dobbert, *B. Z.*, v, 1896, 595.

and in the Psalter of A. D. 1066. in the British Museum, all betray the use of the same method, which appears to have been as follows. The composition was first sketched in with a fine brush or pen, commonly, but not always, in a shade of brown; gold backgrounds were also perhaps applied at an early

FIG. 262.   Our Lord crowning John and Alexius Comnenus: miniature in a Gospel of A. D. 1128 in the Vatican. (*Hautes Études*: G. Millet.)

stage. This preliminary outline was often very carefully done, and the expression of features was rendered with the greatest care. The surface colours were often applied in thin coats so that at first the details of the drawing were visible beneath them. The effect at such an intermediate stage is often remarkable, the drawing lending the contrast of light and shade, so that occasionally the loss of later and denser coats of colour positively improves the effect of the design. But in a Byzantine illumination which has suffered but little from use or from time, all the substructure is hidden beneath masses of rich colour, thrown into relief by the general use of gold-leaf for the backgrounds. Sometimes the accidental removal of surface colours betrays an alteration in the design, the artist having modified the original conception in this or that detail. Thus the abrasion in a Crucifixion miniature in the Paris MS. of the Homilies of Gregory of Nazianzus reveals the fact that the crucified figure was intended to have a short loin-cloth, whereas the finished picture showed a far longer garment.

Byzantine MSS. fall into the two main groups of religious and secular. The former has been conveniently subdivided by M. Millet into six classes : (*a*) Early books of the Old Testament and complete Octateuchs ; (*b*) Psalters ; (*c*) The Prophets ; (*d*) The Gospels ; (*e*) Theological works, editions of the Fathers ; (*f*) Menologies, Church Calendars. The second group is composed of books wholly or partly scientific, such as the medical works of Dioscorides and the Topography of Cosmas Indicopleustes.

FIRST AND SECOND PERIODS

I. Religious Manuscripts.

The important early MS. of the first book of the Bible, commonly known, from the place where it is preserved, as the Vienna Genesis,[1] is closely allied to the Codex Rossanensis and the Sinope fragment (pp. 452, 458), but earlier than either. As later Byzantine miniatures illustrating Genesis are evidently based upon different compositions, it seems probable that this manuscript dates from a time before the general acceptance of a common illustrative cycle. The Octateuchs had a model akin to the Joshua Rotulus (p. 447), and differing in important respects from the Vienna book ; the models in all cases must have been scrolls. Pages have been lost at the beginning and the end, but twenty-four with forty-eight miniatures remain. The text is written in silver letters upon purple vellum. It occupies the upper part of each page, the miniatures being at the bottom in every case. There is no marginal ornament. The colours are white, green, lapis-blue, reddish purple, violet, iron-red, and black. Gold is occasionally used but never polished.

The illustration of the book is the work of several hands.[2] The earlier part of what remains (mins. 1–20 and 21–32) is the work of two different illuminators and their pupils. The first is a literal interpreter of the text, who as a rule leaves the purple page to serve as background for his figures and accessories : his trees are conventional, his environment is suggested by abbreviated features, a segment of a blue circle indicating the sky, a few columns and an architrave a room : atmospheric and perspective effects are rarely attempted. The colours are decided, and black lines are freely used to define contours. Eleven of the pictures appear to be by this illustrator

---

[1] Freiherr von Hartel and F. Wickhoff, *Die Wiener Genesis*, Vienna, 1895 (Beilage to vols. xv–xvi of the Austrian *Jahrbuch*) ; W. Lüdtke, *Untersuchungen zu den Miniaturen der Wiener Genesis*, Greifswald, 1897 ; Kondakoff, *Histoire de l'art byz.*, i. 120 ; D. Ainaloff, *Hellenistic Origins*, &c., 41–2 ; J. Strzygowski, *B. D.*, iii. 68. An early publication of the text was that of R. Holmes, *Epistula complexa Genesim ex codice purpureo argenteo*, &c., Oxford, 1845. Early reproductions of the miniatures are to be found in Lambecius, *Commentarium de augustissima bibliotheca Caesarea Vindobonensi*, Vienna, 1665–79 ; de Nessel, *Breviarium et supplementum Comment. Lambeciani*, &c., Vienna, 1690 ; Kollar, *Commentarii de aug. bibl. Caesarea Vindobonensi*, Vienna, 1766–82. The manuscript is frequently mentioned by the commentators of the Codex Rossanensis (which see). It probably came to Vienna in the second half of the seventeenth century with the Fugger Collection. Fugger may have bought it in Italy (Lambecius, *Commentarium*, as above, 1670, vol. iii).

[2] Wickhoff, as above, 144 and 162 ff.

himself and four designed by him ; four others follow his technical methods, but appear to be inspired by another artist. As a rule each composition is disposed in two zones, one above the other, and the ' continuous' method of narration is adopted.

The second artist also allows the purple page to serve as background, and treats accessories, such as trees, conventionally ; but he is a finer colourist and far more inventive in composition, filling his work with minor episodes and situations unsuggested by the text. He avoids the hard juxtaposition of colours, understands gradation of tone, and paints flesh well.

The remaining pages are the work of three different painters who have more in common with fresco-painters than illuminators, working in a broad impressionist style very different from the minute and finished manner of artists already described.

The subjects depicted are as follows:—
The Fall ; the Expulsion from Eden ; the Flood ; Noah's issue from the ark, and his sacrifice ; God's covenant with Noah ; the Drunkenness of Noah ; Abraham and Melchizedek ; Abraham receives God's promise ; Lot's flight from Sodom ; Intoxication of Lot ; Abraham's return from the attempted sacrifice of Isaac ; Abraham's servant journeys to Mesopotamia ; Rebecca at the well ; the Servant makes gifts to Rebecca ; Esau sells his birthright ; Isaac and Abimelech ; Jacob demands the pied sheep ; the peeled rods ; Laban overtakes Jacob ; Laban searches the tents ; Jacob awaits Esau ; Jacob sends his herds to Esau ; Jacob takes his company across the water, and wrestles with the angel ; God blesses Jacob ; Jacob at Bethel ; burial of the gods of the heathen ; Death of Deborah ; Death and burial of Rachel ; Death and burial of Isaac ; Jacob gives Joseph the coat of many colours ; Joseph's dream ; Joseph's second dream ; the Grazing of the herds in Sichem ; Joseph is sent to his brethren in Sichem ; Joseph and Potiphar's wife ; Joseph falsely accused ; Joseph in prison ; Pharaoh's banquet ; Pharaoh's dream ; Joseph

Fig. 263. Fragment from the Cotton Bible (British Museum, Otho B. VI). P. 446.

interprets the dream ; Joseph recognizes his brethren ; the Return of Joseph's brethren ; the Emptying of the sacks ; Reuben asks permission to take Benjamin to Egypt ; Judah asks for Benjamin ; Jacob permits the departure of Benjamin ; Return of the brethren to Egypt ; the Brethren speak with Joseph's steward ; Jacob blesses Ephraim and Manasseh ; Jacob summons his sons to bless them ; Jacob charges his sons ; Death and burial of Jacob.

The Cotton Bible [1] in the British Museum, almost ruined by the fire in the Cotton Library in A.D. 1731, originally possessed two hundred and fifty

miniatures. Only a hundred and fifty fragments illustrating the Book of Genesis remain, and the majority are so damaged as to be valueless from an artistic point of view. In the general treatment analogies may be traced with the Vienna Genesis, though some would place the date earlier than the sixth century. Probably, in this case also, the illustration is based on earlier work in the form of a scroll. The pictures are sometimes placed two on a page.

The backgrounds are coloured, generally blue, recalling in this those of the earlier mosaics, though they are of a lighter shade. Outlines are heavily drawn; the gestures are natural, and the faces often expressive. The draperies are well executed, but we note that the angel in the Expulsion from Eden has a mantle picked out with parallel gold lines resembling the cloisons of enamel, a feature of frequent occurrence in later miniatures and panel paintings. An interesting feature in connexion with the Cotton Bible is the fact that it, or another book from the same model, was evidently copied by the mosaicists who executed the mosaics in the vestibule of S. Marco at Venice (p. 400).

FIG. 264. Hagar: fragment from the Cotton Bible (British Museum, Otho B. VI).

[1] Cotton MS., Otho B. VI. Bibliographical references will be found in the British Museum Catalogue of Ancient MSS., Part I, Greek, 1881, 20. On the original fly-leaf, now destroyed, was a statement by Dr. James, Cotton's librarian, to the effect that the MS. was brought by Greek bishops from Philippi and presented to Henry VIII; and that it was afterwards given by Queen Elizabeth to Sir John Fortescue, her tutor in Greek, who in his turn presented it to Sir R. Cotton. Some fragments which came into the possession of Dr. Andrew Gifford have been preserved since his death in A.D. 1784 in the library of the Baptist College at Bristol. Reproductions are to be found in Vetusta Monumenta, i, Pl. LXVII, LXVIII; British Museum Catalogue, as above, Pl. VIII (fol. 26 b and 27 a, Gen. xviii. 13 and xix. 1–3); Westwood, Palaeogr. Sacra Pictoria, Pl. III (fol. 24, Hagar). H. Omont in his Fac-similés des miniatures des plus anciens mss. grecs, Paris, 1902, Pl. I, reproduces two surviving copies, made for Peiresc, illustrating: (1) The Almighty with Cherubim (Gen. iii. 24); (2) God's promise to Abraham. The MS. had been lent to Peiresc through the good offices of Camden, and was kept by him for four years.

The Joshua Rotulus in the Vatican Library [1] (Codex Vat. Palat. Gr. 431) is among the most important MSS. now preserved, although it is usually held to be a copy, dating from the period between the seventh and tenth centuries, of an original perhaps as old as the fifth.[2] Two hands have evidently been at work ; an earlier, which has written the short descriptions under or near the figures ; a later, to which the continuous text is due. The earlier

FIG. 265. Joshua pursuing the Gibeonites : miniature from the Joshua Rotulus in the Vatican. (*Hautes Études* : G. Millet.)

may be of the seventh to the tenth century: the later of the tenth. Most critics believe that the copy is traced over an original which had faded : it belongs to the same period as the earlier of the two hands, while the colour, which is thin and pale, is probably of the same date as the later (Figs. 258, 265).

[1] The MS., formerly a long scroll, was in 1902 divided into sections, each separately mounted. In the thirteenth century it was in Greece ; in A. D. 1571 it belonged to Ulrich Fugger, who bequeathed it to Frederick IV, Elector Palatine ; in A. D. 1623 it was taken with other spoils of war by Maximilian I of Bavaria, who presented it to the Pope. The literature is given in the excellent Vatican edition of A. Muñoz, in which the whole Rotulus is reproduced, some parts in colour (*Il Rotulo di Giosuè . . . riprodotto a cura della Biblioteca Vaticana*, Milan, Hoepli. 1905, p. 7). Earlier discussions of the scroll will be found in *Palaeographical Soc.*, i, Pl. 108 ; d'Agincourt, *Peinture*, Pl. LIII ; Labarte, *Histoire des arts industriels*, iii, 1865, p. 27 : Schnaase, *Geschichte der bildenden Kunst*, iii, 1869, p. 239 ; Garrucci, *Storia dell' arte cristiana*, iii. 97–8 ; Kondakoff, *Hist. de l'art byzantin*, i, p. 95 ; Bayet, *L'Art byzantin*, 72, and *Recherches pour servir*, 68 ; E. Frantz, *Gesch. der christlichen Malerei*, i, 1887, 215 ; H. Graeven in *L'Arte*, i, 1898, 227–8 ; F. X. Kraus, *Gesch. der christlichen Kunst*, i. 453 ; Diehl, *Manuel*, 232.

[2] Opinions as to date are divided. Kondakoff ascribes the MS. to the fifth or sixth century, and in this he is followed by Diehl. But there seem to be indications that the work is that of a copyist who has not in all cases fully reproduced his original. It is perhaps more probable that a copy so intelligent and full of life should have been made in the ninth or tenth century, when iconoclasm had given a new impetus to the study of ancient art, than at an earlier period. The frequent resemblances between figures in this or a similar MS. and those on ivory caskets of about the ninth–tenth centuries are rather in favour of this view. But if it can be shown that the earlier of the two hands is of the seventh or eighth century, the earlier time must be adopted.

The original MS. was the work of a Greek artist who probably worked in Alexandria. Details such as the *furcae* in which the King of Ai and the Amorites are hanged, and the type of seat (δίφρος) on which Joshua sits, find parallels in the Vienna Genesis, and in monuments such as an ivory *pyxis* in the British Museum (p. 209), and in a wood carving in Berlin (p. 149). The *furca* replaced the cross in the last years of Constantine's reign.

The Rotulus represents the Hellenic tradition in Byzantine miniature art, and the resemblances in points of detail to the tenth-century Paris Psalter (MS. grec. 139—see below, p. 468) show that both MSS. are of the same artistic descent; the Psalter and its congeners probably reproduce an early model of about the same date as the original of the Rotulus. Both models may have been produced in Alexandria:[1] the copies were possibly made in Constantinople. A number of scenes are missing both from the beginning and end of the scroll, but the Octateuchs (p. 464), which are evidently based upon models of the same kind, permit us to supply the deficiency.[2] From the setting out of the spies, the story runs continuously to the execution of the five kings of the Amorites. We see the Ark crossing Jordan, the erection of the monument at Gilgal, the taking of Jericho, the contest for Ai, the battle with the Amorites. It is noted elsewhere that the Joshua Rotulus or its type was one of the sources from which ivory carvers derived groups or single figures, at a time when sub-classical models were in request (see p. 218).

Among the most important of early MSS. is the Syrian book of the Gospels in the Laurentian Library in Florence,[3] illuminated in the year A.D. 586 by Rabula in the Monastery of Zagba, in Northern Mesopotamia.

The colour is throughout rich, ranking with that of the Codex Rossanensis. The figure subjects are composed strictly to illustrate the Gospel passages and are independent of the early traditions of Christian art in the West. We have here in fact Christian iconography reflected as it were in a new ethnical mirror. A feature which at once strikes the eye is the great fondness of the illustrator for accessories and ornament; in this the book is in absolute contrast to the Codex Rossanensis and the group with which it is associated. Except in the case of the first two and the four last folios, which have full-page illustrations, the ornamental and figure subjects are arranged at the sides of the architectural canon-tables, which are very numerous (Figs. 259, 266). Above the arches are birds and vases, trees, plants, and flowers, peacock's feathers, &c.: to right and left at the bottom various animals and plants. The wealth and variety of this ornament is very striking: the style which it represents must be attributed to Hither Asia, and was the basis of much that became traditional in later Byzantine art. The species of animals and flowers are often rendered with a lively touch and with much fidelity to nature.

The date of this early manuscript being precisely known, and the range of its illustration wide, it will be useful for iconographical purposes to indicate the figure subjects in their order, it being assumed that in every case down to folio 23 the figures are disposed about or within the columns of arches or of Eusebian Canons.

The Apostles elect Matthew in place of Jude; the Virgin standing with the Child; Eusebius of Caesarea and Ammonius of Alexandria; Moses receiving the Tables of the Law, and Aaron with the rod that budded; Samuel with the horn of anointing, Joshua with the sun and moon above him, and the

---

[1] Strzygowski (*Bilderkreis des griechischen Physiologus*, pp. 122 ff.) notes points of resemblance, such as the form of the δίφρος of Joshua, to the Vienna Genesis.

[2] Muñoz, p. 17 and Pl. F, G, &c.

[3] S. E. Assemanus, Archbishop of Apamea. *Bibliothecae Mediceae Laurentianae et Palatinae Codicum MSS. orientalium Catalogus*, Florence, 1742, 1 ff. and Pl. I–XXVI ; Garrucci, *Storia dell'arte cristiana*, Pl. CVII ; Ussoff, in *Drevnosti* (publication of the Moscow Arch. Soc.), vol. xi. For a Syriac MS. (No. 341) with miniatures of the seventh–eighth centuries recently acquired by the Bibliothèque Nat., Paris, see H. Omont, *Mon. Piot.* xvii, p. 85.

Annunciation; Solomon, David, the Baptism, the Massacre of the Innocents; the Miracle of Cana; Abdias, Amos, the Healing of the Woman with the Issue of Blood; Jonah beneath the Gourd, the Woman of Samaria, the Healing of the Lame Man; Zephaniah, Nahum, the Raising of the Widow of Nain's Son; Isaiah, Job, Our Lord standing between two Apostles; Haggai, Habakkuk, the Healing of the Blind Man; Jeremiah, Zachariah, Our Lord with the Sons of Zebedee and their Mother; Daniel, Ezekiel, Our Lord healing the Demoniac;

FIG. 266. Page from the Syriac Gospel of Rabula, A. D. 586, in the Laurentian Library, Florence. (*Hautes Études*: A. Venturi.) P. 448.

Our Lord and the Tribute-money; the Evangelists Matthew and John seated with codex and scroll; Mark and Luke; a miracle (the Loaves and Fishes?); Christ upon the Mount, the Healing of the Lame and Blind; the Entry into Jerusalem, Christ distributing the Bread to the Apostles; the Betrayal, Judas hanging; Our Lord with Matthew at the Receipt of Custom.

With folio 23 begins a series of full-page illustrations.

23. *The Crucifixion*.[1] Holy women at the tomb, and *Noli me tangere*, in a border of step pattern.

In the upper part of the picture Our Lord, in the colobium, is crucified between the thieves, nails being driven through each foot. Below the cross

---

[1] It is maintained by several critics that this and the following miniatures are not of the date of the MS. and are not likely to be earlier than the tenth century (cf. A. Morini, *Origini del culto dell' Addolorata*, Appendix; A. Heisenberg, *Grabeskirche und Apostelkirche*, 1908, 255; G. Stuhlfauth, *Die Engel*, &c., 144, note 5). But Ainaloff has remarked the affinity between the treatment of their subjects and those of the Monza ampullae (p. 623), which are considered to reproduce in outline the early mosaics of the memorial churches in Palestine. Cf. Diehl, *Manuel*, 237.

three soldiers play 'morra' in order to divide the garments. Above the cross are the sun and moon, the former with human features. To right and left are Longinus (ΛΟΓΙΝΟΣ) and Stephaton, with spear, and sponge on reed. Beyond them are five mourning women. the Virgin, who has the nimbus, standing on the extreme left. Below is the Holy Sepulchre, a building with fanciful roof and opened doors, from which issue rays of light. On the left sits the angel discoursing with the two Maries. On the right is Our Lord, while the two Maries kneel before him. In the background is the foliage of trees.

24. *The Ascension.* In the upper part of the picture is a mandorla in which stands Our Lord. It is supported below by the winged beasts and flaming wheels, and at the sides by two angels: to right and left are two other angels with offerings: in the upper corners are the sun and moon with human features. Below stands the Virgin as *orans* between two angels, beyond whom are the Twelve Apostles in two groups. Behind the figures is a hilly landscape.

25. *Christ among the Doctors.* Our Lord is seated in the middle, two doctors standing on each side, two holding books. The scene is beneath an arched canopy surmounted by a cross upon a globe, on each side of which is a long-necked bird with head turned back towards a branch with berries.

26. *The Pentecost.* The Apostles stand before a round hill, on the sides of which are formal plants or trees; flames are depicted above their haloes. In the midst stands the Virgin, above whose head the Dove is seen descending, with flame and rays issuing from its beak.

The miniatures at the beginning of the *Etchmiadzin Gospel*[1] of the year A.D. 989, in the library of the monastery of that name in Armenia, were probably imported into that country from Syria at an early date. The MS. shows more decided Syrian characteristics, but its miniatures, if rough in style, are evidently true copies of Hellenistic originals. They must be considerably older than the text and are regarded as of the sixth century: the subjects comprise Our Lord, the Virgin and Child, the Evangelists, the Sacrifice of Isaac, and a sanctuary symbolizing the Christian Church. Several details in these miniatures suggest the influence of Syria-Palestine. The form of the altar in the Sacrifice of Isaac is found on the ivory *pyxis* of earlier date at Berlin assigned to this region (p. 191, Fig. 115), and its flight of steps may have been suggested by the steps leading up to Calvary often mentioned by early pilgrims. The Adoration of the Magi recalls the type seen on several ivories, on a panel from the Murano diptych in the John Rylands Library, Manchester (Fig. 114), and on a similar panel in the British Museum (Fig. 126). All these panels, from the monumental character of their style, may well reproduce, as has been suggested, the mosaics on the façade of the Church of the Nativity at Bethlehem.[2] In the arcades enclosing the several miniatures and the ornamental details there is close relationship to the Gospel of Rabula (see above), while the iconographical arrangement of several among them also recalls that MS. and the ampullae of Monza, which were made in Syria-Palestine. It can hardly be doubted that the types followed by the Etchmiadzin miniatures are Syrian, and that they go back at least to the first half of the sixth century. The manner in which the school to which they belonged affected early Frankish art is an important instance of the early oriental influence in the West which is elsewhere discussed (p. 85). It is evident in the case of the page with the sanctuary symbolizing the Church, which recalls the shrines represented in the mosaics of St. George's, Salonika, and the Catholic Baptistery at Ravenna.[3]

---

[1] J. Strzygowski, *B. D.*, i, *Das Etschmiadzin-Evangeliar*; Ainaloff, *Hellenistic Origins*, 40.
[2] Ainaloff, p. 41.
[3] D. Ainaloff, *V. V.*, v. 167–8. Ainaloff thinks that this architecture is of Alexandrian inspiration, and compares that of mural paintings of the period of Hadrian and the Antonines on the Palatine at Rome (cf. *Röm. Mitth.*, 1893, 291–2).

Numerous details confirm the Syrian inspiration of the miniatures. The ornament of the arcades is similar to that in the book of Rabula ; the rainbow tinting of one arcade occurs again in the Crucifixion and Ascension miniatures of that book ; the maeander is also common to both MSS. ; so are the birds and plants with which the pages are adorned. There is hardly a decorative feature in Rabula which does not find a parallel in this Gospel. Either,

Fig. 267. Christ before Pilate : page from the Syriac Gospel of Rabula, A.D. 586, in the Laurentian Library, Florence. (*Hautes Études* : A. Venturi.) P. 448.

therefore, the Etchmiadzin miniatures are themselves Syrian of the sixth century, or they copy a work very close in date to the Gospel of Rabula.

Opinions are not unanimous as to the date of all the miniatures. The page with the Virgin and Child has been considered to be contemporary with the Armenian text (A. D. 989).[1]

Fragments from other early Gospels have survived, mostly decorative and without figure subjects. We may especially mention two leaves with rich Eusebian Canons of the sixth century, bound up with a twelfth-century Gospel in the British Museum.[2] The shafts of the columns and the pediments are filled with rich floral and geometrical designs ; in the pediments are medallions with busts of saints on a blue ground ; outside the arches are realistic plants and birds. Interconnected circles, whorls, and rosettes also enter into the

---

[1] O. Wulff, *Die Koimesiskirche in Nicäa*, 267.

[2] Add. MS. 5111, fol. 10 and 11 ; Brit. Mus. *Cat. of Ancient MSS., Greek*, 1881, p. 21 and Pl. II ; H. Shaw, *Illuminated MSS.*, 1833, Pl. I–IV (in colour) ; A. Haseloff, *Codex Purpureus Rossanensis*, 1898, 44–5.

decoration. These leaves should be compared with the pages from an early Gospel at Vienna, which have also rich Eusebian Canons, and wreaths with *lemnisci* enclosing crosses.[1] The ornament in both cases is of Syrian origin.

The Codex Rossanensis,[2] a Gospel in the Cathedral of Rossano in the South of Italy, written in silver letters upon purple vellum and illuminated with miniatures in rich and varied colours, is from the point of view alike of art and iconography so important to the study of early Byzantine art that it must be described at exceptional length. With it must be discussed the fragment of St. Matthew from Sinope now in Paris, which is of the same school, while both have affinities to the Vienna Genesis (p. 444).

The artist who produced the miniatures was a colourist; and the variety and rich tone of the colours employed are in striking contrast to the thin tints of the Joshua Rotulus. In brilliance of tone this book is only second to the Gospel of Rabula.[3] The compositions are well conceived, realistic, and full of detail; they are of fundamental importance for the study of Byzantine iconography, proving as they do that many familiar types (e. g. the Entry into Jerusalem) were already fully developed as early as the beginning of the sixth century, to which period experts in palaeography assign the book.[4] Ornament is sparsely used in this codex and in the volumes artistically related to it, all contrasting in this respect with the Gospel of Rabula and Syrian illuminated books in general. The text is in two columns of silver letters, and there are 188 pages. The miniatures are as a rule divided horizontally into two parts, the lower having half-figures of four kings or prophets of the Old Testament, holding scrolls and bearing witness to the truth of the scene represented above, the upper containing the principal subject. The nature of the illuminated subjects may be briefly resumed.

Fol. 1. The four half-figures below are David, Hosea, David, and Isaiah (here, as elsewhere, David is repeated). The subject above is the *Resurrection of Lazarus.* The upright swathed body of Lazarus is seen in a cave on the right supported by a slave. Christ, as always in this MS., is bearded and clothed in a purple tunic, over which is a gold mantle: he has the cruciferous nimbus. At his feet are Mary and Martha; to right and left, groups of Apostles and spectators.

1 b. David, Zachariah, David, Malachi: *the Entry into Jerusalem.* Christ rides from the left; behind him follow two disciples, while two boys have climbed a tree in the background. From the gates of Jerusalem on the right issue people leading little children and carrying palms: two boys spread garments before the feet of the ass. Within the walls houses are visible: people look from the windows of one, holding palm branches in their hands.

Fol. 2. David, Hosea, David, Malachi: *the Expulsion of the Merchants from the Temple.* On the left is the Temple, a gabled building with projecting portico. Before it Christ, holding a scourge, converses with two priests. On

---

[1] H. Wickhoff, Austrian *Jahrbuch*, xiv, 1893, 196 ff., *Die Ornamente eines altchristlichen Codex der Hofbibliothek* (No. 847). For other early fragments at Paris and St. Petersburg see Cronin, *Codex purpureus Petropolitanus* in *Texts and Studies contributed to . . . Patristic Literature*, v, No. 4, 1899; *Izviestiya* of the Russian Arch. Inst. at Cple., i, 1896, 138 ff.; *Monumenti d' arte*, Fasc. i, Pl. I.

[2] O. von Gebhardt and A. Harnack, *Evangeliorum Codex purpureus Rossanensis*, Leipsic, 1880; A. Haseloff, *Codex purpureus Rossanensis*, 1898; A. Muñoz, *Il Codice purpureo di Rossano e il frammento Sinopense*, Rome, 1907 (the coloured reproductions in this work are the best which have appeared, but all three books contain valuable critical matter). See also Lamprecht in *Bonner Jahrbücher*, Heft LXIX, 1880, 90–98; Zucher in *Göttingische gelehrte Anzeigen*, 1881, 938 ff.; C. Ussoff in *Drevnosti* (*Proc. of the Imperial Moscow Arch. Soc.*), 1902; O. von Gebhardt, *Die Evangelien*, &c., *aus dem Codex purpureus*, Leipsic, 1883; H. Graeven in *Göttingische gelehrte Anzeigen*, 1900, 410 ff.; E. K. Riedin in *V. V.*, 1900, 454 ff.; J. Strzygowski, *B. Z.*, 1899, 589, 590. F. X. von Funk (*Historisches Jahrbuch*, 1896, 331 ff.) ascribes the MS. to the eighth or ninth century.

[3] The colours are applied directly to the purple, though the face of Our Lord is painted over the gold of the nimbus.

[4] The early date assigned by palaeographers is confirmed by iconographical details. The Jewish priests have no special costume, but only tunic and pallium; whereas a distinctive attire characterizes them in the later part of the sixth century.

the right the merchants are retiring. We note a money-changer with his table and *abacus*.

2 b. David (three times), Hosea : *the Parable of the Wise and Foolish Virgins.* In the middle is a panelled door, seen from the side. On the left of it are the five foolish virgins in mantles of various colours, pink, blue, yellow, and black,

FIG. 268. Movement of the heavens round the earth: miniature from the eleventh-century MS. of Cosmas Indicopleustes in the monastery, Mount Sinai (Cod. Sinait. 1186) (*Hautes Études*: N. Kondakoff.) P. 462.

carrying extinguished torches. On the right, in a landscape with a tree bearing golden fruit and a mount from which issues the Four Rivers, are the five wise virgins in white, with burning torches. Christ stands on the inner side of the door.

Fol. 3. David (three times), Zephaniah : *the Last Supper*, and *the Washing of the Disciples' Feet.* A semicircular table with couches at each end, on which Our Lord and Peter recline. Round the table are seated the Apostles, while Judas reaches across for the sop. In the second scene Christ bends over St. Peter's feet.

3 b. David, Moses, David, Isaiah : *Communion of the Apostles, the Distribution of the Bread.* Our Lord stands on the left. Six Apostles in bluish mantles.

4. Moses, David, David, Solomon : *the Dispensation of the Wine.* Here

Our Lord stands on the right, offering a hemispherical golden bowl. The Apostles advance in line from the left.

4 b. David, David, Jonah, Nahum: *Gethsemane.* A rocky landscape: on the left Our Lord bends over the sleeping disciples; on the right he is again seen kneeling in prayer. Above is a band of blue sky, with stars and crescent moon.

5. *Frontispiece to Eusebian Canons.* At four equal points in a circle composed of overlapping disks variegated in blue, pink, and a bluish tint are medallions with busts of the Four Evangelists; each is bearded and nimbed, holding a golden book. The ground is blue, the mantles white. The motive of overlapping disks recurs in the frescoes of Sta Maria Antiqua.

6 b. *Part of Eusebius' letter to Carpianus*, in an ornamental gold border. At the top is a pink rose flanked by doves (?). At the corners are baskets, on the sides pink roses and lotus-like flowers with long stems; at the bottom is a rose flanked by two ducks.

7. David, Sirach, David, Isaiah: *the Healing of the Blind Man.* On the left Our Lord, followed by two disciples, approaches the blind man: on the right the latter bathes his eyes in a quadrangular fountain watched by onlookers.

7 b. David, Micah, David, Sirach: *the Good Samaritan.* On the left the buildings of the city; in the middle the Good Samaritan in the form of Our Lord, and an angel with a golden bowl, lean over the prostrate traveller. On the right Christ leads the ass on which the victim is placed to the door of a house and pays the occupant money.

8. *Christ before Pilate; Judas restoring the Thirty Pieces; Judas hanged.* The governor sits on a high throne before which is a draped table with inkpot and pens. To right and left stand guards wearing golden collars, and holding standards on which are imperial busts. Below, on the left, Christ and two priests advance; on the right stands a group of Roman functionaries. The Judas scenes are below, replacing the usual prophets. On the left the priest, seated in a basket chair with high back beneath a canopy, rejects the silver which Judas offers in the fold of his mantle. On the right Judas is seen hanging from the tree.

8 b. *The Jews choose between Christ and Barabbas.* Pilate is seated as before; on his right stands a group of Jews; on his left a recorder writing in a diptych. Below on the left Christ stands between two functionaries each in chlamys with tablion, one holding a birch: on the right, two slaves in short tunics hold Barabbas. In this miniature also there are no prophets.

121. *St. Mark* seated in a basketwork chair with high back, writing his Gospel. He writes upon a long scroll. Above him is a canopy with an architrave: there are two windows through which the sky is seen. Before him stands a female figure in a blue mantle and with blue nimbus, perhaps a personification of the Divine Wisdom (Ἁγία Σοφία).

Of the above scenes, the Raising of Lazarus occurs here for the first time with the full detail usual in later Byzantine art. The Entry into Jerusalem is also an early example of a type which became traditional. The treatment of the Parable of the Wise and Foolish Virgins varies in art, but the type here seen is similar to that described in the (late) Painter's Manual. The Last Supper and the Washing of the Feet are also compositions which became more or less fixed. The Distribution of the Bread and Wine is a liturgical equivalent of the Last Supper, and does not occur in Western art. The arrangement of the scene in two symmetrical parts suggests imitation of a mosaic, perhaps an early prototype of the version in that of Sta Sophia at Kieff.[1] Of the Parable of the Good Samaritan it may be noted that the representation of the Samaritan under the form of Christ is an oriental feature. The division into two parts of the scene representing Christ before Pilate occurs again on the ciborium columns

---

[1] For the scene see p. 666 and A. Muñoz, *L'Art byzantin à l'exposition de Grottaferrata*, 132 ff.

of S. Marco, which come from the Christian East (p. 155 and Fig. 89) : the same columns are the only other early monuments which present the return of the thirty pieces by Judas in an equally dramatic manner.

The miniature representing St. Mark writing is interesting as an early application to an Evangelist of the type of author's portrait known to have been prefixed to illustrated pagan MSS., and occurring in the sixth-century MS.

Fig. 269. The Ascension of Elijah, from the eleventh-century MS. of Cosmas Indicopleustes in the Monastery of St. Catherine, Mount Sinai. (*Hautes Études* : N. Kondakoff.) P. 462.

of Dioscorides at Vienna (p. 460). It will be remembered that the Gospel of Rabula has two Evangelists represented in a similar way (St. Matthew and St. John).[1]

The female figure before St. Matthew is probably one of those personifications adopted by Byzantine from Hellenistic art. Had the Evangelist been St. John, she might have well been interpreted as the Virgin ; but though the Virgin does occasionally appear under the form of the Divine Wisdom,[2] it is perhaps better to suppose that here only the latter is intended.[3] Various figures representing vehicles of divine inspiration accompany the Evangelists in Byzantine art (e. g. Our Lord in the Clouds, St. Peter, the Virgin): St. John

[1] For the author's portrait, the origin of which is to be sought in Hellenistic bas-reliefs, see Diez in *B. D.*, iii. 38. The portrait of Virgil is seen at the beginning of the famous MS. of the *Aeneid* in the Vatican.

[2] Fresco in Sta Sophia, Kieff ; top of triumphal arch in Cathedral of Monreale, Sicily, where the Virgin *orans* is described as *Sapientia Dei*.

[3] A. Muñoz, *Codex purpureus*, &c., 16.

is often seen dictating to Procorus, though sometimes he is attended by a female figure.[1] Most examples of these attendant figures are late, a fact which makes the present example doubly interesting.

It seems probable that the whole series of illuminations is intended to illustrate the liturgy of Passion Week in the Graeco-Alexandrian Church.[2] Kondakoff is probably right in regarding the codex as a product of a realistic and vigorous monastic art.[3]

The stylistic relations of the Codex Rossanensis with the Vienna Genesis have been discussed by all critics, especially by Ussoff, who considers them in great detail:[4] types of figures, architectural forms, costumes, all offer points of

Fig. 270. The Vision of Isaiah, from the ninth-century MS. of Cosmas Indicopleustes in the Vatican Library. (*Hautes Études*: G. Millet.)

similarity: the colour-scheme is also similar. Affinities less close, but proving the influence of the same artistic current, are found in the Ashburnham Penta-teuch (p. 488), the sepulchral frescoes at Palmyra (Fig. 168), and the apse mosaic at Sinai.[5] The animals represented, such as the humped oxen in the Expulsion of the Money-changers, point to Asia Minor or Syria.

On the whole, Asia Minor appears the most probable place of origin. The Sinope fragments were obtained there, as also were the St. Petersburg fragments (see p. 452). Anatolia is known by documentary evidence to have been rich in painters[6] (see p. 260); and we may note that the distinctive style differs from that of MSS. executed elsewhere. The most serious rival to Asia Minor is the capital,[7] and this is an alternative which will commend itself to many, especially if the book, like the Sinope Gospel, was illuminated for a member of the imperial house.[8]

[1] As on a twelfth-century Italo-Byzantine relief on the outside of the west wall of St. Mark's at Venice.

[2] Muñoz, p. 19. This is also the opinion of Kondakoff, Ussoff, and F. X. Kraus; it is disputed by Haseloff and Pokrovsky.   [3] *Hist. de l'art byz.*, i. 120.

[4] pp. 73 ff. See also Lüdtke, *Untersuchungen zu den Miniaturen der Wiener Genesis*, Greifswald, 1897.   [5] Muñoz, p. 22.

[6] For Asterius of Amasia see Migne, *Patr. Gr.*, vol. xi; J. Strzygowski, *Kleinasien*, 200; A. Muñoz, *Alcune fonti letterarie per la storia dell' arte bizantina*, in *Nuovo Bullettino di arch. crist.*, 1904, p. 222.

[7] O. Wulff, *B. Z.*, xiii, 1904, 573.   [8] E. Cronin, *Journal of Theological Studies*, ii. 590 ff.

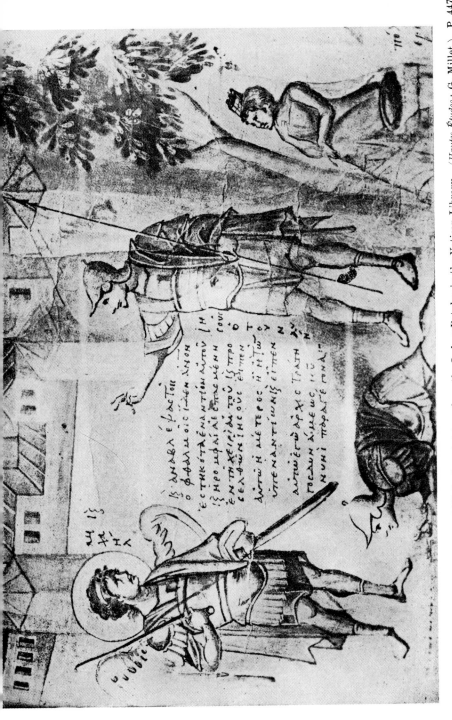

FIG. 271. Joshua at the feet of the Archangel Michael : miniature from the Joshua Rotulus in the Vatican Library. (*Hautes Études* : G. Millet.) P. 447.

The date is generally given as the beginning of the sixth century; but Federici would place it, with the Vienna Genesis, considerably earlier.[1] It has been stated that certain iconographic features, such as the absence of a distinctive costume for the Jewish priests, are held to support this view (p. 452, n. 4).

The fragment of the Gospel of St. Matthew obtained by Captain de la Taille at Sinope, and now in the Bibliothèque Nationale at Paris, belongs to the same school as the Codex Rossanensis, though the execution is inferior and the date perhaps a little later.[2] It comprises Matthew vii, xi, and xiii–xxiv; the miniatures are not placed together at the beginning, as in the case of the Codex Rossanensis, but intercalated in the text, which is written in gold upon purple. A leaf of the book is preserved at Mariopol in Russia. Each miniature is accompanied by two prophets with scrolls, placed not below, but at each end of the picture.

The remaining miniatures are as follows:—

Fol. 10 b. The *Feast of Herod* and *Decollation of St. John the Baptist*, between Moses and David. Herod reclines at table; before him stands Salome, to whom a servant in short girded tunic offers the head upon a golden charger. Behind him is the prison, a roofless enclosure, in which lies the headless body; near it stand two mourning disciples.

Fol. 11. The *First Miracle of the Loaves and Fishes* (Matt. xiv. 19). The accompanying prophets have lost their scrolls; only the upper part of the picture remains.

Fol. 15. The *Second Miracle* (Matt. xv. 32), between Moses and David. Our Lord in gold tunic and mantle with cruciferous nimbus stands between two disciples holding baskets of bread and fish: on the ground are other large baskets of bread. To the right the Israelites are seated eating in two rows in the high grass.

Fol. 29. The *Healing of the Blind at Jericho*, between David and Isaiah. Our Lord touches the eye of the blind man, who supports himself on sticks. Behind him is a disciple, and behind again two Jews in *paenulae*.

Fol. 30. The *Barren Fig-tree*, between Habakkuk and Daniel. Our Lord, followed by a disciple, advances to right towards a solitary fig-tree. In the background is the city with crenellated walls, the interior showing two gabled buildings and one with a dome upon a high drum.

Of these scenes, the first is of a type which persists in later Byzantine art, and occurs in a twelfth-century Gospel in the Laurentian Library at Florence.[3] The Painter's Manual describes the scene in the same way.

The Miracle of the Loaves and Fishes resembles the representation in the Catacombs of Alexandria,[4] though Christ is there seated. The addition of the people eating after the miracle appears to be an oriental feature.

The Miracle of the Barren Fig-tree is not known elsewhere before the twelfth century,[5] unless the relief from Sohag, now in Berlin, represents the scene.[6] The subject is described in the Painter's Manual, and represented in frescoes on Mount Athos. Our Lord in this MS. and in the Codex Rossanensis resembles the Christ of the Gospel scenes in the nave of S. Apollinare Nuovo at Ravenna.[7]

---

[1] See *B. Z.*, 1900, 320; Muñoz, p. 12. The point as to the priestly costume had been raised by Graeven (Austrian *Jahrbuch*, 1900).

[2] H. Omont, *Monuments Piot*, vii, 1900, 175, and Pl. XVI–XIX; *Fac-similés des mss.*, &c., 1902, pp. 1-4; *Journal des Savants*, 1900, 279-85; *Notices et extraits des mss. de la Bibl. Nat.*, xxxvi, 599 ff.; *Compte rendu de l'Acad. des Inscriptions*, 1900, 215-18; A. Muñoz, *Il Codice purpureo di Rossano e il frammento . . . di Sinope*, 16 ff. (reproductions).

[3] Muñoz, as above, p. 16.

[4] *Bull. di arch. crist.*, 1865, p. 63 and Plate; Kraus, *Geschichte der christl. Kunst*, i. 17.

[5] Muñoz, p. 17.

[6] J. Strzygowski, *Hellenistische und koptische Kunst*, Fig. 68. In this sculpture Our Lord is mounted.

[7] As Kondakoff remarked (*Hist. de l'art byz.*, i, p. 120). The type is perhaps Mesopotamian.

II. Secular Manuscripts.

The illuminated *Iliad* in the Ambrosian Library at Milan is considered by some to date from the fourth century, by others even from the third.[1] The Vatican Virgil[2] is not far removed from it in date, both MSS. being apparently copies from older works and purely antique in spirit. Like the frescoes of Pompeii, with which they have been compared, these miniatures descend from Alexandrian art ; Christianity had not modified their pagan inspiration.

The Chronicle of the History of the World in the Golenisheff Collection, written upon papyrus, was evidently executed in Egypt, the date being

FIG. 272.   Scenes from the Life of David : Psalter of A.D. 1066 in the British Museum.
(Add. MS. 19352.)   P. 470.

apparently about A.D. 400.[3] It thus belongs to a time marked by a recrudescence of Egyptian feeling against Hellenic art.[4] The system of illustration is that of pagan Egypt : the pictures are inserted in the text ; they are coloured drawings, the figures arranged in rows without indication of depth or perspective. The colour-scheme is harsh and without variety, the prevailing tones being red and yellow. Plant forms are only used as divisions between the

---

[1] A. M. Ceriani and A. Ratti, *Homeri Iliadis pictae fragmenta Ambrosiana*, Milan, 1905. The earlier edition usually consulted was that of Angelo Mai. The costumes, &c., are studied by A. De Marchi in *Miscellanea Ceriani*, Milan, 1910, 3 ff.

[2] P. de Nolhac, *Le Virgile du Vatican*, Paris, 1897 ; *Codices e Vaticanis selecti*, i.

[3] A. Bauer and J. Strzygowski, *Eine alexandrinische Weltchronik*, in *Denkschriften* of the Vienna Academy (philosophic-historical section), li, 1906, 169 ff.

[4] The most conspicuous example of this recrudescence is found in the frescoes of Kom es-Shugafa (*Zeitschr. für bildende Kunst*, xiii, 1902, 112 ff.).

subjects. There is nothing in the shape of mere ornament, nor are there the decorative borders which appear at an early date in the vellum codices of Asia Minor and Syria: at present we know no Greek or Latin papyrus with such ornamentation.[1] The Asiatic style of illumination with decorative accessories, probably originating in Persia and Mesopotamia, definitely won the day by the beginning of the sixth century: only where an Alexandrian papyrus scroll was literally copied, as in the case of the Joshua Rotulus and the Octateuchs (pp. 447, 464), was the simpler Egyptian manner preserved. The style rich in ornament probably owed its triumph to the spread of the monastic art represented by such books as the Gospel of Rabula and the group of the Codex Rossanensis (see p. 452).

The illustrations of this Chronicle of the World, which was an Alexandrian redaction, need not themselves have been executed in Alexandria. Their crude style, so inferior to that of the Joshua Rotulus, in which Greek influence is evident, points rather to some centre in Upper Egypt where art was modified by indigenous sentiment.

The Vienna manuscript of the medical treatise of *Dioscorides*, a physician of the first century, was executed for Juliana Anicia, daughter of Galla Placidia and wife of the consul Areobindus, in the early years of the sixth century, probably about A.D. 512.[2] The date may be inferred from an acrostic inscription surrounding the central part of the miniature with the princess's portrait described below.

The larger illuminations precede the text of the work. The first shows a peacock with tail displayed; on the next two, groups of doctors are seen in discussion; on the fourth Dioscorides on a folding stool receives the plant mandragora from a female figure personifying Discovery (Εὕρησις), while a dog dies in agony in the foreground. On another page the physician is seen writing, while Discovery holds the mandragora for an artist to draw. The most important miniature is that with a portrait of the princess, to be presently described. When once the book begins, the illustrations are confined to medicinal plants, one of which is accompanied by a nereid with lobster-claws upon her head, riding a marine monster.

The miniature representing the princess shows Juliana seated on a throne, holding in her hand a book or diptych. On either side stand two personifications, Μεγαλοψυχία with a number of gold coins in the fold of her mantle, and Φρόνησις holding an open book, on a page of which is a plant, indicating that the work is probably a copy of Dioscorides. In the foreground on the left a female figure, Εὐχαριστία τεχνῶν, the Gratitude of the Arts, prostrates herself at the princess's feet; between her and Μεγαλοψυχία, Πόθος τῆς φιλοκτίστου, or Love of the foundress, again holds up a book. It is round this scene that the acrostic is inscribed, which, through the mention of a church founded by Juliana at Honoratae, a suburb of Constantinople, gives for the MS. the approximate date of A.D. 512. In the small outer fields with blue grounds surrounding the large composition are putti in grisaille engaged in building operations, again in

[1] St. Jerome mentions vellum as a *substitute* when papyrus is not to be obtained; from the fourth century it must have been in general use outside Egypt. The earliest mention of an illumination on parchment is in Martial (xiv. 186), where there is allusion to a portrait of the author in a MS. of Virgil. It has been suggested that parchment was first commonly used at Pergamum, whence the name. Early examples of painting on papyrus, showing a certain analogy to the designs reserved upon textiles by the wax process (see p. 602), are to be seen in the British and Victoria and Albert Museums (Bauer and Strzygowski, as above, 176).

[2] For the early reproductions and discussions by Lambecius, Du Cange, Gori, d'Agincourt, &c., see the list given by von Premerstein, as below, p. 105. More recent discussions are by J. Strzygowski, *B. D.*, iii, xiv. 57 ff.; D. Ainaloff, *Hellenistic Origin*, &c., 38; N. Kondakoff, *Histoire de l'art byzantin*, i. 108 ff.; F. X. Kraus, *Gesch. der christl. Kunst*, i. 489 and Fig. 345; G. Millet in A. Michel's *Hist. de l'art*, pp. 208–9. Labarte, *Hist. des arts industriels*, gives a good plate in colours of the Juliana miniature (*Album*, ii, 1864, Pl. 78); but the best reproductions, with the most valuable commentary, are those of A. von Premerstein, Austrian *Jahrbuch*, xxiv, 1903, 105 ff., and of the same author with C. Wessely, *Codex Aniciae Iulianae*, &c., 1906.

allusion to the foundation of the church.[1] The purpose of the miniature is to
extol Juliana Anicia as a patroness of the Church and of the arts. The character of the borders surrounding and dividing its surface is oriental, the custom
of enclosing a design within
a border going back to the
ancient art of Mesopotamia.[2]

Of the other miniatures,
we may specially note that in
which Dioscorides is sitting
writing, as it is an early
surviving example of the
author's portrait, later employed for representations of
the four Evangelists at the
beginning of their Gospels.[3]
The type is found on one of
the early sarcophagi from
Konia, and would appear to
have been popular in Hel-
lenistic Asia Minor. Throughout this MS. the Hellenistic
element is predominant ; the
oriental elements are for the
most part decorative only.
The style is distinct from that
of the early MSS. connected
with   Southern   Anatolia,
Mesopotamia,   and   Syria
(Vienna Genesis, Codex Rossanensis, Gospel of Rabula) ;
perhaps the work may have
seen the light in Constantinople itself.

It is noticeable that a
gold background occurs for
the first time in this book.

It will be convenient to
mention here the fifteenth-
century illuminated Dioscorides of the Chigi Library at
Rome,[4] which   reproduces
many of the same subjects
and is clearly a copy of

FIG. 273. The Ascension : illumination in the British
Museum Psalter of A.D. 1066. (Add. MS. 19352). P. 470.

a late Hellenistic original
nearly allied to the Vienna
book. It has numerous pages of coloured plants, trees, and animals, including
birds and insects, the coral, the mandragora scene, the groups of doctors,
Dioscorides with the painter and Epinoia (or Sophia), and (an interesting addition) two views of a nude man, the head being of an antique type.

Other Dioscorides MSS. are the Codex Neapolitanus in the Vienna Library,
the Paris Codex of the ninth century (Gr. 2179), and a MS. in the collection of
Sir Thomas Philips at Cheltenham.

The Christian Topography of *Cosmas Indicopleustes,* who wrote either at Alexan-

[1] We may compare the building scenes of the frescoes of Kuṣeir ʿAmra (see p. 282).
[2] Cf. *B. D.,* iii, p. 57 ; *Orient oder Rom,* 47.
[3] It has been already noticed that the author's portrait, derived from Hellenistic reliefs,
is mentioned by Martial as occurring in a MS. of Virgil (xiv. 186). See Diez, *B. D.,* iii,
pp. 38 ff.   [4] A. Muñoz, *Codici greci miniati delle minori biblioteche di Roma,* Pl. XI–XIV.

dria or on Sinai about A.D. 547, is extant in several illustrated MSS. The oldest, in the Vatican (No. 699),[1] is probably of the ninth century; two others, in the Laurentian Library at Florence and in the monastery on Mount Sinai, are of the eleventh. The work is a curious medley of science and religious doctrine, in which natural history and cosmogony are explained in accordance with the philosophy of Christian belief and Chaldaean legend. The illustration is equally varied, maps from Ptolemy's geography and figures of plants and animals finding their place with miniatures representing scenes from the Old and New Testaments.

The geographical illustrations are the source through which elements of 'pictorial science', Alexandrian in origin, entered the province of later Byzantine art. Such is the representation of the earth as a square flanked by the four personified winds, environed by ocean, or as a mountain similarly surrounded (Fig. 268). The biblical illustrations are chosen to mark the parallelism between the two Testaments: thus Melchizedek is a type of the eternal, the Sacrifice of Isaac and the Escape of Jonah from the Jaws of the Whale typify the Passion and Resurrection, the Ascent of Elijah represents the Ascension of Our Lord. The plants and animals recall the illustrations of the Vienna Dioscorides (see p. 460) and the Smyrna Physiologus (see p. 482).

The three MSS.[2] are all based upon an original contemporary with Cosmas, but their illustrations vary with the taste of the illuminator; thus the artist of the Vatican copy abridges the geographical pictures and dispenses with the animals and plants, while the painters of the other two volumes suppress some of the symbolical illuminations derived from the Bible. It was supposed by various critics that the Vatican MS. might be as early as the seventh century; but the descriptive words placed amongst the illustrations are identical in character with those of the text, which palaeographers assign to the latter part of the ninth. If this is correct the book possesses a commanding interest for Byzantine art. It belongs to a rather obscure transitional time and clearly illustrates the continuity of tradition through the iconoclastic period. On the one hand, many features, such as the zodiac, the personification of Jordan, the heads of seraphs, point back to late classical art; on the other hand, many types and figures are closely related to those in MSS. of the two succeeding centuries.[3] There are many points of analogy with the Vatican Octateuchs, and the conclusion reached by a study of the Joshua Rotulus is confirmed, that the Bible illustration of the eleventh century and later is based upon books of far earlier date. It has been observed that there are repeated parallels between the Vatican book and the Alexandrian Chronicle of the World on papyrus (see p. 459).

Features in the Vatican miniatures suggest an origin in Alexandria: the mummy-like representations of the dead, the figures of Ethiopic type attending Ptolemy, are cited as indications of an Egyptian provenance. It is in itself

---

[1] C. Stornajolo, *Le Miniature della topografia cristiana di Cosmas Indicopleustes* (*Codices e Vaticanis selecti*, Milan, Hoepli, 1908); Garrucci, *Storia*, Pl. CXLII, CXLIII; G. Millet in A. Michel, *Hist. de l'art*, i. 214; Kondakoff, *Histoire de l'art byz.*, Paris, 1886, p. 137 and Figs. on pp. 142–3, 146–7, 149, and *Voyage to Sinai*; Labarte, *Hist. des arts industriels*, iii. 25 and Pl. LXXIX; d'Agincourt, *Peinture*, Pl. XXXIV; J. Tikkanen, *Die Genesismosaiken*, &c., Heisingfors, 1889, 5, 322; D. Ainaloff, *Hellenistic Origin*, &c.; A. Muñoz, *Monumenti d' arte medioevali e moderni*, Pt. II (miniature with Enoch); Diehl, *Manuel*, 224 ff. The text of Cosmas is treated by H. Gelzer in *Jahrbücher für protestantische Theologie*, ix, 1883, 105–41; an English edition by J. W. McCrundle was published by the Hakluyt Society in 1897. There seems to be no proof that Cosmas wrote his work on Sinai; he himself implies that a part at least was composed at Alexandria, of which city he was a native. His own statements suggest that he had some artistic power, and the representations of the monuments at Adulis (Stornajolo, Pl. II) are probably based on his sketches. But it is doubtful whether he could have executed all the miniatures illustrating his work.

[2] For the Sinai Cosmas see Gardthausen, *Cat. codicum graec. Sinaiticorum*, p. 421, Oxford, 1886, and Kondakoff, *Sinaitic Album* (Russian). The Smyrna fragment accompanies the Physiologus in the Library of the Evangelical School (p. 482).

[3] e.g. the type of the old man in Cosmas recalls the Samuel of the Paris Psalter 139 (tenth century); the Isaiah and Elijah resemble figures in the Paris Codex 510 (H. Omont, *Fac-similés*, xxv. 1, xlii. 1).

natural that Alexandria, the centre of ancient science, and distinguished for the attainment of her painters, should have promoted the decoration of works of this character.

It has already been noted in the Introduction (p. 65) that many of the cosmographical features of the Christian topography were derived from Mar-Aba, the Persian Nestorian, and may ultimately be traced to Babylonian sources. The syncretism of the Vatican Cosmas lends it a peculiar importance. By the side

Fig. 274. A Stylite on his column : from an eleventh-century MS.
(British Museum Add. MS. 36636, fol. 48 b.)

of much that is Alexandrian there is plain evidence that the new monumental style is already established, and it has been justly remarked that the miniature in which Our Lord, the Virgin, and three saints are presented in a line before the spectator has all the character of a mural mosaic. Iconographically the book is no less interesting, owing to its introduction of new features and details.

The following is a *résumé* of the chief illustrations. Monuments of Adulis, Ethiopians, &c.; views of the world; planisphere; the high conical mountain with the sun going round it; complete view of the world; the earth and signs of the zodiac; Moses receiving the Law; the Tabernacle of the Jews; the Ark of the Covenant between Abiah and Zachariah; the Court of the Tabernacle; Aaron; Encampment of the Israelites; Abel and his Flock; Enoch and Death; Noah and the Ark; Melchizedek as *orans*; Sacrifice of Isaac; Isaac alone; Judah and Jacob; Moses and the Burning Bush; Moses receiving the Law; David and his Musicians; Ascension of Elijah; Hosea; Amos, Micah, Joel, Obadiah; three scenes of the Story of Jonah; Vision of Isaiah (Fig. 270); Vision of Ezekiel; Vision of Daniel ; Our Lord, the Virgin, St. John the Baptist, Zachariah, and Elizabeth standing in line, with busts of Simeon and Anna above ; Stoning of Stephen ; Conversion of Saul ; the Resurrection of the Dead ; the Cosmos with the Sun ; plan of the world ; the Tabernacle ; the Story of Hezekiah ; the movements of the stars about the world.

In the ninth century, as a result of the changes produced by iconoclasm, there was a revival of the scientific spirit and a consequent predilection for scientific books. In some of these the early Alexandrian style which had presided over the decoration of the earliest illuminated editions is very faithfully revived.[1]

THIRD AND FOURTH PERIODS

I. RELIGIOUS MANUSCRIPTS.

The illustrated Bible appears in the form of an abridgement or series of extracts. The great MS. in the Vatican (Cod. Vat. Reg. Gr. I) is akin to the Paris Psalter (139) and of the same period.[2] It, too, is distinguished by numerous personifications and a similar richness in architectural forms. At the beginning of the book, after miniatures representing the Creation and ornamented with large crosses, the Virgin is seen receiving the book from Leo the patrician. The remaining illustrations represent the Story of Moses ; a Council of Judges ; the Anointing of David ; the Coronation of Solomon ; the Ascension of Elijah ; the Exploits of Judith ; the Maccabees before Antiochus ; Job in his Misery. A seated figure of David introduces the Psalter.

Five illuminated *Octateuchs* have been studied—two in the Vatican Library, one in the Monastery of Vatopedi on Mount Athos,[3] one in the library of the Εὐαγγελικὴ σχολή at Smyrna,[4] and one in the Seraglio, Constantinople :[5] they date from the eleventh and twelfth centuries, the copy on Mount Athos being probably the oldest.[6] Their great interest lies in the fact that they are clearly related to a *rotulus* of earlier date, if not so early as the original of the Joshua Rotulus in the Vatican. Although that famous scroll stands so close in the conception of its scenes to the Octateuchs that the character of its missing miniatures can be inferred from the Octateuch miniatures illustrating the same book, there are yet so many divergences in detail that we cannot suppose it to have itself supplied the model. The occurrence of features indicating a departure from Hellenic ideas and the admixture of oriental characteristics justify the conclusion that the book is based upon a scroll similar to that in the Vatican ; a copy in codex form earlier than any now surviving may probably be assumed.

Of the five MSS., that at Vatopedi is evidently the most faithful copy. Of the two Vatican Octateuchs, one (No. 747) is rather careless, but shows originality in the artist. The other Vatican book (No. 746) is more careful, though the work of a mediocre artist ; the Smyrna book resembles it in both these respects.

There is another Octateuch in the Laurentian Library at Florence (Plut. v, No. 38).

[1] e. g. the Ptolemy of A.D. 813-20 in the Vatican Library, which contains numerous Hellenistic personifications very well executed (Ainaloff, *Hellenistic Origins*, &c.).

[2] *Collezione paleografica Vaticana*, Milan, 1905, Pl. I-XVIII ; Millet in Michel's *Histoire*, i. 228.

[3] N. Kondakoff, *Hist. de l'art byz.*, ii. 275 ; Brockhaus, *Die Kunst in den Athos-Klöstern*, 214 ff.

[4] J. Strzygowski, *Der illustrierte Oktateuch in Smyrna*, Appendix to *Der Bilderkreis des griechischen Physiologus* (*Byz. Archiv*, Ergänzungsheft i), 113 ff. ; D. C. Hesseling, *Miniatures de l'Octateuque grec de Smyrne*, Leyden, 1909 ; H. Graeven, *L'Arte*, i, 1898, 221 ff. ; A. Muñoz, *Il Rotulo di Giosuè . . . riprodotto a cura della Biblioteca Vaticana*, Milan, 1905, Pl. F and G ; O. Wulff, *Izviestiya* of Russ. Arch. Inst. Cple., iii. 201.

[5] Th. Uspensky, *Izviestiya* of the Russian Arch. Inst. at Cple., xii, Sofia, 1907. The book has 352 miniatures, of which about half are reproduced. Cf. G. Millet, *Rev. arch.*, 1910, pp. 71 ff.

[6] Wulff, however (as above), places the Smyrna book in the early part of the eleventh century.

Illustrated Greek *Psalters* fall into two main groups named by Tikkanen the *aristocratic* and the *monastic-theological*.[1] The miniatures of the first group form set compositions occupying the whole page, placed together at the beginning of the volume. The illustrations of the second are marginal, scenes and figures

Fig. 275. David inspired by an allegorical figure: miniature from a tenth-century Psalter in the Ambrosian Library, Milan. (*Hautes Études :* G. Millet.)

upon a small scale surrounding a central text. The first group, of which the famous Paris Psalter of the tenth century (Gr. 139) and its congeners in Rome and Venice are the chief examples (p. 468), shows very clearly the influence of late Hellenistic art ; the style and attitude of the figures, their grouping and disposition in a landscape are all Greek. It owes its origin to a courtly

[1] J. J. Tikkanen, *Die Psalterillustration im Mittelalter.*

art in the service of imperial patrons, whether the artists worked actually in Constantinople or elsewhere. The second group is animated by a different spirit. Here the imagination is more free, the fancy of the artist is allowed a wider range, but theological preoccupations are often betrayed by the choice of subject. It is the art of the monks who worked in the monasteries, at first of Mesopotamia and Syria,[1] later in the widely scattered religious houses which to the last followed the traditions of these precursors. The method of marginal

Fig. 276. The Creation of Man : miniature from the eleventh-century Octateuch in the Laurentian Library, Florence. (*Hautes Études* : G. Millet.)

illustration is known to us from Syrian work of the sixth century; it will be recalled that the Gospel illustrations at the beginning of Rabula's book were all disposed in this way in the border (Fig. 267). The same feature occurs in the early Syrian Gospel at Paris (Bibl. Nat. Gr. 33). Although Psalters fall into these two principal groups, no hard and fast line can be drawn, for sometimes a book with miniatures across the page will be more closely related to the marginal group in artistic details. Nor is it certain that monks confined themselves to the marginal style : they seem to have executed 'aristocratic' Psalters upon occasion.[2]

The oldest surviving Psalter dates from the ninth century, and is known as the Chludoff Psalter, from the collection in which it was formerly preserved : it is now in the Monastery of St. Nicholas at Moscow, and belongs to

---

[1] Cf. Baumstark, *B. Z.*, xvi. 658.
[2] A. Baumstark, *Frühchristlich-syrische Psalterillustration*, &c., *O. C.*, 1905, 295 ff. Baumstark traces a possible evolution of Psalter illustration ; the earlier stages are to be sought in Syria and Palestine, not without Alexandrian influence ; the later stage develops at Constantinople.

the monastic group.[1] Illustrated copies of the Psalms of David begin approximately at the same time both in East and West. But it is certain that late Hellenistic illuminated Psalters must have been in existence at a far earlier period. It is unlikely that the scenes from the life of David which we find in early mural paintings (p. 284) and on silver plate (p. 576) should not have

Fig. 277. David and Goliath : miniature from the Psalter of A.D. 1084 in the Monastery of the Pantokrator on Mount Athos. (*Hautes Études* : G. Millet.) P. 470.

also attracted the illuminator before the iconoclastic period. There is other evidence which leads us to infer that this must have been the case. The 'aristocratic' group of Psalters, dating from the tenth and eleventh centuries, is clearly inspired by lost models, either of Alexandrian or Anatolian origin ; the types, landscape, and composition all point to this descent, while the evident relation of the types to those of the silver plate, which is of the sixth century, carries them back beyond the iconoclastic disturbance. Strzygowski assumes an early original for the Servian Psalter at Munich, as also does Baumstark for another of A.D. 1053 in the Church of the Holy Sepulchre at Jerusalem.[2] Again,

[1] For Byzantine Psalters see J. J. Tikkanen, *Die Psalterillustration im Mittelalter*, vol. i. ; Kondakoff, *Histoire de l'art byzantin*, and *Miniatures of the Greek Psalter in the Chludoff Collection*, 111. The Psalter, as a liturgical book, included the odes, or prayers, derived from the Old Testament, on which see Baumstark in *R. Q.*, xxi, 1907, 157 ff.   [2] *O. C.*, 1905, 295 ff.

the well-known Utrecht Psalter, probably illustrated by an Anglo-Saxon at Haut-villers, near Reims, in the ninth century, has many characteristics which seem to prove that there must at one time have existed a model dating from the fourth or fifth century.[1] The frequent personifications (Earth, Sea, Sleep, &c.) in that book are significant, while in a Passion scene appears the curious machine used to cast lots for the chariot races in the Hippodrome at Constantinople [2] (Fig. 293).

It will be convenient to take as types one or two Psalters representative of

FIG. 278. The Three Children in the Fiery Furnace: miniature from the Psalter of A. D. 1084 in the Pantokrator Monastery, Mount Athos. (*Hautes Études* : G. Millet.) P. 470.

the two groups above indicated. The best known and most beautiful example of the 'aristocratic' group is the tenth-century MS. in the Bibliothèque Nationale at Paris (Grec 139).[3] Most of the full-page miniatures are in almost equal sets at the beginning and at the end : the eight relating to David are at the beginning (7), and at fol. 137. The subjects are : David playing the Lyre among his Flocks, beside him the personification of Melody as a female figure ; David attacks the Lion and Bear, supported by the personification of Strength ('Ισχύς) ; the Anointing of David in the presence of Jesse, Eliab, Aminadab, and others, with the personification of Mildness (Πραότης) ; David, supported by Might (Δύναμις), engages and slays Goliath, who is supported by Braggadocio ('Αλαζονεία) ; David and Saul, with Michael dancing ; Coronation of David, the crown being placed on his head by a nimbed female figure ; David in royal vesture, standing

[1] H. Graeven, *Die Vorlage des Utrecht-Psalters* in *Repertorium*, xxi, 1898, 28 ff.

[2] *Proc. Soc. Ant., London*, N. S., xxi. 188 ff.

[3] Omont, *Fac-similés des miniatures*, &c., Pl. I–XIV ; H. Bordier, *Description des ornements etc. des mss. grecs*, 111 ; Bayet, *L'Art byzantin*, pp. 159, 161, 162 ; G. Millet in A. Michel's *Histoire de l'art*, i. 222, 223 ; Diehl, *Manuel*, 566. Miniatures from this MS. have been very frequently reproduced (Labarte, Schlumberger, Venturi, &c.).

between Wisdom and Prophecy;[1] David rebuked by Nathan, and humbling himself in the presence of Repentance (Μετάνοια).

The remaining miniatures are as follows: the Crossing of the Red Sea,

FIG. 279. David slaying the bear and confronting Goliath: miniature from the Psalter of Basil II in the Marciana at Venice. (*Hautes Études*: G. Millet.)

with four personifications of Night, the Desert, the Deep, and the Red Sea, the Deep, in the guise of a vigorous nude figure, dragging Pharaoh from his horse; Moses receiving the Tables of the Law in presence of the personified Mount Sinai; Anna, mother of Samuel, giving thanks; Jonah; Isaiah between

---

[1] This miniature is reproduced in colours by Labarte, *Hist. des arts industriels*, 1st ed., 1864, *Album*, vol. ii, Pl. 84.

personifications of Night and Dawn ; the sick Hezekiah, behind whom stands the personified Supplication.

It has recently been questioned whether, as in the case of the Etchmiadzin Gospels, these miniatures may not be far older than the text with which they are bound, and represent a very early copy of a Hellenistic original, a copy dating from the fourth to the sixth century.[1] It is not yet, however, established that so excellent a copy as that here presented was impossible at the date when the MS. was written. The costumes are not always understood ; the architecture is fantastic ; the borders are unclassical ; we must await the publication of more detailed evidence before abandoning the attribution hitherto universally adopted. We may remark affinities to the Vienna Dioscorides (see p. 460),[2] and may also compare several Vatican MSS.—a volume of biblical extracts, a Psalter (Gr. 381) of the eleventh century, and an Isaiah, none of which, however, approach its high standard of excellence.[3]

Other well-known illuminated Psalters of the group are a smaller replica of the Paris book in the Monastery of Vatopedi (No. 609), dating from the end of the eleventh century, in which the miniatures are partially repainted ; and the Psalter of the Monastery of the Pantokrator (No. 49), of similar age. These are the only two which are approximately complete in illustration, but the great Psalter of Basil II in the Marciana at Venice is of the same school[4] (Figs. 279, 290). There are numerous other ' aristocratic ' Psalters of which the illustration is imperfect.[5]

As an example of the monastic group we may take the fine MS. in the British Museum, written by Theodore of Caesarea for Michael, abbot of the Monastery of the Studium at Constantinople, and completed in A. D. 1066.[6] A high proportion of the very numerous illustrations are concerned with the life of the Psalmist ; a great number depict those episodes in the Gospel story to which passages in the Psalms allude. Old Testament episodes which have a bearing upon the Psalms are freely introduced, e. g. the Three Children in the Furnace, the Creation of Adam, Daniel in the Den of Lions, Moses striking the Rock, the Plagues of Egypt, the Israelites in the Desert, the Golden Calf, the Sacrifice of Isaac, Abraham entertaining the Angels, Destruction of Sodom, the Ascent of Elijah, and several scenes repeated more than once. Saints and martyrs are very numerous, with occasional representations of martyrdoms. In two places (fol. 27 b, 88), as in other Psalters of the group, there are miniatures relating to the iconoclastic dispute (cf. Fig. 291), the latter example showing iconoclasts engaged in defacing a portrait of Our Lord.[7] Other enemies of orthodoxy who appear are Julian the Apostate dragged off by an angel (fol. 200) and Arius expelled from the Church (fol. 37 b).

Symbolic zoology is represented by the Capture of the Unicorn (fol. 124 b) ; while contemporary geographical ideas find expression in more than one curious figure of the heavens (fol. 135 b, 138). Among the frequent personifications may be mentioned Hades, Helios in his chariot, various rivers, the Four Winds, Orthros with a torch accompanying Isaiah, &c. (cf. the example quoted from the ' aristocratic ' group above). Many of the pictures are literal illustrations of the text (*Wortillustration*[8]): such are a miniature on fol. 10 b, where the ungodly are seen shooting arrows at the righteous ; and on fol. 11 b, where an angel pulls

[1] Dr. R. Berliner's examination of the book, see *B. Z.*, xix. 242 ; G. Millet in A. Michel's *Histoire*, &c., i, p. 224, and *Rev. arch.*, 1910, p. 80.

[2] Some authorities are of opinion that the model was probably of Anatolian origin.

[3] Cf. Diehl, *Manuel*, 571, and the reference there given.

[4] Labarte, *Histoire*, &c., 2nd ed., 1873, Pl. XLIX ; *Collection des Hautes Études*, Series C, No. 535 (David slaying the bear).

[5] Cod. Vat. Gr. 381, see *Collezione paleografica Vaticana*, Fasc. 1, Milan, 1905, Pl. XIX–XXII.

[6] G. F. Warner, British Museum, *Reproductions from Illuminated MSS.*, ser. ii, Pl. 2 and 3 ; F. G. Kenyon, *Facsimiles of Biblical MSS.*, No. vii ; Waagen in *Zeitschrift für Archäologie und Kunst*, i. 97 ; Labarte, *Hist. des arts industriels*, ii. p. 186.

[7] Tikkanen has noted the various known examples of these ante-iconoclastic miniatures.

[8] Cf. A. Goldschmidt, *Der Albanipsalter zu Hildesheim*.

out the tongue of the proud (Fig. 280). The numerous animals are sometimes in the same manner directly illustrative of passages in the accompanying verses.

Like the other monastic Psalters,[1] this book is of the most varied interest: the painter is a man of talent, whose touch is often as delicate as his fancy.

FIG. 280. The angel pulls out the tongue of the proud; David before the Lord: marginal illustrations in the Psalter of A.D. 1066 in the British Museum. (Add. MSS. 19352.) P. 470.

It is to be regretted that the miniatures are for the most part badly rubbed, so that little of the work is seen to advantage.

The Latin Psalter of Melisenda, daughter of Baldwin, King of Jerusalem (A. D. 1118–31), and wife of Fulk, Count of Anjou and King of Jerusalem (1131–

---

[1] The best known of these are the already mentioned Chludoff Psalter and the Pantokrator (No. 61 in the library of the monastery of that name on Mount Athos), dating from A. D. 1084. More nearly allied to the British Museum book are the Hamilton Psalter at Berlin and the Barberini Psalter (twelfth century, E. Dobbert, Prussian *Jahrbuch*, xv. 148). Numerous Russian Psalters produced down to the seventeenth century are descended from books of this type.

44), may be mentioned here in view of the fact that it has a number of full-page miniatures at the beginning which are Byzantine, one being signed by an artist, Basilius.[1] In so far the book might be regarded as a hybrid member of the 'aristocratic' group ; but it differs from the other Psalters of the class not only in the language of its text, but in the subjects of its miniatures, which illustrate the New Testament, with addition of the *Deesis*, and have no connexion with the story of David : they may have been originally painted for another book.

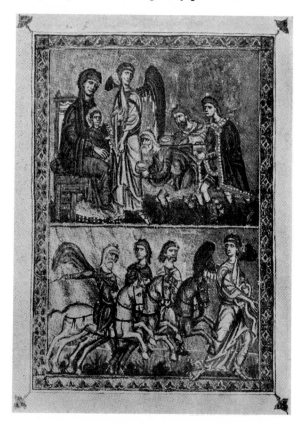

FIG. 281.   The Adoration of the Magi : miniature from the twelfth-century Psalter of Queen Melisenda in the British Museum.   (Egerton 1139.)

The head-pieces in this MS., with their interlacings containing men and monsters, are not Greek, but in the Western Romanesque style, and the smaller illuminated subjects beginning at fol. 202 b, with their ornamental borders, appear to be in like manner by a Western hand, though here and there an Eastern influence is perceptible, as in the representation of St. John the

[1] This Psalter, which is in the British Museum, is numbered Egerton 1139. See *New Palaeographical Society*, 1908, Pl. 140; Du Sommerard, *Les Arts au moyen âge, Album*, 2ᵉ sér., Pl. XXIX, &c. For the carved ivory covers of this MS. see p. 231. The subjects of the miniatures are the Annunciation, Salutation, Nativity, Adoration, Presentation, Baptism, Temptation, Transfiguration, Raising of Lazarus, Entry into Jerusalem, Last Supper, Washing of the Feet, Agony in the Garden, Betrayal, Crucifixion, Descent from the Cross, Entombment, *Anastasis*, Women at the Tomb, Incredulity of Thomas, Ascension, Pentecost, Death of the Virgin, *Deesis*. The iconography is throughout Byzantine : the *Deesis* and *Anastasis* are specifically Byzantine subjects; but in those common to East and West the oriental composition is followed, as in the Last Supper and Pentecost.

Evangelist as a bearded old man. The style of this second artist is very delicate and precise, differing markedly from that of Basilius, which is bolder but less careful, and lacking in the finish of the smaller miniatures. The work of the Greek painter is rough and sketchy in comparison, but his colours are of richer tone. His figures are outlined in black, and their proportions are often faulty ; thus in the Betrayal and Transfiguration, the figures in the foreground are unduly small. The miniatures as a whole are in better condition than those of most Byzantine books ; possibly Basilius may have learned some secrets in the matter of priming and applying gold-leaf from the Western artists with whom he may have associated. The interaction of Western and Byzantine influences in the illustration of this book recalls the same feature in the mosaics of the

Fig. 282. Job's Friends : miniature from the Book of Job of A.D. 905 in the Marcian Library, Venice. (*Hautes Études* : G. Millet.)

Church of the Nativity at Bethlehem, executed a little later and under similar conditions (p. 414).

The fifteenth-century Servian Psalter in the Hof- und Staatsbibliothek in Munich is also worthy of especial mention. It is evidently based upon a much older book which Strzygowski supposes to have been of early Syrian origin.[1] He finds in it motives which he considers only possible in a redaction never influenced by the art of the capital. Baumstark, in his review of Strzygowski's work, strongly supports this view on liturgical and iconographical grounds ;[2] but Millet[3] contests it, believing that the features in question are consistent with a Byzantine origin for the model. In either case, the antique inspiration remains, and the book is a valuable proof of the fidelity to tradition which still influenced the latest phases of Byzantine art within and beyond the frontiers of the empire.

The *Prophets* of the Old Testament are illustrated by various illuminated *catenae*, some of high interest. The *Catena in prophetas* of the Chigi Library in Rome[4] contains figures of the various prophets of a fine statuesque quality, evidently based on good Hellenistic models and suggesting in some cases classical orators : the book dates from the late tenth or early eleventh century. The Prophets of the Laurentian Library, Florence (Plut. v. 9), are distinguished by

---

[1] Strzygowski, *Denkschriften* of the Vienna Acad., vol. 52, *Phil.-hist. Classe*, 1904.
[2] *B. Z.*, xvi, 1907, 644 ff.
[3] *Rev. arch.*, 1908, i. 171-89.
[4] A. Muñoz, *Codici greci miniati delle minori biblioteche di Roma*, Pl. I-V. Only three of the miniatures, Jonah, Micah, and Jeremiah, are unrestored.

a similar dignity, and are of about the same period. The Vatican MS., No. 755, is of the tenth century ; it contains two miniatures representing Isaiah, one showing his martyrdom, the other depicting him between Night and Dawn as in Parisinus 139 and in the Pantokrator Psalter. The large Vatican 1153 [1] is of the twelfth century : it contains miniatures of eleven prophets, also reminiscent of Greek models, while the borders have details of ornament found in early MSS.

FIG. 283. The Angels before the Lord, and before the Devil : miniature from the Book of Job of A.D. 905 in the Marcian Library, Venice. (*Hautes Études* : G. Millet.)

like the Codex Rossanensis and the Gospel of Rabula, and in the frescoes of Sta Maria Antiqua at Rome. The miniatures of the Chigi *catena* have distinct analogies with the tenth-century illuminations of a Gospel of the twelfth century in the Monastery of St. Andrew on Mount Athos.[2] Even closer is the relation to the Gospels (No. 204) in the Monastery of St. Catherine on Mount Sinai [3] of the tenth or eleventh century, which in its turn recalls a Gospel in the Bibliothèque Nationale, Paris (MS. gr., No. 70). The whole group is characterized by the Hellenic influence visible in the figures, and an oriental (Syrian) influence in the ornament : it may be the work of a school working at Constantinople. The surviving illuminated copies of the Book of Job, or fragments of it, are of various dates, the fragment in the Naples Museum (now part of a Coptic Bible) probably belonging to the seventh or eighth century ;[4] the copy at Paris is ascribed to the fourteenth.[5] Intermediate between these are the books at Venice (No. 538), dated A.D. 909 ; Mount Sinai, and Patmos. In the fragment at Naples, the seated figures of Job and his family retain the monumental manner of the art of the early period ; the Sinai book preserves the picturesque tradition of late Hellenistic art, with its pastoral scenes and genre subjects. In the copy in the Marcian Library at Venice, on the other hand (Fig. 283), the picturesque tradition is abandoned, and the figures stand out against a blue background.[6]

The Prophets are finely illustrated in the MS. of the tenth or eleventh century divided between the libraries of Florence and Turin. With the exception of Jeremiah, who is seen in full figure, they are represented in medallions, in a style recalling that of the mosaics at Daphni but more nearly approaching the antique.[7]

Famous examples of illuminated *Gospels* and *Lectionaries* from the First Period have been already noticed. The essential features of the later Byzantine type go back to this time : the architectural canons framing the Concordance,

[1] Muñoz, as above, Pl. VII, VIII.
[2] Ainaloff in *Viz. Vrem.*, vi, 1899.
[3] Kondakoff, *Album* of Mount Sinai, Odessa, 1882, Pl. 32–7.
[4] Kondakoff, *Histoire de l'art byz.*, ii, p. 82.
[5] Kondakoff, as above, ii. 172 ; Diehl, *Gaz. des Beaux-Arts*, 1905, p. 81.
[6] G. Millet in Michel, *Histoire de l'art*, i. 221 ; Bordier, 235 ff.
[7] Millet, as above, 227.

and the figures of the Evangelists, usually seated writing their Gospels, but sometimes standing, are both derived from the older books.[1] The head-pieces with conventional floral designs are of fresh introduction, due to a new oriental influence, though the ornament itself has been developed from vine motives employed in the earlier period in the Christian East. The elaborate pictorial decoration, comprising numerous miniatures with New Testament subjects, seen at its best in the Codex of Rossano (p. 452), is no longer found. There are two

FIG. 284. The Raising of Lazarus: miniature from a twelfth-century Gospel in the Monastery of Iviron, Mount Athos. (*Hautes Études*: G. Millet.)

main types. In the first the four Evangelists are shown writing, while at the beginning of each Gospel is a scene from the New Testament, usually one of the Twelve Feasts. In the second, illustrations of the narrative are introduced in the text, and are often very abundant, as if designed for the use of the unlearned.[2] Head-pieces of the ornamental foliage characteristic of the time are introduced. In the first type the Evangelists are usually beneath canopies, the background being sometimes gilded, sometimes filled with architecture. Figures inspiring the writer are occasionally introduced;[3] the symbols are not found till a late date.[4] The type of seated figure writing is derived, as already stated,

[1] For illustrations from Byzantine Gospels see Kondakoff, Millet, Venturi, S. Beissel, *Vatikanische Miniaturen*, Pl. IX–XI, XIV, and *Gesch. der Evangelienbücher*, &c., 1906.

[2] See the remarks of Kondakoff, *Histoire de l'art byz.*, ii. 137 ff. A fine example of the second type is the eleventh-century Gospel in the Bibliothèque Nationale, Paris (MS. gr. 74), see Omont, *Évangiles avec peintures byz. du XIe siècle*, Paris, 1908.

[3] This feature also occurs in Gospels of the First Period (p. 454). The inspiring figure is found with St. John, but this Evangelist sometimes has the *Dextera Domini*, as in Brit. Mus., Harley 1810, fol. 211 b.

[4] Brit. Mus. Add. 11838, dated A.D. 1326, has the symbols with the Evangelists.

from the antique 'author's portrait' transmitted to later times by MSS. like the Vienna Dioscorides.[1] The canons, which are often decorated with the minute-ness of goldsmith's work, sometimes retain the flowers and animals above the arches and at the corners which we have noted as a characteristic of early Syrian books (e. g. the Gospel of Rabula, p. 448).

The number of Gospel books of the period later than the tenth century is too large to admit even of an attempt at enumeration in a work of this nature : all the important libraries in Europe contain examples of greater or less merit. Several are in the British Museum.[2]

Illuminated editions of the *Fathers* were very popular after iconoclasm, during which period they had been widely read. The favourite book is the Homilies of St. Gregory of Nazianzus, which provided lections for the different feasts of the ecclesiastical year. The large older copies of the Bibliothèque Nationale(No. 510)and the Ambrosiana at Milan—both are of the ninth century—

---

[1] See Diez, *B. D.*, iii. 1–69.

[2] The Byzantine illuminated Gospels and Lectionaries in the British Museum, dating from the tenth–fourteenth centuries, are as follows : *Arundel 547.* Tenth century [F. H. Scrivener, *Collection of MSS. of the Holy Gospels*, 1853, and *Plain Introduction*, 1874, p. 260 ; British Museum, *Cat. of Ancient MSS.*, p. 23]. Seated portraits of the four Evangelists at the beginning of their Gospels ; head-pieces of foliage enclosed in geometrical figures or zigzag ; grotesque initials composed of human limbs, amphorae or jugs suspended from cross-bars, birds, &c. The text is in uncials of Slavonic type, and the character of these initials, reminiscent of Frankish art, points to Western influence.   *Harley 5598.* A lectionary, dated A.D. 995. The illuminations are confined to the head-pieces on fol. 1, 56, and 142, consisting of fine foliate designs geometrically disposed in panels.   *Harley 8785.* A lectionary, tenth–eleventh century. Full-page illustrations of the Evangelists writing their Gospels on gold background ; fine head-pieces fol. 1, 67, 104, 144, 246, 298 b, 642 b, &c. The ornament is of formal foliage ; above the panels in some cases are animal motives, e. g. two lions, two gryphons, peacocks flanking a vase, &c.   *Burney 19.* Gospels, eleventh century ; full-page miniatures representing the Evangelists writing ; delicate foliated head-pieces. (Exhibited.)   *Additional MS. 37001.* Gospels, eleventh century. Ten pages of illuminated Eusebian Canons ; head-pieces. The ornament of the canons is very oriental in character, illustrating the affinities between Byzantine and Saracenic decorative art.   *Arundel 524.* Gospels, eleventh century. A small book, with illuminated Eusebian Canons. The floral ornament again shows oriental affinities.   *Add. MS. 36928.* Gospels, end of the eleventh century.   *Add. MS. 4949.* Gospels, twelfth century. Full-page miniatures of the Evangelists ; head-pieces. The latter are stiff and inferior in execution.   *Add. 1810.* Gospels, early twelfth century. In addition to the usual Evangelists, this book has a number of other figure subjects : the Nativity, Transfiguration, Last Supper, Baptism, Ascension, Annunciation, Presentation, Death of the Virgin, Crucifixion, Descent from the Cross and Entombment, *Anastasis*, Pentecost, Raising of Lazarus, Entry into Jerusalem, Washing of the Disciples' Feet, Incredulity of Thomas, and a martyrdom (fol. 107 b). There are besides several fine head-pieces, with geometrically treated floral ornament. A number of the subjects coincide with those in the Psalter of Melisenda, with which they should be compared, but the rendering of facial expression and the treatment of draperies are finer. The face of the Evangelist St. Mark admirably expresses reflection ; emotion is well given in the miniature of the Descent from the Cross (fol. 205 b). The shading is done with darker tints of the several colours ; high lights are painted on in white.   *Add. MS. 35030.* Gospels, twelfth century ; a small volume, with illuminations of good quality, but much rubbed. The Eusebian Canons are executed in a fine linear style, with animals and plants at the corners ; no gold is used. There are the usual four Evangelists ; St. John stands, dictating his Gospel.   *Add. MSS. 5111.* Gospels, twelfth century. This is the book in which the interesting early illuminated pages mentioned on p. 451 are bound up. In itself it is not remarkable, but possesses one full-page miniature of merit, representing St. Matthew seated writing his Gospel, with a building with an upper loggia in the background.   *Add. MS. 22740.* Gospels of Matthew, Mark, and Luke. twelfth century. Full-page miniatures with the Evangelists ; head-pieces of good quality with formal foliate designs. The proportions of the human figure are faulty, as in the case of St. Mark.   *Add. MS. 5112.* Gospels of St. Luke and St. John, twelfth century. Full-page miniatures of the two Evangelists at their desks ; the work is mediocre.   *Burney 20.* Gospels, dated A.D. 1285. Full-page miniatures of the seated Evangelists, and head-pieces of formal foliate ornament.   *Add. MS. 37007.* Lectionary, thirteenth century. Miniatures of the four Evangelists writing ; the style is coarse. Foliate head-pieces.   *Add. MS. 7170.* Gospels with subjects of Byzantine type, showing, however, Syro-Arabic influence.   *Add. MS. 11838.* Gospels, dated A. D. 1326. Full-page miniatures of the four Evangelists on gold ground, with their symbols in the right-hand corners. Foliated head-pieces of inferior quality. All the great Continental libraries possess examples of Byzantine Gospels.

contain all the sermons, the letters, and the minor works. Later copies are usually of a smaller form, containing sixteen selected sermons beginning with that appointed for Easter.

The Codex Parisinus 510,[1] written between A. D. 880 and 886, is one of the most interesting and important of Byzantine illuminated MSS. It is profusely illustrated, the miniature usually coming at the beginning of the sermon, or division of the text, and sometimes being composed of two or more zones one above the other; a single scene rarely occupies a whole page. In many places the imitation of a much earlier late Hellenistic model is clear, some subjects, such as the Miracle of the Loaves and Fishes, standing nearer to Early Christian types than they do even in the sixth-century Codex of Rossano (p. 452). In some cases, as with the Vision of Ezekiel,[2] the scene is enclosed in an oval frame or border, suggesting the imitation of an ikon. The treatment of the frontispieces recalls the monumental style of contemporary mosaics.

At the beginning of the book, Our Lord is seen enthroned: on two neighbouring pages are the Emperor Basil I, his wife and sons. The emperor stands between the Archangel Gabriel, who places a crown on his head, and the Prophet Elijah, who carries a labarum: the princes carry scrolls.[3]

The remaining illustrations are suggested, directly or indirectly, by passages in the text: the subject of the homily itself may be chosen, or the Church festival which was the occasion of its delivery, or some historical or symbolic allusion admitting parallelism between the two Testaments. Among directly historical miniatures are those depicting episodes in the life of St. Gregory, or contemporary events. Among biblical subjects may be mentioned: the Garden of Eden, the Deluge, Sacrifice of Isaac, Jacob's Dream, Moses, Joshua, Samson, Gideon, the Anointing and Repentance of David, the Judgement of Solomon, scenes from the life of the prophets and kings, Job, the Maccabees, &c. The Gospel subjects include scenes from the childhood of Our Lord, parables and miracles, the Transfiguration, Entry into Jerusalem, Crucifixion, Descent from the Cross, Pentecost, &c. Millet is of opinion that some of the full-page subjects, such as the Transfiguration and Pentecost, are copied from ikons or mosaics. The association on one page of Daniel, the Three Children of Babylon, Manasseh, and Ezekiel suggest a derivation from a Psalter, for they are connected with the illustration of the 'Odes' appended to that book.

The Homilies of the Ambrosian Library are more monotonous in character, every epistle being illustrated by a miniature showing its composition, dispatch, and reception. The illustration of the text is simpler; there are the prophets, the Old Testament scenes, the life of Julian the Apostate. The scenes from the Gospels are proportionately less numerous than those illustrating mythological allusions, as if the secular rather than the sacred subjects had chiefly interested the artist. The illustrations are for the most part in the margins, as in the case of the 'monastic' group of Psalters. The MS. of Gregory at Jerusalem [4] (No. 14, eleventh century) includes a sermon on the Nativity by John of Damascus, freely illustrated with episodes partly biblical, partly derived from secular history (Dream of Cyrus, &c.).

No. 923 of the Bibliothèque Nationale contains a number of parallel passages from the Fathers. The illustration comprises figures of the saints, episodes from the Old Testament and from the New, especially the miracles. There are also genre scenes, showing the activity of the doctor, the painter, the athlete, &c. The book belongs to the same type as the Ambrosian Homilies of Gregory.

It is impossible to describe the later and smaller copies of the Homilies, the illustration of which is influenced by the two types represented in these two

---

[1] G. Millet in A. Michel, i, pp. 239–43; Kondakoff, *Histoire*, &c., ii. 58; Diehl, *Manuel*, 580.
[2] Reproduced by M. Omont, *Fac-similés des Miniatures*, Pl. LVIII; and by Millet, as above, p. 242.
[3] This style of frontispiece perpetuates the late Hellenistic tradition illustrated in the Vienna Dioscorides (see p. 460).
[4] In A. Michel, *Histoire*, i, p. 247.

older redactions.   M. Millet has given a general analysis of their distinguishing features.[1]

The Fonds Coislin of the Bibliothèque Nationale[2] has a fine MS. of the sermons of St. John Chrysostom.   It is remarkable for the introductory miniatures representing the Emperor Nicephorus Botoniates (A. D. 1078–81), for whom it was executed.   The emperor, who is four times represented, is accompanied by

Fig. 285.   Joseph and Mary expelled from the Temple : miniature from the twelfth-century Homilies of James in the Bibliothèque Nationale.   (*Hautes Études* : G. Schlumberger, Hachette.)

the empress, great officers of state, and other persons, the pictures preserving the traditional type of frontispiece-portrait represented in the Vienna Dioscorides and the later Homilies of Gregory.

Two MSS. of the Homilies of Jacobus Monachus in honour of the Virgin may be mentioned.   The Vatican MS. (No. 1162) appears to be an original of the twelfth century ; the Paris MS. (No. 1208),[3] a contemporary replica (Fig. 285).

[1] A. Michel, *Histoire*, i. 243 ff.   The principal MSS. are Bibl. Nationale 543, and Coislin 239 ; Sinaiticus 339 ; Jerusalem No. 14.   For Sinaiticus 339 see N. Kondakoff, *Voyage to Sinai*, pp. 143 ff., Odessa, 1882 ; the MS. is ascribed to the twelfth century.

[2] G. Millet, as above, 247 and Fig. 136 on p. 249.

[3] Schlumberger, *Épopée*, ii, Pl. VIII and pp. 229, 241 ; Venturi, *Storia*, ii, p. 482 ; Kirpičnikoff, *B. Z.*, v, p. 109.

The latter still retains the frontispiece representing Jacobus presented by Chrysostom to Gregory of Nyssa. The illustration of these books consists of whole-page frontispieces and miniatures inserted in the text, with gold backgrounds. They are suggested by allusions in the Homilies, or based upon the parallelism between the two Testaments, or are derived from the story of the Virgin, in which the apocryphal legends play a considerable part ; or, again, they set forth her celestial rank and functions. Irregular arrangement and the detachment of certain scenes from their context suggest that these compositions may be inspired from the frescoes or mosaics of some church decorated in a similar manner to Kahrié Djami at Constantinople.[1]

Fig. 286. Daniel: miniature from the Menologium of Basil II in the Vatican Library.
(*Hautes Études*: G. Millet.)

To the Third Period belongs the illustration of *Menologia* or general liturgical calendars, succeeding the earlier calendars of more local use. The compilation of the lives of the saints by Simeon Metaphrastes was executed in the reign of Constantine Porphyrogenitus (A.D. 912–59): this was abridged in the reign of Basil II, and the most famous illustrated example, that bearing the name of this emperor in the Vatican Library,[2] should strictly be described as a synaxarium rather than a menologium proper.

The endless series of martyrdoms, chiefly by beheading (Fig. 286), represented in a landscape of conventional rocky hills, or before architecture which at first sight seems equally conventional, lends an aspect of monotony to the illustration of this famous book: they are the work of more than one artist.[3] In style the miniatures belong to their time, and are a good example of the contemporary illuminator's art. But the book derives additional interest from its frequent

[1] The decoration both of Kahrié Djami and of the Church of the Peribleptos at Mistra is related to the work of Jacobus Monachus (see p. 416) ; but they date from the fourteenth and fifteenth centuries respectively, and the scenes differ in many ways from those of the MSS.
[2] Il Menologio di Basilio II : *Codices e Vaticanis selecti*, vol. viii, Turin, 1907, where references are given to earlier notices of the MS. See also Millet's remarks in A. Michel, i. 237 ff. Menologia have been treated from the literary side by Ehrhard and Delehaye, see references in *B. Z.*, vii. 231.   [3] Eight artists sign the miniatures, two described as ' of Blachernae.'

loans from antiquity.   It has been pointed out by various scholars that it is very rich in reminiscences of a more ancient art.   Among these may be mentioned the occurrence of sarcophagi with sculptured reliefs, and of nude statues representing idols, derived from pagan art.   The evidence for the copying of Early Christian models is even more direct: thus Joshua before the Archangel Michael reproduces the type seen in the Joshua Rotulus (see p. 457).   M. Millet has drawn attention to the resemblance between the buildings depicted and churches at Salonika, Ravenna, Bethlehem, and Constantinople.   Martyrdoms are often represented near the church consecrated to the martyr, and this is usually a circular building, or a basilica with a circular baptistery attached to it.   The Church of Apamea presents the characteristics of Syrian churches; the building shown in the scene of the translation of St. Timothy to Ephesus resembles that depicted in the translation of St. John Chrysostom to the Church of the Holy Apostles at Constantinople.   Since tradition connects the origin of the latter type with Ephesus, the comparison is interesting, as are those afforded by the representations of St. Simeon Stylites, and the Churches of St. John Studium and Blachernae.   It is argued that the architecture of this manuscript is not conventional but is based upon the actual buildings: the originals from which the artists worked were products of that 'pictorial hagiography' which Asia Minor transmitted to Constantinople.   Reasoning of this kind is certainly seductive; but it is perhaps possible to attach too much weight to these resemblances.

The Menologium in the Synodal Library at Moscow may be compared with the Vatican book for the month of January.   But there are a considerable number of illustrated menologia which do not follow the type of the Vatican book.   The illustrations in many cases are intercalated in the text, instead of being placed at the head of each chapter.   In two examples, those of the Monastery of Esphigmenou on Mount Athos (eleventh century; No. 14), and the Bibliothèque Nationale (No. 580; twelfth century), there are illustrated frontispieces, each divided into several scenes.

The British Museum possesses an illuminated copy of Simeon Metaphrastes' Lives of the Saints for the month of September, dating from the eleventh or early twelfth century (Add. MS. 11870).[1]   It contains more than twenty miniatures, chiefly representing martyrdoms in a conventional landscape, though occasionally the saint appears as *orans*, holding a cross or praying before or in a building.   One subject (fol. 60) depicts a miracle of St. Michael.   In more than one case the saint is seen in a medallion in the centre of four larger medallions in which his story is depicted: there are elaborate head-pieces of the foliate ornament characteristic of the period, often enclosed in circles, lozenges, quatrefoils, &c.   The figures are delicately painted, and the faces often expressive: the scheme of colour is brilliant, the principal tints being blues, greens, purples, browns, and vermilion.

Illuminated copies of theological works have also survived.   Conspicuous among these are the MSS. of the Spiritual Ladder of John Climax, abbot of Sinai, who lived at the close of the sixth century.   The finest copy is that of the eleventh century in the Vatican (Gr. 394),[2] where the miniatures are very numerous and of fine quality, though without variety in subject or conception. The matter is for the most part derived from episodes of religious and monastic life, in which acts of penitence are of especial frequency; and allegorical subjects in great variety accompany the progress of the monk up the 'spiritual ladder'. In the combats of the virtues and the vices, the forces of evil are symbolically distinguished by their black colour and infernal wings.

Another copy of the twelfth century in the Monastery on Mount Sinai is illustrated in a different spirit.   Here genre scenes depict the effects of vice

---

[1] G. F. Warner, British Museum *Reproductions from Illuminated MSS.*, ser. i, 1907, No. 1, Pl. I (St. Euphrosyne).
[2] G. Millet, as above, p. 248.

and virtue; monks are constantly represented, the fact suggesting a monastic origin.

Religious poetry has left less illustration than remains to us in historical works. The Akathistic Hymn (ὕμνος ἀκαθιστός) to the Virgin,[1] considered the work of Photius, who composed it in A.D. 626 to aid in the defence of Constantinople against the Russians, has however survived in illustrated copies. The MS. at Moscow, of the eleventh century, has interesting zoomorphic initials, and each of the twenty-four οἶκοι is preceded by a miniature.

Fɪɢ. 287. An Oecumenical Council : miniature from the Menologium of Basil II in the Vatican. (*Hautes Études* : G. Millet.) P. 479.

The same cycle of subjects is found in the fifteenth-century frescoes of the Church of the Pantanassa at Mistra, and in later frescoes on Mount Athos.

Portraits of imperial persons occur in numerous religious MSS., and some have been noticed above. It may be of interest to mention a typikon of the Monastery of the *Theotokos τῆς βεβαίας ἐλπίδος* at Lincoln College, Oxford, which contains interesting portraits of John Comnenos Ducas Synadenos, his wife, and relatives: it is of the fourteenth century.[2]

II. SECULAR MANUSCRIPTS.

As far as present knowledge goes, illuminated copies of the *Physiologus*, or Book of Symbolic Beasts, were not so popular in the East as were the Bestiaries in the Western Middle Ages. Although the Physiologus itself was probably compiled in Alexandria in the first centuries of the Christian era,[3] no illustrated copies of the First Period are at present known to exist. The origin of the pictorial types at a time preceding the iconoclastic revolution is exceedingly probable, but cannot as yet be proved : animals of a similar kind are used to illustrate the early MSS. of Cosmas Indicopleustes. The earliest examples now

[1] Millet in A. Michel, i. 248.
[2] H. Omont, *Rev. des études grecques*, xvii, 1904, 361–73 ; *B. Z.*, xiv. 1905, 732.
[3] Krumbacher, *Gesch. der byz. Litt.*, 2nd ed., 874 ff. ; *B. Z.*, viii, 1899, 510 ff.

known—for instance, the Smyrna Physiologus of about A. D. 1100 [1]—show an evident affinity with the art of the Psalters of the ' monastic-theological ' school : though their illustrations are not marginal they are similar in style, especially those, common to both books, in which Old and New Testament subjects are introduced for symbolical reasons or to illustrate allusions in the text.   In both we find miniatures relating to the iconoclastic dispute, and to entrance into religious orders : both are conceived in the same theological spirit.   Probably the type of Physiologus containing such supplementary pictures, the earliest type which we now know, was first produced in the ninth century and under monastic influence. [2]

Other illuminated copies of the Physiologus exist, dating from the twelfth century and after.   As time advanced the book became more popular, and the type diverged in some respects from the Smyrna example, possibly as a result

Fig. 288.   A naval battle : miniature from the tenth-century MS. of the Cynegetica of Oppian in the Marciana, Venice.   (*Hautes Études* : G. Millet.)   P. 483.

of influence from the West. [3]   Perhaps the comparative scarcity of Physiologus MSS. is merely due to our ignorance ; if there are other causes, a reason may be sought in the popularity of abridgements of the Natural Histories of Aristotle and Aelian.

It is possible, as Strzygowski has remarked, [4] that there may be interaction between the animal types of the earliest Buddhist art in India and those of the Physiologus, both having a common origin in a Graeco-Asiatic area.   The types of the Physiologus may have affected the treatment of biblical scenes in which numerous animals appear, for example, the naming of the beasts by Adam, and the entry into the Ark.   The same may be said of monstrous and other forms in the illustrated books of Job.

Only a few purely secular illuminated MSS. can be mentioned.   In the Bibliothèque Nationale at Paris there is an eleventh-century copy of the *Theriaca* of Nicander, who lived in the second century. [5]   The illustration comprises three

[1] J. Strzygowski, *Der Bilderkreis des griechischen Physiologus* (Ergänzungsheft i of the *B. Z.*, 1899) ; V. Schultze, *Der Physiologus in der kirchlichen Kunst des Mittelalters* in *Christliches Kunstblatt*, xxxix, 1897, 49–55.   [2] Strzygowski, 95–6.
[3] O. Wulff (*Izviestiya* of Russ. Arch. Inst., Cple., iii. 202) mentions a Physiologus in the Εὐαγγελικὴ Σχολή at Smyrna ' not earlier than the fourteenth century '. This contains features pointing to Western influence.   [4] pp. 92 ff.
[5] The *Theriaca* was a treatise on the remedies to be adopted against poisonous bites.   The picturesque miniature representing the ' Purification of the Gardens ' is reproduced by Millet in A. Michel's *Hist. de l'art*, i. 210.

picturesque miniatures in which the figures are seen in landscapes of Alexandrian type, and a number of other illustrations in the margins without any backgrounds. The work is evidently a painstaking copy of a very early original, perhaps almost contemporary with Nicander himself. It should be compared, as an illustrated scientific work, with the Vienna MS. of Dioscorides (p. 460).

The finest copy of the *Cynegetica* of Oppian dates from the Third Period, and is in the Marcian Library at Venice (tenth century) [1] (Fig. 288).

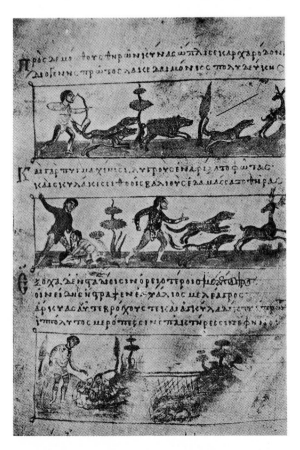

Fig. 289. Scenes from the chase : miniature from the tenth-century Cynegetica of Oppian in the Marcian Library, Venice. (*Hautes Études*: G. Millet.)

It contains numerous historical and mythological illustrations arranged in horizontal bands, usually without borders, hunting-scenes, and figures of animals. Near the beginning we see Oppian presenting his work to Caracalla, and receiving the counsel of Artemis. Among the historical and mythological subjects are Bellerophon and the Chimaera, Achilles on his chariot, and Alexander pursuing Darius,— the very subjects which the hero Digenes Akritas is said to have caused to be represented in mosaic on the walls of his palace at about the time when this book was illustrated. Millet has drawn attention to this relation to monumental art ; probably both versions of the old motives were based upon late Hellenistic models of the third century.

---

[1] G. Millet in Michel's *Histoire de l'art*, i. 212. There is a later (fifteenth century) copy at Paris.

The *Calendar of the Chronographer Filocalus*, written and illuminated in
A. D. 354, is only preserved to us in copies of the fifteenth and seventeenth
centuries from older copies of the Carolingian era.[1] These copies at second
hand possess, however, in so high a degree the characteristics of the fourth
century, that, allowing for the necessary influence of the later style, they still
furnish evidence of great value for the transitional period between pagan and
Christian art. The ninth-century models of surviving editions[2] are either
destroyed or lost, though one was known to the antiquary Peiresc in the first
quarter of the seventeenth century.

The surviving copies are three in number, and are clearly based upon two
different ninth-century models. The earliest copy, that in the Vienna Library
(No. 3416), dates from the second half of the fifteenth century, and is based upon
a redaction like that of an unillustrated fragment at Bern. The other two copies,
those in the Brussels Library and in the Barberini Library at Rome, derive from
a different Carolingian MS. The different copies are complementary to each
other, in so far as miniatures missing in one are still preserved in others, so that
by utilizing all three, Strzygowski has been able to give a fair idea of the
contents of the book, only three illustrated pages remaining blank. The greater
number are taken from the Barberini Codex, and are copies made for Peiresc ;[3]
where a single miniature is represented in more than one MS., it is possible to
draw some conclusion as to the fidelity of the earlier copyists. The title-page
bears an inscription relating to a Valentinus of whom nothing is known ;[4] the
name of the calligrapher Filocalus is given upon one end of the *tabella ansata* on
the same page.[5] The fact that in the pages with the *Natales Caesarum* a Constantius and a Constantine are described as *divi*, while a second Constantius
appears as *dominus noster*, shows that the book was originally written in the
reign of Constantius II (A. D. 350–61): details in the iconography accord with
this conclusion. The actual year must be that of the consulship of the two
princes, A. D. 354.

The book contained a title-page, the *Tychae* of Rome, Alexandria, Constantinople, and Trèves, a Niké, a Victory, a table of the *Natales Caesarum*, or
birthdays of the deified emperors, six pictures representing planets, two of
which did not survive to the second copying, a second title-page (also lost), a
series of miniatures with the emblematical figures of the months and signs of the
zodiac, and two miniatures of imperial persons, one of Constantius II enthroned,
the other of the Caesar Constantius Gallus standing, both with the nimbus.

The calendar was certainly illustrated as well as written in Rome ; but as it
shows various features which became characteristic of East-Christian art, it should
be mentioned in the course of any account of Byzantine miniatures. These
features are a certain relaxation of Roman austerity, the introduction of more or
less 'unorthodox' ornamental motives, some of which—for example, the borders
formed of overlapping heart-shaped figures—bear an oriental impress, the sumptuous costume of the imperial personages recalling in its detail of applied gems

---

[1] J. Strzygowski, *Die Calenderbilder des Chronographen vom Jahre 354*, Ergänzungsheft i of the
Mitth. k. d. A. I., Berlin, 1888 ; N. Kondakoff, *Histoire de l'art byz.*, i. The Vienna copy has been
published more than once, first by Lambecius in the seventeenth century, Bibl. Caes. app.
com., Bk. IV, addit. i ; Kollar, *Analecta Vindobon.*, 1761, i. 946 ff. ; Graevius, *Thesaurus*, vol. viii;
Montfaucon, *Antiq. expl.*, suppl. i, Pl. VI ff. The text of the Calendar was fully discussed by
Mommsen in 1850; see *Abh. der k. sächsischen Gesellsch. der Wiss., Phil.-hist. Classe*, 547 ff.

[2] Only fragments, without illustration, exist at Bern and at St. Gall.

[3] It is clear from Peiresc's letters that these illustrations were sketches provisionally
sent, to be followed at a later time by more exact reproductions. At the same time, the antiquary remarks in a published letter that they follow the original very closely. This was an
outline pen-drawing (Strzygowski, p. 22), but it does not follow that the originals from
which the Carolingian copyists worked were not coloured miniatures.

[4] *Valentine floreas in Deo. Valentine lege feliciter. Valentine vivas, floreas. Valentine vivas,
gaudeas.*

[5] *Filocalus titulavit.* This Filocalus, as a Roman inscription upon stone shows, is probably
the calligrapher who furnished the texts for the inscriptions of Pope Damasus (Strzygowski,
p. 101).

or inwoven figures representations of emperors, empresses, and consuls whose lives were passed in the East-Roman Empire, or in places, like Ravenna, under the influence of its art. The two concluding miniatures, with their portraits of

Fig. 290. The Emperor Basil II : miniature from the Psalter of the tenth century in the Marciana, Venice. (*Hautes Études* : G. Millet.) P. 470.

Constantius II and Constantius Gallus, recall the rather later consular diptychs made for consuls of Constantinople. The fantastic treatment of the architecture in which the *Natales Caesarum* and the calendar tables are framed, a treatment in which structural propriety is abandoned to decorative advantage, marks an early stage of a process which is familiar to students of all the later periods of Byzantine art.

The best example of the illustrated historical book is the history of John Skylitzes at Madrid.[1] It contains nearly six hundred illustrations. The hand is of the fourteenth century, and the history covers the period from the accession of Michael Rhangabé (A.D. 811) to the middle of the eleventh century. The work of several artists may be distinguished. In the earlier part of the book the style is simple and of harmonious colouring ; then follow pictures of larger size and coarser execution ; in the subsequent portion, illustrating the reign of John Zimisces and part of that of Basil II, the subjects are broadly treated in a realistic manner, but the architecture of the backgrounds is more fantastic. In both this and the preceding manner polychrome backgrounds of an oriental character are employed.

The influence of East-Christian illuminated MSS. upon Western mediaeval art was no less powerful and widely extended than that of ivory carvings. It may be assumed in Italy at least from the time of Cassiodorus, who, as is well known, established a *scriptorium* in his Monastery of Vivarium, and probably entertained relations with Mesopotamian centres.[2] The Codex Rossanensis (p. 452) may possibly have entered Italy at quite an early date through relations of this kind, though it is perhaps more probable that it came in with the later influx of Basilian monks. Imported MSS. must have been early imitated by Italians, and the Gospels of Corpus Christi College, Cambridge,[3] are by some considered to be a very early copy from a Greek book of the First Period. In the Third Period, at the time when the great Monastery of Monte Cassino flourished (p. 83), the influence of Byzantine MSS. was continuous. A book of the Gospels (No. 165) in the Biblioteca Casanatense at Rome, with miniatures of the four Evangelists, appears to have been executed in South Italy.[4] It may belong to a rather numerous class of South Italian MSS. of about the year A.D. 1000[5] closely following Byzantine originals. The Gospels in the Ambrosiana at Milan (D. 67) also appear to represent this class, of which Professor Muñoz promises a publication. Late Byzantine books of prayers, of a type to be compared with the Western books of hours, were sometimes copied in Italy for Graecizing princes of the Renaissance. An example is the fifteenth-century book in the Bibliothèque de Ste Geneviève at Paris, written in Greek but possibly illuminated at Milan.[6] The Greek Gospels in the British Museum, written at Rome in A.D. 1478 for Cardinal Fr. Gonzaga by a Cretan priest John, show the interaction of Byzantine and Renaissance styles (Harley, 5790). The number of MSS. in Italy of various periods showing Byzantine influence must be very considerable.[7]

[1] A complete set of photos in the *Collection des Hautes Études* at the Sorbonne. Millet, as above, pp. 213 ff. A MS. of Skylitzes dating from about the beginning of the twelfth century is in the library of the Church of S. Clement at Ochrida in Macedonia (*Izviestiya*, Russ. Arch. Inst. Cple., iv, 1899, 132).

[2] A. Muñoz, *Il Codice purpureo di Rossano*, 29.

[3] H. Wanley, *Cat. librorum septentrionalium*, Oxford, 1705, 151 ; J. O. Westwood, *Palaeographia sacra pictoria* ; Palaeographical Society's reproductions ; Garrucci, *Storia*, iii. 64 ; H. Grisar, *Roma alla fine del mondo antico*, 1899 ; L. Traube, *Abh. der k. bayerischen Akad. der Wiss.*, *Phil.-hist. Klasse*, xxi, 1898, 107. Muñoz (*Codice purpureo*, p. 30) maintains a South Italian, Grisar a Roman origin.

[4] A. Muñoz, *Codici greci miniati delle minori biblioteche di Roma*, 81 ff.

[5] A good example is a Gospel of A.D. 1237 in the *Biblioteca Queriniana* at Brescia, with five miniatures (A. Martini, *Catalogo di manoscritti greci*, &c., i, Pt. II, 223 ff. ; A. Muñoz, *Miniature biz. nella Biblioteca Queriniana di Brescia*, in *Miscellanea Ceriani*, 1910, 172).

[6] A. Muñoz, *Codici greci miniati delle minori biblioteche di Roma*, 90 ff.

[7] A few further examples may be here cited. In a book of sermons in the library of Monte Cassino (MS. 99206) the Annunciation, Adoration of the Magi, and Ascension are affected by the Byzantine types (Prussian *Jahrbuch*, xv. 228 ; see also D. Oderisio Piscicelli Taeggi, *Le Miniature nei Codici Cassinensi*, and E. Bertaux, *L'Art dans l'Italie méridionale*). Though the famous illuminated initials of Monte Cassino are of North European inspiration, oriental types appear in zoomorphic capitals resembling those of books in the Monastery of St. Catherine on Mount Sinai (A. Muñoz, *L'Art byzantin à l'Exposition de Grottaferrata*, p. 85). An exultet-roll in Bari Cathedral, inscribed with the names of Robert Guiscard and his second wife, has minia-

Turning to the countries north of the Alps, we find similar influences at work from the early centuries of the Middle Ages. The ornament of Merovingian MSS. is rich in Eastern motives, both floral and zoomorphic.[1] The Carolingian

FIG. 291. Iconoclasts facing a sacred picture : from the Psalter of A.D. 1066 in the British Museum. (Add. MS. 19352.) P. 470.

era begins under the same auspices.[2] The monk Godescalc, who in A.D. 781–3 illuminated for Charlemagne the remarkable Gospels now in the Bibliothèque Nationale in Paris,[3] must have had for his model a book in the style of the

tures representing Basil II and Constantine (Bertaux, as above, pp. 217 ff.). In the capitular library at Verona there is a bilingual Psalter in Greek and Latin hands of about the seventh century, illustrated with single figures of animals, &c., perhaps of slightly later date. The style is marked by oriental characteristics (Maffei, *Istoria teologica*, Pl. I, Fig. 1 ; Westwood, *Palaeographia sacra pict.*, Pl. X ; A. Goldschmidt in *Repertorium*, xxiii, 1900, 265 ff.). An early Italian MS. in the British Museum has two full-page miniatures representing the Virgin between two archangels (Fig. 295) and the Death of the Virgin, which must be copies of Byzantine originals (Nero, C. 4). [1] See Comte A. de Bastard's reproductions.

[2] Thegan (*Monumenta Germaniae hist.*, ii. 592) relates that before his death Charlemagne collated the Gospels with the aid *of Greeks and Syrians*.

[3] The connexion was first established by Strzygowski, *B. D.*, i. 58 ff. The Gospels of Lothair and of Épernay reveal a certain impressionism perhaps inspired by late Hellenistic art.

Gospels of Etchmiadzin (p. 450). On the reverse of fol. 3 we see a representation of a sanctuary closely resembling that of the earlier Syrian book, the differences chiefly arising from the artist's imperfect comprehension of his original. In the foreground are introduced a variety of beasts and birds of the types which occur in the Syrian Gospel of Rabula (p. 448), betraying the kind of copy which Godescalc had before him. In the later Gospels of St. Médard, written in the time of Louis the Pious (tenth century), a similar motive appears, though the sanctuary has now become a fountain at which the animals drink, and is associated in idea with the Fountain of Life (Jer. i. 13 ; John iv. 13, 14 ; Rev. xxi. 6). In this book the rainbow border, first encountered in early Syrian books, is also reproduced, and so handed on to later Western art.

The large group of early Carolingian illuminated books, known, from a Gospel prepared for the Princess Ada, as the Ada group,[1] shows the evident traces of Syrian inspiration both in ornamental motives and in figure subjects. Between these MSS. and a series of ivory carvings[2] a close relationship exists : ivories and miniatures have common iconographic models, which appear to belong to East-Christian art of the sixth century. Among examples preserved in England, the large composite book-cover in the Victoria and Albert Museum, and the Sneyd *pyxis* in the British Museum,[3] the imitation of oriental types and forms is very evident (Figs. 146, 148). Similar imitation may be assumed in the case of other well-known Carolingian ivories, for example the book-covers from Metz in the Bibliothèque Nationale in Paris.[4]

Peculiarities in the seventh-century Ashburnham Pentateuch[5] justify a similar inference to an early MS. of oriental origin now lost or destroyed. Here details of costume and architecture, showing analogies to the frescoes of Jewish tombs at Palmyra, suggest that the model was of Jewish origin, though the place where the work was executed was very likely Alexandria.[6] It is clear that the painter or painters were familiar with oriental fauna and flora. Other details, such as the architectural ornament of the frontispiece, are oriental in type : the frontispiece, with its windows, recalls the canopy under which St. Matthew sits in the Codex Rossanensis. The MS. has been variously assigned to Upper Italy or Germany.

The Utrecht Psalter,[7] written and illustrated in the early ninth century at Hautvillers in the diocese of Reims, probably by an Anglo-Saxon, is clearly based either upon a model of the fourth or fifth century, or upon an early copy of such a model. The original artist evidently lived in a Greek environment : the division of the Psalms is into two parts after the Greek manner, the second section beginning with Psalm 78 ; there is further an affinity between this MS. and the Joshua Rotulus or its original (p. 447), showing that the model of the Utrecht book was of the same period and character. The backgrounds with their hills and buildings are similarly treated ; the personifications of cities

---

[1] Janitschek, *Die Trierer Ada-Handschrift* and article in *Springer-Festschrift*, 1885.

[2] A. Goldschmidt, Prussian *Jahrbuch*, 1905 ; Vöge, *Repertorium*, xxiv, 1901, 196.

[3] *Catalogue of Ivory Carvings of the Christian Epoch*, No. 43. The question of oriental influence is discussed in the introduction of this catalogue.

[4] Haseloff, Prussian *Jahrbuch*, xxiv (1903), pp. 60 and 61.

[5] The book, which contains the Books of Moses (except Deuteronomy) in Jerome's translation, was formerly at Tours and in the collection of Lord Ashburnham, but is now in the Bibliothèque Nationale at Paris (*Palaeographical Society*, Pl. CCXXXIX ; O. von Gebhardt, *The Miniatures of the Ashburnham Pentateuch*, 1883).

[6] J. Strzygowski, *Orient oder Rom*, pp. 32 ff. ; A. Goldschmidt, *Repertorium*, xxiv, p. 146 ; A. Springer, *Die Genesisbilder in der Kunst des frühen Mittelalters*, in *Abhandlungen der phil.-hist. Klasse der k. sächsischen Gesellschaft der Wissenschaften*, ix, 1884, pp. 663 ff. ; L. Delisle, *Compte rendu de l'Acad. des Inscr.*, Feb., 1883.

[7] Formerly in the Cottonian Library, now in that of the University of Utrecht (W. de G. Birch, *The History, Art, and Palaeography of the MS.* styled the Utrecht Psalter, London, 1876 ; *The Latin Psalter in the University Library of Utrecht*, &c., *photographed and produced in Facsimile*, London, 1875 ; P. Durrien, *L'Origine du Psautier d'Utrecht*, in *Mélanges Julien Havet*, 1895 ; A. Goldschmidt, *Repertorium*, xv, 1892 ; H. Graeven, *Die Vorlagen des U. P.*, ibid., xxi, 1898, 28 ff. ; J. J. Tikkanen, *Die Psalterillustration*, &c., i, Pt. iii).

and places are a conspicuous feature in both cases ; the groups of warriors bear
a resemblance to each other.   Such personifications are especially characteristic
of later Greek art: not only places, but Sun, Moon, Earth, Winds, and Waters,
with abstract qualities like Virtue, Pity, Justice, and Truth, are rendered by
human figures : the whole circle of Nature is in fact personified.   Sleep
(Psalm 75) appears as a small figure hovering like an insect above slumbering
men.   The personification of 'our days' (Psalm 89, v. 8) as *Aeon*, a nude male
figure, points to a Greek original, for the Latin word *Saeculum* is impersonal :
in the same way the bearded half-figure representing Hades (Psalm 114) is more

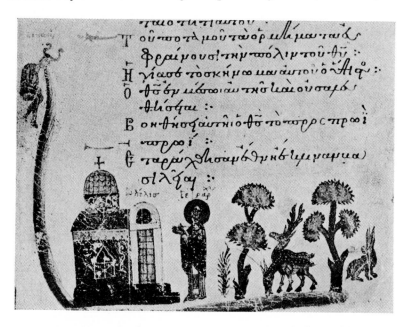

Fig. 292.   Illustration from the Psalter of A.D. 1066 in the British Museum.
(Add. MS. 19352.)

probably derived from the Greek than from the Latin *Infernum*.   More conclusive still is the illustration of the passage in Psalm 21 : 'they parted my
garments among them,' &c., where the curious machine used in the Hippodrome
at Constantinople (cf. Fig. 293) for casting the lots for chariot-races is introduced.[1]
An object of this kind cannot have been known in the west of Europe at the
time when the Utrecht Psalter was written.   Finally we note resemblances
between figures in the Psalter and others on the group of Byzantine ivory
caskets best represented by the Veroli casket at South Kensington (p. 215),
which are themselves partly influenced by the Joshua Rotulus or an early
version of it.   The conclusion is that the artist of the Psalter had before him
a Greek MS. of the Psalms illustrated in the style of the rotulus, and perhaps
of the fourth or fifth century.[2]   The vigorous draughtsmanship is due to the
individual talent of the artist ; the original was probably more classical and
restrained in style, and fully coloured rather than drawn in outline : the linear
style, as in the case of the Calendar of Filocalus, is probably to be ascribed to
the copyist.

---

[1] H. Graeven, as above, p. 34 ; Dalton, *Proc. Soc. Ant. London*, xxi. p. 188.
[2] This conclusion is in contradiction to that of Springer (*Die Psalterillustration im frühen
Mittelalter* in *Abhandlungen der k. sächsischen Gesellschaft, Phil.-hist. Classe*, viii, 1880, pp. 187 ff.).

In the manuscripts of the period of Archbishop Egbert of Trèves there are distinct traces of Byzantine influence, though it is clear that the German artists of the closing tenth century did not rely exclusively upon Eastern sources. Like their contemporaries of the Winchester school in England (see below), they seem to have resorted in great measure to Early Christian models produced in the West.[1] In the Codex of Egbert, as in the Benedictional of St. Æthelwold, the apparent blending of sources is perplexing to the student, because we cannot say what the Western originals really were.[2] General influences of this kind are observed in the group of MSS. of about A. D. 1000 studied by Dr. Vöge, and perhaps produced at Cologne.[3] Here the Byzantine scheme of composition is adopted in some cases, as in the Last Supper and Death of the Virgin ; in others, single Byzantine features are incorporated into a scheme of Western origin, giving rise to a hybrid type. In yet other cases contemporary oriental influence is altogether absent, and the scenes are entirely of Western composition. There

FIG. 293.   The lot-casting machine of the Hippodrome, from a contorniate medal, an ivory carving, and the Utrecht Psalter. (Cf. pp. 143, 468.) P. 489

is an almost exaggerated expression of movement and feeling, in some ways recalling the atmosphere of the Utrecht Psalter. Perhaps these Cologne MSS., like that famous book, reflect the spirit of earlier work based indeed upon the antique, but dating from a period, possibly the fourth century, when the antique had lost its gravity and its repose. Here and there it seems possible to trace a particular feature to Eastern inspiration, as the type of St. Mark as Bishop of Alexandria, which may have been introduced from Egypt.[4]

German art of the Romanesque period is so permeated by Byzantine influences that by the thirteenth century we find a general inspiration and absorption of oriental types, rather than the direct imitation of individual models which had prevailed at an earlier period. Haseloff has demonstrated this in the case of a Saxon-Thuringian school of illuminators working at the beginning of the thirteenth century.[5] The artists adopt Eastern types of faces,

[1] W. Vöge, *Repertorium*, xxiv, 1901, 474, reviewing Sauerland and Haseloff's *Egbert-Psalter*. In the Codex Egberti (see F. X. Kraus's edition) the Washing of the Disciples' Feet, the Pentecost, and the Massacre of the Innocents follow Eastern types.

[2] A clue is perhaps given in the similarity between the gesture of Peter in the scene of the Washing of the Disciples' Feet on a sarcophagus at Arles and in the Gospels at Corpus Christi College, Cambridge (Garrucci, *Storia*, Pl. 141 ; Romilly Allen, *Early Christian Symbolism*, 306).

[3] *Eine deutsche Malerschule um die Wende des ersten Jahrtausends* (Ergänzungsheft vii of the *Westdeutsche Zeitschrift für Geschichte und Kunst*).

[4] Sauerland and Haseloff, *Egbert-Psalter*, 149.

[5] A. Haseloff, *Eine thüringisch-sächsische Malerschule des XIII. Jahrhunderts*, Strassburg, 1897. For other German MSS. influenced by Byzantine models, see E. Dobbert, Prussian *Jahrb.*, xix, 1898, 1 ff., *Das Evangeliar im Rathaus zu Goslar*, and *Gött. gelehrte Anzeigen*, 1890, 883 ff. The *Hortus Deliciarum* of the Abbess Herrade of Landsperg, now extant only in reproduction, is also strongly influenced by Byzantine types.

styles of drapery, even whole compositions, but incorporate them into designs in which, like the Carolingian draughtsmen who produced the Ada group, the English illuminators definitely adopted a linear style, probably because they found colour-shading difficult.[1]

The manner suited their national genius and enabled them to pursue a freer

Fig. 294. Isaiah and Dawn (*Orthros*) : from the Psalter of A. D. 1066 in the British Museum.
(Add. MS. 19352.) P. 470.

and more original path : the excellence of their work was such that it reacted upon continental art.[2] The manuscripts of the Winchester school, of which the Benedictional of St. Æthelwold, in the collection of the Duke of Devonshire, is the most famous example, are executed in a style which has little in common with contemporary Byzantine illumination. Throughout, the artists rely upon mastery of line ; and, though the colours are often rich, the miniatures recall tinted drawings rather than the compositions of the Byzantine illuminator, with their softer outlines, and deeper contrasts of light and shade. The luxuriant foliage which frames the figure subjects, or forms the structure of the initials,

[1] This seems more probable than Haseloff's theory that a vanished early Byzantine linear style, only represented by derivative work in the Etchmiadzin Gospels, actually exerted an influence upon Anglo-Saxon art (*Der Psalter Erzbischof Egberts von Trier*).

[2] There may be ground for Vöge's suggestion that there is a reflection of the Anglo-Saxon linear style in the early sculptures in Bamberg Cathedral (W. Vöge, *Repertorium*, xxiv, 1901).

though conventional in character and doubtless suggested by the vine or acanthus, has little in common with Byzantine foliate design. The iconography of the scenes diverges constantly from that of the Eastern Church, and may rather be connected with the art of Western Europe than that of the new school of Byzantine illumination which began to flourish with the establishment of the Macedonian dynasty. Here and there we find a definitely Eastern feature, such as the Washing of the Child in the Nativity, occurring in the Psalter of Athelstan in the British Museum, a MS. dating from the late ninth century ;[1] such features may have been borrowed from the same early MSS. of the Eastern area which inspired the Carolingian illuminator, but if the Anglo-Saxons had such models they followed them less closely. There may have been intermediate models of continental origin.[2]

The influence of the East-Christian illuminator was naturally felt in the states of the Balkan peninsula. The miniature art of the Southern Slav peoples appears to betray influences coming from different quarters. Bulgaria is more directly affected by the art of Constantinople ; in Servia, which was closely connected with the Monastery of Chilandari on Mount Athos, where Early Syrian MSS. were preserved, the influence of the Early Christian art of Syria and Mesopotamia appears to have lasted until very late. In some parts of the peninsula Byzantine influence was modified by that of Western Romanesque art coming in through Dalmatia or Hungary.[3] The dependence of the well-known fifteenth-century Servian Psalter at Munich[4] on a Byzantine or, as Strzygowski thinks, Early Syrian model has been clearly established. Similar influences are traced by Baumstark in a twelfth-century Gospel in the library of the Greek patriarchate at Jerusalem.[5] Of Byzantine influence in Armenia the Gospels of Queen Mlke (early tenth century) in the Lagoon Monastery at Venice are an important example, though the style depends largely upon the Early Christian art of Mesopotamia and Syria.[6] Armenian illuminated books are enriched with many ornamental motives inherited from similar sources. It has been stated above that the Armenians were important intermediaries between Christian art and that of Persia. Mohammedan MSS. often show in their illumination the influence of Byzantine miniature art.[7]

Western miniaturists copying Byzantine models frequently betray themselves in such details as the rendering of heads and suggestion of motion.[8] It is possible that where, as is often the case, a subject is reversed, e. g. where, in the Entry into Jerusalem, Our Lord rides from the right, instead of from the left as usually in Byzantine art, the copyist may have held the page from the MS. up to the light and traced the design from the back. Although Byzantine influence was thus continually exerted in Europe down to the thirteenth century, we sometimes find a reaction of the West upon the East, or rather the interaction of two styles. The MSS. of Monte Cassino will be at once recalled ; the Servian Miroslav Gospel has already been mentioned (see n. 3). A Western influence is suggested in the Russo-Byzantine miniatures in the Egbert Psalter at Cividale,

---

[1] Westwood, *Facsimiles*, &c., Pl. XXXII.

[2] It may be noted that in the latest Anglo-Saxon period the architecture of Anglo-Saxon churches presents features which have been traced to Germany (Baldwin Brown, *The Arts in Early England*, vol. i).

[3] So in the Miroslav Gospel (late twelfth century ?), which was among the possessions of the murdered King Alexander (Facsimiles by L. Stojanovitch, 1897). Kondakoff and Bus-slaieff have both noted the Western style of the initials.

[4] See Jagitch and Strzygowski in *Denkschriften* of the Vienna Academy, vol. 52, *Phil.-hist. Classe* ; A. Muñoz in *Nuovo Bull. di arch. crist.*, 1906.

[5] Ἁγίου Τάφου, 56 ; see A. Baumstark, *R. Q.*, 1906, 174.

[6] Alishan, *Die Miniaturen des Evangeliars der Königin Mlke*, Venice, S. Lazzaro, 1902. For Syrian influence on Armenian MSS. in the Holy Land see A. Baumstark, *R. Q.*, 1906, 181-2.

[7] E. Blochet, *Rev. arch.*, ser. iv, vol. ix (1907), pp. 193 ff.

[8] E. Dobbert, *Repertorium*, xv, 372-3. Examples of books quoted by Dobbert in illustration are the *Evangelistarium* D. 67 in the Ambrosian Library at Milan (thirteenth century), and the Gospel No. 118 at St. Petersburg (middle of the fifteenth century).

where the symbols of the Evangelists are introduced.[1] The ritual book at Vatopedi of A.D. 1346, with its representations of months and seasons, introduces Western (Italian) types.[2]

Like the ivory carving, the illumination probably provided frequent models for the major arts. It may have assisted the sculptors of the early Romanesque period, especially in Southern France ; we know that an illustrated Bible of the

FIG. 295. The Virgin between Archangels : miniature showing Byzantine influence, from a Western MS. of the twelfth century in the British Museum. (Nero C. 4.)

same style as the Cotton Bible in the British Museum provided the scheme of decoration for the Genesis mosaics in S. Marco at Venice (p. 400); probably an illuminated MS. played the same part in the decoration of Kahrié Djami at Constantinople. On the minor arts, too, the influence of the illuminator must have been considerable. There is an evident analogy between the figure subjects on silver plate and those of miniatures (p. 467); and ivory carvings occasionally suggest the same affinities.

[1] A. Haseloff, *Egbert-Codex* ; N. Kondakoff, *Representations of a Russian Princely Family in Miniatures of the Eleventh Century*, St. Petersburg, 1906 (Russian).
[2] J. Strzygowski, *Repertorium*, xiii, 1890, 241 ff.

Fɪɢ. 296. The Pentecost: head-piece from the twelfth-century Homilies of Gregory of Nazianzus in the Monastery on Mount Sinai. (*Hautes Études*, N. Kondakoff.)

CHAPTER VIII

ENAMEL

THE origin of enamelling in the Christian East is no less obscure than that of the art itself. At first sight it seems strange that this method of decorating metal should not have been invented by the Egyptians. This people had from a very early date been familiar with the process of applying a vitreous glaze to earthenware, and from a period at least as early as the twelfth dynasty had produced gold jewels inlaid with coloured stones very similar in general effect to enamelled ornaments. But though facts of this nature would naturally indicate the Nile Valley as the probable birthplace of enamelling, no enamelled objects from this region are known to be earlier than Roman times. The explanation of this apparent anomaly is perhaps that suggested by Mr. Edward Dillon, who has pointed out that Egyptian glass lacks the lead which is a necessary constituent if this substance is to be successfully fused upon a metal surface.[1] The jewels discovered by Ferlini in 1834–5 in the upper part of a pyramid at Meroe in Nubia [2] were associated with antiquities not earlier than Roman times. If the experience of future excavation corresponds with that of the past, the claims of other countries must be considered superior to those of Egypt. To say nothing of the Aegean peoples whose position with regard to this question is still perhaps uncertain,[3] we find the Greeks and Etruscans enamelling gold jewellery by about A.D. 500 B.C.;[4] and whatever the date of the remarkable barbaric enamels from Koban in the Caucasus,[5] they are certainly older than the objects found at Meroe. The same may be said of the older Celtic enamels of Western Europe, which go back to the early part of the third century before Christ. There is at present practically no evidence on which a theory of origin can be based. The Greeks of the Aegean appear to occupy a strong position, though they may have received the first impulse from the West of Asia, possibly from the Syrian coast. At present, however, we know nothing of early Asiatic enamels. Much of the documentary evidence collected by De Linas and others seems rather to apply to jewellery inlaid with coloured stones ('inlaid jewellery'), of which there are examples as early as the fourth or even the fifth century. Central Asia is still a blank as far as ancient vitreous art is concerned; while enamelling was only introduced into China in the fourteenth century, and then from Constantinople.[6]

These remarks upon the origin of enamelling in general have their bearing upon the history of the art as practised in the Christian East. Perhaps no surviving Byzantine enamel can claim an earlier date than the sixth century A.D., but, as will be noticed below, there is literary evidence

---

[1] *Burlington Magazine*, xi, Sept., 1907, 373.

[2] Ferlini, *Cenno sugli scavi operati nella Nubia*, &c., Bologna, 1837.

[3] The blue substance inlaid in the jewels forming the Aegina Treasure in the British Museum is considered to have been cut and fitted when cold, and not fused in position.

[4] Greek and Etruscan enamelling is delicately applied in compartments of gold wire enriching articles of jewellery (ear-rings from Eretria in the British Museum found in a vase of about B.C. 400, F. H. Marshall, *Catalogue of Jewellery, Greek, Roman, and Etruscan*, Nos. 1267, 1290, 1653–4; fourth-century ear-rings, necklaces, &c., under Nos. 1644–7, 1947, 1951). In the second and third centuries the Greeks coated small figures of animals pendent from ear-rings, &c., with white enamel, a difficult process revived in Europe at the close of the fourteenth century and frequently employed in the Renaissance (examples from Prince Torlonia's excavations at Vulci, &c., in the British Museum appear to be of Greek origin, Marshall, as above, Nos. 1675 ff.). Enamelled jewellery of the fourth and third centuries has also been found in the Greek settlements in the South of Russia (Kondakoff, Tolstoy, and Reinach, *Antiquités de la Russie méridionale*, Index, s.v. *émail*).

[5] Virchow, *Das Gräberfeld von Koban*; *Zeitschrift für Ethnologie*, 1904, 87.

[6] The Chinese name for cloisonné enamel is Fa-lan, a corruption of Fo-lang or Fo-lin, the name of Byzantium in Chinese annals. The Ming Emperor Ching-tai (A. D. 1450–6) took the art under his protection, and the mark of his reign is found upon early examples. See S. W. Bushell, *Oriental Ceramic Art, Collection of W. T. Walters*, Text Edition, 1899, 455.

which makes a knowledge of enamelling in Constantinople probable at least two centuries earlier. When Christian enamels first appear, they are of the cloisonné variety on gold, distinct from the champlevé work upon copper found at Koban and in the Celtic area, and differing also from the wired or encrusted work of the Greeks. Their nearest relations are with the Meroe find ; while to the inlaid jewellery they bear an obvious if only superficial resemblance. It is conceivable that the Persians taught their Western neighbours how to enamel ;[1] but at present there is no satisfactory evidence that at the time of Constantine they knew any other kind of cloisonné work than that in which stones are inlaid *à froid*.[2] The real date of the ewer at St. Maurice d'Agaune[3] in the Valais, enamelled with gryphons and a 'sacred tree' in the Persian style, is uncertain, but no authorities place it earlier than the seventh century, too late to support a Persian claim in the face of the older cloisonné enamels made within the limits of the Byzantine Empire. If Byzantine cloisonné enamel is not of Hellenic origin, suggested to an inventive people already able to fuse glass on metal by the sight of inlaid jewels, the alternative would perhaps be to seek its birthplace in the area embracing Syria, Mesopotamia, and the countries running north to the Caucasus, where, as we shall see (p. 528), it was very popular in the Third Period, and where glass seems to have been manufactured.[4] Upon the evidence at present available it is best to suspend the judgement.

Almost all Byzantine enamels[5] are of the cloisonné variety, that is to say, the enamel is contained within cells composed of thin strips of metal bent to the desired contour and soldered edgeways to the metal base. This kind of enamelling lends itself to minute work, and is practically confined to the precious metals, of which gold was almost exclusively employed in ancient times : it follows that the great majority of Byzantine enamels are of restricted size. They are chiefly small plaques, as a rule rectangular and circular, of such a size that a number may be applied to the decoration of a single object such as a book-cover, reliquary, chalice, or crown, their decoration consisting of figures and busts of sacred persons or saints, and of conventional floral or geometrical designs for use in subordinate positions. In addition to these plaques and medallions, there

---

[1] This is the opinion of Kondakoff and Diehl (*Manuel*, 344).

[2] Too much importance need not be attached to the philological argument based upon the Arabic, Persian, and Turkish words for enamel (*mynâ, mina, mineh*). There seems no satisfactory evidence that the substance so described was introduced to the Arabs by the Sassanian Persians.

[3] M. Dieulafoy, *L'Art antique de la Perse*, v, p. 158 ; S. Guyer, *Christliche Denkmäler des ersten Jahrtausends in der Schweiz*, 102 ; E. Aubert, *Le Trésor de l'Abbaye de Saint Maurice d'Agaune*, Pl. XIX.

[4] Strzygowski has always regarded Armenia as the possible place of origin (cf. *Amida*, 352).

[5] The standard work upon Byzantine enamels is Prof. N. Kondakoff's *Geschichte und Denkmäler des byzantinischen Emails*, an *édition de luxe* in which the Swenigorodskoi collection is described, and a large number of the known enamels in public and private collections are discussed. The work, hereafter cited as Kondakoff, *Enamel*, is also published in a French edition, but is only accessible in large libraries. F. Bock's *Die byzantinischen Zellenschmelze*, &c., covers much of the same ground. See also Labarte, *Recherches sur la peinture en émail*, and *Histoire des arts industriels*, pp. 96 ff. ; Diehl, *Manuel*, pp. 287 ff., 642 ff.

Fig. 297. The Pala d'Oro: S. Marco, Venice. (Alinari.) P. 512.

are in existence a few small articles of jewellery, ear-rings, brooches, so decorated, to which a Byzantine origin is attributed.

There were various methods of producing enamels with figure subjects. If a plain gold background was desired, as was most frequently the case, a thin plate of gold was beaten into a mould having the outline of the figure to be represented, or else, perhaps, the cavity in the required shape

Fig. 298. Agate chalice with enamels, of the eleventh century : in the Treasury of S. Marco, Venice. (Schlumberger : Hachette.) P. 514.

was punched in over a piece of leather. Within this cavity the strips of flat wire which rendered the features, extremities, and folds of drapery were soldered, and the cells thus produced were filled with enamel. This kind of plaque shows at the back the general form of the figure in repoussé. The process may be clearly seen from an examination of such plaques as have lost the whole or a great part of their enamel, such as one of the circular medallions in the Treasury of St. Mark's at Venice and a similar medallion in the Communal Library at Siena. In the medallions of the Swenigorodskoi Collection both the outlines and the principal inner lines appear to have been also punched upon the gold plaque, and can be clearly traced upon the back. Another method is illustrated by medallions in the British Museum (Fig. 304) enamelled upon both sides. Here the background is also covered with enamel contained by a strip of metal soldered round the edges. The same principle is adopted in the case of the medallion from Risano (p. 507) and the example from the Victor Gay Collection now in the Louvre (p. 506, n. 2). When the enamel had received all the firings which it required it was given a high polish which may have added to its durability; but as almost all Byzantine enamels have escaped burial in the earth this point is of comparatively small consequence.[1]

Pure gold is much the best metal for enamelling, as it is ductile, never tarnishes, and only melts at a high temperature, while the glass clings firmly to the surface.[2] The chief objection to it is its softness and excessive malleability, which exposes the finished enamel to the danger of being easily cracked unless very carefully treated. It has been stated that many Byzantine enamels are applied to an alloy of gold and silver (*electrum*) :[3] this would certainly make them stronger; but if strength was required, it is curious that the enamellers should have hardly ever used pure silver, a metal which gives very beautiful blues and greens.[4] Perhaps their neglect of silver may have been due to the fact that it melts at a lower temperature than gold, whereas the coloured glasses which they used, not being of so uniform a quality or fusible at so low a temperature as those now employed, may have fused late and with difficulty: as a consequence of this the whole work might have been imperilled by the premature melting of the silver base. But an alloy of gold and silver actually melts at a lower temperature than pure silver. We must therefore conclude that if the gold used by the Byzantine enamellers is not pure, then their glass must have been of good soft quality, and consequently they could have had no need to fear accidents; their avoidance of it may therefore be merely a matter of taste. But it is curious that they did not sometimes employ the white metal for economy, finally gilding the edges of the cloisons if they wished to produce the effect of gold. They did occasionally use copper, a metal inferior to silver for cloisonné-work, as we see from the above-mentioned medallions in the British Museum and the Louvre:[5] in this they were followed by early makers of cloisonné enamels in Western Europe, for the curious portable altar in the Treasury of Conques and several medallions in various collections are enamelled in cells of the red metal.[6] The champlevé process on copper was very rarely employed, though the practice of

---

[1] For the technical processes of the enameller the reader may consult Mr. H. H. Cunynghame's *European Enamels* in the Connoisseur's Library, and his smaller work on the same subject. Mr. Lewis Day's book on enamelling will also be found useful. The older works by Labarte, de Laborde, Darcel, and others are still valuable ; a bibliography is given by Mr. Cunynghame.

[2] For the comparative merits of the metals which may be used in enamelling see the first chapter in Mr. Cunynghame's *European Enamels*.

[3] Kondakoff, *Enamel*, 102.

[4] Molinier mentions two small silver plaques in the Gréau Collection dating from the tenth or eleventh century, or at any rate in the style of that period, and representing full-length figures (*L'Orfèvrerie*, p. 64).

[5] V. Gay, *Glossaire archéologique*, s. v. *émail* (Fig.) ; *Les Arts*, Jan., 1910, p. 12.

[6] For the Conques altar see E. Molinier, *Histoire des arts appliqués à l'industrie: l'orfèvrerie*, 116.

encrusting silver in bronze might well have suggested its more frequent employment: almost the only example in which it is used to any extent being the large plaque with St. Theodore now in the Hermitage at St. Petersburg[1] (see p. 528). The panel in the *Museo Kircheriano* at Rome would be another instance if it could be proved to be certainly Byzantine (see p. 510). The border of the reliquary at Gran in Hungary has ornament in embossed metal on an enamelled ground (p. 525).

The converse process of applying enamel to surfaces embossed in relief

Fig. 299. Enamelled figure of St. Demetrius on a gold reliquary at Halberstadt. (Schlumberger: Hachette.)

seems also to have been understood by Byzantine enamellers, though they used it rarely. This kind of work, sometimes known as encrusted enamel, is the most difficult of all, and was not attempted by the enamellers of Western Europe until the latter part of the fourteenth century, when it was successfully practised in France. At a later period it formed the principal decoration of the splendid pendent jewels of the Renaissance. The Greeks had produced small ornaments, such as ear-rings, enamelled in this way, in the third century before Christ; but from that time down to the time of Charles V of France the method appears to have been abandoned. The face of the figure of St. Michael upon the enamelled book-cover in the Treasury of St. Mark at Venice (see p. 513) is embossed in gold and covered with enamel; and as this book-cover is not later than the twelfth century, it will be seen that Byzantine art was in this particular some two centuries in advance of that of Europe.

The Byzantine enameller probably worked very much in the fashion described by the eleventh-century author Theophilus, who, though himself of Western origin and writing in the West, was evidently familiar with the methods of the Greeks in more than one of the industrial arts. In the fifty-fourth chapter of the third book of his *Diversarum artium schedula*, he describes the process of making cloisonné enamel, and the description is so good that it might be followed by any amateur desirous of learning the art in our own day. The reader who is interested in the subject is referred to the chapter in question, from which only a few

[1] A. Darcel, *La Collection Basilewsky*, Pl. XIV. For the curious panel in the Museo Kircheriano, Rome, see p. 510. The copper dish at Innsbruck, ornamented in champlevé with the Ascent of Alexander, musicians, dancers, gryphons, eagles, &c., bears an inscription showing that it was made for an Ortukide prince of the twelfth century, perhaps Dawud, who died in A.D. 1144. It may have been made in Mesopotamia, but the Mohammedan craftsman probably learned to use enamel from Byzantine sources. The dish may be regarded as a link with the Mesopotamian metal-work encrusted with silver (Van Berchem and Strzygowski, *Amida*, 120 ff., 353 ff. ; Von Falke, in *Monatshefte für Kunstwissenschaft*, ii, 1909, 234 ff.).

points can here be particularly noticed. The first of these is concerned
with the manner in which ancient enamels were fired. From the earliest
times down to the Renaissance, and even later, the fuel employed was
pure charcoal, which gives off no fumes to tarnish the metal and spoil the
surface of the enamel. According to Theophilus, the powdered glass was
simply put on a plate or in a large kind of ladle made of iron, over which
was placed an iron cover perforated with holes. The charcoal was then
built up about this primitive contrivance and blown to a red heat. More
complicated apparatus was doubtless introduced in time; but down to
the introduction of coal and gas fuel the principle must have been the
same whatever the scale of the operations may have been; under modern
conditions, where coal and gas are used, it is necessary to protect the
object from noxious and sulphur-laden fumes by using a muffle furnace.
After the work had been fired several times, and the enamel renewed until
when cooled it was slightly higher than the edges of the metal cloisons,
the surface had to be first ground down until cells and vitreous surface
were all in one plane, and then polished to give it the requisite lustre.
According to Theophilus the grinding was done with water upon a sandy
stone and the polishing on a lead slab smeared with pulverized pottery
of fine quality mixed with saliva, first rubbed into a paste upon a hard
stone. The final finish was given upon a piece of goatskin similarly
smeared and stretched upon a table. Modern enamellers grind with car-
borundum and emery, and polish with rottenstone or Tripoli powder;
but it is probable that the processes described by Theophilus were very
close to those in use at Constantinople. The glass used for enamels must
have been rendered sufficiently fusible by the addition of a greater or
less quantity of lead oxide, and the even quality attained by the best
Byzantine work proves that the composition must have been scientifically
determined. The colours were given by various metallic oxides. White
was obtained from oxide of tin, blue from cobalt, green from copper, and
so on. The scale of colour was less extensive than that available in our
own day, but comprised several blues, purples, reds, and greens, with
yellow, brown, and flesh-pink. Many colours were preferred translucent,
especially in earlier work. Byzantine enamellers no doubt owed much
to the researches of the chemists who in earlier times had provided recipes
for making coloured glass pastes in imitation of gems.

Literary evidence confirms the conjecture that enamelling may have
been practised in Constantinople in the earliest years after the foundation
of the city. The Anonymus of Banduri says that Constantine set up on
the place called Philadelphion a gilded cross ornamented διὰ λίθων καὶ
ὑέλων; and the passage may refer to enamel, though encrustation of
precious stones and glass pastes is a possible alternative.[1] Evidence
for the time of Justinian is more satisfactory, though far from com-

[1] Kondakoff (*Enamel*, 84) is inclined to accept ὑέλων as referring to enamel. Codinus
repeats the story of the Anonymus.

plete.[1] The accounts of the ornamentation of the altar in Sta Sophia in Paulus Silentiarius, the Anonymus, Cedrenus, and Nicetas Choniates seem to imply that enamel was employed to decorate the altar itself, though not the ciborium above it. It is not until we reach the time of Constantine Porphyrogenitus (A.D. 913–59) that certain literary evidence becomes available. The emperor, in his treatise on the ceremonies of the Byzantine Court, mentions enamels used to decorate the palace or sent as gifts to Mohammedan and barbaric princes,[2] employing the words χύμευσις for enamel and ἔργα χυμευτά for enamelled objects. It would appear from his account that these works of art were set out among other treasures when a display was made on the occasion of great receptions; most probably they were personal ornaments, medallions with portraits, imperial mantles and regalia with enamelled medallions upon them, sacred pictures, crosses, reliquaries, cups, chalices, book-covers—in short, objects belonging to the same categories as those which have come down to our time. Horse-furniture would also appear to have been enriched with enamels, like that of the Celts in earlier days.[3] Goldsmiths and enamellers were accommodated in the building attached to the palace known as the *Zeuxippus*, where the looms of the imperial silk manufactory were established.[4] Residence about the precincts of the royal palace was enforced by the early Teutonic princes in Europe (Franks, &c.), and by the Mohammedan princes of Damascus, Bagdad, and Sicily, in the case of all craftsmen whose work was necessary for the royal luxury. The imperial goldsmiths had, however, no monopoly of the art, which was also practised by independent workmen.

Except in rare instances where historical persons are represented or mentioned by name in inscriptions, or where an enamel has been discovered in the tomb of an identified person, the date of Byzantine enamels can only be approximately given. But there are a few examples which fulfil the above conditions, and they serve as points of comparison for others which resemble them. These are the Limburg reliquary (see p. 522) with its inscription relating to Constantine and Romanus; the cross at Copenhagen, found in the tomb of Queen Dagmar, who died in A.D. 1212, and therefore anterior to that date (p. 527); the crown at Budapest with enamelled representations of the Emperor Constantine Monomachos and the Empresses Zoe and Theodora (p. 525); and the ikon of Chachuli in the church of the Monastery of Gelat (p. 528), with Our Lord crowning the Emperor Michael VII Ducas. But though such precise evidence is rare, indications are not wanting by which the period of a given enamel can be approximately determined. The character of the designs and details of iconography enable us to assign certain outside limits within which most

---

[1] Lethaby and Swainson, *The Church of Sancta Sophia*, p. 70; Labarte, *Hist. des arts industriels*, iii. 67.

[2] *De Caerimoniis*, vol. ii, pp. 566–98 [in the Bonn edition of the *Corpus scriptorum historiae Byzantinae*]. Kondakoff, 110, and Labarte, *Histoire*, &c., iii. 527, both cite the treatise.

[3] Ibid., i. 99, 105. σελοχάλινον χρυσὸν διάλιθον χυμευτόν.

[4] Ducange, *Constantinopolis Christiana*, i. 37. 2.

examples must have been made : comparison with illuminations in MSS. and carvings on ivory establishes these beyond the possibility of error, and we can say with certainty that, with the exception of the Lateran Cross (p. 508), none of the existing specimens with human figures are earlier than the eighth century, very few later than the year A.D. 1200, while the greater part are of the tenth, eleventh, and twelfth centuries, more especially the two latter. It is in attempting to classify enamels within the limits thus described that uncertainty still exists ; for though we note a process of degradation in vigour of design and purity of colour, the work of the tenth century being the best and that of the twelfth inferior, it is often difficult to feel sure of the precise place to which a definite object should be assigned. All attributions are to a certain extent subjective, and the most prudent course is to be content with a latitude of at least a hundred years. After all, we are sure that enamelling reached its zenith at Constantinople during the Comnenian period, and that such specimens as exist from the earlier time between that period and iconoclasm are different in style and character. Whether the art had enjoyed a previous period of excellence under Justinian, relapsing into decadence in the troubled seventh century and during the iconoclastic disturbance, we are hardly in a position to say, though judging from the analogy of other arts it is exceedingly probable. In the work of the twelfth century there is a falling off in the preparation of several colours, notably in flesh-tints, which

Fig. 300. St. Paul : enamel on gold in the Victoria and Albert Museum. P. 506.

from the delicate pink tones of the tenth and eleventh centuries decline into a dead white, much as at Limoges the flesh-tints of late enamellers like Suzanne de Court are lifeless and opaque when compared with those of the Penicauds and their school.

The earliest surviving East-Christian enamels, which do not appear to be earlier than the sixth century,[1] will be noticed below : they are in the British Museum, the Ashmolean Museum, the Louvre, the Vatican, and in Russia. Except in the case of the enamelled cross alluded to above, they bear decorative designs and are without representations of the human figure; but the exception is so remarkable that it would be unsafe to base an argument upon their absence. The existence of certain rude cloisonné enamels with portrait busts made in Europe before A.D. 900 lead to the inference that early Byzantine models with similar subjects must have been known in the West, and that their absence from modern collections is due to their loss and destruction. The most remarkable of the Western productions is the already mentioned Castellani brooch in the British Museum (Fig. 301), containing an enamelled

---

[1] Kondakoff, however, would assign the ear-ring in the Louvre (see below) to the fourth century (p. 82).

medallion with a bust very roughly executed, but apparently showing Byzantine influence.[1] The gold setting of this brooch is identical in character with the work upon the gold cross of the Lombard King Agilulf preserved in the sacristy of the cathedral at Monza, and there would appear to be no serious argument against the attribution of the enamel which it contains to the beginning of the seventh century.[2] If Italian goldsmiths had already learned how to make cell enamel at this period, the production of the busts and other designs on the paliotto of S. Ambrogio at Milan, and of other enamels of the ninth and early tenth centuries in countries further to the west, becomes more comprehensible. For rare Byzantine models may have penetrated beyond the Alps, or there may have been successive imitation, Italian copies of Byzantine work being themselves copied by Ostrogoths or Franks. It seems reasonable to explain the early appearance in Europe of human busts in cell enamel on gold by some such process as this; the coarser designs representing birds and animals, in the style of contemporary inlaid jewellery, as seen on the reliquary of Pepin, which was probably made in the Frankish dominions in the eighth century, may point to a survival of the art of enamelling from Roman times, and to its independent substitution for cell-work with inlay of coloured stones and pastes.

It has been argued by Bock[3] that a knowledge of cell enamelling had been introduced into Rome by the close of the tenth century, and he supposes that the crossed bands of the crown of Stephen of Hungary (crowned A.D. 1000) are by Roman craftsmen; Sylvester II, who sent it, was the art-loving Gerbert, formerly Bishop of Reims and correspondent of Egbert of Trèves. It is conjectured that other crowns dispatched from Rome in the tenth and eleventh centuries were of like origin; even the crown of the Holy Roman Empire may, he thinks, be in part of Roman work. When we remember the Byzantine complexion of Rome in the eighth and ninth centuries (p. 78), and the probable existence within its walls of relics like the enamelled cross of the Sancta Sanctorum (p. 508), there seems no reason why the imitation of Byzantine work should not have begun there quite as early as upon the Rhine. Examples of imitation of earlier Byzantine models may be found in the enamelled book-cover of Archbishop Aribert in the sacristy of Milan Cathedral[4] and the Gospels of Bishop Alfanus (d. A.D. 1182) in that of the Cathedral of Capua.[5] The latter has on one side a Crucifixion, on the other a Christ in Majesty, each side having also ten medallions with busts of saints accompanied by their names in Latin.

---

[1] De Linas, Histoire de l'orfèvrerie cloisonnée, i, Pl. IV, Fig. 3.

[2] Proc. Soc. Antiquaries of London, xx. 65, where the other early Western brooches and ornaments, including the Alfred Jewel, are mentioned. It may be stated here that the lamb which ornaments the large ivory diptych in the treasury of Milan Cathedral is now generally admitted to be constructed of inlaid pastes, and not of enamel (see p. 202).

[3] F. Bock, Die byz. Zellenschmelze, 53 ff.

[4] E. Molinier, L'Orfèvrerie, 118, comparing another book-cover in the Louvre figured by Labarte, Histoire, 1st ed., Pl. XLII.

[5] E. Bertaux, L'Art dans l'Italie méridionale, i. 178-9 and Pl. VII.

Towards the end of the tenth century, Byzantine enamels imported into Western Europe as articles of commerce,[1] or coming as presents from Byzantium to the courts or churches of Europe,[2] served as models for the imitative Western enameller beyond the Alps. Among the most conspicuous examples of such Western imitation are the famous processional crosses in the Münsterkirche at Essen, three of which date from the last quarter of the tenth century, the fourth from about the middle of the century following, and the enamels produced for the art-loving Archbishop Egbert of Trèves.[3] Other examples at Munich and Quedlinburg are noticed below (p. 524). Sometimes the Western artist used copper instead of gold, gilding it on occasion to produce the effect of the more precious metal. Such work may be seen on a portable altar in the Treasury of Conques in Rouergue, which has on the border five busts, the Lamb, and the symbols of the Evangelists. The ground in this case is formed by plain upper medallions from which the busts, &c., are cut out; the medallion so treated is then fixed above a second plain medallion upon which the cloisons representing the details are soldered.

Fig. 301. Gold brooch with enamel in the Byzantine style, probably made in Italy in the sixth or seventh century: British Museum. P. 503.

This process avoids the necessity for beating or punching a cavity in a single plate after the Byzantine manner.[4]

Since the great majority of surviving Byzantine enamels belong to a single period of some three hundred years, it may be convenient to review the principal examples geographically, according to the countries in which they are now preserved; such an arrangement will be complementary to that of Kondakoff, who classifies by the nature of the objects (reliquaries, book-covers, crowns, &c.) which they decorate.

Beginning with our own country, we find that Great Britain is exceptionally poor in these enamels. In addition to a pair of ear-rings of the lunate form popular between the sixth and eighth centuries, enamelled with confronted

---

[1] It is considered that the numerous finely executed diminutive plaques with conventional diaper patterns and floral designs which are set as if they were cabochon stones, on so much Western goldsmith's work of the tenth to the thirteenth century, are in great part Byzantine importations. See Kondakoff, p. 204; De Linas in *Revue de l'art chrétien*, 1887, 421; Molinier, *L'Émaillerie*, Paris, 1891, 50, &c.

[2] Instances such as the reliquary at Poitiers are specially mentioned. But enamels must often have accompanied the textiles and other objects which were so frequently sent in Carolingian and Ottonian periods. On these presents see G. Humann, *Die Kunstwerke der Münsterkirche zu Essen*, Düsseldorf, 1904, 113 ff.

[3] G. Humann, as above; O. von Falke, *Deutsche Schmelzarbeiten des Mittelalters* (examples shown at the Düsseldorf Exhibition of 1902).

[4] E. Molinier, *L'Émaillerie*, 122-4, and *L'Orfèvrerie*, 117 and 176.

birds,[1] and two gold medallions of exceptionally small size, one with a bust of Our Lord, the other with St. Gregory, the British Museum only possesses the copper medallions already alluded to as being enamelled, like the Risano and Louvre examples, upon both their surfaces. This latter peculiarity makes it difficult to guess the purpose for which they were made, for they cannot have been intended to adorn any of the usual objects upon which enamelled medallions were placed.[2] They may perhaps have been pendants of some kind, for even if they had been attached to any vestment or article of apparel, one side would still have been permanently concealed: from the generally excellent style of the workmanship they may be assigned to the eleventh century. As there are traces of iridescence upon the surface, which has also lost all its polish, they must be among the rare examples which have been buried in the ground.

At South Kensington there is a small gold plaque of fine workmanship, with a bust of St. Paul (Fig. 300), and the Beresford Hope Cross,[3] so called because it was at one time in the collection of Mr. Beresford Hope (Figs. 302-3). This cross has on one side the crucified Saviour in a colobium, or long sleeveless tunic commonly found on monuments of the eighth to tenth centuries, and on the other the Virgin, busts filling the vacant extremities. The background, as in other early enamels, is of a translucent green; the cloisons are thick and the drawing of the figures primitive. These facts, together with the presence of the colobium, suggest an early date such as the eighth or ninth century, but Kondakoff inclines to the late tenth or the eleventh century. The

FIG. 302.   Front of the 'Beresford Hope' Cross in the Victoria and Albert Museum.

[1] *Catalogue of Early Christian and Byzantine Antiquities*, No. 267. The coloured substance appears to be true enamel, and the date may quite possibly be the sixth century.

[2] Another medallion, now in the Louvre, is executed in cloisonné work upon copper on both sides (Victor Gay, *Glossaire archéologique*, 615, s.v. *émail*, and *Les Arts*, Jan., 1910, p. 12). It belongs to a class of amulet held to be effective against stomachic disorders (Schlumberger, *Mélanges d'archéologie byz.*, p. 136). It is assigned by Gay and Fröhner (*Philologus, Supplement*, vol. v) to the sixth century, though this appears to be too early a date. It has on one side the usual Medusa-liké head surrounded by radiating serpents, with inscription Ἅγιος ἅγιος ἅγιος, &c.; on the other, the common inscription ὑστέρα μελάνη μελανωμένη, &c., on which see Schlumberger, as above. The border round the inscription is formed of stepped pyramids interlocking, so that dark and light colours alternate. The whole surface is enamelled. Cf. the ring, Fig. 406.

[3] *Arch. Journ.*, viii. 51; *Art Treasures Exhibition*, Manchester, 1857, Section, *Vitreous Art*, Pl. VI, Fig. 1; Kondakoff, 176; Bock, *Die byzantinischen Zellenschmelze*, 340. The cross was originally in the Debruge Duménil Collection (J. Labarte, *Description des objets d'art de la coll. Debruge D.*, No. 681).

work certainly seems more primitive in character than that of known enamels of the eleventh century, but the colobium affords no evidence, as it occurs in eleventh-century MSS.

The early enamel in the Ashmolean Museum at Oxford is of exceptional interest. It is a small circular gold pendant enamelled upon both faces, excavated for Dr. Arthur Evans in a *campagna* at Carina near Risano (*Risinium*) in Dalmatia, in 1878.[1] The town of Risinium was wiped out by the Slavs and Avars in the first half of the seventh century, which gives a *terminus ante quem* for the object. On one face is a leonine quadruped with crested mane in green, yellow, red, and bluish white on a dark blue ground; on the other, a rose with red centre and dark blue and yellow petals on a ground of green.[2] The animal is executed in a conventional style which recalls the creatures of early Persian silk textiles and of the Nagu Szent Miklos treasure; the rose suggests to Dr. Evans Italian influences. It is possible that this most remarkable enamel may have been made during the Ostrogothic dominion in Northern Italy and Dalmatia, under strong oriental influences; and if so it only concerns us here as an additional proof how far enamelling of this kind had already travelled by the time of Justinian. The United States have secured examples of Byzantine enamel which may be described here, as they are now exhibited in England. The silver-gilt reliquary for wood of the True Cross, formerly in the Oppenheim Collection and now in the possession of Mr. J. Pierpont Morgan, is unusually difficult to date with certainty.[3] It is in the

Fig. 303. Back of the 'Beresford Hope' Cross in the Victoria and Albert Museum.

form of a shallow rectangular box enamelled both on the top and round the sides. The subject on the top is the Crucifixion between the Virgin and St. John, with conventional floral designs and inscriptions filling the ground, which is of a rich translucent green. Above are seen the sun and moon. The inscriptions are almost barbarously misspelt, the usual verse 'Woman, behold thy son', &c., being rendered Ιδωυ υι(ο)ϲ ϲου Ιδοι H μιτιρ ϲ(ου); the two lateral figures are described as θεωτωκ(ο)ϲ, Ηωανιϲ. The gestures are clumsy and the faces grotesque. Our Lord wears a violet colobium, and his feet rest upon a red

---

[1] *Archaeologia*, xlviii. 49 ff. (Fig. on p. 50).
[2] Dr. Evans notes that the colours are those of the earlier mosaics at Ravenna.
[3] Bock, *Die byzantinischen Zellenschmelze*, 340 and Pl. VIII ; Molinier, *L'Orfèvrerie*, 43 and 44. The reliquary is at present, 1911, exhibited in the Victoria and Albert Museum at South Kensington. The Hanau triptychs are exhibited at the British Museum.

suppedaneum. A broad border round the central subject contains fourteen busts of saints, each accompanied by his name, and the same kind of ornamentation covers the side edges. The preservation of the work is almost perfect.

Were we to judge by iconography alone, we might assign this curious reliquary to the pre-iconoclastic period, comparing it with the nielloed cross of Adaloald at Monza and the related cross at Goluchow (see p. 548). But this work seems to lack the qualities which give the two crosses the stamp of antiquity in spite of their obvious deficiencies: it is harder in design and more frankly barbaric than either. It may, however, be an early work executed in some outlying part of the empire. The Morgan collection now also includes the triptychs formerly at Hanau (see p. 524).

What was probably a Byzantine pectoral cross of great interest was lost to us at the end of the seventeenth century, though it may yet be in existence in some other country. On June 11, 1685, one Taylour, being in Westminster Abbey, observed through a cranny in the coffin of Edward the Confessor, then exposed, the glitter of a gold chain. He drew it out, and found that it had attached to it an enamelled cross which on one side had the Crucifixion and on

FIG. 304. St. Theodore and St. George, two sides of a medallion enamelled on copper in the British Museum. Pp. 498, 506.

the other a kneeling figure. On the limbs of the cross upon the reverse were inscriptions which the finder considered to be Latin, but which were probably Greek, and seem to have been in all probability meant for ὁ ἅγιος Ζαχαρίας.[1] The cross was given to King James II, who seems to have taken it abroad in his exile and lost it.

Italy is fortunate in possessing Byzantine enamels exceptional both in quantity and quality. In the cypress chest beneath the altar of the chapel of the Sancta Sanctorum at Rome, reopened in 1903 and 1906 after an interval of nearly four centuries, and fully described with illustration for the first time in the latter year, were found several objects ornamented with cloisonné enamel.[2] The earliest in date is the gold reliquary cross (Fig. 305),[3] which may possibly be that discovered by Pope Sergius I (687–701) in the Vatican and by him conveyed to the Lateran.[4] On one side it is now hollow, but if the suggested identification is correct, it was formerly covered with gold plates enriched with gems. On the other side it is covered with five enamelled plaques, that in the centre cruciform, those on the limbs approximately rectangular. The whole surface of each plaque is enamelled and the colours employed are red, orange-red, dull red, lilac, blue, yellow, white, and black. The translucent ground is

---

[1] *Proceedings Soc. Antiquaries of London*, 2nd ser., ix. 227 ; *Archaeologia*, iii, p. 390.

[2] The chest was built into the altar by Pope Leo III (A. D. 795–816), and its contents have been mentioned by writers of the thirteenth, sixteenth, and seventeenth centuries. None of its contents are later than the thirteenth century, and most are much earlier. See P. Lauer, *Le Trésor du Sancta Sanctorum, Monuments Piot*, 1906 ; and H. Grisar, in *Civiltà Cattolica*, year 57, 1906, Pt. ii (June, &c.). The objects are now exhibited in the Museo Cristiano of the Vatican Library.

[3] Lauer, Pl. I ; Grisar, as above, 525 ff. and Figs. 6–8.

[4] Lauer, as above, 36 ff., quoting Duchesne, *Liber Pontificalis*, i. 374.

very badly cracked. Round the side edges runs an inscription in red enamel in Latin letters, with one or two Greek characters, of which it is difficult to make sense, though some words like EPISCOP(VS) (VE)XILLVM (R)EGINA MVNDI are clear : possibly these plaques are additions from other objects; more probably, perhaps, they may be the work of men unfamiliar with the Latin language. The plaque on the upper arm represents the Annunciation,

Fig. 305.   Reliquary cross with cloisonné enamels on gold from the Sancta Sanctorum at the Lateran : now in the Vatican Library.   (After Lauer : *Mon. Piot.*)

that in the centre the Nativity, those on the two arms Joseph and Mary journeying to Bethlehem and the Adoration of the Magi respectively, that on the lower limb the Presentation in the Temple and the Baptism. The subjects are obviously influenced by the Apocryphal Gospels, and are executed in a rude but forcible style, some of the individual figures being very expressive. The whole appearance of this cross is certainly ancient, and there seems no difficulty in accepting it as of the period of Sergius I. As far as descriptions go, it might almost be the cross already in existence in the time of Symmachus (498–514),[1] and M. Lauer rather inclines to this possibility. Whether it is quite so early it is difficult to say in the absence of objects with which it can be compared, for the other enamels which claim an antiquity as high as the sixth century have only animal and floral designs. But the appearance of this cross tends to show that the historical statements as to the early use of enamel

[1] Duchesne, *Liber Pont.*, i. 261.

in the Byzantine Empire are correct. It has been suggested that it may have been brought from the Holy Land, and that it represents the more costly and elaborate mementoes there purchased by pilgrims. The character of the art is East Christian, and if not made in Jerusalem it may have been imported from Syria or even Armenia. Our ignorance of the sites where cloisonné enamel was first produced makes precise attribution for the present impossible.

In the area there was also a rectangular silver casket (Fig. 342 and p. 356), the cover of which is ornamented with enamels.[1] In the centre is a rectangular plaque with the *Deesis*, Christ being seated on a high-backed throne between the standing figures of the Virgin and St. John the Baptist. In a broad border round this plaque are twelve circular medallions, three of which still contain enamelled plaques with SS. Simon, Thomas, and Luke. St. Luke and St. Simon are in the same style, but St. Thomas appeared to M. Lauer to be rather more archaic in treatment. Though these enamels are all of a conventional character they are finely executed, and the colours are rich and good. They date from about the eleventh century, and are probably not much, if at all, older than the box which they adorn.

The Vatican also possesses a gold cross with enamels, by some considered to be as early as the eighth century.[2] A bronze pectoral cross in the same place has on each side five busts in medallions, the ground being also enamelled with geometrical designs. The work has the appearance of champlevé.[3]

The so-called 'encolpion of Constantine' in St. Peter's (p. 550) is enriched with enamelled medallions of the Third Period: it is probably of the twelfth century.

The Stroganoff Collection at Rome[4] contains a flat reliquary with an enamelled representation of the Crucifixion closely recalling that upon the book-cover in the Reiche Capelle at Munich (see p. 524), but inferior in drawing and execution. On each side are plaques with SS. James and Gregory Theologus, while below is Christ in the tomb with Michael and Gabriel on either side. M. Schlumberger would assign it to the end of the tenth or early eleventh century, but it looks as if it might be a hundred years later.

The very curious enamelled panel in the Museo Kircheriano in the same city[5] remains something of a problem. It is a panel of large size (c. 2 ft. high) upon copper, and the enamels are applied both by the champlevé and cloisonné processes. Our Lord stands erect, holding a scroll in his left hand, and with his right making the Greek gesture of benediction. His cruciferous nimbus is jewelled and edged with pearls, the spaces between the cross being filled with floral scrolls. The ground beneath his feet is a broad band enamelled with a series of interconnected circles, each containing a leaf in green and red. This panel, in every way exceptional if an example of the Byzantine enameller's art, is said to have been found near Sta Maria in Trastevere, and is labelled as Byzantine work of the twelfth century. Different as it is from other Byzantine enamels known to us, it diverges almost as much from the style of any contemporary Western school, whether in France or Germany. The type of the figure is Greek, the conventional design of circles containing leaves is oriental, the scheme of colour is not that of Limoges or the Meuse. Perhaps we are here in presence of a work produced by a Greek enameller living in Italy, who had seen examples of the large champlevé panels of Limoges and determined to execute something in the same manner. In this case the date would probably be the early part of the thirteenth century.

---

[1] Lauer, as above, 69 and Plate; Grisar, as above, July, 1906, 172: figured in June, 516-7.

[2] A. Muñoz, *Esposizione italo-bizantina, Grottaferrata*, 54, No. 62.

[3] A. Muñoz, *L'Art byz. à l'exposition de Grottaferrata*, 162, Fig. 127.

[4] G. Schlumberger, *Mon. Piot*, i. 99, Pl. XIII. and XIV; and *L'Épopée*, i, Fig. on p. 520.

[5] A. Venturi, *Le Gallerie nazionali italiane*, iv, 1899, 332-4; J. Strzygowski, *B. Z.*, ix, 1900, 305; Labarte, *Recherches sur la peinture en émail*, p. 42. Labarte thinks the work may be Italian.

FIG. 306. Enamelled book-cover with figure of St. Michael in the Treasury of S. Marco, Venice. P. 513.

The *pala d'oro*[1] in the Cathedral of S. Marco at Venice (Fig. 297) is now a reredos consisting of a large number of enamelled gold plaques in a framework of Western design; it was originally the frontal of the altar, amplified in A. D. 1105 for the Doge Ordelaffo Faliero, and finally rearranged and restored in the thirteenth and fourteenth centuries, the last occasion being in A. D. 1343, when it was enclosed in its present Gothic frame. According to tradition the *pala* was ordered from Constantinople by Doge Orseolo in A. D. 976 ; but the Venetian chronicle of the eleventh century only states that the frontal then ordered was of marvellous workmanship, and makes no direct mention of enamel. This negative evidence would not alone suffice to upset an old tradition ; but a comparison of the enamels among themselves and with others seems to justify the conclusion that only a small number can belong to the close of the tenth century, while the greater part are of the period between the eleventh and the fourteenth. The *pala* must in fact be regarded as a composite work, perhaps owing its chief enrichment to the Venetian share of the spoils in A. D. 1204. The only parts which Kondakoff accepts as possibly belonging to the late tenth and early eleventh centuries are a number of the small medallions ornamenting the jewelled field of the architrave, and the lower border.[2]

The upper band of the *pala d'oro* has upon it the following subjects : in the centre the Divine Wisdom in the form of an angel, and on the two sides of it, beginning from the left : the Entry into Jerusalem, the *Anastasis*, the Crucifixion, the Resurrection, Pentecost, and the Assumption of the Virgin. As the same subjects in the same order are frequent upon iconostases of the Greek churches, it is considered probable that this portion was actually taken from an iconostasis in Constantinople,[3] perhaps from the Church of the Pantokrator. In the lower division immediately above the altar are plaques illustrating the twelve feasts of the Church and scenes from the life of St. Mark, with twelve prophets, twelve Apostles, twelve angels, the Empress Irene, the Doge Ordelaffo Faliero, the *Etimasia* with kneeling angels and the Virgin as *orans*, and (in the centre) Christ enthroned in a mandorla surrounded by the four Evangelists.

The origin and merit of these plaques in the lower part is very various. The enthroned Christ is good Byzantine work of the eleventh or twelfth century, probably by the same master as the Twelve Apostles ; the Evangelists are later and inferior, probably Venetian work of the thirteenth or even fourteenth century.[4] The St. Mark scenes, the Empress and the Doge, and the twelve prophets are also Venetian :[5] the inscriptions and gestures of benediction are Latin. The angels are superior, and appear to be Byzantine work of the early twelfth century.

As already stated, it is among the smaller medallions on the upper and lower borders (thirty-eight in all) that the earliest enamels are to be found. The subjects of some of these show a distinctly oriental influence. Two of them represent a prince hawking, and hounds hunting hares ; another, two gryphons flanking the 'sacred tree', on which is a crowned female head—

---

[1] Alinari, Photos ; Pasini, *Il Tesoro di San Marco*, Venice (Ongania), 1885-7, Pl. XV–XX, account by Veludo ; Labarte, *Recherches sur la peinture en émail*, 17–31, and *Histoire des arts industriels*, iii. 396–412, Pl. LX ; Durand, *Trésor de l'Église de St-Marc*, Paris, 1862; E. Molinier, *Le Trésor de St-Marc*, 1888, 65, and *L'Orfèvrerie*, 65 ff. ; Didron, *Annales arch.*, xx, 1860, 167 ff., and 208–14 : Zanotto, *Venezia e le sue lagune*, 1847, ii, Pt. ii, 82 ff. ; A. Venturi, *Storia*, ii, pp. 645–54, Pl. XV and Figs. The best illustrations are in Pasini. Both he and Labarte (*Hist.*, iii, Pl. LX) give outline sketches showing the relative positions of the subjects.

[2] Kondakoff, 129 ; Veludo in Pasini ; Molinier, *L'Orfèvrerie*, 66.

[3] Kondakoff, 128.   [4] Kondakoff, 131.

[5] Molinier considers that the figure described by the Latin inscription as Ordelaffo Faliero was really made to represent the Emperor John Comnenus (A. D. 1118–43), and that it is genuine Byzantine work, to which the Latin inscription was inappropriately added, perhaps during one of the later restorations. The Empress Irene would then be Irene, daughter of Ladislas I of Hungary, John Comnenus's queen (*Gazette des Beaux-Arts*, Third Period, i, 1889, 43 ; *L'Orfèvrerie*, 65).

perhaps the Woman of the Apocalypse ;[1] another, two peacocks confronted and divided by a sacred tree.

Thus the *pala d'oro*, sumptuous though it appears, is not a homogeneous work: only a part of its enamelled plaques are Byzantine, and a considerable proportion mediaeval Venetian reproductions in the Byzantine style. Although it contains examples of fine workmanship, it does not afford the best opportunities for study, as the light in S. Marco is often dim, and the position of the *pala* itself unfavourable for thorough examination. The student will form a better idea of the character of Byzantine enamels from the book-covers in the neighbouring Library of St. Mark and from a few other examples mentioned below, which are exhibited in a good light and can be examined at leisure.

The first book-cover[2] in the Treasury of S. Marco has in the centre a standing figure of St. Michael in relief and covered with enamel, with an enamelled background ornamented with floral scrolls (Fig. 308) ; he stands on a globe and carries sword and orb. Of six surrounding medallions on the top and bottom of the frame only three remain, with busts of Our Lord, St. Peter, and St. Menas: those from the bottom are lost. Four oval plaques on the sides of the frame have each two saints, Theodore Stratelates and Theodore Tyron, George and Procopius, Demetrius and Nestor, Eustathius and Mercurius. This book-cover is remarkable for having the figure of St. Michael in relief, a very rare thing in Byzantine enamels, while the application of enamel to the face. which is embossed in high relief, shows that Byzantine craftsmen were already masters of a method of enamelling which Western Europe only perfected some centuries later.[3] The work is good, and the date is probably the eleventh century.

The second book-cover[4] in the same place has in the centre a bust of St. Michael in relief, perhaps of the tenth century, and round it fourteen medallions of various periods from the tenth to the fourteenth century. The St. Michael has enamel only on the wings, nimbus, and part of the garments: the body is enriched with gems. Within the inner borders surrounding the figure are eight enamelled plaques: those nearest the figure represent Christ and St. Simeon, the others, SS. Michael, Mark, Luke, Gabriel, John the Baptist, and Bartholomew. Round the frame are fourteen other medallions with the Virgin, SS. John the Evangelist, Matthew, Thomas, James, Philip, Paul, Procopius, Theodore Stratelates, Demetrius, George, Mercury, and Eustace ; the border of the frame in which they are set is covered with very fine repoussé scroll-work. This is one of the most sumptuous examples of the Byzantine goldsmith's art. The back is a fine example of embossed design (Fig. 339). In the middle is a cross with embossed busts of saints in medallions, round the inner border a series of similar busts, outside this an outer border of fine floral scrolls.

The third cover[5] in the Treasury has in the sunk central portion a representation of the Crucifixion between the Virgin and St. John, with two busts of angels, and the sun and moon. All the figures, as well as the usual inscriptions ('Woman, behold thy Son,' &c.), are cut out and applied to the surface of the cover. The surrounding border has in the middle of each side an enamelled plaque with a standing archangel ; along the top of its upper part is added a plaque of the same length with a nielloed inscription.[6] It is clear that this is an object which has been reconstructed, and Durand conjectured that parts of it originally decorated a reliquary for wood of the True Cross.

[1] Kondakoff, 132 ; Venturi, as above, 652-4 (Figs.). These plaques should be remembered in any discussion of the ewer of St. Maurice d'Agaune (p. 496).
[2] Pasini, *Tesoro*, Pl. II ; Durand in Didron, *Annales arch.*, xxi. 101 ; A. Venturi, *Storia*, ii. 656 (Fig.) ; Kondakoff, 189, and Fig. 55 ; Molinier, *L'Orfèvrerie*, 49 ; G. Schlumberger, *L'Épopée*, i, Fig. on p. 89.
[3] The statement of Durand and Pasini that the face is of agate is erroneous.
[4] Pasini, Pl. IV ; Kondakoff, 189 ; Molinier, *L'Orfèvrerie*, 49, 50.
[5] Pasini, Pl. III ; Durand in Didron, *Annales arch.*, 1861, p. 99 ; E. Molinier, *L'Orfèvrerie*, p. 51.
[6]

CT(AY)PЄ КРАТАΙΟΝ ΚΑΤΑ ΔЄΜΟΝШΝ ΚΡΑΤΟС
ΘΗΚΗΝ ΚΑΘΟ ΖШΗС СЄ ΚΑΙ ΘЄΙΟΝ ⟨ΥΛΟΝ+

The fourth example [1] has in the centre a disk of lapis lazuli on which the Crucifixion with the same persons and inscriptions is represented in relief in gold, though the workmanship does not rise above mediocrity. The disk, which is surrounded by a circle of pearls, is in the centre of a rectangular field of fine filigree, on which are carbochon gems and four small enamelled medallions of an archangel, St. Andrew, St. John the Evangelist, and a nameless saint. In the more recent Italian border which surrounds this filigree are four square enamelled plaques with figures of St. Matthew (two), St. Cosmas, and another damaged figure the name upon which is not legible.

Besides the book-covers there is a flat reliquary [2] for the wood of the True Cross with a drawing-out lid. On the front are an enamelled Crucifixion and enamelled medallions, St. John the Baptist, St. John the Evangelist, SS. Thomas, Peter, Paul, and Panteleemon. There are no enamels on the back, which is covered by a plate of silver with a cross rising between two acanthus leaves, and the inscription IC XC NIKA, the whole embossed.

A votive crown (?) of silver gilt ornamented with rectangular enamelled panels bordered with pearls, and incorporated in work of Western origin and later date, also forms part of the treasure. [3] The enamels represent busts of saints and of an emperor described by the name of Leo. Pasini wished to identify this emperor with Leo I (457–74), but even Molinier's attribution to Leo VI (885–911) seems to be too early, the character of the work suggesting the eleventh or twelfth century. It has been suggested that the crown may really be nothing more than the ornamental band once surrounding one of the very large Byzantine chalices, such as some of those actually preserved in the Treasury.

Eight of the Byzantine chalices [4] in the Treasury of S. Marco (Figs. 298, 307) have kept the enamelled plaques which ornamented them. The plaques themselves, which are circular and square, have busts of Christ and of the saints, executed in the usual style of the period to which they belong (tenth to twelfth centuries): the square plaques are probably earlier than the round, which are often framed in borders of pearls. The inscriptions upon two of them are considered to refer to Romanus Diogenes, who came to the throne in A. D. 1068. [5] One chalice has its whole cup covered with enamelled plaques with ornamental designs. [6] A paten has an enamelled medallion of Our Lord with surrounding inscription ΛΑΒΕΤΕ ΦΑΓΕΤΕ, &c., and outer border of precious stones and pearls [7] (Fig. 53).

In the central case in the Treasury are fifteen detached enamelled medallions, [8] said to have come from the decoration of the high altar of the fourteenth century, presumably at the time when the *pala* was being rearranged. They represent Our Lord, saints, and Apostles, and are about two inches in diameter, with the exception of three representing St. Matthew, St. Mark, and St. George, which are considerably larger. They are instructive as illustrating the way in which the cavities in the shape of the contour of the figure were hammered in the gold plate before the cloisons were soldered in. This is very clear in the case of the damaged medallion of St. John the Baptist.

The sacred picture in S. Marco known as the Madonna Nicopea [9] or Bringer of Victory has on its frame sixteen enamelled medallions of a good period—the

---

[1] Pasini, Pl. VII.   [2] Ibid., Pl. XXIII.
[3] Pasini, No. 111, Pl. L ; Molinier, *Le Trésor de Saint-Marc*, No. 100, p. 95, and *L'Orfèvrerie*, 41 ; Labarte, *Histoire*, &c., iii. 396.
[4] These chalices are described by Pasini and Molinier. They have been figured by M. Schlumberger in his *Nicéphore Phocas* and *Épopée*. Several illustrations in the present volume are from the latter work.
[5] Pasini, *Tesoro*, Pl. 41 ; Molinier, *L'Orfèvrerie*, 60 ; Kondakoff, 225-8.
[6] Pasini, Pl. XXXVIII ; Molinier, *Le Trésor de Saint-Marc*, No. 70, and *L'Orfèvrerie*, 61.
[7] Schlumberger, *L'Épopée*, i, Fig. on p. 777 ; Pasini, Pl. XLVIII.
[8] Rosenberg (*Geschichte der Goldschmiedekunst*) has reproduced these medallions.
[9] Pasini, Pl. XXII and XXII a ; Molinier, *Le Trésor de Saint-Marc*, No. 15, and *L'Orfèvrerie*, 56 ; Schlumberger, *L'Épopée*, i, Fig. on p. 665.

tenth or eleventh century. The subjects are Christ, the Virgin, and St. John
the Baptist, together forming the *Deesis*, and SS. John the Baptist (repeated),
John the Evangelist, Eugenius, Damian, Auxentius, Eustace, Nicholas, Paul,
and an Italian repetition of St. Nicholas. They were put upon the frame in
the sixteenth century.

Fig. 307.   Enamelled chalice of the eleventh century : Treasury of S. Marco, Venice.

The Library of St. Mark also contains four very important book-covers
decorated with enamelled plaques. The first of these [1] has plain borders of red
stones or pastes inlaid in cells (*orfèvrerie cloisonnée*), and is decorated with enamels
on both sides. In the middle of the upper cover is a cruciform plaque on which
Christ, in a dark blue colobium and with a yellow nimbus, is represented on
the Cross, which is thrown into relief by a translucent green ground. The
surrounding medallions represent the four Evangelists and SS. John the Baptist,
Peter, Andrew, and three angels, with a single medallion bearing only an ornamental design. The under cover is decorated in a similar manner. In the
middle, on a cruciform plaque, is the Virgin as *orans* between four cruciform

---

[1] Pasini, Pl. **VI** and VIII a; Kondakoff, 185-8, and Fig. 54 ; Molinier, *L'Orfèvrerie*, 42
and 43; Schlumberger, *L'Épopée*, i, opp. p. 188.

monograms, giving the name of Mary and of the donatrix ; round this plaque are ten medallions, of which, however, only three (with SS. Proclus, Philip, and John) are enamelled.

The style represented by this book-cover is very early, and the use of translucent colours throughout, especially green backgrounds, is an early feature. Labarte considered the work as of the ninth century ; both Kondakoff and Molinier regard it as very early. It can hardly be as late as the twelfth century, as the style is more primitive than that of this period, and there can be little hesitation in saying that while it cannot be later than the ninth century, it may be even earlier. It is one of the most precious Byzantine enamelled objects in existence, and its cloisonné border of red stones or pastes lends it an additional interest, for this style of work, as we have seen, was in general superseded by enamel, and its presence here supports the earlier date.[1]

A second book in the Library[2] has also Christ and the Virgin as the central figures on the two covers. Christ is represented standing and holding the book of the Gospels : round him are medallions bordered with pearls containing busts of SS. Andrew, Luke, James, Thomas, Philip, Matthew, Simon, Paul, Elias, and Gabriel ; round the Virgin, who stands with raised hands, are SS. John the Baptist, John Chrysostom, Bartholomew, Peter, Gregory Theologus, Nicholas, Anna, Elizabeth, Joachim, and Basil, similarly bordered with pearls. The work is not of the best quality, and the date is either the eleventh or the twelfth century. The metal-work upon which the enamels are fixed is without engraved or embossed ornament, but is enriched with cabochon gems and rows of pearls. The colours of the enamels are remarkably pale and bright, so that the whole effect is much lighter than usual. The tone is given by a pale lilac contrasting in the drapery with a rich translucent red ; an opaque red and a gamboge yellow are also used (Fig. 308).

A third book in the same place,[3] a Latin Missal of the fourteenth century, has a cover of the same date, also ornamented with cabochon gems and pearls, though here again the principal decoration consists of enamelled plaques. In the middle of one side Christ stands making the gesture of benediction : round the border are rectangular plaques with busts of SS. Peter, Andrew, Paul, Matthew, Luke, Proclus, James, John, Thomas, and Theodore (?). The middle of the back is occupied by the Virgin standing ; round the border are ten enamelled plaques, of which those at the corners, representing the four Evangelists, are of Italian workmanship ; the remaining six are Byzantine, and represent SS. Eugenius, Mardarius, Orestes, Mark, Auxentius, and Simon. The enamels are all of the tenth century and of fine quality : they may be compared with those on the reliquary of Limburg (see p. 522).

A fourth book-cover[4] has six large enamelled medallions round the borders on each side, the principal decoration consisting of reliefs embossed in silver gilt, and representing scenes from the life of Christ and the Virgin. The enamels represent, on one side SS. Michael, Basil, Nicholas, and John Chrysostom, with Moses and David ; on the other the *Etimasia*, David, Solomon, and SS. Gregory of Nazianzus, George, and Demetrius.

The colours are all opaque ; dark blue, dark red, and a thick golden yellow are freely used.

The cover of a book of the Gospels in the Communal Library at Siena[5] has

---

[1] A border of *orfèvrerie cloisonnée* is not in itself conclusive evidence of early date, as the reliquary of Limburg (p. 522) has one. But the work of the present example is in a less finished and more massive style, which really looks as if it might belong to the eighth or even the seventh century. This was the opinion of Molinier, *Gazette des Beaux-Arts*, Second Period, vol. xxxvii, 1888, pp. 388-9.

[2] Pasini, Pl. X and Fig. 13 ; Labarte, *Histoire*, 2nd ed., iii, Pl. 63 ; Molinier, *L'Orfèvrerie*, 51-2 ; Kondakoff, 192 ; Schlumberger, *Nicéphore Phocas*, 449 (after Labarte).

[3] Pasini, Pl. IX and Fig. 12 ; Labarte, as above, Pl. 62 ; Molinier, as above, 51-2 ; Kondakoff, 188. [4] Pasini, Pl. XIII ; Kondakoff, 192.

[5] Labarte, *Histoire des arts industriels*, 2nd ed., iii, Pl. LXI (in colours) ; G. Schlumberger, *Nicéphore Phocas*, 23 ; Kondakoff, 201 ; A. Muñoz, *B. Z.*, xiii, 1904, 707 ; Molinier, *L'Orfèvrerie*, 52.

FIG. 308.   Enamelled book-cover with Our Lord and Apostles : Marcian Library, Venice.
(Alinari.)   P. 513.

about fifty plaques of cloisonné enamel upon it. In the centre of one side is the *Anastasis*, of the other the Ascension, each surrounded by numerous smaller plaques, both round and rectangular. Kondakoff considers that the enamels have come from several different sources and fall into distinct groups. To one group belong Christ as Pantokrator, the Virgin, St. John the Baptist, SS. Peter, Paul, John the Evangelist, and Matthew ; to a second, Christ, St. John Chrysostom, and St. Basil ; to a third, three plaques all representing St. Michael, and allied to which are SS. Theodore, Demetrius, and two seraphim. The dates, according to Kondakoff, vary from the eleventh to the fourteenth century, and he does not believe that any go back to the tenth. Among the best plaques are the archangels ; but the work, though fine in execution, lacks dignity and seems characteristic of a period of decline. The resemblance, however, in style between many of the plaques and those upon the crowns of Monomachos and St. Stephen, the dates of which are confined to a certain period of the eleventh century, suggests that we may have here unequal work of this earlier period rather than an assemblage of pieces of different dates.[1]

It has been suggested that the book-cover was ' made up ' in the Byzantine Empire for sale to Italian merchants.[2] The most prominent colours are lapis and turquoise blue, opaque red, yellow, apple-green, and white. As in the case of so many Byzantine enamels the pupils are frequently represented in the extreme corners of the eyes. On the back of the binding are several small medallions, one of which, representing St. Nicholas, is entirely stripped of its enamel, showing the sunk bust hammered out in the metal. The surface of the two covers is plated with gilt silver which has an ornament of floral designs in relief, possibly of the fourteenth century.

Space forbids the detailed consideration of other Byzantine enamels to be found in Italy, but some of them may just be mentioned. A cross in the Cathedral of Velletri[3] has upon it Christ crucified, between four busts in medallions, two representing the Virgin and St. John. Crosses of a similar kind are preserved at Gaeta and Cosenza ; all three were exhibited at Orvieto in 1896, and at Grottaferrata in 1904. The Cosenza cross, which is ascribed to the eleventh or the twelfth century, has on one side the Crucifixion, with the Virgin and St. John, the *Etimasia* and St. Michael in medallions ; on the other, Christ enthroned amid the four Evangelists, all in circular medallions. The Gaeta cross is much smaller, and has on one side the Crucifixion as in the Cosenza example ; on the other, a standing figure of the Virgin between four busts of saints ; it bears, in addition to the names, a somewhat barbaric inscription relating to one Basil.[4] The pectoral cross of Cardinal Caietano is attributed by some to a date as early as the eighth century.[5] A reliquary for wood of the True Cross, enamelled and bearing inscriptions, is in the Stroganoff Collection at Rome :[6] it has been ascribed to the tenth century.

In the treasury of the Abbey of Nonantola near Modena is a slender silver-gilt cross, on the front of which are applied seven enamelled medallions with busts : the enamels appear to be of about the eleventh century.[7] The rectangular reliquary for wood of the True Cross in the same place has also two small enamelled plaques, one with the *Etimasia*, applied to the double-armed cross in the centre.[8]

[1] Molinier, as above.   [2] Kondakoff, 203.
[3] Bock, *Die byzantinischen Zellenschmelze*, Pl. XXII, XXIII ; Molinier, *L'Orfèvrerie*, 56 ; S. Borgia, *De cruce Veliternâ*, Rome, 1780, pp. xviii ff. ; Didron, *Annales archéologiques*, xx, 1860, 167.
[4] A. Muñoz, *L'Art byzantin à l'Exposition de Grottaferrata*, Rome, 1906, p. 156 and Figs. 119, 120 (cross of Cosenza), pp. 156–7 and Figs. 121–2 (cross of Gaeta) ; *Gazette des Beaux-Arts*, Third Period, xvi, 1896, p. 500, and 1905, p. 506 ; A. Muñoz, *Esposizione italo-bizantina*, Grottaferrata, 1905, 54, No. 55, and *L'Arte*, Rome, 1905, 166–7 and 169 and Fig. ; Molinier, *L'Orfèvrerie*, p. 57.
[5] *B. Z.*, vi, 1900, 719. It was discussed by Ferraro at the Congress of Christian Archaeology at Rome in 1900.
[6] G. Schlumberger, in *Mon. Piot*, 1894.
[7] The same, *L'Épopée*, ii, Fig. on p. 17.
[8] The same, Fig. on p. 81. Cf. also *L'Œuvre d'art*, August, 1897, 147, and Fig. on p. 149.

In Sicily in the twelfth to thirteenth centuries there was a school of enamellers inspired by Byzantine models. Their work, as we know it, chiefly consists of small gold plaques, enamelled with ornamental designs and applied to the crowns or embroidered garments of members of the imperial house. A crown of the Empress Constance of Aragon at Palermo is finely reproduced by Bock in his monumental work,[1] and in the same book may be seen reproductions of an imperial mantle, gloves, and stole to which enamelled plaques and medallions are sewn.[2] These exhibit motives of Byzantine origin, and one of those upon the mantle, with a floriated cross, is almost identical in design with that set in the Towneley brooch in the British Museum. At Capua there is

Fig. 309. The Annunciation : leaves of a triptych enamelled on gold, mounted in a larger triptych of West-European workmanship : Collection of J. Pierpont Morgan, Esq. (Formerly at Hanau.) P. 524.

a Gospel-cover with cloisonné enamel in a purely Byzantine style, but said by Bertaux to be Benedictine work of the late twelfth century.[3]

The cloisonné enamels at Milan and Monza are not of Byzantine workmanship. The enamelled flowers on the famous Iron Crown[4] appear, like the paliotto in Sant' Ambrogio, to be early Western work, probably of the ninth century, while the book-cover in the sacristy of Milan Cathedral[5] is certainly of Italian workmanship imitating the style of the later Byzantine enamellers. Some of the gold panels with which it is decorated have plain metal grounds, others have grounds of enamel in which are Latin inscriptions in gold wire. They comprise scenes from the New Testament and figures of saints, the Crucifixion occupying the centre.

France now possesses hardly any Byzantine enamels, many having disappeared at the time of the Revolution. The most interesting is the portion

---

[1] *Kleinodien des heiligen Römischen Reichs*, Pl. XLIV ; A. Venturi, *Storia*, ii, 667.

[2] Bock, as above, Pl. XXV, VIII. and XIII. Cf. also the ornamental enamels, probably of the twelfth century, on the so-called sword of Charlemagne (ibid., Pl. XXIV), and on the sword of St. Maurice in the Schatzkammer (Pl. XXIII). The enamels on the imperial crown (Pl. I and XXV) are Western work imitating the Byzantine style, with inscriptions in Latin.

[3] *L'Art dans l'Italie méridionale*, i. 276.

[4] Bock, *Kleinodien*; Kondakoff, pp. 236-9 and Fig. 68.   [5] Kondakoff, p. 205.

of a triptych reliquary at the Monastery of Sainte-Croix of Poitiers,[1] which may be one of the earliest Byzantine enamels in existence. It has been identified by French authorities with the reliquary mentioned by Gregory of Tours and Fortunatus[2] as sent by Justin II to St. Radegund in the sixth century. It arrived at Poitiers in the time of Sigebert and before the death of Radegund (†587): its date must therefore lie between A.D. 565, when Justin came to the throne, and A.D. 575, when Sigebert died.

The part preserved is the central panel of the triptych. It has in the middle a cavity for the relic in the shape of a double cross bordered with coloured glass pastes (*verroterie cloisonnée*), set in a single row as in the case of the Limburg reliquary, while the whole field is of dark blue enamel covered with floral scrolls in gold with leaves of turquoise blue and red pistils. From early descriptions made at a time when the reliquary was perfect, we know that each of the two leaves had three superposed busts of saints in enamel; on the outside was a gemmed cross with cabochons at the extremities, and bordered with pearls. The four exterior corners had cavities for relics, bordered, like the interior cross, with coloured pastes.

There are details about this reliquary which make us hesitate to accept the early date claimed for it; for example, the character of the scrolls recalls the ornament of the tenth to eleventh centuries, and the arrangement of superposed busts on the leaves suggests the ivory triptychs of the same period. The history is, however, circumstantial, and as we cannot definitely say that the work could not have been produced in the time of Justin it may be provisionally accepted.

A brooch with a gryphon in the style of the tenth century[3] and the remarkable enamelled amulet already mentioned (p. 506, n. 2) are in the Louvre. Among the enamels lost to France there were reliquaries for wood of the True Cross in the Sainte-Chapelle at Paris, at the Abbey of Grandmont,[4] and at Clairvaux.[5] A gilt-copper chasse with enamels and Greek iambic inscriptions is mentioned by Ducange, and the same author refers to a triptych at Amiens with about twenty enamelled figures.[6]

In Belgium a wooden cross overlaid with silver, on which are filigree and gems of Western thirteenth-century work, is in the treasury of the Sœurs de Notre-Dame at Namur,[7] and is said to have been brought to Belgium by Jacques de Vitry, Bishop of Ptolemais, who died in the Abbey of Oignies. Applied to it are Byzantine enamelled medallions of a good period, perhaps the early eleventh century, representing the *Etimasia*, SS. John the Evangelist, Mark, Matthew, Peter, Paul, Panteleemon, and the Archangel Gabriel. In the Cathedral of the same city is a reliquary for wood of the True Cross, while another appears to have been shown in the exhibition of ecclesiastical art at Malines in 1864.[8] Down to the French Revolution there was at Maestricht a double-armed cross with an inscription relating to a Romanus, given in 1204 by the Emperor Philip of Swabia to the Church of Notre-Dame.[9]

An enamelled picture in the same cathedral (Maestricht) represents the Virgin

---

[1] Barbier de Montault, *Le Trésor de l'abbaye de Sainte-Croix à Poitiers*, Paris, 1883 ; E. Molinier, *L'Orfèvrerie*, 38–40 (Fig.) ; Leclercq, *Manuel d'arch. chrét.*, ii, p. 458. The reliquary is not noticed by Kondakoff and Bock.

[2] *Historia Francorum*, ix, c. 40. See Barbier de Montault, as above, 118–9.

[3] From the Campana Coll., and exhibited in a window of the Galerie d'Apollon in the Louvre ; Kondakoff, as above, 261. E. Gonse (*Exposition universelle de 1878*, ii. 243, 549) and V. Gay (*Glossaire*, s.v. *émail*) refer to Byzantine enamels in French private collections.

[4] Texier, *Dictionnaire d'orfèvrerie*, col. 834 ff.

[5] D'Arbois de Jubainville, *Revue des Sociétés savantes*, 5ᵉ sér., v. 497.

[6] Didron, *Annales archéologiques*, xx, 1860, 166, and xxi, 1861, 123–4. Ducange, in his *Traité du Chef de Saint-Jean*, also mentions an enamelled reliquary for wood of the True Cross at Amiens (*Ann. arch.*, 1862, p. 47). Cf. also R. Mowat, *Bull. Monumental*, 1896, p. 230.

[7] Didron, as above, v. 318 (Fig.) ; Kondakoff, 169 ; *Proc. Soc. Antiquaries of London*, ser. 2, iii. 62 ; Schlumberger, *L'Épopée*, ii, Fig. on p. 193.

[8] W. H. J. Weale, *Catalogue des objets d'art religieux*, Brussels, 1864, 88 and No. 482.

[9] Didron, as above, v. 280 ; Schlumberger, *Nicéphore Phocas*, 477 ; Bock, *Die byzantinischen Zellenschmelze*, 323 and Pl. XX ; Labarte, *Histoire*, &c., 2nd ed., i. 330 ; Molinier, *L'Orfèvrerie*, 56.

Fig. 310. Enamelled triptych of the eleventh century containing wood of the True Cross : mounted in a reliquary of West-European workmanship in the Collection of J. Pierpont Morgan, Esq. (Formerly in the Walz Collection, Hanau.) P. 524.

as *orans* in half-figure and Christ on one side making the gesture of benediction.[1] The inscriptions are very incorrect, and de Linas thought the work due to a Greek artist of the Adriatic or Southern Italy. The date is perhaps the twelfth or thirteenth century. On the back is the Annunciation in repoussé work, probably made for another object.

Germany possesses some exceedingly good examples of Byzantine enamel. The finest is the reliquary for the wood of the True Cross in the Cathedral of Limburg-on-the-Lahn,[2] brought into the West by the knight Heinrich von Uelmen after the sack of A.D. 1204.

It is a shallow rectangular box with a sliding lid. In the interior is a cavity in the form of a cross with double traverse, in which lies a cross containing the relic. The gold covering the back of this cross bears a repousse inscription in nine iambics, showing it to have been made at a time when Constantine Porphyrogenitus and Romanus II were associated in the empire between the years A.D. 948 and 959. The borders of the sliding cover bear similar repoussé inscriptions in larger letters. These are also metrical, and show that 'Basil the Proedros caused the reliquary of the cross to be embellished '.[3] This Basil was either the future Basil II, who during the reign of his stepfather Nicephorus Phocas (A.D. 963–76) held the title of Proedros, or more probably Basil the bastard son of Romanus Lecapenus, the same man who is mentioned on the chalice-reliquary in the treasure of St. Mark. In the latter case the whole object, cross and case alike, would be earlier than A.D. 959, when Constantine died. This is the alternative preferred by Molinier, as against Aus'm Weerth and Labarte.

The upper side of the sliding lid, most conspicuous when the reliquary is closed, has in the middle nine rectangular enamelled plates in three rows of three, together forming a large rectangle (Fig. 311). The central plaque of the middle row represents Christ enthroned, that to the left of it having Gabriel and St. John the Baptist; that to the right, Michael and the Virgin: the figures of the Virgin and the Baptist are nearest to Christ and stand with their hands raised towards him, thus forming the favourite group of the *Deesis* (see p. 664). All the other plaques each contain two figures. On the top row are St. John the Evangelist and St. James, SS. Peter and Paul, Andrew and Mark; in the bottom row, SS. Thomas, Bartholomew, Matthew and Luke, Philip and Simon. Round the large rectangle runs a border of inlaid garnets, round this a narrow band of enamelled ornament consisting of blue lozenges with stepped edges on a white ground; round this in its turn is a broader band of filigree and cabochon gems, interrupted at opposite points by eight small square plaques, six containing enamelled busts—SS. Chrysostom, Theodore, Eustathius, Basil, Nicholas, and George; two squares are occupied by repetitions of St. Basil and St. George without enamel. At top and bottom of this filigree band are broader gemmed bands each containing three large circles of cabochon gems surrounded by borders of garnets.[4] Then comes a broad enamelled border enclosing all four sides, the design consisting of pink lozenge-shaped figures on a white ground. Outside all is an exterior border of silver-gilt with a repoussé band of leaves, and the metrical inscription above referred to.

---

[1] Molinier, *L'Orfèvrerie*, 59.

[2] E. Aus'm Weerth, *Das Siegeskreuz des byzantinischen Kaisers Konstantin VII. und Romanus*, Bonn, 1861, Pl. I; Labarte, *Histoire des arts industriels*, ii. 83–92; Didron, *Annales arch.*, xvii. 377 ff., xviii. 42 ff. and 124 ff.; Kondakoff, as above, 209 ff.; Molinier, *L'Orfèvrerie*, 46 ff.; Schlumberger, *Nicéphore Phocas*, 669 and 672 (Figs. after Aus'm Weerth). The reliquary was given by Heinrich von Uelmen to the Nunnery of Stuben, near Trèves. In 1788 it passed to Trèves Cathedral, but on the outbreak of the French Revolution it was taken to Ehrenbreitstein for safety. In 1815 it became the property of the Duke of Nassau, who in 1827 gave it to Limburg Cathedral. For Heinrich von Uelmen see the references given by Comte Riant, *Dépouilles religieuses*, p. 57; Beyer, *Mittelrheinisches Urkundenbuch*, 275; *Annales Colonienses maximi*, in Pertz, *Scriptores rerum Germ.*, xvii. 824, &c.

[3] ἐκαλλώπισε τὴν θήκην ξύλου.

[4] Cf. the book-cover in the Marciana (p. 516) and the early reliquary at Poitiers (p. 520).

The interior of the case has in the middle a cavity in the shape of a cross with two arms, in which the cross made of the true wood is laid: this cavity extends over the whole field. The greater part of the space between the cruciform cavity and the silver-gilt border is occupied by twenty rectangular enamelled plaques, those nearest the cross having figures of angels, those outside seraphim described by enamelled inscriptions as Ἀρχαί and Ἐξουσίαι. Along the top and bottom of these plaques, and about the upper half of the cross, are bands of enamelled ornament, consisting of series of circles and half circles containing

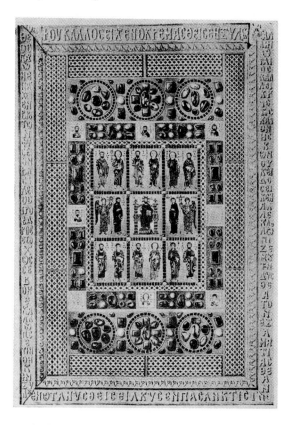

FIG. 311. Enamelled and jewelled reliquary for the wood of the True Cross, tenth century: Cathedral of Limburg-on-the-Lahn. (After Aus'm Weerth.) P. 522.

floral ornament of exquisite quality in very rich colours (green, red, blue, and white).

Both the figure subjects and the conventional ornament on the Limburg reliquary are as fine as any other Byzantine enamels now preserved: the attitudes are as unconstrained as is possible within the limits of such an art; the flesh tints are delicate, the colours of the draperies rich and effective.[1] The presence on the embossed border of an inscription indicating a definite date lends this object a peculiar importance, for while it proves that the close of the tenth century witnessed the highest development of the enameller's art at Constantinople, it furnishes us with a standard with which other Byzantine

---

[1] Four shades of blue are employed—ultramarine, grey-blue, indigo, and sky-blue; two reds, one brownish, the other vermilion; two shades of yellow; a pink flesh-tint, and an opaque white.

enamels may be compared. Among other enamels of similar fine quality are those of Shemokmedi in Ghuria (see below, p. 530).

With the Limburg reliquary may be mentioned two oblong enamelled panels with figures of Constantine and Helena[1] set in a Rhenish reliquary of the thirteenth century, but once belonging to a reliquary of Byzantine origin ; they were probably made for an inscribed cross with the name of Constantine (Porphyrogenitus), now preserved in the above-mentioned Rhenish shrine.

At Munich there are also important enamels. In the Reiche Capelle is a book-cover[2] of the eleventh to twelfth century, the enamels on which are of excellent quality. The subject represented is the Crucifixion, and the realistic treatment of the suffering body of Christ prevents an attribution to an earlier period. By the Cross stand the Virgin, St. John, and Longinus ; in the foreground two soldiers rend the seamless garment, while above are four busts of weeping angels in clouds, and the sun and moon. The reliquary in the Stroganoff Collection at Rome, as already noticed, has points of analogy with the plaque in the Reiche Capelle. The arrangement of the figures is the same, but the work is inferior.

In the Royal Library of the same town the cover of the Gospels of the Emperor Henry II (Cim. 57) is decorated with circular and arched plaques of cloisonné enamel.[3] The arched plaques which represent Our Lord and eleven Apostles have the names in Greek letters, and appear to be Byzantine: the circular, which represent the Evangelists' symbols, suggest German work in the Byzantine manner. All the plaques do not seem to have been designed for the places which they now occupy.[4]

The large triptych by Godefroid de Claire, formerly in the Walz Collection at Hanau,[5] has mounted in the centre two small triptychs enriched with Byzantine enamels of the second half of the eleventh or first half of the twelfth century, the work not rising above average merit. The larger has Constantine and Helena flanking a relic of the True Cross ; on the interior of the leaves are SS. George and Theodore, Procopius and Demetrius; on the exterior, busts of the Evangelists. The smaller has in the interior the Crucifixion ; on the outer side of the leaves, the angel and Virgin of the Annunciation (Figs. 309, 310).

In the Museum of Sigmaringen is a reliquary for wood of the True Cross with enamels ;[6] of another such reliquary in the Church of St. Mary at Cologne[7] only fragments remain. Enamels on book-covers at Gotha and in the library of the Monastery of St. Gall in Switzerland have sometimes been described as Byzantine, but the latter is Western work, and on the former only the small plaques with ornamental design may be Greek.[8]

The treasure of the Cathedral of Quedlinburg contains a Gospel-cover ornamented with filigree and cabochon stones, and having in the centre the Virgin and Child with two bishops. In the filigree border are set nine enamelled plaques and medallions, two of which, with representations of Christ and the Virgin, are Byzantine of the eleventh century, somewhat resembling those upon the cross at Namur.[9] The Byzantine origin of the remaining enamels is doubtful, and the enamelled cross in the same treasure is in the same category.[10] Mention

---

[1] E. Aus'm Weerth, *Siegeskreuz*, &c., 12, Fig. 13.

[2] Zettler, Ensler, and Stockbauer, *Ausgewählte Kunstwerke*, &c., Pl. XXVIII ; Hefner-Alteneck, *Trachten, Kunstwerke und Geräthschaften*, &c., i, Pl. XV (2nd ed., Frankfurt, 1879) ; Kondakoff, 195 ; Schlumberger, *Nicéphore Phocas*, 580 (coloured reproduction, after Hefner-Alteneck) ; C. Becker and J. von Hefner-Alteneck, *Kunstwerke und Geräthschaften des Mittelalters*, ii, Pl. XL.

[3] Labarte, *Recherches sur la peinture en émail*, Pl. C. [4] Kondakoff, 196.

[5] Kondakoff, 220 ; Bock, *Die byz. Zellenschmelze*, 181–4 ; *Archaeologia*, 1910, Pl. V and VI. These enamels were probably brought from Constantinople by Wibald, Abbot of Stavelot, where they were long preserved. Wibald was sent on missions to Manuel Comnenus in A. D. 1155 and 1157. [6] Lehner, *Verzeichniss der Emailwerke*, 1872, p. 1.

[7] Aus'm Weerth, *Siegeskreuz*, &c., 12–13.

[8] Kondakoff, 204. The Gotha cover, from Echternach, is figured by Schlumberger, *L'Épopée*, i. 440.

[9] J. J. Marquet de Vasselot, *Gazette des Beaux-Arts*, Third Period, xx, 1898, 310–11. [10] Ibid.

has been made above of the Rhenish imitations of Byzantine enamels about the year A. D. 1000.

Austria-Hungary also possesses Byzantine enamels of great importance. The reliquary for wood of the True Cross in the cathedral at Gran[1] in Hungary probably came, like that at Limburg, from the crusaders' spoils. It is of the same rectangular form, and is richly ornamented with enamels representing Constantine and Helena with the cross, the journey to Golgotha, and the Deposition. Though not equal to the work at Limburg, these enamels hardly seem to deserve Kondakoff's severe criticism: Molinier found in the scene representing the road to Calvary exceptional movement and originality, and the style recalls to him that of the book-cover in the Reiche Capelle. He points out that the imperial costumes are identical with those upon the crown at Budapest (see below), and would refer both to a good period, presumably the eleventh century.

The border of the reliquary is of embossed silver gilt plaques with fine inter-

FIG. 312. St. Andrew and St. Peter: enamelled medallions of the eleventh century in the Museum at Budapest. P. 526.

laced designs and feeble figures of saints: the interlacings are similar to those on one of the book-covers in the Library of St. Mark[2] and on the frame of a picture of the Virgin at Liége,[3] and they are probably of Byzantine origin. They rise from an enamelled ground, which has been left unpolished like the enamel upon English candlesticks and fire-dogs of the seventeenth century, or the Russian enamels made in the same manner, and thus afford one of the rare examples of champlevé work executed by Byzantine artists.[4]

The National Museum at Budapest possesses a crown,[5] discovered in 1861 at Nyitra Ivanka, consisting of a series of gold plates with enamelled figures of the Emperor Constantine Monomachos (A. D. 1042–54), the Empress Zoe (A. D. 1034–50), her sister Theodora (d. 1042), three female dancers, and personifications of Humility (ταπίνοσις) and Truth (ἀλίθηα): these figures, as

[1] Pulszky, Radisics, and Molinier, *Chefs-d'œuvre d'orfèvrerie ayant figuré à l'Exposition de Budapest*, vol. ii, last plate ; E. Molinier, *L'Orfèvrerie*, 50 and 51, and *Gazette arch.*, 1887, 245 ff. and plate ; *Revue de l'art chrétien*, 2ᵉ sér.. xiv, 1881 ; J. Danks, *Geschichtliches, Beschreibendes und Urkundliches aus dem Graner Domschatz*, 1880 : Kondakoff, 217 ; F. Bock, *Der Schatz der Metropolitankirche zu Gran in Ungarn*, Vienna, 1859 ; Schlumberger, *L'Épopée*, i, Fig. on p. 81. A letter of complaint from Innocent III to the Hungarian prince (dated June 27, 1205) has suggested that this reliquary was among the objects robbed by Hungarians from the envoys of the Cardinal Legate, who carried treasures dispatched to Rome from Constantinople in that year. See *Innocentis III Epistolae*, viii, p. 127 ; Riant, *Dépouilles religieuses enlevées à Constantinople*, p. 43 ; and de Linas, *Origines de l'orfèvrerie cloisonnée*, i. 350.

[2] Pasini, *Tesoro*, Pl. XII (No. 14).

[3] De Linas, *L'Art et l'industrie d'autrefois dans les régions de la Meuse belge* (1881), 81.

[4] Molinier, *L'Orfèvrerie*, 64.

[5] Schlumberger, *Nicéphore Phocas*, Figs. on pp. 517, 521, 523, 525, 527, and 529 ; Molinier, *L'Orfèvrerie*, p. 52–3 ; F. Bock, *Kleinodien*, &c., Pl. 38, and *Mitth. der k. k. Central-Commission*, xii, Vienna, 1867, 85–6 ; de Linas, *Hist. du travail à l'Exposition universelle de 1867*, Paris, 1868, 121–6 ; Kondakoff, 243–9, Figs. 72–7 ; Pulszky, Radisics, and Molinier, *Chefs-d'œuvre d'orfèvrerie ayant figuré à l'Exposition de Budapest*, ii, p. 81 and plates. Filimonov appears to have suggested that this crown was made in Egypt in the fourteenth century. See *Viz. Vrem.*, v. 579–80 and 304–5.

Kondakoff suggests. may have some reference to the coronation festivities at Constantinople. This crown cannot have been made for Monomachos himself, or his portrait would not be on it. It was probably ordered as a gift to some other king, perhaps Andreas I of Hungary (1046–61). The enamels are of fair quality, though somewhat affected by burial in the earth ; the silhouettes of the figures appear to have been stamped with a matrix.[1] The drawing and design are not on a high level, and betray the hand of an artist content with purely industrial aims (Fig. 313).

The Budapest Museum likewise contains two good enamelled medallions[2] representing St. Peter and St. Andrew (Fig. 512). A ring with an enamelled female bust is also referred by Kondakoff to the twelfth century.[3]

In the same museum is the so-called crown of St. Stephen,[4] which is not a king's crown but that of a prince or patrician. The crossed bands or hoops have enamels which Kondakoff assigns to the end of the eleventh or beginning of the twelfth century,[5] refusing to accept them as part of the ornament traditionally recorded by St. Stephen from Pope Sylvester II (†1003). The subjects of the enamelled plaques are Christ enthroned between two cypresses, the Archangels Gabriel and Michael, SS. George, Demetrius, Cosmas, and Damian, and Michael Ducas (A. D. 1071–8) with his son and colleague Constantine, by which emperors the crown was probably sent as a gift, as in the case of that now bearing the name of Monomachos.

In the same museum is a baptismal cross with enamels,[6] made, as the inscription records, by Leontios, a monk of Vatopedi on Mount Athos. The work appears to show Slav or Russian influence and is perhaps later than the fifteenth century.

The treasure of the house of Brunswick-Lüneburg (Welfenschatz) at Gmünden contains an enamelled cross, which, from the primitive character of the figures upon it, may be earlier than the date which Bock assigned to it, namely, the twelfth century. In the same treasure is an ikon of St. Demetrius, partly enamelled in relief like the St. Michael at Venice (p. 513). The work, which is not purely Byzantine, may be of the thirteenth century.[7]

A reliquary for wood of the True Cross is said to be in the Church of Saint Vit at Prague.[8]

In the Schatzkammer at Vienna is preserved the so-called crown of Charlemagne,[9] with four enamelled plaques representing David, Solomon, Isaiah and Hezekiah, and Christ between seraphim. The work is perhaps as late as the beginning of the twelfth century, and may have been executed by Greek workmen in Sicily, where the Western princes employed many Greeks (see below, p. 590).

A similar Siculo-Byzantine origin is suggested for the enamelled medallions on the sword of St. Maurice, also in the Austrian regalia, and for the medallions with conventional cruciform and other designs of fine execution attached to the imperial mantle, dalmatic, and shoes (see above, p. 519). The designs recall ornament in the mosaics of the Cappella Palatina and the Cathedral of Monreale in Sicily.[10]

[1] *Gazette des Beaux-Arts*, xxiii. 374.
[2] Kondakoff, 209.   [3] Ibid., 263.
[4] Ibid., 241 ; Fr. Bock, *Kleinodien*, &c., 79 and Pl. XVI, Fig. 3, and *Die byzantinischen Zellenschmelze*, 234 ff. ; Molinier, *L'Orfèvrerie*, 53–4 ; Schlumberger, *Nicéphore Phocas*, 657 (Fig.).
[5] The plaques on these hoops, with their Latin inscriptions, may be compared with those on the so-called crown of Charlemagne at Vienna. They are very probably of Sicilian workmanship imitating the Byzantine style.
[6] G. Supka, *Archaeologiai Ertesitö*, 1909, 207 ff.
[7] Neumann, *Der Reliquienschatz des Hauses Braunschweig-Lüneburg*, pp. 63, 236; Bock, *Die byzantinischen Zellenschmelze*, 349 ff. and Pl. XXI ; Molinier, *L'Orfèvrerie*, 56. The Welfenschatz was for many years exhibited in the Kunstgewerbe-Museum at Vienna, from which it has now been withdrawn.
[8] Bock, *Mittheilungen der k. k. Commission*, 1870, xv. 16 ; Molinier, *L'Orfèvrerie*, 58.
[9] Fr. Bock, *Kleinodien*, &c., 12 and Pl. I, and *Mitth. der k. k. Central-Commission*, ii, 1857, 89 ; Kondakoff, 249–50.   [10] Bock, *Kleinodien* ; Kondakoff, 254.

The Church of the Holy Cross at Donauwörth once possessed a reliquary with an enamelled cover, now lost.[1]

The head- and arm-reliquaries of St. Blaise in the cathedral treasury at Ragusa have numerous small cell-enamelled plaques with busts and half-figures of saints. The accompanying names are in Latin characters, but the style is Byzantine, and the work is perhaps as early as the late eleventh century; the mountings in which the plaques are set are of the seventeenth.[2]

Denmark has in the cross of Queen Dagmar, now in the Copenhagen

Fig. 313. Figures of dancers enamelled on gold : parts of the crown of Monomachos in the Museum at Budapest. P. 525.

Museum, an exceptionally interesting piece of Byzantine enamel. It was found in the tomb of Dagmar, who died in A. D. 1212, and is to be attributed to the eleventh or twelfth century, probably the latter. On the front, upon a blue ground with white scroll-work punctuated with red, is the figure of Christ as crucified ; on the back a central bust of Christ upon a white ground, with busts of the Virgin, St. John, St. Basil, and St. John Chrysostom upon a ground of blue.[3]

---

[1] F. Schneider, *Mitth. d. historischen Vereins für Donauwörth und Umgebung*, ii. 1–12 ; *B. Z.*, xiv, 1905, 732.

[2] F. Hamilton Jackson, *The Shores of the Adriatic*, ii. *The Austrian Side*, 343–4, and plate.

[3] N. M. Petersen in *Annaler for Nordisk Oldkyndighed*, Copenhagen, 1842–3, Pl. I, Figs. 1[a] and 1[b] ; G. Stephens, *Queen Dagmar's Cross*, London and Copenhagen, 1863 ; *Arch. Journ.*, ii, p. 166 ; Labarte, *Histoire*, &c., 2nd ed., iii. 23 ; Kondakoff, 178, Figs. 51–2 ; Molinier, *L'Orfèvrerie*, 57. The latter rightly points out that Labarte's comparison with the Beresford Hope cross is misleading, the style in the two cases being very different. Queen Dagmar is most likely to have worn a cross made in her own time, i. e. the latter end of the twelfth century.

The enamelled medallions on a mitre from the cathedral at Linköping, now in the National Museum at Stockholm,[1] are probably of German origin, dating from the twelfth century. They represent busts of Christ, the Apostles, angels, and prophets, in the later Byzantine style, the descriptive names being, however, in Latin.

The enamels in various parts of the Russian dominions are very numerous, and can only be briefly mentioned, the student being referred to Kondakoff's work. Among the most interesting is the large rectangular panel in the Museum of the Hermitage, St. Petersburg, executed upon copper with copper cloisons, the main outlines being reserved in the metal ; the work thus combines the cloisonné and champlevé processes, and is very exceptional among Byzantine enamels.[2] The subject is St. Theodore of Heraclea killing a dragon, with the inscription ὁ ἅγιος Θεοδῶρος ὁ Βαθηριάκης (the Dragon-slayer). The style of the work suggests that the panel is comparatively late, and that it was probably made in the twelfth or even in the thirteenth century. St. Petersburg further possesses some interesting early enamels from a Kurgan at Smiela, considered to date from before the eighth century.[3] The Church of Polozk in the Government of Vitebsk has a cross with enamelled plaques of the tenth or eleventh century representing the *Deesis*, two archangels, the four Evangelists, and ten saints.[4] The cross of Archbishop Antonius in the Church of Sta Sophia at Novgorod has the Crucifixion between the Virgin and St. John.[5]

In the Cathedral of St. Michael at Moscow is the interesting book-cover of Prince Mstisslav of Novgorod.[6] It dates from the sixteenth century, but is richly decorated with Byzantine and Russian enamels. Among the Byzantine plaques two standing Apostles are of the tenth century ; the rest are two centuries later. The maniples of the Metropolitans Alexius and Photius, also at Moscow, have enamels sewn upon them.[7] In the armoury at the same place is a fine medallion with a bust of the Virgin.[8] In the Tauric Chersonese a medallion with the Crucifixion now ornaments a mitre.[9] The Palace Church at Livadia has a reliquary for the wood of the Cross with eleven enamelled medallions of saints, good work of the late eleventh or the twelfth century.[10] A cross exhibited at Paris in 1865 by M. Sevastianoff had a figure of Christ crucified, with a white loincloth and green nimbus on a dark ground, with the inscription : Ὁ βασιλεὺς τῆς δόξης.[11] An enamelled medallion found at Kieff has a bust of Our Lord, and appears to be of the eleventh century.[12] A remarkable series of enamelled ear-rings (Kolt), crosses, necklaces, pendants, with cloisonné figures of Our Lord, the Virgin, &c., and an interesting gold crown or diadem with the Ascent of Alexander are in the Khanenko Collection at Kieff.[13]

At the Monastery of Gelat in Mingrelia is an ikon, styled the Virgin of Chachuli, in the form of a triptych enriched with numerous enamelled plaques not altogether homogeneous.[14] In the centre at the top Christ is seen crowning

---

[1] Kondakoff, 257, Fig. 85.

[2] The plaque was formerly in the Pourtalès and Basilewsky Collections (Labarte, *Recherches sur la peinture en émail,* &c., p. 40 and Pl. D, and *Hist. des arts industriels*, Album, ii, Pl. 105 ; Darcel and Basilewsky, *La Collection Basilewsky*, Pl. XIV ; Kondakoff, 163 ; Schlumberger, *Nicéphore Phocas*, 361 ; E. Molinier, *L'Orfèvrerie*, 64 ; A. Darcel, *Gaz. des Beaux-Arts*, xix, 1865, 511).

[3] Bobrinsky, *The Kurgans of Smiela*, 152 and Pl. XX (St. Petersburg, 1887, in Russian).

[4] Kondakoff, 170.

[5] Ibid., 175 ; *Antiquités de l'Empire de Russie*, Atlas, i, No. 25, Moscow, 1849 ; Didron, *Annales archéologiques*, xx, 1860, 166.

[6] G. Filimonoff, *Archaeological Researches*, &c., *The Cover of the Gospel of Mstisslav at Moscow*, Moscow, 1861 (Russian) ; Kondakoff, 198 ; G. Schlumberger, *L'Épopée*, i, Fig. on p. 85.

[7] Schlumberger, *L'Épopée*, i, Fig. on p. 693.

[8] M. Rosenberg, *Geschichte der Goldschmiedekunst*, p. 118, Fig. 131.

[9] Kondakoff, 180 and 255, Figs. 82–4. [10] Ibid., 219.

[11] A. Darcel in *Gazette des Beaux-Arts*, xix, 1865, 510.

[12] G. Schlumberger, *L'Épopée*, i, Fig. on p. 112.

[13] *La Collection Khanenko, croix et images*, 1899 and 1900, and *Époque slave*, 1902, especially Pl. XXVII ff. Most of the objects appear to be of about the twelfth century.

[14] Kondakoff, 135 ff., Figs. on pp. 134 and 135 and 140 ; Durand, *Bulletin monumental*, 1877, 113 ff. ; Schlumberger, *L'Épopée*, vol. i, Fig. on pp. 137, 688.

the Emperor Michael VII Ducas and his wife Maria: other plaques on the central part represent the *Deesis* (three plaques), the four Evangelists, the *Etimasia*, Constantine and Helen with the Cross, two archangels, twelve Apostles (Andrew and Mark each occurring twice), SS. George, Demetrius, Theodore, Procopius, Basil the Great, John Chrysostom, Nicholas the Wonder-worker, Christ Pantokrator, the Virgin (Hodegetria), the Archangel Michael, a medallion of Christ with two crosses, two plaques with figures of bishops, and (on the predella) the Evangelists, St. Theodore Tyron, and a bishop.

On the leaves are the following enamels: the Virgin crowning a king and queen, John the Baptist preaching to a queen, the Virgin alone, SS. Matthew (thrice repeated), John the Evangelist, John the Baptist, Peter, Simon, Thomas, Philip, and Luke; an Annunciation is modern. Besides these there are a number of diminutive plaques with ornamental motives.

Fig. 314. St. George: enamelled gold medallion of the eleventh century in the Swenigorodskoi Collection. (After Kondakoff.) P. 530.

On the left leaf is a very early plaque with the Crucifixion between the Virgin and St. John, Christ being represented wearing the colobium.[1] The ground is translucent green, the cross purple, as also the colobium, the nimbus yellow with a red cross, the flesh-tints milky white. Above the cross is the hand of the Almighty, and flanking the top two angels. Two small medallions with the Virgin and St. Theodore are executed in translucent green, dark blue, purple, yellow, and white.[2] The drawing in these three examples is weak, and there is no attempt at shading or gradation of colour: they are assigned by Kondakoff to the iconoclastic period, or at any rate placed within the limits of the ninth century.[3] On the leaves, one on each side, are also the two halves of an enamelled reliquary cross; one side has St. John the Baptist and the busts of the four Evangelists; the other, Christ on the Cross between busts of the Virgin and St. John. This cross is assigned to the tenth century, to which another, with the cross between Constantine and Helena, also belongs.

It will be seen from the above that this triptych at Gelat is one of the most important monuments for the study of Byzantine enamelling anywhere preserved, and it is to be regretted that it is in so inaccessible a place.

At Gelat there is also an early Georgian ikon of Christ with enamelled nimbus and enamelled medallions round the border (*Etimasia*, an archangel,

---

[1] Kondakoff, Fig. 35 on p. 143.   [2] Ibid., Figs. 39 and 40, p. 146.

[3] Molinier (*L'Orfèvrerie*, 64, note) thinks this early attribution doubtful, and rightly urges the necessity for caution in dealing with work executed in remote provinces where archaistic tendencies may have persisted to a late date.

SS. Peter, Paul, &c.). Most of these are Georgian work in the Byzantine style, characterized by thick bright colours.[1]

The Monastery of Martwili has an enamelled *Deesis* represented in translucent colours on a translucent green ground. The whole work differs from the developed Byzantine style of the tenth century and recalls that of the Gelat-Chachuli ikon (see above) ; it may date from as early as the eighth century.[2] Fixed to the iconostasis of the church in the same monastery is a seventeenth-century triptych, in which are set an enamelled standing figure of the Virgin, and a number of medallions of saints, none later than the beginning of the eleventh century, but some of very fine execution. A small rectangular plaque with a diminutive bust of St. Peter on a green background is thought to belong, like the above-mentioned *Deesis*, to the eight or ninth century.[3] Mart-wili also possesses a remarkable enamelled pectoral cross of almost as early a period, in which Christ is represented wearing the colobium and the ground is enamelled. It has a second enamelled cross among its treasures.[4]

At Chopi in Mingrelia there is an ikon of the seventeenth century on the iconostasis. The enamelled nimbus recalls the work of the first cross of Martwili just described, and should be as early. The remaining enamels, which are round the border, consist of medallions of saints and the *Deesis*, the work perhaps dating from the tenth century.[5] Another ikon at Chopi has preserved eight out of the ten enamelled medallions upon its border : these appear to be of the late tenth or early eleventh century. The case of Queen Tamar's cross in the same place has on the back enamelled medallions of the twelfth or thirteenth century.[6]

Shemokmedi in Ghuria is fortunate in the possession of exceptionally fine Byzantine enamels upon an ikon.[7] These are eight rectangular panels arranged in three rows. In the middle are the *Anastasis* and Annunciation ; the other plaques contain representations of saints. The admirable quality of these enamels and the excellent style of the drawing recall the work of the Limburg reliquary. An ikon at Kozcheri in Mingrelia is similarly adorned with enamels, though of less fine quality.[8]

Other enamels in Imeretia, Swanetia, and Georgia are recorded by Kondakoff,[9] while there are several examples on Mount Athos in the Iberian Monastery and that of Dochiaru. A picture in miniature-mosaic attributed to the time of John Zimisces, but probably rather later, has a number of medallions upon its border (the *Etimasia* and ten saints).[10]

The enamels which form as it were the text of Kondakoff's book are a set of medallions with Our Lord and saints, formerly ornamenting the frame of an ikon of St. Gabriel in the Monastery of Jumati in Georgia. Purchased by M. Swenigorodskoi, they were long known as the enamels of his collection. The work is careful and the colours good, and possibly they may be as early as the eleventh century ; but we cannot rely upon them in the same manner as upon the Limburg reliquary or the Martwili ikon, the date of which is certainly known.[11] In the distribution of the lights and shadows they are inferior to the enamels upon those objects.

[1] Kondakoff, 154.
[2] *Ibid.*, 125 ; but see the opinion of Molinier in note above.
[3] Ibid., 152. [4] Ibid., 171-2.
[5] Ibid., 148 ; Schlumberger, *L'Épopée*, i, Fig. on p. 133. [6] Kondakoff, 222.
[7] Kondakoff, 157 and Fig. 43 on p. 156 ; Schlumberger, *L'Épopée*, i, Fig. on p. 129.
[8] Kondakoff, 158-61 and Fig. 44 on p. 159.
[9] Ibid., pp. 173, 180 : the cross of Nikortzminda, Imeretia, is figured by Schlumberger, *L'Épopée*, i. 125 ; it is of Georgian workmanship with Byzantine medallions of the eleventh century at the extremities. [10] Kondakoff, 207-8.
[11] Ch. de Linas, *Revue de l'art chrétien*, 1885 ; Bock, *Die byzantinischen Zellenschmelze*, &c. ; E. Molinier, *L'Orfèvrerie*, 55. A separate enamelled nimbus and an enamelled face and hand for a figure of the Virgin also form part of the collection, and by their very character suggest a rather later date ; for the custom of applying the nimbus of goldsmith's work to painted ikons suggests the later Russian fashion.

Byzantine enamels were imitated both in Russia and in Georgia at an early date, the imitations preserving the style and character of the originals more closely than those executed under somewhat similar conditions in Italy and on the Rhine.[1] In Russia, crosses, medallions, and gold ear-rings of 'padlock' shape (called *Kolt*) were all enamelled; the results in the latter case were very pleasing, since only decorative designs were attempted. But the Russian artists never quite mastered the processes; their colours, especially the blues, are less durable than those of their masters; their drawing, when they attempt the

Fig. 315. Backs of enamelled gold medallions from which the enamel has been lost: Swenigorodskoi Collection. (After Kondakoff.)

human figure, is defective. Their work all dates from the period between the beginning of the eleventh century and the Tartar invasions of the thirteenth, and has been discovered near Kertch or in the neighbourhood of Kieff. Enamelled medallions to the number of six or eight were worn by the Russian princes upon the *Barmi*, the collars of woven stuff which covered their necks and shoulders. The Georgians had a wider scale of colours than the Russians, and produced figures of better quality.

Byzantine enamels in Greece and the Balkan Peninsula are not numerous.

A pair of silver eucharistic fans (*rhipidia*) belonging to the Cathedral Church of Serres in Macedonia are ornamented with cloisonné enamels which are apparently of the sixteenth century and therefore beyond our period.[2] They are in

---

[1] A special chapter is devoted by Kondakoff to these Russian enamels, while examples of Georgian work which occur on monuments such as the ikon of Christ at Gelat (Kondakoff, p. 154) have been mentioned above. Other Russian enamels in the possession of M. Khanenko at Kieff are reproduced in the finely illustrated catalogue of his collection: they include a number of crosses, ear-rings, and a gold diadem or crown recalling in some ways that of Monomachos in Budapest.

[2] N. P. Kondakoff, *Macedonia*, 154 and Figs. 93, 94; Kondakoff observes that the name ΓΕΝΝΑΔΙΟΥ at the top of the handle of one fan seems to show that the work was done for the Metropolitan Gennadius in the sixteenth century; L. Chesnay, *Monuments Piot*, 1902, 137 ff., and Pl. XIII; G. Millet in A. Michel's *Histoire de l'art*.

the form of lobed disks on straight handles ; one has the Pantokrator surrounded by the symbols of the Evangelists, while the lobes are occupied by busts of angels alternating with cherubim ; the other has Christ Emmanuel in the attitude of benediction with a border of the same celestial beings.   The work, though inferior to that of early periods, is by no means to be despised, and affords an interesting proof of the late survival of the art in the Christian East.   Another

Fig. 316.   Detail of the enamelled reliquary of the tenth century in the Cathedral
of Limburg-on-the-Lahn. Cf. Fig. 311.

pair of enamelled fans of like character, dated A. D. 1592, is in the Church of St. John the Baptist near Serres.   The subjects are similar : in the centre, a half-figure of Our Lord ; round the border, angels and seraphs.[1]

The halo surrounding the head of the Archangel Gabriel, in an ikon attributed to the twelfth century in the Church of St. Clement at Ochrida, is finely enamelled with a diaper of green and red foliage on a white ground.[2]   The date of the enamel should not be much later than that of the picture.

Mount Athos has several Byzantine enamels.[3]

In the border of a mosaic picture are the *Etimasia* and nine saints, attributed to the time of John Zimisces, but probably later.   Other examples are in the Monastery of Dochiaru and the Iberian Monastery.

In the Church of the Holy Sepulchre at Jerusalem there is a painted ikon

[1] Kondakoff, as above, 164 and Fig. 103.
[2] Kondakoff, as above, 268–9 and Pl. XI.
[3] Kondakoff, *Monuments of Christian Art cn Mount Athos*, 207–8 (Russian).

of Our Lord, in a metal frame upon which are eighteen circular and rectangular enamelled plaques of angels and saints, the nimbus round Christ's head being also finely enamelled with scroll designs, and the inscription at the top (ὁ βασιλεὺς τῆς δόξης) decorated in the same way. These enamels are not all of the same date, but the best are ascribed to the tenth and eleventh centuries.[1]

Ebers, in his description of the Church of St. Catherine in the monastery on Mount Sinai, appears to state that there are enamels upon the doors leading from the narthex into the church. Perhaps the statement refers to some other kind of encrustation.[2]

A word may be conveniently added here on the subject of niello. This substance (the name derived from the Latin *nigellum*) was largely used by Byzantine goldsmiths, and its employment will be noticed on a number of metal objects mentioned below.[3] Though, like enamel, it is fused to the surface of the metal which it is desired to ornament, it differs entirely from enamel in being not vitreous but metallic, being composed of four principal ingredients, silver, lead, copper, and sulphur, a combination which fuses at a comparatively low temperature.[4] Byzantine goldsmiths appear to have sometimes used silver or gold in the same cavity which contained the niello in order to obtain a pleasing contrast of colour.[5] It is even said that occasionally enamel and niello are found together in the same bed;[6] if this is really the case, the enamel, which requires a greater heat, must have been fired first and the niello after-wards applied.

The free use of niello on Byzantine plate and jewellery for designs executed by the champlevé process makes it remarkable that champlevé enamelling was not more frequently practised in the Eastern Empire. Figure subjects are rare in niello; they occur on the cross of Adaloald at Monza and one or two other objects (p. 548).

Niello appears to have been occasionally employed in larger masses than is usual. Constantine Porphyrogenitus, describing the oratory or chapel in the Sacred Palace, says that the floor was of massive silver enriched with niello.[7]

---

[1] Kondakoff, *Archaeological Journey to Syria and Palestine*, St. Petersburg, 1904, Pl. LXV; and *V. V.*, iv, 1897, Appendix, p. 40 (both in Russian).

[2] G. Ebers, *Durch Goschen zum Sinai*, p. 261.

[3] It is claimed that the ancient Egyptians used niello in the time of the seventeenth dynasty (axe and dagger of Amosis I, see von Bissing, *Ein thebanischer Grabfund*, and M. Rosenberg, *Geschichte der Goldschmiedekunst*). Greek objects in the Hermitage Museum at St. Petersburg are nielloed, and its employment by the Romans is a matter of common knowledge. Merovingian jewellery and Anglo-Saxon jewellery from the South of England are also ornamented in this way. In mediaeval Europe it was especially used in the Romanesque period.

[4] Comparative tables on the composition of niello derived from the statements in Pliny (xxxiii. 46), Theophilus (*Schedula diversarum artium*, c. 1100 A.D., Bk. III, ch. 28), Cellini (*Trattato della oreficeria*), &c., are given by Rosenberg, as above. The modern processes of employing niello are described by Romain, *Le Bijoutier orfèvre* (1886).

[5] As in the case of the small reliquary in the British Museum, Fig. 332.

[6] Rosenberg thinks, probably correctly, that the second substance on the ring at Palermo (p. 545) is metallic and not vitreous.

[7] Cf. J. Ebersolt, *Le Grand Palais de Constantinople et le livre des Cérémonies*, 1910, and Diehl, *Manuel*, 393.

CHAPTER IX

GOLDSMITH'S WORK AND JEWELLERY [1]

GOLDSMITH'S WORK IN GENERAL.

THE work of the Byzantine goldsmiths offers less variety than that of their mediaeval contemporaries in the West, who for about eight hundred years were occupied with the solution of similar problems. There are several reasons for this comparative monotony. In the West there was a succession of striking and fundamental changes in architecture, an art which has imposed its forms upon ecclesiastical metal-work; at the same time different processes of enamelling succeeded and displaced each other, each requiring a fresh treatment and necessitating a new disposal of the surface to be wrought and decorated. In the Eastern Empire the architectural changes from the fifth century to the fifteenth were less pronounced; there the reliquary in the form of a church would therefore alter far less throughout this long space of time than in a country like France, where the Romanesque style was succeeded by various phases of Gothic with arches, pinnacles, and window traceries of different forms. The style of enamelling in the East remaining constant down to the fall of Constantinople, gold plaques of small size continued to be decorated by the cloisonné process, which meant that they were in all centuries applied to larger surfaces of metal in the same way. But in the West the general adoption of the champlevé process on copper in the twelfth century reacted upon artistic metal-work: the craftsman could now dispense with small plaques treated as if they were merely larger precious stones, and was able to cover considerable surfaces with colour embodied as it were in the very substance of the work. The development of the beautiful translucent enamel upon sunk relief admitted further variety, and the process of painting in enamel still more. Lastly, the restricted use of sculpture in the East debarred the Byzantine goldsmith from many delicate devices known to his Western neighbours. He cast and chased bronze but little, making no such bold and beautiful mouldings as were produced on the Rhine and Meuse in the twelfth century, and confining himself as far as figures were concerned to embossing thin plates of silver or gold. In this respect the stationary character of his work is marked when compared with the continual developments which were taking place in Italy, Germany, and France. In the use of niello he was also conservative, never advancing beyond a few figures on a small scale, or a conventional design. In the application of precious stones he adhered throughout to the plain raised setting (cf. Figs. 308, 316), not attempting the device, known even to the

---

[1] See also, in addition to the references given below, Ch. Diehl, *Manuel*, pp. 287 ff., 635 ff.; H. Leclercq, *Manuel d'arch. chrét.*, ii, pp. 393 ff.

Carolingians, of holding a gem as it were suspended in claws, so that the light might pass completely through it.   Nor did he often mass stones

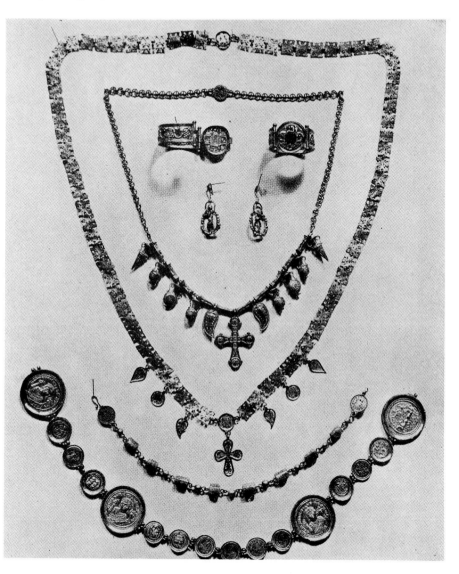

Fig. 317.   Gold jewellery of the sixth century from the neighbourhood of Kyrenia, Cyprus : in the collection of J. Pierpont Morgan, Esq.   P. 541.

together, or arrange them in a close row, except by the old method of *orfèvrerie cloisonnée*, which he maintained after it had been abandoned in Western Europe.   He never faceted his gems or pastes, but in this respect was no more backward than his neighbours, who also contented themselves with cabochon gems down to the approach of the Renaissance. Filigree he occasionally used to cover vacant spaces between the stones or enamels, having no canopies or traceries to perform this office, thus adhering faithfully to a method of ornamentation which the West abandoned with the rise of the Gothic style.   In a word, Byzantine goldsmith's work, though often sumptuous and highly decorative, is perhaps more conservative than any branch of a very conservative art.

Before we examine the more important examples of Byzantine work which have survived to our own day, we may notice some of the literary evidences which prove the magnificence of the treasures once existing in the East-Roman Empire.   John Chrysostom inveighs against the luxury of

FIG. 318.   Silver paten of the eleventh century in the Treasury of the Cathedral of Halberstadt.   (From an electrotype in the Victoria and Albert Museum.)   Pp. 553-4.

the wealthy classes of his day, who covered themselves with jewels and embroidered robes, while their very horses had golden bits.[1]   The descriptions of the gold and silver furniture in the palaces of Constantinople reveal an oriental extravagance.[2]   The *consistorium* or throne-room of the old imperial palace had a throne covered with gold and precious stones beneath a golden canopy upon four columns.   The panegyric of Corippus on Justin II is eloquent with descriptions which would do honour to a goldsmith, and he dwells complacently upon the rich plate and vestments of the royal house.[3]   The accounts left by Constantine Porphyrogenitus and Anna Comnena of the gorgeous displays upon the occasion of imperial receptions complete the tale of the earlier chronicles.[4]   The houses of the

[1] Chrysostom's works in Migne, *Patr. Gr.*, i. 957, v. 515, vii. pp. 501-2.
[2] Labarte, *Le Palais impérial*, 124 ; Diehl, *Justinien*, 82.
[3] iii. 87 ; iv. 103.
[4] Accounts of these splendours will be found (in addition to Labarte's works) in J. Ebersolt, *Le Grand Palais de Constantinople et le livre des Cérémonies*, Paris, 1910, and in Bielyayeff's *Bizantina*, the latter a most valuable work, unfortunately in the Russian language and therefore accessible to few.

wealthy Byzantine nobles, with their silver tables and other furniture, were scarcely less resplendent.

Descriptions of the glittering furniture of churches have been left us both by Greek panegyrists and by pilgrims from other countries. The building which left the most profound impression upon the minds of all who saw it was naturally the Cathedral of the Divine Wisdom in the metropolis.[1] The altar was of gold; the ciborium was splendid with the precious metals and possibly with enamel; the iconostasis, like that of Galla Placidia's Church of St. John at Ravenna, was covered with silver, comprising figures of the Virgin, angels, Apostles, and prophets, either embossed or damascened; the ambo was equally magnificent; the very

FIG. 319. Gold signet of the sixth–seventh century. (British Museum.) P. 540.

FIG. 320. Gold signet of the sixth or seventh century. (British Museum.)

columns and walls within the bema were overlaid with silver. The *polycandela* and other lamps were of silver and gold; the furniture of the altar was of unequalled splendour. Archbishop Anthony of Novgorod, who visited Sta Sophia in A.D. 1200, describes the votive crowns of Constantine and other emperors hanging above the altar, thirty smaller crowns, a suspended golden cross and dove, and behind the altar a golden cross higher than two men.[2] In the sanctuary there were endless gold and silver plates, eighty silver candelabra, and a large number of the most sumptuous chalices and patens. All this might seem exaggeration were it not that we have the testimony of the crusaders of A.D. 1204 and the actual spoils which they took back into the West.[3] And how much even of the spoils has since been destroyed or lost we may learn from the accounts which have come down to us of the indiscriminate

[1] Most of the facts relating to the splendours of the cathedral have been collected by Lethaby and Swainson, who also publish a translation of Paulus Silentiarius. See their *The Church of Sancta Sophia in Constantinople*, 74 ff. The reader may also consult the earlier works of Labarte, *Histoire des arts industriels*, vol. iii, and others, themselves largely based upon the earlier researches of Ducange.

[2] *Itinéraires russes en Orient* (*Soc. Orient Latin, série géogr.*, vol. v); Lethaby and Swainson, 101 ff.

[3] Nicetas describes the destruction of the altar, ciborium, and iconostasis. He mentions no less than forty golden censers, silver candelabra, and other vessels (Lethaby and Swainson, 75). For Robert de Clary's account in the thirteenth century, see his *Prise de Constantinople* in C. Hopf's *Chroniques gréco-romanes*, p. 67.

looting of Constantinople, and of the ultimate official division of what the marauders did not succeed in appropriating for themselves.[1] Nine-tenths of the treasure in S. Marco at Venice comes from the official share of the republic, and even after the disastrous fire of A.D. 1231, which damaged the treasury and destroyed much of its contents, the residue is still of an unequalled interest. M. Molinier, in one of those passages which made his archaeological work so illuminating,[2] warns us, however, to discount in some measure the rather inflated descriptions of Byzantine splendour. He rightly maintains that if the Byzantine work that has survived is to be taken as typical, it is not superior to the Western goldsmith's work of the close of the fourteenth century and later, as revealed to us by such objects as the Royal Gold Cup in the British

FIG. 321. Gold signet of the sixth century with monogram. (British Museum.) P. 540.

FIG. 322. Gold signet of about the fifth century : Our Lord and Apostle (?). (British Museum.) P. 541.

Museum, made for the Duc de Berri, and by the entries in the inventories of that prince and his royal relations. Much that the pilgrims and crusaders saw and described as gold was doubtless really gilt—did not Luitprand in his account of his embassy (A.D. 948–50) assert that the famous mechanical lions of the imperial audience chamber were really made of gilded copper? And the pearls which are such a feature upon the personal ornaments, reliquaries, and chalices are of no great size and quality, and would now command a moderate admiration. Yet, even when due deductions are made for the exaggeration of early historians, the wealth of Constantinople must still have been enormous, and would have been memorable in any age.

In reviewing such work as remains after the destruction of centuries

---

[1] See Comte de Riant, *Dépouilles religieuses enlevées à Constantinople*, Paris, 1875. The Byzantine relics formerly in the Sainte Chapelle at Paris were destroyed during the Revolution. The richest treasure of Byzantine goldsmith's work is in S. Marco (A. Pasini, *Il Tesoro di S. Marco*): it reached Venice as a result of the Crusade. The same cause has enriched the Cathedral of Halberstadt with valuable objects, brought by Bishop Conrad, who accompanied the army (Schatz, *Chronicon Halberst.*, pp. 76–7). Namur received gifts from Henry I, successor of Baldwin (*Ann. de la Soc. arch. de Namur*, ix. 407): an enamelled cross is still preserved (p. 520). The Limburg reliquary (p. 522) was also crusaders' spoil.

[2] *Hist. des arts appliqués à l'industrie : l'orfèvrerie*, 45.

it will be convenient to divide the subject into three sections, the first comprising personal ornaments; the second, objects made and decorated for devotional or ecclesiastical use; and the third, plate. In the second section a few objects not actually of precious metal are included for convenience. Byzantine metal-work, not in gold and silver, has chiefly survived in small objects, mostly of the First Period, found in the greatest numbers in Egypt,[1] or rarely in work on a large scale such as the great bronze church doors. Such of the more important classes as can be conveniently described in groups are briefly noted in a later chapter.

JEWELLERY.

It may be noticed by way of preliminary that Byzantine fashions in the matter of personal ornament differed somewhat from those of the West. In Western mediaeval Europe after Frankish times ear-rings are but rarely mentioned in contemporary literature, and examples are

FIG. 323. Silver ring inscribed : ' Lord preserve the wearer.' (British Museum.)

FIG. 324. Bronze signet of one Stephen. (British Museum.)

never found belonging to any period much earlier than the Renaissance; nor did bracelets, which were common among prehistoric peoples and among the Romans, find much favour before the fifteenth century. In the Eastern Empire this was apparently not the case, though the ear-rings which we possess happen, like European examples, to be of early date. But we know that bracelets continued in use, both through existing examples and through documentary evidence. Thus in A.D. 831 we read that a chief magistrate presented Theophilus with golden brace-lets.[2] The custom of sewing pearls, gems, and even enamelled medallions to the garments may also be conveniently noticed here. The richly embroidered imperial robes were covered in this way until they became so stiff that the grace of draped folds became impossible. Many illumina-tions and mosaics illustrate this magnificence ; while an even better idea may be gained from the royal mantle and other vestures made in mediaeval

---

[1] For these small metal objects see especially Strzygowski's Catalogue, 'Koptische Kunst', O. Wulff's Catalogue of the Collections in the Kaiser Friedrich Museum, Berlin, and the Catalogue of Early Christian and Byzantine Antiquities in the British Museum.

[2] Constantine Porphyrogenitus, *De caerimoniis aulae Byz.*, i. 503.

Sicily under strong oriental influence and now preserved in the Schatz-kammer at Vienna.[1]

Roman jewellery has survived in greater quantities than that of the Eastern Empire, partly because great tracts of that empire have been less accessible to the excavator than the Roman provinces, partly because Byzantium was Christian from the beginning and interments are less likely to yield objects of archaeological interest.

At the beginning of the First Period, as we should naturally expect, there is no clear line of demarcation between late Roman and Byzantine jewellery. The combination of large stones of intense colour, such as plasma or carnelian, with gold of an ever-diminishing solidity is a characteristic which became general in the fourth century. The old Greek insistence on beauty of form was gone: it was no longer necessary to

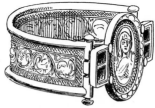

FIG. 325.   Gold bracelet of the sixth century.   (British Museum.)   P. 541.

model well, or to apply to the creations of the goldsmith's craft that fine restraint which preserved the Greeks from the love of empty splendour. What was now required was not work to be picked up and lingered over by the discriminating eye, but something to attract attention from a distance by almost violent contrasts of light and colour. For this purpose fragile gold-work and stones of inferior quality sufficed: with the Greek perfection of detail, the honest solidity of early Roman work was abandoned. Even from the third century the oriental system of massing table-gems or pastes between narrow cloisons had invaded the Roman Empire, and must have obtained early entrance into Constantinople. We may infer this from the survival of the style upon the Limburg reliquary (p. 522) at a time when it had disappeared in Persia and had practically died out in Europe.

The following examples of Byzantine jewellery of the First Period are more or less accessible to students.

Specimens in the British Museum, with their numbers as given in the Catalogue of Early Christian and Byzantine Antiquities, begin with finger-rings.

No. 168 (Fig. 321).   Gold ring with a monogram of the early rectangular form engraved on the bezel (sixth century).

No. 120 (Fig. 319).   Gold ; on the bezel an intaglio bust of Christ with two angels and a cruciform monogram (sixth century).

No. 189 (Fig. 320).   Gold ; on the bezel a head of Christ in intaglio with two adoring angels.   Found with coins of Heraclius (seventh century).

[1] Bock, *Kleinodien des Heiligen Römischen Reichs*, Pl. IV, VI, VIII, XIII, XXV, XXXII.

No. 190 (Fig. 322). Gold ; on the bezel Christ seated ; on the seven connected panels forming the hoop, seven Apostles ; obtained in Smyrna (fifth century).

No. 207. Gold ; on the square bezel two busts of a husband and wife deeply cut in intaglio : between them a cross. The hoop is cut into seven circular panels on which are nielloed busts, male and female alternating (fifth century).

No. 210. Gold ; the bezel set with a coin of Marcian, the shoulders modelled to represent hares (fifth century).

No. 211. Gold ; plain wire hoop ; the bezel a coin of Justinian (sixth century).

All the engraving upon these rings is on the metal, and none of them contain intaglio gems. Several are approximately dated by their association with coins. Of jewellery other than rings belonging to the early period, the more remarkable British Museum examples are as follows :—

No. 252. A rectangular gold panel formed of two pierced plates of scroll-work set back to back. In one of these a mounted Amazonian figure is reserved in the metal. This panel is said to have been found in Asia Minor with six *aurei* of Constantius.

No. 253. A gold plate from a buckle with a circular medallion containing a nielloed bust, from which radiate large lobes. No. 254 is an imperfect buckle of the same kind.

No. 256. Bronze-gilt fibula of the crossbow type, with the sacred monogram and busts in small medallions. This fibula is of a type found with coins from Valentinian I to Arcadius.

No. 264. Gold fibula of the crossbow type engraved with the inscription + ΘY XAPIC (Θεοῦ χάρις) ; not later than the sixth century. The inscription occurs in several objects of about this period.

Nos. 258–261. Four gilt-bronze rectangular plaques from a belt, one with a buckle. They are ornamented with subjects in relief, a male figure standing cross-legged occurring more than once. This type of figure originated in Greek art and was continued in the art of the Syro-Egyptian region.[1] Found in the tombs of the prophets.

No. 267. Pair of gold ear-rings with lunate plaques enamelled by the cloisonné process, the subjects being confronted peacocks. (Cf. p. 505.)

Nos. 268–278. Gold ear-rings (Fig. 328) with lunate plaques of openwork, mostly with confronted birds.[2] Ear-rings of this form have been found not only in Egypt, but also in barbaric graves in Hungary ; apparently of about the seventh century.

No. 279 (Fig. 325). Gold bracelet ; the broad openwork hoop has confronted peacocks separated by a vase, and several geese, all contained in a flowing scroll ; the front, which opens on a hinge, has a circular medallion with a bust of the Virgin in low relief. This bracelet is of the same form as a pair with openwork vine-scrolls and without busts, forming part of the Kyrenia treasure (p. 572) which is dated by the coins found with it to the sixth century. The bracelet is therefore in all probability not later than A.D. 600.

The principal other articles of jewellery found with this treasure consisted of three necklaces, one of large cylindrical plasma beads alternating with pearls, the other two of gold chains with crosses and pendants hanging from them, several pairs of ear-rings, a girdle (?) composed of a number of gold coins and four large gold medals (Fig. 317). The first of these necklaces and the ear-rings are of an early type, and analogous to jewellery ascribed to the Roman period found in Egypt and elsewhere. The two others are interesting from the character of their pendants, which are in the form of little gold amphorae, and of flat open-

---

[1] J. Strzygowski, *Bull. de la Soc. arch. d'Alexandrie*, No. 5, Vienna, 1902, 56–60.

[2] Gold ear-rings, belonging to M. de Nelidoff, were exhibited at the Italo-Byzantine Exhibition of 1904 at Grottaferrata (A. Muñoz, *Esposizione italo-bizantina*, Grottaferrata, 1905, 54).

work plaques, circular and pear-shaped, with confronted birds and conventional patterns. One of the chains has flat rectangular links of quatrefoil design ; both are rather flimsy in construction. The greater number of the coins composing the girdle are of Maurice Tiberius, and all the four large medals, which are stated by numismatists to have been cast and not struck from a die, are of the same emperor : the date is therefore presumably the last quarter of the sixth century. The district of Kyrenia had previously yielded other Byzantine jewels (a chain, ear-rings, &c.), probably of much the same date as the treasure just described ; [1] and to the same period belongs the interesting gold jewellery discovered at Mersina in Cilicia,[2] now in the Hermitage at St. Petersburg, in which the use

Fɪɢ. 326.　Development of gold bracelet of the sixth century.　(British Museum.)　P. 541.

of openwork and the pear-shaped pendants noticed in the Kyrenia necklaces are again conspicuous. The latter feature suggests an oriental (Persian) influence. Another treasure, found at Narona in Dalmatia, included four gold rings and an ear-ring : the coins discovered with it ranged from Justin I (518–27) to Tiberius Constantine (A. D. 578–82).[3] One of the rings was inscribed in Latin letters with the name *Urvece* (Urbica ?), another with a monogram.

Various sites in Sicily have yielded necklaces and ear-rings of a similar style and period. Of a treasure discovered at Pantalica in the valley of the Anapus only a small part has escaped destruction or dispersal ; that which remains, with some objects surviving at least in photographic record, has been described by Orsi.[4] The objects were discovered in 1903 in a bronze vase with many hundred gold coins of Constantine IV, Constans II, Heraclius, and Tiberius,[5] giving the close of the seventh century as the probable date of deposit : Pantalica was probably taken by the Arabs in A. D. 878.

[1] J. L. Myres, *The Reliquary*, 1898, 109–12, Figs. 1–6, and *Catalogue of the Cyprus Museum.*
[2] Kondakoff, *Russkie Kladui* (Russian treasures), 187–92, and Pl. XVIII–XIX.
[3] F. Bulic, *Nuovo Bullettino di archeologia cristiana*, 1902, 234 ff.
[4] *B. Z.*, xix, 1910, 64 ff.
[5] The types are those shown in W. Wroth's *Catalogue of Imperial Byzantine Coins in the British Museum*, i, Pl. XXX, 19, XXXII, 10, and ii, Pl. XXXVI, 2 and 3, XXXVII, 9.

A treasure from Campobello di Mazara,[1] of which the remains are in the museum at Palermo, contains necklaces with openwork disks of gold containing floriated crosses.

What was once the richest treasure of all, that of Syracuse, is now repre-

Fig. 327. Gold ear-rings and other objects of the sixth century from the neighbourhood of Kyrenia, Cyprus. (Museum of Nicosia.) P. 541.

sented only by the nielloed marriage-ring in the Palermo Museum (see below).

Speaking of such finds of Byzantine jewellery of the sixth to seventh centuries M. Smirnoff draws attention to the similarity of their style, however far apart they may be found.[2] This seems to point to one or two important centres of production, of which the work was disseminated in all directions. Both

[1] Salinas, *Le Collane bizantine del Museo di Palermo rinvenute a Campobello.*
[2] *Journal of the Imperial Russian Archaeological Society,* xii (Classical Byzantine and West-European section), 506–10 (in Russian).

Egypt [1] and Cilicia are mentioned as renowned for their goldsmiths, and it is possible that, as in the case of the silver plate found with it, the Cyprus jewellery may have had a continental origin.   The lunate type of gold ear-ring with birds, &c., in openwork which is found in the Mersina treasure, has occurred in Egypt, Cyprus, Asia Minor, and in graves in Hungary.[2]

Of objects probably belonging to the Third and Fourth Periods the British Museum possesses several of considerable interest.

Five specimens are rather massive gold rings with flat hoops and applied bezels, with inscriptions and subjects in niello (Nos. 121 and 129–32 of the catalogue).   One, No. 121, has on the bezel the Annunciation, with the usual inscription from Luke i. 28, Χαῖρε, κεχαριτωμένη, &c. ; the others are marriage-rings having on the bezel figures of Our Lord, or Our Lord and the Virgin, blessing the bride and bridegroom, with the word ὁμόνοια, while the inscription on the hoop is, Εἰρήνην τὴν ἐμὴν δίδωμι ὑμῖν (John xiv. 27).   One has on the hoop, instead

FIG. 328.   Gold ear-ring of the sixth–seventh century.   (British Museum.)

FIG. 329.   Gold marriage-ring with subjects in niello : tenth century or earlier.   (British Museum.)

of the inscription, a series of scenes from the Passion, in this resembling other rings of the class, one of which is in the museum at Palermo.   One reason for supposing that these rings are later than the objects previously mentioned is the debased orthography of the inscriptions ; but it is possible that some may be earlier than has been usually supposed, and date from the sixth or seventh century.[3]   The niello work is not always good and the figures are often mere caricatures, but the restricted space was against the artist.   The same criticism applies to a charming little flat octagonal gold reliquary (Fig. 332), apparently for relics of SS. Cosmas and Damian, whose names are engraved upon it (No. 284).   On the top are the Nativity and Adoration of the Magi in niello, and round the edge the inscription, Ἡ βεβαία σωτηρία καὶ ἀποτροπὴ πάντων τῶν κακῶν, τῶν ἁγίων Κοσμᾶ καὶ Δαμιανοῦ.[4]

Four gold pectoral crosses (Nos. 285–8) may also belong to the Third Period. Fig. 330 (No. 285) has engraved upon the face the verse from Galatians vi. 14 (' God forbid that I should glory,' &c.) ; No. 286 has Our Lord as crucified, in very low relief, and medallions with busts at the ends of the arms (Fig. 331 ; No. 287 has in the centre the Virgin as *orans* ; above her is a standing figure of Christ, and below a military saint (Theodore ?), while on the back is the inscription Γεοργίου Σκοπέλου : the figures were originally nielloed.   No. 288 has the inscription : *Lord, protect the wearer of this (cross).*

[1] The writer has seen a find of gold jewellery said to have been discovered a few years ago at Assiût.   It included a pierced lunate gold collar set with pastes, two medallions with the Annunciation and Miracle of Cana, and a bracelet.
[2] British Museum, *Catalogue of Early Christian and Byzantine Antiquities*, No. 276.   The Cyprus example of the type is figured by Cesnola, Pl. VI.
[3] Dr. Arthur Evans has one from Trapani, Sicily, with Our Lord between two angels, and legend : GLORIA IN EXCEASIS DO ET IN TERRA PAX.   The Latin inscription is in favour of a seventh-century date.   Cf. also Kondakoff, *Enamel*, p. 264.
[4] An interesting nielloed gold reliquary for relics of St. Stephen the younger, son of Basil I, is in the collection of M. Schlumberger, who figures it in his *Nicéphore Phocas*, p. 93.

The Palermo marriage-ring, resembling in style those in the British Museum mentioned above, was found near Syracuse. It has on the bezel Christ blessing an emperor and empress, with the debased inscription ὁς ὧπλον εὐδοκίας, ἐστεφάνοσας ἡμᾶς (Ps. v. 12). The word εὐδοκίας has been thought to imply a reference to the Empress Eudokia Makrembolitissa (A.D. 1068) and the ring referred to the eleventh century, but there is a possibility that it may be older.[1]

Another ring of this class, in the Pichon Collection, has on the bezel Christ blessing a bride and bridegroom, with the word ὁμόνυα and, on the border, *Lord, preserve thy servants Peter and Theodotis.* The hoop has seven Gospel scenes in niello, and on the edges the text: ' Peace I leave with you, my peace I give unto you,' in the usual faulty orthography.[2] The bezel of a ring apparently in this style, with the Crucifixion in niello, and the usual inscription from John xix. 26–7, was described by Sir Charles Robinson before the Society of Antiquaries of London in 1889.[3] A massive gold ring set with a green glass paste is engraved with a head of Christ, round which is an inscription ; on the shoulders, are cruciform monograms with scroll designs continued round the hoop. The inscription relates to a ' Basil the Chamberlain ', whom M. Schlumberger would identify with the Emperor Basil the Macedonian before his accession, thus placing the ring in the ninth century.[4] Another gold ring has a bust of Christ on the bezel and on the shoulders busts of the Virgin and St. John the Evangelist, all apparently in niello. It bears the inscription : *Lord, preserve Aetius protospatharius and drungarius,* &c. This personage is identified by Schlumberger with the Aetius beheaded by the Emir al-Mumenin at Samara on the Euphrates ; if this attribution is correct, this ring also belongs to the ninth century.[5]

Fig. 330. Gold pectoral cross.
(British Museum.) P. 544.

Another octagonal ring of the same metal has on the bezel a monogram and the word Εἰρήνης. Schlumberger deciphers the monogram as Δουκαίνης Αὐτοκρατορίσσης, and ascribes the ring to the Empress Irene, consort of Alexius I Comnenus.[6] Another plain gold ring has on the circular bezel the inscription : *Lord, save Theophano and John.* These persons the same writer conjectures to be the Empress Theophano and John Zimisces (†976), though as they were

[1] G. Romano and A. Salinas, *Archivio storico Siciliano,* New Series, iii, 1878, 92 ff. Other descriptions of this ring will be found in papers by J. Durand, *Bulletin monumental,* 5th series, x, Paris, 1882, 508 ff., and H. Leclercq in Cabrol's *Dictionnaire d'archéologie chrétienne et de liturgie,* s.v. *Anneaux,* col. 2190. The last writer states that it formed part of a rich treasure said to have belonged to the Emperor Constans II, who was assassinated in Syracuse in A.D. 668. Cf. *Bullettino di archeologia cristiana,* 1888–9, 84 ff.
[2] G. Schlumberger, *Nicéphore Phocas,* 389 ; K. Krumbacher, *Sitzungsberichte der k. bayerischen Akad. der Wissenschaften, philos.-philol. und hist. Klasse,* 1906, 439.
[3] *Proceedings,* xi. 89 (no Figure).
[4] G. Schlumberger, *Sigillographie de l'Empire byzantin,* 1884, 562, and *Mélanges d'arch. byz.,* 1895, i. 40 ; Leclercq in Cabrol, *Dictionnaire d'arch. chrétienne,* &c., 1905, s.v. *Anneaux,* col. 2207, Fig. 740.
[5] G. Schlumberger, *Mélanges,* &c., as above, i. 43 ; Leclercq, as above, Fig. 741.
[6] G. Schlumberger, *Compte rendu de l'Académie des Inscriptions et Belles-Lettres,* 1905, 142 (*Quatre bagues d'or*).

never married the attribution seems doubtful.[1] A silver ring, perhaps of the tenth or eleventh century, has an inscription with the name of an imperial spatharius named Theodore: on the sides are monograms reading Θεοτόκε βοήθη and ornamental designs.[2] A gold ring, perhaps a century earlier, has a circular legend on the bezel, Παξῆνος ὁ ἀπελάτης, enclosing a monogram.[3] Sir Charles Robinson in 1889 described a massive gold ring the bezel of which was set with a coin of Michael VII Ducas and his wife Maria (1071-78).[4] A solid gold ring with a large circular bezel bearing an inscription, found a few years ago at Mainz, provides us with a more certain date. The inscription, which is nielloed, consists of two iambics in careless orthography, which, when emended, read as follows:—

Μνῆστρον Στεφάνου Δουκικῆς ῥίζης κλάδου
Κομνηνοφυῆς ταῖν χεροῖν, Ἄννα, δέχου.

Krumbacher[5] showed that the reference can only be to King Stephen Radoslav of Servia (A.D. 1228-34) and his wife Anna Comnena, daughter of the Emperor Theodore Angelus Comnenus Ducas of Thessalonica. As the ring is of a well-known type, it perhaps justifies us in assigning to the thirteenth century others of similar form and appearance, for instance a plain gold ring in the Palermo Museum, with an inscription on the bezel which Salinas reads as Εὐφημίου ὑπάτου,[6] and another ring in the museum of the Principi di Trabia at Palermo with the inscription: *Lord, preserve thy servant Nicetas, imperial protospatharius.*[7]

Of the last centuries of the empire but little jewellery survives, for the times were unsettled, and doubtless, as in the stormier periods of the Middle Ages in the West, objects in the precious metals were freely melted down.

FIG. 331. Gold pectoral cross.
(British Museum.)

A gold ring in the British Museum (*Catalogue*, No. 171), of fourteenth-century type, has engraved on the bezel a cruciform monogram which reads Manuel, and has been supposed, though on insufficient evidence, to have been made for Manuel Palaeologus. Two other gold rings (Nos. 122, 123), one with a bust of Christ in intaglio, the second with a rudely engraved figure of Orpheus, may be of similar date.

In M. Schlumberger's Collection is a small reliquary of the period of the Palaeologi from Palma in Majorca.[8]

LARGER OBJECTS, CHIEFLY ECCLESIASTICAL OR DEVOTIONAL.

If in personal jewellery the Byzantine goldsmith's art is but poorly represented among existing remains, much in the decoration of book-covers, reliquaries, and mounts of chalices has survived to suggest interesting comparison with the contemporary work in Western Europe. Most of these

[1] G. Schlumberger, *Compte rendu de l'Académie des Inscriptions et Belles-Lettres*, 1905, 142; Krumbacher, as above, 439.

[2] Schlumberger, *Quatre bagues d'or*, as above, 143, and *L'Épopée byzantine*, third part, 140.

[3] Ibid., 139.　　　　　　[4] *Proc. Soc. Ant. Lond.*, xi, 1889, 89, No. 4.

[5] *Sitzungsberichte der k. bayerischen Akademie der Wissenschaften, philos.-philol. und hist. Klasse*, 1906, 421 ff. This paper led to various others, on which see *B. Z.*, xix, 1910, 111 ff.

[6] A. Salinas, *Periodico di numismatica e sfragistica per la storia d'Italia*, iii, 1871, 208 ff. and Pl. IX, Fig. 2; Krumbacher, as above, 438.

[7] Salinas, as above, 209 f. and Pl. IX, Fig. 3.

[8] *Compte rendu de l'Acad. des Inscr. et Belles-Lettres*, 1905, 137.

examples are of the Third Period, but at the same time earlier than the thirteenth century, and it is among the products of the late Carolingian and Romanesque periods that they find their nearest affinities.

Flat surfaces were usually ornamented by embossing figures or scroll designs and by the application of filigree or cabochon gems in plain raised settings, sometimes disposed in geometrical groups, as on the reliquary at Limburg (Fig. 316). The use of pearls threaded upon a wire is very characteristic from the time of Justinian down to the twelfth century, if not later : the wire is passed through gold loops placed at frequent intervals, so that when all the spaces are filled with pearls the tops of the loops present the appearance of alternating gold beads. This kind of work, also used for personal ornaments, is seen upon several book-covers and chalice-mounts of the best period (Fig. 340), where enamelled medallions are framed with threaded pearls. It may be regarded as characteristically Byzantine, and is rarely found in Western work except in early Teutonic jewellery made under Byzantine

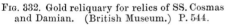

FIG. 332. Gold reliquary for relics of SS. Cosmas and Damian. (British Museum.) P. 544.

FIG. 333. Gold signet with head of Our Lord. (British Museum.)

influence. We find it in Ostrogothic or Lombard jewellery like the cross of Agilulf at Monza, and the Castellani brooch in the British Museum (Fig. 301). It has already been noticed that the massing or alignment in borders of table garnets or glass pastes set in cells formed of fine cloisons was early accepted by the Byzantine jeweller. Conspicuous examples of this are to be seen in the border of the book-cover with remarkable early enamels in the Library of St. Mark at Venice [1] (p. 516), and on the enamelled reliquary at Limburg-on-the-Lahn (p. 522) ; the triptych reliquary of the Monastery of Sainte-Croix at Poitiers, considered to have been sent to Radegund by Justin II, was also ornamented in this way (p. 520). Perhaps the earliest example of all is the lamb which ornaments the leaf of the large composite diptych of the sixth century in the sacristy of Milan Cathedral (p. 202), though here the surfaces of the stones have not been ground flat. It was formerly considered that this ornamentation was enamelled, but it is now held to consist of precious stones fixed without the agency of heat.[2] It has been claimed as of East-Christian rather than Western work, partly owing to its naturalism, the majority of animal forms made by Western barbaric jewellers being highly conventionalized.[3]

Some of the more remarkable examples of devotional or ecclesiastical goldsmith's work may now be considered, postponing enamelled work to another

[1] Pasini, *Il Tesoro di San Marco*, Pl. VI ; Molinier, *Hist. des arts appliqués à l'industrie : L'Orfèvrerie*, p. 43.

[2] Molinier, *Gazette des Beaux-Arts*, 2e Période, xxxvii, 1888, 391, note 1, and Vladimir de Bock, *Proc. of the Imp. Russian Archaeological Soc.*, New Series, viii, 1896, 394–8. See also B. Z., vi, 1897, 467 ; vii, 1898, 249 ; and V. V., vi, 1896, 691.

[3] De Bock, as above. Labarte had already claimed the work as Byzantine, though he regarded the vitreous ornament as enamel.

section. The majority of surviving pieces being of the Third Period, they are here geographically arranged under the countries in which they are now preserved.

The cross of Justin II in St. Peter's at Rome[1] is entirely ornamented on one side with embossed work on thin plates of gold or silver gilt; on the other it is bordered with cabochon stones in raised settings, while the four arms are covered with an engraved inscription upon a plain plate of gold:

Ligno quo Christus humanum subdidit hostem
Dat Romae Iustinus opem et socia decorem.

This seems to imply that the emperor himself was the donor of the relic, while his consort (*socia*) presented the decorated cross. From the arms hang four pendent gems. The embossed side of the cross has a large central medallion

FIG. 334. Gold signet of the fourteenth century with monogram. (British Museum.)   FIG. 335. Gold signet with Orpheus. (British Museum.)

with the Agnus Dei, and four smaller medallions at the extremities: those at the top and bottom containing busts of Christ, those to right and left of the emperor and empress as *orantes*. The rest of the surface is covered with a rich acanthus ornament, recalling the foliage seen upon contemporary Sassanian sculpture. The cross has suffered much from depredation in the course of centuries. Six of the gems have been removed and replaced by pastes, and the pearls which formerly enriched it stripped off. The central medallion on the front was added in the time of Pius IX; the pendent agates are also modern. Bock conjectures that it may originally have been suspended from a *regnum* or votive crown like the cross of Agilulf at Monza; but it may have been made for the relic, and afterwards used as a processional or stationary cross.

The curious embossed silver cross in the cathedral at Ravenna may possibly be as early as the sixth century.[2] The limbs are formed of a series of circular medallions with busts of saints, while at the extremities are foliate designs recalling those upon the cross of Justin. The two large central medallions on either side, representing the Virgin between two cypresses, and the Resurrection, cannot claim so early a date.

The cross of Adaloald in the treasury of the cathedral at Monza is commonly accepted as the actual cross presented to the infant Lombard prince on his baptism in A.D. 603, and referred to in his letter to Queen Theodelinda as *crucem cum signo sanctae crucis Domini.*[3] It is a gold cross with a pearled border,

---

[1] S. Borgia, *De cruce Vaticana*, Rome, 1779 ; Barbier de Montault in Didron's *Annales arch.*, xxvi, 1866, 23, 272 ; Bayet, *Recherches pour servir*, &c., 122 ; Bock, *Kleinodien des heiligen Römischen Reichs* ; Diehl, *Justinien*, 425 ; Ch. de Linas, *Origines de l'orfèvrerie cloisonnée*, i. 303 ff. ; E. Molinier, *Hist. des arts appliqués à l'industrie : L'Orfèvrerie*, 37–8 and Fig. on p. 39 ; A. de Waal, *Die antiken Reliquiare der Peterskirche in R. Q.*, 1893, p. 246 and Pl. XVI, XVII. The cross is kept in the Volto Santo, and is not shown.

[2] Bayet, *L'Art byzantin*, 98 ; Molinier, *L'Orfèvrerie*, 40 ; Garrucci, *Storia*, vi, Pl. 431.

[3] Frisi, *Memorie delle chiese Monzese*, dissertation No. 2 ; Bock, *Kleinodien*, Appendix, p. 35 ;

about four inches long, the face covered by a cruciform plaque of crystal with bevelled edges. Under this is visible the Crucifixion engraved and nielloed. Christ wears the colobium and rests his feet upon a suppedaneum. On the upper limb of the cross is a label with IC XC, and below the arms, IΔЄ O YC CY | IΔY HMP CY. At the extremities of the transverse limb are diminutive figures of the Virgin and St. John in niello, and at the top representations of the sun and moon. On the back is a foliate design boldly engraved. A ring at the top serves for suspension.

Of equally early date may well be another and far more sumptuous cross in the possession of the Countess Dzyalinska.[1] It is a gold encolpium ornamented

Fig. 336. Front of the jewelled gold cross of Justin II in St. Peter's at Rome.
(After Bock.)

with niello, having on the front in niello Christ on the Cross, wearing the colobium as in the Monza example. Above are the sun and moon, and on the titulus at the top of the cross the words +PEΞ PEΓNANTI (*rex regnantium*), a formula occurring on the coins of Justin II. On the back is a bust of Christ in a circular medallion accompanied by two kneeling angels; above it is a half-figure of the Virgin, and below it two standing angels. Round the edges, in niello, is the *Epinekion* hymn of the old Liturgy of St. Basil, and in the interior a cross ornamented with *verroterie cloisonnée* in red and green, having on the back the Assumption in niello. This cross is evidently of very early date. De Linas assigned it to the seventh century, while Molinier argues in favour of the sixth. The inscription may have been used on crosses and other sacred objects before it was adopted on the coinage.

The so-called encolpium of Constantine the Great, in the sacristy of St. Peter's at Rome, is a gold triptych which in reality dates from about the

Molinier, *L'Orfèvrerie*, p. 40. Strzygowski suggests a Mesopotamian influence and a slightly later date (*B. Z.* xiv).

[1] W. Fröhner, *Collections du Château de Goluchow: L'Orfèvrerie*, No. 201, p. 76 and Pl. XVIII (Paris, 1897); C. de Linas, *Émaillerie, métallurgie toreutique, les expositions rétrospectives*, 1880, 179 ff.; Molinier, as above, 41.

eleventh century.[1] The central part, which has along both top and bottom a row of large pearls and rubies, has in the middle the relic of the Cross covered with crystal. In the exterior angles of the cross are four large pearls, and at the extremities of the arms four circular enamelled medallions with white inscriptions on blue grounds : the spaces between these medallions are enriched with ornamental enamels, giving the whole enamelled portion of the triptych somewhat of a lozenge form. In the four corners of the gold plate forming the ground were formerly four applied embossed figures, of which only one, Constantine the Great, remains in the lower left-hand corner. He stands adoring the Cross, and opposite him was doubtless Helena, in the same attitude.

Fig. 337.   Back of the gold cross of Justin II in St. Peter's at Rome. (After Bock.)

The upper corners were perhaps filled with figures or busts of archangels in similar relief, as in the case of the reliquary formerly in the Sainte-Chapelle, which Saint Louis bought from the Emperor Baldwin (see below, p. 560). The inscription upon the four enamelled medallions forms two iambic verses, one defective :

"Ὅρα τι καινὸν θαῦμα καὶ ξένην χάριν
χρυσὸν μὲν ἔξω Χριστὸν ἐν δὲ σκόπει.

The relic seems to have been worn separately, as the receptacle containing it has a ring for suspension ; it may be earlier than the triptych. The back of the central part is embossed with a cross rising from two large acanthus-leaves in the style of the eleventh and twelfth centuries, on an imbricated ground. About the cross are two small medallions embossed with I͞C X͞C and three with ornamental rosettes. On the inner side of the leaves are eight figures in relief, all but one with perfect inscriptions. On one side Christ,

[1] Bock, *Kleinodien*, &c., Pl. XX, Fig. 28, 115 ff. ; A de Waal, *R. Q.*, 1893, p. 250 and Pl. XVIII ; E. Molinier, *L'Orfèvrerie*, 58 (no Fig.) ; G. Schlumberger, *Nicéphore Phocas*, Figs. on pp. 95 and 97.

Demetrius, Barnabas, and Matthew; on the other the Virgin, Panteleemon, Timothy, and Timon: a row of pearls runs across the middle of each leaf.

The treasury of St. Giovanni in Laterano contains a cross-reliquary which has lost its enamels, but retains some cloisonné pastes like those of the Poitiers and Limburg reliquaries and the Venice book-cover; the back has an embossed cross recalling that in the Louvre (Fig. 343).[1] The same treasury has a silver cross of the thirteenth century.[2]

Book-covers and reliquaries of which the enamels are described in another chapter must here be noticed for their metal-work. In the Marcian Library at

FIG. 338.   Cover of a silver reliquary of the eleventh century at Halberstadt : St. Demetrius.
(Schlumberger : Hachette.)

Venice two of the book-covers have plain silver borders with cabochon gems and rows of pearls,[3] and one has the border of *orfèvrerie cloisonnée* already mentioned (p. 515). The two other covers in the same place are good examples of Byzantine embossed decoration ; they have numerous reliefs (scenes from the life of Christ and figures of saints) in the style of the eleventh and twelfth centuries. One has in the border compartments of interlaced scroll-work which occurs upon other pieces of Byzantine goldsmith's work, for instance on the border of the picture of the Virgin in the Cathedral of Liége and the reliquary at Gran in Hungary (p. 525), where the excellence of the scrolls contrasts with

[1] G. de Nicola in *Bollettino d'arte*, iii, p. 19 (1909).
[2] Muñoz, *Monumenti d'arte*, &c., Part II.
[3] Pasini, *Il Tesoro di San Marco*, Pl. IX and X.

the feeble execution of the human figures.[1]   Of the book-covers in the Treasury
of S. Marco the example with the enamelled bust of St. Michael[2] (p. 513) is
specially interesting as being covered with gems, while the border has fine
embossed scrolls : these, unlike those on the border of the other cover with the
complete figure of the archangel, are Byzantine (Fig. 339).   The cover with
the applied Crucifixion upon a ground of lapis lazuli[3] has a border of pearls
round the lapis disk, and round this again an exceedingly fine filigree in which
are set cabochons and diminutive enamelled medallions.   This filigree, in contra-
distinction to the outer border, which is Italian, may well be of Byzantine
workmanship.   Such filigree is also to be seen upon the famous tenth-century
reliquary at Limburg (see p. 522).   The reliquary in the treasure[4] has a plain
border with cabochons like the two book-covers of the library mentioned above,
but on the back is a repoussé cross rising from two acanthus-leaves, with the
inscription IC . XC . NI | K A and an embossed scroll border.

The Byzantine chalices in the Treasury of S. Marco (Figs. 49–52, 298, 307, 340),
thirty-two in number, are in great part agate, sardonyx, or glass in silver-gilt
mounts.[5]   These mounts are not all Byzantine, for after the disastrous fire of the
thirteenth century much of the metal-work had to be replaced by Venetian
goldsmiths, who were doubtless to a great extent influenced by Byzantine models.
To these Western craftsmen are probably due the mounts with filigree scrolls of
a fine bold character, distinct from the other examples of filigree in the treasure
to which a Byzantine origin may be assigned.[6]   Most of the Byzantine mounts
are of plain metal enriched with enamelled medallions, pearls, and cabochon
gems : there are no mouldings or crestings such as would be found upon Western
mediaeval work of the Gothic period.   The chalices are in many cases inscribed
with the words Λάβετε πίετε ; on two of them occurs the name of a Romanus,
who may be Romanus IV,[7] on another that of Sisinnius, a grand logothete.[8]
One has the cup entirely enamelled.   Some of these chalices are of extraordinary
size and larger than any Western examples.   They are of two general types,
the first with a low foot from which a large scrolled handle rises to the rim
on each side (cf. Fig. 51), the second without handles and rising on a higher
foot with short stem and knop.   With them we may note a chalice with its
paten which has been transformed into a reliquary.   It has an agate bowl
without handles, and the rim and foot are connected by silver straps.   Three
small lions upon the rim support the paten, round the border of which is
engraved a pious inscription.   On the foot is another inscription with the name
of Basil the bastard, a partisan of Nicephorus Phocas.[9]

The patens in S. Marco are also very remarkable though less numerous than
the chalices.   They are composed of glass or stone with metal mounts bearing
the consecration formula (Λάβετε φάγετε, &c.).   The most splendid is of fine
alabaster[10] (Fig. 53), enriched with gems and having in the centre a circular
enamelled medallion with a bust of Christ.   It may be of the eleventh century.
In connexion with these examples in S. Marco may be mentioned the paten

[1] Pasini, Il Tesoro di San Marco, Pl. XII and XIII ; Molinier, Trésor de Saint-Marc, No. 10,
L'Orfèvrerie, 63 ; C. de Linas, L'Art et l'industrie d'autrefois dans les régions de la Meuse belge, 81.
[2] Pasini, Pl. IV, p. 73.
[3] Ibid., Pl. VII.   Such application of figures embossed in metal to a stone ground is
very unusual.
[4] Ibid., Pl. XXIII, p. 23.
[5] Pasini, Il Tesoro di San Marco ; E. Molinier, Le Trésor de Saint-Marc, and Gazette des Beaux-
Arts, xxxvii, 1888, 459 ff. ; G. Schlumberger, Nicéphore Phocas, Figs. on p. 21 (agate with name
of Sisinnius) and 253 (sardonyx chalice with name of Romanus) ; the same, L'Épopée, i,
Figs. on pp. 700, 701, 709, 713, 720, 721 ; Rohault de Fleury, La Messe, iv, Pl. CCC–CCCVIII
and Pl. CCCXXV.
[6] Molinier, Gazette, as above, 395, 462, and L'Orfèvrerie, 60 ; Pasini, Pl. XLI.
[7] G. Schlumberger, L'Épopée, i. 705.
[8] Pasini, Pl. XLII ; Molinier, Trésor, No. 72.
[9] Schlumberger, Nicéphore Phocas, 291 (Fig.).
[10] Pasini, Il Tesoro, Pl. XLVIII ; Molinier, Le Trésor de Saint-Marc, No. 94, L'Orfèvrerie, 61 ;
Schlumberger, L'Épopée, i, Figs. on pp. 705 and 777.

FIG. 339.   Back of a book-cover in the Treasury of S. Marco, Venice, with embossed silver
ornament of the eleventh or twelfth century.   P. 552.

(Fig. 318) preserved in the treasury of the Cathedral of Halberstadt.[1] This is not enriched with gems, or partly composed of stone, but of simple silver with embossed ornament in a good style dating from the twelfth or possibly from the eleventh century. In the centre it has a Crucifixion in relief, within a medallion with eight lobes, on each of which is a bust of a saint in relief. Round it runs the formula of consecration. The use of lobes in patens is thus seen to have been adopted in the East at an early date.

The Treasury of S. Marco at Venice also contains an interesting silver reliquary (Fig. 341) in the form of a conventional Byzantine church of the twelfth century, now containing a crystal phial of oriental workmanship with Cufic inscriptions with a relic of the Sacred Blood.[2] This reliquary, like another of similar character and date though less ornate design in the treasury of Aachen Cathedral,[3] was originally an *artophorion* or ciborium for the reserved Eucharistic bread. The Venice example is partially in openwork and the sides are ornamented with repoussé figures of Fortitude and Prudence ; a row of animals in an orientalizing style runs round the base.

S. Marco further possesses a coffer-shaped reliquary of silver with embossed ornament of the eleventh century. On the top is Christ seated, giving crowns to the four martyrs of Trebizond, who stand under an arcade ; on the sides is a nielloed inscription in praise of the martyrs.[4] An embossed book-cover with Crucifixion and *Anastasis* in the Marcian Library may also be mentioned.[5] In the Church of Alba Fucense, north of Lake Fucino, in Italy, is a reliquary for wood of the Cross[6] with sliding lid, having on the top the Crucifixion between the Virgin and St. John, with two busts and angels above, and below, an inscription relating to two donors, John and Maria ; the border is of scrolls with cabochon stones at intervals. Inside are engraved St. Michael and the Transfiguration.

A remarkable example of the silversmith's art, probably of the period between the ninth and eleventh centuries, though not made for a religious purpose, may be mentioned here. It is the small cylindrical silver box, originally made for the pigment of a scribe named Leo, but now used for the chrism in the Cathedral of Padua, where it has probably been from the fifteenth century.[7] It is ornamented with embossed figures, on the hinged lid a Medusa head, round the sides four mythological figures separated by pairs of interlaced serpents— Apollo, a reclining figure, perhaps a listener to his song, Ares, and Eros presenting him with a helmet. Round the top of the box and upon the bottom are inscriptions in two debased iambics :

+ΒΑΦΗС ΔΟΧΕΙΟΝ Ω ΛΕΟΝΤΙ ΠΑС ΠΟΡΟС
+ΛΕΩΝ ΤΟ ΤΕΡΠΝΟΝ ΘΑΥΜΑ ΤΟΝ ΚΑΛΛΙΓΡΑΦΩΝ

Details in the epigraphy of these inscriptions, such as the omega closed at

---

[1] Molinier, *L'Orfèvrerie*, 61 (no Fig.) ; Lessing, *Gold und Silber* (Handbook of the Berlin Kunstgewerbe-Museum), p. 30.

[2] Pasini, *Il Tesoro*, Pl. XXIV ; Molinier, *Trésor*, No. 17, and *L'Orfèvrerie*, 63 (Fig. on p. 61) ; Schlumberger, *L'Épopée*, ii. 485 (Fig.).

[3] S. Beissel, *Kunstschätze des Aachener Kaiserdomes*, Pl. XI (1904), and *Aachenfahrt* (1902) ; Molinier, *L'Orfèvrerie*, 62 ; Schlumberger, *Monuments Piot*, xii, 1905, 201 ff. and Pl. XIV, and *L'Épopée*, i. 461. This reliquary is ornamented on its plain surfaces with nielloed scroll-work and inscriptions, the latter referring to an Eustathius, proconsul and patrician, general of the army of Antioch at some time between A. D. 915 and A. D. 1057. Molinier suggested that the architectural peculiarities of certain Rhenish enamelled reliquaries (in the Victoria and Albert Museum and in the museum at Darmstadt) may be due to imitation of such *artophoria* as those here discussed.

[4] Pasini, *Il Tesoro*, Pl. LXIV ; Molinier, *Trésor*, No. 145 ; Schlumberger, *L'Épopée*, i, pp. 456 and 669 ; ii, p. 669 (Figs.) ; Molinier, *L'Orfèvrerie*, p. 61. The four martyrs are Eugenius, Valerian, Candidus, and Aquila.

[5] Schlumberger, *Épopée*, i, p. 745.

[6] E. Bertaux, *L'Art dans l'Italie méridionale*, pp. 177–8 and Pl. VI.

[7] *L'Arte*, ix, Rome, 1906, 35 ff. and Plate ; article by Toesca. The box is stated to have been presented to the cathedral by Bishop Pietro Donati (A. D. 1428–45), previously Archbishop of Crete. See also *B. Z.*, xv. 701.

FIG. 340.   Chalice of the eleventh century enriched with enamels and pearls :
Treasury of S. Marco, Venice.   P. 552.

the top as seen on the bronze doors of Sta Sophia and on the Limburg reliquary (pp. 522, 618), suggest the tenth century as a possible date.   The figures are of great interest because of their evident relation to those upon the group of ivory caskets mentioned on pp. 215–21, a large number of which derive their subjects in a similar way from classical mythology.   We find the same influences in the casket in the Cathedral of Anagni (p. 557).

FIG. 341.   Silver reliquary in the form of a church of the twelfth century in the Treasury of S. Marco, Venice. (Schlumberger: Hachette.)   P. 554.

The rectangular silver casket in the *arca* of Leo III under the altar of the Chapel of the Sancta Sanctorum at the Lateran is probably a work of about the twelfth century.[1]   It has on each of the two sides two standing figures in relief: on the front St. John Chrysostom and St. Nicholas ; on the back, St. Gregory the Theologian and St. Basil: these all stand, as on contemporary mosaics and ivory carvings, with the letters of their names in vertical lines beside them. The ends are decorated with engraved or punched ornament consisting in each case of a large central medallion containing a cross patée with looped corners to

[1] P. Lauer, *Monuments Fiot*, 1906, 69 and Pl. X and XI, Figs. 6 and 7 ; H. Grisar, *Die romische Kapelle Sancta Sanctorum*, p. 106, and Pl. IV and V, Freiburg, 1908   These objects are now in the Library of the Vatican.

each arm, and circular medallions containing rosettes at each extremity. In the angles of the cross are four ivy-like leaves, and in the spandrels beyond the medallion four disconnected foliate designs. The cover is ornamented with applied enamels described elsewhere (p. 510).

An oval box of copper or bronze in the same place (Fig. 348) has incised ornament apparently filled with niello (?).[1] On the top is the Crucifixion, Christ being represented in the colobium ; on either side stand the Virgin and St. John,

FIG. 342.   Enamelied silver box of the eleventh century from the Sancta Sanctorum at the Lateran, now in the Vatican Library.   (After Lauer, *Mon. Piot*, 1906, Pl. X.)

while below the arms is the usual inscription (ἴδε ὁ υἱὸς σοῦ, &c.) and above the sun and moon. On the sides are the busts of the four Evangelists with their names, and the lid and box have borders of guilloche. From the style of the figures and inscription the date should be about the twelfth century.

Of the same date or perhaps a little later is a smaller oval silver relic-box in the same place,[2] ornamented with engraved design. On the top in three medallions are busts of Christ, St. Peter, and St. John the Baptist ; on the sides the four Evangelists in similar medallions. The remaining surface of the box is covered with vine-scrolls reserved on a nielloed ground.

A casket in the Cathedral of Anagni,[3] formerly entirely covered with silver plates bearing mythological subjects, is important as showing that the silversmith and the ivory carver were inspired by the same models. The casket is rectangular, with cover in the form of a truncated pyramid, and of the rectangular and trapezoidal panels with figure subjects which ornamented its surfaces only

[1] Lauer, as above, 77 and Pl. XII, Fig. 2 ; Grisar, as above, p. 111.
[2] Lauer, 75 and Pl. XII, Fig. 1 ; Grisar, *Civiltà Catholica*, 52 and Fig. 26.
[3] H. Graeven, *Ein Reliquienkästchen aus Pirano*, Austrian *Jahrbuch* ; P. Toesca, *L'Arte*, Rome, 1906, ix, Figs. 3–5, pp. 36 ff.

six remain.   Even the bands of rich foliate ornament which serve as borders
have suffered severely from rough usage : their motives are derived from the
vine and palmette, and are of a bold rich character which suggests a Western
influence of the early thirteenth century.   Ornament of a similar kind is found
on the border of a silver book-cover in the Monastery of Zara,[1] which bears an embossed figure of St. Gregory with a Latin inscription of the thirteenth century ;
also upon a book of the Gospels at St. Aure.[2]   It would seem that stamps for
the production of foliated ornament were distributed from a common centre,
which may have been the north-east of Italy or Dalmatia, regions naturally
penetrated by influences both from East and West.

The figure subjects, which also appear to have been produced by stamps,
represent Hercules with club and lion's skin, and a dancing figure holding a
veil, a group perhaps representing the infancy of Bacchus, a sleeping Silenus,
a putto driving a pair of dolphins, a figure approaching a statue on a high base,
and a youth carrying an offering in veiled hands ; of these subjects, the first two
are of a type frequently occurring on the ivory caskets.   The figures vary considerably in merit, some of the stamps used being apparently much worn.   They
move in a less classical atmosphere than those of the better ivory caskets, and
this later character, with the nature of the ornamental motives, justifies an
attribution to the thirteenth century, though some of the stamps may have been
older than that date, for instance the Hercules.

In Germany and France there are many other examples of Byzantine
ecclesiastical goldsmith's work, mostly derived from the spoils of A. D. 1204.

In the treasury of the Cathedral of Halberstadt is the top of a silver-gilt
reliquary in the form of the tomb of St. Demetrius, with an embossed figure of
the saint as *orans* : in the interior is a repoussé bust of the saint.[3]   The wooden
cross plated with gold and with caps of filigree set with rubies on three
extremities, formerly in the treasure of S. Maria ad Gradus, is now in the
archbishop's palace at Cologne.   Aus'm Weerth considers that, on account of the
abbreviation of the emperor's name in a metrical embossed inscription on the
back, this cross may have been actually the work of Constantine Porphyrogenitus.[4]   In the Church of Jaucourt in the Department of the Aube near Troyes
there is a reliquary for wood of the True Cross with figures of archangels and of
Constantine and Helena.[5]   It is assigned to the twelfth century and now stands
on a French base of the century following.   At Reichenau there is another
reliquary for the wood of the Cross of about the same period.[6]   M. Schlumberger
has described a reliquary bearing the name of Maria Comnena, daughter of
Alexius Comnenus,[7] and also the so-called cross of the family of Zaccaria at
Genoa,[8] with an inscription showing it to have been dedicated by one Bardas,
and renovated in the thirteenth century by Bishop Isaac of Ephesus.   The
reliquary at Brescia,[9] which is rectangular and embossed, has on one side the
Crucifixion, on the other Constantine and Helena on either side of the Cross, with
angels above.

Other references will be found in Molinier's list of Byzantine reliquaries
for wood of the True Cross in the *Gazette archéologique*.[10]   Many examples of
Byzantine work, formerly in the Sainte-Chapelle at Paris, were destroyed at the
time of the Revolution.   The reliquary for wood of the Cross bought by
St. Louis from Baldwin of Constantinople for the *châsse* of the Sainte-Chapelle,

---

[1] *L'Arte*, as above, Fig. 6, p. 39.   [2] *Les Arts*, Paris, 1903, 22.
[3] Schlumberger, *L'Épopée*, ii. 505.
[4] E. Aus'm Weerth, *Das Siegeskreuz der Kaiser Constantinus und Romanus*, 12, 13 (Fig.) ;
Schlumberger, *Nicéphore Phocas*, 421.
[5] Didron, *Annales arch.*, xix, 1859, 46 ; *Gazette des Beaux-Arts*, 3e Période, ii, 1889, 157 ;
Gaussen, *Portefeuille arch. de la Champagne* ; A. Darcel, *Cat. de l'exp. rétrospective*, &c., 1889, No. 283 ;
Schlumberger, *L'Épopée*, i. 501.
[6] *Rev. arch.*, xxxvi, 1900, 176 ff. and Pl. IV.
[7] *Compte rendu de l'Académie des Inscr. et Belles-Lettres*, 1902, 67-71.
[8] *Mon. Piot*, 1895, 131 ff. ; *Mélanges d'arch. byz.*, 275.
[9] Venturi, *Storia*, 66 (Fig.).   [10] *Gazette arch.*, 1887, 245-9.

FIG. 343. Embossed silver-gilt panel of the eleventh century in the Louvre.
(Schlumberger : Hachette.) P. 560.

which has thus disappeared, had on it figures of Constantine and Helena and four archangels, all embossed.[1]   A large silver-gilt panel, which may have been intended for a book of the Gospels, is now in the Galerie d'Apollon in the Louvre, and was formerly at St. Denis.   It is an example of Byzantine embossed work, representing the Holy Women at the Tomb, with a long repoussé inscription from one of the Fathers round the borders.[2]   Though the general effect is good, the style of the figures hardly rises above mediocrity.   The work is perhaps not

Fig. 344.   The Virgin and Child : silver-gilt plaque of the eleventh century.
(Victoria and Albert Museum.)

earlier than the twelfth century,[3] though Labarte and Darcel assigned it to the tenth.   A smaller repoussé panel, also from St. Denis and in the Louvre, has a jewelled cross in repoussé, rising from two acanthus leaves on a background of stars (Fig. 343).   Darcel assigned it to the eleventh century, and it may have been part of the spoil of A. D. 1204.   An embossed medallion with a half figure of a saint was found near Rosières, Jura, in 1891, with a fragment of the skull of St. Akindynos.[4]

The Victoria and Albert Museum, South Kensington, possesses a gilt plaque with the Virgin standing with the Child (Fig. 344), and a triptych with the

[1] Engraved by Morand, *Histoire de la Sainte-Chapelle*, &c., Paris, 1790, 44.   Reproduced by G. Schlumberger, *Nicéphore Phocas*, 171.   Another reliquary, which was lost and destroyed at the Revolution, was that formerly in Notre-Dame at Maestricht.   Ibid., 477.

[2] Labarte, *Histoire*, 1st ed. ; Album, Pl. XXVI ; Schlumberger, *Nicéphore Phocas*, 273 ; Venturi, *Storia*. ii. 657 ; Molinier, *L'Orfèvrerie*, 64.

[3] A. Darcel, *Notice des émaux et de l'orfèvrerie*, No. 710 ; Molinier, *L'Orfèvrerie*, 63.

[4] G. Schlumberger, *Bull. monumental*, 1891, p. 111.

Virgin enthroned between St. Gregory and St. John (Fig. 345). The former, which is stated to have come from Torcello, is a work of considerable merit. A flat reliquary in the collection of M. Martin Le Roy at Paris[1] contains a Byzantine relief in silver gilt upon a small panel, in a frame ornamented with European enamels. The panel has a cruciform cavity for a relic of the True Cross, flanked above by the Archangels Michael and Gabriel, below by the Virgin and St. John; in the field are engraved the inscription H CTA(V)PWCIC and ΕΙΔΕ Ο YOC COY and ΙΔΥ Η MHP COY. The work is good, and appears to be of the eleventh century; the frame is of Italian imitation of Byzantine repoussé. Four silver-gilt plaques with embossed subjects in the same collection (the Annunciation, Virgin and Child, Our Lord among the Doctors, and Pente-

FIG. 345. The Virgin and Child, St. Gregory and St. John : metal triptych of the twelfth century. (Victoria and Albert Museum.)

cost) are evidently based upon Byzantine originals, but probably made in Italy in the twelfth century.[2] They were obtained in Naples.

The following objects in various countries may be noticed: the Monastery of Martwili in Mingrelia has a silver diptych, on the outside of which are two angels in a good style, attributed by Kondakoff to the ninth century.[3] In the same place is a silver-gilt cross, perhaps two centuries later. Several embossed silver frames of ikons in the Church of St. Clement at Ochrida (see p. 318) appear to date from the fourteenth century and even earlier.[4] The grounds are covered with diapers of foliate design or with small panels of interlaced scrolls, and round the frames are in some cases medallions or rectangular plaques with figures of sacred persons, saints, and prophets, or Gospel scenes. Some of these figures are well executed, and present types familiar to us in the art of the period between the eleventh and fourteenth centuries : in one example Kondakoff

[1] *La Collection Martin Le Roy*, vol. i, by J. J. Marquet de Vasselot, No. 12, Pl. X.
[2] Ibid., Nos. 2-5, Pl. II and III.
[3] Kondakoff, *Description of Antiquities in some Churches and Monasteries of Georgia*, St. Petersburg, 1890, 71.   [4] N. P. Kondakoff, *Macedonia*, pp. 250 ff. and Pl. V-XII.

traces the influence of a local Servian style. A Gospel cover in the treasury of the same church has an embossed Crucifixion between the Virgin and St. John. Two flying angels bear small figures in human form, one of which holds a chalice to Our Lord's side ; these figures perhaps represent the Old and New Dispensations. Round the border are pierced panels with interlaced designs.[1] This work is probably late. To these objects we may add the frames of the portable enamels on Mount Athos (p. 433), and two triptych-reliquaries and a book-cover in the monastery of Lavra,[2] and the book-cover with standing figure of St. George and border of floral scrolls enclosing busts at Djumati in Georgia.[3] The number of objects with embossed figures and ornament of this kind still unpublished must be considerable.

FIG. 346. Chalice of Manuel Palaeologus : Monastery of Vatopedi, Mount Athos.
(*Hautes Études* : G. Millet.)

The chalice or cup of Manuel Palaeologus, 1391–1425, in the treasury of the Monastery of Vatopedi (Fig. 346) is an interesting example of the latest period of Byzantine silversmith's work, when the influence of Western art had made itself felt in Constantinople.[4] The cup resembles a chalice with two handles ; its bowl is of jasper, the stem, foot, and handles are of silver-gilt. The foot is octagonal, its surfaces being ornamented with embossed designs, medallions with busts of saints alternating with others bearing the monogram of the emperor, all upon a ground of foliage. The saints are Byzantine in style, and so is much of the ornament upon the knop and elsewhere ; but a Gothic cresting crowns the stem, and the handles are in the form of dragons. If this cup be compared with purely Byzantine work such as some of the chalices in St. Mark's at Venice, the incongruities of its style become apparent.

[1] Kondakoff, *Macedonia*, p. 273 and Pl. XIII.
[2] Schlumberger, *Épopée, iii*, pp. 420, 748, and Pl. III.
[3] Kondakoff, *Georgia*, 107. This is assigned to the eleventh or twelfth century.
[4] Kondakoff, *Monuments of Christian Art upon Mount Athos*, 220 ff. and Pl. XXXVII (Russian).

SILVER PLATE.

This is almost all of the First Period.

The treasure found on the Esquiline Hill at Rome in A. D. 1793, in the British Museum since 1866,[1] contains objects which suggest an origin in the Christian East. The *deductio* of the bride on the large marriage-casket has an oriental appearance, and the figures show an analogy with types of late Hellenistic art. Moreover, an engraved ivory casket of the same form exists in a fragmentary condition in the Cairo Museum,[2] and silver work of this kind was doubtless produced in Alexandria. Other objects of the treasure seem to betray a more definite Eastern influence. The ewer (Cat. No. 307) is of Eastern type ; the vase (No. 306) with animals in the convolutions of spiral scrolls suggests by its ornament the well-known Syrian motive ; and among the silver statuettes (Nos. 332-5) representing the *Tychae* of the four cities, Rome, Constantinople, Antioch, and Alexandria, that of Antioch copies a statue of Eutychides.[3] The treasure, the constituents of which need not be all by the same hand, was

FIG. 347. Silver box of the sixth century from the Sancta Sanctorum of the Lateran ; now in the Vatican Library. (After Lauer, *Mon. Piot*, 1906, Pl. XII.)   P. 564.

probably concealed at some time of danger, perhaps on the occurrence of a barbaric invasion.

Silver boxes, oval and rectangular, with embossed figure subjects, were early used to contain relics. The most ancient, and artistically the finest, is that found in 1894 in a stone urn beneath the pavement near the altar in the Church of S. Nazaro at Milan.[4] On the lid Our Lord is enthroned between the Apostles, with water-jars and baskets with bread before him in allusion to his miracles. On the sides are the Virgin enthroned with the Child, and shepherds who bring offerings ; the Judgement of Solomon ; the Three Children of Babylon in the furnace ; and Daniel judging the Elders. There is a freedom and a sense of style about these groups which point to a period in which classical art was something more than a memory ; and it is probable that the casket was actually used to contain relics at the consecration of the church in the year 382. Graeven saw in it evidence of late Hellenistic workmanship, though Italian archaeologists have claimed it for Rome. The composition of the lid, as Riegl has remarked, recalls the scene of the *Congiarium* on the Arch of Constantine, to which, however, it is superior in its livelier interpretation of a centralized action. The pose of the heads, the expressive features, the telling if summary treatment of the extremities, render this relief a most remarkable example of sculpture in metal in the period of transition between antique and later art.

The best known of these silver relic-boxes is the oval example in the Museo Cristiano of the Vatican, found at Henchir Zirara in Numidia, between Tebessa

[1] *Catalogue of Early Christian and Byzantine Antiquities,* 1905, 61 ff.

[2] Strzygowski, *Koptische Kunst,* No. 7063.

[3] Gardner, *Journal of Hellenic Studies,* ix, 1888, 78.

[4] H. Graeven, *Zeitschrift für christliche Kunst,* 1899 ; A. Venturi, *Storia,* i. 549 and Figs. 445-9 ; A. Riegl, *Die spätrömische Kunstindustrie,* &c., 106.

and Constantine, and presented by Cardinal Lavigerie to Pope Leo XIII.[1] It has on the top a beardless figure in tunic and pallium, holding a wreath with both hands, standing on the mount from which flow the four streams, while on either side is a lighted candle in a tall candelabrum, indicating Paradise: above the head appears a hand holding a wreath. Round the sides of the box are a row of sheep, and a stag and hind drinking at streams issuing from a mount, above which is the sacred monogram. De Rossi was inclined to attribute this reliquary to the fifth century, and in any case it cannot be later

FIG. 348. Bronze box of the twelfth century from the Sancta Sanctorum of the Lateran; now in the Vatican Library. (After Lauer, *Mon. Piot*, 1906, Pl. XII).

than the sixth. Muñoz traces a Syrian influence in the type of the principal figure.

A box of the same form but of ruder workmanship, now in the Louvre, was found in Brianza (Castello di Brivio).[2] It has on the top the Raising of Lazarus, on the sides the Adoration of the Magi and the Three Children of Babylon in the fiery furnace. It is probably also of the fifth century.

At the opening of the relic-chest of Leo III under the altar of the Chapel of the Sancta Sanctorum at the Lateran in 1906, another box of this style (Fig. 347) was discovered.[3] This is stated to have stamped on the bottom a trefoil and a quatrefoil, with the letters HAS in a rectangular border, as well as a St. Andrew's cross between the letters A and Ω. It almost looks as if these were very early 'hall-marks' (see below, p. 568). Another silver box of early

---

[1] De Rossi, *La Capsella argentea africana*, &c., Rome, 1888; Venturi, as above, 552; A. Muñoz, *L'Art byzantin à l'Exposition de Grottaferrata*, 152-3, Rome, 1906.

[2] Venturi, as above, 550 and Figs. 450-2; Muñoz, as above, 153. Other early silver boxes are two found in 1871 under the high altar at Grado, and now in the cathedral treasury; one, which is cylindrical, has in relief the Virgin enthroned with $\overline{\text{MP}}$ $\overline{\Theta Y}$ and names of saints; the other is elliptical, embossed on lid with two lambs on the Mount of Paradise with a gemmed cross between them, and on the sides with medallions with male and female heads of saints with Latin names. Two early silver reliquaries found in 1862 in a stone chest at Pola are now preserved at Vienna. One is hexagonal, with embossed figures, on the sides Our Lord between Peter and Paul with three others; the other is rectangular, with a blue enamelled cross on the lid. The first is claimed for the second century, but is not likely to be earlier than the fifth, while the second must be later.

[3] Ph. Lauer, *Le Trésor du Sancta Sanctorum*, *Mon. Piot*, 1906, pp. 67-8 and Pl. XII, Fig. 3; H. Grisar, *Civiltà Cattolica*, 1906, Pt. iii, Figs. 24-5.

type in the Hermitage Museum at St. Petersburg has upon it busts of Our Lord and Apostles in medallions.   It was found near Sebastopol.[1]

A large silver vase in the Salle des Bijoux in the Louvre, but found near Emesa in Syria,[2] has points of analogy with these early relic-boxes as well as with the Kyrenia censer (p. 573).   Like the latter it has a series of busts in medallions forming a horizontal band, the persons being Our Lord, the Virgin,

FIG. 349.   Silver cover of the fifth century, from Luxor : Cairo Museum.   (Service des Antiquités de l'Égypte : Catalogue, *Koptische Kunst*.)   P. 567.

SS. Peter, Paul, John the Evangelist, and James (?) with the addition of two angels.   The containing band of cable ornament recalls that which runs round the lids and bodies of the reliquaries ; and, as the example on the box from Carthage seems to indicate, was in some cases at least derived from the palm-leaf.   The figures are without the nimbus, and the vase may be as early as the fifth century.   Apart from the single band containing the medallions it is almost devoid of ornament.

A silver treasure, found at Luxor apparently in 1889, once belonged to a church, perhaps to the small basilica discovered in the temples.   It dates from the fifth to the sixth century, and recalls the Church treasures to which allusion

---

[1] *Compte rendu* of the Imperial Archaeological Commission, 1897, 28 and 103, Figs. 87, 88, 213, 214.

[2] H. de Villefosse in *Bulletin des Antiquaires de France*, 1892, 239.

Fig. 350.   Chalice and paten (?) of the sixth century from Lampsacus.
(British Museum.)   P. 567.

is made in the *Liber Pontificalis*: it is now in the Cairo Museum.[1] It consists of a processional cross with a dedicatory inscription, three rectangular covers of book-holders or boxes, ornamented with the sacred monogram in its later forms and a cross (Fig. 349), two censers in the shape of cups on high feet, and part of a third, a silver vase, and one or two fragments. The two book-covers bear inscriptions referring to two bishops named Abraham and Besammon, with the names of silversmiths Gregory and Isidore: all the inscriptions are in Greek.

Next in date to the Luxor treasure perhaps comes the treasure in the British Museum found at Lampsacus on the Hellespont, and probably dating from the sixth century.[2] It consists of a silver lamp-stand of the type resembling

FIG. 351. Silver censer of the sixth century from Cyprus. (British Museum.) P. 573.

that of pricket-candlesticks, a large cup on a low foot, possibly a chalice, two very shallow parcel-gilt silver bowls with monograms in niello (Fig. 350), an openwork lamp-disk or *polycandelon* (Fig. 72), and thirteen spoons with designs and inscriptions in niello (Fig. 56). The inscriptions, which are in Latin and Greek, are secular, being derived from Virgil's Eclogues and from Greek Epigrams on the Seven Sages: they may have been given to a church or monastery, gifts of secular plate and spoons being not uncommon. The lamp-stand and the bowls bear the Byzantine hall-marks mentioned below (p. 568).

A considerable amount of silver plate has been found in Russia and in the island of Cyprus.[3] In the former country the most frequent discoveries have

---

[1] J. Strzygowski, *Koptische Kunst*, Nos. 7201-10, pp. 340 ff., where the objects are fully discussed and photographically reproduced.

[2] *Catalogue of Early Christian Antiquities*, 81-6, Nos. 376 ff. and Pl. XXII and XXIII.

[3] Stephani, in *Compte rendu* of the Imperial Russian Archaeological Commission, St. Petersburg, 1867, 50-2 and 211, 1878, 69, 146, 151-8, and *The Feeding of the Serpents at the Orphic Mysteries*, in *Journal of the Imperial Academy of Sciences*, St. Petersburg, vol. xxv, third paper of the Appendix; Kondakoff, Tolstoy, and Reinach, *Antiquités de la Russie méridionale*, Paris, 1891, 411 ff.; Köhler, *Gesammelte Schriften*, vi. 41-4; de Linas, *Origines de l'orfèvrerie cloisonnée*, ii. 349 ff.; J. Arneth, *Die antiken Gold- und Silber-Monumente des k. k. Münz- und Antiken Cabinettes*, Vienna, 1850, Beilage; A. Odobesco, *Le Trésor de Pétrossa*; Aspelin, *Antiquités du Nord Finno-Ougrien*; Strzygowski and Pokrovsky, *Der Silberschild aus Kertch* in *Materials for Russian Archaeology* (a continuation of the *Compte rendu* mentioned above), 1892, 1 ff.; J. Smirnoff, in the same publication, 1899, 7 ff.; Héron de Villefosse, *Bulletin de la Société des Antiquaires de France*, 1892, 239; A. Venturi, *Storia dell' arte italiana*; British Museum, *Catalogue of Early Christian and Byzantine Antiquities*, 1900, Nos. 376-424; Dalton, in *Archaeologia*, vol. lvii, pp. 159 ff., and lx, pp. 1-24; and *B. Z.*, 1906, 615-17.

been made on the Stroganoff estates in the province of Perm, where Sassanian silver is also found.[1] The presence of such objects in these remote regions is probably to be explained by the fact that they were imported in exchange for furs, as it is well known that the chiefs and princes of barbaric tribes set great store by silver cups and dishes.[2] An historical instance of this predilection is connected with the great Attila, and is related by Priscus in his account of an embassy from the emperor to the Hunnish king, in which he himself took part. The embassy took presents of silver plate with it, and at the banquets at which the envoys were entertained it was observed that, though Attila himself drank from a wooden cup, his guests were supplied with silver vessels. The episode of the church plate of Sirmium, which Attila almost made a *casus belli* against the Western Empire, affords a further illustration of the importance attached by barbarians to silver plate.

Fɪɢ. 352. Silver censer of the sixth century from Cyprus. (British Museum.) P. 573.

This Byzantine silver chiefly consists of dishes or plates of various sizes, parcel-gilt and ornamented with conventional designs in niello and figures in relief. More rarely spoons are found, some of which have inscriptions in niello, others animals, &c., in relief in the bowls. The plates or dishes are massive, and betray their descent from Graeco-Roman silver plate of the imperial period, which is similarly ornamented, though in a more classical style.

Most pieces are marked on the under side with stamps or control-marks (Figs. 353–5, 361), five impressions being the rule, though the same stamp might be used more than once.[3] These stamps are circular, hexagonal, rectangular, or round at the top and square at the base, all much larger than our modern hall-marks. They contain names and monograms which

---

[1] For the Sassanian dishes see the Russian *Compte rendu*, 1878, 145 ff., and Atlas, Pl. VII ; 1883, Pl. X ; Kondakoff, Tolstoy, and Reinach (p. 567, note 3) ; A. Odobesco, *Le Trésor de Pétrossa* ; *The Treasure of the Oxus, British Museum*, 1905, 121.

[2] They were probably brought from the Black Sea up the Volga and Kama. See *Compte rendu de la Commission Impériale archéologique* for 1875 (St. Petersburg, 1878), 69. The Sassanian silver, to which allusion is made below, may have come by way of the Caspian.

[3] It was called ἄργυρον πεντασφράγιστον. See J. Smirnoff, *Zapiski* of the Imperial Russian Archaeological Society, Classical, Byzantine, and West European Section, xii, Pt. v, 506 ff. For these marks see Marc Rosenberg, *Der Goldschmiede Merkzeichen*, new edition, where all the known marks are quoted with abundant illustration.

appear to be those of the controlling officials, and nimbed busts which probably represent imperial persons. Unless the marks [1] upon the early silver reliquary from the *Sancta Sanctorum* (p. 564) should prove to be regular stamps, these Byzantine impressions are the oldest hall-marks known. The Byzantine officials did not confine themselves to the stamping of contemporary plate, but also marked silver of earlier periods. Roman silver at Vienna and St. Petersburg bears the typical Byzantine marks.[2]

Among the so-called votive shields or disks, of which eight are known [3] though one has disappeared, those of Valentinian (A. D. 364–75), found in 1721 in the Arve and now at Geneva, and Theodosius, found in Estremadura in

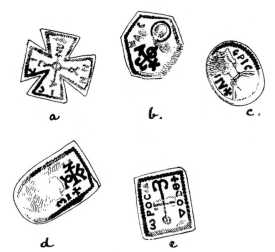

a b. c.
d e

FIG. 353. Stamps of the sixth century on the bottom of a silver dish found in Cyprus and now at Nicosia (Fig. 55).

1847 and now at Madrid (Fig. 356), deserve special mention. The former represents the emperor standing in the middle of six soldiers ; the latter, which is more definitely Eastern in character, shows Theodosius wearing the chlamys and diadem, seated between Valentinian II and the young Arcadius. The group is closed by *protectores* with swords and spears, while an allegorical figure of Spain occupies the space at the bottom of the picture.[4] The shield of Aspar at Florence, dating from the year A. D. 434, shows affinities with the diptychs of Probus and Felix, the style of more than one figure being analogous to that of those upon the ivories.[5] In some ways the most interesting of these shields is that of Justinian in the Hermitage at St. Petersburg, found in a catacomb at Kertch in the year 1891.[6] The emperor is represented on horseback accompanied by guards and a figure of Nike, as on his coins ; the whole design is incised, and not, as usual, in relief. The general scheme recalls that of the Barberini ivory diptych in the Louvre. The emperor wears a diadem without the pearl pendants (ἐνώτια κρεμαστήρια) which were regularly used from the time of Justin II, and a tunic with clavi.[7] The guards (*protectores*) in general

---

[1] Ph. Lauer, *Le Trésor du Sancta Sanctorum* in *Mon. Piot*, 1906, p. 67.

[2] J. Arneth, *Die antiken Gold- und Silber-Monumente*, &c., Pl. S, vii ; *Compte rendu de la Commission Impériale Archéologique* for 1867 (St. Petersburg, 1868), Pl. II, Figs. 1 and 4.

[3] List in Strzygowski and Pokrovsky, *Materials for Russian Archaeology* (*Imperial Arch. Commission*), 1892, 9.

[4] Both shields are figured by A. Odobesco, *Le Trésor de Pétrossa*, 154 and 158.

[5] A. Riegl, *Spätrömische Kunstindustrie*, 118.

[6] Strzygowski and Pokrovsky, *Materials for Russian Archaeology*, 1892, 1 ff. and Pl. V.

[7] Strzygowski, as above, 17–18.

Fig. 354. Stamps on the bottom of a silver dish of the sixth century from Cyprus in the
Collection of J. Pierpont Morgan, Esq.   (Photo communicated by Dr. Marc Rosenberg.)

Fig. 355. Stamps on the bottom of a silver dish from Cyprus (Fig. 360, top).

resemble those upon other monuments and in MSS. of various dates,[1] and, as
at S. Vitale, have the Constantinian monogram upon their shields. The disk
of Justinian is parcel-gilt, and parts of the emperor's head and tunic, as well as
portions of the horse-trappings, are filled with niello.

Among the silver dishes found in Russia are the examples mentioned by
Stephani in the Russian *Compte rendu* (see note 3, p. 567), the best of which

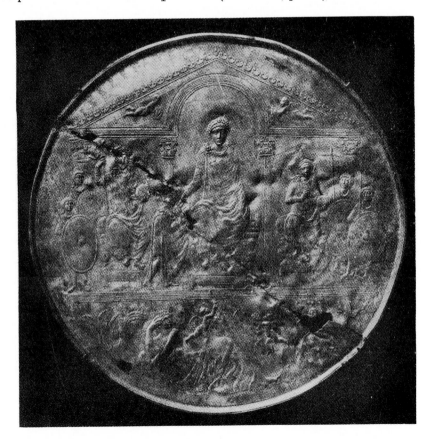

Fig. 356.   Votive disk of Theodosius at Madrid : the Emperor enthroned.
(From an electrotype in the Victoria and Albert Museum.)   P. 569.

have in the centre crosses in niello within circular borders of floral scrolls, and
resemble the dishes with similar subjects found in Cyprus (Figs. 357, 360).[2]
Many of these are at St. Petersburg ; but a dish in the collection of Count
Stroganoff at Rome, found in 1867 in the Berezoff Islands in Siberia,[3] is of
especial interest. It represents a jewelled cross between two angels, fixed
in a starry globe resting upon ground from which flow the four rivers of

[1] e. g. the base of the obelisk of Theodosius at Constantinople, the silver votive shield of
the same emperor at Madrid, the consular diptych at Halberstadt (Fig. 7), the mosaics of
S. Vitale at Ravenna, &c.   See British Museum, *Catalogue of Early Christian and Byz. Antiquities*,
refs. under No. 398, p. 87.

[2] Two more dishes with nielloed crosses were found near the village of Klimowa in
Biarmia in 1907. See *Ath. Mitth.*, xxiii, 1908, 153-4 and Fig. 2.   With them was a dish of
earlier date, with an idyllic scene in relief and Byzantine control-stamps on the base.

[3] De Rossi, *Bullettino*, 1871, 153 ; Garrucci, *Storia*, vi, Pl. 460 ; Kondakoff, Tolstoy, and
Reinach, as above, 433 and 438 ; A. Muñoz, *L'Art byzantin à l'Exposition de Grottaferrata*, Rome,
1906, 149, 150; J. Smirnoff, *Oriental Silver*, Pl. XV (Russian).

Paradise.   The angels recall those of mosaics of the sixth century, and to this
period or to the early part of the seventh century the dish may probably be
assigned.   There is no certainty that it served as a paten, but it may have been
intended for some ecclesiastical use.   The work was perhaps executed in Syria,
where the influence of Persia was strong.   A remarkable dish with the Cruci-

FIG. 357.   Silver dish of the sixth century, with cross and ornament in niello.
(Museum of Nicosia, Cyprus.)   P. 574.

fixion, also found in the Government of Perm, has been discussed by Smirnoff
and others.[1]   It shows the interaction of Christian and oriental influences, and
may be as early as the close of the First Period, though some authorities. think
it later, and would assign it an origin in Central Asia rather than in Persia
or Syria.[2]
    The silver treasures of the First Period from Cyprus have all been found
about six miles west of Kyrenia, the small seaport on the north coast of the
island, at a place called Karavàs (near the site of the ancient Lapithos), and
close to the Monastery of Acheropitia.   The discoveries were made in the last

[1] *Materials for Russian Archæology*, 1899 ; J. Smirnoff, *Oriental Silver*, 1909, Pl. XV.
[2] V. Stassoff, *An Oriental Silver Dish in the Museum of the Hermitage*, St. Petersburg, 1904
(Russian).   M. Stassoff assigns the dish to the thirteenth or fourteenth century, but this
appears unduly late.   Cf. *B. Z.*, xvi. 392.

few years of the nineteenth century and in the summer of 1902. The principal objects of the first find,[1] now in the British Museum, consist of a fine dish with a nielloed cross within a border of ivy-leaves (Figs. 55, 360), a silver bowl with an embossed bust of St. Sergius surrounded by a band of nielloed orna- ment (Fig. 360), a small hexagonal censer (?) (Figs. 351–2) with three loops on the

Fig. 358.   Silver dish of the sixth century found near Kyrenia and now at Nicosia, Cyprus.   P. 576.

rim for suspension and with embossed busts of Our Lord, the Virgin, and saints upon the sides, and a number of spoons with baluster handles and a design of palm- leaves on the backs of the bowls (Fig. 448).   Eight of them are otherwise plain (Fig. 359) ; a ninth has the name Theodoros punched in dots on the side of the handle ; four others have on the upper part of the handle the inscription AY + AΛ in niello, and the remaining eleven have embossed animals (gryphon, leopard, lion, horse, stag, ram, bull, tiger, bear, boar, and hare) in the interior of the bowls. A small silver dish on a low foot, with a nielloed monogram surrounded by a border of vine-leaves, obtained in Cyprus about the same time and now in private hands, may have formed part of the same find.[2]   All the objects

[1] *Archaeologia*, lvii. 159 ff., Pl. XVI–XVIII ; British Museum, *Catalogue of Early Christian and Byzantine Antiquities*, 1905, 86-90, Nos. 396-424.
[2] *B. Z.*, 1906, 615-17 (Fig.).

probably date from the sixth century. The find of 1902 [1] was more important. It consisted of eleven silver dishes of various sizes, nine with embossed subjects illustrating the life of David (Figs. 57–62), two with nielloed designs—a cross and

FIG. 359. Silver spoons of the sixth century from Cyprus. (British Museum.) P. 573.

a monogram—within bands of formal floral design (Fig. 357). With the silver plate was a quantity of jewellery described on another page (p. 541). The adventures of these objects, how they were concealed from the Government of Cyprus,

[1] Dalton in *Archaeologia*, lx, pp. 1–24, and the *Burlington Magazine*, March, 1907 ; Sambon in *Le Musée*, Paris, 1906.

FIG. 360.   Silver dishes of the sixth century from Cyprus.   (British Museum.)   P. 572.

how part were seized by the police while part were smuggled out of the island on behalf of a dealer in antiquities in Paris, make a curious story. The result has unfortunately been to divide the treasure into two parts. One remains at Nicosia ; the other, that taken to Paris, has been purchased by Mr. J. Pierpont Morgan, and is temporarily exhibited in the Victoria and Albert Museum at South Kensington ; both groups have numerous hall-marks.[1] The chief importance of the treasure, however, lies in the scenes from the life of David with which several of the dishes are ornamented. We have here a large part of a cycle which first became popular as early as the fourth century, and is represented on the carved wooden doors of Sant' Ambrogio at Milan (p. 149), in the frescoes at Bawît in Egypt (p. 284), on a later ivory casket in the Museo Kircheriano at Rome (p. 221), and on other monuments. But while evidently deriving from Early Christian models, the subjects of these dishes are as evidently related to what is known as the 'aristocratic' group of illuminated Psalters (p. 467).[2] The close resemblance in the treatment of certain scenes, especially the killing of the lion and the bear, the anointing of David, and the combat with Goliath, seems to show that there must have been an unbroken tradition connecting the Third Period with the First, and that the once popular theory which ascribed the beginning of Psalter illustration to the eighth or ninth centuries is untenable. For the models from which the silversmiths worked are more likely to have been early illuminated MSS. than anything else. The subjects upon the surviving examples are : David killing the lion, killing the bear, summoned by the messenger of Samuel, and conversing with a warrior ; all dishes of small size.[3] On larger dishes[4] we see David introduced to Saul, being equipped with Saul's armour, fighting with Goliath and taking his spoils ; the marriage of David (Fig. 358), and his anointing as king (Fig. 60). The Goliath plate is of still greater size. The marriage scene[5] is of interest as resembling the type on a coin of Theodosius II, where the emperor is seen standing between Valentinian III and Eudoxia (Fig. 402), just as Saul stands between David and Michael. This is an earlier type than that usual in Middle-Byzantine art, in which the third person is usually Our Lord. All the larger dishes, except that with the Goliath scenes, have an architectural background of the same style as that seen on the votive disk of Theodosius at Madrid, but more debased. The foreground is in each case occupied by weapons, bags of money, &c., suggesting the objects of largesse upon consular diptychs, or the attributes of the *Notitia Dignitatum*. The work as a rule lacks life, and both features and drapery are heavy. But the slaying of the lion and the bear have more vigour, and some of the individual figures are not without charm. At the end of this section it may be repeated that the figure-art of East-Christian silver work with figure subjects throughout stands in a close relation to that of miniatures or illuminated books and to carvings in ivory.

FIG. 361. Stamps on base of a sixth-century silver censer from Cyprus (Fig. 351).

---

[1] *Archaeologia*, as above, 13–17.
[3] About 5½ in. in diameter.
[5] Figured, *Archaeologia*, as above, Pl. II.

[2] *Archaeologia*, as above, 17.
[4] About 8 in. in diameter.

Fig. 362. Fragment of tapestry of about the fifth century from a Coptic cemetery in Egypt.
(Victoria and Albert Museum.)

CHAPTER X

TEXTILES

THE figured textiles of the Christian East may be most conveniently divided into two main groups according to the method of manufacture. The first group comprises tapestries and fabrics with inwoven designs; the second is composed of embroideries. Materials occur which fall into neither group (e. g. the printed Egyptian fabrics, p. 602), but the above division may serve in an introductory chapter on the subject.

Figured textiles were used for garments, for hangings or coverings, especially for altars, ciboria,[1] walls, and doorways,[2] and for various subsidiary purposes: the very numerous textiles mentioned in the *Liber Pontificalis* were mostly hangings. Figured stuffs also served as wrappings for the dead,[3] and the large loose tunics in which bodies were interred

---

[1] As in Sta Sophia, Constantinople.
[2] Epiphanius, Bishop of Cyprus (d. A.D. 402), in a letter to John, Bishop of Jerusalem, dated A.D. 394, mentions a figured curtain in the door of the Church of Anablatha in Palestine (Migne, *Patr. Lat.* xxii. 526 : see also de Rossi, *Bullettino*, 1871, 62). The use of curtains in churches is illustrated by mosaics and frescoes, e. g. those of St. George, Salonika (Fig. 221), the Church of the Nativity at Bethlehem, &c.
[3] Ammianus Marcellinus speaks of persons *fulgentes sericis indumentis ut ducendos ad mortem*. Rich textiles were sometimes placed upon the sarcophagus, as in the case of Diocletian. St. Ambrose and St. Basil both mention the usage of interring rich textiles with the dead : the bodies of martyrs were covered with robes of especial splendour. See Cahier and Martin, *Mélanges d'arch. chrétienne*, ii, note on p. 245.

were often enriched with applied figured designs. It is naturally from the Egyptian cemeteries that our principal knowledge of older textiles is derived (Akhmîm, Antinoe, Sakkara, the Fayûm, &c.); but it is increased by documentary evidence. Thus Asterius, Bishop of Amaseia in Pontus (fourth century), a censor of the luxury prevalent in his time, condemns the wealthy for adorning themselves with garments covered with figures, including Gospel scenes and all manner of beasts, 'as if they were frescoed walls in motion.'[1] His descriptions justify the old Roman phrase *acu pingere*, and the classification of tapestry and embroidery as branches of painting. Ausonius on his accession to the consulship received from Gratian a trabea in which a portrait of Constantius was inwoven.[2] Chrysostom, describing the state robes of the emperor, mentions his silk raiment enriched with golden dragons.[3] We may recall the much later royal mantles from Sicily in the Schatzkammer at Vienna, with their inwoven animals, continuing earlier traditions.[4] Paul the Silentiary describes the ciborium curtains of the Cathedral of Sta Sophia at Constantinople as of silk with figures of Our Lord, SS. Peter and Paul, &c.[5] Further evidence is obtained from representations upon surviving works of art. The official mantles of the consuls, as seen upon the consular diptychs, are rich with various designs, mostly conventional floral patterns, but occasionally human figures. Examples of the latter class are those of Areobindus (consul A.D. 506) and Basilius (A.D. 541), which resemble in this respect the earlier trabea sent to Ausonius. On the diptych 'of Stilicho and Serena' in the Treasury of Monza Cathedral, Stilicho's garments show the head of Galla Placidia and the bust of Valentinian beneath canopies.[6] In the well-known ceremonial mosaics in San Vitale at Ravenna, the costume of the Empress Theodora (Fig. 213) has represented upon it the scene of the Adoration of the Magi, thus confirming the statement of Asterius that biblical scenes were depicted upon garments. A similar use of pictured garments among the Sassanian Persians is

---

[1] The passage, which is in a homily (Εἰς τὸν πλούσιον καὶ τὸν Λάζαρον), will be found in Migne, *Patr. Gr.*, xl. 165c ff. See also Kraus, *Geschichte*, i. 389; Ainaloff, *Hellenistic Origins*, &c., 131; J. Strzygowski, *Orient oder Rom*, 116. For the similar strictures of Chrysostom, see the quotations in Cahier and Martin, *Mélanges d'arch.*, ii. 252–3.

[2] 'In qua Divus Constantius parens noster intextus est.' Ausonius calls this *vestis picta* (*Aus. ad Gratianum imp. pro Cons.*, xxi).

[3] Sermon, περὶ τελείας ἀγάπης. *Opera*, ed. Gaume, vi. 348 : δράκοντας ἐν ἱματίοις σχηματιζομένους σηρικοῖς.

[4] Imperial mantles were enriched with applied gems and pearls. Claudian uses the expression *gemmato trabeae cinctu*. In the Calendar of the Chronographer (fourth century; see p. 484) the mantle of the Emperor Constantius II is enriched with gems. Possibly only emperors wore such begemmed garments. Pearls were also sewn upon Carolingian robes (J. von Schlosser, *Schriftquellen zur Gesch. der karol. Kunst*, 408).
The court chlamys was richly woven with peacocks, eagles, &c. Cf. Kondakoff, *Enamels*, 299–300. Constantine Porphyrogenitus especially mentions the peacock (*De Caerimoniis*, i, ch. xxiii).

[5] Paulus Silentiarius, quoted by Lethaby and Swainson, *The Church of Sancta Sophia*, 48–9.

[6] The designs upon these garments were perhaps embroidered and not inwoven. The splendid raiment of Aurelian is also probably to be regarded as embroidered (L. Homo, *Essai sur le règne d'Aurélien*, 193). For embroidery in ancient Rome see M. Besnier's article *Phrygio*, in Daremberg and Saglio's *Dictionnaire des antiquités grecques et romaines*.

proved by the sculptures of Kermanshah, where the king (Chosroes II ?) is apparelled in a figured robe. Mere decorative pattern on garments may be studied in miniatures of MSS.,[1] in mosaics,[2] frescoes,[3] and in representations on silk textiles themselves.[4]

It may be added that figured textiles, woven and embroidered, had been derived by the earlier Greeks from oriental sources, and there are numerous references to them in the classical authors. Euripides describes

Fig. 363. Orpheus: tapestry medallion of about the third century in the Victoria and Albert Museum.

a hanging of oriental workmanship in the temple of the Delphic Apollo [5] with marine battles and mounted hunters. Aristophanes speaks of the ἱππαλεκτρυών and the τραγέλαφος, oriental monsters forming a known pattern on Median carpets.[6]

TAPESTRY.[7]

It is claimed that tapestry was made in Egypt about the year B.C. 1500

[1] e. g. miniatures in the Menologium of Basil (p. 479).
[2] The mosaics in S. Demetrius, Salonika, may be cited as particularly interesting.
[3] Costumes in the frescoes of Kuṣeir ʿAmra may be noted.
[4] e. g. the Günther silk at Bamberg (p. 596).
[5] Ion, 1159 ff.   [6] Frogs, 937 ff.
[7] W. G. Thomson, A History of Tapestry, 1906; W. Lowry, Atti of Eleventh Congress of Christian Archaeology, Rome, 1900, 47 ff.; M. Gerspach, Les Tapisseries coptes, Paris, 1890, and Gazette des Beaux-Arts, 1887, 124 ff. ; R. Forrer, Die Gräber- und Textil-Funde von Achmim-Panopolis, Strassburg, 1891; A. Riegl, Die aegyptischen Textilfunde des k. k. oesterreichischen Museums, Vienna, 1889, and Eranos Vindobonensis, 1893; R. Forrer, Versuch einer Classification der antik-koptischen Textilfunde, Strassburg, 1889 (these and other references are given in the article Akhmîm, sect. ii : Tapisseries, in F. Cabrol's Dictionnaire d'archéologie chrétienne, col. 1049); A. Gayet,

(under the eighteenth dynasty),[1] and that the art of making it was known to almost all the ancient civilizations of the nearer East.[2] The Greek figured stuffs from South Russia, dating from about B.C. 400, are regarded as tapestry.[3] Tapestry was made for the Romans under both the republic and the empire, and great numbers of the tapestry-woven stuffs from the Egyptian sites date from the first three centuries of our era. It is

FIG. 364. Tapestry panel of about the third century from a Coptic cemetery in Egypt. (Victoria and Albert Museum.)

from Egypt that our principal knowledge of early tapestry is derived. Great numbers of specimens have been exhumed from the larger cemeteries, especially that of Akhmîm (Panopolis), which since 1884 has yielded large series to various museums,[4] and that of Antinoe, the city founded by Hadrian in honour of his favourite, Antinous.

Annales du Musée Guimet, xxx. 2 ; J. Baillet, *Les Tapisseries coptes au Musée d'Orléans*, 1907 ; H. Swoboda, in *R. Q.*, vi, 1892, 95 ff., and *Arch. Ehrengabe zu de Rossi's LXX. Geburtstage*, 71 f.; V. de Bock, *Eighth Arch. Congress*, Moscow, 1890 (publ. 1897), 218 ff. (bibliography), and *Trans. Imp. Arch. Soc. of Moscow*, viii, 1897, 1–32 ; E. Schiaparelli, *Di una antica stoffa*, &c., *Bessarione*, Nos. 49–50, 1900, 1–9 ; G. Migeon, *Les Arts du tissu*, ch. iii ; V. de Grüneisen, *Bull. della Soc. Filologica Romana*, x, 1907, 1–24 ; M. Dreger, *Künstlerische Entwicklung der Weberei*, pp. 4 ff. (1904).

[1] Fragments of tapestry-woven linen with design in colours, from the tomb of Thoutmôsis III, in the Cairo Museum (water-colour drawings in the Victoria and Albert Museum. Description in *Cat. gén. des ant. égyptiennes du Musée du Caire*, Nos. 46001–529, *The tomb of Thoutmôsis III*, by H. Carter and P. E. Newberry, 1904, Nos. 46526–9, pp. 143 ff. and Pl. I and XXVIII).   [2] Thomson, 9 ff.

[3] Found in the mound known as the Seven Brothers in the province of Kuban.

[4] Good series are to be seen in this country in the Victoria and Albert Museum (the most considerable), in the British Museum, and at Liverpool. Of collections in foreign

The process by which these Egyptian fabrics were manufactured closely
resembles that by which Gobelin tapestry is produced, and for technical
methods the reader is referred to M. Gerspach's and Mr. Thomson's books.
The warp and woof are sometimes both of linen, at others of linen and

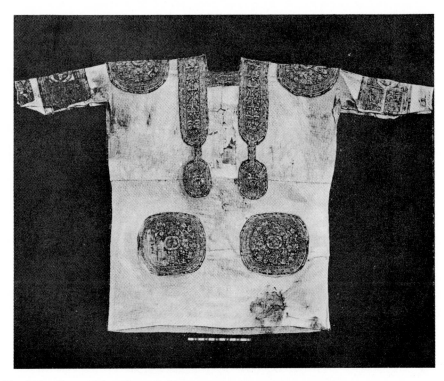

Fɪɢ. 365.   Linen tunic with applied tapestry, about the sixth century, from a Coptic cemetery
in Egypt.   (Victoria and Albert Museum.)

wool; in other cases the weft is of silk, though this is rare in the first
centuries.[1]

museums, those in the Musée Guimet and at the Gobelins in Paris, in the Kaiser Friedrich
Museum and Kunstgewerbe-Museum at Berlin, in the Vienna Museums, and in the Hermitage
and Stieglitz Museums at St. Petersburg are all important.

[1] Gerspach, p. 6. The Coptic loom must have been upright, but of course was much
smaller than those employed at the Gobelins. The most obvious distinction between
tapestry and ordinary shuttle weaving is that in the former the weft or horizontal thread
is pressed down so as to envelop completely and conceal the warp of vertical threads
(Thomson, p. 2). Designs are produced by altering the colour of the weft, and by using
particular threads of the warp. True tapestry is always hand-made. Where, as was
commonly the case in figured garments, tapestry bands or panels had to be introduced
into a woven piece, the process is thus described : (at the requisite point the weaver)
'changed the weft or threads in the shuttle, and working with two or more of the warp
threads combined as one, proceeded with his tapestry weaving, beating down this new weft
with the comb. The ordinary shuttle weaving was continued to right and left of the
insertion, and when the tapestry panel was completed, the warp threads were divided into
their original number, the plain weaving being proceeded with along the width of the loom '
(ibid., 21 and 22). Coptic weavers largely employed the free shuttle (known in France
as the *ressaut* or *crapaud*), and allowed the weft to diverge from the horizontal line in any
direction convenient for the execution of their designs. The fine figures or patterns in
thin linen thread upon dark purple ground in many pieces seem to be executed by the

The colours employed were never more than about twelve. Purples, violet-brown, and reds served for background; for executing the designs, the weaver disposed of violet, indigo, and pale blue, two tones of yellow, orange, several tones of green, and a blue-black. The colours are very fast, and are capable of resisting prolonged action of sunlight.

Large tapestries were used, like silks, as hangings in churches; the

FIG. 366.   The Adoration of the Magi: tapestry medallion from a tunic of about the sixth century, from a Coptic cemetery in Egypt. (British Museum.)

smaller were applied to the garments of the living or served to adorn the great linen tunics in which the bodies of the dead were clothed.

A great number of textiles with tapestry ornament belong to the Egypto-Roman period between the first and third centuries. The subjects and ornament of these are not Christian; where figures occur they are usually mythological, or are concerned with the chase and the games of the circus: an example at South Kensington (2140—1900) shows Vulcan forging the armour of Achilles. There are various female types, often busts, which may be compared to the late Hellenistic figures on the bone carvings from Alexandria. But the commonest pagan subjects are genii on foot or mounted, and the most various animals, fruits, and flowers,

ressaut, and not embroidered by a needle (Gerspach, p. 6): Gayet, however, believes that embroidery was largely used. For the technical process of making tapestry, see also G. Migeon, *Les Arts du tissu*, 174–5.

disposed in compartments or panels of different design. Ornamental motives comprise vine-scrolls and arrangements of vine-leaves, vines issuing from vases, guilloche, wavy lines, lozenges, stepped triangles, rows of hearts, and various geometrical figures for which the Copts had a distinct preference. In these earlier pieces it is very common to find only one colour, a purple or red-brown, contrasting with the buff of the flax which forms the ground and is used to pick out the details. Yellow, green, and red become more common in the Christian period, when the drawing often deteriorates while the general effect grows more brilliant. Christian subjects now become predominant, sometimes easily distinguishable, as in the roundel with scenes from the life of Joseph at St. Petersburg,[1] or that in the British Museum (Fig. 366), at others difficult of interpretation, arrangements of figures as grotesque as any which may be seen on the tapestries of Peru. Throughout the Christian period certain elements of the ancient Egyptian ornament, such as the *ankh*, continued in use, and were incorporated into the symbolism of the new faith; but the motives are chiefly of late Hellenic introduction.

SILK.[2]

All figured silk textiles are included in the class of fabrics with inwoven designs. Even in the area covered by the Byzantine Empire weaving in silk preceded Christianity,[3] and beyond that area it was practised in very remote times.

The antiquity of silk-weaving in China is very great; records exist from which it would appear to have flourished in the third millennium B.C.; in any case, it seems to have been practised in the Far East earlier than in any other part of the world. Raw silk was imported into the West before the fourth century B.C., for the thin *Coa vestis* woven in the island of Cos was of this material.[4] Alexander's general, Nearchos, is stated to have worn silk, and the Greeks of the period following that king's Indian expedition even knew something of the silkworm, Aristotle, who first

---

[1] Strzygowski, *Orient oder Rom*, 113.

[2] J. Lessing, *Die Gewebe-Sammlung*, &c., *des k. Kunstgewerbemuseums in Berlin*; F. Michel, *Recherches sur le commerce*, &c *des étoffes de soie*, 1852; F. Fischbach, *Ornamentik der Gewebe*; F. Bock, *Liturgische Gewänder*; M. Dreger, *Künstlerische Entwicklung der Weberei*, 1904, and *Kunst und Kunsthandwerk*, ii. 330 ff.; Isabel Errera, *Collection d'anciennes étoffes*, 1901; Cahier and Martin, *Mélanges d'archéologie*, ii, iii; J. Strzygowski, Prussian *Jahrbuch*, xxiv, 1903, 147 ff., and *Orient oder Rom*, 90 ff., 114 ff.; R. Forrer, *Römische und byzantinische Seiden-Textilien aus dem Gräberfelde von Achmim-Panopolis*, Strassburg, 1891; A. Cole, *Ornament in European Silks*, 1899; De Caumont, *Bulletin monumental*, xiv. 480; G. Migeon, *Les Arts du tissu*; Diehl, *Manuel*, 248, 600; *Annales du Musée Guimet*, 1902; Ph. Lauer, *Mon. Piot*, 1906, 103 ff.; Gibbon, *Decline and Fall*, v. 57, vii. 12 (Smith's edition), references to various old books.

[3] e. g. Victoria and Albert Museum, No. 334—887, entirely executed in silk tapestry. Egypto-Roman roundels in the same museum are sometimes of linen, tapestry-woven in coloured silks. The combination of linen warp with tapestry-woven silks was favoured after the Saracenic invasion; examples from the cemetery of El-Azam near Assiût.

[4] Aristotle, *Hist. Animalium*, v. 19 (17), 11 (6), relates the tradition that silk was first spun in Cos by Pamphile, daughter of Plates. Were it not that the wearing of silk garments by Nearchos points to their use in Persia, it might have been doubted whether the fine textiles of the early Persian Empire were of silk, as the Zoroastrian regarded such animal products as unclean.

mentions it, perhaps deriving his information from persons who had heard of it in the East. But though the use of silk in the West greatly increased under the Roman Empire,[1] the orientals prevented the export of the silkworm's eggs, and thus preserved for themselves a valuable monopoly. Pliny, writing in the first century A.D., knows no more of the nature of the worm than Aristotle, who wrote four hundred years earlier;[2] we gather from him, however, the interesting fact that Chinese textiles were unravelled and rewoven in occidental designs.[3]

References in classical Latin authors to silk garments are numerous from the first century before our era, but evidently textiles of the material remained very costly for a considerable period, and were only worn by the wealthy. Aurelian is said to have complained that at Rome an ounce of silk could only be purchased by twelve ounces of gold. The silk robes of Theodosius have been already mentioned. At the baptism of Theodosius II, son of Arcadius, the walls of Constantinople were hung with silk fabrics,[4] and it is clear that hangings and garments of this material must have existed in great quantities by the fifth century. The silk-weaving industry in Persia was in a flourishing state in the fourth century, when Shapur II imported weavers into Persis, a district which henceforth became the most important centre; but the geographical position of Iran makes it probable that the material was woven there at an earlier date.

The influence of Persia was early felt in the eastern Byzantine provinces. Oriental fabrics were imported;[5] raw silk was introduced in ever-increasing quantities, to be woven and dyed on the looms of Syria and Tyre. The raw material was absolutely in the hands of Persia, for even when shipped to Ceylon it was controlled by Persian merchants and carried to Persian ports;[6] when it came overland it was sold to the Persians by middlemen of Bokhara and Samarkand. Many of the figured silks belonging to the First Period are of a definitely Persian character, even when they have been found in Coptic cemeteries in Egypt. Most authorities, as Lessing, hold that these silks were actually produced in Persia in the later Sassanian period, chiefly in the sixth century;[7] others,

---

[1] Silk garments remained a mark of effeminate luxury until the fourth century; see Pliny, vi. 20, xi. 26; Cahier and Martin, *Mél. d'arch. chrét.* ii. 241, footnote.

[2] Chinese textiles were imported into Syria (Pliny, vi. 17 (20), 54; xi. 22 (26), 76; F. Hirth, *China and the Roman Orient,* p. 258; H. Semper, *Der Stil,* i. 140).

[3] xi. 76. This was done in Cos.

[4] Ὁλοσηρικῶν. See Bury, *Hist. of the Later Roman Empire,* i. 204.

[5] There may well have been Chinese silks among the number. A passage from Leo Diaconus quoted by Michel (p. 42, *n.* 2) indicates that Chinese silks were among the spoils taken by John Zimisces from the Arabs: ἐκ Σηρῶν ὑφάσματα, but the absence of designs which can be identified as Chinese upon early surviving silks is against the supposition of any important Chinese influence. An exception may perhaps be made in favour of the lattice forming a series of lozenges.

[6] M. Diehl has given a useful summary of the commercial situation in his *Justinien* (iii, ch. iv), where references to ancient and modern writers will be found. That valuable earlier work, Heyd's *Geschichte des Levant-Handels,* may also be consulted. Chinese and Persians used to meet at the harbour of Trincomalee; and this commerce between the Far and Near East is mentioned by Cosmas Indicopleustes.

[7] Sassanian sculptures, as that representing Chosroes II at Kermanshah, show textiles

as Smirnoff,[1] believe that many were made in Mesopotamia under the Arab dominion after the downfall of the Sassanian monarchy. It is in any case certain that Sassanian motives were at an early period copied both within and beyond the limits of the old Sassanian Empire, definitely Persian motives occurring on textiles produced in China and the Eastern

Fig. 367. Silk textile of the sixth–seventh century from Egypt. (British Museum.) P. 592.

Byzantine provinces indifferently (p. 591). In the West, designs of this oriental derivation maintained their popularity through the Middle Ages.

It is not alone in the figures of animals and monsters that this oriental influence is apparent. Upon the silk fabrics of about the seventh century the floral ornament in the borders of the medallions and in the inter-spaces is often composed of Persian derivatives from the palmette,[2] or varieties of the symmetrical 'sacred tree' (hom) which, under so many forms, is of such ancient date in the Nearer East. The influence of Persia is in fact paramount; and it is a curious fact that neither China nor India introduced their motives in this way, though the opportunities of doing so

almost identical with some which have survived (Dreger, *Künstlerische Entwicklung*, &c., Pl. XXXVIII.

[1] *Materials for Russian Archaeology*, xxii. 41.

[2] Strzygowski, Prussian *Jahrbuch*, xxiv. 1903, 157 ff.

must have been very frequent. Some methods of dividing the field of the stuff into a lozenge-diaper have been claimed as Chinese,[1] and there is documentary evidence that Chinese silks were known at the Byzantine court.[2] But any motives and designs which we may regard as peculiarly Chinese seem to be consistently absent.

It was not until the middle of the sixth century that the annoyance caused by the Persian monopoly made the introduction of the silkworm into Byzantine territory a matter of urgent moment. So long as the Christian factories were dependent for their raw material upon countries with which the empire was frequently at war, the prosperity of a great industry might be at any time imperilled by an outbreak of hostilities on the eastern frontier. Whatever may be the truth of the stories told by Procopius and Theophanes of the smuggling of the eggs out of China in hollow staves,[3] it is certain that by some means or other Byzantium became in great measure independent of foreign sources of supply in the reign of Justinian, and that henceforth the workshops were less exposed to the vicissitudes previously affecting the production of their looms. Within the empire, silk was produced during the First Period in Syria and in the imperial manufactories (*Baphia* or *Gynaecea, Zeuxippus*) in Constantinople, which supplied the court and sometimes furnished the public as well. This state of affairs prejudicially affected private enterprise, which could not easily meet such privileged competition. To the last, certain kinds of silk fabrics remained the monopoly of the imperial workshops, and a particular purple might not be produced elsewhere.[4] Before the eleventh century some of the principal centres of the Byzantine silk industry were established in Greece, especially in Thebes and Corinth.[5] It will be noted below that Roger of Sicily transported Greek workmen from Greece to Palermo; and the continuance of the industry in Greece under the Byzantine and Frankish princes is well attested.[6] Silk-weaving

---

[1] Strzygowski, Prussian *Jahrbuch*, xxiv, 1903, 170 ff. The human figures on the painted silk brought by Dr. M. A. Stein from Turkestan are predominantly Chinese, but the ornamental motives seem either of a kind which does not affect Western art, or themselves to bear traces of Western influence (e. g. borders derived from the palmette). Cf. also M. Dreger, *Künstl. Entwicklung*, as above, pp. 35–6.

[2] John Zimisces displayed ἐκ Σηρῶν ὑφάσματα at Constantinople (Leo Diaconus, Bk. X, p. 163, Bonn ed.). Silk with Chinese characters has been found at El Azam ; but its date does not appear to be very early (example in Victoria and Albert Museum).

[3] Gibbon, v. 61 ff. Procopius says that the persons who brought the silkworms were monks resident in Serinda (Khotan (?) or China) : see *De Bello Gothico*, 546–7, and Theophanes, Bonn ed., p. 484. The most generally accepted story is that between the years A.D. 552 and 554 two monks from Serinda offered to bring the emperor eggs from that region, affirming that they could be hatched and fed upon mulberry leaves. The proposal was accepted ; success justified the enterprise ; and large mulberry plantations were soon established in Syria. Justinian had endeavoured without much success to introduce raw silk via Abyssinia, and perhaps round the north of the Caspian, both routes free from Persian control. Officials called *commerciarii* were entrusted with the task of making the necessary purchases in the Persian markets. Much information will be found in the article of Zachariae von Lingenthal, *Eine Verordnung Justinians über den Seidenhandel*, *Memoirs of the Imperial Academy of St. Petersburg*, ser. vii, vol. ix, No. 6.

[4] Code of Justinian, Bk. X, viii, ix ; Theodosian Code, Bk. X, xx, xxi.

[5] For the statement of Benjamin of Tudela (d. A.D. 1173) as to silk manufacture in Central Greece, see G. Mavrojani, Βυζαντίνη τέχνη, 110, 255, Athens, 1893.

[6] For the Frankish period see allusions in W. Miller's *The Latins in the Levant*. For

survived the fall of Constantinople, for we read of Greek weavers summoned to France by Louis XI in A.D. 1480.[1] Some of the most interesting information which we possess with regard to the imperial silk manufactory at Constantinople is derived from the account of his embassy left by Luitprand,[2] who was sent by Otto on a mission to the Emperor Nicephorus Phocas. The envoy had purchased various silk

FIG. 368. Silk textile of about the seventh century with Persian gryphon.
(Victoria and Albert Museum.)

textiles to carry home, but the customs officials compelled him to surrender five pieces of purple fabric, which they informed him were not to be exported, as being κωλυόμενα, or forbidden to foreigners.[3] Those which he was permitted to take with him were marked with lead seals, and the fact reminds us of the conservatism of revenue officers, who still employ the same methods. The account of Luitprand is lively, and deserves perusal.[4]

the silk establishments attached to the palace at Palermo see Falcand, *Hist. Sic.*, in Muratori, *Rerum ital. script.*, vii. 256.

[1] E. Müntz, *Revue de l'art chrét.*, 1893; *Les Artistes byz. dans l'Europe latine du 5e au 15e siècle.*

[2] Pertz, *Mon. Germaniae hist.*, iii. 259; Muratori, *Rerum ital. scriptores*, ii. 447, col. 2 A; Michel, 63.

[3] The emperors used to send these purple silks as gifts to popes and Western princes, as we learn from entries in the *Liber Pontificalis*. For examples see Michel, 64.

[4] It is partly quoted in Cahier and Martin, *Mélanges d'arch. chrét.*, ii. 240.

Though the Italians did not weave silk during the first millennium
of our era, the Rome of the earliest Middle Ages became a distributing
centre where the silk and other textiles of the Orient and the Eastern
Mediterranean were brought for sale or presentation. It was at Rome
that Benedict Biscop obtained the woven fabrics mentioned in Bede's
Life;[1] and the *Liber Pontificalis* is full of entries recording their use
as altar-coverings or hangings in our churches.[2] We hear of gryphons,

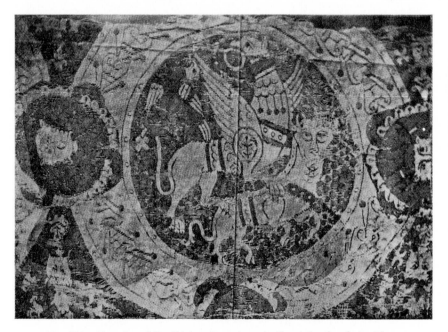

Fig. 369. Tapestry of the thirteenth century, in the style of early textiles.
(Musée Industriel, Lyon.)

peacocks, unicorns, eagles, lions, elephants, leopards, and other beasts,
with various tree-forms, enclosed for the most part in *rotae* or *rotellae*.
By these words are meant circles or medallions, tangent or interconnected
with each other so as to form a network covering the whole stuff, over
which the subject is repeated. (Cf. Figs. 368-9.) These animal and monster
types are of oriental origin, though from a very early period they were
reproduced upon Christian looms. But Christian subjects were not long
in competing with secular designs, and the pages of Anastasius contain
many references to these, for the most part representing episodes from
the lives of Our Lord, the Virgin, the Apostles, and saints. It will be
seen below that a few remarkable fabrics of this type have escaped

---

[1] *Vita S. Benedicti Abb.*, Wearmouth, i. 9. Hangings presented by Egbert, Bishop of York,
are described by an eighth-century poet as *serica peregrinis vela figuris* (Alcuinus Abbas, *Opera*,
ed. Frobenius, ii, Pt. I, 254, col. i). Oswald embellished the church in the same way;
Wilfrid of York and Milfred, King of Mercia, were also donors of silk hangings (Michel,
66 ff.).

[2] See F. Michel, as above, 14 ff.; S. Beissel, *Bilder aus der Geschichte der altchr. Kunst und
Litteratur in Italien*, 260 ff., and *Zeitschr. für Christliche Kunst*, 1894, pp. 357 ff. ; Dreger, pp. 41 ff.

destruction, and are now preserved in churches and museums. Several authorities have justly remarked that some of these ancient textiles may have been made by monks of the Greek colony in Rome. Many have Latin inscriptions; the subjects often reproduce the legends of the patron saints of Roman churches; portraits of popes also occur. Moreover, as the greatest production began precisely at the time of the iconoclast persecution, probability is in favour of manufacture in the West.[1]

The Franks imported silk textiles in even greater quantities than the Anglo-Saxons. Sidonius Apollinaris (d. A.D. 488) mentions the silks of a young Merovingian prince.[2] St. Cloud renounced the use of silk

Fig. 370. Silk textile used for a seal-bag. (Chapter Library, Canterbury.)

garments, but St. Eloi wore them in order to conform to custom; Gregory of Tours speaks of silk altar-hangings in Gaul. Charlemagne himself only used rich textiles for festivals, but presented many to churches.[3]

It has already been noted that figured silks of traditional Persian designs may have continued to be made in Mesopotamia after the Arab conquest of Persia. But from the beginning of the Arab dominion weavers produced designs suited to the taste of the orthodox Moslem. Silk fabrics of this kind were woven by Mohammedans from the early years of their conquests in Egypt and Western Asia: fragments and pieces with inscriptions and geometrical ornament have been found in

[1] Gregorovius, *Gesch. der Stadt Roms*, ii. 378; Labarte, *Hist. des arts industriels*, iv. 334; A. L. Frothingham, *American Journ. Arch.*, x, 1895, 187 ff.
[2] *Epist. IV*, No. 20; quoted by Michel, p. 68.
[3] Dom Ruinart, at the end of his edition of Gregory, gives details showing the abundance of silk textiles in Merovingian times.

early cemeteries in Egypt.[1] By degrees the Mohammedan weavers themselves adopted the heraldically disposed animals and the *hom* of Persian art. In this they only resembled the weavers of the Greek Empire; and it is sometimes a matter of great difficulty to decide to which group of imitators textiles with such designs belong. For example, the fabric with chained leopards at Chinon was not known to be of Mohammedan workmanship until an Arabic inscription was observed upon it (p. 597).

The Moslem had clearly a wide reputation as a weaver in mediaeval Europe.[2] Perhaps the Mohammedan princes of Sicily had workshops for silk manufacture even before Roger, the Norman king, in the middle of the twelfth century, brought back weavers from Corinth, Thebes, and Athens, and established them at Palermo.[3] M. Amari has been followed by more recent authorities in his belief that the Normans only increased the number of weavers, and that the system of the *tiraz*, which corresponded to the Byzantine *gynaeceum*, already existed in the island at the time of the Norman invasion; it may not have been established for any length of time or upon a very extensive scale, and need not have been situated in Palermo itself. Roger's expedition introduced the silkworm into the island, and this must have greatly increased the area of manufacture. He did for Southern Europe what Justinian had formerly done for the Byzantine Empire.

To illustrate the subjects with which figured silks were decorated it will be convenient to mention a few of the more important and accessible textiles, preserved for the most part in museums and the treasuries of churches, and representing the three principal groups with oriental, late Hellenic, and Christian motives.

Subjects upon Silk Fabrics.[4]

(a) Of Persian and Byzantine Origin.

Among the most popular Persian designs is that of a mounted king shooting wild beasts, the whole framed in a medallion and repeated over the surface, the medallions being interlaced or connected by small tangent circles, while the interspaces are filled with formal foliage (Fig. 372).[5] The huntsman is usually duplicated

---

[1] El-Azam, from which site interesting fragments are exhibited in the Victoria and Albert Museum.

[2] Theodulf (xxviii. v. 211) speaks of—
Pallia quae misit, ut puto, torvus Arabs
(von Schlosser, *Schriftquellen zur Gesch. der karolingischen Kunst*, 407). In the *Nibelungenlied* there is mention of Arab silks (Michel, 60).

[3] A.D. 1146–7. See Muratori, *Script. Ital.*, vi. 668; Michel, pp. 73 ff.; Gibbon, vii. 12. Falcandus, a writer of the twelfth century, describes the silks of Palermo.

[4] Migeon, *Essai de classification*, &c., in *Gazette des Beaux-Arts*, 1908; Diehl, *Manuel*, 249.

[5] Some examples of this type may be mentioned : London, British Museum, Department of Egyptian Antiquities ; Victoria and Albert Museum (No. 558, 1893, a lion hunt); another similar; also a fragment from Akhmîm (107—'87) ; St. Servaas, Maastricht (Fischbach, Pl. III); St. Kunibert, Cologne (Schnütgen, *Zeitschr. für christliche Kunst*, xi, Pl. V) ; St. Andrew, Cologne (*Gaz. des Beaux-Arts*, 3ᵉ Période, 1902, 221) ; Sant' Ambrogio, Milan (Venturi, *Le Gallerie nazionali*, iv. 292, and Pl. I and II) ; Paris, Musée Guimet, from Antinoe, Necrop. D : horseman shooting lion ; Berlin, Kunstgewerbe-Museum (No. '78—632), king mounted on a winged horse and holding up cub ; king shooting lions, palmette border (No. '96—630), from Säckingen (Lessing, Pt. III), perhaps made in the sixth–seventh century in the Byzantine Empire ; Tokyo, the example mentioned above, for which also see Lessing, *Gewebe-Sammlung*, Pt. I, Pl. II ; *Annales du Musée Guimet*, xxx, Pt. II, Pl. VI (after p. 152) ; the king represented

so that the composition is symmetrical, the two figures being usually back to back, but turning inwards to release the arrow.   Sometimes the hunter swings aloft the cub of the lioness below him, a motive found on Sassanian silver plate, the designs upon which have affinities with those on these textiles.   It may be remembered that the horse was always the most important animal among the Medes and Persians.[1]

The hunter type was imitated in China in the seventh or early eighth century, as is shown by an example from the treasure of the Horiuji temple at

Fig. 371.   Samson (?) or Hercules (?) : silk textile of about the sixth century in the
Victoria and Albert Museum.   P. 598, n. 1.

Nara in Japan, presented in the eighth century with other objects belonging to the Mikado Shomu (d. A.D. 756) by his consort Kômyô.   In this example, though the composition is Persian the execution is Chinese, and Chinese seals are seen on the flanks of the horses, replacing the Sassanian ' star '.[2]   Most examples of this type were perhaps made beyond the Byzantine Empire, though in the piece in the Musée des tissus at Lyons the costume has Greek

as shown by his head-piece to be Chosroes II (A.D. 591-628).   A variation of the hunter type is seen on a textile from the Church of St. Ursula, Cologne.   Here the king rides a gryphon, and is attacked by a winged monster, while lions are seen below, and ibexes above (No. '81—3, Lessing, Pt. I, Pl. III ; Dreger, as above, p. 40 ; *Gazette des Beaux-Arts*, 3ᵉ Période, 1902, 220).   Sometimes a huntsman is seen on foot armed with a spear ; so in the textile discovered in the Sancta Sanctorum at Rome, where he is seen spearing the lion (H. Grisar, *Die römische Kapelle Sancta Sanctorum*, p. 126 (1908) ; Ph. Lauer, *Mon. Piot*, 1906, Pl. XVIII).   Examples also in Victoria and Albert Museum (2178—1900, 558, 559—1893, Fig. 372).

[1] For the hunter motive see *L'Arte*, ix, 1906, 193 ff. (G. Sangiorgi) ; Strzygowski, Prussian *Jahrbuch*, xxiv, 1903, 151 ; F. Justi, in *Zeitschr. für Christl. Kunst*, 1898, pp. 361 ff. ; Dreger, as above, pp. 32, 37, &c.

[2] *Toyei Shukoi, An Illustrated Catalogue of the Ancient Imperial Treasury called Shoshoin*, 1909, Pl. XCIV ; *Japanese Temples and their Treasures*, Pl. CCIII (1910).   It may be noted that the Chinese equally reproduced later designs on silk brocade produced under the Mameluke sultans in the thirteenth and fourteenth centuries.   For an example, with addorsed eagles, in the Kunstgewerbe-Museum at Berlin, see Lessing, Pt. I, Pl. I.

elements.[1] The derivative type, in which both mounted and unmounted horse-men appear, and the name ZAXAPIOY is inwoven above, must be Christian. Examples are in the British and Victoria and Albert Museums, and Berlin[2] (Fig. 367).

Monsters, beasts, or birds confronted or addorsed within medallions, and separated by some variety of formal foliage representing the *hom* or sacred tree,

Fig. 372. Silk textile of the eighth or ninth century. (Victoria and Albert Museum.)

are also of Persian derivation; like the hunter motive they appear to have been also reproduced beyond the limits of the Sassanian Empire. Such motives were adopted not only by Byzantine and Greek, but by Saracenic and Sicilian weavers; they ultimately passed into the stock of subjects reproduced in Central and Western Europe. The tradition was persistent, and the date of some pieces is often difficult to determine. The borders of the medallions are usually of motives based upon the palmette: they are often reduced to sequences of heart-shaped figures; foliate designs of similar origin fill the interspaces. Here again, in a Berlin example with gryphons reproduced by Lessing, the Chinese are found reproducing, about the ninth or tenth century, a Persian

[1] Migeon, *Arts du tissu*, 26–7; Dreger, as above, p. 37. The piece was formerly in the Church of Mozac, Puy-de-Dôme.

[2] Brit. Mus., Christian Room; V. and A. Mus., 303—1887 (from Akhmîm), 2063—1900, 2150—1900, 2067—1900, 769 —1893. Cf. A. F. Kendrick, *Burlington Magazine*, 1905, p. 238.

original perhaps three hundred years older. Among the most remarkable fabrics of this class which may perhaps be regarded as Christian rather than Persian is the splendid piece with yellow eagles on a purple ground in the Church of St. Eusèbe, Auxerre,[1] and the cope at Metz, known as the Chape de Charlemagne, also with eagles,[2] on a ground of red. The pieces at Aix-la-Chapelle with swans and ducks[3] may also have been produced in the Christian East. The winged gryphons of the 'Suaire de Saint Siviard'[4] at Sens may be pseudo-Sassanian rather than actually Persian; the same may be the case with the nimbed cocks

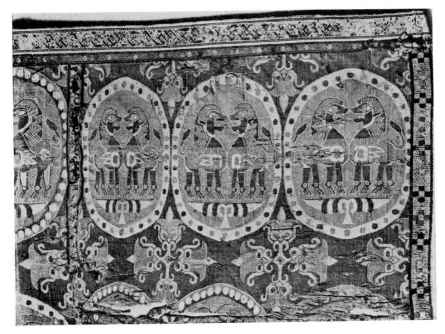

Fig. 373. Silk textile of the sixth–seventh century found in the Sancta Sanctorum, now in the Vatican Library.

and formal lions of the treasure of the Sancta Sanctorum[5] (Fig. 373). The number of textiles with animals dating from the First and Second Periods is considerable.[6]

The heraldic treatment of beasts or monsters, within or independent of circles or *rotellae*, was retained by the Byzantine weavers of the middle period,

[1] Migeon, 29 (Fig.); Schlumberger, *L'Épopée*, i. 409.
[2] Migeon, 30 (Fig.).
[3] Cahier and Martin, ii, Pl. XII; Schlumberger, *L'Épopée*, ii. 325.
[4] E. Molinier, *Exposition rétrospective*, 1900, 47.
[5] Ph. Lauer, *Mon. Piot*, xv, Pl. XVI and XVII; M. Dreger, in H. Grisar, *Die römische Kapelle Sancta Sanctorum*, p. 155.
[6] The following are prominent examples : —Victoria and Albert Museum, Nos. 8562–3—1863, 1241–64, No. 761—1893, the Sassanian bird-tailed gryphon ; No. 764—1893, fragment with head of a gryphon; No. 613—1891, fragment with eagles ; No. 753—1893, confronted lions with pairs of dogs set tail to tail; No. 2066—1900, formal 'tree' in medallion; another, from Akhmîm, with same design, No. 355—1887, &c. Paris, Musée Guimet : From Antinoe, Egypt, Necropolis C. and D., ibexes on buff ground; conventional trees and zebus: the trees buff, green, and red, the zebus red, on blue ground ; peacocks and peacocks' heads, confronted birds, winged horse. Sens : confronted lions on red ground (Cahier and Martin, ii, Pl. 39). Berlin : Kunstgewerbe-Museum, gryphons (Lessing, Pt. I, No. '84—226), the contours are 'curly' in the Chinese manner; the foliate ornament of the background is Chinese in character. Hildesheim Cathedral : Pairs of eagles, each separated by a 'tree'; in spandrels foliate ornament derived from the palmette, possibly a Western imitation of a Persian original (Lessing, Pt. II).

and with great success. A magnificent example is preserved in the Katholische Pfarrkirche at Siegburg. It is a silk fabric with great lions of a yellowish tint upon a purple ground, and the inscription, 'In the reign of Romanus and Christophorus, the most Christian emperors.'[1] The piece is thus dated at the close of the first quarter of the tenth century, as Romanus was crowned in A.D. 920, while his son Christophorus, named joint emperor in the following year, died in A.D. 931. The treatment of the lions is full of force and vigour; the conventional style is here used with all its effect.

Another dated piece of almost equal age is in the Kunstgewerbe-Museum at

Fɪɢ. 374. Silk textile, with names of Constantine VIII and Basil II, at Düsseldorf, made between A.D. 976 and A.D. 1025. (From a water-colour by Herr Paul Schulze in the Victoria and Albert Museum.)

Düsseldorf.[2] It also has lions upon a purple ground, and an inscription mentioning Constantine VIII and Basil II, showing that it must have been made between A.D. 976 and A.D. 1025 (Fig. 374).

Equal certainty is not to be attained with regard to the silk fabric with yellow elephants upon a red ground discovered in the shrine containing the remains of Charlemagne in the Cathedral of Aix-la-Chapelle.[3] Each elephant stands alone with a formal tree behind it in a medallion with a border of debased palmettes (Fig. 375); oval ornaments with similar palmettes fill the interspaces; green and blue are freely used for details. In one part of the stuff upon the red ground is a Greek inscription:—

'Under Michael, chief chamberlain and keeper of the privy purse, Peter

---

[1] Found in the shrine of St. Anne. Inscription: Ἐπὶ Ῥωμανοῦ καὶ Χριστοφόρου τῶν φιλοχρίστων δεσποτῶν. Lessing, *Gewebesammlung*, Pt. III; F. Bock, *Gesch. der liturgischen Gewänder*, iii. 167; *Bonner Jahrbücher*, Heft 46, 161, Pl. X; P. Clemen, *Die Kunstdenkmäler der Rheinprovinz*, v, Pt. IV, 1907, Pl. XX; G. Schlumberger, *Nicéphore Phocas*, 109, and *L'Épopée*, ii. 293 (figure only); *Gazette des Beaux-Arts*, Third Period, xxviii, 1902, 208; G. Migeon, *Les Arts du tissu*, 16.

[2] H. Frauberger, *Bonner Jahrbücher*, Heft 93, 1892, 224 ff.; Lessing, *Gewebesammlung*, Pt. III. Inscription: Ἐπὶ Κωνστα(τίν)ου καὶ Βασιλείου τῶν φιλοχρίστων δεσποτῶν. Other fragments at Berlin and Crefeld; G. Schlumberger, *L'Épopée*, 293.

[3] Cahier and Martin, *Mélanges d'arch. chrét.* ii. 234 ff. and Pl. IX–XI; F. Bock, *Zeitschrift des bayerischen Kunstgewerbe-Vereins*, 1894, 65 ff.; G. Schlumberger, *Nicéphore Phocas*, 437; M. Dreger, *Künstlerische Entwicklung*, &c., p. 64. Another smaller fabric of a violet colour was also found in the shrine.

being Archon of (the Manufactory) of Zeuxippos. In the second indiction.'[1] The identity of the officials mentioned cannot be determined with certainty, so that it is impossible to decide upon the precise indiction. It was formerly thought that the stuff might be almost of Charlemagne's time; but few are now disposed to ascribe it to so early a period. The shrine is known to have been opened about A.D. 1000 under the Emperor Otto, and again in the fifteenth century

FIG. 375. Part of the silk textile from the shrine of Charlemagne at Aix-la-Chapelle. (From a water-colour by Herr Paul Schulze in the Victoria and Albert Museum.)

at the orders of Louis XI,[2] so that a fabric of later date than the remains may well have been introduced. Opinions vary between the tenth and twelfth centuries. A fragment (Fig. 47) with an elephant motive allied to the preceding is in the Kunstgewerbe-Museum at Berlin.[3] Elephants are mentioned

---

[1] Ἐπὶ Μιχαὴλ πριμι(κηρίου) κοιτ(ωνίτου) καὶ εἰδικοῦ Πέτρου ἄρχοντ(ος) τοῦ Ζευξίππου ἰνδ. ιβ.

[2] It was opened again in 1810, and once more in recent years, when the latest reproductions (Lessing's) were taken. M. Diehl, at the Archaeological Congress held at Cairo in 1909, suggested that the textiles were probably inserted in the time of Otto, and that they date from the latter part of the tenth century. He points out that the title εἰδικός is first found in the middle of the ninth century, and that κοιτωνίτης never occurs in the eighth (*Compte rendu du Congrès International d'archéologie classique*, Cairo, 1909, 267).

[3] Lessing, *Gewebesammlung*; Prussian *Jahrbuch*, 1900, xxi and xxii (Museum Report); Smirnoff, in *V. V.*, vii. 609–10.

in mediaeval inventories as forming part of the decoration of various silk fabrics now destroyed. One such mention occurs in the inventory of St. Paul's Cathedral, London, dating from the latter part of the thirteenth century.

The textile found in the tomb of Bishop Günther in the Cathedral of Bamberg [1] was probably placed there at the time of the bishop's interment in the second half of the eleventh century; it may have been made only a few years earlier. When discovered it was in a great number of fragments; but after these had been pieced together it was found that only the heads of the emperor and his horse were destroyed.

The subject is a nimbed emperor [2] riding a white horse, richly caparisoned, to left, holding a jewelled labarum in his left hand, and wearing a crown, a long purple tunic, and blue mantle, with red buskins. Before and behind him stand

Fig. 376. Silk textile found in the coffin of St. Cuthbert, Durham, and now in the Chapter Library. (From a water-colour by J. J. Williamson in the Victoria and Albert Museum.)

two female personifications of cities in mural crowns, one offering a diadem, the other a crested helm. The ground is a diaper of green circles on purple, each circle containing a figure somewhat resembling the spade in cards, alternately pink and blue, the interspaces being filled with yellow lozenges. Above is a broad ornamental border in several zones, the larger filled with interconnected circles containing formal floral designs, and with similar but smaller circles containing debased palmettes. The emperor's purple tunic is diversified with 'clubs' and 'spades', and the borders, like the horse's trappings, are richly jewelled. Short jewelled streamers are attached to the animal's legs and tail.

Among the stuffs of the Third Period with heraldic animals, to be regarded

---

[1] Cahier and Martin. *Mélanges d'arch.*, ii. 251 ff., and Pl. XXXII-XXXIV; G. Schlumberger, *Nicéphore Phocas*, 365. Michel, 34 ff., doubted whether the subject is really inwoven and not rather embroidered. He noted a textile having a *historiam imperatoris* in Anastasius. An interesting fragment with an emperor in a chariot, perhaps of earlier date, is in the Victoria and Albert Museum (No. 762—1893).

[2] Kings and emperors are often represented with the nimbus in East-Christian art, even when their careers had made them detested by Christians. Thus in the Menologium of Basil (p. 479) Herod and Julian the Apostate are both nimbed.

as Saracenic rather than Byzantine reproductions of early Persian types, must be included that with confronted and chained tigers in the Church of St. Étienne, Chinon, if the inscription inwoven in it is Arabic.[1]   It is needless to linger over the numerous examples of this class, which are well represented in Lessing's work : M. Migeon has also discussed these fabrics.[2]

It remains to notice another textile which, though oriental, may not be Asiatic, and appears to be inspired by other artistic influences than those hitherto described.

The silk fabrics found in the coffin of St. Cuthbert at Durham include an example (Fig. 376) of an exceptional character, perhaps even as old as the fourth or early fifth century.[3]   A large medallion with a border of grapes and

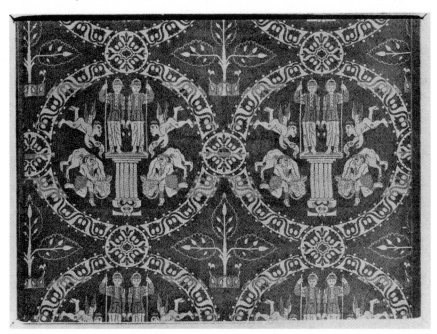

Fig. 377.   Silk textile of the sixth–seventh century with the Dioscuri : Crefeld.   (From a water-colour drawing by Herr Paul Schulze in the Victoria and Albert Museum.) P. 598.

other fruits encloses a ceremonial vessel (?) draped at each end, and containing other fruits.   It rises from water in which ducks and fish are swimming, while the interspaces between this and the other medallions which once covered the complete fabric were occupied by larger ducks, as two surviving examples prove.   This type of design seems essentially Egypto-Greek, recalling the Nilotic scenes of early mosaics (p. 328) ; it has little in common with Mesopotamian or Persian art, and is therefore an object of exceptional interest and importance. The other silks at Durham do not so directly concern us here.

[1] Michel, 40, 50 ; V. Luzarche, *La Chape de Saint Mesme de Chinon*, Soc. arch. de Touraine, March, 1851 ; Cahier and Martin, iii, Pl. XIII ; Migeon, *Les Arts du tissu*, 44–5.

[2] As above, ch. iv.   Cf. also 'Suaire de St. Potentien ', Sens (Schlumberger, *Nicéphore Phocas*, 133).

[3] J. Raine, *Saint Cuthbert*, 1828, Pl. V ; Dreger, as above, p. 32.   The ground is red, the principal other colours being yellow and purple.   The arguments used by Dr. Raine to prove that this textile was made for St. Cuthbert have no scientific value.   It seems to be certainly older than the time of the saint's death, and was probably one of the fabrics originally interred with the body.   Another fabric figured by Raine (Pl. IV), representing a mounted huntsman with a hawk and dog, is of Saracenic type, and must have been one of the stuffs placed with the body in A. D. 1104, when the tomb was opened (Raine, 196).

(b) Late Hellenic Motives.

Important as was the Persian inspiration, it naturally did not suffice for the requirements of Greeks, or Christians brought up in an atmosphere of Greek tradition. In all subjects requiring the introduction of the human figure late Hellenic influence was necessarily prominent. Subjects from pagan Greek mythology are not infrequent, and may have been introduced by the weavers of Syria and Asia Minor,[1] though even in these pieces ornamental motives of Persian origin often accompany figures of Greek derivation.[2] The fabric from the shrine of St. Servatius at Maestricht with the Dioscuri (?) is among the earliest.[3] The surface is covered by a continuous series of medallions connected at the four opposite points by small circles, and each containing a repetition of the same design. This consists of the Dioscuri standing side by side on an altar, to right and left of which fly genii pouring libations ; below, symmetrically disposed, are two men with steers for sacrifice. This piece has been described as work of the fourth century from Asia Minor, but may be conjectured to be of rather later date. A second example[4] with the same design is at Crefeld (Fig. 377). Another piece has a representation of Ganymede.[5] The busts and figures of Hellenic type upon Egyptian textiles have been already noticed, but the material is usually other than silk.

(c) Christian Subjects

As in the case of tapestry, distinctively Christian subjects soon found a place by the side of those of pagan origin ; examples of about the sixth century are preserved, and it is clear from their character that they must have been produced in a Christian community. At one time figured silks with sacred or scriptural subjects must have been very numerous :[6] they are now of great rarity. Most remarkable is the fragment in the treasury of the cathedral at Sens, with scenes from the life of Joseph in two zones, with accompanying Greek inscriptions.[7] The Daniel between the lions in the Benedictine Nunnery of Eichstädt in Bavaria is of later date.[8]

Special mention must be made of the beautiful Annunciation and Nativity fragments discovered in the relic-chest in the Sancta Sanctorum in the Lateran,[9] neither of which can be later than the sixth century (Fig. 378).

EMBROIDERY.

The method of working with the needle upon a finished textile with gold or coloured thread dates from very ancient times,[10] and accompanied the weaving

---

[1] For late Hellenic motives see Strzygowski, Prussian *Jahrbuch*, as above, and M. Dreger, as above, pp. 25, 35, &c. Cf. textile, man driving quadriga, in Louvre (Cahier and Martin, *Mélanges d'archéologie*, iv, Pl. XX) ; at Aix-la-Chapelle (S. Beissel, *Kunstschätze des Aachener Kaiserdomes*) ; Collection Liénard (G. Schlumberger, *L'Épopée*, ii. 36). The winged horse, seen on fragment from the Sancta Sanctorum (*Monuments Piot*, xv, 1906, 115, Fig. 19) and in a fabric from Antinoe in the Musée Guimet at Paris, is perhaps an oriental form rather than a representation of Pegasus. The ' Samson ' forcing open a lion's mouth, described as Christian, may possibly have been intended for Hercules (H. Semper, *Der Stil*, i. 437). Examples of this are in the Victoria and Albert Museum (Fig. 371), the Vatican (*Mon. Piot*, xv, 1906, Pl. XVIII), &c. Cf. Dreger, pp. 27, 31.

[2] On this mixture of influences see Strzygowski, *Jahrbuch*, as above, 166 ff.

[3] F. Fischbach, *Ornament of Textile Fabrics*, Pl. III ; A. Migeon, *Les Arts du tissu*, Fig. on p. 22.

[4] Fischbach, Pl. III.   [5] Lessing, Prussian *Jahrbuch*, i, 1880, 119–26.

[6] Anastasius mentions a great number of scenes from the life of Our Lord and the Virgin, enumerated by Michel, 22 ff. Old Testament subjects are far less frequent.

[7] Strzygowski, *Orient oder Rom*, 117 : Chartraire et Prou, *Mém. de la Soc. des Ant. de France*, lviii, 1899 ; Ch. de Linas, *Revue des Sociétés savantes*, ii, 1857 ; Ch. Diehl, *Justinien*, 399, Fig. 138 ; Gaussen, *Portefeuille archéologique de la Champagne* (coloured plates).

[8] Cahier and Martin, ii. 250, and Pl. XVIII. Cf. the piece with similar subject at Sens, the ' Suaire de Saint Victor ' (Schlumberger, *L'Épopée*. i. 405).

[9] Ph. Lauer, *Mon. Piot*, xv, 1906, Pl. XV and XVIII ; H. Grisar, *Die römische Kapelle Sancta Sanctorum*, Pl. VI, VII.

[10] Embroidery was in great request under all the early civilizations in Babylonia, Egypt, Phoenicia, and the Mediterranean. About the fifth century B.C. figured garments went out

of figured stuffs throughout the period with which we are concerned. While silk-weaving and tapestry-weaving flourished it was, however, of less conspicuous importance than it became in the later centuries. Akhmîm and other sites have furnished a number of examples, chiefly with human figures, some dating perhaps from the century before the Arab occupation.[1] The most important surviving examples of embroidery date, however, from the twelfth to the fourteenth centuries. A few of these may be mentioned.

Fig. 378. The Annunciation: silk textile of the sixth–seventh century from the Sancta Sanctorum, now in the Vatican Library.

The *omophorion* at Grottaferrata,[2] by some still ascribed to a date as early as the twelfth or thirteenth century, is by others placed as late, or almost as late, as the inscription upon it (A.D. 1618). It is embroidered with New Testament scenes: the Annunciation, Nativity, Baptism, Entry into Jerusalem, Transfigura-

of fashion in Greece, but after Alexander's time they regained favour, and were increasingly used under the Roman Empire. See article *Phrygio* in Daremberg and Saglio. For Byzantine embroideries once belonging to Pope Paul II, see Muntz, *Les Arts à la Cour des Papes*, ii, p. 207. also F. Bock, *Gesch. der liturgischen Gewänder*, ch. ii.

[1] Examples in Victoria and Albert and other great museums. Figs. in R. Forrer, *Römische und byz. Seiden-Textilien aus . . . Achmim-Panopolis*, 13 and plates.

[2] Farabulini, *Arch. ed arte rispetto ad uno raro monumento greco*, Rome, 1883 ; *Gaz. des Beaux-Arts*, 1905, 501 ; *R. Q.*, 1905, 205 ; Muñoz, *L'Art byz. à l'Exposition de Grottaferrata*, 141–2 and Fig. 100 ; H. Grisar, *Civiltà Cattolica*, 1897, 220 ; N. Kondakoff, *Monuments d'art chrét. du Mont Athos*, 1902, 249. The *omophorion*, which roughly corresponds to the *pallium* of the Roman Church, is of white silk, and the embroidery is upon appliqué bands and panels, four of which are cruciform.

tion, Ascension, Pentecost, and Death of the Virgin. There is also a Panto-krator between angels, saints, and prophets.

A similar divergence of opinion has existed with respect to the so-called 'Dalmatic of Charlemagne' (Figs. 45, 380) in St. Peter's, Rome.[1] This famous

FIG. 379. Embroidery in silk, of sixth or seventh century, from **Egypt**.
(Victoria and Albert Museum.)

embroidery, which is of great beauty, was formerly assigned to any date from the time of Charlemagne down to about the eleventh century. As long as it was commonly believed that Byzantine art was incapable of producing anything

[1] A bibliography of the earlier literature is given by A. Colasanti, *Nuovo Bullettino di archeologia cristiana*, 1902, 155. The principal earlier publications are: S. Boisserée, *Über die Kaiser-Dalmatika*, &c., Munich, 1842; Didron, *Annales archéologiques*, i. 151, and xxv. 288; Bayet, *L'Art byz.*, 219; Pérate in *Gazette des Beaux-Arts*, Second Period, xxxvi, 1887, 166. See also *B. Z.*, ix, 1900, 606–7; Braun, in *Revue de l'art chrétien*, 1901, 52–4; *Arch. Journal*, iv. 286. A coloured reproduction is given in the *Art Workers' Quarterly*, Jan., 1906. But the finest is still that in F. Bock's *Kleinodien des Heiligen Römischen Reichs*. The principal defenders of an earlier date are Pérate and A. Colasanti, the latter arguing in favour of a period not later than the end of the eleventh or beginning of the twelfth century. On the other side are Braun and Dobbert (*Repertorium*, xv. 515). See also the ref., *B. Z.*, 1900, 606–7.

of merit after the sack of Constantinople in A. D. 1204 there was force in the
argument that such fine work as this could not be posterior to that date.   But
now that this belief has been abandoned the dalmatic is ascribed to the
fourteenth century, when embroidery was very extensively practised.   This is
the opinion of perhaps a majority among modern critics.

Four subjects are embroidered upon the dalmatic in gold and coloured silk

Fig. 380.   Embroidered dalmatic of the fourteenth century in the sacristy of St. Peter's,
Rome.   Cf. Fig. 45.   (Moscioni.)

thread upon a dark blue ground.   On the front Our Lord, beardless (Emmanuel
type, see p. 672), is seated on the globe holding an open book on which are
inscribed the words of Matthew xxv. 34 ; before him are the choirs of angels
and the orders of the saints.   The inscription is Ἡ ἀνάστασις καὶ ἡ ζωή.   On the
back is the Transfiguration.   On the two shoulders is seen the Communion of
the Apostles, on the back the Transfiguration (Fig. 45).

Two pieces of embroidery now forming an antependium belonging to the
Collegiate Church of Castell' Arquato were bequeathed in A.D. 1314 by the
Patriarch of Aquileia.[1]   The subjects are the two phases of the Communion of

---

[1] A. Muñoz, *L'Art byz. à l'Exposition de Grottaferrata*, 130 ff., and *L'Arte*, 1905, 165 ; Baumstark, *R. Q.*, 1905, 206 ; A. Venturi, *Storia*, ii. 355-6.

the Apostles. The ground is of red silk, the embroidery of gold and blue silk, the borders showing interlaced designs in green and two shades of blue. These embroideries, the original use of which is uncertain, may perhaps be reckoned among the earlier surviving examples of such work. The latest date as yet assigned them is approximately that of the death of the patriarch in A.D. 1314, while some suggest that they were already of some age at the time of the bequest and that they may go back to the eleventh or twelfth century.

Among the finer pieces of embroidery are various *epitaphioi* or 'shrouds', used in the Eastern Church upon Good Friday to cover the ceremonial bier of Christ. The central subject embroidered upon them is the dead Christ mourned by angels, the Virgin, St. John, other Apostles, and holy women. One in the Church of St. Clement at Ochrida, Macedonia, has the name of Andronicus II Palaeologus, and is of his time (A.D. 1282–1328).[1] The Christ lies on the bier, behind which are angels with *rhipidia* or liturgical fans. Another at Salonika is of the fourteenth century at latest.[2] More recent examples of the sixteenth and seventeenth centuries are in the Monasteries of Dionysiu, Dochiaru, and Chilandari on Mount Athos.[3] Shrouds and other embroideries of Moldavian, Servian, and Russian origin are discussed and reproduced by Kondakoff.[4]

In the Treasury of S. Marco at Venice there is an *epitaphios*, while in the same place is another embroidery on violet silk with SS. Michael and Gabriel holding sceptres and orbs, and an inscription describing it as the gift of Constantine Comnenus, cousin of the Emperor Manuel.[5] Most of the old oriental textiles in S. Marco were destroyed in the fire of A.D. 1234.

FABRICS WITH PRINTED DESIGNS, AND OTHER STUFFS.

Very interesting among East-Christian textiles, and perhaps among the earliest of Christian figured stuffs, are the linen fabrics printed by reserve, found in Egyptian cemeteries (chiefly Akhmîm) and represented in various large collections. Some of the finer specimens in Germany and Austria have been discussed by Strzygowski,[6] who observes that they were produced by a process known to Pliny as practised in Egypt. The subjects are represented or outlined in the natural colour of the linen upon grounds dyed blue or red, and it is clear that before the stuff was immersed in the dyeing bath they were in some way protected from contact with the colour. Pliny[7] says that they were treated by an agent which counteracted the effect of the dye. An ethnographical parallel suggests that what was used was not any mysterious *medicamentum*, but simply wax. In Java and Sumatra the method of ornamenting figured cloths (*batik*)

---

[1] Miliukoff, in *Izviestiya* of the Russian Arch. Inst. at Cple., iv, 1899 ; N. Kondakoff, *Monuments of Christian Art on Mount Athos*, 1902, 263 (Russian), and *Macedonia*, 1909, 243, Pl. IV. This shroud has Evangelists' symbols at three corners, that of St. Mark being replaced by a figure of a ciborium, with Greek inscriptions. The inscription is :

Μέμνησο ποιμὴν Βουλγάρων ἐν φυσίαις
Ἄνακτος Ἀνδρονίκου Παλαιολόγου.

[2] Kondakoff, *Athos*, p. 266 ; Letourneau and Millet in *B. C. H.*, xxix, 1905, 259 ff.

[3] Kondakoff, *Athos*, Pl. XLI–XLIII.

[4] *Athos*, 264–5, 267 ff., Pl. XXXIX, XL, XLIV, XLV ; *Macedonia*, 243 ff. See also D. V. Ainaloff, *Transactions of the Eighth Arch. Congress held at Moscow in 1890* (Moscow, 1897), 220 ff. and Plates.

[5] Ongania, *Il Tesoro di San Marco*, 77–8 and Pl. XIX ; *Gaz. des Beaux-Arts*, Second Period, xxxvii, 1888, 392.

[6] *Orient oder Rom*, 90 ff. ; Dreger, pp. 30 ff. ; Diehl, *Manuel*, p. 78.

[7] Cf. *Inlinentes non coloribus sed colorem sorbentibus medicamentis* (*Nat. Hist.*, xxxv. 42). It seems probable that Pliny was not altogether clear as to the process. He says that the fabric, when the design has been protected, is plunged for a short time *in cortinam pigmenti ferventis*. There is no reason why the dye should be boiling ; on the other hand, a second immersion in boiling *water* would be necessary to remove the wax. Pliny appears to have misunderstood his informant, and compressed two distinct parts of the process into one. See Sir Stamford Raffles, *History of Java*, 2nd ed., i. 188.

Fig. 381.   Linen cloth of about the fifth century, printed by reserve, from Egypt.   (Victoria and Albert Museum.)

is as follows.[1]   The part intended to form the background is painted over with hot wax.   The cloth is then dipped in the dye, which stains every part not covered with wax.   When the dye is fast, the cloth is boiled, by which means the wax is removed and the pattern appears in the chosen colour in strong relief against the light ground.   The Javanese do not rest content with two colours, but produce polychrome designs, repeating the process already described, but now waxing the whole ground and only leaving unwaxed such portions of the design in neutral tint as they wish to stain red, or whatever the second colour may be.   The method may obviously become a three or four-colour process ; but as it is very tedious the number of tints is not usually large.   In the Egyptian examples only one bath of dye appears to have been used as a rule.

The more remarkable examples of these printed textiles are worthy of special attention.   They include large fragments at Berlin with Daniel[2] and Peter[3] receiving a book (the Psalter) from Our Lord, the subject being apparently akin to the *Traditio Legis* (see p. 664), fragments (all from one stuff ?) in the Victoria and Albert Museum (Nos. 721–3—1897, 1103—1900), in Berlin and Leipzig with the Virgin and Child, the Annunciation, saints, and scenes including Moses ;[4] the healing of the man with the dropsy ;[5] a piece in the collection of Dr. J. P. Richter, London, with SS. Mark, Peter, and Thomas on a blue ground ;[6] a large piece with figures before an altar belonging to Dr. Forrer ;[7] a piece on a green ground, now lost, with a scene from the life of Joseph.[8]

We may in conclusion allude to another kind of work frequently found in Coptic cemeteries.   The surface of the linen textile is worked into loops at frequent intervals, giving the whole a towel-like appearance.   Upon this a pattern is worked in coloured wool, frequently purple, drawn into long loops and tufts, again giving the effect of a thick towel.   The style was especially employed for hangings, such as the large example with *gammadia* at the corners in the Victoria and Albert Museum, attributed to the period between the sixth and ninth centuries ; other examples are assigned to the Roman period.

Influence of Textiles on the Arts.

It has already been remarked (pp. 88, 93, 103, 165, 182) that on account of their portability textiles at various times exerted an important influence upon other arts, more especially those of mosaic, mural painting, and sculpture : among such textiles those woven of silk were probably the most important.   It has often been observed that such mosaics as those in the vaulted roofs of Sta Costanza at Rome bear a resemblance to those silk textiles in which the field is divided into lozenge-shaped compartments each containing its own subject ; some of the early frescoes have a similar affinity, for example at Kuṣeir ʿAmra (p. 280), while mosaic pavements may have been first suggested by the figured carpets produced in ancient times in the Nearer East.   We seem to trace a similar influence in enamels ornamented with beasts and trees of oriental type, such as those on the *pala d'oro* in S. Marco, Venice (p. 512).

---

[1] A photograph of Javanese women making *batik* is published in *The Women of all Nations*, ed. by T. A. Joyce and N. W. Thomas, 181.

[2] *Orient oder Rom*, Pl. IV.   The background red.   In the Kunstgewerbe-Museum.

[3] Ibid., Pl. V.   In very bad condition.   As Strzygowski notes, the same subject adorned one of the curtains suspended from the ciborium of Santa Sophia at Constantinople.   See Paulus Silentiarius' metrical description in Salzenberg's *Altchristliche Baudenkmale*, xviii, and *Orient oder Rom*, 100, 101.

[4] A Moses fragment in the collection of Dr. Reinhardt is figured by Strzygowski, Pl. VI. Moses receives the Tables of the Law ; in an upper zone there appears to have been subjects from the New Testament.   The background is blue.

[5] *Orient oder Rom*, Pl. VII.

[6] R. Forrer, *Die Zeugdrucke der byzantinischen Kunstepochen*, 11 and Pl. II. 2, and *Kunst des Zeugdruckes*, 10.

[7] *Zeugdrucke*, 11 and Pl. II, Fig. 2.

[8] *Orient oder Rom*, 109.

The early sculptured slabs in low relief which were produced throughout the Mediterranean area from the sixth to the eleventh century (p. 165) certainly owe much to figured hangings.[1]   The effect of textile motives upon minor sculpture in ivory is apparent in the case of the ivory casket at Darmstadt.[2]

The ornament of Western Romanesque sculpture probably owes much to the influence of oriental models transmitted by means of textiles produced in Persia or the Byzantine provinces from the sixth to the twelfth century.[3]   This is especially evident in the case of capitals of columns, where confronted beasts and 'sacred trees' betray their Iranian or Mesopotamian origin.   An example specially quoted is a capital in the Church of Urcel, with two confronted lions recalling such textiles as that at Le Mans.[4]   We have already seen that Sassanian textiles were copied by the Chinese about the seventh century (p. 591), and it is possible that the Chinese conception of the lion was modified by Persian models woven in silk.[5]

[1] W. Lowrie, *Atti* of the Eleventh Int. Congress of Christian Archaeology held in Rome, 1900 (Rome, 1902), 43 ff. (especial reference to a large curtain with *gammadia* from Egypt, resembling carved slabs in S. Clemente, Rome, &c.); Sesselberg in *Zeitschrift des deutschen Palästina-Vereins*, xxiv. 152.

[2] H. Graeven, *Bonner Jahrbücher*, xii, 1903, 431.

[3] Lenormant in Cahier and Martin's *Mélanges d'arch. chrétienne*, i ; A. Springer, *Ikonographische Studien* in *Mitth. der k. k. Central-Commission*, Vienna, 1860, v. 66 ff. ; Durand in Didron's *Annales archéologiques*, xxv, 1865, 152 ; *B. Z.*, 1908, 293.

[4] *Gazette des Beaux-Arts*, 1876, 402–3, the Fig. reproduced from Ch. Cahier's *Nouveaux Mélanges d'archéologie*.

[5] Metal-work probably shared in the dissemination of Persian influence.   A Sassanian ewer of metal is in the same Japanese treasure-chamber where the silk is preserved.

CHAPTER XI

VARIOUS: POTTERY AND GLASS, METAL-WORK, WEIGHTS, COINS, SEALS, ENGRAVED GEMS, &c.

POTTERY.

THE ceramic art of the Christian East is most abundantly illustrated by unglazed ware of the First and Second Periods: later periods are at present imperfectly illustrated.

The plain red or buff earthenware employed for common utensils in Roman and earlier times naturally continued to be made in later cen-

FIG. 382.   Pottery ampulla of the sixth century from Egypt : St. Menas between two monsters.   (British Museum.)

turies; it is the material of the innumerable lamps and ampullae yielded by excavations in all the Mediterranean countries, the latter group being chiefly represented by the flasks brought by pilgrims from the well-known shrine of St. Menas at Alexandria.[1]   Certain votive terra-cotta disks found in the Tauric Chersonese and bearing figures of saints seem to have also belonged to the class of εὐλογίαι, but since the designs are sunk, they

---

[1] See Index to *B. Z.*, 1909, s.v. *Ampullen* ; M. A. Murray, British Museum, *Catalogue of Early Christian and Byz. Ant.*, 54 : Wulff, *Berlin Catalogue*, i. 263 ff. ; K. M. Kaufmann, *Ausgrabung der Menas-Heiligthümer*, Cairo, 1906, and *Die Menasstadt*, 1910.   Kaufmann believes that the flasks were filled with water.   For St. Menas and his legend see *Revue de l'orient chrétien*, 1908, 212 ff. The ' camels ' to right and left of St. Menas are now explained as sea monsters.   See E. A. W. Budge, *Texts relating to St. Mena*, 1909 ; and Chaine in *Rev. de l'orient chrét.*, 1908, 212–18 ; *B. Z.*, xix, 1910, 157.

may have been used to stamp cakes given to pilgrims.[1] These may be also of about the sixth century.

A finer red ware with impressed designs was also made in Egypt,[2] where also ware with figure reliefs resembling *terra sigillata* occurs at an early date (Fig. 386). Excavations in the same country have given us a paler unglazed ware with figures painted in black outline, sometimes on a white slip. Such are numerous vases and vessels in the Kaiser Friedrich Museum and at Cairo, and fragments from Bawit painted with

FIG. 383. Pottery lamps of about the sixth century: that on the left an Egyptian or Syrian type; that on the right, with Jonah and the monster, of a type common in Carthage. (British Museum.)

human heads, birds, fishes, &c.[3] A fragment in the British Museum has a figure of a saint.

The number of lamps of unglazed red ware, chiefly dating from the fourth to the seventh centuries, is extremely large, and all great museums contain examples.[4] They are especially numerous from North Africa, Egypt, and Syria-Palestine, those with inscriptions in relief usually coming from Egypt or Palestine. Three terra-cotta medallions in the Treasury of Monza with figure subjects were probably brought from the

---

[1] Latysheff in *V. V.*, vi. 344 ff. SS. Phocas and George, with Greek inscriptions.

[2] Examples in the British Museum, *Catalogue*, Nos. 923 ff. and refs.; Garrucci, *Storia*, Pl. 466.

[3] J. Clédat, *Mém. de l'Inst. franç. d'arch. orientale du Caire*, xii, 1904, 12, 66–7, 71, 147.

[4] British Museum, *Cat. of Early Christian and Byz. Ant.*, pp. 138 ff., with references; Wulff, *Berlin Catalogue*, i. 243 ff.; Garrucci, *Storia*, Pl. 473–6; O. Pelka, *Koptische Altertümer im German-ischen National-Museum*, 1906, &c.

Holy Land, like the well-known metal ampullae.[1] The large disk in the
Barberini Library, with Christ seated among six Apostles, while in
the foreground people stand with suppliant gestures, may also be noticed.[2]

Small pottery figures of men and animals, apparently votive, have
been found in numbers on the site of the Menas shrine.[3]

The bricks and tiles used in East-Christian buildings were often
stamped with marks and monograms;[4] but these marks belong to the
province of epigraphy rather than to that of art; and the material
composition of the bricks has little interest for the study of ceramics.
The same may be said of the clay sealings of wine jars, not strictly
pottery, since they were not fired.   Impressions with figure subjects
on pottery fragments, apparently of the sixth century, are of interest,
as for example one in the British Museum with St. Michael (Fig. 387).[5]

Great as is the variety of these objects of unglazed ware, their artistic
quality is seldom high, and perhaps the most attractive are the painted
jars and other vessels from Egypt, most of which are of the First Period.
East-Christian ceramic art becomes more interesting with the appearance
of wares covered with a vitreous glaze.

Siliceous glazes had been employed from very early times in Egypt,
and the blue or greenish Ushabti figures and other small objects so covered
go back to the third millennium B.C.   Pottery with a lead glaze[6] is thought
to have been first made in the first century B.C., when it appears on
various sites, at Alexandria, Tarsus in Asia Minor, and in the Allier district
of Gaul.[7]

It is interesting to note that green-glazed ware came into vogue in
China under the Han dynasty (B.C. 206–A.D. 220); and that a ceramic
revival of the fifth century is ascribed to potters from the Indo-Scythian
kingdom, who are reported to have improved the methods of producing
coloured glazes.[8]

Prof. Petrie's discovery in 1909–10, at the south end of Memphis, of
kilns for baking glazed pottery, with a large number of fragments of
vessels, is of much interest for the early history of glazing ware.[9] The date
is considered to be between A.D. 1 and A.D. 50, a fragment of a lamp of
known type permitting this conclusion.   The glazed sherds are of great
interest both from their colouring and their design.   The chief colour is
a deep indigo blue, lighter blues, manganese purple, and apple green.

---

[1] X. Barbier de Montault, *Bulletin monumental*, 5ᵉ série, xi, 1883, 144.

[2] Garrucci, *Storia*, Pl. 465–6.   [3] O. Wulff, *Berlin Catalogue*, i. 282 ff.

[4] Cf. tile in British Museum, *Cat. of Early Christian Antiquities*, No. 928.   Dr. Mordtmann's
Collection from Constantinople is in the Kaiser Friedrich Museum, Berlin, but not at present
catalogued (cf. O. Wulff, *Berlin Catalogue*, i. 298).   At the Mosque of Eski Djuma (Church of
Hagia Paraskevi), Salonika, the 'rectangular' monograms of early sixth-century type occur
upon loose bricks detached from the original building.

[5] *Catalogue*, No. 930.

[6] H. Mazard, *De la connaissance par les anciens des glaçures plombifères*, 1879.

[7] British Museum, *Catalogue of Roman Pottery*, by H. B. Walters, 1908, p. xi.

[8] S. W. Bushell, Introduction to the Catalogue of the J. P. Morgan Collection of Chinese
porcelain, 1907.

[9] W. M. F. Petrie, *Memphis and Meydum*, 1910.

The designs are almost entirely Persian, showing little, if any, direct Greek influence. Winged bulls, confronted beasts, 'sacred tree', &c., all occur; and the problem arises whether this Persian character points to some oriental revival of the art of making glazed pottery. A question of even greater interest concerns the employment of tin glaze. There seems no particular reason why such a glaze should not have been used about the beginning of our era, as it was certainly known in more ancient times.[1] It is possible that the Constantine bowl in the British Museum [2] may

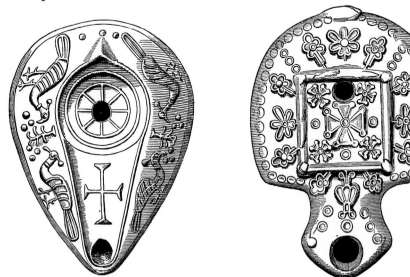

FIG. 384.   Two terra-cotta lamps of about the sixth century : that on the left from Beyrut, that on the right from Abydos, Egypt. (British Museum.)

afford an example of this, though the opaque white of its surface may be produced by applying a clear glaze over a white slip. The bowl has in the interior (Fig. 385), under the glaze, an incised figure of Our Lord and an inscription relating to Constantine and Fausta, showing it to have been made before A.D. 329. The exterior is ornamented with a chequer of blue and white.

The Constantine bowl stands alone, and we know little of the art of making fine glazed ware in Early Christian times. But as glazed pottery appears at the beginning of the Arab occupation in Egypt, and lustred glazed ware with Cufic inscriptions not later than the tenth century has been found in the ruins of Fostât,[3] the conclusion is suggested that an

---

[1] Oxide of tin was used for glazing Babylonian bricks (De la Beche and Reeks, *Catalogue of Specimens illustrative of the Composition and Manufacture of British Pottery and Porcelain*, 30–2).

[2] *Catalogue of Early Christian and Byz. Ant.*, No. 916. The authenticity of this bowl, once doubted by Strzygowski (*Orient oder Rom*, 61 ff.), is now accepted by him (*B. Z.*, x. 734, xi. 671), and he has defended it against a more recent attack by Mgr. Wilpert. Ceramic experts who have examined this interesting object do not believe it to be of modern date.

[3] Dr. F. R. Martin considers that the oldest lustred ware was intended to imitate gilding (*Burlington Magazine*, xvii, April, 1910, 46). He says that in the oldest pieces no Mohammedan ornament is seen, only such designs as occur on the Coptic red earthenware painted in black (fish, birds, &c.). Arab examples occur of the Tulunid, or at any rate pre-Fatimite, period. Dr. Martin thinks that the makers of the beautiful Fatimite lustre were probably Copts.

advanced ceramic art flourished in the country without intermission, and that the Saracenic potters were instructed by the Copts. Dr. A. J. Butler, who developed this view,[1] rightly supported it by allusion to the general prosperity of industrial Egypt in the period just prior to the Moslem invasion.[2] It seems quite probable that the finer ceramic products of Syria and Persia, dating from the thirteenth and later centuries, were first inspired by Egyptian potters who left the Nile valley after the

Fig. 385.   Interior of the ' Constantine bowl' of glazed earthenware: fourth century.
(British Museum.)   P. 609.

destruction of Fostât in the middle of the twelfth century. The mounds of Fostât have yielded, in addition to these finer wares, bowls and fragments of glazed sgraffiato ware, in which the clay body is first coated with a slip, the design then incised in the slip so as to expose the ground, and the whole finally covered with a lead glaze. It is remarkable that while Mohammedan potters in Asia continued the finer Egyptian process of lustre, the Christian potters of the Mediterranean area seem to have confined themselves to such incised and lead-glazed pottery. This is almost all that we have to show as 'Byzantine', though much of it seems by no means exclusively Greek. It is widely diffused, being found at Con-

[1] *Burlington Magazine*, October, 1909, 19 ff.
[2] See his earlier work, *The Arab Conquest of Egypt*, ch. vii and xxiv, and p. 490.

stantinople itself,[1] on the Black Sea[2] (Chersonese, Theodosia, &c.), in the Caucasus, at Ephesus, at Salonika, at Sparta, and bears a close resemblance to the *tazze* found in Cyprus and the Italian sgraffiato ware of the period between the thirteenth and fifteenth centuries.[3] Less common than the sgraffiato fragments are those with a similar glaze but with subjects in relief apparently impressed with a mould.[4]

It seems reasonable to infer that Egypt was the centre from which

Fig. 386. Terra-cotta relief of the fourth–fifth century, perhaps imitating a figure on an ivory diptych : Cairo Museum. (*Catalogue-général : Koptische Kunst*, No. 8978.) P. 607.

this glazed ware spread to the various countries where Egyptian commerce penetrated. The style of decoration is everywhere similar; and though Constantinople itself and parts of Anatolia are at present regarded as the chief centres of its later production, it may well be that it was

---

[1] J. Ebersolt, *Cat. des poteries byz. et anatoliennes du Musée de Constantinople*, 1910.

[2] Examples in the Stieglitz Museum at St. Petersburg. Cf. V. de Bock, *Poteries vernissées du Caucase et de la Crimée* in *Mémoires de la Société des Antiquaires de France*, lvi, 1897, 1–62; Von Stern, *Theodosia and its Ceramics*, Odessa, 1906 (German and Russian). The route from Egypt to Russia may have been via Syria and Arménia. Cf. also N. Kondakoff, *Russian Treasures*, i. 41, and *B. Z.*, xvii. 282.

[3] Orvieto, Viterbo, and Siena appear, by civic records, to have been the most ancient centres of mediaeval ceramic art in Italy (A. Imbert, *Ceramiche Orvietane dei Secoli XIII e XIV*, Rome, 1909 : M. Solon's review, *Burlington Magazine*, October, 1909, 10 ff.).

[4] Examples in the Victoria and Albert Museum and at Berlin have been finely reproduced by Mr. Henry Wallis in his *Byzantine Ceramic Art*. The same author has discussed other pieces of interest in *Persian Ceramic Art in the Collection of Mr. F. Ducane Godman*, 1891, Appendix, 39 ff. For the Berlin examples see O. Wulff, *Berlin Catalogue*, ii, 1911, nos. 2002 ff. and Pl. XVIII, XXIX.

produced at a number of different sites situated at considerable distances from each other. The common feature lies in its somewhat primitive character. Pottery of this kind is easy to make, and is apt to appear at any period when the manufacture of superior wares is either unknown or in abeyance: the sgraffiato slip-wares made in England in the seventeenth century afford a case in point. Probably the mediaeval potters of the Mediterranean countries made this simple ware because they were unable to rival the fine pottery which Egypt,

FIG. 387. Stamp of the sixth century on red pottery fragment. (British Museum.) P. 608.

Syria, and Mesopotamia had long manufactured; and if such pottery really represents Byzantine achievement in the Third and Fourth Periods, then the East-Roman Empire was behind the Mohammedan states in ceramic art and in no sense their teacher. It may be that far finer wares may be discovered when systematic excavations are undertaken; and it is difficult to believe that so elaborate a civilization as that of the East-Roman Empire, so luxurious, so distinguished for skill in other industrial arts, should have remained content with a proficiency in ceramics of which a Persian would have been ashamed.[1] Future research may have surprises in store; if it leads to no more profitable results than those at present attained, it will be necessary to conclude that the people of the Byzantine Empire preferred to make all their finer vessels of other materials than clay. The circular disks or dishes of faience inlaid in the walls of churches in parts of Greece,[2] especially the Morea and Mount Athos,[3] and ornamented with rosettes, concentric circles, floral and geometrical designs, are attributed to Rhodes or Constantinople, but it seems probable that they are of Mohammedan origin.

GLASS.

(See also chapter on *Enamel*, p. 494.)

Of East-Christian glass we know even less than of East-Christian pottery. More fragile and far more subject to decay, it has survived in lamentably few examples.

In the vitreous, as in the ceramic art, Egypt led the way. It is well known that Roman Italy developed the manufacture of glass through her close connexion with that country,[4] and the influence of Alexandria

---

[1] Theophilus (*Diversarum artium schedula*, ii, ch. xvi) ascribes painted ware to 'the Greeks', the designs being 'circles or arches or squares, and in them beasts, birds, or leaves'. The description cannot refer to the sgraffiato wares, as there is mention of colours, ground singly, with which the painting is done. Cf. H. Wallis, *Persian Ceramic Art* (Godman Collection), as above, 45.

[2] Luka, Chrysapha, Mistra; in Argolis at Merbaka, &c. (A. Struck, *Vier byz. Kirchen der Argolis* in *Ath. Mitth.* 1909, 227. See also Karabacek, *Zur muslimischen Keramik*, in *Oesterr. Monatsschriften für den Orient*, 1885).

[3] Iviron, Lavra, &c. (H. Brockhaus, *Die Kunst in den Athosklöstern*, 254 ff.).

[4] E. Dillon, *Glass* (The Connoisseur's Library), ch. iii. After Justinian's edict of A.D. 529, Egyptian glass-makers are said to have dispersed themselves over the empire (Kondakoff, *Enamel*, 78).

extended through the Asiatic no less than through the European provinces. In Roman times the Holy Land and Syria were great centres of production, but the plainer kinds of glass must have been produced in many places. Documentary evidence is not abundant. The Theodosian Code mentions, among craftsmen exempt from certain taxation, *Vitrearii, vasa vitrea conflantes*;[1] while Constantine Porphyrogenitus states that the Emperor Romanus Lecapenus sent seventeen glass vessels to Italy, though he omitted to describe their nature.[2] Illustrations of vessels, which from their transparency are presumably of glass, are not infrequent in illuminated

Fig. 388.   Glass bowl with enclosed gold ornament from Canosa, probably made in Egypt in the third century A. D.   (British Museum.)

MSS., mosaics, and frescoes. Such are the small phials with globular body and straight neck seen upon the desks of the seated Evangelists whose portraits are placed at the beginning of their Gospels.[3]   In the mosaics on the north wall of the Church of St. Demetrius at Salonika, which are not later than the sixth century, we see a hanging lamp apparently of glass. This object has a foot, and bears a general resemblance to Saracenic and Turkish mosque lamps of the thirteenth and later centuries, though it is apparently of plain undecorated glass.

The well-known gilded glasses of the Roman catacombs need not all be of Egyptian origin, though the connexion of this kind of decoration with Egypt is demonstrated by the existence of pre-Christian examples which can only have been made in Alexandria; such are the bowls from Canosa (Fig. 388) now in the British

---

[1] Cf. Dillon, as above, 96.
[2] *De Caerimoniis,* ii, xlv, p. 661 (Bonn edition).   Cf. also J. Fowler, *Archaeologia,* xlvi, p. 93.
[3] e. g. British Museum, Arundel MS. 547, Gospels of the tenth century, miniature representing St. Mark.

Museum.[1] But the iconographical types bear evidence of oriental influence, for instance the scene known as the *Traditio Legis* (p. 664).[2] Theophilus, the mediaeval writer on technical processes of the industrial arts, asserts that in his time gilded glass cups were still made 'by the Greeks', who protected the gilded designs by an upper layer of glass in the old fashion.[3] It is possible that work of this kind may have come to his notice in Sicily.

Certain objects disinterred from cemeteries in the district of Caltagirone in Sicily are perhaps typical of the kind of glass-ware in use in the Mediterranean in the earlier Middle Ages.[4] The types include plain beakers and jugs, and there are beads of various forms and colours. In the cemeteries have occurred coins of Maurice Tiberius (A.D. 582–601), and the interments are considered pre-Mohammedan. The beaker with expanding lips, a type known on other sites of Roman date, assumes a form recalling that of the richly enamelled Saracenic glasses of later times, to which it probably formed a transition. It may well be, as Orsi maintains, that the great centre of diffusion for glass vessels and beads was Syria ; it was to Syrian technical traditions that both the Venetian and the Saracenic glass-workers owed their inspiration. Polychrome beads from these Sicilian interments are rare ; but they exist, and present an analogy to those of Castel Trosino and of early Teutonic graves in Central and West Europe and in England ; a similar analogy exists in the case of bronze buckles, which in Sicily are sometimes ornamented with Greek cruciform monograms.[5] Of other glass belonging to the First Period we know little or nothing. The small glass money-weights,[6] of which examples are found in several museums,[7] are chiefly of the sixth century, and are of interest from the names of the officials moulded in relief upon their upper surfaces ; but technically they are unimportant, being composed of a common greenish glass of a single tint (Fig. 389). Similar in character are certain small flat circular pendants for necklaces, found chiefly in Syria, with the Good Shepherd and other early subjects.[8]

The most remarkable of the rare surviving examples of Byzantine glass are of the Third Period, and preserved in the Treasury of S. Marco at Venice. We may notice in the first instance the fine cup with enamelled and gilded ornament.[9] The method of decorating glass by designs painted upon the surface and fixed by a subsequent firing had been employed in Roman times. But in the examples presumed to be of Roman date the designs are thinly applied ; they lack the gem-like brilliance and depth of the oriental enamelled glass, which began in the twelfth century and reached its climax in the beautiful mosque lamps, bowls, beakers, flagons, and candlesticks of the two centuries which followed.[10] These qualities the cup in San Marco in some measure possesses, and this perhaps affords some reason for ascribing it to a later date than the Roman period.[11] The cup, which is of purple glass, is of small size (height,

[1] H. Vopel, *Altchristliche Goldgläser* (in J. Ficker's series) ; Dalton, in *Archaeological Journal*, lviii, 1901, 225 ff., where the Canosa bowls are figured. In the 'gilded glasses' the subjects are reserved in gold-foil, in which the details are etched, and the whole is protected by a second layer of glass fused to the first.
[2] O. Wulff, *Repertorium*, xxiii. 318 ff.
[3] *Schedula diversarum artium*, ii, ch. 15. Published in R. Hendrie's London edition, 1847, and by Ilg in Eitelberger's *Quellenschriften*, vii, 1874.
[4] Orsi, *B. Z.*, 1910, 70 ff.   [5] *B. Z.*, as above, 72.
[6] A useful list is given by Seymour de Ricci, *Proc. Soc. Bibl. Arch.*, xxiv, 1901, 56–7 and 97–107. See also *B. Z.*, vii, 1898, 603 (Mordtmann) ; *B. C. H.*, xxxi, 1907, 321 ff. (Grégoire) ; *Échos d'orient*, 1907, 199, 302 (L. Petit).
[7] Those in the British Museum are described in the *Catalogue of Early Christian and Byzantine Antiquities*, Nos. 660 ff.   [8] Ibid., Nos. 697 ff.
[9] Ongania, *La Basilica di San Marco*, Pl. XL, No. 78, and XLI, No. 82; Molinier, *Le Trésor de la basilique de Saint-Marc*, 58 ff. ; E. Dillon, *Glass*, 66 and 102. See also J. Tikkanen, *Acta Societatis Scientiarum Fennicae*, xvii. 321.
[10] Oriental enamelled glass was probably first made in Egypt, but Syria soon became distinguished for its manufacture. Venice learned to enamel glass in the fifteenth century.
[11] Most earlier critics, and lately Mr. Dillon, have maintained the Roman date. Molinier, Tikkanen and others consider it Byzantine.

0·080 m. ; diam. 0·120 m.) and mounted in silver-gilt in a Byzantine style. Round the body are seven enamelled medallions containing figure subjects of a purely pagan character, and in the interspaces between these are smaller medallions each containing a head in profile with golden diadem, and suggesting the imitation of coin types. In the interior of the rim, and at the base of the cup, are bands of pseudo-Cufic inscription, thinly applied and not laid on in impasto like the remaining decoration. The classical style of the figure subjects has doubtless decided many in favour of the first centuries of our era. The early date granted, it is easy to suppose the inscriptions a later addition, especially as they differ somewhat from the figures in the manner of their application. But the non-Christian character of the figures is not itself an important factor : it is found on the well-known Byzantine ivory caskets, which it seems impossible to assign to so early a period as the fourth century (p. 214) ; and these caskets are also decorated with heads resembling coin types in small medallions. In addition to this, the Cufic inscriptions appear to be illegible, as if they had been used as mere decoration by an artist who did not understand their meaning. But as such use of Cufic is a recognized feature in Byzantine ornament (p. 711), it appears on the whole preferable to follow Molinier in giving

Fig. 389.   Glass money-weights of the sixth century.   (British Museum.)

the cup to Byzantine rather than Roman art, and ascribing it to the ninth or tenth century.

The Treasury of S. Marco contains, among many chalices, bowls, lamps, and patens,[1] several of glass which are probably of Byzantine origin. They are of clear or greenish glass, the ornament, where it exists, taking the form of conical or button-like projections, apparently applied, or ringed disks and other motives sculptured in the glass body. Some are sculptured with animals in relief; these are of oriental appearance and perhaps of oriental origin, recalling similar objects carved in rock crystal. The patens assume the form of the plate or the shallow bowl ; the lamps are bucket shaped or resemble a balance-pan.[2] One has an inscription on its silver mount mentioning Zachariah, Archbishop of Iberia, a fact which may possibly connect this group of glass vessels with Georgia. The conical glass cups used for insertion in the metal *coronae* or *polycandela* (cf. Fig. 395) suspended in churches, and probably also in houses, are not represented in the treasury ; they must have been in use from the early centuries of our era, as they are mentioned by Paul the Silentiary as contributing to the illumination of Santa Sophia in A.D. 563.[3] As small, common, and easily broken objects they were naturally more exposed to

---

[1] *Lamps*—Pasini, Pl. LIV, Nos. 123–7 ; Dillon, Pl. XI. *Patens*—Pasini, Pl. XLIX, Nos. 107–10. *Chalices*—Pasini, Pl. XXXI, Nos. 76 and 77. M. Schlumberger has figured many, if not all, of these chalices and patens in his *Nicéphore Phocas* and *L'Épopée*. Mr. Dillon, pp. 100 ff., gives a convenient list of those vessels in Pasini's work which he regards as possibly of Byzantine manufacture. They are also enumerated, with references to Pasini's plates, in Molinier's *Le Trésor de la basilique de Saint-Marc*, Venice, 1888.

[2] The resemblance of certain lamps to a balance-pan is noted by Paul the Silentiary in his description of Sta Sophia. He says that such lamps had a single central light, and this may have been the earliest arrangement.

[3] 'Shaped like the οὐρίαχος or butt of the spear.' The passage is given in Lethaby and Swainson's *The Church of Sancta Sophia*, 50 ff. This form was used independently of a metal mount in the early Middle Ages in the West ; it is frequently seen suspended from ciboria or arches in illuminated MSS. of Carolingian or Romanesque date.

destruction than vessels of greater worth, and would not have been brought to Italy by crusaders. The small apertures in the pierced marble plates filling church windows were probably filled with glass.

Glass pastes simulating engraved gems, familiar to the Greeks and Romans, were probably known in the East-Roman Empire as long as intaglio and cameo gems remained popular ; but actual examples are practically unknown in the First Period. To the Third Period belongs a class of rather large cameo pastes, usually oval, with figures of Our Lord, the Virgin, and saints with their names beside them. Some examples have the descriptive names in Greek, others in Latin, yet the style is in both cases very similar. They have been discovered in the most widely distant sites : at Akhmīm (Panopolis) in Egypt, at Smyrna, at Athens ; and we may perhaps surmise that the manufacture began in the East, providing models imitated by contemporary Western glass-makers. These pastes, which are to be found in most large museums, are for the most part of about the twelfth century. Greek examples in the British Museum represent Our Lord, the Virgin, and SS. Theodore, Demetrius, and Nicholas.[1]

Fig. 390.   Cameo glass pastes of about the twelfth century.   (British Museum.)

Bronze Doors: Various Metal-work.

It may appear incongruous to include in a chapter containing miscellanea objects of so monumental a character as these church doors. But since Byzantine metal-work on a great scale is exceedingly rare, while on the other hand smaller objects in bronze are too miscellaneous, and often of too small merit, to call for description in a special chapter, the incongruity may perhaps be allowed to pass.

The decoration of the doors is chiefly by encrustation with silver, after the style illustrated on a small scale by the *exagia* (p. 621). The method, if not already practised on large objects as early as the sixth century, had certainly been extended to them by the ninth century, to which date the door of Ma'mun in the Mosque of Omar at Jerusalem is ascribed.[2] This style of damascening may well have been of Eastern introduction, and have been adopted in the empire in the First Period. Whether this

---

[1] *Catalogue*, Nos. 686 ff. Wulff, *Berlin Catalogue*, ii, p. 65, assigns these reliefs to Venice.

[2] A. D. 831 (Becker in *Zeitschrift für Assyriologie*, 1904, 105 ; M. von Berchem, *Inscriptions arabes de Syrie*, 8, and Pl. II, 4).

FIG. 391. Bronze door of the ninth century, Sta Sophia, Constantinople, with monograms
inlaid with silver. (Sébah and Joaillier.)

was so or not, it was always popular among the Moslems of Mesopotamia, Syria, and Egypt from the thirteenth century onwards, and was by them transmitted to Italy.[1]

The oldest and most beautiful of the Byzantine bronze doors are those of Sta Sophia, Constantinople, with inscriptions mentioning the Emperors Theophilus and Michael and the year A.D. 838.[2] The panels, which bear monograms and other ornament damascened in silver, are framed in borders cast in relief and enriched with bosses and scrolls, the whole in an admirable style (Fig. 391), suggesting that the founders, had they devoted themselves to the production of figures, would probably have left us work of no inconsiderable merit.

The examples still preserved in Italy[3] were mostly given by a rich merchant of Amalfi named Pantaleon, and by his son and grandson. This family possessed a house in Constantinople, and its members were familiar with contemporary Byzantine art. Those of Amalfi are composed of twenty-four plaques, twelve fixed upon the wood of each valve and framed by bands of metal fixed by nails. On sixteen of the plaques are nailed bronze crosses rising from divergent foliage. The four middle compartments bear the figures of Our Lord, the Virgin, St. Peter, and St. Andrew engraved or punched in outline. The lines are filled partly by hammered silver, partly by red and green enamel (?), and the faces and extremities are covered by thin plates of silver on which the features and details are first engraved, then filled with a black substance. A long inscription under the figure of St. Andrew indicates that the doors are the gift of Pantaleon, son of Mauro ; and as this personage is known to have been dead in A.D. 1066, the doors must be rather earlier than this date.[4] Six lions' heads with rings in their mouths serve as handles.[5] These were the doors which in A.D. 1066 must have excited the admiration of Desiderius, Abbot of Monte Cassino,[6] who ordered another pair for his own monastery, through Mauro, son of Pantaleon. His doors, still at Monte Cassino, are of a simpler design than those of Pantaleon. The decorated panels bear nothing but crosses like those at Amalfi ; on those undecorated is a long inscription giving the names of all the churches subordinated to the abbey.

In the year A.D. 1070 Pantaleon the younger, son of Mauro, presented to the Church of St. Paul without the Walls at Rome, served by Benedictines depending upon Monte Cassino, a pair of doors of far finer quality.[7] Here all the ornamentation was damascened or filled with niello (?). There was a whole series of figures of apostles, saints, and prophets, and scenes from the New Testament, from the Nativity to the Descent into Hell ; several compartments were occupied with crosses ; another had a long Latin inscription with the names of Pantaleon, Pope Alexander II, and the Archdeacon Hildebrand. Pantaleon himself was represented kneeling at the feet of St. Paul. These doors were seriously damaged by fire and now only fragments remain.

Six years later, in A.D. 1076, the same Pantaleon presented bronze doors to Monte Gargano.[8] The compartments are filled with damascened figures of

---

[1] 'Saracenic' metal-work (cisterns, bowls, candlesticks, salvers, writing-boxes, tables, &c.) is represented in the great museums in London, Paris, Berlin, and other cities, as also are the derivative products of the Venetian *azziminist.*

[2] Salzenberg, *Altchristliche Baudenkmäler von Constantinopel* ; Lethaby and Swainson, *The Church of Sancta Sophia at Constantinople.*

[3] E. Bertaux, *L'Art dans l'Italie méridionale,* i. 403 ff. ; H. W. Schulz, *Denkmäler der Kunst des Mittelalters in Unteritalien,* ii. 228–45.

[4] Bertaux, as above, 405.

[5] There is some doubt whether these were also made in Constantinople.

[6] See Wattenbach's edition of the Chronicles of Monte Cassino, *Mon. Germ. Script.,* vii. 711.

[7] D'Agincourt, *Histoire de l'art par les monuments,* iv, Pl. XIII–XX ; Bayet, *L'Art byzantin,* 206, Fig. 69 ; Bertaux, as above, 405–6 ; Nicolai, *Della basilica di San Paolo,* Rome, 1815, Pl. 11–17.

[8] Bertaux, 406 ; Schulz, i. 243 ff. and Atlas Pl. XXXIX ; Huillard-Bréholles, *Monuments des Normands,* &c., Pl. V ; S. Borgia, *Memorie di Benevento,* Rome, 1763, i. 177.

angels representing episodes from the victory over Lucifer down to the appearance of St. Michael to the Bishop of Siponto. The inscription mentions Pantaleon by name, states that the doors were cast in Constantinople, and contains a recommendation that they should be cleaned once a year in the manner explained by the donor.

In A. D. 1087 the son of this Pantaleon, himself bearing the same name, presented to the Church of Atrani near Amalfi doors almost identical with those given to the cathedral of that town about twenty years before:[1] the principal difference is that the figure of St. Sebastian replaces that of St. Andrew.

FIG. 392. Bronze weights, inlaid with silver : that on the left, 2 oz., that on the right, 3 oz. (British Museum.) P. 621.

In the same period of the eleventh century a noble of Salerno named Landulf Butromile, determined to rival the munificence of the patricians of Amalfi, presented to the cathedral of his native city bronze doors in like manner ordered in Constantinople.[2] These doors are also an imitation of the doors given to Amalfi by the first Pantaleon: the crosses in relief are identical in each case. But the Salerno doors are far larger, with fifty-four panels to twenty-four. Eight have designs damascened in silver; one bears the inscription in six hexameters dedicating the gift to St. Matthew; on another, two gryphons drink at a fountain; the rest have figures of Our Lord, the Virgin, SS. Peter, Paul, Simon, and Matthew, the names of the last four being in Latin: the donor and his wife Guisa are seen to right and left of St. Matthew. The inlay in the figure subjects is now for the most part lost.

The makers of this series of doors are only recorded in two cases. On one of the crosses of the Amalfi doors it was formerly possible to read the name of Simeon.[3] On the doors of St. Paul without the Walls the name of Staurakios was engraved in a cursive hand.[4]

The doors of the narthex in the Cathedral of S. Marco at Venice are held by some to be a gift of the Emperor Alexius Comnenus, by others to have formed part of the spoil of A.D. 1204.[5] Each valve has fourteen panels framed in borders

[1] Schulz, ii. 259 and 285, Fig. 116.
[2] Schulz, as above, ii. 285, Fig. 115; Pl. LXXXV, Figs. 4 and 5; Bayet, L'Art byzantin, 205, Fig. 68; G. Clausse, Basiliques et mosaïques, &c., ii. 14 ff.
[3] Camera, Storia d'Amalfi, 2nd ed., i. 155.
[4] Ἐκαμώθη χειρὶ ἐμοῦ Σταυρακίου τοῦ χύτου· οἱ ἀναγιγνώσκοντες εὔχεσθε ὑπ' ἐμοῦ.
[5] Ongania, La Basilica di S. Marco, v, Pl. 191, A¹; Ch. Errard and A. Gayet, L'Art byzantin, Pt. I, Venise, Pl. II and III.

with conventional foliate designs, of which the upper twelve have each a saint standing beneath a rounded arch, the lower two, animals, birds and foliate designs in geometrical compartments. The figures are damascened in silver, and each is accompanied by a name similarly encrusted. Other doors after the Byzantine style were made for S. Marco in the twelfth century.[1] The damascened doors of the Mausoleum of Bohemond at Canosa, by Roger of Amalfi,[2] introduce ornament of a Saracenic character; those of the Cathedral of Troja, by Oderisius of Benevento, also retain the method of encrustation. In the second

Fig. 393.   Bronze censer of about the seventh century.   (British Museum.)

half of the twelfth century, Italians preferred to decorate their doors with figures in relief, though even here they resorted to Byzantine ivories as models for their subjects (cf. p. 220).[3]

The Byzantine style of damascening bronze doors was imitated in Russia, where gold was employed as well as silver, and the scenes represented are more elaborate. The finest doors are at Suzdal, and are of the thirteenth century. Those from Novgorod, now at Alexandrova,[4] are a century later, and already show a more decidedly Russian character. On Mount Athos there are finely damascened doors with very elaborate ornamentation of animals, monsters, and scrolls.[5]

---

[1] Venturi, *Storia*, ii. 656; E. Bertaux, *L'Art dans l'Italie méridionale*, 409. One door was made for Leo di Molino, procurator of the fabric; another, with crosses in relief, is of the twelfth century.   [2] Bertaux, as above; Diehl, *Manuel*, 684; Venturi, ii. 552.

[3] Doors at Trani, &c. (Venturi, ii. 553 ff.; Bertaux, 421).

[4] G. Millet in A. Michel, *Hist. de l'art*, iii. 960.

[5] N. Kondakoff, *Monuments of Christian Art on Mount Athos*, Pl. XXXVIII; Diehl, *Manuel*, 809, 810.

The bronze *exagia* [1] or metal money-weights (Figs. 42, 392) deserve mention because the denomination was so frequently deeply engraved and inlaid with silver, and this process is essentially the same as that adopted on a larger scale upon the bronze doors. The unit is the *solidus* or νόμισμα, and both the Greek and Latin denominations are employed; the weights range from fractions of the solidus, to the ounce (six *solidi*), the pound, and two or three pounds, the abbreviations NO or SOL usually representing the unit, Γ the ounce, and Λ the pound. Besides these signs they bear the names or monograms chiefly of prefects or proconsuls, but

FIG. 394. Development of the censer, Fig. 393.

occasionally of princes. Sometimes there are busts which may be imperial, and more rarely figures of saints, a remarkable pound weight with two military saints being in the British Museum (Fig. 42). The date of most examples is the sixth century : examples of the later periods do not appear to be known. They are usually flat, and either rectangular or circular. Some weights, however, are of the spheroidal form of Roman times. *Exagia* were used by Theodoric in Italy, and several examples bear his name.[2]

OTHER SMALL OBJECTS OF METAL.[3]

The *censers* which have been preserved belong chiefly to the First and Second Periods, and have globular or hexagonal (cf. Figs. 351, 393) bodies and low foot-rims, for which three separate feet are sometimes substituted. Most of them are

---

[1] Examples in the British Museum, see *Cat. of Early Christian and Byz. Ant.*, Nos. 425 ff. and references there given. Examples in Algerian museums, *Rev. arch.*, July–December, 1903, p. 80. Cf. also *B. Z.*, ix (1900), pp. 477, 668 (Papageorgiu and Papadopoulos Kerameus); Ἀθηναῖον, vii, 1878, p. 263 (Papadopoulos Kerameus); G. Schlumberger, *Monuments byzantins inédits* in *Florilegium Melchior de Vogüé*, 562, &c.

[2] Brit. Mus. *Catalogue*, No. 444 ; another with monogram of Theodoric (?) is in the Dutuit Collection, Petit Palais, Paris.

[3] See especially the Catalogues of the British, Cairo, and Kaiser Friedrich Museums.

without covers, and suspended from chains; but in a few examples a handle is used instead of chains and there is a pierced domical cover.[1]   A considerable group of bronze censers with New Testament subjects in high relief (Fig. 393) appears to date from the sixth or seventh century, and perhaps originated in Palestine. Examples of this type, represented in many museums, come from Egypt, Syria, Anatolia, and even the Crimea.[2]   In later times, if we may judge from repre-

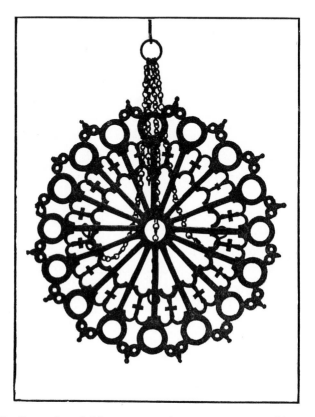

Fig. 395.   Bronze lamp-holder (*polycandelon*) for glass lamps.   (British Museum.)

sentations in miniatures, the usual type of censer resembled a cup or chalice with a rather high foot : it also seems to have had no cover.

Metal *lamps* in the First Period continued the traditions of Early Christian times : they preserve in general the old forms, and are often provided with stands.   Such lamps were in use at any rate down to the seventh century.[3]

Church lamps for numerous lights (*polycandela*) often took the form of a pierced disk or *corona* suspended by chains and containing a number of separate receptacles for oil, probably of glass.[4]   These are also represented in museums (cf. Fig. 395) ; one at Cairo has the apertures not in the circle itself, but at the extremities of radiating projections.[5]

[1] Wulff, *Berlin Catalogue*, i, No. 980.
[2] The example in the British Museum (*Catalogue*, No. 540) is from Syria.   For other examples see Wulff, *Berlin Catalogue*, i, Nos. 967 ff.
[3] Numerous examples in the British Museum (*Catalogue*, Nos. 495 ff.) ; Kaiser Friedrich Museum, Berlin (Wulff, *Catalogue*, Nos. 760 ff.) ; Cairo Museum (Strzygowski, *Koptische Kunst*, Nos. 9124 ff.).
[4] For the variety of lamps in churches see the description of the interior of Sta Sophia by Paulus Silentiarius, quoted in Lethaby and Swainson.   [5] No. 9153.

The number of *bronze vessels* and utensils of various sizes and forms is considerable : a high proportion comes from Egypt. These also may be studied in the catalogues already so frequently cited. Only one type can here be noticed, a kind of bowl with two swinging handles on a low pierced foot. The interest of this type lies in the fact that while the earliest examples presumably come from Egypt, almost identical specimens have been exhumed from Anglo-Saxon cemeteries in England,[1] and in early Teutonic graves in Germany.

The variety of bronze crosses and other small objects is too great for consideration in this place. We may note a type of reliquary cross (Fig. 397) with figures rudely engraved or in relief. Some of these are assigned to the sixth or seventh century, but the ruder examples may extend into the Third Period. They may have been made for pilgrims to the Holy Land.[2]

Ampullae.

The sixteen ampullae of base metal, with subjects in relief upon both sides, preserved in the cathedral at Monza,[3] whether or not the gift of Gregory the Great to Theodelinda the Lombard queen, are certainly of the sixth century and, as their inscriptions prove, brought from the Holy Land. These inscriptions: ΕΛΕΟΝ ΞΥΛΟΥ ΖΩΗϹ ΤѠΝ ΑΓΙѠΝ ΧΡΙϹΤΟΥ ΤΟΠѠΝ, or ΕΥΛΟΓΙΑ[4] ΚΥΡΙΟΥ ΤѠΝ ΑΓΙѠΝ ΤΟΠѠΝ. repeated with varying orthography, clearly relate to the sacred sites in Palestine, and show that the flasks were made to contain the miraculous oil from

Fig. 396. Bronze lamp of the sixth century on pricket-stand, probably from Egypt. (British Museum.)

[1] Strzygowski, *Koptische Kunst*, No. 9044; Wulff, *Berlin Catalogue*, i, No. 1014.

[2] Wulff, as above, Nos. 918 ff. ; British Museum, *Catalogue of . . . Byz. Ants.*, Nos. 558 ff. A number of crosses allied to this type are in the Khanenko Collection at Kieff (*La Collection Khanenko, Croix et images*, 1899, Pl. X ; 1900, Pl. XIX, &c.).

[3] Photos : *Hautes Études*. Photographic reproductions : A. Heisenberg, *Grabeskirche und Apostelkirche*, i, Pl. VIII–IX ; H. Kehrer, *Die heiligen drei Könige in der Litteratur und Kunst*, ii, Figs. 31–3. Other descriptions and illustrations : Frisi, *Memorie storiche di Monza*, i, 1794 (inaccurate reproductions of six examples) ; Garrucci, *Storia*, vi, Pl. 433–5 (drawings of all the types represented, and descriptions on pp. 46 ff.) ; F. Kraus, *Geschichte der christl. Kunst*, i. 524 ; V. Schultze, *Arch. der christl. Kunst*, 302 ; de Rossi, *Roma sotterranea*, iii. 505, and *Bull. di arch. crist.*, i. 36 ; G. Stuhlfauth, *Die altchristliche Elfenbeinplastik*, 148 ; J. Strzygowski, *B. D.*, i. 71 ff., 105 ff. ; N. Kondakoff in Glubokovski's *Orthodox Encyclopaedia*, vi. 87 ff. ; D. Ainaloff, *Hellenistic Origins*, 168 ff. (Russian), an important discussion of these interesting objects. The small group of repoussé gold *encolpia* in various museums may be compared with the Monza ampullae in that they also have figure subjects of iconographical interest, and are of quite as early a date (Strzygowski, *Zwei Goldenkolpien aus Adana*, in *B. D. I.*).

[4] The word εὐλογία, literally blessing, was given to any object which had been blessed, especially those associated with tombs of martyrs (Garrucci, 47). Cf. the flasks associated with the tomb of St. Menas.

the wood of the Cross carried away by pilgrims from all parts of the Christian world. The nature of the scenes represented confirms this origin. The Crucifixion, Holy Women at the Tomb, Ascension, and Incredulity of Thomas point to Jerusalem : the Annunciation, Salutation, Nativity, Adoration of the Magi, to Bethlehem. The treatment of these subjects offers many points of interest. The Crucifixion is never realistic, Our Lord being represented in several cases simply by the nimbed bust placed above the Cross, while the two thieves are seen in full figure ; or, where the whole body is shown, the arms are half extended while no cross is visible: in this case a long garment falls to the ankles. Two small figures, presumably Adam and Eve, kneel to

right and left, and beyond them stand the Virgin and St. John. The sun and moon appear either as busts with rayed crown and crescent upon the head, or as a simple star and crescent. In the scene on Easter morning (Figs. 39, 398) the angel is usually seated by the tomb, which is a columnar structure, apparently circular, with conical or domed roof [1] surmounted by a cross, double doors, and openwork *cancelli* : the foremost of the two women carries a censer. The inscription for the scene, which is sometimes on the same side of the ampulla as the Crucifixion, is ANECTH O KVPIOC variously spelled. In the Ascension, Our Lord, holding the Gospel and raising the right hand in benediction, is seated on a throne in a mandorla supported by four angels ; below stands the Virgin flanked by the Apostles. In one case (Garrucci, Pl. 434. 3) a *Dextera Domini* issues from beneath the mandorla, and a dove descends above the Virgin's head. In the Incredulity of Thomas (Fig. 399) Our Lord stands between two groups of six Apostles, holding a book of the Gospels, while Thomas approaches from the left ; the accompanying inscription is O K̄C̄ MOY KAI O ΘEOC

FIG. 397. Incised bronze reliquary cross. (British Museum.) P. 623.

MOY ; the closed doors which appear as a background in later art are absent. In the Annunciation the Virgin stands with the spindle in her hand and the woolbasket beside her. In the Nativity the manger is in the centre, with the ox and ass and star above, while the Virgin lies on the mattress to the right, and St. Joseph sits, head supported on hand, on the left. In the Baptism Christ stands up to the ankles in Jordan, the Baptist is on the left, and one angel holding a garment on the right. The Adoration of the Magi is usually combined with the Annunciation to the Shepherds, the three kings standing on one side, three shepherds on the other, of the throne on which the Virgin is seated facing, with the Child held straight before her. The monumental type of these figures, as mentioned elsewhere, has suggested that the group may repeat upon a small scale the mosaic which once stood on the exterior of the Church of the Nativity at Bethlehem. As on some of the sixth-century terra-cotta lamps,[2] busts of the Twelve Apostles in medallions form a border to a central subject in more than one case ; a circle of six-pointed stars is also used for the purpose. One flask has in the centre a cross with loops at all extremities ; and all have crosses within round-headed arches on the necks.

The British Museum possesses a lead ampulla of a similar type to those at Monza with scenes and inscriptions of the same character : on one side is the Incredulity of Thomas (Fig. 399), on the other the Women at the Tomb ; the ampulla was obtained in Egypt, but must have been brought from Palestine.

[1] In one case (Garrucci, Pl. 43. 1) three lamps seem to hang in the interior.
[2] e. g. Garrucci, *Storia*, Pl. 473. 1.

In the British Museum are also three other lead ampullae,[1] apparently of rather later date, with figures of military saints. There is no evidence that these examples are connected with Palestine. There is also a curious little lead triptych in openwork with three single figures, and above the middle part a round arch flanked by two birds recalling Syrian art of the late sixth century.

Coins (Figs. 400-3).

The coinage of the Byzantine Empire will disappoint the eye trained to appreciate the variety of design and the fine modelling which distinguish the coins of Greece. It is more monotonous than we might have

Fig. 398.   The Maries at the Tomb ; the Ascension : lead ampullae of the sixth century from the Holy Land in the Cathedral of Monza.   (*Hautes Études* : G. Millet.)

expected even from a people to which sculpture meant comparatively little; and even at times of renaissance it hardly shows the vitality manifested in other arts. Glancing over the work of a thousand years, the eye is rarely arrested by a graceful or a powerful design: for the most part all is mediocre and conventional, as if the officers of the mints were influenced by the feeling that money was a sordid necessity which should not be made unnecessarily attractive. Yet here and there the exception appears; and in the tenth and eleventh centuries there is a period of respectable achievement. Mr. Wroth, who has done so much to re-establish the study of Byzantine numismatics, gives it as his verdict that though the execution is often careless or unskilful, and though the choice of types is limited in range, yet it is not hard to find individual specimens possessing

---

[1] *Catalogue, Early Christian and Byz. Ant.*, Nos. 997-9.

a distinctive charm, while at most periods the currency displays, if not the qualities of great art, at any rate a certain numismatic propriety.[1]

Coins were minted in gold, silver, and bronze, those of silver being now the rarest. The gold coins are as a rule the least worn, a fact probably to be explained on the theory that they were issued for the most part for the payment of taxes and tribute, and were less constantly in circulation than those of less precious metal; the bronze coinage, which was at its best in the sixth and seventh centuries, is often much defaced by continuous usage. The principal gold coin was the *solidus* or *nomisma*,[2] which weighed about 70 grains; its fractions, the *semissis* and *tremissis* (half and third), were issued down to the tenth century. The standard was maintained until the eleventh century, when, in the reign of Michael VIII, there was a tendency to supersede gold by electrum. The 'scyphate' or saucer-shaped *nomisma* begins early in the same century, existing side by side with a lighter flat coin of about 63 grains. About A.D. 1081 the latter disappears, leaving the heavier scyphate form in possession of the field.

The chief silver coin down to Heraclius was the *miliaresion* of about 70 grains: that emperor introduced the hexagram of about 100 grains. From Constantine V to Alexius I, coins of thin fabric were struck, weighing about 40–50 grains; Alexius issued thicker coins similar to the bronze currency, and Michael IX imitated the Venetian *matapans*.

From the time of Anastasius down to the last quarter of the seventh century the bronze coinage bore on the reverse conspicuous marks of value, M signifying the *follis* of 40 *nummia*, and K, I, and Є pieces of 20, 10, and 5 respectively. The weight varies considerably; the *follis*, which under Justinian weighed about 300 grains, fell towards the eighth century as low as 50, rising and falling irregularly in subsequent reigns.

As a rule, all coins bore on the obverse the image of the emperor as bust or full figure; he is seen alone, or with members of his family, but occasionally with figures of Our Lord or the Virgin, who set the crown on his head (Constantine Porphyrogenitus; John Zimisces; Romanus III). The reverse varies considerably. The figure of Victory occurs in the early period under Anastasius and his successors. Justin II introduced the Tyché or Fortune of Constantinople. Tiberius II (A.D. 578–82) first used the cross potent standing on steps, a design which had a very long career. The rarer patriarchal cross with double traverse appears under Theophilus in the ninth century. Leo VI (A.D. 886–912) introduced the Virgin in half-figure as *orans* with the inscription MARIA; an ivory carving at Berlin (p. 226) probably shows this emperor being crowned by the Virgin. Under Alexander (A.D. 912–13), the first saint (St. Alexander) appears on

---

[1] *Imperial Byzantine Coins* (British Museum Catalogue, 1908), p. lxxxv. In this work will be found references to Sabatier and other early writers. For coins of Trebizond, &c., see W. Wroth, *Coins of the Vandals, Ostrogoths and Lombards, and of the Empires of Thessalonica, Nicaea, and Trebizond*, British Museum Catalogue, 1911; O. Retowsky, *Die Münzen der Komnenen von Trapezunt*, Moscow, 1910.

[2] The *nomisma* circulated widely in Europe as the *bezant*.

a coin.[1] The full figure of the Virgin with the Child was used by Romanus IV, the standing Virgin as *orans* by Constantine IX; the Virgin with the Child before her in a medallion first appears under John Zimisces.

The bust of Our Lord in two types, one bearded, the other beardless, is seen for the first time on coins of Justinian II in the seventh century (A.D. 685-95). Intermitted in the iconoclastic period, it was again used by Michael III, Constantine VII, and Nicephorus Phocas. The enthroned figure of Our Lord, a type which long continued popular, makes its first appearance under Basil I, the Macedonian. The rule that the emperor alone, with members of his family, or with Our Lord and the Virgin, should occupy the obverse is not universal. Constantine V omitted the imperial portrait, placing a cross upon the obverse, and an inscription in several lines on the reverse: on the silver coins of Constantine VII the same arrangement is found. On the other hand, Theophilus places imperial portraits on both sides of the coin. Barbarian rulers often placed the head of the reigning Byzantine emperor on their coins: this was done by the Ostrogoths in Italy, and probably by the Vandals in Africa, who used the head of Justin I.

Fig. 399. Lead ampulla of the sixth century from the Holy Land, found in Egypt. (British Museum.) P. 624.

The portraiture of the coins is for the most part conventional. A real likeness is seldom attempted, and heads which appear to have individual character are made to serve for more than one emperor, so that all real claims to likeness have to be abandoned. Where the heads of different rulers are characterized by distinct features or attributes, it is still impossible to say whether the differentiation implies resemblance, unless the coin can be compared with a contemporary portrait of another kind, e. g. a representation in an illuminated manuscript. But manuscript or other portraits are rare; and even when the comparison can be effected, the very conventional way in which on the coins the eyes are rendered by a circle or a pellet makes it in most cases difficult to decide in favour of a faithful representation. The coins of the early emperors to Justinian have conventional heads. In Justinian's case it is possible that the full-

[1] Afterwards St. George was adopted by John II, and SS. Theodore and Demetrius by Manuel I.

faced head introduced in A. D. 538 may be a portrait, as it agrees in general with the description of Procopius.[1] Phocas seems to be really portrayed[2] as the face with its short pointed beard differs materially from those of his predecessors. The obverse of one of Heraclius' coins may also be a portrait.[3] Constans II and Constantine IV are characterized, but we cannot be sure whether their features are faithfully rendered. From their time down to the tenth century, including the iconoclastic period, all heads appear to be conventional, except possibly that of Leo III.[4] Constantine Porphyrogenitus is seen in a bust executed with the fineness of a gem,[5] but the head is so like that of Leo VI that its authenticity must be doubted. In the same way we are obliged to reject as true presentations the heads of Nicephorus Phocas and John Zimisces. From this time down to the sack of Constantinople in A.D. 1204 there are a few attempts at characterization, but no reliable portraits. The Latin emperors used imported Venetian coins, and struck none with their own effigies. There is little to chronicle after the restoration. The coins are carelessly struck and feebly designed, so that even where, as in the case of John VIII, a portrait may be intended, we learn little by comparing it with Pisanello's famous medal. It may be noted that there is no authentic portrait of an empress on the coins. Theodora does not appear at all ; other empresses, Sophia, wife of Justin II, Anastasia, consort of Tiberius II, Leontia, wife of Phocas, are conventional figures, perhaps in some cases reproducing statues.

Thus the coins do little to make the princes of the East Roman Empire live for us; or if they make an emperor more real, as in the case of Justinian, they make him at the same time less heroic. We would have given much to know the features of the greater rulers, of Leo, conqueror of the Saracens, of Basil, founder of a dynasty, of Nicephorus Phocas and John Zimisces, the leaders of undefeated armies, of Constantine Porphyrogenitus the artist, and Alexius the diplomat. It is a record of lost opportunities similar to that of our own coinage before Tudor times.

The inscriptions[6] on the coins are short and vary little. Down to Justinian II the obverse usually has the emperor's name preceded by DN (*Dominus noster*), and followed by PP AVG (*Perpetuus Augustus*). When the Greek inscriptions came in at the end of the eighth century, BACIΛEVC, BACIΛEVC PWMAIWN or AVTOKPAT (Αὐτοκράτωρ) often replaced the Latin titles, which, however, continued to be used until the middle of the eleventh century. From the time of Romanus IV (A.D. 1067–71), the word ΔECΠOTHC was alone used.

The reverses in the early centuries bear such legends as *Victoria Aug.*,

---

[1] Wroth, *Catalogue*, as above, xci, and Pl. IV, 11, 12 ; VII, 1, 3; VIII, 4. The lost gold medallion of A. D. 534 (?) (Wroth, frontispiece to vol. i) had already introduced a characterization of Justinian's features.

[2] Ibid., Pl. XX, 4, 5, 12 ; XXII, 16.

[3] Ibid., Pl. XXIII, 4, 8 ; XXVIII, 3, 4. In the last years of his reign Heraclius has a huge full beard and moustache.

[4] Ibid., Pl. XLII, 7, 8.   [5] Ibid., Pl. LIII, 7.

[6] For the more remarkable inscriptions see Wroth, ii. 664 ; and for the epigraphy, i, cv.

Gloria Romanorum. Heraclius introduced *Deus adiuta Romaniṣ,* and ЄΝ ТΥТΟ ΝΙΚΑ—the earliest of the Greek inscriptions. Justinian II used IHC CRISTOS REX REGNANTIVM, a form which persisted in later reigns : Constantine V (A.D. 751) introduced IHSVS XPISTVS NICA, a barbaric formula in which, as in later issues, Greek and Latin are confused. 'Mixed legends,' in which Greek words were partly written in Latin letters, continued down to the third quarter of the eleventh century. Monograms, so universal on the lead seals, are very rare on coins, and chiefly occur on the bronze pieces of Cherson.[1] A few of the rectangular form (cf. Figs. 387, 389) occur in the time of Justinian. Where they are found later they are cruciform, the letters being attached to the extremities of a cross (cf. Figs. 334, 392). Dates, almost always giving the regnal years, occur on the bronze coinage from Justinian to Constans II (A.D. 641–68) : after this reign they are rarely found.

The sacred monogram (Chi Rho) sometimes occurs in both its commoner forms (✶ and ☧); the former or 'Constantinian' type, which on works of art and monuments is seldom later than the fourth century, is found on coins of Maurice Tiberius and Heraclius.

FIG. 400. Coins. 1. Constantius II ; 2. Valens ; 3. Constantius Gallus ; 4, 5. Julian II ; 6. Jovian ; 7. Valentinian I. (British Museum.)

The principal mint throughout the history of the empire was that of Constantinople, where coins of all denominations were struck : for many centuries, indeed, the metropolis was the only place where money was coined.[2] Before Justinian, Nicomedia and Antioch were the only additional mints ; but after the conquests of that emperor we find, in addition to these, Thessalonica, Cyzicus, Alexandria, Carthage, Sicily, Rome, Ravenna, and Cherson. In the seventh century Cherson drops out, but Isaura and Cyprus are added.[3] In the eighth century only Sicily, Rome, and Ravenna remain beside Constantinople ; in the ninth and tenth only Cherson. After

[1] A list of the monograms is given by Wroth, as above, ii. 761–2.
[2] For the mints, their mint-names, and officina marks see Wroth, i, xcix ff.
[3] The coins which Mr. Wroth describes as 'Provincial' and 'Italian' were also issued in the seventh, eighth, and ninth centuries, but their exact locality is unknown. The former may have been issued in Sardinia and Sicily, the latter are assigned to Central and Southern Italy.

this the metropolis coined alone down to the fall of the empire. Of all these mint places few coined in gold and silver. Carthage from about A.D. 534 to 698 was one. Rome coined gold from Constans II (A.D. 641–68) to the death of Constantine V (A.D. 775): so did Ravenna, from its capture by Belisarius to its final loss to the empire (A.D. 555–741). The 'Provincial' and 'Italian' mints also issued gold. Thessalonica, Nicomedia, Cyzicus, Antioch, Isaura, Cyprus, Alexandria, and Cherson minted nothing but bronze.

Fig. 401. Coins. 1. Valentinian II; 2. Theodosius I; 3. Arcadius; 4. Eudoxia; 5. Honorius; 6. Valentinian III; 7. Theodosius II; 8. Marcian; 9. Eudocia; 10, 11. Pulcheria. (British Museum.)

The Byzantine coinage influenced in many curious ways that of the earliest Mohammedan dynasties. In the first century after the Hegira Greeks were employed to make the dies, and sometimes bungled the Cufic inscriptions.[1] In the second half of the seventh century under the Khalif Abd-el-Melik (d. A.D. 705), the familiar cross raised upon three steps occurs; but it degenerates until the vertical limb finally carries a crescent. An example of this is seen on a copper coin of Homs (Emesa) in Syria, which bears on the obverse a standing figure of the khalif.[2] Some of the Ortukid princes in the twelfth century did not disdain to place figure-designs of Christian origin on their coinage: Christ enthroned or the bust of Christ, imitating Byzantine types, thus occur.[3]

SEALS.[4]

Byzantine seals offer this distinction from those of mediaeval Europe, that almost without exception they were impressions upon metal and not

[1] Karabacek, Kuṣejr 'Amra, 216.

[2] H. Lavoix, Cat. des monnaies musulmanes de la Bibliothèque Nationale, No. 70, p. 21.

[3] S. Lane Poole, The Coins of the Turkuman Houses of Seljook, Urtuk, Zengie, &c., British Museum, 1877, Nos. 324 ff., and the same, Numismata Orientalia, Pl. IV.

[4] G. Schlumberger, Sigillographie de l'empire byzantin, Paris, 1884; Mordtmann, Conférence sur des sceaux et plombs byzantins; Sorlin Dorigny in Revue arch., 1877, and Bulletin critique, 1884, 272 ff.; R. Paribeni, Bullettino dell' Archivio paleogr. italiano, i, Perugia, 1908, 77–94 (contains a bibliography of the work done in connexion with seals since the publication of Schlumberger's work); B. A. Pančenko, Izviestiya of the Russian Arch. Inst. at Constantinople, xiii, 1908; W. de Gray Birch, British Museum Catalogue of Seals, v, pp. 1–72; articles by K. M. Konstantopoulos in Svoronos' Journal International d'Archéol. Numism. from vol. ii (1899) onward.

upon wax, the latter material being less suitable for use in a hot climate. In this connexion it may be noted that the East has seldom made use of wax: the Chaldaeans used clay, a substance also employed by the inhabitants of Turkestan down to the eighth century; while since the introduction of paper, the oriental has always impressed directly upon the document a matrix smeared with ink or other colouring matter. A very few matrices of bronze, stone, &c., apparently cut for use with wax, belong to the Christian East, and these are small in diameter; the larger bronze examples must be as a rule assigned to the period after the fall of Constantinople and to places where Western influence was strong.[1] Under the Byzantine Empire matrices for wax were so few as to be a negligible quantity.

It will thus be seen that the Byzantine seal is what we know as a *bulla*, made in the following manner. If the metal employed was gold or silver,[2] two thin circular sheets were impressed with the obverse and reverse design and joined together with overturned edges, the space between them, except where the suspending cords ran through, being filled with some kind of mastic, so that the whole had the general form of a thick medallion. If

Fig. 402. Coin of Theodosius II: the emperor between Valentinian III and Eudoxia.

lead was used, as was usually the case, two disks, each with a central groove already prepared, were placed one upon the other, and the suspending cords laid in the grooves. They were then pressed or struck between the two faces of a double matrix in which the design was engraved[3] until they were welded together into a single disk firmly enclosing the cords. It is supposed that the matrices may have been of iron, and that they may have been worked by handles like wafering irons, as were the bronze instruments used in making lead papal bulls. In any case, their material would seem to have been more perishable than bronze, for although the seals themselves have been preserved in thousands, only a single iron matrix appears to be known. Curious as this is, it has been pointed out that a similar anomaly exists in the case of the dies of early coins, and of the stamps used to impress the handles of amphorae in ancient times: though the impressions are numerous, the stamps themselves have disappeared.[4] Owing to the rapid disintegration of the surface of lead when exposed to a damp atmosphere, Byzantine seals are difficult to preserve, and in wet northern climates they

---

[1] e. g. the large circular matrix of a Cretan monastery in the collection of M. Schlumberger, figured in his *Sigillographie*, p. 202. For small earlier matrices (eleventh century?) of steatite, see Brit. Mus. *Catalogue of Early Christian and Byz. Ant.*, Nos. 97–100, and Schlumberger in *Florilegium Melchior de Vogüé*, 564.

[2] Only the emperors used gold, and gold seals were only used for rescripts, donations to monasteries, and letters to great vassals, the weight of gold being proportionate to the dignity of the recipient of the document. When the appearance only of precious metal was desired without its cost, a lead seal was covered with a thin foil of gold or silver. For ordinary documents and correspondence the emperors, like the popes in the West, used leaden seals.

[3] Called βουλλωτήριον.

[4] A certain number of lead disks exist, bearing effigies and inscriptions, very like seals,

sometimes crumble away if kept in drawers, where there is no free play of air. The only remedy in this case is to cover them with a fine varnish. The majority of existing specimens were obtained at Constantinople during the reconstruction of buildings round the Seraskierat and during the construction of that part of the Adrianople railway which runs through the city: the great number found in or near one spot perhaps points to the existence in this place of the Imperial Archives. But though as yet the metropolis has yielded the greatest number, numerous specimens have been found in other cities, notably Smyrna, Beyrut, Salonika, Athens, Naples, Palermo, and Carthage.[1]

These unassuming lead seals or *bullae* are of the greatest interest to the historian: in some ways they are more important than the coins, on account of the greater variety of the persons and places commemorated by their legends. These throw light upon almost every phase of Byzantine society, upon the court, the nobility, the civil and military administration, upon ecclesiastical organization, and upon the life of private citizens: it has been remarked with justice that they provide a continuous commentary to the *De Caeremoniis* of the Emperor Constantine Porphyrogenitus and the *De officiis* of Codinus. There is hardly a high office in court, Church, or army which is not commemorated by a seal; eparchs, generals, protonotaries, protospatharii, archbishops, and abbots have all left their titles inscribed upon these disks of lead; as we read the infinitely various styles and designations, the men who guided the great machine of government seem to defile before us in their orders and degrees. Nor is the light cast upon the geography of the empire less important than that which throws the official hierarchy into strong relief. We learn in their proper form the names of towns, fortresses, bishoprics, convents, churches, and institutions, while all the themes of the empire are represented in the list. The names of great families are given in the accepted orthography of the times in which they lived. Finally, the figures represented are of considerable iconographical interest; for though the portraits of imperial persons are fewer in number than on the coins, the representations of saints are more frequent, and the Virgin and Our Lord are seen in a greater variety of types. All these points lend the large series of Byzantine seals a considerable historical importance, though it must be admitted that in strength and sculptural beauty, as well as in variety of design, they cannot compare with the seals of the Western Middle Ages. The noble matrices of England, France, and Germany in the thirteenth and fourteenth centuries, with

---

but clearly made for other purposes. Some of these were devotional medallions to be worn round the neck; others were tokens entitling poor people to doles. See Schlumberger, as above, 78.

[1] The *bullae* from Carthage and neighbourhood have been treated by R. P. Delattre in his *Culte de la Sainte Vierge en Afrique*, 88 ff., where a large number are reproduced, all of earlier date than the eighth century. The frequent occurrence in this series of the cruciform monogram seems to indicate that some at least of M. Schlumberger's examples may be rather earlier than was formerly supposed. Delattre's seals have also been described by M. P. Monceau in *Bull. de la Soc. d'Ant. de France*, 1908, 219 ff. and other pages in the same volume.

their presentment of kings and mounted knights, churches and abbeys, ships and cities, bishops and abbots, and armorial bearings, are the expression of a more vigorous and accomplished talent than that which stood at the disposal of the Eastern Empire.

Compared with our finer Western seals, the best work of the Byzantine engravers is lacking in power : it often has neatness and elegance, never the amplitude and majesty of an occidental seal of the period of St. Louis.

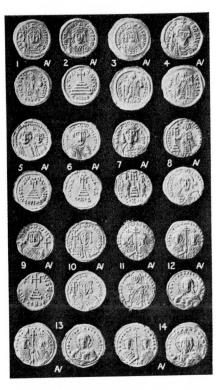

In the majority of cases the types figured upon the obverse of Byzantine seals are of a religious character. Upon about half the examples known we see the Virgin [1] alone or with the Child, or more rarely accompanied by saints; next in order of frequency come figures of saints, St. Michael being especially prominent.[2]

After these the cross is most often reproduced, in the great majority of cases the patriarchal cross with double traverse, standing upon steps, and rising from divergent foliage ; next in frequency are figures of Our Lord, usually busts, dating, like similar representations on the coins, from the reigns of Nicephorus Phocas, John Zimisces, Basil II, and Constantine XI. The Virgin and

FIG. 403. Coins. 1. Justin II ; 2. Tiberus II ; 3. Maurice Tiberius ; 4. Phocas ; 5. Heraclius ; 6. Constans II ; 7. Constantine IV ; 8. Justinian II ; 9. Leo III ; 10. Constantine V ; 11. Basil I and Constantine VII ; 12. Nicephorus Phocas ; 13. John Zimisces ; 14. Basil II and Constantine VIII. (British Museum.)

Our Lord together or accompanied by saints ; or two or more saints together ; or religious scenes, are rarer.[3] Less common still are figures of an angel, of the Lamb, or of the emperor or empress. Then come representations of animals and monsters ;[4] rarest of all are effigies of the owners of the seals.

The legends of the vast majority of seals are all in Greek, the chief exceptions being some examples of the pre-iconoclastic period, where

---

[1] Especially frequent are the types Blachernitissa and Hodegetria (p. 673), though other titles, derived from the names of convents, or particular aspects and qualities of the Mother of God, are comparatively frequent.

[2] Other popular saints in order of their frequency are : St. Nicholas of Myra ; the military saints George, Demetrius, and the two Theodores ; SS. Basil, John Chrysostom, John the Baptist, John the Evangelist, Peter, and Procopius.

[3] The scenes chiefly found are : the Annunciation, Baptism, Presentation, Transfiguration, Crucifixion, Death and Assumption of the Virgin, Daniel in the Lions' Den, &c.

[4] Lion, gryphon, wolf, leopard, eagle, hare, peacock, pelican, &c.

there may be a Latin inscription on one side and a Greek on the other; specimens dating from a later period under the Norman princes of Sicily, and a third class made for oriental subjects of the empire between the ninth and twelfth centuries, where Greek and Arabic are found together.[1] The legends usually surround the figures; but where they occupy the whole field, as they often do in the Comnenian and iconoclastic periods, they fill the field in horizontal lines. In iconoclastic seals, on which sacred subjects were abandoned, the legend upon one side commonly took the form of a monogram, the letters of which were disposed at the extremities and centre of a cross (Fig. 404). Most frequently the monogram gives the invocation Θεοτόκε (or Κύριε) βοήθει, in which case the supplementary words τῷ σῷ δούλῳ are placed within the angles, the name and titles of the owner finding a place on the reverse. In later seals which bear effigies, the formula is generally written in full as part of the legend. The space occupied by titles tends to increase with the centuries, for the simple honours of early days were no longer sufficient in a decadent society greedy of hierarchical distinctions: under the Palaeologi such titles as πανυπερπρωτοσεβαστουπέρτατος were conceived, though nothing quite so absurd occurs on the legends of seals. It is generally possible to date seals within comparatively narrow limits, sometimes from the mention of historical personages, sometimes from their resemblance to coins, sometimes, again, from the mention of places the relation of which to the empire or Church changed at known times; a town, for example, may be mentioned as the seat of a bishopric which at a certain date was raised to metropolitan rank, so that the use of the word bishopric gives a *terminus ante quem*. Cases in which seals remain attached to the documents which they originally attested are far more rare than in the West, for the archives of the Byzantine Empire have almost all perished, and only a few sealed documents remain in the Convent of Patmos, at Naples, Bari, and La Cava.[2]

As a rule the name of the signatory is set out in full, whether it is that of an individual or a corporation. But sometimes it is only indicated by allusions which are obscure to us. More rarely a seal will be anonymous, or the name may be the same as that of the saint represented on the obverse, who is then invoked for the protection of his namesake. Very often, as in the West, the seal is personified, and the legend is in the first person: ἐγὼ σφραγίζω τὰς γραφὰς 'Αλεξίου (or τηρῶ or βεβαιῶ, &c.), recalling the *secreta tego*, &c., of the Western Middle Ages. Legends are frequently difficult to decipher owing to decay of the surface, faulty striking, or even to careless orthography or lettering of the matrix. From the eleventh century down to the middle of the thirteenth, legends are constantly in iambic trimeters of execrable style, in which the quantities all appear to be false until we remember that the syllables have the accents of the spoken language.

---

[1] Schlumberger, as above, 74. [2] Ibid., 90.

As in the West, one person might have more than one seal in virtue of several offices held successively or at the same time; or again, he might have a larger official seal, and a smaller seal for private use, analogous to the *secretum* of our own Middle Ages. Women of the upper classes had their own seals, of which a considerable number have survived.

Fig. 404. Lead seals of the sixth century and later. (British Museum.)

M. Schlumberger has classified Byzantine seals under five main heads :—

A. *Geographical*—seals of officials of themes, cities, monasteries, &c., and seals of bishops.

B. *Naval and military.*

C. *Ecclesiastical* (other than those of bishops).

D. *Seals of civil functionaries.*

E. *Seals of private persons*, giving family names.

It is not necessary in the present place to recapitulate the territorial divisions of the empire from Greece and the Balkan Peninsula to the eastern frontiers; but as the administration of all themes was organized upon a common model, it may be useful to mention the titles of the principal officers whose seals have survived to illustrate Constantine's work.[1] As the theme was primarily a military unit, its highest official was the *strategos*, enjoying the rank, if at the head of a great theme, of *protospatharios*, or general; if of a minor theme, of *spatharios* or *spathariocandidatos*, a grade approximately corresponding to that of a lieutenant-colonel. His principal assistants were the *protocancellarios*, a chief of the chancellary, and *protomandator*, or chief of the messengers. The principal civilians of the theme were the chief treasury official, or *protonotarios*, and the judge, or *krites*, whose functions were sometimes performed by a single person; the *commerciarii* were responsible for the customs and land revenue. The chief military officers inferior to the *strategos* were the *turmarchs*, ranking as *spathariocandidati*, *merarchs*, *drongarii*, *counts*, and *centarchs*; where the theme was maritime, the fleet also had its *drongarios*. The military treasurers were *logothetae* and *chartularii*. Officers outside the usual hierarchy were *dukes*, commanding forces in frontier districts, *catapans*, commanding fortified places, and *archons* of the cities. The ecclesiastical hierarchy is chiefly represented by seals of archbishops, bishops, presbyters (priests), abbots (*hegoumenoi*) and *archimandrites*, placed over several monasteries. The archives and treasuries of churches and abbeys were under the charge of the *chartophylax*, *chartularius*, *cimeliarch*, and *skenophylax*. The officials responsible for orphanages and hospitals (*orphanotrophoi* and *xenodochoi*) were usually clerics.

The persons attached to the imperial court were naturally very numerous. There were the officers of the various troops of guards, *manglavrites*, *silentiarii*, and *excubitores*, who usually, like most officials of distinction, bore the honorary title of *spatharii*, corresponding, in a general way, to the membership of the *Légion d'honneur* or the Order of the Bath. Then there were a host of civil functionaries from the court marshal, or *curopalates*, to the great falconer, the *vestiarii* in charge of the wardrobe, and the *cursores*, or imperial messengers. The empress, in like manner, had her household, the members of which had their seals. The *zôstae*, or women of the bedchamber, and *nymphae*, or maids of honour, are both represented in the list of impressions. In fine, the sigillography of the Byzantine Empire illustrates the life of a highly organized and carefully policed state, where functions were infinitely multiplied and the official element was very conspicuous. The administration was bureaucratic, and we picture to ourselves a society in which almost every one wore a uniform. But though there was perhaps too much officialism, not all seals claim for their owners official titles or rank. A number even of those preserved were used by private persons; far greater numbers, especially those of simple design and small size, have undoubtedly perished.

[1] M. Alfred Rambaud, in his *Empire grec au Xe siècle*, gives a lucid account of the themes in the time of Constantine Porphyrogenitus.

Seals with family names, which have survived in quantities, bear many interesting and familiar surnames, such as Botoniates, Bryennius, Cantacuzenus, Comnenus, Lascaris, and Scleros.

Engraved Gems.

The engraving of gems never attained to such popularity in the Byzantine Empire as the carving of ivory.[1] A great number of Roman gems were taken from Italy by Constantine upon the foundation of his new city, and his example was doubtless followed by the patricians who migrated with him. Some of these stones were preserved in Constantinople until the sack of A.D. 1204, when they were brought back once

FIG. 405. *a.* Intaglio on crystal, sixth–seventh century. (British Museum.)
b. The Virgin and Child: intaglio on chalcedony. (British Museum.)

more to Western Europe: like other antique gems treasured by the Middle Ages, their classical subjects had often been made to serve as representations of Christian persons or scenes. But the art was already decadent when the new metropolis was built; though the contemporary cameos have their attractive qualities, they could not compete for the favour of connoisseurs with the finer work executed in earlier times. Nevertheless engravers seem to have been at work in the Eastern Empire during the whole period of its existence; for although surviving examples of their gems are not numerous, they cover a great number of centuries, from the fourth to the fourteenth. As a rule, the work does not rise above mediocrity, often falling distinctly below it; in this it resembles the average gem-cutting of the Sassanian Persians, who were also influenced by the late Graeco-Roman art, and while their empire lasted produced gems differing but little from Christian stones except in the purely oriental nature of their subjects. But the Sassanians at their best produced gems of considerable merit, like the cameo with the capture of Valerian by Sapor in the Cabinet des Médailles at Paris,[2] and the fragment of a man with a bull in the same collection. We have no work of equal

---

[1] E. Babelon, *Catalogue des camées antiques et modernes de la Bibliothèque Nationale, Paris*, lii ff., Paris, 1897, and *La Gravure sur pierres fines* (*Bibl. de l'Enseignement des Beaux-Arts*), 184 ff. ; A. Furtwängler, *Antike Gemmen*, vol. iii, 373–5.

[2] Babelon, *Camées*, lvii. 357, and Pl. XLII, No. 360 ; also reproduced in *Mon. Piot*, i, 1884, Pl. XII, Fig. 1.

vigour from Byzantine artists, and though they occasionally produce results which are not unpleasing, their gems are poor indeed by the side of those cut by the ancient Greeks or the craftsmen of the Augustan age. They worked both in cameo and in intaglio, using the same stones which were in favour under the Early Roman Empire (carnelian, chalcedony, heliotrope, haematite, jasper, lapis lazuli, sardonyx); they employed the drill in the same careless manner,[1] seldom attaining precision or delicacy of line. The contrast between the average Byzantine work and that of the finer Roman period is very similar to that observed between Byzantine and Roman silver plate. In the one case the figures stand out in sharp relief, finely articulated and full of life; in the other they are nerveless, producing an effect which is at once heavy and soft. Compare the figures on the silver dishes from Cyprus illustrated in Figs. 358, 360 with those upon the Roman treasures from Hildesheim or Bernay, and you have the distinction between Roman and Byzantine cameos reproduced in another medium and upon a larger scale. Before passing to the actual gems, we may recall the fact that, like their predecessors, Byzantine lapidaries fashioned numerous chalices, cups, &c., out of agate, chalcedony, and crystal. The best-known examples of these are in the Treasury of St. Mark's at Venice,[2] to which allusion is made in another section (Figs. 49–54). The onyx bowl of a chalice in the treasure of the Sacristy of the Patriarchs at Moscow may be of Byzantine workmanship.[3]

To the transitional period at the beginning of Byzantine history probably belong various stones, with inscriptions, usually in cameo, such as μνημόνευε, λέγουσιν ἃ θέλουσιν, λεγέτωσαν, οὐ μέλ(ε)ι μοι, &c.[4] A sardonyx cameo at Munich, representing an emperor, probably a successor of Constantine, is of about the same period.[5] To the period between this time and the Macedonian revival of the ninth century belong a considerable number of gems in various large collections. Among these may be noted some gems in the British Museum: a rock crystal intaglio with a rider preceded by a winged figure, with a cross above (*Catalogue of Early Christian and Byzantine Antiquities*, No. 84); an onyx cameo with a charioteer (No. 101); a cameo with a head resembling Alexander, with a horn of Ammon above the ear and the inscription τῆς καλῆς τύχης μνημόνευε, &c. (No. 103); a cameo with two angels each grasping the shaft of a cross standing between them (No. 89) (for examples with a similar subject in the Cabinet des Médailles at Paris see below); three intaglios

---

[1] For technical processes of gem-engraving, which have remained very much the same from ancient to modern times, see Furtwängler, as above; Babelon, as above, p. xxiii; Blümner, *Technologie*, iii. 279 ff.; C. W. King, *Antique Gems and Rings*, pp. 20 ff.; H. Middleton, *The Engraved Gems of Classical Times*, ch. ix, pp. 103 ff.; L. Claremont, *The Gem-cutter's Craft*, London, 1906. [2] See also Babelon, *Camées*, p. lv.

[3] F. de Mély, *Mon. Piot*, xii, 1905, Pl. XV, Fig. 5.

[4] British Museum, *Catalogue of Gems* in the Department of Greek and Roman Antiquities, No. 2154 ff.; *Cat. of Early Christian and Byzantine Antiquities*, Nos. 7, 8; Babelon, as above, Nos. 346 ff.

[5] Furtwängler, as above, Pl. LXVII, Fig. 4. Baron Gustave de Rothschild possessed a cameo of this period with two imperial busts, described by an added inscription of later date as SS. Sergius and Bacchus.

on nicolo and haematite with angels bearing crosses (Nos. 85–7); a jasper intaglio with the Entry into Jerusalem (No. 90); three jasper intaglios with monograms (Nos. 93–5); a sapphire with a monogram (No. 96), recalling a carnelian in the Cabinet des Médailles with a similar type of monogram (Babelon, *Pierres fines*, p. 186).

Two sardonyx cameos at Munich[1] are assigned by Furtwängler to this early period; one has the Apostles in two rows on either side of a disproportionately large cross; the other, Christ enthroned between the Apostles.

The following gems in various collections seem to belong to the Third Period, from the tenth to the thirteenth centuries.

In the British Museum: a chalcedony intaglio with the Virgin and Child (No. 92); a sard cameo with a horse and surrounding inscription: *O Lord, help Julianus* (No. 102); an onyx cameo in two layers, with the Annunciation, remarkable for the fact that the Angel Gabriel is represented as a small nude winged figure like a genius or *putto*;[2] a sardonyx cameo with St. John the Baptist standing with an inscribed scroll (No. 105).

In the Cabinet des Médailles, Bibliothèque Nationale, Paris, are the following:—A sardonyx cameo of three layers representing two angels holding wands in their left hands and with their right hands supporting a long cross, at the top of which is a medallion with a bust of Our Lord: in the exergue a design resembling a patera flanked by ears of corn;[3] an amethyst cameo with Our Lord standing and making the gesture of benediction;[4] a sardonyx cameo of three layers with the Annunciation, and inscription, χαῖρε κεχαριτομένη ὁ κϲ (κύριος) μετὰ σοῦ;[5] another sardonyx cameo with a similar Annunciation;[6] a third cameo with the same subject, the inscription χέρε καιχαριτομένη, also in relief, and on the back an intaglio representing the *Deesis* (p. 664) inscribed θκε βοηθι τὴν δουλιν σ' Ανα (θεοτόκε βοήθει τὴν δούλην σοῦ 'Αννα), perhaps referring to Anna Comnena (†1108);[7] sardonyx cameo of three layers with SS. George and Demetrius, above whom is a half-figure of Our Lord in benediction;[8] chalcedony cameo with a dolphin and a debased inscription beginning κυρία χαῖρε,[9] a heliotrope cameo with a bust of Our Lord holding the book and making the gesture of benediction;[10] a jasper cameo with the same subject;[11] a heliotrope cameo with half-figure of the Virgin with the Child;[12] a green jasper cameo with St. John the Evangelist seated with the book of his Gospel and his name in Greek characters;[13] a cameo on the same stone, with a half-figure of St. Demetrius and inscribed name.[14]

Among intaglio gems in the same collection is a half-figure of the Virgin issuing from a fountain inscribed ΜΡ ΘΥ Η ΠΗΓΗ in allusion to the Virgin of

---

[1] Furtwängler, Pl. LXVII, Figs. 6 and 7.
[2] *Proc. Soc. Ant. London*, 2nd ser., xviii, p. 365.
[3] E. Babelon, *Catalogue des Camées*, Pl. XXIX, No. 333. A cameo with the same subject, inscribed with a prayer for one Leontios, is in the cathedral at Moscow (Garrucci, *Storia*, vi, Pl. 479, Fig. 13. Another very similar, now in the Cook Collection, has the inscription ΕΞΟΥΕΙΕ (ἐξουσίαι) (C. H. Smith and A. Hutton, *Proc. Soc. Ant. London*, 2nd ser., vol. xi, p. 89, No. 3). [4] Babelon, as above, No. 332, Pl. XXXIX.
[5] Ibid., Pl. XXXIX, No. 336; G. Schlumberger, *Nicéphore Phocas*, 101.
[6] Babelon, No. 337; Garrucci, *Storia*, vi, Pl. 478, Fig. 30.
[7] Babelon, No. 338, Pl. XXXIX, and *Pierres fines*, p. 191.
[8] Babelon, No. 342, Pl. XL, and *Pierres fines*, Fig. 143; Schlumberger, *Nicéphore Phocas*, 91.
[9] Babelon, No. 340, Pl. XXXIX.
[10] Ibid., No. 333, Pl. XXXIX; Schlumberger, *Nic. Phocas*, 91.
[11] Babelon, No. 334, Pl. XXXIX.   [12] Ibid., No. 339.   [13] Ibid., No. 341.
[14] Ibid., No. 343, Pl. XL. Cf. cameo with St. Nicholas at Lyons (A. Blanchet, *Mon. Piot*, xvii, p. 75).

the church founded by Justinian and containing a fountain ;[1] a red jasper with the Nativity.[2]

In the Galerie d'Apollon at the Louvre there is a cameo on lapis representing the Virgin as *orans* between two formal plants inlaid with gold. The letters MP ΘY are similarly inlaid, as well as the nimbus and the ornament upon the mantle. In the same place there is another relief of the same subject on heliotrope.

The Imperial Historical Museum at Vienna possesses the only dated Byzantine gem, a cameo in green jasper with a bust of the Virgin full face, with surrounding inscription naming the Emperor Nicephorus Botoniates (A.D. 1078–81).[3]

In the treasury of the Sacristy of the Patriarchs at Moscow is an onyx cameo of fine workmanship, representing the Virgin standing as *orans* with the Child in a medallion upon her breast: it seems to belong to the eleventh or twelfth century.[4]

The collection of Mr. Maxwell Somerville at Philadelphia contains a few Byzantine gems, including a jasper (?) cameo with a bust of Our Lord.[5]

It is possible that the emerald with the portrait of Our Lord, sent by Bajazet to the Pope in A.D. 1492, may be identical with that which Anthony of Novgorod saw, in A.D. 1200, set in the centre of a silver dish presented in the tenth century to the patriarch of Constantinople by the Grand Duchess Olga of Russia, who died in A.D 968. Her gem may have reproduced the Edessa portrait of Our Lord, which was translated to Constantinople in A.D. 944.[6]

A green marble paten (?) in the Monastery of Xeropotamou on Mount Athos has in the centre the Virgin censed by angels, surrounded by angels vested as priests and bearing liturgical objects, and (in an outer row) by Apostles kneeling before the Throne (cf. *Divine Liturgy*). This remarkable work is ascribed to the twelfth century.[7]

AMULETS.[8]

Amulets, chiefly prophylactic against disease or magic, were evidently popular; they were plaques or medallions worn as pendants or finger-rings.

Fɪɢ. 406.   Silver signet with 'Medusa' head and inscription : *Lord, preserve the wearer*, worn as an amulet.   (British Museum.)

The former class were mostly of bronze or copper, though a rare enamelled medallion is now in the Louvre (p. 499). They bear inscriptions warning the spirit of the disease to take flight, often in the name of Solomon, who

[1] Garrucci, *Storia*, vi, Pl. 478, Fig. 36.   [2] Ibid., Pl. 478, Fig. 31.
[3] De Mély, *Le Camée byzantin de Nicéphore Botoniate*, in *Mon. Piot*, vi, 1900, p. 195 ff.
[4] F. de Mély, *Mon. Piot*, xii, 1905, Pl. XV, Fig. 1.
[5] Maxwell Somerville, *Engraved Gems, Their History and Place in Art*, Philadelphia, 1889, Nos. 575, &c.
[6] G. F. Hill, *The Reliquary*, July, 1904, 190. See also F. de Mély, *Gazette des Beaux-Arts*, 1898, 492, and E. von Dobschütz, *Christusbilder*, 1899, 149 ff.
[7] Kondakoff, *Mon. of Christian Art on Mt. Athos*, Pl. XXX and p. 225.
[8] On this subject see G. Schlumberger, *Mélanges d'archéologie byzantine*, 117 ff. ; M. Siebourg, *Bonner Jahrbücher*, Heft 118, pp. 158 ff.

is seen mounted and transfixing a prostrate figure with his lance, or on foot, menacing a nude figure with a whip. Another type has a Medusa-like head surrounded with serpents, and in the border : + ΑΓΙΟϹ ΑΓΙΟϹ ΑΓΙΟϹ ΚΕ ϹΑΒΑШΘ ΠΛΗΡΗϹ ΟΥΡΑΝΟϹ (ΚΑΙ ΓΗ) : on the reverse is a denunciation of a disease—apparently colic. An example made of gold, found at Tchernigoff in 1821, is now in the Hermitage at St. Petersburg.[1] The Medusa head is found upon a ring in the British Museum (Fig. 406), which, however, has on the hoop the ordinary inscription : *Lord, preserve the wearer*. A gold amuletic ring is in M. Schlumberger's collection,[2] and silver bracelets and other amulets at the Cairo Museum show the mounted lance-bearer transfixing a figure on the ground.[3] The superstitions to which these objects bear witness probably spread from Alexandria about the beginning of our era.

[1] Derivatives of this type are numerous in Russia. Cf. *La Collection Khanenko* (Kieff), *Croix et images*, 1899, Pl. IX, 1900, Pl. XXIX, and *Époque slave*, 1902, Pl. XIII.

[2] *Mélanges*, Fig. on p. 131.

[3] J. Maspéro, *Bracelets-amulettes d'époque byzantine* in *Annales du Service des Antiquités de l'Égypte*, ix, 1908, 246 ff.

FIG. 407. Head-piece with the Descent into Hell : from a MS. of the twelfth century in the Monastery, Mount Sinai (Sinait. 339). (*Hautes Études*: N. Kondakoff.)

CHAPTER XII

ICONOGRAPHY

IT is impossible in a general work like the present to deal with all the subjects represented in Byzantine art. An attempt will, however, be made to describe those which were most important or most popular, to note the points in which the Eastern treatment differs from that adopted in the West, and to suggest the sources from which the types were originally derived.[1]

[1] Among the most valuable accounts of Byzantine iconography are Prof. N. Pokrovsky's *The Gospel in the Monuments, chiefly Byzantine and Russian*, St. Petersburg, 1892, vol. i of *The eighth Arch. Congress*, Moscow, 1890, and *Sketch of the Monuments of Orthodox Iconography and Art*; but they are unfortunately written in Russian, as are the treatises of other Russian writers who deal incidentally with the subject (Smirnoff, Ainaloff, Riedin, &c.). Kondakoff, however, discusses many iconographical points in his *Histoire de l'art byzantin*, &c., published in French, and his work on the Swenigorodskoi enamels, which appeared both in French and German. O. Wulff's *Koimesiskirche in Nicäa* also contains much valuable information in German. Strzygowski's many books and pamphlets are also full of iconographical matter, as also are those of Millet. Eduard Dobbert, in his articles on S. Angelo in Formis in the Prussian *Jahrbuch* (vol. xv) and on the Last Supper in the *Repertorium für Kunstwissenschaft*, contributed greatly to our knowledge of the subject, especially to the comparative study of Eastern and Western types. In this he has been followed by A. Haseloff and W. Vöge, who approach the subject from the Western side, and their studies on the early schools of German miniature painting abound in iconographical information.

It is a commonplace that the Early Christians did not introduce a new art with a new religion; they adapted to new ends existing forms and compositions. The frescoes of the catacombs, the earliest mosaics like those of Sta Costanza, the Christian sarcophagi, all continue without any violent rupture the traditions of pagan art. Even where innovation could not be avoided, as in scenes for which antique art afforded no precedent, individual figures are copied from earlier models, the representations of sacred persons are based upon pre-existing types. In religious art the costume of pre-Christian times was preserved. The tunic and mantle, characteristic of Christ and the Apostles, are inherited from the pagan Roman period, but they were the dress of the Greek portion of the empire. It is not the Roman toga which we see, but the pallium or himation of the Hellenistic world.

This point, small as it is, suffices to introduce a general statement as to the iconography of the Christian East. It is not Roman in origin. Iconography is concerned not with ornament but with figure art; and this, in Early Christian times, was inspired in much that concerned the matter, in almost all that concerned the manner, from Hellenistic sources. Rome made significant additions, perfecting portraiture and giving a new importance to the historical point of view; but though the masculine Roman spirit might impose a direction or suggest a mood, it could not romanize all execution. A high proportion of the work was done by immigrant Greeks, whose models were naturally derived from the creations of their own race. The ceremonial scene, the representation of a battle or a triumph, might bear the peculiar Roman quality; in the genre scene or the mythological figure the artist was free to follow his own bent, to reproduce the idyllic pastoral of Alexandria or embody the Hellenistic conception of human beauty. But these painters and sculptors were not pure Hellenes: they came from centres long penetrated by oriental influences. Many of them had Egyptian or Syrian blood in their veins, and were quick to graft upon the Hellenic stock much that would have been abhorrent to the spirit of the older Hellas. To the end Greece controlled the composition and inspired the attitude or gesture; but at an early period the East imposed aspects, such as the oriental conception of Christ (p. 671), or introduced scenes and subjects like the *Anastasis* (p. 663) or *Deesis*, which bear no trace of a Hellenic origin.[1] Of subjects adapted from Hellenistic sources we may cite the episode of the Washing of the Child, so constant in Byzantine Nativities, probably borrowed from the similar scene as it occurred in pagan life. Models were not wanting in contemporary art: one is found in a relief in the Museum of the Capitol at Rome.[2] More familiar is the adoption of Orpheus charming the beasts with his lyre, a common subject in the art of the Roman Empire; the legendary musician was connected with

---

[1] A theory which has received considerable support derives the type of the Virgin with the Child from Isis and Horus; the type of St. George mounted and attacking the dragon has been associated with Horus (Clermont Ganneau, *Horus et Saint-Georges*, 1877).

[2] *Museum Capitolinum*, iv, Pl. 60. See also G. Salomon, *La Statue de Milo*, ii, Pl. XI, Fig. 47.

ideas of death and the life to come, and thus by an almost natural
transition came to be regarded as a type of Christ.[1] The iconographical
debt to classical art apparent in the episode is even clearer if we descend
to the attitude or the gesture. The Christian gestures of benediction [2]
were originally positions of the fingers indicating that the person represented was engaged in conversation with another. The so-called Latin
benediction, in which the third and fourth fingers are bent down upon the

FIG. 408.   The Pentecost : miniature from the Syriac Gospel of Rabula (A. D. 586) in the
Laurentian Library, Florence. (*Hautes Études* : A. Venturi.) P. 662.

palm, while the first and second are extended, is most commonly found in
pagan art with this general and secular meaning. The Greek benediction,
in which the third (more rarely the second) finger joins the thumb so as
to form a circle, while the other fingers remain extended,[3] is rarer as a mere
sign of discourse. The mourning attitude, in which the head of a standing
person is supported upon the hand, characteristic of the Virgin and St. John
in Crucifixion scenes, originated in Greek art. It occurs, for example, on

[1] Cf. Heussner, *R. Q.*, iv. 104 ff. ; *Zeitschr. des deutschen Palästina-Vereins*, xxiv. 139 ff.
[2] N. P. Kondakoff, *Enamels*, 292 ; H. von der Gabelentz, *Die kirchliche Kunst im italienischen Mittelalter*, 67. In Early Christian art there is no distinction between the Latin and Greek gestures (Kraus, *Realencyklopädie*, ii. 751).
[3] So in the Egbert Codex, where it is frequent (*Göttingische gelehrte Anzeigen*, 1890, pp. 880-1), and in the Alcuin Bible in the British Museum.

the well-known sarcophagus of the Mourning Women from Sidon, which is of the fourth century B. C.[1] Another, but less common attitude expressive of grief, in which both arms hang at full length before the body while the hands are joined, is derived from the same Hellenistic source. The touching of the chin with the hand, as a sign of reflection, is also Greek.[2] It is often Peter's attitude at the Last Supper, and appears as early as the

FIG. 409. The Pentecost : miniature of the early twelfth century in the Psalter of Queen Melisenda in the British Museum. (Egerton 1139.) P. 662.

sixth century in the Cotton Bible. The position of the right hand just issuing from the fold of the mantle, which almost appears to restrain it, as in the case of the 'Sophocles' in the Lateran Museum, is characteristic of the orator in classical times. The attitude was probably transmitted to the West by Byzantine art.[3] The familiar recumbent position at meals was retained by the artists of the Christian East, and is always seen in the case of the front figures in the Last Supper. It was not adopted in the West, where Christ and the disciples are all seated upright.

---

[1] Studnicka, *Rev. arch.*, 1905, Pl. XII, XIII.   [2] Baumeister, *Denkmäler*, i. 589.
[3] It is used by Duccio, and occurs in Italian mosaics and early German MSS. influenced by Byzantine art (Dobbert, Prussian *Jahrbuch*, xv. 220).

Down to the fifth century subjects derived from the chase and country life, animals, fruits, and motives without any obvious religious significance were employed to decorate sacred buildings. Although religious symbolism lent many of these a new meaning,[1] they belonged to the picturesque art which especially flourished in Alexandria. We see them in the early mosaics, as well as in the paintings of the Catacombs; they covered the walls or vaults of churches in the First Period, and their character is preserved in the paintings of Kuṣeir 'Amra (p. 282). In the fifth century, when the desire to see sacred history openly represented had triumphed over symbolism, the pagan element declined and scenes from the Old and New Testament became general. Both in East and West we read of decoration in this new 'historical' style,[2] which soon brought in its train the representation of more recent events and the introduction of secular persons: in this way the portrait became more and more popular. The mosaics in San Vitale and at Parenzo, where Justinian, Theodore, Archbishop Maximianus, and Bishop Euphrasius are depicted, illustrate the growth of this tendency,[3] which continued until the last period of Byzantine art, and is instanced by the figure of Metochites at Kahrié Djami (Fig. 245). In secular art it was naturally of more frequent occurrence. The representation of the triumphs of Belisarius in the imperial palace of Chalce at Constantinople included much portraiture, and in the hall and chambers of the Kainourgion Basil I was seen enthroned among the generals of his army or surrounded by the members of the imperial family. The princes of later dynasties commanded historical frescoes in which portraits were freely introduced (p. 261).

With the progress of time the symbolism of the earliest period and the historical treatment which succeeded it were blended in the service of the liturgical idea, by which the mind and eye of the worshipper were directed toward the contemplation of the sacred mysteries. The mosaics and paintings upon the church walls are sometimes inspired by the liturgy performed within them, as in the early case of S. Vitale at Ravenna.[4] As the idea of sacrifice was elaborated, the scenes from the Passion, avoided by Early Christian art, took a conspicuous place in fresco and mosaic. The Crucifixion itself was naturally the last of these scenes to be represented, and though it was certainly known in the sixth century, it was still with

---

[1] Thus the parable may well have contributed to the popularity of the fishing scenes; the vine has an equally obvious application; the flowery meadows and palm-trees suggest the joys of Paradise, &c. Animal and bird decoration was still used, though rarely, in the Third Period. Cf. frescoes of a rock-hewn church in Cappadocia about eleventh–twelfth century (H. Rott, *Kleinasiatische Denkmäler*, 232).

[2] The Gospel scenes were represented in the church at Blachernae, built by Pulcheria in A.D. 451. In Cyprus, at Patras, &c., we read of the same thing. Cf. G. Millet in A. Michel's *Histoire de l'art*, i. 177.

[3] The destruction of so many early mural paintings has involved the ruin of many painted fresco portraits. Here again the mural paintings of Kuṣeir 'Amra, with their group of sovereign princes, represent the practice of an earlier art.

[4] Quoted by Millet in A. Michel, *Histoire de l'art*, i, Pt. I, 181. It has been observed elsewhere (pp. 358 ff.) that the decorations of S. Vitale may have a direct relation to the Monophysite controversy.

comparative frequency replaced by such compromises as those seen on the ampullae of Monza,[1] or by the simple cross without the figure of the Crucified.[2] In the series of Gospel pictures in the mosaics of S. Apollinare Nuovo at Ravenna, the Crucifixion scene is altogether omitted.[3] The iconoclastic dispute arrested the progress of this development, and reduced the decoration of churches to simpler forms. The iconoclasts did not object to figure subjects, but were determined to prevent what they regarded as

Fig. 410. Joseph's Dream, the Flight into Egypt, the Baptism, the Transfiguration, the Raising of Lazarus: mosaics of the twelfth century in the Cappella Palatina, Palermo. (*Hautes Études*: G. Millet.)

idolatry. Deriving their inspiration from oriental sentiment, they wished to restore to Christian art the characteristics which had marked it at its birth. The iconoclastic interlude was not an outbreak of Puritanism: many of the subjects tolerated by the destroyers of images would have displeased the Puritan even more than ikons: it meant a temporary return upon an abandoned point of view. It enlarged the range of secular subjects, and in this way compensated for its neglect of those bearing a religious character.[4]

The triumph of the venerators of images under Irene and Theodora

---

[1] Where the bust of Christ is, in all cases but one, seen above, and detached from the cross. This idea was continued in the Roman churches, as at S. Stefano Rotondo.

[2] As in the mosaics of St. Irene at Constantinople (Fig. 226).

[3] It may have been reserved for some other place, though of this there is no evidence.

[4] Schnaase, *Gesch. der bildenden Künste*, 2nd ed., iii. 227 ff. The well-known 'Palatine' MSS. (the Paris Psalter, Homilies of Gregory, &c.) of the tenth and eleventh centuries may have been influenced by the monumental work of this time, as well as by late Hellenic models of earlier date. For these MSS. see Kondakoff, *Histoire de l'art byz.*, ii. 57–8, 102 ; J. J. Tikkanen, *Die Psalterillustration*, &c., 135).

restored the union between liturgy and art.   From the second half of the
ninth century the concordance between the spoken word and its translation
into visible form becomes more and more precise, until in about a hundred
years the final phase of Byzantine iconography was established in all its
essential features.   Most frequent and conspicuous is the group of subjects
illustrating the principal feasts of the liturgical Calendar, while the
apocalyptic figures of earlier symbolism were retained and amplified,
especially those illustrating the Last Judgement.   The figure of Christ
becomes predominant, no longer the Christ of the Gospels, but the Pantokrator or image of the invisible God, the visible expression of that union
in one form of the divine and human natures which the Councils of Ephesus
and Chalcedon had established as an article of belief.[1]   He looks down from
the top of the principal dome, which represents the celestial Church, while
in the central apse the Virgin stands as representative of the Church on
earth interceding for sinful mankind.   For in the Third Period the decoration of churches was regulated according to an elaborate theological system :
the church represented the cosmos, and every corner of it had its appropriate ornament.[2]   By the eleventh century a complete scheme was established over which the influence of the liturgy was predominant ; in the
Fourth Period, as at Mistra, that influence had become supreme.   Old
Testament subjects yield place to those depicting the life of Christ and the
Virgin.   In middle and later Byzantine art the Old Testament is chiefly
represented by the single figures of prophets or priests whose message or
whose function brings them into relation to the story of Christ.   In the
mosaics these figures are constantly found, and in the conspicuous positions
which their character requires.   They were commonly placed round the
lower zone of the principal dome, in the top of which was throned the
Pantokrator: in the intermediate zone between them and this central
figure stood a line of angels.   The commanding place given to St. John
the Baptist, who sometimes occupies the centre of a group even when Our
Lord is also present, may be explained by the fact that he is regarded,
with Zachariah, Simeon, and Anna, as among the last of the prophets,
while at the same time he is the Baptist of the New Messiah.[3]   On the
front of the chair of Maximianus (Fig. 122) and in the miniature of the
Vatican Cosmas representing the last prophets, St. John occupies the
central position.   Even once-popular subjects from the New Testament
were neglected if they had no liturgical significance.[4]   The miracles play

---

[1] The Council of A.D. 692 forbade the representation of Christ under the image of a lamb.

[2] The most perfect remaining examples are St. Luke in Phocis, Daphni, and the Sicilian churches.   For the usual arrangement of subjects the reader may consult ch. iv of Bk. III in M. Diehl's *Manuel* (pp. 448 ff.).

[3] Strzygowski, *Denkschriften* of the Vienna Academy, li, 1906, 163.

[4] The New Testament scenes most frequently found are the 'Twelve Feasts' of the Calendar : The Annunciation, Nativity, Presentation, Baptism, Transfiguration, Raising of Lazarus, Entry into Jerusalem, Crucifixion, *Anastasis*, Pentecost, Ascension, and Death of the Virgin.   It may be noted that in the rock-cut chapels of Cappadocia (p. 268) the Miracles are still found, as well as apocryphal subjects equally popular in the art of the First Period.   In this respect these frescoes are curiously conservative.

a very small part after the establishment of the new iconography. Although from the Third Period onwards the tendency to impose a rigid scheme of composition for all religious scenes increased, it is a mistake to suppose that the rules were always obeyed. Doubtless painters usually conformed to precedent, but compulsory uniformity could never be enforced. The 'Painter's Manual', discovered on Mount Athos, and published in the first instance by Didron, is now known to be of much later date than was originally supposed. The writer, Dionysios of Furna, lived in the early eighteenth century, and his oldest sources do not go further back than about two hundred years.[1] It is not easy to say at what time the individual subjects composing Byzantine iconography assumed a stereo-typed form. Some had already become fixed in the sixth century; of this the miniatures of the Codex Rossanensis (p. 452) afford important proof.

Fig. 411. Christ before Pilate ; the Crucifixion : miniature from a twelfth-century Gospel in the Laurentian Library, Florence. (*Hautes Études* : G. Millet.)

In that MS. the Raising of Lazarus, the Entry into Jerusalem, and the Last Supper already have, with other subjects, the essential features which they retain in late Byzantine art.[2]

The influence of East-Christian iconographical types was almost con-tinually felt in one or the other part of Europe down to the thirteenth century; the principal vehicle was the illuminated manuscript. But this influence was often indirect, and the Western artist shows a constant tendency to diversify the theme by original traits of his own invention. The study of early German mediaeval MSS. seems to show that about A.D. 1200 the Eastern types were more followed than they had been two hundred years earlier. Byzantium was most influential just at the moment when she herself was about to enter upon her decline, and Europe to begin the development of the Gothic style.[3]

---

[1] A. Papadopoulos Kerameus, *Denys de Fourna, Manuel d'iconographie chrétienne,* &c., St. Peters-burg, 1900, and the same author's later Διονυσίου τοῦ ἐκ Φουρνᾶ Ἑρμηνεία τῆς ζωγραφικῆς, &c., St. Petersburg, 1909. A principal source drawn upon by Dionysios was an anonymous painter's book of A.D. 1566.

[2] Haseloff, *Codex purpureus Rossanensis,* 127 ff. Heisenberg assigns an equal importance to the lost mosaics of the Church of the Apostles at Constantinople : this they would certainly possess were their origin in the sixth century beyond dispute (A. Heisenberg, *Grabeskirche und Apostelkirche,* ii. 140 ff.).

[3] A. Haseloff, *Eine Thüringisch-Sächsische Malerschule,* pp. 217–18, Strassburg, 1897.

It may be useful to pass in review a selected number of scenes and types of habitual occurrence or especial interest. But the following pages can offer little more than a series of notes, only developed in the case of certain New Testament subjects.

(a) COMPOSITIONS AND SCENES.

It will be necessary to pass rapidly over scenes from the Old Testament. The Book of Genesis provided many themes illustrated in Bibles, Octateuchs,

FIG. 412. Abraham entertaining the angels, symbolic of the Trinity : illumination in the Psalter of A. D. 1066 in the British Museum. (Add. MS. 19352.) P. 652.

Psalters, and other MSS., and in the decoration of churches, as in Sicily and Venice. Among cycles, the story of Joseph was early popular. It furnishes numerous illustrations in the Vienna Genesis (p. 445) and covers a large part of the ivory episcopal throne at Ravenna (pp. 205–6): it continued to attract during later periods, for the career of the Jewish hero was considered typical of that of Christ. The ivory casket of which the scattered parts are in the British and the Berlin Museum (Fig. 137) shows that it was familiar to the carvers of the twelfth century. Episodes from the story of Moses, especially the Passage of the Red Sea, were continually repeated, but rather to illustrate passages in the

Psalms than as parts of the original history. A cycle rivalling that of Joseph depicted the exploits of Joshua. Like the story of Abraham, it had formed part of the scenes in the nave mosaics of Sta Maria Maggiore at Rome; and the Joshua Rotulus at the Vatican, whatever its own date, is evidently a copy of an original perhaps as early as the fourth century. Jonah, so frequently found in Early Christian art, is rarer after the First Period: he is now usually clothed instead of naked.[1] The life and exploits of David, though not frequent in Early Christian art,[2] are found in the frescoes of Bawit in Egypt (p. 284), which are of the First Period. They have been noted above on the silver dishes from Cyprus and other works of the minor arts (p. 576). The

Fig. 413. The Arming of David : silver dish of the sixth century from Cyprus. (Collection of J. Pierpont Morgan, Esq.)

David cycle is the most frequent of all those derived from the Old Testament on account of the popularity of the Psalter.[3] This book is really a link between the iconography of the Old and New Testaments, for it incorporates many scenes from other early books of the Bible, and inserts amongst them, especially to illustrate the prophetic passages, scenes from the life and Passion of Christ.

Individual scenes from the Old Testament survived in iconography as possessing a particular liturgical or theological significance. Episodes in the life of Abraham, for example, were important from this point of view. One of these is the Sacrifice of Isaac, typical of the Lord's Supper;[4] another, the

---

[1] For Jonah in Early Christian art see O. Mitius, *Jonas auf den Denkmälern*, &c., 1897 ; the story is represented in frescoes in the oases of the Libyan Desert. See V. de Bock, *Matériaux pour servir à l'archéologie de l'Égypte chrétienne*, Pl. X. See also Strzygowski in *Denkschriften* of the Vienna Academy, *Phil.-hist. Klasse*, 1, 1904, 148.

[2] David with the sling is found on the roof-frescoes in the cemetery of Calixtus, on the ivory reliquary at Brescia (see p. 192), and on sarcophagi from Gaul (E. Le Blant, *Sarcophages*, &c., p. viii, note 8, and p. xx).

[3] The Creation cycle is found at Monreale, in the Cappella Palatina at Palermo, and the Baptistery at Florence. It also occurs in Italo-Byzantine art on the ivory paliotto of Salerno, in the frescoes of Ferentillo and Assisi, &c.

[4] This scene was a favourite in Early Christian art. Its directly symbolical nature is emphasized in the sixth century, as in the mosaics of S. Vitale at Ravenna (p. 358). See J. Wilpert, *Das Opfer Abrahams in der altchristlichen Kunst*, R. Q., i, 1887, 130 ff.

Entertainment of the three Angels (Fig. 412), which came to represent the Trinity in the art of the Eastern Church.[1]

Subjects illustrating the lives of Our Lord and the Virgin are of more frequent occurrence, and a selection from among them may be more particularly described, attention being called, where possible, to analogies or differences between Eastern and Western modes of treatment.

Annunciation.[2]

(Cf. Figs. 6, 95, 149, 155, 189, 219, 246, 254, 305, 309, 378, 414.)

The angel advances, usually from the left, carrying a rod or wand in his left hand. The Virgin is either seated upon a cushioned bench, or has

FIG. 414. The Annunciation : miniature in a Gospel of the twelfth century in the British Museum. (Harley 1810.)

just risen from it. She holds the spindle with the red or purple thread, and by her side is a basket.[3] Behind are buildings, but the scene passes in the open.

[1] The so-called Ἁγία Τριάς, mentioned in the ' Painter's Manual ' of Mount Athos, but occurring far earlier in Byzantine art and frequent in the frescoes of the Cappadocian churches (see p. 268).

[2] J. Strzygowski, B. D., i. 42–4 and 101 ; G. Millet, B. C. H., xviii, 1895, 453 ff. ; Pokrovsky, Gospel, &c., pp. 3 ff. ; J. Stuhlfauth, Die Engel in der altchristlichen Kunst, 58–78 ; A. Heisenberg, Grabeskirche und Apostelkirche, ii, 1908, 221 ff. ; V. de Grüneisen, Scritti di storia di filologia e d'arte, Rome, 1907, 15–37 ; Th. Schmidt, Izviestiya of the Russian Arch. Inst. at Cple., xi, 1906, p. 153.

[3] The Virgin is supposed to have been occupied in weaving a purple veil for the Temple when the angel appeared. The basket is not usually found after the eleventh century.

The rarer type, in which the angel finds the Virgin drawing water from the well, also based upon the apocryphal Gospels, is not favoured by later Byzantine artists.

In the later periods the Virgin is commonly seated; the standing type, which is found on the early ampullae at Monza (p. 623), and has been specially associated with Syria-Palestine, was not abandoned. The dove is sometimes represented above the Virgin's head.

In the West, with the fourteenth century, the angel gradually assumes more

Fig. 415. The Nativity, Washing of the Child, and Annunciation to the Shepherds: mosaics of the fourteenth century in Kahrié Djami, Constantinople. (Sébah and Joaillier).

animation, and is seen as it were flying forward or kneeling;[1] the wool and basket are absent, and the scene is usually enacted under a roof. The lily in the pot is Western, and becomes common in Italy in the fourteenth century.[2]

Nativity.[3]

(Cf. Figs. 149, 155, 254, 305, 415.)

In this scene the Virgin usually lies upon a kind of mattress, while the Child is in a manger of masonry with the ox and ass behind it. In the fore-

---

[1] In quite early Italian pictures, such as Duccio's Annunciation in the National Gallery, the Byzantine type is retained. The angel has the collected manner usually seen in Byzantine Annunciations, from which the example at Kahrié Djami markedly differs (Fig. 246).

[2] H. von der Gabelentz, *Die kirchliche Kunst im italienischen Mittelalter*, 99.

[3] See Max Schmid, *Die Darstellung der Geburt Christi in der bildenden Kunst*, Stuttgart, 1890; A. Heisenberg, *Grabeskirche und Apostelkirche*, ii. 223 ff., Leipsic, 1908; Pokrovsky, *Gospel*, &c., 48 ff.

ground Joseph is seated on one side resting his head on his hand,[1] while on the other side the nurses are seen preparing a bath for the Child.   Behind the manger is the mouth of a cave[2] in the side of a hill, on the slopes of which are shepherds with their flocks receiving the message from the angels, who appear in the sky.   A shaft of light often descends from a segment of a circle above.

The episode of the Washing of the Child is a very constant feature in Byzantine Nativities, while in the West this is not the case.   It is probably derived from the apocryphal Gospels,[3] but, as already mentioned, the actual models may have been classical, and connected with the legend of Bacchus.[4]

The episode of the incredulous midwife Salome extending her withered hand to touch the Child is also based upon apocryphal and oriental sources.   It has been commonly thought not to occur much before A.D. 800.[5]   In Western Nativities some kind of stall is almost invariably shown above the manger.

Adoration of the Magi.[6]

(Cf. Figs. 36, 84, 114, 126, 232, 281, 305, 366.)

In this scene, a favourite in Early Christian art, the Magi are represented in Persian costume, with tight hose and ' Phrygian ' caps.[7]   By the sixth century it had become common to introduce an angel, who presents the kings to the Virgin and Child.   Joseph is also introduced, standing in a subordinate position behind the chair.[8]   The arrangement is in early examples often symmetrical, the Virgin sitting full face, the angel and the kings grouped on either side : this appears to be characteristically Syrian.[9]   The distinction of the Magi according to their ages, the first an old man, the second of middle age, the third young, is adumbrated on the sixth-century ampullae at Monza, where two of the kings appear bearded and the third beardless.[10]

The Persian costume was retained in Carolingian art, which was largely based upon Early Christian and early Byzantine models.   Crowns first appear in the West in the twelfth century.   In the East they seem to be rather earlier, occurring in the Paris Gregory Codex (No. 510) and the Vatican Menologium.

Baptism.

(Cf. Figs. 95, 111, 155, 254, 305, 410.)

This subject has been well treated by Strzygowski,[11] and more recently by C. F. Rogers,[12] A. Jacoby,[13] and Heisenberg in the work already cited.[14] John the Baptist almost always stands upon the left, and, after the eleventh

---

[1] The features mentioned thus far occur on the Monza ampullae of the sixth century. The Washing of the Child is not there found.

[2] The cave is mentioned in the apocryphal Gospels.

[3] Dobbert in Prussian *Jahrbuch*, vi, 1885, 159–60, though the first definite literary mention appears to be in Symeon Metaphrastes.   See also the same writer, *Ueber den Styl Niccolò Pisano's*, &c, 81.

[4] F. Noack, *Die Geburt Christi in der bildenden Kunst*, Darmstadt, 1894 ; *B.Z.*, iv, 1895, 601 ff. ; A. Kirpičnikoff, *Memoirs of the Imperial Russian Arch. Soc.*, vii ; Heisenberg, ii. 227.

[5] Schmid, as above, 39 and 125.

[6] Pokrovsky, *Gospel*, &c., 113 ff. ; Lehner, *Die Marienverehrung in den ersten Jahrhunderten*, Stuttgart, 1881 ; Liell, *Die Darstellung der allerheiligsten Jungfrau*, &c. ; Rohault de Fleury, *L'Évangile*; A. Heisenberg, as above, ii. 229 ff. ; H. Kehrer, *Die Heiligen Drei Könige*, &c., 1908.

[7] It will be remembered that when Chosroes captured Jerusalem he is said to have spared the mosaic upon the Church of the Nativity representing the Adoration because he recognized the Magi as Persians.

[8] But there is no angel on the sixth-century Monza ampullae, on which the Adoration is combined with the Annunciation to the Shepherds.   The introduction of Joseph is due to the influence of the apocryphal Gospels (Ainaloff in *V. V.*, v. 171, note).

[9] See Heisenberg, Pt. II, 231.

[10] Garrucci, *Storia*, 433, Fig. 9.   The sixth-century Gospels of Etchmiadzin show a distinction of age (J. Strzygowski, *B. D.*, i, Pl. VI, Fig. 1).

[11] *Ikonographie der Taufe Christi*, 1885.   [12] *Baptism and Christian Archaeology*, Oxford, 1903.

[13] *Ein bisher unbeachteter apokrypher Bericht über die Taufe Jesu*, Strassburg, 1902.

[14] *Grabeskirche und Apostelkirche*, ii 236.

century, always on a higher level than Our Lord, on whose head he lays his hand. Christ stands approximately full face ; he is bearded, and usually makes the gesture of benediction with his right hand, which, however, is not raised. On the opposite bank of the river stand angels holding cloths or towels, or extending the ends of their mantles, to dry the body of Our Lord. In the eleventh century there are usually two angels ; later three or even more.[1] The dove descends in a shaft of light issuing from a segment of a circle at the top : in the background to right and left are symmetrical rocks between which the river flows. St. John and the angels are often represented in a posture suggesting energetic action. Behind the Baptist is often a small tree with the axe at its root (Matthew iii. 10), which appears as early as the sixth century.[2]

A personification of Jordan, based on the classical type of river-god, is often seen in the foreground, recumbent upon his urn. Occasionally a cross is represented in the water. The personification of Jordan was already common in the sixth century ; cf. the Orthodox Baptistery at Ravenna.

The points in which the Byzantine scheme influenced European representations in the twelfth century have been fully discussed by Haseloff.[3]

Transfiguration.[4]

(Cf. Figs. 79, 149, 155, 184, 225, 254, 410, 416.)

Christ stands on the central of three summits ; on the other two stand Moses (young) and Elias (old) inclining their heads towards him. Usually Christ is alone in a mandorla, and light radiates from his body : sometimes all three figures are in one large glory. In the foreground are Peter, James, and John in attitudes of amazement and fear, sometimes expressed by exaggerated gesture. A shaft of light descends from a segment above as in the Baptism. The subject is not certainly represented in Christian art before the sixth century, when it occurs in the Syrian Gospel of Rabula and in the apse mosaic of S. Apollinare in Classe at Ravenna. But in neither of these cases is the composition of the traditional Byzantine type described above, which is first known to us from the lost mosaics of the Church of the Apostles at Constantinople.[5]

In the West the Transfiguration, though it is found by exception in earlier times, is not a common subject until rather late : it only became popular after A.D. 1457, when the Feast of the Transfiguration was universally observed.[6] The figures of the Apostles are not in such strained attitudes as in the East.

The rays issuing from Our Lord's body are a Byzantine feature, as also is the marked difference between the ages of Moses and Elias.[7]

Raising of Lazarus.[8]

(Cf. Figs. 80, 149, 254, 284, 410)

Lazarus is seen swathed as a mummy in a vertical rock-tomb, in which he stands erect. His form is supported by a man, who, in later representations, begins to unbind the wrappings : a second man sometimes holds the removed door of the tomb. Before him are Mary and Martha kneeling, while Christ advances usually from the left, followed by a crowd. More rarely the personification of Hades is introduced.

---

[1] Strzygowski, 22, 24. On the Monza ampullae there is one angel only.

[2] Garrucci, *Storia*, vi, Pl. 447. Ivory panel in the Victoria and Albert Museum.

[3] *Eine Thüringisch-Sächsische Malerschule des 13. Jahrhunderts*, 115 ff., Strassburg, 1897.

[4] Dobbert in Prussian *Jahrbuch*, xv, p. 135.

[5] As described by Mesarites, see Heisenberg, as above, ii. 181.

[6] Augusti, *Denkwürdigkeiten aus der christlichen Archäologie*, iii. 292 ; Pokrovsky, *Iconography*, 202.

[7] The relations of the Western and Byzantine types are discussed by Haseloff, *Thüringisch-Sächsische Malerschule*, &c., 124–7.

[8] Pokrovsky, *Gospel*, &c., 249 ff. ; Dobbert, as above, 146 ; Heisenberg, ii. 241.

The subject, which occurs in Early Christian art, is frequent in later times. An interesting early Byzantine example is in the Codex Rossanensis, where the ampler and more historical treatment first appears.

Entry into Jerusalem.[1]

(Cf. also Figs. 13, 143, 149.)

Christ usually rides from the left, always sitting sideways.[1] People issuing from the gate of Jerusalem on the right spread garments before him and carry branches; others who have mounted trees in the background cast branches

Fig. 416. The Transfiguration: miniature of the early twelfth century in the Psalter of Queen Melisenda, British Museum. (Egerton 1139.) P. 655.

down. These people are represented as of childish stature, though their proportions and expressions are those of adults: possibly this feature may be due to the description of the scene in the apocryphal Gospels,[2] though, as children are specially mentioned in Matthew xxi, the explanation does not seem necessary.

The essential details appear early in Christian art, but the sideways position of Our Lord, and the childish proportions of the persons who greet him, belong to Eastern Christianity. In the West, Christ frequently rides from the right; the

---

[1] Dobbert, as above, 149; A. Haseloff, *Codex Purpureus Rossanensis*, 91 ff.; Ussoff, *Drevnosti* (Moscow), ix, p. 43; Pokrovsky, *Gospel*, &c., 258 ff.; Heisenberg, ii. 247.

[2] Tischendorf, Apocryphal Gospels, *Gesta Pilati*, i. 3.

people who meet him are adult ; and he almost invariably rides astride.[1] The fact that he does so on Early Christian sarcophagi is an argument in favour of their Western origin.[2]

Fig. 417. The Entry into Jerusalem : mosaic of the eleventh century in the Monastery Church of Daphni, Attica. (*Hautes Études* : G. Millet.)

The Washing of the Apostles' Feet.[3]

(Cf. Fig. 229.)

On the left the Apostles are seated on a bench : Peter sits at its left end, one foot over a vessel of water, above which Christ bends. Peter raises his right hand to his forehead to express the sense of his unworthiness.

In the Western version this type is often closely followed, though the position

[1] Where the sideways position appears in the West, as in the Sacramentary at Bamberg of the eleventh century (ed. iii. 11), there are other indications of direct oriental influence. Childish figures also occur in certain Western MSS.; but here again their elderly appearance suggests a Byzantine influence. There are several Western examples of the thirteenth century (Haseloff, *Thüringisch-Sächsische Malerschule*, 137).

[2] He is seen so riding on the well-known sarcophagus of Junius Bassus, and on a Lateran sarcophagus (Garrucci, *Storia*, Pl. 313. 4), &c. [3] Dobbert, as above, 151.

of the personages is sometimes reversed, Christ being on the right, the Apostles on the left.

The Agony in the Garden.[1]

Christ is seen praying on the right; and by an example of the 'continuous' narrative method reappears on the left awakening the sleeping disciples. Sometimes an angel appears to the kneeling Christ: sometimes the whole group of the Apostles is substituted for the three.

The scene is already treated by the continuous method in the Codex Rossanensis.

The Betrayal.[2]

Here all the essential features are common to East and West, except as regards particular attitudes and gestures. But in Byzantine art Judas usually approaches Christ with a hurried and rapid movement. Peter is always seen cutting off Malchus' ear: the crowd always carry lights in the background. Duccio, in his Maestà at Sienna, has given an ideal rendering of the scene.

The Last Supper.[3]

The Byzantine composition shows a semicircular table with the chord towards the spectator; round it the Apostles recline. At the end to the spectator's left Christ reclines[4] in the antique fashion with St. John near him, while in the corresponding position on the right is St. Peter. Further back on the right Judas reaches over the table towards a dish upon which a fish is commonly seen. This type begins in the First Period (Codex Rossanensis).

In illuminated Psalters the Last Supper frequently occurs as an illustration to Psalm xl. 10. The Communion of the Apostles (see p. 666) is a symbolic version of the Last Supper, and is also found in the Rossano Codex.

The Last Supper in Western mediaeval art is based on John xiii. 21-30. The participants do not recline, but are seated at the table; in front of it Judas is seen receiving the sop from Our Lord, who sits in the middle on the other side.

The Crucifixion.[5]

(Cf. Figs. 140, 149, 164, 187, 188, 192, 193, 252, 261, 318, 348, 411, 418.)

The representation of Christ upon the Cross was not tolerated by the sentiment of the earliest centuries. The oldest examples known to us, of which the door of Sta Sabina at Rome and the ivory panel in the British Museum are the most prominent, show Our Lord as still living: the Virgin and St. John are already present,[6] though not in the symmetrical positions occupied by them at a later time. It is with the sixth century that the subject begins to appear with greater frequency, though in some examples we still meet with a reluctance to represent Christ actually upon the Cross: on the ampullae from the Holy

---

[1] Dobbert, 152.   [2] Dobbert, 152 ; Heisenberg, as above, ii, p. 249.
[3] E. Dobbert, *Repertorium*, xv, 1892, 357–84 (for Last Suppers in Early Christian art see his earlier publication on the subject, printed in 1872). See also Prussian *Jahrbuch*, xv. 130.
[4] More rarely Our Lord is seen sitting, a posture in which St. Peter is more frequently represented.
[5] Dobbert, Prussian *Jahrbuch*, vol. i. p. 41 ff. ; J. Reil, *Die frühchristliche Darstellung der Kreuzigung*, Leipzig, 1904 ; Zestermann, *Die bildliche Darstellung des Kreuzes* ; Forrer and Müller, *Kreuz und Kreuzigung Christi in ihrer Kunstentwicklung* ; L. Bréhier, *Les Origines du Crucifix dans l'art religieux*, 1904 ; Strzygowski in *B. Z.*, xiv, 1905, 363, and xiii, 1904, 662.
[6] As indicated by the version in the Gospel of St. John, which artists evidently followed.
     e. g. on the Monza ampullae (p. 624). This in spite of the fact that Choricius of Gaza and Gregory of Tours both allude to representations of the Crucifixion publicly shown in churches. Both of these writers lived in the sixth century, and Choricius in the early part of it. The ampullae at Monza, which represent types of the same century, show us as a rule the bust of Christ above the Cross, from which it is quite detached. Perhaps the designs on the ampullae reproduce those of lost Palestinian mosaics.

Land at Monza, the thieves are represented upon their crosses; but the central cross is merely surmounted by a medallion containing the head of Christ, or else by a standing figure in long raiment with the arms extended.[1] Of other actors in the drama, the Virgin and St. John stand to right and left.

FIG. 418. The Crucifixion : mosaic of the eleventh century in the Monastery of Daphni.
(*Hautes Études* : G. Millet.)

though two kneeling figures sometimes appear at the foot of the Cross, possibly representing Adam and Eve. The sun and moon, henceforth regularly present, are personified as busts, as usually down to the thirteenth century. The most elaborate of the early Crucifixions is the miniature in the Gospel of Rabula (p. 448), which, however, is not certainly of the same date as the book (A.D. 586).

---

[1] Garrucci, *Storia*, vi, Pl. 434. 2. For the whole figure with extended arms, see ibid., 434. 4; Cabrol, *Dictionnaire d'arch. chrétienne*, s.v. *Ampoules*.

Here not only are the Virgin and St. John, the mourning women, the thieves, and Longinus present, but the sponge-bearer (Stephaton) is for the first time introduced, as well as the soldiers casting lots (by the game of *morra*) for the seamless garment.   The sun and moon are a disk and crescent, features being drawn upon the sun.[1]

Although the historical, as opposed to the 'liturgical' treatment, is not that generally adopted in later centuries, it yet occurs long after the early period.[2] Symbolic figures recalling those so commonly found in Carolingian Crucifixions are also found.   A figure kneeling at the foot of the Cross, and representing either Faith or (less probably) the Church, is seen receiving the blood in a chalice in several illuminated manuscripts.[3]   The church and synagogue, in like manner very popular in Carolingian times, also occur in Byzantine Crucifixions, though very rarely.   One example is on an enamel in the Botkin Collection, reproduced by Kondakoff in his work on the Swenigorodskoi Collection (Pl. XIII) ; Kondakoff sees in these figures Mary Magdalen and Mary, wife of Cleophas.[4]   Another is in a Syrian MS. of the thirteenth century in the British Museum.[5]   Others are found in the eleventh-century Gospel in the Bibliothèque Nationale at Paris (see note 3, below), and in a Bulgarian MS. in Lord Zouche's Collection.   In Byzantine art these figures are introduced by angels, a feature which in Western art is chiefly found in Italy, where it may be due to Byzantine influence ; it is so characteristic of the Eastern versions that these can hardly be derived from early Western art, as Weber[6] was inclined to suppose.   Further, the distribution of the MSS. showing these figures is very wide among Eastern nations. The historical treatment, which from its wealth of detail reminds us of the Carolingian Crucifixions, is not that which became typical in the art of later centuries.[7]   As a rule only the Virgin and St. John stand on either side of the Cross, below which the skull of Adam is commonly seen.[8]   Above the arms are two half-figures of angels, with the sun and moon represented as a radiate disk and a crescent, both on a small and inconspicuous scale.   The feet of Our Lord always rest upon a *suppedaneum* ; his head, which is surrounded by a cruciferous nimbus, is inclined over his right side, and the arms are only slightly bent.   Though the eyes are closed, and the figure is represented as dying or dead, there is no suggestion of agony, but rather of final repose.   The long hair falls over the shoulders ; the face is always bearded ; a loincloth reaches from the waist to the knee and the body is rather emaciated.   The colobium, or long sleeveless tunic, is seen in the Rabula miniature, and frequently occurs in examples of the eighth to tenth centuries (Figs. 188, 302). But the colobium is not a proof of early date: it occurs for example in the British Museum Psalter of A.D. 1066, where there are also other Crucifixions in which the short loincloth is used.   It is only by exception that any of the other

---

[1] Features are not so common upon the representation of the two luminaries in Byzantine art as in the West.   They occur in the Russo-Byzantine Crucifixion miniature of the eleventh century interpolated in the Psalter of Archbishop Egbert of Trier now in Cividale.

[2] e. g. MS. gr. 1156 in the Vatican Library, where the holy women, John, the captain, and the skull of Adam are all seen (Rohault de Fleury, *La Sainte Vierge*, i, Pl. 48 ; d'Agincourt, *Painting*, Pl. 57 ; Pokrovsky, *The Gospel in the Monuments*, &c., 329).

[3] Gospels of the eleventh century in the Bibliothèque Nationale (MS. grec, 74, f. 59 and 207 : R. de Fleury, *La Sainte Vierge*, Pl. XVI).   Also in the eleventh-century Physiologus MS. at Smyrna (Strzygowski, *Der Bilderkreis des griechischen Physiologus*, &c., Pl. XXIII), and two later MSS. connected with it, one in Russian (Pokrovsky, as above, 328) and one (written in Bulgarian) in Lord Zouche's Collection (R. Curzon, *Catalogue*, 1849, 33).   The earliest known example of this figure is, however, to be found in an eleventh-century Anglo-Saxon Gospel at Holkham Hall.   On the whole subject, see A. Haseloff, *Der Psalter Erzbischof Egberts zu Trier*, 180–1 and 213.
[4] Against this see Haseloff, as above, 181.
[5] Add. MS. 7110.   [6] *Geistliches Schauspiel*, &c., 133 f.
[7] The eleventh-century type is described by Millet, *Monastère de Daphni* (cf. Fig. 418).
[8] The tradition that Adam was buried on Golgotha is recorded by the Fathers (cf. S. Jerome, Letter XLVI, and *Commentary on S. Matthew*, iv, ch. xxvii).   Honorius of Autun, *De Imagine Mundi*, iii (in Migne, *Patr. Lat.*, 172), says *In loco Calvariae sepultus* (Adam) *aliquamdiu requievit*.

figures are represented. Longinus is sometimes seen, not piercing Our Lord's side, but standing with his right arm raised in admiration. Sometimes a kneeling figure (an adoring emperor or empress) is introduced. More rarely still the soldiers appear, casting lots. In Western Crucifixions [1] after the eighth century we still meet with complicated historical versions with numerous accessory figures and personifications. Towards the latter part of the tenth century there is a tendency to adopt the simple group with the Virgin and St. John, or at the

FIG. 419. The Descent from the Cross: miniature of the early twelfth century in the Psalter of Queen Melisenda in the British Museum. (Egerton 1139.)

most, Longinus and Stephaton. At this period a long tunic is worn by Our Lord, but it differs from the colobium in having long sleeves. In the eleventh century Christ is often beardless and youthful, though not invariably so : his eyes are almost always closed, though there are examples of opened eyes as late as the beginning of the thirteenth century.[2] About A.D. 1200 the West intro-

---

[1] For purposes of comparative study the following references to works on Western Crucifixions may be useful : Carolingian Period, Cahier and Martin, *Mélanges d'archéologie*, ii. 39 ff. ; Rhenish Crucifixions of about A.D. 1000, W. Vöge, *Eine deutsche Malerschule um die Wende des ersten Jahrtausends*, Trier, 1891, 265 ; German Crucifixions of the late twelfth and early thirteenth centuries, A. Haseloff, *Eine Thüringisch-Sächsische Malerschule*, Strassburg, 1897, 143 ff. ; English Crucifixions anterior to the thirteenth century, *Proc. Soc. Ant. London*, N. S., xxii. 225 ; Italian Crucifixions, H. von der Gabelentz, *Die kirchliche Kunst im italienischen Mittelalter*, 73.

[2] e. g. Haseloff, as above, 148.

duced the custom of representing the two feet as fastened by a single nail ; this remains almost universal through the Gothic period.   In the fourteenth century began the realistic treatment of the dead Christ, whose body is emaciated and contracted with agony.   The actions of the Virgin and St. John now become dramatic : the Virgin yields altogether to her grief, and is supported by the attendant women (the *spasimo* or *svenimento* of Italian art).

Anastasis.[1]

(Cf. Figs. 149, 157, 407, 420.)

This term is used in East-Christian art for the scene which in the West is described as the Harrowing of Hell.   It is symbolic of, and a substitute for, the Resurrection, which is a less popular subject in the East.[2]   The *Anastasis* is usually connected with the apocryphal Gospel of Nicodemus[3] (ch. xviii), where John the Baptist is said to have foretold the descent of Our Lord into hell.   But it is very probable, as Strzygowski has suggested, that early Egyptian legend and belief affected the typical representation of this subject.   One of the romances of Setne Khamuas, popular in Roman Egypt, describes the visit of Setne to Amenti, the underworld.   In the fifth hall of Amenti they see the wicked rich man, in whose right eye the bolt of the door of the hall is fixed. Mr. Scott Moncrieff[4] has published the whole passage, as it may affect the type of the *Anastasis*, pointing out that the figure of the wicked man grovelling in Amenti with the long door-post fixed in his eye must have been familiar to Roman Egypt, and as a signal example of retribution may have been adopted in Christian iconography.   At any rate, in *Anastasis* pictures Christ is sometimes seen driving his long staff into the eye of Hades, who lies prostrate before him. The mouth of hell, where shown at all, is indicated by a cavernous entrance, not by the open jaws of a monster, as in Western mediaeval art.   Christ advances over the broken valves of the door, holding a long cross in one hand.   With the other he raises Adam from a sarcophagus-tomb ; behind Adam appear Eve, David, Solomon, and other righteous persons of the Old Testament.   Near Our Lord stands John the Baptist ; behind him are grouped figures of the righteous under the Old Dispensation.   In the foreground, below Christ's feet, lies the figure of Hades as an old bearded man whose hands and feet are chained (cf. Fig. 420).   Sometimes angels are seen fastening the chains.   St. John the Baptist is not found in this scene before the eleventh century.   The ivory carving in the British Museum (*Catalogue of Early Christian and Byzantine Antiquities*, No. 299) is now held to represent another subject.

The Pentecost.

(Cf. Figs. 149, 243, 296, 408, 409.)

The usual Byzantine scheme shows the Virgin and Apostles seated about a space in the form of a round-headed arch, in which appear a figure or figures representing the World which the Apostles were to evangelize (Fig. 409).[5]   Another type is represented by Fig. 408, from the Gospel of Rabula, where the tongues of flame descend upon a group of Apostles, in the centre of whom is the Virgin.

[1] G. Millet, *Mon. Piot*, ii. 209, and *Monastère de Daphni*, s.v. *Limbes* ; Ch. Diehl, *Mon. Piot*. iii. 232 ; H. von der Gabelentz, *Die kirchliche Kunst im italienischen Mittelalter*, 119.   Some authorities consider that the *Anastasis* may have originated in the Holy Land (Baumstark, *R. Q.*, xx, 1906, 125).

[2] Though occurring in miniatures of the MSS. of the middle Byzantine period and later (e. g. the Psalter, eleventh century, in the British Museum, Add. MSS. 19352).   In the First Period, the scenes of the Holy Women at the Tomb often indicate the Resurrection.   These also persist in late times, e. g. Servian Psalter at Munich.

[3] Tischendorff, 83 ff.

[4] *Church Quarterly Review*, Oct., 1909, in the article *Gnosticism and Early Christianity in Egypt*.

[5] In the west cupola at S. Marco, Venice, the Descent of the Holy Spirit is accompanied by figures of sixteen pagan nations.

The Dormition of the Virgin.

(Cf. Figs. 149, 161, 180, 185, 421.)

Here the body of the Virgin lies on a bier round which the Apostles are grouped. Behind it, in the middle, Christ stands holding in his arms the soul

Fig. 420. The *Anastasis*: mosaic of the eleventh century in the Monastery of Daphni.
(*Hautes Études* : G. Millet.)

of his mother, represented as a diminutive human figure. The subject, which is based upon the apocryphal Gospels, is more popular in Byzantine than in Western art, which probably borrowed it in the first instance from Eastern sources.[1]

[1] According to Nicephorus Kallistos, the festival was introduced in the reign of the Emperor Maurice (A. D. 582–602). See *Nuovo Bullettino di arch. crist.*, iv. 53 f. ; Dumont in *Rev. arch.*, 1871. Examples in art are not known until after iconoclasm. One of the earliest appears to

The story was known before the time of Gregory of Tours, who transmitted it in an abridged form to the Church of Gaul. It was subsequently incorporated by Vincent de Beauvais and Jacques de Voragine in their encyclopaedic works. In both East and West we find the episode of the Jewish high-priest who, stopping the funeral procession and endeavouring to obtain possession of the coffin, had his arms withered and fixed to its side until he abjured his unbelief.

The Tree of Life.

On account of its oriental origin it may be of interest to include in this list of selected subjects one of far less frequent occurrence. It is derived from the (Buddhist) story of Barlaam and Joasaph,[1] in which a man, pursued by Death in the form of a unicorn, takes refuge in a tree, and forgetful of pursuit eagerly seeks the honey on the branches. Meanwhile the unicorn waits below, and two mice (one white, the other black, symbolical of day and night) gnaw the roots of the tree, under which are seen Hades and a dragon. The subject illustrates the transience of mortal life, and the carelessness of mankind. It is frequently used in Byzantine Psalters to illustrate Psalm 143. (144.) 4: 'Man is like to vanity; his days are as a shadow that passeth away.' It so occurs in the Psalter of A. D. 1066 in the British Museum, the Barberini Psalter in the Vatican,[2] &c.

Traditio Legis.[3]

(Cf. Fig. 422.)

This is the scene in which Our Lord as the central figure gives the Law to SS. Peter and Paul, who stand to right and left, the book or scroll being actually handed to St. Peter. The *Traditio* first occurs on sarcophagi,[4] originally as part of a fuller scene in which Our Lord appears among the whole group of Apostles in the New Jerusalem, the latter being indicated by a wall or gateway: the version with the three figures is probably an abridgement of this. Christ is sometimes represented upon the Holy Mount from which the four rivers issue (Fig. 37), or else the lamb stands upon the mount, while the twelve lambs issuing from Jerusalem and Bethlehem are seen in a space below. Sometimes, as in mosaics, he points with his right hand to a palm on which is seated the phoenix, emblem of immortality.[5] The *Traditio Legis* is probably of Syrian origin.[6] On Ravenna sarcophagi Christ sometimes gives the scroll to Paul and not to Peter, a feature which suggests to Wulff that these particular monuments depend upon the art of north-west Asia Minor rather than that of Antioch, Asia Minor being the scene of St. Paul's missionary activity.[7]

Deesis.[8]

(Cf. Fig. 342.)

This is a symbolical group of Christ, the Virgin, and St. John the Baptist. Our Lord is enthroned in the centre; the two other figures stand turned towards

---

be the apse fresco in the church at El-Hadra (*O. C.*, i, 1901, 358 ff.). The type is thought to have originated in Jerusalem (A. Baumstark, *O. C.*, 1904, 1–22). There are, however, several in Western cathedrals and churches. See E. Mâle, *L'Art religieux du XIIIᵉ siècle*, 321 ff.

[1] The romance was brought to Jerusalem from India in the seventh century by a monk of St. Sava named Johannes. See Krumbacher, *Gesch. der byz. Litteratur*, 2nd ed., 887. The Greek version prepared by Johannes soon became popular, and illuminated copies exist (Paris, Bibl. Nat., gr. 1128). For the similar westward progress of the poem of Sakuntala see *B. Z.*, 1905, 653.   [2] Muñoz in *L'Arte*, vii, 1904, 139.

[3] Duchesne, *Origines du culte chrétien*; A. Baumstark, *O. C.*, iii, 1903, 173 ff.; O. Wulff, *Die Koimesiskirche in Nicäa*, 219.   [4] Garrucci, *Storia*, 326 ff.

[5] Ainaloff in *Journal of Ministry of Public Instruction*, St. Petersburg, 1895, 262.

[6] Baumstark, as above; *B. Z.*, xiii, 1904, 661.

[7] *Repertorium*, xxxi, 1908, 282–3.

[8] Kondakoff, *Enamels*, German ed., 272; A. Kirpičnikoff, *Journal of the Ministry of Public Instruction*, St. Petersburg, November, 1893, 1–26. The *Deesis* was also known as Τριπρόσωπος παράστασις.

him, each holding out both hands in an attitude of supplication (δέησις). Kondakoff
has derived the scene from a court ceremony of the ninth century, in which a

FIG. 421. The Death of the Virgin: mosaic of the twelfth century in the Martorana,
Palermo. (Brogi.) P. 663, and cf. Figs. 180, 185.

special hymn of praise was chanted before the emperor by two officials standing on
either side ; but others have seen in it a development of the *Traditio Legis* (which
see).[1] But whatever the origin, the group ultimately became apocalyptic, and

[1] *Orient oder Rom*, 100 ff. ; *Denkschriften* of the Vienna Academy, *Phil.-hist. Klasse*, vol. lii,
93 ; *O. C.*, iii. 173. Ainaloff dissents from this view (*V. V.*, 1907, p. 616).

forms the centre of the Last Judgement. The Virgin was held to represent the Church of the New Dispensation mediating between the Saviour as Judge and the world: St. John represented the Old Dispensation. Examples of this subject, which was especially popular from the tenth century onwards, occur in mosaics, enamels, and ivory carvings.[1] The *Deesis* appears in Western art as a result of Byzantine influence.[2] Christ, the Virgin, and St. John the Baptist in the *Deesis* arrangement appear in a few Western Dooms.[3]

Etimasia.[4]

The *Etimasia* (ἐτοιμασία) or ' preparation of the throne ' is suggested by passages in the Psalms (especially ix. 8), alluding to the coming of Our Lord as Judge. The sense is apocalyptic. The earlier and simpler allusion, however, is rather to the exaltation of Christ to the throne of his Father than to the Last Judgement, though from the eleventh century the throne forms part of Eastern representations of the Doom.[5] In early examples,[6] where the throne stands for the invisible but present Godhead, it has upon it a sacred monogram or a scroll; then an open book replaces the scroll; later a diadem and instruments of the Passion are added, and so it appears in the Judgement scenes.[7]

The story told in the Golden Legend that Chosroes, when in Jerusalem, seated himself on a throne with a cross, a dove or cock, may point to the existence of an actual throne.[8]

The Communion of the Apostles.[9]

(Cf. Figs. 233, 423.)

In this symbolical scene, which is unknown to Western art and may be regarded as the Last Supper in its liturgical aspect, Our Lord is seen administering the bread and wine to the Apostles, who advance from either side; his figure is twice repeated, in order that the gift of the two elements may be represented (Figs. 233, 423). The origin of the scene goes back to the First Period; it occurs, as well as the Last Supper, in the Codex Rossanensis of the sixth century (fol. 3). In later periods it appears in its developed form, and is a favourite subject in the apses of churches, though it is occasionally found in domes, as in the Monasteries of Vatopédi and Chilandari on Mount Athos.

---

[1] De Linas notes five examples on carved ivories (*Ivoires sculptés*, Paris, 1885, 5).

[2] The example over the portal at Grottaferrata near Rome may be classed as actually Byzantine (*Gazette arch.*, 1883, 348 f. and Pl. 57-8; E. Bertaux, *L'Art dans l'Italie méridionale*, 143, Paris, 1904).

[3] A. Haseloff, *Eine Thüringisch-Sächsische Malerschule*, &c., 181 and 195.

[4] Durand, *Étude sur l'etimasia, symbole du Jugement dernier*, &c., Paris, 1867; De Rossi, *Bullettino*, 1879, 126 f. ; F. X. Kraus, *Realencyklopädie*, i. 432, and *Geschichte der christlichen Kunst*, ii. 17 and 20; *Rev. arch.*, xxv, 1894, 330; G. Millet, *Monastère de Daphni*, 84 ff. ; O. Wulff, *Die Koimesiskirche von Nicäa*, 211 f. and 221 ff. ; Kondakoff, *Swenigorodskoi Enamels*, 129. In addition to the passages in the Psalms referring directly to the Judgement, cf. Daniel vii. 13, 14 ; Matthew xxv. 31 ; Mark xiv. 62 ; Luke xxii. 69 ; Hebrews viii. 1 and x. 12 ; Rev. iv. 2-8,v. 6 ff.

[5] In early representations of the Judgement the throne is not present; e. g. MS. of Cosmas Indicopleustes, Garrucci, *Storia*, Pl. 153.

[6] e. g. on gilded glasses, mosaics of Sta Maria Maggiore (additions made here to the primitive design).

[7] e. g. at Torcello (p. 404) ; in the Vatican and Paris Psalters of the eleventh century ; in the Western MS. (now destroyed) known as the *Hortus Deliciarum* by Herrad of Landsperg, a book in which Byzantine influence was distinct; in the frescoes of the Uspenski Cathedral at Vladimir (fifteenth century), &c. We learn from Arculph (*De locis sanctis*, ch. ix) that the instruments were exhibited for veneration at Jerusalem in the seventh century. On the mosaics of the triumphal arch of S. Michele in Affricisco (p. 364), a work probably of the sixth century, the two archangels on either side of Our Lord carry the lance and the reed with the sponge and hyssop.

[8] *Legenda aurea*, xiv. 9 ; Wulff, *Koimesiskirche*, 225.

[9] E. Dobbert, *Über die Darstellung des Abendmahls durch die byzantinische Kunst*, 22, 1872; A. Muñoz, *L'Art byzantin à l'Exposition de Grottaferrata*, 132 ff. ; *B. Z.*, 1896, 599 ; A. Baumstark, *R. Q.*, 1905, pp. 206-7.

Well-known examples of the subject are in the cathedrals at Kieff [1] and Serres; it is also found in frescoes of churches in Cappadocia and Lycia.[2]   In the West it is seen in Southern Italy, in the frescoes of Sant' Angelo and Monte Raparo in the Basilicata,[3] both within the radius of Byzantine influence.   It is rarer in the minor arts, but is seen on the Vatican dalmatic (see p. 601).

The Divine Liturgy.[4]
('H Θεία Λειτουργία.)

In this mystical scene, which belongs to the later periods of Byzantine art, Our Lord is represented standing before the altar, while angels ecclesiastically

Fig. 422.   The *Traditio Legis*, sarcophagus of the fifth century : S. Apollinare in Classe, Ravenna.   (Alinari.)

vested approach from both sides and bear to him the sacred utensils—vessels, book, vestments, censers, &c., down to the water and towel for cleansing the hands of the celebrant.   Good examples occur among the frescoes of Mistra.

In the West the Divine Liturgy, treated with an even more extended symbolism, but not compressed into a single scene, is found in the sculpture of Reims Cathedral.

Last Judgement.[5]
(Cf. Figs. 424, 427.)

The Judgement was only known to Early Christian art in the form of the separation of the sheep from the goats [6] or of a group in which Christ is seated alone with Apostles or saints.[7]   The first approach to a representation of a Doom

---

[1] Rohault de Fleury, *La Messe*, iv, Pl. CCLX.

[2] Chiefly of the eleventh and twelfth centuries (H. Rott, *Kleinasiatische Denkmäler*, 138, 144, 338).   [3] E. Bertaux, *L'Art dans l'Italie méridionale*, 122.

[4] Didron, *Manuel d'iconographie chrétienne*, pp. xxxvi and 229.

[5] Pokrovsky, *The Last Judgement in Byzantine and Russian Art*, in Transactions of the Sixth (Russian) Archaeological Congress, vol. iii ; O. Wulff, *Die Koimesiskirche in Nicäa*, 240 ; Voss, *Das Jüngste Gericht in der Kunst des frühen Mittelalters* in *Beiträge zur Kunstgeschichte*, 1884, vol. viii ; P. Jessen, *Die Darstellung des Weltgerichts in der Kunst des Abendlandes* ; Frimmel, *Die Bilderhand-schriften der Apokalypse* ; G. Scharf in *Archaeologia*, xxxvi ; F. X. Kraus, *Die Wandgemälde in der S. Georgskirche zu Oberzell*, 15 ff. ; A. Baumstark, *R. Q.*, 1905, 204.

[6] Sarcophagi, Garrucci, *Storia*, 304. 3 ; mosaics of S. Apollinare Nuovo (cf. Fig. 211).

[7] Fresco in the Catacombs, Wilpert, *Malereien der Katakomben*, 403, Pl. 75.

is in the miniature of the Vatican Cosmas (p. 462)[1] which is divided into several zones; Christ is enthroned above with the Book of Life; below are eight angels; below these, living men; at the bottom is the resurrection of mankind. There is no indication of hell, of the blessed, or of the angels blowing the last trump.

FIG. 423. Figures of Our Lord in the mosaic representing the Communion of the Apostles in the Cathedral of Serres, Macedonia : eleventh century. (*Hautes Études* : Perdrizet-Chesnay.)

In the typical Byzantine scheme Christ is seated upon a throne, below which are burning wheels and from which issues a stream of fire (Daniel vii. 9 and 10) descending to the lower right-hand corner, where the torments of the damned are depicted. Beneath Our Lord is set the empty throne (see *Etimasia*), on which lies the Bible, and round which are instruments of the Passion.[2] As assessors appear

---

[1] Garrucci, Pl. 153. 2.

[2] The preparation of the throne in the Judgement is mentioned by Ephraim Syrus (d. A.D. 378). Cf. Matthew xxiv. 30 ; Psalm ix. 8. The apologia against Constantine Copro-

the Twelve Apostles on either side of the Judge, while the Virgin and St. John the Baptist intercede for mankind before him (cf. *Deesis*). The archangels stand by in an attitude of repose, while other angels and the company of the blessed

FIG. 424. Details of the twelfth-century mosaic representing the Last Judgement in the Cathedral of Torcello. (Alinari.)

complete this portion of the scene, prominent among them being those blowing the trumps. Among the blessed in Paradise the seated figure of Abraham holding the soul of Lazarus in his bosom is occasionally seen.[1] The figure bearing a cross, which sometimes (as at Torcello) appears before the celestial gate, is that

nymus, which refers to pictures of the Doom, makes no mention of this throne, nor do the accounts of a picture painted by a Greek artist for Boris I (d. A.D. 888) of Bulgaria (Pokrovsky, p. 296). The *Etimasia* throne does not appear to have been added to the scene much before the eleventh century. The earliest examples with *some* of the instruments of the Passion are in the Paris Gospel (No. 74) and in the Paris and Vatican Psalters of the eleventh century. The instruments had been represented earlier alone, e.g. mosaics of S. Michele in Affricisco (q.v.). The relics brought by Heraclius in A.D. 634 may have suggested their introduction.

[1] Torcello mosaic (p. 404), Paris, Bibl. Nat., MS. gr. 74, fol. 13 b and 51 b; frescoes in Cappadocia of eleventh–thirteenth centuries, H. Rott, *Kleinasiatische Denkmäler*, 144, 246.

of the repentant thief, whose representation in art results from the Gospel of Nicodemus. In the lower part of the scene the dead rise from their graves,[1] while the wild beasts of the land and the great monsters of the deep each give up their dead. The classification of the blessed and the damned according to their earthly rank or condition, kings, bishops, laymen, &c., is a comparatively late addition. It may be noted that the retributory angels are sometimes coloured red, as in the Paris Gospel (No. 74) of the eleventh century; in Genesis pictures the angel who expels Adam and Eve from Paradise, e. g. the Greek Bible of the Laurentian Library (Plut. v. Cod. 38), is coloured in the same way.

In Western Dooms uninfluenced by Byzantine models the *Etimasia* throne and the fiery stream are not found,[2] while the Virgin and St. John usually kneel as intercessors instead of standing. On the other hand, the binding of the sinners in chains is peculiar to the art of Western Europe. The weighing of the souls by the Archangel Michael has also been considered of Western origin, but it occurs on the walls of churches in Asia Minor,[3] among the Copts, and in the Armenian churches of Jerusalem.[4]

The *Etimasia* is not seen in the Utrecht Psalter, though there is an illustration of the very verse (Psalm ix. 8) in which the word occurs.

(b) Representations of Individual Figures.

The Almighty.

The First Person of the Trinity is usually represented by the *Dextera Domini*, as constantly in the early Byzantine MSS. (Vienna Genesis, &c.). The 'Ancient of Days' (ὁ παλαιὸς τῶν ἡμερῶν) is a conception of the Godhead as an aged man in which the attributes of Creator and Saviour are united. It may have originated at the time of iconoclasm, and was established in Byzantine art in the eleventh century, occurring in MSS. of that date.[5] In the Smyrna Octateuch this type is seen in a circle filled with stars.[6] He holds in his left hand a circle on which are sun and moon and signs of the zodiac: on his nimbus are the words ὁ ὤν (the Eternal). In mural decoration the Ancient of Days is seen in the triumphal arch of the Basilica of St. Paul at Rome, and in the frescoes at Nereditsi in Russia (about A. D. 1200), &c.[7] The Trinity is commonly represented by the scene in which Abraham entertains the three angels under the oak at Mamre (Fig. 412). The scene in the Barberini Psalter in the Vatican, where we see the Virgin and Child in a medallion upon which the dove descends in rays of light from the hand of the Almighty, is rather the Immaculate Conception than the Trinity.[8]

Types of Christ.[9]

Apart from symbolic figures, as the Lamb or the Good Shepherd,[10] the repre-

---

[1] A. Springer, *Repertorium*, 1884, 387.

[2] Evidences of such Byzantine influence are seen in the book of Herrad of Landsperg, and in a MS. at Wolfenbüttel (Cod. Helmst, 65). For the chief distinctions between Byzantine and Western Last Judgements, A. Haseloff, *Eine Thüringisch-Sächsische Malerschule*, &c., 180 ff., may be consulted.

[3] H. Rott, *Kleinasiatische Denkmäler*, 246 and 270-1. The episode is found in the Karshikilisse near Arebsun on the Kizil Irmak in Cappadocia, dating from the early thirteenth century, and in the Yilianikilisse at Peristrema, the frescoes of which are of about the same age.

[4] A. Baumstark, *R. Q.*, 1906, 170.

[5] e. g. Bibliothèque Nationale, Paris, MS. grec 74, fol. 1 (Bordier, *Description des peintures*, &c., 133).

[6] J. Strzygowski, *Der Bilderkreis des griechischen Physiologus*, 114.

[7] Here the inscription says: *Jesus Christ, the Ancient of Days.*

[8] J. Strzygowski, *Denkschriften der k. Akad. der Wissenschaften*, vol. 52, Vienna, 1906, Phil.-hist. Klasse, p. 90.

[9] *B. Z.*, xii, 1903, 669; Dobbert, Prussian *Jahrbuch*, xv, 211, and *Christus-Bilder*; N. Kondakoff, *Iconography of Our Lord and Saviour Jesus Christ*, St. Petersburg, 1905; J. Weis-Liebersdorf, *Christus- und Apostelbilder*, Freiburg, 1902; Th. Schmit, *Kahrié-Djami*, 170 ff. (*Izviestiya*, Russian Arch. Inst. Cple., xi, 1906). For Christ-types on Byzantine coins see W. Wroth, *Imperial Byzantine Coins* (British Museum Catalogue, 1908).

[10] The Good Shepherd type dies out in the seventh century, and was forbidden by the

sentations of Our Lord may be divided into two main types, the Hellenistic, in which the Saviour is youthful and beardless,[1] and the oriental, in which he appears as a man of about thirty, with a moustache and short beard.   In the latter type the hair is always long, falling over the shoulders; in the former it is sometimes long and sometimes short.

The bearded type has often been described as the Nazarene type, and supposed to have originated in Palestine.   There does not, however, appear to be sufficient ground for confining it to so narrow an area: it may possibly have been affected

FIG. 425.   Christ Pantokrator: mosaic of the eleventh century in the dome of the Monastery of Daphni, Attica.   (*Hautes Études*: G. Millet.)

through Edessa by the art of Sassanian Persia.   Early examples are a bust in the Catacombs, and the figure on the Constantine Bowl (Fig. 385).   It occurs throughout in the Codex Rossanensis of the sixth century, which is thought to have been painted in Asia Minor (p. 452).

The Hellenistic type is common upon the sarcophagi and early ivories; but a slight beard is seen on the Berlin sarcophagus from Sulu Monastir (Frontispiece). Sometimes the beardless and bearded types occur in the same place, for example in the mosaics of S. Apollinare Nuovo, and of S. Michele in Affricisco.   In all cases the bearded face is typical of the historical Christ; the beardless adult face soon came to indicate the celestial being.   The beardless type is found in certain Old Testament scenes where Christ represents the Father;[2] but more often in

Council of A. D. 692.   The type seems to belong to Hellenistic Anatolia, and has, so far, not occurred in Syria or Egypt.   See *R. Q.*, iv, 1890, 97 f. ; Ainaloff, *Hellenistic Origins, &c.*, 164 ; Strzygowski, *Orient oder Rom*, 59, and *Denkschriften* of the Vienna Academy, *Phil.-hist. Klasse*, li, 1906, 156.   Cf. Fig. 209.

[1] H. Dütschke, *Ravennatische Studien*, 99 ff.

[2] This conception of Christ is based on various Biblical passages (Colossians i. 1–16 ; John x. 30), amplified by passages from the Fathers (St. Ambrose, St. Augustine, &c.).   See H. von der Gabelentz, *Die kirchliche Kunst im italienischen Mittelalter*, 31–2.   Our Lord is thus

his purely symbolic aspect as Emmanuel, the ideal or pre-existent Godhead (Isaiah vii. 14). The usual attribute is then a scroll carried in one hand: the right hand makes the gesture of benediction.[1] It is naturally the type employed when Our Lord is seated upon the globe: one of the oldest examples of this representation appears to be that of the *Traditio Legis* (q.v.) in the cemetery of S. Priscilla, which is of the middle of the fourth century.[2] It is also found in the early mosaics of Ravenna[3] and Rome,[4] but becomes rare in Byzantine art after the iconoclastic period. An ivory in the Carrand Collection at Florence shows it;[5] but it is essentially a motive of the earlier centuries.

In early mediaeval Western art of the Carolingian, Anglo-Saxon, and Romanesque periods there sometimes appears to be a confusion between the top of the globe and a segment of a circle regarded as a rainbow.[6] The two came to be distinct, for they sometimes occur together,[7] while in rare instances Christ is seated on the 'rainbow' with a small globe beneath his feet. The idea of the rainbow may sometimes have been suggested by the upper part of the globe, but there is mention of a rainbow in Rev. iv. 3 ('there was a rainbow round about the throne'), though not in the familiar position. In the Last Judgement, and as the Pantokrator, Christ is bearded, because in his function as Judge he is regarded as merely continuing his earthly mission: the severity of his countenance is then perhaps to be ascribed less to the ascetic tendencies of Byzantine art than to deliberate intention of suggesting severity.[8]

Dr. Hans Graeven raised an interesting question when he suggested a relation between certain types of Buddha in the sculptures of Gandhara, on the north-west frontier of India, and the Christs of the late Hellenistic sculpture of Asia Minor,[9] such as that of the Berlin sarcophagus. There is certainly reason to believe that the sculpture of Gandhara may have been inspired by that of Asia Minor; but as it chiefly flourished in the first and second centuries of our era it is difficult to suppose a Christ-type developed sufficiently early to have affected the types of Buddha. Resemblance may perhaps be more safely explained by descent from a common Hellenistic pagan type. The type of the Good Shepherd has analogies in the East.[10]

The subject of Our Lord treading on the lion and dragon, or asp and basilisk, popular in pre-Gothic times in Western Europe,[11] is found upon Early Christian lamps[12] and on the Pignatta sarcophagus at Ravenna (p. 137). An early example

seen on Early Christian sarcophagi, and later, e. g. in the Genesis mosaics at S. Marco, Venice (J. J. Tikkanen, *Die Genesis-Mosaiken*, &c., 222). The type also occurs in Carolingian Creation scenes.

[1] O. Wulff, *Die Koimesiskirche in Nicäa*. 272; E. K. Riedin in *Journal of the Ministry of Public Instruction*, St. Petersburg, 1891, 308 ff.; N. Kondakoff, *Enamels*, 288 (German edition). Sometimes a long cross is held (Riedin, *Proc. Imp. Russian Arch. Soc.*, N.S., ix, 1897. 240).

[2] It recurs on later frescoes representing the same subject in the Basilica of SS. Felix and Adauctus in the cemetery of Commodilla, assigned by Wilpert to the sixth century (*Nuovo Bullettino di arch. crist.*, 1904, 165).

[3] Apse of S. Vitale.

[4] S. Lorenzo and S. Teodoro; lost mosaics of S. Agatha; S. Costanza (Garrucci, *Storia*, 207). It is rarely found where Christ is represented as miracle-worker; an example occurs on the diptych with scenes from the life of Christ in the treasury of Milan Cathedral, thought by some to be as early as the sixth century. In the frescoes of S. Angelo in Formis (p. 316) Our Lord is on the globe when he speaks to the woman of Samaria and the woman taken in adultery.

[5] Labarte, *Hist. des arts industriels*, i, Pl. IX.

[6] Strzygowski, however (*B. Z.*, x, 1901, 719), holds that the globe and the rainbow are distinct.

[7] e. g. in a charter of the foundation of New Minster at Winchester by Edgar, A. D. 996 (Brit. Mus., Cotton MSS., Vespasian A. viii).

[8] Dobbert in Prussian *Jahrbuch*, xv. 214.

[9] *O. C.*, i. 159. See also *B. Z.*, xi, 1902, 662; xiii, 1904, 290.

[10] Jacoby in *Monatsschrift für Gottesdienst und kirchliche Kunst*, viii, 1903, 269.

[11] Merovingian stoup or bucket from Miannay near Abbeville; Carolingian ivory carving (book-cover in Bodleian Library and panel from Genoels-Elderen, Brussels); Northumbrian sculpture (crosses of Bewcastle and Ruthwell). In Gothic art, cf. the Beau-Dieu of Amiens.

[12] *Catalogue of Early Christian and Byzantine Antiquities*, No. 721.

of its occurrence was in the frescoes of the Catacombs at Alexandria, and this has suggested to M. Émile Mâle[1] that the type originated in the old Egyptian representations of Horus trampling upon dragons.[2]

The famous early pictures of Our Lord, such as those of Edessa and Kamulia (in Cappadocia), were probably first heard of in the sixth century.[3]

The Virgin.[4]

Except in the scriptural scenes in which she plays a part, and in the *Deesis*, the Virgin is usually seen with the Child. This association of mother and infant is found in the frescoes of the Catacombs ; but Smirnoff has suggested that the personification of *Pietas Augusta* on Roman coins may have influenced the type.[5] Others believe that it was affected by the Egyptian representations of Isis and Horus, and certainly the resemblance is so strong as to be almost convincing.

The place consecrated to the Virgin, in the apse of the church, was already hers as early as the fifth century.[6] In the representations of this period the frontal position is rigidly maintained.[7]

At a very early date the attitude of the *orans* (cf. Fig. 426), probably of pagan Egyptian origin,[8] and most frequent in representations of women, was given to the Virgin ; at a later time it was given to her even when the Child was present, either by seating her with the Child on her knee, or by representing the Child conventionally in a circular medallion over her breast (cf. *Platytera*, below). In a transitional form she holds the medallion, as in Sta Maria Antiqua at Rome.[9] The seated *orans* goes back to the First Period.[10]

The famous pictures of the Virgin in various churches and monasteries, often regarded as miraculous or 'not made with hands', established certain definite types which remained popular for centuries in Byzantine art.[11] Among these the *Hodegetria* and the *Blacherniotissa* are the most widely known. The former,[12] or 'she who points the way', is a type very probably of Egyptian derivation : the Virgin either sits or stands, with the Child on her left arm, and holding her open right hand before her breast. Of the *Blacherniotissa* there appears to have

---

[1] *Compte rendu du Congrès International d'archéologie classique*, Cairo, 1909, 270 ; Néroutsos Bey, *Ancienne Alexandrie*, 46 f.

[2] In these the subsidiary animals at the sides are seen with the heads downwards, and the repetition of this feature in the case of the asp and basilisk, which at Alexandria were similarly placed in the composition, is used by Mâle to enforce his argument.

[3] On the subject of the *verae icones* of Our Lord see E. Dobbert, *Christus-Bilder* ; G. F. Hill, *The Reliquary*, x, 1904, pp. 173 ff.

[4] G. B. de Rossi, *Imagines selectae Deiparae Virginis*, 1863 ; R. de Fleury, *La Sainte Vierge*, Paris, 1878 ; V. Schultze, *Archäologische Studien über altchristliche Monumente*, 1880, 177 ff. ; F. X. Kraus, *Realencyklopädie*, ii. 361-5, s.v. *Marienbilder* ; A. Venturi, *La Madonna*, Milan, 1900, 1-80 ; Th. Schmidt, *Kahrié Djami*, 125 ff. (Russian) ; J. Strzygowski in A. de Waal's *Archäologische Ehrengabe zum 70. Geburtstag G. B. de Rossi's* (Rome, 1892), 394 ff. ; H. von der Gabelentz, *Die kirchliche Kunst im italienischen Mittelalter*, 170 ; A. Muñoz, *Iconografia della Madonna*, Florence, 1905 ; A. Baumstark, *R. Q.*, xix. 201, xx. 159.　　　　[5] *V. V.*, iv, 1897, 52.

[6] O. Wulff, *Die Koimesiskirche in Nicäa*, 246. The selection of this position may go back even beyond the Council of Ephesus (A. D. 436).

[7] J. Strzygowski, *Cimabue und Rom*, 49.

[8] J. Strzygowski, *Denkschriften* of the Vienna Academy, *phil.-hist. Klasse*, li, 1906, 155 ff. ; W. E. Crum, *Proc. Soc. Bibl. Arch.*, 1899, 251 ; O. Marucchi, *Atti della Pont. Acad. Rom. di Arch.*, 1906, 353 ff.

[9] *B. Z.*, 1905, 582.

[10] *R. Q.*, 1893, 9 ; *B. D.*, i. 65. For the Virgin as *orans*, see also D. Ainaloff and E. Riedin, *The Cathedral of Sta Sophia at Kieff* (Russian), 38-44 ; J. Strzygowski, *Archäologische Ehrengabe zum 70. Geburtstag G. B. de Rossi's*, 1892, 394, and *Denkschriften* of the Vienna Academy, as above ; J. Wilpert, *Ein Zyklus christologischer Gemälde*, 30 ff., &c.

[11] Strzygowski, *Archäologische Ehrengabe*, &c., as above.

[12] Baumstark, *O. C.*, iii, 1903, 235 ; Wulff, as above, 244 ff. ; Strzygowski, *Denkschriften*, as above, 158-9 ; *Arch. Journal*, xxxix, 1882, 131. The picture of the Hodegetria, formerly preserved in Kahrié Djami at Constantinople, and destroyed by the Turks in A. D. 1453, is reproduced (from a copy) by d'Agincourt, *Painting*, Pl. LXXXVII.

been more than one variety. As a rule the Virgin holds the Child with both hands; but sometimes a figure in the attitude of the *Deesis* (p. 664) is inscribed *Blacherniotissa*.[1] Probably there were several famous ikons in the Monastery of Blachernae, to all of which the title was given.[2] The *orans* type holding the

Christ-medallion over the breast (see above) is sometimes described as Blacherniotissa, while that in which the Virgin stands and the medallion is unsupported is known as *Platytera*: this first appears in church apses in the twelfth century. Another well-known type was the *Kyriotissa*, named from the Kyros Monastery in Constantinople.[3] It represents the Virgin standing with the Child, and may have resembled the better-known form of the Blacherniotissa. The type known as Ζωοδόχος Πηγή belongs to later Byzantine art.[4] The Γαλακτοτροφοῦσα is usually late, but cf. Fig. 174.

The ideal Madonna of early Italian art was suggested by Byzantine types; and in many Italian pictures of the thirteenth century we may still note the absence of any close and human relation between mother and child. The infant Christ makes the gesture of benediction, and preserves the serious attitude of an adult. But although the usual Byzantine representation is of a somewhat formal hieratic character, the human aspect of their relationship was occasionally expressed.[5] Sometimes the Virgin is identified with the Divine Wisdom (Ἁγία Σοφία), as at the top of the triumphal arch at Monreale[6] and in Santa Sophia at Kieff. Some have suggested the same identification in the case of the female figure standing before the seated figure of St. Mark in the Codex Rossanensis[7] (see p. 454).

In middle and later Byzantine times the descriptive legend placed on either side of the Virgin's head is M̅P̅ Θ̅Y̅ (Μήτηρ Θεοῦ). But in the early centuries Ἡ ἁγία Μαρία is found, as in the fifth-century papyrus History of the World in the

Fig. 426. Marble relief of the Virgin: S. Marco, Venice. (Alinari.)

Golenisheff Collection (p. 459), and in the frescoes of the church at El-Hadra by the Natron Lakes.[8] It was common in Egypt, where there was a popular

---

[1] e. g. an enamel at Maestricht (Bock & Willemsen, *Antiquités sacrées de S. Servais*, &c., p. 230).

[2] O. Wulff, *Koimesiskirche*, p. 263.

[3] Ducange, *Constantinopolis cristiana*, Bk. IV, p. 87.   [4] *B. Z.*, xviii, 183.

[5] J. Strzygowski, *Cimabue und Rom*, 49; A. Haseloff, *Eine Thüringisch-Sächsische Malerschule*, &c., 199.

[6] The accompanying inscription is *Sapientia Dei*. Most instances in which the Divine Wisdom is seen inspiring an Evangelist are late. An Italo-Byzantine relief outside the west wall of St. Mark's at Venice has St. John inspired by a female figure. In late Slav Gospels the personification is sometimes winged.

[7] A. Muñoz, *Il Codice purpureo di Rossano*, 16.

[8] *Denkschriften*, as above, 153 and Pl. VII. For El-Hadra, see *O. C.*, i. 358.

objection to the description Μήτηρ Θεοῦ.[1]   The form Ἡ ἁγία Μαρία is not always
a proof of early origin, for it appears to persist as an exception in later times,
occurring on the ivory with the Annunciation in the Trivulzio Collection at
Milan, which is considered by some as late as the eleventh century.[2]

Angels.[3]

In the earliest Christian art angels were represented as beautiful youths
without wings, draped in the tunic and long mantle or *pallium*.   It is probable
that the wings were added in imitation of the figures of Niké or Victory,[4] for among

Fig. 427.   The Descent into Hell and Last Judgement : mosaic of the eleventh century in
the Cathedral of Torcello.   (Alinari.)

the early representations of winged angels are those holding a medallion or wreath
in the same manner as the confronted Victories on antique monuments (cf.
Figs. 124–5).   Winged angels were general in the fourth century and universal
from the sixth.   As early as the latter century we find the archangels occasionally
distinguished by imperial costume,[5] consisting of the long chlamys with the

---

[1] Sharpe, *Hist. of Egypt*, 262, 264, 267 ; Smirnoff in *V. V.*, iv, 1897, 39 f.   The form was
naturally preferred by Monophysites.

[2] Venturi, *Storia*, ii. 611 and Fig. 43.

[3] F. J. Turmel, *L'Angélologie depuis le faux Denys l'Aréopagite*, in *Rev. d'histoire et de littérature
religieuse*, iv, 1899, 289 ff. ; J. Stuhlfauth, *Die Engel in der altchristlichen Kunst* ; J. Strzygowski,
Orient oder Rom, 1901, 28.   V. de Grüneisen, in *Scritti di storia di filologia e d'arte*, Naples, 1908,
25 ff., draws attention to the marked Hellenistic character of an angel (?) painted on part of a
mummy-cover found at Antinoe.

[4] This theory is more probable than that of Stuhlfauth, which derives the wings from
those of the symbol of St. Matthew (*Die Engel*, &c., 244).   The staff given to the angel as
messenger recalls the fact that the original function of Niké was to bring news of victory.
In the Vienna Genesis, the angel who appears to Abraham in the sky resembles a figure of
Niké (Hartel and Wickhoff, *Die Wiener Genesis*, Pl. XI).

[5] e. g. the five-part diptych leaf at Ravenna (p. 210) and the mosaics of S. Apollinare in
Classe.

rectangular patch known as the *tablion*; in later centuries, when this kind of distinction became usual, they wear the embroidered imperial costume (Fig. 427). The archangels hold the orbs perhaps as early as the fourth century;[1] in later periods they sometimes carry the *labarum* as well. Unlike emperors, however, they keep their feet bare, as almost invariably do sacred persons and Apostles throughout Christian art. The Archangel Gabriel, when, as in the Annunciation, he acts as the heavenly messenger, carries a long wand or staff. Sometimes, however, Michael also carries it when in repose, as for instance in mosaics of S. Michele in Affricisco or the British Museum ivory diptych-leaf. The Divine Wisdom (Ἁγία Σοφία) appears to have been at times personified as an archangel, occasionally with the crucigerous nimbus indicating identity with Our Lord.[2]

Michael and Gabriel are most commonly represented, Raphael and Uriel are infrequent; the latter occurs at Bawît.[3] The cult of the Archangel Michael received a new stimulus under Justinian, who built numerous churches in his honour, and encouraged their erection by others.[4]

The seraphs, thrones, principalities, and all the hierarchy of heaven entered into the scheme of Byzantine iconography. The cherubim are especially conspicuous:[5] they are found in the Gospel of Rabula and the ninth-century Vatican MS. of Cosmas (p. 456). On coins they first appear in the reign of Andronicus II.[6] The *tetramorph*, or composite winged figure formed of the lion, ox, eagle, and man, of Ezekiel's vision is rarer.[7]

A most exceptional treatment of an angel as a small nude figure resembling a genius or *putto* is found on a remarkable cameo in the British Museum.[8]

Devils.

Devils are dusky human figures with wings: they are most frequently seen in the Temptation of Our Lord, and appear as early as the ninth-century Paris MS. of Gregory, No. 510[9] (see p. 477; cf. Fig. 428).

Apostles, Evangelists, Saints, Ecclesiastics.[10]

The principal Apostles are distinguished by varying age, or by the colour and arrangement of the hair. Thus St. Paul is bald upon the top of the head and has a rather long pointed beard; St. Peter has thick hair clustering over the forehead and a short round beard. The same person may be differently represented under different aspects. Thus St. John when regarded as Apostle is young and beardless; when as Evangelist, as an elderly bearded man. St. John the Baptist is sometimes given wings in late representations of the *Deesis*, especially in Palestine; but most examples are too late for our periods.[11] The Greek picture of St. John in the Wilderness in the Accademia at Florence,

---

[1] e. g. the ivory diptych in the British Museum (*Cat. of E. C. and Byz. Antiquities*, No. 295).

[2] Cf. p. 392 above. N. Kondakoff, *Enamel*, 189, *Byzantine Churches of Constantinople*, 115–16, 124, and *Histoire de l'art byz.*, ii. 135. Ἡ ἁγία Σοφία in the fourteenth-century frescoes of S. Stefano, Soleto (Otranto), is represented as an angel with a cruciferous nimbus (Ch. Diehl, *L'Art dans l'Italie méridionale*, 96).

[3] Clédat, article *Baouit* in Cabrol's *Dict. d'arch. chrét.*, 234.

[4] Procopius, *De aed.*, i. 3, 8, 9; ii. 10; v. 3, 9; Ch. Diehl, *Études sur l'administration byzantine dans l'exarchat de Ravenna*, 266.

[5] Didron, *Annales archéologiques*, vii. 152.

[6] W. Wroth, *Imperial Byzantine Coins*, pp. xcviii and 623.

[7] e. g. frescoes of the rock-hewn Church of St. Barbara in the Soandere Valley, Cappadocia, dated A. D. 976–1028 (H. Rott, *Kleinasiatische Denkmäler*, 1908, 147–8).

[8] *Proc. Soc. Antiq. Lond.*, 2nd ser., xviii, 365; *Cat. of Early Christian and Byz. Antiq.*, No. 104.

[9] Cf. also Paris MS. of Gregory of Nazianzus, fol. 165, reproduced by H. Omont, *Fac-similés des MSS.*, &c., Pl. XXXV. See further Th. Schmidt, *Kahrié Djami*, 191–2; N. Pokrovsky, *The Gospels*, &c., 192–3.

[10] J. Ficker, *Darstellung der Apostel in der altchristlichen Kunst*; Weis-Liebersdorf, *Christus- und Apostelbilder*; Heisenberg, *Grabeskirche und Apostelkirche*, ii. 208 ff.; A. Muñoz, *Codice purpureo di Rossano*, 115 ff.

[11] Examples were shown at the Grottaferrata Exhibition. See A. Baumstark, *R. Q.*, 1905, 205.

where the Baptist is shown with wings, is assigned to the sixteenth century.[1] Wings are given to St. John on account of the prophecy of Malachi.[2]

The frequent representation of the Evangelists seated at desks writing at the beginning of their Gospels is derived from the custom of placing the author's portrait in this attitude at the beginning of his work.   The idea was derived

Fig. 428.   The Temptation: miniature of the early twelfth century in the Psalter of Queen Melisenda.   (British Museum: Egerton 1139.)

from Hellenistic bas-reliefs, and is found in the early Virgil in the Vatican Library.[3]   Among the earlier Christian MSS. in which it occurs are the Vienna Dioscorides and the Codex Rossanensis (pp. 452, 456).

The saints of the Eastern Church are exceedingly numerous, and the calendars recording their feast-days were volumes of considerable size.[4]   It is usual to

---

[1] A. Muñoz in *Rivista d'arte*, 1909, 119 and Fig.
[2] iii. 1 ; repeated in Matthew, xi. 10 : 'I will send my messenger,' &c.
[3] E. Diez in *B. D.*, iii. 38 ; A. Muñoz, *Il Codice purpureo*, &c., 15.
[4] The most famous is the Menologium of Basil in the Vatican Library (p. 479).   For Byzantine hagiology see H. Delehaye, *Les Légendes hagiographiques*, Brussels, 1905.   The great Byzantine compiler of 'Acts of the Saints' was Simeon Metaphrastes, who lived in the second half of the tenth century, and is first mentioned in an epitaph composed by Nicephorus Uranos in the reign of Basil II (*B. Z.*, vii, 1898, 473).   See also H. Delehaye, *Analecta Bollandiana*, xvi, 1897, pp. 311 ff., and A. Ehrhardt, *R. Q.*, 1897, 537 f.

find the saints of the same profession grouped together: thus the great Fathers of the Church often occur together, as do episcopal and ecclesiastical saints. The military saints in like manner form pairs or groups, among the most popular being the two Theodores (Tyron and Stratelates), George, Demetrius, Procopius, and Sergius and Bacchus, the officers of the imperial guard. Cosmas and Damian, the Anargyri, or doctors who healed without fee, are also invariably associated and universally popular. As in the West, local saints were chiefly honoured

Fɪɢ. 429.   St. Matthew writing his Gospel : miniature in Gospel of the eleventh century in the British Museum.   (Burney 19.)

in the cities or countries where they were born, worked, or died. Sometimes a saintly type owed its origin to a particular region. The type of the equestrian saint, of which St. George is the most conspicuous example, appears to have spread from Egypt, and to have typified the triumph of faith over infidelity.[1] The vestments of ecclesiastics are essentially similar to those of the Orthodox Greek Church.[2]

Personifications.

The personification of rivers, mountains, and other natural features, of cities, or of abstractions such as Prudence, Melody, &c., was inherited by Byzantine from Hellenistic art. The most familiar of these personifications are those of the Jordan in the scene of the Baptism, where the river is seen leaning upon

[1] J. Strzygowski, *Zeitschrift für ägyptische Sprache*, xl, 1903, 49–60 ; *B. Z.*, xii, 1903, 699 ; *Materials for Russian Archaeology*, viii. 29 (St. Petersburg, 1892, in Russian). There does not seem to be sufficient reason to derive St. George from the Egyptian figures of Horus, as Clermont Ganneau (*Horus et Saint-Georges*, Paris, 1877) was disposed to do. He might equally well originate from a late Hellenistic type. The Barberini diptych, with its mounted emperor (p. 199), is associated by Strzygowski with the idea of Christian triumph.
[2] Cf. Figs. 287, 345. See J. Braun, *Stimmen aus Maria-Laach*, 1900, pp. 167 ff. ; P. Bernardakis, *Échos d'Orient*, v, 1901, pp. 129 ff.

his urn,[1] and of Hades in the *Anastasis,* the city of the dead being represented by a grey-haired and grey-bearded man.[2]

Life (*Bios*) and Opportunity (*Kairos*) are personified as youths[3] (Figs. 65, 91). The Year is represented by a female figure in a thirteenth-century commentary on Job in the National Library at Paris (MS. gr. 134): she is red, as is the Day in the contemporary Vatican Job Codex (No. 1231), the colour being symbolic of light. The corresponding personifications of Night in these manuscripts are similarly blue.[4]

FIG. 430.   Personifications of Humility and Truth : enamels on gold from the crown of Constantine Monomachos in the museum at Budapest.

In the fine tenth- and eleventh-century Psalters in Paris and elsewhere Night and Dawn, Melody, Wisdom, &c., are depicted as female figures (see p. 468).

In the early mural paintings at Bawit (p. 284) we find Faith and Hope personified.

As in Western mediaeval art, the soul is represented by a diminutive human form.[5] The soul of the Virgin held by Our Lord in the Dormition is always thus treated, but is there commonly swathed (Fig. 421).

The *Months and Seasons*[6] were represented by busts or complete figures with

[1] e. g. mosaics of the Orthodox Baptistery at Ravenna; ivory carving in the British Museum (Fig. 111), &c. The rivers of Paradise are personified in the Genesis mosaics in S. Marco at Venice. The horn-like projections on the head of Jordan in the Baptistery are crab's claws; they are found on the head of the personification of the Sea in the Vienna Dioscorides (p. 460), occur upon a sarcophagus at Rome (Tikkanen, *Die Genesismosaiken,* &c., p. 224, note), on Carolingian ivory carvings (Cahier and Martin, *Mélanges d'archéologie,* vol. ii), and in the Anglo-Saxon Benedictional of St. Ethelwold, belonging to the Duke of Devonshire.
[2] J. Strzygowski, *Koptische Kunst,* p. xviii ff.; *B. Z.,* xiii, 1904, 291. The Nymph of the Well from which Rebekah draws is twice repeated in the Vienna Genesis leaning upon her urn.   [3] A. Muñoz. *L'Arte,* 1904, 130.   [4] Tikkanen, as above, 235.
[5] Ibid., 236. In the S. Marco Creation of Adam, the soul of the first parent has wings like Psyché.
[6] J. Strzygowski, *Das Calenderbild des Chronographen,* in *Ergänzungsheft I des k. deutschen arch.*

suitable attributes. At an early period a scene of rural or domestic life suitable to each month was introduced into illustrated calendars. So in the Calendar of Filocalus (p. 484).

In some examples, as for instance the mosaic discovered by Renan in 1861 near Tyre, busts of indistinguishable type do duty for the months. The sun and moon are often represented by busts, the one with a radiate crown, the other with a crescent upon the head. They so appear within disks in the starry segment representing the heaven in the miniature of the Vienna Genesis in which Joseph explains his dream to his father and brothers.[1] But sometimes the sun is realistically treated, as in the same MS., where Jacob watches the luminary rise after wrestling with the Unknown.[2]

The symbols of the Evangelists seem to be a Western feature, and do not appear with any frequency in Byzantine art until a late period, when Western influence had made itself felt.[3] They are found in very early monuments in Italy[4] and Gaul,[5] in some of which oriental influence is possible, though not necessarily affecting this particular feature.

They occur in the earliest Western MSS., for example in the Lindisfarne Gospels (about A. D. 700) in the British Museum (Cotton MS., Nero D. 4), and were afterwards continuously employed in all Western countries, whereas in the East they are infrequent down to about A. D. 1300.[6] It may be noted, however, that Our Lord is seen enthroned between the four beasts in the mural painting in the twenty-sixth funerary chapel at Bawit, which is probably not later than the seventh century,[7] and that in the apse painting in the White Monastery at Sohag (p. 287), a painting considered to date from the eleventh century, the same beasts flank the mandorla in which the figure of Our Lord is enclosed.[8] They are found in the Ascension-miniature in the Gospel of Rabula (p. 450), also in the frescoes of the rock-cut Church of St. Barbara in the Soandere Valley in Cappadocia, dated A. D. 976–1028, and in other rock churches at Susam Bayry and Gereme in the same province.[9] They are further found in Italo-Byzantine wall-paintings in South Italy.[10]

(c) Symbols, &c.

The Sacred Monogram and Cross.

In the first four centuries of our era the various forms of the sacred monogram were generally used for the cross, which was not universally employed as a symbol of the Crucifixion before the sixth century.[11]

Inst., xiii, 1890, 241 ff. (on a fourteenth-century MS. with calendar, from Trebizond), Denkschriften der k. Akad. der Wissenschaften, phil.-hist. Klasse, 1, 1904, 144, and R. Q., xii. 6 ; Davis, Archaeologia, xxxviii (1860), 224 f. and Pl. IX–XII (mosaics at Carthage, the types corresponding to those of Filocalus) ; A. Riegl, Mittheilungen des Inst. für österreichische Geschichtsforschung, x, 1889. See also Gazette arch., 1879, xxii ; Monuments Piot, iii, 1896, 202 (mosaics in North Africa).

[1] Hartel and Wickhoff, Die Wiener Genesis, Pl. XXIX.   [2] Ibid., Pl. XXIV.

[3] J. A. Herbert, Burlington Magazine, xiii, June, 1908, p. 162. It is believed, however, that the symbols may have originated in the liturgical cycle of Egypt (B. Z., xv. 702).

[4] Mosaics of St. Restituta, Naples (p. 369), ivory in the Trivulzio Collection (p. 191); in both cases the symbols have each six wings, as on the cipollino chair in the Treasury of S. Marco at Venice, believed to be that given by Heraclius to Grado.

[5] Stone relief from Aquitaine (Le Blant, Nouveau Recueil des inscriptions chrétiennes de la Gaule, 1892, 269).

[6] A. Muñoz, Miscellanea Ceriani, 1910, p. 173 (Gospel of late eleventh or early twelfth century at Brescia) ; N. Kondakoff, Geschichte und Denkmäler des Byzantinischen Emails, 177. They are found on the embossed silver frame of a fourteenth-century ikon in the Church of St. Clement at Ochrida ; the frame appears to be contemporary (Kondakcff, Macedonia, 260 and Pl. X).

[7] J. Clédat, Mémoires de l'Institut français d'arch. orientale du Caire, 136 and Pl. XC–XCI.

[8] V. de Bock, Matériaux pour servir, &c., 58. De Bock mentions the apocalyptic beasts, though they are not very visible on his Plate XXI. The beasts also occur in similar positions at Esneh (Bock, as above, Pl. XXX).

[9] H. Rott, Kleinasiatische Denkmäler, 1908, 147, 207, 232.

[10] Diehl, L'art byz. dans l'Italie méridionale, 154.

[11] See British Museum, Guide to Early Christian and Byzantine Antiquities, p. 19.

In Egypt the old Egyptian symbol of life, the *ankh* (☥), frequently stood for the cross upon textiles discovered in cemeteries;[1] on similar textiles, as also on Early Christian reliefs in Asia Minor,[2] the *swastika* is found, evidently with a religious significance (cf. also p. 687). This figure persisted later, and is found in the ornament of Sta Sophia, Constantinople (cf. pp. 696, 713).

The sacred monogram of the Constantinian form persisted in Byzantine art until the seventh century: it is found on coins of Heraclius.[3] The cross itself had appeared as early as the fourth century, and it may here be noted that the Byzantine cross is not always equal-armed, but constantly has the lower limb longest like the so-called Latin cross[4] (cf. Figs. 226, 339, &c.). The expanding extremities of the top and arms, very characteristic throughout the whole period,

Fig. 431. Sarcophagus of St. Felix: S. Apollinare in Classe, Ravenna. (Alinari.)

are of quite early introduction: they are seen in the apse mosaic of Sta Pudenziana at Rome, where the large cross is thought to represent that erected by Constantine at Jerusalem (p. 335).[5] The cross covered with jewels is of equally early date; and that emitting rays, or displayed in a field of stars (Fig. 343), comes in about the same time. This mode of representation has been associated with the vision of a radiant cross in the sky between Jerusalem and Golgotha reported in the fourth century.[6] The cross raised upon steps, or rising from two acanthus leaves, also appears in the First Period. The cross with double traverse, often called the patriarchal cross, is also early. It is found on the reliquary at Poitiers

---

[1] Akhmîm and elsewhere. See P. Scott-Moncrieff in *Church Quarterly Review*, October, 1909.
[2] On textiles at Antinoe see *Annales du Musée Guimet*, 1902, Pl. I and II (after p. 152). For the *swastika* on Early Christian tombs in Pisidia, Lycaonia, and Isauria, see A. Margaret Ramsay in Sir W. M. Ramsay's *Studies in the Eastern Provinces of the Roman Empire*.
[3] W. Wroth, *Imperial Byzantine Coins in the British Museum*, i. 253. The form with limbs at right angles, commonest in the fifth century, occurs on the sculptured slab in the roof of one of the chambers in the base of the Column of Arcadius at Constantinople (*Ath. Mitth.*, 1893, 233–4). Here the P has the loop open, a feature which may be peculiarly Eastern, as it occurs not only on the Golden Gate at Constantinople (A. D. 388–91), but also at Hierapolis, Thebes (in Boeotia, &c.). De Rossi (*Bullettino*, 1880, 144) also considered the open loop Eastern. Cf. Figs. 349, 456.
[4] The long cross is found from the fifth century (C. Bayet, *De titulis Atticae crist.*, 57 ff.; De Vogüé, *Syrie Centrale*, 51 and 66). After the sixth century its use is continuous.
[5] See also H. Grisar, *Analecta Romana*, 468. Disks at the ends of the arms may represent globes and signify dominion (G. de Nicola, *Bull. d'Arte*, iii, p. 29, 1909). Cf. Figs. 86, 339.
[6] O. Wulff, *Die Koimesiskirche in Nicäa*, 243. The cross amidst stars is seen in the mosaics of S. Apollinare in Classe and of S. Gennaro at Naples.

said to have been presented by Justin II and Sophia to St. Radegund (p. 548). It appears on Byzantine coins in the reign of Theophilus (A. D. 829–42).

The elevation of the cross in presence of Helena and Macarius is found in the Vatican Menologium of Basil (tenth century). It probably goes back to an earlier time.[1] The *labarum* is the name given to the standard on which the sacred monogram is represented (Fig. 432). It has been so often described[2] that it is needless to do more than mention it here. An interesting comparison has been made by F. Sarre between this Christian standard and those of the Parthians.[3]

Cruciform monograms, in which letters are disposed about the extremities of a cross (e. g. Figs. 321, 355 *a*), apparently begin in the sixth century, and continue to the Fourth Period. The rectangular type of monogram (e. g. Figs. 321, 355 *d*) begins earlier, and falls into disuse after the sixth century. In the West it lasted longer, having been adopted by the Franks and handed down by them to their successors. The European examples are, however, clumsier and larger than their Byzantine prototypes.

The Nimbus.

This distinctive mark of pre-eminence was probably adopted in Christian art from the representation of emperors.[4] Although even the cruciferous form given

Fig. 432. Medallion of Valens, illustrating the *labarum*.

to Our Lord occurs as early as the beginning of the fourth century,[5] it continued to be assigned or withheld with some irregularity down to the sixth century: thus the angels in the Vienna Genesis (p. 444) are not nimbed. In the First Period the nimbus was often of a blue or a bluish-green colour,[6] as we sometimes see it in Western miniatures of Romanesque times. But from the eighth century it was usually golden. It would seem that the nimbus first became general in the Syro-Egyptian area.

The square nimbus, though it appears to occur in the mosaics of St. Demetrius, Salonika, is not characteristic of East-Christian iconography.[7] It was introduced by the popes to meet iconoclastic criticism, which objected to the use of the circular nimbus in representations of living persons.

The mandorla,[8] or 'glory' surrounding the whole body, encloses the figure of

---

[1] D. Ainaloff, *V. V.*, v, 1899, 71.

[2] Smith and Cheetham, *Dictionary of Christian Antiquities*, s.v. *labarum*; F. X. Kraus, *Realencyklopädie*, &c.

[3] *Beiträge zur alten Geschichte*, iii, 1903, 333–71. The article is illustrated by twenty-five figures.

[4] A. Krücke, *Der Nimbus und verwandte Attribute in der frühchristlichen Kunst*, and the review in *B. Z.*, xv. 694; N. Müller, *Realencyklopädie für protestantische Theologie und Kirche*, 3rd ed., 559–66; *B. Z.*, ix, 1900, 599. Cf. the imperial coinage, the figures of Constantius II and Constantius Gallus in the Calendar of Filocalus (p. 484), &c.

[5] On the sarcophagus from Sulu Monastir at Berlin (p. 128) and on the Constantine Bowl in the British Museum (Fig. 385) (*Cat. of Early Christian and Byz. Antiquities*, No. 916); and see A. Muñoz, *Nuovo Bullettino di arch. crist.*, xiii. 301 ff.

[6] So in the niche-mosaics of Sta Costanza, and in SS. Cosmas and Damian at Rome; S. Apollinare Nuovo, S. Vitale, Archiepiscopal Chapel, and S. Apollinare in Classe at Ravenna. The late mosaics of various Roman churches also retained the coloured nimbus; an example occurs in the mosaics of S. Venanzio (J. Smirnoff, *V. V.*, iv, 1897, pp. 48–9).

[7] For the square nimbus, see V. de Grüneisen, *Tabula circa verticem*, in *Archivio della R. Soc. rom. di Storia Patria*, xxix, xxx; Sauerland and Haseloff, *Der Psalter Erzbischof Egberts von Trier*, 52 ff.; and Ph. Lauer, *Mém. Soc. Ant. de France*, lxxvii, 1907, 55–71. Its use is most common between the eighth and thirteenth centuries.

[8] Clédat in *Mém. de l'Inst. français d'arch. orientale du Caire*, xii, 1904, Pl. XCVI. The painting in the twenty-sixth chapel at Bawit (Clédat, Pl. XC and XCI) shows Our Lord enthroned and surrounded by a bluish mandorla.

the infant Christ in his mother's arms in the Gospels of Etchmiadzin and in frescoes at Bawît;[1] the Virgin herself is thus distinguished in the apse mosaic of Panagia Kanakaria in Cyprus (p. 384). It is thus at any rate as early as the sixth century.

SECULAR ICONOGRAPHY.

Important work in this province has been done by M. Lambros, who has collected material from monuments of art illustrative of the types of the various emperors.[2] In preceding chapters imperial portraits in mosaic have been noted (cf. Figs. 5, 213, &c.), and a greater number of imperial personages are represented in illuminated MSS.[3] (cf. Fig. 290). Exigencies of space make it impossible to do more in the present chapter than add a few short notes on costume.

Fig. 433.   The Emperor Julian: miniature of ninth-century MS. of the Homilies of Gregory in the Ambrosian Library, Milan.   (*Hautes-Études*: G. Millet.)

The dress of the Byzantine lower classes did not differ essentially from that of similar classes in the West: a girded tunic reaching to the knees, with occasionally a mantle, and boots with leg coverings, are its essential features.

In the dress of the wealthy classes and court officials, the *chlamys* played an important part, and different forms with various distinguishing ornaments were worn by different ranks. Our principal authority for court costume, apart from the evidence of such monuments as the mosaics in S. Vitale at Ravenna (p. 356), various miniatures and ivories, &c., is the book of the Emperor Constantine

---

[1] See note 8 on previous page.

[2] An international committee was appointed to undertake this work at the first Congress of Classical Archaeology. At the Cairo Congress M. Lambros read an account of the progress made; the work seems to have chiefly devolved upon him (*Compte rendu du Congrès International d'arch. classique*, Cairo, 1909, p. 267).

[3] M. Diehl cites some of the more important MSS. (*Manuel*, 590): Bibl. Nat., 510, much damaged figures; Psalter in the Marciana, with Basil II (Fig. 290); eleventh-century *Exultet* roll of Bari, with Basil II and Constantine VIII; Bibl. Nat., gr. 922, with Constantine Ducas and Eudoxia crowned by the Virgin; Vatican, gr. 666, with Alexis Comnenus (*Manuel*, Fig. 184); MS. of St. John Chrysostom in the Bibl. Nat., with Nicephorus Botoniates (*Manuel*, Fig. 183); Vatican, *Urb.* 2, with John Comnenus. The Vatican Barberini Psalter shows an imperial family of three persons (*Manuel*, Fig. 185).

Porphyrogenitus.[1] The dress both of patricians and great ladies[2] was of the most sumptuous description, and was often composed of figured silks (p. 584).

The imperial robes,[3] adopted from Persia, were thickly embroidered with pearls and precious stones: none but rulers might wear boots of the imperial red. In the period from the fifth to the seventh century the long chlamys with rectangular patch of a different colour (*tablion*) (Figs. 118, 224) was worn by both emperors and empresses, as we see it in the S. Vitale mosaics, in the representation of David in the Vatican Cosmas (fol. 63 b), &c. Kings in the biblical narrative are shown in early MSS., like the Vienna Genesis, in the chlamys. In these MSS. a gold diadem with an aigrette of stones or pearls in the centre completes the royal costume (cf. also Figs. 128, 138–40, 213, 216, 262, 290, 356).

A few words may be added on military equipment. The soldiers of the Byzantine army were protected for the most part by scale armour, though, if we may judge from quite early monuments, ring or chain mail was sometimes used.[4] Helmets[5] have crests or spikes, either with or without plumes. Shields are either oval, or pointed at the bottom, resembling the kite-shaped shield of Western Europe. Weapons of offence were straight swords with guards only slightly projecting on either side, and long spears[6] (cf. Figs. 10, 11, 42, 59, 93, 144, 230, 279, 306).

The bow, apparently of the 'composite' oriental type, was in general use (Figs. 145, 372).

---

[1] *De Caerimoniis aulae byzantinae* (Bonn edition), vol. i. See also N. Kondakoff, *Enamel*, 299 ff. J. Wilpert, *Bessarione*, x, 1905, fasc. 86, argues that the chlamys with *tablion* is the *pallium discolor* of the law of A. D. 382.

[2] See A. von Premerstein, Austrian *Jahrbuch*, 1903. M. Molinier discusses modes of dressing the hair in *Études d'histoire du Moyen Âge dédiées à G. Monod*, Paris, 1896, 61–70 : ' La coiffure des femmes dans quelques monuments byzantins.' Shoes of pierced and gilded leather were worn, numerous examples of which have been found in Egypt.

[3] Pokrovsky, in *Materials for Russian Archaeology*, viii, 1892, 18 (Publ. of the Imperial Russian Academy), discusses the imperial chlamys and tunic of the sixth century. Cf. also Strzygowski on the silver shield from Kertch (p. 569).

[4] Strzygowski, *Orient oder Rom*, 67.

[5] Cf. the Joshua Rotulus (Figs. 265, 271), silver plate (Fig. 59), &c.

[6] On the Byzantine army see Diehl, *L'Afrique byzantine*; H. Gelzer, *Genesis der byz. Themenverfassung*; C. W. Oman, *The Byzantine Empire*. On the navy, C. Neumann, *Die byz. Marine*, in *Hist. Zeftschrift*, 1898, pp. 1 ff.; C. de La Roncière, in *Le Moyen Âge*, 1897, pp. 201 ff.; Cecil Torr, *Ancient Ships*, pp. 16 ff.; J. B. Bury, in his edition of Gibbon's *Decline and Fall*, Appendix to vol. vi, in which Greek fire is discussed. For ships in battle, cf. Fig. 288.

Fig. 434. Illuminated head-piece from a Gospel of the eleventh century in the British Museum.

CHAPTER XIII

ORNAMENT

It has been well remarked that when higher forms of artistic expression decline or die out, ornament, which is the possession not merely of the cultured but of the average population, shows a superior power of resistance; it is handed on from generation to generation, when the figure-art which may have originally accompanied it has been long forgotten. It thus possesses an ethnological value, and the analysis of its elements will often throw unexpected light upon phases in the history of nations. That the Byzantine Empire stood in some relation to Greece, Egypt, Syria, and Persia, might be deduced from a study of its ornament alone, if all written historical documents had been destroyed. It is rather under an historical than an artistic aspect that Byzantine ornament will be discussed within the short limits of the present chapter. To deal effectively with so wide a subject from the purely artistic point of view would require not only very special qualifications, but also a wealth of detailed illustration beyond the possibilities of this volume. The origin, development, and distribution of certain selected motives will be briefly stated, while a few remarks of a more general application will be prefixed by way of introduction.

Of Byzantine ornament in general it may be said that even when executed in relief it almost always aims at a colouristic effect, or imitates a model executed in colour; and that it shows a predilection, first for covering void spaces with continuous ornament disposed on geometrical principles, secondly for framing designs in formal borders. These charac-

FIG. 435. Carved ornament of the sixth century, Sta Sophia, Constantinople.
(After Salzenberg.)

teristics are oriental; for the Greek, and the Roman while still under Greek influence, did not seek so much a contrast of colour as beauty of line and form, and where any considerable space was to be decorated, insisted upon a central figure-subject standing out upon a background free from ornament distracting to the eye. Classical feeling did not suffer the secondary element, i. e. the geometrical or floral design, to encroach upon or monopolize any such important space; and although, as Riegl has shown, the oriental style began to creep in during the late Roman period, it was not until about the time of Justinian that it achieved a permanent victory. Such a treatment of a considerable space as that of the spandrels in Sta Sophia (Fig. 435) might have shocked a Greek even of the Hellenistic period: it marks the triumph of these purely Eastern methods which find their late development in Mohammedan art. We find 'repeating' or continuous ornament extending its sphere in the centuries immediately preceding. The covering of columns with a network of continuous pattern, forming lozenges, imbrications, and connected *swastikas*, appears in the columns of the mosque façade of Diarbekr (Amida), which are probably not later than the fifth century. One column has the combination of hexagons and crosses round a central octagon which has always been popular in the East for the arrangement of glazed tiles and inlaid carving in wood,[1] and appears both in the Early Christian art of Egypt, as in the tympanum of the Djami Ali at Dashlut,[2] and in the mosaics of Sta Costanza at Rome (p. 333). A similar treatment of columns is found in the remains of the Coptic monasteries of S. Apollo at Bawît[3] and S. Jeremias at Saqqara[4] (cf. Fig. 267).

The framing of ornamental subjects in formal borders is first introduced

Fig. 436. Nielloed ornament on a silver dish of the sixth century, from Cyprus, in the British Museum.

in the ancient art of Mesopotamia, and may have become extensively known through its adoption by the textile art. It spread rapidly westward under the Roman Empire, being largely used in those mosaic pavements which were in their origin carpets translated in terms of stone. The sculptured slabs in low relief which themselves imitated textiles (p. 165) adopted borders very generally (Figs. 99, 439), as did ivory carvings (Figs. 8, 9, 122–5, 132, &c.); while the fresco-painter, the illuminator, and the worker in mosaic employed them to define the spaces which they had to decorate. Their utility was so generally recognized that they established a firm footing in the Western art of the Middle Ages, were taken over by the Carolingians, and never afterwards fell completely out of favour.

To those unfamiliar with the conservatism of design, there are few things more remarkable than the persistence of ornamental motives throughout the centuries. Once well planted, they appear almost ineradicable; they survive political changes, and are handed on from

[1] Van Berchem and Strzygowski, *Amida*, 153 ff.
[2] Originally part of the decoration of the monastery at Bawît.
[3] Possibly as early as the fifth century. Represented in the Pavillon de la Trémouille at the Louvre. See J. Clédat's accounts of the excavations. Other forms of continuous geometric ornament are common to Egypt and the ruined cities of Syria (*Amida*, 157).
[4] See J. Quibell, *Service des antiquités de l'Égypte, Saqqara*, Pt. II.

one empire to another until their origin is forgotten by those who employ them. They may indeed be so modified that at first sight they are hard to recognize; they may suffer a process analogous to that which in comparative mythology is known as contamination,[1] but, in spite of all changes, they persist, and a patient investigation will discover their true descent. The classical example of such persistence is the lotus, with its principal development, the palmette: the acanthus and vine are later than these, and to a certain extent grafted on them; but all have enjoyed

FIG. 437.   Nielloed ornament in the centre of a silver dish of the sixth century from Kyrenia. (Nicosia Museum, Cyprus.)

a popularity which has lasted with a few breaks from antiquity to the present day. A decided geographical barrier, or the rise of a strong indigenous artistic movement, may indeed divert the influence of these hereditary motives. For instance India, though a borrower from Persian art, developed a naturalistic ornament derived from her own flora as early as the second century before Christ, and the ornamental motives of Bharhût and Sanchi are for the most part purely Hindu. The mediaeval artists of the thirteenth century in like manner cast themselves free from the designs which Romanesque art inherited from the antique, and reproduced their own plants and foliage from nature. In these ways the old designs are superseded; but sooner or later some revival or other will often bring a rejected ornament once more into consideration, and after a long exile it may find the gates no longer barred against it. This conservatism, with the contamination of one ornamental motive by another, often led to curious results. The acanthus developed out of the palmette, the

[1] When figures or episodes from one story are bodily removed to another to suit the purposes of the artist.

palmette being first 'acanthized' and the complete acanthus following later. Not far from the beginning of our era, the vine coming from Hither Asia established itself in Roman art, though its principal development was in Syria and Egypt. But after a time a new contamination arose; the palmette annexed the vine. The vine, in short, was 'palmettized'; and out of the resulting hybrid arose not only the typical Byzantine floral designs of the Third Period (Figs. 64, 160), but also the foliate arabesques of Saracenic art. Palmettes and acanthus-leaves of comparatively un-

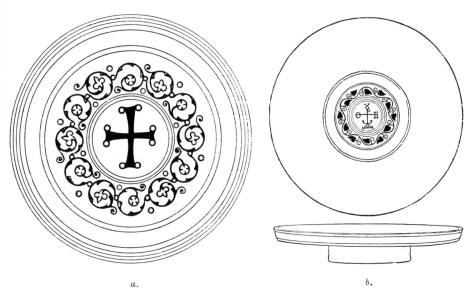

a.   *b.*

FIG. 438. *a.* Nielloed ornament in the centre of a silver dish of the sixth century found at Kyrenia. (Nicosia Museum, Cyprus.)
b. Small silver dish of the sixth century with monogram and ornament in niello.

modified form survived to a late date side by side with the hybrids; but, contrary to the rule which obtains in nature, it was the hybrid which proved the most prolific.

The ornamental designs used in the Christian East fall into two main classes: those received through Hellenistic sources, and those introduced from the East. The latter group includes a number of designs originally borrowed from the Hellenic area and returned with or without modification during the earlier Christian centuries.

MOTIVES ADOPTED FROM HELLENISTIC SOURCES.

The Acanthus.

In the second half of the fifth century B.C. the lotus-palmette[1] began to receive 'acanthizing' modifications which ultimately led to the birth of the

---

[1] For the palmette, in addition to Goodyear, *The Grammar of the Lotus*, see Riegl, *Stilfragen*, 1893; Furtwängler, *Sabouroff Collection*, introduction to the sculpture, 6 ff.; Brückner, *Ornament und Form der attischen Grabstelen*, 4 ff.

acanthus as an independent motive. For there is reason to believe that the masters of ornament did not, as Vitruvius relates,[1] copy the plant from nature. Insensibly their experiments with the leaves of the palmette assumed a form resembling the acanthus-leaf; the resemblance was observed and consciously improved, until at last the plant itself was deliberately taken as a model. We need not mention all the stages in the development of the acanthus. After the sixth century it lost in relief and character, and the work of the ninth century and later is mostly without the strong effects of light and shade which the undercutting of earlier times had produced. A more important point is the habit of dismembering the plant, a custom which was foreshadowed when the Greeks split the palmette into two halves.[2] By the fifth century the Sassanian Persians and the Eastern Greeks had carried this dismemberment further; they cut off leaves and parts of leaves to be employed as new units; they associated these units in combinations inconceivable in nature, produced such impossibilities as a continuous band or scroll of acanthus (Fig. 439),[3] and finally, as in the spandrels of Sta Sophia, made scroll-work of this kind range all over considerable spaces. Treatment of this kind recalls the liberties taken with figures of animals by the early Teutonic craftsmen, who so dismembered and compounded beast-forms that at last only a practised eye can discern an animal at all. The acanthus remained popular even in the Fourth Period, being found in considerable variety in the sculptured ornament at Mistra; but in the Third Period it found a rival in the palmettized vine, which was especially popular with illuminators and workers in metal (Figs. 64, 339).[4]

In the early centuries it was used for borders, framing geometrical panels with a continuous band of leaves: so on the marble doors in the gallery in Sta Sophia[5] (Fig. 3) and on the diptych of the Consul Boethius in the museum at Brescia (Fig. 8). This fashion was adopted by Carolingian artists, who constantly employed it as a border for miniatures and ivory carvings.

The Ivy-leaf.

The ivy-leaf and ivy-scroll, like the acanthus, probably assumed a naturalistic form very gradually: there seems reason to believe that it began as a lotus-leaf.[6] It appears independently in Mycenaean and Greek art, but was perhaps not finally identified with the ivy until the naturalizing Hellenistic period. In Byzantine art it is chiefly characteristic of the First and Second Periods, becoming rare with the ninth century; an example is seen on the silver dish from Cyprus (Fig. 438, a). The heart-shaped form which a conventional leaf may readily assume is not always connected with the ivy, even as derivative of the lotus-leaf. The 'hearts' which are so common on Sassanian and Italo-Byzantine sculpture, and on textiles (Fig. 440), are probably derived from the palmette-top (see p. 692); while the leaves which appear when the *lemnisci* of wreaths were

---

[1] Vitruvius, iv, c. 1. The sculptor Callimachus is said to have been so struck by the effect of a basket lying upon an acanthus plant that the idea of the Corinthian capital arose in his mind. The story has all the marks of a fiction invented to explain a forgotten genesis. As a matter of fact the acanthus appears on *acroteria* at a date when Corinthian capitals were either non-existent or at any rate exceedingly rare. Another explanation suggests that the acanthus, which appears upon palmettes of the Athenian gravestones of the fourth century, was placed there because it grew in the rocky ground where cemeteries were situated. But the earlier stele discovered by M. Place at Khorsabad negatives this view also. See P. Gardner, *Sculptured Tombs of Hellas*, 121. [2] A. Riegl, *Stilfragen*, 211.
[3] As at St. John of the Studium at Constantinople. The Copts early made long bands of acanthus interlace, and produced many hybrid forms, examples of which are to be seen in the Cairo and other museums, coming from various early sites.
[4] Strzygowski has maintained against Riegl that the familiar leaves of Mohammedan arabesques are debased vine forms and not acanthus.
[5] Prussian *Jahrbuch*, xiv, 1893, 75 ff.
[6] Goodyear, *Grammar of the Lotus*; Riegl, *Stilfragen*, 117, 126, 177; O. Wulff, *Die Koimesis-kirche von Nicäa*, 200.

converted into tendrils, are perhaps very generalized vine-leaves (cf. Fig. 81).
It may be conveniently mentioned here that all the four suits of our
playing-cards, three of which must be derived from leaves (one, the spade,
somewhat resembling a conventional ivy-leaf), occur in Byzantine ornament,
usually upon textiles.[1]   In the ceremonial book of Constantine Porphyrogenitus
the ' spades ' upon garments are called κισσόφυλλα.[2]

The Palmette.

This motive was inherited by Byzantine art in various forms, some of which
are of quite an early type.   Ornament in which the anthemion alternates with

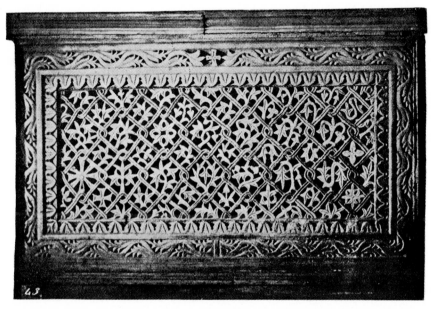

FIG. 439. Transenna, S. Vitale : showing various treatment of acanthus and its use as a scroll.

the lotus occurs carved in stone at Kaisariani in Attica, before the cave at
Athens containing the spring known as the Clepsydra, and on various fragments
of uncertain provenance discovered on the Acropolis.   The association of these
sculptures with crosses of peculiar form has led Strzygowski to date them about
the beginning of the fifth century.[3]   On the back of the Limburg reliquary,
which is of the tenth century, there is an embossed border of debased palmettes
alternating with three-pointed lotus, clearly derived from a Greek original.[4]
In ornamental borders of the Daphni mosaics (eleventh century) the palmette
or anthemion is still unmistakable, although treated in a careless and schematic
fashion.[5]   But like other designs of the earlier tradition it was no longer a very

---

[1] The *heart* is especially common upon the mantles of saints in enamels ; hearts and
clubs occur together on the garments of the Emperor Nicephorus Botoniates in the MS. in the
Bibliothèque Nationale, Paris ; they occur in juxtaposition on the silk textile of Bishop Gün-
ther (p. 596).   The spade is seen on the costumes of the guards in the Justinian mosaic in
S. Vitale at Ravenna, and on the hangings of St. Anne's bed in the mosaics of Daphni
(Millet, Pl. XVIII).   Cf. Figs. 199, 304, 314, 440.

[2] Riedin in *Trans. of Imp. Russ. Arch. Soc.*, N.S., ix, Pt. II, 205, St. Petersburg, 1897.

[3] ’Εφ. ’Αρχ., 1902, 82–90.

[4] E. Aus'm Weerth, *Das Siegeskreuz*, &c., Pl. III.

[5] Millet, *Daphni*, 107, Fig. 49.   Here, as on the abacus of the columns on the north portal
of the Church of St. Godehard at Hildesheim, we find a type of palmette scroll with alternating anthemion and trefoiled bud which recalls Greek types.   For the Hildesheim example

conspicuous motive, nor did it enjoy the position which it once held in the arts of Egypt, of Hither Asia, and Greece. Its importance in Byzantine art lies rather in the transmission of its characteristics to forms of a quite different origin, in the 'palmettizing' to which it gave rise at a comparatively early date, and in the dismemberment and recomposition of its several parts. This hybridization was carried out both upon the acanthus and the vine-leaf. Examples of acanthus-leaves recompounded into palmette-like forms are found upon the façade of the

FIG. 440.   Silk textile of the sixth–seventh century found in the Sancta Sanctorum, now in the Vatican Library, showing palmettes and heart-shaped leaves.

Mshatta, which no one would date later than the seventh century and some assign to the fourth. It is difficult to see in what quarter except Mesopotamia this characteristic hydrid can have originated. Acanthus ornament showing similar tendencies is found upon capitals of Sassanian origin; and it seems not unlikely, as Strzygowski has suggested, that the Sassanians derived the classical motives with which they took such liberties, not from the Mediterranean cities, but from the Greek colony at Seleucia. Probably the similar ornament upon the Tulunid gravestones in Egypt reached the Nile via Mesopotamia and Syria, and had a like Persian origin.[1]

As an example of detached fragments of the palmette independently used, we may notice the *hearts* which singly, or in long bands forming borders, occur upon Sassanian textiles of the fifth to seventh centuries (Fig. 440). These are originally nothing more than the two upmost incurving leaves of the palmette,

see A. Zeller, *Die romanischen Baudenkmäler von Hildesheim*, Berlin, 1907. Something of the same sort survives in the fourteenth century in the mosaics of Kahrié Djami (Th. Schmidt, Pl. XXXI). For a fine Greek example see the stele from Aegina of the time of Pheidias (P. Gardner, *Sculptured Tombs of Hellas*, Pl. XIV).

[1] J. Strzygowski, *Mshatta* (Prussian *Jahrbuch*, 1904), 280 ff.

with the space which they enclose, detached and filled with a solid colour.[1]
They either form continuous bands, as upon the Persian textiles,[2] or are dispersed among other ornamental motives.[3]

The large leaf with curved sides, and almost pear-shaped in contour, which is such a familiar feature in later oriental, especially Persian, art is in

FIG. 441. The Virgin and Child(?): silk textile of the sixth–seventh century; the border shows degraded palmettes. (Victoria and Albert Museum.)

like manner a palmette derivative.[4] It also occurs on the slab at Torcello already mentioned. A somewhat similar form, though less flamboyant, had been in use in Mycenaean times.

But perhaps the most interesting, as it was certainly the most widespread form of the palmette, is that which is known as the 'enclosed palmette'.[5] This

---

[1] Strzygowski, in Prussian *Jahrbuch*, xxiv, 1903, 158. The derivation is clear because the detached ornaments and the complete palmettes sometimes occur on the same piece of stuff, and the upper parts of the latter are identical with the former.

[2] R. Cattaneo, *L'Architettura in Italia*, &c., Fig. 102 and p. 157. Carved slabs of the ninth century at S. Maria degli Angeli at Assisi and Torcello Cathedral. A similar treatment on a carved sarcophagus at Nicaea (O. Wulff, *Die Koimesiskirche in Nicäa*, 184).

[3] As in the mosaics of Sta Sophia, Constantinople (Salzenberg, Pl. XXIV). It is not, however, certain whether in cases like this the form may not derive from the 'ivy-leaf'.

[4] *Jahrbuch*, as above, 157.   [5] Cf. Fig. 94 above.

ornament, which was of Greek origin, has an almost continuous history in the East; but though adopted by the Celts [1] was never a Roman motive, a fact which is of some importance to the question of artistic influences in mediaeval Europe. It is found in the Syrian area at At-Tûba,[2] on capitals of the fifth to sixth century at Daphni,[3] as well as in mosaic borders of the eleventh century at the same place [4] and frequently at Mistra.[5] It occurs on Sassanian capitals, on ninth-century stone reliefs on the larger door of S. Marco dei Partecipazi at Venice,[6] and on sculpture of the Visigothic period at Toledo.[7] Such examples explain how it became such a very common ornament all over Europe in Romanesque times.[8]

The Laurel.

The laurel-wreath, commonly used for the wreaths which enclose sacred monograms or busts upon sculptured slabs or ivories, became less common in the middle and later periods. It did not, however, fall into disuse. It is found as a border for illuminated miniatures, e.g. in a Vatican Psalter of the twelfth to thirteenth century.[9] Cf. Figs. 76, 77, 81, 121, 204, 456.

Scrolls.

The narrow floral scroll, consisting of a continuous undulating line from the upper and lower sides of which single leaves issue alternately but always in the same direction, is a motive which persisted through all centuries. It occurs on capitals and transennae at San Vitale,[10] in the stone sculpture at Nicaea,[11] and the Monastery of Lavra on Athos:[12] in the Fourth Period we find it again at Kahrié Djami and Mistra. The motive passed into the Italo-Byzantine art of the dark ages [13] and also into France.[14] It is frequently found in later Western mediaeval art. The type of leaf employed is not always the same; sometimes it seems to approximate to the acanthus, at others to the vine (Figs. 25, 86, 88, 106, 125, 438, 442).

Cornuacopiae.

The cornucopiae, which perhaps first became common in the time of the Diadochi, is an ornament frequently used in the First Period. It occurs on the façade of Mshatta,[15] and is especially conspicuous in the mosaics of S. Vitale [16] at Ravenna, where it is arranged in pairs. It is also found on consular diptychs (e.g. that of Areobindus, c. A.D. 506, at Lucca), and on capitals at Ravenna, Parenzo, and Philippi,[17] in the ruined towns of Syria,[18] and in Egypt.[19] It was early introduced into Frankish art.[20]

---

[1] British Museum, *Guide to the Iron Age*, p. 17.
[2] A. Musil and others, *Kusejr 'Amra*, Fig. 130, p. 207, Vienna, 1907.
[3] G. Millet, *Daphni*, Fig. 2, p. 8.   [4] Ibid., Fig. 38, p. 66.
[5] Millet, *Monuments byz. de Mistra*, Pl. XL, XLV, XLVI, &c.
[6] Cattaneo, as above, Fig. 139, p. 245.
[7] A. F. Calvert, *Toledo*, Pl. 438, Fig. 2 (1907).
[8] A few examples are : the front of the sarcophagus of St. Agricola in S. Stefano, Bologna (Cattaneo, Fig. 54, p. 112); the large Kronleuchter at Hildesheim (A. Zeller, *Romanische Baudenkmäler von Hildesheim*); the early rood in Stepney Church (*Proc. Soc. Ant. of London*, xxii. 226); the Norman font at Bishopsteignton (J. C. Cox and A. Harvey, *English Church Furniture*, 196), &c.
[9] *Cod. Vat. Palat. Gr.*, 381. Reproduced in *Collezione paleografica Vaticana*, Fasc. 1, Milan (Hoepli), 1905.
[10] Venturi, *Storia*, i. 93, 99.
[11] O. Wulff, *Die Koimesiskirche in Nicäa*, Fig. 36, p. 185.
[12] Brockhaus, *Die Kunst auf den Athos-Klöstern*, Pl. VII and VIII.
[13] Slab at Cividale (Venturi, *Storia*, ii. 131).
[14] Gospels of Godescalc (eighth century) (Venturi, ii. 131).
[15] Prussian *Jahrbuch*, 1904, 310. For other examples see O. Wulff, *Berlin Catalogue*, i.
[16] Diehl, *Ravenne*, 80.   [17] *B. Z.*, 1902, 487, Pl. III.
[18] Lintel of church at Chirbet Tezin in North Syria (Prussian *Jahrbuch*, 1904, Fig. 32, p. 250).   [19] Architrave at Deir er Rife near Assiut (ibid., Fig. 87).
[20] Gospel of St. Médard. See p. 488.

The Fret.

The fret is also an ornament chiefly dating from the early period.   It is seen in many varieties at Bawit, some of them representing the ' ribbon fret '[1] (as if

Fig. 442.   Pierced marble transenna, S. Apollinare Nuovo, Ravenna ; sixth century ; fret-like border producing *swastikas*.   (Ricci.)

made of a stiff ribbon set up on edge) so popular in early mediaeval Western art from Carolingian to Gothic times.   Sometimes it is broken up after a fashion found in early Frankish and Christian Celtic art.   A tendency to treat the

---

[1] J. Clédat, *Mém. de l'Inst. franç. d'arch. orientale du Caire*, Pl. XIII and XIV.   This kind of fret is at least as early as the third century, as it occurs in the mural paintings (Fig. 168) at Palmyra of that date (Strzygowski, *Orient oder Rom*, p. 11).   It is also found on the ivory vase in the British Museum (p. 214).   A border of undulating ribbon found in the sixth-century Gospel of Rabula and the Vienna Gospel of about the same date was copied in much later times, as in the twelfth-century Vatican MS. of the Prophets (No. 1153).   See A. Muñoz, *Codici . . . delle minori biblioteche di Roma*, Pl. VIII.

fret as an independent ornament, qualified to fill principal spaces instead of merely surrounding them, is seen in the frieze of the great temple at Palmyra, which is of the third century.[1] The resemblance of this early example of fret diaper to that employed by Saracenic artists in Mesopotamia in the thirteenth century is remarkable, and it is probable that we have here the inheritance of an ancient motive which had never completely died out. The fret does not disappear in the Third and Fourth Periods. It is found, for example, on the exterior of Greek churches,[2] in the decoration of Kahrié Djami,[3] &c. In some cases fret-like designs have lines crossing each other at right angles, producing series

Fig. 443.   Marble ambo of the sixth century in S. Apollinare Nuovo at Ravenna : showing
dentils, astragalus, and other mouldings.   (Ricci.)

of connected *swastikas* as at Ravenna (Fig. 442), Amida (p. 713), and Saqqara (Quibell, i, Pl. XXXI).   A tendency to incline the angles of the fret is observed in the First Period (Fig. 449).

The Step-pattern.

If not connected with the fret, this motive, very frequent in the borders of Byzantine illuminated MSS. and mosaics of the tenth century and later, may possibly be derived from the mural crenellations of Hither Asia.[4]   Such battlements are reproduced in the background of a miniature in the early fragment of the Gospels from Sinope now in Paris, though there they are

---

[1] *Proc. Soc. Ant. London*, xxii, p. 216.
[2] A. Struck, *Ath. Mitth.*, 1909, 226 ; G. Lampakis, *Mém. sur les antiquités chrétiennes de la Grèce*, 44.
[3] Th. Schmidt, Pl. XXIII, XXVIII.
[4] The step-pattern occurs in the mosaics of Sta Sophia, Constantinople (Salzenberg, Pl. XXIV, XXVI), and at Nicaea (Wulff, *Koimesiskirche*, 200).

in their proper place upon a building.[1] The fact that step-patterns occur on the Hindu sculptures at Sanchi (third century B.C.) may perhaps be regarded as an argument in favour of the architectural origin: similar designs occur in the art of ancient Peru. More important, perhaps, is the use of the motive in an ornamental band on the Parthian Palace of Hatra, where it may very well be regarded as brought down from the cresting of a crenellated wall.[2] Step-patterns occur in the borders of the eighth-century Frankish Gospel of Godescalc,[3] which betrays oriental influences, as well as on the English eighth-century Gospels of St. Augustine's Abbey in the British Museum.[4]

Mouldings.

Familiar types (oves, astragalus, dentils, &c.), though commoner in the First Period,[5] survived to much later times: examples occur in the string-courses of St. Luke of Stiris in Phocis, on sculptured reliefs (Torcello, &c.), and on ivories (caskets, triptychs), &c., all of the Third Period; but at this time they are no longer motives of primary importance. Cf. Figs. 119, 123, 124, 128, 140, 443, 450.

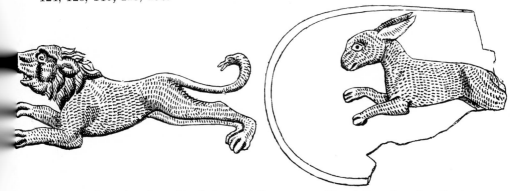

FIG. 444.   Animals embossed in the bowls of silver spoons of the sixth century from Cyprus. (British Museum.)

Animals and Monsters.

Quadruped monsters with human heads, recalling the ancient Mesopotamian sphinx, are found at Mshatta, where the creature wears a pointed cap.[6]

The sphinx continued to be reproduced in the mediaeval period, appearing on the reliefs upon the Gorgopico Church at Athens,[7] at St. Luke of Stiris, in Aegina, &c.   Mshatta can also show the centaur, who stands opposite a gryphon at the base of one of the great sculptured triangles.   The appearance

---

[1] A. Muñoz, *Codice purpureo di Rossano e il frammento Sinopense*, Plate B, Rome, 1907. In later MSS., such as the Menologium of Basil in the Vatican Library, bands of stepped ornament traverse the architectural background at levels where they would be structurally out of place.

[2] Dieulafoy, *L'Art antique de la Perse*, v. 20.

[3] Comte A. de Bastard, *Peintures des manuscrits*, &c., Pt. III; A. Venturi, *Storia*, ii. 285.

[4] G. F. Warner, *Reproductions of MSS. in the British Museum*, Series III, Pl. III. The crenellations upon the Franks casket of whale's bone in the British Museum (eighth century) may actually represent crenellations on a wall. But if so the idea may well have been suggested by an oriental model.

[5] Mshatta (Prussian *Jahrbuch*, 1904, 276); plaster string-courses of St. Luke's (Schultz and Barnsley, Pl. XXVIII); cf. also examples in the ninth-century church at Skripu (*B.Z.*, iii, 1894, 11).

[6] Prussian *Jahrbuch*, 1904, 309.

[7] Rivoira, *Origini della architettura lombarda*, 205-6. A sphinx in the claws of a gryphon is seen on a capital of the Church of Kutais in Georgia (begun A.D. 1003) (*Jahrbuch*, as above, Fig. 86).

of this figure seems to indicate classical influence. Strzygowski has noted that in representations of Orpheus produced in the Syro-Egyptian region, the musician is usually accompanied by a centaur.[1] The dolphin, though not frequent, is found in Byzantine ornament.[2] Byzantine animal-ornament is for the most part of oriental origin (p. 706); even in the above cases the Hellenistic source may only be secondary.

Fig. 445. Carved slab from a well-head of the eleventh century from Italy : showing whorls, rosettes, &c., in interconnected circles. (Victoria and Albert Museum.)

ORIENTAL MOTIVES.

The various motives composing Courajod's *Grammaire orientale*[3] passed into the ornament of Europe after the fifth century, and were especially popular throughout the period (seventh–tenth centuries) when sculpture was at its lowest. They are most frequently found on the ambon, the ciborium, the closure slab, and the sarcophagus of this time, more particularly in Italy, so much so that they used to be regarded as characteristically Lombardic. But

[1] *Jahrbuch*, 313, and *Zeitschr. des deutschen Palästina-Vereins*, xxiv. 143 ff.

[2] e.g. on the marble revetment of Sta Sophia at Constantinople (Lethaby and Swainson, 244-5).

[3] The substance of M. Courajod's lectures at the Louvre is given by A. Marignan, *Un Historien de l'art français : Louis Courajod*, Paris, 1899.

our knowledge of the art of Hither Asia in the first five centuries of the Christian era now enables us to trace them for the most part to Syria, the ruined cities of which were first made familiar to archaeologists through the researches of de Vogüé.[1] The Jewish art of the beginning of the Christian era as exemplified on the ossuaries is expressed in a similar grammar.[2] The most conspicuous elements are the whorl, the rosette, the interlaced band, and the series of interconnected circles. This Neo-Greek or Graeco-Asiatic style is cosmopolitan in the First and Second Periods, spreading not only in Greece and Italy, but also in North Africa[3] and the South of France: to the influence of this style may be ascribed the adoption of a new and purely ornamental style of sarcophagus at Arles, in which the human figure is abandoned.[4] The Goths and Lombards became acquainted with its elements perhaps even before they entered Italy, for it doubtless penetrated far inland from the Adriatic coasts. Details appear in early Frankish MSS. Though commonest in the earlier centuries, designs of the 'oriental grammar' continued in use in the two later periods.[5]

The Sacred Tree.

Allusion has already been made to the connexion between the 'heart' and Sassanian modifications of the palmette. More important, because far more general, are the various types of conventional plant or tree commonly represented between the pairs of confronted beasts. Such types are all comprehended under the generic term 'sacred tree',[6] because they all ultimately descend from a well-known feature of ancient Mesopotamian art. But as the original sacred trees were never real trees of any known species, but artificial compounds of lotus elements, so its descendants in later centuries are always composite. Their elements may ultimately be derived from the lotus-palmette, but are modified by additions derived from the acanthus and the vine, so that in late examples there remains nothing of the Mesopotamian sacred tree except its formal symmetry and its central position between the confronted animals or monsters. The most curious examples occur in Sassanian and Coptic art, the stem often presenting the appearance of a candelabrum from which stems with leaves issue in symmetrical pairs. At the top there are often upturned stems recalling the upmost leaves of the anthemion, or sometimes there will be a debased representation of the whole palmette as a crown or finial. The Sassanian examples sometimes terminate in the eagles' wings found on the head-dresses of kings of the house of Sassan; and this type occurs on Mshatta.[7] Through Syria it reached

---

[1] La Syrie centrale. The American Expedition of 1899–1900 covered part of the same ground as M. de Vogüé. Its numerous photographs are published in the archaeological volume of the expedition by Mr. Howard Crosby Butler.

[2] See Clermont Ganneau, Rev. arch., 1873, 398 ff.; 1878, 320, &c.; De Saulcy in Gazette arch., 1879, Pl. XXXV, p. 261 (Fragments d'art judaïque).

[3] Marignan, 135 (references to Annales de la Société arch. de la province de Constantine, 1870, Pl. III); Bulletin de l'Académie d'Hippone, xviii, Pl. 36, p. 72; xvii. 16 and 17, Pl. IV and Pl. VII; Annuaire de la Soc. arch. de la province de Constantine, 1870, 61; Recueil de la Soc. arch. de Constantine, 1878; Bulletin des Antiquaires de France, 1880, p. 270; Rohault de Fleury, La Messe, iv, Pl. 275, 290, &c.

[4] E. Leblant, Sarcophages chrétiens de la Gaule, Pl. 33, 36, 46. For the Regio Gothica in the South of France and its sculpture, see Marignan, 148. Marignan's list of pre-Romanesque sculptured fragments in France (pp. 163–87) is valuable. Among the motives may be noticed gryphons, peacocks, whorls, rosettes, &c. A lead coffin at Nimes has winged lions; a lead sarcophagus at Lyons (Museum) from Sidon is covered with a variety of Neo-Greek designs. The Merovingian sarcophagi in the Musée Carnavalet at Paris have 'toute la grammaire néo-grecque'.

[5] e.g. at Nicaea (Wulff, Koimesiskirche, 200), at Kahrié Djami, &c.

[6] On the development of the sacred tree see Riegl, Stilfragen, 99 ff.; W. H. Goodyear, The Grammar of the Lotus, 179 ff.

[7] Prussian Jahrbuch, 1904, 314.

Palestine,[1] Egypt, and North Africa.[2]   Sacred trees of purely vegetable type,
without the wings, but still having something of the stiff candelabrum form,
passed from Syria and Egypt to Italy, Merovingian and Carolingian France,[3]
Visigothic Spain, and Anglo-Saxon England, while they naturally held their
ground in Mohammedan art.   One interesting example in our own country
is the design on the back of the Alfred Jewel in the Ashmolean Museum at
Oxford.[4]

Another interesting example occurs on the horn of Ulphus in York Cathedral,
where the 'tree' has upon it the pine-cones characteristic of Mesopotamian art[5]
(cf. p. 705).

The Vine.

This is among the most important of all motives, for not only does it pervade
the reliefs, mosaics, frescoes, manuscripts, and minor works of art of the Christian
East, but by transmission from early Byzantine sources exerted a powerful influence upon the decorative art of Western Europe in Carolingian and Romanesque

Fig. 446.   Mosaics of the twelfth century in the nave of the Church of the Nativity at
Bethlehem, showing fantastic forms of the 'sacred tree', with wings, vases, &c.   (From a
drawing by W. Harvey : Byzantine Research and Publication Fund.)

periods.   It will therefore be necessary to follow its history in rather greater
detail.

The vine and its schematized forms do not belong to classical ornament ; they
lie outside the stock motives employed by the Greek and early Roman artist.
The plant is represented upon Assyrian sculptures sometimes as appropriate to
the scene, sometimes decoratively.[6]   Its popularity as decoration probably
originated in Mesopotamia ; it extended to the Mediterranean by the fourth
century B.C.   It was from the provinces of Iran that in the second century B.C.
the Chinese first imported both the vine itself and its use in ornament.   This
was the result of the expedition conducted by General Chang Kien in the reign

[1] Curious combinations of vases, foliage, wings, &c., in the general form of the sacred
tree are found in the nave mosaics of the Church of the Nativity at Bethlehem (twelfth
century) (Fig. 446); in those of the Dome of the Rock at Jerusalem (De Vogüé, Le Temple de
Jérusalem, p. 87) of the late seventh and eleventh centuries, and of the Mosque of El-Aksa at
Jerusalem (ibid.).   [2] Jahrbuch, 322.

[3] Cf. Sacramentary of Drogo, Comte de Bastard, Peintures des Manuscrits, Pt. V, and
Gospels of Gaignières, ibid., Pt. VIII.   [4] Proc. Soc. Ant. of London, xx. 76.

[5] Journ. Brit. Arch. Assoc., xlviii, p. 251.   The pomegranate or pine-cone as terminal ornament is found on symmetrical vines of the early eleventh century, e.g. on a pluteus of the
Cathedral of Torcello (A.D. 1008).

[6] Relief from Koyounjik in the British Museum.

of the Emperor Wu-ti, of which we have historical record.[1] Material evidence
is afforded by the appearance of the vine-scroll, sometimes with birds and

Fig. 447.   Part of the façade of the Palace of Mshatta : Kaiser-Friedrich Museum, Berlin,
showing elaborate vine-scrolls, birds, &c., with large band of zigzag, rosettes, &c.   P. 704.

animals in its convolutions, upon the small bronze mirrors of the period.
Chinese documents tell us that the region from which the vine came was the
land of Ta Yüan, which can only have been a province of Iran and is probably

[1] F. Hirth, *Ueber fremde Einflüsse in der chinesischen Kunst*, **12 ff.**

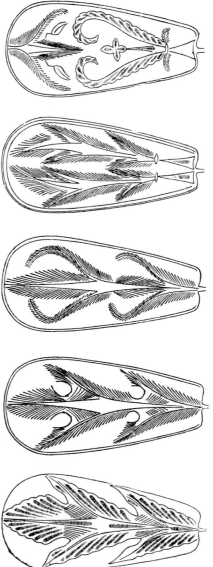

Fig. 448. Designs on backs of silver spoons of the sixth century from Cyprus. (British Museum.) P. 573.

to be identified with Fergana. The same region must also have given the vine to India. If, therefore, the vine as ornament was not used either east or west

FIG. 449. Ornament on one of the 'Pilastri Acritani' in the Piazzetta, Venice : Syrian work of the sixth century, showing vine and acanthus motives, inclined fret, &c. (Alinari.)

of Hither Asia before a period well within Hellenistic times, while within that region it certainly occurs at a far earlier date, it may be regarded as an Asiatic motive, probably of Mesopotamian origin.

The most characteristic and one of the earliest types of vine-scroll is that in which the convolutions enclose animals and birds. The idea of inserting human and animal figures in floral scrolls was not new: it occurs in early Greek vases. But where it thus occurs, the foliage is composed of palmettes, and descends from the lotus, not the vine.[1] Examples of the vine enclosing animals begin to be numerous from about the fourth century A.D. Some of them are fairly true to nature in the treatment of leaves and stems; others are more openly conventional, and set out on a geometrical plan. To the first class belong the relief in the Lateran Museum at Rome,[2] the two drums of columns in the Ottoman Museum mentioned elsewhere (p. 154), a part of a wooden architrave from Egypt now in the Kaiser Friedrich Museum at Berlin,[3] the ivory-covered throne at Ravenna (Fig. 122). To the second class belong the façade of Mshatta (Fig. 447), the Pilastri Acritani (Fig. 449 and p. 170), an ivory panel from Egypt at Berlin,[4] another ivory panel in the Cairo Museum,[5] and two of the curious ivory panels now set in the sides of the pulpit in the choir of the Cathedral at Aix-la-Chapelle,[6] which have obvious affinities to the foregoing. The ivory vases in the British Museum (see p. 214), the Victoria and Albert Museum, the Beuth-Schinkel Museum at Berlin, and the collection of the Comtesse de Béarn at Paris[7] all show various degrees of conventionalization, and are not very easy to date. Perhaps the whole group should be assigned to the Mesopotamian area, for the popularity of the vine-scroll in early Mohammedan art is probably to be traced to that part of Mesopotamia which was once under Sassanian rule: we may suppose that the motive came into both Christian and Arab art from this province of Persia.

The vine was a favourite ornamental motive in the early Third Period, occurring on the capitals of the Bible House cistern at Constantinople, assigned to the reign of Basil I,[8] but it becomes debased in the eleventh century:[9] its later destinies in ornament are not without interest. The 'Byzantine' floral scrolls illustrated in the head-piece, Fig. 64, typical of the decoration in vogue between the tenth and the thirteenth centuries, are really composed of conventional vine-leaves;[10] their structure proves this origin, though the fact that they are constantly parti-coloured is apt to mislead the eye. The small red dots in the centres are perhaps descendants of the dots placed at the junction of stem and stalk in the earlier carved representations of the plant. Conventional vine-scrolls and leaves based upon Byzantine originals appear in West-European MSS. from the eleventh century, and are a feature in the background of Limoges enamels in the thirteenth.[11] The artists of Islam treated the vine with the utmost freedom, sometimes adopting the principle of contamination, by means of which the vine-leaf becomes a curious composite, 'palmettized,' and built up out of old Persian palmette elements such as the heart and the pear-shaped leaf;[12] at others, showing a half-naturalistic vine-leaf issuing from palmette volutes.

[1] Riegl, *Stilfragen*, 205-8. For animals in foliage cf. Figs. 24-5, 122. Early examples occur at Spalato.
[2] Wickhoff, *Die Wiener Genesis*, Fig. 11 ; Riegl, *Die spätrömische Kunstindustrie in Oesterreich-Ungarn*, 71.
[3] Strzygowski, *Hellenistische und koptische Kunst*, Fig. 56, p. 63 ; O. Wulff, *Berlin Catalogue*, i, No. 263.
[4] Strzygowski, *Hell. und kopt. Kunst*, Fig. 51, p. 64 ; Wulff, *Berlin Catalogue*, No. 619. The bone carvings with vine designs so common among Coptic antiquities are offshoots of the same group.
[5] Strzygowski, as above, Figs. 52 and 53, p. 65, and *Koptische Kunst*, No. 7116.
[6] *Hell. und kopt. Kunst*, 50.
[7] Brit. Mus., *Catalogue of Ivory Carvings of the Christian Era*, No. 15 and references there given.
[8] J. Strzygowski, *B. D.*, ii. 100, 228.
[9] In Italy (Cattaneo, *Architettura*, &c., 76, 154) ; on sarcophagus of Yaroslav at Kieff (Ainaloff and Riedin, *Anc. Mon. of K.*, 52).
[10] Prussian *Jahrbuch*, as above, 333 (illustration from the Codex Vaticanus Urb. 2, painted in A.D. 1128, under John Comnenus). Designs of the same character were repeated in repoussé metal-work, e.g. on the triptych from Chakhuli, now at Gelat (Kondakoff, *Enamels*, German ed., 133-4).
[11] Cf. J. Marquet de Vasselot in A. Michel's *Histoire de l'art*, ii. 952.
[12] e.g. the Fatimid frieze at Cairo, reproduced in the same place, Fig. 101, p. 332. Cf. also the inscribed rosettes on the façade of the Mosque of Muayyad (el-Aḥmar), also at Cairo, figured by Van Berchem, *Corpus*, &c., Pl. XXI, No. 2, p. 71 ; the sculptured slabs at Torcello, A.D. 1008.

The vine and not the acanthus forms the staple of the 'arabesque': the story of Mohammedan floral ornament is, as Strzygowski has shown, the story of the palmettizing of the vine.

Fig. 450.   Sculptured ornament of the eleventh century on the ambo in the Cathedral of Torcello: mouldings, late 'sacred-tree' design with cone at top.   (Alinari.)

The Pine-cone.

The pine-cone (cf. p. 700), derived from ancient Assyrian art, is used in building up the centres of the great rosettes in high relief on the Mshatta façade.[1]

[1] Prussian *Jahrbuch*, 1904, 295, Fig. 75.

It is not an important feature in later art, though there are examples of derivative forms, e. g. in the mosaics of Sta Sophia,[1] and it is used as a top or finial to
'sacred-tree' types of the eleventh and twelfth centuries (Fig. 450). It was
most popular cast in bronze in the round, when it served upon fountains as
the base from which the central jet of water issued. The bronze cone in the
Cathedral of Aix-la-Chapelle is an example of this.[2]

NATURALISTIC FORMS.

The naturalistic or only half-conventionalized flower is to be found in
Byzantine ornament of various periods, but is especially prominent in the
Syrian MSS. of the sixth century (p. 448). In the Fourth Period appear new
and interesting forms, such as the bell-shaped flowers of Kahrié Djami[3] and
the blossoms arranged in a vase of Mistra.[4]

Ornament of Animals and Monsters.

'Heraldic' and confronted animals, or animals in procession, are an inheritance of Mesopotamian art which passed into the Byzantine culture-area, first in
the Sassanian period, and by a second wave in the time of Mohammedan
dominion from about the tenth century.[5] Examples of the First and Second
Periods are common both on sculptured slabs and in textiles (pp. 165 ff., 593).
Examples of the Third are especially frequent in Mesopotamia, the old home
of this style, in Greece, and in the Balkan area,[6] the beasts being often
disposed within interconnected circles. Such beasts, as well as monsters
with human heads, occur equally in Armenian MSS.

Thanks to the occurrence of a very early Cufic inscription on the Kharput gate
of Amida (A. D. 909–10),[7] Strzygowski's derivation of this animal ornament from
Mesopotamia is confirmed. This may be compared with one on a slab from the
Acropolis Church in the National Museum at Athens, in which confronted lions are
contained within a border of Cufic letters [8] combined with split palmettes of early
Islamic style ; and with the Cufic ornament on the sarcophagus of 'Romanus II'
(A. D. 959-63) in the lower church of St. Luke of Stiris. Beasts, birds, and
monsters are all treated in this symmetrical fashion, and it would be tedious to
enumerate examples. We may, however, in passing, note that the gryphon,
which was always popular, was a creation of ancient Mesopotamian fancy, and
in early Greek art had more than one variety. After the Christian era such
eccentric types as the lion-gryphon [9] dropped out ; and both in Persia and among
the later Greeks the variety with the eagle's head is universal (Fig. 452). As it is
common upon silk stuffs of Persian origin or affinity, it may have owed some
of its renewed popularity to the influence of textiles. This winged monster
penetrated into barbaric Europe, the principal entrance being perhaps through
Cherson in the south of Russia.[10]

---

[1] Salzenberg, *Altchristliche Baudenkmäler*, xxiii, Pl. XXIV.

[2] Strzygowski, *Der Dom zu Aachen und seine Entstellung.*

[3] Th. Schmidt, Pl. XXIV.

[4] G. Millet, *Mon. byz. de Mistra*, Pl. LX. This design has an almost Indian appearance.

[5] The earliest Mohammedan ornament, as e.g. that on the Mosque of Tulun, is devoid of
animal motives.

[6] Well-known examples are on the façade of the Metropolitan Church at Athens, Mount
Athos (Lavra), and the Church of Skripu ; there are Hither-Asiatic examples from Miafarkin
near Diarbekr (Strzygowski, *Amida*, 366), Konia (Prussian *Jahrbuch*, xxvi. 79), Myra (Rott,
Kleinasiatische Denkmäler, 341), &c.

[7] *Amida*, 370.   [8] Ibid., 371.

[9] On this type of gryphon see *The Treasure of the Oxus*, British Museum, 1905, 87. The
gryphon occurs on more than one iconostasis, e.g. in St. Luke of Stiris in Phocis (Schultz and
Barnsley, Pl. XXII). Here he has the nimbus (*Archaeologia*, LV, Pl. XXXIV).

[10] Hampel has collected much evidence for the influence of the East upon early Hungarian industrial art. See *New Researches upon Monuments of the Time of the Hungarian Conquest.*
Budapest Acad. of Sciences, 1907 (Magyar), and the review in *B. Z.*, xvii. 650.

The eagle also deserves special mention. It is a common feature in the ornamental sculpture of the sixth century,[1] and was perpetuated both in Greece and in Italy,[2] becoming a very favourite feature in Italian Romanesque churches: in later times (eleventh to fourteenth century) it is also common, being frequent in Macedonia and (Old) Servia.[3] The two-headed variety does not seem to have been adopted in the Byzantine Empire before the tenth century:[4] it occurs especially in connexion with the Emperor Theodore Lascaris, and is found both on textiles and on coins. It was common in Trebizond, and is seen carved in relief at Mistra (Millet, *Mon. byz. de Mistra*, Pl. XLVII). It appears to have been originally the symbol of the Babylonian town of Lagash, and was later adopted by the Hittites, being found upon 'Hittite' monuments of Cappa-

Fig. 451. End of the ivory casket in Troyes Cathedral. (From an electrotype.) P. 708.

docia.[5] It may have become Byzantine through the fact that Theodore Lascaris was despot of Nicomedia, in which province Bogaz Keui and other Hittite cities were situated. It appears in Saracenic art,[6] and passed into Russia. Perhaps the crusaders brought it into Central Europe, for the German double-headed

[1] Ambo of Salonika (p. 147); numerous capitals of columns (cf. Fig. 20); stone 'doors' at Constantinople (Prussian *Jahrbuch*, xiv, 1893, 76, Fig. 4).

[2] Between crosses on carved slabs at St. Luke of Stiris (Schultz and Barnsley, Pl. XIII, Fig. B); door of S. Ambrogio, Milan (ninth century) (Cattaneo, *Architettura in Italia*, &c., Fig. 117, p. 196). For South Italian examples see E. Bertaux, *L'Art dans l'Italie méridionale*.

[3] e.g. sculptured slabs at Sta Sophia, Ochrida (Miliukoff, *Izviestiya*, Russ. Arch. Inst. Cple., iv, 1899, Pl. XXVI).

[4] S. P. Lambros in *Proceedings of the Cairo Archaeological Congress*, pub. 1910; Lethaby and Swainson, *Church of Sancta Sophia*, 68. The two-headed eagle also occurs on a carved stone fragment at Daphni (Millet, *Daphni*, 69), &c.

[5] Perrot and Chipiez, *Histoire de l'art*, &c., *Sardinia, Judaea*, &c., ii, Fig. 343, p. 176, and Pl. VIII. It has often been remarked that the custom of supporting columns on the backs of animals (lions) is also found among the Hittites.

[6] Seljuk sculpture at Konia, &c. (Max van Berchem, *Amida*, 99), and on the incense-burner of the Emir Baisari (fourteenth century) in the British Museum.

eagle does not appear before 1345.[1] But it occurs in illuminated MSS. of earlier date.[2]

The birds represented in early Coptic art with medallions round their necks (Fig. 86) are in some cases eagles. An example painted on the wall of one of the funerary chapels at Bawît has the word ἀετός painted immediately above it.[3] A bird on one end of the ivory casket at Troyes bears a resemblance to the Chinese phoenix (Fig. 451).

In the Early Christian centuries, as is well known, many animals, confronted

FIG. 452. Marble relief with gryphons, of the eleventh century : S. Marco, Venice.
(Alinari.)

or disposed singly, had a symbolic meaning in ornament (harts, peacocks, doves, &c.). In some cases this meaning survived late, but as a rule after the First Period the animal becomes simply decorative, and has no more mystical significance than the majority of the beasts and birds which ornament such early Syrian MSS. as the Gospel of Rabula[4] (p. 448). The symbolic beasts of the Physiologus (p. 482) were not so popular with the Eastern designer as they were in the West. We do not find, for example, the pelican in her piety or the unicorn with the same frequency. The stylization of animal forms, and their confusion with floral designs, as in Romanesque times, is not common in Byzantine art ; as a rule each retains its individuality. Whether East-Christian illuminators originated the fashion of forming initial letters from combinations of fish, birds, and human limbs we cannot say with certainty. The curious fact that such capitals occur both in early Lombard and Merovin-

---

[1] F. Sarre in Prussian *Jahrbuch*, xxv, 1904, 64 ff.

[2] e. g. the Bible of St. Martial in the Bibliothèque Nationale, Paris ; Comte de Bastard, *Peintures des manuscrits*, &c., Part IX, British Museum copy.

[3] J. Clédat, *Mém. de l'Inst. franç. d'arch. orientale du Caire*, Pl. XCIII.

[4] The same remark applies perhaps to most of the animals represented even within the First Period. Apart from the MSS. mentioned, we may note such examples as the beasts of the mosaic pavements, silver-work (Fig. 444), &c.

gian MSS., and in Coptic and Armenian, Bulgarian and Russian MSS. of the eleventh century and later, seems to point to a common model originating in some central region before the eighth century.[1] They may belong to an early Graeco-oriental art and have been probably disseminated by Syrian maritime trade. Their persistence at so late a period as the eleventh century may

Fig. 453. Inscription and ornament in mosaic, of the eighth–ninth century: Church of St. Irene, Constantinople, showing leaves in band of zigzag. (Byzantine Research and Publication Fund.)

possibly be explained by the fact that they belong to a popular art unaffected by newer styles. M. Bordier has suggested that beast-capitals were the earliest illuminated initials of the Christian East.[2] For animals, cf. also Figs. 104, 151, 162, 266, 275, 384, 456.

GEOMETRICAL ORNAMENT.

The varieties of this ornament are too numerous to be severally discussed, but the following may be noted. The network of interconnected circles found in early mosaics, carved transennae, &c., is a motive conceived in the oriental spirit, the circles being frequently filled by animal or floral motives. This method of covering an extended surface was already very common by the sixth century,

[1] N. Kondakoff, *Zoomorphic Initials in Greek and Glagolitic MSS. of the Tenth and Eleventh Centuries in the Library of the Monastery of St. Catherine, Sinai* (Russian); the same, *Macedonia*, 1909, 57 ff.; *B. D.*, i. 92 ff.

[2] *Description des ornements des mss. grecs de la Bibliothèque Nationale*, 24.

and is found in carved reliefs,[1] mosaics,[2] and textiles.[3] It may have originated with the textile art, as also may the similar device of covering the field with a diaper of lozenges, each lozenge also filled with an animal, plant, or human figure. The motive exists both in textiles and in frescoes, doubtless inspired by woven fabrics.[4]

The band of lozenges, which may be resolved into two bands of zigzag, though of early introduction (Figs. 32, 454), is more frequent in the two later periods,

FIG. 454. Carved impost capital of the sixth century : Cathedral of Parenzo, showing acanthus within double zigzag. (Alinari.)

each lozenge sometimes enclosing a leaf or flower, as at Mistra.[5] The single zigzag, which forms so striking a feature in the frieze of Mshatta (Fig. 447), is used in the middle Byzantine period to form borders (cf. Fig. 453), frequently sur-

---

[1] Especially on transennae or closure slabs.
[2] Pavements both of the First Period (e.g. that in the Louvre from Tyre) and of the Third and Fourth Periods (St. Luke (Fig. 251), S. Marco, Mistra, &c.).
[3] Especially figured silks of Persian affinities (Ch. X).
[4] Prussian *Jahrbuch*, xxiv, 1903, 173 ff. Frescoes in one of the smaller chambers at Kuṣeir ʻAmra (Fig. 170) ; frescoes, funerary chapels at Bawit (J. Clédat in *Mém. de l'Inst. français d'arch. orientale*, xii, 1904, Pl. XXII, XXIII, XXIV). A lozenge-diaper on a smaller scale, the lozenges being merely filled with dots, is frequent in the frescoes of Cappadocian churches, dating from the Third Period (H. Rott, *Kleinasiatische Denkmäler*).
[5] A lozenge band enclosing rosettes, on a wooden seat of the third century found by Dr. Stein in Turkestan and now in the British Museum, is almost identical with that seen in Fig. 32. The resemblance may be perhaps explained as the result of Hither-Asiatic influence working in two directions.

rounding medallions, &c., on carved ivories. It also occurs in brick on the exterior of churches in Greece.[1]

At an earlier date we find it similarly employed, as in the frescoes of Kuṣeir 'Amra, and on the shafts of columns in Egypt, as in those of the portal of the south church at Bawît.[2] In painting and mosaic it will often run through or divide a band of floral ornament or of chequers (Kahrié Djami).

Large single lozenges are often used as the central feature of a carved closure slab or ambo panel both in the First and later periods (Fig. 443), but especially between the ninth and twelfth centuries.[3] On such slabs a large figure, lozenge, circle, &c., may be combined with smaller figures, or else contain them.

FIG. 455. Carved marble slabs of the eleventh century on the fountain in the Monastery of Lavra, Mount Athos. (*Hautes Études* : G. Millet.)

Interlacings, double or multiple, are so continuous a feature that they can only receive a general notice. The double interlaced band began early and lasted late. Of ancient Mesopotamian origin, it was common in the First Period, but equally found in the Third (brick ornament on the exterior of Greek churches, &c.),[4] and after. Interlacings of many varieties, including the loose-knot type, are found in the frescoes of Bawît.[5] Combined with foliate ornament, they remained a feature of Armenian art through the Middle Ages until modern times. The interlaced band is equally persistent in Syrian, Mesopotamian, and Jewish ornament.[6] Cf. Figs. 18, 68, 91, 97, 176, 348.

[1] G. Lampakis, *Mém. sur les antiquités chrétiennes de la Grèce*, Athens, 1902, 44, &c.

[2] J. Clédat in Cabrol's *Dict. d'arch. chrétienne*, s.v. *Baouit*, 215–16. This treatment recalls the ornamentation of columns in the Romanesque period.

[3] Schultz and Barnsley, *Mon. of St. Luke of Stiris*, Pl. XXII and XXV ; *Archaeologia*, 1897, Pl. XXXIV ; Wulff, *Die Koimesiskirche*, 164 ff.

[4] G. Lampakis, *Mémoires sur les antiquités chrétiennes de la Grèce*, pp. 44 ff.

[5] Clédat in *Mém. de l'Institut franç. d'arch. orientale*, xii, Cairo, 1904, Pl. XI, LIX–LXI, LXXVI ff.

[6] A. Baumstark, *R. Q.*, 1906, 178, 180. For interlacings in Europe in the early centuries of the Middle Ages see J. Romilly Allen, *Celtic Art in Pagan and Christian Times*, ch. viii.

Decorative Script.

Though Greek inscriptions were often placed in prominent places in association with ornament, the actual letters were regarded as more than decoration. But it was different with Arabic characters when they became known. Byzantine artists seem to have been impressed, like the Italians at a later date, with the decorative qualities of the Cufic script,[1] and used it for bands of ornament on the exterior of their churches.[2] In Italy such designs are familiar to us on the borders of robes in the paintings of the earlier Renaissance; but they had been used from the twelfth century in mosaic pavements and in the south of the peninsula.[3] Floriated Cufic appears to have come in towards the end of the first millennium, possibly introduced by Moslem artists who followed the Bulgarian armies into Greece. It is noteworthy that the

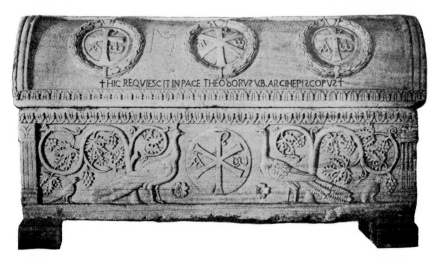

FIG. 456. Sarcophagus of Archbishop Theodore in S. Apollinare in Classe, Ravenna.
(Ricci.)

decorative use of Cufic script only occurs on Byzantine monuments in Greece, and is apparently not represented in Constantinople.[4]

The Cross and Swastika.

The cross, though used from the fourth century, was not common in ornament before the sixth century. Previous to this its place was taken by the various forms of the sacred monogram or Chi-Ro (Fig. 456), which in the Eastern Empire did not disappear so early as in the West, but survived on coins of Phocas and of Heraclius, and in sculpture, to a late period.[5] (Cf. p. 681.)

---

[1] For decorative Cufic ornament see A. de Longpérier, Œuvres, ed. Schlumberger, i. 381 ff. ; Van Berchem and Strzygowski, Amida, 20 ff., 370 ff.

[2] e.g. St. Luke of Stiris in Phocis (Schultz and Barnsley, Monastery of St. Luke, Pl. XI); Daphni (G. Millet, Le mon. de Daphni, p. 66, Fig. 36 ; Prussian Jahrbuch, 1904, Fig. 104. See also G. Lampakis, Mémoire sur les antiquités chrétiennes de la Grèce, pp. 27, 42).

[3] e. g. pavements of St. Nicholas at Bari (A. D. 1105–23) and Sta Maria del Patir near ˹R˺ossano (E. Bertaux, L'Art dans l'Italie méridionale). For the employment of oriental characters as decoration in Western churches see de Longpérier, Rev. arch., 1846, Pt. II, p. 700.

[4] Strzygowski, Amida.

[5] Flanked by A and ꞷ in carved ornament of the Metropolitan Church at Mistra (Millet, Mon. byz. de Mistra, Pl. XLVI). The complex form without the loop occurs in the fourteenth-century mosaics of Kahrié Djami (Pulgher, Anciennes églises, &c., Pl. XXX).

The cross issuing from a pair of acanthus-leaves does not appear to begin before the seventh century, after which it was continually employed (Figs. 343, 445), and was of very wide distribution.[1]

The floriated cross with equal arms, especially enclosed within a circle, is common in the Third Period. The cross rising from a globe appears on coins, and on marble reliefs of the First Period[2] (see also p. 681).

The *swastika* as ornament is found independently, as in the mosaics of Sta Sophia, Constantinople; it is also formed by the intersection of lines at right angles in continuous fret-like designs, as on fifth-century columns at Amida,[3] a transenna in S. Vitale (Fig. 442), &c.

[1] *B. Z.*, iii, 1894, 12 ; *B. D.*, i. 121. It is frequent in the interesting mediaeval sculpture of Armenia.

[2] e.g. in the gallery of Sta Sophia (Lethaby and Swainson, Fig. 61).

[3] Strzygowski, *Amida*, 1910.

INDEX I. GENERAL

INDEX II. ICONOGRAPHY

INDEX III

MUSEUMS, LIBRARIES, TREASURIES, AND COLLECTIONS

INDEX IV. AUTHORITIES

Dover Books on Art

AFRICAN SCULPTURE, Ladislas Segy. 163 full-page plates illustrating masks, fertility figures, ceremonial objects, etc., of 50 West and Central African tribes—95% never before illustrated. 34-page introduction to African sculpture. "Mr. Segy is one of its top authorities," NEW YORKER. 164 full-page photographic plates. Introduction. Bibliography. 244pp. 6⅛ x 9¼.

T396 Paperbound $2.00

CALLIGRAPHY, J. G. Schwandner. First reprinting in 200 years of this legendary book of beautiful handwriting. Over 300 ornamental initials, 12 complete calligraphic alphabets, over 150 ornate frames and panels, 75 calligraphic pictures of cherubs, stags, lions, etc., thousands of flourishes, scrolls, etc., by the greatest 18th-century masters. All material can be copied or adapted without permission. Historical introduction. 158 full-page plates. 368pp. 9 x 13. T475 Clothbound $10.00

A DIDEROT PICTORIAL ENCYCLOPEDIA OF TRADES AND INDUSTRY. Manufacturing and the Technical Arts in Plates Selected from "L'Encyclopédie ou Dictionnaire Raisonné des Sciences, des Arts, et des Métiers," of Denis Diderot, edited with text by C. Gillispie. Over 2000 illustrations on 485 full-page plates. Magnificent 18th- century engravings of men, women, and children working at such trades as milling flour, cheesemaking, charcoal burning, mining, silverplating, shoeing horses, making fine glass, printing, hundreds more, showing details of machinery, different steps in sequence, etc. A remarkable art work, but also the largest collection of working figures in print, copyright-free, for art directors, designers, etc. Two vols. 920pp. 9 x 12. Heavy library cloth. T421 Two volume set $18.50

SILK SCREEN TECHNIQUES, J. Biegeleisen, M. Cohn. A practical step-by-step home course in one of the most versatile, least expensive graphic arts processes. How to build an inexpensive silk screen, prepare stencils, print, achieve special textures, use color, etc. Every step explained, diagrammed. 149 illustrations, 8 in color. 201pp. 6⅛ x 9¼. T433 Paperbound $1.55

METALWORK AND ENAMELLING, H. Maryon. Probably the best book ever written on the subject. Tells everything necessary for the home manufacture of jewelry, rings, ear pendants, bowls, etc. Covers materials, tools, soldering, filigree, setting stones, raising patterns, repoussé work, damascening, niello, cloisonné, polishing, assaying, casting, and dozens of other techniques. The best substitute for apprenticeship to a master metalworker. 363 photos and figures. 374pp. 5½ x 8½.

T183 Clothbound $8.00

PRINCIPLES OF ART HISTORY, H. Wölfflin. This remarkably instructive work demonstrates the tremendous change in artistic conception from the 14th to the 18th centuries, by analyzing 164 works by Botticelli, Dürer, Hobbema, Holbein, Hals, Titian, Rembrandt, Vermeer, etc., and pointing out exactly what is meant by "baroque," "classic," "primitive," "picturesque," and other basic terms of art history and criticism. "A remarkable lesson in the art of seeing," SAT. REV. OF LITERATURE. Translated from the 7th German edition. 150 illus. 254pp. 6⅛ x 9¼.   T276 Paperbound $2.00

FOUNDATIONS OF MODERN ART, A. Ozenfant. Stimulating discussion of human creativity from paleolithic cave painting to modern painting, architecture, decorative arts. Fully illustrated with works of Gris, Lipchitz, Léger, Picasso, primitive, modern artifacts, architecture, industrial art, much more. 226 illustrations. 368pp. 6⅛ x 9¼.   T215 Paperbound $1.95

SHAKER FURNITURE, E. D. and F. Andrews. The most illuminating study of Shaker furniture ever written. Covers chronology, craftsmanship, houses, shops, etc. Includes over 200 photographs of chairs, tables, clocks, beds, benches, etc. "Mr. & Mrs. Andrews know all there is to know about Shaker furniture," Mark Van Doren, NATION. 48 full-page plates. 192pp. 7⅞ x 10¾.   T679 Paperbound $2.00

PRIMITIVE ART, Franz Boas. A great American anthropologist covers theory, technical virtuosity, styles, symbolism, patterns, etc. of primitive art. The more than 900 illustrations will interest artists, designers, craftworkers. Over 900 illustrations. 376pp. 5⅜ x 8.   T25 Paperbound $1.95

ON THE LAWS OF JAPANESE PAINTING, H. Bowie. The best possible substitute for lessons from an Oriental master. Treats both spirit and technique; exercises for control of the brush; inks, brushes, colors; use of dots, lines to express whole moods, etc. 66 illus. 272 pp. 6⅛ x 9¼.   T30 Paperbound $1.95

DESIGN FOR ARTISTS AND CRAFTSMEN, L. Wolchonok. The most thorough course on the creation of art motifs and designs. Shows you step-by-step, with hundreds of examples and 113 detailed exercises, how to create original designs from geometric patterns, plants, birds, animals, humans, and man-made objects. "A great contribution to the field of design and crafts," N. Y. SOCIETY OF CRAFTSMEN. More than 1300 entirely new illustrations. xv + 207pp. 7⅞ x 10¾.
T274 Clothbound $4.95